FINANCIAL REPORTING AND GLOBAL CAPITAL MARKETS

Financial Reporting and Global Capital Markets

A History of the International Accounting Standards Committee 1973–2000

KEES CAMFFERMAN AND STEPHEN A. ZEFF

OXFORD
UNIVERSITY PRESS

This book has been printed digitally and produced in a standard specification in order to ensure its continuing availability

OXFORD
UNIVERSITY PRESS

Great Clarendon Street, Oxford OX2 6DP
Oxford University Press is a department of the University of Oxford.
It furthers the University's objective of excellence in research, scholarship,
and education by publishing worldwide in
Oxford New York
Auckland Cape Town Dar es Salaam Hong Kong Karachi
Kuala Lumpur Madrid Melbourne Mexico City Nairobi
New Delhi Shanghai Taipei Toronto
With offices in
Argentina Austria Brazil Chile Czech Republic France Greece
Guatemala Hungary Italy Japan South Korea Poland Portugal
Singapore Switzerland Thailand Turkey Ukraine Vietnam

Oxford is a registered trade mark of Oxford University Press
in the UK and in certain other countries

Published in the United States
by Oxford University Press Inc., New York

© Kees Camfferman and Stephen A. Zeff 2006

The moral rights of the author have been asserted

Database right Oxford University Press (maker)

Reprinted 2009

All rights reserved. No part of this publication may be reproduced,
stored in a retrieval system, or transmitted, in any form or by any means,
without the prior permission in writing of Oxford University Press,
or as expressly permitted by law, or under terms agreed with the appropriate
reprographics rights organization. Enquiries concerning reproduction
outside the scope of the above should be sent to the Rights Department,
Oxford University Press, at the address above

You must not circulate this book in any other binding or cover
And you must impose this same condition on any acquirer

ISBN 978-0-19-929629-3

Contents

List of Figures	xv
List of Tables	xvi
Foreword	xvii
Preface	xix
List of Abbreviations	xxi

1. Introduction and Overview — 1
   1.1. Approach — 2
   1.2. Overview — 4
      1.2.1. The Antecedents and Founding of the IASC — 5
      1.2.2. The IASC to 1987 — 6
      1.2.3. The IASC from 1987 to 2000 — 9

PART I. ORIGINS

2. Origins of International Accounting Harmonization — 21
   2.1. International Economic Integration and Accounting Harmonization — 21
   2.2. The Creation of Regional Accountancy Bodies — 23
   2.3. Calls for Uniformity of Accounting Standards — 23
   2.4. International Accounting in the United States — 25
   2.5. Accountants International Study Group — 26
      2.5.1. National Programmes for Establishing Accounting Principles — 27
      2.5.2. Formation of the Study Group — 29
      2.5.3. Benson's Motivations — 30
      2.5.4. The Initial Work of the Study Group: The Inventories Booklet — 31
      2.5.5. The Remaining Work of the Study Group — 32
   2.6. An International Accounting Secretariat — 37
   2.7. Accounting Harmonization in the EEC and the Role of the UEC — 38
   2.8. The Stage for the IASC — 41

3. The Founding of the IASC — 43
   3.1. The Initiative to Form an International Accounting Standards Committee — 43
   3.2. Benson's Role and Motivation — 44
   3.3. General Reactions to the IASC Proposal — 46
   3.4. Main Features of the 1973 Agreement and Constitution — 48
      3.4.1. Participating Countries and Accountancy Bodies — 48
      3.4.2. Relations with ICCAP — 49
      3.4.3. Objective and Scope of Activities — 51
      3.4.4. Compliance, 'Best Endeavours', and Voting — 52

	3.4.5. Financing	53
	3.4.6. Location	53
3.5.	Reactions to the Founding of the IASC	54
	3.5.1. Reactions within the UEC	55
	3.5.2. Impact on the Accountants International Study Group	57

PART II. 1973–87

4.	The People and the Structure of the IASC	61
	4.1. The Chairmen	61
	4.2. Composition of the Original Delegations to the IASC	64
	4.3. Evolution of the Delegations to 1987	67
	4.4. Delegations Subsequently Added	71
	4.5. Incorporation of Associate Members	73
	4.6. The Technical Staff	74
	4.7. The Official Language(s)	77
	4.8. Link with the ICAEW	78
	4.9. The Early Plan for the Approval and Production of Standards	79
	4.10. Composition of the Project Steering Committees	79
	4.11. Communications	80
	4.12. Meetings of the Committee (from 1977 Onwards, the Board)	80
	4.13. Finances	82
	4.14. Changes in 1977 in the Agreement and Constitution	84
	4.15. The Organisation and Planning Committee (OPC)	85
	4.16. The Consultative Group	86
	4.17. Changes in 1982 in the Agreement and Constitution	87
	4.18. IASC/IFAC Co-ordinating Committee	89
	4.19. The IASC's Major Reassessment of Its Future Plans in 1987	89
5.	'Compromise to Harmonise': Setting the IASC's Early Standards	90
	5.1. Overview	90
	5.2. Working Arrangements and Composition of Steering Committees	90
	5.3. Review of the Technical Projects 1973–87	93
	5.4. The First Standard: IAS 1	93
	5.5. Tempered Ambitions: IAS 2 to IAS 5	96
	5.5.1. IAS 2: Inventories	97
	5.5.2. IAS 3: Consolidated Financial Statements and the Equity Method	99
	5.5.3. IAS 4: Depreciation Accounting	101
	5.5.4. IAS 5: Information to be Disclosed in Financial Statements	102
	5.5.5. The IASC's Policy Takes Shape	103
	5.6. A Non-starter: Auditing Standards	104
	5.7. Inflation Accounting: IAS 6 and IAS 15	105
	5.7.1. IAS 6: Accounting Responses to Changing Prices	106
	5.7.2. A Discussion Paper without Discussion	108

	5.7.3. IAS 15: Accounting Responses to Changing Prices Revisited	109
5.8.	Stocking the Shop: IAS 7 to IAS 13	110
	5.8.1. IAS 7: Statement of Changes in Financial Position	111
	5.8.2. IAS 8: Unusual Items and Accounting Changes	111
	5.8.3. IAS 9: Research and Development	113
	5.8.4. IAS 10: Contingencies and Events after the Balance Sheet Date	114
	5.8.5. IAS 11: Construction Contracts	114
	5.8.6. IAS 12: Accounting for Income Tax	115
	5.8.7. IAS 13: Presentation of Current Assets and Current Liabilities	117
	5.8.8. IAS 7–13: Concluding Remarks	118
5.9.	Foreign Currency Translation: The Long Road to IAS 21	119
	5.9.1. E11: An Unsuccessful Attempt	119
	5.9.2. A Breakthrough and a Crisis	121
5.10.	A Courageous Discussion Paper on Banks	123
5.11.	Showing Leadership: IAS 14, 17, and 19	125
	5.11.1. IAS 14: Segment Reporting	126
	5.11.2. IAS 17: Accounting for Leases	127
	5.11.3. IAS 19: Retirement Benefits	129
5.12.	Antecedents of a Conceptual Framework: IAS 16, 17, and 18	131
	5.12.1. Fair Value	131
	5.12.2. Other Issues in IAS 16	132
	5.12.3. IAS 18: Revenue Recognition	133
5.13.	The End of the Beginning: IAS 20, 22, and 23–6	134
	5.13.1. IAS 20: Government Grants	135
	5.13.2. IAS 22: Business Combinations	135
	5.13.3. IAS 23: Capitalization of Borrowing Costs	138
	5.13.4. IAS 24: Related Party Transactions	138
	5.13.5. IAS 25: Investments	140
	5.13.6. IAS 26: Retirement Benefit Plans	141
5.14.	Conclusion	142
6. The IASC Labours to Gain Recognition		144
6.1.	The Best Endeavours Undertaking	144
6.2.	An Important Endorsement from the FIBV	146
6.3.	European and World Surveys of Financial Reporting: A Boon for the IASC	147
	6.3.1. The Lafferty/*Financial Times* Volumes	147
	6.3.2. Two Further Surveys	148
6.4.	Impact on Country Members of the IASC Board	149
6.5.	United Kingdom & Ireland	150
	6.5.1. Action Taken by the CCAB	151
	6.5.2. Action Taken by the London Stock Exchange	154
	6.5.3. Responses to the IASC's Surveys	155

6.6.	United States	155
	6.6.1. AICPA's Responses to the IASC's Surveys	157
	6.6.2. A Conflict between the FASB, FEI, and the SEC over the IASC's E3	157
	6.6.3. Criticism of the IASC by Two US Big Eight Accountancy Firms	160
	6.6.4. Approaches to the FASB Relating to IASC Standards	161
	6.6.5. FASB's Ambivalence towards International Standards under Kirk	162
6.7.	Australia	164
6.8.	Canada	165
6.9.	France	166
6.10.	Germany	169
6.11.	Japan	171
6.12.	Mexico	172
6.13.	The Netherlands	172
6.14.	Nigeria	174
6.15.	South Africa	175
6.16.	Italy	176
6.17.	Taiwan	176
6.18.	Discussion of Selected Associate Members Not Serving on the IASC Board	177
	6.18.1. Pakistan	177
	6.18.2. India	178
	6.18.3. Singapore	178
	6.18.4. Hong Kong	179
	6.18.5. Malaysia	179
	6.18.6. New Zealand	179
6.19.	Non-participation by Central and South American Countries	180
6.20.	General Assessment of the Impact of the IASC's Standards up to 1987	181
6.21.	The IASC Seeks Support through Visits and Liaison	182
6.22.	The IASC's Contacts at the European Level	184
6.23.	The IASC's Contacts with the SEC	185
6.24.	The IASC's Initial Contact with IOSCO and Its Portent	186
7. The IASC Copes with Its Political Environment		187
7.1.	The Developing World and the United Nations	187
	7.1.1. Sensitivity to the Aspirations of Developing Countries	189
	7.1.2. The Ad Hoc Working Group and ISAR	190
7.2.	The OECD	192
7.3.	Integration with IFAC: 1973–82	195
	7.3.1. The Founding of IFAC	195
	7.3.2. Failure of a Proposed Integration Agreement	197
	7.3.3. Towards the Mutual Commitments	200

7.4. Origins of the Consultative Group and Outside Board Members	202
7.4.1. Early Stirrings	203
7.4.2. Formation of the Consultative Group	204
7.4.3. Financial Analysts, but Not Financial Executives, Join the Board	205
7.5. The Last Attempt at a Merger with IFAC: The Bishop Working Party	206

PART III. 1987–2000

8. The Changing Look of the IASC: People, Structure, and Funding	213
8.1. Chairmen and Vice-Chairmen	213
8.2. Changing Composition of Board Membership	218
8.2.1. Involvement of National Standard Setters	219
8.2.2. Financial Analysts	220
8.2.3. Financial Executives	220
8.2.4. Other Delegations	222
8.2.5. Staff Observers/Technical Advisers	225
8.3. Challenges Facing Some Delegations During the Activist 1990s	226
8.4. Voting Practices of the Board Delegations	228
8.5. Guests and Observers at Board Meetings	228
8.6. Venues, Frequency, and Length of Board Meetings	230
8.7. Opening Board Meetings to the Public	231
8.8. Observers on Steering Committees	232
8.9. Sir Bryan Carsberg Succeeds David Cairns as Secretary-General	233
8.10. The IASC Augments Its Research Staff	235
8.11. The IASC Expands Its Support Staff and Requires More Office Space	236
8.12. Executive Committee Replaces the Organisation and Planning Committee	237
8.13. The Board Establishes the Standing Interpretations Committee	238
8.14. Significant Growth in the IASC's Budget	239
8.15. The IASC's Foundation Working Party: Charting the Course Towards a Vehicle for Fund-Raising	240
8.16. The Advisory Council	246
8.17. Fund-Raising	247
8.18. Amending the IASC Constitution in 1992	249
8.19. Relations with IFAC	250
8.20. Consultative Group	250
9. The IASC Fortifies Its Standards: The Framework, and the Comparability and Improvements Projects	253
9.1. The Building Blocks and the Framework	254
9.1.1. Hesitant Steps towards a Framework	254
9.1.2. The Building Block Projects	256

9.1.3. From Building Blocks to the Framework	259
9.1.4. The Framework and the Reduction of Options	262
9.1.5. The Balance-Sheet Approach	263
9.2. The IASC Reviews Its Previous International Accounting Standards	264
9.2.1. Reluctance to Revise Existing Standards	264
9.2.2. Group Accounting: The Revision of IAS 3 Leads to IAS 27, 28, and 31	266
9.3. Comparability and Improvements	269
9.3.1. The Comparability Project: Towards E32	270
9.3.2. The IASC Seeks the Limelight with E32	274
9.3.3. From E32 to the *Statement of Intent*	275
9.3.4. Start of the Improvements Project	280
9.3.5. Scope of the Improvements Project	281
9.3.6. Closing the 'Package'	282
9.3.7. The Ten Revised Standards	285
9.3.8. Muted Reactions to the Completion of the Improvements Project	286
9.4. Other Projects	287
9.4.1. Cash Flow Statements: The Revision of IAS 7	287
9.4.2. Developing Country Issues	288
9.4.3. IAS 30: Bank Disclosures	291
10. Raising the Stakes: The IASC Responds to IOSCO and the SEC	293
10.1. The Emergence of IOSCO	293
10.2. The IASC Establishes Contact with IOSCO via the SEC	295
10.3. The Comparability Steering Committee: E32	298
10.4. The Resolutions Taken at IOSCO's 1988 Annual Conference	300
10.5. The Inception of the IASC's Improvements Steering Committee	305
10.6. Developments at IOSCO	306
10.7. The Role of IOSCO in the Improvements Steering Committee	309
10.8. The SEC's Cautious Response to Capital Market Pressures	311
10.8.1. Acceleration in the New York Stock Exchange Listings of Overseas Companies	311
10.8.2. Rule 144A: SEC Waives Disclosure Requirements for Private Placements of Securities by Foreign Companies	312
10.8.3. SEC's Unprecedented MJDS Arrangement with Canada	312
10.8.4. IOSCO and SEC Endorse IAS 7	313
10.8.5. Daimler-Benz Becomes the First German Company to List in New York	314
10.8.6. The New York Stock Exchange Supports IASC Standards	316
10.8.7. SEC Allows Foreign Registrants to Adopt Parts of Three IASC Standards	317
10.9. IOSCO Official Defines the Qualities Required in the IASC's Revised Standards	318

	10.10.	IOSCO Identifies the Core Standards It Expects from the IASC	320
	10.11.	IOSCO's Rebuff to the IASC	321
	10.12.	The IASC and IOSCO Chart the Way Forward	325
	10.13.	The IASC Accelerates Its Target Date to March 1998 for Completing Its Core Standards	328
	10.14.	The SEC Announces the 'Three Key Elements' to be Reflected in Acceptable IASC Standards	331
	10.15.	A Closer Working Relationship Between the IASC and IOSCO	334
	10.16.	The New York Stock Exchange Pressures the SEC to Accept the IASC's Standards	335
	10.17.	The FASB Questions the IASC's Due Process	338
	10.18.	The IASC Board Completes the Core Standards	340
	10.19.	IOSCO Endorses the IASC's Core Standards	341
	10.20.	The SEC Issues a Major 'Concept Release' in February 2000	343
	10.21.	The European Commission Proposes to Require EU Listed Companies to Adopt IASC Standards	347
11.	Putting Teeth in Harmonization: The IASC Completes Its Core Standards	348
	11.1.	Introduction	348
	11.2.	Development of the Technical Agenda	348
	11.3.	The Standard-Setting Process	352
		11.3.1. Due Process and Short Cuts	352
		11.3.2. Steering Committees and Technical Staff	353
		11.3.3. Involvement of National Standard Setters	354
		11.3.4. Comment Letters	355
	11.4.	Income Tax: Revision of IAS 12	357
		11.4.1. Eliminating the Deferral Option	357
		11.4.2. E49: Closer to the United States, Away from the United Kingdom	358
		11.4.3. Final Difficulties	360
	11.5.	Financial Instruments	361
		11.5.1. The Hopeful Start of a Long Journey	361
		11.5.2. Identifying the Issues	363
		11.5.3. Failure to Issue a Comprehensive Standard	367
		11.5.4. Reorganization of the Project	370
		11.5.5. The IASC Makes Time for a Fundamental Study	370
		11.5.6. The Core Standards Target Date Necessitates an Interim Solution	371
		11.5.7. IAS 39 Completes the Set of Core Standards	374
		11.5.8. The Joint Working Group and the 'Permanent Solution'	376
	11.6.	Intangible Assets and Impairment	378
		11.6.1. An Unsatisfactory First Exposure Draft	378
		11.6.2. Impairment First: IAS 36	380
		11.6.3. Goodwill and Other Intangibles	382

11.7.	Other Core Standards on New Topics	383
	11.7.1. IAS 33: Earnings per Share	384
	11.7.2. IAS 34: Interim Reporting	385
	11.7.3. IAS 35: Discontinuing Operations	386
	11.7.4. IAS 37: Provisions	388
11.8.	Revisions of Standards	389
	11.8.1. IAS 1: Presentation of Financial Statements	390
	11.8.2. IAS 14: Segment Reporting	393
	11.8.3. IAS 19: Employee Benefits	395
	11.8.4. IAS 17: Leases	397
11.9.	Post-Core Technical Work	398
	11.9.1. IAS 40: Investment Property	399
	11.9.2. IAS 41: Agriculture	401
	11.9.3. Unfinished Projects	404
11.10.	Conclusion	407
12. The World Wakes Up to the IASC		408
12.1.	Introduction	408
12.2.	A Mixed Record of Acceptance in Europe	408
	12.2.1. France	409
	12.2.2. Germany	411
	12.2.3. The Netherlands	414
	12.2.4. Nordic Countries	415
	12.2.5. Switzerland	416
	12.2.6. United Kingdom	417
12.3.	The European Commission's Gradual Conversion to IASC Standards	418
	12.3.1. Warming of Relations between the IASC and the European Commission	418
	12.3.2. The European Commission Seeks to Reinforce the European Voice in the IASC	422
	12.3.3. The Commission Places the IASC at the Centre of its Harmonization Effort	423
	12.3.4. FEE Promotes a 'European Accounting Research Foundation'	427
	12.3.5. The Pace of European Companies Listing in New York Drives the European Commission's Evolving Accounting Policy	428
	12.3.6. FEE Proposes a 'Financial Reporting Strategy within Europe'	429
	12.3.7. The European Commission Calls for a Required Use of IASC Standards by EU Listed Companies	430
12.4.	Impacts Outside of Europe	432
	12.4.1. Australia	433
	12.4.2. Canada	435

	12.4.3. Japan	436
	12.4.4. South Africa	437
	12.4.5. United States	438
12.5.	Support for the IASC from International Financial Institutions	441
	12.5.1. Impact of the World Bank on the Diffusion of IASC Standards among Developing Countries	441
	12.5.2. The International Financial Stability Forum	442
12.6.	The G4+1	443
	12.6.1. Early Evolution of the G4+1	443
	12.6.2. The Continuing Development of the G4+1	444
	12.6.3. European Interests Establish E5+2 to Counter the G4+1	445
13. Towards a World Standard Setter: The Restructuring of the IASC		447
13.1.	Formation of the Strategy Working Party and Its Membership	447
13.2.	Meetings During 1997 and Successive Drafts of the Discussion Paper	450
	13.2.1. July 1997 Meeting	450
	13.2.2. September 1997 Meeting	454
	13.2.3. Reactions to the 17 November Draft from Outside the Working Party	457
13.3.	The Working Party's Deliberations During 1998	459
	13.3.1. January 1998 Meeting	460
	13.3.2. April 1998 Meeting	462
	13.3.3. July 1998 Meeting	463
13.4.	The Discussion Paper Published in December 1998	463
13.5.	Comment Letters on the December 1998 Discussion Paper	466
13.6.	The Advisory Council, Executive Committee, and Board Take Up the Working Party's Proposals in March 1999	470
13.7.	Enevoldsen and Carsberg Table Their Own Proposal in Warsaw in June/July 1999	472
	13.7.1. The Proposals	472
	13.7.2. The Executive Committee Considers the Proposal	473
	13.7.3. The Board Meets with the Working Party in June 1999	474
	13.7.4. The Working Party Meets in July to Consider the 'Single Board' Proposal	475
13.8.	Developments Following Warsaw	478
	13.8.1. Consultations	478
	13.8.2. Turner's Letter	480
	13.8.3. Mogg's Letter	481
	13.8.4. Prada's Letter	482
13.9.	Working Party Meets in September 1999	483
13.10.	Run-up to the Board's November 1999 Meeting in Venice	485
	13.10.1. The Working Party Confers to Make Further Revisions	485
	13.10.2. Enevoldsen and Carsberg Pre-Empt the Working Party	486

13.11. The Executive Committee's and Board's November 1999
       Meetings in Venice 488
       13.11.1. The Enevoldsen and Carsberg Note: Circumventing
                the Working Party 488
       13.11.2. Fateful Decision at the Executive Committee Meeting . 489
       13.11.3. 'The Deal' 490
       13.11.4. The Board Meeting 491
13.12. Transition from the Old to the New IASC 493
       13.12.1. Development and Issue of the Working Party's
                Final Report 493
       13.12.2. The Selection of Members of the Nominating
                Committee 493
       13.12.3. The Board's December Meeting in Amsterdam . . . 494
       13.12.4. IASC Nominating Committee Selects the Trustees for
                the New Regime 495
       13.12.5. Funding Requirements 496
       13.12.6. IASC Board Approves the Constitution 496
       13.12.7. IASC Member Bodies Approve the IASC's
                Restructuring 496
       13.12.8. The Trustees Choose the New Members of the
                Restructured Board 497
       13.12.9. The IASC Reaches the End of Its Life 498

Appendix 1: Text of the 1973 Agreement and Constitution 500
Appendix 2: Chairmen and Senior Staff 504
Appendix 3: Members of the Delegations to the IASC, 1973–2000 . . . 506
Appendix 4: Technical Projects, Exposure Drafts, and Standards 513
Appendix 5: Venues and Dates of Board Meetings 524
Appendix 6: Interviewees 527
Appendix 7: Use of, and References to, Unpublished Sources 529

Notes 530
Index 656

List of Figures

2.1.	Sir Henry (later Lord) Benson	27
4.1.	IASC chairmen and secretaries, IASC tenth anniversary dinner, 15 June 1983	62
4.2.	IASC chairmen and secretary, Toronto, June 1984	62
4.3.	IASC delegates and staff, London, January 1975	64
4.4.	IASC delegates, International Congress of Accountants, Munich, October 1977	68
4.5.	IASC delegates and staff, Edinburgh, July 1987	72
4.6.	David Cairns	76
4.7.	Meeting of IASC board in the Council Chamber of the ICAEW, London, March 1978	81
5.1.	Sir Henry Benson presents IAS 1 to the press, London, January 1975	95
7.1.	IASC chairmen and IFAC presidents at the Arthur Young Professors' Roundtable, London, May 1980	198
8.1.	IASC Chairmen Eiichi Shiratori and Arthur Wyatt at the World Congress of Accountants, Washington DC, October 1992	214
8.2.	IASC chairmen, IASC twentieth anniversary conference, 29 June 1993	215
8.3.	Michael Sharpe	216
8.4.	Stig Enevoldsen	217
8.5.	Tom Jones	218
8.6.	IASC delegates and staff, Singapore, November 1990	219
8.7.	IASC delegates, observers, and staff, Amsterdam, May 1995	221
8.8.	IASC delegates, observers, and staff, London, December 2000	224
8.9.	Meeting of IASC board in São Paulo, March 2000	231
8.10.	Sir Bryan Carsberg	234

Note: All illustrations reproduced with permission of the International Accounting Standards Foundation, London.

List of Tables

2.1. Publications of the Accountants International Study Group	32
3.1. Membership of the IASC in 1973	49
4.1. IASC revenue and expenditure, 1974–87	83
8.1. IASC revenue and expenses, 1988–2000	241
9.1. Revisions of International Accounting Standards during Comparability and Improvements	273
11.1. The 'core' standards work programme	351

Foreword

This book was conceived at IASC's farewell dinner in December 2000. Hans Burggraaff, a former chairman of IASC, announced that he thought that the history of the Committee should be written while so many of the participants in its success were still active and could be interviewed to give their perceptions of IASC's ambitions, and the difficulties it had faced in achieving them. We were very fortunate to find two such outstanding academics as Professors Kees Camfferman and Steve Zeff to undertake the tasks of sifting through IASC's records and interviewing so many of those involved with IASC, and, above all, of interpreting their research results in the light of the economic history of the time.

IASC, the brainchild of Lord Benson, will always have a secure place in the history of the globalization of the accounting profession. It grew out of the Accountants International Study Group, consisting of representatives of the British, Canadian, and US accountancy institutes—a group that was an early forerunner of the G4+1, which consisted of members and staff of the major standard setters of the 1990s (Australia, Canada, New Zealand, the United Kingdom, and the United States) and IASC staff.

All along, those responsible for the management of IASC shared a vision of a world in which a transaction would be accounted for in a similar manner no matter where it took place. Persuading others to support that objective was the role of IASC over the twenty-seven years of its existence.

From its modest beginnings as not much more than a collector of various existing best practices IASC developed into a body that determined which practice was to be regarded as the best and should become the world standard. In its later years it worked with the securities regulators to try to ensure that its standards would be accepted anywhere in the world without the need for reconciliation to the local jurisdiction's accepted practices or standards. Its final act was to decide the shape of its successor organization—the standard-setting IASB and its supervisory body of trustees. IASC approved its successor's constitution; and it appointed the nominating committee that in turn chose the IASC Foundation's trustees, who then selected the members of the new IASB. Several of those who served part-time on the Board of IASC became full-time members of the new IASB. These themes have been brought out clearly by those who were heavily involved in the debates of the time.

This book will be the definitive history of IASC from its inception to its transformation from a part-time to a full-time organization. Its readers will understand how the idealism and dedication of generations of professionals nurtured and sustained the vision of a single set of high-quality global standards and created, in the IASB, a means of achieving it. That vision has yet to be realized. But IASC lit a beacon on a path that the IASB is following—a path that I and my fellow Board members are convinced will, ultimately, lead to achievement of the objective set by IASC's founders.

We are all grateful to Professors Camfferman and Zeff for their scholarship, insight and sheer hard work in producing such a fine history of a unique organization.

Sir David Tweedie
Chairman, International Accounting Standards Board

Preface

In response to a commission from the International Accounting Standards Board (IASB) in December 2002, we began working on a major history of its predecessor body, the International Accounting Standards Committee (IASC), from 1973 to 2000. The IASB reimbursed us for our travel costs and sundry expenses, while allowing us complete editorial freedom in design and execution of the research project.

The book is intended to be of interest to all who are participants or observers of the development and application of International Financial Reporting Standards: accounting practitioners, capital market regulators, company financial executives, financial journalists, students, and academics. We discuss not only the development of the IASC's standards but also the increasing maturity of the IASC and the economic and regulatory forces that impinged on its work and productivity. In the final analysis, history is about people, and this book is no exception.

We owe a debt of gratitude to the IASB for generously providing us with office facilities and enabling us to make use of its extensive archive of IASC materials. The Koninklijk Nederlands Instituut van Registeraccountants, in Amsterdam, the Institute of Chartered Accountants of Scotland, in Edinburgh, and the Canadian Institute of Chartered Accountants, in Toronto, allowed us to use their valuable collections of files. The Institute of Chartered Accountants in England and Wales, in London, kindly enabled us to use its library's collections of serials. The Japanese Institute of Certified Public Accountants provided a major service in facilitating the series of interviews in Tokyo.

We wish to acknowledge the substantial assistance provided by our universities, the Vrije Universiteit and Rice University.

We are deeply grateful to our many interviewees and to those who commented on various drafts. In addition, we are indebted to many organizations and people who assisted us in a variety of ways, including data collection, retrieving documents, and establishing contact with interviewees. Foremost among those who assisted us is David Cairns, who provided numerous documents from his extensive personal files, participated in two lengthy interviews, commented in detail on drafts, and responded cheerfully to a great many requests for additional information and insights.

We, as authors, are solely responsible for this work.

Kees Camfferman
Stephen A. Zeff

List of Abbreviations

AARF	Australian Accounting Research Foundation
AASB	Australian Accounting Standards Board
AcSB	Accounting Standards Board (Canada)
AICPA	American Institute of Certified Public Accountants (United States)
AIMR	Association for Investment Management and Research
AISG	Accountants International Study Group
AP	Agenda Paper (in references to IASC archival sources)
APB	(1) Accounting Principles Board (United States)
	(2) Accounting Practices Board (South Africa)
APC	Accounting Practices Committee (South Africa)
ASB	Accounting Standards Board (United Kingdom)
ASC	Accounting Standards Committee (United Kingdom), from 1976 onwards
ASSC	Accounting Standards Steering Committee (United Kingdom), until 1976
ASX	Australian Stock Exchange
BADC	Business Accounting Deliberation Council (Japan)
CAR	Council on Annual Reporting (the Netherlands)
CCAB	Consultative Committee of Accountancy Bodies (United Kingdom)
CGAA	Certified General Accountants' Association (Canada)
CICA	Canadian Institute of Chartered Accountants
CNC	Conseil National de la Comptabilité (France)
COB	Commission des Opérations de Bourse (France)
Consob	Commissione Nazionale per le Società e la Borsa (Italy)
CPA	Certified Public Accountant
CRC	Comité de la Réglementation Comptable (France)
E	Exposure draft, of the IASC (followed by number)
ED	Exposure draft, of the ASC or the AARF (followed by number)
EEC	European Economic Community
EU	European Union
FAF	Financial Accounting Foundation (overseeing the FASB)
FAS	(Statement of) Financial Accounting Standards (United States)
FASB	Financial Accounting Standards Board (United States)
FEE	Fédération des Experts Comptables Européens
FEI	Financial Executives Institute (United States)
FIBV	Fédération Internationale des Bourses de Valeurs

FIFO	First-in, first-out (inventory flow)
FRED	Financial Reporting Exposure Draft (of the ASB)
FRS	Financial Reporting Standard (of the ASB)
FSA	Financial Services Authority (United Kingdom)
FSR	Foreningen af Statsautoriserede Revisorer (Denmark)
GAAP	(1) Generally Accepted Accounting Principles (United States) (2) Generally Accepted Accounting Practice (United Kingdom and some other countries)
HGB	Handelsgesetzbuch (Commercial Code, Germany)
IAFEI	International Association of Financial Executives Institutes
IAS	International Accounting Standard(s)
IASB	International Accounting Standards Board (successor to IASC)
IASC	International Accounting Standards Committee
ICAA	Institute of Chartered Accountants in Australia
ICAEW	Institute of Chartered Accountants in England and Wales
ICAI	(1) Institute of Chartered Accountants in Ireland (2) Institute of Chartered Accountants of India
ICANZ	Institute of Chartered Accountants of New Zealand
ICAS	Institute of Chartered Accountants of Scotland
ICC	International Chamber of Commerce
ICCAP	International Co-ordination Committee for the Accountancy Profession (1972–7)
ICCFAA	International Co-ordinating Committee of Financial Analysts' Associations
IdW	Institut der Wirtschaftsprüfer in Deutschland (German Institute of Auditors)
IFAC	International Federation of Accountants
IMA	Institute of Management Accountants (United States)
IOSCO	International Organization of Securities Commissions
ISAR	Intergovernmental Working Group of Experts on International Standards of Accounting and Reporting (United Nations/Unctad)
IWP	International Working Party (of accountancy bodies, 1967–72)
JICPA	Japanese Institute of Certified Public Accountants
JWG	Joint Working Group (of standard setters on financial instruments, 1997–2000)
JWP	Joint Working Party (of IASC and IFAC, 1977–82)
LIFO	Last-in, first-out (inventory flow)
NAA	National Association of Accountants (United States)
NASB	(1) Nigerian Accounting Standards Board (2) Norwegian Accounting Standards Board

NIVRA	Nederlands Instituut van Registeraccountants (Netherlands Institute of Registered Auditors)
NYSE	New York Stock Exchange
OECD	Organisation for Economic Co-operation and Development
OPC	Organisation and Planning Committee (of the IASC)
OSC	Ontario Securities Commission (Canada)
PCG	Plan Comptable Général (France)
PSASB	Public Sector Accounting Standards Board (Australia)
SAICA	South African Institute of Chartered Accountants
SDC	Standards Development Committee (as proposed by the IASC's Strategy Working Party, 1997–9)
SEC	Securities and Exchange Commission (United States)
SIC	Standing Interpretations Committee (of the IASC)
SIB	Securities and Investment Board (United Kingdom)
SFAC	Statement of Financial Accounting Concepts (United States)
SMAC	Society of Management Accountants of Canada
SSAP	Statement of Standard Accounting Practice (United Kingdom)
SWP	Strategy Working Party (of the IASC, 1997–9)
TSG	Tripartite Study Group (the Netherlands)
UEC	Union Européenne des Experts Comptables Économiques et Financiers
UN	United Nations
WP1	Working Party No. 1 (of IOSCO)

1

Introduction and Overview

The formation of the International Accounting Standards Committee (IASC) in 1973 was the organized accountancy profession's most important and enduring response to the growing internationalization of capital markets following the Second World War. It was an ambitious private-sector initiative whose members performed as part-time standard setters in addition to their full-time jobs as partners in accountancy firms, company financial executives, university academics, and staff members of accountancy bodies.

The IASC was the brain child of Sir Henry Benson, one of the leading lights of the British accountancy profession. With the rise of multinational enterprise in the 1960s and the consequent need to compare financial statements from different parts of the world, he realized that an effort had to be launched to harmonize the vastly different accounting practices across countries. The resourceful and determined Benson secured the support of the principal accountancy bodies in Australia, Canada, France, Germany, Japan, Mexico, the Netherlands, the United Kingdom, and the United States to establish a body that would narrow the differences across national accounting standards.

The IASC's office was established in London, and the funding provided by the participating accountancy bodies was sufficient to secure a skeletal staff consisting of a secretary, an assistant secretary, and a typist.

From this meagre beginning, the IASC began issuing a series of mostly flexible accounting standards, which, in its formative years, were taken more seriously in developing than developed countries. But as the pace of globalization picked up in the 1980s and especially in the 1990s, the IASC, with strong encouragement from major securities market regulators, began improving its standards to a level of quality that commanded the attention and respect of national and regional regulators, national standard setters, major multinational companies, and leading accountancy bodies. Finally, in 1999–2000, the IASC restructured itself under the eventual name of International Accounting Standards Board (IASB), a body with mostly full-time members and a considerably larger staff. The IASB enjoys the international recognition and acceptance which the IASC had earned, and today it sets International Financial Reporting Standards for private-sector enterprise around the world.

In our view, an understanding of the functioning and impact of the IASB and its standards can be enhanced through an appreciation of what has gone before. Some of the most vexing problems relating to the IASB's standards and structure can be traced back to similar questions raised in the 1990s and before. Those who interact with the IASB, or researchers who wish to study aspects of the IASB's work and impact, can clearly benefit by coming to appreciate how the IASC faced and resolved comparable challenges.

It is our aim in this book to tell the story of the formation and evolution of the IASC from 1973 to 2000. In this introductory chapter, we first describe the approach we have taken to study and present the IASC's history. Secondly, this chapter provides an overview and synthesis of the major ideas, trends, and developments, keyed to the respective chapters in which they are treated in depth.

1.1. APPROACH

Our intention in writing this book has been to present a general history of the IASC, that is, a history covering the origin, work, and impact of the IASC, as well as the forces that shaped the IASC and its mission. We have been interested not in pure chronology but in a balanced and well-documented study of the causes and effects of the IASC's evolution and of its increasing role on the world stage, as well as the motivations of its leading figures. In designing and carrying out our study, we have endeavoured to be sensitive to the ever-changing economic, political, and regulatory environments, nationally as well as internationally.

Even those who want to write general histories bring certain assumptions to their work, and we are no exception. Our main premise, which is implicit throughout the book, is that we accept the IASC's stated purpose of setting accounting standards in the public interest. In other words, we take it as given that a high standard of accounting and financial reporting is an important factor in the proper functioning of capital markets and in strong corporate governance. Because of the complexity and changing nature of business, and because interested parties can have real but conflicting interests in selecting accounting policies, 'high quality accounting' is a somewhat elusive concept. A consensus on what accounting ought to be is typically slow to emerge. Accounting standards have the potential to contribute significantly to an improved quality of financial reporting by playing an educational role, by encouraging the resolution of differences of view through discussion and debate, and by imposing a more or less arbitrary but nevertheless useful consistency in treatment in cases where a consensus has not yet emerged.

Our understanding of the history of the IASC is that it was this public-interest perspective which motivated many of those who were the most active in its standard setting. There was always more than a tinge of idealism about the IASC which, in our view, should be considered in any evaluation of the body. This provided part of the drive to keep going, first during the 1970s and 1980s, when the IASC produced little perceptible impact and was treated with condescension by some national standard setters and other participants in the accounting process, and subsequently during the 1990s, when success seemed to be within its grasp but only after completion of a grinding work programme.

Another factor that shaped our approach, and therefore should be acknowledged at the outset, is that our writing is inevitably coloured by our Dutch and

US backgrounds, in particular our grounding in the financial reporting traditions of our home countries. We are conscious of at least one area where this has had some effect on our writing. Some readers may notice our implicit approval of the overall direction in which the IASC's standards evolved, especially during the 1990s. Clearly, our task in writing this book has been to understand rather than to endorse, and even if it were the latter, we would, with many other people, be able to find fault with numerous specific elements of the IASC's technical output. Nevertheless, we cannot help believing that the IASC's standards generally developed in the right direction, and we think it is proper to point that out here.

Although our combined European and North American backgrounds helped us to appreciate a wider range of perspectives than either of us could have managed alone, we could never hope to understand in depth all of the national backgrounds of the participants in the IASC. As a result of our linguistic limitations, our discussion of the roles of the English-speaking countries and of France, Germany, and the Netherlands is better developed than that of other countries. However, the fact that throughout the book we focus in particular on the United Kingdom and the United States is not merely a question of the abundance and accessibility of sources from those countries, but primarily because, in our view, these two countries were in fact of primary importance.

The IASC had both a technical and a political dimension. A large part of its energy was absorbed by the discussion of technical accounting issues, but there was always an awareness of the need to ensure that the IASC's output, and indeed the IASC itself, found and maintained its place in the wider world. We have noted that former IASC delegates tended to classify their colleagues in terms of 'technicians' and 'politicians', as well as the rare individuals who excelled in both domains. In our book, we have attempted to do justice to both aspects. This posed a challenge in how to treat the IASC's process for resolving the technical issues. We decided not to limit ourselves to generalized statements on the standard-setting process, but to discuss each of the technical projects on its own merits. In our view, an understanding of the IASC cannot be achieved without an appreciation of what its members spent most of their time talking about, and of the rich variety of factors that influenced the IASC's work. For that reason, readers without a background in accounting should not be deterred from reading the approximate one-third of the book (Chapters 5, 9, and 11) which deals with the standard-setting process. When discussing each of the board's many projects, we have endeavoured to focus on the essential ideas and controversies without burdening the reader with dizzying detail.

We have researched the IASC's history by drawing on a wide array of source materials. We have studied the extensive archive of drafts, correspondence, and internal communications currently housed in the office of the IASB in London. We have also examined archival materials in those few accountancy bodies that have both preserved their records and made them available to us, notably the Koninklijk Nederlands Instituut van Registeraccountants in Amsterdam, the Institute of Chartered Accountants of Scotland in Edinburgh, and the Canadian Institute of Chartered Accountants (CICA) in Toronto. While we devote a considerable portion of our book to the interaction over a long time between the IASC and the International Organization of Securities Commissions (IOSCO), we were not permitted to see the minutes of IOSCO's working parties and committees or other documents that were not on the public record. We overcame this restriction by arranging interviews with key participants in the work of IOSCO.

More generally, we have created our own research database by conducting more than 135 interviews around the world. A list of interviewees is included as Appendix 6. Most of the interviewees were members of one or more of the IASC's board, steering committees, working parties, Consultative Group, Advisory Council, and Strategy Working Party, or who served on its support staff. We also interviewed or solicited the views of many individuals who dealt with the IASC on behalf of such bodies as Canada's Ontario Securities Commission, France's Commission des Opérations de Bourse, the US Securities and Exchange Commission (SEC), the European Commission, the World Bank, the Australian, London, and New York Stock Exchanges, the International Federation of Accountants (IFAC), the Fédération des Experts Comptables Européens (FEE), the Union Européenne des Experts Comptables, Economiques et Financiers (UEC), and the US Financial Accounting Standards Board (FASB).

In many cases, we contacted our interviewees following the interview to provide clarification or to answer additional questions. Some were interviewed a second or third time. Almost all interviews were recorded and transcribed. The interviews were typically conducted on the basis of confidentiality, which means in practice that we tend to refer to interviews mainly to support relatively straightforward factual statements for which no documentary evidence is available. In instances when we drew more substantively on the interviews in our writing, we obtained the interviewee's express permission to do so. Yet the significance of the interviews has been greater than would be suggested by the frequency of the references in the notes. The interviews have played a crucial role in helping us judge causes and effects, in the selection of material to discuss, and in identifying the issues and events that really mattered.

We exposed drafts of our manuscript to numerous of our interviewees and others for comment. In addition, we have drawn on the published literature, both professional and academic, in English, French, German, Dutch, and Spanish, and we arranged for translations of selected writings in Japanese and Italian. For the benefit of scholars, we have been generous in citing our unpublished and published sources as well as in supplying collateral reference materials of possible interest.

1.2. OVERVIEW

As indicated above, the history of the IASC is complex, because it was connected with the development of financial reporting in at least a dozen key countries and in many other countries as well. The IASC interacted with the accountancy bodies which made up its membership (known as its member bodies), with national standard setters, with securities market regulators, and with organizations like IFAC, the United Nations (UN), the Organisation for Economic Co-operation and Development (OECD), and the European Commission. This means that, at any time, the IASC was involved in a multiplicity of 'story lines', of which some were more technical, and others more political. In this book, we have chosen to emphasize the individual story lines. To do so, we have divided the book in three main parts. Part I deals with the antecedents and the founding of the IASC. Part II takes up the history to 1987, and Part III covers the period from 1987 to the winding up of the IASC. The year 1987 represents a turning point in the IASC's history for several reasons. The most important was the emergence of IOSCO and its growing impact on the work of the IASC. Another was the board's strategic decision to begin ridding its standards of as many optional accounting treatments as practicable and therefore to increase the usefulness of its standards.

Within Parts II and III, the individual chapters have a thematic focus, dealing separately with organizational issues, the technical standard-setting work, the impact of the IASC in various countries, and its relationships with other organizations. Inevitably, this means that each of the chapters provides only a partial view of the IASC during that period. We have attempted to assist the reader to arrive at a more general understanding by the inclusion of cross-references among the chapters.

1.2.1. The Antecedents and Founding of the IASC

The key to understanding the IASC prior to 1987 is to recognize its close connection with the accountancy profession. It was an initiative taken by national accountancy bodies, it was almost exclusively composed of accountants, and its modest impact on practice reflected the limited power of the accountancy profession in most countries to impose accounting standards on reporting companies.

Chapter 2 shows how internationalism gripped the accountancy profession, or at least its leadership, in a number of countries during the 1960s. Accounting practice differed significantly around the world, and professional leaders began to express the view that enhanced cooperation among accountancy bodies was a necessary first step to narrowing the international differences in accounting practice. The necessity for narrowing the differences was demonstrated by references to the growth of international trade and investment in the post-war period, and the consequent needs of investors and other users for comparable financial information. Yet, while international economic integration was clearly important during the 1950s and 1960s, it does not appear that investors and other users were putting much pressure on the accountancy profession to deal with the consequences. It was mainly on the initiative of the accountancy profession itself that several attempts at international cooperation among accountants were made. The IASC was the most successful of these ventures. In Europe, the Americas, and the Asia-Pacific region, regional bodies of accountancy institutes had been set up. The UEC, the regional European body, made a half-hearted attempt to develop accounting standards. From the late 1960s onwards, there were moves towards establishing a worldwide organization to represent accountancy bodies, finally resulting in the formation of IFAC in 1977.

The initiative that can be seen as the direct precursor of the IASC was the establishment of the Accountants International Study Group (AISG) in 1966, set up to collate information about accounting practice in three countries—Canada, the United Kingdom, and the United States—as well as make useful comparisons and point towards desirable avenues of improvement. The Study Group's series of informational booklets represented the first programme of continuing cooperation between accountancy bodies in the three countries. The driving force behind the formation of the Study Group was Henry Benson, the president of the Institute of Chartered Accountants in England and Wales (ICAEW).

The Study Group's publications were not intended as binding on anyone; so the next logical step was to form a body possessing greater authority to shape best accounting practice around the world. In the United Kingdom and Ireland, the idea of issuing such guidance under the rubric of 'accounting standards' had led to the establishment of a 'standard-setting' body in 1970. In May 1972 in the United States, the American Institute of Certified Public Accountants (AICPA) endorsed the creation of an independent FASB to replace its Accounting Principles Board. In this climate, Benson (by then Sir Henry Benson) envisaged the creation of a similar standard-setting body at the international level, including a broader array of countries than the Study Group. In 1972–3, the ICAEW invited a selection of leading national accountancy bodies in nine countries to found the IASC. The countries were Australia, Canada, France, Germany, Japan, Mexico, the Netherlands, the United Kingdom and Ireland (counted as one country), and the United States. Benson installed himself as the IASC's first chairman and quickly became the indispensable leader in its early development.

The founding of the IASC is treated in Chapter 3, which shows that very little persuasion was required to induce the invited bodies to join. Despite the considerable cost of membership, none wanted to be left out, although there was the inevitable discussion about the structure and authority of the new body. Defining the relationship between the IASC and the nascent IFAC was particularly controversial, and it was effectively deferred for later consideration.

1.2.2. The IASC to 1987

Part II of the book discusses the IASC's organization (Chapter 4), its standard-setting process and the contents of its standards (Chapter 5), the impact of its standards in countries around the world (Chapter 6), and its relationship with other organizations, including IFAC, the UN, and the OECD (Chapter 7). These themes were related in the following way.

In regard to organization, the IASC's support staff was tiny to begin with and did not really grow during this period. Initially all the members of its technical staff served for short periods on the basis of secondment, but in 1984 a permanent secretary-general was appointed. The significance of this change was not immediately apparent, because the first secretary-general, Geoffrey Mitchell, stayed on for just one year after his initial two years as a seconded secretary. The next secretary-general, David Cairns, remained at his post for almost ten years, from April 1985 to December 1994, and became almost the embodiment of the IASC. Nevertheless, for most of the time before 1987, the main organizational feature of the IASC was the committee itself (known as the board after 1977, and referred to as such in the remainder of this chapter), on which the founding national accountancy bodies were represented in nine delegations of three members each. Generally speaking, the member bodies took their responsibilities seriously, and they dispatched senior and highly competent people to compose their delegations. The chairmen succeeding Benson—until 1987 these were Joseph Cummings (United States), John Hepworth (Australia), Hans Burggraaff (the Netherlands), Stephen Elliott (Canada), and John Kirkpatrick (United Kingdom)—had all held leadership positions in their national professions. Nevertheless, the IASC's collective expertise was not a sufficient answer to the question of how the member bodies, none of which (but the CICA) had regulatory power over financial reporting in their home countries, could secure companies' compliance with IASC standards. At the time of the founding of the IASC, this question was probably not acutely felt, because most of those involved seemed to accept Benson's characterization that accounting harmonization was 'an urgent international need'. If so, all that was needed was a supply of international accounting standards, and compliance would almost take care of itself. Yet it soon became clear that this was not the case, and that none of the member bodies was willing, let alone able, to insist on compliance with the IASC's standards as a condition for an unqualified audit opinion.

The result was that, prior to 1987, there were very few listed companies in the home countries of the founder member bodies which referred to the IASC's standards in their annual reports. Any illusions the board members may have had regarding the worldwide status of the IASC's standards were dispelled by a series of surveys which clearly revealed the IASC's lack of progress in securing adherence. By 1980, it was clear that the IASC faced a serious compliance problem, despite numerous initiatives undertaken by the IASC's successive chairmen and secretaries to promote the IASC's standards in countries around the world. In the first part of the 1980s, Canada was a major exception, as the CICA managed to persuade a significant number of companies to refer to IASC standards in their annual reports to shareholders. Indeed, the Canadian delegation to the board, and especially the CICA, were the most enthusiastic supporters of the work of the IASC, from the beginning to the end of the board's tenure.

Compliance was a problem for the IASC, but not because its early standards were very demanding. The IASC's Canadian success must be judged in the light of the fact that most companies satisfying Canadian 'generally accepted accounting principles' (GAAP) would not have to make a major effort to comply with IASC standards as well. According to its founding Constitution, the IASC was set up to issue 'basic' accounting standards. This meant, for one thing, that the twenty-six standards issued until 1987 dealt mainly with topics that were common to most enterprises, such as accounting for inventories, depreciation, income tax, or revenue. With a few exceptions, the IASC did not attempt to issue industry standards. The standards were also basic in the sense that the board tacitly agreed on an approach to standard setting that would not make adoption too difficult. The IASC's pre-1987 standards were based on the principle that accounting practices widely seen as unacceptable should be prohibited, but that the standards did not necessarily have to prescribe a single accounting treatment for each topic. Most standards allowed a choice among two or more treatments, and so were compatible with national requirements or majority practice in the home countries of all the founder members who actively sought to ensure such compatibility. This approach exposed the IASC to the charge that it was seeking the lowest common denominator. It is true that most of the early standards contained little that was new for countries with the most developed national requirements. Yet, for most board member countries, full compliance with IASC standards would have brought about at least some improvements in accounting practice.

The original IASC was the exclusive preserve of accountancy bodies. Its membership was limited to a 'closed shop' of founder members, whose selection was agreed after some bargaining between the ICAEW and the AICPA. The original Constitution opened the possibility of associate membership, and scores of accountancy bodies joined as associate members. This entitled them to a degree of participation in the work of the IASC, particularly through membership of the steering committees which prepared the draft standards as input for the board's deliberations. Some of these associate members resented their exclusion from full membership, particularly when they believed that their secondary status was based on a perception of inferior professional standards. As it happened, the IASC's more notable early successes were scored in some of the countries represented by associate members, rather than in the founder member countries. For developing countries that lacked the capacity to develop their own standards, the IASC's output was a convenient resource. In 1978, the IASC reduced its exclusivity by modestly expanding and diversifying the membership on its board. In that year, delegations arrived from Nigeria and South Africa, increasing the number of seats from nine to eleven.

IFAC came into being in 1977. Several of the accountancy bodies which were excluded from full IASC membership played important roles in IFAC, and this was one of the reasons why there was constant pressure from IFAC for closer integration, or even a merger of the IASC into IFAC. This was, however, resisted by the IASC. One of the reasons was simply the desire of the founder members to retain control. Another was the view that the IASC might secure a higher degree of compliance with its standards if it were to expand its membership beyond accountancy bodies to include ones representing the preparers and users of financial statements. A merger with IFAC, on the other hand, would mark out the IASC even more clearly as an organization of accountants. The advocates of wider membership could point to serious challenges to the IASC coming from the UN and the OECD. By the late 1970s, both the UN and the OECD had begun to involve themselves with financial reporting by multinational enterprises. Within both organizations, it was argued that the IASC lacked legitimacy because it represented only accountants, and that international accounting standards had to be set by an intergovernmental body. Even though it was never very likely that such an intergovernmental body might be created, the mere discussion of it encouraged the IASC to reconsider its organization and membership.

Under the leadership of Chairman Hans Burggraaff and Secretary Allan Cook, the various pressures on the IASC were resolved in a series of negotiated agreements enshrined in the IASC's Constitution as revised in 1982. IFAC and the IASC remained formally independent organizations, but a pact of so-called Mutual Commitments gave IFAC certain rights over the appointment of IASC board members. The number of seats for accountancy bodies was increased by another two to thirteen. The founder members gave up the right to their permanent seats but were effectively assured of reappointment. IFAC and the IASC declared their intention to increase the number of delegations from developing countries. In addition, up to four seats were reserved for other organizations 'having an interest in financial reporting'. In 1983 and 1984, delegations from Italy and Taiwan, respectively, were seated at the board. In 1986, a delegation composed entirely of financial analysts was appointed to the board. A further exposure of the IASC's work to interested parties beyond the accountancy profession was the creation of a Consultative Group in 1981, on which a broad and ever-widening range of organizations, such as the World Bank and the International Chamber of Commerce, was represented.

These changes were sufficient to free the IASC from significant pressure from IFAC, the UN, and the OECD, but not sufficient to ensure widespread compliance with its standards. By 1987, the IASC was ready to embark on a new course. Instead of relying on voluntary adoption of basic standards allowing optional treatments, it changed its approach to standard setting in a way to gain the support of securities market regulators in countries with well-developed capital markets.

1.2.3. The IASC from 1987 to 2000

Part III of the book is again divided into thematic chapters, covering the IASC's organization (Chapter 8), its standards (Chapters 9 and 11), its relations with the outside world and its impact (Chapters 10 and 12), and, finally, its restructuring into the IASB (Chapter 13). As in Part II, these themes are intertwined.

In 1987, the IASC was still a body that was not widely known outside the accountancy profession. It had little, if any, impact on accounting practice in the developed world, and some might have said (and indeed some did) that it had become introverted or even sleepy. Yet within and without the IASC a number of developments were gaining momentum.

Most importantly, the internationalization of capital markets was accelerating. As a result, the demand for international accounting standards finally acquired some of the urgency which had been postulated rather than proven when the

IASC was founded in 1973. In 1987, the IASC established contact with IOSCO, which was just emerging as a force in the world of securities market regulators. The IASC and IOSCO reached an understanding that, if the IASC were to improve its standards to an acceptable level of quality, IOSCO's member bodies would consider endorsing the IASC's standards as the basis for reporting by foreign companies seeking stock exchange listings in their jurisdictions. This promised, at long last, authoritative recognition for the IASC's standards.

The understanding with IOSCO came at a time when the IASC itself was already reconsidering its approach to standard setting. Since 1982, the IASC had been reviewing its earlier standards, and it had very tentatively embarked on a project to develop a conceptual framework to guide its standard-setting work. Some delegations were initially reluctant to support these initiatives, and by 1987 few standards had been revised and no conceptual framework documents had been published. Yet, at a pivotal meeting in March 1987 in Sydney, the board reached the conclusion that the IASC's original approach had run its course and that it was time for a change. The board decided to move ahead full speed towards completing its conceptual framework, as well as to launch a major 'Comparability project' to reduce the number of options in the existing standards.

Although the Comparability project emerged from within the IASC itself, the Holy Grail of IOSCO endorsement quickly became its main driver. Within IOSCO, the powerful US securities regulator, the SEC, held a dominant position because of the importance of the US capital market and the SEC's enormous size and reputation. What mattered to the IASC was that the most vociferous demand for international accounting harmonization stemmed from non-US companies seeking a stock exchange listing in the United States. Unlike the situation in the European Union, for instance, where the 'mutual recognition' of financial reporting practice was already well established, the SEC required all foreign registrants to file financial statements prepared in accordance with the challenging norms of US generally accepted accounting principles (US GAAP) or to provide at least a reconciliation of earnings and shareholders' equity to US GAAP. In the view of the IASC, the endorsement of its standards by IOSCO would be tantamount to the SEC dropping its reconciliation requirement for IASC standards.

As it soon became clear that endorsement by the SEC and the other members of IOSCO would require more than just the elimination of options, the Comparability project was shortly succeeded by an 'Improvements' project, which greatly broadened the scope of the board's review of its previously issued standards. This resulted in a major revision of ten of the IASC's standards by the end of 1993. However, the IASC was severely disappointed when IOSCO informed it in 1994 that it was not prepared to endorse the revised standards, both because of specific objections and because it wanted to act on the IASC's standards as a comprehensive set, rather than on a piecemeal basis. This was a troubling issue, because several important elements were still missing from the set of IASC standards. The most important gap was a standard on financial instruments. The IASC had begun work on this topic as far back as 1988, but by 1994 the project had virtually run aground with no solution in sight.

Despite this disappointment, the relations with IOSCO had by the middle of the 1990s already brought about a considerable change in the IASC's fortunes, as well as in its mode of operation. The IASC began to be taken more seriously by national accounting standard setters, companies, and governments in the developed world. Several national standard setters in Europe adopted a policy of incorporating IASC standards in their national standards, albeit typically with a proviso such as 'to the extent possible'. The FASB began to express concern that it might be constrained in its own standard setting by the IASC's work on new topics, particularly financial instruments. Leading companies in France, Germany, and Switzerland embraced the IASC's standards. In some European countries, IASC standards began to be seen as the only realistic hope of ever gaining access to the US capital markets without adopting, or reconciling to, US GAAP. Even the European Commission, which had traditionally been very cool towards the IASC, recognized that there was little future for a European programme of accounting harmonization. It shifted to a position of supporting the IASC, if only to prevent a de facto worldwide accounting harmonization on the basis of US GAAP over which Europe would have no influence whatsoever. This latter prospect was by no means unimaginable. In 1993, the German icon Daimler-Benz had become the first German multinational to list on the New York Stock Exchange. Daimler and a number of other major European multinationals adjusted their financial reporting, in different degrees, to US GAAP.

The increased significance of the IASC had its consequences for the way it operated. Until the early 1990s, the preponderance of the delegates was accountancy firm partners, with a sprinkling of financial executives, academics, and officers of professional institutes, comparatively few of whom had standard-setting experience. In the 1990s, the IASC board came to include an enlarged component of financial executives and members of national standard setters. In addition, observer delegations from IOSCO, the US FASB, and the European Commission began to attend board meetings. Two other non-accountant delegations were added to the lone financial analysts' delegation: one representing the Federation of Swiss Industrial Holding Companies, and another from the International Association of Financial Executives Institutes. The effect of all these changes was an increased sophistication of the technical debate, even though the quality of the board's deliberations had never been poor to begin with, as well as a more explicit focus on the practical requirements of the companies that actually applied the standards.

Other implications of the higher stakes were a greater awareness of the need to follow a well-defined due process, greater transparency in the form of open meetings, as well as a more active fund-raising effort. Initially, the IASC had been financed almost entirely by the membership fees of the bodies represented on the board. In addition, a large part of the actual costs of the IASC was borne by the member bodies and the accountancy firms. These paid for the time and some of the travel costs of the people attending board and steering committee meetings, as well as most of the costs of translating and distributing the IASC's standards and exposure drafts. Right until the end, the IASC continued to be an organization resting largely on such 'volunteer' efforts, but from the early 1990s onwards additional funding was raised by actively soliciting donations from companies, business organizations, and financial institutions. To assist in the fund-raising, an Advisory Council was created in which senior business executives and stock exchange representatives from a range of countries were gathered. A more professional approach to publishing and marketing the standards also raised significant amounts of money.

Until the end of 1994, the IASC's technical staff remained very small, consisting mostly of Secretary-General David Cairns and a few people seconded for short periods from accountancy firms. There is no doubt that Cairns's ability and dedication were invaluable to the IASC during this crucial period. His immersion in all aspects of the IASC's work enabled it to achieve much with slender resources. But with the changing composition of the board's membership and the lifting of its sights, the IASC could not continue to rely, in essence, on a single gifted individual. Cairns was succeeded in 1995 by Sir Bryan Carsberg, a senior British civil servant with a strong background in accounting as well as in regulatory circles. He continued as secretary-general until the tenure of the IASC expired. Under Carsberg, the IASC finally acquired a more sizeable technical staff, although it continued to fall short of the requirements of the IASC's ambitious work programme.

Carsberg's entrance onto the stage coincided with the succession of the Australian Michael Sharpe to the chairmanship of the IASC. Sharpe's immediate predecessors—Georges Barthès de Ruyter (France), Arthur Wyatt (United States), and Eiichi Shiratori (Japan)—had each in their different ways served the IASC well. Nevertheless, Sharpe surpassed them in his fervid belief in the cause of international accounting harmonization, and for the next two-and-a-half years, he and Carsberg proved to be a very effective team. Together, they gave the IASC a new sense of direction and drive at a time when it risked faltering in the aftermath of IOSCO's refusal to endorse its standards.

One of their first achievements was to reach a new agreement with IOSCO. According to this agreement, announced in July 1995, the IASC committed itself to complete a specified set of 'core' standards, covering all the major financial statement issues, including accounting for financial instruments. The standards were to be completed according to a tight schedule, ending in 1999. If the IASC could deliver the core standards in time, IOSCO would seriously consider giving its endorsement.

The core standards were essentially completed in December 1998, after three-and-a-half years of work under intense pressure. This was a year before the original target date. In 1996, with encouragement from the SEC, the IASC had decided to accelerate the already fast pace of its core standards programme. For most board delegates, it was a real struggle to combine the gruelling pace of work for the IASC with the senior jobs they held at home. Yet the board and its staff persisted, and they looked back with fondness on the period as one in which the board really became a cohesive unit. Many delegates increasingly felt that their role was no longer one of defending their national customs and practices, but rather that they were working together towards a common goal of great significance.

Despite the time pressure imposed by the core standards agreement, the IASC took its standard setting very seriously. The IASC had left behind its earlier approach of merely eliminating accounting practices at the fringes of acceptability, as in its early days, and the pragmatic elimination of commonly used options, as in the Comparability project. The IASC's conceptual framework, which had been completed in 1989, provided a basis for making principled choices among alternatives, and it led to standards that departed sometimes quite radically from established practice in most developed countries, as opposed to being mere codifications of best practice.

In general, the framework pointed towards a balance-sheet-oriented approach to accounting, in which profits and losses were defined in terms of changes in the values of assets and liabilities. This was quite different from the income-statement-oriented approach that had dominated financial reporting for most of the twentieth century and which consisted essentially of allocating cash flows to accounting periods. Related to this change to a balance-sheet orientation was an increasing reliance on fair values, or market values, as a basis of valuing assets, instead of the traditional historical cost basis. By no means were all board delegations willing to go very far in following the logic of the framework, the balance-sheet approach, and fair value accounting. But some national standard setters, particularly from the English-speaking world, were travelling down the same road on the basis of similar conceptual frameworks. Their increasingly influential representatives in the board, either as members of delegations or as observers, did not tire of reminding the IASC board of the implications of its framework.

Some of the standards of the 1990s were messy compromises, notably IAS 39 on the recognition and measurement of financial instruments. This was a complex mixture of the more traditional and the new approaches, which satisfied very few people. Nevertheless, IAS 39 was approved by a narrow majority as the last of the core standards. Other standards, like IAS 37 on provisions and IAS 41 on agriculture, could more aptly be described as pure specimens of the new approach to financial reporting that was gradually gaining ground around the world.

During this period, the core standards agreement was generally interpreted with considerable optimism. The belief that before long IASC standards would be endorsed by IOSCO, and perhaps even by the SEC, encouraged voluntary adoption of these standards by multinational companies in many countries. In some countries, particularly in Continental Europe, legislation was passed that allowed companies to report on the basis of IASC standards instead of according to national accounting law or national accounting standards. Other countries did not go so far, but their national standard setters adopted policies to align their national accounting standards as much as possible with IASC standards.

However, not all countries embraced IASC standards. Those that did were typically countries without a strong national tradition of accounting regulation, such as Switzerland, or countries which had a strong national tradition, but one which was breaking down under the influence of globalization. The prime example of the latter category is Germany, where an elaborate but strictly national approach to financial reporting had evolved, based on a link between financial reporting and taxation and an important role for accounting in terms of company law but a limited role in public capital markets. With the advent of an internationally oriented public capital market and the concomitant demand for much more informative financial reporting to investors, the German system was opened up in 1998 to allow all listed companies to report on the basis of IASC standards as well as according to US GAAP.

A few countries, above all the United Kingdom and the United States, but also Australia and Canada, had strong national standard setters in the same capital market-oriented tradition as the IASC. These countries were far less, or not at all, inclined to grant the IASC an equivalent position to its national standard setter. In 1993, the standard setters from these four countries began to form a group to hold informal meetings to discuss solutions to contemporary accounting issues, and quickly found that their common conceptual outlook made their cooperation very effective. The participating standard setters issued a series of jointly published, but not jointly written, discussion papers on important accounting issues, generally acknowledged to be of a high quality, and which tended to advocate the above-mentioned shift towards a balance-sheet-oriented fair value model of financial accounting.

The group became known as the G4, or as the G4+1 when the IASC was allowed to attend its meetings. This was in deference to the moral obligation of the IASC's member bodies from these countries, though strictly speaking not of their standard setters, to keep the IASC's other member bodies informed of international initiatives in the area of financial reporting. Despite the IASC's representation at G4+1 meetings, typically by Secretary-General Carsberg, there was some resentment and suspicion of the G4+1 in the IASC board. Resentment, because the cooperation in the G4+1 increased their representatives' dominance of the IASC board meetings, and suspicion, because some believed that the G4+1 would not remain content to issue discussion papers, but would in effect become an international standard setter that could supplant the IASC.

Whether or not the G4+1 members harboured any such designs, it became clear by 1996 that a reconsideration of the relationship between the IASC and these influential national standard setters was in order. The objective of international harmonization required their cooperation. But it was unlikely that, in the long run, the most effective approach was for them to participate simply as members of national delegations (as the Australian, Canadian, and UK standard setters), or as observers to board meetings (as the FASB). None of them would ultimately be willing to harmonize their national standards with those issued by a board in which they were a small minority, particularly not if they had doubts about either the technical ability of other members or their commitment to set standards on the basis of conceptual soundness rather than political expediency. In addition, the IASC had to consider what would happen after the completion of the core standards. It was becoming clearer that IOSCO, and the SEC in particular, might not be willing to endorse the standards if it had misgivings about the quality of the IASC's due process as the world standard setter of the future. During 1995 and 1996, certain members of the FASB had publicly and repeatedly criticized the IASC's working methods. Although the SEC had not made any comparable public statements, the IASC was aware that it shared to some extent the FASB's concerns.

For these reasons, the IASC board decided in September 1996 to install a heavyweight Strategy Working Party (SWP) with a broadly worded charge to come up with recommendations for the IASC's future strategy and structure. Throughout 1997 and 1998 the SWP, ably chaired by Edward J. Waitzer (former chairman of Canada's Ontario Securities Commission), wrestled with the problem of how to reconcile technical expertise with representativeness. The national standard setters, that is, those who formed the G4+1, argued for a dominant role for their members in a restructured IASC. Most of the IASC member bodies, as well as national governments of non-G4 countries and the European Commission, argued that they would be unwilling to accept the IASC's standards if they were excluded from any meaningful role in their formulation. At the end of 1998, the SWP produced a proposal for a two-tier body with a delicately balanced representative board, like the old IASC board, and a Standards Development Committee consisting mainly of standard-setter representatives. The heavily compromised proposal pleased few people. To right the ship, IASC Chairman Stig Enevoldsen (representing the Nordic Federation of Public Accountants), who had succeeded Sharpe as board chairman in 1998, and Secretary-General Carsberg became involved in tense negotiations throughout 1999 with stakeholders in the board's future, mostly parallel to the deliberations actually going on in the SWP. The SEC played an increasingly active role in these negotiations, and it did not disguise the brute fact that it would insist on a restructuring based on an 'independent expert model', in fact a model very much like that of the FASB. The IASC member bodies accepted—although some only reluctantly—that the IASC would have to be cut loose from the accountancy profession, and a degree of consensus emerged around a model of a relatively small group of experts, appointed by independent trustees. Towards the end of the year, the main unresolved difficulty was whether the group of experts should be geographically balanced and whether they should all be full-time, or a mix of full-time and part-time, members of the standard-setting body. Both a geographical spread and part-time membership could be seen as introducing a greater degree of representation on the board of the IASC's main constituents.

These issues were dramatically resolved at the IASC board meeting of November 1999 in Venice. During the meeting, the IASC's executive committee, together with the secretary-general, overturned the objections of those who argued for a larger, mostly part-time board attuned to geographical representation. Believing that the IASC could not become a viable standard setter on the world stage without the support of the SEC, the executive committee decided to resolve the impasse by inviting the SEC to state its terms. The result was a proposal for an independent board without any prescribed geographical representation and with only a small minority of part-time members, two out of fourteen. A degree of representativeness was provided at the level of the trustees, who would appoint the board members, and who would themselves be appointed by co-optation. This proposal was presented to the IASC board as a non-negotiable recommendation which it could either accept or reject. Realizing that there would be little point in continuing the IASC without SEC support, the board voted unanimously in favour of the proposal. As a result, the IASC was replaced by the IASB in 2001. In December 2000 the IASC board held its last meeting, presided over by Thomas Jones (from the financial executives delegation) who had succeeded Enevoldsen as an interim chairman when the latter's term ended in June 2000.

In May 2000, a few months after the IASC board had taken its fateful decision on its restructuring, IOSCO announced its long-awaited decision to endorse the IASC's core standards. In fact, the endorsement was less than full-throated, as it allowed IOSCO's members to require 'supplementary treatments' such as a reconciliation to national standards and the imposition of additional disclosures and interpretive detail. These were already part of the SEC's arsenal for dealing with foreign companies that did not use US GAAP. So far, the endorsement has not made a difference to the SEC's position on foreign listings, which has led to its characterization as a 'hollow' victory for the IASC. In fact, the SEC had issued a concept release in February 2000 in which it listed formidable conditions relating to the quality of auditing and supervision of compliance in third countries which would have to be met before the SEC could accept financial statements based on IASC standards without a reconciliation to US GAAP.

With nothing more than the heavily conditioned endorsement by IOSCO, the IASC might have seen little more than a bleak future. In most developed countries, US GAAP might easily have become the de facto standard for large enterprises, because of the irresistible pull of US capital markets. But coming on the heels of IOSCO's decision on endorsement, the European Commission unveiled a major initiative of its own in June 2000. It announced a bold proposal to require all listed companies in the European Union to prepare their consolidated financial statements according to IASC standards commencing in 2005. The proposal was breathtaking in its potential impact. IASC standards would have to be adopted by thousands of European companies, rather than being merely an option for the few hundred which had listings outside the European Union. None of the IASC's previous successes in gaining recognition for its standards had even remotely approximated the scale of the Commission's endorsement. The required use of IASC standards in the European Union probably was a major factor in encouraging many other countries, apart from the United States, to take similar measures in the following years, leading to the present position of the IASB as an acknowledged leader, together with the FASB, in the field of financial reporting.

The irony of this outcome is that the IASC was, in the end, raised to prominence by the European Commission, which, at best, had ranked low in the IASC's scale of priorities during the 1990s. Throughout the 1970s and 1980s, the European

Commission had responded with disdain to the IASC's initiatives. Only during the 1990s did the Commission gradually adopt a more supportive attitude, if only to forestall an invasion of US GAAP. By then, however, the IASC was focusing unswervingly on IOSCO, and it largely ignored the European Commission. The Commission was one of the most outspoken opponents of the new structure adopted by the IASC at the end of 1999. Yet the Commission soon afterwards became the new IASB's most important customer.

Part I
Origins

2

Origins of International Accounting Harmonization

2.1. INTERNATIONAL ECONOMIC INTEGRATION AND ACCOUNTING HARMONIZATION

Following the Second World War, a period of rapid growth in international trade and investment set in. It has been estimated that between 1950 and 1965, the value of total external capital movements grew by a factor of between three and four. An increasing share of this expanding capital flow consisted of foreign direct investment, as opposed to portfolio investment. The growth in foreign direct investment was strongly related to the rise of the multinational corporation. By the late 1960s, a great majority of the large multinationals were American or British, which collectively accounted for some four-fifths of the stock of foreign direct investors. However, Japanese and German companies had by that time also become significant overseas investors. And, given their small domestic economies, countries like Switzerland and the Netherlands may not have been so important in absolute terms, but revenues from their foreign direct investment were rather more significant to their economies than they were in the United States and the United Kingdom.[1] The rise of the multinational, and in particular of the US multinational, captured the imagination of many and was both celebrated and feared. In 1967, Jean-Jacques Servan-Schreiber, a leading French journalist, warned Europe in a widely read book that mounting American investment was coming to dominate its economy.[2] American companies were taking over European companies, setting up European headquarters, capitalizing on their flexible organizations and openness to innovation, and empowering their subsidiaries to engage in cross-border trade with far greater ease than their European counterparts. This view was certainly not without a factual basis, although it should be noted that at the same time there was also a steadily expanding reverse stream of European investment in the United States.[3]

Another aspect of international economic integration in the post-war years was the elimination of barriers to trade and investment by the formation of international trading blocs. The most significant developments, at least in the context of this book, occurred in Europe. In 1948, the Benelux Customs Union was formed, embracing Belgium, Luxembourg, and the Netherlands. Three years later, the European Coal and Steel Community (ECSC) was launched. Conceived as an effort to join the production capabilities of France and Germany,[4] it included

Belgium, Luxembourg, the Netherlands, and Italy as well. In 1957, the same six countries signed the Treaty of Rome, forming the European Economic Community (EEC), also known as the Common Market, which built upon the ECSC. And in 1960, seven countries—Austria, Denmark, Norway, Portugal, Sweden, Switzerland, and the United Kingdom—created the European Free Trade Association, as a defensive move. In 1973, the EEC became the dominant group when it was joined by Denmark, Ireland, and the United Kingdom.

The International Accounting Standards Committee (IASC) came into existence against this background of growing cross-border movements of capital, the unique position of the United States in the post-war world economy, and the developing EEC. It was not too difficult to see that economic integration had potential consequences for financial reporting. Although in all developed countries financial reporting had a common basis in double-entry bookkeeping, by the middle of the twentieth century financial reporting practices differed considerably among countries.[5] These differences were related to such factors as company law, company finance, taxation, and the strength of the accountancy profession. Removing such differences through harmonization of accounting would, at least in theory, facilitate international trade and investment. Not only would it be easier for investors to compare the results of companies in different countries, it would also ease the burden on multinational companies which had to prepare financial statements for subsidiaries according to different local regulations.

Yet, at the same time as economic integration made accounting harmonization more urgent, it became more difficult to achieve. A gradual expansion of accounting regulation in many countries gave a clearer outline to hitherto vaguely defined traditions and common practice, thus sharpening international differences in accounting.

The IASC was neither the first nor the only initiative to grapple with the accounting implications of the post-war trend towards international economic integration. From the 1950s to the early 1970s, a number of organizations were set up that preceded or would impinge on the work of the IASC. These initiatives are discussed in this chapter. First, there was the growth of regional accountancy bodies. Second, repeated calls for international uniformity of accounting principles, in particular at the international congresses of accountants, set in motion a train of events leading eventually to the formation of the International Federation of Accountants (IFAC) in 1977. Simultaneously, these calls for uniformity provided the impetus for collaboration among a much smaller group of countries in the Accountants International Study Group (AISG), founded in 1966. This Study Group can be seen as a lineal predecessor of the IASC. It should be noted that all these initiatives, including the IASC, originated within, and were carried out by, the accountancy profession. Simultaneously, there was a movement at governmental level towards harmonization of company law, including accounting, within the EEC. As this European programme of accounting harmonization was to be a significant factor in the IASC's work, its origins are discussed in this chapter as well.

2.2. THE CREATION OF REGIONAL ACCOUNTANCY BODIES

In 1951, accountancy bodies in ten central and southern European countries—Austria, Belgium, France, Germany, Italy, Luxembourg, the Netherlands, Portugal, Spain, and Switzerland—formed the Union Européenne des Experts Comptables Economiques et Financiers (known as the UEC). It held periodic congresses, published a quarterly journal, and sponsored study committees on a wide range of subjects. In 1963, the leading accountancy bodies of Denmark, Ireland, Norway, Sweden, and the United Kingdom as well as two Dutch institutes agreed to join the UEC.[6]

Regional accountancy bodies were also set up in the Americas and Asia, but their activities were mainly limited to holding periodic congresses. The Conferencia Interamericana de Contabilidad (Inter-American Accounting Conference) was founded in 1949 in San Juan, Puerto Rico, and its conferences have been held throughout the Americas every two or three years.[7] As its name implied, its activities largely centred on its conferences. During the 1960s and 1970s, quite a few papers presented at these conferences focused on solutions to accounting for inflation. It was later renamed the Asociación Interamericana de Contabilidad (Inter-American Accounting Association).

In 1957, a Far East Conference of Accountants met in Manila. It was renamed the Conference (and later Confederation) of Asian and Pacific Accountants, and it held gatherings every two or three years throughout the region.[8]

Neither of these two regional bodies undertook to standardize accounting, auditing, or terminology. Yet Washington SyCip, a leader of the Philippines accountancy profession, argued in his opening address at the 1957 conference that 'The gathering of accurate statistics which is so vital to the economic growth of the Far East will be much easier if the accountants in this area can have more uniform standards in the preparation of financial statements.'[9]

Thus, it can be seen that national accountancy bodies were looking beyond their borders, and one of the insistent calls beginning in the late 1950s was for uniformity or harmonization of accounting and auditing practices around the world.

2.3. CALLS FOR UNIFORMITY OF ACCOUNTING STANDARDS

At the Seventh International Congress of Accountants in 1957, held in Amsterdam, the president of the congress, Jacob Kraayenhof, cited the 'divergencies on auditing standards in the various countries' as a problem to be faced.[10] In an address to the AICPA's (American Institute of Certified Public Accountants) annual meeting two years later, he was obviously preoccupied with the implications of the recent founding of the European Common Market, and he repeated this call and argued as well for steps to be taken towards achieving international 'uniformity' of accounting principles.[11] He drew attention to the increasing flow of capital, especially from America into Europe, bringing into focus the disparities between the accounting used by the American parent and by the overseas subsidiaries. He said that 'mergers and amalgamations are effected, in certain cases, at what can be said to be a feverish tempo' and that there was a need for 'comparable data in respect of net equities and results'.[12] He closed his speech by issuing a challenge to the AICPA: to invite other countries to set up standing committees for the research and study of accounting principles with a view towards achieving greater international uniformity.[13] His message may well have registered with some of the leaders of the US accountancy profession. Partners in the big firms were following their major clients overseas, either setting up offices in other countries or forging links with the overseas offices of their international affiliates.

In the early 1960s, Price Waterhouse & Co. felt the need for guidance in how it should attest to 'present fairly' or 'give a true and fair view' when the financial statements of the many foreign subsidiaries to be consolidated with a US or UK parent company had been prepared in accordance with significantly different local accounting norms. The firm invited Professor Gerhard G. Mueller, of the University of Washington, to serve as an International Accounting Research Fellow in the firm's New York City office from June 1962 through August 1964 to assist it in coping with these disparities in national accounting practice. Mueller had completed a Ph.D. thesis at the University of California, Berkeley, in 1961 on the international accounting practices in six European countries.[14]

It was not until 1962 that the US accountancy profession itself adopted a more internationalist view. Although the AICPA was a founder member of the Inter-American Accounting Conference, the US profession had remained largely parochial.[15] In a book published in 1962 on behalf of the AICPA's committee on long-range objectives, nothing was said about any role the Institute might play on the world stage.[16] But in September of that year, the AICPA hosted the Eighth International Congress of Accountants, in New York, the theme being the 'world economy' in relation to accounting, financial reporting, and auditing. In the opening session, Jacob Kraayenhof, speaking as the president of the last congress, again pointed to the need for international uniformity in accounting principles.[17] He added, prophetically, 'May I express the sincere hope that internationally co-ordinated research, study and discussion may soon be organized.'[18] His view was echoed, even more strongly, by a plenary speaker, P. F. S. Otten, the chairman of Philips' Gloeilampenfabrieken, which happened to be an audit client of Kraayenhof's firm.[19]

Paul Grady, a senior partner in Price Waterhouse & Co. and a leading member of the US profession, had the task of summarizing the technical sessions of the congress. He reported that 'Many of the papers presented to this Congress urge that steps be taken to hasten the further development, understanding and acceptance of standards of auditing, accounting and reporting on an international basis.'[20] Grady referred favourably to an article by Alvin R. Jennings, the Institute's 1957–8 president and a senior partner in Lybrand, Ross Bros. & Montgomery, in which he appealed for steps to be taken towards the development of international accounting and auditing standards.[21] The Jennings article, together with the clear messages received from those attending the international congress, did much to broaden the thinking of the Institute's leadership.

An influential voice in the Canadian Institute of Chartered Accountants (CICA) also supported steps towards international standards of accounting and auditing practice. In August 1963, almost a year after the eighth international congress, the editor of the Institute's journal complained that 'no discernable progress has been made' towards carrying forward Kraayenhof's 1959 proposal to establish standing committees for the research and study of accounting principles on a global stage.[22] While this complaint may have been correct in a literal sense, namely, there was as yet no international standing committee, the next sections show that there were nevertheless several initiatives during the mid-1960s to find an appropriate organizational vehicle to deal with international issues.

2.4. INTERNATIONAL ACCOUNTING IN THE UNITED STATES

While the United States was not the only and probably not even the first country where an interest in international accounting issues arose, it was probably ahead of others in developing a research infrastructure in the area. The AICPA, following the 1962 international congress, took a first step. The Institute's executive director, John L. Carey, later wrote, 'Through a reactivated Institute committee on international relations, a vigorous program was undertaken to encourage international co-operation among professional accountants, to improve exchange of information, and eventually to agree on common standards.'[23] All of the Big Eight accountancy firms were represented on the committee. In 1964, the committee published a thick volume, *Professional Accounting in 25 Countries*. The Big Eight firm partners had called on their offices around the world to draft chapters that included sections on the organized accountancy profession, auditing standards, and accounting principles and practices. It was the first such volume to be produced by a professional accountancy body. In its Introduction, the committee referred to the demands for 'improvement and greater uniformity in international accounting and professional standards ... which were voiced by many participants in the Eighth International Congress held in New York in September 1962'.[24] The committee added that such a need was also 'expressed by representatives of international financing and lending institutions such as the World Bank, the International Finance Corporation, the Inter-American [Development] Bank, and various individual and corporate investors'.[25] The committee was reluctant to embrace international uniformity as an attainable (or even desirable) goal, yet it viewed the compilation of norms and practices in its book as 'a prerequisite to constructive action' in that direction.[26]

By 1965, the Institute's committee on long-range objectives acknowledged the importance of internationalism. In a major book published that year, *The CPA Plans for the Future*, written by John L. Carey in collaboration with the committee, a considerable section was devoted to 'The Movement to Internationalism'.[27]

Carey wrote, 'Any effort to obtain international agreement on accounting principles and auditing standards would confront enormous difficulties; yet it would clearly be a highly desirable development.'[28] All of this is evidence of the international awakening of the AICPA.

In addition to the initiatives from the AICPA, US business schools began turning their attention abroad in the 1950s and 1960s: actively studying international business, and providing technical assistance to nascent business programmes overseas.[29] Early in the 1960s, international accounting emerged as an important object of study by US accounting academics. In the 1960s, articles began appearing in North American accounting journals drawing attention to the problems flowing from the lack of international comparability of financial statements.[30] In 1962, the University of Illinois established a Center for International Education and Research in Accounting, and in that year it held an International Conference on Accounting Education, timed to dovetail with the international congress in New York.[31] The Center proceeded to sponsor an annual series of Seminars on International Accounting, it began to publish a series of monographs, and in 1965 it launched a semi-annual research journal, the first of its kind devoted to international accounting.

Professor Gerhard Mueller Berkeley's doctoral thesis, as well as research he conducted during 1962–4 in the New York office of Price Waterhouse & Co., led to a series of monographs on the accounting practices in the Netherlands, Sweden, Argentina, Germany, and Japan, published between 1962 and 1968.[32] In the mid-1960s, he established the International Accounting Studies Institute at his university, which sponsored a series of research studies. In 1967, Mueller, a pioneer in the field of international accounting,[33] wrote the first textbook treating the subject.[34]

In 1963, a new scholarly journal with international credentials was founded at the University of Chicago. Entitled the *Journal of Accounting Research*, its senior editorial staff, for the first time in a United States accounting academic journal, spanned two countries, the United States and the United Kingdom.[35] It was envisaged that Australia would be a third participating country, but in 1965, Professor R. J. Chambers, of the University of Sydney, opted to found his own academic journal, *Abacus*, which began publishing comparative and international articles.

Thus, it can be seen that accounting academics were beginning to look beyond their borders in the 1960s.

2.5. ACCOUNTANTS INTERNATIONAL STUDY GROUP

While these activities in the United States might be said to be unilateral, an example of truly international collaboration was developed in the form of the Accountants International Study Group. The initiative to found this group was taken in 1966 by Sir Henry Benson (Figure 2.1), a progressive thinker in professional matters and the president of the Institute of Chartered Accountants in England and Wales (ICAEW). He took the lead by promoting the establishment of a study

Figure 2.1. Sir Henry (later Lord) Benson

group composed of representatives from institutes in the United Kingdom, the United States, and Canada. Before treating Benson's proposal and discussing the work of the study group, it is well to review the state of the national programmes for establishing accounting principles and auditing procedures in the middle of the 1960s.

2.5.1. National Programmes for Establishing Accounting Principles

The professional accountancy bodies in the United States, England and Wales, and Canada, in 1939, 1942, and 1946, respectively, were the earliest in the world to initiate programmes to give official guidance on what constitutes accepted accounting practice, which eventually became known as 'generally accepted accounting principles' (GAAP) in the United States and Canada and as 'generally accepted accounting practice' (also GAAP) in the United Kingdom. In the United States, the Securities and Exchange Commission (SEC) made it known that publicly traded companies were, with rare exceptions, expected to follow the *Accounting Research Bulletins* of the AICPA's Committee on Accounting Procedure and, beginning in 1959, the *Opinions* of its successor body, the Accounting Principles Board. The ICAEW's series of *Recommendations on Accounting Principles* constituted, apart from those that were incorporated in the Companies Act 1948, informed opinion and did not oblige Institute members to accept their advice. The CICA's series of *Bulletins* were not mandatory, but, because of the rigorous regime in its neighbour to the south, the pressure to comply was probably a good deal stronger than in Britain.[36] By the middle of the 1960s, therefore, a substantial body of recommended GAAP had been published in the three countries. However, in Canada and the United States, companies and their auditors focused mainly on conforming with recommended GAAP, while in the United Kingdom the overriding concern was that the financial statements give 'a true and fair view', as required by the Companies Act.

Because the CICA's *Financial Reporting in Canada*, its biennial summary and analysis of the financial reporting practices of Canadian industrial and mercantile companies, regularly compared Canadian GAAP with those in the United States and the United Kingdom (as well as their historical development), it had the least to gain from, and probably the most to contribute to, a study group bridging the three countries.[37] The CICA has traditionally been attentive to accounting and auditing developments in the United States and the United Kingdom.

By the middle of the 1960s, the professional accountancy bodies in Australia and New Zealand were adapting the ICAEW's series of *Recommendations* to their respective circumstances or, in a few instances, innovating on their own.[38] No comparable programmes for giving guidance on accounting principles were in effect on the European Continent. In France, guidance on accounting had a clear public-sector character, and was provided through successive revisions of the Plan Comptable Général.[39] In Germany, guidance on accounting developed in the form of a system of legal interpretation. Under this system, the published commentaries by leading authorities on the accounting provisions in company law were accorded considerable authority, supplementing the binding interpretations provided by jurisprudence.[40] In the Netherlands, prior to a major revision of company law in 1970, accounting practitioners looked to the occasional reports of ad hoc committees of experts formed by employer federations.[41] Nascent programmes for establishing accounting principles may have existed in a few other countries.

On the subject of auditing, the United States also was a pioneer. In 1939, spurred by the SEC's reaction to the McKesson & Robbins scandal, the Institute formed a committee to issue statements on auditing procedure, and in 1948 it approved a set of auditing standards. In Canada, the CICA's *Bulletins* dealt both with accounting and auditing. In the United Kingdom, it was not until 1961 that the Council of the ICAEW began to issue *Statements on Auditing*.[42] In the 1960s, the scope of judgement left to English and Scottish chartered accountants in their conduct of external audits was much more expansive than that accorded their brethren in North America. The range of topics, as well as the specificity of instruction, reflected in accounting and auditing pronouncements in North America well exceeded that in Britain.

In the early 1960s, as viewed from the United Kingdom, the programmes for establishing accounting principles and auditing procedures in North America were well in advance of those in Britain. The ICAEW was still issuing its voluntary *Recommendations* after twenty years and had finally overcome a historical aversion to advising its members on auditing practice. Benson later said, 'Certainly until an appreciable time after the Second World War, there was a clear feeling that it was not the task of the Institute to write Auditing Standards, or indeed to publish anything on the subject at all.'[43] In other respects as well, the Institute was an insular body, steeped in tradition. Benson, the senior partner in Cooper Brothers & Co., who, it has been said, 'helped shake up the old firm "until it rattled"',[44] could not have watched submissively as his Institute's Council continued in its time-honoured ways. At long last, the operation of the staid Institute underwent numerous reforms during the middle 1960s, opening itself to the world.[45] It is difficult to believe that Benson, a domineering figure who had served on Council since 1956, did not have a large hand in bringing about these changes.

2.5.2. Formation of the Study Group

One such change, which Benson himself initiated as Institute president in 1966, was to urge the AICPA and CICA to join the ICAEW in creating a study group to draw together the best accounting and auditing practices from the three countries and report their findings to the world. Zeff wrote, 'For the Institute, which had until then shunned collaboration on technical accounting matters even with accountancy bodies in the United Kingdom, a collaborative effort such as the Study Group marked a major shift in policy.'[46] When Benson made the proposal, he was speaking on behalf of his own Institute only, as he had not yet formally consulted the Scottish and Irish institutes about their possible participation.[47]

Benson broached his proposal first in Canada and then in the United States. Both Benson and the AICPA president, Robert M. Trueblood, of Touche Ross & Co., attended the CICA annual conference in Regina, Saskatchewan in August 1966. It was then the custom of these and other Institutes to invite other Institutes' presidents to their annual meetings. Benson addressed the annual meeting of members as follows:

The accountants in Canada, the United States and the United Kingdom report each year on the truth and fairness of balance sheets and profit and loss accounts involving thousands of billions of dollars. Nevertheless, the rank and file of us in our respective countries are inclined to pursue our separate ways with comparatively little regard to, or indeed knowledge of, accounting and auditing developments in other countries. I am not for a moment advocating regimentation or uniformity. I am saying no more than that a careful study of the developments in the other two countries at regular intervals would, I think, be helpful to all of us. For example, I have in mind the publication jointly by our three Institutes, yearly or perhaps every two years, of a paper which would be issued to all our members indicating the lines of thought of our colleagues in the other two countries. As far as the United Kingdom is concerned I know that this would be stimulating. If you think there is any merit in this suggestion we might take it further.[48]

At the conference in Regina, Benson met with Trueblood as well as with Jack Wilson, of Clarkson, Gordon & Co., the incoming CICA president, to discuss his proposal. Benson has written that, following that meeting, 'We agreed quickly that such an enterprise would be worthwhile.'[49] Yet Wilson and apparently also Trueblood were cool to the suggestion. Wilson was concerned about its cost and likely usefulness. One could well have expected them to wonder what the Americans and Canadians could learn from the British, as the latter's *Recommendations* and *Statements on Auditing* were, in point of coverage and firmness, well behind those issued in North America. Yet neither country wanted to be left out.[50]

At the AICPA's annual meeting in Boston, held in October 1966, Benson placed his proposal before the Institute's executive committee and Council, and he ventured the view that 'The publications to be issued by the "study group" might bring about a reassessment of present practices and future plans in the three countries.'[51] In January 1967, it was announced that the International Study Group had been approved by the governing bodies of the cooperating institutes and would have its first meeting in February. Its terms of reference were: 'To institute comparative studies as to accounting thought and practice in participating countries, to make reports from time to time, which, subject to the prior approval of the sponsoring Institutes, would be issued to members of those Institutes.'[52]

Representatives to the Study Group were named by the AICPA and CICA as well as by the ICAEW, the Institute of Chartered Accountants of Scotland (ICAS), and the Institute of Chartered Accounts in Ireland (ICAI). *The Accountant* reported that 'Topics to be discussed cover a wide field, from education and training to professional relations and auditing procedures.'[53] In fact, while all of these topics were discussed during the meetings of the Study Group, its publications were intended to deal solely with issues of accounting and auditing. Benson attended only the first meeting of the Study Group, although not as a member of the UK delegation, and, at his suggestion, Robert Trueblood, the immediate past AICPA president, was elected as chairman.[54]

2.5.3. Benson's Motivations

Why did Benson advocate the establishment of the Study Group? One clear reason was his fervent desire to gain acceptance in the United Kingdom for the required attendance at stocktaking by the auditor. In a major speech in 1958, Benson had argued that it was 'indefensible' for UK auditors not to verify the existence and value of inventories, a practice that he knew had long been mandatory in North America.[55] Above all, Benson wanted to see a Study Group publication on the subject, drawing on the North American practice of physical attendance by auditors at stocktaking, which he hoped would then secure the necessary support for that practice in the United Kingdom. In the end, as will be seen below, he succeeded in his aim.

Benson may also have been concerned at the state of financial reporting in the United Kingdom. He had served as a joint inspector into the affairs of Rolls Razor Ltd., which suddenly collapsed a few weeks after publication of its annual accounts in 1964. Questions were raised in the press about the adequacy of its published accounts.

He himself stated a third motivation, which was a lesson he learned in Cooper Brothers & Co.: 'After the war, when I was helping to build my firm's national and international practice, I realized that it would be quite impossible to do so without clear manuals of procedure and principles for the guidance of partners and staff world-wide who were engaged in professional work.'[56]

A fourth motivation was his belief that a genuine synergy could be realized by taking advantage of the best accounting and auditing thought in the United Kingdom, Canada, and the United States, and that this would confer benefits in all countries in which accounting was practised.[57]

2.5.4. The Initial Work of the Study Group: The Inventories Booklet

Undoubtedly owing to Benson's influence, the United Kingdom was selected as the first country to coordinate the preparation of a booklet, and its choice of topic was inventories. The resulting booklet, entitled *Accounting and Auditing Approaches to Inventories in Three Nations*, was published in January 1968. It appeared as a publication of the 'Accountants International Study Group', the full name by which the Study Group would become known. The print order was for 55,000 copies, of which 30,000 were to be dispatched to the subscribers of *Accountancy*, the ICAEW's journal.[58] Benson had probably given orders that the booklet was to achieve maximum impact among the Institute's members. Indeed, the print order for the inventories booklet exceeded the sum of those for the next four booklets in the series,[59] evidently because of Benson's personal interest in the outcome.

In the booklet, the Study Group concluded that 'Attendance to observe physical inspection of inventories is a most significant verification procedure for audit purposes. This practice has received more forceful emphasis in North America than in the United Kingdom. We endorse its desirability and commend its adoption as internationally recognised standard practice.'[60] This was the vigorous endorsement that Benson had expected to see in the publication.

Less than five months after publication of the Study Group's booklet, the ICAEW's Council rushed out a special guidance statement that, without mentioning the booklet, specified definitive steps to be taken by an auditor to verify the amount attributed to a company's inventory balance.[61] Benson had won the day.

2.5.5. The Remaining Work of the Study Group

From 1967 to 1977, when the Study Group was disbanded, it produced a total of twenty booklets. It never revisited a subject after a booklet had been issued. Table 2.1 shows the titles of the studies, their years of publication, and the nation that was in charge of the drafting.

Members of the Study Group were nominated by the five institutes, and its 'plenary' meetings were held twice a year. Each nation could designate a maximum of three delegates to the Study Group, and it was agreed that the UK delegation would consist of two members from the ICAEW and one member representing both ICAS and the ICAI. Until the latter years of the Study Group, the Scottish Institute supplied the representative, while the Irish Institute was only slightly involved. At each of its meetings, the members of the Study Group would exchange information on developments concerning the accountancy profession in their respective nations. In fact, the contacts and general exchange of information during the Study Group's semi-annual meetings proved to be useful to the

Table 2.1. Publications of the Accountants International Study Group (by year of publication, showing drafting nation)

Year	Nation	Title
1968	United Kingdom (ICAEW)	Accounting and Auditing Approaches to Inventories in Three Nations
1969	United States	The Independent Auditor's Reporting Standards in Three Nations
1969	Canada	Using the Work and Report of Another Auditor
1971	Canada	Accounting for Corporate Income Taxes
1972	United States	Reporting by Diversified Companies
1973	United States	Consolidated Financial Statements
1973	Canada	The Funds Statement
1974	United States	Materiality in Accounting
1974	United States	Extraordinary Items, Prior Period Adjustments and Changes in Accounting Principles
1974	United Kingdom (ICAEW)	Published Profit Forecasts
1975	Canada	International Financial Reporting
1975	United Kingdom (ICAEW)	Comparative Glossary of Accounting Terms in Canada, the United Kingdom and the United States
1975	United States	Accounting for Goodwill
1975	Canada	Interim Financial Reporting
1975	Canada	Going Concern Problems
1976	United States	Independence of Auditors
1977	Canada	Audit Committees
1977	United Kingdom (ICAS)	Accounting for Pension Costs
1978	United States	Revenue Recognition
1978	Canada	Related Party Transactions

participating institutes above and beyond the value of the publications themselves. During the meetings, draft texts would be discussed and, when appropriate, new topics would be selected for study. An Institute would then volunteer to draft a study. The Institute responsible for drafting would actively consult the institutes in the other nations, as each booklet was to represent an integrated whole of the views and experiences supplied by the institutes in all three nations.[62] The opinions expressed in the booklets were those of the Study Group, not of the drafting Institute.

The Study Group debated whether to describe its opinions as 'Conclusions' or 'Recommendations'. Since December 1968, the CICA's pronouncements were known as 'research Recommendations' or '*Handbook* Recommendations'. The CICA's Thomas wrote, 'The Canadians have been most insistent that the results of studies should be called conclusions and not recommendations, because of our concern about developing two sets of recommendations—one nationally and one internationally—with the inevitable confusion that would result.'[63] The Study Group settled on Conclusions.

Eleven of the twenty booklets dealt primarily with accounting issues: inventories, corporate income taxes, segment reporting, consolidated statements and the equity method of accounting, the funds statement, materiality, extraordinary items and changes in accounting principles, goodwill, interim reporting, pension costs, and revenue recognition. Several of the booklets on accounting also treated auditing issues. Most of the other studies dealt principally with auditing issues or matters of financial statement presentation, and one consisted of a comparative glossary of 160 accounting, auditing, and financial terms. Two booklets treated published profit forecasts and audit committees.

The CICA and the AICPA each supplied draftsmen for eight of the studies, and four were drafted by members or staff of the English or Scottish institutes. In addition, the English and Scottish institutes worked on two other projects that were never completed. Hence, the two institutes in North America assumed the larger share of the drafting responsibilities, even though the impetus for setting up the Study Group had come from Benson, when he was president of the ICAEW. One supposes that the much longer experience with issuing accounting and auditing pronouncements at the CICA and AICPA, compared with that at the English and Scottish institutes, may explain this disparity. The ICAEW had particular difficulties in bringing its project on published profit forecasts to completion. This was the Study Group's longest running project, which went through many drafts. There were signs that the ICAEW was operating at the limit of its capacity around 1970, as its international and domestic commitments began to multiply.[64] It therefore had to ask ICAS to take over the responsibility for one of its Study Group projects.[65]

The rate of production of booklets increased over time. Only four booklets were published during the Study Group's first four years, while ten were issued in the last four years. This was due at least in part to the efforts by the CICA's research studies staff to assist the UK draftsmen and encourage the US draftsmen (audit managers seconded by the major firms) to complete their projects.[66] The CICA was the most enthusiastic contributor of the drafting bodies to the work of the Study Group. The ICAEW accorded the Study Group, perforce or by choice, the lowest priority of the drafting bodies.[67]

The successive chairmen of the Study Group were rotated among the three nations, as follows:

1967–8	Robert M. Trueblood (United States)
1968–9	Ronald G. Leach (United Kingdom, ICAEW)
1969–70	John R. M. (Jack) Wilson (Canada)
1970–1	Theodore L. Wilkinson (United States)
1971–2	Douglas S. Morpeth (United Kingdom, ICAEW)
1972–3	Robert M. Rennie (Canada)
1973–4	R. Kirk Batzer (United States)
1974–5	George D. H. Dewar (United Kingdom, ICAS, also representing the ICAI)
1975–6	John W. Adams (Canada)
1976–7	Edwin W. Macrae (United States)

Adams was the only chairman from industry. All of the others were partners in major accountancy firms.

As might be imagined, an issue arose over whether other nations' accountancy bodies should be represented in the Study Group, and one or two may have been miffed at being excluded. An informal approach to the president of the Canadian Institute, Jack Wilson, was made in 1967 by a representative of the Nederlands Instituut van Registeraccountants (NIVRA). While Wilson's initial reaction was positive, Benson made it known that three nations was the limit.[68] Benson later wrote, 'We felt that if this exercise was to get off the ground, the maximum number of nations who should initially be involved was three, and they should start with the advantage of all speaking a common language.'[69]

At the Study Group's meeting in June 1968, it was tentatively proposed by the US delegation that Australia be invited. But once the implications for the travel cost of all parties had been discussed, as well as the political ramifications of accepting Australia, but not New Zealand, other British Commonwealth nations, or the Netherlands, the motion was withdrawn.[70] Benson himself envisaged that other nations might be added at a later date, but this did not occur during the life of the Study Group.[71]

Some of the salient conclusions—sometimes firm, sometimes bland—contained in the series of booklets may be summarized as follows. As will be seen in subsequent chapters, many of these conclusions were to be the starting point of the IASC's work.

In the accounting section of the booklet on inventories, the use of 'lower of cost and market' (as in the United States) or 'lower of cost and net realizable value' (as in Canada and the United Kingdom) were supported practices. The position on 'direct' or 'variable' costing in the booklet was equivocal, and no conclusion was issued on the use of LIFO, which was practised only in the United States (paragraph 100). The booklet ended with a plea for a reduction in the number of deviations from standards of best practice (paragraph 101).

The booklet on corporate income taxes touched on a vexed subject in all three countries. By 1971, when the booklet was issued, all three nations had pronouncements dealing with deferred tax (or tax allocation) accounting, and those in Canada and the United States were passed 'against much opposition' (paragraph 46). The only substantive conclusion in the booklet dealt with a choice of method and was cautiously expressed: 'On balance, it is concluded that the deferred method is to be preferred in practice to the accrual method, and that the accumulated balances should be regarded as deferred credits or debits rather than accrued liabilities or assets' (paragraph 46). Under the deferred method, subsequent changes in the tax rate are ignored. In Canada and the United States, the deferred method was recommended, while the position in the United Kingdom favoured the accrual method (paragraph 22).

The booklet on diversified companies, another topic of controversy, advanced a bold conclusion: 'Financial statements of diversified companies should include information on separate segments, and that information should be examined and reported upon by independent auditors' (paragraph 86). The two most important Canadian corporations acts and the British Companies Act 1967, as well as the SEC (but not the Accounting Principles Board), required diversified companies to disclose certain types of information on material segments. But only in Canada was it required that the auditor's report cover such information.

On consolidated financial statements, the Study Group's position was that, when both consolidated and parent company statements were provided, the former should be considered the primary financial statements. While this position would not have been controversial in the three nations, in most of the rest of the world in 1973, consolidated statements were just beginning to become more commonplace. The implication was that they should be prepared. The Study Group also concluded that, although the generally used criterion for preparing consolidated statements was the investor's ownership of more than 50 per cent of the voting shares of an investee, 'There may well be circumstances, however, where effective control with 50% or less of voting equity would be the determining factor' (paragraph 73). This latter provision would have been at variance with US practice. The Study Group also called upon corporations to make a number of significant financial disclosures in relation to their inter-company holdings (paragraph 73).

On the funds statement, a financial report that had recently become required only in Canada and the United States, but was still not required and was 'not too commonly found' in the United Kingdom,[72] the booklet, issued in 1973, said, 'The Study Group endorses its desirability and commends its adoption as an internationally recognized financial reporting practice' (paragraph 104).

The booklet on international financial reporting, issued in 1975, provided guidance on how auditors should report on 'secondary financial statements', that is, those prepared specifically for use in countries other than the company's home country. It dealt with the appropriate accounting principles and auditing procedures to use when reporting in an international environment, the need to distinguish between primary and secondary financial statements, and the importance of disclosing the nationality of the principles or procedures used. Mueller called this study 'a truly pioneering piece of work, since there exists virtually no literature on this specific topic and since the recommendations put forward are original with the AISG'.[73]

In the booklet on goodwill, also issued in 1975, it was concluded that 'Goodwill should be accounted for as an intangible asset which has a limited life and should be amortized to income on a systematic basis over its estimated life' (paragraph 27). This position accorded with recommended practice in Canada and the United States. In the United Kingdom, the accounting treatment of goodwill was still being studied by the standard-setting body, but it was clear that the Study Group's conclusion was at variance with the common practice of writing off goodwill against reserves.

The booklet on interim reports, issued in 1975, concluded that such reports should 'preferably' be published every quarter (paragraph 82), yet interim reports as often as quarterly were the practice only in Canada and the United States. Interim reports, the Study Group said, should report sales or gross revenues as well as net income (paragraph 82). In many countries of the world at that time, sales or gross revenues were not reported even on an annual basis, and such reporting had been required in the United Kingdom only since 1967.

In 1977, the Study Group issued a booklet on pension costs, a subject on which there was a 'relatively wide disparity in accounting' in the three nations (paragraph 48). It concluded that 'neither the Terminal Funding nor the pay-as-you-go method is appropriate for accounting for pension costs' (paragraph 50).

Not all of the projects selected for study led to booklets. A project on 'Accountants and the Smaller Business', which was being drafted by the ICAEW, was abandoned because it was seen to be directed at auditors' clients rather than auditors, which was not a priority for the Study Group at the time.[74] A project on 'Accounting for Foreign Currency Items' was characterized as 'covering one of the most difficult subjects on the Study Group's agenda' by its draftsman, George Dewar, the former ICAS president.[75] Although it went through a number of drafts, it never resulted in a publication. As will be seen below, the IASC would find this to be one of the most intractable projects on its early agenda as well.

The disbandment of the Study Group in 1977 is discussed in Section 3.5.2 in relation to the founding of the IASC. But at this point the following assessment can be made. Whatever the impact of its booklets on practice and national standard setting,[76] the Study Group did perform the vital role of bringing leaders of the accountancy profession in the three nations into closer contact and cooperation, and of acquainting them and the readers of the booklets with the diversity of practice and the reasons for that diversity. In this respect, the Study Group took an important stride in the direction of a meaningful international dialogue on accounting standards.

2.6. AN INTERNATIONAL ACCOUNTING SECRETARIAT

The AISG was by design a select club, embracing the countries with the most advanced standard-setting programmes. But the sentiments expressed at the time of the 1962 international congress gave rise to attempts to set up a truly international body that would also look after the interests of countries where accountancy was less developed. In 1977, these attempts would result in the creation of the IFAC. As opposed to the relatively tranquil world of the regional accountancy bodies and the Study Group, the political dimension of international accounting clearly came into view in this setting.

In 1965, John L. Carey wrote in the above-mentioned publication *The CPA Plans for the Future*: 'It has also been suggested that an international information center be established by the professional accounting organizations of the world, with a full-time secretariat charged with the duty of distributing professional publications and disseminating technical information on an international scale. Such an international center might also offer guidance to newly developing professional societies in countries where a well organized profession does not yet exist.'[77]

The idea of an international professional entity took hold in a number of countries, and it surfaced in 1967 at the Ninth International Congress of Accountants in Paris. In a session devoted to 'the international harmonization of accounting principles', the international rapporteur, Tom K. Cowan, a New Zealand professor, made a plea for an 'international accounting bureau',[78] and it appears that quite a number of national rapporteurs made similar suggestions in their papers. The French congress president, François-Maurice Richard, encouraged discussion of this idea with a view towards adoption of a resolution establishing an international secretariat at the meeting of the heads of delegations near the end of the congress.[79] At this point, however, Benson stepped in. Supported by the US and Dutch representatives, he thwarted this initiative and proposed instead the installation of a working party to study the idea of an international secretariat. The opposition to an international secretariat by the United States, the United Kingdom, and the Netherlands was based on the apprehension that an association with other accountancy bodies of perceived lower standing might imply a degree of recognition of these other bodies that they were unwilling to give, or might even entail in the future a threat to their own high standards.[80] As the strong support for an international secretariat in many other countries could not be ignored altogether, a compromise had to be found. As proposed by Benson, the heads of delegations instead created an International Working Party (IWP) to study the proposal for an international secretariat and report to the next international congress, in Sydney in 1972. The IWP consisted of representatives of the institutes that had hosted the post-war congresses (the ICAEW, ICAS, the ICAI, the NIVRA, the AICPA, and the Ordre des Experts Comptables) and of the co-sponsors of the next congress, the Institute of Chartered Accountants in Australia and the Australian Society of Accountants. Representatives from India and Mexico were added subsequently. Benson and the secretary of the ICAEW represented the three institutes from the United Kingdom and Ireland on the IWP.

Ostensibly, the principal task of the IWP was to consider the role and future plan of the international congresses. In fact, its main topic was whether and how to establish an international secretariat. Benson continued to press for delay and was reported to have said at the first meeting of the IWP that it would take 'at least ten years' before such a secretariat could be established.[81] During the IWP's tenure, however, the AICPA changed its position. In 1969, Robert L. May of the AICPA's Committee on Overseas Relations advised the Institute's Council:

We of the American Institute have for good reasons resisted the development of an international secretariat or its equivalent. It is time, however, that we stop merely opposing the concept, but rather start developing specific proposals which will result in a meaningful form of international accounting cooperation. In my opinion, we have no choice in this matter. We must either develop a form of participation *suitable* to our interests, or else we will be excluded from an organization which will undoubtedly be *inimical* to our interests.[82]

Henceforth, the AICPA favoured establishment of an international secretariat as a means of facilitating the harmonization of accounting principles and auditing procedures, yet it still had its concerns over how the body would be set up and who would run it.[83]

In the end, the English position to defer a decision prevailed.[84] The IWP, in its report to the Tenth International Congress of Accountants in 1972, in Sydney, advised that it would be 'premature' to set up an international secretariat. Instead, it said that 'leadership in the development of [professional] standards must come from individual countries, rather than from a supra-national administrative body.'[85] In addition, it encouraged the establishment and development of regional associations such as the UEC. Finally, the IWP was to be given another five-year term to prepare the way for an international secretariat. The IWP was to be renamed as the International Co-ordination Committee for the Accountancy Profession (ICCAP), and its membership was to be expanded to include Canada, Germany, and the Philippines. The recommendations of the IWP were accepted at the Sydney congress. The first meeting of ICCAP was scheduled for April 1973. Benson was succeeded as the representative from the United Kingdom and Ireland by Douglas S. Morpeth, the ICAEW's 1972–3 president, and John P. Grenside (who would become the ICAEW's 1975–6 president).

2.7. ACCOUNTING HARMONIZATION IN THE EEC AND THE ROLE OF THE UEC

In a sense, a European influence on accounting can be traced to the early 1950s. Mueller wrote that 'The genesis of consolidated financial statements requirements in Europe is found in the early agreements among the ECSC signatories.'[86] His reference was to the financial statistics the ECSC gathered and reported which were aggregated across parents and subsidiaries and across countries, and which reflected adjustments to eliminate intercompany transactions.[87] More important consequences for accounting were to follow from the Treaty of Rome (1957), which envisaged the free movement of persons, goods, services, and capital across the member states of the EEC. On this basis, the EEC started work on a series of directives aimed at harmonizing company law, including financial reporting requirements. The First Company Law Directive, published in 1968, established the principle of mandatory publication of financial statements by limited liability companies. The contents of financial statements were to be governed mainly by the Fourth and Seventh Directives. Work on these two Directives was begun in 1965. At the request of the European Commission, accountancy bodies from the member states formed a working party chaired by a former president of the Institut der Wirtschaftsprüfer (IdW), Wilhelm Elmendorff. This working party produced a draft Directive on the annual accounts of limited liability companies in 1968. In 1970, it completed its work with a proposal for a Directive on consolidated financial statements and the accounts of private companies. Both of these formed the basis of the EEC's own draft Directives. A first draft of the Fourth Directive by the European Commission was published in November 1971.

The UEC, of which Elmendorff was a prominent member, recognized the importance of this development at an early stage. In 1958, it formed a working party chaired by the Belgian Léon Saxe, in order to ensure that the accountancy profession could make its voice heard in the process of company law harmonization, and in the accompanying process of opening up the market for audit services across the EEC. The 'Commission Saxe' was indeed recognized as interlocutor by the EEC. Because not all of the countries represented in the UEC were EEC member states, the Commission Saxe was changed into an independent body in 1961, known as the Groupe d'Études des Experts Comptables de la C.E.E. Supported by the major accountancy bodies in the EEC member states, the Groupe d'Études became a recognized advisory body of the EEC on accounting and auditing matters.[88]

Despite its eagerness to be involved with European company law harmonization, the UEC represented a yawning diversity of views. Especially after the British, Scandinavian, and Dutch institutes joined the UEC in 1963, the Continental, law-based approach to accounting regulation was confronted by the inductive, case-by-case approach to establishing accounting practice favoured in Anglo-American countries. McDougall has caricatured the adherents of both approaches as the 'pseudo-scientists' (according to the law) and the 'pseudo-artists' (true and fair, or fairly present).[89] Within the UEC, a certain tension remained as the new entrants tended to look with some condescension on the older members, whereas the latter referred ironically to the former as 'the Northern Lights'.[90]

This division made it virtually impossible for the UEC to arrive at a common position on harmonization or uniformity of accounting principles. The UEC's original articles of association had listed as one of its objectives 'the progressive unification of the most rational and effective practices applied in the different countries' and 'the harmonisation of codes of professional duties' (article II, paragraphs 2 and 3). Indeed, this one clause was the reason why the UK and Dutch institutes had declined to join the UEC during the 1950s, as they feared that it might lead to a lowering of their professional standards to the level of what were seen as the weaker European institutes.[91] Their accession to the UEC in 1963 was therefore preceded by difficult negotiations, which led to the elimination from the articles of association of all indications that the UEC might impose rules or standards on its members.[92] Instead, the UEC embraced the principle of 'non-commitment', implying that the UEC 'is not entitled to elaborate or impose directives on its member-organizations'.[93]

The divide in Europe became particularly clear when successive drafts of the Fourth Directive appeared. The Elmendorff committee 'did not consider it to be its task to put forward new, possibly better rules for the publication of accounts'.[94] As it merely looked for harmonization of existing practices, its proposals and the corresponding EEC draft Directive of 1971, mainly reflected the law-based approach to accounting as known in Germany and France. When it became clear that Denmark, Ireland, and the United Kingdom were to join the EEC, which they did in 1973, strong objections to the proposed Fourth Directive were raised in particular by the British profession. By the end of 1972, wrote *The Economist*, 'The British accountancy profession had worked itself into a lather about the horrors of joining the community.'[95]

On the Continent, it was acknowledged that the British could legitimately claim that their distinctive approach to accountancy should be recognized now that the United Kingdom was about to join the EEC. However, there was also a belief that the British were overstating the differences. One German author pointed out that, with the formation of the Accounting Standards Steering Committee in 1970, a new era had begun in the United Kingdom in which the 'true and fair' view was being evermore circumscribed by accounting standards.[96] Another saw it as ironic that UK auditors were binding themselves more closely to rules than the German auditors had ever been.[97] The UK attitude was therefore seen as inspired as much by a British sense of superiority as by any substantial defects of the proposed Fourth Directive.

One of the initiatives taken by the UK accountancy profession was to encourage the UEC to play a more active role in the hope that the British could influence the course of the accounting directives programme in the EEC through its participation in the UEC.[98] Henry Benson was a member of the UEC's executive committee from 1967 to 1973, and its vice-president during 1970. During this period, he began to urge the UEC to move in the direction of issuing accounting and auditing norms. In the light of the UEC's earlier history, it is ironic that this initiative came from a past president of the ICAEW, and that his efforts were resisted by most of the Continental countries.[99] But attitudes towards standards in the United Kingdom had changed rapidly in the late 1960s, owing in part to a number of corporate scandals that were associated with questionable accounting practices. The impending entry of the United Kingdom into the EEC was clearly a new factor of great importance as well.

The objections raised by the other UEC members may have had less to do with the merits of publishing accounting standards than with a suspicion of Benson's motives or a dislike of his attitude. Benson was seen by some as representing the international accountancy firms that formed an increasing threat to the small and local firms which formed the backbone of the UEC's constituency. International norms of practice might weaken the national institutes, which formed the small firms' main line of defence.[100]

That Benson's views and the way they were expressed caused resentment in Europe was shown in December 1972, when the ICAEW organized a conference on 'The British Company in Europe'. Benson, as one of the speakers, rounded off a survey of European accounting practice with the conclusion that, 'Taken as a whole, the UK is in the lead by a large margin.'[101] This prompted a reply by the Dutch UEC President Aad Tempelaar, who argued that claims of exclusive leadership by one country would lead only to chauvinistic reactions by the others, without furthering the cause of harmonization: 'If our British friends feel that UK accounting practices are the best in Europe, they will achieve their ends far better by not stamping them with the label "Made in Britain".'[102]

This exchange alerted some in Britain to the 'annoyance and resentment' that the British attitude was causing on the Continent.[103] One of the internationalist voices was that of Edward Stamp, who commented: 'Sir Henry's pride in British accomplishments is of Churchillian proportions. I admire and respect it, and I believe we need more of it. We must also be prepared to recognise and accept that comparison is inevitably a two-way process and there is much that we can learn from others.'[104]

Despite the friction, Benson succeeded in bringing about a change in the UEC's constitution, which allowed it to issue non-mandatory Recommendations.[105] In November 1972, he urged the UEC's executive committee to begin issuing recommendations during the next year.[106] By then, as is discussed more fully in Chapter 3, he was also spearheading the establishment of the IASC. As will be seen, the reaction to Benson's plans for the IASC was coloured by surprise at the discovery that he had been active on two fronts simultaneously. It is likely that, by 1972, Benson had lost most of his confidence that he could turn the UEC into an effective source of authoritative guidance, and was focusing on an extension of his earlier creation, the AISG.[107]

2.8. THE STAGE FOR THE IASC

When the IASC was formed in 1973, it did not emerge from a vacuum. For at least a decade, the international dimension of accounting had been recognized. Various and sometimes conflicting approaches had been taken to develop organizational forms in which international issues could be researched, discussed, or resolved. It is interesting to note the pivotal role played by Henry Benson around 1970. He was the founder of the AISG. He was at the centre of ongoing discussions about an international secretariat for the accountancy profession. He was a prominent exponent of the UK point of view concerning the EEC's programme of accounting directives. And he was behind the UEC's somewhat reluctant move towards issuing recommendations. As will be taken up in Chapter 3, in 1972 Benson was about to take on another role, as the founder of the IASC.

3

The Founding of the IASC

3.1. THE INITIATIVE TO FORM AN INTERNATIONAL ACCOUNTING STANDARDS COMMITTEE

As discussed in Chapter 2, the idea of international harmonization of accounting and auditing principles was very much alive in the world of accountancy bodies during the late 1960s and the early 1970s. Naturally, it was also a prominent topic at the Tenth International Congress of Accountants held in Sydney in September 1972. Looking back at the congress, the president of the American Institute of Certified Public Accountants (AICPA), LeRoy Layton, wrote:

> There was one consistent thought, expressed in almost every study group—that there should be established, without delay, some body of experts (a study group, a working party, or an international committee) that would tackle, on a continuing basis, the very difficult task of establishing international standards of accounting and auditing, or at the very least, bringing our varied national standards into much closer agreement.[1]

The congress was in fact the birthplace of not one, but two international committees, which would maintain a close and sometimes complicated relationship for almost thirty years. One, the International Co-ordination Committee for the Accountancy Profession (ICCAP), was created at the formal meeting of the heads of delegations. The formation of ICCAP was prominently announced as the next step towards an international secretariat for the accountancy profession (*see* Section 2.6). From ICCAP, the International Federation of Accountants (IFAC) was to emerge in 1977. The formation of the other committee, the International Accounting Standards Committee (IASC), was discreetly discussed at an informal meeting of high-level representatives of the four institutes that, since 1966, participated in the Accountants International Study Group (AISG, *see* Section 2.5). This meeting brought together the presidents, secretaries, and two past presidents of the English, Scottish, Canadian, and American institutes, with the Scots representing the Institute of Chartered Accountants in Ireland (ICAI) as well.[2] The Australian bodies sponsoring the congress apparently 'put in a token appearance'.[3] The meeting had been arranged in advance by Sir Henry Benson on behalf of the Institute of Chartered Accountants in England and Wales (ICAEW). It was intended to be confidential, and no publicity was given to it during the congress.[4]

During this meeting, it was agreed in principle to expand the role of the Study Group. Instead of, or in addition to, publishing study booklets it would undertake to formulate international accounting standards and to ensure their worldwide acceptance. It was also agreed to invite new country members to the Study Group and to strengthen its organization and finances.[5] Henry Benson wrote, 'there was no difficulty in reaching agreement in principle' on these points.[6] Although there were still many differences of opinion to resolve concerning the practical arrangements, all present felt that the time was ripe for international accounting standards, and therefore this meeting is rightly considered as the origin of the IASC.

In summary, the course of events over the next months was as follows. The participants at the Sydney meeting held a second meeting in London in December 1972. This resulted in a concrete proposal to be put before the councils of the institutes participating in the Study Group. By this time, it was proposed to set up a new body, tentatively called the IASC, alongside the existing Study Group.[7] The councils of these institutes gave their approval by the end of January 1972. Early in February, the three UK and Irish institutes invited and obtained the support of the three other UK accountancy bodies that hitherto had not participated in the Study Group.[8] Towards the end of February, invitations were sent out to selected accountancy bodies in Australia, France, Germany, Japan, Mexico, and the Netherlands.

These institutes were invited to attend a meeting in London, together with representatives of the American and Canadian institutes and the six UK and Irish bodies, on 19 March 1973. This paved the way for a final meeting in London on 28 June 1973, where the text of an 'Agreement to establish an International Accounting Standards Committee' was made final. The Agreement, consisting in fact of an Agreement and a Constitution, was signed the following day at a ceremony in Chartered Accountants' Hall. After a press conference, the newly established IASC held its first meeting on the afternoon of the same day.

3.2. BENSON'S ROLE AND MOTIVATION

There is general agreement that Henry Benson was the guiding spirit behind the founding of the IASC. Yet he acted throughout in close consultation with the ICAEW, and the IASC at the time was seen at least as much as an initiative of the ICAEW as of Benson himself. The initiating correspondence sent out to the participating accountancy bodies between September 1972 and March 1973 was signed by Douglas Morpeth in his capacity of president of the ICAEW. It was only at the March 1973 meeting that Benson visibly took the lead by assuming the chairmanship of that meeting. It was Benson who signed the agenda papers for the founding meeting of June in his capacity of 'chairman'. It is possible that, in the earliest stages, the leadership of the ICAEW had not quite decided who would take the lead in the new body. Morpeth has claimed that he himself might have assumed the chairmanship but that he chose to support Benson instead.[9] It is unlikely that Benson himself entertained any doubts about who should lead the IASC. Yet it is clear that, as regards the IASC initiative, Benson's personal motivations and those of the ICAEW cannot easily be disentangled.

As to the motives that the ICAEW and Benson may have had in common, there is no reason to doubt the motive most often given by themselves and by many others: the fact that, internationally, the growth of international trade and the rise of the multinational company had resulted in a groundswell of opinion in favour of concrete action to formulate international accounting standards. This development had come to a head during the Sydney congress where, as Benson put it, the widespread demand for internationally accepted standards became clear in a way that was 'almost telepathy'.[10] Following the Sydney congress, the staff of the ICAEW elaborated the proposals in a document with a title that seemed to capture the mood of the times: 'Basic Accounting Standards—An Urgent International Need'.[11] The growth of interest in international accounting from the 1950s through the 1960s has been documented in Chapter 2 to show that this was, in fact, a well-established theme in the early 1970s. The ICAEW was by this time in a good position to take a leading role. During the 1960s, it had gone through a period of revitalization and modernization. Prompted by a number of accounting scandals, it had become sensitive to the importance of accounting standards. In 1970, it had taken the lead in setting up a standard-setting body in the United Kingdom, the Accounting Standards Steering Committee (ASSC).[12]

Given a consensus that international accounting standards were desirable or at the very least inevitable, the ICAEW may have found it in its interest to ensure that it could make its mark on such standards. On the one hand, an international accounting standard-setting body in which the British took the lead might prevent a predominance of US GAAP.[13] On the other, it has been argued that the UK accountancy bodies set up the IASC out of concern over the programme of accounting harmonization of the European Economic Community (EEC).[14] As noted in Section 2.7, there was indeed considerable commotion within the UK profession over the EEC, and this motive clearly did play a role in establishing the IASC, at least in the perception of the ICAEW. However, there is little evidence that this aspect of the IASC proposal raised great concerns on the Continent. Arguably, the direct participation of the United Kingdom in negotiations over the EEC's accounting Directives, which started on its accession to the EEC in 1973, had a far greater impact than any indirect influence exercised through the IASC.[15]

There were also signs in 1971 and 1972 that the United Nations might become active in the area of international accounting standards (see Section 7.1). In its document 'Basic Accounting Standards—An Urgent International Need', the ICAEW seemed to hint darkly at this possibility when the need for quick action was emphasized 'before other agencies come to the conclusion that the accountancy bodies jointly are incapable of solving [the problems of harmonization] and take the matter into their own hands'.[16]

In addition to these general motives, there may also have been personal ambitions on the part of Benson. A credible possibility is that Benson was motivated by a widely acknowledged rivalry between himself and Sir Ronald Leach. The origins of this rivalry are not clear but are likely to be found in the fact that Benson, together with John Pears, aggressively built up Cooper Brothers into a serious challenge to Peat Marwick Mitchell, of which Leach was the senior partner. Moreover, Leach was the founder and first chairman of the UK Accounting Standards Steering Committee, established in 1970. In addition to all other considerations, the IASC may have been attractive to Benson as a means to establish parity between himself and Leach in this area.[17]

In the end, though, no explanation of the origins of the IASC would be complete without recognizing the importance of Benson's vision. Even those who resented his autocratic manner respected him for his truly long-term view of the importance of international accounting standards. With a certain prescience, he said in 1975:

Bit by bit, gradually, I think…that as the prestige and the importance of the I.A.S.C. will grow, this body will be recognised in the international field, and one can expect that modifications of national laws will be necessary to conform to international accounting norms. But let's be realistic on this subject, it will take us many years before arriving at the necessary harmonisation. My point of view is the following: I think that we shall see, during the next five years, great successes, the effects of which will not make themselves felt until the year 2000. Don't laugh when I mention the year 2000, twenty-five years is nothing in the life of a great profession.[18]

Benson's drive was of crucial importance in transforming generally held but inchoate feelings about the necessity of international harmonization into a concrete programme of action.

3.3. GENERAL REACTIONS TO THE IASC PROPOSAL

The general tenor of the reactions of the accountancy bodies that were approached to participate in the IASC was positive. This applied both to the institutes that had already participated in the Study Group and to the others that were asked to join in 1973. In general, the flattering thought, or the assumption as a matter of course, of being included among the leading countries was sufficient to overcome concerns about the costs and various reservations about the way the new entity was to be set up. As outlined below, the generally positive reaction was coloured by the specific circumstances of the prospective members.[19]

According to Wallace E. Olson, then the AICPA's executive vice-president, the AICPA differed strongly with Benson and the ICAEW over the relationship between the new body and ICCAP. Yet, on the whole, it favoured the plan because 'U.S. interests coincided with those of the United Kingdom in regard to the type of accounting standards that might be mandated by the Common Market.' It supported the proposal '[t]o avoid a potential collision between the standards of the English-speaking countries and those of the Common Market'.[20]

The leadership of France's Ordre des Experts Comptables was interested to join the IASC because it was seen as an opportunity to 'open the windows'.[21] In the early 1970s, the Ordre began to realize that the French profession risked falling behind internationally. The Plan Comptable Général had insulated France from accounting practices abroad, and it was found that French accountants were not well represented in the international accountancy firms in France.[22] Joining the IASC became a part of the effort to reinvigorate the French profession.

In its initial reaction, Germany's Institut der Wirtschaftsprüfer (IdW) supported the notion of international accounting standards.[23] The leadership of the IdW was keen to join the IASC even though its general membership was said to be sceptical.[24] As will be seen, the IdW strongly favoured a close relationship between the IASC and ICCAP, not least because the ICCAP chairman, Reinhard Goerdeler, was a prominent IdW member and the IdW provided the ICCAP secretariat.

The Japanese Institute of Certified Public Accountants (JICPA) was aware that the Japanese economy had become more open to international investment and foreign trade during the 1960s. In retrospect, the listing of Sony Corporation on the New York Stock Exchange in September 1970 was cited as an important symbol of this trend.[25] If asked, the JICPA would probably have subscribed to Benson's view that international accounting standards were 'an urgent need'. Nevertheless, the understanding of developments outside Japan was generally limited, and the precise implications of the IASC initiative may not have been well understood. The JICPA's willingness to join the IASC was therefore also a matter of not wanting to 'miss the bus',[26] even though it may not have been quite clear where the bus was heading.

In the early 1970s, the leadership of the Instituto Mexicano de Contadores Públicos was active in developing its international relations. The Institute believed it had presented itself as a strong candidate to host the 1977 international congress of accountants. Even though, in the spring of 1973, it lost out to the IdW which was to organize the 1977 congress in Munich, its international credentials were sufficient for it to be awarded the 1982 congress, which was held in Mexico City. As the only member of ICCAP from Latin America, the Mexican Institute was keen to play a leadership role in Latin America and the Spanish-speaking world, not least because it felt that it was ahead of Spain in the area of accounting. From this perspective, joining the IASC was natural even though the Council of the Institute was concerned about the costs.[27]

The Nederlands Instituut van Registeraccountants (NIVRA) had been eager to join the Study Group ever since its inception, and had in fact included an item in its policy plan for 1973 'to find a form in which European organisations could join the so-called North Atlantic Triangle'. After the IASC was founded, the NIVRA noted with satisfaction that 'Few plans [of the NIVRA Board] can have had such a successful and easy outcome.'[28] Nevertheless, there was concern whether the exclusive set-up of the IASC might interfere with other more broadly based attempts at international cooperation, such as ICCAP. To be sure, the NIVRA decided at an early stage to make its decision to join contingent on whether the French and the Germans would join.[29]

3.4. MAIN FEATURES OF THE 1973 AGREEMENT AND CONSTITUTION

Between the Sydney congress in September 1972 and the inaugural meeting in June 1973, the proposed IASC was extensively discussed within and among the participating accountancy bodies. The representatives of the institutes that participated in the Study Group met in London in December 1972, and representatives of all of the bodies invited to join the IASC, except for the Japanese, met in London in March 1973. There were numerous informal contacts as well. During this period, the IASC Agreement and Constitution gradually took shape.[30] The main features of the Constitution (reproduced in Appendix 1) are discussed in the following sections.

3.4.1. Participating Countries and Accountancy Bodies

In Sydney, Benson had proposed that Australia, France, Germany, and the Netherlands join the expanded Study Group. LeRoy Layton and Wallace Olson, the chairman and executive vice-president, respectively, of the AICPA, argued in favour of inviting Mexico and Japan as well. They feared that Benson's proposal would allow the United Kingdom, via the Commonwealth contingent, to dominate the organization. Benson agreed to Mexico, but whether to invite Japan remained an open question until the meeting in London in December 1972. As in the case of the Study Group, Benson wanted to have a compact committee. In the United Kingdom and other countries, there were doubts about the technical contribution that Japan could make, but in the end the argument prevailed that Japan could not be ignored because of its economic significance.[31] Because there were no Japanese representatives at the London meeting of March 1973, there was speculation until May that the Japanese might not take their seat.[32] In that case, the United Kingdom, French, German, and Dutch institutes would have proposed that the seat be offered to one or more of the Nordic countries.[33] These speculations proved groundless, however, and the JICPA took its place among the founder members of the IASC.

With the addition of Mexico and Japan, the composition of the IASC was nearly identical to that of ICCAP, except that India and the Philippines were represented on the latter but not on the former.[34] While the addition of both countries to the IASC would have been attractive to those who argued in favour of integration of the IASC with ICCAP, a further extension of the membership beyond Japan and Mexico was not acceptable to the United Kingdom. As a compromise, Benson introduced the concept of 'associate' membership, by which accountancy bodies from other countries might become involved in the work of the IASC even though they did not have a vote and could attend meetings of the Committee only by invitation.[35] The Indian Institute let it be known that it had no objections to being left out, provided the Philippines also was not invited.[36]

Table 3.1. Membership of the IASC in 1973

Australia	The Institute of Chartered Accountants in Australia
	Australian Society of Accountants
Canada	Canadian Institute of Chartered Accountants
France	Ordre des Experts Comptables et des Comptables Agréés (Order of Accounting Experts and Qualified Accountants)
Germany	Institut der Wirtschaftsprüfer in Deutschland (Institute of Auditors in Germany)
	Wirtschaftsprüferkammer (Chamber of Auditors)
Japan	Nihon Kouninkaikeishi Kyoukai (Japanese Institute of Certified Public Accountants)
Mexico	Instituto Mexicano de Contadores Públicos (Mexican Institute of Public Accountants)
Netherlands	Nederlands Instituut van Registeraccountants (Netherlands Institute of Registered Auditors)
United Kingdom & Ireland	Institute of Chartered Accountants in England and Wales
	Institute of Chartered Accountants of Scotland
	Institute of Chartered Accountants in Ireland
	Association of Certified Accountants
	Institute of Cost and Management Accountants
	Institute of Municipal Treasurers and Accountants
United States of America	American Institute of Certified Public Accountants

At the time, the discussions were typically worded in terms of which countries should join the IASC, and the Constitution (article 3) specified that each country was to have one vote. Yet in fact the membership of the IASC consisted of accountancy bodies.[37] Most of the original delegations represented a single accountancy body. But in Australia, there were two member bodies, as was true in Germany, once it had been agreed that the Wirtschaftsprüferkammer would be a joint signatory with the IdW.[38] In the UK and Ireland, there were no fewer than six member bodies, but in the IASC Constitution (article 1(a)), they all were considered as coming from one country. Table 3.1 lists the membership of the IASC at its founding. All countries were to have one vote, even though they could send two representatives and a staff observer to Committee meetings.

3.4.2. Relations with ICCAP

Whether and how the IASC should be related to ICCAP was the most contentious issue during the run-up to the founding of the IASC.[39] As will be seen in subsequent chapters, this was the prelude to a complicated relationship between the IASC and ICCAP, and its successor, IFAC.

ICCAP was created at the Sydney congress in September 1972 upon the recommendation of the International Working Party (IWP). It was a further step towards setting up a permanent international secretariat of the accountancy profession, which had begun at the international congress of accountants in Paris, in 1967 (*see* Section 2.6). Within the IWP, the AICPA had argued in favour of creating an international secretariat immediately, but Benson, on behalf of the UK profession, had opposed this step. The creation of ICCAP was a delaying compromise that postponed a decision on the creation of an international secretariat while keeping the issue on the agenda.

When, at the Sydney congress, Benson proposed to expand the Study Group, it is understandable that the AICPA wanted to ensure that ICCAP, the embryonic international secretariat, was not fatally weakened before it was even born by the creation of a parallel but independent organization. LeRoy Layton and Wallace Olson insisted that the proposed standard-setting body be established as part of ICCAP.[40] Benson, on the other hand, had no intention of making ICCAP more important than it had to be, nor of involving more than a compact group of countries in the IASC. The main argument that he used was the as-yet unsettled state of ICCAP. Hinting at his experiences in the Union Européenne des Experts Comptables (UEC), he said: '[Letting ICCAP assume responsibility for international accounting standards would] expose [this] initiative to the political ambitions and problems of participation from countries which could make little or no contribution. The delays and manoeuvrings the British have experienced in comparable situations leads them to the conclusion that such delays and manoeuvrings would fatally weaken the initiative under consideration.'[41]

The AICPA, supported by the Canadians, responded by pressing for fast progress in ICCAP. In January and February 1973, even before the first meeting of ICCAP in April 1973, the AICPA circulated proposals among its fellow ICCAP members for rapidly transforming ICCAP into an 'International Institute of Public Accounting'. One of the goals of this institute would be to '[e]stablish international standards of accounting and auditing and promote their adoption by national bodies when reporting international operations'.[42]

Once Germany was invited to join the IASC, it allied itself to the United States and Canada by making its participation conditional on the IASC being made part of ICCAP. As indicated above, the IdW had a strong interest in the success of ICCAP. Together with Mexico, these four countries strongly supported integration of the IASC within ICCAP. France and Japan did not have an outspoken position on the issue, while the Netherlands and Australia favoured integration in principle but were willing to postpone this in order to avoid delaying the start of international accounting standards.[43] Since the ICAEW maintained its opposition against integration, a deadlock ensued that could not be broken by informal consultation nor at the meeting of 19 March 1973 in London.[44] At that meeting it was agreed to defer the question of the relationship between the IASC and ICCAP until ICCAP had had a chance to discuss the issue at its first meeting.

This by itself did not help move matters forward, as the membership of ICCAP was by and large identical to the proposed membership of the IASC. During the first ICCAP meeting on 26 and 27 April 1973 the same impasse over the position of the IASC reappeared. It seems, though, that ICCAP Chairman Goerdeler was able to work out a compromise along the following lines. The AICPA proposal to move rapidly towards an 'International Institute of Public Accounting' was still on the table. It received support from a number of countries, but it also faced determined UK opposition. The proposal was, for the time being, put on hold by entrusting it to a working party. Apparently in exchange, the United Kingdom was willing to give its consent to the following resolution:

ICCAP endorses the endeavours that have resulted in the formation of IASC. ICCAP formally invites IASC to be part of the world attempt to develop the accountancy profession.

ICCAP requests IASC to recognise in its charter that it is part of the ICCAP organisation although it is autonomous in its issuance of exposure drafts and recommendations.

ICCAP further agrees that the IASC basic Charter shall not be reviewed until the end of 1976 without the agreement of IASC and ICCAP.[45]

This settled the matter, at least for the time being. When the IASC Constitution was finalized on 28 June, wording directly copied from this resolution was included in the 'Agreement to Establish an International Accounting Standards Committee' (article 2).

3.4.3. Objective and Scope of Activities

Compared to the protracted negotiations over ICCAP, the participants easily reached agreement on the objectives of the IASC. According to the final text of the Agreement (article 1(a)), the IASC was set up:

to formulate and publish in the public interest, basic standards to be observed in the presentation of audited accounts and financial statements and to promote their worldwide acceptance.

The notion of 'basic' standards originated with Benson and was accepted without apparent discussion by the other accountancy bodies. Benson later observed: 'I meant to convey the impression that the standards issued would be simple and straightforward, on topics that went to the root of published financial statements.'[46]

There was more resistance to Benson's suggestion that the IASC should set auditing standards as well as accounting standards. Earlier versions of the objectives clause were drafted in terms of 'basic international standards in accounting, auditing and financial reporting'.[47] One of the early lists of possible topics to be addressed by the Committee did include 'minimum audit requirements' and 'form and purpose of the audit report'.[48] Yet in the end, the wording was modified to the more equivocal 'standards to be observed in the presentation of audited accounts and financial statements', and the issue was left open with the understanding that the Committee would initially concentrate on accounting standards.[49] Benson did not give up, and at the press conference where the founding of the IASC was announced, he mentioned minimum auditing requirements as one of the topics that might be addressed.[50]

3.4.4. Compliance, 'Best Endeavours', and Voting

An important but difficult issue was to define the obligations of the participating institutes with respect to ensuring compliance with the published standards. These institutes came from countries with widely different regulatory cultures. There were significant variations in the legal regulation of the accountancy profession and of financial reporting, in the power of the institutes over their members and over the setting of national standards, and in the influence of auditors on the reporting practices of companies. In recognition that some institutes might be able to achieve more than others, the Agreement did not directly require the institutes to ensure compliance with the IASC's standards, but to use their best endeavours to ensure such compliance.

More specifically, the best endeavours were defined with respect to three groups: reporting companies, auditors, and other groups whose support for international accounting standards should be sought, such as governments, regulatory bodies, and securities markets.

With respect to companies, it was fairly easy to reach agreement on the objective, yet it would subsequently prove difficult to achieve. In the Agreement, the institutes undertook 'to use their best endeavours to ensure that published accounts comply with [the] standards, or that there is disclosure of the extent to which they do not' (Agreement, article 1(c)(i)).

Defining the obligation for auditors proved to be more difficult. A first draft of the Constitution required (always, of course, to the extent of a member body's best endeavours) that 'audit reports explicitly affirm that the auditors have satisfied themselves that the accounts comply with [the] standards'.[51] Australia, France, and the United Kingdom did not see a problem, but the IdW and the NIVRA objected to imposing such a requirement on their membership. The CICA and the AICPA 'were prepared to go that way', even though the AICPA preferred to limit it to auditors' reports destined for an international public.[52] To meet the objections, the clause was modified to say that only non-compliance should be mentioned in the auditor's report.

The NIVRA preferred to qualify this clause even further by limiting the requirement to those standards that had secured 'general acceptance and observance...by governments, authorities controlling securities markets and other regulatory agencies...and by the industrial and business community in a wide sense'.[53] This reflected the consensual approach to issuing accounting norms in the Netherlands, and a belief that such norms could not be imposed unilaterally on companies by the accountancy profession. In the words of Pieter Louwers, chief internal auditor of Philips and one of the first two Dutch representatives on the IASC, the IASC should avoid looking like 'a power-grab by the auditors'.[54] Although this modification was not acceptable to the other institutes, the wording of the Agreement (article 1(c)(i)) was revised to stress that ensuring acceptance and compliance should be seen as 'joint major objectives' of the IASC.[55] As is discussed in Chapter 7, this issue would come back in later years. It would then lead to the creation of the IASC's Consultative Group and to the addition of board members from other organizations than accountancy bodies.

An issue arose as to whether the best endeavours should include taking disciplinary action against auditors who fail to insert the required statement on compliance in the auditor's report. Although agreement was reached to include a clause calling for disciplinary action, this was changed to 'appropriate action' in the final version on the basis of legal advice obtained by the ICAEW (Agreement, article 1(c)(iii)).[56]

France's Ordre expressed the view 'that it would be difficult for a country which has voted against a basic standard, to require from its nationals that they abide by this standard', and they therefore argued that standards had to be approved by a unanimous vote. This was not acceptable to the other delegations, but it was agreed to raise the threshold by requiring a vote of three quarters (or seven out of nine votes), instead of two-thirds, before a standard could be published. For exposure drafts, a two-thirds majority was sufficient.[57]

3.4.5. Financing

The financial arrangements (Constitution, article 6) specified that each country would contribute one-ninth of the annual budget. The budget would be used to cover the costs of the permanent staff and the travel and accommodation expenses of one member of each country's delegation. The rent, rates, and taxes of the office housing the IASC's secretariat would be borne by the country where the office was located. These arrangements were accepted without difficulty, even though the concerns of smaller countries (the Netherlands) and countries with high travelling costs (Australia) were noted.[58] The budget for the first full year (1974) was tentatively set at £62,400.

3.4.6. Location

In advocating the establishment of the IASC, the ICAEW intended from the beginning that its secretariat should be located in London. The AICPA, however, decided to press for New York, and the location of the secretariat became a matter of discussion. Douglas Morpeth tried to win support for London from the Germans, the Dutch, and the French, because the ICAEW was reported to be 'very anxious' to avoid a US location.[59] The French Ordre, which was not keen on either London or New York, and presumably realizing that Paris would not be an acceptable candidate, tried to enlist support for Amsterdam. But since the NIVRA, unlike the ICAEW, was unwilling to bear all of the costs of housing the secretariat, Amsterdam was never a serious alternative.[60] As, apart from the AICPA, there was no strong support for New York either, it was agreed that the secretariat should be based in London.

3.5. REACTIONS TO THE FOUNDING OF THE IASC

The IASC initiative was not made public until June 1973. Yet Benson wrote in *The Accountant* in December 1972 that the Sydney congress might provide the momentum for establishing and accepting basic accounting and auditing standards.[61] Morpeth and Mackenzie gave similar comments on the Sydney congress.[62] Just days before the founder members of the IASC met in London on 19 March, Morpeth 'stressed the need for international co-operation and for international accounting standards' in his opening remarks to the ICAEW's annual conference.[63] When the IASC was formally founded, due care was taken to ensure that the event would not pass unnoticed. On 29 June 1972, the Agreement and Constitution were signed during a public ceremony in the Council Chamber of the ICAEW at Chartered Accountant's Hall. Benson had arranged for the Parliamentary Under-Secretary of State for Trade, the Earl of Limerick, to be present and address the meeting prior to the signing. Rising to the occasion, Lord Limerick, a Scottish chartered accountant, endorsed the IASC by stating that his government was 'wholeheartedly and unreservedly in favour of this splendid effort'.[64] In another effort to garner support for the IASC, David Leroy-Lewis, the deputy chairman of the London Stock Exchange, was invited to have dinner with the newly formed Committee on 28 June. His speech, in which he expressed the Exchange's 'good wishes... stemming from a certain identity of interests', was circulated to the press.[65]

Benson had urged the participating bodies to arrange 'opportunities for extensive publicity' in their home countries. A press conference was held after the signing ceremony, and a press release was distributed with a view towards achieving wide international coverage. As a result, the founding of the IASC was quite extensively covered in the British and Irish press, but coverage in most other member countries seems to have been much less.

Coverage in the general press mainly reflected the contents of the press release and Benson's opening speech as chairman. As a result, the IASC was characterized in a positive vein as a 'major move' or a 'major step towards the harmonization of international accounting practice'.[66] Benson's remark that eventually forty to fifty countries might become associated with the IASC was widely quoted, as well as his prediction that it would have 'a profound effect' within ten years.[67] *The Wall Street Journal*, in a long article, quoted Wallace Olson as saying that the IASC's standards 'won't be terribly inconsistent with the basic standards that exist in the U.S.'[68] *The New York Times* ran a brief article, apparently drawn from the AICPA's press release.[69]

The professional press provided additional commentary. *Accountancy Age* called the formation of the IASC 'a very welcome move'. It added: 'Hopefully the IASC will be able to claim a more lasting claim to fame than the old study group. Although this group cannot be faulted for its effort, the results of its work have often fallen on stony ground.... It is important that the IASC should be able to produce the dramatic progress Sir Henry predicts.'[70] *The Accountant* spoke confidently of a 'Historic Agreement', and even 'possibly one of the most significant in the whole long history of international business'.[71]

Outside the United Kingdom, the amount of coverage in the professional literature varied considerably, perhaps reflecting different degrees of enthusiasm in the various participating bodies. The NIVRA included a twelve-page insert in its journal, containing a photographic reproduction of the Agreement and Constitution and some articles. NIVRA Chairman Jan Schoonderbeek described how his institute's 'dream' of joining the Study Group had come true. In a more sober mood, accurately anticipating the IASC's overriding problem of the 1990s, he added: 'It will be quite a different challenge to have the norms accepted by governments, by bodies such as the Securities and Exchange Commission (S.E.C.) in the U.S.A. and by the various constituent parts of the business community. Will there be willingness to adjust laws, regulations and traditions to the developing international insights of the I.A.S.C.?'[72]

At the other extreme, the journal of the IdW did not mention the IASC until its December 1973 issue, and then only in passing in a news item on ICCAP. The IASC was described as a 'part of ICCAP' and as part of the initial steps taken towards an ambitious 'international organization of accountancy institutes'.[73] The AICPA's journal and newsletter both included a short factual note.[74] The French, Canadian, and Australian institutes occupied a middle ground by giving a factual account, the Agreement and Constitution, or both, without making significant comment.[75]

3.5.1. Reactions within the UEC

The swift emergence of the IASC during the spring of 1973 was noted with particular acuteness within the UEC. As shown in Section 2.7, the UEC had only just embarked on a programme of issuing recommendations on accounting and auditing. Moreover, the UEC had done so at the urging of Henry Benson. Some accountancy bodies who were also members of the UEC reacted to the IASC proposal with surprise, if not annoyance. In its initial reaction, the IdW wrote to Morpeth in February 1973 as follows: 'We do, however, want to convey our surprise insofar as since Sydney numerous meetings between representatives of our organisations have taken place, some of them having dealt with partly similar initiatives in the European area, but at these occasions your plans have neither been mentioned nor even been hinted at.'[76]

On 30 April and 1 May 1973, when the IASC was still the subject of intense discussions between the participating institutes, the UEC executive committee met in London. Henk Volten reported on this meeting to the NIVRA board:[77]

Last November, the initiative came from England (Sir Henry Benson) to develop U.E.C. recommendations. As became clear subsequently, the initiator was then already aware of the preparation of the I.A.S.C.-proposal. Pressure from various sides (Netherlands, Sweden, but also Scotland) to create clarity in this situation has now led the successor of Sir Henry in the Executive Committee... to plead in favour of a kind of liaison between I.A.S.C. and U.E.C.

Why the Scots would have been upset is not clear, because ICAS had been involved in all of the talks on the IASC since the Sydney congress. But it is natural that the other accountancy bodies would have been mystified by what appeared to be a kind of double dealing on the part of the ICAEW. Given that Benson was heavily involved with so many of the important developments at this time, such as the UEC, the IWP and of course the IASC, he must have considered the effects that his actions in one arena would have in the others. One might speculate, for instance, that his efforts to develop the UEC were intended to support his argument in the IWP that an international secretariat would be premature before the regional bodies had had a chance to develop.[78] However, it is likely that the course of events was influenced less by English deviousness than by the fact that, late in 1972 and early in 1973, the situation was still fluid and it was difficult to see which route, if any, would lead to effective international standards. This is illustrated by a discussion at a meeting of the ICAEW's overseas relations committee on 23 January 1973. The committee was at that time informed for the first time about the IASC initiative. It also discussed the UEC's ongoing preparations for drafting recommendations on accounting and auditing:[79]

> It was...agreed that the Institute should continue to maintain pressure for the special [UEC] committee to start work even if this were subsequently to be superseded by the work of the International Accounting Standards Committee...The committee took the view that only by continued pressure on a number of fronts was progress likely to be made in establishing basic international standards.

This last observation was apparently the basis of agreement within the UEC as well. In fact, it was never likely that the formation of the IASC would be hindered by the UEC. Apart from the UK and Irish bodies, the only other UEC members among the proposed IASC members were the IdW and the NIVRA.[80] Of these latter two, the NIVRA was probably the strongest supporter of a more active UEC, partly because a former NIVRA president, Aad Tempelaar, was president of the UEC in 1973. Yet there was never any doubt within the NIVRA leadership that it should join the IASC, even though there were some scruples about possible reactions of other UEC members.[81] Like the ICAEW, the NIVRA had its doubts whether the UEC could be developed into an effective standard setter, as 'past experience with the U.E.C. does provide little ground for optimism'.[82]

A meeting was held in Amsterdam on 19 May of the UEC presidency and the UEC members that were to be part of the IASC. It was decided that the UEC would continue 'on its own' and would act quickly to prepare recommendations. A technical committee (with representatives from France, Germany, the United Kingdom, and the Netherlands) would meet on 19 June to discuss two drafts 'on the topics suggested in Lisbon (November 1972) by Sir Henry Benson'.[83] One of these topics was 'disclosure of accounting policies', and the other was the 'object and content of the auditor's report'. Progress on the first of these topics was rapid. A draft recommendation on disclosure of accounting policies was published in October 1973, followed by a definitive version in January 1974.[84] The UEC moved faster than the IASC, which did not publish its first exposure draft, on the same topic of disclosure of accounting policies in March 1974, and its standard (IAS 1) in January 1975 (*see* Section 5.4). Yet this did little to strengthen the hand of the UEC. It was fairly obvious that something had to be done to prevent confusion and duplication of effort, and it was equally obvious that the UEC had to give way. *The Economist* had described the UEC's plan for issuing recommendations as half-hearted, which was borne out by the fact that the first draft recommendation was accompanied by a letter from the UEC secretary-general stating that the UEC executive committee was 'studying' the continuation of its programme on recommendations.[85] The UEC did not, in fact, issue any recommendations on accounting after the first, although it went on to develop a rather elaborate series of guidance statements on auditing issues. In 1987, the UEC and the Groupe d'Études were combined into the Fédération des Experts Comptables Européens (FEE). Given that there were grave doubts within the UEC itself about its role as an accounting standard setter, it can be understood that feelings towards Benson were not particularly hard. Even though he effectively nipped the UEC's accounting recommendations in the bud, after he had been pushing hard to persuade the UEC to issue such recommendations in the first place, it was recognized that he should receive credit for attempting to strengthen and activate the UEC. When he left the UEC executive committee in the spring of 1973, two years before his term ended, he did not leave under a cloud but received a tribute to his efforts by UEC President Aad Tempelaar.[86]

3.5.2. Impact on the Accountants International Study Group

As indicated above, the earliest plans for the IASC were couched in terms of expanding the AISG. The London meeting of December 1972, at which the IASC proposal was discussed, was held one day before a regular meeting of the Study Group, also in London. At that stage, it was decided that the IASC would be a new organization, set up apart from the Study Group. Wallace Olson, the AICPA's executive vice-president, had attended the meeting on the IASC and also attended the Study Group's meeting on the next day. He was reported in the minutes of the Study Group as saying that, as the IASC would concentrate on basic standards, the Study Group should continue to work on more sophisticated topics. The delegates from the American, Canadian, English, and Scottish institutes at the Study Group meeting 'strongly recommended' that the Study Group continue its important work, 'while recognizing that its recommendations would be of interest mainly to accountants in Canada, the USA and the United Kingdom'.[87]

Yet a few years later, in June 1976, the Study Group recommended to its sponsoring institutes that no new projects be added to its present programme, and said that it would endeavour to complete its ongoing projects within the next eighteen months.[88] John W. Adams, of Canada, the Study Group's chairman in 1975–6, said that this decision was taken to lend 'moral support to the IASC, which was struggling to get recognition internationally. We felt that the English-speaking countries represented by our Group should support them.'[89] An additional consideration was the imminent founding of IFAC in 1977, which would require a reallocation of resources by the participating institutes.[90] Accordingly, at the end of 1976, the sponsoring institutes voted to disband the Study Group, if the plans for IFAC were to go ahead. The decision was not announced until September 1977, when the last doubts about the founding of IFAC had been dispelled.[91] The demise of the Study Group was not widely lamented, but some paid tribute to its pioneering work in comparative studies.[92] Joseph Cummings, then the chairman of the IASC which had effectively taken over the Study Group's mantle, wrote, 'The AISG lacked two ingredients of success: one, participation by representative membership, and two, procedures for enforcing recommendations which were included in the published studies.'[93] As shown in subsequent chapters, these issues remained fundamental to the IASC throughout its life, and they dominated the restructuring of the IASC at the end of the 1990s (*see* Chapter 13).

Part II

1973–87

4

The People and the Structure of the IASC

This chapter discusses the organization of operations and early evolution of the International Accounting Standards Committee (IASC), paying attention to its structure, the leadership, the composition of the delegations, and its finances. The initial structure of the IASC was determined by the 1973 Agreement and Constitution, as discussed in Chapter 3. The Constitution was modified in 1977 and 1982, on the occasion of the international congresses of accountants in Munich and Mexico City, respectively. Reference is made to the impact of these constitutional changes. As is discussed more fully in Chapter 7, the 1982 Constitution was accompanied by a Mutual Commitments pact between the IASC and the International Federation of Accountants (IFAC), which contained several important provisions bearing on the organization of the IASC.

Readers should consult Appendices 1–3 and 5 in conjunction with this chapter: a reproduction of the 1973 Agreement and Constitution, a chronological list of IASC chairmen and senior staff, a list of members of delegations, and a list of venues and dates of IASC Committee/board meetings.

4.1. THE CHAIRMEN

Sir Henry Benson (1910–95), the founding chairman from June 1973 to July 1976, was the senior partner of Coopers & Lybrand, in London, and served as a path-breaking president of the Institute of Chartered Accountants in England and Wales (ICAEW) in 1966–7. By all accounts, he was a dominant figure both in his firm and in professional circles. His considerable public service earned him a life peerage in 1981.[1] Benson was originally to retire as IASC chairman in 1975, but the members of the IASC expressed the 'overwhelming sentiment' that he should continue as chairman for a further term of up to two years.[2]

Joseph P. Cummings (1919–2000), chairman from July 1976 to June 1978, was deputy senior partner of Peat, Marwick, Mitchell & Co., in New York City, in charge of the firm's international operations. He had been a member of the Accounting Principles Board (APB) of the American Institute of Certified Public Accountants (AICPA) from 1966 to 1973, serving as its vice-chairman for six years.

John A. Hepworth (born in 1919), chairman from July 1978 to June 1980, was a partner in Yarwood, Vane & Co., in Melbourne, which was associated

Figure 4.1. IASC chairmen and secretaries, IASC tenth anniversary dinner, 15 June 1983. *Left to right*: Paul Rosenfield, John Hepworth, Sir Henry Benson, Stephen Elliott, Hans Burggraaff, Washington SyCip (IFAC), Geoffrey Mitchell

Figure 4.2. IASC chairmen and secretary, Toronto, June 1984. *Left to right*: Stephen Elliott, John Kirkpatrick, Geoffrey Mitchell, Georges Barthès de Ruyter

internationally with Deloitte Haskins & Sells. In 1974–5, he was president of the Institute of Chartered Accountants in Australia (ICAA).

J. A. (Hans) Burggraaff (born in 1920), chairman from July 1980 to October 1982, was a partner in Binder Dijker Otte & Co., in Amsterdam. He chaired the Dutch Tripartite Study Group on financial reporting from 1972 to 1975, and he served a two-year term as chairman of the Nederlands Instituut van Registeraccountants (NIVRA) in 1977–8.

Stephen Elliott (1920–2002), chairman from November 1982 to March 1985, was born in London and studied in England. He served as the managing partner for Canada in Arthur Andersen & Co., based in Toronto, for twenty-one years, retiring in 1982. He chaired the Accounting and Auditing Research Committee of the Canadian Institute of Chartered Accountants (CICA) from 1970 to 1972.[3]

John L. Kirkpatrick (1927–2002), chairman from April 1985 to October 1987, was deputy chairman of the UK firm of KMG Thomson McLintock, in Glasgow. He was president of the Institute of Chartered Accountants of Scotland (ICAS) in 1977–8.[4]

Thus, after Benson's three-year term, Cummings and Hepworth served for two years, Burggraaff for two years and three months, and Elliott and Kirkpatrick for two-and-a-half years, which became the standard term for the chairman following the approval of the amended Constitution in October 1982.

Henry Benson was designated as the first chairman during the process of organizing the IASC. His successors were elected by the Committee (or board, as it was known as a result of the revision of the Constitution in 1977) as chairman designate between nine and fifteen months before their term as chairman was to begin, in order to ease the transition. With one exception, all of the chairmen succeeding Benson were elected by acclamation.

The exception occurred in 1984, when John Kirkpatrick, representing the UK & Irish delegation, and Rolando Ortega, of the Mexican delegation, vied for the position. Kirkpatrick, who believed that his name would be the only one put forward for chairman designate, took a year's temporary leave from his delegation beginning in the spring of 1983 in order to manage some professional affairs at home prior to his expected ascendancy to the chair. He was replaced in the delegation by Jeff Pearcy, also a member of the Scottish Institute. When Kirkpatrick learned that the election would be contested, he returned to attend part of the October 1983 and March 1984 meetings, held in Paris and London, respectively.[5] The election was between a representative of the IASC's host country, which was one of the dominant members of the board, and one from a founder country that was not one of the major world players in standard setting. There was no rancour over the contest; it was just that there were two candidates for the position. Chairman Stephen Elliott conducted the election, by secret ballot, at the March 1984 meeting, and he announced that Kirkpatrick had won. It is believed that the vote was eight to five.[6]

4.2. COMPOSITION OF THE ORIGINAL DELEGATIONS TO THE IASC

The purpose of this section is to convey an impression of the composition of the original delegations to the IASC as well as how the members of each delegation were appointed. A review of the members who attended the first eight meetings, from June 1973 to April 1975, excluding those who attended only the signing ceremony on 29 June 1973, may give some impression of how the several delegations were constituted (the figure in parentheses is the number of meetings attended):

— Australia
   Dick Burgess (3)
   Harry Levy (1)

Figure 4.3. IASC delegates and staff, London, January 1975. *Front, left to right*: Seigo Nakajima, Sir Henry Benson. *Middle, left to right*: Howard Lyons, Tony Kewin (*behind Nakajima*), Henk Treffers (*behind Benson*), Robert Mazars (*behind Treffers*), Wendy Neave, Alexander Mackenzie. *Back, left to right*: Doug Thomas, Jeremy Winters, John Hepworth, Is Kleerekoper, Manuel Galván (*behind Kleerekoper*), Henk Volten, Bob Sempier, Paul Rosenfield, Joe Cummings, Richard Simmons, Krafft von der Tann

John Hepworth (5)
Ron Munro (4, of which one meeting as staff observer)
Tony Kewin (staff observer) (4)

— Canada
Howard Lyons (8)
Doug Thomas (8)

— France
Robert Mazars (8)
André Henrot (3)
Alfred Cordoliani (staff observer) (8)

— Germany (Federal Republic)
Krafft Freiherr von der Tann (6)
Hans Havermann (3)
Horst Kaminski (staff observer) (7)

— Japan
Shozo Tatsumi (5)
Junichi Kawaguchi (5)
Seigo Nakajima (staff observer) (6)

— Mexico
Manuel Galván (8)
Julio Freyssinier (1)
Alfonso Campala (staff observer) (1)

— Netherlands
Henk Treffers (8)
Pieter Louwers (4)
Is Kleerekoper (2)
Henk Volten (staff observer) (8)

— United Kingdom & Ireland
Sir Henry Benson (Chairman) (8)
Alexander Mackenzie (8)
Gerry Slator (staff observer) (1)
Jeremy Winters (staff observer) (6)

— United States
Joseph Cummings (7)
Robert Sempier (staff observer) (8)

Under the Constitution, each country's accountancy body (or bodies) could select a maximum of two members of their delegation to the Committee, accompanied by a staff observer. Until 1984, during Stephen Elliott's term, the IASC chairman constituted one of the members of his country's delegation.

Only one of the original members was a financial executive: Pieter Louwers, the chief internal auditor of Philips, who had to withdraw from the Committee in 1974 because of ill health. Virtually all of the other voting members were partners in accountancy firms.[7] All of the staff observers but two were employees of the sponsoring accountancy bodies.[8]

In the UK & Irish delegation, whose members were chosen by the Consultative Committee of Accountancy Bodies (CCAB) beginning in 1974, it was for many years a practice that both the English and Scottish institutes were represented in the delegation (Benson and Mackenzie, respectively, at the outset).[9] The initial staff observers, Gerry Slator and Jeremy Winters, came from the staff of the Accounting Standards Steering Committee (ASSC), which was renamed the Accounting Standards Committee (ASC) in 1976.

Joseph Cummings, as noted above, had been vice-chairman of the APB, and Robert Sempier, the staff observer, was the AICPA's director of international activities, later to become executive director (1977–91) of IFAC. As early as 1974, the National Association of Accountants (NAA), now the Institute of Management Accountants, complained that the US delegation omitted any representation from management accountants.[10] It was not until 1986 that the NAA became a co-sponsor with the AICPA of the US delegation, and John F. Chironna, of IBM, became its first representative on the IASC board in that year.

In the Canadian delegation, Howard Lyons had been chairman of the CICA's Accounting and Auditing Research Committee, and Doug Thomas, formerly the CICA's executive director, was its general director of research.

In the French delegation, Alfred Cordoliani, the staff observer, was the secretary-general of the Ordre des Experts Comptables, and Robert Mazars was a partner in an important accountancy firm bearing his name.

Krafft Freiherr von der Tann was the only member of the Committee who held a hereditary title (Freiherr is the equivalent of baron). Von der Tann was a sole practitioner. Hans Havermann was a partner in a major accountancy firm, and Horst Kaminski was on the staff of the Institut der Wirtschaftsprüfer (IdW).

In the Dutch delegation, Henk Treffers was at that time the accounting adviser to the Ministry of Justice. Previously, he served as chairman of the NIVA (predecessor of the NIVRA) and president of the Union Européenne des Experts Comptables, Economiques et Financiers (UEC). He was a partner in Moret & Limperg. Kleerekoper, a partner in Klijnveld, Kraayenhof & Co., had been deputy chairman of the NIVA. Louwers had also been chairman of the NIVRA.

The Australian delegation was led by members of the Institute of Chartered Accountants in Australia, but the Australian Society of Accountants, whose membership was composed mostly of company accountants and small practitioners, also participated. The Institute and Society agreed at the outset that the Institute would compose the IASC delegation and that the Society would look after the International Co-ordination Committee for the Accountancy Profession (ICCAP) and then, beginning in 1977, after IFAC. (E. H.) Dick Burgess was the Institute's president, but, owing to ill health, his service on the Committee was short-lived. Harry Levy attended one meeting on behalf of the Society, whose executive director, Ron Munro, attended several. Tony Kewin represented the Institute.

Both of the voting members of the Japanese delegation were partners in firms. Seigo Nakajima, a member of the Business Accounting Deliberation Council (BADC), was the first full-time accounting academic to form part of a delegation to the IASC. The BADC was the advisory body to the Ministry of Finance on accounting standards.

In the Mexican delegation, Manuel Galván, a partner in González Vilchis (associated with Price Waterhouse & Co.), was chairman or a member of the Comisión de Principios de Contabilidad (Accounting Principles Committee) of the Instituto Mexicano de Contadores Públicos (Mexican Institute of Public Accountants) during his service on the IASC. He served in the Mexican delegation until 1978, attending all seventeen meetings during his tenure, fourteen of them as the lone Mexican present.

4.3. EVOLUTION OF THE DELEGATIONS TO 1987

Of all the delegations, the one from the Netherlands had the least amount of turnover and therefore, on average, the longest terms of service. Henk Volten, the general director of the NIVRA, served as staff observer for fourteen years, although he attended less frequently in the later years, when he had become more active in IFAC. Most of its members were rightly regarded as among the most respected figures in the accountancy profession: Henk Treffers, Pieter Louwers, Is Kleerekoper, Hans Burggraaff, Jan Uiterlinden, Herman Marseille, and Frans Graafstal. Louwers, from Philips, was the only company executive in the Dutch delegation. Uiterlinden and Graafstal were partners in Klijnveld, Kraayenhof & Co., and Marseille was a partner in Van Dien & Co., which was affiliated with Deloitte, Haskins & Sells. Clearly, the Dutch profession and the NIVRA made a substantial commitment to the IASC.

After Louwers in the Dutch delegation, the US delegation was the next to appoint a company executive, this time as a matter of policy for the delegation: Eugene J. Minahan, who was succeeded by company executives Willis A. Smith, Ralph L. Harris, and John F. Chironna. In 1976, when Minahan was appointed, the AICPA approached the Financial Executives Institute (FEI) for a nominee who was also an AICPA member.[11] At that time, Minahan, who was about to retire as vice-president and controller of Atlantic-Richfield, a major oil company, was an active member of FEI's Corporate Reporting Committee, which, among its other duties, responded to Financial Accounting Standards Board (FASB) initiatives. Minahan had extensive overseas experience with his company.[12] Smith was comptroller of CPC International and had extensive experience in South America; he was also a member of both the AICPA and the FEI. Subsequent to Smith's appointment to the IASC board in 1979, the FEI named him to its Corporate Reporting Committee. At its March 1980 meeting, the IASC board encouraged the member bodies

Figure 4.4. IASC delegates, International Congress of Accountants, Munich, October 1977. *Left to right*: Horst Kaminsky, Wallace Olson, John Brennan, a Japanese delegate, Geoff Vincent, Hugh Richardson, Roy Nash, Joe Cummings, Robert Mazars, Hans Havermann, Masayaki Iwanami, Hans Burggraaff, John Hepworth, Seigo Nakajima, Doug Thomas, Henk Treffers, Morley Carscallen, Otto Grünewälder, Yukio Fujita, Krafft von der Tann, Dominique Ledouble, John Grenside, Nick Reece, Henk Volten, Eugene Minahan, Alexander Mackenzie, Reinhard Goerdeler (IFAC), Robert Sempier (IFAC)

represented on the board to consider including an accountant from industry in their delegations.[13]

The succession of practitioner members on the US delegation all came from big accountancy firms: Cummings (Peat Marwick Mitchell), Donald J. Hayes (Arthur Young), Roger Cason (Main Hurdman), Dennis R. Beresford (Ernst & Whinney) and Ralph E. Walters (Touche Ross). Cummings and Hayes had been members of the APB, and Walters had served for seven years on the FASB.[14] Paul Rosenfield, who distinguished himself as the IASC's inaugural secretary, having been seconded by the AICPA, returned to the IASC board in 1978 as staff observer to the US delegation, remaining until 1985. Rosenfield was employed in the accounting standards division of the AICPA and had previously served on the research staff of the APB.

The UK & Irish delegation, as indicated above, continued its duality of membership from the English and Scottish institutes. The string of members from the ICAEW came from the Big Eight firms: John P. Grenside (Peat Marwick Mitchell), David C. Hobson (Coopers & Lybrand), and Christopher J. Stronge (Deloittes). Grenside and Hobson served on the UK & Irish ASC during periods that overlapped their service on the IASC board, and Stronge had been an ASC member prior to his IASC service. Grenside had been president of the ICAEW in 1975–6. The Scots who succeeded Alec Mackenzie on the board were John Kirkpatrick and, briefly, Jeff Pearcy (from ICI), who was a former member of the ASC. The CCAB selected an Irish banker, Gerard Murphy, to succeed Pearcy. Murphy was the only Irishman from the Republic ever to serve in the delegation between 1973 and 2000. Ironically, it was during Murphy's tenure, in 1988, that the UK & Irish delegation was renamed the UK delegation. The delegation's staff observers, with the exception of David Tweedie, who was the technical director of the Scottish Institute, came from the ASC's staff at the ICAEW.

In the French delegation, Dominique Ledouble, the secretary-general of the Ordre, succeeded Alfred Cordoliani as the staff observer. In turn, he was succeeded as staff observer by Patrice Cardon and then by Jean-Claude Scheid, both of whom were employees of the Ordre. In 1982, Georges Barthès de Ruyter, a partner in Frinault Fiduciaire, joined the delegation, and in 1985 Jean-Luc Dumont, a partner in the Salustro firm, began twelve years of service in the delegation, one of the longest in the IASC's history. Jean-Pierre Lagarrigue's tenure in the delegation, begun in 1984, was cut short in 1985 by his death.

In the Canadian delegation, the successors to Howard Lyons (Haskins & Sells) were Morley Carscallen (Coopers & Lybrand) and Stephen Elliott. In 1981, the CICA appointed its first financial executive, Douglas R. Hagerman (NOVA Corporation), who had served on the CICA's Accounting Research Committee. The Society of Management Accountants of Canada (SMAC) and the Certified General Accountants' Association (CGAA) joined the CICA as sponsors of the Canadian delegation in 1978.[15] Hagerman was succeeded by Bruce Irvine, an accounting professor, who was the first member appointed by SMAC, and then by another financial executive, J. Michael Dawson (Consolidated-Bathurst, Inc.); Dawson had chaired the CICA's Accounting Standards Committee in 1982–3. The first CGAA representative did not join the delegation until 1988. The long-serving members of the delegation, Doug Thomas and John Denman, both came from the CICA's full-time staff; on a few occasions, an incoming member was labelled a staff observer as he transitioned to membership.

The Australian delegation was hampered by the long distances to attend board meetings, and several representatives (e.g. John Balmford, Douglas Rickard, and Rex Thiele) attended because they happened to be near the meeting site on other business, or they were filling in for a member who could not attend (such as David Boymal for Kenneth Spencer in June 1984).[16] The succession of members representing the Institute, following John Hepworth, was Phillip C. E. Cox (a company director), John N. Bishop (Peat Marwick Mitchell), and Spencer (Peat Marwick Mitchell). By 1985, however, the Institute had come to regard IFAC as an important force in the international accountancy profession, and it wanted to appoint one of its members to IFAC Council in succession to Peter Agars, a past national president of the Society. In an unusual 'swap' between the rival bodies, the Institute thereupon named John Bishop, who was conveniently a member of both bodies, to IFAC Council, and the Society appointed Ronald J. Cotton (1985–7), a past national president and the first financial executive to serve as a regular member of the delegation, to the IASC board.

It was the practice in Australia for one or both members of the delegation to the IASC to attend meetings of Australia's Accounting Standards Board as observers. In the 1980s, moreover, there was a trend towards appointing delegates having standard-setting experience or a technical background. Cotton was, at the time of his appointment, a member of the Accounting Standards Review Board (the standards oversight committee), and Boymal (also a member of both accountancy bodies), who was appointed to the delegation in 1987, had been a member of the Accounting Standards Board (ASB). Warren McGregor, the technical director–accounting at the Australian Accounting Research Foundation, became the first regularly attending staff observer in 1986, following years in which a staff observer would attend only sporadically, perhaps because of cost.

For the first seven years, the German delegation was composed of Krafft von der Tann, a founding member who served until his death in 1980, accompanied by Hans Havermann (1973–5), Otto Grünewälder (1975–80), and a staff observer, Horst Kaminski succeeded by Peter Marks, from the IdW. From 1980 to 1993, when the first member from industry was appointed, only one voting member attended. It was a deliberate policy to leave one seat open for a company executive, but it was not until the 1990s that company executives evinced any interest in the work of the IASC.[17]

The apparent policy of the Japanese delegation was to use the staff observer's position as a training ground for future members. Seigo Nakajima and Yukio Fujita were university accounting professors, while the other members of the delegation were drawn from accountancy firms. Nakajima became a delegation member in 1975 and remained in the delegation until 1988, having thus served on the IASC board longer than anyone else in its history, fifteen years in total.

At most of the meetings during the 1970s, only one member of the Mexican delegation, Manuel Galván, was in attendance. All of the members and staff observers were from accountancy firms. In those years, the Instituto Mexicano de Contadores Públicos did not employ any technical staff. The members who succeeded Galván were Leopoldo Romero (1979–83) of the firm of Galaz, Carstens, affiliated internationally with Touche Ross & Co., Rolando Ortega (1982–6), of Coopers & Lybrand, and Jesús Hoyos (1982–7), of Gonzalez, Vilchis, affiliated with Price Waterhouse. Romero had been a member of the Mexican Institute's Comisión de Principios de Contabilidad (Accounting Principles Committee) during most of the 1970s. In the 1980s, Hoyos was also a member of the Comisión. Several members of the delegation, including Hoyos, served as the Institute's vice-president for legislation, who oversaw the work of the Comisión.

Owing to severe economic problems in Mexico, including a major devaluation of the peso in 1982 as well as the financial problems that were claimed by the Mexican Institute, the Mexican delegation requested some financial relief from its obligations to the IASC so that it might remain on the board. The delegation members found it difficult to obtain foreign currency to finance overseas travel, and the Institute argued, in regard to its annual fee to the IASC, that the IASC should take the fee out of its surplus, to which the Institute had contributed in past years.[18] Although the IASC board did not want to set a precedent, it did not want to see the departure of the Mexican delegation before the end of its term either. At its March 1986 meeting, the board approved a limited financial concession, being careful not to set a precedent, so that the delegation could remain on the board to the end of 1987.[19] Later in 1986, a desperate board agreed to an unprecedented decision to waive the Institute's contributions to the 1986 and 1987 IASC budgets so long as its contributions in arrears were paid.[20] With this agreement, the Mexican delegation could remain on the board to the end of 1987, when its term expired. In 1988, under the revised Constitution, the Mexican delegation, as with all founder bodies, had to apply for reappointment to the board, which, in the end, it elected not do. Beginning in 1988, therefore, Mexico no longer had a delegation on the board, but the delegation returned to the board in 1995 (*see also* Section 8.2.4). Mexico was the only founding member whose service on the board of the IASC was ever interrupted.

4.4. DELEGATIONS SUBSEQUENTLY ADDED

The 1973 Constitution said that only the nine countries whose accountancy bodies were signatories to the Agreement and Constitution could be represented on the Committee. The amended Constitution in 1977 (*see* Section 4.14) provided that two additional member countries could appoint representatives to the IASC board. The board acted promptly to instruct the secretariat to write to the associate member bodies for expressions of interest in becoming board members on a rotation basis.[21] At its March 1978 meeting, the board agreed to issue invitations to Pakistan and South Africa to join as voting members for four-year terms.[22] Pakistan, however, withdrew its candidacy, evidently for financial reasons.[23] Nigeria was swiftly approved for the opening, and its representative attended the next board meeting, in November 1978, when the three representatives of South Africa also made their debut.

The South African delegation's two voting members all came from major accountancy firms and typically were very senior and influential members of the National Council of Chartered Accountants (SA). Most of them served for fairly long terms on the IASC board. Warwick G. Thorby (1978–86), of Peat Marwick Mitchell, and J. A. (Jock) Porteous (1978–83), of Goldby, Compton & Mackelvie, which was affiliated with Touche Ross, formed the initial delegation. Thorby was then the chairman of the National Council, and Porteous was a past chairman. At the time of his appointment, Porteous chaired the National Council's Accounting Practices Committee (APC). The APC drafted the standards, and the Accounting Practices Board decided whether to confirm them as statements of 'generally accepted accounting practice'. Rick G. Cottrell (1983–9), of Coopers & Lybrand, succeeded Porteous. The staff observers were the successive technical directors

Figure 4.5. IASC delegates and staff, Edinburgh, July 1987. *Front, left to right*: Rick Cottrell, Peter Wilmot, Ayodeji Oni, John Kirkpatrick, George Barthès de Ruyter, Alfonso Campaña, Jean-Claude Scheid, S. T. Chiang. *Middle rows, left to right*: Eiichi Shiratori, David Damant, Gerard Murphy, John Chironna, Wilhelm Tjaden (*in front of Chironna*), Christopher Stronge, Herman Marseille, Geoffrey Mitchell, Frans Graafstal, Bruce Irvine, Michael Dawson (*behind Barthès*), Ronald Cotton, Olusegun Osunkeye, Gillian Bertol, Tadaaki Tokunaga, John Denman. *Back row, left to right*: Jean-Luc Dumont, Giancarlo Tomasin, Giuseppe Verna, Tom McRae, David Cairns

of the National Council, which became the South African Institute of Chartered Accountants in 1980.

In the Nigerian delegation, Michael Ayodeji Oni, a partner in a predecessor firm of Ernst & Young, proved to be a leader during his four-year term (1983–7). C. Oyeniyi O. Oyediran, a partner in Coopers & Lybrand, had been president of the Institute of Chartered Accountants of Nigeria in 1976–7, and two other regular members of the delegation, including Oni, subsequently became presidents of the Institute.

The Constitution as amended in October 1982 expanded the number of rotating seats for non-founder members to four. Anticipating this change, the board agreed in a postal ballot, conducted after its June 1982 meeting, to the nomination of Chile and Italy as new board members as well as to a re-election of South Africa and Nigeria to new five-year terms.[24] Under the 1982 Constitution, new board members were appointed by IFAC Council, but the IASC/IFAC Mutual Commitments pact (*see* Section 4.17) provided that 'IFAC Council will seek the advice of the outgoing [IASC] Board as to all nominations' (article B8). It turned out that Chile, ostensibly for financial reasons, had to withdraw.[25] At the June 1983 board meeting, it was announced that IFAC Council had nominated Taiwan for the fourth opening, and the selection was ratified by the board.[26] Taiwan's term was to be only four years, as it was taking its seat a year after the opening arose. The members of the Italian delegation were all from accountancy firms,[27] as was the sole representative, S. T. Chiang, in the Taiwanese delegation.

Another innovation introduced with the 1982 Constitution was a provision for up to four organizations 'with an interest in financial reporting', that is, non-accountancy bodies, to be elected to board membership. This change marked a signal departure from the model of the IASC adopted in 1973, when the Agreement and Constitution was signed exclusively by national accountancy bodies. This facility was first used in October 1985, when an invitation was extended to the International Co-ordinating Committee of Financial Analysts Associations (ICCFAA). The ICCFAA accepted forthwith. David C. Damant, the first member of the financial analysts' delegation to attend meetings of the board, had been a leader of the European Federation of Financial Analysts' Societies as early as the 1960s. He had actively sought to remain in touch with the IASC ever since it was founded, and had been one of the initial members of the IASC's Consultative Group, created in 1981 (*see* Section 4.16).

By 1986, the number of delegations had increased to fourteen. Of the delegations added between 1977 and 1986, only South Africa and the financial analysts were retained as member delegations until 2000. Damant remained a member of the delegation until 2000, becoming the longest serving voting member of the board.

The IASC's leadership would have liked to attract a preparer organization to board membership as well, the leading candidate being the International Association of Financial Executives Institutes (IAFEI). From 1981 onwards, IAFEI did belong to the Consultative Group, yet by 1987 all of the IASC's attempts to bring IAFEI onto the board had failed.[28] Chairman Kirkpatrick wrote that IAFEI's 'German brethren are proving a sticking point so far, as they find it difficult to contemplate sitting down with "the auditors"—how sad if the German profession's élitism should cause this initiative to fail!'[29] IAFEI also seemed to be concerned that its delegation would regularly be outvoted by the delegations dominated by the practising accountants.[30]

4.5. INCORPORATION OF ASSOCIATE MEMBERS

Under article 1(b) of the Constitution, the Committee decided to write 'urgently' to professional accountancy bodies around the world, inviting them to join the IASC as associate members.[31] In December 1973, a scant five months after the IASC's founding, letters were mailed to seventy-four accountancy bodies in fifty-nine countries. Between 1974 and 1981, a total of forty-six associate members were admitted, including some which were invited subsequently.[32] In 1982, under the IASC/IFAC Mutual Commitments pact, all members of IFAC automatically were enrolled as members of the IASC.

Curiously, of the thirty-six invited accountancy bodies that decided not to join the IASC by 1981, twenty-one were from the twenty-five that were invited from Central and South America. The lack of interest by the Central and South American countries in the IASC is discussed in Section 6.19.

Candidates for associate membership were expected to be capable of meeting the membership fee, which was set originally at £1,000 but then was scaled down according to the membership size of each body.[33] To be eligible, they had to be entitled to participate in the quinquennial international congresses of accountants. Like the founder members, all of the associate members agreed to undertake the 'best endeavours' obligation set out in the IASC Agreement.

As soon as the accountancy bodies became associate members, their countries were eligible to be represented on project steering committees, and all of the associate members were invited to discuss the revised IASC Agreement and Constitution during the Munich international congress in October 1977, once the founder members had approved all of the modifications.

4.6. THE TECHNICAL STAFF

Reflecting the ICAEW's paternal view, the Constitution provided that 'The accountancy bodies in the United Kingdom and the Republic of Ireland will be responsible, subject to the approval of the Committee, for recruiting staff for the permanent office in London.' The Canadian representatives suggested that the AICPA should select the inaugural secretary.[34] In the interests of international harmony, the ICAEW, one supposes, acceded to this suggestion. Thus, an English chairman of a body based in London could be balanced with an American head of staff. The AICPA seconded Paul Rosenfield to be the secretary for two years. Rosenfield had spent eight years with Price Waterhouse & Co. until 1965, when he joined the Institute's Accounting Research Division, servicing the APB. He was an author of a number of journal articles and was the principal draftsman of the APB's Statement No. 4, *Basic Concepts and Accounting Principles Underlying Financial Statements of Business Enterprises*, issued in October 1970. After interviewing candidates for the two-year position as assistant secretary, Rosenfield recommended Richard J. Simmons, a manager in the London office of Arthur Andersen & Co., as his choice, and Benson extended the offer. Both Rosenfield and Simmons completed their service in June 1975. Rosenfield returned to the AICPA as director of technical research, and Simmons rejoined his firm. Succeeding Simmons as assistant secretary was Christopher J. Relleen, who was seconded by Deloitte & Co., where he was working in both the London and Brussels offices. Relleen returned to Deloittes in March 1977.

In 1975, the Canadians were asked to choose the secretary. As the chairman and the assistant secretary, Chris Relleen, were from the United Kingdom, and the United States had contributed the first secretary, there was a need to find a secretary from somewhere else than the United Kingdom and the United States. Canada had been an active and enthusiastic member and had a candidate: W. John Brennan, who was seconded by the University of Saskatchewan, where he was an accounting professor.[35] He began as secretary in July. Brennan had served on the CICA's Accounting and Auditing Research Committee from 1969 to 1972. He served for more than two years, until November 1977, when he returned to his university.

In December 1977, Roy C. Nash, an American who was a principal with Arthur Young & Company in Madrid, became IASC secretary, returning to his firm as a partner in September 1979. Prior to 1975, he had worked in the firm's Boston office. He was the last North American to head the secretariat. Hugh F. Richardson, seconded by the London office of Coopers & Lybrand, became assistant secretary in April 1977, remaining until May 1979, when he returned to his firm.

In October 1979, Allan V. C. Cook became not only the first non-North American secretary but also the first staff member to come from industry. Prior to joining the IASC, he was with Unilever, in London, where 'He was actively involved in the development of accounting policies for the Unilever Group and the appraisal of international accounting developments and their impact on Unilever.'[36] In June 1979, an Australian, E. Peter Akins, of Yarwood, Vane & Co. (Hepworth's firm), in Sydney, became assistant secretary. Akins had been director of research and education in his firm. In December 1981, Cook left to become head of accounting research at the Royal Dutch/Shell Group of Companies, in London. In May 1981, Akins returned to his firm in Sydney.

When Cook's term expired, the board's leadership considered recruiting a successor from a non–English-speaking country but, in the end, concluded that any such candidate would probably not have a sufficient command of the English language.[37] Instead, they turned to Geoffrey B. Mitchell, a reader in accounting at Flinders University of South Australia, in Adelaide. In January 1982, he became secretary, being seconded by his university. In March 1985, after more than three years' service, he left to become the ICAEW's technical director. It was during Mitchell's period of service that the position of secretary became the secretary-general. It was stated in the minutes of the board's meeting in June 1983 that 'While the principle of rotation of secretariat staff on secondment had had much to recommend it in the early years of IASC, the extensive liaison activities of IASC today required a continuity in the office of Secretary.'[38] As Mitchell satisfied the board's criteria for the appointment, at the expiry of his secondment he was offered the position of secretary-general, which he accepted as of January 1984.[39]

Brian R. Shearer was seconded as assistant secretary by Thornton Baker, London, where he was a manager. In May 1983, he returned to his firm, by then known as Grant Thornton, as partner and director of the national technical department. In June 1983, John R. Bloxsome, an audit manager with Spicer & Pegler, in London, internationally associated with Spicer & Oppenheim, was seconded by his firm to serve as assistant secretary. He returned to his firm in September 1985.

David H. Cairns, a technical partner in Stoy Hayward, London, became secretary-general in April 1985. In his firm, he had been chairman of the international accounting and auditing committee of Horwath and Horwath International (HHI), which developed international accounting and auditing standards for HHI member firms. He had co-authored three major surveys of international financial reporting practices between 1979 and 1984 (*see also* Section 6.3). He had, by far, the longest tenure in the secretariat, serving until the end of 1994.

Brian A. Rutherford, an accounting lecturer at the University of Kent at Canterbury, became assistant secretary in October 1985 'on a permanent basis'.[40] He returned to his university in March 1987, being the last of the assistant secretaries. The successor title for this backup to the secretary-general became known as research manager.[41]

Figure 4.6. David Cairns

Six of the seven secretaries and secretaries-general were British, American, or Canadian, and all of the assistant secretaries, save one, were British. The two exceptions were Australian. One could infer that their national backgrounds might have served to promote an Anglo-American influence in the work of the IASC.

A major function of the technical staff was to assist the project steering committees with the research and drafting of exposure drafts and standards. But it also handled the bulk of the IASC's correspondence, arranged for meetings of the IASC board and its steering committees, attended the meetings and accompanied the chairman on official visits, managed the printing and distribution of exposure drafts and standards, and wrote the periodic *IASC News*.

The IASC staff produced the English-language version of each standard and exposure draft, but until 1987, the member bodies and not the IASC were largely responsible for their circulation. The member bodies were responsible for preparing and publishing translations into their national languages. The accountancy bodies also gathered and transmitted to the IASC the comments submitted in their respective countries on the exposure drafts. More generally, as David Cairns has written, 'all contact between the IASC and national standard setting bodies, companies, stock exchanges and regulators had to be made through the appropriate accountancy bodies—the IASC was not allowed to have direct contact' with these entities.[42] The practical impact of this restriction probably varied over time and from country to country. Benson himself set a precedent by seeking to establish contacts with many organizations, not necessarily through the intervention of the relevant member bodies.

4.7. THE OFFICIAL LANGUAGE(S)

From the beginning, there was some controversy over the language, or languages, to be used. The draft Constitution, prepared by the ICAEW after the December 1972 meeting, at which Canadian, UK, and US representatives alone were present, specified that 'The Committee shall conduct its discussions and issue its exposure drafts and statements for publication in the English language' (article 6(b)). At the March 1973 meeting, to which all of the founder bodies were invited, the issue was addressed anew. Although it was then agreed that the Committee's discussions should be conducted in English, it was argued that 'To confine the publication of exposure drafts and standards to an English language version would tend to prejudice and delay the widest dissemination of these documents and it was accordingly agreed that the Committee should assume responsibility for their translation into the French, Spanish and German languages so that they could be published in that form in different countries.'[43]

At the foundational meeting, on 28 June 1973, the French proposed that the Committee's discussion be conducted in French as well as English and that the definitive text of exposure drafts and standards shall be published in both languages.[44] In the end, this proposal was not accepted, although the chairman was authorized to accept contributions at meetings made in another language so long as the statement was translated at the same time by another member of that delegation. It was again confirmed that the definitive text of exposure drafts and standards was to be in English. The member bodies were authorized to arrange for and distribute translations into other languages, at their own expense.[45]

At the Committee's November 1973 meeting, confirming an agreement made at the planning meeting the previous March, it was agreed that 'The definitive version of each IASC document will be circulated worldwide in English'.[46] At the July 1974 meeting, however, the French delegation, led by Alfred Cordoliani, pressed for agreement that 'the IASC should consider adopting French, German, Spanish, Japanese, and Dutch in addition to English as official languages', but this was, again, not accepted.[47] Those familiar with the 'sort of Babel' encountered during deliberations in the UEC,[48] where all documents had to be rendered in three languages, presenters at congresses could speak in any of the three languages, and committee chairmen could adopt their preferred language of the three, wanted to avoid a similar experience in the IASC.

4.8. LINK WITH THE ICAEW

With help from the ICAEW, the IASC obtained office space at 3 St. Helen's Place, in Bishopsgate in the City of London (i.e. London's financial community), a quarter of a mile from Chartered Accountants' Hall, the edifice housing the Institute's secretariat, which had been built for the Institute in 1893. The Institute, under the terms of the 1973 and 1977 Constitutions, paid the rent, rates, and any taxes on the IASC's permanent office.[49] Hans Burggraaff has written that 'It was a great convenience for Board and Chairman that all domestic issues in running a secretariat were taken care of by knowledgeable people who were available on the spot. For the same reason there was always a seat on the [Organisation and Planning Committee, see below] for the UK. For the secretary too it was a convenience that he had a "godfather" next door, especially when that secretary was non-British. In addition: IASC was, or so I understood, not a legal entity that could enter into contracts in the UK. We needed the intermediary of ICAEW for such contracts.'[50]

The ICAEW generously made its facilities—library, dining room, meeting rooms, and Council Chamber—available to the IASC secretariat. The secretaries also had access to the Institute's technical staff. For the first three secretaries, who were North Americans and therefore not members of the Institute, these privileges, almost as if they were members of the Institute, were welcome indeed. Roy Nash recalled the splendour of attending the Institute's annual dinner in the Guildhall.[51]

In 1978, the IASC moved its office outside of the City to a more capacious location, 49–51 Bedford Row. Four years later, when the IASC realized that it required even larger premises for the expanding needs of the secretariat in London, the UK & Irish delegation made it known that it would continue its rent subsidy at the current level, thus obliging the IASC board to budget £5,000 as a supplement to cover the additional rent for 1983, when the office was moved to 41 Kingsway.[52]

4.9. THE EARLY PLAN FOR THE APPROVAL AND PRODUCTION OF STANDARDS

The Committee's plan was to issue its first standard by April 1975, 'with other standards following at 3 or 4 monthly intervals, in order publicly to demonstrate the resolve of the profession to make progress on basic international standards'.[53] In the end, the IASC bettered the deadline for its first standard by three months, and the completion of the next dozen standards required just under five years, remarkably close to the average pace envisaged at the inaugural meeting.

The Constitution provided that at least two-thirds of the IASC must vote in favour of exposure drafts and that at least three quarters must approve the standards. Each delegation had one vote. These voting thresholds were not changed in the subsequent revisions of the Constitution. Dissenting views, and even the tally of the vote, were not to be placed on the public record. A more extensive discussion of the early plan for the production of standards may be found in Chapter 5.

4.10. COMPOSITION OF THE PROJECT STEERING COMMITTEES

The IASC chose the countries to be represented on the project steering committees, whose task was to draft the proposed standards, but it fell to the respective countries' accountancy bodies to name their representatives. The first half-dozen project steering committees were composed solely of representatives from the founder countries. The first associate member to sit on a steering committee was approved at the April 1974 meeting, the same meeting at which the initial list of associate members was approved.[54] At the following meeting, in July, the Committee discussed four new steering committees, two to be composed solely of founder member countries and two that would each consist of two founder members and one associate member.[55] The first associate member countries to be represented on steering committees were Israel, South Africa, New Zealand, Belgium, and India, in that order, all appointed in 1974 or 1975.

The chairmen of the steering committees were always from a country represented on the Committee. With but one exception, the person chairing the steering committee was also serving on the board.[56] By 1983, the policy was that, in addition to the chairman, the other two steering committee members were in most instances from non-board countries, of which one would be from a developing country.[57]

On the projects dealing with some of the more complex and controversial issues, such as on accounting for inflation and pensions, the board appointed a larger steering committee.

As is discussed more extensively in Chapter 5, the membership of the steering committees was carefully planned to ensure that the founder members all served on an approximately equal number of committees, as well as to provide opportunities for participation to associate members who expressed an interest to do so.

4.11. COMMUNICATIONS

At the suggestion of Secretary Paul Rosenfield, the IASC began issuing a periodic, mimeographed *IASC News* in September 1973. It represented a bulletin board of information on Committee and steering committee meetings, the names of new associate members, changes in the chairmanship and the secretariat, news about the recognition or acceptance of IASC standards in member countries, and, eventually, extracts from speeches by the chairmen. In 1976, *IASC News* was upgraded into a more comprehensive news source.

In 1987, the IASC published the first bound volume of its standards. The ICAEW also published a volume of the IASC standards in 1987, which included the prefaces to the standards explaining the applicability of the standards in the UK and Ireland.[58] In following years, such compilations of its standards were published annually by the IASC. Previously, most of the paper copies of the IASC's standards and other publications had been distributed solely by its member bodies, yielding no income for the IASC itself. The bound volume of standards was the first publication actually sold by the IASC.[59]

The year 1987 also marked the issue of the IASC's first annual report as a separate publication, in order to make its presence better known to the worldwide accountancy profession.[60] Following ratification of the IASC/IFAC Mutual Commitments pact during the 1982 international congress in Mexico City, IFAC's own annual report had included an elaborate section on the IASC's activities. From 1988 onward, this section in IFAC's annual report continued but in an abridged format.

4.12. MEETINGS OF THE COMMITTEE (FROM 1977 ONWARDS, THE BOARD)

The Committee (or board) met four times in each of 1974 and 1975, three times a year from 1976 to 1986, but only twice in 1987. It was decided in late 1973 to hold one meeting per year outside of London,[61] but from 1978 to 1987, except for two years, the board met twice a year in venues other than London. By 1981, the board had met at least once in each of the founder members' countries.

Attendance at the meetings was generally high. Most of the delegations had two or three members in attendance at most meetings. Yet for long periods, Mexico, Japan, Australia, and Germany were exceptions. In seven of the eight board meetings from June 1978 to the end of 1980, Mexico continued to send only

Figure 4.7. Meeting of IASC board in the Council Chamber of the ICAEW, London, March 1978

one representative, the only exception being the February/March 1978 meeting held in Mexico City, when there was a full delegation. In 1981, Mexico began a practice of sending at least two members to each meeting.

Japan sent only one delegate to just over 40 per cent of the meetings from 1973 to 1987. Following John Hepworth's term as chairman in 1980, only one Australian delegate attended most meetings during the next five years. During Taiwan's brief term on the IASC board, from 1984 to 1987, only one delegate, always the same person, attended all of the meetings. No one from France attended the June 1978 meeting in Perth, Australia, and Italy was absent at the March 1987 meeting in Sydney. The long distances may have been a problem.

As mentioned above, from 1980 onwards Germany held one seat open in its delegation for a financial executive.

At the March 1979 meeting, Chairman Hepworth mentioned that a request had been received 'that observers from national and international organizations be allowed to attend meetings of the Board', which were always held in camera.[62] Nothing more was reported on this matter until the June 1980 board meeting, when it was revealed that the board had 'decided not to invite the FASB as an observer to IASC Board meetings', and that it had also decided not to seek observer representation from 'a group representing EEC interests'. The board decided as well not to invite regional accountancy organizations to be observers at its meetings. In March 1981, Chairman Burggraaff persuaded a reluctant board to authorize the chairman, at his discretion, 'to invite a limited number of guests to board meetings', so long as the IASC member body representing the guest's country concurs, with the proviso that guests would not normally have the privilege of the floor.[63]

The decisions taken in 1980 and 1981 suggest a tension between opening a window to the outside and keeping it closed. The meetings of the Consultative Group, also established in 1981, provided a convenient middle ground.

4.13. FINANCES

At the inaugural meeting in June 1973, the Committee set the budget for the first calendar year, 1974, at £62,400, but by September 1974 the estimate of the gross expenditure to be incurred during the year had increased by more than one-third, to £85,000.[64] This run-up in cost precipitated a cash shortage, which was partially relieved in 1974 by a £7,000 grant from the Leverhulme Trust.[65] The Committee boldly agreed a gross expenditure budget of £107,300 for 1975 so that there would not be 'a material reduction in the impetus and effectiveness of the work of IASC'.[66]

Under the IASC's Constitution, each of the nine founder countries was to contribute one-ninth of the operating cost; hence, the increased financial burden on each delegation became an immediate issue. In July 1974, the Committee decided to recommend a two-tier fee structure for the founder members, to take effect in 1974: (*a*) all of the nine founder members would bear a 'fixed basic charge' of £7,000 per year, adjusted in later years for inflation, and (*b*) the balance of the IASC's yearly budget would be covered by the founder members using a formula based on their respective membership sizes. Under this formula, the delegations whose accountancy bodies had aggregate membership sizes of under 10,000 would collectively contribute 10 per cent of the balance. The remaining 90 per cent of the balance would be shared by the delegations whose accountancy bodies had a membership of more than 10,000. The UK & Irish delegation and the US delegation, whose aggregate membership sizes were by far the largest, would each bear 36 per cent of the balance, and Australia, Canada, and France would contribute 16, 8, and 4 per cent, respectively, of the balance.[67]

The expenditure incurred to operate the IASC during its first fourteen years was generally on the rise, initially fuelled by the high inflation in the 1970s and into the early 1980s, and especially as reflected in international air fares. Other reasons were not hard to find: the costs of travel for the growing number of steering committees as well as for the board meetings, which were gradually increasing in length and at which the number of delegations in attendance was rising from nine to eleven and then to thirteen and fourteen.[68] Even so, a substantial part of the total travel costs was not borne by the IASC but by the member bodies. The IASC reimbursed the costs of only one delegate for each country attending a board or steering committee meeting.[69]

Table 4.1. IASC revenue and expenditure, 1974–87 (£1,000)

Year	Revenue[a]	Of which: IFAC contribution	Expenditure[b]	Surplus[c]
1974	89	—	75	13
1975	124	—	110	15
1976	117	—	112	5
1977	122	—	129	(7)
1978	161	—	130	31
1979	170	—	153	17
1980	186	—	146	39
1981	214	—	195	19
1982	218	—	203	15
1983	258	27	249	10
1984	304	31	272	32
1985	325	30	331	(5)
1986	325	32	291	33
1987	317	31	350	(33)

[a] Includes 'Sale of standards': £1,647 (1986); £7,868 (1987).
[b] Includes 'Exchange gains and losses'.
[c] Differences due to rounding.
Source: IASC's financial statements included with agenda papers.

The sequence in the figures for annual revenue and expenditures from 1974 to 1987 is shown in Table 4.1. During this period, the IASC secretariat consisted of but two technical staff (including the secretary or secretary-general) and one clerical staff, becoming two in 1987.

The IASC's annual budget for gross expenditure, which rose steadily to £348,207 by 1987, about one-quarter of which represented the cost of international travel to attend board meetings, could be compared with an expenditure budget of £440,000 for 1989 for the UK & Irish ASC.[70] The Dearing Committee, which in 1988 recommended creation of an ASB, with two of its members to be full-time and an enlarged staff, proposed an annual budget of £1.5 million for the new body.[71] The 1987 budget for Canada's Accounting Standards Board and Advisory Board, summed, was Can$745,000 (£350,000).[72] The 1987 budget of expenditures for the US FASB was US$11 million (£6.9 million), with seven full-time board members and a full-time research and technical staff of about forty.[73] In comparison with these national counterparts, the IASC was a much smaller enterprise.

The annual fees received from the burgeoning number of associate members helped to defray the costs of operation. The budgeted income from associate member fees rose from £4,000 for 1975 to £11,250 for 1977 and finally to £19,000 for 1982, when, beginning in 1983, under the IASC/IFAC Mutual Commitments pact, this fee income was replaced by an annual contribution by IFAC of 10 per cent of the IASC's budget to defray the costs of non-board members' service on the steering committees. The budgeted contribution from IFAC for 1983 was £26,700. Under the Mutual Commitments pact, IFAC's membership of eighty-eight accountancy bodies representing sixty-four countries automatically became members of the IASC.[74]

The IASC continued to approach charitable foundations for assistance in meeting its escalating costs.[75] A number of smaller grants were received from a few foundations, and the Nuffield Foundation contributed £5,900 towards the IASC's project on inflation accounting, payable over three years, 1974 to 1976. Applications were made to the Ford Foundation and Carnegie Corporation, apparently without effect.[76] In 1975, the Wolfson Foundation promised £21,000 payable over three years.[77] It seems likely that Henry Benson was instrumental in securing a number of the grants from UK sources.

The Group of Ten Bank Governors, which had approached the IASC in 1976 to ask that it undertake a project on the minimum disclosures and presentation in the financial statements of banks, promised a contribution of £10,000 towards the cost of that project.[78] The cheque was received in 1979, a year prior to publication of the IASC's discussion paper, *Disclosures in the Financial Statements of Banks*.

4.14. CHANGES IN 1977 IN THE AGREEMENT AND CONSTITUTION

At the IASC meeting in July 1974, it was proposed to set up a working party to 'review the future programme, working procedures, and possible future changes in the Constitution of the IASC'. Alec Mackenzie was selected to chair the working party, the other members being representatives from Australia, Germany, and the United States. The original members representing these countries were John Hepworth, Hans Havermann, and Robert Sempier (the staff observer), respectively. Among the issues it was to consider were the terms of office of the Committee members and the chairman, the status of associate members, the basis of the appointments to secretary and assistant secretary, the frequency and length of Committee meetings, the formation and composition of steering committees, and the country location of the secretariat, which was a matter of great sensitivity to the UK & Irish delegation.[79]

The steering committee (renamed from working party, yet subsequently called a subcommittee) presented its recommendations to the Committee in October 1975.[80] As amended by the Committee in October 1977, at the time of the Munich international congress, they became part of the IASC's Agreement and Constitution by vote of the IASC's founder bodies.

One consequential recommendation was to delete 'basic' from 'basic standards' in article 1(a) of the Agreement and in the IASC's 'Preface to Statements of International Accounting Standards', published in January 1975. The steering committee may have believed that the term basic might be misinterpreted as 'elementary' or 'rudimentary'. It was made clear at a later meeting that the change 'would not, by itself, indicate any change in the procedures of IASC'.[81] Yet, by 1975, it was evident that the IASC was beginning to tackle standards that went beyond basic.

As mentioned above (Section 4.4) the Committee, now to be called the board, could have as many as two non-founder members on a rotation basis, but the founder members themselves were not to be subject to re-election.

The steering committee rejected a proposed change in the best endeavours clause in the Agreement. In regard to compliance with the IASC's standards, the steering committee recommended not to add 'directors' and 'officers' (of companies) to auditors as the members of the professional accountancy bodies who were expected to satisfy themselves that the accounts complied with the IASC's standards.

The steering committee also recommended that, as a part of the best endeavours obligation, the auditor need not refer to non-compliance if 'the circumstances are adequately explained in the financial statements'. The auditor should refer to non-compliance, the committee said, in the absence of an adequate explanation in the financial statements. But the notion of 'adequate explanation' was dropped by the Committee, perhaps because it was too subjective. The Committee decided to say instead that 'In the event of non-disclosure [in the financial statements] reference to non-compliance is [to be] made in the audit report.' The adequacy of the disclosure in the financial statements was not mentioned. The steering committee's recommendation, as modified by the Committee, was approved by the founder member bodies.

In line with the decision already taken in 1974, the previous provision in the Constitution that each founder country must contribute one-ninth of the annual budget each year was changed to authorize the IASC board to determine the contribution formula.

Also of interest was the amendment to redefine the IASC's membership as consisting of all of the professional accountancy bodies that were signatories to the revised Constitution in 1973 or that subsequently become members. The term 'associate member' was dropped.

4.15. THE ORGANISATION AND PLANNING COMMITTEE (OPC)

Following the Munich international congress in October 1977, the steering committee that had recommended revisions in the Agreement and Constitution proposed to the IASC board that it be reconstituted as an 'Organisation and Planning Committee', with rotating membership, and that it would convene the day before each board meeting. Its role would be to 'keep under review the organization, plans and structure of the IASC'.[82] The board approved the steering committee's proposal with minor changes at the following meeting. One change was that the board chairman's country could not serve on the OPC, as it came to be known, during his term of office, but the chairman attended OPC meetings, and, it was said, was very influential there.[83] The new OPC would be composed of representatives from three countries (increased to four in 1982), to become effective following the March 1978 board meeting.[84]

Whether it was intended or not, the OPC became a kind of executive committee. At every subsequent board meeting, without fail, a number of agenda items dealing with 'the organisation, plans and structure of the IASC' were brought forward by the OPC for discussion.[85] Among its responsibilities was to recommend the country members of the new steering committees, to recommend country members to fill vacancies on the board, to nominate a chairman-designate of the IASC board, to recommend the annual budget for approval, and to monitor developments relating to board members' contacts with governments and national standard-setting bodies. These were hardly inconsequential matters.

During its first two years, the OPC was chaired by John Grenside, the Peats senior partner who had replaced Henry Benson in the UK & Irish delegation.[86] The host country, which was paying the IASC's rent, proved to be first among equals in the work of the OPC, for, from 1978 to 1990 but for two years, the UK & Ireland (renamed the UK delegation in 1988) was always one of the three delegations represented on the committee. The UK & Irish delegation had to withdraw from the OPC during 1985–7 during John Kirkpatrick's chairmanship according to the board's agreement that the chairman's country may not also sit on the OPC. One consideration for retaining the UK & Irish delegation on the OPC, it was mentioned, was that there were 'advantages to the Secretariat of administrative oversight being exercised by a member [of the OPC] within easy reach of the IASC offices'.[87] The chairmen of the OPC, with the names of the other delegations represented until 1987, were as follows:

1978–9	John Grenside, UK & Ireland; United States, the Netherlands
1979–80	John Grenside, UK & Ireland; Canada, the Netherlands
1980–1	Stephen Elliott, Canada; Japan, UK & Ireland
1981–2	Stephen Elliott, Canada; Japan, France, UK & Ireland
1982–3	Seigo Nakajima, Japan; France, Mexico, UK & Ireland
1983–4	Georges Barthès, France; Mexico, South Africa, UK & Ireland
1984–5	Rolando Ortega, Mexico; South Africa, Nigeria, UK & Ireland
1985–6	Warwick Thorby, South Africa; Nigeria, Italy
1986–7	M. Ayodeji Oni, Nigeria; Germany, Australia, Italy

4.16. THE CONSULTATIVE GROUP

In 1981, the IASC formed a Consultative Group composed of representatives of various organizations with an interest in financial reporting. This was a major step towards expanding the IASC's reach to worldwide bodies beyond the accountancy profession. The first Consultative Group contained representatives of the following bodies:

— Fédération Internationale des Bourses de Valeurs (FIBV)
— International Association of Financial Executives Institutes (IAFEI)
— International Chamber of Commerce (ICC)

— International Confederation of Free Trade Unions
— International Co-ordinating Committee of Financial Analysts' Associations
— The World Bank

The United Nations (UN) and the Organisation for Economic Co-operation and Development (OECD) had also been invited to join the Consultative Group, but both declined to be formal members.[88] Representatives of the secretariat of the OECD and the UN Centre on Transnational Corporations did attend meetings of the Consultative Group as observers.

The Consultative Group met with the board twice each year, directly preceding a board meeting, to discuss the agenda papers for the upcoming meeting as well as any other matters facing the IASC. The Consultative Group held its inaugural meeting in public, the first time an organ of the IASC had done so.[89] In the years following its initial gathering in June 1981, however, the Consultative Group conducted all of its meetings in private.

As is discussed more fully in Chapter 7, the Consultative Group was the first step in a process of opening up the IASC board to participation by organizations from outside the accountancy profession. The Group was viewed as a kind of 'training ground' for future board delegations, and, indeed, the three non-auditor delegations that eventually joined the board (the financial analysts' delegation, the delegation from IAFEI, and the delegation of the Federation of Swiss Industrial Holding Companies) all had their origins in the Consultative Group.[90]

Between 1981 and 1987, other bodies joined the Consultative Group, including the International Bar Association, a delegation representing the international banking associations, and the International Organization of Securities Commissions (IOSCO). At the Mexico City international congress in 1982, Chairman Elliott said, 'At the next Congress in 1987, I hope that my successor can report to you that it is an accomplished fact that International Accounting Standards are not set in isolation by accountants but in a spirit of partnership with both users and preparers.'[91]

Quite apart from its contribution to the standard-setting process, the Consultative Group proved its worth during the OECD Forum on Harmonization of Accounting Standards in 1985. As it happened, a number of individuals who expressed their support for the IASC during that conference were also members of the Consultative Group. In this way, they made a significant contribution to enhancing the IASC's legitimacy in the eyes of the OECD.[92]

4.17. CHANGES IN 1982 IN THE AGREEMENT AND CONSTITUTION

During the Mexico City international congress in October 1982, not only was the IASC/IFAC Mutual Commitments pact approved but also the IASC's Agreement and Constitution were amended once again.[93] The new Constitution eliminated the distinction between founder and non-founder members, and ended, at least in principle, the perpetual board membership of the founder members. Instead, the new Constitution provided that the IFAC Council was empowered to nominate and appoint as many as thirteen country members of IFAC to serve on the IASC board, and that the board itself could co-opt to its membership as many as four other organizations possessing an interest in financial reporting (article 4). These changes reflected the desire, in particular of Chairman Burggraaff, to expand the board's horizons beyond the accountancy profession and the founder countries. His aim was to achieve the worldwide adoption, application, and enforcement of the IASC's standards, matters which the accountancy profession was largely powerless to influence.

It was also stated that the term of appointment of all members serving on the board, including founder members, was five years (Constitution, article 5(a)), and all of the board members were eligible for reappointment. As this new provision took effect on 1 January 1983, the founder members knew their reappointment would come up for discussion in 1987. The Mutual Commitments provided that that 'At least 9 countries nominated [by the IFAC Council] will be selected from among the most significant countries in terms of the status and development of the accountancy profession or that are of significant importance to international commerce and trade' (article 8), thus virtually assuring the reappointment of the founder members. In the event, all but Mexico renewed their seats at that time.

The best endeavours clause was moved from the Constitution to the Mutual Commitments pact and reproduced in the revised Preface to Statements of International Accounting Standards. The original best endeavours clause, conceived in 1973 and reaffirmed as amended in 1977, adjured members 'to ensure that published accounts comply with these standards or that there is disclosure of the extent to which they do not'. In the 1982 revision, the best endeavours obligation became that of IFAC's member bodies. As then IASC Chairman Burggraaff has written, 'IFAC wanted to appoint the professional members of the IASC Board; in return, IFAC should undertake, on behalf of the profession, to get the standards adopted, applied and enforced, in as much as the profession was able to do so.'[94] Under the 1982 revision included in the Mutual Commitments, IFAC member bodies were charged 'to ensure that published financial statements comply with International Accounting Standards in all material respects and disclose the fact of such compliance' (article 7). Non-compliance no longer had to be disclosed. Nobes observed that this 'gradual weakening of the commitments required from member bodies' was a 'tell-tale sign of the problems of enforcement'.[95] These problems are discussed more fully in Chapter 6. It was also a sign that the IASC board was tackling some difficult and controversial issues.

A major change in the new Constitution was that all of the members of IFAC automatically became members of the IASC (Mutual Commitments, article 3). And, as noted above, IFAC agreed to contribute 10 per cent of the IASC's annual budget (Mutual Commitments, article 14(b)).

4.18. IASC/IFAC CO-ORDINATING COMMITTEE

One outgrowth of the Mutual Commitments pact was the formation in late 1982 of the IASC/IFAC Co-ordinating Committee. IFAC appointed its president, Washington SyCip, of the Philippines, and its deputy president, Russell E. Palmer, of the United States, to the committee. The IASC named as members its chairman, Stephen Elliott, of Canada, and John Kirkpatrick, of Scotland.[96] The committee was not mentioned in the Mutual Commitments pact or in the revised Agreement and Constitution of the IASC. In the section of IFAC's 1983 annual report containing the IASC's report on its activities for the year, it was stated, immediately following a reference to the committee, that 'IFAC and IASC are working closely together to achieve enhanced compliance with IASC Standards and IFAC Guidelines.'[97] The committee met once a year; in addition, there was attendance at each other's meetings, and there was contact at the secretariat level. In future years, the IASC's chairman and secretary-general were joined on the committee by IFAC's president and executive director. In each year, the two IASC members attended a meeting of IFAC's Council, and the two IFAC members attended a meeting of the IASC board.

4.19. THE IASC'S MAJOR REASSESSMENT OF ITS FUTURE PLANS IN 1987

The March 1987 meeting of the IASC board, held in Sydney, represented a watershed in the development of its programme to issue standards. (See Chapters 9 and 10 for a more extensive discussion.) The central decision in Sydney was for the board to begin a process for improving its standards. The board also resolved to seek closer contact with regulatory authorities and multinational enterprises as well as with national standard setters, all to promote a greater degree of acceptance of its standards worldwide. In due course, these decisions would result in important consequences for the IASC's organization and effectiveness. As is described in Chapter 8, it would lead to a broadening of the composition of the board delegations beyond an almost exclusive reliance on national accountancy bodies in order to bring in the representatives of other interested parties. Following the board's approval of its new direction in March 1987, together with the more active involvement in its work by securities market regulators, the IASC entered an era in which the impact of its standards commanded the attention of a much wider audience.

5

'Compromise to Harmonise': Setting the IASC's Early Standards

5.1. OVERVIEW

The International Accounting Standards Committee (IASC) was set up to produce International Accounting Standards, and it embarked upon its task with alacrity. Between its founding in 1973 and the end of 1987, it published a total of thirty-one exposure drafts and two discussion papers. By the end of 1987, the exposure drafts had resulted in twenty-six standards. No revisions of any of these standards had been published, but one of them, IAS 6 on price changes, had been superseded by IAS 15.

The IASC managed to maintain a steady rate of production. New projects were started at a regular pace, most of which resulted in the publication of a standard in three to five years' time (*see* Appendix 4 for an overview of the IASC's technical projects). Between 1975 and 1980, following an inevitable accumulation of projects, the IASC typically attended to around eight projects simultaneously, and at any one time some four exposure drafts were outstanding. Around 1980, the portfolio of projects was reduced, and, with some delay, the number of outstanding exposure drafts declined as well. For a brief period in 1984, no exposure drafts were outstanding at all. By 1985, the project portfolio was back at its former level. This fluctuation in output can partly be related to the greater challenge posed by some of the subjects taken up by the IASC in the late 1970s, such as segment reporting, leases, retirement benefits, and business combinations. These projects led to standards that broke new ground in most countries, including those of several founder members. In addition, by the early 1980s the IASC began to review existing standards, but little of this work led to any revised standards.

Throughout this period, the IASC's operating procedures for developing its standards changed little. These will be treated first, followed by a discussion of the standards themselves.

5.2. WORKING ARRANGEMENTS AND COMPOSITION OF STEERING COMMITTEES

The IASC's working arrangements were agreed at the Committee's first meeting on 29 June 1973. The full Committee (known as the board after the revision of the

Constitution in 1977) was to choose the subjects on which standards were to be issued and to determine the objectives and scope of each standard. The Committee 'should not act as a drafting committee' but would appoint steering committees for each subject. Initially, steering committees consisted of three members, all or most of them members of the full Committee. The steering committee, assisted by the secretariat, was responsible for producing preliminary drafts. When amended and approved by the full Committee, these would be published as exposure drafts, and comments would be invited. Based on these comments, the steering committee would submit a draft standard to the full Committee for approval.[1]

This was essentially the procedure followed throughout the period 1973–87, although in practice the board did get involved in drafting to a considerable extent. Throughout the 1970s and 1980s, it was customary for the IASC secretary or the chairman of the steering committee to prepare revised drafts during the board meetings on the basis of comments by the board. In this way, the board could often discuss the comment letters on an exposure draft and approve the final standard for publication during a single board meeting.[2]

Inevitably, the procedures were modified on the basis of experience. For instance, in April 1974 it was agreed that henceforth each steering committee would submit a point outline of the proposed standard before preparing a draft of the complete standard. Over the next years, as the point outlines became more and more elaborate and often began to contain large sections of the proposed text, the original idea behind the point outlines was resurrected in 1981 by introducing 'issues papers' to precede the point outlines.[3] Another elaboration of the procedure, adopted from 1978 onwards, was to circulate 'preliminary exposure drafts' for comment among the member bodies during the drafting stage.[4] As is shown in Chapter 7, this change was a response to criticism expressed by some associate members about the lack of opportunities for non-board members to participate in the IASC's work.

These procedures probably were drawn from the experience of the American, Canadian, and UK & Irish delegations, based on the process adopted by their respective standard-setting bodies. In this regard, Paul Rosenfield, who had served on the research staff of the US Accounting Principles Board (APB), was probably influential.

The IASC did not follow American practice in that, unlike the APB or the Financial Accounting Standards Board (FASB), it did not publish dissenting views or even make known the vote on each exposure draft and standard. The FASB opened its meetings to public observation at the beginning of 1978, but the IASC did not do so until March 1999. In the 1970s, such a degree of openness would have been unthinkable in member countries other than the United States. Nevertheless, the IASC was hardly a secretive body. As it consisted of a considerable number of delegations, many with their own support groups at home, its agenda papers circulated widely. This became even more the case after the creation of the Consultative Group in 1981.[5]

The actual as opposed to the intended composition of the steering committees cannot in all cases be reconstructed with certainty. In some cases, members sent replacements, ceased attending, or came accompanied by staff observers. In the discussion of the standards in this and subsequent chapters, the steering committee chairmen are indicated in the text. The membership of the steering committees, to the extent that it can be reconstructed, is in each case indicated in a note following the first reference to the steering committee chairman.[6]

Until 1980, the steering committees typically retained their original size of three members, although one or two members might be added on particularly difficult topics (inflation accounting, foreign currency translation). In 1980, the steering committee on related party transactions (IAS 24) was set up with four members 'to balance developed and developing countries in this project'.[7] But whatever the particular reason was in this case, all subsequent steering committees consisted of at least four members.

The board decided on the composition of the steering committees in terms of countries, and decided which country was to provide the chairman. The chairman would normally be a board representative. The member bodies that were invited to contribute the other members of the steering committee selected the individuals who would serve. From about 1975 onwards they would typically not be board representatives.

In selecting the member bodies to serve on steering committees, the board was guided by the secretariat, which would regularly prepare tabulations of the number of steering committees in which each member body had participated. The intention was to ensure that all members bodies represented on the board would take on a roughly equal share of the work, and that the other member bodies with an interest in steering committee work and with qualified individuals to serve would have a regular opportunity to participate. Apart from sharing the workload, this policy might enhance the likelihood of broader acceptance of the resulting standards, beyond the countries represented by the founder bodies.

With respect to the founder members, the idea of equal participation was approximately achieved. Between 1973 and 1987, each of the founder members served on nine (Australia, Mexico) to thirteen (UK & Ireland, the Netherlands) steering committees, but the United States served on fifteen.

With respect to the associate members, the picture was inevitably more diverse. Between 1973 and 1987, twenty-nine countries out of a total of at least fifty-five eligible countries served on at least one steering committee.[8] The most active were South Africa (five committees) and Nigeria (four committees), which is clearly related to the fact that these countries were the first to occupy the rotating board positions created for non-founder members in 1977.

Typically, the countries serving on steering committees were also the ones that were most active in sending comment letters on exposure drafts. This was true, for instance of Denmark, New Zealand, and Sweden. Sweden, which served on three committees, was a particularly faithful correspondent, as the Föreningen Auktoriserade Revisorer failed to comment on very few of the exposure drafts issued by the IASC between 1974 and 1987, or indeed between 1974 and 2000.

The availability of suitable individuals was a limiting factor for some countries, although it was found that, because of the presence of the international auditing firms, many small countries could send well-qualified and knowledgeable people to the steering committees.[9]

5.3. REVIEW OF THE TECHNICAL PROJECTS 1973–87

The following sections discuss the technical projects undertaken by the IASC during the period 1973–87. This discussion must, for each standard, of necessity be brief and selective. Even though the IASC's first standards may now appear to be very simple documents, they were prepared in a quite elaborate process in which many people had their say and which involved meticulous attention to detail. We discuss those aspects of the successive standards that throw light on the way in which the IASC's agenda, its ambitions, its working arrangements, and the constraints under which it operated evolved during this period.

5.4. THE FIRST STANDARD: IAS 1

The subject of the IASC's first standard, 'disclosure of accounting policies', was already mentioned as one of the leading candidates for the first standard shortly after the 1972 Sydney congress.[10] Its attraction as the first topic must have been that it was unquestionably 'basic', in whatever way that phrase from the IASC's founding Agreement (article 1) might be interpreted. Moreover, it was unlikely to be controversial and it could therefore be expected that a standard would be ready for publication before long.[11] Sir Henry Benson believed it was essential to produce the first standard as soon as possible, to show that the IASC was making tangible progress, and he started work before the IASC was even founded. In May 1973, Benson instructed the staff of the Institute of Chartered Accountants in England and Wales (ICAEW) to write to the proposed member bodies to send copies of pronouncements, recommendations, legislation, and other relevant materials relating to four topics listed in the 'Basic Accounting Standards' document circulated to the invited bodies in February 1973.[12]

Alexander Mackenzie, the outgoing president of the Institute of Chartered Accountants of Scotland, was chosen as chairman of the first steering committee.[13] In approaching its topic, the steering committee could obviously draw on the standards on disclosure of accounting policies issued by the UK & Irish Accounting Standards Steering Committee (ASSC) and the US APB in December 1971 and April 1972, respectively. Several other bodies were working on the subject at the same time as the IASC, suggesting that it may have been basic, but not trivial or out of date. As described in Section 3.5.1, the Union Européenne des Experts Comptables (UEC) rushed out a document on the subject in January 1974. Other comparable standards issued around the time of IAS 1 include an ED on Disclosure of Accounting Policies issued by the Accounting Research Committee of the Canadian Institute of Chartered Accountants (CICA) in June 1974 (issued as an unnumbered Research Recommendation in December 1974); the Australian Statement of Accounting Standards DS11, *Disclosure of Accounting Methods Used in Preparing Financial Statements*, issued in November 1973; and Statement of Standard Accounting Practice 1, *Disclosure of Accounting Policies*, issued in October 1974 by the Council of the New Zealand Society of Accountants.

IAS 1, published in January 1975, had drawn on several of these sources.[14] It distinguished between fundamental accounting assumptions and accounting policies. The former were identified as going concern, consistency, and accrual. As long as these assumptions were followed in the financial statements, this fact did not need to be disclosed. Accounting policies were defined as the 'principles, bases, conventions, rules and procedures' adopted by management in preparing and presenting financial statements (paragraph 8). The key recommendation of IAS 1 was that financial statements should include 'a clear and concise disclosure of all significant accounting policies' (paragraph 18).

During the drafting stage, Benson put his mark on the proceedings by rewriting the draft prepared by the steering committee and by submitting both versions simultaneously to the Committee. Although Benson courteously noted that he had obtained the permission of the chairman of the steering committee, the gesture left little doubt, if any remained, about the proprietary feelings of Benson for his Committee.[15] In general, Benson took great pride in his drafting skills, honed in his meticulous supervision of the writing of a large number of government and other reports, and it is apparent that he wanted to follow his customary approach to collective authorship in the IASC as well.[16] The first exposure draft, E1, and IAS 1 were mainly based on Benson's draft.

His was not the only influence, however. The Dutch delegate Pieter Louwers was behind the clause that wrong or inappropriate treatment of items in the financial statements is not to be rectified by disclosure of accounting policies, notes or explanatory material (paragraph 20). In this way, Louwers scored a point in a domestic discussion in the Netherlands, where this position was not yet generally accepted.[17] The French delegation also took an active part and proposed a considerable number of amendments. Some of these, like the requirement to disclose post–balance sheet events, were not evidently related to the subject of the standard, and thus were discarded. Nevertheless, some were adopted, such as the requirement that 'Financial statements should show corresponding figures for the preceding period' (paragraph 21).[18] The Institut der Wirtschaftsprüfer (IdW) argued repeatedly in favour of raising prudence to the status of a fundamental concept, to bring IAS 1 in line with the Fourth Directive. This was not supported, and it caused some annoyance to the IdW that some countries which had supported prudence in the Groupe d'Études and in the UEC now voted against this proposal.[19] In the end, though, IAS 1 was unanimously approved for publication.[20]

Benson placed his stamp on the publicity surrounding the publication of IAS 1, just as he had on the text itself. To ensure maximum attention, he orchestrated a carefully planned press conference, preceded by private meetings with selected

Figure 5.1. Sir Henry Benson presents IAS 1 to the press, London, January 1975

newspapers.[21] The IASC press release carried the title, 'Sir Henry Benson Launches the First International Accounting Standard.'[22] Benson's prominent role at the press conference was reflected in some of the media coverage, which, at least in the UK, was truly extensive. *The Times*, under the heading of 'High-Speed Sir Henry', wrote that 'Much of the celerity' with which IAS 1 was produced 'must be credited to the account of Sir Henry Benson, the chairman, who has so vigorously promoted the IASC around the world.'[23] The *Daily Express* did not get all its facts right, but it captured the flavour of the proceedings when it wrote: 'There are 23 different nations on the committee and the British are in the lead.' But when it came to the question of what it all meant, *The Wall Street Journal* observed: 'Most members of the committee said adoption of the new standard wouldn't make much difference in their countries. But Robert Mazars, the French delegate, said it represented a step forward in France.'[24]

To the English-speaking world, IAS 1 was a symbolic standard, even though it contained a few elements that went beyond current practice or current requirements.[25] IAS 1 was the IASC's signal that it had begun its task and was capable of producing standards within a reasonable time frame.[26]

Benson opened his speech at the press conference with the words: 'When the history of the accounting profession comes to be written, I think that today may well be thought to have been a turning point, or epoch, on which the future depended.'[27] Yet, in the next sentence, he announced that he was not going to discuss the standard itself, and he devoted the remainder of his talk to the IASC, its organization, and its future plans. Chief among the latter was the IASC's intention to issue three or four standards each year. Beyond giving the title of the standard, the press release announcing IAS 1 did not give a clue as to its contents. While Benson was active in promoting the IASC in speeches and articles during 1975, the only comment made with respect to IAS 1 was to announce the simple but significant fact that it had been published.[28] This was how IAS 1 and the preceding E1 were typically seen in the English-language press: 'Tame stuff, but it is the beginning of some hard international give and take'.[29]

But from a French perspective, IAS 1 was not at all a simple restatement of the familiar. In a thoughtful essay, Dominique Ledouble, a French auditor who had assisted Mazars in the work of the steering committee and who was to be the French staff observer from 1976 to 1981, pointed out that IAS 1 essentially reflected statements of the US and UK standard setters. Indeed, the very list of examples of accounting policies showed an 'exact correspondence' with the topics covered in US pronouncements on accounting principles. Therefore, it was 'the adaptation of Anglo-Saxon texts to an international level'. This was a different set of ideas than the French were familiar with, as was brought home by the fact that it proved difficult to choose the right phrase from the French accounting vocabulary to translate the 'accrual concept' mentioned in IAS 1. Even more difficult was the idea of substance over form. While not difficult to translate, it fitted awkwardly in the institutional framework of French financial accounting. The French Plan Comptable embodied a decidedly legalistic approach to financial reporting, on the basis that uniformity was worth the price of strict compliance with occasionally arbitrary rules.[30] The French reaction to IAS 1 was the first in a long line of claims, not without justification, that the IASC's approach to standard setting was dominated by the traditions of the Anglo-American countries.

5.5. TEMPERED AMBITIONS: IAS 2 TO IAS 5

While IAS 1 was moving rapidly and without great problems to completion, the Committee began to work in earnest on the next standards. IAS 1 was largely self-evident and did at any rate not have implications for the income or financial position of reporting enterprises. It could therefore be prepared without raising many questions about the IASC's procedures or objectives. But during the work on the next standards, the IASC was forced to grapple with a number of fundamental issues. How should a committee composed of leading figures from nine countries' accountancy bodies, meeting in this way for the first time, proceed to set up and then to deal with a technical agenda? What topics should it deal with? Should its standards break new ground? Should they allow alternative accounting treatments for the same events or transactions? Should decisions be reached by consensus?

The Constitution and Agreement provided partial answers to these questions. The IASC was to promulgate basic standards, and approval of a standard for publication required a vote of at least three quarters of the number of voting rights. But it was essentially up to the Committee to reach agreement on the kind of standards it wanted to publish.

In doing so, it also had to take note of the world outside. For outside parties, even after E1 was published, the IASC was an unknown quantity with a considerable potential influence. The exposure drafts of the first few standards following IAS 1 were therefore an occasion to gauge the IASC's intentions and, where necessary, to inform it of the lines it should not cross or to urge it to take a firmer stance.

It seems that the work on IAS 2 to IAS 5 brought home to many members of the Committee and the various subcommittees that setting international accounting standards required more concessions than they had expected. In order to deal both with differences of opinion within the Committee and with comments from outside, it had to be accepted that strongly worded positions found insufficient support and that minority views could not be ignored. Henk Volten, the Dutch staff observer, wrote that, by the end of 1975, 'A period of getting acquainted, involving inevitable struggles, has led to mutual understanding of the various points of view.... The emphasizing of conflicting positions has changed to a large extent into an expressed desire for unanimous acceptance [of proposed standards].'[31]

The subjects chosen for the next four standards were inventory valuation (IAS 2), consolidated statements (IAS 3), depreciation of fixed assets (IAS 4), and basic disclosure in the financial statements (IAS 5). All were seen as basic rather than 'sophisticated' topics.[32] Progress on all four was smooth, so that in 1976 the IASC achieved for the first time its stated goal of publishing 'three to four standards a year'. Three standards a year, however, turned out to be the maximum the IASC could regularly manage prior to 1987. Only in 1983 was it able to publish four new standards.

It was noted with satisfaction that the exposure drafts attracted a considerable volume of comment letters.[33] As the IASC's secretariat prepared typewritten verbatim transcripts of the contents of the letters, sorted by topic, the volume of comments can be compared across standards. The comment letters on each of the four exposure drafts amounted to more than one hundred transcript pages. With 183 pages, E3 set a record that was not to be broken until E32 was published in 1989. From E3 to E32, the only exposure drafts to attract more than one hundred pages of comment letters were those preceding IAS 12, on accounting for taxes, and IAS 17, on accounting for leases.[34]

5.5.1. IAS 2: Inventories

The subject of this standard was originally described as 'valuation of stock and work in progress',[35] yet the language used in the final standard was 'valuation of inventories'—the American term, not the British. This potentially wide-ranging subject was soon brought down to manageable proportions by a proposal from the steering committee to exclude construction contracts, and by a decision of the full Committee to limit the standard to the valuation of inventories in the context of the historical cost system. This last decision was disappointing to the Dutch delegation, as there was a strong tradition of replacement value accounting in the Netherlands, and the Nederlands Instituut van Registeraccountants (NIVRA) was very active in propagating that system abroad.[36] Given these limitations, two main issues remained to be solved between the start of the project and July 1975, when IAS 2 was approved for publication. The first was the status to be accorded to alternatives to first-in, first-out (FIFO), in particular last-in, first-out (LIFO) and the base stock method. The second issue was whether direct costing should be allowed.

LIFO was used widely in the United States, for tax-related reasons. Internationally, it was often seen as a typically American method even though it was known in several other countries as a minority practice.[37] In 1971, the European Economic Community (EEC) published a draft of its Fourth Directive, in which LIFO and FIFO were accorded equal status (article 37). In Continental Europe, however, the base stock method was traditionally used to achieve results similar to LIFO.

The steering committee, chaired by Howard Lyons (Canada), and the full Committee wavered on LIFO.[38] The steering committee, in which the United States was not represented, argued for a secondary status for LIFO as an 'other acceptable practice' next to the 'preferred practice' of FIFO. The full Committee favoured a version in which LIFO and FIFO were granted equal status. A compromise was reached in which LIFO was not explicitly presented as a 'less preferred' or 'other acceptable' practice, but in which the use of LIFO required some additional disclosures.[39] As pointed out in a Canadian comment letter on the exposure draft (E2, published in September 1974), 'It would appear that the inclusion of LIFO is a concession to our friends to the South who have, of course, embraced LIFO for tax rather than accounting reasons.'[40] While it is true that LIFO was popular in the United States, so that it is likely that the US delegation would have argued in its favour, it was not a majority practice for large companies in that country during the early 1970s.[41] Moreover, it was used in other countries as well. For instance, the Greek and Indian institutes referred to practice in their country when they expressed support for LIFO in their comment letters. Hence, opponents and supporters of LIFO were not neatly grouped by country, and opposition to LIFO was expressed in comment letters from the United States as well.

The steering committee was firm that the base stock method 'should not be used', and this view found its way into the exposure draft. This raised questions in Germany why LIFO would be allowed but not the base stock method, which was well known in Germany.[42] It also proved difficult to swallow for the Dutch delegation, which regarded the base stock method as a pragmatic approximation of replacement cost accounting in the income statement. The Dutch therefore considered voting against the standard. A number of UK companies also lobbied for the base stock method, not least because its acceptance by the IASC might help to overturn the UK standard SSAP 9 on this point.[43] Faced with this pressure, the IASC accorded the base stock method the same treatment as LIFO in IAS 2.

The steering committee preferred absorption costing, with direct costing (also known as variable costing) mentioned as an acceptable alternative. In Mexico, represented on the steering committee, direct costing was allowed, as well as in Australia.[44] It was prohibited in the United States and in a draft standard published by the UK and Irish ASSC, and this position was adopted in E2 as well, which required the use of absorption costing.[45] But in May 1975, two months before IAS 2 was approved, the ASSC had issued SSAP 9, which, in contrast to the corresponding exposure draft, was silent on the acceptability of direct costing. The ASSC had changed its position, and the ICAEW now supported the equivalence of absorption costing and direct costing in its comment letter on the IASC's E2. Support for direct costing also came in comment letters from South Africa and Australia, and in the end, IAS 2 allowed both methods.

5.5.2. IAS 3: Consolidated Financial Statements and the Equity Method

By the mid-1970s, the practice of consolidated financial reporting was by no means universal among listed companies in all IASC member countries, but it was clear that the practice was spreading rapidly. With IAS 3, published in 1976, the IASC could take up a position somewhat ahead of practice on a major accounting topic, without the risk of backing a wrong horse.

Consolidated reporting had been required of companies subject to the Securities and Exchange Commission in the United States since the 1930s and in the United Kingdom since the Companies Act 1947. In other countries consolidation had only recently become mandatory (as in Germany in 1965, although for domestic subsidiaries only, and in the Netherlands in 1971) or was still not mandatory at all, as in France and Japan.[46] A Seventh Directive on consolidated financial statements was in preparation but would not be published until 1983. One of the attractions to the IASC of dealing with consolidated financial reporting at an early stage was that it might hope to have some influence on the development of the Seventh Directive.

Knowing that in countries like France the adoption of consolidated financial reporting was only a matter of time, the IASC found it fairly easy to reach agreement on the central requirement that all parent companies should issue consolidated financial statements (paragraph 34). While it was clear on this central issue, IAS 3 was rather flexible on the choice of consolidation principles. There were two main issues in this regard. The first was whether or not subsidiaries with 'dissimilar' activities might be excluded from the consolidation, as in the case of a finance subsidiary of an industrial parent. The second was whether a 'subsidiary' company was to be defined as one in which the parent had more than half the voting rights, or whether a more general definition should be used, based on control of the financial and operational policies of the subsidiary.

In both cases, the steering committee, chaired by Joe Cummings (United States), advocated clear rules: no exclusion of dissimilar activities, as this would lead to subjective interpretation, and subsidiaries defined in terms of voting rights, as this was considered to be 'unambiguous'.[47] But this would have brought the standard in conflict with regulations and practice in a number of countries. Therefore, the full Committee decided that both voting rights and other means of control be considered in determining which investee companies should be classified as subsidiaries, in line with practices in several European countries. On dissimilar activities, the steering committee proposed, and the full Committee agreed, to require the consolidation of all subsidiaries, regardless of their activities. This position, which was at variance with US generally accepted accounting principles (US GAAP), was included in the exposure draft E3 (published in December 1974).

An interesting feature of E3 was that it required that working capital, long-term assets, and long-term debt of the group 'should be analysed by major geographical areas, by continent or by country' (paragraph 64). This casual venture into the area of segment reporting was remarkable. In the United States and the United Kingdom, mandatory segment reporting had been introduced only recently.[48] The 1974 draft of the EEC's Fourth Directive included a requirement for geographical and line of business segmentation, but this was not unopposed.[49]

On the whole, E3 could be expected to draw attention, and it did. As indicated above, E3 attracted the largest volume of comment letters of all pre-1987 exposure drafts. The bulk of these came from the UK & Ireland, Australia, Canada, and South Africa. The United States, the Netherlands, Japan, Sweden, Sri Lanka, and India also provided extensive comments. Relatively little comment came from Germany, France, and Mexico. The comments ran the gamut from full approval to complete rejection. Recurrent criticisms were that E3 was too lengthy, too detailed, not basic, and in conflict with local standards or law.

The stiffest opposition to E3 came not from countries where consolidation was not yet part of established practice, but from the United Kingdom and the United States. The British responses in particular were notable for their almost shocked reaction to the idea that the IASC might presume to impose changes on UK practice. The chairman of the UK ASSC, Sir Ronald Leach, wrote in response to E3:

I was urged by my Committee to write to you...to report in the clearest terms that in our view the paper was not suitable in its present form for publication as an international standard.... My Committee were also concerned at the inclusion in the exposure draft of proposals that would deny to companies in the UK the right to avail themselves of alternative forms of presenting group accounts at present specifically permitted by law.[50]

Other UK respondents also argued that international standards should not curtail the flexibility allowed by law. Taken literally, this could not have been acceptable to the IASC. It might be wise for the IASC to ensure, as it typically would do over the coming years, that its standards were compatible with at least one option in each of the various national requirements. But to accept that its standards had to accommodate all options in all countries would preclude it from issuing meaningful standards at all. Some concessions had to be made, however, and the most contentious issue for the United Kingdom was the mandatory consolidation of dissimilar activities.

As is discussed more extensively in Section 6.6.2, this aspect of E3 was opposed in the United States as well. In the words of Cummings, the proposal to require the consolidation of dissimilar activities 'hit the fan in the U.S.' and alerted many people to the possible domestic impact of the IASC.[51] In the end, IAS 3 accommodated the UK and US position by exempting subsidiaries with dissimilar activities from mandatory consolidation (paragraph 37).

Many respondents commented on the proposed geographical segmentation. Perhaps surprisingly, rather few rejected segmentation in principle. A typical comment, however, was that this issue should be dealt with in a separate statement. The IASC acted on that suggestion. The final wording of IAS 3 (approved in March 1976) was much more restricted than E3, merely calling for disclosure if this was necessary for a 'fair disclosure of the exposure to exceptional risks of operating in other countries' (paragraph 47e). Yet a project to draft a standard on segment reporting was added to the agenda in July 1976.

In retrospect, IAS 3 stands out as arguably the most important standard issued by the IASC in the pre-1987 period.[52] It was the first standard that tested the will of the international accounting community to support the IASC's standards. It provided clear guidance on a significant issue that was highly topical in many countries. It has been asserted, for instance, that IAS 3 was frequently consulted during the preparations for the Seventh Directive. Moreover, by drawing widespread attention, IAS 3 greatly enhanced the IASC's visibility.

In terms of working arrangements, IAS 3 showed that the IASC already began to be less dominated by its founder. Henry Benson had personally intervened in the process of drafting IAS 1, by rewriting the steering committee's draft. With IAS 3, which was the second subject in the IASC's original programme of work, Benson attempted to do the same. But unlike the chairman of the first steering committee, Cummings refused to give his permission and thus caused a 'minor explosion'. Reportedly, Cummings was the only member of the IASC who could stand up to Benson. Afterwards, Benson no longer took a hand in the drafting of standards.[53]

5.5.3. IAS 4: Depreciation Accounting

Compared to IAS 3, IAS 4, *Depreciation Accounting* (approved in July 1976) was a simple standard calling for systematic depreciation of all depreciable assets. It did not prescribe or discuss particular depreciation methods. In addition, it called for certain basic disclosures by type of assets, such as the depreciation method and depreciation rate, the gross book value of assets, and accumulated depreciation.

Initially, IAS 4 was not intended to be such a modest standard. The point outline proposed that it would deal with depreciable amounts, depreciation methods, investment grants, tax issues, and changes in depreciation methods.[54] The first draft specified straight-line depreciation as the standard method, with required disclosure of the difference if another method were used.[55] The Committee agreed, and ruled in addition that certain depreciation methods would not be allowed at all, in particular those resulting in increasing charges over time. However, further reflection led the steering committee, chaired by Tony Kewin (Australia), to the insight that 'To exclude the use of certain methods currently used in practice goes beyond the brief of the IASC to concern itself with basic standards.'[56] Hence, the exposure draft E4 (approved in April 1975) no longer specifically ruled out any depreciation methods. Moreover, the identification of methods resulting in 'even charges' as a benchmark was dropped, apparently because the Committee was unable or unwilling to state that straight-line depreciation was superior.

With the comment letters, the first signs came in that some observers thought the international standards were becoming too basic and that there should be at least some guidance in the choice of a depreciation method. The Zambian Association of Accountants wrote that it was 'disappointed' because E4 'merely restated the principles which had been applied and implemented by practicing accountants for a number of years'.[57] Coming from a country that potentially would have more use for the IASC's standards than the founder member countries themselves, this was a signal to note. On the basis of comments like this, the steering committee proposed an insertion in the standard gently encouraging companies to choose 'a method that most appropriately reflects the expected consumption of its service potential during each accounting period'.[58] But this was not accepted by the Committee. After all, the general nature of E4 could also be seen as a virtue. A 'professional organisation' from the United States wrote: 'We believe this proposed statement is at a level of generality appropriate to the objectives of your committee.'[59]

But despite comments that IAS 4 might be too bland, it contained at least one element that later was to become quite controversial. In December 1977, the UK standard setter, known since 1976 as the Accounting Standards Committee (ASC), published SSAP 12, *Accounting for Depreciation*. Like IAS 4, SSAP 12 considered all property to be depreciable assets. However, the ASC suspended the application of SSAP 12 to investment properties. This temporary exemption of investment property from the requirement to depreciate was made permanent with the publication of SSAP 19, *Accounting for Investment Properties* in September 1980. Hence, from the end of 1977 onwards, there was a significant conflict between IAS 4 and UK and Irish accounting standards (*see also* Section 6.5.1). When it was completing SSAP 19, the ASC did not fail to inform the IASC of its view that reconsidering IAS 4 was 'essential' and 'a more vital project than some of the esoteric subjects which you are now considering'.[60]

5.5.4. IAS 5: Information to be Disclosed in Financial Statements

IAS 5 resembled IAS 4 in that a reasonably ambitious start resulted in a modest standard, which in turn gave rise to comments that the IASC had swung too far

'Compromise to Harmonise' 103

in the direction of basic standards. The objective of this project was to create a standard which listed the basic disclosures in financial statements. The standard consisted, first, of a general requirement to disclose all material information 'necessary to make the financial statements clear and understandable'. The British and the Dutch would have preferred to use 'true and fair view' as the central criterion, but this evidently did not get sufficient support.[61] Following the general requirement, the bulk of the standard consisted of a list of required headings and subheadings, mainly concerning the balance sheet, as well as additional footnote disclosures for some items.

The first draft prepared by the steering committee, chaired by Manuel Galván (Mexico), was rather more lengthy than the final standard, and it contained some disclosures that went beyond the self-evident.[62] One was, again, a requirement to break down sales turnover by major classes of business, and another was to give 'an analysis of taxation on corporate results showing the amount payable currently and the deferred charge or credit'.[63] The line of business segmentation requirement came up for discussion in November 1974, just weeks after the Committee had approved E3 on consolidated statements, which contained a requirement to provide geographical segment information.[64] While the Committee cannot, therefore, have been opposed to segmentation in principle, it nevertheless removed the segmentation clause from the draft. The tax disclosure did not appear in E5 either, which was approved in April 1975.

E5 again proved to be a disappointment to the Zambian Association of Accountants, which thought it was 'cautious in the extreme'. Similar criticisms came from founder member countries. A Canadian body wrote: 'We are struck by the fact that in both [E5] and others we have read, the statements seem to be very general and sweeping and perhaps one is inclined to consider them somewhat insignificant.' From the UK & Ireland came the verdict that E5 was 'fairly elementary' and was characterized by a 'broad brush approach'. The Society of Investment Analysts informed the IASC that it was disappointed: '[E5] asks far too little and in particular its treatment of the income statement was so sketchy that we wondered why it had been included.'[65] Nevertheless, IAS 5 was approved in July 1976 without major changes from E5. And despite criticisms that it was too elementary, it was not altogether without effect. It was noted, for instance, that some of its requirements led to changes in France's Plan Comptable.[66]

5.5.5. The IASC's Policy Takes Shape

By the time IAS 5 was published in October 1976, the IASC had started to find its bearings. Whereas IAS 1 had been non-controversial, the exposure drafts leading to IAS 2 and especially IAS 3 encountered serious opposition. In the United Kingdom, there had been vocal resistance to the idea that the IASC might curtail some of the flexibility of local regulations. In the United States, the first exposure drafts had caused 'resentment and opposition' which was not dispelled by the fact that the standards in the end had accommodated the US position.[67] IAS 4 and IAS 5, on the other hand, had perhaps not been ambitious enough. Joe Cummings, taking over the chairmanship of the IASC in November 1976, attempted to summarize the experience:

> One thing we learned quickly is that enthusiasm for straightening out the world has to be tempered somewhat. An international committee is better off keeping its standards rather basic, uncomplicated, and probably not beyond the standards that now exist in the sophisticated market countries.[68]

The IASC's strategy for the 1970s and most of the 1980s began to take shape. It was, essentially, to eliminate practices that were widely regarded as unacceptable without trying to choose between practices that were seen as valid alternatives or that were firmly enshrined in the more advanced accounting environments. The policy would sometimes be referred to as 'to cut off the edges of the omelette'.[69]

IAS 1 had already laid the basis for this approach, by asserting that 'There are many different accounting policies in use even in relation to the same subject; judgment is required in selecting and applying those which, in the circumstances of the enterprise, are best suited to present properly its financial position and the results of its operations' (paragraph 8). At this stage, the objective was to limit the diversity and to make it transparent, but not to impose uniformity.

This policy was most clearly, and most consistently, put forward in many speeches and articles by Chairman Hans Burggraaff in the early 1980s.[70] It was also expressed, sometimes more tentatively, by several participants in the IASC during the later 1970s.[71] Although some participants would have been comfortable with a policy of this kind all along, to others it was something of a climbdown. Among these others was Henry Benson, who observed in 1980:

> The device of providing alternatives is in any event contrary to the whole concept of IASC at least as it existed in its formative stages. The object of IASC was to cut out alternatives and choices so as to ensure a reasonable degree of uniformity or comparability. I am an absolutist in this respect. I believe that once the principle of alternatives is admitted, worthwhile standards go by the board.[72]

The scope for compromise allowed by the claim of being 'absolutist' both in cutting out alternatives and in aiming for 'a reasonable degree of uniformity' presumably allowed Benson to accept such things as the inclusion of both FIFO and LIFO in IAS 2. Still, there was a note of disappointment when Benson complained on the same occasion: 'I don't think the determination is there to bring about comparability.'[73]

5.6. A NON-STARTER: AUDITING STANDARDS

As noted in Section 3.4.3, the question of whether the IASC should concern itself with auditing standards had been raised in the preparatory discussions of 1972 and 1973. At that time, the question was left open for future resolution. In the founding stage, it was Henry Benson who had advocated the inclusion of auditing subjects in the IASC's agenda, and he continued to do so over the following years. His list of possible topics submitted to the Committee in January 1974 included seven auditing subjects in addition to twenty accounting topics. In the accompanying note, he advised that it should be decided 'whether to spill over into the audit field. There may be divided views on this; for myself I veer in favour of an audit subject fairly soon.'[74]

It is likely that one of the reasons why Benson was keen to begin work on auditing at this time was the same reason why some other IASC members wanted to defer it. At this stage, negotiations were going on in ICCAP about setting up a permanent International Secretariat or International Federation of Accountants (*see* Section 7.3). If the IASC were to stake out a claim in the auditing field, the potential significance of the new organization would be substantially reduced. Similarly, those European IASC members who retained a loyalty to the UEC, or at least wanted to give it another chance, saw auditing as an area where the UEC could develop a meaningful presence alongside the IASC. In effect, an agreement that implied a division of labour along these lines was reached between IASC and UEC in 1974.[75]

Nevertheless, Benson did not give up on auditing. Early in 1976, towards the end of his chairmanship, he conducted informal talks with the Basel Committee of banking supervisors on a possible role for the IASC in setting standards for banks (*see* Section 5.10). The matter was discussed at the March 1976 IASC meeting, and Benson persuaded an apparently reluctant Committee to let it be known informally to the Basel Committee that the IASC was willing to carry out work in auditing.[76] But in the summer of 1976, Benson's term as chairman ended and he was unable to see the matter to fruition. When, in the autumn of 1976, the Basel Committee formally wrote to Joe Cummings with reference to Benson's encouragement, to invite the IASC to discuss the possibility of setting accounting and auditing standards for banks, the IASC decided to engage in discussions on accounting standards only.[77] After that, with Benson gone and with the establishment of IFAC in 1977, the suggestion that the IASC might concern itself with auditing standards did not recur.

5.7. INFLATION ACCOUNTING: IAS 6 AND IAS 15

Accounting responses to changing prices had received considerable academic attention in the English-speaking world during the 1960s. In Germany and the Netherlands, such attention could be traced back to the 1910s and 1920s, and in the Netherlands replacement value accounting had gained a considerable number of adherents in practice as well. Yet it was only in the 1970s that inflation accounting vaulted to the top of the international accounting agenda.[78] The reason was the sharp increase in inflation in 1974 as a result of the first oil shock. Throughout the 1960s, the rate of general price level increases in the IASC founder member countries had gradually crept up to reach an average of around 6–7 per cent in 1970–73.[79] In 1974, it jumped to an average of around 15 per cent. Ironically, inflation rates in countries with a tradition of inflation accounting, notably Germany and the Netherlands, remained fairly low or returned quickly to lower levels. But the United Kingdom and Ireland were particularly hard hit with rates occasionally exceeding 20 per cent in the mid-1970s. In the United Kingdom, inflation accounting became a matter of serious political attention, epitomized by the 1975 Sandilands report. Although not quite as severe, inflation was persistent in Australia, France, and the United States.

5.7.1. IAS 6: Accounting Responses to Changing Prices

Inflation accounting was not mentioned as a potential topic during the founding stages of the IASC. Even though Henry Benson had been aware of it at least since 1971, he first brought it up in the IASC in his January 1974 list of possible subjects for future standards. However, in that list inflation accounting was included among the sophisticated topics that might be considered after progress had been made with more basic subjects.[80] Yet, in April 1974 the topic had apparently acquired such urgency that a steering committee on 'accounting in the face of inflation' was formed, even though the agenda for that IASC meeting did not include the choice of a new topic.[81] Whereas prior steering committees had consisted of three members, this was a five-member committee. Apart from the unavoidable Dutch, the steering committee consisted of representatives from Canada, the UK & Ireland, and the United States. The Institute of Certified Public Accountants in Israel (an associate member), a country where inflation was to reach around 40 per cent in 1974, also nominated a member when it was invited to do so. The committee's chairman was Howard Lyons (Canada).[82]

At the press conference marking the publication of IAS 1 in January 1975, Benson mentioned the fact that inflation accounting had risen to the top of the IASC's agenda. As a result, *Forbes* warned against complacency with regard to the IASC, as 'It could...turn into a surprising game for U.S. companies.' It pointed out that 'many Dutch companies' including Philips were already using inflation accounting: 'If the IASC adopted the Dutch replacement-cost approach and could make it stick, companies all over the world could see their earnings drop dramatically.'[83]

Although this scenario did not materialize, it was not for want of trying on the part of the Dutch. The Dutch representative on the steering committee was Wessel van Bruinessen, a partner in one of the leading Dutch firms who was considered to be a fervent advocate of replacement value accounting, even by the standards of the NIVRA at that time. Within the steering committee, he had to 'fight a tough battle over principles' from the first meeting onwards.[84] The problem was not so much that the other steering committee members were less keen on producing a forceful standard, but rather that they were committed to a different approach. The US and UK & Irish representatives thought of inflation accounting in terms of general price level adjustments, which the Dutch adherents of replacement value accounting had always rejected as theoretically unsound. In this way, the IASC steering committee was the stage for a miniature version of the ongoing debate over these two main approaches to accounting for inflation. The IASC's challenge was to find an acceptable position even as accounting standard setters and other bodies around the world were still coming out in favour of one method or the other, or were changing their positions.[85]

To start with, the steering committee presented the IASC with a complex package, consisting of three draft documents.[86] A draft standard on 'accounting treatment of changing prices' would require all enterprises using the historical cost basis in their financial statements to publish supplementary data or key figures based on general purchasing power adjustments. However, enterprises recording specific price changes in their primary financial statements (as some Dutch companies did) should provide a reconciliation to historical cost. They might present purchasing-power adjusted data as an option. A second draft standard described in considerable detail how general purchasing power adjustments would have to be made. The third document was not a draft standard but a draft 'discussion memorandum' on replacement value accounting. This amounted to an exposition of replacement value theory as traditionally taught in the Netherlands. As a whole, the package looked more like a reflection of the current battle lines than an expression of an emerging consensus.

The IASC failed to reach a decision on the package at its April 1975 meeting, and decided to defer consideration for a year 'in view of the present uncertainty concerning inflation accounting in many countries'.[87] The steering committee was, however, united in its view that deferral was unwise, as the present rate of inflation made financial statements that ignored price changes misleading. It urged the IASC to reconsider its decision, and submitted a revised draft standard.[88] This draft would require all enterprises to present a systematic response to specific or general price changes, or both, but did not describe any such responses in detail. The information could be supplied either in the financial statements or in a supplement. In October 1975, the IASC approved an exposure draft, E6, along these lines.

Van Bruinessen described this as a breakthrough. Whereas in the IASC's previous thinking replacement value accounting had had the status of an allowed alternative, E6 meant the 'absolute equivalence' of purchasing power accounting and replacement value accounting. He ascribed it, apart from Dutch tenacity, to his perception that internationally the tide was turning away from purchasing power adjustments.[89] Late in 1974, the IdW had produced a draft recommendation on accounting for specific price changes.[90] This was followed by a comparable draft by the Australian Accounting Research Foundation in June 1975.[91] Even more significantly, the SEC issued a draft release favouring the required disclosure of replacement cost data in August 1975,[92] while the September 1975 Sandilands report also came out in favour of current cost.[93]

As Van Bruinessen put it, the NIVRA was now faced with a tactical choice. It could be content with E6, or press on, backed up by the 'moral authority' of the

SEC and Sandilands, and accept current cost only. The NIVRA publicly opted for the latter course.[94] As it turned out, this was perhaps not the better choice in terms of supporting accounting for changing prices in general. When the comments on E6 came in, they were about evenly divided between favourable reactions and responses advising that issuing a standard would be premature before a degree of international consensus on the issue was reached. Allowing both approaches now, so the argument went, would make it more difficult to reach harmonization at a later stage. Comments of the latter kind came in particular from Australia, New Zealand, the UK and Ireland, and the United States, and it would appear that some respondents were only too happy to emphasize the significance of the international differences of opinion. By taking an uncompromising stance, the NIVRA played into the hands of those who argued that the enduring controversy was sufficient reason to defer an international standard.

And then there was, of course, downright opposition to any form of mandatory inflation accounting. One group of US respondents warned the IASC that it would put 'the growing goodwill and support for IASC in the US business community' at risk if it were to issue a standard by which that community 'would be thrown automatically into a non-compliance posture'. The Japanese Institute of Certified Public Accountants advised more gently that the IASC was 'taking a risk and might lose its prestige' by 'being very unrealistic'.[95]

On the basis of these comments, the steering committee concluded that it would be 'inappropriate' at this time to require enterprises to adopt a systematic approach to changing prices, that is, one of the two alternatives of current value accounting and purchasing power accounting. Fear of large-scale non-compliance with a negative impact on the IASC's status was a major factor.[96] It therefore recommended a revised draft, which would in essence be accepted for publication as IAS 6 in March 1977. IAS 6 merely required enterprises to disclose which procedures had been adopted to reflect the impact of general price rises, specific price rises, or both. If no such procedures had been adopted, then that fact should be disclosed. In view of the steering committee's original enthusiasm, this was a very weak standard indeed. The NIVRA, whose delegation had accepted the result with great reluctance, published IAS 6 in the Netherlands with the exhortation 'that the more advanced national views on the subject should be fully adhered to'.[97]

5.7.2. A Discussion Paper without Discussion

Between the publication of E6 and the approval of IAS 6 (October 1975 to March 1977), the steering committee worked on a discussion paper, intended as a contribution to the ongoing debate on accounting for changing prices. This was the first publication by the IASC that was neither a standard nor an exposure draft. The original idea was, rather ambitiously, to prepare 'a detailed example of a hypothetical company which will be used to demonstrate the essential characteristics of the many proposals made to solve the problem of accounting for changing prices. The example will be based on a set of economic data that covers fifteen years.'⁹⁸ Yet no such comprehensive example was ever submitted to the board. The discussion paper, 'Treatment of Changing Prices in Financial Statements: A Summary of Proposals' (published in March 1977), consisted of a brief treatment of the main issues involved in accounting for specific price changes and general price level adjustments. This section was largely taken from earlier drafts of E6. In addition, the discussion paper contained a lengthy appendix, summarizing recent standards, discussion drafts, and other guidance on the subject from twelve IASC member countries.

The discussion paper contained no invitation to submit comments, and it appears that none were received or at least discussed by the board. Apart from providing a useful summary of information on national attempts to deal with inflation accounting, it did not contribute significantly to the international debate.

5.7.3. IAS 15: Accounting Responses to Changing Prices Revisited

The international debate certainly did not subside after IAS 6 was published. Particularly in the United Kingdom, where inflation remained at a high level, the drama continued to unfold. Following the Sandilands report, the ASC published an exposure draft (ED 18) in November 1976, which contained far-reaching proposals to apply current cost accounting in the primary financial statements. However, it prompted strong resistance, culminating in the passage of an extraordinary resolution by the membership at a special meeting of the ICAEW in July 1977 that current cost accounting statements should not be made compulsory. After this setback, the ASC published an 'interim recommendation'—known as the Hyde Committee Guidelines—in November 1977, which called merely for disclosure of current cost adjustments to cost of sales and depreciation, and of a gearing adjustment. Backed by growing support for current cost accounting in practice, the ASC published a standard (SSAP 16) in 1980, which required a current cost balance sheet and income statement, although this might be in the form of a condensed supplementary presentation.

Outside the United Kingdom and the Netherlands, though, the practice of inflation accounting made little headway in Europe. National guidance issued in France and Germany during the 1970s had little if any impact on practice.⁹⁹ In the United States, the SEC's Accounting Series Release No. 190 of March 1976, which required supplementary information on a current replacement cost basis, led the FASB to issue Statement of Financial Accounting Standards No. 33 in September 1979. FAS 33 required supplementary disclosure of both price level-adjusted data and current cost data.

In March 1977, the IASC created a new steering committee charged with 'maintaining a watching brief' in the area of inflation accounting. It was to be a small committee in which the Netherlands, the United Kingdom & Ireland, and the United States were represented.¹⁰⁰ The steering committee regularly informed the board of developments, and in March 1978 it was decided that the time was ripe to ask the steering committee for a new draft standard. With a steering committee that had put itself on a 'pragmatic rather than theoretical basis', the atmosphere was rather different than during the preparation of IAS 6.[101] In a succession of drafts, the board and the steering committee carefully crafted an exposure draft that would be compatible with both the US and UK approaches.[102] E17 (approved in March 1980) and the resulting IAS 15 (approved in June 1981) were relatively simple documents. Yet IAS 15 did go a step beyond IAS 6, which it replaced. It required disclosure of adjusted depreciation and cost of sales, and of adjustments relating to monetary items if these were part of the accounting method adopted. The standard avoided stating a preference for a current cost approach or the use of price level adjustments.

In view of the heated debates on inflation accounting in the 1970s, it is striking to see that the response to E17 bordered on indifference. The volume of comment letters (thirty-three transcript pages) was the lowest of any exposure draft issued prior to 1987, and it came from an unusually narrow range of respondents. Whereas it was usual for most founder member countries to send in a reaction, this time responses were received from Germany, the Netherlands, the UK & Ireland, and the United States only, as well as from four other countries. Apparently, interest in inflation accounting was dying out except in the small number of countries where it was actively practiced. Given the fact that the standard had been tailored to the UK and US situations, it is not surprising that most responses from these countries, which made up the bulk of the total, were positive. The most common negative comment was the warning that, without further guidance, the standard was likely to remain 'academic' in countries with little or no practical experience in this area.

It is doubtful whether IAS 15 made any serious impact anywhere. Not long after it was published, inflation accounting disappeared as a major issue in the United States, the United Kingdom, and other countries as a result of falling inflation rates. In the United Kingdom, current cost accounting was characterized as a 'dead duck' by 1983.[103] SSAP 16 was suspended in June 1985, after several years of large-scale non-compliance, and was withdrawn in April 1988. In the United States, the requirement to disclose price level-adjusted data was withdrawn in 1985, and disclosures on inflation accounting were made voluntary in 1986.[104] By 1987, only a handful of Canadian companies still provided the supplementary current cost data called for by the *CICA Handbook*.[105] In 1989, the IASC recognized that inflation accounting was a 'lost cause'[106] and inserted a revised preface in IAS 15 which made its application non-mandatory.[107]

5.8. STOCKING THE SHOP: IAS 7 TO IAS 13

Even though inflation accounting was the most glamorous topic of the late 1970s, it was not where the IASC would build its reputation. Rather, the IASC earned its place in the sun by issuing in rapid succession a series of standards on relatively elementary subjects. The successive chairmen of the IASC, at least up to Stephen Elliott in the early 1980s, were keen to increase the number of extant standards. As the public face of the IASC, travelling the world to urge endorsement and adoption of international standards, they wanted to have a 'product to sell', rather than the mere promise of future standards.[108] With IAS 7 through 13, issued between 1977 and 1979, the body of IASC standards grew too large to be ignored.

5.8.1. IAS 7: Statement of Changes in Financial Position

The topic of 'source and application of funds' was presented to the Committee in a secretariat note as a 'relatively straightforward subject'.[109] And indeed, the development of the standard proceeded very smoothly, taking somewhat less than three years from the decision to start the project in November 1974. The funds statement had rapidly been adopted during the 1960s on a largely voluntary basis in Canada and the United States, and a similar adoption process was going on in France, Germany, and the Netherlands in the mid-1970s.[110] There were few difficult decisions for the steering committee, chaired by Alfred Cordoliani (France), or the IASC to take.[111] One of the significant issues relating to the funds statement, whether to define funds in terms of cash and cash equivalents or working capital, was resolved by prescribing no funds concept at all.[112] As in the case of IAS 2, the IASC had some difficulty whether to choose UK or US terminology for the title of the statement: Statement of Source and Application of Funds (Canada and United Kingdom), or Statement of Changes in Financial Position (United States). In the end, as in IAS 2, it chose the American wording.

The exposure draft E7, approved in March 1976, was well received. Most comment letters were favourable or very favourable. A number of UK & Irish respondents declared that E7 presented the matter better than the ASC's SSAP 10 (published in 1975).

IAS 7 (approved in July 1977 and essentially similar to E7) required that a statement of changes in financial position should be included as an integral part of the financial statements. Within the statement, funds from operations should be presented separately from other sources, and unusual items should be disclosed separately.

5.8.2. IAS 8: Unusual Items and Accounting Changes

In the early years of the IASC, the procedures for choosing new topics were not very elaborate. The secretariat would prepare a list of possible topics for the full Committee to choose from, but it was free to modify topics on the spot or even to come up with completely new ones during its meetings. In November 1974, at the start of the project leading to IAS 8, the Committee chose to combine two topics suggested by the secretariat, extraordinary items and accounting changes, and to entrust them to a single steering committee. A third topic, prior period items, was added, and the entire package was described as 'presentation of the income statement'.[113]

The US chairman of the steering committee, Joe Cummings, had been involved with the subject during his years as a member of the APB.[114] He knew from experience how controversial income statement presentation, with its direct impact on 'headline' earnings, could be.[115]

As with other standards, the steering committee's first pass at the subject was more wide-ranging and bolder than the final standard. In its point outline, the committee had considered the issue of unrealized surpluses (revaluations) and was groping for what might be called, with hindsight, a statement of comprehensive income.[116] The Committee did not follow this lead, and unrealized gains and losses were left outside the scope of IAS 8.

Another issue on which the standard was not so forthright as the steering committee had intended was direct charges to equity. In its first draft submitted to the full Committee, the steering committee included a discussion of the difference between the all-inclusive and the current operating performance concepts of income, and the proposed standard announced that the income statement should include all changes in equity apart from transactions with owners and two other exceptions.[117] The full Committee did not want to go as far as that, and it took the sting out of the proposal by an expedient that it was to use on other occasions as well. Until a new format was adopted in 1991, all 'Statements of International Accounting Standards' consisted of two sections. One section, headed 'International Accounting Standard', was printed in bold type. This section was the accounting standard proper in that it stated the allowed or prescribed treatments and the required disclosures. This section was preceded by a section in normal type, headed 'Explanation', in which the issues covered in the standard were discussed and some of the choices made in drafting the standard were explained. The relation between the boldfaced standard section and the preceding explanation was somewhat ambiguous, and this allowed the IASC to make pronouncements on contentious issues without clearly committing itself. When approving E8 (July 1976), the Committee eliminated the reference to the all-inclusive concept of income from the boldfaced standard, while maintaining the discussion of the all-inclusive and current operating concepts of income in the explanation. As with other standards, the lack of a clear link between the standard and the explanation puzzled some comment letter writers.[118]

On accounting changes, E8 introduced the criterion that non-mandatory accounting changes might be made only when they gave rise to a 'fairer presentation'. Possibly, this reflected the influence of Joe Cummings. If accepted, this would have been the first appearance of a general 'fairness' criterion in the IASC's standards. However, respondents from Canada and the United States pointed out that, in the context of financial statements, 'fair' did not allow a distinction of degrees, and that audit reports could state only whether something was fair or not. Therefore, in IAS 8, the wording 'more appropriate presentation' was used.[119]

Although some respondents criticized E8 as vague and representing 'the lowest common denominator', the desirability of a standard on these issues was not questioned.[120] E8 and IAS 8 did indeed allow a number of options, notably in regard to accounting changes, but they also included several straightforward requirements or prohibitions. Following IAS 8, enterprises would have to show income from ordinary activities as a line item in the financial statements, and would not be allowed to take unusual items directly to equity.

5.8.3. IAS 9: Research and Development

In the free style of its early days, the IASC decided to add accounting for research and development costs to its agenda in November 1974 without any prompting from the secretariat. Progress was swift, and the resulting standard, IAS 9, was approved for publication in March 1978. IAS 9 provides a good illustration of the pragmatic approach by which the IASC was quite willing to change its views in order to ensure compatibility with requirements in the founder member countries. As would have been clear to the steering committee's Canadian chairman, Doug Thomas, the countries to be kept particularly in mind were the United Kingdom and the United States.[121]

The main issue was whether to allow or require the capitalization of development costs. Initially, the steering committee proposed to allow no capitalization at all, with the possible exception of expenditures on tangible assets such as laboratory buildings and equipment. If these could be used for other purposes than research and development, the expenditures might be capitalized and depreciated. In this, the steering committee suggested that it followed the line of both the United States (FAS 2) and the UK & Ireland (ED 14).[122] However, the ASC's ED 14, published in January 1975, ran into considerable opposition. The influential British aerospace industry in particular argued that the capitalization of development expenditure was appropriate in certain circumstances. Yielding to this pressure, the ASC issued a new exposure draft, ED 17, in April 1976, which required capitalization of development expenditures in certain cases.[123] This happened a month after the IASC's steering committee had presented its own first draft, rejecting capitalization, to the full Committee. The need for a change of position was evident, and by November 1976 the steering committee had produced a draft that allowed, but did not require, the capitalization of development expenditures when certain stated conditions were met. For good measure, the steering committee also produced a table showing that the draft was essentially compatible with draft or final requirements in the United States, the United Kingdom, Australia, and France, as well as with the draft Fourth Directive.[124] The steering committee's draft was, with some modifications, approved as E9 (November 1976). E9 did go further than the UK standard and the Fourth Directive in that it required disclosure of the amount of research and development costs whereas the latter two did not.

Given that E9 was drafted with a close eye on the major national requirements, it comes as no surprise to find that most of the respondents to E9 thought the draft was at least acceptable. The most significant negative comment came from Denmark and Belgium. In two identical reactions, foreshadowing the asset-based approach of the IASC's Framework, it was pointed out that 'Only resources that [are] exchangeable (i.e. are separable from a business and have value in and of themselves) should be reported as assets.'[125] Many UK & Irish respondents objected to the required disclosure of research and development costs, but the general tone of their reactions was positive. Hence, E9 was made final with minor changes as IAS 9 in March 1978.

5.8.4. IAS 10: Contingencies and Events after the Balance Sheet Date

By July 1975, the IASC was in the midst of the inflation accounting debate, and it was getting bogged down on the issue of foreign currency translation (*see* Section 5.9). It is therefore understandable that the secretariat was cautious when it recommended three new topics. It commented: 'The subjects suggested are ones on which it should be relatively easy for IASC to reach agreement at this stage in its development. Subjects in which serious differences exist on matters of principle within or between countries have been avoided.'[126] The Committee showed more confidence in its own capabilities than the secretariat by combining two topics, 'accounting for contingencies' and 'events occurring after the balance sheet date', into one. It also chose, on its own initiative and without prompting by the secretariat, to start a project on the non-trivial subject of 'accounting for taxation'. The third topic, 'accounting for long-term contracts', was chosen on the recommendation of the secretariat (the last two subjects are discussed in the next subsections).[127]

Contingencies and events after the balance sheet date did in fact turn out to be an area where agreement was easily reached. The exposure draft, E10 (approved in March 1977), was well received, and no respondents opposed the publication of the standard.[128]

Even though the steering committee did not include any North Americans, IAS 10, approved for publication in June 1978, clearly echoed FAS 5, *Accounting for Contingencies*, issued by the FASB in March 1975.[129] Using by and large the same wording as FAS 5, IAS 10 stated that contingent losses should be accrued if it is probable that future events will confirm that an asset has been impaired or a liability incurred at balance sheet date, and that a reasonable estimate of the resulting loss can be made. Again in keeping with FAS 5, contingent gains should not be accrued, and provisions for general or unspecified business risks were ruled out.[130] On events after the balance sheet date, IAS 10 ruled that assets and liabilities should be adjusted in so far as these events provided additional evidence of conditions on the balance sheet date.

5.8.5. IAS 11: Construction Contracts

In accounting for construction contracts, the main issue was the choice between the completed contract method, where all profits are deferred until the end of the project, and the percentage of completion method, in which profits are recognized as the work progresses. In the early 1970s, the more conservative completed contract method appears to have been dominant in Continental Europe, if only for income tax reasons. While the percentage of completion method was not unknown in Europe, it was associated with US financial reporting practice.[131] In the United States, Accounting Research Bulletin No. 45 (1955) expressed a mildly worded preference for percentage of completion when there are dependable estimates. The UK's SSAP 9 (1975) came out more clearly in favour of percentage of completion.

The steering committee, which was the first to be composed wholly of 'non Anglo-Saxons'—Mexico, France, and India[132]—proposed to require application of the percentage of completion method, except in 'circumstances where dependable estimates of future costs cannot be made, or there are significant unresolved factors in the nature of the work to be performed or the revenue attributable to the contract'. In its first drafts, the steering committee used a mode of argument that would become common in the IASC only after the adoption of its conceptual framework in 1989. The steering committee stated confidently that the accrual assumption of IAS 1 'requires the use of the percentage of completion method'.[133] At this point, though, the full Committee was not yet prepared to accept this deductive approach. 'Because of the opinions expressed by several members of the Committee', the steering committee had to revise its proposals considerably. In E12, approved for publication in July 1977, the choice of methods was left to the reporting enterprise, with the single limitation that the percentage of completion method could be used only in case of sufficient certainty about the outcome of the project.[134]

E12 attracted the largest volume of comments since E3. But, although the large volume might suggest controversy, the majority of the responses were favourable, not least because E12 was again compatible with UK and US requirements.[135] Many UK respondents, both from business and the accountancy profession, compared E12 favourably with SSAP 9, and expressed the hope that the UK standard would be brought into line with the international standard. On the other hand, one UK respondent thought E12 was 'a masterpiece of compromise'. The authors of another UK letter wrote that they were 'of course, aware of the political reasons for this approach, but we repeat our dislike for any proposed standard offering a choice of two quite different methods'.[136] These respondents would have preferred the steering committee's original approach, but at this stage the IASC was not yet prepared to eliminate options that had strong support in the home countries of its member bodies. IAS 11, published in March 1979, was similar to E12 on the issue of completed contract versus percentage of completion.

5.8.6. IAS 12: Accounting for Income Tax

The problems of the IASC's strategy of cutting off the 'bad' edges while retaining the acceptable practices of most major countries came to light with the standard on accounting for income taxation. On this issue, the United Kingdom stood alone in espousing partial allocation. By this approach to accounting for the difference between taxable and reported income, only those differences that are expected to reverse in the near future are accounted for as deferred taxes. In the other IASC member countries that were familiar with deferred taxation, partial allocation was considered to be conceptually unsound. In these countries, comprehensive allocation was the norm, as in APB Opinion No. 11, *Accounting for Income Taxes* (1967). The IASC could not afford to reject a prominent feature of UK practice, but could only include it as an acceptable alternative at a considerable risk to its credibility.

Just how tightly the IASC's deliberations were tied to developments in the United Kingdom is shown by a chronological comparison. When the IASC's steering committee on accounting for taxation was set up in July 1975, the UK's ASSC was about to issue SSAP 11, *Accounting for Deferred Tax* (August 1975). In line with the preceding exposure draft, SSAP 11 required comprehensive tax allocation. The IASC steering committee's first drafts, submitted up to March 1977, therefore did not mention partial allocation, except in dismissing it as 'too detailed a point' for inclusion in the proposed standard.[137] But following the publication of SSAP 11, rather intense pressure by business and the UK government led the ASC to publish ED 19 in May 1977, which allowed partial tax allocation as well as comprehensive allocation.[138] In the words of steering committee member Hans Burggraaff, this presented the IASC with 'no small difficulty'.[139] Over the summer, the steering committee had to prepare a revised draft that allowed partial allocation as well. The steering committee, which did not include any UK representatives, observed in October 1977, when it presented the revised draft to the board: 'The Steering Committee did not support the idea underlying this concept but recognised that its acceptance in some countries required its recognition in the international standard.'[140]

The steering committee did attempt to limit the application of the partial method by requiring 'assurance beyond reasonable doubt that the timing differences not accounted for will result in no payment or reduction of taxes in the foreseeable future'. Under these conditions, partial allocation was introduced as an allowed alternative in E13 (approved for publication in October 1977).

Quite apart from the issue of partial allocation, E13 and the resulting IAS 12 were complicated documents, the longest issued by the IASC until then. The fact that it unambiguously required tax effect accounting was by itself seen as a major step forwards. In some member countries it was not uncommon to treat taxes as a form of profit distribution rather than as an expense item, and, even where it was treated as an expense the taxes payable, or 'flow through', method was often used.[141] Other substantial issues addressed were: the choice between the deferral method, common in the United States, and the liability method, common in the United Kingdom, to determine the tax expense for the period (in the end, both were allowed); whether deferred receivables might be accrued (only in case of 'reasonable expectation of realisation'); the treatment of loss carry-forwards; the disclosure of tax expenses relating to accounting changes, unusual items and prior period adjustments; the tax effects of the revaluation of assets, and the reconciliation of the reported and effective tax rates. IAS 12 was therefore no insignificant standard, and hardly basic. Particularly with respect to disclosure, it probably went beyond the majority practice in most member countries.

Primarily because it allowed partial allocation, E13 came in for considerable criticism in the comment letters and the press.[142] One US respondent observed that 'To propose widely differing options for similar situations tends to make a mockery of the entire standards setting process.' Another US respondent, equally unconcerned by the fact that the IASC had accommodated the United States over LIFO not all that long ago, was 'disillusioned by the fact that the Committee provides a choice of accounting methods'. Similarly critical comments came from Canada, the Netherlands, Singapore, and even the United Kingdom.

Yet most respondents from the United Kingdom and Ireland were positive, even though some demanded that the criterion of 'assurance beyond reasonable doubt' be relaxed. One respondent objected to the fact that E13 considered comprehensive allocation as the normal method: 'The U.K. would not wish to be seen as adopting as a standard an "abnormal" method.' The steering committee allowed itself to refuse this final concession to UK sensibilities, but it felt it had to give way on the criterion for applying partial allocation. IAS 12 required no more than 'reasonable evidence' that unrecognized timing differences would not reverse within a three-year period. After mentioning the criticisms that E13 allowed too many options, the steering committee observed resignedly: 'The Steering Committee believes that the IASC has to allow all of these options, in the light of current world practice regarding tax effect accounting, even the option of allowing the partial concept under both the deferral and liability methods.'[143]

One notable innovation in IAS 12 was that it contained a transitional provision. In order to make the standard more palatable, reporting enterprises that had not previously recorded accumulated tax balances were given the option either to follow the provisions on accounting changes in IAS 8 or to charge (credit) these items directly to retained earnings when the timing differences reversed. For these items, the income statement, but not the balance sheet, would be based on IAS 12. Once a precedent had been created by IAS 12, transitional provisions of this kind would appear in other standards as well.

5.8.7. IAS 13: Presentation of Current Assets and Current Liabilities

The topic of 'accounting for working capital' was not intended to be controversial. The issue was essentially whether enterprises should group current assets and current liabilities in the balance sheet and, if so, what criterion should be used to distinguish current from non-current assets and liabilities. An exposure draft, E14, was approved for publication in March 1978. Exceptionally, the draft was approved for publication at the same board meeting where it was first tabled.[144]

Although relatively few comment letters were received, the steering committee felt obliged to conclude that 'There was no broad general support for the Exposure

Draft.'[145] ED 14 had recommended, but not required, that enterprises apply the current–non-current distinction in their balance sheets, and that, in general, the distinction should be made by grouping items with a duration or time to conversion into cash or cash equivalents of one year or less. From the comment letters, it appeared that outside Europe, the need for a standard on this issue was not widely felt. Some even opposed it for perpetuating a 'meaningless' distinction that could be positively harmful if it led investors to incorrect conclusions about an enterprise's liquidity. Respondents from Continental Europe showed themselves more receptive to the notion of mandatory balance sheet classifications. However, this created problems as well, as these respondents pointed out conflicts with the balance sheet schedules that formed the core of the Fourth Directive.

The steering committee, chaired by the Canadian Morley Carscallen but with a majority of European members, put the question of whether a standard should be issued at all before the board, accompanied by a positive recommendation.[146] It made the best of the criticisms by arguing that 'If we issue the Statement we will be the first major accountancy body to officially raise the conceptual problems of making the distinction.'[147] The board agreed, and IAS 13 was approved in June 1979 after the general one-year criterion and possible conflicts with the Fourth Directive had been eliminated.

5.8.8. IAS 7–13: Concluding Remarks

A few months after IAS 13 was published, former IASC Secretary Roy C. Nash wrote:

At first glance, it would appear that tremendous progress has been made in harmonising international accounting and reporting standards.... In a relatively short time, the IASC has issued 13 international accounting standards and two discussion papers, and it has 11 more topics under study as possible future standards. However, in reality, universally agreed accounting and reporting standards are far from fruition.[148]

Nash mentioned the lack of support for international standards in IASC member countries as a significant problem. Another major problem noted by Nash was that the IASC 'has found it increasingly difficult to achieve agreement on basic principles'. This appears to be belied by the fact that all of the exposure drafts and standards discussed in this section were approved by a unanimous vote.[149] But the voting record may in several cases not reflect the remaining differences of opinion. Apparently, delegations would drop their opposition when it became clear that a standard had gathered sufficient support to be passed in a formal vote.[150] To the outside world, it could still be argued that the unanimous support of the delegations enhanced the credibility of the standards.

As the preceding discussion of IAS 7–13 has shown, there were several instances of strong differences of opinion that could be resolved only by compromise. Even on relatively uncontroversial topics like the funds statement or the definition of current assets and current liabilities, the IASC was unable to come up with unequivocal guidance. The need to accommodate both the UK and the US positions was an important reason for this, and the board was not oblivious of requirements in other board member countries either.[151] The preponderant influence of the British point of view became evident in particular in the case of IAS 9 and IAS 12. What is notable is that the other board members were willing to go to great lengths to adjust the IASC's standards to the requirements of the United Kingdom and the United States.

5.9. FOREIGN CURRENCY TRANSLATION: THE LONG ROAD TO IAS 21

In 1976, Alister Mason, a research officer at the University of Lancaster, conducted a survey to elicit the views of informed respondents on international financial reporting standards. One anonymous US respondent commented on the agenda of the IASC: 'Some topics should be avoided like the plague. Issuance of our Statement of Financial Accounting Standards No. 8—"Accounting for Translation" has resulted in irreconcilable differences between accounting in the US and elsewhere, differences that defy standardization unless somebody changes his local rules.'[152]

The advice, if it ever did reach the IASC, came too late. In January 1974, the IASC decided to set up a steering committee on 'translation (conversion) of foreign accounts in financial statements'. It was to become the most intractable topic on the IASC's pre-1987 agenda. It was not until March 1983 that IAS 21, *Accounting for the Effects of Changes in Foreign Exchange Rates*, was approved for publication. As predicted, the US position on the issue turned out to be a critical piece in the puzzle.

5.9.1. E11: An Unsuccessful Attempt

The steering committee, initially consisting of Chairman Henk Treffers (the Netherlands) and representatives from Japan and the United States, ran into difficulties almost from the start.[153] In its first draft, submitted in July 1974, it distinguished between accounting for transactions in foreign currency on the one hand and the translation of the financial statements of subsidiaries expressed in foreign currency, for the purposes of consolidation or application of the equity method, on the other. For transactions, it advocated conversion at closing rates, with the differences taken to income. Although this conflicted with the traditions of some countries (in particular Germany, where strict observance of the realization convention was given much weight), this position was adopted at an early stage of the project and was not seriously challenged afterwards. However, the steering committee was unable to recommend a single approach to translating long-term balance-sheet items associated with transactions: it could not decide on the exchange rate to be used, nor could it agree on the treatment of any of the resulting translation differences. The committee was also divided on the translation of the financial statements of foreign subsidiaries and associates. It recognized the existence of two methods. The 'historical rate approach', essentially similar to what would become known as the temporal method, required the conversion of amounts stated at historical costs against historical exchange rates. Alternatively, the closing rate method involved conversion of all balance-sheet items at current exchange rates. There was support for both methods in the steering committee, and it could not agree on recommending a single method nor on criteria to signify when one or the other should be used. The only conclusion on which the steering committee could agree was that to leave the matter undecided 'tends to destroy the usefulness of the proposed standard', and it therefore asked the full Committee for guidance.[154]

The full Committee found it as difficult to choose as had the steering committee. The treatment of long-term items and the translation of financial statements in foreign currency were debated in a series of inconclusive discussions between 1974 and 1977. The only result was that the discussions became evermore intricate and complicated. On the translation of financial statements, the choice between the temporal method and the closing rate method became entangled in debates about whether all or some translation differences resulting from either or both methods should go through income or be taken directly to equity. Matters were further confused by the introduction of variants of the historical rate method, such as the current–non-current and the monetary–non-monetary methods. Moreover, by March 1976, the steering committee had discovered forward contracts, which it saw as a 'very difficult' topic.[155] For some time, the steering committee grappled with the issue that would afterwards become known as hedge accounting and was tentatively finding its way in and around issues like hedge effectiveness. Several expedients were tried in order to move matters forward, but to no avail.[156]

Meanwhile, in October 1975, the FASB had nailed its colours to the mast by issuing FAS 8, *Accounting for the Translation of Foreign Currency Transactions and Foreign Currency Financial Statements*, which firmly embraced the temporal method as the only allowed approach to translating financial statements in foreign currency. FAS 8 required that translation differences be taken to income, which led to large swings in reported income. As the closing rate method was used to varying degrees in other countries, and as few companies anywhere would have liked to see the IASC follow the FASB on the treatment of translation differences, the IASC's dilemma became even harder to resolve.[157]

The obvious way out was to allow both the temporal and closing rate methods, and this approach was in fact chosen in E11 (approved in July 1977). What is less obvious, but more interesting, is that it took the IASC a number of years to reach this conclusion. In 1974 or 1975, the idea that the IASC should publish standards with unambiguous guidance was still held by at least some members of the Committee and some of the steering committees. But by 1977, most members of the Committee seem to have accepted the view that the IASC did not necessarily have to make a choice among alternatives that all received substantial support in practice.

The draft on which E11 was based was not prepared by the steering committee, but by the secretariat, IASC Chairman Joe Cummings, and the US representative on the steering committee, Bob Sempier.[158] E11 left almost all of the major issues unresolved. Not only did it allow a choice between the closing rate and temporal methods, but it also gave no firm prescriptions on how translation differences arising out of both methods should be handled. E11 was equally unclear about the treatment of translation differences on long-term balance sheet items. The steering committee's excursion into hedge accounting was cut short by a simple statement that forward rates 'may' be used to record transactions if the amount of foreign currency at settlement date has been established by a forward contract (paragraph 28).

Predictably, many of the respondents to E11 took issue with the almost complete lack of guidance provided by the draft standard, even though some recognized that the IASC could do little else under the circumstances. The IASC could perhaps draw some comfort from the fact that a number of respondents observed that E11 had at least set out the issues more clearly than, for example, FAS 8 or the UK's ED 21.[159]

The steering committee attempted to address the criticisms of E11. It placed a revised draft before the board, which ruled out some options in dealing with translation differences and tentatively linked the choice between the temporal and closing rate methods to the nature of the subsidiary, along the lines subsequently followed in IAS 21.[160] But this merely reopened the previous, inconclusive discussions, and in November 1978 the board sent the draft back to the steering committee, which it expanded with one member.[161]

5.9.2. A Breakthrough and a Crisis

In the spring of 1979, events took a different turn. The FASB announced that it would reconsider the much-criticized FAS 8, which led the IASC to suspend its work on currency translation.[162] Meanwhile, the standard setters in Canada, the UK & Ireland, and the United States agreed that UK and Canadian representatives would be added to the FASB task force charged with reconsidering FAS 8. On behalf of the IASC, Secretary Allan Cook participated in the task force as well, and, as he believed that the IASC would gain much from the publicity, he agreed that the FASB would mention the cooperation with the IASC in its publication.[163] The task force laid the basis for FAS 52, for which a first exposure draft was published in August 1980. FAS 52 prescribed the closing rate method for most subsidiaries, with most translation differences taken directly to equity.[164] An essentially similar exposure draft (ED 27) was published in the United Kingdom in October 1980, leading to SSAP 20 in April 1983.

The IASC's steering committee had been well aware of these developments and in the course of 1980 the committee prepared a draft that closely followed the newly emerging consensus. This draft was circulated with the agenda papers for the November 1980 board meeting in Dublin. At that point, the French and German member bodies lodged a strongly worded protest, claiming that the IASC was presented with a fait accompli. Prior to the November meeting, the Ordre des Experts Comptables, the Wirtschaftsprüferkammer, and the IdW wrote to IASC Chairman Burggraaff that it was 'extremely regrettable' that the agreement on currency translation had been reached outside the IASC's normal procedures. The Ordre remarked that 'Such a separate initiative gives credit to those who see I.A.S.C. as a mere channel for world implementation of "anglosaxon standards"', and it threatened that 'Any other move of the same kind would definitely ruin the credibility of this committee. It would regretfully lead the French Ordre to consider whether its membership is still appropriate.' The German bodies intimated that they did not want to continue their participation in the IASC if decisions were reached outside the board and the remaining IASC members 'are merely charged with the translation into their national languages'.[165]

The issue raised by the French and German reaction was not seen as a minor dispute but as a serious threat to the very existence of the IASC.[166] An indignant Dominique Ledouble, secretary of the Ordre, was quoted in the press as saying, 'I wonder why the IASC exists if such negotiations take place independently of it.' France's Commission des Opérations de Bourse called for a European accounting standard setter to counter US dominance.[167] Yet one might ask why the French and the German member bodies were so incensed in this case. As discussed earlier in this chapter, the French and German delegations had acquiesced throughout the 1970s in the dominance of the IASC's standard-setting process by developments in US and UK domestic standards. The fact that the IASC had to bend over backwards to accommodate the UK position on deferred taxation could hardly have been any less damaging to the IASC's credibility than the tripartite agreement between Canada, the United Kingdom, and the United States on currency translation. This agreement could even be seen as a cause for rejoicing, because it opened the way for the IASC to produce a stronger standard than E11.[168]

One aspect that played a role was that Canada, the United Kingdom, and the United States had collaborated in the Accountants International Study Group, which had only recently been disbanded. It was therefore easy to suspect that a structural rather than an incidental cooperation among these countries was intended.[169] The chairman of the UK ASC, Tom Watts, certainly helped to fuel such concerns. Apart from making disparaging remarks about the IASC in the press, Watts personally and rather publicly approached the European Commission to present the newly developed approach to currency translation and to offer his services to the Commission as interlocutor on international cooperation in setting accounting standards.[170]

A related cause for annoyance was that the cooperation among the three English-speaking countries led to press comments that the IASC consisted of first- and second-rate members. The September 1980 issue of *World Accounting Report* put the matter in such a way that it could hardly be ignored by the countries involved:

Anyone reading the reports that accounting standard-setters in the USA, the UK and Canada have agreed a common approach to the problem of currency translation might be forgiven for imagining that these were the only countries that mattered in the field of international accounting. This is far from the truth.

...

It is regrettable that the international accounting world still splits all too easily in the Anglo-Saxons and the rest. Language and history are the main reasons for this .... And there is that all too popular belief that the continental Europeans—barring the Dutch, of course—are far too backward to be considered in these matters.[171]

At the November 1980 board meeting, the French and German delegations insisted that their complaint be resolved before the draft could be discussed at all. Thereupon, the board passed a resolution that its 'members have agreed that IASC is the appropriate forum for the development and publication of International Accounting Standards'. Moreover, it was agreed that 'When any discussions on accounting standards are proposed between two or more countries that do not share common legislation, IASC is invited to participate therein on the understanding that any such participant does not have the authority to commit IASC in such discussions without the express authority of the Board of IASC.'[172]

The French and German member bodies had no objections to the overall approach of the proposed standard. Once their procedural complaint was addressed, the IASC could proceed. Although no major disagreements were left, the IASC waited until October 1981 to approve its exposure draft, E23. The main reason was that the FASB's draft had been approved by a narrow four votes to three, and the IASC did not want to expose itself to the risk of another switch in the FASB's position.[173] Shortly before FAS 52 was issued in December 1981, the IASC approved its exposure draft, followed by the final standard, IAS 21, approved in March 1983. Both E23 and IAS 21 were largely in agreement with FAS 52.

Quite apart from the French and German complaints, IAS 21 provided a straw in the wind, showing that the mood at the IASC was gradually changing, and that its members set less store by unanimity. E23 was the first exposure draft for which a dissenting vote was recorded, in this case cast by Mexico. The reasons for Mexico's objection were not recorded.[174] IAS 21 was also approved with one dissenting vote, not by Mexico but by Germany, which objected to a perceived violation of the prudence principle in the treatment of unrealized translation gains and losses.[175]

5.10. A COURAGEOUS DISCUSSION PAPER ON BANKS

As mentioned above in relation to the subject of auditing standards, Henry Benson was informally approached in February 1976 through the Bank of England by the Basel Committee on Banking Regulation and Supervisory Practices. The Basel Committee had been set up in 1974 by the central banks of the so-called Group of

Ten industrialized countries and Switzerland in response to several bank failures which showed the need for international cooperation in banking supervision. As it informed Benson, the Basel Committee saw the promotion of the standardization of accounting and auditing standards for banks as one of its possible tasks.[176] In September 1976, the Basel Committee made a formal request for assistance in the area of the 'contents of bank's financial statements', and this led to the creation of a steering committee in March 1977. The steering committee, composed of representatives from Germany, the Netherlands, the UK & Ireland, and the United States, was notable for being the first to contain no individuals who also served simultaneously on the full Committee.[177] The Group of Ten central banks agreed to make a substantial contribution of £10,000 to the IASC's budget.

With this project, the IASC embarked on its first attempt to issue a standard for a specific industry. The idea of issuing industry standards resurfaced periodically in the IASC's discussions during the 1970s and the 1980s, and it was never ruled out altogether. Yet apart from its work on banks and its projects on extractive industries, insurance, and agriculture during the 1990s, the IASC preferred to focus on standards for general application.

The original intention of the project on banks was that it should result in an IASC standard on disclosure in the financial statements of banks. Moreover, it was to be a standard that would be ahead of practice, rather than following it. The steering committee was aware that some of its proposals would be controversial, and it included with one of its earlier drafts a list of the 'areas in the proposed draft Statement which are likely to encounter the greatest resistance'. These included sensitive items like a paragraph in the Explanation section declaring that undisclosed reserves were 'unacceptable' if financial statements were to give a true and fair view, disclosure of a substantial concentration of assets and liabilities with single debtors or creditors, disclosure of the amount of, and movements in, provisions, and disclosure of the amount of uncovered dealing positions.[178] The board supported this approach but thought it necessary to ensure the backing of the Basel Committee. The Basel Committee was therefore asked whether it would be willing to lend its name as a 'co-promotor' to the proposed exposure draft. However, after considering the draft, the Basel Committee informed the IASC in July 1978 'that the proposed statement was not one which they could formally endorse as a basis for an accounting standard but that they were pleased to see the IASC addressing themselves to this subject and consider the paper, as a discussion document, to be a useful contribution to the general debate on these matters'.[179] This reply was disappointing, even though the IASC had already received earlier signals of reservations from within the Basel Committee, emanating apparently from some of the EEC Central Banks.[180] And although the steering committee had suggested that the IASC might go it alone and issue an exposure draft for a standard without the backing of the Basel Committee, the board opted instead for a discussion paper which was approved for publication in October 1979.

Presumably because it was merely a discussion paper, it retained most of the controversial disclosures initially proposed by the steering committee. Regarding undisclosed reserves, it was stated that financial statements 'cannot present a true and fair view...if there are undisclosed overstatements of liabilities, undisclosed understatements of assets or undisclosed accrual of amounts for general or unspecified business risks'.[181] The IASC kept its options open by noting in the preface to the discussion paper that it might in due course issue a standard on the subject.

The discussion paper did attract attention, but perhaps not as much as desired. One observer commented that 'Very few banks...appeared to have heard of the IASC discussion paper.'[182] Yet *World Accounting Report*, never averse to stirring up controversy, described it as a 'surprise attack on leading banks' accounting', and it was noted that the recommendations did not merely go beyond customary practices in countries like Switzerland, but also went beyond practices in the United Kingdom and the United States.[183] *WAR* also obtained a copy of the transcribed comment letters and took the unusual step of publishing an extensive report on them.[184] It commented in shocked tones that, given the number of banks that were potentially affected by the discussion paper, the response rate had been 'ridiculously low'. Only thirty-three comment letters had been received, of which three were from banks. In fact, the response rate was not at all unusual for the IASC at that time, and Secretary Allan Cook declared that the IASC was quite satisfied.[185] But even if the IASC itself might have grown accustomed to this level of response, it should have been clear that the excitement with which some of the IASC's earlier exposure drafts, such as E3, had been received had worn off. *WAR*'s reaction underlined that the IASC still had some way to go in attracting the attention commensurate to its aspirations as an international standard setter.[186]

Perhaps surprisingly, the general tone of the responses was positive, even though there were some defenders of hidden reserves. Many respondents praised the quality of the IASC's discussion paper and expressed their sympathy with the notion of international harmonization. But a common theme was that the IASC should not proceed to develop a standard without the cooperation of national legislators and the Group of Ten. The IASC should also await the completion of the EEC's banking Directive. Given the evident reluctance of the Group of Ten to endorse the IASC's proposals, and the fact that an EEC directive was hardly imminent, this could not be construed as an encouragement to proceed. The IASC board, following the recommendation of the steering committee, concluded that the time was not yet ripe for a standard. It did decide to publish a 'Summary of Responses' in order to do justice to the comment letter writers and to announce its general intention to 'review the situation from time to time'.[187] As is discussed in Section 9.4.3, the IASC resumed work on financial reporting by banks in 1984, leading ultimately to the publication of a standard (IAS 30) in 1990.

5.11. SHOWING LEADERSHIP: IAS 14, 17, AND 19

In the early 1980s, the IASC reached the high-water mark of its performance during the pre-1987 phase. Quantitatively, there was a surge of output culminating in a record of four new standards published in 1983. In terms of quality, a number of the standards published around this time were ahead of practice in many countries. These standards dealt with topics on which, in most countries, there was little or no guidance and on which a clear international consensus was lacking. Nevertheless, the IASC managed to produce standards that, unlike the standard on inflation accounting, contained some firm guidance to practice.[188] While the drafting process of these standards was lengthier than that of most previous standards, there was nothing like the inordinate delay seen in the production of the standard on currency translation (IAS 21).

5.11.1. IAS 14: Segment Reporting

The idea of providing information by line of business and geographical areas was not altogether new when, in 1976, the IASC placed segment reporting on its agenda. In several countries, such as France, Sweden, and the United Kingdom, there were generally worded legal requirements for companies that were active in more than one line of business to provide additional information.[189] As indicated above, the IASC's own E3 (published in 1974) had contained a loosely worded segmentation requirement. But stricter standards, specifying the nature of the information to be disclosed and the determination of segments were only a very recent phenomenon. In the United States, the SEC had required segment reporting in annual reports to stockholders since 1974, and the first accounting standard on the issue, FAS 14, was published in December 1976.[190] Perhaps to draw on the US experience, Eugene Minahan, a financial executive in the US delegation, was made steering committee chairman.[191]

Against this background, and perhaps with the recent barrage of comment letters on E3 fresh in their minds, the steering committee began on a cautious note. The first question it raised in its issues paper to the full Committee was: 'Are current requirements and current practices in IASC countries on the reporting of Diversified Operations...such that an IASC standard can be devised and issued without undue shock?'[192] Apparently, the full Committee answered in the affirmative, and the steering committee produced its first draft. But it described its proposal as 'a modest "entry-level" standard', which would do no more than require diversified companies to provide unspecified information about segments of their business, without clear guidance in identifying segments.[193] The full Committee was no more keen than the steering committee to move forward, and both seemed happy to put the project on hold for a year while a survey was carried out on the reporting practices in thirty-five countries where segment reporting was said to be at least a minority practice. When the project was taken up again in June 1978, Minahan reported his impression of an 'emerging IASC consensus that the world is not ready for a full-blown standard', and again offered the alternative of 'a "soft" introductory standard'.[194] But time had done its work, and the full Committee, now known as the board, had emboldened itself. If nothing else, the entry of the Oganisation for Economic

Co-operation and Development (OECD) and the United Nations (UN) into the area of accounting standards during the later 1970s helped push matters along. The publications by both bodies on information disclosure by multinational companies, discussed more fully in Chapter 7, made segment reporting a very topical and unavoidable issue. IASC Chairman Cummings had, as a member of the UN's Group of Experts, assisted in the preparation of one of these publications and would have been as aware as anyone of the need to move forward on this issue.

Hence, without specifying in so many words whether it wanted a 'full-blown' or an 'introductory' standard, the board agreed in October 1979 to an exposure draft (E15) which was loosely modelled on FAS 14. The exposure draft called for segment reporting along both industry and geographical lines. Although E15 did not go beyond timid suggestions on the identification of reportable segments, it did require, for each segment, disclosure of sales, segment results, and segment assets employed, as well as the basis for inter-segment pricing. In contrast, the revised draft of the Fourth Directive published in July 1978 had included a limited segmentation of sales only, as the segmentation of operating profit, included in earlier drafts, had been eliminated. When the comment letters came in, those from Europe tended to warn that compliance with this standard 'might not be as general as usual in the EEC countries'.[195] Some of the respondents called for an 'escape clause' for cases where the disclosure of segment information might be detrimental to the reporting enterprise. The steering committee observed that the insertion of such a clause 'would not enhance the image of IASC in the eyes of such bodies as UN and OECD', and advised against it. As a result, IAS 14 was approved in March 1981 without major changes from E15.

Despite the fact that IAS 14 was subsequently much criticized for containing a fair amount of soft language, it was welcomed at the time as 'a bold move', which showed that the IASC began to attach more weight to showing leadership than to obtaining consensus.[196] Henry Gold, Shell's head of accounting research and a member of the IASC's Consultative Group, noted that 'This would perhaps be the first time that an international standard has run ahead of UK practice in such a significant way.'[197] In a reversal of roles, the ASC set up a working party to consider a standard that would bring United Kingdom reporting in line with IAS 14.[198] Yet a comparable UK standard, SSAP 25, was not approved until 1990. Presumably because of the absence of a UK standard, the London Stock Exchange, in 1983, excluded IAS 14 from its general requirement that foreign listed companies comply with IASC standards (*see* Section 6.5.2).

5.11.2. IAS 17: Accounting for Leases

A simple but telling indication that, with lease accounting, the IASC was definitely moving into 'non-basic' areas is provided by the number of definitions in the opening paragraphs of the final standard. Whereas previous standards typically had no more than two or three definitions, IAS 17 contained seventeen definitions, including highly technical items such as 'contingent rental' and 'unearned finance income'.[199] A recurring complaint in the comment letters on the preceding exposure draft, E19, was that the draft was complex and required repeated reading. Another indicator that leasing was an unusual subject was that the chairman of the steering committee, Paul Rutteman, was simultaneously chairing a UK steering committee that prepared SSAP 21, *Accounting for Leases and Hire Purchase Contracts* (issued in August 1984).[200] As IASC Secretary John Brennan observed in 1977, the fact that the IASC started to address issues at the same time that the national standard-setting bodies were taking them up provided new possibilities for the IASC to act 'as a catalyst in the harmonisation of domestic standards'.[201] Yet, although IAS 17 and SSAP 21 had much in common, and progress on SSAP 21 was said to have benefited from the prior publication of IAS 17, they were not identical, and their publication was not synchronized.[202]

Although IAS 17, *Accounting for Leases* dealt with a range of issues, including the treatment of sale and leaseback transactions and accounting by lessors, the fundamental issue was whether certain assets should be capitalized or not in the financial statements of lessees. The steering committee consistently advocated that a distinction be made between finance leases and operating leases and that capitalization of the former should be required. This approach was finally adopted in IAS 17 (approved in February 1982).[203] In this way, the steering committee followed the approach of FAS 13, *Accounting for Leases* (issued in November 1976). Yet both the steering committee and the board were aware that FAS 13 was a contested standard, and that capitalization was still unusual or unknown in many other countries. It was still fiercely debated in the United Kingdom, where the leasing industry vociferously opposed the ASC on this issue.[204] Therefore, the question of how to make capitalization palatable continued to be discussed in the IASC until the very end of the project. Part of the solution was the well-tried expedient of moving controversial material to the explanatory section of the standard.

In line with FAS 13, the steering committee had favoured quantitative criteria to distinguish between finance and operating leases (particularly a rule that a lease should be classified as a finance lease if the present value of the minimum lease payments is equal to or greater than 90% of the fair value of the leased object). Yet the board preferred a 'substance over form approach' and, in the end, the criteria, shorn of their quantitative thresholds, were relegated to a footnote in the explanatory section as 'examples of situations where a lease would normally be classified as a finance lease'. Following the precedent set by IAS 12, the standard was also made more acceptable by a four-year transitional period, during which enterprises might opt not to apply the standard in its entirety, provided that certain disclosures were given. That such measures were not superfluous was shown by the large volume of comment letters. Many of these, particularly the unusually large number of letters from Germany and the reaction by the industry association Leaseurope, were distinctly hostile.[205] Yet the IASC stuck to its position, and its resolve was strengthened by support from its newly established Consultative

Group.²⁰⁶ Clearly, it was believed in the board at this point that producing a good standard was more important than gaining maximum compliance. An IASC spokesman was quoted in the press saying that the IASC was aware that 'Some EEC states won't be able to implement the standard since it will be in flat contradiction to their legislation, but it will be up to the accountancy bodies in those countries to use their "best endeavours"...to bring their governments into agreement in the long term.'²⁰⁷ The result was a standard that proved to be remarkably robust. IAS 17 was not revised until 1997, and even after the revision it still bore a strong resemblance to the original standard.

5.11.3. IAS 19: Retirement Benefits

When, in 1977, the IASC added the subject of accounting for retirement benefits in the financial statements of employers to its agenda, it entered unsettled and to some extent uncharted waters. As was the case with other issues, the United States was at that time the only significant country where a standard with more than just disclosure requirements was in force.²⁰⁸ But even APB Opinion No. 8, *Accounting for the Costs of Pension Plans* (issued in 1966) did not provide a stable point of reference. In 1974, the FASB had begun a massive project on accounting for pensions which, after more than a decade, was provisionally concluded with FAS 87, *Employers' Accounting for Pensions* (issued in 1985). The intervening period witnessed a succession of discussion papers, exposure drafts, re-exposure drafts, and interim standards, including FAS 36, *Disclosure of Pension Information* (issued in 1980). The Fourth Directive wisely said very little on the subject, given the considerable diversity of institutional arrangements concerning pensions within Europe.²⁰⁹ The first UK standard on the subject, SSAP 24, was issued in 1988 after a gestation period of about ten years.

Hence, pensions was a subject, like leasing, on which the IASC could cooperate with national standard setters who were developing new standards in the area. The steering committee chairman was Doug Thomas, the CICA's general director of research, who ensured that the IASC project was coordinated informally with the CICA's own project on pensions.²¹⁰ Highlighting the specific nature of the project was the fact that the steering committee consulted closely with the Consultative Group of Actuarial Associations from the European Community Countries during the course of the project.

Conceptually, IAS 19 shaped the issues in terms that had become customary in the United States. It distinguished between defined benefit plans and defined contribution plans. For the former, it required that current service costs be charged systematically to the expected remaining working lives of the employees. The costs were to be determined on the basis of either an accrued benefit valuation method or a projected benefit valuation method. For defined contribution plans, the required contribution should be charged against income for the period.

As seen from the United States, IAS 19 was broadly in line with current accounting standards, and for that reason it suffered from some of the deficiencies that had prompted the FASB to start a revision of these standards: IAS 19 accepted a variety of actuarial methods, it offered little guidance on actuarial assumptions, and it did not call for the recognition in the balance sheet of unfunded vested benefits.

In contrast, by explicitly ruling out the pay-as-you-go and terminal funding approaches to determining periodic costs, IAS 19 conflicted with practice in many countries, particularly in Europe. In that light, the reactions to the exposure draft (E16, approved in October 1979) coming from Europe were remarkably restrained. Not only was the volume of comment letters fairly low, there were also few outright negative reactions.[211] One reason for this may have been the generous proposed transitional provision, which allowed first-time adopters to accrue any previously unrecorded liability gradually. The steering committee had observed that it 'would have preferred not to have any transitional provisions, but believes that the precedent of IAS 12...gives us no alternative in order to encourage adoption of the Statement'.[212] But another factor was that, by 1980, if not before, a more relaxed attitude towards 'best endeavours' and compliance with international standards seems to have become prevalent in a number of countries. Such an attitude was at any rate shown by the Danish reaction, which was quite positive about the standard but noted dryly that 'We foresee that it will be some time before the proposed standard will be generally accepted, not only by the profession but also by the business community.'[213]

Even though IAS 19 was a fairly flexible standard, it was significant in that it was published well before the major national standard setters had completed their own projects on this issue.[214] As if in recognition of this leadership, the IASC was asked a few years later to play a coordinating role during the closing stages of the Canadian, UK, and US projects on pensions. At an April 1985 OECD forum on accounting harmonization (*see also* Section 7.2), the three national standard setters were called upon to harmonize their efforts on pensions. Heeding this call, Peter Godfrey, the chairman of the UK Accounting Standards Committee, asked the IASC to set up a working party.[215] The IASC secretariat, apparently still remembering the ruffled feathers over the Canadian, UK, and US initiative on currency translation, approached the French and German member bodies for a chairman. When they declined, the Dutchman Herman Marseille (who had been a member of the IAS 19 steering committee) was made chairman.[216] As it happened, the working party met only once. It appeared that, particularly, Canada and the United States were not keen to change their approach.[217] The working party diplomatically concluded that there had been 'some reduction in the degree of conflict', so that bilateral contacts and monitoring by the IASC would henceforth be sufficient. Despite this limited result, the IASC board concluded that 'It was a good and positive thing to have done.' If nothing else, the working party was a signal that the IASC might move away from a role in which it essentially followed the existing accounting standards of the leading national standard setters.[218]

5.12. ANTECEDENTS OF A CONCEPTUAL FRAMEWORK: IAS 16, 17, AND 18

In three standards published in 1982—IAS 16, *Accounting for Property, Plant and Equipment*; IAS 17, *Accounting for Leases* (already discussed above), and IAS 18, *Revenue Recognition*—the IASC attempted to define more general concepts that could be used across several standards. In that way, they foreshadowed the IASC's 1989 *Framework for the Preparation and Presentation of Financial Statements*, although it must be emphasized that, in the early 1980s, there was as yet no conscious effort to develop such a Framework.

5.12.1. Fair Value

The element that all three standards had in common was the notion of 'fair value', which during the 1990s was to play an increasingly prominent role in the standards of the IASC and several national standard setters. According to IAS 16, assets acquired in exchange for other assets might be recorded at the fair value of the assets given up, and a similar requirement applied to assets acquired in exchange for shares. In IAS 17, fair value played a role in determining the classification of a lease as a finance or an operating lease, as well as in the determination of profit or loss in sale and leaseback transactions. Finally, IAS 18 observed that the amount of revenue in an exchange of non-monetary assets is normally determined using the fair value of the assets exchanged. Fair value was first mentioned in 1977, in drafts of IAS 17. As the drafting of the other standards (and of IAS 22, *Accounting for Business Combinations*, which also included a reference to fair value) proceeded, it was noted by the secretariat that they all referred to fair value. In March 1980, it therefore put a proposal to the board to agree on a definition that could be used in all future standards.

The fact that fair value appeared more or less simultaneously in four different projects is less miraculous than it might seem at first sight. Typically, all steering committees would pay close attention to the relevant US accounting standards, and in these cases they all found references to fair value. In this case, the relevant standards were FAS 13, *Accounting for Leases* (1976), APB Opinion No. 29, *Accounting for Nonmonetary Transactions* (1973, with regard to property, plant, and equipment, as well as revenue recognition), and APB Opinion 16, *Business Combinations* (1970). Of these US standards, only FAS 13 contained a definition of fair value: 'the price for which the property could be sold in an arm's length transaction between unrelated parties'. Among the IASC steering committees there were differences of opinion about the definition to adopt. Some wanted a reference to 'open and unrestricted markets' as a reference point, while others wanted to elaborate on the required qualities of the buyer and the seller by such adjectives as 'willing', 'knowledgeable', 'not anxious to buy (sell)'.[219] In the end, the board agreed on the definition that, in substance, was used by the IASC since then: 'Fair value is the amount for which an asset could be exchanged between a knowledgeable, willing buyer and a knowledgeable, willing seller in an arm's length transaction'.[220]

E18, on property, plant, and equipment was the first exposure draft to be published with the new definition, and the reactions were awaited with interest. But it turned out that the only substantial comment came from the European Group of Valuers of Fixed Assets, a regional association representing the professional property valuation industry. Its response to E18 touched on a sore point that had already been raised within the IASC: the definition was not specific on the kind of market conditions it assumed to prevail and could therefore lead to undesirable outcomes in the case of weak demand or demand by buyers with a special interest. After further deliberation, however, the board decided to leave the definition unchanged. It followed the lead of the IASC secretariat, which observed that, so far, the objective of using fair value in IASC standards was to provide a reasonable basis for a journal entry in case of non-cash transaction or in case a transaction needed to be divided up. Unlike valuers, accountants did not seek to establish potential disposal proceeds or the cost of potential replacements.[221]

E18 led to an increasingly close relationship between the IASC and the property valuation industry. Copying the IASC's model, the International Assets Valuation Standards Committee was formed in 1981, and it became a member of the IASC's Consultative Group in 1990.[222]

5.12.2. Other Issues in IAS 16

Fair value was a relatively subordinate element of IAS 16, which was prepared by a steering committee chaired by Leopoldo Romero (Mexico).[223] Because depreciation had already been treated in IAS 4, the main focus of IAS 16 was on determining the depreciable amount and accounting for the disposal of fixed assets. The scope of IAS 16 was further restricted as the project continued. The treatment of government grants and the capitalization of interest costs were taken out, as they were to be dealt with in separate standards (IAS 20 and IAS 23, respectively).[224] The exposure draft (E18, approved for publication in March 1980) intended the standard to be applied both in historical cost and in current cost financial statements, but the final standard was limited to historical cost systems only.

In other respects, IAS 16 (approved in October 1981) again displayed a desire to accommodate a wide range of national practices. It allowed the revaluation of property, plant, and equipment (still within the overall context of a historical cost system). In this respect, IAS 16 reflected practice in countries like the United Kingdom and the Netherlands, where revaluations, particularly of land and buildings, were rather common. IAS 16 did impose some limitations, in particular that revaluations should be systematic, that the net carrying amount should not exceed the recoverable amount, and that upward revaluations should be credited directly to equity under the heading of revaluation surplus. IAS 16 also reflected the practices of countries, such as Germany, where revaluations were rare. In particular, it allowed enterprises to state assets acquired in exchange for other assets at the book value of the assets given up, rather than at the fair value of the assets exchanged. This option, which allowed the perpetuation of conservative valuations, was criticized in comment letters from Canada, Sweden, the United Kingdom, and the United States, but was retained in the final standard.

5.12.3. IAS 18: Revenue Recognition

The IASC's standard on revenue recognition was smoothly produced between 1979 and 1982, without noticeable controversy. This may have been due to the capable hand of Stephen Elliott, the future IASC chairman, who chaired the steering committee.[225] It was perhaps also due to the fact that the board had instructed the steering committee to follow 'a basic approach'.[226] In other words, the standard did not deal in a detailed and potentially controversial way with specific types of transactions or with conventions in specific industries. IAS 18 did include a lengthy appendix discussing the appropriate accounting treatment for a wide range of specific situations, such as consignment sales, subscriptions, and financial services, but it was firmly indicated that the appendix was illustrative only and not part of the accounting standard.

The standard itself dealt with revenue recognition at a fairly high level of abstraction. Its chief feature was that it identified the transfer of 'the significant risks and rewards of ownership' as the main criterion for the recognition of revenue, supplemented with criteria concerning uncertainty regarding collection, associated costs, and possible returns (paragraph 23). The steering committee was aware that it was moving away from a 'traditional' approach based on the passing of legal title, to a 'broader' approach having regard to 'commercial substance and financial reality'.[227] In the exposure draft (E20, approved in November 1980) and in IAS 18 (approved in June 1982), no explicit attention was drawn to this shift in emphasis, although it was observed rather neutrally that the passing of risks and rewards might occur at a different time than the passing of legal title (paragraph 7). This break with tradition was commented upon in a few comment letters, but not in the letters from Germany and Austria, where substance over form was traditionally not strongly established.[228] The volume of comment letters, most of which were favourable, was almost at a record low, so the steering committee advised to make only minor changes in the final standard.[229]

The significance of IAS 18 should not be judged by the somewhat desultory response to the exposure draft. After it was completed, it helped to bring about the idea within the IASC that it should develop a set of building-block standards on basic elements of financial statements, such as assets, expenses, liabilities, and equity. Having such building blocks would ultimately provide the IASC with a more conceptually sound basis for standard setting, compared to its approach so far of eliminating the evidently bad practices while allowing several that each had widespread support. A series of projects to draft such standards started in 1982, which ended with the publication of the IASC's Framework in 1989. This development is discussed more fully in Section 9.1.

5.13. THE END OF THE BEGINNING: IAS 20, 22, AND 23–6

From 1983 onwards, the IASC's productivity as measured by the number of completed standards began to fall. Whereas four standards were published in 1983, only two were published in 1984, none in 1985, one each in 1986 and 1987, and none in 1988. In at least one sense, the IASC was reaching the natural end of a cycle, as it began to run out of basic topics. Although the secretariat had never found it very easy to elicit suggestions for topics from the member bodies, it always managed to compile long- and shortlists of topics for consideration by the board. But by the end of 1983, the most obvious or pressing topics had been covered or were being dealt with, as the secretariat noted in a reflective agenda paper for the October 1983 board meeting.[230]

The secretariat supported its view by drawing on an academic research study by Frederick Choi and Vinod Bavishi, who had empirically demonstrated which areas of financial reporting were most in need of harmonization, and who had urged the IASC to take a leadership role.[231] The researchers had identified consolidation practices, goodwill, deferred taxes, long-term leases, discretionary reserves, inflation, and foreign currency translation as areas in which major differences existed. But, as the secretariat observed, almost all of these topics had already been addressed. The secretariat therefore advised the board to shift its attention to reviews of existing standards, to the building-block standards mentioned above, and to standards for specialized areas, notably those dealing with issues relevant to developing countries, and occasional industry standards. Essentially, this was the course adopted by the board during the next few years, although it remained reluctant to issue industry standards and did not, during this period, deal specifically with developing country problems.

In addition, it was recognized within the IASC that another possible approach was to shift to a lower gear. This possibility was suggested by an ad hoc committee created in 1983 to consider the development of the IASC in the medium term.[232] The suggestion also came from some member bodies which were concerned about the costs of participation in international organizations, as well as about the accumulation of international norms and standards, not just from the IASC, but also from the UN, the OECD, and the EEC.[233] Reflecting these views, IASC Chairman John Kirkpatrick summarized the resulting IASC position in 1985 as follows: 'There will be a change of emphasis. We have covered a vast area in our standards. We will slow down now. The world does not need more standards than are absolutely necessary, although we will produce them in areas where there is demand.'[234] That, of course, was one way of putting it. It was put another way by the veteran Dutch staff observer Henk Volten, who complained around the same time to Secretary David Cairns about the 'light agenda' for the board meetings in October 1984 and March 1985, and suggested that the NIVRA had begun to see the IASC as less interesting and relevant.[235] In fact, the NIVRA had recently decided that it would no longer publish translations of exposure drafts and standards, something which it had done faithfully since 1974. One of the reasons it cited was that the costs were no longer justified by 'decreased interest, reflected by a sharp decline in the number of reactions from individual members, firms and [companies'] accounting staff'.²³⁶

This is the background against which the declining number of standards were produced during the mid-1980s. It is also the background that shows why these standards, which are discussed in the next paragraphs, tended to deal with relatively specialized issues, excepting of course of the perennially controversial subject of business combinations.

But these standards also show how the IASC was reaching the end of an era in another sense. Several board delegations showed themselves more willing to vote against proposed exposure drafts or standards, and sometimes because the standards contained too many rather than too few options.

5.13.1. IAS 20: Government Grants

IAS 20, *Accounting for Government Grants and Disclosure of Government Assistance*, was an uncontroversial standard that was produced relatively swiftly in slightly over three years. What helped was that several potentially difficult issues related to tax-based assistance were excluded from the scope of the standard.

The topic came to the IASC's agenda when the steering committee on accounting for property, plant, and equipment (IAS 16) proposed to deal with it in the context of its standard. In June 1979, the board decided instead to set up a separate project.²³⁷ At that time, there was a tentative understanding that the FASB might consider approving a standard identical to the eventual IASC standard. In the end, the FASB decided against this, contrary to the recommendation of its own staff (*see also* Section 6.6.5).²³⁸ IAS 20 (unanimously approved in November 1982 after generally supportive reactions to E21, approved in March 1981) required government grants to be recognized in income on the basis of a matching with the costs which they were intended to compensate. Crediting such grants directly to equity was ruled out, as well as recognition as income in the period in which the grant became receivable, unless it related to past losses or expenses. On this point, the project was a good example of the generally weak link between the composition of steering committees and the contents of the standards. Apart from Warwick Thorby, the South African chairman, the steering committee consisted of Wilhelm Tjaden (Germany) and M. Drake (Norway). When it recommended to prohibit the direct recognition of tax-free grants in income, the steering committee noted that this method was usual in both Germany and Norway.²³⁹

5.13.2. IAS 22: Business Combinations²⁴⁰

The topic of business combinations was placed on the agenda in June 1978 with some apprehension that it would be a difficult project, but in the belief that it could no longer be postponed.²⁴¹ The project was complicated by a simultaneous and tortuous attempt to develop a UK accounting standard. The IASC also had to take account of the hard-won compromise position that had been reached in the United States in 1970 with APB Opinions No. 16, *Business Combinations*, and No. 17, *Intangible Assets*.[242] And then there were various European traditions to accommodate, as well as the forthcoming Seventh EEC Directive. The IASC steering committee, chaired by the Australian John Bishop, had its work cut out.[243]

There were two main issues. The first was, under what conditions, if any, should pooling of interests accounting be allowed. The other was the accounting treatment of goodwill arising upon application of purchase or acquisition accounting. In the United States, APB Opinion No. 16 had reduced but by no means eliminated the situations in which pooling of interests might be applied, after earlier attempts to eliminate pooling altogether had been opposed by the business community. In Europe, pooling was rare in practice, as far as the steering committee could ascertain, and it was believed that the Seventh Directive would allow purchase accounting only.[244] In the United Kingdom, the ASSC's ED 3 (1971) would have required pooling in some instances, but before ED 3 could be turned into a final standard, doubts emerged whether pooling was allowed by law. ED 3 was allowed to lapse, and the uncertainty was not resolved until pooling (or merger accounting as it was known in the United Kingdom) was legalized by the Companies Act 1981 (section 37).

On accounting for goodwill, positions were even more diverse. APB Opinion No. 17 required capitalization and amortization over a period not exceeding forty years. The Fourth Directive, on the other hand, included a rebuttable presumption that the useful economic life would not exceed five years. The Seventh Directive, still in the drafting stage, allowed goodwill to be charged directly to retained earnings. The latter practice was common in the United Kingdom and the Netherlands.

In tackling this difficult subject, the steering committee recognized that compromise was inevitable.[245] Although it was not keen on pooling of interests, it never proposed to rule it out altogether, not least because pooling was introduced into the Seventh Directive as a result of strong UK pressure.[246] Throughout the drafting process, it was recognized that there was a subgroup of business combinations, referred to as a 'uniting of interests', for which pooling might be appropriate. Initially, the steering committee sought to limit the number of such cases by a strict definition of uniting of interests. Then, the committee gradually discovered the merits of a third method of accounting known as the new entity approach (in which the assets and liabilities of both entities are revalued to fair value).[247] By restricting pooling to a group of rare 'unitings of equal interests' and allowing a choice between purchase accounting and new entity accounting for other 'unitings of interest', the steering committee thought to save pooling in principle while virtually eliminating it in practice.[248] But the board did not accept this. E22 (approved for publication in March 1981) veered the other way. Rather than imposing strict conditions to determine whether a business combination was a uniting of interests, the board ruled that it was sufficient if a business combination was effected by an exchange of shares. In that case, E22 allowed a choice between purchase, pooling, and new entity accounting.

It is interesting to note that new entity accounting figured so prominently in the IASC's considerations, given that it was not a part of regulation or practice in any country represented on the IASC board.[249] For that reason, it was not enthusiastically received by the respondents to E22, who thought that including a third approach was unlikely to contribute to harmonization. The steering committee thereupon proposed to de-emphasize it by presenting it as an extension of the pooling method, but the board removed it from IAS 22 altogether.[250]

On the core issue of pooling itself, the reactions were mixed. The US respondents used E22 to continue their domestic discussion as to whether pooling was fundamentally unsound. Reactions from Continental Europe warned against possible conflicts with the forthcoming Seventh Directive. Reactions from the United Kingdom showed anxiety that the recently achieved legal recognition of merger accounting in the Companies Act 1981 might be curtailed by the different definition of uniting of interests in E22.

In the end, IAS 22 contained ostensibly tightened criteria for the application of pooling of interests accounting in order to reduce the possibility that a combination of companies of very unequal size would be classified as a uniting of interests. But although it was asserted that a uniting of interests was likely in 'rare circumstances' only (paragraph 36), the criteria used to define a uniting of interests allowed a wide range for interpretation.[251]

In regard to goodwill, the steering committee was distinctly averse to the option of charging it directly to equity. Initially, it wanted to allow immediate expensing or amortization only. However, the UK & Irish and Dutch delegations, supported by South Africa and Italy, made it clear that they would not support a standard that did not allow charging goodwill to equity. The option was duly introduced into the exposure draft, but with the restriction that it was allowed only when there was uncertainty over whether, and to what extent, goodwill represented future profits.[252]

The steering committee preferred a five-year limit to amortization in order to bring the standard in line with the Fourth Directive.[253] The board, however, decided that no time limit should be specified apart from the general requirement to amortize over the useful life of the goodwill.[254]

The treatment of goodwill was the issue that exercised the respondents to E22 the most, but their reactions were by no means unanimous. Almost every conceivable position on capitalization, amortization periods, and charging to equity was forcefully advocated. Although the conditions imposed by E22 on charging goodwill directly to equity were hardly restrictive, the steering committee felt it had to go one step further by including it as a free option in the final standard. A clearly reluctant steering committee advised the board to make this change 'because many wanted this treatment, although the Steering Committee could not see any good arguments in support of the practice'. It underlined its distaste by stating that the revised draft 'presents such arguments as can be put in its favour. [If the option is permitted] the Board may wish to supply arguments to support such a practice.'

In June 1983, IAS 22 was approved with nine votes in favour, the smallest possible majority and the most divided vote so far. That the standard passed at all was due only to the inconsistency of the Mexican delegation. When the option to charge goodwill to equity had been inserted, Germany and Mexico had indicated they would vote against the final standard for this reason. In the final vote, Germany abstained, Canada voted against, and the Italian delegation, according to its pattern of erratic attendance at board meetings, was absent. The Mexicans, however, voted in favour.[255]

5.13.3. IAS 23: Capitalization of Borrowing Costs

Following on the heels of IAS 22, IAS 23 also scraped through with three dissenting votes in October 1983.[256] The no-votes can hardly have been inspired by conflicts with national practices or requirements, because few of the more outspoken suggestions made during the drafting stage had survived in the final standard.

On the most basic issue, the steering committee had suggested in its point outline that, subject to conditions, interest costs should be capitalized. The steering committee, chaired by Willis Smith (a financial executive and member of the US delegation), had the recently issued FAS 34, *Capitalization of Interest Cost* (October 1979), in mind.[257] However, this proposal was modified by the board on the first possible occasion, when it laid down the rule, subsequently included in IAS 23, that enterprises should adopt a consistent policy of either capitalizing or not capitalizing borrowing costs associated with assets that take a long time to get ready for intended use or sale.

Another issue where the board did not take a clear position was whether capitalization should also apply to inventories. This was thought to be particularly relevant in developing countries, but it was objected to by the UK & Irish delegation. As a result, attempts to distinguish between various classes of assets in the boldfaced standards section of IAS 23 were dropped, although the Explanation did discuss interest costs related to inventories in a tentative way. The UK & Irish delegation also objected to a proposal which would have required enterprises that expensed their interest costs to disclose the amounts that would have been capitalized under the alternative treatment. This disclosure did not make it into IAS 23 either.[258]

The result of the whittling away of the more salient features of the proposed standards was predictable. Some comment letter writers urged the IASC to come out clearly in favour of capitalization, some argued the same for non-capitalization, and others wished the IASC would just choose any of the two as long as a clear choice was made.[259] Most likely, the three no-votes against IAS 23 indicated concerns that the standard was too permissive.

5.13.4. IAS 24: Related Party Transactions

Like IAS 14 on segment reporting, IAS 24 was developed partly in response to concerns originating among developing countries about financial reporting by multinational enterprises. For that reason, the steering committee consisted of four rather than the usual three members, in order to balance the developed (Germany and the Netherlands) and developing countries (Brazil and Nigeria) on the committee.[260] Against this background, it was clear that there were expectations to meet on the user side, but there were few precedents that could be followed to determine a level of disclosure that might be acceptable to reporting companies. The steering committee noted that only Canada had issued guidance in the area (*CICA Handbook*, section 3840). The steering committee observed:

The Steering Committee is therefore inclined to be cautious in its approach to this subject and not to go too far in its proposals. Nevertheless, it is recognised that the document produced will need to meet an adequate standard so as to be in keeping with other International Accounting Standards and acceptable to such bodies as OECD and UN, who no doubt will be invited to comment on the paper at an early stage in its development.[261]

As IAS 24 was to be a disclosure standard, the main task before the IASC was to define, in carefully crafted language, the circumstances in which the disclosure of related party transactions was to be required and which information was to be disclosed. In the process, most of the substantial content proposed by the steering committee was transferred to the Explanation section, making the boldfaced standard, with just over a hundred words, one of the shortest ever to be issued by the IASC. One of the key items that was eliminated from the text altogether was the idea, let alone the requirement, that related party transactions should be restated to arm's length conditions. The steering committee concluded this would be 'too radical' as a requirement, even though it was reluctant to remove all references to the notion.[262] The standard merely required that 'related party relationships' should be disclosed where control exists, regardless of whether actual transactions have taken place. In addition, where transactions have taken place, the nature of the relationship, the type of transactions, and other information 'necessary for an understanding of the financial statements' should be disclosed (paragraph 26). The Explanation section included a definition of related parties taken from the *CICA Handbook*.[263] It also contained a discussion of the information that 'normally' would have to be disclosed in the case of related party transactions, such as the volume of the transactions, the outstanding items, and pricing policies. This information was labelled as 'elements necessary for an understanding of the financial statements' after the wording 'effects of transactions' was found to be too suggestive of quantified information.[264]

The exposure draft was not particularly liked by the writers of comment letters, either because it was too vague or because it imposed too great a burden on companies. A UK respondent characterized the proposed standard as 'creating work for those who have nothing to hide, while having no impact on those who do'. A number of respondents pointed out that the matter might better be left to a political organization such as the OECD or the UN, and that the OECD's *Guidelines on International Investment and Multinational Enterprises* did in fact already take it up.[265] In the end, the board was not quite comfortable with the standard, either. After extensive editing, it was approved with two votes against.[266]

5.13.5. IAS 25: Investments

If one standard is to be chosen to mark the end of the IASC's first phase, it would probably be the unloved IAS 25. That it was unloved was not because the steering committee that produced it lacked talent. It contained no less than two future IASC chairmen. But one of them, Georges Barthès, who also chaired the committee, recalled the experience as 'awful'.[267] IAS 25 illustrated how the IASC's customary approach to harmonization was breaking down, an approach that was summed up by the steering committee itself as 'to prohibit accounting treatments that are generally agreed to be bad, and to permit alternatives where there is no general consensus as to the most appropriate method'.[268] The problem with investments, and more generally with valuation of assets and the treatment of gains and losses on revaluation, was that there was no consensus on what was bad, and that the range of possible alternatives was wide indeed.

IAS 25 started out in 1981 as a not-too-ambitious project on accounting for marketable securities. But on the recommendation of the steering committee, the scope was soon expanded to include all investments, including investments in subsidiaries and investment properties.[269] This decision introduced insuperable complications, and, after a few years, the board decided, against the wishes of the steering committee, to refer accounting for subsidiaries to the steering committee that was reviewing IAS 3 on consolidated financial statements and the equity method (see Section 9.2.2). Nevertheless, investment properties remained within the scope of the investments project, and this meant that the simmering conflict between IAS 4, *Depreciation Accounting*, and the UK accounting standards over whether investment properties were depreciable assets had to be confronted (see the discussion of IAS 4, above). The steering committee was quite clear in its preference for internal consistency. It argued that because investments, including investment properties, were typically held with a view to expected appreciation in value, it made sense to choose an accounting treatment that showed such value changes in income when they occurred. However, neither the board nor the member bodies, which were consulted in a postal ballot, were convinced. E26 (approved in June 1984) allowed investment properties to be treated either as properties (and depreciated) or as investments (at market value).

As the exposure draft neared completion, more and more options were added, not just with regard to investment properties. In the end, E26 would allow investments classified as current assets to be valued either at market value or at the lower of cost and market value. If the latter, there was a choice between a portfolio approach or an approach based on the valuation of individual assets. Long-term investments were to be valued at cost or at revalued amounts, with the lower of cost or market value a third option in the case of marketable securities. Investment properties might be treated either according to IAS 4 and IAS 16, or as long-term investments. It would be incorrect to say that all conceivable treatments of realized and unrealized gains and losses were acceptable, but for certain classes of assets there were major options that allowed a choice between including value changes in income or applying them directly to owners' equity. Despite, or because of, the options, E26 was approved with the votes of Australia, Mexico, and South Africa against, making it the least supported exposure draft so far.[270]

The good news on E26 was that it attracted a fair number of comments, most of which were in favour of an international standard on the issue. The problem was, as the steering committee noted, that many respondents wanted a reduction in options but they did not agree among each other on which options to remove.[271] As the board could not agree on substantial changes either, IAS 25 (approved in October 1985 with the US voting against),[272] did not differ greatly from E26. But against the wishes of the steering committee, yet another option was introduced. If investment properties were treated as long-term investments, the full range of treatments for long-term investments applied, including valuation at cost without depreciation. The steering committee argued in vain that this was inconsistent with the main argument advanced for not charging depreciation, that is, that changes in the fair value of such investments were more significant than their depreciation.

So, in the end, IAS 25 came to include a very wide range of options. To US delegate Ralph Walters, who was later to chair the Comparability steering committee that was to prepare the way for a reduction of options, IAS 25 symbolized the weakness of the IASC's traditional approach. He commented: 'We really shot ourselves in the foot with that one.'[273] Other board members also cited IAS 25 as an important factor in bringing about a change of approach in the IASC that began with the start of the Comparability project.[274]

5.13.6. IAS 26: Retirement Benefit Plans

The subject of 'accounting for pension plans' was one of the last to be chosen by the ad hoc approach occasionally used by the IASC, when it had not yet developed more elaborate procedures to set its agenda. It was decided in March 1982 to set up a steering committee on this topic even though it was not included in the secretariat's list of possible topics that was on the table for that meeting.[275] IAS 26 was also reminiscent of earlier standards because it was heavily influenced by UK concerns. It was unusual, however, for being applicable to a different type of entity than the previous standards. With the exception of its limited foray into bank accounting, the IASC had so far eschewed 'industry' standards.

In general, views on reporting by defined benefit plans—defined contribution plans provided few difficulties—could be characterized by reference to two poles. On the one hand were those who thought that the reporting should focus on the 'fund', that is, on showing the assets and changes in assets and thus giving a report on the management of the plan assets. On the other hand, there were those who wanted to report on the 'plan', that is, the plan assets and the obligations under the pension plan, thought of as a single reporting entity. The most extreme plan position was that both the plan assets and obligations should be reported in a single balance sheet. Intermediate positions included showing obligations in a footnote to the financial statements or in an actuarial report attached to the financial statements. The extreme fund position was not to disclose obligations, or more specifically, the actuarial present value of promised retirement benefits (APVPRB) altogether. The latter view was motivated by a concern that an APVPRB based on projected salaries was not strictly speaking a liability, while a disclosure of APVPRB on the basis of current salaries might incorrectly suggest the existence of a surplus. Roughly speaking, most interested parties in the United Kingdom (including the insurance industry and the Institute of Actuaries) favoured a fund approach. On the other hand, FAS 35, *Accounting and Reporting by Defined Benefit Pension Plans* (1980), prescribed a plan approach, but a dissenting opinion in the US standard along fund lines was a reminder that this conclusion had been contested.

The problem for the IASC was that there was not much common ground and no consensus on unacceptable practices to be eliminated. Instead, advocates of the more extreme versions of each approach considered the opposite approach to be wholly unacceptable. Even though the steering committee's chairman, Ralph Harris, came from the United States, it favoured the view prevalent in the United Kingdom.[276] It was supported by a vociferous response from the United Kingdom to the preliminary exposure draft and to E27 (approved in March 1985).[277] The rest of the board was willing to look for a compromise, but it drew the line when the steering committee proposed to make APVPRB disclosure optional, in evident deference to the UK position.[278] On the other hand, a plainly reluctant steering committee had to accept that most variants of the plan approach were allowed in IAS 26.[279] Hence, almost anyone could find something objectionable in IAS 26 (approved in June 1986), as it allowed APVPRB to be calculated both on the basis of current and projected salaries, and allowed it to be included in the financial statements, the notes, or a separate actuarial report. It passed with one vote against and one abstention.

5.14. CONCLUSION

An oft-repeated characterization of the pre-1987 standards was that the IASC was seeking the 'lowest common denominator'.[280] This chapter suggests that such a dismissive assessment is not justified. Obviously, the IASC's first twenty-six standards did contain many options on important accounting issues. Yet these standards also ruled out practices that were by no means uncommon in several member countries. Examples included: not presenting consolidated financial statements, the taxes payable method, and not capitalizing leases at all. Moreover, several of the standards called unambiguously for significant disclosures. Had the IASC truly sought the lowest common denominator, there would have been no serious concerns over non-compliance with its standards (as is discussed in Chapter 6).

One reason why the standards had to include options was because the IASC's Constitution ruled that at least three quarters of the delegations had to vote for the publication of a standard. Including options was a way to secure sufficient votes, a process summarized by Chairman Hans Burggraaff as 'compromise to harmonise'.[281] But a more fundamental reason was simply that, at the time, options as such were acceptable. Domestic accounting standards or laws in most board member countries were by no means free of options in the 1970s and 1980s. Some of the IASC's early standards included options even though they were approved unanimously. So when the IASC did begin to eliminate options after 1987, it was not because the voting arrangements had been altered. It was because views on the acceptability of options had changed.

Before 1987, the IASC's strategy was not to seek uniformity. It was 'to outlaw the unacceptable, and allow the acceptable'.[282] It should be recalled that, during this period, before the development of its conceptual framework, the IASC did not have a clearly articulated set of criteria for eliminating accounting alternatives, had it wanted to do so. As long as some board members, most of whom were well-qualified individuals holding senior positions in their home countries, were willing to advance serious arguments in support of, say, partial tax allocation, the board was not inclined to make arbitrary decisions in favour of one particular approach.

This policy was not always understood by the IASC's outside critics and respondents to exposure drafts, who continued to berate the IASC for allowing a range of choices for most accounting issues. Within the IASC itself, there was occasional disappointment, and to some extent, expectations really had to be lowered. When the IASC was founded, Henry Benson's public utterances if not his personality suggested that the IASC would be aiming for more clear-cut and less ambiguous guidance.

But by 1987, the IASC's first phase was passing. That it was a first phase, and that there were to be other phases ahead, had been understood ever since the days of Henry Benson. Burggraaff, who had been the most eloquent defender of the IASC's initial strategy, remarked in 1982 that 'We are not writing standards for eternity; we may come back to existing standards when the time is right.'[283] Chairman John Kirkpatrick captured most of the history of the IASC when he said in 1986: 'I would say that harmonization means compatibility today. Tomorrow it means comparability. The day after tomorrow, conformity.'[284] He may not have been aware how soon tomorrow was to begin.

6

The IASC Labours to Gain Recognition

The purpose of this chapter is twofold: to review the disappointing performance, on the whole, of the members and associate members of the International Accounting Standards Committee (IASC) in fulfilling their 'best endeavours' undertaking, and to trace the efforts of the IASC to secure recognition and, even more important, acceptance of its standards by national regulators and standard-setting bodies.

The chapter begins by reviewing the IASC's best endeavours undertaking and then proceeds to present evidence of progress towards fulfilling this obligation in board-member countries and in a sampling of other countries. The chapter concludes by discussing the IASC board's efforts to improve its liaison with accountancy bodies, other organizations interested in financial reporting, and securities market regulators.

6.1. THE BEST ENDEAVOURS UNDERTAKING

One of the key planks in Sir Henry Benson's platform for the IASC was that a means be found for securing compliance with the Committee's standards. Apart from the United States, where the Securities and Exchange Commission (SEC) rigorously enforced compliance with the pronouncements of the national standard setter, in other countries compliance was largely left to each company's external auditor. In the light of this state of affairs, the IASC Agreement and Constitution was boldly ambitious. The sixteen sponsoring (or founder) accountancy bodies, as signatories to the Agreement and Constitution, undertook

(a) to support the standards promulgated by the Committee;
(b) to use their best endeavours:
  (i) to ensure that published accounts comply with these standards or that there is disclosure of the extent to which they do not and to persuade governments, the authorities controlling securities markets and the industrial and business community that published accounts should comply with these standards;
  (ii) to ensure that the auditors satisfy themselves that the accounts comply with these standards. If the accounts do not comply with these standards the audit report should either refer to the disclosure of non-compliance in the accounts or should state the extent to which they do not comply;

(iii) to ensure that, as soon as practicable, appropriate action is taken in respect of auditors whose audit reports do not meet the requirements of (ii) above;

(c) to seek to secure similar general acceptance and observance of these standards internationally.

Each founder body, as well as each body subsequently admitted as an associate member, was left to decide how it would implement the best endeavours clause in the IASC Agreement and Constitution. An IASC explanatory statement, *Commentary on the Statements of International Accounting Standards*, issued on 6 March 1974 together with its first exposure draft, emphasized that 'the most important and serious obligation which Founder and Associate Members of IASC have undertaken' was stated in (b)(ii) and (iii), above (paragraph 17). This point was repeated in a subsequent brochure, *The Work and Purpose of the International Accounting Standards Committee*, issued in January 1975. Yet, by the latter part of the 1980s, as will be seen, none of the accountancy bodies in the countries represented on the IASC board could affirm that they had imposed such an obligation, with any significant amount of enforcement follow-up, on members who were auditors. Two stock exchanges, in London and Amsterdam, stated an expectation that listed companies disclose their compliance with IASC standards, but neither exchange offered a plan for securing compliance, and their stated expectation was itself rescinded only a few years later. Canada was alone in successfully persuading a significant number of companies on the Toronto Stock Exchange to disclose whether they complied with IASC standards.

For listed companies on the Toronto Stock Exchange, as well as on the London and Amsterdam exchanges, the requirement to disclose conformity with IASC standards was more symbolic than a challenge to the companies, because the IASC standards issued during the years of the exchanges' respective requirements or recommendations were largely compatible with national standards. Nonetheless, the IASC would have welcomed these endorsements of its standards by the three important stock exchanges.

Less than two years after the IASC was founded, Benson began to exhibit a degree of impatience with the slow pace at which some of the founder bodies were fulfilling their best endeavours undertaking. The following passage appears in the minutes of the April 1975 IASC meeting:

The Chairman appreciated that [some founder members] were facing various difficulties [in their home countries]. However, he pointed out that the words 'best endeavours' in the Agreement to establish IASC were not put in as an excuse for inaction. He also stated that sooner or later the press or public will inquire as to the extent to which IASC standards are being enforced by the participating bodies. Furthermore smaller countries want international accounting standards and wish to enforce them but before doing so they will want to be sure that the major countries are enforcing them.[1]

Benson took an uncompromising view of the position IASC standards should occupy in relation to national standards. The minutes of the IASC's April 1975 meeting report his opinion that 'A national standard should be withdrawn in cases in which it is less restrictive than an international accounting standard dealing with the same subject.'² This is not a view that would have gone down well with national standard setters in the major countries, especially at a time when the reputation of the IASC rested only on one published standard, on the disclosure of accounting policies. In an agenda paper for the November 1974 board meeting, Benson wrote, 'Our International Standards will be made a laughing stock if they are not enforced.'³

Yet Benson and his colleagues knew, or should have known, that the signatories could have done little more than launch a process of promoting awareness of the IASC's standards in their respective countries. Of the founder countries having an accounting standard setter, only the United States had an effective process for securing compliance with the standards. In countries such as the United States and Canada, a body of well-developed standards already existed, and a new set of IASC standards could not have easily competed with them for national acceptance. In the United Kingdom, the first genuine standard-setting body had been set up only three years earlier, and it was proceeding about its work earnestly. In other countries, such as France and Germany, the financial reporting culture was not yet attuned to the need to provide equity investors with financial information. And, above all, each country's accountancy body, or bodies, may have possessed limited, if any, legal authority to change the map of accounting practice.

Henk Volten, the staff observer to the Netherlands delegation from 1973 to 1987, pungently characterized the original best endeavours clause as follows:

This statement of the objectives is of a pure principled beauty, but it appeared that it could not be realized in the rough and tumble of practice. The negative approach did not work. In no country did enterprises show themselves willing to proclaim their departures from IAS, not least because they would as a rule consider that they had good grounds for their departures. The accountancy bodies, let alone the individual auditors, did not insist.⁴

6.2. AN IMPORTANT ENDORSEMENT FROM THE FIBV

Henry Benson believed that the stock exchanges could provide critical support for the IASC standards. An early endorsement came from the Fédération Internationale des Bourses de Valeurs (FIBV, International Federation of Stock Exchanges, currently known as the World Federation of Exchanges). Its general assembly, held in Madrid on 8–10 October 1974, passed the following resolution:

Member Exchanges of the Fédération Internationale des Bourses de Valeurs situated in countries whose professional accountancy bodies are either Founder or Associate members of the International Accounting Standards Committee should take steps to include in their listing requirements reference to compliance with Standards issued by the International Accounting Standards Committee.⁵

An IASC discussion paper said that the FIBV's action resulted from 'discussions with the stock exchanges in the major business centres of the world'.[6] Although the resolution was jointly sponsored by the London Stock Exchange and the Amsterdamse Effectenbeurs (Amsterdam Stock Exchange),[7] it was Henry Benson who, as early as January 1974, wrote the president of the FIBV about 'co-ordinating the work of the Federation and IASC in the area of disclosure'.[8]

Although it was reported in 1978 that the majority of IASC member bodies were 'involved in consultations with stock exchanges in their own countries, seeking to achieve requirements that financial statements filed with those exchanges be prepared in conformity with IASC standards',[9] as noted above only two stock exchanges had done so, and then only for a few years, prior to 1987.

6.3. EUROPEAN AND WORLD SURVEYS OF FINANCIAL REPORTING: A BOON FOR THE IASC

Six European and world surveys of company financial reporting yield an interesting overview of the degree to which IASC standards were having an impact.

6.3.1. The Lafferty/*Financial Times* Volumes

The IASC received an unexpected boost from Michael Lafferty, who, until 1981, was the banking and accounting correspondent of the *Financial Times*. Between 1979 and 1984, Lafferty, assisted by colleagues, published three volumes surveying the financial reports of, successively, 100 major European companies, 200 major world companies, and 250 major world companies.[10] In each of these substantial volumes, the authors selected IASC standards as the yardstick against which to gauge the adequacy of company financial statements, which would have done much to promote the work of the IASC in the eyes of company chief financial officers and CEOs around Europe and the rest of the world.[11] Indeed, the 1980 volume contained a short article by IASC Chairman John Hepworth, as well as short articles by Eng Howe Wong, of the United Nations Centre on Transnational Corporations; Charles G. Wootton, deputy secretary-general of the Organisation for Economic Co-operation and Development (OECD); and Robert Coleman, of the European Commission.

The 1983–4 volume reproduced the following quotation from remarks made by Henry Benson at the IASC's tenth anniversary celebration in 1983, in which he repeated his prophetic outlook for the IASC (*see also* Section 3.2):

I hope that by the year 2000, the impact of the IASC will be of dominating importance in the presentation of financial statements. The first and immediate task is to ensure that all listed companies state affirmatively whether their statements comply with international standards, and that this be made a condition of listing on stock exchanges and bourses.[12]

The authors of the survey thereupon remarked: 'As the survey shows, there are several countries where the first task is well on its way to being achieved. Unfortunately, the United Kingdom (Lord Benson's own country) is not one of them.'[13] By 1983, as will be noted below (see Section 6.5.2), the London Stock Exchange had rescinded its requirement that listed companies disclose their non-compliance with any IASC standards. Yet Italy's Commissione Nazionale per le Società e la Borsa (Consob) had 'signed on' to IASC standards, and it was reported that no fewer than eighty-seven Canadian companies had signified their adherence to IASC standards in their 1981 annual reports.[14]

The *Financial Times* also began publishing a monthly news bulletin, *World Accounting Report*, in 1976, which proceeded to give extensive coverage to international accounting issues, including the work of the IASC. Benson wrote a letter to Michael Lafferty, its editor, for publication in the first issue in which he welcomed the new venture.[15]

After Lafferty left the *Financial Times*, the newspaper sponsored a survey in 1984 of some 175 companies of 'international importance', also using IASC standards to frame the analysis, because, as the authors wrote, 'We believe the standards provide an independent and skilfully developed set of yardsticks'.[16]

6.3.2. Two Further Surveys

In 1979, Price Waterhouse International published a survey of financial reporting practices in sixty-four countries. On compliance with IASC standards, it concluded as follows:

There are nine countries included in this survey which can be classified [as ones where IASC standards are accorded the same status as domestic standards] and where compliance can be deemed mandatory, although the situation in each is not identical. These are Bahamas, Fiji, France, Malaysia, Nigeria, Pakistan, Singapore, Trinidad and Zimbabwe Rhodesia. In the tabulations, these nine countries have cited IASC Standards, where appropriate, as the authority for requirements or prohibitions. In some of these countries, however, practice is in an evolutionary stage and the Standards may not always be followed in every detail in every case.[17]

This quotation from the Price Waterhouse survey is diplomatically phrased, as it seems improbable that compliance was actually mandatory in any of the listed countries. France was a founder member and Nigeria was a member of the IASC board from 1978 to 1987. They are both discussed below.

In a 1984 survey of thirty countries' financial reporting practices, Gray, Campbell, and Shaw found that five countries (Malaysia, Mexico, Thailand, Zambia, and Zimbabwe) responded that the IASC had 'significant influence' on external financial reporting, while a dozen reporting jurisdictions (Belgium, Channel Islands, Denmark, France, Hong Kong, Indonesia, Ireland, Italy, New Zealand, Philippines, South Africa, and the United Kingdom) reported that the IASC had 'moderate influence'.[18] The following countries represented on the IASC board reported no influence: Australia, Japan, and the United States.

Until the latter part of the 1980s, as will be seen below, the major impact of IASC standards on financial reporting occurred in developing countries in Africa and Asia. For reasons that are unclear, there was no reported impact in Central and South America (*see* Section 6.19).

Another point worth noting is that few companies mentioned compliance or non-compliance with IASC standards in their annual reports, at least until the early 1980s, and they were mostly in Canada, as will be seen. The 1979 survey of 100 European company annual reports, cited above, found that 'References to IASC are few and far between.'[19] The world survey in 1980 of 200 major quoted companies, also cited above, observed that 'Only a handful of annual reports include reference to IASC.'[20]

When interpreting the results of surveys such as those by Price Waterhouse and Gray, Campbell, and Shaw, which was based on data supplied by the accounting firm of Deloitte Haskins & Sells, one must appreciate that, in every country, it is impossible to know what practices are followed by all companies, including the large number of companies whose financial statements are not deposited in a public registry. The weighting of preponderant practice in a country (e.g. by number of companies, relative sales volume of companies, total asset value of companies) is entirely subjective. Moreover, it is implausible to believe that the country reporters personally examined hundreds or thousands of company annual reports; instead, the data are most likely the impressions held by informed observers, such as accounting firm partners in each country.

6.4. IMPACT ON COUNTRY MEMBERS OF THE IASC BOARD

In the following sections, we discuss the impact of the IASC and its standards on accounting developments, first, in the countries represented on the board and, second, on a sampling of non-board countries both in the developed and developing world.

From the very outset, the secretariat regularly surveyed IASC members on the steps that had been taken to incorporate IASC standards into national norms and practice. The most extensive survey, including replies from board and non-board members around the world, was conducted in 1988, although others, to which only the board members responded, occurred in other years, especially in 1979 and 1983–4. Extracts from these surveys are reported below, in the country sections.

When interpreting the results of these surveys, one must take into account that all of the data were self-reported by the several accountancy bodies and were therefore subject to several forms of reporter bias, including the care with which each responding body gathered and classified the data as well as any desire by a body to impress the IASC with the fulfilment of its best endeavours obligation.

Also, the fact that many of the IASC standards permitted optional treatments facilitated a conformity with national requirements or practice even in areas where the IASC standards were not consulted for either.

The IASC's survey in 1979 of the eleven board-member countries found that every one of the sponsoring accountancy bodies had adopted a plan for disseminating standards, as well as exposure drafts, to its members.[21] Indeed, as early as February 1978, the IASC secretary confirmed that IASC exposure drafts and standards were being published in thirty countries, including those of the founder members.[22]

In non–English-speaking countries, the drafts and standards were translated into the local language. By 1987, IASC standards had been translated into twenty languages: Arabic, Chinese, Danish, Dutch, French (different versions produced in Canada and France), German, Greek, Hebrew, Indonesian, Italian, Japanese, Korean, Malay, Norwegian, Portuguese, Serbo-Croat, Spanish, Swedish, Thai, and Turkish.[23] Some bodies reproduced the drafts or standards in their membership magazine or in a bound volume, while others distributed them, free or at a price, to selected parties and to those requesting copies. The bodies' general response to a question concerning the authority of IASC standards in their country was that they were not equal in standing to the national guidance or the law, as the case may be, but that they recommended that the national standard setter take account of the IASC standards in their deliberations.

The following is a review of the steps taken in countries represented on the IASC board between 1973 and 1987, by which their professional accountancy bodies carried out their best endeavours undertaking. Apart from the American Institute of Certified Public Accountants (AICPA), all of the professional accountancy bodies in the founder countries actually distributed IASC standards in one form or another. The professional accountancy bodies in several of the countries, including Australia, Canada, Germany, Mexico, and the United Kingdom, periodically published comparisons between their national standards and IASC standards. This review also recites initiatives taken by securities market regulators and stock exchanges to encourage compliance with IASC standards; in some cases, these initiatives may have been precipitated by professional accountancy bodies.

6.5. UNITED KINGDOM & IRELAND

Standard setting in the United Kingdom and Ireland had begun in 1970, with the founding by the Institute of Chartered Accountants in England and Wales (ICAEW) of the Accounting Standards Steering Committee (ASSC), which proceeded to draft Statements of Standard Accounting Practice (SSAPs).[24] Subsequently, the Institute of Chartered Accountants of Scotland (ICAS) and the Institute of Chartered Accountants in Ireland (ICAI), as well as the Association of Certified Accountants, the Institute of Cost and Management Accountants, and the Institute of Municipal Treasurers and Accountants,[25] joined the committee, and all six bodies formed the Consultative Committee of Accountancy Bodies (CCAB), an umbrella group, in 1974. These were the same six bodies that signed the IASC Agreement and Constitution in 1973. The SSAPs were formally issued once approval had been given by the governing Councils of the six bodies.

There was no statutory requirement until 1989 that UK companies disclose that they had not complied with applicable accounting standards. The overriding legal obligation on the auditor was, and is today, to affirm that the accounts give a 'true and fair view'.

6.5.1. Action Taken by the CCAB

In December 1974, the ICAEW, together with the other UK and Irish accountancy bodies that had formed the CCAB, approved an 'Introduction to Statements of International Accounting Standards'. The ICAEW's version said, 'The Council expects members to observe International Accounting Standards.' It added that the provisions of the Explanatory Foreword to the UK and Irish SSAPs 'apply equally' to IASC standards. This meant that, 'If the accounts do not comply with International Accounting Standards the audit report should either refer to the disclosure of non-compliance in the accounts or should state in the audit report the extent to which they do not comply.'[26] Yet Michael Renshall, the ICAEW's technical director during the first half of the 1970s and chairman of the Accounting Standards Committee (ASC) during its concluding years, from 1986 to 1990, has written, 'So far as I know, no member [of the ICAEW] was disciplined for breaching accounting standards per se during the ASC's 20 year existence.'[27]

When IAS 1 was issued in January 1975, the CCAB began a practice of publishing a Preface to each IASC standard when it was distributed in the UK and Ireland by the CCAB bodies. The Preface explained the applicability of the IASC standard in the UK and Ireland. The CCAB's general policy on IASC standards in the UK and Ireland, which was repeated in its Preface to each standard, was stated as follows:

International Accounting Standards (to the extent they are not already covered by legal requirements or national standards) come into effect when their provisions are incorporated into SSAPs issued by the Councils of the UK and Irish bodies: they do not override UK and Irish law and SSAPs.[28]

The CCAB then proceeded to advise whether, and to what extent, compliance with company law and the SSAPs would automatically ensure compliance with the IASC standard.

Beginning with SSAP 14, on group accounts, issued in 1978, the SSAPs regularly contained a note comparing the SSAP with the corresponding IASC standard. Perhaps it was not a coincidence that IAS 3 was said to be 'a major influence on the development of SSAP 14'.[29]

The new UK and Irish standard-setting programme suffered a number of embarrassing reversals during the 1970s, as a result of which Edward Stamp wrote in 1979: 'The whole accounting standards programme is now bogged down in confusion, acrimony, and dissent.... In fact, the output of the ASC does not compare very favourably with that of [the IASC] ... the IASC has often been much quicker in producing standards on the more important subjects.'[30] Already in 1978, a committee was looking into possible improvements in the effectiveness of the ASC.

Bearing out Stamp's observation, by 1985 the IASC had issued standards on seven subjects for which there were no equivalent UK and Irish standards: presentation of current assets and current liabilities (IAS 13), segment reporting (IAS 14), accounting for property, plant, and equipment (IAS 16), revenue recognition (IAS 18), accounting for retirement benefits by employers (IAS 19), capitalization of borrowing costs (IAS 23), and related party disclosures (IAS 24).[31] When Ian Hay Davison became ASC chairman in July 1982, he concluded that 'The efforts of the [IASC] were in danger of outrunning our work at home and indeed there were one or two topics where the IASC had already issued Exposure Drafts which had not yet been touched upon by us in the UK.' He said that his policy was 'to encourage the IASC to hasten slowly and to give more time to persuading member bodies to implement their proposals'.[32]

Of the first twenty-six IASC standards, issued through 1987, only one, IAS 4 on depreciation, published in October 1976, created a serious conflict with UK and Irish practice, which was that annual valuations, not annual depreciation charges, should be recorded on investment properties, while IAS 4 required that depreciation be recorded on all properties.[33]

In March 1978, the CCAB replaced its 'Introduction' of December 1974 with an almost identical version of the IASC's 'Preface to Statements of International Accounting Standards', which had just been approved by the IASC.[34] As with the previous Introduction, the 'Preface' reproduced the IASC members' best endeavours obligation. Evidently, the auditor's obligation to disclose non-compliance was the same as before, because an ICAEW publication asserted in 1979 that 'It is required that non-compliance with international standards should be disclosed in the financial statements or, if not disclosed, should be referred to in the audit report, but there is no requirement to quantify the effect of non-compliance.'[35] But actual compliance with this obligation by auditors was another matter. In the ICAEW's *Survey of Published Accounts 1978*, it was reported that forty-nine companies to which IAS 4, *Depreciation Accounting*, was applicable had provided no depreciation on some or all of their properties, thus not complying with the standard. Yet, of the forty-nine companies, only twenty-three specifically referred to their non-compliance with IAS 4. None of the auditors of the other twenty-six companies disclosed the fact of non-compliance in their report.[36]

In 1981, the ASC issued SSAP 19, *Accounting for Investment Properties*, which stated that investment properties should not be subject to periodic charges for depreciation. SSAP 19, therefore, was in conflict with IAS 4. Paul Rutteman, a partner in the UK firm of Arthur Young, has written, 'When we introduced a standard saying that investment properties should not be depreciated, we immediately sought and won a change in IASs to accept our practice.'[37] That UK victory occurred in 1986, when the IASC acknowledged in IAS 25, *Accounting for Investments*, that investment properties did not have to be depreciated. Rutteman's point was that 'As individual countries develop their standards in isolation, the pressures for dilution of IASs will increase. There will be more options, not less.'[38]

In 1986, the position of the CCAB bodies towards IASC standards was still very much like it was in 1975. The 'Explanatory Foreword' to the SSAPs, which had previously been silent on the standing of IASC standards in the United Kingdom and Ireland, was revised in August of that year to state, in somewhat restrained language, that 'The accountancy bodies attach importance to fostering the harmonisation of accounting standards internationally. To this end, they have collectively undertaken to support the work of the International Accounting Standards Committee.' But, it added, 'If, in rare cases, [an SSAP and an IASC standard] were to differ significantly, the United Kingdom and Irish accounting standard would prevail.'[39]

During the last two years of John Grenside's term (1976–80) on the IASC board, he was also a member of the ASC. David Hobson, who succeeded Grenside on the board in 1980 and remained until 1985, served on the ASC from 1970 to 1982, and Ian Hay Davison, who became the ASC chairman in 1982, asked Hobson to continue to attend ASC meetings as an observer.[40] Christopher Stronge, who succeeded Hobson in 1985, also attended ASC meetings as observer until 1990. Hence, there was an attempt by the ASC chairman to manage relations between the two bodies. But Tom Watts, of Price Waterhouse & Co., the ASC chairman from 1978 to 1982, was decidedly pessimistic about the prospects for international harmonization. Although conceding that 'IASC has done, and is still doing, sterling work', he said, 'I am personally doubtful about its ability to procure the harmonization of standards among those countries and areas which already have established machinery for setting standards.... There is a tremendous difference between a direct responsibility for setting standards in a territory and proposing solutions without having that responsibility.'[41] In another interview, he said prophetically, 'The only way to get international harmonisation is by agreement between the national Standards-setting bodies.'[42]

A minor crisis occurred in 1980, when IASC Secretary Allan Cook was taken aback to discover that the ICAEW, which had the responsibility for distributing IASC standards in the United Kingdom, had stopped publishing the standards when there was no UK and Irish SSAP on the same subject. He learned from a remark made by Tom Watts at a recent conference that, as the UK policy on IASC standards was that they 'have no status within the UK until they are adopted by incorporation into a domestic standard',[43] it was decided not to publish those standards until they had been incorporated in the ASC's standards. Cook thereupon reminded the ICAEW's staff of the need to get out the backlog of undistributed standards.[44] This change in policy may well have been precipitated by the conflict with IAS 4. Perhaps as an act of expiation, the ICAEW published a bound volume in 1981 of IASC standards 1–13.[45]

6.5.2. Action Taken by the London Stock Exchange

During the 1970s, the London Stock Exchange acted to lend support to the IASC. In 1972, the Exchange had already given backing to the UK and Irish SSAPs in its booklet, *Admission of Shares to Listing*, two years after the ASSC began operations, when it said that it 'will expect the accounts of listed companies to be drawn up in accordance with the standards approved by these [five] accountancy bodies; any departure from these standards must be disclosed and explained.'[46] On 23 October 1974, at the urging of Henry Benson and less than two weeks after promulgation of the FIBV's recommendation to its members, the Exchange extended its support to the IASC and announced that UK listed companies must prepare their accounts also in conformity with IASC standards. The eventual provision said that 'Any significant departure from or non-compliance with these standards [IASC standards as well as SSAPs] must be disclosed and explained.'[47] Listed companies incorporated outside the United Kingdom did not need to comply with SSAPs but were expected to have their accounts prepared in conformity with IASC standards. Any significant departure from, or non-compliance with, the applicable IASC standards was to be disclosed and explained.[48]

The Exchange's decision to require its companies to disclose departures from two different sets of accounting standards would not have gone down well with Sir Ronald Leach, the chairman of the ASSC. In April 1977, Leach's successor as chairman, Sir William Slimmings, said, 'I think it is quite clear that we must aim to have only one "book of rules" to which reference need be made in ensuring that accounts comply with all relevant standards.'[49] Benson had apparently approached the Exchange without consulting the ASSC or the ICAEW in advance, which would not have been well received by those who were turning out SSAPs.[50]

In April 1979, the London Stock Exchange retreated from its strong position on compliance by UK listed companies with both IASC standards and SSAPs. Gavin Fryer, then the head of the quotations department at the Exchange, recalled that companies complained that it was an unreasonable burden to have to disclose departures from both SSAPs and IASC standards, especially as there had recently been some divergences between the two. In 1974, he said, the Exchange's decision was taken to show support for the IASC, but by 1979 it was evident that UK standards were stronger than IASC standards.[51] Although it continued to express support for the IASC's programme of formulating and publishing standards, the Exchange announced that it would no longer expect UK companies to comply with IASC standards or to disclose instances of non-compliance. Its expectation with respect to listed companies incorporated outside the United Kingdom was retained without change.[52] In the space of just six years, therefore, the Exchange first imposed and then rescinded its stated expectation that UK listed companies adhere to IASC standards. The Exchange offered no explanation for its volte-face, although one supposes that the ASC and the ICAEW, as well as some of its listed companies, had lodged a complaint with the Exchange.

Reliance on a stock exchange for securing compliance with accounting standards can lead to disappointment. The London Stock Exchange's expression of support for IASC standards probably had more value as an exhortation than as an instrument of proactive oversight. In 1979, several of the major UK accountancy firms remarked that the Exchange had done little to enforce compliance with the UK and Irish SSAPs;[53] the Exchange must have done even less on compliance with IASC standards. Indeed, the Exchange registered its opposition to IAS 14, *Reporting Financial Information by Segment*, issued in 1981, apparently because companies incorporated outside the United Kingdom and Ireland found some of the required disclosures, including 'the basis of inter-segment pricing', to be anathema. In 1983, the Exchange acted to exempt non-UK companies from compliance with IAS 14.[54]

6.5.3. Responses to the IASC's Surveys

In early 1975, all six accountancy bodies in the United Kingdom and Ireland replied to the IASC, mostly with similar responses. Members had already been, or shortly would be, notified that their compliance with IASC standards was expected. The body would communicate with members who audited, or were officers or board members of, companies where non-compliance with standards was evident.[55] In the IASC's 1988 survey of the use and application of its standards, the United Kingdom replied that its national requirements, developed separately, conformed in all material respects to twenty extant IASC standards, while four standards dealt with subjects for which there were no national requirements but agreed with practice, one (segment reporting) disagreed with national requirements, and one disagreed with practice (effects of changing prices).[56]

6.6. UNITED STATES

The best endeavours undertaking by the IASC's founder members was awkward, to say the least, for the US sponsoring organization, the AICPA, because the SEC, not the AICPA, was the body authorized by law to secure compliance with US accounting norms, and the independent Financial Accounting Standards Board (FASB), not the AICPA, would be setting US standards beginning on 1 July 1973, two days after the IASC Agreement and Constitution was signed and went into effect. There was no point in asking the New York Stock Exchange to modify its listing agreement in regard to IASC standards, because the ultimate decision on such matters belonged to the SEC, which regulates the US securities exchanges and possesses statutory authority to establish accounting standards. In Accounting Series Release No. 150, issued in December 1973, the SEC recognized the FASB as the principal private-sector accounting standard setter in the United States. Wallace E. Olson, the AICPA's full-time chief staff officer in the 1970s, recalls that he apprised those attending the IASC's organizational meeting in March 1973 that, because of the institutional structure for standard setting and securing compliance in the United States, the Institute was in a position only to do its best 'to coordinate with the IASC'.[57] If an IASC standard were to be in conflict with an FASB standard, the Institute could hardly counsel its members to adopt the IASC standard.

In fact, a search of the *Fortune* 500 companies' financial statements between 1978 and 1980 turned up no references to the IASC or to its standards.[58] But in 1984, General Electric Company (GE) affirmed in its annual report to share owners that the accounting principles used in the company's financial statements 'are consistent in most important respects' with IASC standards. GE opted to make this disclosure in order to give a boost to the cause of international harmonization. It discontinued making this affirmation in 1991. A factor in its decision was that a year earlier, the IASC proposed to eliminate last-in, first-out (LIFO), which GE was using, as an allowed alternative treatment.[59] Although LIFO was not, in fact, disallowed, GE did not resume its reference to IASC standards. In 1986, IASC Secretary-General David Cairns wrote, 'There are, in fact, no material respects in which the standards issued by the FASB do not conform with international accounting standards. As a result, all US listed companies comply with all international accounting standards. Unfortunately, only one, GE, says so.'[60]

In fact, unknown to Cairns, Exxon Corporation had, five months earlier, in its 1985 annual report, inserted the following passage in its 'Summary of Accounting Policies':

The corporation's financial reporting is in alignment with the Organization for Economic Cooperation and Development guidelines for multinational enterprises and with the standards of the International Accounting Standards Committee.

Beginning in its 1986 annual report, Exxon appended 'with minor exceptions' at the end of its reference to IASC standards (which it called 'guidelines') and it dropped the reference to the OECD's guidelines. Exxon continued to affirm that its financial statements were 'consistent' with IASC standards through its 1991 annual report, following which the reference disappeared. Exxon also used LIFO.

FMC Corporation, also a LIFO user, referred to consistency with IASC standards from its 1986 to 1998 annual reports to shareholders (omitting 1994). From 1987 to 1991, CPC International, another user of LIFO, stated that its financial statements were drawn up in conformity with IASC standards. Salomon Inc. referred to compliance with IASC standards from 1988 to 1993. Moreover, Arthur Andersen & Co., its auditors, said in its opinion that the financial statements were fairly presented in conformity with both US generally accepted accounting principles (GAAP) and IASC standards, which was a rarity. Salomon's chief financial officer, Donald S. Howard, had joined the IASC's Consultative Group in June 1987 to represent the International Banking Associations. He was a staunch supporter of IASC standards. The Salomon reference to IASC standards was discontinued once he retired from the company in 1994.[61]

These were the only major US companies that mentioned IASC standards in their annual reports during the 1980s. There was at least one other reference to IASC standards in a set of financial statements prepared in the United States.

Beginning in the 1986 annual report of the International Federation of Accountants (IFAC), the local firm in the United States that audited its financial statements affirmed that they were prepared in conformity with both US GAAP and IASC standards. That may have been a 'first' in the United States. In IFAC's 1991 annual report, the auditor said that its financial statements were in conformity with IASC standards alone, with no reference at all to US GAAP. This reference to IASC standards continued in the auditor's report until 2001, when the reference was changed to international public sector accounting standards.

6.6.1. AICPA's Responses to the IASC's Surveys

In early 1975, the AICPA said that, under existing policy, it would not distribute copies of the Preface and IASC standards to each member of the AICPA; nor did it say it would publish them in its journal. It would, however, give them considerable publicity.[62] It observed that it treats many other AICPA publications and the FASB's standards in the same manner. When the IASC standards were 'significantly different' from US GAAP, the AICPA would 'exhort' the FASB, the SEC, and the stock exchanges 'to give early consideration to such differences with a view to achieving to the extent practicable harmonization of those areas in which a significant difference exists'.[63]

In the IASC's 1988 survey of the use and application of its standards, the United States replied that its national requirements, developed separately, conform, in all material respects, to twenty-three of the twenty-five extant IASC standards, the exceptions being IAS 12, *Accounting for Taxes on Income*, and IAS 15, on accounting for price changes.[64]

6.6.2. A Conflict between the FASB, FEI, and the SEC over the IASC's E3

There was an interesting contretemps between the FASB, the Financial Executives Institute (FEI), and the SEC over the SEC's support of a recommendation in an IASC exposure draft that was at variance with US GAAP. It occurred in 1975 and well demonstrates the fervour of a national standard setter to defend its turf from an outside challenger.

In this unusual episode, the IASC's effort to develop and issue even a 'basic' accounting standard led to strong reactions in the United States. In December 1974, the IASC issued E3, 'Consolidated Financial Statements', which implied that all subsidiaries, not excepting the banking, insurance, and finance subsidiaries of industrial parents, be consolidated (*see also* Section 5.5.2). Accounting Research Bulletin No. 51, *Consolidated Financial Statements*, issued in 1959, had countenanced an exception for dissimilar subsidiaries. On 10 June 1975, John C. Burton, the SEC chief accountant, writing to the AICPA on behalf of the Commission, praised the IASC's proposal, saying,

> The principles set forth [in E3] are not inconsistent with generally accepted accounting principles in this country and do reflect what we believe to be preferable accounting practice.... If the International Accounting Standards Committee issues a final statement embodying these principles and if no contrary statement has been issued by the Financial Accounting Standards Board, the Commission will propose for comment amendments to its Regulation S-X which will conform its consolidation rules to those set forth in the statement.[65]

Marshall S. Armstrong, the FASB chairman, upon seeing Burton's letter, protested to Ray Garrett, Jr., the SEC chairman, on behalf of the FASB:

> The Board is greatly concerned about the consequences of the action proposed in that letter.... If carried out, the proposed action could seriously undermine the effectiveness of the Board as a significant factor in the improvement of financial reporting. The organizations sponsoring the Board and their membership may well view the proposed action as circumvention of the Board, the standards-setting group they have pledged to support. The result would be a weakening in the generally recognized authority of the Board to establish accounting standards and more than likely a loss in more financial support for the board.[66]

The FASB was not quite two years old, as was the IASC, when Armstrong wrote the letter.

Two months before Armstrong had written his letter, the FEI, one of the FASB's sponsoring organizations, had expressed anxiety at the possible role of the IASC in influencing US GAAP. The FEI's full-time president, Charles C. Hornbostel, wrote to Philip L. Defliese, chairman of the board of directors of the AICPA, the US signatory of the IASC agreement, as follows:

> We understand consideration has been or is being given to the issuance of a Statement on Auditing Standards which would require disclosure of non-compliance with IASC Standards. Any such requirement or similar recognition of IASC pronouncements would present clients of U.S. accounting firms with potentially serious problems.... Given the circumstances existing in the United States, we think the commitment of the AICPA to support the implementation of IASC standards should be explicitly limited to circumstances where such standards coincide with generally accepted accounting principles in this country, as recognized by the FASB.[67]

Hornbostel's concerns were based on a decision by the AICPA's board of directors in December 1974,

> to recommend to the Auditing Standards Executive Committee that it consider adopting a standard imposing an obligation on auditors either to require disclosure or to disclose in their opinions noncompliance with pronouncements of the International Accounting Standards Committee in financial reports destined for international use, provided the Financial Accounting Standards Board takes no exception to such action.[68]

In another pre-emptive strike, Hornbostel inserted the following sentence in the 28 May 1975 issue of the *FEI Bulletin*, its membership newsletter: 'Standards promulgated by the IASC which are inconsistent with or beyond the scope of FASB standards cannot be accepted by U.S. enterprises or by their independent accountants.'[69]

In reply to Hornbostel, Defliese assured him that the question of conformity with IASC standards was not on the active agenda of the Institute's Auditing Standards Division. He added, in line with the AICPA's recent response to the IASC's survey,

Where pronouncements of the IASC are significantly different from effective pronouncements (or established practice) in the United States, the AICPA (which no longer has the power to set accounting standards) will urge those organizations involved in setting U.S. standards, principally the Financial Accounting Standards Board, to give early consideration to such differences with a view to achieving, to the extent practicable, harmonization of those areas in which a significant difference exists.[70]

This reply satisfied Hornbostel,[71] but just before answering Defliese's letter he had written to SEC Chairman Garrett, endorsing the position expressed in Armstrong's letter, and added:

The transition from a general proposition that the need for international standards has wide support to specific statements and proposed actions to support the IASC, as indicated in the June 10 letter [from Burton], fails to comprehend the fact that the IASC is an unsanctioned body with little general acceptance by its constituency. On the contrary, due to IASC operating methods, there is strong evidence that the initial support for the Committee has decreased.[72]

Although Henry Benson, the IASC's chairman, had not been copied on Hornbostel's letter to Garrett, a copy of the letter came to his attention, and he pointed out in a letter to Garrett, with copies sent to Hornbostel and Armstrong (among others), that the IASC's Agreement and Constitution was 'signed by and on behalf of sixteen of the leading professional accountancy bodies of the world' and that twenty-three other accountancy bodies had since endorsed the agreement.[73] He took issue with the assertion that the IASC was an 'unsanctioned body'. In his letter, Benson also defended the IASC's operating methods.

In his reply to Armstrong, SEC Chairman Garrett wrote as follows:

It seems clear that all efforts at an international level cannot be expected to adopt an American solution. It seems even clearer that proposed solutions at such a level may be considered for possible adoption [in the US] without upsetting the authority of the Board when the Board has not yet decided to deal with the issue. In this regard we believe that there is enough work for everybody and that efforts by both bodies can be combined to the benefit of world capital markets in general and U.S. shareholders in particular without jeopardizing the authority of either body.[74]

Armstrong and his FASB colleagues would not have been pleased with this advice from the SEC chairman, as they probably had believed that the IASC would not be competing with the board for primacy in setting US accounting standards.

In the same letter, Garrett revealed the SEC's strong interest in the international harmonization of accounting standards[75] and its support of the IASC:

The Commission believes that the articulation of meaningful international accounting and disclosure standards is a matter of great importance in improving international capital markets. We are witnessing an influx of foreign registrants at the Commission and the adoption of international standards will achieve improved comparability in an environment which is currently riddled with exceptions. We therefore have viewed with great favor the development of the IASC and our letter [of 10 June] was designed to express our support for their international objectives.

Garrett replied to the FEI as follows, supporting the position espoused by Benson:

Inasmuch as the leading professional accounting organizations of most major free-world countries have formally agreed to make their best effort to support the work of the IASC, it is far from evident that the IASC lacks standing although it is equally evident that the nature of that standing has not been determined in detail at this time. Accordingly, we are not prepared to conclude that the IASC is an unsanctioned body nor that it has little general acceptance by the international financial community.[76]

AICPA Chairman Defliese, who was a partner in Coopers & Lybrand (Benson's firm), advised Benson that the reaction by the major accountancy firms and by industry to the SEC chief accountant's letter of 10 June 1975 'has been quite unfavorable from all directions'. But he added that, while he himself had originally been in favour of full consolidated statements 'from a theoretical point of view', he now believed that the inclusion of banks, insurance companies, and finance companies 'would be undesirable because from a practical standpoint, the resources of these companies are not readily available to the consolidated group, and their debts are usually not assessible against the group. In my view, consolidated accounts infer such availability.'[77] It would seem as if Defliese and his firm had heard from some of their clients.

In the end, the IASC modified its final statement, IAS 3, issued in June 1976, to provide that 'A subsidiary may be excluded from consolidation if its activities are so dissimilar from those of the other companies in the group that better information for the parent company shareholders and other users of the statements would be provided by presenting separate financial statements in respect of such subsidiary' (paragraph 37). In a letter to Robert Sempier dated 19 December 1975, Chief Accountant Burton expressed his disappointment with the changes reflected in the final standard.

This episode may have served to sensitize the FASB, the SEC, the major accountancy firms, and the FEI to the possible implications for US GAAP of the AICPA's best endeavours agreement with the IASC.

6.6.3. Criticism of the IASC by Two US Big Eight Accountancy Firms

Early in 1975, both Price Waterhouse & Co. (PW) and the chairman of Arthur Andersen & Co. warned that the IASC's standards would not be well received in the United States. A third firm, Touche Ross & Co., worried over the proliferation of standard setters.[78] Under the title 'One Cook Too Many?' the editor of PW's newsletter asserted that any requirement for US companies to disclose departures from IASC standards 'would be so disruptive and unpopular with business and the profession alike as to be unenforceable.... Even if conflicts [between

IASC and FASB standards] do not arise, we will resist strongly any attempt in this country to require disclosure of departures from IASC pronouncements.'[79] Harvey E. Kapnick, the Andersen chairman, said in a speech on 2 May 1975 that, once the IASC begins issuing standards that differ from US requirements, 'Utter chaos will occur. Why? Because business will start to react with horror at how such new requirements could be established without their knowledge and participation.... How can one person [in the US delegation] represent all of the diverse business, professional and governmental interests in this country?'[80]

Like the FEI's Hornbostel in his letter to AICPA Chairman Defliese, they both were probably reacting to the suggestion by the AICPA's board of directors in December 1974 of an auditing standard requiring an opinion on compliance with International Accounting Standards. In the event, no such auditing standard was ever issued. Instead, on 24 July 1975, the AICPA's board of directors reacted to the controversy, recited above, over the IASC's exposure draft on consolidated financial statements. It proceeded to tone down its support for IASC standards by formally resolving—as the AICPA had already written to the IASC and to Hornbostel—that 'To achieve acceptance of international accounting standards in the United States will require their specific adoption by the Financial Accounting Standards Board.... If there is a significant difference between [an IASC standard and US practice], the Institute will urge the FASB to give early consideration to such difference with a view to achieving harmonization of those areas in which the difference exists.'[81] Such was the intensity of concern over the prospect of an auditing standard on the disclosure of non-compliance with IASC standards that 'The heads of major CPA firms discussed the [AICPA] resolution... and agreed to support it and future activities of the IASC, provided it continues along the moderate path it seems to be currently following.'[82] The AICPA's modified position was apparently enough to satisfy the critics, and shortly afterwards Defliese could write to John Grenside that 'All major firm leaders agreed to refrain from publicly opposing the aims of IASC.' To Benson, Defliese wrote: 'This is the best that can be done at the moment, at least until we can persuade the FASB to become more involved with IASC.'[83] But, as was noted above, the FASB in 1975 did not evince much interest in international harmonization.

By 1986, however, Arthur Andersen & Co.'s Public Review Board did not merely refrain from criticism, but opined that 'It is desirable for the standard-setting bodies in individual countries to work closely with IASC as they develop the standards applicable in their countries.' It added that 'Another positive role for the IASC may be to serve as codifier of the best of present international practices.'[84] Hence, the view coming from Arthur Andersen & Co. had changed, perhaps influenced by the IASC's record of progress since 1975.

6.6.4. Approaches to the FASB Relating to IASC Standards

The IASC's first official contact with the FASB was on 23 March 1976, when Alec Mackenzie, who was chairing a special steering committee on the organization and structure of the IASC (*see* Section 4.14), met in the FASB's offices with two staff members and had lunch with the members of the board. Mackenzie reported that FASB Chairman Marshall Armstrong had said, 'As regards the problem of reconciling domestic and international standards his approach was "conference and not confrontation".'[85] Nonetheless, Henry P. Hill, a senior technical partner at Price Waterhouse & Co., could say in May 1976 that 'The FASB has made no pledge to support [the IASC's] pronouncements as has the AICPA, and has been unwilling to subordinate its agenda priorities to those of the IASC.'[86]

Yet the wheels began turning at the FASB and at the AICPA in 1976. In November 1976, the FASB's director of research and technical activities performed an analysis for the board of the differences between US GAAP and IASC standards 1–5 and IASC exposure drafts 6–8. In July 1977, William P. Hauworth, II, the chairman of the AICPA's international technical standards subcommittee (which regularly met with the US delegation to the IASC board), dutifully wrote a four-page letter to the FASB, reciting the differences between US GAAP and IASC standards 1–6, and asked the board to consider taking steps with a view towards harmonizing the differences.[87] Following a meeting in November 1977 between FASB and IASC representatives, FASB Chairman Armstrong sent a constructive reply to Hauworth on 9 December 1977, saying that the meeting was helpful and that the positions reflected in IASC standards 1–6 'and the underlying reasoning will be considered whenever the Board undertakes a project in which those positions are relevant'. As reported in the FASB's newsletter, however, the purport of Armstrong's letter was to decline to take any action on the differences.[88]

6.6.5. FASB's Ambivalence towards International Standards under Kirk

Donald J. Kirk, who succeeded Armstrong as FASB chairman in January 1978, seemed to be less interested than even Armstrong in the work of the IASC. In the next several years, the IASC was rarely mentioned in *Status Report*, the FASB's newsletter. Yet in 1979, the FASB did name an IASC representative, probably the first such appointment, to be an observer on its advisory task force on foreign currency translation (*see* Section 5.9.2).[89] Also in 1979, Donald J. Hayes, an Arthur Young & Company partner who had joined the US delegation to the IASC board in 1978, was named to the FASB's advisory council. It is not known if this was a coincidence or an endeavour to open a line of communication.

In 1981, when the IASC issued E21, 'Accounting for Government Grants and Disclosure of Government Assistance', the AICPA's international technical standards subcommittee 'urged the FASB to address the topic and to issue a pronouncement similar to any final IASC standard'. But the FASB decided that any possible differences with US GAAP did not justify adding the subject to its agenda (*see also* Section 5.13.1).

So long as, in Kirk's perception, the SEC, to which the FASB looked for the enforcement of its standards, had not marked out 'international' as an important issue for the board to take up, Kirk and his board colleagues concentrated on producing standards for domestic use. In an interview in late 1983, he said, with finality,

We have our plate full with the problems just in this country. I personally am very pessimistic about any super-national [sic] standard setting. It's just beyond my term of office, that's for sure, and I'll leave that to my successor to struggle with.[90]

Cairns, Lafferty, and Mantle—two Britons and an Irishman—have remarked, 'The American coolness [towards the IASC] is, perhaps, understandable given the frequently parochial attitude of companies and standard setters in the United States.'[91] On the other hand, one could argue that, as the differences between US GAAP and the early IASC standards were largely inconsequential, there was little reason for the FASB to attend to the deliberations of the IASC board. This was the task of the AICPA's delegates to the board.

Kirk's view was not shared by all of the members of the FASB. One of his colleagues on the board, Ralph E. Walters, a former partner in Touche Ross & Co. and an FASB member since 1978, complained in 1984 that 'The FASB's attitude toward the IASC has been a mixture of unofficial encouragement, moral support, and benign neglect.... International harmonization has a low priority at the FASB.'[92] In reply, Kirk wrote, 'Because of legal requirements and the expectations of the American community, the FASB must concentrate on its mission to develop standards for entities that issue financial reports in accordance with generally accepted accounting principles in the U.S.... It would be awkward at [the] least, in view of the FASB's responsibilities in the U.S., for the Board to participate in setting standards that inevitably would differ in important respects from our own standards.'[93]

A reason for Kirk's reluctance to become involved at that time with the work of the IASC might well have been his anxiety over the criticisms in the United States of the slow progress of the FASB in addressing issues. These criticisms led to reform measures taken in 1977 by the board of trustees of the foundation overseeing the FASB. Kirk, therefore, would have been preoccupied with the need for the FASB to demonstrate the effectiveness of its new procedures.[94]

A search of the annual reports of the FASB and of its advisory council from 1973 onwards shows that their first reference to the IASC did not appear until 1985. This mention in 1985 related to the FASB's participation with the IASC at a major OECD forum on international harmonization (*see* Section 7.2), as well as to recent instances of liaison between the two bodies at the FASB's offices in Stamford, Connecticut. At the forum, Kirk gave a talk in which he did not seem to foresee a day when the FASB might reconsider one of its standards in the light of an IASC standard.[95] One participant recalled Kirk's speech as 'probably the most negative about the IASC by any national standards setter at that symposium'.[96]

Interestingly, FASB Vice-Chairman Robert T. Sprouse served on an informal IASC working party beginning in 1982 to enable the standard setters in the United States, United Kingdom, and the Netherlands 'to seek a common approach' to accounting for deferred income tax.[97] The working party's report, completed in 1984, would, it was decided, 'be taken into account' when IAS 12 is reviewed (*see* Section 11.4).[98]

6.7. AUSTRALIA

In Australia, the Councils of the Institute of Chartered Accountants in Australia and the Australian Society of Accountants (known today as CPA Australia), the sponsors of the Australian delegation to the IASC board, jointly promulgated Statements of Accounting Standards (each known as an AAS). The Councils' general policy beginning in 1976 and continuing into the 1980s was that the two bodies' members should refer only to Australian standards in company annual reports, but there was an exception, noted below. Conformity with Australian standards was presumed to imply compliance with IASC standards.

The essential position of the two Councils was that IASC standards not conforming to Australian standards would be referred to the two bodies' drafting committee for its consideration. Each AAS would disclose how it compared with the corresponding IASC standard.[99] When an IASC standard did not conform to an AAS, and the Councils concluded that the former was not appropriate for Australian practice, auditors were expected to disclose a departure from the IASC standard at the same time as affirming adherence to the AAS. The Councils reached such a conclusion only once: when AAS 13, on research and development costs, was issued in 1983, they stated that 'IAS 9 is not appropriate for Australian practice at the present time'. In the addendum to a number of other Australian Standards, substantive differences with the corresponding IASC standard were duly noted.

Yet an active participant in Australian standard setting has advised, 'I don't ever recall members disclosing departures from IASs prior to 1987, nor do I recall the local standard setting body modifying its standards because of differences with IASs'.[100] It has been suggested by some that the Councils really did not contemplate that auditors would need to disclose deviations from IASC standards.[101] None of the stock exchanges or state registrars of companies had taken a position on IASC standards, and Australia did not then have a securities commission.

In the IASC's 1988 survey of the use and application of its standards, Australia replied that sixteen of the IASC's extant standards conformed to national requirements, while seven dealt with topics on which there were no national requirements but nonetheless agreed with practice, and two did not agree with practice in areas where there were no national requirements.[102] Curiously, Australia affirmed that the national requirement on research and development costs conformed, in all material respects, to the corresponding IASC standard.

6.8. CANADA

In the 1970s, Canadian accounting principles came under explicit government regulation. In December 1972, Canada's provincial securities commissions announced that they would recognize the Canadian Institute of Chartered Accountants' (CICA) accounting Recommendations as constituting 'generally accepted accounting principles' (GAAP) when applying the terms of provincial laws and regulations.[103] By 1987, this policy that the CICA's accounting Recommendations would constitute GAAP in Canada had been endorsed in Regulation 44 under the Canada Business Corporations Act 1975 (for federally chartered corporations) and by the Corporations or Securities Acts in eight of the ten provinces.[104] Hence, this legal authority conferred on the CICA's accounting Recommendations meant that, for IASC standards to find legal acceptance in Canada, they had to be incorporated in the pronouncements issued by the CICA. This meant that the CICA was the only one of the IASC's founder members which had the legal authority to shape its national GAAP, and therefore could have acted to incorporate IASC standards into Canadian practice.

By 1977, the CICA had established an elaborate process for dealing with new IASC projects and exposure drafts, which could lead either to changes in its accounting Recommendations or in the advice given to the Canadian representatives on the IASC board.[105] Indeed, in the late 1970s and into the 1980s the CICA's Accounting Research Committee (renamed the Accounting Standards Committee in 1982) 'streamed' the drafts on a few of its standards projects with comparable IASC exposure drafts so as to minimize differences between the two, as far as practicable.[106] An example was the impact of the IASC's E9, on research and development costs, on Canadian GAAP. Even before E9, issued in February 1977, led to the publication in 1979 of IAS 9, the CICA's Accounting Research Committee incorporated the essence of E9's paragraph 18 on the criteria to be met for capitalizing certain development costs in its accounting Recommendation, issued in August 1978. E9's paragraph 18 was equivalent to IAS 9's paragraph 17. Another example was IAS 18, *Revenue Recognition*, upon which the CICA said it drew 'extensively' in the preparation of its own exposure draft on Revenue in 1985.[107] In 1984, the CICA issued a loose-leaf publication that, with periodic supplements, compared IASC standards with Canadian GAAP.[108]

As suggested above, the CICA's accounting staff was in touch with the Canadian delegation to the IASC board to ask that it try to remove any incompatibilities between evolving IASC standards and Canadian GAAP.[109] The active attempt to align Canadian GAAP with the IASC standards would have been welcome to the IASC, but it could also be yet another source of the 'free choices' that populated quite a few of IASC's standards, as Paul Rutteman suggested earlier in the case of the United Kingdom. This was most notably the case with the deferral and amortization of foreign currency gains and losses on long-term debt.

Moreover, in December 1975, the CICA's Accounting Research Committee issued guidance to the effect that, for companies reporting 'in an international environment, it is desirable... that they disclose conformity with or identify deviations from' IASC standards.[110] But this action did not lead to any actual disclosures in company annual reports.[111] The provincial institutes, not the CICA, were, and are, responsible for enforcing the Rules of Professional Conduct.

By 1980, the view was held within the IASC that compliance with IASC standards needed strengthening, and the board resolved in June 1980 that the member bodies should contact multinational companies and urge them to disclose compliance with the IASC's standards.[112] Of all the members, the CICA was the most active, and the most successful, in carrying out this resolution. In November 1980, Stephen Elliott and Douglas R. Hagerman, the members of the Canadian delegation to the IASC board, wrote to the CEOs of companies in the Toronto Stock Exchange's 300 Index, asking them to support the IASC by referring to its standards in their annual report. Annually thereafter, until at least 1987, the Exchange's president and CEO wrote a similar letter to the CEOs of listed companies.[113] It was reported in 1988 that the chairman of the ASC 'also writes to the senior partners of all major accounting firms urging them to encourage their audit clients to comply with International Accounting Standards and disclose the fact of such compliance in their financial statements'.[114] As a result of these initiatives, the CICA reported that ninety-two companies in 1981 and 105 companies in 1982 referred to IASC standards in their annual report to shareholders.[115] The CICA's biennial survey of 325 companies' financial statements reported that only a few of these companies signified a departure from IASC standards.[116] In 1987, Canada reported that 102 out of a sample of 129 of the larger Canadian companies listed on the Toronto Stock Exchange reported compliance with IASC standards in their 1986 annual report.[117] No other country matched Canada's record in persuading domestic companies to refer to their compliance with IASC standards in their annual report to shareholders. Of course, as borne out in the IASC's 1988 survey of the use and application of its standards, IASC standards largely conformed to national requirements; hence, a company's reference to IASC standards came at a low cost.[118]

6.9. FRANCE

Between 1973 and the mid-1980s, efforts to further the cause of IASC standards in France were a part of wider moves to redefine and modernize French accounting. Traditionally, accounting had been seen primarily in terms of its legal functions concerning dividends and taxes, and in terms of generating statistics for government use. Gradually, however, the emphasis was shifted to providing information for investors. An early sign of this development was the creation of a securities regulator, the Commission des Opérations de Bourse (COB), in 1967. From the start, the COB emphasized the importance of financial information, for instance by strongly encouraging the publication of consolidated financial statements.[119] The movement continued with revisions of the Plan Comptable in 1979 and 1982, and the accounting laws of 1983 and 1985 implementing the Fourth and Seventh Directives.[120]

In general, the leadership of the Ordre des Experts Comptables et des Comptables Agréés supported the change towards investor-oriented financial reporting, and it saw its participation in the IASC as a means of changing attitudes in France.[121] Robert Mazars, a member of the French IASC delegation, explained in 1976 to an audience of French auditors:

> One of the most interesting contributions of the IASC has been to restore our confidence, of us, Frenchmen, in the role and significance of accounting. The negative attitude towards accounting that we have in France does not exist in most other member countries of the I.A.S.C., and particularly not in the Anglo-Saxon countries where there is great respect for accounting.... What we can conclude is that these [International Accounting Standards] will modify the spirit in which we, in France, all too often look at accounting, that is to say, in a rigid framework, tied to taxation or to the obligations of national accounting and statistics. What is needed is to put accounting back into its natural sphere, which is to provide information on the situation of an enterprise to third parties.[122]

Apart from this educational approach, the Ordre had limited opportunities to promote the use of IASC standards directly. In its reply to the IASC's survey in 1979, the Ordre reported that it had not issued any official statement on the status of IASC standards. Like the domestic documents issued by the Ordre, the international standards were in general considered as recommendations.[123] It might have added that even its own recommendations 'were not very frequently followed'.[124] One reason for this was that statutory audits were not the preserve of the Ordre but of the Compagnie Nationale des Commissaires aux Comptes. The Compagnie was not a signatory of the IASC Agreement and was not represented on the IASC board until 1983. The Ordre therefore focused its attention on the indirect application of IASC standards, by advocating that the legislator adopt the standards or at least their essentials in law or in the ongoing project to revise the Plan Comptable.[125] The 'legislator' in this case was the Conseil National de la Comptabilité (CNC, National Accounting Council), the standard-setting body affiliated with the French Ministry of Economics and Finance. In 1976, it was reported that the CNC, 'accepted the need to study the first five International Accounting Standards with a view to identifying differences with the national Plan Comptable'.[126]

The Ordre had an ally in the COB which was sympathetic to the aims of the IASC.[127] Like the Ordre, the COB also had limited power to set reporting requirements, and had to rely mainly on persuasion.[128] In 1976, the COB declared its support for the work of the IASC, and, referring to IAS 1, *Disclosure of Accounting Policies*, issued in January 1975, counselled that a 'positive attitude by French companies is desirable'.[129] *World Accounting Report* said that the COB reminded French accountants that 'They are now required to refer in their audit reports to any departures from IASC standards', and that 'It will attentively observe the manner in which IAS 1 is applied in 1976.'[130] In 1979, the Price Waterhouse International survey report said that the COB 'has recommended compliance with IASC Standards but at present the Commission does not insist on disclosure of departures from certain of these standards. The degree of compliance was weak at first but is strengthening.'[131]

Apart from limitations to its formal powers, the Ordre had to contend with a sceptical attitude among both auditors and companies. A significant issue was that the IASC was clearly seen as an Anglo-American body. This was admitted, for instance by Mazars, who tried to present the fact in a positive light. He pointed out that it was useful to take a different angle to familiar accounting issues, and that, after all, France had arrived on the scene rather late so that it would be 'absurd' not to profit from the experience of Anglo-American standard setters.[132]

The notion of Anglo-American domination was always present as a potential source of irritation, although the Ordre 'accepted the principle that we were playing a game where we were clearly a minority'.[133] The issue flared up in 1980, when both the COB and the Ordre publicly criticized the IASC. As discussed more fully in Section 5.9.2, the Ordre was offended by the fact that a working party formed by Canada, the United Kingdom, and the United States had worked out a common approach to foreign currency translation, and in particular that considerable publicity had been given to the result before it had been discussed within the IASC. Referring to this development, Dominique Ledouble, the secretary of the Ordre, publicly called into question whether the IASC should continue to exist.[134]

In July 1980, the monthly bulletin of the COB contained an overview of international efforts to harmonize financial reporting.[135] After discussing the efforts by the United Nations (UN), the OECD, and the European Economic Community (EEC) as the most important initiatives, the unsigned article turned to the IASC. It commented on the 'very unequal' effectiveness of its standards across countries, and construed the IASC's 1979 survey as a recognition by the IASC that it had a serious compliance problem. As a diagnosis, the article observed that 'While, moreover, the harmonisation sought is very much impregnated with American methods and ideas, sharply different from those that are current in the majority of European countries, difficulties are inevitable.' In order to prevent the gradual global imposition of US accounting standards through the mechanism of the IASC, the EEC member states were called upon to develop a 'European model of company accounts' so that the IASC could limit itself to the task of developing a system of reconciliations between the US and European systems.

Exactly why the COB and the Ordre chose to take a critical attitude towards the IASC at this time is not clear. Playing to the domestic political galleries may have been part of the explanation.[136] It should also be borne in mind that the legitimacy of the IASC was quite widely challenged around 1980, not just in France (*see* Chapter 7). But perhaps it is best to see these incidents, which in the end did not affect the relations between the Ordre and the IASC, as not significant in themselves. Rather, they might be seen as indications of regained confidence in French accounting, a belief that France had learned the lessons that needed to be learned from abroad, and that the French institutional framework was now capable of producing high-quality, informative accounting on its own.[137]

This attitude is shown most clearly on the subject of consolidated financial statements, where, it was said, France could pride itself on rapidly having closed a wide gap.[138] In October 1983, the French accountancy bodies held a seminar on consolidated financial statements to coincide with a meeting of the IASC board in Paris, so that all of the board members could attend.[139] While the timing of the seminar was a sign that relations between the French profession and the IASC were cordial enough, the seminar also made it evident that the IASC had had relatively little impact on French financial reporting. Despite IAS 3 (issued in 1976), approximately 25 per cent of listed companies did not publish consolidated statements in their annual reports by 1983. Moreover, the substantial rise in consolidated reporting that had taken place over the previous decade was attributed to the influence of the COB rather than to the IASC.[140] Until 1985, when the Seventh Directive on group accounts was adapted into French law, there was no legal requirement to publish consolidated financial statements. The CNC's president, Jean Dupont, acknowledged later in 1983 that the CNC 'prepares comparisons between International Accounting Standards and French Accounting Law with a view to harmonisation'.[141] But the CNC did, in the end, prefer to make up its own mind. It had never issued an 'opinion of conformity' as between the Plan Comptable and IAS 3, and there was no doubt that it was the Seventh Directive rather than IAS 3 that shaped the French law on consolidation.[142]

By the mid-1980s, the situation in France might be characterized as one of mild interest in the IASC. There was little coverage in the literature, but there were some signs that companies were beginning to apply IASC standards.[143] In 1984, the international accountancy firm of Ernst & Whinney reported that 'multinational groups follow US GAAP or IASC standards while medium-sized groups generally have a preference for the 1968 recommendations of the CNC.'[144] In 1986, it was reported that an increasing number of French companies, including the recently denationalized Saint-Gobain, were publishing consolidated statements that disclose conformity with IASC standards.[145] In the IASC's 1988 survey of the use and application of its standards, France replied that national requirements accord with eighteen of the then extant IASC standards, while three of the standards are ones on which there are no national requirements but agree with practice, three do not correspond with national requirements or practice, and one differs from national requirements.[146]

6.10. GERMANY

Early in 1975, when the IASC's first standard had just been published, it was already pointed out that the Institut der Wirtschaftsprüfer (IdW) and the Wirtschaftsprüferkammer, the two German bodies that appointed the delegation to the IASC board, had very little scope for using their best endeavours to promote the application of IASC standards. Hans Havermann, the German delegation's staff observer, wrote that it had to be expected that the IASC's standards would depart in 'not a few' respects from German law and practice. But, he added, 'There can be no doubt that in such cases of collision, national rules take precedence over IASC standards.' It was true, Havermann conceded, that the IdW was bound by the IASC's Constitution to encourage German auditors to mention departures from IASC standards in their report, but as the wording of published audit reports and the reasons for issuing modified reports were closely circumscribed by law, non-compliance with IASC standards could in practice only be reported in the management letter.[147] Perhaps because of this expectation of limited practical significance, interest in the IASC in Germany was not strong, and Havermann called on his colleagues to increase the apparently disappointing number of comment letters on IASC exposure drafts written from Germany.[148] Yet the IdW itself was also slow to draw attention to the IASC in its comprehensive annual reference work, the *Wirtschaftsprüferhandbuch*. The first reference to the IASC did not appear until the 1977 edition, and it was only from 1981 onwards that a section on the IASC and its standards was included on a regular basis.[149]

In 1978, Havermann reported that the German business world had 'not at all responded to the IASC and its standards with enthusiasm or unconditional approval'. According to Havermann, businesses were not prepared to accept standards produced in a process in which they were not represented. The possibility of commenting on exposure drafts did not make up for this deficiency, and therefore German enterprises had sent in only very few comment letters.[150] But this procedural objection may merely have been a symptom of a more general lack of interest. From 1983 onwards, the German IASC member bodies left one of the two seats in their delegation vacant as a standing invitation to send an industry representative. The offer was not taken up, however, until 1993.[151]

While the reporting companies were not responsive, the IdW and the Wirtschaftsprüferkammer also had to report in their reply to the IASC survey in 1979 that their best endeavours to persuade the authorities that published financial statements should comply with IASC standards had been without success so far. The two bodies said that 'The German stock exchange is not inclined to advocate unilaterally on the national level compliance with IASC Standards. They would, however, prefer if this question could be resolved also by the stock exchanges in the international field', that is, by the FIBV. Evidently, the German stock exchange did not regard the FIBV's resolution of October 1974 (*see* Section 6.2) as sufficiently authoritative.[152]

In short, despite the IdW's efforts, the IASC's standards were seen by many in Germany as 'merely of a theoretical nature'.[153] During the first half of the 1980s, as measured by coverage in the professional journals, interest in the IASC ran at a very low level. This situation lasted as long as the legal framework imposed tight restrictions on the applicability of international standards.[154] In the IASC's 1988 survey of the use and application of its standards, Germany was the 'extreme value', as it reported that seventeen of the twenty-five extant IASC standards conflicted with its national requirements.[155] Germany was the only founder member of the IASC to report that none of the financial statements of listed enterprises conformed, in all material respects, to IASC standards. Thirty-three of the thirty-seven other responding countries with stock exchanges reported that 'all or most' listed companies, or 'a majority' of listed companies, conformed.[156] One is inclined to discount this comparatively unfavourable picture of Germany; it seems likely that the other member bodies, when formulating their replies to the IASC's surveys, may not have taken as strict a view of compliance as the IdW.

6.11. JAPAN

In June 1976, the Business Accounting Deliberation Council, an advisory body to the Ministry of Finance, issued a Financial Accounting Standard on consolidated financial statements which, it was said, 'takes into consideration the requirements of International Accounting Standard No. 3, "*Consolidated Financial Statements*"'.[157] However, the pressing need to enable Japanese companies to list in New York, where consolidated statements were required, and to allow US multinationals to list on the Tokyo Stock Exchange by publishing consolidated statements, which were previously illegal in Japan, was a much more powerful influence on this development than was IAS 3.[158]

In its reply to the IASC's survey in 1975, the Japanese Institute of Certified Public Accountants (JICPA) said that it had established a special committee 'to discuss and to advise on problems related to IASC, and has been very active in every aspect of its service'.[159] When departures from IASC standards come to the Institute's attention, it would send a letter to the member who served as the company's auditor.

In its reply to the IASC's survey in 1979, the JICPA reported that the Tokyo Stock Exchange had amended its listing requirements on 28 February 1979 to allow foreign companies to prepare their financial statements on the basis of IASC standards instead of in accordance with Japanese regulations.[160]

In 1985, Sasebo Heavy Industries Co., a major shipbuilding and marine engineering company, included a disclosure in its annual report which was written in English and prepared for users abroad that its consolidated statements were in conformity with IASC standards. Sasebo appears to have been the first Japanese company to apply IASC standards in its English language financial statements. In 1985, the JICPA affirmed that it had issued a report on the differences between the first twenty-one IASC standards and Japanese GAAP 'together with proposals for the adoption of International Accounting Standards'. It was affirmed that the JICPA's ASC had been active in promoting the acceptance of IASC standards in Japan.[161]

In the IASC's 1988 survey of the use and application of its standards, Japan replied that its national requirements conformed to the extant IASC standards on seventeen issues but that five of the standards differed from national requirements, and three corresponded with practice but were on topics on which there were no national requirements.[162]

As late as 1991, Campbell wrote, 'Although Japan is represented on the International Accounting Standards Committee (IASC), the latter is considered to have had little influence on Japanese financial reporting. The primary reason for this is that the IASC seeks to implement its standards through the efforts of the national professional accounting bodies and, as mentioned earlier, the JICPA has a relatively weak influence on the standard-setting process in Japan.'[163]

6.12. MEXICO

In 1975, the Instituto Mexicano de Contadores Públicos (Mexican Institute of Public Accountants) reported that it had created an ad hoc committee to study the status of IASC standards in relation to the Institute's requirement that its members comply with Mexican accounting pronouncements. The Bolsa de Valores de México (Mexico Stock Exchange) had already acted to require listed companies to comply with the Institute's pronouncements, and the Institute added, 'If and when IAS's have equal force as Mexican pronouncements, departures observed would be communicated to the Exchange'. As with the Canadian provincial institutes, disciplinary action against auditors breaching the code of conduct was, and is, taken by the affiliated *colegios* around the country, not by the Institute.[164]

In 1979, the Institute reported that its approach was gradually to eliminate the differences between Mexican GAAP and IASC standards, and that its representative on the IASC board met regularly with a subcommittee of the Institute's accounting principles committee to discuss the drafts. In general, the Institute said that its disclosure requirements were not as ample as those of the IASC, but there was, with a few exceptions, a compatibility between the Mexican pronouncements and IASC standards.[165]

Mexico replied to the IASC's 1988 survey of the use and application of its standards that nine of the extant IASC standards conformed to national requirements, yet ten differed from national requirements; three were on topics for which there were no national requirements, but they nonetheless agreed with practice, and three were at odds with national requirements and practice.[166] Mexico replied that only a 'majority', not 'all or most' of the financial statements of enterprises listed on the country's stock exchange generally conformed in all material respects to IASC standards.[167]

6.13. THE NETHERLANDS

In 1976, the management board of the Nederlands Instituut van Registeraccountants (NIVRA, Dutch Institute of Registered Auditors) boldly announced a procedure by which IASC standards would become binding in the Netherlands. The first step in the procedure would be adoption of a standard by the Tripartiete Overleg (TSG, Tripartite Study Group), an independent body composed of representatives of financial statement preparers, auditors, and users. The NIVRA contributed the delegation of auditors to the TSG. Henk Volten, the long-time staff observer of the Dutch delegation to the IASC board, wrote, 'In 1977, the Tripartite Study Group stated publicly that it was of the opinion that IAS 1 through 6 conformed with Dutch regulations as comprised in the law or in the *Considerations* [the TSG's guidance statements]; later IAS 7 through 12 were also deemed acceptable.'[168] The second step in the procedure was acceptance by the NIVRA itself. The NIVRA would 'accept' IASC standards only after they had been found to be acceptable by the TSG or its successor, the Raad voor de Jaarverslaggeving (CAR, Council on Annual Reporting).

The Amsterdam Stock Exchange had been one of the sponsors of the FIBV's 1974 resolution, discussed above, but the Exchange required several years to give effect to it. In August 1978, the Exchange amended its rules to require listed companies to prepare their financial statements in conformity with IASC standards to the extent that they had been accepted by the NIVRA.[169] By July 1983, when the Stock Exchange rescinded this requirement (very much as the London Stock Exchange had done four years earlier), the NIVRA had not formally accepted any of the IASC's standards.[170] In fact, the NIVRA never did accept any IASC standards. Instead, beginning in 1980, the TSG and then the CAR regularly disclosed which IASC standards were at variance with their recommendations.[171] They also reviewed their own recommendations, where appropriate, to bring them into line with the IASC standards. In the IASC's 1988 survey of the use and application of its standards, the Netherlands replied that sixteen of the extant IASC standards conform to national requirements, but that three IASC standards are ones on which there are no national requirements but nonetheless agree with practice, and four do not conform to national requirements.[172]

Hans Burggraaff and Jan Uiterlinden, both members of the Dutch delegation to the IASC board, persuaded a very limited number of Dutch companies to state in their annual report that they complied with IASC standards. But Royal Dutch/Shell would not agree to do so, because, so it was said, it wanted its annual report to be comparable with those of the important sisters in the oil industry, all of which were using US GAAP.[173]

In its survey of the annual accounts of 120 quoted companies for 1981, the NIVRA found only four references to IASC standards.[174] In each of two subsequent surveys covering 1984 and 1986, only one company out of 120 was found to refer to IASC standards.[175] The NIVRA had taken no steps to oblige auditors to disclose departures from, let alone follow, the recommendations issued by the TSG and the CAR. As a result, references to these national recommendations in companies' annual reports were almost as scarce as those to IASC standards.

In 1984, the NIVRA announced that it would no longer prepare translations of IASC exposure drafts and would no longer print both the IASC's exposure drafts and standards in its journal because of its cost and because 'A lack of interest was indicated by a strongly decreased number of reactions from individual members and firms to international exposure drafts.'[176]

In 1986, the Dutch government introduced a minor reference to IASC standards into Dutch law.[177] The European Seventh Directive (1983) on consolidated financial statements included an exemption for intermediate holding companies. These did not have to prepare consolidated financial statements provided that, among other things, the ultimate parent company prepared consolidated financial statements in accordance with the Seventh Directive. In a 1986 legal interpretation, the Dutch government expanded the coverage of this clause to parent companies from outside the European Community and declared that, for the purpose of applying this clause, IASC standards were seen as equivalent to the Seventh Directive. The Dutch board member Herman Marseille had been instrumental in preparing this policy, and when the IASC board was informed in March 1986, it congratulated the NIVRA 'on its achievements in this respect'.[178] David Cairns made sure the new Dutch policy was prominently reported in *IASC News*.[179] The European Commission, however, was not pleased. As is discussed in Section 12.3.1, by 1986 it was not yet prepared to recognize the IASC as a body of equal standing. Nor did it want member states to develop their own policies in this respect. The Commission put considerable pressure on the Dutch government, including the threat of legal action.[180] The Dutch government therefore rescinded the decree in 1988, citing as the main reason that virtually all of the differences between the Seventh Directive and the IASC's standards on consolidation had been eliminated, so that there was no need for an additional interpretation.[181]

6.14. NIGERIA

The Institute of Chartered Accountants of Nigeria became an associate member of the IASC in 1976 and was a member of the IASC board from 1978 to 1987. In its 1979 reply to the IASC survey, the Institute reported that it had not issued standards but instead adopted IASC standards. It added that it had directed its members to observe these standards.[182] On the initiative of the Institute, the independent Nigerian Accounting Standards Board (NASB) was set up in 1982, and IASC standards were, together with those of a number of countries, examined by the board when it drafted its standards. By 1987, the NASB had issued six standards, which were said to conform to the corresponding IASC standards. The NASB had no means for securing compliance with its standards, and it appeared that the general level of compliance was low.[183]

The first chairman of the NASB, from 1982 to 1985, was Adedoyin Ogunde, who served in the Nigerian delegation to the IASC board from 1979 to 1983. Ogunde's successor as NASB chairman was Oyeniyi Oyediran, who served on the IASC board from 1979 to 1982.[184] Hence, the NASB was well connected with the work of the IASC.

In the IASC's 1988 survey of the use and application of its standards, Nigeria replied that five IASC standards had been used as the basis for national requirements, and it ventured the view, perhaps a shade hopefully, that, for thirteen of the extant IASC standards, there were no national requirements but that national practice generally conformed with the standards.[185]

6.15. SOUTH AFRICA

The National Council of Chartered Accountants (SA) became an associate member of the IASC in 1974 and joined the IASC board in 1978. It was stated in 1975 that, to carry out its best endeavours, the National Council anticipated that, 'Although the development, exposure and acceptance of [the Accounting Practices Committee's and Accounting Practices Board's] statements will continue as before, they will, so far as practicable, be developed in parallel with those of the IASC.'[186]

In its reply to the IASC's survey in 1979, the National Council reported that IASC standards were compatible, with only a few exceptions, with South African accounting pronouncements. The Companies Act 1973 stipulated that financial statements shall be prepared 'in conformity with generally accepted accounting practice'. The Council ventured the view that, 'In the absence of a codified domestic standard it is considered that codified International Accounting Standards would constitute persuasive evidence of a "generally accepted accounting practice" unless the preparer could establish otherwise on a domestic basis.'[187] In 1980, the National Council was renamed the South African Institute of Chartered Accountants (SAICA).

In 1984, South African Breweries said in its annual report that its principal accounting policies 'conform in all material respects' to IASC standards. It continued to make this affirmation for at least the next ten years. It was the first major South African company to do so. The company's finance director, Selwyn MacFarlane, a chartered accountant who subsequently became chairman of the Accounting Practices Board and president of SAICA, is credited with giving this early boost to IASC standards in South Africa.[188]

It was reported in 1986 that one of the members of the South African delegation to the IASC board 'personally contacted the senior partners of the major professional firms in South Africa and has impressed upon them the desirability of financial statements making reference to compliance with International Accounting Standards'.[189]

In the IASC's 1988 survey of the use and application of IASC standards, South Africa reported that it had used as many as eight of the twenty-five extant IASC standards as the basis for its national requirements.[190] Like Mexico, South Africa replied that a 'majority', not 'all or most' of the financial statements of enterprises listed on the country's stock exchange generally conformed in all material respects to IASC standards.[191]

6.16. ITALY

The Consiglio Nazionale dei Dottori Commercialisti joined the IASC board in 1983 and remained until 1995.

In 1984, Cairns, Lafferty, and Mantle asserted that 'The IASC's biggest success is in Italy.'[192] This referred to an ordinance issued in April 1982 by the Commissione Nazionale per le Società e la Borsa (Consob, National Commission on Companies and the Stock Exchange), which stipulated: 'In areas where [Italian accounting] standards are incomplete or have yet to be issued, the principles established by the IASC constitute the basic terms of reference for listed companies, unless they clash with Italian law.'[193] This decision by the Italian stock exchange regulatory body represented, until then, the strongest official support for IASC standards in any country.

The Consiglio Nazionale insisted that external auditors refer to IASC standards in their report on companies' statutory financial statements, and it was reported that this practice was being followed.[194]

In its reply to the IASC's 1988 survey of the use and application of its standards, Italy said that fourteen of the extant IASC standards corresponded with national requirements, while two agreed with practice but were not subjects on which there were national requirements, two differed from national requirements, and six were at odds with practice but were not subjects on which there were national requirements. Italy said that IAS 21, *Accounting for the Effects of Changes in Foreign Exchange Rates*, served as the basis for a national requirement.[195] Like Mexico and South Africa, Italy replied that a majority of, not all or most, the financial statements of enterprises listed on the country's stock exchange generally conformed, in all material respects to IASC standards.[196]

6.17. TAIWAN

The National Federation of Certified Public Accountants Associations of the Republic of China became a member of IFAC Council in 1983 and in 1984 began a three-year term as the second accountancy body from East Asia, after Japan, represented on the IASC board.

S. T. Chiang, the lone Taiwanese delegate to the IASC board, reported in 1985 that the IASC was 'little known' in his country prior to the signing of the IASC/IFAC Mutual Commitments pact in October 1982, when the National Federation automatically became a member of the IASC. He continued to report a number of interventions he had made to bring IASC standards very much to the fore in his country.[197]

By 1987, the independent Financial Accounting Standards Committee had issued twelve Statements of Financial Accounting Standards (SFASs), and they have generally conformed to IASC standards.[198] Nonetheless, as borne out in the IASC's 1988 survey of the use and application of its standards, Taiwanese standards

Gaining Recognition 177

had not been issued on most of the subjects taken up in IASC standards. Taiwan replied that ten of the IASC's extant standards conform to its SFASs, but for most of the subjects on which Taiwan had no national requirements, the IASC standards agreed with practice.[199] Like Mexico, South Africa, and Italy, Taiwan replied that a 'majority', not 'all or most' of the financial statements of enterprises listed on the country's stock exchange generally conformed in all material respects to IASC standards.[200]

6.18. DISCUSSION OF SELECTED ASSOCIATE MEMBERS NOT SERVING ON THE IASC BOARD

Several of the early associate members of the IASC actively drew on its standards in their respective countries. Allan Cook, the IASC secretary from 1979 to 1981, has said that some associate members 'showed a huge interest', and he cited Pakistan, India, Singapore, Hong Kong, and especially Malaysia.[201] While many associate members responded to the IASC's series of surveys, these five countries and New Zealand will be treated here. A final observation will be made about the absence, in large measure, of Central and South American countries from the work of the IASC.

6.18.1. Pakistan

The Institute of Chartered Accountants of Pakistan and the Pakistan Institute of Industrial Accountants (now the Institute of Cost and Management Accountants of Pakistan) both became associate members in 1974. They were invited to sponsor a delegation to the IASC board in 1978 but had to withdraw 'due to factors unforeseen at the time they had expressed an interest in joining the Board'.[202] As discussed in Section 4.4, the problem was that the two bodies were unable to raise the significant financial contribution expected from board members.

The two bodies co-sponsored a seminar on International Accounting Standards in May 1976 in Karachi, followed by the publication of articles discussing IAS 1 and IAS 2 in *The Pakistan Accountant*. In a speech at the seminar, the president of the Karachi Stock Exchange confidently predicted that the first two IASC standards 'will receive the approval of our Government, and if necessary, suitable provisions will be introduced in the Companies' Act or Securities & Exchange Ordinance, to make the application of these Standards obligatory'.[203]

The same two bodies held a professional development seminar in January 1980 on IASC standards, at which one speaker said that 'The financial statements of Pakistan companies were now being submitted to international agencies and that for this reason it was essential that they should comply with international accounting standards.'[204]

Pakistan's Companies Ordinance, 1984 required listed companies to follow those IASC standards in their financial statements that were notified for the purpose by the federal Corporate Law Authority.[205] With only three exceptions, all of the IASC's first twenty-four standards were adopted in Pakistan.[206]

The Pakistan Accountant regularly reprinted the contents of *IASC News*.

The IASC's 1988 survey of the use and application of its standards reported that Pakistan had adopted twenty-four of the twenty-five standards as its national requirement.[207] It is interesting to note that, in the IASC's 1988 survey, Botswana, Cyprus, Malawi, Malaysia, Oman, and Zimbabwe also reported strong records of adoption of IASC standards, which were comparable to that of Pakistan.

6.18.2. India

The Institute of Chartered Accountants of India (ICAI), which became an associate member in 1974, decided two years later 'because of membership of IASC...to seriously undertake the task of setting accounting standards in India'.[208] Kamal Gupta, the ICAI's technical director, has said, 'Apart from providing this basic impetus for [Indian] standard setting, the work of the IASC has also proved to be of great assistance in formulating individual standards.'[209]

The ICAI's Accounting Standards Board, established in 1977, proceeded to issue a series of 'recommendatory' standards. Its first ten standards, completed by 1985, closely followed the topics on which the IASC had issued standards, and it has been reported that the ICAI used the IASC standards as a basis for formulating them. With respect to the IASC standards for which there were no Indian equivalents, the ICAI encouraged companies to adopt them.[210] The Institute organized a series of seminars and workshops to discuss the IASC's exposure drafts and standards.[211] Yet, in the IASC's 1988 survey of the use and application of its standards, India reported that it had used only one IASC standard as the basis for one of its own, and that ten of the twenty-five extant IASC standards did not agree with practice and were topics on which there were no national requirements.[212]

6.18.3. Singapore

In 1975, the Singapore Society of Accountants (today part of the Institute of Certified Public Accountants of Singapore) became an associate member, and, beginning in 1977, the Society relied heavily on IASC standards when issuing Singaporean standards.[213] By 1 January 1987, twenty-two of the first twenty-four IASC standards (all but IAS 5 and IAS 15), as modified to suit local conditions, were approved as standards in Singapore.[214] In the IASC's 1988 survey of the use and application of its standards, Singapore reported that it had used twenty-four of the twenty-five extant IASC standards as the basis for its national requirements.[215] David Cairns has written, 'In practice, the Singapore standards were identical to IAS, but the Society objected to our saying that it used IAS as national standards. It adopted the identical text as Singapore standards.'[216]

6.18.4. Hong Kong

Beginning in 1983, it was the practice of the technical director of the Hong Kong Society of Accountants, an associate member since 1975, to prepare draft accounting standards 'on the basis of a brief provided by the [Accounting Standards Committee] which is usually to "Hongkongize" an IAS'.[217] The SSAPs largely conformed to IASC standards, but with fewer free choices than in the latter.[218] Yet, in the IASC's 1988 survey, Hong Kong replied that there were no national requirements corresponding to twelve of the IASC's extant standards, of which eight were in conformity with practice and three differed from practice. Only one IASC standard was used as the basis of the Hong Kong standard.[219]

6.18.5. Malaysia

The Malaysian Association (now Institute) of Certified Public Accountants (Institut Akauntan Awan Bertauliah Malaysia) became an associate member in 1975 (later joined by the Institut Akauntan Malaysia, the Malaysian Institute of Accountants), and by 1978, IAS 1 to 4 had become approved accounting standards in Malaysia. Ten of the next twelve IASC standards became operative in Malaysia by 1983.[220]

In March 1980, the Malaysian Association of CPAs held a professional development seminar on IASC standards.[221] In 1986, it was said that IASC standards were the 'backbone of standard setting in Malaysia'.[222] The Malaysian standard setter would 'top and tail' each IASC standard by writing a Malaysian introduction and noting at the end any paragraphs that did not apply because they contravened Malaysian law.[223] The IASC's 1988 survey of the use and application of IASC standards reported that Malaysia had adopted eighteen of the twenty-five extant IASC standards as it national requirements.[224]

6.18.6. New Zealand

In New Zealand, the Financial Accounting Subcommittee of the New Zealand Society of Accountants (today the Institute of Chartered Accountants of New Zealand), an associate member since 1974, concluded in 1975 that IAS 2, on inventories, represented a better draft than its own subcommittee on inventories had prepared. Consequently, the Society's Board of Research and Council adopted IAS 2 in full as the New Zealand standard.[225]

In its response to the IASC's survey in 1975, the Society said it had 'written to Government, Stock Exchanges, [the] Bankers Association, Financial Executives

Institute, and other similar organisations, drawing attention to IASC, the Society's obligations in relation thereto and seeking their support for the adoption of the International Standards'. It also said that its Professional Standards Committee will write to auditors in regard to any lack of disclosures of non-compliance with IASC standards.[226] In the IASC's 1988 survey, New Zealand replied that its national requirements conformed to sixteen of the IASC's extant standards, while four of the standards agreed with practice but were not treated in national requirements, and five differed from practice and were not the subjects of national requirements.[227]

6.19. NON-PARTICIPATION BY CENTRAL AND SOUTH AMERICAN COUNTRIES

The general disinterest in the IASC by the professional accountancy bodies in Central and South America has been a puzzle.[228] When it became clear in 1974 that most of the invited South American bodies did not respond to the invitation, or declined to apply for associate membership, Henry Benson, as well Joe Cummings (of the US delegation) and Manuel Galván (of the Mexican delegation), sought to discuss the matter with their contacts in the region. Galván agreed to confer with those active in the Inter-American Accounting Conference with a view towards securing a country member from South America, preferably Argentina or Brazil.[229] Finally, after numerous entreaties, the Instituto dos Auditores Independentes do Brasil joined in 1977. By March 1978, of the forty-one countries whose accountancy bodies were IASC members, only one, Brazil, was from South America.[230]

In the Gray, Campbell, and Shaw world survey conducted in 1984, mentioned above, Brazil, Chile, and Uruguay reported no IASC influence.[231] The aforementioned 1979 survey conducted by Price Waterhouse covered the following seventeen Latin American countries, none of which was singled out by the firm as ones where 'compliance [with IASC standards] can be deemed mandatory': Argentina, Bolivia, Brazil, Chile, Colombia, Dominican Republic, Ecuador, El Salvador, Guatemala, Honduras, Mexico, Nicaragua, Panama, Paraguay, Peru, Uruguay, and Venezuela.[232]

After the IASC/IFAC Mutual Commitments pact went into effect in 1982, all IFAC members, including seven from South America, automatically became members of the IASC. Yet only one South American country, Brazil, participated in the IASC's 1988 survey on the use and application of its standards around the world. While Brazil reported that nineteen IASC standards conformed to its national requirements, it said that no national requirements corresponded to five of the IASC standards. No replies were received from non-board members Chile, Colombia, Ecuador, and Paraguay.[233] Argentina and Uruguay had been members of IFAC, and therefore also of the IASC, but they were suspended from IFAC in 1986 because of the non-payment of their contributions.[234] Venezuela, also a member of IFAC, allowed its membership to lapse in 1988. Among the possible reasons for the lack of participation by South America may have been the professional institutes' straitened financial condition, as well as language and culture, including a perception that the IASC (and IFAC) were the domain of the English-speaking countries.[235]

6.20. GENERAL ASSESSMENT OF THE IMPACT OF THE IASC'S STANDARDS UP TO 1987

None of the founder members of the IASC reported in 1988 having adopted any of the IASC's standards as their national requirement, and only Canada, in one instance, reported that it had used an IASC standard as the basis for fashioning its national standard.[236] The founder countries with active equity capital markets—Australia, Canada, the United Kingdom, and the United States—also had well-established national standard setters, and they may have felt that they had little to learn from the IASC. Among those four countries, Ralph E. Walters, a long-time FASB member and a member of the US delegation to the IASC board from 1984 to 1987, said, 'The Canadians, in particular, were the most dedicated to the harmonization theme.'[237] This was illustrated clearly by the CICA's prompt action following the board's June 1980 decision to approach multinational companies in the member bodies' home countries about disclosing compliance with the IASC's standards. In contrast, it was reported in March 1981 that in six out of eleven countries represented on the board, no action had yet been taken.[238] The generally limited impact of the IASC's standards in the founder members' countries may probably be ascribed in part to a certain reticence on the part of some of the member bodies in advocating the cause of the IASC in their home countries. However, it should be noted that the formal powers of most member bodies to ensure compliance with the IASC's standards, or to incorporate these standards into national standards, was limited.

Apart from the limited powers of the member bodies, the generally muted impact of the IASC's standards was due to coolness on the part of companies. In countries with developed financial reporting standards, such as the United States and the United Kingdom, companies were understandably wary of submitting themselves to another layer of standards. In respect of other countries, the IASC was supplying a product for which there was as yet little demand. Most European countries had equity capital markets, but during the 1970s and the early 1980s companies typically did not rely on these markets as their main source of finance; instead, they looked to banks, families, and the state. Candid reporting was for insiders, and the financial reports to be filed in a public record office were prepared strictly in accordance with the law, which, depending on the country, protected various needs for non-transparency.

In 1976, when he stepped down as IASC chairman, Henry Benson drew on his three years' experience to characterize the challenge as follows:

The step from national standards to international standards looks to be a short one but it has grievous pitfalls. Nationals of every country prefer their own ways just as they prefer their own food, wine and customs. There is an even more formidable obstacle: national governments. No government will willingly give up its sovereignty and yield the right to decide what will happen in its own country.[239]

In developing countries, the IASC was rather more successful. In 1986, Secretary-General David Cairns reported that IASC standards 'are used as national standards in Malawi and Zimbabwe and as the basis for standard-setting programmes in Nigeria and Kenya', which he learned during visits to those countries.[240] Many developing countries were borrowing from development banks and thus were required to file periodic reports reflecting high standards of accounting and auditing (*see* Section 12.5.1). The World Bank's need for reliable information on projects it was financing was the main reason for its decision to join the IASC's Consultative Group in 1981.[241] In 1983, the International Finance Corporation (IFC), which is affiliated with the World Bank, made it known that borrowers from the IFC should, in the summary of accounting policies presented in the opening note to their financial statements, refer, wherever applicable and practicable, to IASC standards.[242] Because of this pressure from the development banks, the possible influence of IASC standards may have percolated into the private sector and thus into the agenda of the national accountancy bodies. Richard Simmons, the IASC's first assistant secretary, aptly observed that the associate members were, in many ways, much stronger advocates of international accounting standards than the founder members.[243]

In 1987, the board received a reminder of how its relatively modest success so far had heightened expectations about its future role in the process of harmonization. Paul Rutteman, an Arthur Young partner in London and the former chairman of the Groupe d'Études, wrote (prophetically) as follows:

IASC's work and standards have already acquired a reputation that ensures that it cannot be ignored. But harmonisation must be achieved internationally and success must be judged in terms of harmonisation between the major capital markets—rather than by the number of countries with relatively small capital markets that have adopted IASs as their own. There is still a long way to go and, in the long term, the IASC itself will have to be modified so that it comprises the organizations responsible for setting the standards in different countries, rather than just the accounting profession.[244]

6.21. THE IASC SEEKS SUPPORT THROUGH VISITS AND LIAISON

IASC Chairmen Henry Benson, Joseph Cummings, and John Hepworth promoted the IASC around the world at meetings and in frequent speeches and published articles. On one evening, following a board meeting, the chairman would typically invite local executives, regulators, and leaders of the accountancy profession to a dinner.[245] In 1978, Secretary Roy Nash paid calls on IASC associate member bodies in Southeast Asia and New Zealand in connection with his attendance at IASC meetings.[246] This process of outreach accelerated in 1980 under the chairmanship of Hans Burggraaff. Beginning with Burggraaff, the chairman and secretary undertook a series of visits to the professional accountancy bodies, standard setters, government regulators, and major corporations in IASC member countries, as well as to national and regional accounting congresses.[247]

In response to criticism by the OECD and others that the IASC board was 'too narrowly based in that it represents only the accounting profession',[248] the IASC in 1981 launched a Consultative Group, also a Burggraaff innovation, with membership drawn from the preparers and users of financial statements (*see* Section 4.16).

By 1984, the IASC chairman or secretary, or both, had visited national standard-setting bodies in the Netherlands, Canada, France, Australia, New Zealand, Mexico, and South Africa, and plans were laid for visits to Nigeria, Italy, the United Kingdom, Ireland, and Japan.[249] In 1985–6, visits were made to India and Pakistan.[250] During 1986 and 1987, Secretary-General David Cairns undertook an extensive tour of Africa.[251] Cairns made these stops on trips he had already arranged to attend board and steering group meetings.[252]

Burggraaff began to give talks at an array of international and national conferences, using these platforms to explain the objectives and operation of the IASC to a wider range of audiences. He also began a practice, continued by his successors, of inviting important figures in the accounting world to be guests at board meetings, beginning with the FASB chairman, Donald J. Kirk, in June 1981 (again in June 1985); Tom Watts, chairman of the UK ASC, in March 1982; and Jan Schoonderbeek, chairman of the Netherlands Council on Annual Reporting, in June 1982. Typically, the guests were invited to make a short presentation to the board during the meeting. Further invitations were extended to the following:

- IFAC President Washington SyCip and IFAC Executive Director Robert N. Sempier (June 1983 and June 1984)
- Professor M. N. K. Kinzonzi, secretary-general of the African Accounting Council (October 1983)
- Raymond C. Lauver, FASB member (June 1984)
- Hermann Niessen, of the European Commission, and Herbert Biener, of the German Justice Ministry (October 1984)
- IFAC President Robert L. May and IFAC Executive Director Robert N. Sempier (June 1985 and June 1986)
- Peter Godfrey, chairman of the UK ASC (October 1985)
- Robert C. Spinosa Cattela, finance director of Philips' Gloeilampenfabrieken, of the Netherlands (June 1986)
- John Miles, chairman of the Australian Accounting Standards Board (March 1987)[253]

The IASC did not overlook the influence of educators. At the board's June 1983 meeting, 'It was agreed that the Secretariat should write to member bodies asking them to make contact with universities and colleges in their own country and to ensure that all universities and colleges have adequate copies of IASC material.'[254]

The idea for this initiative may well have come from Secretary Geoffrey Mitchell, who was himself an accounting academic on leave from his university in Australia.

6.22. THE IASC'S CONTACTS AT THE EUROPEAN LEVEL

Despite the alleged importance of the EEC's programme of Directives as a factor in its establishment, the IASC promoted only sporadic contacts during the 1970s with bodies active at the European level. In 1974, Benson met a few times with the chairmen of the Union Européenne des Experts Comptables Economiques et Financiers (UEC), E. Pougin, and of the Groupe d'Études, A. Reydel,[255] but it appears that, after Benson left, these relationships were allowed to lapse, perhaps because the IASC's next two chairmen were not Europeans. In February 1980, Allan Cook, the first secretary who was a European, wrote to the then chairman of the Groupe d'Études, G. J. Kramer, in line with the board's October 1979 decision to involve other organizations at the start of new projects, but Kramer declined other than on an ad hoc basis owing to a lack of resources.[256]

In its June 1980 meeting, when the board held a lengthy discussion of its future, including its outside relationships, Secretary Cook recommended that it seek an observer 'representing EEC interests' to attend board meetings. Seigo Nakajima, the senior board member from Japan, said, however, that such an invitation would not be favourably received in Japan. Accordingly, the invitation was not extended. The EEC was not, unlike the UN and the OECD, invited to join the Consultative Group, because it was envisaged at the time that only worldwide organizations would be eligible for participation.[257]

This did not mean that the IASC neglected the European Commission. In December 1981, IASC Chairman Hans Burggraaff, accompanied by Secretary Cook and Secretary Designate Geoffrey Mitchell, met with Hermann Niessen and members of his staff in Brussels. Niessen was the top official dealing with accounting matters in the Commission's Directorate-General for Internal Market and Industrial Affairs. Owing to the pertinacity of Secretary Mitchell, the IASC held follow-up meetings with Niessen and his staff on a six-monthly basis during the next few years. Mitchell prepared detailed minutes of the meetings, and IASC drafts were regularly supplied to Niessen. The topics discussed at the meetings covered a wide range.[258] In 1984, Chairman Stephen Elliott invited Niessen to attend the October board meeting as a guest, which, as indicated above, he did. The next meeting between the IASC and the European Commission did not occur until eighteen months later, again at the suggestion of the IASC. None of the IASC's contacts with the Commission were initiated by the latter.

In May 1986, IASC Chairman John Kirkpatrick and Secretary-General David Cairns met with Niessen and Karel Van Hulle at the European Commission. They discussed two proposed European Community Directives, the Dutch initiative to declare the IASC's standards equivalent to the Seventh Directive on consolidated accounts (*see* Section 6.13), and IASC's work programme. *IASC News* carried the following conclusion from the meeting: 'It was generally agreed that although differences between European Community Directives and International Accounting Standards are small, greater conformity was a desirable objective.'[259]

6.23. THE IASC'S CONTACTS WITH THE SEC

In 1980, John L. Kirkpatrick, then a member of the UK & Irish delegation to the IASC board, displayed his awareness of the significance of the US SEC to the IASC, when he said in a speech: 'If the IASC's worldwide accounting standards seriously transgressed the SEC's rules as to what should, and what should not, appear in financial statements, the value of the IASC, and its work, could be so severely damaged as to render it a body not entitled to use the word "international" in its name.'[260]

Several years later, in March 1984, the IASC established its first formal contact with the SEC in an open meeting in Washington on 26 March. IASC Chairman Stephen Elliott was accompanied by IASC Secretary-General Geoffrey Mitchell; FASB Chairman Kirk; AICPA President Philip B. Chenok; Ralph L. Harris (of IBM), a member of the US delegation to the IASC board; and Willis A. Smith (of CPC International), the chairman of the AICPA's international technical standards subcommittee and a former IASC board member. They met with the members of the Commission, Chief Accountant Clarence Sampson, and Assistant Chief Accountant Clarence Staubs. The agenda covered a broad array of issues, including the case for international harmonization, the IASC's operating procedures and the role played by its member bodies, the differences between IASC standards and US GAAP, the possible acceptance of IASC standards for securities registration purposes, and the role of intergovernmental bodies (such as the UN and the OECD). It was reported that SEC Chairman John S. R. Shad had recently testified that the SEC 'is interested in, and supportive of, the development of international standards of accounting and auditing.'[261]

In his prepared remarks at the meeting, Kirk gave the IASC no more than tepid support, pointing out that international harmonization was, as Shad had said in recent Congressional testimony, a 'long-term process'. He cited some of the obstacles to harmonization (repeated from an earlier paper[262]), and he drew attention to the fact that the AICPA, not the FASB, was the US member of the IASC. At the close of his remarks, he reiterated his view that the mission of the FASB was to attend to financial information that is relevant to users in the United States.[263] The lack of enthusiasm on the part of the FASB was subsequently confirmed by an FASB spokesman: 'We were invited and couldn't really decline. But [FASB] felt like a fifth wheel at the meeting.'[264]

During the meeting, Elliott invited Shad 'to consider ways in which your support could be made more manifest to the world of international accounting.'[265] It was reported that, at the meeting, 'Shad asked SEC Chief Accountant Sampson to look into whether the SEC could give greater support to the efforts of the IASC.'[266] One of the SEC's self-imposed norms, namely, that it did not comment formally on drafts, whether issued by the FASB or the IASC, may have hampered its ability to give explicit support to the IASC.[267] The meeting with the SEC was a valuable opportunity for the Commission and its senior staff to 'get acquainted' with the leaders of the IASC, and vice versa.

A year after the meeting with the SEC, the IASC commented on the SEC's concept release 33-6568 on Facilitation of Multinational Securities Offerings, issued on 28 February 1985. The SEC had sought views on how best to harmonize the disclosure and distribution practices for offerings of securities by multinational corporations in the United States, the United Kingdom, and Canada. The options were a 'reciprocal approach', by which the offering document in one country would be accepted in the others, or a 'common prospectus approach', by securing an international agreement on the disclosures and distribution standards. The IASC recommended that 'A "common prospectus approach" based on conformity with International Accounting Standards should be the ultimate objective.' But in the short and medium runs, the IASC said, practicalities would require use of a reciprocal approach.[268]

Curiously, the SEC's accounting staff concluded from a review of the comments received on the SEC's February 1985 concept release that 'There is little evidence to suggest that the reconciliation requirement [i.e., to US GAAP] has provided a serious obstacle to foreign issuers entering U.S. markets.'[269] The New York Stock Exchange Advisory Committee on International Capital Markets was among the commentators which, it said, 'envisioned the necessity for a reconciliation'.[270] In the 1990s, the Exchange tried in vain to persuade the SEC to eliminate the reconciliation requirement (*see* Section 10.16).

In 1987, the SEC's Office of the Chief Accountant published a descriptive chapter entitled 'Accounting and Auditing Standards in Relation to Multinational and International Issues of Securities', as part of a report to Congress on the internationalization of the securities markets.[271] The chapter included several pages on the work and impact of the IASC, but the staff study, which was not a statement of the Commission's views, offered no policy recommendations.

6.24. THE IASC'S INITIAL CONTACT WITH IOSCO AND ITS PORTENT

SEC Commissioner Charles C. Cox, who attended the March 1984 meeting with the IASC representatives, took the initiative at a meeting three years later to bring the IASC into contact with the International Organization of Securities Commissions (IOSCO), which proved to be a turning point in the IASC's relations with securities market regulators, including the SEC. This meeting and its profound implications for the work of the IASC are discussed in Chapter 10.

7

The IASC Copes with Its Political Environment

The International Accounting Standards Committee (IASC) had been formed as a purely private-sector initiative by an exclusive group of accountancy bodies. With the arguable exception of Mexico, these bodies represented the developed world only. The early years of the IASC were a time when the idea of expanding political or social control over business was in the ascendancy in most countries. In many developing countries, this idea was reinforced by a desire to assert national independence. Against this background, it is not surprising that the IASC was subjected to critical scrutiny from various quarters.

During the 1970s and early 1980s, the IASC had to deal with a number of challenges. These were various expressions of a single underlying notion, which was that the IASC's composition and procedures did not allow all of those with an interest in international accounting standards an appropriate participation. The parties taking an interest in the work of the IASC were by no means homogeneous. They divided along the lines of developed versus developing nations, governments versus the private sector, and accountants versus the users and preparers of financial statements. Another line of tension was that between accountancy bodies that were represented on the IASC board and those that were not. This was a sensitive division, as bodies that were left out sensed quite rightly that this was not merely a matter of restricting the board to a manageable size, but also related to perceptions of their quality.

This chapter deals with the course the IASC tried to steer among these conflicting forces. The story in this chapter is structured around three developments that were closely interconnected: relations with the United Nations (UN), relations with the Organisation for Economic Co-operation and Development (OECD), and attempts to bring IASC under the control of the International Federation of Accountants (IFAC).

7.1. THE DEVELOPING WORLD AND THE UNITED NATIONS

The possibility that the UN might play a role in the setting of international accounting standards had already been voiced before the IASC was founded. During the October 1971 Jerusalem Conference on Accounting, Edward Stamp, a prominent British accounting academic, had suggested that the UN should be approached with a proposal for a 'world consultative body of accountants' to develop accounting standards.[1] In fact, the issue of international accounting standards had already surfaced at the UN. In December 1971, the International Labour Organisation (ILO) organized a conference in Turin on universal standards and conventions in accounting, and the UN was said to consider a 'summit of leading accountants' for 1972 to discuss 'the chaos of international accounting methods'.[2] But when the UN did take action, it was not through the ILO, and it was with a somewhat different emphasis. In 1972, a Group of Eminent Persons was appointed by the UN secretary-general to study the impact of multinational corporations on development and international relations. Behind the creation of the Group were concerns on the part of developing countries about loss of sovereignty because of the operations of multinationals in their midst.

The Group's report, published in 1974, concluded in general that 'Host country bargaining power should be increased.' A conclusion with potential relevance to accounting and financial reporting was that 'Developing countries need to develop the capacity to monitor the pattern of the distribution of benefits between themselves and the multinational corporations which operate in their economies.'[3] The report also recommended the continuous involvement of the UN with issues involving the activities of multinational corporations. As a result, the UN set up a Commission on Transnational Corporations, as well as a Centre on Transnational Corporations, with the task of collecting data. The Group of Eminent Persons emphasized the 'pivotal importance of information disclosure' and recommended developing an 'international standard' for company reporting. This standard should lead to internationally comparable information, geared in particular to the information needs of governments. The international standard might therefore coexist with existing national standards for reporting to shareholders. The Group of Eminent Persons recommended the creation of an expert group on international accounting standards to determine the information on multinational corporations required by host and home country governments.[4]

The Group of Eminent Persons did its work during the fall of 1973 and the early months of 1974, and it may not have been aware of the recently founded IASC. No representative of the IASC testified before the Group. Yet, by November 1974, the UN had been in touch with the IASC to discuss the possibility 'of the U.N. entrusting the setting of accounting valuation rules to IASC and the payment of a grant by the U.N. towards the work of the IASC'.[5] These discussions apparently came to naught, because in March 1975 the UN Commission on Transnational Corporations decided to form its own Group of Experts in line with the recommendation of the Eminent Persons.[6] This created a potential problem for the IASC, as the Group of Experts might become active in setting accounting standards itself.[7] The IASC therefore took the initiative to create a liaison with the Group of Experts, with the result that Joe Cummings, the IASC chairman-designate, was appointed as a member of the Group of Experts.[8]

The Group of Experts met twice during 1976 and 1977, after which it submitted a report to the Commission on Transnational Corporations.[9] The report was perhaps reassuring to the IASC in that it mentioned the 'valuable work being carried out by IASC in developing international standards in respect of valuation and other standards'. It mentioned the work of the IASC as one of the reasons why the Group had decided to limit itself to the question of disclosure. The report also concentrated on general purpose financial reports, so that the issue of separate reporting standards for reporting to governments had disappeared. Nevertheless, the report was controversial in its recommendation that standards be developed for the disclosure of a wide range of financial and non-financial information.[10] The International Chamber of Commerce and the International Organisation of Employers mounted a campaign against the report, and several multinational enterprises expressed concern about the difficulties of implementing the proposals and their possible political ramifications.[11]

Sir Henry Benson clearly saw the proposals in a political light and went on the attack in an article in the *Financial Times* of 22 March 1978. According to Benson, the presence in the UN of a wide range of countries, including 'far-Left Communist republics' ensured that the project was 'fraught with political danger'. There was a real danger, he said, that states with no commitment to transparency 'will support proposals for increased corporate disclosure in order to use them as a political weapon, either against mixed economies in general or in order to obtain particular advantages'. Moreover, 'The task of drawing up long lists of disclosure requirements is easy work but doctrinaire proposals which take no account of realities are more likely to invoke ridicule than compliance.' In contrast, Benson lauded the 'short, clear and uncomplicated' standards published by the IASC and suggested that the UN ask the IASC to incorporate the UN's concerns in its own programme of work.[12]

The IASC did not follow the lead of its former chairman. It preferred to follow the line of Edward Stamp who, in a rebuttal of Benson's views, had expressed the hope for a 'fruitful partnership' between the IASC and the UN.[13] When the UN established a successor committee, the 'Ad Hoc Intergovernmental Working Group on International Standards of Accounting and Reporting', in May 1979, the IASC offered its cooperation.[14]

7.1.1. Sensitivity to the Aspirations of Developing Countries

It is possible that, by 1979, the IASC had become more sensitized to the demands of developing nations than it had been in the days of Benson. The dissatisfaction of the developing countries with their lack of representation in the IASC had come to the surface during the Eleventh International Congress of Accountants in Munich, in 1977. The presentation of the IASC's revised Constitution had been somewhat marred by the criticism from some associate members that they had had no voice in the revision. During the congress, Dr. O. Van der Meulen, the president of the Belgian Institut des Réviseurs d'Entreprises, coordinated a more general protest against the dominance of the IASC by the founder members. Although the discontent was probably most keenly felt by some associate members in developed countries, such as Belgium and the Scandinavian countries, the issue of the developing countries was raised as well. It was argued that, because of the activities of multinational corporations in their countries, they had a particular interest in international standards, but that their specific economic and social circumstances were typically not taken into account by the IASC.[15]

Around the same time, the IASC was rather embarrassed by the failure of Pakistan to take up the rotating seat offered to it with the implementation of the Constitution of 1977 (*see* Section 6.18.1). The two Pakistani bodies that were to occupy the seat jointly discovered too late that they would be unable to pay the fee expected from board member bodies, and they had to withdraw their acceptance of the seat offered to them.[16] In a confidential report, Secretary Roy Nash observed that 'The IASC could be subject to criticism for changing its Constitution to allow more Board memberships but effectively eliminating most Members from Board positions because of the financial requirements.'[17] Fortunately for the IASC, it turned out that the Institute of Chartered Accountants of Nigeria, which was offered the Pakistani seat after a secret ballot, had understood the financial implications when it applied for a board seat.[18]

Developing-country participation remained a sensitive issue during the next few years. When a steering committee was set up to review the existing IASC standards in March 1982, the Organisation and Planning Committee (OPC) observed that, 'from a public relations point of view' it would be useful if the composition of the new steering committee indicated 'to the outside world that an independent review was being commenced. Thus, the appointment of two non-board member countries [to the steering committee], one being a developing country, is essential'. The OPC recommended this policy even though it noted that board member countries might be able to contribute well-experienced members or staff observers to the review steering committee, whose help would have been welcome.[19]

7.1.2. The Ad Hoc Working Group and ISAR

Meanwhile, the UN's Ad Hoc Working Group met six times between March 1980 and April 1982. The IASC, which was allowed to send an observer, was represented during most meetings by one or two board members, the secretary, and occasionally its chairman. The political dimension of international accounting standards emerged more clearly in the thirty-four-member Ad Hoc Working Group than it had in the thirteen-member Group of Experts. The Group was deeply divided between the developing countries, which made up the majority of the Group, and the member states of the OECD. In general, the developing countries (organized in the UN as the Group of 77) pressed for wide-ranging financial and non-financial disclosures, which the OECD countries tended to resist.[20]

The position of the IASC in this dispute was somewhat delicate. On the one hand, it had to be sufficiently responsive to the views of the developing countries, because an aloof attitude on the part of the IASC might lead to calls for the UN to develop a fully fledged international accounting standard-setting arm. This remained a possibility for so long as the IASC could be criticized for having an inadequate number of developing countries on its board.[21] As discussed above, the IASC was aware of this weakness. Therefore, Chairman Hans Burggraaff gave a commitment to the UN that, of the four seats on the IASC board becoming available in 1982, three would be allocated to developing countries.[22] In 1982, Nigeria and South Africa were reappointed, while Italy and Taiwan were appointed for the first time.

On the other hand, the IASC could not afford to antagonize the developed countries forming the OECD. As is discussed below, the OECD was also becoming active in the area of international accounting standards around 1980, and it might well take action that would undermine the position of the IASC.

In trying to remain in good standing with both sides, the IASC seems to have succeeded somewhat better with the developing than with the developed countries. The Canadian representative on the Ad Hoc Group of Experts, John Denman, observed that, 'In general, this group [of developing countries] is much more receptive than the OECD Group to the work of the IASC.'[23] In September 1982, the IASC came under attack when an article in *World Accounting Report* charged the IASC with being 'extremely naive' in letting themselves be used for the political purposes of some of the developing countries. The IASC, it was said, 'has attempted to upgrade its own status by getting in on the act but has succeeded only in incurring the wrath of governments of all political persuasions'.[24] This caused some soul-searching at the IASC, and some national representatives on the Ad Hoc Working Group were consulted to gain another perspective on events. The UK representative, George Smith, commented that the IASC 'went overboard' at the Group's second meeting [November 1980] by asking 'that the UN give its seal of approval to IASC standards'. At that time, the IASC 'was thought to be buttering up to the Group of 77'. However, Smith noted that, in later meetings of the Ad Hoc Working Group, the IASC had gained credit with its 'helpful interventions of an authoritative and professional nature'.[25] Canadian representative John Denman conceded that 'To some, the IASC did appear to be turning itself into the conscience of the Third World,' but he defended Burggraaff and Secretary Allan Cook, who 'had achieved a great deal, particularly by their frankness, clarity of expression and obvious technical expertise'.[26] Fortified by these comments, Secretary Geoffrey Mitchell wrote a reply appearing in *World Accounting Report* that the IASC 'has not been able to find one country whose wrath it has incurred', and that it welcomed the support for its work in the report of the Ad Hoc Working Group.[27]

The Ad Hoc Working Group remained divided until the end. Its final report, submitted to the Commission on Transnational Corporations after its last meeting in April 1982, did contain a guideline on reporting, including lists of minimal disclosures.[28] But the report was 'marred by the evident lack of unity in the group'.[29] The group was unable to present a unanimous recommendation on whether it should continue to meet, and, if so, when. Nevertheless, in October 1982 the Economic and Social Council created a successor group, the

Intergovernmental Working Group of Experts on International Standards of Accounting and Reporting (also known as ISAR).

So far, ISAR has proven to be the most long-lived UN group in the area of financial reporting. It was set up to meet annually, initially for three years, but in 2005 it held its twenty-second meeting. It was established with wide-ranging terms of reference: to review, consider, and recommend on issues of accounting and reporting. However, its mandate did not include the setting of accounting standards. The founding resolution recognized that 'The process of setting standards for accounting and reporting...takes place primarily at the national and sometimes regional levels.'[30] This reticence effectively removed any threat to the IASC.[31]

Although the split between the OECD countries and the Group of 77 reappeared at ISAR's first meeting, its members found sufficient common ground to agree on a programme of studying topics such as transfer pricing, goodwill, depreciation, and provisions.[32] While the IASC continued to maintain good relations with ISAR and the UN Centre on Transnational Corporations, the UN gradually figured less prominently in the IASC's activities as the 1980s progressed. Throughout the 1980s, the IASC was represented at all the meetings of ISAR, typically by its chairman or secretary-general. But 'liaison with the UN' was dropped as a regular item on the IASC agenda in 1985, and there were occasional concerns about the costs of the IASC's involvement with ISAR.[33]

7.2. THE OECD

The Paris-based OECD entered the area of financial reporting in 1976, and like the UN it threatened to develop into a possible rival of the IASC. Yet, when the IASC was being founded, the suggestion had been made by the Nederlands Instituut van Registeraccountants (NIVRA) to involve the OECD as an ally. In March 1973, the NIVRA had, on its own initiative, discussed the matter with the Dutch Foreign Ministry, which expressed its willingness to instruct its permanent representative to the OECD to 'put out his feelers'.[34] There are no indications that further steps were taken, and it is not known whether this was because of reluctance on the part of the OECD or on the part of the other IASC members.

Probably independently of any steps taken by the Dutch, the OECD took an interest in international financial reporting as early as 1973.[35] In June 1976, the OECD adopted a 'Declaration on International Investment and Multinational Enterprises', which included a set of 'Guidelines for International Enterprises: Disclosure of Information'. Among the recommended disclosures were the expenditure on research and development for the enterprise as a whole and sales turnover and operating results segmented by geographical area. In July 1978, the OECD set up an 'Ad Hoc Working Group on Accounting Standards'. This was a time when the business world was waking up to the implications of the report of the UN Group of Experts, and the OECD shared some of the concerns.[36] The Working Group was to report in the fall of 1979 on the need to undertake further work in the area of accounting standards. In particular, it was to review the work of the UN and the IASC and to report on whether the OECD should become permanently involved in establishing accounting and disclosure standards.

From the late 1970s onwards, expressing one's bewilderment or annoyance with the proliferation of organizations involved with accounting standards became a staple of the literature.[37] The UN, the OECD, the IASC, and the EEC were frequently mentioned together with the implied or explicit recommendation that one or more of these bodies should cease their activities in this area. Moreover, it was not evident to everyone that the IASC should or would take the lead in international standards.[38] As discussed above, the business world was not enthusiastic about the work of the UN Group of Experts, and some might have seen the OECD as a more dependable counterweight to the UN than the IASC.[39] Moreover, in many Continental European countries there was a strong tradition to see accounting regulation as a government responsibility. From that perspective, the OECD, as a body whose membership consisted of governments, was a more natural alternative than the private-sector IASC, not least because the difficulties of the IASC in ensuring compliance were becoming more and more evident (*see* Chapter 6).[40] Because of the prevalence of this attitude, there was a 'genuine fear' in the IASC that the OECD, even if it did not set standards itself, might seriously interfere with the IASC's work.[41]

Against this background, the invitation to the IASC to present its work to the Ad Hoc Working Group was of great importance. The presentation was made on 4 April 1979 by John Grenside, the OPC chairman, standing in for IASC Chairman John Hepworth. In his presentation, Grenside emphasized the expertise and apolitical nature of the IASC, and the problems the OECD would face if it were to involve itself in setting accounting standards. It was a frank presentation, in which Grenside did not gloss over the weaknesses of the IASC, such as the flexibility of its standards and the problem of ensuring compliance.[42] It appears that the presentation was quite effective. Hans Burggraaff and Doug Thomas (Canadian IASC staff observer), who represented their respective countries in the Working Group, reported back to the IASC on the 'favourable impression' made by Grenside.[43] Meanwhile, some IASC delegations successfully tried to enlist the support of their national governments.[44] The result was that, in October 1979, Burggraaff could report that, although the Ad Hoc Working Group was to be succeeded by a permanent OECD Working Group on Accounting Standards, this new body was not to set accounting standards itself.[45]

While this must have been gratifying to the IASC, it did by no means imply that it could henceforth ignore the OECD. As Burggraaff continued to report, the Ad Hoc Working Group believed 'that the exclusion of governments and governmental standard setting bodies from membership of IASC weakened the effectiveness of the International Accounting Standards'. The OECD therefore saw a role for itself in 'energizing' international standard setting by ensuring that the views of governments, the international business community, national and international standard setting bodies, as well as those of the accountancy profession would be taken into account.[46] The permanent OECD Working Group was therefore set up as a kind of permanent coordination committee in which the IASC would be just one participant, representing the accountancy profession, next to representatives from governments, business, and trade unions.[47]

Put differently, the OECD's willingness to recognize the IASC as a leading force in the area of international accounting standards was conditional on the willingness of the latter to broaden its base and to give up the idea that setting accounting standards was the preserve of the accountancy profession. The IASC, of course, sought to defend itself publicly against criticism of its working procedures and to present itself as the most suitable body to work for international harmonization.[48] But the OECD's pressure nevertheless led the IASC to make a number of significant changes in its operations. As early as June 1980, the IASC adopted a policy of developing contacts with national standard setters by means of a series of visits (*see* Section 6.21).[49] The secretariat observed:

This decision must be seen in the context of the comments by the OECD Working Group on Accounting Standards, which concluded that the present Constitution of IASC, as an organisation of professional accounting bodies, presents significant difficulties to the task of setting international accounting standards as many of the members of IASC are not directly responsible for implementing and enforcing national standards.[50]

Other changes that were related to the OECD's pressure included the establishment of the IASC's Consultative Group in 1981 and the allocation of board seats to organizations other than professional accountancy bodies, starting in 1986. Both developments are discussed more fully below.

The Ad Hoc Working Group's report had more or less instructed the IASC to participate in the work of the successor Working Group.[51] Careful to heed that call, the IASC maintained regular contacts with the OECD and its Working Group on Accounting Standards throughout the 1980s and into the early 1990s. Initially, there was some concern on the part of the IASC that the Working Group's review of the OECD's Guidelines for Multinational Enterprises might evolve into standard setting.[52] But these fears proved unfounded. The Working Group or its subgroups discussed accounting topics such as the relationship between tax accounting and financial reporting, foreign currency translation, and consolidation. It published a series of reports and incidental papers, and it organized conferences and round tables. The reports of the OECD Working Group drew quite heavily on the IASC standards, and the IASC believed that this provided a welcome advertisement and enhanced its authority.[53] Hence, successive IASC chairmen and secretaries invested a considerable amount of time in contacts with the OECD.

Over time, the OECD clearly moved to a more peripheral position, as seen from the IASC's perspective. If there was any single event that marked this development, it was the 'Forum on Harmonization of Accounting Standards', hosted by the OECD in Paris on 23 and 24 April 1985.[54] At the conference, participants from a wide range of backgrounds expressed support for the IASC to play a leading role in international harmonization. By that time, the original reason for the OECD's involvement with accounting standards had by and large disappeared, as the possibility that the UN would be able to develop into a significant force had diminished. This fact, in conjunction with the positive views on the IASC expressed by many at the conference, allowed the OECD to relax its attention to international accounting standards. After 1985, therefore, the OECD began to recede more into the background from the point of view of the IASC. But its continuing significance can be seen from the fact that an OECD symposium on financial instruments in 1988 was instrumental in bringing that important topic onto the agenda of the IASC (*see* Section 11.5.1).

7.3. INTEGRATION WITH IFAC: 1973–82

The IASC's relations with the UN and the OECD, and in particular the underlying issues of developing country representation and the participation of non-accountants in the work of the board, were key factors in discussions over a possible integration of the IASC with IFAC, formed in 1977. The less the IASC would be an organization of accountants only, the more difficult it would be to integrate it with IFAC. IFAC was a relatively open organization in which accountancy bodies from developing countries played a significant role. The IASC, on the other hand, was controlled by its founder members from developed countries, and aligning the two organizations in this respect would not be easy.

As discussed above, these two factors came into play during the late 1970s. But, by then, the relationship between the IASC and IFAC was already burdened by quite a long history of struggles within the worldwide accountancy profession, going back to the Ninth International Congress of Accountants (1967) in Paris (*see* Section 2.6). Against this background, it is not surprising that the IASC/IFAC relationship was one of the most complex issues confronting the IASC around 1980.

7.3.1. The Founding of IFAC

As discussed more fully in Section 3.4.2, one of the major difficulties faced by the founders of the IASC was to define its relationship to the International Co-ordination Committee of the Accountancy Profession (ICCAP). ICCAP had been founded at the international congress of 1972, in Sydney, as an interim step towards the creation of a permanent international secretariat for the accountancy profession. The creation of such a secretariat was supported by the US, German, and French accountancy bodies, who also argued in favour of a close relation between the IASC and ICCAP. The Institute of Chartered Accountants in England and Wales (ICAEW) and the Institute of Chartered Accountants of Scotland (ICAS) were opposed to the creation of a secretariat and, if one were to be created, they certainly wanted the IASC to remain independent of it. In 1973, a compromise had been reached which, in effect, deferred the creation of a secretariat by calling for further study of the issue by ICCAP, while on the other hand the IASC Agreement acknowledged in somewhat ambiguous wording that IASC was 'part of' ICCAP but 'autonomous in the issue of exposure drafts and standards' (paragraph 2).[55] The same paragraph also linked the IASC with

ICCAP by an even more ambiguous clause that the Constitution of the IASC 'shall not be reviewed until the end of 1976 without the agreement of the [IASC] and [ICCAP]'.

Within ICCAP, troublesome negotiations took place between the spring of 1973 and the middle of 1975 about the creation of a permanent organization which, from this stage onwards, was referred to as an 'International Federation' rather than an 'International Secretariat'. Douglas Morpeth, representing the ICAEW, strongly but single-handedly opposed such a move, in line with the position taken by Henry Benson ever since the Paris congress of 1967. The other members of ICCAP, in particular Wallace Olson, the AICPA's chief staff officer, argued in favour. In June 1975, agreement was reached in principle that an International Federation would be created at the international congress of 1977, to be held in Munich. The agreement could be reached because the AICPA gave assurances with respect to two major British concerns: the International Federation would be run on a limited budget, and the IASC secretariat in London was not expected to be combined with the secretariat of the Federation in New York.[56]

Up to this point, the possible relations between the IASC and the proposed Federation, apart from the location of the secretariat, did not figure prominently in the discussions within ICCAP. Nor was the issue actively considered by the IASC. But between July 1975 and March 1976 the relationship between the new Federation and the IASC had to be worked out, in order to enable ICCAP to present a complete proposal for the new Federation in an interim report. It appears that Benson, in consultation with Morpeth, attempted to gain the initiative by scheduling a discussion of a possible revision of the IASC's Constitution for the October 1975 meeting of the IASC. In a note to the IASC, Benson argued for a close liaison with IFAC while maintaining the independence of the IASC: 'There is nothing to be gained by altering something which is working satisfactorily.'[57] When ICCAP's chairman, Reinhard Goerdeler, learned that the IASC was starting to reconsider its Constitution, he wrote to Benson prior to the October meeting to remind him that revisions of the IASC Constitution required the agreement of ICCAP.[58] Goerdeler, who was to become IFAC's first chairman, was in favour of the closest possible relationship between the IASC and IFAC, or even an amalgamation of the two bodies. In fact, this position was shared to some extent by all members of ICCAP, except for the United Kingdom.

To Benson, the integration of 'his' IASC with IFAC, whose founding he had strongly opposed, was anathema. He clung tenaciously to the apparent right of the IASC to exercise a veto over changes in its own Constitution.[59] He obtained the IASC's agreement to the position that the relationship between the IASC and IFAC 'should be maintained on the same general basis as that which currently exists between IASC and ICCAP', and the Committee authorized him to negotiate with ICCAP on this basis.[60]

Lengthy discussions in ICCAP followed, as well as between Benson and Goerdeler.[61] The final result was that the ICCAP Interim Report of March 1976 and the Final Report of March 1977 declared that '[ICCAP's] relationship with IASC should be carried forward to IFAC on the same general basis'. Benson's views prevailed even to the extent that the Interim and Final Reports did not explicitly repeat that the IASC was part of ICCAP. Nor did they reflect Goerdeler's wish that the membership of the IASC and IFAC should be identical.[62]

The outcome was another illustration of Benson's formidable qualities as a negotiator. But he was greatly assisted by the unwillingness of the other members of ICCAP to put the grudging acceptance of IFAC by the ICAEW at risk by insisting on subordination of the IASC to IFAC.[63]

It is noteworthy that the other delegates on the IASC generally supported Benson, even though their national organizations might be in favour of integration of IASC and IFAC. They drew the line, however, when Benson and Alexander Mackenzie (IASC member for the UK & Ireland) attempted to weaken the link between IFAC and the IASC beyond the text of the ICCAP Interim Report. Since 1974, Mackenzie had chaired a working party on the 'Organisation and Future' of the IASC (see Section 4.14), and in that capacity he had prepared a draft of a revised Constitution.[64] In his draft, Mackenzie had merely written that the signatories 'recommend that arrangements should be made to establish and maintain a continuing liaison between the two bodies'.[65] He motivated this by stating:

I would be very reluctant to incorporate in [the] Agreement words which could be interpreted differently on such an important matter as whether IASC is or is not part of IFAC. It is already clear that one interpretation of 'the existing relationship' is that IASC will be 'a part of' IFAC, and I think we must clarify once and for all that, initially at any rate, IASC is not part of IFAC.[66]

This gave rise to protests from the French Ordre and, when this had no great effect, from the German delegation as well. Joe Cummings, who had succeeded Benson as chairman in July 1976, joined in by declaring that he was 'bothered' by the fact that the precise wording agreed to in the ICCAP Interim Report had not been used.[67] In the end, despite protests by Mackenzie, the 1977 Agreement and Constitution included the phrase that the existing relationship between ICCAP and the IASC would be 'carried forward' to IFAC. Whether or not this meant that the IASC was part of IFAC was not spelled out.

7.3.2. Failure of a Proposed Integration Agreement

The relation between the IASC and the newly created IFAC was given shape in 1978 by means of a high-level liaison committee which would become known as the Joint Working Party (JWP). Apart from secretaries, its initial members were Reinhard Goerdeler and Gordon Cowperthwaite for IFAC and John Hepworth and John Grenside for the IASC.[68] Cowperthwaite was a past president of the Canadian Institute of Chartered Accountants (CICA) and a senior partner of Peat Marwick in Toronto, who was to become chairman of IFAC in 1980. He became a staunch advocate of the integration of IFAC and the IASC.

After an uneventful first year in the relations between the IASC and IFAC, the question of integration was brought onto the agenda again when, in June 1979, the IASC members of the JWP expressed their surprise on learning that IFAC had conducted a straw poll among its members about merging IFAC and the IASC. The timing was significant because, as discussed above, in April 1979 John Grenside

Figure 7.1. IASC chairmen and IFAC presidents at the Arthur Young Professors' Roundtable, London, May 1980. *Left to right*: Washington SyCip (IFAC), John Hepworth, Joe Cummings, Reinhard Goerdeler (IFAC), Sir Henry Benson, Hans Burggraaff, Gordon Cowperthwaite (IFAC).

had given a presentation on the IASC before the OECD's Working Group, and had been interrogated about the lack of involvement of non-accountants in the IASC's work. This was echoed in the reaction by the IASC members in the JWP. They stressed the need for an independent IASC and remarked that 'If IASC were being set up ab initio today, it would probably incorporate non-accountants.'[69]

But IFAC pressed for progress on a closer relationship, and the IASC members on the JWP seemed disposed to cooperate. Initially, relatively modest plans were discussed, such as common membership and more formalized liaison procedures. But evidently the IASC members on the JWP were unable to resist pressure from the IFAC members to accept more radical proposals.[70] The result was a draft 'integration agreement', to be put before the IASC board and the IFAC Council in October and November 1979 for preliminary discussion.

The draft integration agreement intended to end the IASC's independent existence on the occasion of the international congress in Mexico City in 1982. The IASC would be reconstituted as the 'accounting standards setting arm' of IFAC. One of the main arguments put forward to support this move was that contacts with the UN, the OECD, and other organizations had shown that the outside world was 'confused' about the relations between the IASC and IFAC.[71] Even though there does not appear to have been much evidence that the outside world was in fact very confused, the argument was often used over the next few years, also couched in terms of the need for the 'profession to speak with one voice'.

When the draft was discussed at the IASC board and the IFAC Council, two issues arose.

First, the Dutch delegations at both meetings strongly opposed the proposal, because it would tend to preclude the participation of non-accountants in the IASC's work. In the Netherlands, there was a general tradition of broad-based cooperation in social and economic life. When a Dutch body charged with recommending accounting norms, the Tripartite Study Group (TSG), was set up in 1970, it was only natural that the body would represent the interests of employers' organizations, the trade unions, and the NIVRA.[72] The Dutch had questioned the dominance of the IASC by accountants already in 1973, when the IASC was founded (see Section 3.4.4), but now they insisted even more strongly. Their argument was reinforced by the fact that Hans Burggraaff, who had been elected chairman-designate of the IASC at the same October 1979 meeting, had been the chairman of the TSG from 1972 to 1975. Moreover, because Burggraaff was also a member of the OECD Working Party, he could speak with authority on the urgency of acting on the OECD's suggestions to broaden the base of the IASC beyond accountants. Nevertheless, the other IASC members did not see this as a reason to reject the integration agreement even though the UK & Ireland, Germany, France, and Mexico made their agreement conditional on keeping the option open to involve other parties in the work of the IASC.[73]

The second issue was raised at the IFAC Council by Washington SyCip, of the Philippines. The draft integration agreement intended to leave control over the composition of the IASC board in the hands of the founder members, all from developed countries. SyCip drew attention to the increasing criticism by the developing countries of the IASC's 'undemocratic structure'.[74] On a subsequent occasion, Gordon Cowperthwaite would observe:

There is a feeling of distrust amongst developing nations towards I.A.S.C., because it is dominated by the developed nations and not by the 'worldwide profession'. The L.D.C.'s [less-developed countries] should not be tempted to draw away from I.A.S.C. and support instead a U.N.-sponsored body.[75]

The JWP attempted to deal with these comments and presented a revised integration agreement to IFAC and the IASC for discussion in March 1980. A key element of the proposal was that founder members would continue to serve, but only until 1987. After that, the composition of the board would be gradually changed, as all seats would be held on a rotating basis. The two seats for non-founder members, created in 1977, would be continued, and, starting in 1982, up to four seats might be made available to 'non-accounting organisations'.[76]

At the March 1980 meeting of the IASC board, however, integration was halted in its tracks. A blocking minority emerged, as the UK & Ireland, Australia, and South Africa joined the Netherlands in rejecting the JWP's revised proposals. Formally, the board decided to 'defer' further consideration of the proposals 'pending exploration of the possibilities for restructuring the Board to include other parties'.[77] This had been the issue on which the Netherlands had rejected an earlier version, and, as is discussed more fully below, the IASC board had in fact begun considering participation by non-accountants in the later part of 1979.

For the UK & Irish delegation, participation by non-accountants was not the critical issue. On that score, the original proposal had been acceptable in principle. Their main objection was to the new possibility that founder members might be rotated off the board:

> [W]hile the preservation of the nine reserved seats on the Board of IASC may no longer be acceptable, any alternative arrangements must reflect the dependence of IASC upon the active participation firstly of countries which have experience of, and a capability in, standard setting and secondly of countries which could exercise influence on the recognition of international standards in the major regions of the world.[78]

Although there was no formal vote on a UK & Irish resolution to defer consideration of the integration agreement, this was in fact decided as it became clear that the draft integration agreement was not supported by the required qualified majority of the IASC board. At the JWP meeting held the day after the IASC's board meeting, Gordon Cowperthwaite summed up the position: 'We seem to be back at square one.'[79]

7.3.3. Towards the Mutual Commitments

It was not perhaps as dramatic as Cowperthwaite suggested. But the initiative had clearly shifted from IFAC to the IASC. The series of draft integration agreements had been driven by IFAC's strong push towards amalgamation. But after March 1980, the next major step in the negotiations would be taken only when the IASC had made up its mind.

The IASC's self-declared time out lasted until January 1981, when the JWP reconvened to discuss new proposals. In the meantime, the IASC did indeed proceed with considering the involvement of non-accountants, which was the stated reason for deferring talks on integration. Work proceeded on proposals for a Consultative Group. Under the influence of Burggraaff, the idea of integration was discarded to avoid criticisms that the IASC would become even more dominated by the accountancy profession.[80] Even Gordon Cowperthwaite, with whom Burggraaff stayed in close touch during this period, was willing to concede this point:

> G. C. admitted that we were looking for something like a chameleon: IFAC and IASC should be capable of being seen united by those who want so, and at the same time as being separate by those who prefer it that way. G. C. was prepared to consider a better word than 'integration', but so far had not discovered one.[81]

But an acceptable phrase was found by Secretary Allan Cook, who developed the idea of 'mutual commitments'. Under this formula, the IASC and IFAC would each retain their independent existence and their respective Constitutions but would bind themselves by a written agreement that specified the obligations both bodies would undertake towards each other. Any suggestion of subordination or takeover was thereby avoided.

This proved to be a fruitful approach to defining the relationship between the IASC and the accountancy profession. But it left the contentious issue of control over IASC board seats undecided. The positions of various member bodies on this point were made clear at the June 1980 board meeting.[82] Nigeria was the strongest proponent of rotation, or the required re-election, of all members. The Netherlands declared that it was not keen on rotation but that it would be prepared to be rotated off the board to address the complaints of countries like Denmark and New Zealand which believed that they did not have a significant opportunity to participate. For similar reasons, South Africa was in favour of rotation. The opposite point of view was expressed by Seigo Nakajima of Japan: 'The only reason for rotation is to introduce a new viewpoint, a new capacity or experience.... Experts should not be selected on a democratic basis.' John Grenside for the UK & Ireland insisted that 'Present founder members should remain because some of them are key accounting nations.... IASC will lose credibility if it drops certain core countries.' Burggraaff attempted to counter this by arguing that the IASC's credibility would also be impaired if no rotation was introduced. But Chairman John Hepworth addressed the essence of Grenside's concerns: 'I don't believe that IASC could afford to lose the US and the UK, and that for technical reasons, not political or commercial ones.'

The result of these discussions was that the board agreed, with Nigeria dissenting, that 'It did not wish to agree to a re-election requirement for founder members.'[83] On this basis, a proposal structured according to the concept of mutual commitments was prepared in which the IASC went no further than including as one of the commitments that it would 'undertake to reconsider' its election procedure.

This document was discussed by the JWP at its meeting of 14 January 1981, in Toronto. This was the first meeting of the JWP since discussion of the integration agreements had been called off, and it was regarded as 'critical'.[84] On the table were the mutual commitments proposal from the IASC, as well as a revised integration proposal prepared by Cowperthwaite. As it happened, none of those present remembered whose turn it was to chair the meeting, so a coin was tossed to determine the chairman. Burggraaff won. So he was able to decide that the mutual commitments proposal would be discussed first. This had a major influence on the course of the meeting.[85]

At first, though, the meeting threatened to become acrimonious when the IFAC delegation declared that the IASC's mutual commitments proposal was unacceptable.[86] According to Cowperthwaite, the proposal 'appears to go back beyond 1973 and casts in stone the position that IASC is not a part of IFAC'.[87] Burggraaff reiterated the essential element of his position:

that there had been one major change to the environment since the arrangements about integration that took place in 1973. It was the criticism that was developing from OECD and to a lesser extent the UN, from FEI [Financial Executives Institute[88]], and to a lesser extent the business community generally that accounting standards were too important to be left to the experts.

When the issue of rotating the founder members was brought up again, the meeting appeared to be heading for a deadlock. However, Burggraaff created a breakthrough by venturing a personal suggestion that had not been discussed in the IASC. He asked whether IFAC would accept an arrangement by which all IASC board members would be appointed by the IFAC Council, with safeguards in the Mutual Commitments pact that the founder members could retain their seats. This cleared the air immediately as Cowperthwaite 'welcomed the proposal heartily'.

This comparatively simple formula proved to be a framework within which the complex set of issues facing the IASC could be solved.[89] The continued existence of the IASC as a separate body, coupled with the possibility of board seats for non-accountants, made the IASC less of an instrument of the accountancy profession. On the other hand, the right of IFAC to appoint board members went some distance towards satisfying those who favoured integration of the two bodies. As to founder member rotation, it was agreed in the Mutual Commitments that founder members would continue until 1987 and that subsequently at least nine members would be 'the most significant countries in terms of the status and development of the accounting profession or that are of significant importance to international commerce and trade'.[90] The wording was deliberately chosen to allay any doubts that not only the United States and the United Kingdom, but also countries like Japan, France, and Germany would retain their seats. The aspirations of the developing countries were addressed by the commitment that 'preferably not less than three' board seats would be given to developing countries. In addition, a clause was inserted in the IASC's Constitution that IFAC would contribute 10 per cent of the IASC's budget to defray the costs of the participation in steering committees by members who were not represented on the board. It was understood that this contribution was intended to help the developing countries in particular.

Although it required extensive consultations to agree the details of the new IASC Constitution and the Mutual Commitments, the essentials of the accord reached by the JWP in January 1981 were accepted without great difficulty by the IASC and IFAC. The new Constitution was formally approved by the original founder members at the Mexico City congress of October 1982.

7.4. ORIGINS OF THE CONSULTATIVE GROUP AND OUTSIDE BOARD MEMBERS

From the previous discussion, it is evident that the effort to involve non-accountants in the IASC's work was partly a tactical response to political pressures facing the IASC around 1980.[91] Yet, the loosening of the ties between the IASC and the accountancy profession, which started with the formation of the Consultative Group and the subsequent allocation of board seats to other organizations, was a more fundamental process, that went on long after the pressures that set it in

7.4.1. Early Stirrings

When the IASC was founded, the ICAEW probably took it for granted, on the analogy with its Accounting Standards Steering Committee, that the individuals on the IASC should all be members of the founder accountancy bodies. The AICPA, which had just lost the task of setting domestic standards to the independent FASB, preferred to keep the IASC under the control of the accountancy profession. But as indicated above, it was self-evident to the Dutch delegation that other parties should be involved, in keeping with their national background. When the NIVRA received the invitation to join the IASC, one element of its reaction was to argue that 'Auditors cannot lay down the law for society.'[92] It apparently informed the Dutch trade unions about the IASC initiative, because these in their turn wrote to the International Confederation of Free Trade Unions and the World Confederation of Labour to suggest that these bodies should approach the IASC in order to be invited to participate in standard setting.[93] There is no sign, however, that these international labour organizations actually took any steps towards the IASC.

The NIVRA did achieve some result, though. It was behind the insertion of a clause in the IASC Agreement which expanded the 'best endeavours' undertaking to persuading governments and the industrial and business community that published accounts should comply with the IASC's standards (paragraph 1(c)(i)).

Another initiative in this area was taken by the Mexican delegate Manuel Galván. In 1974, he arranged a meeting between Henry Benson and his compatriot Alfredo Améscua, who was the chairman of the International Association of Financial Executives Institutes (IAFEI). The IAFEI had set up a committee on international financial reporting in 1973 as a reaction to the establishment of the IASC, and it expressed a desire for coordination with the IASC.[94] Although Benson expressed the view that 'The more people think about international standards and work on the subject the better,' he did not expect much from the IAFEI initiative.[95] Contacts with IAFEI did indeed lapse shortly afterwards.

When the IASC's first exposure draft was published in 1974, some efforts were made to compile a list of about twenty international organizations that were added to the mailing list.[96] As discussed in Chapter 6, Henry Benson and the succeeding IASC chairmen devoted considerable energy to stimulating the interest of other organizations in the work of the IASC. However, these efforts were directed towards gaining recognition of IASC standards rather than direct participation in standard setting. Moreover, although contacts were developed with some of these organizations, many were infrequent and informal, some lapsed, and in other cases the contacts remained limited to a mere inclusion in the mailing list.[97] As shown in Chapter 5, a variety of individuals and organizations in the member countries commented on IASC exposure drafts, but these were indirect contacts, funneled through the member bodies.

7.4.2. Formation of the Consultative Group

Throughout the 1970s, most member bodies seem to have been content with this situation, even though the NIVRA occasionally raised the point of participation by other than accountancy bodies.[98] The Dutchman Hans Burggraaff, who succeeded to the chairmanship in July 1980, was personally convinced of the need to provide the IASC with a broader basis, but it required pressure from the outside, in particular from the OECD, to prod the IASC into action.

In October 1979, following the IASC's presentation before the OECD Working Group in April that year, the board began to discuss the involvement of other organizations in earnest. Initially, the board was not keen to make drastic changes. It preferred to work within the limits of the present Constitution, and it was reluctant to take measures that would inhibit free discussion at board meetings. After reviewing its existing contacts, the board agreed that it was important to 'monitor' developments at organizations such as the UN, the OECD, the EEC, and national standard setters. Of the other contacts, only the ICC was considered sufficiently close to the IASC in its views on international accounting standards to warrant closer ties. This belief was largely inspired by the public stance taken by the ICC over the report of the UN Group of Experts in 1978 (*see* above).[99] But even in the case of the ICC, no closer ties were envisaged than consultation on responses to UN initiatives or encouraging coordinated responses to IASC drafts by ICC members. In the case of other organizations, invitations to discuss point outlines or drafts would be sent out on a case by case basis, depending on the nature of the standards projects at hand.[100]

But after March 1980, when the IASC decided to defer discussions with IFAC over integration, more radical changes in the IASC's procedures began to be discussed, including group consultations with interested parties, observers at board meetings, more outsider participation in steering committees, and the allocation of board seats to other organizations.[101] At that time, France, the Netherlands, and the United States had accounting standard setters which were not controlled by the accountancy profession, and which included non-accountants. The UK and Irish Accounting Standards Committee was, until 1982, composed exclusively of nominees of its accountancy body members, but in 1982 its membership arrangements were completely overhauled. The new focus was on seeking a balance between preparers, auditors, and users of accounts.[102] Although there were therefore precedents for opening the IASC to non-accountants, the IASC's member bodies did not necessarily wish to copy their national situation to an international level. As François-Maurice Richard, representing the French profession on the IFAC Council, expressed it, the IASC should remain 'of the profession, for the profession'.[103] On balance, the IASC board was not immediately willing to adopt the most far-reaching change, the involvement of outside parties as board members. Apart from reservations on the part of the member bodies, there was also the practical problem that the IASC had in fact very little information about the extent to which outside parties actually wanted to be involved with the IASC. In June 1980, it was therefore agreed to sound out a number of organizations about the possibility of setting up a consultative group. A list of eight potential members was compiled, consisting mainly of those organizations from the 1974 mailing list with which the IASC had maintained some form of contact.[104] Burggraaff and Cook visited these organizations in person and found that the idea was favourably received.[105] In March 1981, it was therefore decided to establish the Group, and it was convened for the first time on 13 October of that year. The composition and subsequent operations of the Consultative Group are discussed in Section 4.16.

The idea of a consultative group, while it was an important step for the IASC in opening to the outside world, was not without precedent. In 1972, the Wheat Study, which recommended the establishment of the Financial Accounting Standards Board in the United States, proposed that it works closely with a Financial Accounting Standards Advisory Council (FASAC), which was to be composed of representatives from a wide range of organizations interested in financial reporting.[106] From the beginning, FASAC has met quarterly in joint sessions with the board and its technical staff. In the United Kingdom, the Accounting Standards Committee had set up a Consultative Group in 1976 with 'representatives of finance, commerce, industry and government and other persons concerned with financial reporting'.[107]

7.4.3. Financial Analysts, but Not Financial Executives, Join the Board

For the time being, setting up a consultative group was as far as the IASC would go. When it was decided to discuss the idea of such a group with outside organizations, it was agreed that these organizations would not be involved as full board members. However, Burggraaff believed that 'IASC should have non accountants on its Board.'[108] In the Mutual Commitments proposal developed towards the end of 1980 this idea was put before the board again. By that time the board members had apparently become more receptive to the idea. Therefore, the 1982 Constitution did indeed allow the board to invite up to four organizations 'having an interest in financial reporting' to be represented on the board (paragraph 12(a)).

When the IASC began to give effect to this clause, it did not directly consider the financial analysts as the most likely candidate. Initially, it was believed that the ICC was the most promising organization with which to develop further contacts, but, in the end, the ICC did not wish to extend its participation beyond membership of the Consultative Group. Like other Consultative Group members, the ICC believed that it was not authorized to commit its members and that it did not have adequate arrangements for consultation and debate.[109] When, in 1980, the list was drawn up of organizations to be approached for developing further contacts, the financial analysts were ranked last and were subject to the proviso that none of the other organizations could be assumed to represent them.[110]

However, the IASC might have known better. As early as November 1973, David C. Damant, the vice-president of the European Federation of Financial Analysts' Societies, had written to Secretary Paul Rosenfield to express his interest in the work of the IASC.[111] Over the next years, Damant continued to write to, and call on, the IASC secretariat, attempting in various ways to establish a liaison between the IASC and the International Co-ordinating Committee of Financial Analysts' Associations (ICCFAA, established in 1974). It is not surprising that the ICCFAA was the first to respond, and with great enthusiasm, to the IASC's invitation to join the Consultative Group.[112]

In June 1984, the IASC decided to invite ICCFAA and the IAFEI to join the IASC board. The ICCFAA accepted forthwith.[113] Damant, according to Secretary-General David Cairns, 'was totally committed to the thing, very supportive, wanted it to happen, made it happen, as a result of which the board made the decision, and they came on with effect from 1 January 1986'. IAFEI was, Cairns said, more difficult: 'Part of the problem was that the FEI institutes in France and Germany perceived the IASC as a body of auditors, because the institutes that were members of IASC in their countries were also auditors,' and they had picked only auditors as members of their delegations. Also, finance was a problem, which was not solved until 1996, when the IAFEI finally joined the IASC board.[114]

7.5. THE LAST ATTEMPT AT A MERGER WITH IFAC: THE BISHOP WORKING PARTY

Following the signing of the 1982 Constitution and the Mutual Commitments, relations between the IASC and IFAC settled down to a largely uneventful routine. The chairmen of both bodies occasionally attended meetings of the other body and an exchange of information was maintained. IASC annual reports were included in the IFAC annual report beginning in 1983. As specified in the Mutual Commitments, a high-level Co-ordinating Committee was set up which met, as a rule, once a year. Its main task, as stated in its terms of reference, was to monitor the progress made in gaining compliance with IASC standards, and to develop plans to further promote acceptance and compliance.[115] As shown in Chapter 6, compliance with IASC standards, or rather the increasingly evident lack of it, had become an important topic for the IASC in the early 1980s. Yet it seems that the Co-ordinating Committee achieved little more than an exchange of information on efforts taken by each of the two bodies individually.

But the idea of a merger did not go away. Although IFAC, and in particular its Executive Director Robert Sempier, denied that it was aiming for a merger, IFAC continued to express its concern over the confusion that the separate existence of IFAC and the IASC was said to be causing in the outside world.[116] The idea of a merger was effectively brought back on the agenda in the run-up to the Thirteenth World Congress of Accountants[117] in Tokyo by Raymond G. Harris. In August 1987, Harris, a partner in Deloitte Haskins & Sells Samson Belair and the Canadian representative on the IFAC Council, circulated a letter calling for a meeting during the upcoming Tokyo congress to discuss a review of the Mutual Commitments. He cited the concern of a number of unspecified IFAC member bodies about the representation of the accountancy profession by two organizations and the confusion which this had caused. In addition, Harris pointed out the possibility of cost savings by combining the operations of the two bodies.[118] The meeting did take place on 13 October and discussed Harris' proposal to establish a review working party with terms of reference clearly pointing towards a merger.[119]

Harris' letter was, on the face of it, a private initiative, but subsequently he claimed that he had obtained prior informal agreement from the Canadian, Australian, UK, and US accountancy bodies.[120] He must have been aware that some of the forces that had blocked a merger in 1980 had been weakened since then. In 1980, the Netherlands and the United Kingdom led the opposition to the integration proposals. But in 1987, the incoming IFAC chairman was a past president of the ICAEW, Price Waterhouse partner Richard Wilkes, who was greatly in favour of a merger. This would make it difficult for the ICAEW to put up strong opposition. Given that, in the context of a merger, the location of the IASC secretariat might well come up for discussion, the ICAEW still favoured the IASC's independence.[121]

In the Netherlands, the NIVRA's influential General Director Henk Volten had, by 1986, come to the conclusion that there were no objections for the IASC and IFAC to share a secretariat. Volten was also dissatisfied with the strategic choices made by the IASC in March 1987, when the board agreed to reduce the number of options in its standards (*see* Section 9.3). According to Volten, if the IASC had indeed largely completed a set of basic standards, the proper response would be to reduce the staff and the frequency of meetings, not to seek new tasks. In particular, he thought the IASC, as a 'technical committee', should not have much to do with encouraging compliance with the standards. This was a task for the 'administrative' body, IFAC. During the spring of 1987, Volten persuaded the NIVRA to encourage international initiatives in this direction. Naturally, Volten welcomed Harris' letter and replied that his Council had decided 'that it would be highly desirable to investigate the possibility of a merger'.[122]

Those who wanted to maintain the independence of the IASC took the Harris initiative very seriously. During August and September 1987, IASC Secretary-General David Cairns actively sought declarations of support for the IASC's independence from IASC board member bodies and members of its Consultative Group. By the time of the Tokyo congress, both the advocates and opponents of a merger were mobilized, and the congress was said to be the scene of some quite intense political activity.[123] In the end, the twenty member bodies that met at Harris' invitation agreed to set up a working party to review the aims, effectiveness, and relationship of IFAC and the IASC. But the terms of reference actually given to the working party, as opposed to those proposed by Harris, focused mainly on improving the cost-effectiveness and financing arrangements of both organizations, and placed little emphasis on the possibility of a merger.[124] The choice of John Bishop, a former IASC board member for Australia as well as a former member of the IFAC Council, did not predispose the working party to press for a merger, either. In Bishop's view, controlling the costs of the profession's international activities was the real issue, not merger.[125] The outcome of the Tokyo congress was therefore seen as a compromise, if not an actual victory for those who advocated the IASC's independence.[126]

As is discussed in Chapter 8, financing was indeed a serious concern for the IASC by the late 1980s. But these concerns were not such that they could be alleviated by cost savings following from joint activities or a merger with IFAC. Compared with IFAC, the IASC was already a highly efficient organization which achieved much with a small staff. Rather, the IASC's financial problems were caused by the increase in the volume and pace of its work that was the result of its strategic reorientation during 1987 and 1988. Assisted by its new links with the International Organization of Securities Commission (IOSCO), the IASC was finally beginning to be seen as the potential accounting standard setter for international financial markets (*see* Chapter 10). This change in the work and the position of the IASC was going on while the Bishop Working Party went about its work, and the change made the working party seem increasingly anachronistic.

John Bishop saw the question of the IASC's autonomy as a key issue, and also a sensitive one. As he wanted to have the IASC's views at the earliest opportunity, he met with members of its board and with the Consultative Group in June 1988.[127] In the Consultative Group, he was given to understand in no uncertain terms that a review of the relations between the IASC and IFAC was very inappropriate at that juncture. In particular, the representatives from IOSCO, Paul Guy and Bertrand d'Illiers, made it clear that it was incompatible with the IASC's new ambitions and work programme to be moved back into the fold of the accountancy profession.[128] Not least because of the strong support of the Consultative Group, Cairns felt confident to conclude in September 1988 'that the threat of merger, or perhaps takeover, has disappeared. This will allow us to concentrate on the far more important matters ahead of us.'[129]

From this point onwards, the IASC essentially went on to pursue its own agenda, including its plans to set up a fund-raising foundation (discussed in Section 8.15). From the IASC's point of view, the main function of the working party was now to endorse this suggestion. In May 1989 Chairman Georges Barthès de Ruyter wrote somewhat impatiently to John Bishop that, while the IASC had decided to wait with a decision on the planned foundation until the working party had reported: 'The Board needs to know, and know fast, whether additional funding will be available from 1990—or whether it has to slow down at the very moment that it is achieving greater recognition and success than ever before.'[130]

The final report of the working party, bearing a December 1989 date, was highly satisfactory to the IASC. The working party concluded that 'Any development in this direction [of emphasizing or increasing the dominance of the accounting profession over IASC's activities] would be highly undesirable and should be avoided if at all possible.' Moreover, the working party concluded on the basis of a survey that the IASC was a well-run and highly regarded organization, and it welcomed the IASC's own plans for obtaining more funding.[131] That the relation between the IASC and IFAC was no longer the burning issue as it had been in the 1970s and early 1980s is suggested by the tepid reactions to the report. It appeared to be impossible to convene a meeting of the commissioning bodies to receive and discuss the report, and therefore it was agreed, rather weakly, that the IASC and IFAC would make presentations during the 1992 international congress in Washington on the steps they had taken, or would take, to implement 'those recommendations made by Bishop with which they were in agreement'.[132] The knotty question of relations between the IASC and IFAC had not so much been resolved as simply overtaken by events.

The final severing of the link between the IASC and IFAC occurred in May 2000, when IFAC's member bodies approved a restructuring of the IASC to become a body independent of the accountancy profession (*see* Chapter 13).

Part III
1987–2000

8

The Changing Look of the IASC: People, Structure, and Funding

This chapter focuses on issues relating to the operation of the International Accounting Standards Committee (IASC). Considerable attention is devoted to the IASC's leading figures, the broadening composition of the board delegations, the conduct of board meetings, the IASC's finances, and the organizational units that complemented the work of the board. As in Chapter 4, readers may wish to consult Appendices 2, 3, and 5 in conjunction with this chapter.

8.1. CHAIRMEN AND VICE-CHAIRMEN

The IASC continued its practice of having each chairman serve for two-and-a-half years.

Georges Barthès de Ruyter (born in 1931) became IASC chairman in October 1987, succeeding John Kirkpatrick, and he served until June 1990. He had joined the IASC board in 1982. Barthès was an audit partner of Arthur Andersen & Co. in Paris.[1] He was a member of the French standard-setting body, the Conseil National de la Comptabilité. Kirkpatrick, who had won his chairmanship in a contested election, counselled Barthès to choose his successor at an early stage. Because of his belief that the chairmanship should reflect a diversity of accounting cultures, Barthès with support from John Kirkpatrick devised a policy, carried forward by successive boards, of rotation between Anglo-American chairmen and non–Anglo-American chairmen,[2] which proceeded as follows:

John Kirkpatrick, United Kingdom (1985–7)
Georges Barthès de Ruyter, France (1987–90)
Arthur Wyatt, United States (1990–2)
Eiichi Shiratori, Japan (1993–5)
Michael Sharpe, Australia (1995–7)
Stig Enevoldsen, Nordic Federation (1998–2000)
Thomas Jones, International Association of Financial Executives Institutes (2000–1)

Arthur R. Wyatt (born in 1927) was the chairman from July 1990 until December 1992. He joined the US delegation to the IASC board on 1 January 1988. In

Figure 8.1. IASC Chairmen Eiichi Shiratori and Arthur Wyatt at the World Congress of Accountants, Washington DC, October 1992

1953, he received a Ph.D. in Accountancy from the University of Illinois and thus became the only IASC chairman with an earned doctorate. He was a principal in the Accounting Principles Group of Arthur Andersen, in Chicago. Previously, he had been a full-time accounting professor at the University of Illinois, a technical partner in Arthur Andersen, chairman of the Accounting Standards Executive Committee of the American Institute of Certified Public Accountants (AICPA), a member of the AICPA's board of directors, and, from 1985 to 1987, a member of the Financial Accounting Standards Board (FASB). Following his surprise resignation from the FASB, Wyatt was appointed to the IASC board in 1988 with the intention that he might succeed to the chairmanship two years later. But his was not the shortest board service prior to becoming chairman. Hans Burggraaff became chairman in July 1980 only sixteen months after his first board meeting.

Eiichi Shiratori (1934–98) became chairman in January 1993 and served until June 1995. He was a member of the IASC board from 1983 to 1988 and rejoined it in 1990. After attending graduate school at Northwestern University, near Chicago, he returned to Japan in 1962 to help open Arthur Andersen & Co.'s office there. He became a partner in the worldwide firm in 1971. After spending most of his career in the Arthur Andersen & Co. organization, he left in 1990 to become chief executive officer of IONA International Corporation, based in Japan. From 1976 to 1980, he was a member of the Business Accounting Deliberation Council, which was the accounting standards adviser to the Ministry of Finance.

Figure 8.2. IASC chairmen, IASC twentieth anniversary conference, 29 June 1993. *Left to right*: Eiichi Shiratori, Sir Henry Benson, John Hepworth, Georges Barthès de Ruyter

Michael J. Sharpe (born in 1937) was chairman from July 1995 to December 1997. He was national audit partner and a member of the executive committee of the Australian firm of Coopers & Lybrand, in Sydney, and was senior technical partner (accounting and auditing) for Coopers & Lybrand International. He joined the IASC board in 1990. Sharpe was president of the Institute of Chartered Accountants in Australia and a member of the Australian Securities and Investments Commission's Takeover Panel. He was a director of State Super, which was Australia's largest superannuation fund, and served on the board of the Australian Stock Exchange. Henry Benson, under whom he worked in the firm's London office in the 1960s, was his mentor over many years, and it was Benson who urged Sharpe to accept the invitation to represent Australia on the IASC board.[3]

Stig Enevoldsen (born in 1950) served as chairman from January 1998 to June 2000.[4] He was an audit partner in Deloitte & Touche, Copenhagen. He joined the IASC board in 1989, first as a member of the Danish delegation and then representing the Nordic Federation of Public Accountants, serving until 2000. From 1987 to 1996, he was a member of the Regnskabsteknisk Udvalg (Danish Accounting Standards Committee), serving as chairman the last six years. He was an adviser to the Danish government on the implementation of the European Economic Community's Seventh Directive.[5]

Figure 8.3. Michael Sharpe

Thomas E. Jones (born in 1938) became the chairman during the second half of 2000, awaiting implementation of the decision to restructure the IASC board. He joined the IASC board in 1996, representing the International Association of Financial Executives Institutes (IAFEI). A Briton by birth and a member of the Institute of Chartered Accountants in England and Wales (ICAEW), he had held positions in Italy and Belgium before joining Citicorp, in New York City, where he was successively the chief financial officer and an executive vice-president.[6] Jones was a member of the board of trustees, 1991–8, including service as its vice-president in 1996–8, of the Financial Accounting Foundation (FAF), which oversees the FASB. He served on the FASB's Emerging Issues Task Force from 1985 to 1989. He had been chairman of the Committee on Corporate Reporting of the Financial Executives Institute (FEI), and he also chaired the Chief Financial Officers Committee of the American Bankers Association. Jones was the only IASC chairman not to have been a partner in an accountancy firm.

Eiichi Shiratori, Michael Sharpe, and Stig Enevoldsen were elected as chairmen-designate between twenty-three and thirty-two months before the beginning of their respective terms as chairman, the election of Sharpe and Enevoldsen even preceding the installation of their predecessor. Unlike the earlier chairmen-designates, Sharpe and Enevoldsen also carried the title of deputy chairman, which implied no additional duties, yet they were participants in virtually all of the correspondence between the secretary-general and the chairman.[7] Hence, Sharpe

Figure 8.4. Stig Enevoldsen

and Enevoldsen, compared to the earlier chairmen, had a smooth transition into the chairmanship. In previous years, the chairman-designate had been elected nine to fifteen months before the beginning of their term.

At the IASC board's October–November 1997 meeting, held in Paris, it elected two vice-chairmen: Patricia McConnell, a member of the financial analysts' delegation, and Thomas Jones, from the financial executives delegation. Both were based in the United States. Their terms began in January 1998, coincident with Stig Enevoldsen becoming chairman. Hence, the elected deputy chairman was replaced by two elected vice-chairmen. The reason given for this departure was the board's reluctance to elect a new chairman-designate cum deputy chairman because of the uncertainty over the future role of the chairman in the light of the ongoing strategy review and possible restructuring of the IASC.[8] Both McConnell and Jones were widely respected members of the board.

Figure 8.5. Thomas Jones

8.2. CHANGING COMPOSITION OF BOARD MEMBERSHIP

As with the chairmen, the board delegates continued to be appointed for two-and-a-half-year terms. In 1987, the board was composed of thirteen country delegations and the financial analysts' delegation. Under article 4 of the IASC's Constitution, approved in 1982, the board could co-opt to its membership as many as four organizations possessing an interest in financial reporting. As will be seen, the IASC added two such organizations to the board in 1995–6, bringing its total membership to sixteen.

The sponsor of each delegation to the board had the unfettered right to select the members of the delegation, subject to the limit on the number who could attend. There is no evidence that questions arose over the identity or background of any of the delegates.

Figure 8.6. IASC delegates and staff, Singapore, November 1990. *Front, left to right*: Patricia McConnell, Eiichi Shiratori, Peter Wilmot, Gillian Bertol, Christopher Stronge, Arthur Wyatt, David Cairns, Giuseppe Verna, Ambrogio Picolli, Jean-Luc Dumont. *Middle, left to right*: Johan van Helleman, Raymond Béthoux, Michael Sharpe, John Hudson, Dietz Mertin, John Chironna, Yukio Ono, Brigid Curran, David Damant, Erik Mamelund, Geoffrey Mitchell, Ron Murray. *Back, left to right*: Richard Golikoski, Cor Regoort, Doug Brooking, Herman Marseille, Gilbert Gélard, Rolf Rundfelt, Paul Cherry, Fouad Alaeddin, Art Guthrie, In Ki Joo, John Denman, John Carchrae

8.2.1. Involvement of National Standard Setters

Encouraged by a recommendation of the IASC's Foundation Working Party in 1994 (*see* Section 8.15), the leadership of the board, especially Chairman Michael Sharpe, actively sought to encourage the accountancy bodies to nominate a member of their national standard setter to the board, so as to take advantage of their technical expertise as well as enlist their support.[9] The following newly appointed board members, by year, reflected that policy:

1995 David Tweedie, chairman of the UK Accounting Standards Board (ASB); Ian Hammond, member of the Australian Accounting Standards Board (AASB); Rafael Gómez Eng, retiring chairman of Mexico's Accounting Principles Committee; Reyaz Mihular, chairman of Sri Lanka's Accounting Standards Committee; and Alex Milburn, immediate past chairman of Canada's Accounting Standards Board

1996 Per Gunslev, chairman of Denmark's Accounting Standards Committee

1997 Peter Wilmot, chairman of South Africa's Accounting Practices Board; Leslie Anderson, member of Zimbabwe's Accounting Practices Board; and Michael Crooch, retiring chairman of the AICPA's Accounting Standards Executive Committee

1998 Kenneth Spencer, chairman of the Australian Accounting Standards Board; and Jean den Hoed, chairman of the preparers' delegation of the Netherlands' Council on Annual Reporting

The most pivotal of these appointments was David Tweedie. Michael Sharpe intervened personally to persuade the president of the ICAEW to arrange Tweedie's appointment to the IASC board.[10]

Throughout the 1990s, a member of the FASB attended board meetings as a guest and then as an observer (*see* below).

To be sure, a number of members of the board appointed in prior years, such as Seigo Nakajima, Joe Cummings, Hans Burggraaff, David Hobson, Doug Hagerman, Stephen Elliott, Ralph Walters, Peter Stilling, Stig Enevoldsen, Sigvard Heurlin, and Chris Nobes were either current or former members or chairmen of national standard setters. Several of the staff observers, including Doug Thomas, John Denman, Paul Rosenfield, and Warren McGregor, were at the same time providing technical support for national standard setters. But by the middle of the 1990s, when the board had risen to the challenge set by the International Organization of Securities Commissions (IOSCO) to fashion standards on complex and controversial subjects, a policy of tapping such expertise and collaboration became all the more important.

8.2.2. Financial Analysts

The financial analysts' delegation continued to be very active on the board, and, as mentioned above, one of its members, Patricia McConnell, became vice-chairman in 1998. With David Cairns's encouragement, David Damant often invited one or more local analysts to attend board meetings as part of the delegation.[11] From 1991 onwards, it was usual for the financial analysts to have a delegation of four to six persons at board meetings. Among other things, this practice helped the IASC spread the word about its work, and Damant raised the funds necessary to pay the analysts' board contribution.

The members of the delegation were very active in board discussions, and considerable attention was paid to their views. The lone financial analyst to serve in a country delegation, Doug Brooking of South Africa, was also a chartered accountant. He joined the board in time to chair the steering committee on earnings per share, leading to IAS 33.

8.2.3. Financial Executives

The US delegation included a preparer without interruption from 1976 to 2000, a record not even approached by any other delegation. Preparers began to appear

Figure 8.7. IASC delegates, observers, and staff, Amsterdam, May 1995. *Front, left to right*: Terry Harding, Arlene Rodda Thomas, Albrecht Ruppel, Bernard Jaudeau, Jim Leisenring, Jean-Luc Dumont, Roberto Tizzano, Hank Howarth, Liesel Knorr, Eiichi Shiratori, Monica Singer, Judith Cunningham, Jan McCahey, Narendra Sarda, Munir Al-Borno. *Back, left to right*: Cees Dubbeld, Paul Pacter, Karel Van Hulle, Barry Robbins, Sigvard Heurlin, Harald Brandsås (*behind Heurlin*), Peter Stilling, Rolf Rundfelt, Gilbert Gélard, Jan Klaassen, Heinz Kleekämper, Ian Somerville, Ray De Angelo, Patricia McConnell, Etsuo Sawa, Jay Perrell (*behind Sawa*), Michael Sharpe (*in front of Sawa*), John Denman, David Damant, Bruce Picking (*in front of Damant*), Stig Enevoldsen (*next to Damant*), Christopher Nobes (*next to Enevoldsen*), Paul Cherry, Yukio Ono, Johan van Helleman, Herbert Biener

in delegations that previously had had only partners of accountancy firms or representatives of the professional institutes. In 1992, Bernard Jaudeau, of Thomson, became the first preparer to form part of the French delegation. In 1993, Bernd-Joachim Menn, the chief accountant at Bayer, became the first to occupy the seat set aside for a preparer almost ten years previously in the German delegation. Also in 1993, Ian Somerville, of South African Breweries, became the first preparer in the South African delegation. In 1995, Geoff Heeley, of Broken Hill Proprietary, became the first preparer in the Australian delegation since 1987. As the IASC was recording improvements in its standards during the 1990s and had begun to command the attention of the world's securities market regulators, listed companies began to take its work seriously.

In 1995–6, the IASC secured two preparer delegations for the board, increasing the size of the board to sixteen delegations. In 1995, the Federation of Swiss Industrial Holding Companies became the board's second delegation, after the analysts, not representing one or more professional accountancy bodies. The IASC had invited the Schweizerische Kammer der Bücher-, Steuer- und Treuhandexperten

(Swiss Institute of Certified Accountants and Tax Consultants) to send a delegation to the board, but it declined, much to the annoyance of a number of the large Swiss multinational companies. More and more of these companies were using IASC standards (see Section 12.2.5) but complained that they were not involved in the process.[12] Probably because of the active role that Harry K. Schmid, of Nestlé, played in the delegation of the International Chamber of Commerce (ICC) in meetings of the Consultative Group, the IASC then turned to the Federation, whose members accounted for about half of the total capitalization of the Swiss stock market, and it accepted the invitation to send a delegation to the board formed around Schmid.[13] The Swiss accounting Institute agreed to fund one-third of the delegation's costs, and it supplied the technical adviser to the delegation, a partner in KPMG. The IASC explained that the appointment of the Federation to a board seat was 'in recognition of the great interest' by Swiss companies in the use of IASC standards.[14] Peter Zurbrügg, of Hoffmann-La Roche, followed by Malcolm Cheetham, of Novartis, accompanied Schmid in the Swiss delegation.

In 1996, following ten years of spurned invitations (see Section 7.4.3), the IASC finally succeeded in persuading the IAFEI to join the board.[15] It is interesting to note, however, that the German multinational, Siemens, attended meetings of the IASC's Consultative Group (see below) in the IAFEI delegation from 1988 to 1992. Attitudes had changed, the stakes were higher for industry in the mid-1990s, and, owing to the initiative of Thomas Jones, Citicorp provided funding to support IAFEI's participation. Jones, as noted above, was elected vice-chairman in 1998 and was elected chairman in 2000 to serve until the IASC was succeeded by the International Accounting Standards Board in early 2001. David C. Potter, of British American Tobacco, and L. Nelson Carvalho, of the Universidade de São Paulo, Brazil, also formed part of the delegation.

By 1996, the number of preparers in board delegations had increased markedly, which meant that the burden on company executives of proposed new disclosure requirements was discussed with greater feeling. Harry Schmid, together with Bernd-Joachim Menn, the financial executive in the German delegation, became the most active critics of proposed new disclosures. Schmid, in particular, carried weight because he represented the biggest constituency of users of IASC standards. But the addition of the Swiss preparer delegation and the financial executives delegation was important in terms of their impact on the voting, because a single preparer in a country delegation might not always have significant influence on the vote cast by the delegation.[16]

8.2.4. Other Delegations

The South African delegation, which had joined the board in 1978, remained through 2000 and was by far the longest-serving non-founder delegation. Because of the country's international isolation until the early 1990s, and even afterwards, the South African Institute of Chartered Accountants (SAICA) believed it was important to retain its seat on the board and not lose touch with international developments in accounting. SAICA therefore regularly sent a highly qualified delegation, which behaved in a non-confrontational manner during board meetings so as not to give offence.[17] In 1995, the South Africans began sharing their representation on the board with the Institute of Chartered Accountants of Zimbabwe.

In 1990, the Nordic Federation of Public Accountants became a member, following two years in which Denmark served under its own flag. The delegation was always composed of Danes, Swedes, and Norwegians, because the Finns, also a member of the Federation, never evinced an interest in participating. Iceland, also a member of the Nordic Federation, never participated. An original member of the delegation, Stig Enevoldsen, became IASC chairman in 1998.

A delegation from India joined the board in 1993. The sponsoring body, the Institute of Chartered Accountants of India, sent one representative only, either the current or immediate past president of the Institute. In 1995, India began sharing the delegation with Sri Lanka, and the Institute of Chartered Accountants of Sri Lanka contributed one member, Reyaz Mihular, who remained in the delegation until 2000.

The inclusion of Zimbabwe and Sri Lanka in shared delegations was intended to diversify the board's membership in the developing world.[18] Delegations representing Jordan, Korea, and Malaysia (see below) were similarly intended to expand the reach of the board into the Middle East and Asia, and to encompass emerging economies. The IASC was never successful in attracting a delegation from the Americas south of Mexico, although Peru was considered as a candidate in 1994.[19] As noted in Section 4.4, Chile had been invited to send a delegation in 1982, but declined. The board did not get round to holding a meeting in South America until March 2000, when it met in São Paulo, Brazil.

A Jordanian delegation served on the board from 1988 to 1995, which was constituted by the Arab Society of Certified Accountants, a body based in London but, at the request of Council of the International Federation of Accountants (IFAC), established a base also in Jordan.[20] The leading figure in the delegation during the first two years was Talal Abu-Ghazaleh. At the beginning of the board's April 1989 meeting in Brussels, he read a strongly worded statement to the board in which he complained that the IASC had spurned Jordan's invitation that the board hold a meeting in an Arab country. The country in question was Bahrain, and the leadership decided that it could not meet in a country whose member body had not issued the invitation and was not the 'home' country of the Arab Society.[21] Abu-Ghazaleh also argued for the appointment of members of his delegation to steering committees and to the Organisation and Planning Committee (OPC), and that a member of his delegation be elected to a new post, vice-chairman of the IASC.[22] He pleaded the case of developing countries and specifically of the Arab world. His oration was not well received,[23] yet Jordan was appointed to the OPC in 1990, and members of the Jordanian delegation were promptly named to two steering committees, including one on the development of accounting standards for developing and newly industrialized countries. The board held a meeting in Amman in June 1992. Creation of the position of vice-chairman at that time was not seriously considered.

Figure 8.8. IASC delegates, observers, and staff, London, December 2000. *Front, left to right*: Sir Bryan Carsberg, Thomas Jones, Patricia McConnell. *Middle row, left to right*: Magnus Orrell, Peter Clark, Angus Thomson, Ruud Vergoossen (*in front of Thomson*), Helmut Berndt, Makoto Shinohara, Christophe Patrier, Brian Morris, Toshihiko Amano, Tony Seah Cheo Wah, Jim Saloman, Jim Gaa, Elizabeth Fender (*in front of Gaa*), Kurt Ramin, Paul Cherry, Colin Fleming, Carlos Buenfil, Luis Moirón (*behind Buenfil*), Frank Palmer, Rieko Yanou, Shozo Yamazaki, Francis Desmarchelier, Patricia Walters, Narain Gupta, Susan Koski-Grafer, Leslie Anderson, Erna Swart, Kathryn McArdle. *Back, left to right*: Martin Noordzij, Jean den Hoed, Bob Rutherford, Christopher Nobes, Jean Keller, Sigvard Heurlin, Philipp Hallauer, Anthony Carey, Rolf Rundfelt, Tatsumi Yamada, John Smith, Nelson Carvalho, Harry Schmid, Jerry Edwards, Tony Cope, Per Gunslev, Peter Wilmot, David Damant, Malcolm Cheetham, Reyaz Mihular, Jochen Pape, Jan Klaassen, Karel Van Hulle, Gilbert Gélard, Martin Faarborg, Klaus-Peter Naumann

Korea sent a delegation from 1988 to 1992, but its senior member, who decided on how the delegation would vote, apparently had no facility with spoken English, and he had to rely on a younger colleague for translations during the board meetings.[24]

The IASC leadership was periodically concerned about the lack of full participation by the Italian delegation, which had joined the board in 1983.[25] No one from the Italian delegation turned up at the March 1987 board meeting in Sydney, where the board's future strategy was approved, or at the March 1993 meeting in Tokyo, where decisions were made on the drafts of several Improvements projects and on financial instruments. By the board's rules, an absence was the same as a 'no' vote. At only one other board meeting in the history of the IASC had a delegation been absent (France, in June 1978). It was not uncommon for some members of the Italian delegation to attend for only part of a board meeting. The delegation was removed from the OPC in 1986 after only two years, apparently because of poor attendance. The delegation came close to being rotated off the board in 1988.[26] In 1995, it was succeeded on the board by Malaysia.

Malaysia's delegation continued on the board until 2000, in which Tony Seah was a particularly active member. In 1997–8, the Securities Commission of Malaysia seconded a staff member, Azizah Mohd Jaafar, to the IASC research staff, which was arranged by Secretary-General Bryan Carsberg.[27]

The Mexicans, who were required to withdraw from the board at the end of 1987 for non-payment of dues, resumed sending a delegation in 1995. In order to raise the funds necessary to settle its unpaid dues of about £27,000, the Mexican Institute's Accounting Principles Committee held a major conference in 1994, at which representatives from the US Securities and Exchange Commission (SEC) and the FASB attended. The conference attracted a large attendance of accounting practitioners as well as companies thinking of listing in the United States. The conference succeeded in raising more funds than were necessary, and the Institute accepted an invitation received the following year to resume sending a delegation to the IASC board. Financial executives were invited to be part of the Mexican delegation, but they declined.[28] In the end, the IASC forgave Mexico's unpaid dues.[29]

Other countries that applied for board membership 'were not appointed because they had not demonstrated their interest in the work of the IASC by, for example, commenting on IASC exposure drafts or volunteering for steering committee membership'.[30]

8.2.5. Staff Observers/Technical Advisers

Each delegation was entitled to have a staff observer in addition to two voting members. The title of staff observer was changed to technical adviser in November 1990.[31] Even though they were known as observers, several distinguished themselves over long periods by the contributions they made at board meetings and their service on key steering committees, including John Denman (1983–95), of Canada; Gilbert Gélard (1988–97), of France; Warren McGregor (1986–99), of Australia; and Etsuo Sawa (1992–9), of Japan. Denman was instrumental in arranging the active collaboration of the Canadian Institute of Chartered Accountants (CICA) in the IASC's major project on financial instruments.

8.3. CHALLENGES FACING SOME DELEGATIONS DURING THE ACTIVIST 1990s

As the IASC's standards were being improved so as to be more prescriptive and less flexible, and as globalization began to change the business and economic conditions in which accounting functioned in some countries, the members of some delegations had to come to terms with a new reality in their deliberations and voting in the IASC. A question that was answered differently by different delegations, and sometimes differently by different members of the same delegation, was whether their mission was to vote at board meetings to defend their country's accepted accounting practice or, if it were different, whether they should instead vote for what they regarded, in the light of the board's technical papers and discussions, as being in the public interest. Furthermore, differences in culture and accounting traditions placed some delegations at a disadvantage during the discussions in board meetings.

In twenty votes on final standards or revisions of standards between 1995 and 2000, the US delegation voted twice against and abstained six times, which under the IASC's rules had the effect of a no-vote.[32] No other delegation cast fewer yes-votes during the same period. Yet the US delegation was not simply blocking departures from US generally accepted accounting principles (GAAP). At the October 1992 board meeting, as is discussed in Section 9.3.6, the US delegation had to decide whether to support the Improvements steering committee's proposed elimination of last-in, first-out (LIFO) as an allowed alternative treatment in the revision of IAS 2 despite its entrenched position in US GAAP. In the end, the US delegation surprised many by voting with the steering committee. The US delegation faced a confrontation with the FASB at the IASC board's April 1998 meeting, when its members had been urged by the FASB chairman to vote against E62 on financial instruments. Instead, the delegation decided to vote in favour of the draft. In March 2000, the US delegation agreed to the use of fair value in IAS 40, on investment property, even though this was contrary to US GAAP (see Section 11.9.1).

In contrast, the leadership of the Japanese Institute of Certified Public Accountants (JICPA) was of the view that its delegation was there to protect Japanese interests, that is, not to vote for the elimination of accounting practices from IASC standards that were accepted in Japan.[33] For that reason, the Japanese delegation was one of those which, in 1992, voted against the elimination of LIFO. Yet the Japanese delegation voted for all but one of the standards and exposure drafts approved by the board since 1995, even though several standards must have been at variance with Japanese regulation or accounting practice.[34]

For the Germans, as perhaps also for some other delegations, service on the IASC board was a challenge in several dimensions.[35] One was language. Those who dominated the board's fast-paced discussions tended to be the Americans, the Canadians, the British, the Australians, the South Africans, and even the Dutch, who had an Anglo-American outlook and could speak fluent English.[36] These countries all had national standard setters, and most had an agreed conceptual framework, as the IASC board had its own Anglo-American Framework, put in place in 1989. The members of their delegations usually could understand the accounting and financial jargon, such as that relating to securitization and other financial instruments, which was regularly being spewed forth in their richly inventive equity capital markets. Their standard setters spoke the language of US GAAP even if they did not follow US GAAP. Yet the Germans had no standard setter until 1998. Their accounting norms were laid down in statute law and were traditionally geared to the needs of income taxation and dividend distributions. A hierarchy of interpretive literature, ranging from court opinions to treatises and journal articles written by acknowledged experts, had come into existence to deal with the many practical issues not covered by the statutory norms.[37] And the German equity capital market was not a factor in financing the needs of major enterprise.

When, in the early 1990s, the German delegation to the IASC board raised objections during board discussions by citing German law, their arguments were often seen as reflecting the values of a self-contained world having few points of contact with Anglo-American accounting. As the IASC had, in effect, committed itself to Anglo-American accounting, other board members saw little to be gained by a closer scrutiny of the German system. Within Germany, on the other hand, the Ministry of Justice, industry, the major accountancy firms, and leading academics were still strongly committed in the early 1990s to maintaining their national approach. Thus, the German delegation found itself caught in the middle.

In 1993, there was a major breakthrough in Germany. Daimler-Benz negotiated a surprise listing on the New York Stock Exchange (NYSE)—the first German company ever to do so—and German industry was shocked into realizing that it had to begin taking the IASC seriously, if only as a line of defence against an invasion of US GAAP. German industry promptly appointed a representative, Bernd-Joachim Menn, of Bayer, to the German delegation to the IASC board. In 1994, Bayer, along with Schering and Heidelberger Zement, began using IASC standards in their consolidated accounts, thus leading to a quickened pace of a movement towards a dilution in the impact of German GAAP on financial reporting by listed companies. By 1995, the gathering change in posture of industry towards the need to reform German financial reporting influenced the Ministry of Justice, the accountancy firms, and academics to warm to the work of the IASC, believing that its standards were preferable to a submission to US GAAP. The European Commission's decision in November 1995 to sign on to the IASC's standards programme confirmed the momentum (*see* Sections 12.2.2 and 12.3.3). In the 1990s, as is noted in Section 10.8, globalization was enveloping Germany, and at the IASC board the German delegation was hurrying to catch up with this new reality, in effect undergoing a crash course in internationalization. Their traditional accounting system was being displaced before their eyes.

8.4. VOTING PRACTICES OF THE BOARD DELEGATIONS

One can only generalize about how the various board delegations cast their votes on all or parts of standards. Their practices may have changed over time with the changing composition of their membership. Some delegations were instructed on how to vote, on some or all issues, by their sponsoring professional body or by their Ministry of Finance. Others were advised by a committee in their home country but were left free to vote their convictions. Most delegations, it seems, decided themselves on their vote.

How did the delegations vote when the views of their two voting members differed? The IASC's Constitution specified that each delegation had one vote, but there was no rule on how the delegations should decide on their vote. Some delegations left the voting decision in such cases to the senior member. Others, such as the US delegation, abstained in the event of a disagreement. An abstention was, in effect, a negative vote. In some delegations composed of one member from an accountancy firm and another from industry, the former could overrule the latter. At least one delegation rotated the vote: on one issue, member 1 casts the vote, and on the next issue member 2 casts the vote.

8.5. GUESTS AND OBSERVERS AT BOARD MEETINGS

In 1988, the FASB accepted IASC Chairman Georges Barthès de Ruyter's invitation and began attending as a guest at board meetings.[38] Ray Lauver, a member of the FASB, attended until March 1990, when he retired from the FASB. He was succeeded at the following meeting by the FASB's vice-chairman, James Leisenring, and in 1996 by FASB Member Anthony Cope. Leisenring earned a formidable reputation as an incisive interlocutor during the meetings and breaks, and his pointed remarks (and those of Michael Crooch, a member of the US delegation) during meetings often provoked quick-witted ripostes from David Tweedie. Not all of this verbal jousting was comprehended by board members and observers whose first language was not English.

In 1989, the IASC board invited Japan's Business Accounting Deliberation Council, which advised the Ministry of Finance, to join the Consultative Group and attend board meetings as a guest, but the invitation was declined.[39]

In 1990, after some initial reluctance, the European Commission accepted Chairman Barthès' invitation to begin attending board meetings as a guest.[40] Hermann Niessen attended two meetings in 1990, just prior to his retirement from the Commission's staff, and he was succeeded the following year by Karel Van Hulle. With effect from the beginning of 1992, the status of the FASB and

European Commission representatives was upgraded to observer, with the right to join in the board's discussions. IASC Chairman Arthur Wyatt said, 'Initially [the FASB and European Commission representatives] were invited to listen but we gradually realised that we could benefit from their observations so now they are active participants.'[41] Allister Wilson began accompanying Van Hulle as an adviser to board meetings in 1996.

In 1996, IOSCO began sending an observer delegation to the board. IOSCO apparently had been approached earlier to send a delegation, but declined.[42] It was already sending observers to virtually all of the IASC's steering committees, which may have been seen as sufficient involvement in the board's work. In February 1996, when the SEC approached Bryan Carsberg to give strong encouragement to the board to accelerate its core standards programme while maintaining high quality, Carsberg replied that IOSCO could send an internationally representative observer delegation to board meetings so that its members could see for themselves how the board maintained high quality.[43] The offer was accepted, and the IOSCO delegation attended for the first time in June 1996. The delegation from IOSCO regularly ranged between three and six members, by far the largest of any observer delegation. It always included representatives from the SEC's Office of the Chief Accountant (Mary Tokar occasionally accompanied by Chief Accountant Michael Sutton, followed by D. J. Gannon), France's Commission des Opérations de Bourse (Francis Desmarchelier), and Japan's Ministry of Finance (Mikio Nakaune and Toshiyuki Kenmochi, followed by others). Until the end of 1998, the German Ministry of Justice (Herbert Biener) and the Ontario Securities Commission (OSC)(James Saloman succeeded by John Carchrae) also formed part of the delegation, but they stopped attending once the core standards were completed in December 1998.

At the board meeting in July 1997, held in Beijing, an observer delegation from the Chinese Institute of Certified Public Accountants (CICPA) began attending, the culmination of efforts by Secretary-General Cairns and Chairmen Wyatt and Shiratori, who attended major international conferences in China in 1992 and 1995.[44] China could not be invited to send a delegation, because it was not a member of IFAC. It was not until May 1997 that the CICPA joined IFAC. The CICPA had declined IFAC membership until Taiwan, an IFAC member since 1988, was renamed Chinese Taiwan. This was a sensitive and contentious issue, but in the end Taiwan agreed to this change.[45] Once the CICPA joined IFAC, Chairman Michael Sharpe acted to engage China in the IASC's work. Sharpe knew that China had been experimenting with IASC standards but was not yet prepared to make a commitment. He believed that China was too important an economic power to be left outside the tent.[46] In March 1996, when the executive committee discussed the proposal to invite China to become an observer, it also considered extending a similar invitation to Russia.[47] At the board meeting in June 1996, the proposal to invite China was approved by a bare majority (nine votes for, none against, and seven abstentions), but a similar proposal to invite Russia was defeated (six votes for, eight against, and two abstentions).[48] The members of the Chinese delegation spoke very little during meetings.

From 1998 to 2000, the Basel Committee on Banking Supervision attended most board meetings as a guest. IFAC was entitled to attend as an observer and occasionally sent a representative. The Basel Committee had also been involved in topics of special interest to it, notably IAS 30 on bank disclosures and IAS 39 on financial instruments. It even provided funding for the early work on IAS 30 (*see* Section 5.10).

With this considerable increase in the number of observers, meeting in a large room also occupied by as many as three persons in each of sixteen delegations, and the chairman, the secretary-general, any guests, one or more consultants from the collaborating standard setters, and the IASC staff, the number of those in attendance, many obliged to listen and speak in a second language, exceeded seventy.[49] The sheer size of these meetings, usually lasting four to five days, became a challenge to all in attendance, especially the chairman. It was one of the factors propelling the establishment of a Strategy Working Party (SWP) in 1997 to recommend a better structure for the IASC (*see* Chapter 13).

8.6. VENUES, FREQUENCY, AND LENGTH OF BOARD MEETINGS

The venues of board meetings were rotated around the world. Of the forty-four meetings held by the board from 1987 to 2000, only five were held in London. All told, twenty-eight meetings were held in Europe, five took place in North America, two were held in each of Sydney and Tokyo, and single meetings occurred in Amman, Beijing, Johannesburg, Kuala Lumpur, São Paulo, Seoul, and Singapore. Typically at board meetings, the board members and senior staff would meet with the local representatives of the international organizations serving on the Consultative Group as well as with leaders of the national accountancy body and other entities of strategic importance in the country.[50]

As the pressure began to build on the IASC to provide IOSCO with standards it could endorse, the frequency and length of board meetings increased in the 1990s. The number of meeting days ascended to a peak of twenty-five in 1998, the year in which the board rushed to complete the core standards. The trend from 1987 to 2000 is shown below:

1987	2 meetings, 7 days	1994	2 meetings, 8 days
1988	3 meetings, 9 days	1995	3 meetings, 11 days
1989	2 meetings, 5 days	1996	3 meetings, 14 days
1990	3 meetings, 9 days	1997	4 meetings, 20 days
1991	3 meetings, 9 days	1998	5 meetings, 25 days
1992	3 meetings, 9 days	1999	4 meetings, 18 days
1993	3 meetings, 9 days	2000	4 meetings, 18 days

Board members recall the seven-day meeting in April 1998 in Kuala Lumpur, when the more than sixty persons in attendance debated a large number of draft

Figure 8.9. Meeting of IASC board in São Paulo, March 2000

standards under difficult conditions. Chris Nobes, a member of the UK delegation, reported on the meeting with some feeling:

> This was the Board's longest meeting in history: seven days, with extra meetings before and after for many Board representatives. There were other unusual elements. The venue was arranged at short notice, the IASC having earlier cancelled its plans to meet in Tel Aviv when Israel was preparing for war. The Malaysians were well-organised and hospitable, but seven hours of jet lag were compounded by an element of surreality by our being in an enormous freezing hotel surrounded alternately by tropical sun and tropical storms, and by having to work long hours in sight of one of the world's largest artificial beaches. Added to the strain of this, the official evening receptions were non-alcoholic, given Malaysia's state religion.[51]

Moreover, Chairman Stig Enevoldsen was so adversely affected by the conditions that he fell ill and was incapacitated for twenty-four hours.[52]

8.7. OPENING BOARD MEETINGS TO THE PUBLIC

As early as January 1996, Secretary-General Carsberg posed the question of whether board meetings should be held in public.[53] Until then, only the FASB, among national standard setters, held its meetings 'in the sunshine'. In March 1997, the G4+1 began opening its meetings to the public so long as the host country's facilities enabled such attendance.[54]

In 1998, the IASC decided to become the second standard setter to do so. The previous year, the board had formed a SWP to review and make recommendations on the IASC's strategy and structure (see Chapter 13). In an early draft of its discussion paper, circulated internally in October 1997 and reaffirmed in the widely circulated draft of 17 November, the working party made known its belief that board meetings should be open to the public.[55] During 1998, the executive committee unanimously agreed to recommend adoption of this view to the board, and the Advisory Council expressed strong support.[56] At its November 1998 meeting, the board unanimously voted to open its meetings to the public,[57] which became effective with the March 1999 meeting in Washington, DC.[58] The IASC thus responded to a criticism of the IASC's due process by former FASB Chairman Dennis R. Beresford: 'Perhaps the most fundamental difference [between the FASB and the IASC] is that the FASB's deliberations are open to public observation and the IASC's are not.'[59] In May 1997, SEC Chairman Arthur Levitt struck the same chord: 'We expect the IASC to conduct its dialogue in the most open way possible.'[60]

Chris Nobes reported on the first experience of an open meeting:

About 20 observers attended the four-day meeting, although not all at the same time. They were a mixture of Big Five accountants, journalists and regulators. Their presence seemed to make little difference to the willingness of the Board to engage in detailed arguments or to the willingness of the Americans, Australians and British to amuse the rest by being rude to each other.[61]

The IASC's decision to conduct its meetings in the sunshine was important in persuading the AASB to do likewise in October 1999. The Australian Urgent Issues Task Force had been holding open meetings since its establishment in 1995.[62]

8.8. OBSERVERS ON STEERING COMMITTEES

As is mentioned in Sections 10.3 and 10.7, IOSCO sent as many as four representatives to the Comparability and Improvements steering committee meetings from 1987 to 1993, and they participated actively in the debate and even voted on the drafts. They were the first officially designated observers to attend steering committee meetings.[63] In October 1994, the IASC's executive committee formally invited IOSCO to send one observer to all steering committee meetings.[64] The practice of inviting observers expanded in the mid-1990s, as part of the board's outreach to interested parties, especially those with specialist knowledge. From 1995 onwards, such bodies as the ICC, the World Bank, the Basel Committee on Banking Supervision, the Fédération des Experts Comptables Européens (FEE), the Fédération Internationale des Bourses de Valeurs, the European Federation of Equipment Leasing Company Associations, UNCTAD, the International Finance Corporation (IFC), the International Actuarial Association, and the International Association of Insurance Supervisors (IAIS)—in addition to IOSCO and the European Commission—attended steering committee meetings as observers. Almost

Changing Look of the IASC 233

all of these organizations were also members of the IASC's Consultative Group. The IASC believed that it was essential to tap the expertise and gain the support of these influential bodies.

8.9. SIR BRYAN CARSBERG SUCCEEDS DAVID CAIRNS AS SECRETARY-GENERAL

David Cairns became the secretary-general in 1985, at a time when the board was disposed to allow the secretariat to drive most of its initiatives. Cairns managed the transition from the board's initial programme of issuing a steady stream of mostly permissive standards to a phase where it began tightening and improving the standards. He also strongly supported the need for a conceptual framework. Cairns immersed himself in all aspects of the IASC's work, and he emphasized the importance of developing and adhering to a strategic plan. He wrote and spoke extensively on behalf of the IASC. He travelled the world to tell the IASC's story and to secure support for its standards, both in developed and developing countries.

Cairns's tireless dedication to the cause of international accounting harmonization and to the aims of the IASC was second to none. During his almost ten years as secretary-general, Cairns, with only a slender full-time staff at his command, enabled the IASC to take major strides towards achieving its objectives. The high level of the productivity of the research staff was traceable mainly to his strong hand. He was the force behind the launching of the *Annual Review*, the conversion of the modest *IASC News* into the richly informative *IASC Insight* and *IASC Update*, and the major expansion of the IASC's publications. These included the annual handbook containing all of the board's standards as well as the innovative subscription package for IASC publications, which became profitable ventures. He warned of the need for a significant fund-raising initiative to support the IASC's heightened aspirations. He also pushed hard for a closer involvement between the IASC and national standard setters, in the face of opposition by some professional accountancy bodies that were concerned about the preservation of their turf.

With the board's major effort to pursue its Comparability and Improvements projects, spanning 1987 to 1993, and its increasing determination to persuade IOSCO and the SEC that it was developing sound standards, an increasing number of other strong figures with their own visions and independent wills assumed major roles within the IASC. Inevitably, there was a clash of styles and personalities. There was also some tension between Cairns and some members of board delegations. Perhaps his long tenure as secretary-general imbued him with a sense of ownership of the process and its aspirations. At a time of difficult relations with the leadership, in March 1994, he resigned from the IASC but remained in his capacity of secretary-general until the end of December 1994. At the time of his departure, Cairns wrote, with full justification, 'We have built an IASC which has a well earned place at the top table with other standard setting bodies and other organisations around the world.'[65]

Following an extensive search process, Cairns was succeeded in May 1995 by Sir Bryan Carsberg, who had been the UK's first director-general of the Office of Telecommunications (a regulatory body known as Oftel) from 1984 to 1992, and since 1992 was director-general of the UK's Office of Fair Trading. He had previously been an accounting professor at both the University of Manchester and the London School of Economics. From 1978 to 1981, he was an academic fellow and assistant director of research and technical activities for the FASB. He served as a member of the UK ASB Board from 1990 to 1994 and was its vice-chairman between 1990 and 1992.[66]

Between 1995 and 1997, Carsberg and Chairman Michael Sharpe worked as a team to give innumerable speeches and confer with important figures in the accounting, financial, and regulatory arenas around the world. They were on the road incessantly. Sharpe has written that his partnership with Carsberg 'was one

Figure 8.10. Sir Bryan Carsberg

in which we both rejoiced'.⁶⁷ Carsberg was often invited to meetings of IOSCO's Working Party 1. His background as a regulator enabled him to relate well to IOSCO and other regulatory bodies.

Stig Enevoldsen's working relationship with Carsberg was more difficult. Language was a problem, and they differed in manner and in their approach towards leading the board. During the taut negotiations over the restructuring of the IASC in 1999, Enevoldsen defended the model favoured by the Continental Europeans, while Carsberg was more preoccupied with the need to keep the SEC on board and with the importance of developing a working relationship between the IASC and the FASB (*see* Chapter 13).

8.10. THE IASC AUGMENTS ITS RESEARCH STAFF

In April 1987, after Assistant Secretary Brian Rutherford returned to the University of Kent, Secretary-General David Cairns abandoned the practice of having an assistant secretary, who, except for Rutherford, had always come on a two-year secondment.⁶⁸ The assistant secretaries had handled administrative tasks and had been assigned to steering committees to incorporate the members' views into draft standards following their meetings. Cairns wanted the staff to be project managers rather than note-takers at steering committee meetings. Not all board members agreed with this enhancement in the role of the staff; some believed that the staff should attend to administration and not engage in technical work at all.⁶⁹ Beginning in 1987, Cairns gradually managed this shift towards research management. Between 1987 and 1990, a total of four staff members served on secondment, never more than two simultaneously. Of these four, Angus Thomson, who was seconded by the Australian Accounting Research Foundation (AARF), came with direct experience of research for standard setting. Cairns had to deal with a budget that did not allow much expansion in the size of staff. To be sure, the salaries of seconded staff might be partially, or perhaps even totally, covered by their employers. Such staff also had the advantage of their acknowledged technical competence, but their short terms of service, usually no more than two years, had the disadvantage of disrupting the continuity of some projects.

In 1990, Cairns advertised for a technical director. From the middle of 1991 to the end of 1992, Robert Langford and then Brigid Curran, the latter seconded by AARF,⁷⁰ served successive terms as technical director, Langford for a much shorter period than Curran. Brigid Curran served for about fifteen months, as it was always her plan to return to Australia by the end of 1992. Some six other appointments were made to the research staff between 1991 and 1993, usually on secondments, and most of them remained for about a year to fifteen months for a variety of reasons, including the lack by some of any standard-setting experience and a tight budget.⁷¹ Cairns himself was apparently responsible for some of the turnover, because he was not an easy supervisor. Not all of the staff were willing or able to work to his exacting standards.

There was no technical director again until July 1994, when Liesel Knorr, a partner in the Köln office of KPMG Deutsche Treuhand, was seconded to the position by her firm for a five-year term. She left in June 1999 to become secretary-general of the Deutsche Rechnungslegungs Standards Committee, the newly established German Accounting Standards Board. During May and June 1994, there was a dearth of research staff support. Upon her arrival, Knorr found that the full-time research staff consisted of one person, Terry Harding.[72]

From 1994 onwards, aided by the success in raising funds, the research staff gradually rose to six and seven. In addition to a number of staff seconded from accountancy firms and other employers, the senior staff included Peter Clark, who joined in September 1994 and remained through 2000 and beyond with the International Accounting Standards Board, Laurence Rivat (seconded by the Paris office of Deloitte Touche Tohmatsu) from December 1995 until September 1998, and Paul Pacter from July 1996 to 2000. From 1993 to 1996, Pacter, a freelancer who had formerly worked on the FASB's technical staff, had managed the IASC's segment reporting project on a part-time basis. Thus, as the work of the IASC picked up pace in the middle and latter 1990s, the number of research staff eventually grew with it. In addition, during the 1990s the board benefited from research staff, including importantly John Carchrae and then Ian Hague loaned by the CICA, as well as from the UK ASB, on collaborative projects.[73]

Knorr was succeeded in September 1999 by James S. Saloman, who was seconded to the IASC from PricewaterhouseCoopers, in Toronto, where he was a partner in the national accounting and auditing services group. He had served as chief accountant of the Ontario Securities Commission from 1994 to 1996. In that capacity, he had been a member of IOSCO's Working Party 1 on multinational disclosures and accounting and chaired its Accounting and Auditing Subcommittee.[74]

8.11. THE IASC EXPANDS ITS SUPPORT STAFF AND REQUIRES MORE OFFICE SPACE

During the 1990s, the range of activities requiring attention at the IASC increased. In 1991, Gillian Bertol, who had been David Cairns's executive assistant, was appointed to the new position of publications director. In January 1997, Kurt Ramin joined the IASC in the new position of commercial director, on a two-year secondment from the New York City office of Coopers & Lybrand. He began dealing with a host of issues, including expanding the sale of publications, developing new products, managing the development of the IASC's infrastructure, arranging for the translation of IASC publications, and licensing the IASC's copyrighted publications to accountancy firms and other organizations. Sales of translations of the IASC publications had the potential of being a major source of receipts. Paul

Pacter created and managed a website for the IASC. In 1999, Ramin extended his secondment for another two years.

Because of its expanding activities, the IASC twice sought a more capacious suite of offices. Moves to larger quarters occurred in 1991 and again in 1997, from space in Kingsway to two successive suites in Fleet Street, one next door to the other. The IASC's revised Constitution in October 1992 stipulated that the secretariat could be located elsewhere than in London, but no other venue was ever seriously considered.

It was always necessary for the IASC to persuade the English Institute to sign as lessee on its office space, as the IASC itself was an unincorporated association.

8.12. EXECUTIVE COMMITTEE REPLACES THE ORGANISATION AND PLANNING COMMITTEE

From 1978 to 1993, when it was replaced by an executive committee, the OPC had steered the affairs of the IASC board. Beginning in 1987, it was ordinarily composed of four of the board's delegations (but five in 1988–90), with a yearly rotation on and off the OPC of two delegations, respectively; the IASC chairman was an ex officio member. For most years from 1978 to 1990, the UK & Irish delegation (the UK delegation since 1988) held permanent membership on the OPC, mainly because of the proximity of members of that delegation to the IASC office in London. Also until 1990, the OPC chairman was drawn from a different delegation each year. Beginning in 1990, the IASC chairman also chaired the OPC. The composition of the OPC from 1987 to 1993, including the OPC chairman each year until 1990, was as follows:

1987–8	Wilhelm Tjaden, Germany; Australia, United States, UK & Ireland
1988–9	David Boymal, Australia; United States, Netherlands, Canada, Germany, United Kingdom
1989–90	John Chironna, United States; Netherlands, Canada, Germany, United Kingdom
1990–1	Netherlands, Canada, Jordan, Japan
1991–2	Canada, Jordan, France, Financial Analysts
1992–3	Jordan, France, Financial Analysts, Nordic Federation

For some years, the board and the OPC had reconsidered the role of the OPC in relation to the board. In 1991, the secretariat suggested, as one option, the creation of an 'Executive Group', similar to one installed by IFAC in succession to its planning committee.[75] The IASC secretariat said that the current system was 'inefficient and unbusinessmanlike', because virtually all matters taken up by the OPC were reconsidered anew by the board; and, as members of the delegations represented on the OPC did not feel bound by its recommendations, they would feel at liberty to speak against them in board meetings. The OPC was also reluctant, it was said, to 'deal with substantial issues'.[76]

After October 1992, when Michael Sharpe was named the deputy chairman as well as chairman-designate, he, Chairman Shiratori, and Secretary-General Cairns began meeting on a regular basis, and it apparently seemed wise to bring those meetings within the frame of an executive committee. Finally, at the board's June 1993 meeting, it decided that the OPC should be replaced by an executive committee composed of the three senior officers and three members of the board.[77] Its initial composition was of Chairman Shiratori, Deputy Chairman Sharpe, Secretary-General Cairns, and individuals from three delegations: Fouad Alaeddin, of Jordan; Stig Enevoldsen, of the Nordic Federation of Public Accountants; and Peter Stilling, of the United Kingdom. The new executive committee commenced operations on 1 July 1993, and the OPC went out of existence.

8.13. THE BOARD ESTABLISHES THE STANDING INTERPRETATIONS COMMITTEE

For reasons discussed in Section 10.14, the board voted in September 1996 to set up a Standing Interpretations Committee (SIC).[78] IOSCO, and in particular the SEC, believed a procedure to deal with interpretations was needed. At the board's meeting in January 1997, it approved the twelve members of the SIC, representing users, preparers, and auditors of financial statements. Paul Cherry, until 1995 a member of the Canadian delegation to the board, was named the chairman.[79] A staff member was assigned to support the SIC's work.

All but two of the SIC's twelve members were from accountancy firms. In addition, representatives of IOSCO and the European Commission, as well as the IASC chairman, attended as observers. Harry Schmid, a member of the Federation of Swiss Industrial Holding Companies' delegation, was the only board member to be appointed to the SIC in 1997. In subsequent years, two additional board members, Patricia McQueen and John T. Smith, also served on the SIC, and another board member, Peter Wilmot, attended SIC meetings as an observer to liaise with the board.

Under the arrangement approved by the board, the SIC submitted proposed interpretations to the board following an exposure process. The board voted on the text as put forward by the SIC. Approval of an interpretation required that three quarters of the delegations vote in favour, just as was required for the approval of an IASC standard.

In July 1997, the IASC began publishing a two-page update, *News from the SIC*, immediately following every SIC meeting. The IASC then began selling a looseleaf binder containing draft and final SIC Interpretations.

When the board revised IAS 1, *Presentation of Financial Statements*, in 1997, it inserted a provision stating that compliance with IASC standards was intended to mean compliance with each applicable standard as well as with each applicable SIC interpretation, thus endowing the interpretations with official recognition.

8.14. SIGNIFICANT GROWTH IN THE IASC'S BUDGET

Chairman-Designate Arthur Wyatt said in 1989 that 'People are always amazed at how much IASC achieves with so little.'[80] A comparison between the IASC's total expenditures (figures are rounded to the nearest £1,000) with those of the FASB and the UK ASB in 1992 and 1995 is instructive:[81]

	IASC (£)	FASB (£)	ASB (£)
1992	975,000	7,184,000	1,893,000
1995	1,259,000	9,834,000	2,247,000

When interpreting these comparisons, one must factor in the international travel cost incurred by the IASC. Each delegation paid for the travel of two of its members, while the IASC covered the cost for the third. The ASB compensated its part-time members a modest amount, and it paid full salaries to its chairman and technical director. For the IASC, unlike the FASB, the time spent by the board members, all of whom served on a part-time basis, was not compensated for by the standard-setting body. The ASB had two paid board members in 1992 and 1995. The IASC had no paid board members.

The IASC's burgeoning responsibilities from 1987 onwards, driven mainly by the challenge laid before it by IOSCO and the SEC, inevitably meant the incurrence of additional costs, chiefly for the increased number of steering committee meetings, the more frequent and longer board meetings (*see* Section 8.6), the enhanced technical and support staff, and the growing number of publications (the newsletters, draft statements of principles, exposure drafts, and the standards themselves). In 1988 and 1989, the number of pages in *IASC News* expanded considerably. In 1991, David Cairns replaced it with a more substantial periodical, *IASC Insight*. He added *IASC Update*, which was sent out following each board meeting, because of a growing number of requests for the prompt communication of board decisions. The increasing pace and scope of board activity led to a considerable expansion of the number of pages in *IASC Insight* and thus required more editorial attention by the IASC's small research staff. In 1995, the draft statements of principles, exposure drafts, and final standards began being published in glossy covers, thereby taking on a more professional appearance. Moreover, in the mid-1990s there was a substantial increase in the number, extent of circulation, and number of pages in the discussion papers and issues papers.

The IASC had been distributing *IASC News* as well as the exposure drafts and final standards gratis to its member bodies, which had the right and obligation to publish and distribute IASC standards in their respective countries. In 1987, the IASC's leadership began looking for ways and means of generating publication revenues for the IASC. In that year, David Cairns arranged for the publication and sale of the first bound volume of IASC standards, which the IASC began producing and selling annually. In 1991, the IASC announced a subscription scheme by which subscribers would pay in advance to receive all of the IASC's publications at a package price. Beginning with E32 in 1990, the board also began selling the sets of comment letters received on exposure drafts and issues papers. These developments from 1987 onwards, both on the cost and revenue sides, were also intended to raise the profile of the IASC.[82] The new publications programme, under the direction of Gillian Bertol, began raising significant revenues by 1991, as shown in Table 8.1.

Because of the expanded scale of the IASC's operations since the late 1980s, there emerged a great need for aggressive fund raising, which eventually became the major assignment entrusted to the Advisory Council, which was formed in 1995 (and discussed below).

8.15. THE IASC'S FOUNDATION WORKING PARTY: CHARTING THE COURSE TOWARDS A VEHICLE FOR FUND-RAISING

In June 1988, the OPC asked the secretariat 'to prepare a paper on the establishment of a Foundation that would obtain financial contributions from accountancy firms, the business community, financial institutions and other interested organizations'. In April 1989, the secretary-general prepared and submitted that memorandum. He said that, for 1989, the budgeted amount to be funded by the IASC's member bodies and IFAC was £376,000. This amount represented the excess of expenditures over revenues (mostly from publications), and, according to the IASC's Constitution, 90 per cent was to be borne in equal shares by the thirteen countries and the one organization represented on the board. The remainder was covered by the annual contribution from IFAC. In view of the board's ambitious plan to move its standards programme to the next level, Cairns foresaw that it would require an additional £200,000 a year until 1995 to enable the IASC to recruit additional staff, pay for research assistance on specific projects, and cover the cost of the necessary steering committee meetings. On the assumption that the member bodies would be unwilling or unable to provide this additional funding, he advanced a proposal that the IASC, an unincorporated association, should establish an 'International Accounting Research Foundation' to raise the necessary funds with effect from 1990. Cairns recommended in his memorandum that the Foundation should be organized so that contributors could obtain tax relief on their contributions and that the Foundation not be taxed on the contributions received or on any interest or other investment income it receives.

Table 8.1. IASC revenue and expenses, 1988–2000 (£1,000)

	Revenue						Expenses			
	Board members	IFAC	Other contributions	Publication	Other[a]	Total	Secretariat	Other[b]	Total	Surplus or deficit
1988	316	35	0	10	18	379	217	164	381	−2
1989	338	38	3	33	23	435	252	167	419	16
1990	359	40	142	27	36	604	350	200	550	54
1991	388	43	219	84	28	762	571	244	815	−53
1992	484	54	279	124	46	987	670	305	975	12
1993	504	56	306	267	13	1,146	672	481	1,153	−7
1994	522	58	296	407	14	1,297	735	470	1,205	92
1995	555	60	284	294	129	1,322	720	539	1,259	63
1996	631	70	932	384	189	2,206	1,170	653	1,823	383
1997	653	72	742	588	149	2,204	1,249	768	2,017	187
1998	674	75	820	884	167	2,620	1,362	740	2,102	518
1999	694	77	663	1,026	177	2,637	1,322	746	2,068	569
2000	929[c]	—		1,111	161	2,201	1,823	1,276[d]	3,099	−898

[a] Mainly interest income after tax and, after 1995, World Bank grant for project on agriculture.
[b] Mainly cost of meetings of IASC board and the various committees.
[c] Combined figure for contributions from all sources.
[d] Includes costs of trustees and fund-raising for restructured IASC.

Source: IASC financial statements as included with board agenda papers.

The Bishop Working Party, which had been studying the relationship between IFAC and the IASC (*see* Section 7.5), had been apprised of the proposal for a foundation and had informally signified its support. When it rendered its report in December 1989, the working party said it was 'most supportive of the funding initiatives being considered by IASC, and in particular the concept of the International Accounting Research Foundation (IARF)'.[83] Progress had been delayed because the IFAC member bodies wanted to see the Bishop report before acting on the initiative.

Cairns strongly favoured the setting up of a foundation, but the board was reluctant. The IASC continued to debate the proposal for a foundation in 1990, by which time it was renamed the International Accounting Standards Foundation. A critical funding initiative was taken at the board's March 1990 meeting in Amsterdam. Chairman Georges Barthès decided that the IASC could wait no longer. As a result, Arthur Wyatt, the chairman-designate and member of the US delegation, got in touch with Robert Mednick, a senior partner in the Chicago executive office of Arthur Andersen, about making an approach to the Big Six accountancy firms for funding support. Mednick invited Wyatt to make a presentation at the next meeting of the Big Six firms' chief executives. His request was quickly agreed, and the IASC received a substantial contribution, £25,000 from each of the firms, almost immediately.[84] The firms continued making the same contribution on an annual basis.

At its November 1990 meeting, perhaps to see if an alternative to a foundation could be devised, the board set up a high level Funding steering committee, which was chaired by Georges Barthès de Ruyter, the immediate past IASC chairman. Its dual task was to raise finance as well as to decide whether to proceed with forming a foundation. All of its members were currently serving on the board or had recently retired from the board, and included Arthur Wyatt, the current IASC chairman. The steering committee's vice-chairman, Christopher Stronge, who retired as a member of the UK delegation to the board in November, agreed to organize and coordinate the fund-raising activity in the United Kingdom, which he did until at least 1992.[85]

In July 1991, the Funding steering committee decided against moving ahead with a foundation and instead continued its fund-raising activities.[86] It appeared to some that the idea of a foundation was dead. To some, the envisaged foundation might have brought IFAC, the spokesman for the world accountancy profession, too centrally into the affairs of an IASC that, since the early 1980s, had been bringing non-accountancy bodies into its orbit. Rather than risk a closer association between IFAC Council and the IASC, some board members preferred instead to emphasize the IASC's links with its member bodies.

While the Funding steering committee did not believe that the IASC's Constitution needed to be changed in order that the IASC might obtain external funding, it concluded that it may be desirable to do so.[87] There was no actual provision to authorize outside funding in the IASC's Constitution, which had last been amended in 1982. Secretary-General Cairns obtained advice from a solicitor that the Constitution did, in fact, give the board the power to raise external funds, but some board members did not accept this interpretation.[88] A process began of amending the Constitution to deal with a number of issues, and at the World Congress of Accountants held in October 1992 in Washington, DC, the IASC member bodies approved a revised Constitution, which, among other things, contained the following new paragraph under the head of the board's responsibilities and powers:

The Board shall have the power to:

...

(h) seek and obtain funds from Members of IASC and non-members which are interested in supporting the objectives of IASC provided that such funding is organised in such a way that it does not impair the independence, or the appearance of independence, of IASC.

It is not clear how long the Funding steering committee continued in operation. It was reported in January 1993 that the IASC had approached accountancy firms and the business community for additional funding, and it received £150,000 in 1990, £219,000 in 1991, and an expected £300,000 for 1992.[89] The IASC's *Annual Review* for 1991–2 identifies the financial contributors by magnitude of contribution.

Cairns persisted in his belief that the IASC required a foundation to coordinate the fund-raising effort, and he believed that it should be considered as part of a general restructuring of the IASC to meet the heightened challenges it was facing from IOSCO and regulatory bodies such as the SEC and the OSC. In October 1992, acting on the basis of the secretariat's submission, the board agreed to set up a working party on the establishment of an International Accounting Standards Foundation and on the future structure and organization of the IASC. It had the following terms of reference:[90]

The Working Party should review the structure and organisation of IASC in order to ensure that:

- IASC has the right structure and organisation to maintain and enhance its role as [the] recognised body for the development of International Accounting Standards;

- the accountancy profession, through IFAC and its Member Bodies and through the regional bodies, continues to recognise and support IASC and play a full part in the work of IASC;

- the preparers and users of financial statements, national standard setting bodies and other interested organisations play an appropriate and full part in the work of IASC; and

- IASC has sufficient funding to carry out the necessary research and consultations that are essential to its work and recruit and retain high quality staff.

The Working Party will also consider IASC's earlier proposal to establish an International Accounting Standards Foundation. This proposal was supported by the IASC/IFAC (Bishop) Working Party which reported in 1989. The review will consider the role of that Foundation and its relationship with the IASC Board. In particular, the review will consider whether any responsibilities should be transferred from the Board (or elsewhere) to the Foundation.

The Working Party will make recommendations to the Board of IASC by the end of 1993. Any consequential changes in the IASC Constitution will be dealt with at a meeting of Member Bodies in mid-1995.

The members of the working party were promptly appointed, and its first meeting was held in January 1993. The chairman, as with the Funding steering committee, was Georges Barthès de Ruyter. The other eight members were Ger Verhagen, of the Netherlands; Ulyesse LeGrange, of the United States; Jens Røder, of Denmark and incoming vice-president of FEE; Juan Herrera, of the Dominican Republic and deputy president of IFAC; Frank Harding, of the United Kingdom and a member of IFAC Council; Michael Sharpe, an IASC board member from Australia and deputy chairman of the IASC; John Denman, technical adviser of the board's Canadian delegation; and Tsuguoki Fujinuma, of Japan. Herrera and Harding were appointed by IFAC, and the other members were named by the IASC.

The working party held three meetings during 1993. Its initial recommendation was that a Foundation or Council would oversee the work of the IASC board as well as raise funds. An alternate version of the recommendation was that the new body's oversight function would require a Constitutional change, as it would empower the Foundation or Council to select the members of the IASC board. The working party agreed at its first meeting that each country sending a delegation to the board should be encouraged to include at least one person who is directly involved in the work of the national standard setter. The working party's tentative recommendations were discussed at the board meeting in March 1993 in Tokyo. There was reluctance to accept the alternate version because of the risk that the accountancy profession would lose control of the IASC. Views were expressed on both sides of bringing national standard-setting bodies, or members of those bodies, more closely into the work of the IASC. Christopher Nobes, of the UK delegation, advanced a suggestion which was minuted as counselling 'a need for delicacy in dealing with those standard-setting bodies that are part of national governments'.[91]

The working party completed its assignment by the end of 1993, and its final recommendations were reported in February 1994.[92] It proposed creation of 'a high level, international Advisory Council consisting of outstanding individuals in senior positions from the accountancy profession, the business community, the other users of financial statements and other backgrounds'. The overall objective of the Council was 'to promote the acceptability of International Accounting Standards, enhance the credibility of the work of the IASC and ensure that the necessary level of funding is available for IASC's work'. The Council's functions were, in addition to raising funds, (*a*) to review and comment on the board's strategy 'so as to satisfy itself that the needs of IASC's constituencies are being met', (*b*) to prepare 'an annual report (which would be included in the IASC's *Annual Review*) on the effectiveness of the Board in achieving its objectives and in carrying out its due process', (c) to promote 'participation in, and acceptance of, the work of IASC by the accountancy profession, the business community, the users of financial statements and other interested parties', and (d) to review the IASC's budget and financial statements. The working party also recommended that the Council be consulted on the appointment of the country members of the board.

The working party recommended that, where practicable, each board member country include at least one person who is directly active with national standard setting and at least one from the business community. It also recommended a closer involvement between the board and national standard setters,[93] by sponsoring annual meetings of standard-setting bodies, encouraging cooperation between such bodies and with the IASC, and by encouraging 'direct involvement of standard-setting bodies in the work of IASC'.

Finally, the working party envisaged a 'further evolution' in which the Advisory Council would be replaced by a Foundation having certain powers and responsibilities even more extensive than those delegated to the Council, including the selection and appointment of board members, which would require a revision of the IASC's Constitution.

The Council was to be composed of three representatives drawn from different backgrounds in the worldwide accountancy profession 'and proposed by the Council of IFAC', three representatives of the international business community, and a financial analyst, a stock exchange official, a lawyer, and a securities regulator from an IOSCO member body.

Secretary-General Cairns sent the working party's report to board members for their comments as well as to all of the IASC's member bodies and to the Consultative Group.[94] At the June 1994 meeting of the executive committee, Cairns reported that the written responses received 'support the appointment of an Advisory Council, and the main thrust of the Report, but some concerns have been raised about the role of the Advisory Council, in particular its involvement in the appointment of Board Representatives and Technical Advisers'.[95] Some members of the board, at its July 1994 meeting in Edinburgh, were not ready for the creation of an oversight body.[96] In the absence of the working party chairman, Michael Sharpe presented its report at the board meeting. Cairns has written that Sharpe 'made a significant attempt to water down the proposals'.[97] According to Cairns, Sharpe proposed:[98]

- greater emphasis should be given to the fund raising role and less emphasis should be given to the other activities of the advisory council;
- board member countries and organizations should be 'free to consult' rather than 'should consult' the advisory council about the composition of their delegations;
- the advisory council should 'monitor' the work of the board rather than 'prepare an annual report on' the work of the board; and
- the number of business representatives on the council should be reduced.

The board approved the appointment of an Advisory Council and the other recommendations in the working party's report, subject to three amendments.

Mainly, the board stipulated that 'Each country on the Board should not be required to include at least one person who is directly involved in the work of the national standards setting body.'[99] Cairns has written that several board members attempted to delete the 'further evolution' section of the working party's report. He said, 'Many board representatives wanted nothing to do with a proposal that may result in their own demise as well as a reduction in the powers of the accountancy bodies and other organizations which they represented.'[100]

As is seen in Chapter 13, some of the proposals of the Foundation Working Party and the reaction they evoked in the board foreshadowed the subsequent debate over the restructuring of the IASC. This debate was concluded in December 1999 with the approval by the IASC board of a far more radical restructuring than envisaged by the Foundation Working Party.

8.16. THE ADVISORY COUNCIL

To implement the recommendation of its Foundation Working Party, the IASC board set up an Advisory Council with effect from 1 July 1995. Its functions were set out as follows:[101]

- to review and comment on the strategy of the IASC Board, to ensure that the needs of its constituencies are being met;
- to prepare an annual report for publication in the IASC Annual Review on the effectiveness of the Board;
- to promote participation in and acceptance of the work of IASC by all interested parties;
- to review IASC's budget and financial statements; and
- to assist with the raising of finance to enable IASC to carry out its activities, while ensuring IASC's independence.

The Advisory Council was seen within the IASC as 'a high level' body 'to promote the acceptability of International Accounting Standards, enhance the credibility of IASC and provide the funding that IASC requires'.[102] The report and membership of the Council were prominently displayed in the IASC's *Annual Review* each year.

Fund-raising was arguably the most important function because of the increasing demands of the IASC's work programme. The Advisory Council's chairman, Stephen Eccles, a Briton who had worked at the World Bank for twenty-eight years and eventually became the Bank's vice-president and controller, was resourceful and pertinacious in leading the fund-raising effort. It was Eccles, with the support of Randolph Andersen, who was responsible for a $531,000 (£350,000) World Bank grant in 1994 to the IASC for a project on agricultural issues. The members of the Council were drawn preponderantly from the user community. The other members were as follows:[103]

Richard Grasso*—chairman of the New York Stock Exchange (Grasso never attended any of the meetings, and James L. Cochrane, senior vice-president of the Exchange, attended in his place)

Frank Harding—vice-president of IFAC and partner in KPMG, London

Juan Herrera*—president of IFAC and partner in KPMG, Santo Domingo

Boudewijn F. Baron van Ittersum* – chairman of the Amsterdam Stock Exchange

Jürgen Krumnow—member of the board of managing directors, Deutsche Bank

Jean Saint-Geours*—former president of France's Commission des Opérations de Bourse

Eiichi Shiratori*—the immediate past IASC chairman

Al Sommer Jr.*—former member of the US Securities and Exchange Commission, chairman of the US Public Oversight Board, and securities lawyer

Jean-Guy de Wael*—chairman of the European Federation of Financial Analysts' Societies and chairman of Paribas Group

The members whose names are followed by an asterisk served on the Council only until the end of 1997, following which they were succeeded by James Cochrane; Michael Cook of the US firm of Deloitte & Touche and former chairman of the US FAF; Linda Quinn of the law firm of Shearman & Sterling, New York, and former director of the SEC's Division of Corporation Finance; Gérard Worms, partner of Rothschild Bank, France; Antonio Zoido, president of the Madrid Stock Exchange; Stig Enevoldsen, IASC chairman; and Michael Sharpe, the immediate past IASC chairman. During 1998, Kimiaki Nakajima, of the Corporation Finance Research Institute (COFRI), Japan, was added to the Council.[104]

The Advisory Council met twice yearly through June 1999. The IASC's chairman, deputy chairman, and secretary-general regularly attended the Council's meetings as observers or members. At each meeting, it heard and discussed reports on the IASC's strategy, plans, activities, and financing, and it discussed the progress on fund-raising. Each year the Advisory Council rendered a report, describing how it carried out its functions and expressing support for the IASC's objectives and aims, which was published in the *Annual Review*. The Council was peremptorily terminated in the second half of 1999, when it became evident that a decision to restructure the IASC board was imminent. There was no mention of the Advisory Council in IASC's *Annual Review* for 2000.

8.17. FUND-RAISING

The IASC had begun its fund-raising in earnest in 1990, six years before the Advisory Council was formed. In that year, the Big Six international public accountancy firms gave £25,000 each to the IASC, a contribution they continued to make in every year through 1998. Following the merger of Price Waterhouse and Coopers & Lybrand in 1998, the Big Six became the Big Five, and contributions of £25,000 arrived from each of the five remaining firms during 1999 and 2000.

From 1993 to 1999, the IASC's fund-raising efforts produced the following receipts (rounded to £1,000):[105]

1993	£306,000	1997	£742,000
1994	£296,000	1998	£820,000
1995	£284,000	1999	£663,000
1996	£932,000		

It would appear as if the fund-raising initiatives of the Advisory Council, which commenced during the second half of 1995, had an effect. Over the seven-year period, the leading countries by percentages of total contributions were the United Kingdom, 19 per cent; United States, 14 per cent; Germany, 8 per cent; Switzerland, 6 per cent; Australia and France, 5 per cent each; and Japan and the Netherlands, 4 per cent each. The vast majority of the UK contributions were from companies, usually around £5,000 each, while in the US financial firms and securities exchanges were significant sources. In 1996, when the total US contribution according to the IASC's fund-raising report was £279,000, which was 35 per cent of the sum received that year by the IASC, more than £230,000 came from the financial community, notably the investment banks, with an additional £16,000 coming from the Inter-American Development Bank (based in Washington). The NYSE contributed £45,000 over a three-year period.

Contributions from Germany were virtually nil until 1997, when they vaulted to £100,000 per year, with most companies or commercial banks giving £5,000 each. Jürgen Krumnow, of Deutsche Bank, was instrumental in the German fund-raising.[106] More than half of the contributions from Japan came from the JICPA, which gave £15,000 a year for six years. The total contributions over the period from Italy and Denmark almost doubled those from Canada and South Africa. The only contribution from Singapore, £15,000, came from the national accountancy body. The balance of funding among countries varied significantly over the years.

The United Kingdom was a negligible contributor in the early years, but, mainly because of the efforts of Secretary-General Carsberg, who led the fund-raising in the United Kingdom, it became the largest contributor in the later years. He sent out a joint letter with Frank Harding to the top 250 companies by London Stock Exchange quotation. They requested a commitment of £10,000 for five years. The success of UK fund-raising was, in part, because the IASC was better known than in other countries and the contacts were already established.[107] Council Chairman Stephen Eccles believed that a different approach was needed in the United State, where the IASC was hardly known among companies and the financial institutions. In general, he focused on the firms and companies that would view the development of International Accounting Standards as being in their interest. This meant financial firms, especially the investment banks, which, as noted above, became major contributors, chiefly because of the efforts of Jim Cochrane. Eccles undertook to exploit his contacts with the international development banks, although the results were disappointing. Cochrane and Richard Grasso, at the NYSE, used their contacts as well. At Eccles' request, Carsberg produced a promotional brochure that described the work of the IASC. Plans were laid as well for fund-raising in other parts of the world, but the results were, in general, not up to expectations.

US corporations and mutual funds, as it happened, saw little reason to contribute. Among the more generous companies, but still less than £5,000 per year, were Johnson & Johnson and General Electric. Both companies had referred in their annual report to compliance with IASC standards, the latter from 1984 to 1990 and the former from 1991 to 1993. Other companies that had made such references (*see* Section 6.6), as Exxon, FMC, and CPC, contributed a very small amount or nothing at all. Salomon, which had also made such a reference, contributed £46,000 in the banner year of 1996. Eccles encountered one mutual fund executive in New York City who professed no interest in International Accounting Standards, because he wanted his firm to continue to take advantage of its private access to financial information of Japanese companies that other investors could not decipher from the companies' obscure financial statements. Greater transparency in financial reporting would lose the firm its competitive edge when making investments.

When the IASC announced in March 1996 that it was accelerating its process of issuing standards (*see* Section 10.13), which would add about £700,000 per year to its costs, the Advisory Council, led by Eccles, promptly assured Carsberg that it would raise the needed funds and that the board should 'get on with it'.

8.18. AMENDING THE IASC CONSTITUTION IN 1992

Several issues arose that seemed to call for amendments to the IASC's Constitution, which dated from 1982. The most important of the amendments, which granted explicit power to the IASC to raise funds, was discussed in Section 8.15.

One inconsequential amendment, mentioned above, had been suggested by the Bishop Working Party: the stipulation that the IASC's administrative office is to be located in London 'should be removed to overcome any constraint on future consideration' (paragraph 18).[108]

The previous reference that up to thirteen countries may be nominated and appointed by IFAC Council and shall be representatives of 'the professional accountancy bodies that are members of IFAC in these countries' was changed to 'Members of IASC in these countries' (paragraph 5(a)). Thus, the notion that the countries represented on the IASC were drawn from IFAC's membership, which was introduced in the 1982 Constitution, now reverted to members of IASC itself. The number of country members was unchanged. The term 'staff observer' in board delegations was changed to 'technical adviser' (paragraph 6). It was also made clear that, at plenary meetings of the members of the IASC, each member body will have one vote, which can be cast by proxy (paragraph 17).

At the meeting of member bodies of the IASC held on 11 October 1992 in Washington, DC, the proposed Constitution 'was approved on a show of hands without a dissenting vote'.[109] This was the IASC's fourth Constitution, following those approved upon its inception in 1973 and at the international congresses of accountants in 1977 and 1982.

8.19. RELATIONS WITH IFAC

Once or twice a year, the IASC/IFAC Co-ordinating Committee met in order to exchange information and views on issues of common interest, including especially IFAC's nominations of new or modified delegations to the IASC board. The members of the committee were the chairmen of the two bodies, the IASC secretary-general, and the IFAC secretary.

In 1993–4, a sensitive subject arose. IFAC's International Auditing Practices Committee (IAPC) proposed to change its name to the International Auditing Standards Board (IASB), and IFAC sought the IASC's views. The new initials, some thought, could be confused with the IASC. In February 1994, David Cairns surveyed the views of the IASC board, and eight of the ten delegations that responded opposed the change. Only Canada and South Africa supported it. Three of those who opposed the change—Michael Sharpe, Stig Enevoldsen, and Sigvard Heurlin (Swedish delegation)—envisaged that one day the IASC might well change its name to the International Accounting Standards Board (IASB).[110] In the end, the IAPC did not change its name to IASB. In July 1995, the IASC's executive committee contemplated a possible change in name to IASB, but the matter died for lack of sufficient support.[111]

8.20. CONSULTATIVE GROUP

The Consultative Group, founded in 1981, was part of the IASC's ongoing programme for meeting with international organizations of users, preparers, standard setters, regulators, and other interested parties. The aim was to obtain the advice and support of these influential bodies. There is no doubt that the Group was important to the IASC during the 1980s and into the 1990s. In the 1980s, Group members did provide considerable advice during meetings on both technical and strategic matters.[112] But gradually doubts about its usefulness began to surface.[113] In 1996, Secretary-General Carsberg observed that 'the members of the Consultative Group are not the kind of people who are practised in the business of discussing technical accounting issues. They may occasionally be able to alert us to concerns of a broad strategic nature. But it is unlikely that we would not have heard of these through other channels—comments on Exposure Drafts and so on—and the main benefit of our Consultative Group is in fostering a relationship with other important international organizations.'[114]

Consultative Group members were also tapped to provide specialist assistance in some of the technical projects.

Between the founding of the Group and the time of Carsberg's comments, two members of the group—the international organizations of financial analysts and financial executives—had taken seats on the board. Harry Schmid, who had represented the ICC, had moved to the board on an individual basis, as the leader of the delegation of the Federation of Swiss Industrial Holding Companies. The European Commission, the FASB, and IOSCO had begun as members of the Consultative Group, but soon began to make technical contributions as observers at board or steering committee meetings. Other members of the Consultative Group also served as observers on steering committees in their area of expertise. In this way, the Consultative Group was drained of some of its most active and technically competent members, while those who remained did not necessarily have to rely on the joint meetings of the Consultative Group with the board to convey their views.

When Carsberg made his remarks in 1996, there was more general agreement that simply going over the agenda for the coming board meeting was no longer the most effective use of the time of either the board or the Consultative Group, and there was some experimentation with different formats for the meetings. Until 1997, the Group typically met twice a year for one day each with the board and its senior staff. But in 1997, the meetings began to be held once a year with only a subset of the board. Yet this did not make the meetings more effective, and in 2000, the final year of the IASC, no meeting was called at all.[115]

From 1987 onwards, the following members were added to the Group:

1987	International Bar Association
	International Banking Associations
	International Organization of Securities Commissions (IOSCO)
	International Finance Corporation
1988	Financial Accounting Standards Board (FASB)
1990	European Commission
	International Assets Valuation Standards Committee
	Basel Committee on Banking Supervision
1991	Fédération Bancaire de la Communauté Européenne
1996	International Association for Accounting Education and Research (IAAER)
1997	International Association of Insurance Supervisors
	International Forum of Actuarial Associations

In November 1995, when the board voted to invite the IAAER, a worldwide association of accounting academics, to join the Group,[116] it was minuted that 'The Board also decided that although consideration may be given to granting IAAER observer membership of the Board after three years, no commitment should be given at this stage.'[117] No such further consideration was given, and it is supposed that the cost of serving as an observer at board meetings prevented the academic body from pursuing such a suggestion.

The original role of the Consultative Group was to stimulate interest in the work of the IASC among major international organizations in the private and public sectors. That the role of the Group diminished in importance somewhat in the 1990s is explained by the increasing prominence of the IASC in the eyes of most of the interested parties. The IASC no longer found it necessary to stimulate interest by international organizations in its work, because they were knocking on its door.

9

The IASC Fortifies Its Standards: The Framework, and the Comparability and Improvements Projects

The technical work of the IASC (International Accounting Standards Committee) from the late 1980s onwards was different from that during the 1970s and early 1980s. As noted in Chapter 5, the IASC certainly showed leadership in some of its early standards, but, on the whole, its approach to standard setting had been to eliminate practices that were generally agreed to be unacceptable, and to accept all those practices which one or more board member bodies were prepared to defend with plausible arguments. Both the IASC's leadership and most members of the board were willing to accept—at least for the time being—that this led to the inclusion of numerous options in the IASC's standards. It was also accepted that the IASC often made its choices on a pragmatic basis in which compromise played an important role.

But from 1987 onwards, the reduction of options in order to further the cause of international harmonization became the primary focus of the IASC. The Comparability and Improvements projects dominated the IASC's agenda between 1987 and the end of 1993. Another important change was that, from 1989 onwards, the IASC could refer to its *Framework for the Preparation and Presentation of Financial Statements* as a basis for deciding which options should be removed or retained, and for developing new standards.

As is detailed in Chapter 10, these changes were closely related to the cooperation that grew up since 1987 between the IASC and the International Organization of Securities Commissions (IOSCO), in the sense that a reduction of options was a central criterion in determining the acceptability of IASC standards for cross-border securities offerings. Yet, as will be seen, the reduction of options had already become an important theme within the IASC prior to its first contacts with IOSCO. This theme had emerged from the reviews of earlier standards, carried out by the IASC from 1982 onwards. Similarly, the idea of a conceptual framework can also be traced back to the IASC's agenda of the early 1980s.

The main sections of this chapter discuss, first, the Framework project and its antecedents, second, the reviews of standards during the 1980s and early 1990s, followed by the Comparability and Improvements projects, concluded in November 1993. The chapter concludes with a discussion of a small number of other projects taken up by the IASC during this period (*see* Appendix 4 for an overview of the IASC's technical projects).

Obviously, the IASC's standard-setting activity cannot be divided into neat chronological stages. This chapter therefore partly deals with events prior to 1987. Similarly, some of the IASC's standards published after 1993 had their origins prior to that year, but are discussed in Chapter 11.

During the period discussed in this chapter, the IASC's working arrangements, such as the role of steering committees and the steps taken in the production of each standard, were largely similar to the arrangements of the 1970s and early 1980s discussed at the beginning of Chapter 5. Naturally, there were gradual changes, and some are noted in the course of this chapter. Section 11.3 contains a more extensive discussion of the standard-setting process as it evolved from 1987 onwards.

9.1. THE BUILDING BLOCKS AND THE FRAMEWORK

9.1.1. Hesitant Steps towards a Framework

In 1978, when the IASC was deeply mired in its project on foreign currency translation, a US comment letter on the exposure draft (E11) pointed out that the IASC was unlikely to make headway 'without some explicit or implicit framework of objectives for the financial statements. Such a framework is missing in the deliberations of the IASC, as well as the deliberations of the FASB.'[1] At that time, the Financial Accounting Standards Board (FASB) was about to publish its Statement of Financial Accounting Concepts (SFAC) No. 1, *Objectives of Financial Reporting by Business Enterprises* (November 1978). No other standard-setting body, or legislator, had developed a complete and operational conceptual framework, and it was probably too early for the IASC to contemplate doing so. The comment was passed over without apparent discussion.

Yet the question did not go away. When, in April 1979, John Grenside made a presentation on the IASC to the critical Ad Hoc Working Group of the Organisation for Economic Co-operation and Development (OECD, *see* Section 7.2), he was asked if the IASC had a conceptual framework project on its agenda. Grenside replied that this was not the case, and that the IASC was waiting to see how the FASB's framework project would develop.[2] Yet it was realized within the IASC that this might not be good enough. Later that year, Chairman John Hepworth went on record saying that 'Possibly, the Board will consider a conceptual framework project on an international level.'[3] Early in 1980, the lack of a conceptual framework was already recognized as a recurring, although perhaps unfair, criticism of the IASC.[4]

The topic of 'objectives of financial statements' began to appear in 1979 in the lists of possible topics which the secretariat prepared when the board had to choose new projects, but it was not adopted until November 1982.[5] This decision was made without evident enthusiasm on the part of the board, and certainly not with the idea that the IASC was entering a new chapter in its history. In a postal ballot among members of the board and the Consultative Group prior to the November 1982 meeting of both groups, 'Objectives' ranked ninth in importance out of twelve possible topics, and two respondents had indicated the topic was not suitable for study by the IASC.[6] That it was nonetheless chosen was not least because Chairman Stephen Elliott and Secretary Geoffrey Mitchell were able to point out that this topic had attracted the support of the Consultative Group.[7] Yet both the Consultative Group and the board agreed that the project, modestly entitled 'Aspects of the Objectives of Financial Statements', 'should be a limited study and not lead to an international "conceptual framework"'.[8]

In the face of the hesitant attitude of the board, the idea of a framework did not go away, but it took on a subtly different form. A concept that floated around during 1983 and 1984 was that of the 'framework of Standards'. This did not refer to a separate document, such as the FASB's Statements of Financial Accounting Concepts, but to the implicit structure and internal consistency of the extant IASC standards. The idea originated in an October 1983 paper by the secretariat in which it discussed the selection of new topics for the next years. It proposed a strategy by which the board would select topics that would 'fill in the gaps in the existing standards as they relate to a typical income statement and balance sheet. Major gaps which currently exist are: Owners' Equity, Liabilities, Assets/Expenses—Definition and Recognition, Purchased Goodwill.'[9] This idea was picked up by an ad hoc advisory committee to the Organisation and Planning Committee (OPC), which had been set up in June 1983 to consider the work of the IASC in the medium term (1985–90).[10] The views of two committee members, Kenneth Spencer (Australia) and Dennis Beresford (United States), were echoed in the committee's report, when it advised that:

The first priority of IASC in adopting new topics for study should be to fill the gap in the existing framework of Standards, such as 'liabilities' and 'shareholders' interests'. The Committee recommends that a review of the existing framework be undertaken, both to confirm what the gaps are and to determine whether the Standards in issue form a cohesive whole—that is, whether there is an overall logic and consistency of approach that underlies them.[11]

The idea of filling in the gaps was innocuous enough. But by introducing the notion of cohesiveness or consistency, potentially more far-reaching changes to the IASC's customary approach were intimated. Yet, by suggesting that the IASC already had a framework, one that was implicit in the existing standards, the objections of some board members to a conceptual framework project were circumvented.

The ad hoc committee, supported if not encouraged by Secretary Mitchell, took a leaf from the book of the Australian Accounting Research Foundation (AARF), which had deliberately embarked in a low-key fashion on a conceptual framework project in 1980. The AARF's approach had been to start with research on the 'key elements' of financial statements such as assets, liabilities, and revenues, before announcing publicly that it was working on a conceptual framework. Mitchell himself, before he joined the IASC, had agreed to write a monograph on 'liabilities' for the AARF.[12]

On a suggestion by the secretariat, the IASC board agreed to set up steering committees on liabilities and on owners' equity in March and June 1984, respectively. In both cases, the secretariat explained its recommendation in terms of 'filling in the gaps in the existing framework of standards'. In both cases, the proposal was not presented as a novelty but as of one kind with the recently published IAS 18 on revenue recognition which, it was observed, had attracted 'widespread favourable comment' (see Section 5.12.3).[13]

By the end of 1984, partly as a result of the work of the objectives steering committee, the idea of 'filling in the gaps' had evolved into one of developing a series of 'building blocks'. The idea was that the statements or standards on objectives, liabilities, and owners' equity, together with IAS 18, would contain the basic concepts that would be used in the drafting of other standards on more specialized topics.[14] Following this line of thought, a fourth, and, as it turned out, last 'building block' project on assets and expenses was started in June 1985 at the urging of Spencer.[15] As discussed below, the next step would be taken in November 1986, when the building block projects were combined into a single project to prepare a Framework document.

9.1.2. The Building Block Projects

9.1.2.1. Objectives of Financial Statements

The steering committee on objectives of financial statements, the first of the building block projects, was chaired by M. A. Oni (Nigeria).[16] The project moved on at a measured pace between November 1982 and November 1986. The steering committee presented a point outline to the board in March 1984, in which it proposed a document on Objectives of Financial Statements which would stand apart from the other IASC standards, and which was to deal with the users of financial statements, the fundamental objectives of accounting, and the qualitative characteristics of accounting information.[17]

In drafting this document, the steering committee had clearly drawn on the FASB's Statements of Financial Accounting Concepts (SFAC). The steering committee's proposal to define the basic qualitative characteristics of accounting as 'relevance' and 'reliability' was an evident reflection of SFAC 2, *Qualitative Characteristics of Accounting Information*, issued in 1980. Yet the steering committee had adapted the FASB's ideas to suit the range of views represented in the IASC. For instance, the dominant concern for the information needs of investors in the FASB's Conceptual Framework was modified by the steering committee, which prominently included 'accountability' as a fundamental objective of financial reporting, next to 'economic decision-making'. This suggested a broader range of users, or stakeholders, and different kinds of information needs.

This March 1984 point outline set the terms for ongoing discussions in the board and the steering committee during 1984 and 1985. Despite extensive adjustments and modifications, the basic structure of the point outline remained visible. The editing process is illustrated by the peregrination of 'prudence'. Reflecting fundamental differences of opinion in which the Continental Europeans were traditionally ranged against the English-speaking delegations, prudence was in various stages considered as a fundamental accounting assumption, as an element of reliability, taken out altogether because it was seen to conflict with neutrality and fair presentation, and put back in as a factor contributing towards reliability.[18]

As the project progressed, the steering committee advised that work should be started on a revision of IAS 1, on disclosure of accounting policies, to bring it in line with the draft on objectives. The board charged the objectives steering committee with this task, and this produced a draft standard on 'Objectives of General Purpose Financial Statements and the Disclosure of Accounting Policies', which was circulated as a preliminary exposure draft among the member bodies during the latter part of 1985.[19] In general, the responses were favourable to the idea of issuing an exposure draft. The National Association of Accountants (United States) observed that the draft 'quite closely tracks the concepts statements issued by our FASB over the years', but this was not intended as a criticism.[20]

Despite the positive response, the board started to doubt the wisdom of aiming to issue the material in the form of an International Accounting Standard. These doubts were resolved in November 1986, when the project was transferred to the newly formed Framework steering committee.

9.1.2.2. Liabilities

Meanwhile, the project on liabilities had started in March 1984 on the basis of the recommendations of the objectives steering committee. It was seen as a companion project to IAS 18 on revenue recognition. In contrast to the objectives project, it was the intention from the start to produce a regular standard. The steering committee, chaired by the South African Rick Cottrell, put forward a draft that dealt extensively with definitions, recognition, measurement, and disclosure.[21] One of the main problems that the steering committee ran into, and one that was highly significant for the work of the IASC during the 1990s, arose from the fact that it was seeking to define liabilities in terms of obligations. But in that case, what should be done with items such as provisions for repairs and deferred credits, which were not obligations? Should these be considered as a separate class of elements, or building blocks, of financial statements, next to liabilities? The board ruled that there should not be a separate class of elements and ordered the steering committee to liaise with the recently created steering committee on owners' equity, in the apparent hope that the two committees, which between them were to cover the entire right-hand or credit side of the balance sheet, could find a place for deferred credits. However, by deciding that provisions for major repairs should be allowed, the board ruled out a pure obligations-only approach to liabilities.[22] Before this discussion could be carried to completion, the project was handed over to the Framework steering committee in November 1986.

9.1.2.3. Owners' Equity

The project on owners' equity was taken up shortly after the project on liabilities, but it encountered more difficulties in coming to grips with the subject matter. For one thing, the steering committee (chaired by Giancarlo Tomasin, Italy) observed that the impact of accounting laws was greater for equity than for many other topics.[23] Another problem was how to define equity. The steering committee proposed to define equity independently, that is, without referring to other balance sheet elements. But the board, perhaps alerted by the discussion about deferred credits a few months earlier, ruled that equity should be defined as a residual (assets minus liabilities).[24] One of their concerns was that, with independent definitions of both equity and liabilities, items might come up that fitted neither definition. Once this fundamental decision was taken, there was little left for the steering committee to do but to consider the classification and presentation of various items within equity. Although it came up with a number of specific proposals (such as allowing treasury stock to be treated as an asset governed by IAS 25, *Accounting for Investments*), none of these were carried forward to either the Framework project or subsequent standards. The project on owners' equity was therefore one of the few IASC projects not to result in any publication.

9.1.2.4. Assets and Expenses

In contrast to the project on owners' equity, the assets and expenses project was of major significance for the subsequent Framework. This was true even though it was the last of the building block projects to be launched, and the board had merely discussed a point outline when the board decided to merge the building blocks into a single Framework. The steering committee on assets and expenses was chaired by Ron Cotton (Australia), who was heavily assisted by Warren McGregor.[25] McGregor, who produced the point outline, had served with the AARF since 1980 and was a 'real convert' to the idea of conceptual frameworks.[26] In writing the point outline, McGregor was apparently drawing on ongoing research in Australia, on behalf of the AARF, on the definition and recognition of assets. The point outline was a memo of twenty-eight pages containing an anthology of definitions of assets and expenses taken from the English-language accounting literature, from Sprague's *Philosophy of Accounts* (1907) onwards.[27] On the basis of this review, McGregor, with the assent of the steering committee, went right to the essentials of the definitions adopted in the subsequent Framework. Assets were defined as 'expected future economic benefits controlled by the enterprise as a result of past transactions and events'. An item was to be recognized as an asset if it meets this definition, if it is probable that the future economic benefits will arise, and if it has a cost or other value which can be quantified with sufficient reliability. Expenses and losses were defined in terms of using up an asset or incurring a liability, and the steering committee proposed not to give separate recognition criteria for expenses or losses, as they 'flow directly from the definitions of an expense and a loss and the recognition criteria for assets and liabilities'.[28] The board agreed with this approach but made sure that potentially radical conflicts with current practice would be muffled by deciding that 'Debit balances that do not meet the definition of an asset but are not recognized, for the time being, as expenses should be discussed but not explicitly defined or given a name.'[29]

9.1.3. From Building Blocks to the Framework

By the summer of 1986, it had become clear that decisions had to be taken on the way forward for the four building block projects. One problem was that these four projects—especially the three on assets, liabilities, and equity—required careful coordination, because it was hard to deal with any one of the three without reference to the other.[30] The board therefore agreed during its meeting of June 1986 to delay any publication until all four exposure drafts were approved. But there were also other, more fundamental concerns expressed during the June meeting. Particularly with regard to the draft on objectives, it was seen as a problem that the draft contained material that was unsuitable for inclusion in a standard, because it would be difficult to write it in terms with which a preparer could comply. In addition, it was noted that the definitions of elements of financial statements conflicted with some treatments prescribed in extant standards. It was possible, for instance, that research costs might meet the general recognition criteria in the proposed standard on assets, yet IAS 9 prohibited capitalization.[31] Therefore, the board agreed to conduct a review of the building block projects. Members of the board who had serious concerns with the proposed documents could attend the November 1986 meeting of the OPC where the matter would be discussed.

Attendance at the November 1986 OPC meeting showed that concerns over the building blocks were mainly held by the representatives of the English-speaking countries. If the IASC ever lived up to its reputation as an Anglo-American organization, it was surely during this meeting. Australia, Canada, South Africa, the UK & Ireland, and the United States all attended. The secretariat was represented by two Britons. No other countries were there, except France and Nigeria (whose representatives attended ex officio).[32]

Some of those present were clearly in favour of a conceptual framework. These included not only Warren McGregor but also Secretary-General David Cairns. Cairns had succeeded Geoffrey Mitchell as secretary-general in 1985 and was willing to push more openly towards such a framework than Mitchell had done.[33] As early as August 1986, well before the board had had a chance to discuss the matter, Cairns publicly expressed his hope that an exposure draft of a single framework document, resulting from a combination of the building blocks, might be published sometime in 1987.[34]

And indeed, at the November 1986 OPC meeting and at the follow-on board meeting, it was agreed to accept a proposal prepared by Cairns to create a new steering committee to draw up a conceptual framework that would include the materials covered by the building block projects. The framework was to be a separate document, with a different status both from the 'Preface to Statements of International Accounting Standards' and from the standards themselves. In its proposal to the board, the secretariat suggested a modest role for the proposed framework: 'A frame of reference for the board in its thinking but which is not a Standard. The Framework should not bind the board to adopt conceptual solutions. The board should be able to adopt practical or politically acceptable solutions rather than those required by the Framework.'[35] Both the OPC and the board made sure that the minutes recorded that the Framework would not bind the board to particular solutions.[36] Given the nature of the proposed Framework, the revision of IAS 1 was taken out of the brief of the new steering committee and placed on hold until completion of the Framework.

Unlike all but the earliest IASC steering committees, the Framework steering committee was to be composed of board members only. While this suggests that this was an unusually significant project, it was in fact primarily a practical measure that would allow the steering committee to respond quickly to board decisions.[37] The committee consisted of the chairmen of the four disbanded building block steering committees, to which David Damant, of the financial analysts' delegation, was added. It fell to Canada to chair the committee, and Michael Dawson, an English-born Montrealer from industry who was attending his first board meeting in November 1986, was its choice as chairman. Dawson had served on the Accounting Research Committee of the Canadian Institute of Chartered Accountants (CICA) from 1977 to 1983 and became its chairman during 1983.[38] Warren McGregor served as the principal draughtsman of the steering committee, supported by Kevin Stevenson, the director of the AARF.[39] As the building block committees had already prepared the ground, the Framework project was able to proceed rapidly. In little over a year, the board was able to approve an exposure draft with a unanimous vote (March 1988).

The first drafts of the Framework foreshadowed the final (1989) version to a considerable extent, with main sections on the objectives of financial statements, qualitative characteristics of financial statements, elements of financial statements, recognition of elements, and measurement of elements. With this structure, the IASC Framework was strongly reminiscent of the FASB's Statements of Financial Accounting Concepts No. 1, 2, 3, and 5 (1978–84).[40] Because of this, but also because of the nationality of its supporters within the IASC, the Framework project had an undeniable Anglo-American flavour about it. The secretariat had already shown its awareness of this when it suggested that the Framework could 'reflect the different influences on financial reporting around the world and so help rebut the criticisms that IASC is biased in favour of both Anglo-Saxon and developed countries'.[41] A French member was added to the Framework steering committee in March 1987 'in order to increase the representation on the Committee of countries from outside the Anglo-Saxon tradition of accounting'.[42]

This was Francis Bastien who, notwithstanding the general policy in regard to this committee, was not a board member, but who was put forward because he had been an active member of the steering committee on assets and expenses.[43] Bastien, a former chief accountant of the French Commission des Opérations de Bourse (COB), did not share the French delegation's scepticism concerning the need for a conceptual framework.[44]

The steering committee did its best to avoid the impression of depending too much on the US Conceptual Framework by including elements drawn from different accounting traditions.[45] This resulted in differences of emphasis given to such topics as reporting on stewardship, the true and fair view, prudence, and maintenance of physical capital. On the whole, however, the similarities with the US Conceptual Framework were more apparent than the differences, as was pointed out repeatedly after the Framework was published.[46] And even if the IASC Framework was not a linear descendant of the US Framework, it was clearly a member of a family of kindred documents that appeared more or less simultaneously at the end of the 1980s in Australia, Canada, and the United Kingdom.[47] These projects were linked through individuals who participated in more than one of them, such as Warren McGregor who was closely involved in the Australian Framework project. David Solomons, an emeritus professor of the Wharton School, University of Pennsylvania, served as a consultant to the IASC project.[48] Solomons had drafted the FASB's SFAC 2 and he prepared the report *Guidelines for Financial Reporting Standards* (1989) for the ICAEW. Michael Dawson, the chairman of the IASC's Framework steering committee, had acted as an adviser to the CICA project that added elements of a conceptual framework to the *CICA Handbook*.[49]

By association, if nothing else, the IASC Framework could not fail to be seen as representing the Anglo-American element within the IASC. Nevertheless, the French delegation was able to accept the Framework after some debate. In the French tradition, accounting regulation was part of the general hierarchy of legal texts, with general laws creating the legal framework for more specific laws, regulations, and decrees. In this line of thinking, a Framework that was drafted after a number of standards had already been completed and with which these standards were not necessarily in agreement was somewhat odd. Nevertheless, the delegation was able to see that, in the future, the Framework might play a role that was familiar to them, as the basis for a deductive approach to standard setting.[50]

The German delegation, and its home constituency, had different concerns. While they were quite comfortable with the idea of a Conceptual Framework, they found that the contents of the IASC Framework differed from the framework implicit in German accounting. In general, it was believed that the IASC's Framework focused mainly on providing useful information to equity investors, while German accounting was grounded in accountability and creditor protection. While this view led to criticism of the IASC Framework in Germany, it did not prevent the German delegation from voting for the exposure draft and the final Framework.[51] Similarly, the Dutch delegation voted in favour, despite concerns in its home constituency that the Framework offered insufficient scope for the application of the matching principle.[52]

Despite reservations of various kinds, the responses to the exposure draft of the Framework were generally positive and supportive. Successive drafts were also favourably received by the Consultative Group. As a result, the Framework was approved unanimously by the board in April 1989.[53]

9.1.4. The Framework and the Reduction of Options

In March 1987, shortly after the building blocks were combined into a single Framework project, the IASC launched its Comparability project, aimed at reducing the number of options in its extant standards (discussed more fully below). As the Comparability project got under way, the idea emerged that the Framework might have an important role to play in the elimination of options. This idea was not clearly associated with the Framework project from the beginning. As discussed above, the original idea behind the building block projects was to fill in the gaps between the standards rather than to close the options in the standards. Although it is true that Spencer and Beresford had emphasized, in 1983, the need to review the 'overall logic' and 'coherence' of the standards, these notions were only indirectly related to a reduction of options and were, at any rate, only loosely attached to the building block projects. But with the transition to the consolidated Framework project, the idea of reducing options moved quickly to the foreground. The secretariat paper of November 1986, which proposed the Framework project, tentatively suggested that the building blocks 'might help reduce the number of options in Standards'. But the March 1987 secretariat paper, which proposed the Comparability project, stated more confidently: 'The development of the Framework for Financial Reporting should help to reduce options.'[54] A corollary of this view was that the Framework had to be finished as soon as possible once the Comparability project had started.[55]

The March 1988 exposure draft and the final version of the Framework described the purpose of the Framework as 'providing a basis for reducing the number of alternative accounting treatments permitted by International Accounting Standards' (paragraph 1(b)). But the exposure draft did go a step further. It identified a final objective by stating that 'The reduction, and ultimately the elimination, of free choices of accounting treatments for like transactions and other events in national and International Accounting Standards will improve the comparability of financial statements' (paragraph 41). This last sentence proved too much for some respondents, notably some Dutch industry associations, Royal Dutch/Shell, and the American Institute of Certified Public Accountants (AICPA). It was therefore removed even though the US Financial Executives Institute agreed that an elimination of options would 'substantially improve the utility and value of international financial statements'.[56]

The expected 'major' role of the Framework in reducing options was commented on more than once around the publication of the Framework by David Cairns and others.[57]

9.1.5. The Balance-Sheet Approach

An aspect of the Framework that gained increasing importance during the 1990s and beyond was its balance-sheet approach (also known as asset and liability approach). That is, the Framework was seen to support a shift away from a traditional emphasis on income determination based on realization and matching, towards an approach in which income was considered as a derivative of changes in assets and liabilities. The Framework did not address this explicitly, but in its section on the elements of financial statements, the balance sheet elements (assets, liabilities, and equity) were discussed first, while the elements of performance (income and expenses) were defined in terms of changes in assets and liabilities.

In this respect, the IASC's Framework clearly mirrored the FASB's SFAC No. 3, *Elements of Financial Statements of Business Enterprises* (1980), which also shifted the emphasis to a balance sheet, or asset and liability, view of accounting.[58] Yet to some extent, the balance-sheet orientation of the Framework flowed naturally from the building blocks on liabilities, equity, and assets. There was no separate building block project for expenses, as it was included in the project on assets. As discussed above, the liabilities and assets steering committees were thinking of definitions in terms of 'obligations' and 'expected future economic benefits', and it was recognized that a strict application of such definitions would eliminate a number of items from the balance sheet, such as deferred revenues and expenses, which were associated with an income statement approach to financial accounting. Yet, during the building blocks phase, the question of a balance-sheet versus income statement approach was not explicitly raised. It should be kept in mind that, during this phase, IAS 18 on revenue recognition was seen as one of the building blocks. As IAS 18 had a clear income statement orientation, there was no reason at that time to think of the building block projects as a whole having a pronounced balance-sheet orientation.

However, with the transition to a single Framework, the issue became clearer. At one point, the steering committee proposed, with reference to the elements of assets, liabilities, and equity, the inclusion of a sentence, 'The balance sheet is composed of these, and only these, elements.'[59] While this sentence did not appear in the exposure draft or the Framework, the thinking was clear enough. The exposure draft and the Framework did serve notice that, while balance sheets drawn up in accordance with current standards might include items that did not satisfy the definitions of the elements of financial statements, these definitions would underlie new standards and future reviews of existing standards (Framework, paragraph 52).

On the basis of the IASC's discussions of early 1987, Peter Wilmot (a member of the South African delegation) welcomed the IASC's decision to base its Framework on the fundamental accounting equation (assets minus liabilities equals shareholders' funds), and wrote that 'The so-called fourth element of balance sheets representing deferred gains and losses has no conceptual validity.' Although he expected only a 'minimal' impact of the Framework on financial reporting in the short term, he suggested an increasingly significant impact in the future.[60]

The same point was also made in a few of the comment letters on the exposure draft of the Framework, but, unlike Wilmot, in a cautionary rather than welcoming tone. Royal Dutch/Shell noted that, if the balance-sheet approach of the Framework were 'applied in an unbending fashion to such difficult areas as accounting for pensions, this new approach could have troublesome consequences for the realistic and relevant reporting of results'.[61] Similar comments were made by the Accounting Standards Committee (United Kingdom), Arthur Young (United Kingdom), and the Financial Executives Institute (United States).[62] The latter observed that the IASC exposure draft 'continues the balance sheet bias that pervades the U.S. conceptual framework, which we continue to have serious reservations about; however, in the interest of harmonization, we do not [object] to issuance of this Exposure Draft.'[63] Responding to these comments, the steering committee replied with the hardly reassuring observation that the proposed framework was consistent with other frameworks in this respect. On the whole, the steering committee concluded that the Framework 'has respect for the balance sheet but not a balance sheet bias, and therefore, the definitions of elements are appropriate'.[64] This was apparently enough to remove any reservations there may have been in the board.

9.2. THE IASC REVIEWS ITS PREVIOUS INTERNATIONAL ACCOUNTING STANDARDS

9.2.1. Reluctance to Revise Existing Standards

By the middle of 1979, the IASC had produced about a dozen standards, and the idea of reviewing them began to be mooted. From June 1979, the secretariat routinely included 'review of existing standards' in the lists of potential new topics it prepared for the board. Yet, until 1982, no action was taken despite occasional urging from the outside. In their 1980 *Financial Times* survey, Michael Lafferty and David Cairns recommended that the IASC review all of its existing standards and that 'It should commit itself to developing more precise standards in the areas of consolidation, depreciation and inventories within two years.'[65]

In March 1982, the board selected the review of existing standards as one of its new projects, with strong support from the IASC's Consultative Group.[66] The steering committee to review the first standards consisted of Jesús Hoyos Roldán (chairman, Mexico), A. B. Frielink (the Netherlands), Rick Cottrell (South Africa), and Khoo Eng Choo (Malaysia).[67] Its initial task was to review IAS 1, *Disclosure of Accounting Policies*, IAS 2, *Valuation and Presentation of Inventories under the Historical Cost System*, IAS 4, *Depreciation Accounting*, and IAS 5, *Information to be Disclosed in Financial Statements*. Subsequently, it was asked to review IAS 7, *Statement of Changes in Financial Position*, and IAS 8, *Unusual and Prior Period Items and Changes in Accounting Policies* as well. (IAS 6, *Accounting Responses to Changing Prices*, had already been replaced by IAS 15.) The review of IAS 3,

Consolidated Financial Statements, was entrusted to a separate steering committee in 1983. IAS 3 was easily the most significant of the IASC's early standards, and surveys had shown a considerable number of problems in compliance and in incorporation in local law or standards. As is discussed later in this chapter, the review of IAS 3 turned out to be a major project, resulting in three new standards.

The review of IAS 1, 2, 4 5, 7, and 8, however, did not lead to any changes. This was not because the steering committee did not identify any meaningful potential changes. On the contrary, in June 1983 it presented a formidable list of possible modifications. Apart from many editorial changes, these included the radical proposal to consider 'whether a narrowing of options previously given may be appropriate'. As a first step, it might be desirable to 'invite countries whose practice was different from the substantial majority practice to justify their positions'. Specifically, the steering committee proposed to eliminate the base stock method from IAS 2 (on inventories) and to reconsider the permission to use the last-in, first-out (LIFO) method of inventory valuation. A fundamental suggestion, carefully phrased as a question, was 'Whether the overriding concept that financial statements should show a true and fair view (or similar wording) should be articulated somewhere in the IASC literature.' IAS 1, *Disclosure of Accounting Policies*, might be a possible place to do so. The steering committee also proposed to settle a long-standing conflict between IAS 4, *Depreciation Accounting*, and UK accounting standards (*see* Sections 5.5.3 and 6.5.1) by allowing exceptions to the general requirement to depreciate in the case of investment properties.[68]

In the end, the board struck out the idea of a true and fair override and the elimination of LIFO. It also decided that it wanted to proceed with revisions only 'where there were changes of major importance' and that the remaining changes proposed by the steering committee 'did not present a prima facie case for amending those standards'.[69] An important argument was that re-exposure would be quite costly. For several member bodies, each standard and exposure draft entailed translation costs.[70] The board ordered the steering committee to reconsider whether there were in fact major amendments to be made. Before the steering committee could report, the review of IAS 1 was handed over to the steering committee on objectives (discussed above).[71]

The review steering committee made a second attempt in March 1985. It concluded with apparent regret that there was as yet insufficient international support for 'outlawing' LIFO and the base stock method, so that a revision of IAS 2 was not appropriate. It did propose 'substantive changes' to IAS 4 and IAS 5, but the board again concluded that these changes were not required at this time.[72]

The steering committee had, to no avail, prefaced its proposals with a note of urgency. It expressed appreciation for 'the Board's concern that revisions to International Accounting Standards will result in much additional work and expense for Member Bodies and users', but it advised nevertheless that 'If International Accounting Standards are not kept relevant and up-to-date there will be increasing danger of interference by government and intergovernmental organisations in the setting of accounting standards.'[73] As discussed in Chapter 7, the possibility that the OECD or the United Nations would seriously interfere with the IASC's work was beginning to become quite remote by the mid-1980s. The board may therefore have been less impressed with this threat than with its own apprehensions about the costs of reviews. In June 1985, the board decided not to revise IAS 2, 4, and 5.[74]

Similarly, the board saw no need to revise IAS 7, *Statement of Changes in Financial Position*, even though, in March 1985, the steering committee had pointed out that this was a good opportunity for the IASC to 'take a leadership role in the setting of Standards'. The steering committee noted that a cash approach to preparing statements of changes in financial position was gaining ground and that IAS 7 should be revised accordingly. The FASB added a project on cash flow reporting to its agenda in April 1985, but the IASC board declined to do so.[75] The steering committee and the board agreed that there was no need to revise IAS 8, *Unusual and Prior Period Items and Changes in Accounting Policies*, at this time.

Other standards were reviewed by a different procedure, adopted by the OPC in October 1983.[76] Five years after the publication of a standard, the secretariat would send out a questionnaire to the member bodies seeking opinions about the standard in question. A board member would be asked to review the responses and make a recommendation to the board as to whether a project should be initiated to revise the standard. During 1986 and 1987, IAS 9 through 13 were subjected to this procedure. Only in the case of IAS 12, *Accounting for Taxes on Income*, did this lead to a decision, in March 1987, to set up a steering committee to prepare a revised standard. As this turned out to be a lengthy project that was not completed until the approval of a revised IAS 12 in October 1996, it is discussed in Section 11.4.

The member bodies were generally in agreement that there was no need to revise IAS 9, 10, and 13. They were divided over IAS 11, *Accounting for Construction Contracts*. About half indicated that it would be appropriate to require the application of the percentage of completion method in certain circumstances, instead of allowing a free choice between the percentage of completion and completed contract methods. Canadian board member Bruce Irvine, who reported to the board concerning the responses, noted that this, again, would be an opportunity for the IASC to show 'leadership'. However, it would create problems in terms of acceptability, as it would not reflect accepted practice in many countries. On balance, he made a 'marginal' recommendation not to revise IAS 11, and the board followed his advice.[77]

9.2.2. Group Accounting: The Revision of IAS 3 Leads to IAS 27, 28, and 31

Apart from IAS 12, the only standard which the IASC agreed to revise prior to its Comparability and Improvements projects, was IAS 3, *Consolidated Financial Statements*. IAS 3 was replaced by three closely related standards: IAS 27, *Consolidated Financial Statements and Accounting for Investments in Subsidiaries* (approved in June 1988); IAS 28, *Accounting for Investments in Associates*

(November 1988); and IAS 31, *Financial Reporting of Interests in Joint Ventures* (November 1990).

The drafting process for IAS 27, 28, and 31 was quite complicated. Initially, in March and June 1983, two steering committees were set up. One, chaired by Seigo Nakajima (Japan), was to deal with the review and revision of IAS 3.[78] The other, chaired by Doug Hagerman (Canada), was to prepare a standard on accounting for joint ventures.[79] Subsequently, it was decided to add the treatment of subsidiaries and associates in parent company financial statements to the revision of IAS 3. Still later, the treatment of associates was transferred to the steering committee on joint ventures. The exposure draft produced by this latter committee, E28 (approved in March 1986) dealt with both associates and joint ventures, but the board then decided to separate the two subjects. In November 1988, it approved IAS 28 (Associates) based on E28, and installed a new steering committee to deal with joint ventures. This steering committee prepared the way for IAS 31 with an exposure draft (E35) approved in October 1989. These three standards are discussed below.

9.2.2.1. IAS 27: Consolidated Financial Statements

IAS 3 had been one of the most successful early standards, at least in terms of attracting attention and generating controversy. In particular, the IASC's original proposal to require the consolidation of all subsidiaries, including those with dissimilar activities, was badly received in the United States. In the end, IAS 3 allowed such subsidiaries to be excluded from consolidation. To see whether this exception could be removed or limited was one of the objectives when the board agreed in principle, in June 1982, to review IAS 3.[80] The IASC was probably encouraged by the fact that, in January 1982, the FASB had decided to begin a project on the reporting entity, including consolidation, partly in response to a proliferation of unconsolidated finance subsidiaries. This resulted in the publication of Statement of Financial Accounting Standards (FAS) No. 94, *Consolidation of All Majority-Owned Subsidiaries* (October 1987), which opened the way for the IASC to eliminate the exception for dissimilar activities in IAS 27.

While the IASC kept one eye on the United States, it kept another one on Europe while it was reviewing IAS 3. IAS 3 had also been a successful standard in that it was used as an important point of reference for the European Seventh Directive on consolidated financial statements.[81] IAS 3 included a 'group' concept that allowed, albeit as an exception, to use criteria other than voting rights in determining which companies were controlled by the parent and therefore had to be included in the consolidation. 'In rare circumstances' it might be appropriate, according to IAS 3, to consolidate companies where the parent has a statutory or contractual right to control the operating and financial policies, even though it does not have more than one half of the voting rights in that company. The Seventh Directive, approved in 1983, took this a step further by basing consolidation on a generalized control concept in which ownership of more than half the voting rights was just one of the possible means of realizing control. Adjusting IAS 3, in turn, to the

Seventh Directive was an important reason for the IASC to revise the standard.[82] There were close contacts between the IASC and the European Commission while work on IAS 27 was in progress, much closer than on any previous standard.[83] Reflecting these consultations, the definition of a subsidiary in IAS 27 was based on a control concept that referred to the power to govern operating and financial policies, rather than voting rights.[84]

Given that the exposure draft (E30, approved in March 1987) was in line with European and US developments, it was generally well received. IAS 27 was approved with one abstention.

9.2.2.2. IAS 28: Accounting for Associates

IAS 3 required the use of the equity method to account for investments in associated companies, and IAS 28 did not change this. The improvement brought by IAS 28 was that it refined the guidance (for instance, by specifying more clearly when application of the equity method had to begin and end). As did IAS 27 regarding subsidiaries, IAS 28 addressed the treatment of associates in both the consolidated and in the parent company financial statements. This extension to the parent financial statements came at the cost of more options. In order to accommodate the different legal requirements in different countries, both IAS 27 and IAS 28 allowed a choice between the equity method, cost, or revalued amounts.[85] At this stage, with the Comparability project barely under way, this was apparently not yet seen as problematic. The parts of the exposure draft (E28) dealing with associates attracted few comments, and IAS 28 was approved unanimously.

9.2.2.3. IAS 31: Joint Ventures

Compared to the well-known concept of associates, joint ventures were a novel phenomenon in the mid-1980s. As the steering committee observed at the outset, the practice of using joint ventures was still developing rapidly, and a diversity of meanings was attached to the term 'joint venture'.[86] It took the IASC several years to work out the classification of the various forms of joint ventures that finally appeared in IAS 31 (jointly controlled operations, jointly controlled assets, and jointly controlled entities). To understand the subject, the IASC engaged in extensive consultations with joint venture operators.[87] The main question, however, was whether jointly controlled entities should be accounted for by the equity method or by means of proportional consolidation. For incorporated joint ventures, the equity method was the preferred or required method in Canada, the United Kingdom, and the United States, while proportional consolidation was allowed in several European countries and Canada, and required in France.[88] Initially, the IASC tended towards the equity method. E28 (approved in March 1986) required the equity method, although proportional consolidation might be used as well under rather vaguely defined circumstances. But, following a slim set of comment letters, the board and the steering committee began to move towards the opposite position.[89]

At this point, it was decided to set up a new steering committee on joint ventures, chaired by Arthur Guthrie (Canada). This committee turned out to be highly critical of the equity method.[90] Hence, E35 (approved in October 1989) required the use of proportional consolidation, as this was believed to reflect the substance and economic reality of the joint venture.[91] This gave rise to a considerable volume of comments from UK and US companies, but also from the AICPA, the US Securities and Exchange Commission (SEC), and the UK Accounting Standards Committee (ASC), all of which advocated the equity method. The IASC thereupon modified its position by making the equity method an allowed alternative next to the benchmark method of proportional consolidation.[92] The steering committee remained unconvinced of the merits of the equity method, yet it accepted that the fact that it was used and required in many countries needed to be taken into account.[93] That this created another substantial option contributed to the steering committee's lack of enthusiasm. Nevertheless, it was also possible to put a more cheerful face on the matter. The French delegation's technical adviser, Gilbert Gélard, presented the fact that the standard, in its choice of benchmark, was at odds with the traditional UK and US position as evidence that the IASC was 'a truly international body'.[94]

9.3. COMPARABILITY AND IMPROVEMENTS

As discussed in the previous section in connection with IAS 31, the IASC still found it necessary to include options in its standards, even as it entered the 1990s. Yet dissatisfaction with options had begun to make itself felt long before. One milestone along that road was IAS 25, *Accounting for Investments* (approved in October 1985), with its plethora of options (*see* Section 5.13.5). The building block projects were seen by some as steps towards a conceptual framework that might provide a basis for clear choices among alternatives, but this was not yet the IASC's stated policy. In the short term, there was frustration on the part of at least some board members that the substantial effort of reviewing the earlier standards had so far left most standards, and their options, unaffected.[95] Moreover, there was a growing realization that the IASC had dealt with most of the basic topics.

Towards the end of 1986, these issues were drawn together in a comprehensive review of the future work of the IASC. Successive versions of a strategic discussion paper were tabled during the board and OPC meetings in November 1986 (London) and March 1987 (Sydney).[96] During the pivotal Sydney meeting, the board made a number of key decisions concerning its standard-setting agenda:

Firstly, the board agreed that it had completed 'the substantial majority of basic Standards and, hence, it will spend less time in developing new Standards'.

Secondly, the board agreed to continue its policy of reviewing existing standards, and to spend more time doing so.

Thirdly, the board would set out to reduce the number of options, or to eliminate options, in the existing standards. This task should be given a 'high priority', and it was agreed that 'No new topics should be selected at the present time in order that energies may be directed towards the reduction of options.'[97]

These decisions marked the start of the Comparability project which, together with the subsequent Improvements project, was to dominate the IASC's agenda until the end of 1993. Although it has sometimes been surmised that these projects were started at the request of IOSCO, it can be seen from the preceding discussion that they had their origins within the IASC itself. Nevertheless, it is true that in March 1987, a process was in train to bring the IASC in touch with IOSCO, which coalesced with the internally generated discussion about the IASC's future direction. Although no agreements of any kind had so far been reached with IOSCO, the IASC had been informed by the SEC, IOSCO's leading member, that a reduction of options in the standards would be important in gaining recognition for the IASC from securities regulators.[98] The contacts with IOSCO, discussed more fully in Chapter 10, came therefore at a very opportune moment.

9.3.1. The Comparability Project: Towards E32

At the same meeting of March 1987, when it was agreed to reduce the number of options, the board set up a steering committee for this task. This Comparability steering committee was chaired by Ralph Walters (United States), a former member of the FASB. The other members were Jean-Luc Dumont (France), Herman Marseille (the Netherlands), Eiichi Shiratori (Japan), and Peter Wilmot (South Africa), all of whom were at that time members of the IASC board. In October 1987, a few months after the steering committee's first meeting in July, relations with IOSCO had developed to such a point that it was agreed that IOSCO would send representatives to attend the meetings of the Comparability steering committee. As its representatives, IOSCO chose three chief accountants: Bertrand d'Illiers (COB, France), Paul Cherry (Ontario Securities Commission, OSC), and Edmund Coulson (SEC).

The steering committee set itself a tight deadline by aiming for approval of an exposure draft by the board in November 1988. This deadline was achieved when, at that meeting, the exposure draft E32, 'Comparability of Financial Statements' was approved. The swift progress reflected the high priority given to the project by the board, but also Walters' personal commitment.[99] Walters was strongly dissatisfied with some of the standards issued by the IASC, in particular IAS 25, *Accounting for Investments*. It was known that IOSCO would hold its annual conference in Melbourne in November 1988, just after the IASC's board meeting, and that it would be very helpful if the IASC could announce substantial progress in reducing options.[100]

Research published in the late 1980s probably served to embolden the IASC to rid its standards of optional treatments. An article published in December 1987, which David Cairns had seen, calculated the net incomes for a hypothetical company according to the prevailing US, UK, Australian, or German accounting standards for the treatment of extraordinary items, discontinued operations, changes in accounting policies or principles, and changes in estimates and errors. The range of resulting net incomes by use of the four countries' accounting norms was $35,000, $261,000, $241,000, and $10,000, respectively, thus rendering comparisons difficult.[101] In 1989, Touche Ross Europe published a case study in which it recast the financial statements of a multinational group using the prevailing accounting practices of seven countries in the European Economic Community (EEC), and concluded that the resulting financial statements could hardly be compared. The range of 'maximum achievable' and 'minimum achievable' net incomes, as well as the 'most likely' net income, varied significantly from country to country.[102]

Prior to the steering committee's first meeting, Cairns provided it with an extensive analysis of the thirty-five major options in IAS 1 through 25. In the note, Cairns gave information on which options were allowed or required in a wide range of countries, and he added summaries of comments received during earlier reviews of these standards.[103] The steering committee's task was to go through the list and decide on a recommendation in each case. Chairman Walters observed that 'His favoured approach was to eliminate an option where two or more alternatives existed. He suggested that this might only be [feasible in] the minority of cases. [An a]lternative would be to identify one option as a benchmark or as a preferred treatment.'[104] A third alternative would be, of course, not to make a recommendation at all. The steering committee considered this possibility in the case of IAS 25, 'as these [options] had recently been discussed and agreed by the Board', and some were reluctant to reopen the somewhat painful discussions. But for others, IAS 25 epitomized the need for change, and so IAS 25 was included within the scope of the Comparability project.[105]

In going through the list of options, the steering committee was able to reach agreement fairly easily on which options it preferred. The members understood, as Walters emphasized, that a willingness to compromise was indispensable to the success of the project.[106] But it also turned out that the committee members shared a reasonably similar view of trends in accounting practice and on which practices would, in the long run, be untenable.[107] They differed, however, in their estimates of the feasibility of banning certain options immediately. So when, for instance, Walters proposed to eliminate pooling of interests altogether, his view was sympathetically received by the steering committee, but not supported.[108] What also proved difficult, both in the steering committee and in the board, was agreeing on the designation of alternative treatments, and on whether the effect of alternative treatments and the reasons for using them should be disclosed.

On the whole, Walters and Wilmot preferred to be bold by eliminating options wherever possible, and, as a second-best alternative, to express a preference where alternatives were to be allowed. The IOSCO observers—but not necessarily all of the IOSCO member bodies—were also strong supporters of the drive to eliminate options.[109] The Dutch, on the other hand, came from a background where flexibility was valued and seen as a sine qua non of sound financial reporting. They were not keen on eliminating options altogether and were against onerous disclosure requirements for companies choosing alternative treatments.[110] The Japanese had a similar point of view.[111]

In cases where a choice between treatments was to be preserved, the board vacillated on whether it should express a preference, or use neutral wording to designate the two treatments. In the end it decided to use the terms 'preferred treatment' and 'allowed alternative treatment' in E32.[112] Although Walters had suggested the word 'benchmark', his proposal was not adopted, partly because several delegations had indicated that it might be a difficult term to translate into their own languages.[113] Benchmark may also have been seen as a too emphatic expression of superiority. The board carefully avoided the suggestion that the 'preferred' treatment was superior by explaining that the preferred treatments had been chosen on pragmatic grounds, as 'the most likely and practicable way of achieving greater comparability of financial reporting on a timely basis' (E32, paragraph 21).[114] E32 contained a proposed requirement to reconcile balance sheet and income statement amounts based on an allowed alternative treatment to the amounts that would have resulted from the application of corresponding preferred treatment.

In preparing E32, the IASC's draft Framework played a modest role.[115] E32 probably reflected the steering committee's genuine priorities when it mentioned conformity with the Framework as the second criterion used as the basis for selecting among alternatives. The first was 'current worldwide practice and trends in national accounting standards, law and generally accepted accounting principles' (paragraph 19).[116] E32 acknowledged that in some cases, a preferred treatment was chosen that did not fully conform with the definitions or recognition criteria in the draft Framework. This was the case, for instance, with IAS 23, *Capitalisation of Borrowing Costs*. The immediate expensing of interest costs was chosen as the preferred treatment, even though such costs might meet the recognition criteria for assets. The general reason given for departures from the Framework was pragmatic: the board believed that the objective of 'comparability on a timely basis' would be better achieved by following current practice in such cases (paragraph 20). In the case of IAS 23, a further pragmatic reason was that reconciliation from capitalization to expensing was easier than the other way round. Within the board, the main objections to this pragmatic approach came from the Australian delegation, which had been one of the strongest advocates of embarking on a Framework project.[117]

E32 as published in January 1989 proposed amendments to thirteen of the IASC's standards. These proposals, and their subsequent results, are summarized in Table 9.1. Of the twenty-eight standards published to date, IAS 26–28 were considered too recent for inclusion in the Comparability project. Three standards (IAS 3, 12, and 15) were the subject of separate reviews when the Comparability project began. One standard (IAS 6) had already been replaced, and eight standards (IAS 1, 4, 7, 10, 13, 14, 20, and 24) were judged to have no major options affecting net income or equity. Of these, however, IAS 7 was shortly afterwards to be the subject of a separate revision. In twelve of the thirteen standards affected by E32, the proposed changes had the effect of curtailing the number of options. The

Table 9.1. Revisions of International Accounting Standards during the Comparability and Improvements Projects

Standard/topic	Status at start of Comparability project (1987)	E32 recommendation (1989)	Statement of Intent (1990)	Status end of 1994
IAS 1 Accounting Policies	No major options			Reformatted
IAS 2 Inventories*		Revise	Revise but reconsider	Revised
IAS 3 Consolidation	Already replaced			
IAS 4 Depreciation	No major options			Reformatted
IAS 5 Disclosure		Revise	Do not revise	Reformatted
IAS 6 Inflation	Already replaced			
IAS 7 Funds Statement	Separate revision			Revised
IAS 8 Accounting Changes*		Revise	Revise	Revised
IAS 9 Research and Development*		Revise	Revise but reconsider	Revised
IAS 10 Contingencies	No major options			Reformatted
IAS 11 Construction Contracts*		Revise	Revise as in E32	Revised
IAS 12 Income Tax	Separate revision in progress			Reformatted, revision in progress
IAS 13 Current Assets and Liabilities	No major options			Reformatted
IAS 14 Segment Reporting	No major options			Reformatted, revision in progress
IAS 15 Inflation	Separate revision in progress			Reformatted, application optional
IAS 16 Property, Plant, and Equipment*		Revise	Revise as in E32	Revised
IAS 17 Leases		Revise	Defer revision	Reformatted
IAS 18 Revenue*		Revise	Revise as in E32	Reformatted
IAS 19 Retirement Benefits*		Revise	Revise as in E32	Revised
IAS 20 Government Grants	No major options			Reformatted
IAS 21 Currency Translation*		Revise	Revise as in E32	Revised
IAS 22 Business Combinations*		Revise	Revise as in E32	Revised
IAS 23 Borrowing Costs*		Revise	Revise but reconsider	Revised
IAS 24 Related Party Transactions	No major options			Reformatted
IAS 25 Investments		Revise	Defer revision	Reformatted, revision suspended
IAS 26 Retirement Benefit Funds		Excluded as too recent		Reformatted
IAS 27 Consolidation	Not yet approved	Excluded as too recent		Reformatted
IAS 28 Associates	Not yet approved	Excluded as too recent		Reformatted
IAS 29 Hyperinflation	Not yet approved	Not yet approved		Reformatted
IAS 30 Disclosure by Banks	Not yet approved	Not yet approved		Reformatted
IAS 31 Joint Ventures	Not yet approved	Not yet approved		Reformatted

* The package of ten standards revised as part of the Improvements project.

thirteenth standard, IAS 5, *Information to be Disclosed in Financial Statements*, would not be changed because it included significant options, but in order to introduce the reconciliation requirement, applying to all standards with allowed alternative treatments.

In all, E32 dealt with twenty-nine situations where the standards allowed a choice between two or more alternatives. In fourteen situations, E32 proposed to leave a choice between a preferred and an allowed alternative treatment, and in fifteen situations it proposed a single treatment. Inevitably, given the number of topics involved, there had been many differences of opinion within the board on individual issues. Some of the options nominated for elimination were still widely used in some countries, or had been inserted as hard-won compromises in the IASC's original standards. These included the option to choose the completed contract method for the recognition of revenue on all construction contracts and transactions involving the rendering of services (IAS 11 and 18), the deferral of foreign exchange gains and losses on long-term monetary items (IAS 21), charging goodwill directly to equity (IAS 22), and taking changes in the market value of current investments directly to equity (IAS 25). In some cases, E32 did not merely propose to eliminate options but also proposed restrictions on the remaining options. The most conspicuous instance of this was the insertion of a maximum amortization period for goodwill. IAS 22 had merely required that goodwill be amortized over its useful life. E32, in line with the Fourth Directive, now proposed a default amortization period of five years, to be extended to a maximum of twenty years if a longer period was justified.[118]

But despite the significant potential for disagreement, and the serious debate on many issues, E32 was approved unanimously for publication.[119] Looking back, steering committee Chairman Ralph Walters said:

I am so proud of the performance of the Steering Committee and the Board. The Committee met just four times for a total of eight days, and just 20 months elapsed from the approval of the idea to approval for public exposure. It's most significant to note that no single member of the Steering Committee and no member of the IASC Board agreed with all the proposals, yet each member of the Committee and all 13 countries represented on the IASC voted to approve the ED. We all realized that in order to harmonize each must sacrifice for the greater good of all.[120]

The board realized that, with E32, it would send an important signal to the world that it intended to seek a new and more significant role for itself. If possible, the signal should be free from the noise of dissenting opinions.[121]

9.3.2. The IASC Seeks the Limelight with E32

Before the start of the Comparability project, public interest in the IASC was flagging somewhat. As documented in Chapter 5, the number of responses to exposure drafts had declined after the first standards of the mid-1970s. While some exposure drafts, like that on leasing, attracted somewhat wider attention, the response on others had been limited. The publication of the draft Framework had rekindled some interest in wider circles, but by and large the IASC's discussion papers circulated within a comparatively narrow group in which the member bodies dominated. With E32, the IASC made a determined and successful effort to attract the attention of a wider audience, in particular financial executives. The publicity surrounding E32 was carefully planned, and much energy was invested in providing information and encouraging debate.

Another reason to pay careful attention to publicity was that E32, with fifty A4-pages, was a complex document, far longer than any of the IASC's preceding A5-booklets. There was a risk that the message about the IASC's new strategy might be obscured, and the response rate lowered, if the world were to get the impression that all the IASC had to offer was a mass of accounting detail. At the request of the steering committee, Cairns approached two academics, Christopher Napier and Michael Bromwich, of the London School of Economics, to comment on the clarity and consistency of the draft.[122] Moreover, a firm of public relations consultants was retained to advise on the format and style of the exposure draft, its distribution, and the media strategy.

While the Comparability steering committee was at work, the IASC board members and staff already tried to draw attention to the venture in speeches, articles, and in the IASC's first published annual report, for 1987.[123] In January 1989, when E32 was published, the effort to reach out was intensified. Hundreds of 'key people' in a number of countries, particularly the members of the boards of directors of listed companies, were identified with the help of the member bodies, and copies of E32 were sent to them.[124] *IASC News* was restyled with higher quality paper and a more professional layout. David Cairns embarked on a series of trips taking him all over the world to give speeches and discuss E32 with a wide range of audiences. These included stock exchanges, national standard setters, member bodies, and financial executives institutes, as well as multinational bodies such as the OECD and the European Commission. IASC Chairman Georges Barthès, Ralph Walters, and other members of the Comparability steering committee did their part in this extensive round of consultations.[125]

9.3.3. From E32 to the *Statement of Intent*

In terms of attracting attention, the publicity surrounding E32 was highly successful. The volume of comment letters received greatly exceeded the previous record set by E3, on consolidated financial statements, in 1975.[126] The IASC staff was overwhelmed by the response, even though two audit firms had made extra staff available to assist in reviewing the letters. Cairns warned the steering committee that it might not be possible to review the letters with the customary care.[127] As will be seen, this was but one element of concern over the IASC's 'due process' that emerged in the course of the Comparability and Improvements projects.

In all, over 160 comment letters were received, including forty-one from member bodies and accountancy firms, forty-nine from individual enterprises, seventeen from industry associations and financial executives institutes, and the remainder from stock exchanges, regulators, professional associations, and individuals.[128] To the IASC, this marked a real turning point, as it had succeeded in attracting the serious attention of the business world.[129]

With E32, the IASC embarked upon a new policy of publishing the comment letters it received. The steering committee had proposed that the IASC publish a summary of the responses. Reacting to some of the due process concerns, the steering committee argued that this would 'help demonstrate the efforts that the Board has undertaken and the difficulties that it has faced'.[130] In July 1990, the board decided to go one step further by making photocopies of the responses available, to the extent that the respondents gave their permission. The board also agreed that a similar policy would be followed with future exposure drafts.[131]

9.3.3.1. General Nature of the Reactions to E32

In general, the IASC's intention to reduce the number of options in its standards was favourably received, and agreement on the objective of greater comparability was 'virtually unanimous'.[132]

Nevertheless, there were some critical comments on this basic level as well, notably from the Netherlands and Japan. Both the Dutch standard setter, the Council on Annual Reporting, and the Japanese Institute of Certified Public Accountants questioned what they saw as the overriding priority given to comparability in E32. They argued that fair presentation, taking into account the circumstances of the individual enterprise, or specific national environments, should be the paramount consideration. Both organizations warned that enforced uniformity of method does not necessarily yield comparability.[133]

Obviously, respondents who agreed with the general approach of E32 could still find fault with the board's choices on individual issues, and many, often conflicting, comments of this nature were received. These might take the form of a general unease that E32 seemed to be biased in favour of Anglo-American options, or against Continental European traditions.[134] However, as responses from the Anglo-American world outnumbered those from Continental Europe by four to one, this opinion was expressed by a minority of respondents only.[135] To the extent that respondents from the English-speaking world commented on the general drift of the proposals, a recurring complaint was that E32 gave too much weight to the status quo. The apparent low priority given to the IASC's own Framework in deciding on preferred or alternative treatments also came in for substantial criticism.

9.3.3.2. Charting the Way Forward

By July 1989, six months after the publication of E32, the IASC had committed itself in public to taking the next step in the Comparability project by June 1990. However, it had not yet specified clearly what that step would be.[136] As the deadline for comment letters had been extended from 30 September to, in effect, the end of 1989, it had to make up its mind under considerable time pressure. E32 (paragraph 9) had suggested that the board might proceed to reissue revised standards on the basis of E32 and the comments received, without re-exposure. This raised a considerable volume of criticism and due process concerns, both in the comment letters and during the various visits and conferences attended by IASC representatives during 1989. From several quarters, it was pointed out that there had been no preliminary exposure draft, that it was improper to approve changes on so many issues in one package, and that E32 did not show the proposed changes to the explanation sections of the affected standards. The IASC was therefore asked to re-expose all of the standards affected by E32.[137]

During 1989 and into 1990, several ways forward were discussed in the board. One possibility was to implement E32 by issuing an international accounting standard on 'Financial Statements of Multinationally Listed Enterprises'. This would leave the extant standards intact but would specify which options from these standards had to be chosen by enterprises with international listings.[138] Another option, favoured by some board members, was to issue an 'IAS 32', that is, a standard modelled after E32 which would be directly binding on all enterprises. In the end, the board followed the preference of the steering committee, which advocated issuing a 'statement of amendments'. This would list all agreed amendments of the standards as a package. It would be binding on the board in revising the affected standards, but, until the standards were revised, reporting companies would not need to take the amendments into account in order to report in conformity with the IASC's standards.[139] The discussion on how to proceed with the Comparability project was complicated by the fact that the board wished to reconsider some issues in E32. Moreover, the board began to realize that an endorsement by IOSCO would require more changes to the standards than envisaged by E32, and that for these additional changes some form of exposure would be required.[140]

It was not until March 1990 that the board finally agreed on the procedure to be followed.[141] At its next meeting, in June, it accordingly approved for publication the *Statement of Intent: Comparability of Financial Statements*. This was a document showing how the IASC meant to deal with the twenty-nine options covered by E32. For most options, the *Statement of Intent* confirmed the position in E32. On some, it indicated a new tentative position by the board, and in some cases it announced that the matter was being deferred for later consideration. Except for these latter cases, the *Statement of Intent* announced that exposure drafts would be issued for all standards affected by E32, and that the board considered itself bound by the position taken in the *Statement of Intent* if this confirmed the position of E32. In other words, the exposure of the draft standards was not meant to reopen the debate on the decisions confirmed by the *Statement of Intent*. Exposure would allow the IASC to make additional changes which were considered necessary to improve the standards to a level acceptable to IOSCO. Any revisions would take effect only when the standards themselves were revised. The *Statement* was silent on whether or not the revised standards would be voted on as a package.

9.3.3.3. The IASC Changes Its Position on Some of the E32 Issues

As might be expected, several of the E32 proposals attracted widespread disapproval. Generally speaking, the IASC did not allow itself to be swayed from its chosen course by these criticisms. It acted in line with the advice given by Morley Carscallen, a member of the Canadian delegation to the IASC from 1976 to 1979. Recalling the IASC's earlier days, Carscallen wrote to the board on E32: 'There will be comments that the proposed approach will discourage enterprises from attempting to comply with International Accounting Standards and thus be a Bad Thing. I suggest you ignore such comments.... I think that the IASC has done well, and is certainly past the stage when it has to consider making its standards acceptable by trying to keep everybody happy.'[142]

In particular, the proposal to eliminate the direct charging of goodwill to equity drew strong dissents from many respondents from Continental Europe and the United Kingdom, where it was accepted practice.[143] Of all the E32 proposals, this was probably the one with the greatest potential impact on reported profits. As Carscallen predicted, several companies threatened or hinted that this would prevent them from adopting or continuing to use IASC standards.[144] But within the steering committee and the board there was general support for requiring the capitalization of goodwill, although there was much 'wringing of hands' over the appropriate length of the amortization period.[145] In the end, the position of E32 was maintained (a five-year amortization period, unless a longer period can be justified, but never more than twenty years).

Similarly, the IASC maintained the position of E32 on most other issues. But there were some where it either deferred a decision or changed its position.

On leasing, there was considerable opposition from the United Kingdom, focused on the somewhat specific point of recognition of finance income by lessors. This had already been a point of UK concern when IAS 17 was approved in 1982. The board still found the issue difficult to grasp, and it agreed to defer a conclusion until further study could be made.[146] Similarly, there was opposition, particularly from the banking and insurance sector, on the proposals for IAS 25, *Accounting for Investments*. By early 1990, the IASC's project on financial instruments was well on its way. The board was aware that this was going to cover not just 'new' financial instruments, but also the more traditional investments covered by IAS 25.[147] It therefore made sense to postpone a decision on revising IAS 25 until the completion of the financial instruments project, which at that time was expected to happen within a few years (*see* Section 11.5.1).

There were three issues on which the IASC changed its position between E32 and the *Statement of Intent*. With all three the effect was to restrict the options open to enterprises even further. The most controversial decision was made on LIFO. The board proposed in the *Statement of Intent* to eliminate LIFO altogether, while in E32 it had been an allowed alternative. LIFO had already been controversial when the original IAS 2 was prepared. The method was seen by many as conceptually unsound, and its acceptance in IAS 2 was perceived as a concession to the United States, where the acceptability of LIFO for tax purposes was conditional on its application in the financial statements (*see* Section 5.5.1). Similar reactions were received on E32. Hence, the secretariat had concluded in its summary of comment letters on E32 that the reactions justified the elimination of LIFO. This proposal was carried by a vote of four to three in the Comparability steering committee.[148] However, the secretariat may have overstated the case somewhat. Paul Cherry, one of the IOSCO observers on the steering committee had advised in favour of eliminating LIFO. Yet he began to waver after a second reading of the comment letters had revealed to him that 'Support for LIFO is more widespread geographically than I thought and may well increase.'[149] There were in fact only about twenty comment letters that were unambiguously critical of LIFO, and one-third of these expressed a willingness to accept that the United States might have to be accommodated. Almost half of the letters that were critical of LIFO came from Australia, and all but a few of the remainder came from English-speaking countries other than the United States.[150] In contrast, about ten responses from the United States, Germany, and Japan argued that LIFO and FIFO should be seen as equally valid alternatives. Most other US respondents did not raise the issue and appeared to be content with the fact that E32 recognized LIFO as an allowed alternative. In all, it could hardly be said that the comment letters showed that there was a strong call for the abolition of LIFO. Nonetheless, the board decided to propose the elimination of LIFO, even though a significant number of delegations had misgivings. In a March 1990 straw poll in the board, the proposal was carried by seven votes to five.[151]

The other two points on which the *Statement of Intent* differed from E32 were less controversial, at least in the board. On IAS 9, *Accounting for Research and Development Costs*, and IAS 23, *Capitalisation of Borrowing Costs*, E32 had proposed immediate expensing—of development costs and borrowing costs, respectively—as the preferred treatment, with recognition as assets allowed as alternative treatment for qualifying items. On both issues, the board was attacked from two sides. From the more principled side it was argued that this recommendation was inconsistent with the IASC's own Framework, and that a conceptually sound approach would be not merely to allow but to require capitalization if an item met the relevant conditions. From the pragmatic side, the proposal was criticized by enterprises with high levels of development cost or high levels of investment in self-constructed assets.[152] As criticism on both counts was not restricted to particular geographical areas, and as the conceptual arguments were not easy to ignore, the board changed its position. But whereas many respondents had merely wanted a reversal of the preferred and alternative treatments, the steering committee and the board went further by eliminating the option of immediately expensing items that qualified for recognition as assets.[153]

9.3.3.4. Other Changes in the Statement of Intent

E32 would require companies using an allowed alternative treatment to disclose the difference between the preferred and alternative treatments for the affected balance sheet and income statement items. That this point was untenable became clear during the extensive consultations on E32 which the IASC organized around the world during 1989. It was also made clear by the comment letters.[154] During the October 1989 board meeting, several delegations including the Dutch, the Germans, and the French reported strong opposition in their countries to reconciliation. Moreover, it was argued that reconciliation was really a matter for securities market regulators, not standard setters. The IOSCO representatives agreed. They pointed out that IOSCO's members, when and if IOSCO were to endorse the IASC's standards, could themselves require reconciliation if the preferred treatments were not used.[155] Having the reconciliation requirement in the standard itself would be helpful, but 'If . . . the reconciliation in E32 hinders its acceptance, IOSCO would not be concerned if it was dropped provided IASC identified the benchmark treatments.'[156] With this encouragement, the board agreed in March 1990 to eliminate the reconciliation requirement.[157]

Many respondents to E32 took issue with the 'preferred treatment'/'allowed alternative treatment' wording. The statement in E32 that the preferred treatments were not necessarily better than the alternatives was not always understood or accepted. Some companies complained that their practices would be stigmatized as second-rate, and other respondents argued that many of the preferred treatments were not better.[158] Responding to Cairns' suggestion, the board decided in March 1990 to revert to the word benchmark, as had been advocated by Walters at the start of the Comparability project.[159]

As a result of the various changes made to the E32 proposals, the *Statement of Intent* was not approved unanimously, as E32 had been. The Italian, Japanese, and Korean delegations voted against, or abstained. As will be seen, this proved to be a signal of further difficulties ahead.

9.3.4. Start of the Improvements Project

In the early stages of the Comparability project, many within the IASC believed that eliminating most of the options from the existing standards would be sufficient to make them acceptable to IOSCO. Yet, as the project progressed, as the contacts with IOSCO and individual securities regulators intensified, and as IOSCO's own views on the subject began to be better articulated, it became clear that completing the Comparability project would not be enough to persuade IOSCO to accept the IASC's standards. A particularly clear signal came from IOSCO's Annual Conference in November 1988 (*see* Section 10.4). A resolution was passed encouraging the IASC 'to pursue its project to eliminate accounting alternatives and to ensure that its standards are sufficiently detailed and complete, contain adequate disclosure requirements, and are prepared with a visible commitment to the needs of users of financial statements'.[160]

Taking this and other signals into account, not least those emanating from the SEC, the IASC discussed its work programme in depth during the board meeting of April 1989 in Brussels.[161] Based on a lengthy paper by David Cairns, the board agreed that it had to do three things. Firstly, it had to implement the Comparability proposals. Secondly, taking its cue from the IOSCO resolution, it had to improve all of the existing standards, not just those affected by E32, to ensure that they were 'sufficiently detailed and complete and contain adequate disclosure requirements'. Finally, it had to fill the major gaps by addressing issues not yet covered by the set of IASC Standards.[162] The board agreed to entrust the first two tasks to a new steering committee. This project became known as the 'Improvements' project, which is discussed in this chapter. The attempt to fill the remaining gaps in the set of standards dominated the IASC's technical agenda during the remainder of the 1990s. The resulting new standards are discussed in Chapter 11.

Although it was agreed in April 1989 that the Improvements project was to be completed by the end of 1992, the steering committee did not actually begin its work until September 1990, that is, after the publication of the *Statement of Intent*.[163] Ralph Walters was to chair the Improvements steering committee, but the chairmanship passed instead to Paul Cherry (Canada) well before September 1990. Cherry had by then returned to Coopers & Lybrand from the OSC and had become a member of the Canadian IASC delegation. Apart from Cherry, the steering committee consisted of Tadaaki Tokunaga and Etsuo Sawa (Japan), Fouad Alaeddin (Jordan), Johan van Helleman (the Netherlands), and Ron Paterson (United Kingdom), as well as their technical advisers. IOSCO was represented by a large contingent of up to five observers. The European Commission, which had not had an observer on the Comparability steering committee, was also represented.[164]

9.3.5. Scope of the Improvements Project

In November 1990, the board discussed and agreed the Improvements committee's ambitious work programme.[165] Its most straightforward task was to implement the changes envisaged in the *Statement of Intent*. Its second, and more difficult, task was to reconsider all standards and, where necessary, to clarify and expand the implementation guidance provided by the standard, 'so that different enterprises applying the Standard achieve substantially similar accounting results for like transactions and events'. This was one of IOSCO's major concerns, but, being essentially open-ended, it was not easy to deal with. Finally, the steering committee was asked to revise all standards in terms of format and style in order to eliminate inconsistencies and to bring the standards in line with the wording used in the Framework. The style revision was also intended to eliminate the remnants of the IASC's previous, more circumspect approach. Wording such as 'desirable' and 'commonly used' were to be replaced by clear prescriptions.

In November 1990, the board agreed to revise nineteen standards before April 1993. The other extant standards were either very recent (such as IAS 29), not directly relevant for companies with multinational listings (such as IAS 26 on retirement benefit plans), or would be dealt with in due course, for instance as part of the financial instruments project (IAS 25, on investments). To complete the revision of nineteen standards, including an exposure draft stage for each standard, in the course of seven board meetings between February 1991 and

April 1993 was a huge challenge. The steering committee's work plan envisaged several board meetings during which no fewer than seven exposure drafts or final standards had to be debated and, more critically, approved. It soon became clear that this was impossible. In January 1991, Cairns informed the board that 'The amount and complexity of the work on the Improvements project is far greater than expected,' and that revisions of all standards would 'take much longer than we originally envisaged.' Staff work on all projects other than Improvements was suspended, with the exception of financial instruments, where the staff work was being done by the CICA.[166] Still, the Improvements project quickly fell far behind the original schedule, prompting repeated changes in the timetable.[167] Revision of the standards not covered by the *Statement of Intent* was first postponed, and then removed from the scope of the Improvements project altogether. Ultimately, the project was limited to revising ten standards covered by the *Statement of Intent*, and the IASC had to work very hard just to complete this smaller task by the end of 1993.

9.3.6. Closing the 'Package'

The IASC had dealt with E32 and the *Statement of Intent* as a package. Chairman Wyatt in particular had insisted on this approach, and it turned out to be vital.[168] In this way, the delegations disciplined themselves to make the concessions on individual standards that were necessary to achieve a significant reduction of options. The same logic required that the final revised standards should also be approved as a package. However, given that three issues were left open for reconsideration by the *Statement of Intent*, the board had to decide at some point what the package exactly contained by taking a final position on each of these issues.[169]

Between February 1991 and March 1992, the board approved and issued exposure drafts for eight of the ten standards affected by the *Statement of Intent*. All, including the three exposure drafts dealing with the issues to be reconsidered, were in agreement with the positions in the *Statement of Intent*. However, at the June 1992 meeting it became clear that the standards on inventories and borrowing costs were running into difficulties. The reservations about these standards shared by the German, Italian, Japanese, and Korean delegations began to coalesce into serious opposition. The four delegations came from countries where prudence in accounting was traditionally valued, not least because of links between financial reporting and taxation.

The board had been aware of these reservations, but the voting pattern so far had shown that these delegations were, as all other delegations, to some extent prepared to put their objections aside in the light of the overall objectives of the Comparability and Improvements projects. Italy, Japan, and Korea had voted against the *Statement of Intent*, or had abstained, for reasons related to the three reconsidered standards. Korea and Japan had voted against the exposure draft on inventories (E38). One delegation, probably Japan, voted against the exposure draft on interest costs (E39). In the case of development costs (E37) the vote had been unanimous. Germany—where LIFO had become generally acceptable for tax purposes only as recently as 1990—had confined itself to stating its objections, but had voted in favour in all cases.[170]

However, in April 1992 it suddenly became known that IOSCO favoured the retention of LIFO (*see* Section 10.7), which probably encouraged the four delegations.[171] In June 1992, preliminary votes showed that the standards on inventories and borrowing costs could not count on the required number of eleven votes of fourteen.[172] Therefore, at its next meeting in October 1992, the board had to reconsider the Improvements package.

Because of what was at stake, and because of the uncertainty of the vote, the October 1992 board meeting was awaited with some suspense.[173] Particularly in the case of LIFO, the position of the US delegation was watched with some interest. It was well known that, in the United States, LIFO had similar tax consequences as in Germany. Even though the US delegation to the IASC had not indicated that it would vote against the abolition of LIFO, not everyone was prepared to predict confidently that it would indeed acquiesce in its removal as an option. In March 1992, FASB Chairman Beresford had pointed out that doing away with LIFO 'would be devastating to the U.S. . . . Particularly in the United States, companies may decide that harmonization isn't worth the costs of losing LIFO tax benefits.' As the IASC needed the votes of all but three of its members to issue a standard, Beresford predicted that 'They will have a hard time doing away with LIFO.'[174] The AICPA, in its comment letter on E38, had written that it had been unable to reach a consensus on whether the final standard should prohibit LIFO, and it confined itself to noting the 'considerable implementation difficulties for United States companies' that would result from such a prohibition.[175] The financial analysts' delegation supported the elimination of LIFO but observed that this was against the wishes of US financial analysts, who believed that earnings based on LIFO were more useful for predicting cash flows.[176]

At the October board meeting, though, it was not the US but the German delegation which joined forces with the Italian, Japanese, and Korean delegations to block the abolition of LIFO. The German position was not only that taxes were an issue, but also that the required disclosure of the difference between the LIFO effects and the benchmark treatment meant that, from an investor point of view, there was no urgent reason for eliminating LIFO. Moreover, there was a more general feeling of disaffection in the German delegation that E32 and the *Statement of Intent* showed a one-sided disposition in favour of Anglo-American accounting practices.[177] It is possible to question this view, for instance in the light of utterances by FASB Chairman Dennis Beresford that E32 would, for the first time, establish international standards that conflicted significantly with US standards.[178] But what mattered was the perception, and this led the German delegation to seize the opportunity and to help in the formation of a blocking coalition. As a result, the board approved, in October 1992, a revised version of IAS 2, which gave LIFO the status of allowed alternative treatment.

The backtracking on LIFO was highly visible because it was a well-known and clear-cut issue, with the added interest of the unusual US position. But it differed in degree rather than kind from the IASC's decisions on capitalizing borrowing and development costs. At the same October 1992 board meeting, it became clear that there was also insufficient support for eliminating the option of immediately expensing borrowing costs. A revised version of IAS 23, *Borrowing Costs*, was therefore approved. It identified immediate expensing of all borrowing costs as the benchmark treatment and capitalization of qualifying costs as allowed alternative. This was directly opposite to the position in the *Statement of Intent*, which had proposed the elimination of immediate expensing as an option. But, unlike LIFO, there was intermediate ground between the two positions. Before it agreed to the final position in October 1992, the board had already agreed in June that the criteria for 'qualifying costs' should be modified to emphasize that capitalization would be exceptional.[179] As on LIFO, Germany and Japan supported the proposed move away from capitalization, because it would be more in line with their domestic practices. This time, they received support from the delegations of the Nordic Federation and the United Kingdom. The United States opposed the proposal because it would maintain the free choice on capitalization in IAS 23.[180]

Even less conspicuous was the way the IASC dealt with capitalization of development costs. On this issue, the IASC ostensibly maintained the position of the *Statement of Intent*. IAS 9 (revised), *Research and Development Costs*, required the capitalization of development costs meeting certain criteria. Germany, which opposed capitalization on the grounds that this was not prudent, felt free to agree with the standard because it had helped to ensure that the criteria were sufficiently strict.[181] It could be argued that, in essence, reporting enterprises still had a largely free choice, as they had under the previous version of IAS 9. It was, after all, up to the reporting company to make and support the claim that the criteria for capitalization had been met.

Formally, the board agreed in October to revise the package of changes listed in the *Statement of Intent* on LIFO and borrowing costs, and then recommitted itself to the revised package. This time, the United Kingdom voted against, because of the retention of LIFO.[182] The board also agreed that all of the ten standards would need eleven votes in favour, and would not come into effect until all ten would be approved.[183]

In a way, the dealings over E37, E38, and E39 were simply a continuation of the IASC's tradition of compromising and adjusting to obtain the necessary support. But there was a certain symbolic quality about the three standards that made it more than business as usual. Because the three standards had been singled out as a group in the *Statement of Intent*, because the discussions on all three came to a head in the same board meeting of October 1992, in Chicago, and because the nucleus of opposition was in all three cases formed within the same group of non–English-speaking countries, it was easy to see the decisions on the three standards as a significant turning point. As the German delegate, Heinz Kleekämper, put it, Germany and 'a small group of allies' had 'succeeded one last time' to 'save LIFO' and stem the tide on capitalization of development and borrowing costs. But he knew that, already with the publication of E32, 'The power of the fact, that is, the comfortable Anglo-Saxon majority in the places where the decisions are made, had won the battle.'[184]

9.3.7. The Ten Revised Standards

The Improvements project was completed in November 1993, when the last of the ten revised standards was approved and the package was put to a final vote. In this final vote, the Japanese delegation voted against. It emphasized, however, its support for the revised standards, and it pledged once more to use its best endeavours to ensure that published financial statements conform with these standards.[185] The ten revised standards were IAS 2 (inventories), IAS 8 (unusual and prior period items and changes in accounting policies), IAS 9 (research and development costs), IAS 11 (construction contracts), IAS 16 (property, plant, and equipment), IAS 18 (revenue recognition), IAS 19 (retirement benefit costs), IAS 21 (foreign exchange rate changes), IAS 22 (business combinations), and IAS 23 (borrowing costs).

The main changes, of course, were the elimination of options, or the designation of some options as allowed alternative treatments, in line with the positions in the *Statement of Intent*, as modified by board's decisions of October 1992. Another significant change, called for by IOSCO, was an expansion of the disclosure requirements included in the standards. In addition, the format of the standards had been revised. Until then, the IASC's standards had consisted of two separate sections: an 'explanation' section in normal type, containing definitions, background material, and sometimes implementation guidance, followed by the 'standard' section in bold type. In the new format, the distinction between the boldfaced standard and explanation was retained, but the explanatory material was now printed directly behind the corresponding boldfaced paragraphs.

The explanatory material was expanded to include guidance on a range of issues that had not been dealt with by the original standards. For instance, IAS 21, *The Effects of Changes in Foreign Exchange Rates*, now dealt with the treatment of goodwill arising on the acquisition of foreign entities, and IAS 22, *Business Combinations*, now discussed the treatment of stepwise acquisitions. Many of these additions had been suggested by the IOSCO representatives on the Improvements steering committee.[186] Some had a European origin, such as the requirement to reverse the write-down of inventory to net realizable value when the net realizable value subsequently increases.[187] However, because all these additions were printed in normal rather than bold type, differences of view concerning their status could persist. IOSCO, and the SEC in particular, insisted that compliance with IASC standards included compliance with both the 'grey-lettered' and the 'black-lettered' sections, a point of view shared by the IASC staff, whereas several delegations assumed a difference in status between the two.[188] The IASC refrained from mentioning the difference in type in its Preface to Statements of International Accounting Standards. Users of the standards continued to express uncertainty over the significance of the distinction until the dissolution of the IASC.[189]

During 1994, the IASC reformatted its remaining standards, not covered by the Improvements project. This was a limited operation to ensure that all standards followed the same style of boldfaced paragraphs interspersed with explanations and further guidance in normal type. Cairns sternly warned the board members that they should resist any temptation to 'tinkering' with the substance of the standards on this occasion.[190]

Mainly because of an expansion of the explanatory material and the inclusion of appendices with illustrative examples, the total length of the ten revised standards increased by 70 per cent compared to their predecessors.[191] Whether that provided enough implementation guidance to satisfy IOSCO was an open question. In 1991, Brigid Curran, the IASC's technical director, had summarized the key difficulty of the Improvements project for the benefit of the board: 'It is impossible to know when to cease work on an amendment of a Standard since we have been formally advised by IOSCO that the adoption of International Accounting Standards requires a certain quality to be attained. Unfortunately, there remains significant ambiguity as to what quality is necessary.'[192] The IOSCO representatives, particularly those from North America, were respected for their technical expertise, and their views on what would be acceptable to the securities regulators in their countries could not be dismissed lightly. Yet there was awareness within the IASC that, in the end, they were speaking on a personal basis rather than with clear instructions from IOSCO.[193]

9.3.8. Muted Reactions to the Completion of the Improvements Project

For a project that, together with the Comparability project, had been at the centre of the IASC's activities for almost seven years, the end of the Improvements project was announced by the IASC in a rather low-key fashion. The December 1993 issue of *IASC Insight*, which was published after the final approval of the package of ten revised standards, briefly mentioned the completion of the project on page 2 in the list of items dealt with at the last board meeting, and again on page 8 in a matter-of-fact statement preceding a summary of the last two standards to be approved.[194] Nor did the professional press devote extensive coverage to the completion of the project. It was duly reported but hardly with the sense that a milestone had been reached.[195] By late 1993 and early 1994, it was widely realized that it was not so much the completion of the Improvements project that was decisive, but IOSCO's endorsement of the IASC's standards, and that the latter was by no means guaranteed by the former.[196] Nevertheless, Arthur Wyatt had been right when, as IASC chairman-designate, he had written in 1989 that the Comparability project 'will likely come to be seen as the watershed event in the history of the IASC'.[197] But it was the beginning rather than the end of the project that marked the turning point.

9.4. OTHER PROJECTS

The following sections discuss the IASC's remaining projects from the late 1980s and early 1990s that were not directly related to the Comparability and Improvements projects.

9.4.1. Cash Flow Statements: The Revision of IAS 7

As shown in Section 9.2.1, the IASC had seen no need in 1985 to revise IAS 7, *Statement of Changes in Financial Position*. However, during the Comparability project it changed its view. When the Comparability steering committee determined its position on each of the substantial options in the extant standards, it found that IAS 7 was essentially a single large option. The key phrase of that standard (paragraph 22) read: 'Each enterprise or group of enterprises should adopt the form of presentation for the statement of changes in financial position which is most informative in the circumstances.' While this degree of flexibility might have been acceptable to the board as late as 1985, in the new perspective of the Comparability project it was decidedly anachronistic. The Comparability committee advised the board that IAS 7 should be dealt with, but also indicated that it could not do so itself. The removal of this option would require a complete rewriting of the standard, which was not an appropriate task for a steering committee charged solely with identifying options for removal.[198]

Hence, the board set up a separate steering committee for the revision of IAS 7 in April 1989, chaired by Peter Wilmot (South Africa).[199] An exposure draft, E36, was soon agreed (February 1991, with publication following in July), and a revised standard was unanimously approved in October 1992.[200]

Since the publication of the original IAS 7 in 1977, there had been a movement, particularly in the English-speaking countries, away from a statement of changes in financial position (or statement of sources and application of funds) based on working capital, and towards a statement based on cash flows.[201] The most prominent, although not the first, milestone in this movement was FAS 95, *Statement of Cash Flows* (November 1987).[202] FAS 95 introduced a cash-based rather than a working-capital-based statement, as well as a division of the statement into sections on cash flows from operating, investing, and financing activities. By the early 1990s, comparable cash-based standards were issued or in preparation in other countries as well. Like FAS 95, the revised IAS 7 prescribed a cash flow statement based on cash and cash equivalents, with the same tripartite classification. Beyond these main features, different views continued to be held. This was true within countries, as shown for instance by the fact that FAS 95 allowed a choice between the direct and indirect methods of presenting operating cash flows. Between countries, there were differences on the type of activity with which dividends paid should be classified. IAS 7 reflected these differences by allowing enterprises a choice on several of these issues. Apart from these options, IAS 7 contained unambiguous guidance on many points. In this respect, it was radically different from the original IAS 7, and was a good example of the way the IASC was changing. That IAS 7 (revised) was a much more rigorous standard than its predecessor, and in fact rather close to FAS 95, was confirmed when, in October 1993, IAS 7 became the first of the IASC's standards to be endorsed by IOSCO for use by internationally listed companies (*see* Section 10.8.4).

9.4.2. Developing Country Issues

Almost from its inception, the IASC was criticized for issuing standards without regard for the needs of the developing world. The criticism was somewhat inappropriate, because in practice developing countries were more eager to adopt the IASC's standards than the developed countries represented on the board. The criticism nonetheless resurfaced periodically. In this section, two of the IASC's responses are discussed: first, its standard on financial reporting in hyperinflationary economies (IAS 29), and, second, its aborted project on the reporting needs of developing and newly industrialized countries.

9.4.2.1. IAS 29: Hyperinflation

The IASC board decided in October 1983 to add a project on 'accounting in high inflation economies' to its agenda. It did so in response to requests from developing countries, particularly from Latin America.[203] During the course of the project, the World Bank also expressed a strong interest, as the Bank was under some pressure to provide guidance in this area.[204] The five-member steering committee was composed largely of countries that had experienced high inflation, although in the case of Germany the experience was rather distant. Apart from Wilhelm Tjaden, the German chairman, the steering committee included representatives from Argentina, Israel, and Mexico. The United States was added, not because it was experiencing high inflation, but presumably in order to ensure that the committee could draw on the required technical expertise.[205]

The project resulted in a standard, IAS 29, *Financial Reporting in Hyperinflationary Economies*, which was approved for publication in April 1989. IAS 29 required that the primary financial statements of an enterprise reporting in the currency of a hyperinflationary economy should be stated in terms of monetary units current at the balance sheet date. To this end, the amounts for non-monetary items in financial statements should be restated by applying a general price index. IAS 29 also provided more specific guidance on issues such as the choice of index, corresponding figures for prior periods, and the treatment of gains and losses on the net monetary position.

The practical significance of IAS 29 must have varied considerably across the developing world. In the exposure stage, it was confirmed that the approach of the standard was in keeping with national requirements or approaches in many Latin American countries, especially Argentina and Brazil. However, it also became clear that several of these countries had already developed more elaborate guidance themselves, while it was feared that other countries would lack the expertise to apply the rather general prescriptions of IAS 29 in practice.[206]

IAS 29 was of some significance for the IASC itself in laying to rest the ghost of its difficult and ultimately fruitless efforts on accounting for inflation. As discussed in Section 5.7, these efforts had culminated in 1981 with the publication of IAS 15, *Information Reflecting the Effects of Changing Prices*. This standard required economically significant enterprises to provide certain minimum disclosures based on either a current cost or a general purchasing power approach. IAS 15 reflected an uneasy compromise among three groups: the proponents of the two main approaches to accounting for inflation (current cost accounting and the general purchasing power approach) and those who were not convinced that the IASC ought to issue a standard on the issue at all. Because, at a conceptual level, there was no clear partition separating accounting for inflation from accounting for high inflation, the new project threatened to reopen some of the old discussions. Indeed, some members of the board believed that the IASC should issue a revised version of IAS 15 dealing with all levels of inflation. Others, however, pointed out the low levels of compliance with the original IAS 15, and they warned of the risk that international corporations would not be able to disclose compliance with IASC standards solely because of IAS 15.[207] By 1987, when the IASC was focusing its strategy on this type of company, that must have been an unbearable prospect. The board therefore gradually disconnected IAS 15 from what was to become IAS 29. In the end, IAS 29 contained no direct references to IAS 15, even though the basic approach of IAS 29 was essentially identical to what was described, in IAS 15, as the general purchasing power approach. In the title of the standard, 'high inflation' was replaced by 'hyperinflation', presumably to underscore that the standard was applicable in the most exceptional circumstances only.[208] As a result, shortly after it had approved IAS 29, the board was free to decide in October 1989 that application of IAS 15 was no longer mandatory.

IAS 29 was clearly intended as a more peripheral element in the IASC's collection of standards. Nevertheless, it acquired some additional significance when it was included in the small set of IASC standards accepted by the SEC in 1994 (*see* Section 10.8.7).

9.4.2.2. Reporting Needs of Developing Countries

In April 1989, the same meeting at which IAS 29 was approved, the board agreed to set up a steering committee to undertake a 'comprehensive review of the financial reporting needs of developing and newly industrialized countries and the way which IASC can help meet these needs'.[209] The board appointed Talal Abu-Ghazaleh (Jordan) as chairman of the steering committee. The other members represented a mixture of developed and developing countries, as well as international organizations such as the United Nations and the World Bank.[210] R. S. Olusegun Wallace, a Nigerian academic at the University of Exeter, was hired as an 'International Research Fellow' to assist the steering committee.

On earlier occasions, Abu-Ghazaleh had shown himself ready to question the IASC's established ways, and the draft working programme for his steering committee reflected a similar drive to move beyond the status quo. According to this proposal, circulated early in 1990, the committee was to deal not only with financial reporting, but also with the organization of the accountancy profession and with professional education in developing countries.[211] Not surprisingly, Abu Ghazaleh's proposal—which may not have had the full support of the steering committee[212]—provoked considerable resistance, both in the International Federation of Accountants (IFAC) and in the IASC. It was remarked that this would bring about the merger between IFAC and the IASC by the back door, just after the Bishop Working Party had put an end to discussions of a merger (*see* Section 7.5). Eyebrows were also raised by the proposals to set separate standards for developing countries and to include the People's Republic of China in the steering committee, even though that country was a member of neither IFAC nor the IASC.[213]

In the light of reactions in IFAC and the informal comments from the IASC's member bodies prior to the IASC board meeting of March 1990, the draft working programme was withdrawn. It was replaced by a proposal from the Jordanian delegation that the IASC should take the initiative to set up an independent advisory board on the reporting needs of developing and newly industrialized countries. This board would be sponsored by the IASC and other organizations, such as IFAC and the United Nations. The board would consist of the members of the IASC steering committee, with the addition of other international organizations and accountancy bodies from developing countries.[214] Although the IASC board approved the project in principle, it was effectively put on hold indefinitely, pending the results of consultations between IFAC and other potential sponsors. As advised by IFAC, the IASC board decided that its own steering committee on developing countries should meanwhile continue under its original terms of reference.[215] Abu-Ghazaleh thereupon resigned, in June 1990, both as chairman of the steering committee and as a member of the Jordanian delegation to the IASC.[216]

The steering committee continued to function, first under Jordanian, then under French chairmanship. But the project languished because staff resources were withdrawn to concentrate on the Improvements project. Although a fresh start was attempted in 1992, and the board agreed that the project had a high priority, little progress was made.[217] In July 1993, the project was abruptly terminated.

A major weakness of the project throughout its life was that many in the board were not convinced that developing countries had reporting needs that should be addressed by separate standards.[218] It was agreed, though, that small companies or specific industries might have reporting needs where the IASC could play a useful role. In this respect, the project would bear fruit later in the 1990s. In the course of consultations with regional accountancy bodies and other organizations that arose out of the project on financial reporting in developing countries, David Cairns noted that there would be great support for IASC projects on agriculture and extractive industries.[219] As is discussed in Chapter 11, these issues were taken up by the IASC. Nevertheless, for the rest of its life, the IASC had to endure sporadic criticism that it 'ignored' the developing nations.[220]

9.4.3. IAS 30: Bank Disclosures

In 1981, the IASC had decided to put on hold its project on disclosures in the financial statements of banks, in order to await developments in the official regulation of bank accounting, particularly in the EEC (*see* Section 5.10). The IASC resumed work on banking in 1984, encouraged by progress on a European Directive on financial reporting by banks.[221] The European Directive was approved in 1986, and it was an important point of reference for the IASC, although, of course, it also paid attention to best practices and regulations in countries such as the United States and Australia.[222]

The IASC appointed a new steering committee for the revived banking project, chaired initially by David Hobson and subsequently by Gerard Murphy, of Anglo Irish Bank, Dublin.[223] An accountant from industry, Murphy presided over the completion of the IASC's first industry standard. In this way, he symbolized how the IASC in the second half of the 1980s was broadening its base beyond the accountancy profession and was beginning to move beyond basic standards. The Basel Committee, which in 1976 had invited the IASC to take its first steps in the area of bank accounting, showed a strong interest during this second phase. By 1988, it had set up its own task force on accounting, one of its representatives participated in the work of the steering committee, and in 1990 the Basel Committee joined the IASC's Consultative Group.[224]

It took two exposure drafts (E29, approved in November 1986, and E34, approved in April 1989) before the IASC could complete IAS 30, *Disclosures in the Financial Statements of Banks and Similar Institutions* (approved in June 1990). Although the first exposure draft was generally well received, it was felt within the IASC that substantial revisions were in order to address concerns that national regulations in various countries might hinder the application of the standard in practice.[225]

The most sensitive element of the standard was that it banned, in effect, secret and hidden reserves.[226] IAS 30 prevented the overstatement of liabilities, as it required that charges for expected losses on loans in excess of specifically identified probable losses should be presented as appropriations of retained earnings (paragraph 58). So, even though IAS 30 was ostensibly concerned with disclosure, it did have important consequences for the determination of income.

During the 1980s and early 1990s, support for the traditional use of secret reserves by European banks was eroding. According to the European bank accounting Directive of 1986, EEC member states could still allow secret reserves in the form of undervaluation of certain assets, but only within the limits prescribed by the Directive.[227] At the time that the IASC was completing IAS 30, it was not clear how many member states would actually use this option, but there were signs that only a minority, consisting of Germany, Luxembourg, and the Netherlands, might do so. Within the IASC, the German delegation took the position that the exception that allowed banks to form undisclosed reserves was no longer tenable, and it voted in favour of IAS 30. This isolated the Dutch delegation both in the board, where all other delegations voted in favour, and at home, where the Dutch banks and many auditors wanted to retain the secret reserves or at least to delay their abolition. In the end, the Dutch delegation abstained from voting, but it defended the standard in public and called upon Dutch banks to follow it.[228]

When E29, the first exposure draft on banks, was approved, the IASC board instructed the steering committee to continue work on recognition and measurement issues for banks. However, it soon became clear that these issues were inseparably linked to the problem of accounting for what were known as 'new financial instruments'. When the second exposure draft, E34, was approved, the IASC had just embarked on a financial instruments project, and it therefore decided to defer work on recognition and measurement issues for banks. In June 2000 the IASC set up a new steering committee to work on bank disclosures and presentation, but this was too near the IASC's dissolution to have any practical consequences (*see* Section 11.9.2).[229]

10

Raising the Stakes: The IASC Responds to IOSCO and the SEC

At its meeting in March 1987 in Sydney, discussed below and in Chapter 9, the IASC board took stock of its standards programme and proceeded to develop a strategic plan. The leaders of the board were troubled that the IASC's standards were, for the most part, being adopted or adapted only in developing countries. The board's standards were registering very little impact in the developed, industrialized countries, especially in those with well-developed equity securities markets. The leaders felt it was essential that, to have any real impact in the developed world, the board had to establish a closer relationship with securities market regulators, national standard setters, and major preparers. They also came to believe, with a nudge from the US Securities and Exchange Commission (SEC), that real progress towards international harmonization would not occur until most of the optional treatments in the board's standards were removed.[1] This chapter shows how the International Organization of Securities Commissions (IOSCO) occupied the centre stage in the IASC's aims and deliberations between 1987 and 2000. A first phase in the relationship between the two organizations ended in a difficult period during the second half of 1994. The relationship was then set on a new footing in 1995, and a more promising phase began. These two distinct phases are covered in Sections 10.1–10.11 and 10.12–10.21, respectively.

10.1. THE EMERGENCE OF IOSCO

The prospects for the IASC establishing closer contact with securities market regulators took on a new dimension on 17 July 1986, when an article and editorial appearing in the *Financial Times*[2] disclosed the existence of a hitherto obscure body known also as the IASC, the International Association of Securities Commissions. The body had just begun its annual conference in Paris, which was its first such meeting held outside the Americas. It was founded in Caracas in 1974 as the Interamerican Conference of Securities Commissions and Similar Organizations (Conferencia Interamericana de Comisiones de Valores y Organizaciones Similares), and its sole activity was to hold annual conferences. During the body's conference in April 1983 held in Quito, Ecuador, the by-laws were changed to adopt a new name, the International Organization of Securities

Commissions and Similar Entities (Organización Internacional de Comisiones de Valores y Entidades Similares), and it began admitting members from outside of the Americas.[3] Prior to its 1986 conference, the body's only European involvement was the London Stock Exchange and France's Commission des Opérations de Bourse (COB).[4] The *Financial Times* reporter said that the body 'has always had the reputation of being a rather sleepy organization whose annual get-togethers gave the opportunity for jamborees rather than jaw-boning' and that it 'has traditionally been dominated' by the SEC. But it awakened with a start in Paris.

One can only surmise that the Paris hosts in July 1986 chose the name, International Association of Securities Commissions (IASC), for their conference as an improvement over the cumbersome name selected in 1983, yet the by-laws were not changed accordingly. Hence, the official name adopted in 1983 remained in effect. In 1987, the by-laws were changed to drop the appendage, 'and Similar Entities', and the body became known as IOSCO.[5]

On the first day of its conference in Paris, 'Delegates agreed on a fundamental reform of the organisation's structures destined to turn it into a genuine international securities watchdog.'[6] At the conference, the body agreed to establish a permanent secretariat in Montréal. It was reported that Yves Le Portz, chairman of the COB and also chairman of the conference, 'has played an important part in steering the IASC towards a more effective role'. Both SEC Chairman John S. R. Shad and SEC Commissioner Charles C. Cox addressed the conference. Le Portz performed a key role in energizing the body, and Shad committed the SEC to be an active player.[7]

This 'other' IASC's awakening occurred at a time of growing international capital movements. Between 1980 and 1985, cross-border transactions in bonds and equities had increased, as percentage of gross domestic product, from 9 to 35 per cent in the United States, and from 7 to 33 per cent in Germany. Although these were seen at the time as sizeable changes, they were, as it turned out, merely the first stirrings of a spectacular and sustained increase in cross-border investment, lasting throughout the 1980s and into 1990s. By 1997, these percentages had become 213 and 253 per cent, respectively. Other countries registered even larger increases.[8]

After seeing the *Financial Times* article, Secretary-General David Cairns began making enquiries about this other IASC. On 28 July, he wrote Chairman-Designate Georges Barthès de Ruyter that 'This is an organization [with] which we ought to have contact.' He asked Barthès, based in Paris, whether he knew Le Portz and if he could facilitate a meeting between him and Cairns.[9] Apparently, this meeting did not occur.

During the latter 1980s, both the IASC and IOSCO had small secretariats and were only beginning to make an impact. David Cairns, in London, and Paul Guy, in Montréal, were the embodiment of their respective secretariats.[10] Both bodies made extensive use of volunteers as members of their committees. As shown in Chapter 6, the IASC's some two dozen accounting standards had gained degrees of acceptance only in a number of developing countries. Of the countries represented on the IASC's board, virtually none of the Anglo-American countries and only a few of the other developed countries were importing any of its standards into its national accounting standards or laws.

IOSCO's membership rose from twenty in 1983 to fifty-six in 1990 and to seventy-three in 1995.[11] The SEC was by far the most powerful regulator among IOSCO's members. Perhaps no other country had a securities market regulator with a sizeable technical staff or one that was so undeviatingly attentive the setting of, and compliance with, accounting standards.

Both the IASC and IOSCO became much more consequential in the 1990s. By stages, the IASC intensified its standard-setting programme so as to elevate its standards to a level of quality that might secure the endorsement of IOSCO, which, as a practical matter, meant endorsement also by the SEC. The IASC secretariat expanded its technical staff to achieve that aim. For its part, IOSCO received fresh impetus and enhanced gravitas by the reorganization of its Technical Committee in 1990 under the leadership of SEC Chairman Richard C. Breeden, which is discussed in Section 10.6.

10.2. THE IASC ESTABLISHES CONTACT WITH IOSCO VIA THE SEC

In August 1986, Chairman John L. Kirkpatrick and Secretary-General Cairns spoke at a major international conference in Princeton, New Jersey, bringing together some sixty accounting policymakers, including national standard setters, from twenty-three developed and developing countries and from international organizations such as the United Nations (UN) and the Organisation for Economic Co-operation and Development (OECD).[12] The three-day conference would have enabled Kirkpatrick and Cairns to have useful conversations with a wide range of individuals interested in the board's programme or work. Following the conference, Cairns went to Washington for an informal meeting with SEC officials, including a chat with Commissioner Cox.

A motive behind the SEC's interest in harmonizing international accounting standards was expressed by Chief Accountant Clarence Sampson in a speech in 1987: 'Are US investors deprived of investment opportunities because more stringent accounting, auditing and disclosure requirements in the US act as a deterrent to capital raising efforts of foreign issuers?'[13] The standards of accounting, auditing, and disclosure in other countries were also a concern to the SEC's Division of Enforcement.[14]

En route to the board's March 1987 meeting in Sydney, Kirkpatrick and Cairns stopped in Washington to meet with the SEC on 11 March. Clarence Sampson, Clarence Staubs, and Edmund Coulson, all staff members of the SEC's Office of the Chief Accountant, as well as Commissioner Cox, attended the meeting. After hearing from Kirkpatrick about the recent work of the IASC, Chief Accountant Sampson pointedly referred to the optional treatments in the IASC's standards. He asked whether they could be narrowed, and, if so, how fast. He asked whether the IASC could identify one option as a 'reconciling method' so that different companies around the world could reconcile to that treatment. Cox added that this would be better than reconciling to the requirements of one country, the evident reference being to US generally accepted accounting principles (US GAAP). Kirkpatrick readily agreed and said that there would be an instant reaction against such a reconciliation, and he undertook to explain the reasons for options in the IASC standards. Staubs said that the reconciling standard could become a common frame of reference for international capital markets. Kirkpatrick added that the reconciling standard might be seen as the preferable standard.[15]

During the meeting, Commissioner Cox said that it would be useful for the IASC to work closely with IOSCO and participate in its meetings, as it had begun to deal with such topics as accounting and enforcement. Such participation would, he said, enable the IASC to become acquainted with securities market regulators from around the world and to discuss accounting problems and related issues. He said that he would arrange for the IASC to be issued an invitation to attend IOSCO's next annual conference, in Rio de Janeiro in September 1987.[16]

A month after the meeting with the IASC, Sampson went public with his concern about the number of options in IASC standards. In an interview with the Bureau of National Affairs, published on 10 April 1987, Sampson said, 'Until the IASC reaches the point where they can have a set of standards which eliminates most of the alternatives, I don't think they will be accepted as an international accounting standard body—a body of standards that [would]...be sufficient for an offering anywhere in the world...and which can give you some assurance of comparable reporting.'[17]

The enquiry by the SEC chief accountant about optional treatments lent a degree of urgency to a discussion held at a meeting the previous October of the IASC's Organisation and Planning Committee (OPC) about whether to launch a project that would reduce or eliminate options in existing IASC standards. As viewed from the SEC, the IASC was seeking to be recognized as a 'player', but the SEC was not about to confer such recognition until its standards were revised and strengthened; they had too many options, and they were too general.[18]

Also en route to the board's Sydney meeting, Kirkpatrick and Cairns attended a UN meeting in New York City and then paid a call on the Financial Accounting Standards Board (FASB), where they 'discussed the possibility of regular gatherings of standard-setters in conjunction with IASC Board meetings' and also 'considered ways in which IASC and the FASB could work closer together, possibly through international task forces on emerging topics of international interest'.[19] The renewed effort to promote closer contacts with national standard setters was beginning.

At its meeting in Sydney, the IASC board devoted a full day to devising a strategic plan for its future work, thus building on the OPC's discussion of the previous October. Cairns had sent a substantial memorandum on strategy to the board members prior to the meeting. Also included in the agenda papers was a memorandum written by Cairns on his and Kirkpatrick's meeting earlier that month at the SEC. It stated, 'If consensus could be achieved on a single basis for "reconciliation" the SEC would be receptive to a proposal to allow foreign companies to reconcile to that standard rather than US generally accepted accounting principles.'[20] This was the carrot.

The board decided that, as it had completed 'the substantial majority of basic Standards, it will spend less time in developing new Standards'.[21] Instead, the board accorded a 'high priority' to reducing or eliminating the number of options in existing standards. It voted to set up a steering committee composed solely of board members to 'examine each option and recommend whether it could be eliminated or some preference indicated'.

Obviously concerned about the need for a greater impact in developed, industrialized countries, the board decided that it should 'hold discussions with regulatory authorities and multinational enterprises and so achieve a greater influence with national standard-setting bodies'. It also favoured greater contact with the standard-setting bodies themselves. These positions stood in stark contrast to the long-standing view within the board that the IASC was not to have any direct contacts with regulators, companies, and national standard-setting bodies without first obtaining permission from the country's one or more accountancy bodies.

Following the Sydney meeting, Ralph Walters, a former FASB member who was to retire from the IASC board in July after three years of service, agreed to chair the IASC's newly established 'Comparability' steering committee, which was charged with reducing or eliminating the options in the IASC standards. Others observed that he was the 'driving force' in this endeavour.[22] Walters has characterized the temper of the times as follows:

The purpose of the IASC is to improve the usefulness of accounting internationally. To succeed in this, one needs to harmonize existing national standards to eliminate, or at least minimize, free choice alternatives. Pressure was building from IOSCO, in which the SEC was most influential. Both the UN and OECD were making noises about getting involved, and I think most thoughtful people wanted to head them off. It was clear that if the IASC was to have any effect on this area, because it had no authority or powers of enforcement, it would be necessary to obtain the recognition and acceptance of the IOSCO group (e.g., SEC). The US delegation was exerting much pressure to move ahead with the Comparability project. I agreed to accept the chairmanship only with the understanding that representatives of IOSCO be included on the steering committee, because I knew that if our recommendations were not acceptable to the controlling bodies, the whole project would be simply an exercise in futility.[23]

In Sydney, the IASC board also decided, on Chairman Kirkpatrick's recommendation, to invite IOSCO to join its Consultative Group 'and so build a bridge with regulators'.[24] IOSCO promptly accepted the invitation[25] in time for it to be represented at the next meeting of the Group in Edinburgh on 30 June 1987. In accepting the IASC's invitation to join its Consultative Group, Paul Guy, IOSCO's secretary-general, wrote,

Provided some important changes could be made to the international standards, they could eventually be accepted in prospectuses of multinational offerings. It is therefore essential that a close association be put in place between IOSCO and your committee.[26]

At the IASC's suggestion, IOSCO named three representatives, mentioned below, to attend the meetings of its Comparability steering committee. For their part, Kirkpatrick and Cairns attended IOSCO's annual conference in Rio de Janeiro in September, at which the members in attendance 'recommended that regulatory authorities should examine practical means of promoting the use of common standards of accounting in prospectuses'.[27] With strong interest thus expressed on both sides, the IASC and IOSCO began to forge a working relationship that would lift the IASC's aspirations and lay the groundwork for a number of ambitious initiatives during the final decade of the century.

In May 1987, IOSCO's Executive Committee agreed to set up a Technical Committee,[28] which included representatives from the thirteen largest capital markets in the world.[29] According to IOSCO's 1991 annual report, 'Representatives from securities commissions, governments and self-regulatory organizations ("SROs") from the following jurisdictions comprise the Technical Committee: Australia, France, Germany, Hong Kong, Italy, Japan, Ontario, Québec, Spain, Sweden, Switzerland, The Netherlands, the United Kingdom, and the United States.'[30] By 1993, the Technical Committee had sixteen members, as Mexico and the US Commodity Futures Trading Commission had been added.

The Technical Committee in turn created a working party on accounting and auditing,[31] chaired by Paul G. Cherry, the chief accountant of the Ontario Securities Commission (OSC). It came to be numbered as Working Party 2, and its members began attending meetings of the IASC's Comparability steering committee as observers.

With these steps, the IASC and IOSCO launched thirteen years of intense and sometimes difficult discussions and negotiations, eventually leading up to IOSCO's endorsement of a core set of IASC standards in May 2000.

10.3. THE COMPARABILITY STEERING COMMITTEE: E32

During 1988, the IASC's Comparability steering committee, chaired by Ralph Walters, held a series of 'fast track' meetings to produce a major draft that would cut back significantly on the number of permitted options. (*See* Section 9.3.1 for a more extensive treatment of the Comparability committee.) The three chief accountants constituting IOSCO's Working Party 2 on accounting and auditing standards—Paul Cherry, of the OSC, Edmund Coulson, of the SEC, and Bertrand d'Illiers, of the COB[32]—attended meetings of the steering committee as observers on behalf of IOSCO, yet they participated in the meetings as if they were full members, Cherry being outspoken on the need to eliminate alternative treatments.[33] During the committee's deliberations, the chief accountants made it clear that the committee's proposal for an exposure draft represents a useful first step, provided that there is agreement in principle on the ultimate objective:

- completeness of general principles (short-term)
- key disclosure items (medium-term)
- supplementary guidance/interpretation on implementation matters (medium/ long-term).[34]

As will be seen, the 'ultimate objective' was a comprehensive set of standards with enhanced disclosures and ample interpretive guidelines.

The Comparability committee held four meetings from July 1987 to September 1988, when it completed its proposal for an exposure draft.[35] Coulson's strategy, he said, was 'to get them to come up with the toughest standards they possibly could. One of the concerns I had, and I laid this out to the Commission, if this [set of IASC standards] was ever accepted and the standards were somehow viewed to be weak, then all the US companies would want to use all these perceived weak standards.'[36] This has always been a fundamental issue in the eyes of the SEC: there must be equitable treatment for all companies in the US capital market. In June 1989, Linda Quinn, the director of the SEC's Division of Corporation Finance, said, 'If domestic companies must account on a more stringent, burdensome, costly basis, how can you say that a foreign issuer can come to the United States using a system that the US companies would love to use and sell to exactly the same investor?'[37] This argument has been a principal reason that the SEC has insisted that foreign registrants not using US GAAP must reconcile their earnings and shareholders' equity to US GAAP.

OSC Chief Accountant Cherry waxed optimistic with the progress he had witnessed in the Comparability steering committee. In September 1988, just prior to returning to his accountancy firm, Coopers & Lybrand, he drafted a proposed four-page statement of 'endorsement' by the Technical Committee that would urge IOSCO's member organizations 'to accept compliance with or reconciliation to IASC standards'.[38] SEC Chief Accountant Ed Coulson disagreed, writing to Cherry, 'I believe that [your] draft is much too detailed and premature given the relatively early stage of the IASC project.' In his own redraft, Coulson bespoke caution, proposing that the Technical Committee say in one page only that the Comparability committee's exposure draft 'represents an important first step in assessing the feasibility of the IASC project'.[39] So, in October 1988, even before the IASC board could consider the steering committee's proposal at its November meeting, IOSCO's Technical Committee jumped the gun by issuing a guarded statement of support for the committee's draft, using Coulson's proposed wording.[40]

At its meeting, the IASC board made only minor changes in the draft before approving it unanimously for exposure as E32, 'Comparability of Financial Statements', to be published on 1 January 1989.[41] E32 proposed to eliminate twenty-three alternative treatments, by now labelled 'free choices', in twelve of the IASC's previously issued standards. It apportioned the allowed treatments into two categories: required or preferred treatment, and 'allowed alternative treatment'. The importance to the steering committee of the SEC's and IOSCO's views is made clear in the following list of four criteria that the board said were used to decide which of the alternative treatments should be designated as required or preferred:

(a) current worldwide practice and trends in national accounting standards, law and generally accepted accounting principles;
(b) conformity with the proposed IASC Framework for the Preparation and Presentation of Financial Statements ('proposed Framework');
(c) the views of regulators and their representative organizations, such as the International Organisation of Securities Commissions; and
(d) consistency within an International Accounting Standard and with other International Accounting Standards.[42]

An important proviso in E32 was the following: 'An enterprise that presents financial statements which use allowed alternative accounting treatments but purport to conform with International Accounting Standards should reconcile its reported net income and shareholders' interests to those amounts determined using the preferred treatment' (paragraph 22). The Comparability committee's decision to create the classification of preferred and allowed alternative treatments was in response to the disclosure at the board's March 1987 meeting in Sydney that the SEC sought a reconciliation to a single standard.[43]

The most critical of the letters of comment received from securities market regulators came not from the SEC but from the OSC. The OSC's new chief accountant, Michael Meagher, wrote that, 'At this time we would not accept financial statements prepared in accordance with IASC standards in lieu of financial statements prepared in accordance with Canadian standards.' But he held out the hope that 'Filling in the gaps, eliminating alternatives in like situations and providing more detailed guidance is an approach that eventually should allow us to accept financial statements prepared according to IASC standards as the primary financial statements for certain classes of foreign companies.'[44] One notes that neither the SEC nor the OSC was contemplating the use of IASC standards by domestic companies in their primary financial statements. Evidently, Meagher was more cautious than his predecessor as OSC chief accountant, Paul Cherry, in characterizing the support that should be given at this stage to the IASC.

10.4. THE RESOLUTIONS TAKEN AT IOSCO'S 1988 ANNUAL CONFERENCE

As the Comparability committee was pursuing its agenda, an obvious need arose to secure an official statement from IOSCO on its expectations for the IASC's revised standards. IOSCO had not yet formally articulated the qualities it was seeking in the IASC's revised standards except for the expectation that fewer options be permitted, although, as noted, above, the three chief accountants had outlined the ultimate objective in June 1988.

IOSCO had held its 1987 annual conference in Rio de Janeiro. No one from the senior staff of the SEC's Office of the Chief Accountant or Division of Corporation Finance had attended the 1985 through 1987 conferences, and, while the harmonization of accounting and auditing standards was discussed, no progress towards an articulated consensus was made.[45] At the 1987 conference, the Presidents Committee adopted an important recommendation: 'They [i.e., securities administrators] should examine practical means of promoting the use of common standards and auditing procedures.'[46] This was a start, but it did not point to an agreed source of 'common' accounting standards.

IOSCO held its 1988 annual conference on 14–17 November in Melbourne, Australia, which occurred a week after the IASC board approved E32, its first utterance on the elimination of optional accounting methods. At that conference, Donald J. Moulin, a partner in the Washington office of KPMG Peat Marwick and chairman of the SEC Regulations Committee of the American Institute of Certified Public Accountants (AICPA) since 1987, presented an important paper at Workshop No. 4 on Harmonization of Accounting and Auditing Standards. At the previous conferences he had attended, Moulin was troubled that 'The accounting discussions lacked direction and a sense of purpose.'[47] That no senior representative from the SEC's accounting staff had attended previous IOSCO conferences had been a contributing factor to this lack of progress. He sensed that a disagreement within the SEC had been an obstacle. He recalls as follows:

The US SEC was sending mixed signals because the Commissioners and the staff had not agreed on a single approach. The SEC would accept international accounting standards (IASs) if the IASs conformed to US GAAP. Yes, IASs were incomplete, were not sufficiently detailed, and allowed alternatives that limited comparability. However, it appeared that some persons at the SEC were using these reasons, perhaps disingenuously, to justify their opinion that only US GAAP was acceptable.[48]

Reacting to Moulin's recollection, the then SEC chief accountant, Edmund Coulson writes as follows:

However, it was clear that at the present time and for the foreseeable future, that in fact was the case given the state of affairs with respect to the set of IAS that existed. And the SEC understood that even with the plans for improvement, much work remained in order to develop a sufficiently robust set of standards that could even be considered in an environment that commanded investor protection. At the SEC, it was unclear whether the IASC was up to that task, given their past history of compromise and developing standards that embraced virtually all practices. The attitude was 'show us you can do it', and then we will consider it.[49]

At the Rio conference, Moulin approached Henry Bosch, the chairman of Australia's National Companies and Securities Commission, who was to be the host for the 1988 conference, and secured approval to prepare and present a paper in a workshop that would recommend using the standards of the IASC and the International Auditing Practices Committee (IAPC) of the International Federation of Accountants (IFAC). Bosch reacted positively, but he deferred formal acceptance of Moulin's proposal until after an exchange of correspondence.

Moulin informed Edmund Coulson, the SEC chief accountant, of his plan. He also discussed his initiative with IASC Chairman John Kirkpatrick and IASC Secretary-General David Cairns, as well as with Robert Sempier, the IFAC executive director, and he received their support. In June 1988, he completed the first draft of his paper, and he sought comments from a wide circle of interested parties, including Bosch, Cairns, Ralph Walters, Paul Cherry, and Coulson. The recommendations in Moulin's paper were therefore widely known before it was presented in Melbourne.

Moulin's paper, entitled 'Practical Means of Promoting Common Accounting and Auditing Standards', led to the adoption by IOSCO of its first resolutions on accounting and auditing standards. He was, in effect, serving as an 'honest broker' between SEC/IOSCO and the IASC and as the catalyst to elicit an articulation from IOSCO of what qualities it sought in the IASC's revised standards and thus apprise the IASC of how to proceed to gain support from the regulator community. In the final version of his paper, he proposed several key prerequisites for revised IASC standards so that they might serve as a 'reconciliation benchmark' in multinational prospectuses or be used to prepare financial statements in multinational prospectuses, paraphrased as follows:

- They must provide sufficiently detailed guidance so that different preparers' interpretations of the standards do not lead to non-comparable financial statements.
- They must be sufficiently complete so that multinational preparers do not rely heavily on individual country guidance on subjects not covered by IASC standards, thus impeding comparability.
- They must contain sufficient disclosure requirements that would provide information on material issues that may bear on the use, understanding, and interpretation of the financial statements.

A fourth prerequisite, more a matter of process than content, was that the revised standards 'must be perceived as developed with sufficient mindfulness of the needs of users of financial statements'.[50]

Moulin closed his paper of twenty double-spaced pages by proposing two resolutions for the Workshop panel to consider, and he included references as well to the IAPC of IFAC:

- IOSCO encourages the IASC to improve International Accounting Standards and pursue its project to eliminate accounting alternatives with an agenda to ensure that its standards are sufficiently detailed and complete, contain adequate disclosure requirements, and are prepared with a visible commitment to the needs of users of financial statements; and encourages the IAPC to develop guidance on the independence of auditors and common requirements for auditor's opinions for use in audits of multinational issuers.
- [A]ssuming that international accounting and auditing standards are appropriately improved by the IASC and IAPC, respectively, IOSCO member governments should, by the year 1994, permit financial statements in multinational prospectuses and

subsequent periodic financial reports that are audited in accordance with IAPC auditing standards and that are prepared either (a) in accordance with the standards of the country in which the company is domiciled and reconciled to IASC standards or (b) solely in accordance with IASC standards.

This second of the two draft resolutions clearly established Moulin as an enthusiast for the work of the IASC and the IAPC, and, as will be seen, his intervention at the IOSCO conference had a positive effect.

Henry Bosch selected the panel for Workshop No. 4, at which Moulin presented his paper, and his choices virtually assured that the panel would be sympathetic to Moulin's message. He chose Georges Barthès de Ruyter (by then the IASC chairman) to chair the panel; together with Ralph Walters, Paul Cherry, and Kenneth Spencer, of Australia (a former IASC board member and a former member of Australia's Accounting Standards Review Board).[51] After hearing and discussing Moulin's paper, the panel issued its report to the Presidents Committee. In a decisive tone, it said, 'The panel agreed that IASC and IAPC are the appropriate bodies [to set international standards]...and strongly urged IOSCO to support and endorse these bodies as the appropriate standard setters and to support their acceptance by IOSCO's members.' It added, 'The panel stressed the urgency of the matter. The [European Economic Community's] free flow of capital by July 1, 1990, and a single market by January 1, 1993, were described as examples of the need for prompt action.'[52]

The panel proposed two formal resolutions for adoption by the Presidents Committee. The first resolution was virtually identical to Moulin's first resolution, reproduced above. The second resolution was as follows:

IOSCO continues to strongly support the work of both the IASC and IAPC by providing assistance through working groups in their respective projects that affect the development of common accounting and auditing standards.[53]

This second resolution fell well short of Moulin's proposed second resolution. Moulin's recommendation of an endorsement (without actually using that term) if the standards are suitably improved by 1994 was dropped entirely.

Of the four resolutions adopted by the Presidents Committee, reproduced below, the first was added by the Committee but was entirely consistent with the report of Workshop No. 4, and the remaining three were the same, word for word, as the Workshop's two but were reorganized into three points. But there was no hint of a possible future endorsement of the standards by IOSCO. The four resolutions by the Presidents Committee were as follows:

- IOSCO encourages the IASC (International Accounting Standards Committee) and IAPC (International Auditing Practices Committee) to act promptly to facilitate the establishment of improved international accounting and auditing standards.
- IOSCO encourages the IASC to improve International Accounting Standards and pursue its project to eliminate accounting alternatives and to ensure that its standards are sufficiently detailed and complete, contain adequate disclosure requirements, and are prepared with a visible commitment to the needs of users of financial statements.

- IOSCO encourages the IAPC to improve international auditing standards including requirements on the independence of auditors and on auditor's opinions.
- IOSCO continues to strongly support the work of both the IASC and IAPC by providing assistance through working groups in their respective projects that affect the development of common accounting and auditing standards.[54]

Why was the second of the panel's resolutions a retreat from the one recommended by Moulin? David S. Ruder, the SEC chairman, served on the Presidents Committee, and it was reported that he was not willing to accept the idea of an endorsement, as was implied in the second of Moulin's draft resolutions.[55] During the conference, IOSCO Secretary-General Paul Guy discussed Workshop No. 4's draft conclusions with Ruder and learned of his aversion to an endorsement. Even though it was clear that the Workshop panel strongly favoured an endorsement, it was reported that the intervention of 'some influential members of the Presidents Committee' led to a toning down of the conclusions so that the Presidents Committee could accept them *in toto*.[56] Representatives of the IASC attending the conference were disappointed that IOSCO was unwilling to go as far as to support a 'prospective' endorsement.[57] The ever-cautious SEC, which had legal responsibility for assuring a high standard of quality in US financial reporting standards, preferred to render its own assessment of the IASC's improved standards, once they were completed, before it could support a decision by IOSCO to issue an endorsement.

While Moulin did not obtain the approval of his visionary second resolution, his paper did contribute importantly to the start of the process by which IOSCO formally looked to the IASC for progress towards the international harmonization of accounting standards.

Less than a week after the IOSCO conference, the SEC went on record to support the movement towards international accounting standards. In its first official utterance on international accounting standards, the SEC said, 'Mutually acceptable international accounting standards are a critical goal because they will reduce the unnecessary regulatory burdens resulting from current disparities between the various national accounting standards.'[58] The SEC had a clear motivation to push for the harmonization of accounting standards: the challenge of regulating in a market that was increasingly becoming global.

In September 1989, IOSCO's Technical Committee published a 103-page report, *International Equity Offers*. It had been prepared by Working Party 1 on multinational securities offerings, chaired by Stewart Douglas-Mann, of the London Stock Exchange, and it was accepted and approved by the Technical Committee, which endorsed its recommendations. The report encouraged regulators to enable issuers to use one disclosure document for all jurisdictions in which they elect to sell securities, and it concluded that a 'critical factor' towards this end 'is the acceptability of financial statements in multiple jurisdictions. Development, or recognition, of adequate internationally acceptable accounting, auditing and independence standards would greatly facilitate the development of the use of a single disclosure document.'[59]

10.5. THE INCEPTION OF THE IASC'S IMPROVEMENTS STEERING COMMITTEE

The Comparability steering committee continued its deliberations, taking note of the letters of comment received on E32 as well as other feedback (e.g. from the SEC and IOSCO). In July 1990, the IASC board voted to publish its follow-up report, labelled *Statement of Intent: Comparability of Financial Statements*. In this *Statement of Intent*, the board reaffirmed most of the recommended proposals in E32, made a number of modifications, and formally proposed that ten standards be revised. Reacting to the many critical comments received, the board also decided that companies adopting an allowed alternative treatment in financial statements purporting to conform to IASC standards should not be required to reconcile their net income and shareholders' interests to those amounts using the 'benchmark' treatment (as the 'preferred' treatments had become known).[60] Cherry has written that 'Part of the problem was that IOSCO members were divided, and they needed unanimous agreement; so acceptance by IOSCO seemed very problematic. This way, individual IOSCO members could choose which "benchmarks" [they would use] for national reconciliation purposes'.[61]

In its *Statement of Intent*, the board declared that it would disallow a further alternative treatment, last-in, first-out (LIFO), which was permitted in IAS 2. E32 had already recommended that the base stock method be disallowed. As is discussed below, the disallowance of LIFO became a matter of controversy in October 1992, when the board adopted the revision of IAS 2.

The implementation of the positions enunciated in the *Statement of Intent* was assigned to an Improvements steering committee. This committee had already been created by the board in its April 1989 meeting, in response to the message received from IOSCO's November 1988 conference. SEC Chief Accountant Edmund Coulson had made the point repeatedly that getting rid of options was not enough; another problem was the absence of implementation guidance. His insistence on the need for explicit guidance, he said, was not well received by the leadership of the IASC, as it was felt that reducing or eliminating options would be enough to move the revised standards to the level of recognition and endorsement.[62] Nevertheless, the charge of the Improvements steering committee was to revise most of the IASC standards before the end of 1992 by building on E32 and to ensure that the revised standards 'are sufficiently detailed and complete and contain adequate disclosure requirements'.[63] As discussed in Section 9.3.4, the Improvements committee did not begin its work until 1990, and its charge was soon limited to revising the ten standards proposed for revision by the *Statement of Intent*.

In *International Equity Offers*, IOSCO set out its expectation for the work of the Improvements committee:

This Improvements Project will attempt to respond to the concerns expressed by [IOSCO's] Working Party No. 2 that the present IAS are incomplete and do not provide sufficient detailed guidance on the implementation of certain principles. The objective is that they should stand on their own as a comprehensive set of accounting standards.[64]

In an article published in 1991, Paul Cherry, who had been a major participant in the Comparability project, sought to allay fears that 'International harmonization must necessarily lead to U.S.-style reporting practices,' or to 'a codification or rule book style of standardization', which typified US GAAP.[65] Anxiety was apparently palpable that the FASB's pronouncements would become the template for the revised IASC standards.

10.6. DEVELOPMENTS AT IOSCO

By the middle of 1989, Paul Cherry had resigned from the IOSCO working party, and his place was taken by Michael Meagher, his successor as OSC chief accountant in September 1988, on a two-year secondment from Thorne Ernst & Whinney.

In October 1989, Richard Breeden succeeded David Ruder as SEC chairman. Breeden viewed the Commission as having been overwhelmingly focused on domestic concerns. He believed that the growth in international markets and the pace of globalization should be reflected in the SEC's policies, and he communicated this view forcefully to the staff.[66] Previously, the SEC had sent staff members to attend meetings of IOSCO's Technical Committee, but Breeden attended the Committee's February 1990 meeting himself and did not miss a meeting during his SEC chairmanship. He wanted to send a signal that the SEC regarded the Committee's work as important, thus making it harder for other country members of the Committee to send staff if the SEC chairman was sitting at the table. Breeden became immediately concerned that the Technical Committee did not exist as a functioning deliberative body of securities market supervisors. Half of its members, including those representing the Germans, the British, and the Swiss, were trade associations with no governmental power at all. He wanted to see it become the counterpart for securities market regulators of the Basel Committee on Banking Supervision.[67] At his direction and with the cooperation of other key agencies in IOSCO, the SEC wrote a Strategic Assessment of the Technical Committee's role in IOSCO, which led to a major reorganization of the Committee.[68] Breeden thereupon became chairman of the Technical Committee.[69] Under the new plan of organization, only securities market supervisors could serve on the Committee, and Working Party 2 on accounting and auditing was merged into Working Party 1 (WP1), on multinational securities offerings under the chairmanship of Linda C. Quinn, the powerful director of the SEC's Division of Corporation Finance.[70] The title of WP1 was referred to variously as 'multinational securities offerings' (by the IASC) or 'multinational disclosures and accounting' (by the SEC).[71] Quinn's background was as a securities lawyer, and she had joined the SEC's staff in 1980. She became director of Corp Fin (as the division was known) in 1986. As the IASC's Improvements committee was moving ahead with the process of proposing revisions in IASC standards, the SEC wanted its own person to chair IOSCO's oversight committee. WP1 then set up an Accounting and Auditing

Subcommittee, whose chairman has always been the current or immediate past chief accountant of the OSC,[72] initially Michael Meagher, with a member of SEC's Office of the Chief Accountant, at the outset Richard Reinhard, also sitting on the committee. Since 1990, WP1 itself has always been chaired by an SEC staff member, and Linda Quinn held that position until February 1996, when she resigned from the SEC to enter law practice. Breeden put the SEC's best people at the disposal of IOSCO.

For his part, Breeden expressed optimism about the IASC's productivity. At a Congressional hearing in May 1991, he said, 'I do believe that we will have a nucleus of international accounting standards sometime in 1992.'[73]

Changes during 1989 in the membership of IOSCO's Working Party 2 on accounting and auditing standards (that is, prior to the reorganization) raised a question of whether members who at the time were employed in the private sector could truly convey the views of public-sector regulators that had chosen them as their representatives. One would expect that IOSCO, being a federation of securities market regulators, would compose its working parties with the members or staff of the regulators themselves, or at least those who had previously been regulators. But in 1989, the UK Securities and Investments Board (SIB), a government body whose remit did not include accounting or auditing and did not oversee foreign companies listed on the London Stock Exchange,[74] nonetheless wanted to become a member of the working party and to attend meetings of IASC's Comparability steering committee and later its Improvements committee. A country as important as the United Kingdom could hardly be ignored, but the SIB realized that its representative had to be someone with an accounting or auditing background. The SIB chose Kenneth Wild, a London partner in Touche Ross & Co., and he was to be assisted by Geoffrey Mitchell, then the technical director of the Institute of Chartered Accountants in England and Wales, and also the staff observer to the UK delegation to the IASC board. Moreover, Paul Cherry continued to chair the working party even though he was no longer the OSC chief accountant; in September 1988 he had completed his secondment and returned to his accountancy firm, Coopers & Lybrand. Between 1991 and 1993 (during a critical period), Michael Meagher continued as chairman of Working Party 1's Accounting and Auditing Subcommittee after he had returned to his accountancy firm following two years' service as OSC chief accountant. But Cherry and Meagher had previously been regulators. David Cairns raised a question of the propriety of these appointments, especially those made by the SIB; his expressed concern did not allude to the technical competence of the people involved but only to the authority they would carry, or at least the regulatory experience upon which they could draw, when speaking on behalf of the regulatory bodies they were representing.[75] The practice of regulators appointing representatives from outside of the regulatory body was not limited to these instances. A precipitating problem was that a number of national regulators, as with the SIB, did not have accounting staff, or if they did, they could not be made available to IOSCO.

During the first half of the 1990s, WP1 and its Accounting and Auditing Subcommittee played the decisive roles in IOSCO's communications with the IASC. In both the working party and the Subcommittee, the SEC and OSC representatives were clearly the most active and influential, as will be seen. In addition to the United States and Canada, other countries represented on the Subcommittee during 1993, a pivotal year, were the United Kingdom and France, the members being Geoffrey Mitchell on behalf of the SIB and Pierre Chaput (Bertrand d'Illiers' successor at the COB), respectively. The countries other than the United States, Canada, the United Kingdom, and France that were represented on WP1 were Australia, Belgium, Germany, Hong Kong, Italy, Japan, Luxembourg, the Netherlands, Spain, and Switzerland. Herbert Biener, representing the German Ministry of Justice, and Carlo Biancheri, of Italy's Commissione Nazionale per le Società e la Bolsa (Consob), played active roles in the deliberations. WP1 made its decisions by consensus, without taking actual votes. The members of WP1 represented their national regulators, and most were not especially versed in accounting and auditing.[76] The representatives of Japan's Ministry of Finance were accompanied by an accounting adviser, Atsushi Kato, a partner in Chuo Audit Corporation, affiliated with Coopers & Lybrand.

WP1 relied heavily on its Accounting and Auditing Subcommittee. The Subcommittee reviewed the IASC's work on its ongoing projects in considerable depth. In July 1993, its chairman, Michael Meagher, requested that the IASC furnish the Subcommittee with an extensive list of internal board documents: all technical papers, background matter, and responses to exposure drafts that were circulated to individual steering committees, all IASC board papers, and copies of all IASC board minutes.[77] Clearly, the Subcommittee proposed to oversee the IASC board's every step instead of being content with vetting the IASC's process and allowing it to produce the final standards. The leadership of the IASC believed that this request was excessive and unnecessary, but in the end it agreed on a compromise that seemed to satisfy both parties.[78]

In 1994, Edward Waitzer, the chairman of the OSC, said that he believed that IOSCO should be endorsing the IASC's process, rather than endorsing the particular positions taken in its standards.[79] Stuart Grant, the executive director for accounting policy of the Australian Securities Commission and a member of WP1, agreed.[80] But he was in a small minority on WP1.[81] WP1's Accounting and Auditing Subcommittee, whose chairman represented the OSC, had taken a markedly different tack. Indeed, the Subcommittee went so far as to second-guess the IASC board even on whether revised exposure drafts should be re-exposed.[82] At a meeting of WP1 in December 1993, which David Cairns attended by invitation, both Linda Quinn and Michael Meagher complained that the IASC was too secretive, making it difficult for IOSCO to learn the reasons for the decisions reflected in the IASC's draft standards as well as for IOSCO to acquaint IASC steering committee members with IOSCO's views at an early stage.[83] It was evident that both Quinn and Meagher sought an even closer oversight of the IASC's standard-setting process.

10.7. THE ROLE OF IOSCO IN THE IMPROVEMENTS STEERING COMMITTEE

Paul Cherry became chairman of the Improvements steering committee, which held its first meeting in September 1990. Its deliberations proceeded apace on revising ten IASC standards with a view towards securing IOSCO's endorsement. After Cherry had returned to his accountancy firm in late 1988, he was working full-time as a special adviser to the chairman of the OSC as well as continuing to chair IOSCO's Working Party 2 on accounting and auditing standards until the middle of 1989. Then, in mid-1989, he became even more active in the work of the IASC: he replaced Michael Dawson as a board member from Canada.

As discussed in Chapter 9, the steering committee embarked upon its work diligently to enhance the implementation guidance and expand the disclosure requirements in the designated set of ten previously issued standards. As occurred in the Comparability phase, representatives from the SEC, OSC, and the COB—Richard Reinhard, Michael Meagher, and Bertrand d'Illiers, respectively—attended the meetings of the Improvements committee as observers but participated fully in the discussions. As noted in the Section 10.6, the UK SIB also began sending observers to the committee's meetings.

Linda Quinn wanted to see the IASC move swiftly. In response to her urging, the IASC leadership tried, albeit ultimately without success, to accelerate the timetable by which the Improvements project would be completed.[84] She was a major supporter of the IASC's standards programme and hoped to see the revised standards through to their eventual endorsement as soon as practicable.[85]

Yet the Improvements steering committee had difficulty interpreting the signals from WP1. Accounting standards were not the only item on WP1's agenda, and the working party seemed to be falling behind in its work. There was a growing concern that WP1 was holding the IASC to a higher standard than it expected of itself and that it was setting a constantly moving target. The big impediment was WP1's need for unanimous agreement on any official positions; so that any official communications were lengthy and very carefully worded, taking into account all of the disparate views of the fourteen members on WP1. Often, what WP1 did not say in its communications seemed to be more important than what it did say.[86]

Revised drafts of the ten standards resulting from the work of the Improvements committee were exposed for comment by the board in 1991 and 1992 and, after amendments were made in the light of the comments received, were approved by the board in stages in 1992 and 1993. They were published by the IASC in a 209-page volume, *Comparability of Financial Statements: Revised International Accounting Standards 1993*. The following were the ten revised standards:

IAS 2, *Inventories*
IAS 8, *Net Profit or Loss for the Period, Fundamental Errors and Changes in Accounting Policies*

IAS 9, *Research and Development Costs*
IAS 11, *Construction Contracts*
IAS 16, *Property, Plant and Equipment*
IAS 18, *Revenue*
IAS 19, *Retirement Benefit Costs*
IAS 21, *The Effects of Changes in Foreign Exchange Rates*
IAS 22, *Business Combinations*
IAS 23, *Borrowing Costs*

One of the standards, IAS 2 on inventories, provided the occasion for a notable misreading by the IASC of IOSCO's intentions. E32 proposed that LIFO should be retained as an allowed alternative treatment. After reviewing the comment letters on E32 in January 1990, the Comparability steering committee agreed to recommend to the board that LIFO should be eliminated, and no objections were raised by IOSCO at that meeting. The board approved this decision, and the *Statement of Intent* specified that LIFO should be removed from the list of allowed alternative treatments.

The Improvements steering committee duly recommended in its draft revision of IAS 2 that LIFO should be eliminated, and the board approved a corresponding exposure draft in June 1991. Yet at the April 1992 meeting of the Improvements steering committee, Michael Meagher announced that IOSCO believed that the steering committee had gone too far by eliminating LIFO.[87] To everyone's surprise, the body that had been pressing the IASC to remove alternatives was arguing for the retention of an option.

At the board's October 1992 meeting in Chicago, when it was taking final action on IAS 2, four country delegations—Germany, Italy, Japan, and Korea—voted against the elimination of LIFO. The four negative votes were sufficient to prevent a three-fourths vote in favour of elimination.[88] David Cairns wrote, 'Those who obstructed the removal of the choice did so because companies were allowed the same choice in their own countries (often by tax law).'[89] Ever since the first version of IAS 2 (in 1975), the United States had been seen as the major obstacle to the elimination of LIFO. In the United States, companies were permitted to enjoy the tax benefits of LIFO only if they used it in their published financial statements. Yet to the pleasant surprise of the other board members, the US delegation had decided that it would vote for the elimination of LIFO, to demonstrate its support of harmonization.[90]

This was an embarrassing setback for the IASC board. But it was also an embarrassment for IOSCO. It was IOSCO, after all, that had been prodding the IASC to reduce the number of alternative accounting treatments. The IASC had approved a conceptual framework, and it was working assiduously to respond to IOSCO's demands on behalf of investors. One might have expected that the taxation implications of financial reporting norms would no longer govern the board's decisions. The October 1992 meeting of the board was Arthur Wyatt's last as chairman, and in a speech at the 14th World Congress of Accountants, held in Washington just afterwards, he emphasized the difficulties facing the 'internationalization of accounting standards'. Incoming IASC Chairman Eiichi Shiratori spoke more hopefully but also warned that the process had a long way to go.[91]

10.8. THE SEC'S CAUTIOUS RESPONSE TO CAPITAL MARKET PRESSURES

Within IOSCO, the SEC clearly occupied a unique position. Not only did it supervise the capital market which was the most attractive destination for many major companies seeking an international listing, it also imposed the most stringent financial reporting requirements which it expected both domestic and foreign issuers to observe. Foreign companies were expected to report on the basis of US GAAP or to provide a Form 20-F reconciliation of their earnings and shareholders' equity to US GAAP. In most other countries, foreign companies from developed countries could obtain listings on the basis of financial statements prepared according to the GAAP of their country of origin with no, or few, requirements for additional information. Throughout the 1990s, the key question was whether and when the SEC would allow foreign companies to list on a basis other than US GAAP. This section considers the SEC's policy on this point during the early 1990s, before continuing the discussion of the relation between the IASC and IOSCO in Section 10.9.

10.8.1. Acceleration in the New York Stock Exchange Listings of Overseas Companies

When, in the late 1980s, as a result of its collaboration with IOSCO, the IASC sought to become much more responsive to the needs of internationally listed companies, the number of foreign companies listed in the United States was still relatively small.[92] The United Kingdom traditionally was the most important market for international listings. In 1988, there were 526 foreign companies listed on the London Stock Exchange, which was 26 per cent of 2,054 domestic companies. In absolute numbers, this made London the most important international market. In contrast, the New York Stock Exchange (NYSE) counted seventy-seven foreign listings (5 per cent of domestic listings), rather less than the number of foreign companies listed on the Tokyo (112) or Paris (221) stock exchanges. The bulk of the foreign companies listed in New York were from Canada, with UK companies making up most of the rest. This situation changed dramatically during the early 1990s, as the US capital markets became attractive to many of the world's leading companies. From 1988 to 1992, the number of foreign companies listed on the NYSE gradually rose from 77 to 120, and the number of countries represented on the exchange increased to more than thirty. In 1993 alone, the Exchange listed another forty-five companies. Several of these were flagship companies in their home countries, including Ahold, Argentaria, Australia and New Zealand Banking Group, Daimler-Benz, Fletcher Challenge, Midland Bank, and Zeneca. The Exchange aggressively sought to increase the number of world-class foreign companies in its list.

The SEC was aware of the concern expressed by companies and regulators overseas about the restrictions it placed on the financial reporting by foreign companies. In 1990–4, the SEC announced several concessions for foreign companies issuing securities in the United States.

10.8.2. Rule 144A: SEC Waives Disclosure Requirements for Private Placements of Securities by Foreign Companies

In April 1990, the SEC adopted Rule 144A under the Securities Act 1933, which, among other things, exempted foreign companies from the costly disclosures required when registering securities with the SEC, so long as they place their securities privately with major financial institutions, such as the large pension funds. The institutions, in turn, could resell the securities to other qualifying institutions, thus enhancing the liquidity for privately placed securities in the United States. In this way, foreign issuers of securities could raise capital in the United States without submitting to the SEC's accounting and disclosure requirements if they were to sell only to qualifying institutions and not to retail investors. Rule 144A, which has been adjudged to be a success, was intended to make the US capital market more easily accessible to foreign issuers.[93]

10.8.3. SEC's Unprecedented MJDS Arrangement with Canada

In June 1991, the SEC announced an arrangement with Canada's provincial securities regulators for a 'multijurisdictional disclosure system' (known as MJDS),[94] allowing companies in both countries to issue securities in the other by using their home country prospectus, without reconciliation except for common equity and non-investment grade securities. This historic arrangement could be consummated only because of the close comparability of US and Canadian accounting and disclosure norms. In 1985, when the SEC had made known its intention to harmonize with other countries' disclosure and distribution practices for offerings of securities by multinational corporations, the United Kingdom was mentioned along with Canada. But after a considerable period of discussion and extended consideration, the SEC could see that, together with other problems, the UK's membership in the European Economic Community (EEC) precluded it from entering into such an agreement unilaterally.[95] Any such arrangement involving the United Kingdom would perforce need to apply to all countries in the EEC, and that, to the SEC, would have gone far beyond what it was prepared to do. Consequently, the proposal, issued in 1989,[96] was limited to Canada. The SEC's proposal did not contemplate a reconciliation requirement for either debt or equity securities, but Linda Quinn, a cautious policymaker on accounting and disclosure issues, imposed one for equity in the agreement announced in 1991.[97]

The MJDS represented the SEC's only foray into the sphere of 'mutual recognition' between countries, at least as regards accounting and disclosure norms. In 1992, the Japanese Ministry of Finance approached the SEC to accept mutual recognition on accounting issues, but the discussions led to naught.[98] As is noted below, in 1993 the German Finance Minister pressed the US Secretary of the Treasury to accept mutual recognition on accounting, but the offer was firmly declined.

This MJDS evinced the SEC's desire, at a time of the increasing globalization of capital markets, to promote a limited harmonization of accounting and disclosure without sacrificing its principles. As will be seen in its communications to the IASC board, the SEC was committed to the aim of harmonization, but it proceeded, as always, by cautious steps.

10.8.4. IOSCO and SEC Endorse IAS 7

In December 1992, the IASC issued a revised IAS 7, on cash flow statements, which did not form part of the set of standards on which the Improvements steering committee was working. The revised standard supplanted its predecessor, issued in 1977, which called for the mandatory publication of a funds statement. IOSCO took advantage of the revised standard to announce at its eighteenth annual conference in Mexico City in October 1993 its endorsement of IAS 7 for use by its regulator members.[99] In November 1993, the SEC, under newly appointed Chairman Arthur Levitt, announced a number of accommodations, including IAS 7, for foreign companies.[100]

IAS 7 was the first IASC standard to be formally embraced by IOSCO. The initiative that led to the endorsement was taken early in 1993 under SEC Chairman Breeden's watch, jointly by the SEC's Division of Corporation Finance and Office of International Affairs, headed by Linda Quinn and Michael Mann, respectively. It was intended as a confidence-building measure, as an incentive to the IASC to continue to improve its standards.[101] Breeden believed that, if regulators wanted bodies like the IASC to get greater resources and more talented people, they had to be perceived as institutions that mattered.[102] The decision was a sign of the SEC's and IOSCO's willingness to reach out. The IASC welcomed the decision, and it led the IASC to believe that IOSCO would, in future, endorse its revised standards one at a time, which, as will be seen, was not at all the intention of the SEC.

For the SEC, the decision to urge IOSCO to endorse IAS 7 for foreign registrants was not a difficult one to make. It was a matter of disclosure, not measurement or recognition. IAS 7 closely paralleled FAS 95, issued by the FASB in 1987. And, importantly, it had no bearing on the SEC's required reconciliation of earnings and shareholders' equity. It was viewed as a stand-alone standard, and in many countries there was not a requirement for a cash flow statement.[103] Nonetheless, IOSCO's action, which could not have been done without the backing of the SEC, was a signal event. SEC Chairman Arthur Levitt described it as a 'landmark step of accepting, without supplement, modification or reconciliation, cash flow statements prepared in accordance with International Accounting Standard number 7 for use by foreign companies'.[104] Levitt said that the acceptance of IAS 7 for use by foreign registrants was one of several initiatives the SEC had just taken that will 'lower regulatory costs, facilitate the transition into the US disclosure system and accommodate foreign practices, without compromising the fundamental principle of full disclosure and investor protection mandated by federal securities laws'.[105]

Trevor Harris, a Columbia University accounting professor and a close student of international accounting developments, was reported to say that '[The SEC's action on IAS 7] was no big deal, other than as a token gesture, because the standard is essentially the same as US GAAP.' He added, 'From a signaling point of view, it was good, but in terms of substance, it's not going to make much difference.'[106]

10.8.5. Daimler-Benz Becomes the First German Company to List in New York

In 1991, a group of major German companies—BASF, Bayer, Daimler-Benz, and Hoechst—met with the SEC to seek approval for a New York listing based on their German GAAP financial statements, without a reconciliation to US GAAP. Somewhat earlier, Volkswagen had approached the SEC on similar terms. But the SEC was adamant that it would not waive the reconciliation requirement.[107] Then in March 1993, the SEC approved the NYSE listing of Daimler-Benz, which became the first German company to list in the US market and therefore was required to reconcile to US GAAP. Linda Quinn recalled that '[Daimler's listing] was a huge, huge event in Germany' as well as being important to the SEC, to show that it was not impossible for a company to do this.[108] It met with 'angry reaction' from other German multinationals, which accused Daimler of 'surrendering' to Anglo-US accounting practices.[109] It meant that German companies lost whatever leverage they had in seeking SEC recognition for German GAAP. Daimler, according to the requirement of German law, used German GAAP in its annual financial statements, and it submitted to the SEC's requirement to reconcile its earnings and shareholders' equity to US GAAP.[110]

The Daimler listing came after several years of persistent pressure on the SEC from the NYSE to relax its accounting requirements in order to enable more foreign multinationals to obtain listings without the need to reconcile their earnings and shareholders' equity to US GAAP equivalents. SEC Chairman Breeden regarded these efforts as an 'outrageous' attempt to 'eviscerate the disclosure system in the United States and the protection of American investors, in order to enhance the profits of the traders on the Stock Exchange'.[111] At a 1993 conference, James Cochrane, senior vice-president and chief economist of the NYSE, said that the Exchange 'has had some difficult discussions' with the SEC in the past few years 'on the issue of requiring foreign companies to quantitatively reconcile their financial statements' to US GAAP.[112] The then SEC chief accountant, Edmund Coulson, has said, 'There was an absolute *battle*.'[113]

After the SEC had approved the listing of Daimler-Benz, the German Finance Minister, Theo Waigel, called upon the US Secretary of the Treasury, Lloyd Bentsen, to agree to mutual recognition between US and German accounting standards. He said that other German companies, unlike Daimler-Benz, would not agree to produce financial statements according to both US and German GAAP in order to be listed in US markets.[114] When the same issue was raised in April 1992, SEC Chairman Breeden was quoted as saying, 'It is inconceivable that we would have mutual recognition with Germany.'[115] For her part, SEC Commissioner Mary L. Schapiro was quoted as saying in September 1993 that the SEC would insist that foreign companies conform with US GAAP when seeking a listing in US markets.[116] The entreaty from Waigel went nowhere.

For his part, William Donaldson, then the chairman and CEO of the NYSE, took advantage of the listing to call for flexibility so as to enable other major multinationals to list in New York. His undisguised purpose was to press the SEC to be more relenting when meeting with any of the 'more than 2,000 companies around the world that meet the NYSE standards of size, share ownership and earnings'.[117] A few months after he departed as SEC chairman, Richard Breeden characterized the Exchange's high-pressure campaign 'to give a "free pass" exempting all so-called "world class" companies from all U.S. disclosure, accounting and auditing standards' as 'a serious mistake'.[118]

Partly as a result of this pressure, SEC Chairman Breeden, as well as his predecessor and successor as SEC chairmen, David S. Ruder and Arthur Levitt, took a number of senior SEC staff members on tours around the world to meet with major banks and companies, to discuss the SEC's regulations in relation to possible listings in the United States. The SEC's then director of the Office of International Affairs, Michael Mann, recalls that Linda Quinn and he tried to communicate the SEC's 'openness to flexibly applying its requirements. Our goal was to demonstrate to companies seeking U.S. registration that the SEC would take a principled approach to applying its rules. We needed to show that we were reasonable and that, where comparability between differing standards could be achieved, accommodations could be worked out and therefore compromise would be possible.'[119] In the early 1990s, the SEC made a number of 'ad hoc accommodations' to non-US issuers,[120] but Chairman Breeden insisted that US GAAP be the required standard for foreign companies listing in the United States.[121]

While the Daimler listing did not have a direct impact on the work of the IASC, it was nonetheless an important turning point in the development of European financial reporting. It eventually led other Continental European companies to reassess their own interest in a New York listing, which in turn led the European Commission to support the IASC, as a counterweight to US GAAP (*see* Section 12.3). David Cairns, the IASC's secretary-general, drew attention to the great disparity between Daimler's German and US GAAP profits (which turned out to be a DM 615 million profit according to German GAAP and a DM 1,839 million loss by use of US GAAP) to press the point that the adoption of IASC standards by securities market regulators without reconciliation to another GAAP, which he expected would occur 'very soon', would obviate the need for investors to understand such 'inexplicable differences'.[122]

10.8.6. The New York Stock Exchange Supports IASC Standards

As a result of the NYSE's frustrations in trying to persuade the SEC, and especially Chairman Breeden, to accept their home country financial statements for world-class multinationals based overseas, the Exchange began warming to the use of IASC standards as, 'perhaps, the most promising route' by which to overcome the SEC's US GAAP reconciliation obstacle to the attraction of foreign listings.[123] At a conference in November 1993, the NYSE's James Cochrane spoke glowingly about the promise of IASC standards:

IASC has demonstrated a tremendous amount of leadership and is beginning to make real progress. The IASC progress now has momentum behind it under the new SEC Chairman, Arthur Levitt. The SEC's recent acceptance of International Accounting Standard No. 7 on cash flow was a symbolic gesture on the part of the SEC that there is a serious effort underway to move towards International Accounting Standards. We take that as a very strong sign of encouragement. As IASC principles are adopted by more major non-U.S. issuers—and as these principles get closer to U.S. GAAP—financials done by a foreign issuer using them will be sufficient for U.S. investors to make completely informed judgments about the issuer's state of health. European companies have indicated that all they need is U.S. acceptance of IASC principles and they'll be knocking down the door of the NYSE and U.S. capital markets.[124]

In March 1995, the Exchange and Coopers & Lybrand co-sponsored a major conference in New York City at which the promise of using IASC standards was explored. At the conference, Trevor Harris presented his findings from a study of the differences for eight companies based in seven countries between their use of the IASC's revised standards and the requirements of US GAAP.[125] He found that, 'At least for firms utilising the IASC's revised international accounting standards, there are few instances, especially from an investor's perspective as opposed to a technical accounting perspective, where the companies' compliance with IASs would not meet US GAAP.'[126] His conclusion was that the differences were not as problematic as was commonly believed, a finding that would have been welcomed at the Exchange. As noted in Section 8.16, in 1995 the Exchange signed on to the IASC's new Advisory Council, and James Cochrane helped with fund-raising in the United States.

10.8.7. SEC Allows Foreign Registrants to Adopt Parts of Three IASC Standards[127]

In April 1994, the SEC issued rule proposals to allow foreign registrants to use portions of three IASC standards: IAS 21, *The Effects of Changes in Foreign Exchange Rates* (revised in 1993), IAS 22, *Business Combinations* (revised in 1993), and IAS 29, *Financial Reporting in Hyperinflationary Economies* (issued in 1989).[128] The final rules were approved in December 1994. Again, this decision gave evidence of the SEC's willingness to acknowledge areas of agreement between IASC standards and US GAAP, but, as with IAS 7, which did not represent much of a departure from US GAAP, the portions of these three standards were also compatible with the policies of the SEC's accounting staff. Even before this action, the SEC had allowed foreign registrants in highly inflationary economies to use their general-price-level (GPL) restated financial statements, without modification, in their filings with the Commission. The SEC's acceptance of portions of IAS 21 and 29 applied this policy as well to foreign registrants with subsidiaries operating in hyperinflationary economies, in effect allowing the restate-translate procedure in place of translate-restate.[129] But the SEC rejected the option in IAS 29 that current cost be accepted in lieu of GPL-restated historical cost.[130]

In regard to business combinations, for both domestic and foreign registrants the SEC's accounting staff had already favoured a more limited availability of the 'pooling of interests' treatment than under Accounting Principles Board (APB) Opinion 16, and the more restrictive 'uniting of interests' approach of IAS 22 was compatible with that position. On goodwill, also taken up in IAS 22, the SEC's accounting staff had informally come to favour a maximum useful life closer to twenty years, believing that it was the judgement being made by the securities market; therefore, IAS 22's limit of twenty years, compared to the protracted term of forty years allowed by APB Opinion 17, would have been compatible with this position.[131]

Trevor Harris, who had played a key role in advising Daimler-Benz on the accounting aspects of its 1993 listing in New York, said that the SEC's acceptance 'of the use of IAS 21 and IAS 22 by non-US registrants is truly significant', because 'In those cases, there are significant differences from US GAAP.'[132] Yet Michael Sutton, the SEC chief accountant from June 1995 to January 1998, said that the SEC's actions on IAS 21 and 22 were 'a non-event in the US community', that US companies did not feel they were disadvantaged by those concessions. They were Linda Quinn's way, he said, of tossing the foreign companies a bone.[133] Quinn's view was that these were 'big cost' issues or were otherwise troublesome to foreign issuers, and she felt that the IASC standards would serve just as well as US GAAP.[134]

It was only the SEC, not also IOSCO, which accepted the portions of the three standards. By doing so, the SEC wanted to demonstrate that it was supportive of the IASC's process, as two of the standards had recently been revised, but also to help foreign issuers reduce the cost of keeping two sets of books, especially in regard to accounting for business combinations and with respect to hyperinflationary economies.[135] As far as is known, the issue of accepting portions of the three standards never came before IOSCO for its consideration.

Another accommodation conceded by the SEC in 1994 was, like the SEC's acceptance of IAS 7 for foreign registrants, made easier because it did not alter earnings or shareholders' equity: 'Foreign private issuers that prepare financial statements on a basis of accounting other than U.S. GAAP using proportionate consolidation for investments in joint ventures may, in certain cases, omit differences from U.S. GAAP in classification or display if the investment would be accounted for using the equity method under U.S. GAAP.'[136] This accommodation was not limited to foreign registrants using IASC standards. In IAS 31, issued in 1990, proportionate consolidation was set as the benchmark method when accounting for joint ventures, with the equity method as the allowed alternative treatment. Proportionate consolidation was an option to the equity method in Canadian GAAP but has never been acceptable under US GAAP.

10.9. IOSCO OFFICIAL DEFINES THE QUALITIES REQUIRED IN THE IASC'S REVISED STANDARDS

Linda Quinn and others from the SEC did not elaborate in speeches and other public utterances on their expectations of the IASC. Michael Meagher, the chairman of WP1's Accounting and Auditing Subcommittee, did make such a presentation in March 1993, although it was not published. It is important to examine the contents of Meagher's presentation carefully, as it was the only written record of a significant public utterance during the first half of the 1990s by an IOSCO official who was vetting the IASC's revised standards. The last official statement by IOSCO on its expectations of the IASC had been made at its November 1988 conference in Melbourne.

Meagher was the OSC chief accountant from September 1988 until December 1990, when he returned to his Toronto firm of Peat Marwick Thorne, as its name had become. But he carried on as chairman of the subcommittee, and in his speech he drew attention to the essential qualities that IOSCO was seeking in the IASC's revised standards:[137]

> Such standards must ensure there is a high level of consistency in accounting treatment for like transactions.
>
> ...
>
> Such a set of international accounting standards must be sufficiently complete and detailed to achieve the overriding requirement of consistency and comparability in accounting treatment for like transactions.

'The overriding principle', he said, 'is that financial statements must fairly portray like transactions in a relevant and reliable manner.' In regard to completeness, he identified a number of 'mainstream accounting issues', which, he said, may not be completed by the IASC for some time. Standards on such subjects as accounting for segment reporting, earnings per share, financial instruments, intangible assets, and income taxes, he said, might well need to be completed before IOSCO can give its endorsement to the product of the board's work. (*See* Section 10.10 for a treatment of IOSCO's expanded list of standards.)

While Meagher said that he himself favoured a piecemeal acceptance of the IASC's standards, others, he said, would delay any further endorsement until all of the requirements were satisfied. Meagher believed that IOSCO should consider accepting all of the IASC's revised standards resulting from its Improvements project, once it is concluded. 'Thereafter', he added, 'as new or revised standards are issued, these standards should also be subject to review and acceptance by IOSCO.' As will be seen, Meagher's preference for a piecemeal approach towards the standards was decidedly not shared by the SEC, which was the dominant player in WP1 and its subcommittee.

In his speech, Meagher complained that the IASC, in its past standards, had designated the section entitled 'Explanation' as guidance that was not mandatory. In the drafts of the newly revised standards, he said, the board had intermingled the explanatory paragraphs with the exposition of the standard itself, but only the material in bold typeface was said to be mandatory. Meagher said that 'No real measure of reliability and consistency of accounting treatment will be obtained unless the explanatory material must also be followed.' He pointedly said that unless the IASC makes the explanatory material mandatory, 'Individual securities regulators may be forced to make adherence to all explanatory material a precondition to their acceptance of the accounting standards.' IOSCO, and especially the SEC, were adamant from the outset that compliance with IASC standards meant all of it, including the explanatory material in light face.[138] In May 2000, Paul Pacter, a senior member of the IASC's research staff, wrote, 'Since the IASC Standards were reformatted in the early 1990s, the Board has used bold type to express matters of general principle. . . . Normal type has been used to express finer points of detail. Both, however, are part of the International Accounting Standard.' And, he added, 'The IASC Board votes on the Standard in its entirety'. He said that the secretariat regards paragraphs written in both the bold and normal types to possess 'equal authoritativeness'.[139]

Recognizing that the IASC's Comparability project had not been able to eliminate all optional treatments, Meagher said that the IASC board's decision in its *Statement of Intent* not to impose a requirement on companies to reconcile the results obtained by adopting an allowed alternative treatment to the benchmark treatment 'has not been entirely satisfactory for securities regulators'. In E32, the IASC had said that companies would be obliged to present such a reconciliation in their financial statements. Yet, as noted in Section 10.5, the IASC's decision to dispense with a reconciliation requirement had been taken with the acquiescence of IOSCO.

10.10. IOSCO IDENTIFIES THE CORE STANDARDS IT EXPECTS FROM THE IASC

The IASC leadership met in May 1993 with SEC representatives and became aware of a tentative list of core standards that was being compiled so as to constitute a complete set of accounting standards. To their consternation, the list included a number of specialized projects such as accounting for commodities, environmental issues, and special purpose entities as well as for the accounting issues in certain industries.[140] In June 1993, IASC Chairman Shiratori wrote an anguished letter to SEC Chief Accountant Walter Schuetze and Linda Quinn. In the letter, he argued that the SEC's list of proposed standards represented an unreasonable request. Schuetze replied that the staff study had in mind only the IASC's completed standards and ongoing standards projects, plus an expected project on interim reporting.[141] The IASC leadership must have been relieved upon receiving this response. If the SEC was actually thinking of imposing a requirement that such specialized standards should be included in the core set, Shiratori's letter sought to urge them not to do so.

In August 1993, WP1 informed the IASC of an extensive list of forty-one topics which it expected the IASC to address as 'the necessary components of a reasonably complete set of accounting standards (core standards) that would comprise a comprehensive body of principles for enterprises undertaking cross-border offerings and listings'.[142] WP1 had accepted the list in June, and it was announced at IOSCO's annual conference in October. By announcing this list of topics, IOSCO for the first time specified the scope of coverage it expected in any set of accounting standards proposed for its endorsement. It was made known to the IASC that the list of core standards had its origin in an SEC staff report.[143]

Upon receiving the recommended list of core standards from WP1 in August 1993, David Cairns wrote to Eiichi Shiratori and Michael Sharpe, 'The list is interesting in that it contains little that is not covered by existing International Accounting Standards or by our current work programme. This is encouraging.'[144] At IOSCO's annual conference in Mexico City in October 1993, Cairns, in a speech, enthusiastically welcomed Linda Quinn's announcement at the congress of IOSCO's endorsement of IAS 7, on cash flow statements, and of the list of necessary components of a core set of standards, as 'a necessary step' towards getting its standards accepted worldwide.[145] In her own remarks, Quinn was reported to have expressed IOSCO's 'concerns' about the draft of IAS 9, on research and development, which the IASC board was set to approve, and did, in a few weeks' time.[146] The concern, which Cairns said had not previously been communicated, apparently was over the draft's requirement for the capitalization, in certain conditions, of development costs.

In his speech, Cairns expressed confidence 'that further progress can be announced in Tokyo next year—that progress will be significant, even if it does not take us to the end of our journey'. As is noted in Section 10.11, Jean Saint-Geours, the chairman of IOSCO's Technical Committee, had told Shiratori that he favoured a staged endorsement process, rather than delaying any further endorsement until all of the core standards were revised to IOSCO's satisfaction. But, as will be seen, this did not correspond with the view from the SEC.

In December 1993, after the secretariat had conducted an extensive analysis, the IASC concluded that nineteen of IOSCO's forty-one topics were covered by the ten revised standards in its Comparability/Improvements projects which the board approved in November 1993 (on three of these topics the IASC said that further work was indicated), eleven were treated in other standards issued previously, and one was dealt with by the recently revised IAS 7. The remaining ten topics, with one exception, were the subjects of the IASC's ongoing standards projects. Only one topic, on interim reporting, had not yet been addressed by any completed or ongoing project.[147]

10.11. IOSCO'S REBUFF TO THE IASC

Prior to the arrival of two fateful letters from IOSCO in June 1994, the IASC had received mixed signals from IOSCO representatives about whether further endorsements would be made on a piecemeal or rolling basis or would not be made until the entire set of core standards were completed to IOSCO's satisfaction. In October 1993, IOSCO's endorsement of IAS 7, with identical action by the SEC, created an impression that IOSCO would follow the former of the two approaches. Then, in April 1994, the SEC announced its intention to endorse portions of three other IASC standards (*see* Section 10.8.7), but without IOSCO collaboration. At the World Congress of Accountants in October 1992 in Washington, IOSCO Secretary-General Paul Guy said that he favoured an endorsement by stages.[148] Michael Meagher, in his March 1993 speech at Fordham, had said, 'I favor a piecemeal acceptance of the IAS's.' He recommended that, following completion of the IASC's Improvements project, 'IOSCO should consider accepting all the revised standards from that specific project.'[149] Jean Saint-Geours, the chairman of the COB and of IOSCO's Technical Committee, favoured a seriatim, or staged, endorsement process, a view which he conveyed in two meetings during 1993 with Chairman Shiratori.[150] Early in 1994, Edward Waitzer, the chairman of the OSC and a member of IOSCO's Technical Committee, said that he favoured a step-by-step endorsement process by IOSCO.[151] Because of these statements from authoritative figures in IOSCO, IASC board members expected a stepwise endorsement process.[152]

One of the difficulties in interpreting the signs coming from the Technical Committee was that most of its members were lawyers who had little accounting background. During his work on the Improvements project, Paul Cherry was concerned that most members of the Technical Committee seemed not to understand his briefings on the revised standards, which, he believed, may have impeded progress.[153]

It was reported that a lobby in France was writing members of IOSCO's Technical Committee to urge endorsement of the revised IASC standards as early as its annual conference in October 1993.[154] Indeed, several European countries on WP1—France, Germany, and Italy—favoured a step-by-step endorsement process.[155] Yet word had reached David Cairns as early as April 1993 that Linda Quinn was 'fairly negative' towards endorsement in the short term and felt that 'It would not be until 1996, 1997 or even 2000 before IOSCO was able to endorse International Accounting Standards.'[156] In January 1994, Quinn told Cairns during a conversation in Washington that there would be no further IOSCO endorsement of IASC standards until the entire core set were produced and approved as a package.[157]

For his part, Eiichi Shiratori had made it known in early 1993, upon becoming IASC chairman, that he wanted to see an endorsement from IOSCO 'as soon as possible',[158] one reason being that such an imprimatur would better enable the board to raise needed finance from companies around the world.

During the early months of 1994, the IASC's leadership anxiously awaited the news from IOSCO's working party. IASC Deputy Chairman Michael Sharpe had actually seen a draft of the letter from WP1 to IASC Chairman Shiratori but was not allowed to keep a copy.[159] Finally, two lengthy letters dated 17 June 1994 to IASC Chairman Shiratori and signed by Linda Quinn and Michael Meagher (known as the 'Shiratori letters') conveyed the assessment by WP1 and its Accounting and Auditing Subcommittee of the IASC's work thus far, including the ten revised standards that had emerged from the Improvements project.[160] The letters represented a setback for the IASC. They reported that eight of the ten revised standards (all but IAS 9, on research and development, and IAS 19, on retirement benefits costs) were found to be acceptable. On IAS 9, WP1 said that it could not reach a consensus on the acceptability of the required capitalization of development costs when certain criteria were met, a treatment to which the SEC would certainly have objected. WP1 did, however, identify 'suspense issues' on all ten of the revised standards. In the letter, WP1 said that suspense issues 'include items that generally are encountered infrequently, often are complex, and would not need to be addressed before IOSCO would consider recommending acceptance of IASC standards'.

Of the IASC's other published standards, Quinn and Meagher did not raise any 'essential' issues (that is, ones that must be resolved prior to endorsement), on the following:[161]

IAS 20, *Accounting for Government Grants and Disclosure of Government Assistance*
IAS 24, *Related Party Disclosures*
IAS 27, *Consolidated Financial Statements and Accounting for Investments in Subsidiaries*
IAS 28, *Accounting for Investments in Associates*
IAS 29, *Financial Reporting in Hyperinflationary Economies*
IAS 31, *Financial Reporting of Interests in Joint Ventures*

On all of the foregoing six, except for IAS 29, 'suspense' or other issues were raised. On a further eight standards (IAS 1, 5, 10, 12, 13, 14, 17, and 25), they either gave encouragement for the efforts currently in train to develop revisions or made specific suggestions for improvement. Three standards were not considered by IOSCO: IAS 15 on the effects of changing prices; IAS 26, on accounting and reporting by retirement benefit plans; and IAS 30, on financial statement disclosures by banks. Quinn and Meagher advised the IASC that 'the necessary components of a core set of standards' identified by WP1 in its letter of 16 August 1993 included certain topics that were not yet covered by the IASC's existing standards: most financial instruments, intangible assets, earnings per share, employee benefits, and interim reporting. In addition, they said that 'Recognition and measurement issues for discontinued operations and hedging for commodities have not been addressed in a comprehensive manner in any existing standard.' IASC Chairman Shiratori later said, 'In broad terms, 14 of the 24 Standards are acceptable, four Standards are unacceptable to varying degrees, and six Standards are already subject to review by IASC.'[162]

David Cairns, Paul Cherry, and IASC Deputy Chairman Michael Sharpe believed that the letters from Quinn and Meagher were encouraging, especially compared to what they had feared.[163] Indeed, at a conference they both attended in September 1994, Quinn told Cairns that the Shiratori letters should be regarded as 'good news letters'. The suspense issues, she said, were necessary to get EU and Japanese approval to the letters.[164] Yet there were a number on the board who mistrusted the SEC, if only because of the Shiratori letters. Would the SEC ever deliver? In the Shiratori letters, the SEC had clearly prevailed within WP1. As indicated above, IOSCO's decision not to move towards endorsement of any further standards at this time, while a keen disappointment, did not come as a surprise. Yet the IASC's leadership had hoped that IOSCO would endorse the IASC's process, not each of its standards one by one. The major task facing the board was to address the topics on which standards had not yet been issued, by far the most daunting of which was financial instruments.

World Accounting Report described IOSCO's unwillingness to endorse any further IASC standards until the entire core set is complete as a 'blow' to the IASC.[165] And, to be sure, the IASC leadership was disappointed that WP1 would not proceed to recommend endorsement of the standards it found to be acceptable.

Chairman Shiratori was the most keenly disappointed of all. At IOSCO's annual conference in October 1994 in Tokyo, he gave a 'hard-hitting' address, drafted by David Cairns,[166] which was critical of IOSCO's endorsement process.[167] He said that IOSCO's approach to the further endorsement of IASC standards was 'unsatisfactory', in part because it 'implies that IOSCO expects IASC to have dealt with issues that have not been, and perhaps cannot be, resolved by national standard setting bodies', and he referred specifically to financial instruments. He pointed out that the SEC continues to 'endorse' FASB pronouncements 'even though the FASB is a long way from completing its Financial Instruments project'. He argued that IOSCO should endorse the IASC's process and not review each standard in detail, 'something which most of its members do not do in their own jurisdictions'. He pointed out that IOSCO had been a member of the IASC's Consultative Group since 1987, and that its representatives have regularly taken part in the meetings of the IASC's steering committees and have been invited to comment on all of the IASC's exposure drafts and draft statements of principles. He was annoyed that IOSCO had raised the spectre of suspense issues on the ten revised standards even though IOSCO's views 'were taken into account at every stage' of the IASC's deliberations on those standards. 'IOSCO', he said, 'should accept all the revised Standards without qualification.'

Clearly, Shiratori was exasperated, and this airing of his views at IOSCO's annual conference may, in the eyes of some, not have made relations between the two bodies any easier. Cairns recalls that 'The speech was widely supported by regulators and other participants although there were clearly some who disagreed with its aggressive tone.'[168]

Many of Shiratori's points were understandable and well taken. IOSCO had indeed set the bar very high for the IASC to surmount. WP1's endorsement of its standards required the unanimous consent of all of its—by then—fourteen members,[169] who represented the very different regulatory cultures and experiences of their countries. Unanimity was essential to the SEC, because it would not accept being outvoted by other regulators. Furthermore, the SEC was not prepared to support a prospective endorsement, but insisted that no judgement could be rendered until the entire core set of standards were completed and could be evaluated in regard to all of the qualities that the SEC believed they must possess, in terms of the number of options, the degree of specificity, the adequacy of the required disclosures, and the breadth of coverage. To the SEC, this was a substantive policy issue.[170] As noted above, the SEC was especially guarded because it knew that, if it were to allow foreign registrants to adopt IASC standards that were more flexible and yielding (for example, with more options and fewer required disclosures) than US GAAP without a reconciliation requirement, it could not prevent US registrants from likewise adopting IASC standards by switching from US GAAP.[171] Linda Quinn herself expressed this anxiety as far back as 1989.[172] In such an event, if US GAAP were to become markedly less pervasive among US registrants, questions could be raised about the future viability of the FASB as the purveyor of US GAAP. The SEC had no intention of swapping its 'oversight authority' over the FASB for a more uncertain relationship with an international standard setter based in London.

Shiratori's speech in Tokyo notwithstanding, Secretary-General Cairns led an effort to re-establish a positive dialogue with Working Party 1. In September 1994, he communicated Shiratori's request to all of the IASC board members and technical advisers 'to contact the members of IOSCO Working Party 1 in your country to discuss the [Shiratori letters] and their attitude to further endorsement of International Accounting Standards by IOSCO'.[173]

The secretariat conducted an extensive analysis of the Shiratori letters and especially WP1's conclusions. In close coordination with Shiratori, it devised a new work programme that, it was believed, would be acceptable to WP1 in the light of its demands, in order to contribute constructively to cooperation between the IASC and IOSCO towards an eventual endorsement of the IASC standards. At its meeting in November 1994 in Budapest, the IASC board approved the revised work programme and authorized Shiratori and Cairns to respond to the Shiratori letters 'along the lines set out in the Chairman's paper for the IOSCO Annual Meeting in Tokyo in October 1994'. This was done in a letter signed by Shiratori, dated 28 December 1994, to Linda Quinn and James Saloman, who had just succeeded Michael Meagher as chairman of WP1's Accounting and Auditing Subcommittee.[174] The letter, which would have been developed and drafted by the secretariat, was sent three days before David Cairns' last day at the IASC. While it repeated the criticisms of IOSCO's current approach and his proposed reforms of this approach contained in Shiratori's speech, it presented and explained its revised work programme and proposed steps to 'open channels of communication' between the IASC and WP1. Shiratori concluded the latter by saying, 'We look forward to discussing these and other issues at our meeting on 2 February in Zurich.'

10.12. THE IASC AND IOSCO CHART THE WAY FORWARD

Following receipt of the two Shiratori letters of 17 June 1994 and Shiratori's critical speech at IOSCO's annual conference in October 1994, it became necessary to agree a plan with WP1 under which the IASC could formulate a programme of work to fulfil the expectations of IOSCO within a time frame satisfactory to both bodies. The first step had been taken by Shiratori in his letter of 28 December 1994. At the IASC, there were bruised feelings and even some antagonism towards IOSCO, which the latter believed were due to faulty communications.[175] Although there was no disruption in the work programme of either body, the principals wanted to reach an understanding on where everything stood and how to make the relationship work better.[176]

The search for agreement may have been eased by a changing of the guard at the senior levels of both bodies in 1994–5. At the end of 1994, David Cairns, the IASC's secretary-general, departed. He was succeeded in May 1995 by Sir Bryan Carsberg, who brought valuable experience as a regulator to the IASC. Eiichi Shiratori's term as IASC chairman was to end in June 1995, and he would be succeeded by Michael Sharpe, of Australia, who had been the IASC's deputy chairman as well as chairman-designate—and thus very active in the IASC's leadership affairs—since October 1992.

After Edward Waitzer, the OSC's chairman, succeeded the Frenchman, Jean Saint-Geours, as chairman of IOSCO's Technical Committee at the Tokyo conference in October 1994, he was quoted as saying that 'I sat down with Shiratori and his successor, Michael Sharpe, and we talked about how to get the relationship on a more constructive footing.'[177] One of Sharpe's first tasks, as he saw it, was to reach an agreement with WP1 on the way forward towards securing IOSCO's endorsement of the IASC's standards.

Sharpe's opportunity came early in 1995, several months before he became chairman. At IOSCO's Tokyo conference, Sharpe, Shiratori, and several members of the European delegations to the IASC were invited to attend a meeting on 2 February of WP1 in Zurich (mentioned at the end of Shiratori's letter of 28 December). On the morning of the meeting, prior to the arrival of the IASC delegation, WP1 Chairman Linda Quinn and James Saloman, the chairman of WP1's Accounting and Auditing Subcommittee, agreed on the idea of proposing a phased work plan for the IASC to complete the remaining core standards within a determinable period, leading to endorsement by IOSCO and the SEC. Linda Quinn was committed to moving the process forward. During the morning session with the IASC delegation, Sharpe tried to argue, without success, that WP1 should reconsider its position on the standards. Then, on the way to the luncheon venue, Saloman floated the idea of the work plan with Sharpe, knowing that the strategy was that Sharpe and Quinn would be seated next to each other at lunch.[178] Sharpe recalls the lunch conversation, during which he and Quinn agreed a way forward, which contemplated a work plan leading to the eventual endorsement of the core standards. She thereupon wrote out the basis of this agreement on a linen napkin, or serviette. Sharpe refers to it as the 'Zurich napkin' agreement.[179] Sharpe proposed to complete the remaining core standards in the next several years, and Quinn assured him of a close working relationship towards that end. To Quinn, it was important to inform the public that IOSCO and the IASC were continuing to work together and that there had not been a fracture in the relationship. The work plan would give the public an idea of the time frame, which, she believed, 'also gave real visibility and credibility to the IASC process, in that this was being dealt with substantively'.[180]

After endorsing the idea of the work plan, WP1 proposed a press release for the approval of IOSCO's Technical Committee, which was to meet in mid-March in Sydney. But the Technical Committee balked.[181] The issue was highly controversial in the Technical Committee, as a number of its members were not confident they could gain acceptance for such a commitment in their home countries.[182] In the end, the Technical Committee reached agreement that a press release should be deferred until the IASC and IOSCO were in a position to announce an actual work plan, or programme, to accompany it. The work plan was to be based on the Shiratori letters, with eventual completion in three to five years. The Technical Committee wanted the press release and the agreed work plan to be announced following its next meeting, to be held in July during IOSCO's annual conference in Paris. The news of this decision did not allow the IASC much time to elaborate the work plan. As it happened, the IASC's board and executive committee were to meet at the end of March and again in May. During its meeting at the end of March, the executive committee agreed that such a work plan should be developed in time for a press release to be issued in July, and it was agreed to enlist Paul Cherry's assistance in developing the work plan.[183] Cherry and James Saloman, the chairman of WP1's Accounting and Auditing Subcommittee, knew each other well and were both resident in Toronto, which facilitated a rapid resolution of differences. Cherry and Technical Director Liesel Knorr, who was also serving as acting secretary-general until Bryan Carsberg's arrival on 22 May, exchanged drafts of the proposed work plan. John Denman, the long-time technical adviser in the Canadian delegation, joined Cherry in his meetings with Saloman. Chairman Shiratori, the executive committee, and Carsberg monitored developments in May and June, and the proposed work plan was completed to Saloman's satisfaction in time for the IOSCO conference. In May, Shiratori pointedly wrote to Saloman that the IASC's position was that IOSCO should endorse at least the fourteen standards which were acceptable.[184] But Sharpe was aware that, while many, if not most, members of WP1 favoured a step-by-step process of endorsement, the SEC was opposed.

The IASC scheduled a meeting of its executive committee in Paris to coincide with IOSCO's conference in July, and they were both in the same hotel. It was Sharpe's first month as IASC chairman. Negotiations over the final terms of the agreement were still being conducted between the two bodies at the eleventh hour.[185] In the end, Bryan Carsberg secured the executive committee's approval of the work plan, with completion scheduled for June 1999, carrying forward the agreement in principle between Sharpe and Quinn in Zurich.[186] On 11 July, both bodies issued a joint press release and held a news conference. In the release it was stated that 'The Board has developed a work plan that the Technical Committee agrees will result, upon successful completion, in IAS comprising a comprehensive core set of standards. Completion of comprehensive core standards that are acceptable to the Technical Committee will allow the Technical Committee to recommend endorsement of IAS for cross-border capital raising and listing purposes in all global markets.'[187] In the release, Sharpe was quoted as saying, 'Companies should now feel confident the IASC and IOSCO are fully committed to developing IAS that will be acceptable everywhere in the world and recognize the efficiencies that may be obtained from using IAS.' Edward Waitzer, the chairman of IOSCO's Technical Committee, was quoted as saying, 'IOSCO is committed to working with the IASC to ensure a successful completion of the work plan on a timely basis.'[188] The IASC's 'Work Programme 1995–1999' was attached to the release (see also Table 11.1). Yet Bryan Carsberg's minuted remark at the meeting of IASC's Advisory Council on 8 July 1995 betrays a residue of a distrust of IOSCO: 'The press release has been drafted by IOSCO, and it will be very difficult for IOSCO to renege on endorsement in 1999 after such publicity.'[189] Carsberg realized that to push for immediate IOSCO endorsement, as Shiratori had urged, would have led to an internal split in WP1, between the SEC and other regulators. He said, 'I decided that the right thing to do was to go for the 1999 target rather than press for immediate recognition. It seemed to me that having the IOSCO agreement based on that work programme would provide the signal to companies that was needed. They could sensibly start using international standards now because the path is clear and eventual recognition is now virtually certain.'[190] He was minuted as saying that, as a result of the agreement, 'The relationship between IASC and IOSCO has greatly improved.'[191]

The agreement between the IASC and IOSCO represented more than a reaffirmation of cooperation between the two. *World Accounting Report* said,

The 'new deal' [announced by IOSCO and IASC in July] is a typically bold move by the fairly formidable IASC team of Sharpe and Carsberg. It puts the IOSCO/IASC alliance back on the rails; it sets a timetable leading to worldwide use of IASC standards; by clear IOSCO endorsement it implies a major breakthrough in gaining US acceptance of IASC standards—and challenges the SEC to deny this; it tells multinationals looking for access to use of financial markets that a move to use of IASC standards will provide access in the medium term, without the embarrassments suffered by Daimler Benz of US GAAP reconciliations.... And certainly this is a way for the IASC to emerge into the twenty-first century as a dominant force in world standard-setting.[192]

Michael Sutton, the SEC's chief accountant, called the agreement a 'major milestone'.[193] Paul Leder, the deputy director of the SEC's Office of International Affairs who became chairman of WP1 in 1997, said that the latter's work on the IASC's standards 'began in earnest' upon the signing of the agreement.[194] The focus shifted from the strategic to the technical issues.[195] And, as is brought out in Section 12.3, the July 1995 agreement prompted the European Commission to look to the IASC as the source of a comprehensive set of international accounting standards. For his part, Sharpe was reported as saying that he was confident that the revised standards would be approved by IOSCO in 1999. Sensing the accelerating globalization of the capital markets, especially on the European Continent, Sharpe said, 'The pressure from the marketplace is on our side. One business language is so important when everybody seems to want access to world capital markets.' Ever the enthusiast for IASC standards, he said that 'The whole matter of the [IASC–IOSCO] announcement really says that the IASC is going to be the leading standard-setting body in the world. And we have to behave like that to deliver the goods. We are going to need a lot of help from other standard setters and a lot of support generally—including financial support.'[196]

Former IASC Secretary-General David Cairns characterized the challenge that lay ahead of the IASC as follows:

In practical terms, to win IOSCO's endorsement of the core standards, the IASC has to do enough to satisfy Canada, Japan and the USA, the three countries which opposed the further endorsement of IASs in [July] 1995. At the same time, the IASC has to avoid doing so much that it loses the support of those who favoured further endorsement or even endorsement of the process of setting IASs—Australia, Europe and Hong Kong.[197]

10.13. THE IASC ACCELERATES ITS TARGET DATE TO MARCH 1998 FOR COMPLETING ITS CORE STANDARDS

There were those who expressed scepticism that the IASC could complete the core standards as soon as the middle of 1999. It was a daunting task for a part-time body with a fairly small technical staff to produce the standards to IOSCO's satisfaction in a scant four years. Therefore, the IASC's announcement in April 1996, nine months into the four-year period, that the target date was being accelerated to March 1998 came as a surprise to many. This was, in Bryan Carsberg's view, the 'shortest feasible time for completion of the projects required by IOSCO', which was fifteen months earlier than the programme approved by the board at its November 1995 meeting in Sydney.[198] An IASC press release said that the IASC board's approval of the 'fast track work programme' was 'contingent upon IASC's success in raising additional funds with a target of about £700,000 per year for two years'. The additional funds were to cover the costs of extra board meetings and meetings of the steering committees, as well as 'the extra staff required to enable us to handle more projects simultaneously'.[199] The acceleration in its pace of work was also facilitated by cutting back on the number of steps required by the board's 'due process' procedures.[200]

In an April 1996 press release, the IASC explained that a major reason why it opted to advance its already tight schedule was to accommodate the financial reporting needs of major multinationals, especially a number based on the European Continent, that 'foresee the desirability of having additional stock market quotations and will face additional costs if they are not able to use International Accounting Standards for all their reporting purposes'. 'Significant encouragement to accelerate the work programme', the press release continued, 'also came from members of IOSCO, including the European members, the Canadian members and the US SEC.'[201] Bryan Carsberg reported to the board in March 1996 that the requests from Canada and the SEC originated with OSC Chairman Edward Waitzer and SEC Chairman Arthur Levitt, evidently because European companies were pointing towards listings in Canada, Japan, and the United States. If the companies were to list in the United States soon and adopt US GAAP as an interim solution until IASC standards were accepted by the SEC for foreign registrants, they would face transition costs in later switching to IASC standards, or they might postpone seeking a listing. Furthermore, to European companies and their governments the use of US GAAP was politically indefensible, if only because they were set entirely in the United States with no participation in the process of interested parties overseas.[202]

Despite the barrier of the reconciliation to US GAAP, the number of foreign companies listed on the NYSE almost doubled, from 165 to 304, between the end of 1993 and the end of 1996. New listings included such high-profile European companies as AXA, Cadbury Schweppes, Deutsche Telekom, Elsevier, ENI, Gucci, Jefferson Smurfit, Nokia, Pechiney, Scania, and SGS-Thomson.[203] Over the same period, the total number of foreign companies registered with the SEC increased from 588 to 1,019.[204]

Among the reasons was the gathering pace of globalization, leading executives to come to the belief that a listing in New York raises a company's stature to one of worldwide prominence. *The Wall Street Journal* editorialized that '[Foreign] companies want not just exposure to U.S. money that a [New York] listing would bring, but the imprimatur of the NYSE for all it means to investors the world over.'[205]

New York's deep and liquid capital market for public offerings must have been a significant draw in itself. Deutsche Telekom was one such company, a recently privatized segment of Deutsche Bundespost, which announced in February 1996 its plan for an initial public offering of US$13 billion (the largest IPO ever in

Europe), about one-fourth of which was destined for the US capital market. In November 1995, the European Commission wrote, 'As more and more Member States are implementing important privatisation programmes and as the capital needs of the companies concerned are increasing, the number companies facing [the need to conform with US GAAP] is growing.'[206]

Allister Wilson, of Ernst & Young UK, took note of the changing capital market scene on the European Continent:

the traditional sources of finance for continental European companies—for example, banks and private investors—are no longer able to fully satisfy multinational companies' capital requirements. As a result, more and more European companies are having to look to the international capital markets for their funding. This, in turn, has been facilitated by the creation of a European capital market by means of simplified listing procedures aimed at encouraging companies to seek multiple listings in the [European Union].[207]

The growing interest of European multinationals in the US capital market developed against a background of a general surge in capital market activity. Between 1993 and 1997, the market value of the world's stock markets approximately doubled.[208] All the major Continental European markets shared in this trend, but the changes in Germany amounted to nothing less than a revolution in the thinking of major multinationals and banks. The big ('universal') banks that traditionally sat on the multinationals' supervisory boards had suffered a drop in their lendable funds owing to their increasing loan activity in the former East Germany.[209] Former SEC Chairman Richard Breeden said the following at a conference in 1993:

Even in Germany and Japan (though for very different reasons), the traditional system of relationships is changing between a universal bank in Germany, and the companies in which it holds stakes, and the 'main bank' in Japan and its relationship to a group of companies within a *keiretsu*. The German banks have been fairly quiet about it, but nonetheless the steps of Deutsche Bank and others to reduce the size of their industrial equity holdings suggests the beginning of a profound change in the capital market systems in Germany.[210]

Furthermore, by the beginning of the 1990s the big private German banks began to see their future less as *Hausbanken* and more in investment banking.[211] An active equity capital market was finally coming to Germany, as some two million Germans purchased Deutsche Telekom shares in November 1996, which must have been a signal occurrence in German stock market history: the large-scale emergence of retail equity investors.

Even if a company did not need to raise capital overseas, a US listing was viewed by major German companies as strategically important, especially for making acquisitions through exchanges of shares.[212] After having vilified Daimler's executive management for submitting to a US GAAP reconciliation in 1993,[213] a number of the very same German multinationals began to use US GAAP or IASC standards themselves.[214] From 1996 onwards, other German companies followed Daimler to the NYSE.

Whatever the reasons for these fundamental changes in the European capital markets, major European multinationals in several countries shortly found it necessary to become well acquainted with US GAAP, if only to prepare their Form 20-F reconciliation on instruction of the SEC—the 'additional costs' mentioned in the IASC's April 1996 press release. If, by the time they went to New York, IOSCO had endorsed IASC standards and thus the SEC had signified its acceptance of the standards for use by foreign registrants without the need for a reconciliation, the multinationals could lower their cost of entry into the US market. The IASC's leadership did not want to risk 'losing' these major multinationals to US GAAP, for once they were to come to know and use US GAAP, they might not want to shift again to IASC standards. Hence, it became essential to accelerate its agreed deadline for completing the core standards and thus secure IOSCO's endorsement more quickly. From the point of view of the SEC, which was forced to deal with a rapidly increasing number of different national GAAPs, the apparent surge of interest in a US listing on the part of European companies increased the potential usefulness of the IASC's standards.

The OSC's Waitzer and the SEC's Levitt were apparently willing to help the IASC board raise the additional funds it would need to accelerate its schedule.[215] If the IASC were to accelerate its pace, Levitt said that the SEC would increase the resources it devotes to international accounting matters.[216] Accordingly, SEC Chief Accountant Michael Sutton promptly designated Mary Tokar as the member of his staff to devote all of her time to international accounting issues. In September 1997, she was promoted to senior associate chief accountant for international accounting and auditing standards, a new position.[217] In May 1996, furthermore, the SEC announced that Arthur Wyatt, a former IASC chairman, would begin serving as special advisor to the SEC on international accounting.[218]

The political climate had changed from the early 1990s, when SEC Chairman Breeden took an uncompromising stance with respect to the applicability of US GAAP to foreign registrants. In 1996, the NYSE, under Chairman and Chief Executive Richard Grasso, was actively lobbying both the SEC and the Congress, and conservative members of Congress, such as Phil Gramm (Republican of Texas), chairman of the Senate securities subcommittee, were receptive to arguments to open up the US capital market. Foreign securities regulators, through IOSCO, were also applying pressure on the SEC to be more flexible in its requirements (*see* Section 10.16).[219]

10.14. THE SEC ANNOUNCES THE 'THREE KEY ELEMENTS' TO BE REFLECTED IN ACCEPTABLE IASC STANDARDS

The IASC–IOSCO agreement signed in July 1995, foreshadowed by the entente between Michael Sharpe and Linda Quinn five months earlier in Zurich, meant that the SEC would soon be facing a decision about implementing an IOSCO endorsement of the IASC's core standards. Furthermore, with SEC encouragement, the IASC had just announced a fifteen-month acceleration in its target date for completing the core standards. It was time for the SEC to make known its own expectations for the IASC's revised standards. It did so in an important press release issued on 11 April 1996. In the release, the SEC affirmed that it 'supports the IASC's objective to develop, as expeditiously as possible, accounting standards that could be used for preparing financial statements used in cross-border offerings. From the Commission's perspective, there are three key elements to this program and the Commission's acceptance of its results':[220]

- The standards must include a core set of accounting pronouncements that constitutes a comprehensive, generally accepted basis of accounting;
- The standards must be of high quality—they must result in comparability and transparency, and they must provide for full disclosure; and
- The standards must be rigorously interpreted and applied.

When the SEC's press release appeared, Bryan Carsberg wrote to the members of the IASC Advisory Council and executive committee, 'I understand that its genesis was in discussions between our US Advisory Council [members] and the SEC officials which noted that it would be useful to have a statement which we could quote about SEC support for our activities.'[221] This view is not confirmed by SEC Chief Accountant Sutton, who recalls that the release was originally developed by Michael Mann, director of the Office of International Affairs, and that he himself drafted the 'the three key elements'. Sutton writes, 'It was a way to frame the debate and also make clear that the Commission would be unwilling to compromise the integrity of financial reporting in the US capital markets.'[222]

The first of the three elements in the SEC's release, completeness of coverage, had already been mentioned several times recently by IOSCO officials. The second element introduced the term 'high quality' into the discourse over the setting of accounting standards.[223] In expanding on this term, the SEC referred to the three qualities, 'transparency, comparability and full disclosure', which it has regularly cited over the years as the hallmarks of sound financial reporting. The third element, that the standards should be 'rigorously interpreted and applied', addressed the SEC's concern that the interpretations and applications might vary across countries. As is mentioned below, this third element played a role in prompting the IASC board to create a committee to give interpretive advice. As to 'applied', the IASC probably thought that the issue of companies' compliance with its standards fell within the province of auditors and regulators, not its own. As is brought out in Section 10.20, the SEC raised this issue again, with even greater emphasis, in its concept release of February 2000.

The SEC's news release concluded with the following assurance: 'As soon as the IASC completes its project, accomplishing each of the noted key elements, it is the Commission's intention to consider allowing the utilization of the resulting standards by foreign issuers offering securities in the U.S.'[224] The term 'consider allowing' bespeaks the SEC's characteristic caution. The agency concedes very little. Observe also that the SEC did not propose to extend the use of acceptable

IASC standards to domestic issuers. US GAAP would continue to apply to US companies whose securities are publicly traded in US capital markets that are subject to the SEC's jurisdiction.

What criteria would the SEC invoke when assessing whether the revised IASC standards possess high quality? SEC Chairman Arthur Levitt said in a December 1996 speech, 'There's no doubt in my mind that [the IASC standards'] acceptability to US investors will depend on how well those standards measure up to our own.' This remark tended to support the view of some Europeans that the SEC was comfortable only with US GAAP. In the same speech, Levitt said that an important message in the SEC's April press release was that 'Acceptance of IASC standards by the SEC is not a foregone conclusion.'[225] This remark may have been intended to respond to the statement attributed to IASC Secretary-General Carsberg three months earlier that the IASC is 'fairly confident' of the SEC's support of its standards for use by foreign companies listing on the NYSE.[226] The SEC continued to make this point: in October 1997, it wrote, referring to the prospect of eventual endorsement, 'At this point, the resolution of the core standards project remains uncertain.'[227] At a meeting in June 1997 at the SEC offices in Washington, Chief Accountant Sutton remonstrated with Carsberg for taking the SEC's eventual endorsement of the IASC standards for granted.[228]

Sutton amplified on Levitt's characterization of high quality standards by saying, 'SEC acceptance of IASC standards has not already been agreed to.... We need to be willing to evaluate the [IASC's] proposals objectively, measuring them not by whether they are identical to US GAAP, but rather by how well they would resolve problems that we have experienced.... We remain firmly committed, however, to the proposition that, to be accepted in US markets, international standards should result in the same credibility and integrity that are produced by US standards. As the IASC goes through its standard-setting process, the staff will continue to express reservations about provisions that we feel are not appropriate, or when we feel that the coverage is not adequate.'[229] Sutton made it clear that the FASB would continue to play a leading role in the setting of 'conceptually sound accounting standards for US issuers' as well as play an active role in the dialogue over the setting of international standards. He emphasized that the SEC was doing no more than considering the use of acceptable IASC standards by foreign issuers only.[230]

At its June 1996 meeting in Stockholm, the IASC board decided to establish a procedure for issuing interpretations of its standards.[231] Bryan Carsberg, upon becoming secretary-general in May 1995, believed that the IASC should, like other standard setters, have an interpretations committee, but resources were a limiting factor.[232] By the middle of 1996, such a committee became inevitable. At the June meeting, Carsberg informed the board that 'IOSCO strongly want us to establish [a system for issuing interpretations] and members of the IOSCO Working Party 1 said, at my meeting with them in January, that their experience of our operating such a system could be a material factor in contributing to their confidence in us and therefore influencing their decision on endorsing our standards when we have completed the work programme.'²³³ The third of the SEC's three key elements conveyed its own view, and the SEC was, of course, a force within WP1.²³⁴

The proposal for an interpretations committee was heavily controversial at the board, especially among the Europeans. Some members worried that it would become another standard setter. Yet the clear desire by IOSCO for a procedure to deal with interpretations won the day.²³⁵ In September, the board set up the Standing Interpretations Committee (SIC), whose recommendations were to be subject to board approval. Paul Cherry, who had retired from the Canadian delegation to the IASC board the year before, became its chairman and remained in that capacity until 2001. Further discussion of the SIC appeared in Section 8.13.

10.15. A CLOSER WORKING RELATIONSHIP BETWEEN THE IASC AND IOSCO

In 1996, it became evident that the relations between the IASC and IOSCO were warming. This development owed its genesis to the July 1995 announcement by the IASC and IOSCO that pointed towards an eventual decision by IOSCO on the acceptability of the IASC's core standards, once they were completed. Edward Waitzer, chairman of IOSCO's Technical Committee, wrote in May 1996:

> At the IOSCO annual meeting in Tokyo, not quite two years ago, the then Chairman of the IASC [Eiichi Shiratori] delivered a scathing keynote address, entirely uncharacteristic of his usual manner, but reflecting IASC's cumulative frustration of dealing with a process that they perceived to be characterized more by anti-responses than productive dialogue. Rather than deny or escalate the conflict, we set about to develop a workplan that would focus on core international accounting standards and a reasonable timeframe for devising them.²³⁶

Also, in 1996, there was a change in SEC personnel who were involved with IOSCO. In February 1996, Linda Quinn left the SEC,²³⁷ and the SEC's principal liaison with IOSCO shifted from the Division of Corporation Finance to the Office of the Chief Accountant, as the remaining issues were less strategic and tactical than technical.²³⁸ By then, Michael Sutton was the SEC chief accountant. In June 1996, at the IASC's invitation, IOSCO began sending observers to board meetings. WP1 decided that, of its some seventeen member jurisdictions, only the United States, France, Germany, Japan, and Ontario could send observers to board meetings. Paradoxically, the United Kingdom and Italy, which were both represented on WP1's Accounting and Auditing Subcommittee, did not go to the board meetings. Germany and Japan went to the board meetings but were not on the Subcommittee.²³⁹

The regular attendance at board meetings by the SEC observer, Mary Tokar, promoted a better understanding on both sides. Tokar, a member of the staff of the SEC's Office of the Chief Accountant, had just been assigned full-time responsibility for developments on international accounting matters, and she began serving on both Working Party 1 and its Accounting and Auditing Subcommittee, thus becoming the principal staff link between the SEC and both IOSCO and the IASC. In 1999, she became the chairman of WP1.

Unlike his predecessor, IASC Secretary-General Bryan Carsberg was regularly invited to attend meetings of IOSCO's Working Party 1. At a meeting of the IASC's Advisory Council in June 1996, it was noted in the minutes that Carsberg had also attended a meeting of IOSCO's Technical Committee, 'and this had demonstrated good communication and warm support from IOSCO for the objectives of IASC.... In discussion, it was noted that the working relationship between IASC and IOSCO, particularly IOSCO's acceptance of observer membership of the Board, provided a basis for confidence about the prospects. The formal statement made by the SEC [in April 1996] was strong evidence of their position as was their appointment of Art Wyatt as an adviser on International Accounting Standards. The US members confirmed their view that there had been a genuine change in attitudes in the United States.'[240]

10.16. THE NEW YORK STOCK EXCHANGE PRESSURES THE SEC TO ACCEPT THE IASC'S STANDARDS

As has already been noted, the NYSE had been urging the SEC to be more 'flexible' so as to enable more world-class multinationals to seek a listing. The pace of increase in foreign listings on the NYSE during the 1980s was slow, and it retarded the Exchange's ambition to be known as the premier international capital market in the world. As noted earlier, the number of foreign listings on the Exchange was growing rapidly during the 1990s, and by the end of 1997 as many as 343, or 11 per cent, of its 3,046 listed companies were of foreign origin.[241] Yet this still placed the NYSE behind the London Stock Exchange's main market which, at the end of 1997, had 526 foreign listings, which represented 20 per cent of the 2,683 total listed companies.[242] A comparison of the total market value of the equity capital of domestic and foreign companies listed on the two exchanges at the end of 1997 reveals the relative dominance of foreign listings in London compared to New York as well as London's larger market capitalization for foreign companies (amounts in billions):[243]

	New York	London
Domestic	US$8,900	£1,300 (US$2,100)
Foreign	US$2,800	£2,400 (US$3,800)

The NYSE believed for some time that one of the obstacles to attracting more foreign multinationals to its list was the SEC's Form 20-F reconciliation, which obliged the companies to report two measures of earnings, according to their national GAAP and by US GAAP, which was believed to confuse investors and the press.[244] The London Stock Exchange accepted IASC standards, US GAAP, and, because of the principle of mutual recognition, also the GAAPs of the other fourteen member states in the European Union. The London Exchange did not require non-UK companies using their own country's GAAP or IASC standards to reconcile to UK GAAP. The NYSE sought a means of placing pressure on the SEC to move faster towards acceptance of the revised IASC standards for use by foreign registrants in US capital markets without the need to reconcile to US GAAP. Because it viewed the SEC as no more than a cautious participant in the international harmonization process, the Exchange turned to Congress. During 1996, a bill entitled the National Securities Markets Improvement Act was being considered by Congress. It contained no provisions dealing with financial reporting. The Exchange got in touch with Senator Phil Gramm, who chaired the securities subcommittee, which oversees the SEC, and persuaded him to introduce a provision on financial reporting in the bill,[245] which eventually formed part of the final legislation approved by Congress and signed by the President. The provision added by the senator charged the SEC to move forward with its support for international accounting standards with greater alacrity. This was Congress' first utterance on the subject of international accounting standards, and the main thrust of the provision was as follows:

> It is the sense of the Congress that...the [Securities and Exchange] Commission should enhance its vigorous support for the development of high-quality international accounting standards as soon as practicable...[and should report to Congress within a year] on progress in the development of international accounting standards and the outlook for successful completion of a set of international accounting standards that would be acceptable to the Commission for offerings and listings by foreign corporations in United States markets.[246]

The SEC's report to Congress in October 1997, which was mandated by the 1996 Act, contained a narrative summary of the SEC's efforts to achieve international harmonization and a series of documentary appendices.[247] Echoing, but slightly softening the remark made by SEC Chairman Levitt in December 1996 (*see* Section 10.14), the SEC said, 'One important, though not determinative, issue [in the SEC's consideration of the IASC's revised standards] will be differences between international accounting standards and U.S. accounting standards.'[248]

The SEC's October 1997 report pointed out why its cautious approach to vetting the IASC's standards was justified:[249]

> If IASC standards are not judged, either in principle or in application, to be of comparable quality to U.S. standards, adoption of those standards for use by foreign registrants without reconciliation or supplemental disclosure could have the following results:
>
> - investors may begin to question the transparency of financial reporting in U.S. markets, with a resulting reduction in the stability of the markets or efficiency of pricing of capital for both domestic and cross-border issuers; and
> - domestic registrants would be put at a competitive disadvantage because application of U.S. accounting and reporting requirements would impose higher disclosure requirements on them than on foreign enterprises competing for capital in the same markets.

Therefore, the Commission will have to consider carefully the extent to which current requirements for presentation of U.S. GAAP information by foreign private registrants should be modified.

One observes, again, that the SEC did not propose to consider changing the current reporting requirements for domestic registrants.

In its 1997 report to Congress, the SEC gave a rare glimpse into the magnitude of its dedication to international accounting and auditing. In the Office of the Chief Accountant alone, it said, three accountants—a fourth was just added—focus primarily on international accounting, reporting, and auditing issues, representing more than 4,000 hours during the financial year ending 30 September 1997. It pointed out that 'Staff members from the Division of Corporation Finance and the Office of International Affairs are also active participants in Working Party No. 1.'[250]

In the report, the SEC evinced a degree of frustration in working with the IASC. It pointed out that the advice received from 'IOSCO and its members' (i.e. including the SEC) on draft standards 'is not determinative in any of the IASC's decisions' and that 'neither IOSCO nor any individual regulatory group has oversight authority over the IASC'.[251] This relationship differs very much from the one to which the SEC has long been accustomed with the FASB, where the former has exercised what it terms oversight authority over the latter as well as over its predecessor bodies, the AICPA's Committee on Accounting Procedure and APB. Implied in these relationships has been a continual process of communication between the SEC's accounting staff and the standard setter. In rare instances, the SEC or its staff or the Commission itself has imposed its own view on the standard setter.[252]

The SEC itself obeys elaborate procedures, dictated by the relevant federal legislation, when making changes in its rules, such as a change in the Form 20-F reconciliation requirement for certain foreign registrants. In 1994, it took the SEC eight months to compose, expose for comment, and finally formulate and approve rules on the portions of the three IASC standards that were to be accepted for use by foreign registrants without the need to reconcile to US GAAP (*see* Section 10.8.7). Mary Tokar outlined the procedure that must be followed once IOSCO were to endorse the IASC's core standards:[253]

If, after assessment of the completed core standards, the SEC staff concludes that the current reconciliation requirements should be reduced or removed, the staff will need to bring a rule proposal to the Commission to amend the current filing requirements for foreign private issuers. If the Commission supports the staff's recommendations it would publish proposed amendments for public comment. The staff would then analyse the comments received and make final recommendations to the Commission, which would then be included, if approved by the Commission, in an adopting release. This procedure of announcing proposed rule changes, allowing time for public comment and then publishing final rules is mandated by US law and applies to any SEC rules and regulations.

When one judges the IASC's standards approved between 1973 and 1992 as well as the ten revised standards approved by the IASC board in 1993, which still contained a number of allowed alternative treatments, it is well to remember that flexible standards with more than one option were prevalent in US GAAP as recently as the 1960s, and quite a number of options continue to be found in today's US GAAP. Prior to the issue of a series of APB Opinions in 1966–70, US GAAP allowed optional treatments in a rather flexible format on accounting for business combinations, intangibles, leases, deferred taxes, pensions, and extraordinary items, as well as on funds statements. Moreover, the SEC did not support the APB's valiant attempt in 1962 to prescribe only one method of accounting for the investment tax credit. In early 1963, after the APB had approved only a single accounting treatment for the tax credit, the SEC insisted that an alternative treatment be allowed. It is easy to forget that the widespread availability of options and flexible formats, with comparatively little interpretive guidance, was once the norm in US GAAP.[254]

10.17. THE FASB QUESTIONS THE IASC'S DUE PROCESS

As the IASC was constantly aware of its need to obtain the SEC's approval, it must have been a matter of concern that the US national standard setter, the FASB, repeatedly and publicly questioned the quality of the IASC's procedures and its standards.

In 1995, FASB Chairman Beresford was pointedly critical of the IASC because 'Some issues have been dealt with at a more superficial level than we believe is appropriate.' He urged the IASC to deal explicitly with detailed implementation issues. He said that many IASC standards 'are so broad that they wouldn't be considered operational in the US'.[255] The following year, after the IASC announced an acceleration of the target date for completing the core standards, Beresford, speaking at the third annual conference of world standard setters in Copenhagen, criticized the IASC's new target date as 'highly unrealistic' and 'hopelessly optimistic' in view of the heavy workload, including financial instruments, which lay ahead.[256] He was reported to have 'lambasted' the board's due process.[257] Beresford seemed to be saying that the IASC board was placing speed ahead of quality. Barry Robbins, a member the US delegation from 1994 to 1997, indeed said that speed was being placed ahead of due process, as the board's leadership, Sharpe and Carsberg, rushed the drafts into standards before the steering committees could run their course.[258]

FASB Vice-Chairman Jim Leisenring was also critical of the IASC, and was quoted in September 1996 as saying, 'We've often complained to the IASC about loose drafting. We are concerned that these standards are not being scrutinised properly.'[259] In March 1998, he said, 'While the lowest common denominator is not the target of IASC standards, the standards often contain so much purposeful ambiguity that when applied, they will not enhance comparability.'[260] Indeed, in a tense meeting in June 1997 at the SEC offices in Washington with Carsberg, SEC Chief Accountant Michael Sutton said he had a concern that the IASC was making compromises which produced weak standards.[261]

In December 1996, the FASB published a voluminous and detailed analysis of the 'variations' between IASC standards and US GAAP. The FASB's 426-page study referred to 255 variations on matters of approach and/or guidance, which, it said, 'will be an important tool for [the SEC's] assessment of the completed core set of standards'.[262] The FASB study indeed contained a thorough and useful examination of the variations, so that 'an enhanced understanding of the differences' between IASC standards and US GAAP could 'guide future efforts toward greater comparability of accounting standards and financial reporting worldwide'.[263] Yet it almost seemed designed to catalogue every conceivable difference, major and minor, between the two GAAPs, as if to suggest that the IASC had a very long way to go. For its part, the IASC preferred to cite the opinion of Morgan Stanley Dean Witter's equity research group that 'Many investors would find most of [the 255 differences] meaningless. For reflecting economic substance in most industries, IAS is easily of comparable quality to US GAAP, if auditors do their jobs.'[264] Trevor Harris, who wrote the Morgan Stanley report, had conducted a series of case studies, cited above, in which he found that non-US companies' use of the revised IASC standards did not produce differences from US GAAP that should have troubled investors.

IASC Technical Director Liesel Knorr said, '255 is a lot of differences but it is not meaningful to number them', as they were a mixture of substantive and minor differences, some the IASC would defend and others it would not.[265]

At a meeting of the IASC's Advisory Council in January 1997, Secretary-General Carsberg emphasized the positive side of the FASB's comparative study. It was noted in the minutes that he 'said that he did not see [the study] as a reason for great concern. The SEC had long been aware that IASC's standards would not be as detailed as those of FASB. The position was that IOSCO had accepted that some IASC standards were satisfactory without further improvement and other specialised industry standards covered by FASB were not on our work programme and not part of the IOSCO requirement. The other standards covered by the study were under review in IASC and the study would be helpful in providing a checklist of issues which should be considered by IASC.'[266] For its part, *IASC Insight* did not publish any comment on the FASB study.

The press continued to draw attention to the FASB's sour view of the IASC. In January 1998, *The Economist* reported that officials at the FASB 'are privately scathing about the work of the IASC. They accuse its secretary-general, Sir Bryan Carsberg, of "manipulating the press" into thinking that the SEC has agreed to the new standards. The FASB claims that the standards are too flexible, giving firms too much discretion over what they report; that their meaning is often ambiguous; and that there are big uncertainties about how—if at all—they will be enforced.'[267] It was a time when some at the FASB may have viewed the IASC as a competitor, perhaps even threatening its survival.

Jim Leisenring was reported as saying at a conference in late 1998 that he did not think that IASC standards made the grade as 'global standards'. He suggested that the IASC is 'sacrificing quality for the sake of convergence'. The article went on,

Global standards should meet four key criteria, delegates were told. They should be consistent with the framework; offer minimum alternative accounting procedures ('because comparability is crucial'); be unambiguous and comprehensible; and be capable of rigorous interpretation and application.

'In my opinion [Leisenring said], there are no international standards that meet these requirements—nor are there likely to be in the near future'.[268]

Yet the IASC moved more swiftly on some issues than the FASB because the latter was, inevitably, slowed by the very size of its operations and its elaborate due process. Sometimes the less expensive system can overtake the more expensive system. Peter Zurbrügg, of Hoffmann/La Roche and a member of the Federation of Swiss Industrial Holding Companies' delegation to the IASC board, said in January 1998, 'In two and a half years [the IASC] has accomplished something that would have taken the FASB at least a decade'.[269] Ralph Walters, a former member of the FASB who joined the IASC in 1984, reflected in a similar vein about his experience at the board in the 1980s:

I thought [the IASC] did a remarkable job with a three- or four-person staff. I came from [the FASB] where we had this staff in the neighbourhood of a hundred people, changing all the time, and it took them *forever* to get anything to us. Yet [David Cairns and] three or four people were churning out stuff, and most of it was high quality.[270]

10.18. THE IASC BOARD COMPLETES THE CORE STANDARDS

At its December 1998 meeting in Frankfurt, the IASC completed the last of the core standards, IAS 39 on the recognition and measurement of financial instruments, and transmitted the entire set to IOSCO in the hope that they would all be endorsed for use by securities market regulators around the world.[271] Although the board had set March 1998 as the target date for completing the standards, it had to be delayed by nine months in order to deal with all of the complicated and controversial issues on the intractable subject of financial instruments.[272] At its meeting in November 1997, IOSCO's Technical Committee, recognizing the difficulty of the financial instruments project, confirmed the IASC's revised timetable.[273]

There was a time in 1997 when a concern over how long it might take the IASC to deal with financial instruments led the Europeans, keen to defend themselves against an invasion of US GAAP, to give some thought to breaking ranks and endorsing the IASC's standards ahead of the other IOSCO members, but this split within IOSCO never eventuated.[274] In 1996, Veba and Deutsche Telekom had decided to reconcile to US GAAP, and in 1997 a considerable number of emerging technology companies listed on Germany's newly created Neuer Markt adopted US GAAP.[275]

The board held five meetings in 1998, the most in any year, in order to assure completion of the core standards by the end of the year. During its December meeting, the board received a facsimile message from Gordon Brown, the UK

Chancellor of the Exchequer, reminding it of the declaration by the G7 finance ministers and central bankers of 30 October 1998, calling on the IASC 'to finalise by early 1999 a proposal for the full range of international agreed accounting standards', and that 'IOSCO and the Basle Committee should complete a timely review of these standards' (*see also* Section 12.5.2).[276]

Warren McGregor, the long-time technical adviser of the Australian delegation, wrote, 'There is no doubt that the IASC has performed a small miracle in completing its core standards program in the short period of time it allowed itself. And it is fair to say that the body of standards now comprising IASs is a significant improvement over those in place prior to the commencement of the improvements program.'[277]

A full discussion of the board's work on the development and completion of its standards from 1987 to 2000 may be found in Chapters 9 and 11.

10.19. IOSCO ENDORSES THE IASC'S CORE STANDARDS

WP1's formal process of assessing the core standards began in January 1999 and entailed a thorough examination over the course of many meetings.[278] The process began under the chairmanship of Paul Leder, who was succeeded as chairman in July 1999 by Mary Tokar, both of the SEC. IOSCO's publication which it issued to support the endorsement was a 126-page report by its Technical Committee.[279] It summarized the recommendations of WP1, which was by then composed of representatives from seventeen jurisdictions, but whose identities were not disclosed in the report.[280]

WP1 began its assessment 'by considering over 850 issues that had been raised over the course of the core standards project'. It was stated in the assessment report that 'Supporting material includes over 700 pages of comment letters prepared by the Working Party, as well as other correspondence with the IASC about the components of the core standards work program.'[281]

Following the evaluation, the working party concluded that 'The majority of their concerns had been addressed and the range of concerns had been narrowed significantly.'[282] The bulk of the report consisted of an extensive enumeration of about 120 substantive issues which was what was left of the 850 issues raised by WP1 over the years in its correspondence with the IASC. For each of the 120 issues, one or more jurisdictions believed that their concerns had not been completely removed by the IASC's core standards programme and therefore justified a supplementary treatment. At a late stage, WP1 decided not to show for each issue which jurisdictions maintained their objections. It is understood that the SEC above all, but also the OSC, France's COB, Italy's Consob, and Japan's Financial Services Agency, were the sources of most of the substantive issues raised, and that one or more of them did not want to be identified as such. The other jurisdictions had comparatively few reservations about the endorsement. Germany, the Netherlands, and the United Kingdom reportedly had none.[283] No substantive issues were raised for six standards, and a further six standards attracted only one substantive issue each. Not surprisingly, IAS 39, on financial instruments, had by far the greatest number of issues raised by the working party.

The report was received at IOSCO's annual conference in May 2000 in Sydney, and a resolution was passed that IOSCO recommend 'that its members allow multinational issuers to use 30 IASC standards, as supplemented by reconciliation, disclosure and interpretation where necessary to address outstanding substantive issues at a national or regional level'.[284] Of the thirty standards, fourteen were 'new or substantially revised as a result of the core standards work program', with effective dates ranging from 1998 to 2001.[285] The thirty standards encompassed the following (in their latest revisions, where applicable): IAS 1, 2, 4, 7, 8, 10–12, 14, 16–24, 27–9, and 31–9. Seventeen SIC Interpretations, produced by the IASC's Standing Interpretations Committee, were comprehended in the endorsement.

IAS 40, on investment properties, was one of the core standards, but it could not be completed in time. The Technical Committee said, 'The Working Party intends to assess the investment properties standard as soon as possible after its completion.'[286]

The 'supplemental treatments', which enabled the national regulators to deal in their own way with the outstanding substantive issues, were set out as follows:

- **reconciliation:** requiring reconciliation of certain items to show the effect of applying a different accounting method, in contrast with the method applied under IASC standards;
- **disclosure:** requiring additional disclosures, either in the presentation of the financial statements or in the footnotes; and
- **interpretation:** specifying use of a particular alternative provided in an IASC standard, or a particular interpretation in cases where the IASC standard is unclear or silent.[287]

These supplemental treatments were already what the SEC had been insisting upon in the financial statements of foreign registrants for all material departures from US GAAP, and it is clear that IOSCO could not have secured the SEC's support for its endorsement without stipulating these exceptions. It is known that the SEC insisted on the reconciliation.[288] While Tokar made it clear that the IASC had made progress by completing the core standards, she cautioned that 'IASC standards still need improvement before they are accepted without supplemental treatments.'[289] Yet one member of the working party recalls that the reconciliation was not meant to be a reaffirmation of what the SEC was already doing. Not all the 'outstanding substantive issues' qualifying for supplementary treatment came from the SEC, and, critically, the SEC committed itself to move from full to partial reconciliation, that is, for the outstanding substantive issues only.[290]

To some, IOSCO's endorsement decision disproved the belief that it was incapable of committing itself to anything. The decision gave heart to its members, because it was seen as an action that, finally, had 'bite'.[291] Yet some regarded

IOSCO's endorsement as 'hollow', especially as the SEC did not retreat from requiring a full reconciliation for all material deviations from US GAAP.

10.20. THE SEC ISSUES A MAJOR 'CONCEPT RELEASE' IN FEBRUARY 2000

The IASC was first informed that the SEC was planning to issue a concept release on international accounting standards at a meeting on 2 September 1998 between Bryan Carsberg and SEC staff members Paul Leder, then the chairman of IOSCO's Working Party 1, and Mary Tokar, then a member of WP1's Accounting and Auditing Subcommittee.[292] Leder and Tokar explained that the SEC's purpose in issuing the release, which was timed for the first quarter of 1999, was to assure itself that, by participating in an endorsement of the IASC's core standards, it would not be moving too far ahead of, that is be out of touch with, the views of users, preparers, and auditors in the United States. If the reaction from within the United States were positive to such an endorsement, the SEC could eventually move ahead with rulemaking to meet the formal requirements of accepting the standards for cross-border listings.

The concept release was to be a further stage in an evolution from the SEC's April 1996 news release, which called for a comprehensive set of high quality accounting standards that could be rigorously interpreted and applied, constituting the three key elements which the SEC expected to find in the IASC standards.

In a speech on 10 February 1999, SEC Chief Accountant Lynn E. Turner unveiled the proposal for a concept release as follows:

If, after assessment of the completed core standards, the SEC staff concludes that the current reconciliation requirements should be reduced or removed, the staff will need to bring a rule proposal to the Commission to amend the current filing requirements for foreign private issuers.

The Commission then could publish proposed amendments for public comment. If it did so, the staff would analyse the comments received and develop final recommendations for the Commission, which then would be issued, if approved by the Commission, in an adopting release.

This procedure is mandated by U.S. law and applies to any SEC rules or regulations.

One step that is being planned, is a concept release to seek public input regarding some of the key issues that have been identified to date. Let me talk for a few moments about some of those issues.

When the Commission considers changes to its accounting and disclosure requirements, it must evaluate the impact of potential changes on capital formation, including the possible impact on the cost of capital for domestic companies, and, critically, on investor protection. These basic concerns helped shape the three criteria for assessment of the completed standards identified in the SEC's April 1996 press release.[293]

He then referred to the need to build an international financial reporting 'infrastructure' comparable to the one that supports the high quality of financial reporting in the United States. He signalled the need for regulatory oversight of the setting of accounting standards and for regulatory involvement in enforcing compliance with the standards. Included in the infrastructure, he said, were 'auditing, quality control and independence standards that will result in high quality audits on a worldwide basis', which he linked to the concerns recently raised by the World Bank. In a speech in December 1998, Turner had said,

> I must mention the concerns that have been expressed by the World Bank with respect to the quality of audits in some foreign countries. They are concerned that if a major accounting firm uses its own name on the audit opinion of a foreign company's financial statements, but has not applied rigorous audit standards indicative of a high quality audit, investors and lenders may be misled. I share the concern of the World Bank regarding this issue.[294]

Turner alluded not only to the Asian financial crisis of 1997 but also to the Russian and Brazilian financial crises of 1998 and 1999, respectively, which raised serious questions of transparency in international financial markets.[295] A study conducted for the United Nations Conference on Trade and Development (UNCTAD) also dealt with the criticisms raised about the lack of transparency.[296] Thus, in addition to treating in the concept release the issue of a US GAAP reconciliation if foreign company financial statements were prepared in accordance with IASC standards, it was also evident, partly influenced by a series of world financial crises, that other issues, such as auditing standards, worldwide quality control in the major audit firms, and regulatory enforcement, could not be divorced from the question of the acceptability of international accounting standards.[297] Also, it became clear that it was integral to the endorsement of the IASC's core standards that, going forward, the IASC was restructured in such a way that it could be counted upon to continue to issue high quality accounting standards. All of these matters came under the head of the financial accounting infrastructure.

Mary Tokar began drafting the concept release in early 1999,[298] but its completion was put off until after the IASC board had completed action on its restructuring (*see* Chapter 13). If the IASC board had opted to restructure itself along lines that were not acceptable to the SEC, the concept release might well not have viewed the board as a source of high-quality standards.[299] Once the IASC board had, in November 1999, approved a restructuring plan that satisfied the SEC, the concept release could be readied to solicit the views of commentators on whether, and to what degree, reliance should be placed on IASC standards and on the IASC as a high-quality standard setter. All that remained for the restructuring plan to become final was the approval by the IASC's member bodies, which occurred in May 2000.

The concept release was issued on 16 February 2000.[300] The basic issue raised in the release was whether there exists a 'supporting infrastructure' to assure that the IASC standards would be rigorously interpreted and applied, which was the third element in the SEC's April 1996 news release. In the release, the SEC argued that high-quality accounting standards must be supported by an infrastructure that ensures that the standards are rigorously interpreted and applied, and that issues and problematic practices are identified and resolved in a timely fashion. Elements of this infrastructure include:

- effective, independent and high-quality accounting and auditing standard setters;
- high-quality auditing standards;
- audit firms with effective quality controls worldwide;
- profession-wide quality assurance; and
- active regulatory oversight.[301]

When composing the release, the SEC was troubled by evidence of a wide-ranging lack of compliance with IASC standards. Among non-US companies that claimed they were using IASC standards, many were found not to be following all of the standards, and often their auditors did not disclose this deviation. An extensive survey of 125 adopters of IASC standards conducted by David Cairns, which was cited in the release, depicted the extreme variability of such compliance by companies and their auditors.[302] In a March 2000 speech, SEC Commissioner Isaac C. Hunt, Jr. struck a cautionary note. He said that the SEC itself had 'identified a number of situations involving inconsistent application of IASC standards, and even misapplication of the standards. This history', he added, 'raises the possibility that even the most comprehensive, consistent set of accounting standards can still result in poor quality financial reporting.'[303]

During 1999, the SEC may have acquired first-hand evidence of the lack of regulatory oversight and auditor compliance even with national accounting standards in a major European country. *The Economist* reported that Hans Havermann, the chairman of the German Accounting Standards Board (DRSC), made a special trip to the SEC in 1999 to complain 'that German companies and their auditors were ignoring domestic standards. When the companies listed in America, he asked plaintively, could the SEC please try to get them to behave?'[304] Lynn Turner, who said he met with Havermann and with Karl-Hermann Baumann, the deputy chairman of the DRSC and chairman of Siemens' supervisory board, recalls assuring them that the SEC would 'absolutely and unequivocally' support the DRSC and enforce its standards.[305] Havermann denies that the purpose of the visit was other than to acquaint the SEC with the recently founded DRSC.[306]

An unchecked discretion by companies in their adoption of IASC standards and even of national standards was, in the SEC's view, an obstacle to comparability, thus justifying the need for its multifaceted financial reporting infrastructure.

In the concept release, the SEC posed twenty-six questions on which it sought comments from companies, investors, securities professionals, accountancy firms, and other interested parties. Twelve were questions addressing whether the IASC standards constituted a comprehensive set, were of high quality, and could be rigorously interpreted and applied. Most of the remaining questions dealt with a series of auditing and regulatory issues, including the usefulness of the SEC's reconciliation requirement. No. 14 in the list asked whether the SEC's acceptance of IASC standards should be predicated on the IASC's successful restructuring in line with the SEC's expectations. In the discussion leading up to the question, the SEC said:

At this time, we do not anticipate adopting a process-oriented approach (like our approach to the FASB) to IASC standards. Instead, we expect to continue a product-oriented approach, assessing each IASC standard after its completion. Nonetheless, the quality of the standard-setter has relevance to our consideration of the IASC standards, particularly with respect to implementation and interpretation questions. [footnote omitted]

The key question, No. 4, was, 'Are the IASC standards of sufficiently high quality to be used without reconciliation to U.S. GAAP in cross-border filings in the United States?'

As always, the SEC was a reluctant partner. *IASC Insight* observed that 'The SEC is venturing into what are, for it, unfamiliar waters... [and is] understandably wary of opening the door to any system where its responsibilities to the US capital markets might be compromised.'[307]

In his March 2000 speech, SEC Commissioner Hunt emphasized a view that Chief Accountant Michael Sutton had expressed in 1996: 'To be acceptable [to the SEC], the IASC standards must be able to require the same *quality* of reporting as U.S. GAAP, but need not mirror U.S. GAAP.'[308] *IASC Insight* reported in 2000, 'When replying to Invitations to Comment during the core standards project, the SEC staff's comments to IASC have tended to focus on the quality of the proposed standards rather than the differences between the proposed standards and US GAAP.'[309]

After the comments on the release were received and analysed, an SEC deputy chief accountant, John M. Morrissey, reported the following summary of the range of views expressed:

On the issues of whether or not IAS are now of sufficiently high quality and whether the SEC should accept IAS without reconciliation to U.S. GAAP, most Europeans say 'yes, definitely' while most U.S. respondents say 'not yet.'

Inside the U.S., the Business Roundtable and several large and prominent U.S. registrants cited the strength of the U.S. capital markets and the importance of high quality information in preserving investor confidence. They reiterated the need to maintain high quality standards to ensure the success of our markets, and said that international accounting standards have improved, but are 'not there yet.' They urged that the existing requirements for reconciliation be continued until the international accounting standards—and the necessary interpretation and auditing infrastructure—reach a higher level of quality.[310]

The FASB and its oversight body, the Financial Accounting Foundation, in their joint letter of comment, urged a continuation of the reconciliation requirement.[311] Even the president and chairman of the AICPA, a founder member of the IASC, wrote, 'Although individual IAS may be of high quality, we do not believe the body of IAS is of sufficiently high quality to be used without reconciliation to U.S. GAAP in cross-border filings in the U.S at this time.'[312]

The concept release has not led to further SEC rule making on international accounting standards. For its part, the SEC has encouraged the International Accounting Standards Board (the restructured IASC, renamed in January 2001) and the FASB to converge their standards at a high level of quality.[313] As a result, one day, there might be no material differences to be reconciled.

Within the IASC, Europeans viewed the concept release as evidence that the SEC will never be satisfied.[314] It was seen as a sign that the SEC was imposing even more conditions.[315]

10.21. THE EUROPEAN COMMISSION PROPOSES TO REQUIRE EU LISTED COMPANIES TO ADOPT IASC STANDARDS

Coming on the heels of IOSCO's endorsement decision, the European Commission announced in June 2000 its surprise recommendation that all listed companies in the European Union adopt IASC standards in their consolidated statements. As a result of this action, IOSCO's endorsement of the IASC standards lost most of its relevance for the European members of IOSCO. The European Commission's recommendation is treated in Section 12.3.7. The coincidence of these two historic decisions, together with the SEC's concept release and the ratification by the IASC member bodies of the restructuring of the IASC (reported in Chapter 13), made 2000 a pivotal year in the history of the IASC. The old era was ending, and a new one was about to begin.

11

Putting Teeth in Harmonization: The IASC Completes Its Core Standards

11.1. INTRODUCTION

Continuing the theme of Chapters 5 and 9, this chapter concludes the discussion of the technical work of the International Accounting Standards Committee (IASC) by treating the standards completed after 1993. That year marked the end of the Comparability and Improvements projects, which had shaped the IASC's agenda from 1987 onwards. As described in Section 10.12, the IASC's failure to obtain the endorsement of the standards revised under the Comparability and Improvements projects by the International Organization of Securities Commissions (IOSCO) was followed by an agreement between the IASC and IOSCO on an IASC work programme that might in due course lead to the desired endorsement. Most of the standards covered in this chapter were part of this 'core' standards agreement of July 1995. The agreement was a turning point in the IASC's history, but important elements of the work programme underlying the agreement had already been in place for some years. For several standards covered in this chapter the discussion will start well before 1993. The treatment of the individual standards in Sections 11.4–11.9 is preceded by an overview of the development of the technical agenda (Section 11.2), and by general comments on the standard-setting process during this period (Section 11.3).

11.2. DEVELOPMENT OF THE TECHNICAL AGENDA

The starting point for all of the IASC's technical work during the 1990s was the review of its strategy conducted at the board meeting of March 1987, in Sydney. This pivotal meeting has already been taken up in Chapters 9 and 10. At that meeting, it was decided that the revision of the IASC's existing standards, rather than issuing standards on new topics, was henceforth to be an important part of its work. The immediate results of that decision were the Comparability and Improvements projects, resulting in the revision of ten standards by the end of 1993.

Apart from the Comparability and Improvements projects, the work of the IASC can be summarized in the following round numbers. Between 1988 and

2000, the IASC initiated twenty-five projects. Of these, one-third consisted of revisions of existing standards, and two-thirds dealt with new topics or with the expanded topical coverage of existing standards. Most of these topical areas were, at least in part, already envisaged in the discussion paper tabled at the March 1987 board meeting.[1] This paper contained a list of topics based on suggestions made by board representatives at various times. The major exception that was not already contemplated in 1987 was the project on intangibles other than goodwill, and the related project on impairment of assets (resulting in IAS 38 and IAS 36, respectively).[2]

The secretariat's agenda paper for the March 1987 meeting also listed some topics that were not subsequently adopted by the IASC. The apparent reason was that these topics were at best peripheral to financial reporting practice in the 1990s (costing, value-added statements, and forecast statements), or dealt with public-sector and not-for-profit accounting. The IASC had never seriously considered not-for-profit accounting. It had indeed been represented by Secretary-General David Cairns on the Public Sector Committee of the International Federation of Accountants (IFAC), since that committee was founded in 1986. The Bishop Working Party (*see* Section 7.5) had recommended in 1989 that the IASC should take over responsibility for public sector accounting from IFAC, a point of view that several Australians who were active in the IASC or in IFAC urged the IASC to accept.[3] Cairns was heavily involved in the preparation of International Public Sector Guideline 1, *Financial Reporting by Government Business Enterprises* (issued in 1989).[4] This Guideline required government business enterprises to use the same accounting standards as private-sector business enterprises. Yet for practical purposes the IASC left the public sector area to IFAC during the 1990s.[5]

The close correlation between the 1987 proposals and the actual work completed during the 1990s was related to the persistent efforts of David Cairns to convince the board of the need for systematic planning of its work programme. From March 1987 onwards, Cairns repeatedly urged the Organisation and Planning Committee (OPC) and the board to approve a multi-year plan of its activities, and he provided a series of draft business plans and five-year plans, all tracing their origin to the March 1987 strategy review. The board did approve a five-year plan in June 1990, but felt so little committed to it that Cairns concluded that the plan had already been effectively abandoned by 1991.[6] Nevertheless, his efforts brought a degree of continuity to the IASC's planning that contrasts strongly with the ad hoc choice of topics characteristic of the IASC's early years. Cairns continued to supply the OPC (subsequently the executive committee) and the board with frequently updated plans for the technical work, and this practice was continued by his successor, Sir Bryan Carsberg.

The need to satisfy IOSCO exerted a crucial influence over the IASC's planning during the 1990s. In August 1993, Chairman Eiichi Shiratori was informed that IOSCO's Working Party 1 (WP1) had agreed on the necessary components of a core set of standards (*see* Section 10.10). Although IOSCO's list of thirty-seven topics was not keyed to specific IASC standards, it would have been clear that all but a few of the topics were to some degree covered either by existing standards, current projects, or by projects marked for future action by the board. At a general level, the core standards list was in harmony with the IASC's own planning. The list did not indicate whether IOSCO was prepared to endorse the existing standards on core topics, or the ones about to be finished with the conclusion of the Improvements project in November 1993 but, at the IASC it was expected that IOSCO would endorse some of these standards in 1994.[7] For this reason, and also because the IASC's limited resources were fully tied up in a number of major projects that would continue to run for several years (in particular, financial instruments, intangibles, and income taxes, but also segment reporting, earnings per share, and presentation of financial statements), the August 1993 advice from WP1 on the core standards list had no immediate impact on the IASC's work programme.[8]

This changed following the so-called 'Shiratori letters', sent by IOSCO to the IASC in June 1994. These letters specified in far greater detail than the August 1993 communication what the deficiencies, from IOSCO's point of view, in the extant IASC standards were. It became clear that the IASC would have to revisit some of the recently revised standards, as well as to complete its ongoing projects. As detailed in Section 10.10, the IASC prepared a revised work programme on the basis of the 'Shiratori' letters during the second half of 1994. After some modifications, this formed the basis of an agreement between the IASC and IOSCO, announced in July 1995, that successful completion of this work programme would result in 'a comprehensive set of standards' which IOSCO would consider for endorsement.[9]

The programme on which the agreement was based listed sixteen projects to be completed by June 1999 (see Table 11.1, as well as the listing of projects in Appendix 4). The relation of these projects to the IASC's ongoing work at the time can be summarized as follows:[10]

Three difficult and complex projects (financial instruments, income taxes, and intangibles) had already been on the IASC's active agenda since the late 1980s. These projects are discussed in Sections 11.4–11.6. As will be seen, the IASC combined its project on intangibles with the required revisions to existing standards on research and development, impairment, and goodwill, which were listed as three separate projects in the core standards work programme.

Five projects dealt with topics not yet covered by existing standards. Projects on earnings per share and agriculture were already under way. Projects on interim reporting, discontinued operations, and provisions and contingencies still had to be initiated. It may be noted that agriculture and provisions were included in the work plan even though IOSCO had not asked for these projects. The project on agriculture grew out of the IASC's own wish to do something of particular relevance to developing countries. In practical terms, the project resulted from an agreement between the IASC and the World Bank. Provisions had been added at the initiative of the IASC itself, and it was combined with IOSCO's request for a revision of the standard on contingencies (IAS 10). Provisions, interim reporting, and discontinued operations had been on the IASC's lists of possible future topics since 1987. Apart from agriculture (Section 11.9.2), these new projects are treated in Section 11.7.

Table 11.1. The core standards work programme

Topic[a]	Start date[b]	End date		Impact on standards		
		Planned[c]	Actual[d]	Revised	Withdrawn	New
A. Projects in progress by July 1995						
Income taxes	3/1987	11/1995	9/1996	IAS 12		
Financial instruments	6/1988	11/1997	12/1998			IAS 32, IAS 39
Intangibles	4/1989	6/1996	7/1998	IAS 22	IAS 4, IAS 9	IAS 36, IAS 38
Earnings per share	3/1990	3/1997	1/1997			IAS 33
Segments	3/1992	3/1997	1/1997	IAS 14		
Presentation	3/1993	11/1997	7/1997	IAS 1		
Agriculture	6/1994	11/1998	12/2000			IAS 41
Retirement benefit costs, etc.	11/1994	3/1999	1/1998	IAS 19		
B. Projects started after July 1995						
Interim reporting	11/1995	3/1999	1/1998			IAS 34
Discontinued operations	11/1995	11/1998	4/1998			IAS 35
Provisioning & contingencies	3/1996	6/1999	7/1998			IAS 37
Leases	6/1996	6/1999	11/1997	IAS 17		
Research & development revision	6/1996	6/1998	7/1998	combined with intangible assets		
Impairment revision	6/1996	6/1998	7/1998	combined with intangible assets		
Goodwill revision	6/1996	6/1999	7/1998	combined with intangible assets		
Investments revision	11/1997	6/1999	3/2000		IAS 25	IAS 40

[a] Topic descriptions as in 'Draft IASC Work Plan—1995–1999', attached to 'IASC and IOSCO Reach Agreement', IASC press release, 11 July 1995.

[b] Board meeting (month/year) in which project was added to agenda.

[c] Planned end dates as in 'Draft IASC Work Plan—1995–1999', 11 July 1995.

[d] Board meeting in which final standard was approved for publication.

The remaining projects were revisions of existing standards. Of these, the revisions of the standards on segment reporting (IAS 14) and retirement benefits (IAS 19) were seen as more challenging than the revision of IAS 1, *Presentation of Financial Statements*, and the limited revision of IAS 17, *Accounting for Leases*. By July 1995, the revisions of IAS 1 and IAS 14 were already in progress. These revision projects are discussed in Section 11.8. The required revision of IAS 25, *Accounting for Investments*, was initially seen as a limited revision following completion of the financial instruments project. It would subsequently develop into a major separate standard on investment properties (IAS 40, discussed in Section 11.9.1), but by that time the standard was no longer regarded by IOSCO as an indispensable component of the core package.

In sum, the core standards agreement did not dramatically alter the direction of the IASC's work. Nor, as shown by the standards on agriculture and provisions, did it dominate the agenda to the exclusion of all other concerns. Yet it was undoubtedly of great significance for setting a specific target date for completion. To complete the core standards on time, or rather to obtain IOSCO's endorsement as soon as possible, became urgent as more and more multinational companies were seen to adopt US generally accepted accounting principles (US GAAP) rather than IASC standards. As discussed more fully in Section 10.13, the IASC responded to this pressure by accelerating its work programme in March 1996, when it shifted the planned completion of the core standards from mid-1999 to March 1998. In the end, the last standard of the core package was completed in December 1998. This was a miraculous achievement for a part-time board with limited staff support.

From the middle of 1997 onwards, the IASC began to prepare for the post-core period. It gradually began to add projects to its agenda that were outside the core, beginning with a project on insurance. This was followed by projects on discounting, emerging markets, extractive industries, business combinations, reporting financial performance, and bank disclosures. Apart from discussion papers on insurance and extractive industries, none of these projects, discussed in Section 11.9.3, resulted in IASC publications.

11.3. THE STANDARD-SETTING PROCESS

During the 1990s, the IASC's standard-setting process was in essence still based on the procedures described in the 1973 Constitution. Standards were approved for publication by a vote of at least three-quarters of the delegations. Standards were preceded by the publication of an exposure draft, approved by at least two-thirds of the delegations. Although not envisaged in the 1973 Constitution, the IASC had begun in 1978 to precede exposure drafts by the limited circulation of preliminary exposure drafts (*see* Section 5.2). Starting with the project on financial instruments, this stage was replaced by the circulation of a (draft) statement of principles, as used by the Canadian Institute of Charted Accountants (CICA).[11] Once approved by the board, a statement of principles became the basis for preparing an exposure draft.

All drafts were prepared by steering committees, of which often only the chairman was a member of a board delegation, and which were supported by IASC staff. Despite the basic continuity in procedures, the way this basic framework was put to use during the 1990s differed in several respects from earlier periods. The differences were partly the result of gradual evolution, and partly of deliberate decisions. Chapter 8 described important aspects of these changes, in particular the growing size and changing composition of the IASC board and the increase in the IASC's technical staff. This section comments on some of the more specific features of the IASC's standard-setting process during the 1990s that, together with the discussions in Chapter 8, serve as a common background to the individual standards discussed in this chapter.

11.3.1. Due Process and Short Cuts

One characteristic of the IASC during the 1990s was a greater awareness of the significance of defining its own due process, and of adhering to it. The heightened interest in due process was inspired at least in part by the growing importance to the IASC of gaining recognition in the United States. As viewed by Arthur Wyatt, just before he assumed the IASC's chairmanship in 1990, the IASC's operating procedures were not unlike those of the Accounting Principles Board (APB) (1959–73), the predecessor of the Financial Accounting Standards Board (FASB),[12] which may well have been a gentle way of saying that there was scope for improvement. Growing contacts with the North American securities regulators in IOSCO also made the staff and at least some board members more conscious that the IASC's procedures resembled the more relaxed approach to standard setting found in most board member countries rather than the more rigorous North American tradition.[13] But the increasing workload and greater time pressure on the IASC also raised due-process questions. Whereas during the 1970s and 1980s it had not mattered greatly whether a standard was delayed for half a year or more, in the context of the Improvements project, and even more so during the core standards phase, it was vital that the IASC adhered to its tight schedule. A decision, for instance, whether changes to a draft were significant enough to require another round of exposure demanded a careful evaluation of what exactly the IASC owed its constituents in terms of the opportunity to comment on drafts.

Hence, the same factors that made the IASC more aware of the importance of due process also tempted it to simplify its procedures. The board's decision of March 1996 to advance the planned completion date of the core standards included the adoption of a 'fast-track' procedure. Following this procedure, all revision projects would move directly to an exposure draft, without a preliminary discussion document such as a draft statement of principles. All other projects would be limited to one preliminary discussion document (in some earlier cases both an issues paper and a draft statement of principles had been circulated) and an exposure draft. The exposure period for preliminary documents and exposure drafts—which in the previous years had ranged from three to eight months for exposure drafts, depending on the complexity of the topic, was limited to three months.[14] When the IASC published its proposals, it was careful to anticipate criticism and to emphasize that the fast-track procedure did not impair its due process.[15] Nevertheless, the IASC remained vulnerable on this issue, and criticism continued to emanate both from Europe and the United States, as well as from the board delegations themselves.[16]

11.3.2. Steering Committees and Technical Staff

The trend towards larger steering committees, which gradually began in the 1980s, continued in the 1990s. The IASC's first steering committees had consisted of three members, including the chairman. From 1990 onwards, steering committees had at least five members. When IOSCO and the European Commission began to send observers to steering committee meetings, the number of people attending could exceed fifteen. As in Chapters 5 and 9, the members of the various steering committees are mentioned in the notes following the first reference to each steering committee chairman in the text.

Service on steering committees became more popular as the IASC gained in visibility, and by 1996 the IASC's staff had some difficulty in handling the large numbers of nominations for steering committee membership.[17] Prior to 1994, the IASC selected the member bodies to be represented on the steering committees, and left the selection of the individuals to these member bodies. From 1994 onwards, the IASC allowed all member bodies to nominate individuals for each steering committee. The executive committee would then make a recommendation on the composition of the steering committee for approval by the board.[18] For the steering committee on provisions, no fewer than thirty-eight individuals were nominated by the various member bodies.[19]

Despite this popularity, the usefulness of steering committees was occasionally called into question. Throughout his period of service, Secretary-General David Cairns played a prominent role in the IASC's technical work. Gradually, other staff members, including Peter Clark, Terry Harding, Liesel Knorr, Paul Pacter, Laurence Rivat, Paul Sutcliffe, and others were indispensable as project managers to bring the increasingly complex standards projects to completion. The idea that the staff might take over a larger part of the drafting role or even make steering committees redundant had its supporters. In addition, there was occasional friction over the degree to which steering committees were authorized to issue preliminary documents, such as draft statements of principle, without approval by the board or clearance by the technical staff.[20] During the early 1990s, when the IASC's staff was still quite small, ideas about an enhanced role for the staff were perhaps somewhat premature. Nevertheless, Cairns raised these issues with the executive committee and the board in 1994. Apart from minor modifications of procedures, the result was a confirmation of the general principles that steering committees would as a rule be appointed for all projects.[21]

Cairns' successor Carsberg also favoured a strengthening of the staff relative to the steering committees, and he had more staff at his disposal than Cairns ever had. Although this did not lead to major changes in the formal definition of steering committee roles and procedures, it did mean that he was not reluctant to economize on steering committee work in order to meet the tight deadline of the core standards programme. The most notable instance, to be discussed below, was the final stage of the financial instruments project, when the staff completely supplanted the steering committee and worked directly with the board. As some board delegations set much store by the steering committee system, there were occasional tensions when it was believed that steering committees were not allowed to play their proper role.

11.3.3. Involvement of National Standard Setters

As discussed in Section 8.2.1, the 1990s saw a growing involvement by national standard setters in the work of the IASC. A member of the FASB attended board meetings from 1988 onwards, first as a guest and then as an observer. The number of representatives from national standard setters in country delegations increased over time. It was generally agreed by board members and staff that the direct participation of the members of national standard setters in board meetings helped to bring the level of technical discussions, although not necessarily low to begin with, to very respectable heights.

The enhanced ties with standard setters also took the shape of a number of collaborative projects. The project on financial instruments was, in its early stages, undertaken in cooperation with the CICA, which provided the staff resources. The project on earnings per share was carried out in cooperation with the FASB. The project on provisions ran parallel with a similar project of the UK Accounting Standards Board (ASB), and the ASB again provided most of the staff work. The revision of IAS 14, *Reporting Financial Information by Segment*, was coordinated with a subsequently started project of the FASB and the CICA.

Despite the significance of other national standard setters, in particular from Australia and Canada, it is fair to say that the most persistently influential standard setters during the later 1990s were the FASB and the ASB. The FASB's significance, as always, was based on its unquestioned superiority over all others in terms of resources, experience, and the volume and rigour of its extant accounting standards. In comparison, the ASB was a recent creation which was still reshaping financial reporting in the United Kingdom. Its influence in the IASC was perhaps less due to its accumulated body of standards than to the fertility of its thinking and the debating skills of the UK delegation.

As is seen in this chapter, in several of the IASC's technical discussions during this period the UK and the US delegations, or the ASB and the FASB, took different positions, and the IASC sometimes veered towards the one, and sometimes towards the other. Whenever discussions about the alleged Anglo-American dominance of the IASC flared up, the frequent differences of opinion between the United Kingdom and the United States would be cited to reassure the sceptics that there was no such thing as a unified Anglo-American bloc, or Anglo-American accounting. To the sceptics, of course, this was beside the point, as divisions among the United States and the United Kingdom did not prevent that, together, the English-speaking delegations made a disproportionately large contribution to the debates in the board.[22]

11.3.4. Comment Letters

An analysis of the comment letters received by the IASC on its exposure drafts of the 1990s illustrates the growing interest in the IASC's activities in widening circles.[23] As noted in Chapter 5, the volume of comment letters had settled at the modest level of thirty to forty for each exposure draft during the 1980s. The bulk of the responses typically came from the national accountancy bodies that made up the membership of the IASC, although in some countries there were consultative arrangements to ensure that the comments from the accountancy bodies reflected a wider range of views. E32, 'Comparability of Financial Statements' (published in 1989), broke that pattern by attracting more than 160 comment letters, including many from companies and other business organizations. That level would never be reached again by the IASC. The next fifteen exposure drafts (E33–E47), issued between 1988 and 1992 and which included the ten exposure drafts of the IASC's flagship Improvements project, resulted in between thirty and fifty-five comment letters each. In that sense, E32 had not immediately set off a sustained wider interest in the work of the IASC. The exception was E40 on financial instruments on which the IASC received more than seventy comment letters (not counting the more than 110 letters received by the CICA from Canadian respondents). With the second exposure draft on financial instruments, E48 (1994), there was a definitive shift to a higher volume of responses. The IASC and the CICA each received about eighty comment letters, and for the IASC's remaining twenty exposure drafts (E49–E68), the amount of comment letters typically was between seventy and one hundred.[24] Although the IASC staff would have appreciated a greater number of comments as vindication of the IASC's aspiration to be a world-wide standard setter, it was generally felt that the comments it did receive provided sufficient input for the board's deliberations. No systematic attempts were made to increase the number of responses.[25]

Throughout the 1990s, the accountancy bodies remained the most reliable respondents to the IASC's exposure drafts, providing, on average, above a quarter of all comments. Financial analysts' organizations, particularly the Security Analysts Association of Japan and the Association for Investment Management and Research (AIMR), made up a small but faithful group of respondents. The delegation of financial analysts had been the first board delegation not representing a national accountancy body. From the early 1990s onwards, after they had accepted observer status, the European Commission and the FASB also regularly provided comments.

Over time, responses from the business community (individual companies and representative organizations) increased from about 25 to 50 per cent of the responses. Until 1994, a large proportion of business comments came from US companies, many of which commented only once or sporadically. After 1994, however, responses from individual US companies all but ceased, in marked contrast to the increasing interest in the IASC in the rest of the world.

Of the handful of companies that commented regularly on the IASC's exposure drafts during the early 1990s, most were represented on the board or the Consultative Group. Staff of the Royal Dutch/Shell Group (the Netherlands and the United Kingdom), including former IASC Secretary Allan Cook, were members of the IASC's Consultative Group for most of the 1980s and 1990s. Nestlé (Switzerland) also became a regular respondent when it was represented in the Consultative Group by Harry Schmid. BHP (Australia) was among the earliest corporate contributors to the IASC. In 1995, one of its directors, Geoffrey Heeley, became a member of the Australian delegation. From 1993 to 1997, South African Breweries, another regular respondent, enabled Ian Somerville to serve as a member of the South African delegation.

After 1994, the pattern of comments from business began to correspond more closely with their actual application of international standards, or with the specific issues at stake. The exposure drafts on financial instruments, employee benefits, and leases brought predictable concentrations of responses from banks and insurance companies, from leasing associations, and from actuarial bodies and firms. The Swiss multinationals formed a distinct group of consistent respondents from business. Since 1995, they were directly represented on the board through the Federation of Swiss Industrial Holding Companies, and, as a group, they were for some years among the most prominent users of IASC standards.

11.4. INCOME TAX: REVISION OF IAS 12

The remainder of this chapter discusses the IASC's standard-setting activity in more detail.[26] An appropriate start is the revision of IAS 12, *Accounting for Taxes on Income* (published in 1979). This revision had its origins in the early 1980s, was actively begun in 1987, and resulted in a new standard, IAS 12, *Income Taxes*, in 1996. This long and difficult project provides a good illustration of the changes in the IASC's standard-setting process as it began to transform itself into a standard setter for global capital markets.[27]

11.4.1. Eliminating the Deferral Option

As discussed in Section 9.2, the IASC followed a policy of periodically reviewing its published standards from the early 1980s to 1987. These reviews did not convince the board of the need to revise any standards, with the exception of IAS 3, *Consolidated Financial Statements*, and IAS 12. At the same board meeting, in March 1987, when the revision of IAS 12 was agreed, the board set out on a new course by launching the Comparability project in which all of its other standards would be revised in order to eliminate options.

It would perhaps have been more logical to include IAS 12 in the Comparability project, but the revision of IAS 12 had probably already established itself in the minds of the board members as a distinct project.[28] Nonetheless, in the initial stages, the revision of IAS 12 was simply aimed at eliminating options, and the approach taken was indistinguishable from that of the parallel Comparability project.

IAS 12 as approved in 1979 did contain several major options (*see* Section 5.8.6). The most important was that reporting companies had a choice between the deferral method, required in the United States and Canada, and the liability method, which was commonly used or required in most other countries with a published norm on the subject. In addition, IAS 12 allowed a choice between comprehensive and partial tax allocation. The United Kingdom in particular had insisted on the inclusion of partial allocation. When a questionnaire on IAS 12 was sent out in 1986, when it was due for periodic review, nineteen out of twenty-two member bodies, including the American Institute of Certified Public Accountants (AICPA), had indicated that IAS 12 should allow the liability method only. Apparently, a belief that the time had come for the IASC to begin reducing options was widely shared by the member bodies. Only the Dutch took the position that had hitherto prevailed in the IASC. The NIVRA, in words reminiscent of former IASC Chairman Hans Burggraaff, wanted to retain both methods, 'as good reasons can be given for different methods and, depending on circumstances, the most appropriate method may differ'.[29] The comments from the member bodies had indicated rather less support for the elimination of partial allocation. Not just the United Kingdom, but also others, including France, the Netherlands, New Zealand, and Hong Kong, wanted to retain a choice even though they might prefer comprehensive allocation.[30]

The steering committee, initially chaired by the French delegate Raymond Béthoux, succeeded in 1994 by Bernard Jaudeau, developed proposals that closely matched the views expressed by the member bodies.[31] In a short time, it prepared an exposure draft which was approved by a unanimous vote of the board in November 1988 as E33, 'Accounting for Taxes on Income'. This exposure draft was an edited version of the old IAS 12, but with the deferral method eliminated. Partial allocation would still be allowed, but only if additional disclosures were provided.

The steering committee cited two main considerations underlying the proposal that led to E33.[32] One was in line with the IASC's traditional approach of ensuring compatibility with the most important national standards: the steering committee noted that the FASB had abandoned the deferral method, implying that this removed an important reason for maintaining the option. In December 1987, the FASB had issued FAS 96, *Accounting for Income Taxes*, to replace APB Opinion No. 11, which had mandated the deferral method.

The second reason was representative of the IASC's new approach: the steering committee argued that the liability method was in keeping with the 'asset and liability orientation in accordance with the IASC Framework for the Preparation and Presentation of Financial Statements'.[33] This was one of the first occasions when the IASC's emerging Framework (of which an exposure draft had been approved in March 1988) was put to use in choosing among alternatives. Conveniently, the traditional and the new approach yielded the same result in this case, as the FASB's change in position followed from the definition of a liability in the FASB's Conceptual Framework, which had served as the main source of inspiration for the IASC's Framework (*see* Section 9.1).[34]

11.4.2. E49: Closer to the United States, Away from the United Kingdom

Unfortunately, the situation in the United States following FAS 96 was not stable. FAS 96 was heavily criticized as difficult and costly to implement, but also as conceptually flawed.[35] Its effective date was deferred three times, until it was superseded in February 1992 by FAS 109, *Accounting for Income Taxes*. Because of this uncertainty, the IASC's steering committee recommended in June 1990 to defer the revision of IAS 12, even though the responses to E33 were generally favourable. An additional reason to delay the project was that, by mid-1990, it had become clear that IOSCO did not merely want to see the elimination of options in the standards, but also additional guidance on many issues. Because of this, the Improvements project had been set up to extend and complete the Comparability project. As the revision of IAS 12 had been running parallel to Comparability, it made sense to see how the Improvements project would work out before redrafting the text of IAS 12.[36] As the Improvements project consumed nearly all the IASC's resources during 1991 and 1992, this meant that the income tax project was put on hold until the end of 1992.

Early in 1993, the opinion within the board was that the publication of FAS 109 had 'unblocked' the situation, and the project began to move forward again.[37] Exposure draft E49, 'Income Taxes', was approved in June 1994. By this time, the IASC's thoughts on the subject had evolved significantly, with the result that E49 moved closer to the US position and away from the United Kingdom.[38]

In 1993, Barry Robbins, a technical partner in Price Waterhouse in San Francisco, joined the steering committee, which was believed to need strengthening, in particular with regard to its knowledge of the complex FAS 109.[39] In 1994, Robbins became a member of the US delegation in the IASC board. In addition, the steering committee obtained the assistance of Raymond Simpson, the FASB's project manager on the income tax project. Profiting from this infusion of experience, the steering committee advised the board that the earlier exposure draft, E33, had not fully captured the shift towards an asset and liability approach that was reflected in FAS 96 and FAS 109. In particular, the board was told that the liability method of accounting for deferred tax was not automatically consistent with an asset and liability approach as embodied in the Framework, because 'liability method' could mean different things.[40] As described in IAS 12 (1979) and E33, and as practised in most countries, the liability method was based on the difference between taxable income and accounting income (timing differences), and on the expected reversal of these differences in the future. Under this approach, the main difference between the liability and deferral methods was that deferred tax assets and liabilities were adjusted for changes in the tax rate under the liability method but not under the deferral method. In FAS 96 and FAS 109, the starting point was not the income statement, but the difference between the book values of assets and liabilities and their 'tax base', that is, their values for tax purposes. The FASB introduced the term 'temporary differences' to distinguish these differences from the traditional 'timing differences'. In practical terms, the difference between the two approaches was that all timing differences were also temporary differences, but not the other way round.

The IASC board agreed with the steering committee that, in order to be true to its Framework, it should move from the 'income statement liability approach' of IAS 12 and E33 to the 'balance sheet liability approach' of FAS 109. This included adopting the FASB's wording in terms of temporary differences and tax base.[41] E49 reflected these decisions. It had taken the IASC board some time to grasp the difference between the two liability approaches. Probably assuming that others might experience similar problems, the board decided that a background paper should be published together with E49 in which the change in approach was explained in detail.⁴²

Another important change in E49, relative to E33, was that it would no longer allow partial tax allocation. This change was suggested to the board by the steering committee on the basis of the comments received on E33. In addition, it was noted that in most countries comprehensive allocation was now required. The major exceptions were South Africa and New Zealand, which permitted partial allocation, and the United Kingdom, where it was required.⁴³ The IASC's intention to eliminate partial allocation was greeted in the UK press in the somewhat dramatic terms of the UK's impending 'international ostracism' and the ASB having 'to toe the line'.⁴⁴ Yet, for the UK delegation and for the ASB, partial allocation—which had been forced on its predecessor, the Accounting Standards Committee (ASC), by political pressure—was no longer a key issue.⁴⁵ To the dismay of the UK business community, the ASB published a discussion paper in 1995 in which it tentatively proposed 'full provisioning' (comprehensive allocation).⁴⁶

11.4.3. Final Difficulties

Between the end of the exposure stage in May 1995 and the approval of the revised IAS 12 in September 1996, the income tax project absorbed a considerable fraction of the IASC's energy, even though, in the end, the final standard did not differ greatly from E49.

At this late stage, a problem emerged over the concept of the tax base, which the IASC believed it had borrowed from FAS 109.⁴⁷ The concept might have been unambiguous in a US context, but the comment letters showed that it was not necessarily true in all jurisdictions that assets and liabilities had clearly defined values for tax purposes.⁴⁸ Although most board delegations were by this stage quite committed to following FAS 109, that standard did not even define the concept of tax base. To solve the problem, the board wrestled inconclusively with a variety of increasingly complex definitions of tax base. An attempt was made to rewrite the standard without using the tax base concept.⁴⁹ In the end, the board decided not to make major changes to E49 on this point, effectively sweeping the issue under the carpet.

Yet not all delegations supported the approach of FAS 109. As indicated above, by 1995 the UK delegation's opposition to the proposed standard had shifted from the traditional issue of partial allocation to criticism of E49's 'balance sheet liability method'. This opposition focused in particular on the question whether the deferred tax liability arising from a revaluation of assets met the definition of a liability in the IASC's Framework. On this point, the United Kingdom was supported by the South African and Swiss Industrial Holding Companies delegations, while the delegation of the International Association of Financial Executive Institutes (IAFEI) was also critical of the standard.⁵⁰ This meant that it would be a close-run vote, but the South African delegation allowed itself to be persuaded that the standard was on balance acceptable.⁵¹ ASB Chairman David Tweedie, who had joined the IASC board in November 1995, realized it might be too late to alter the standard, but he made sure his objections were understood. The result was one of the passionate debates between Tweedie and Jim Leisenring, the FASB observer, which to some extent became part of the IASC's folklore.[52] Subsequently, Tweedie claimed that the experience with IAS 12 alerted him to the need for the ASB to 'get ahead of the game' in order to influence the debates in the IASC.[53] As the standard mustered just enough votes to pass, the IASC was able to announce with some pride that the revised IAS 12 was the first standard to be completed under the core standards agreement.[54]

11.5. FINANCIAL INSTRUMENTS

11.5.1. The Hopeful Start of a Long Journey

The project on financial instruments was unquestionably the most challenging in the IASC's history. It would also become the most controversial element of the legacy of standards bequeathed to the IASC's successor, the International Accounting Standards Board (IASB).

The project began in 1988 and was only provisionally concluded with the approval of IAS 39 in December 1998. There had been other long projects of up to ten years or more, such as foreign currency translation (IAS 21), disclosures in the financial statements of banks (IAS 30), and the revision of IAS 12 on income taxes. But in these cases, there had been periods when work was suspended or carried on at low levels of intensity. With financial instruments, there was hardly any respite, as the subject came up during almost every board meeting between June 1988 and December 2000.

When the IASC decided to work on financial instruments, financial innovation had been proceeding at a swift pace for more than a decade. But it was only in the second half of the 1980s that a sense of urgency began to develop concerning the accounting implications of 'new' or 'exotic' financial instruments, as part of wider concerns over the hidden risks of these instruments to individual businesses and the financial system.[55] As often occurred, the FASB led the way by launching a project on financial instruments in May 1986. The IASC did not immediately give the issue a high priority, although new financial instruments were recognized as an important part of the project to develop a recognition and measurement standard for banks, which had been added to the IASC's agenda in 1987 (*see* Section 9.4.3).[56] In March 1988, the board agreed on a work programme for the period up to 1992, in which a project on financial instruments was scheduled to commence in 1990. At that time, the IASC's immediate priorities were the Framework project and the reduction of options (Comparability project).[57] However, at the next board meeting, in June 1988, the secretariat argued for the immediate inception of a project on financial instruments. The arguments it gave, for instance that 'Many financial instruments are international in character,' and that 'It is desirable that common solutions are obtained at an early stage in the standard-setting process,' would have been as valid in March as they were in June.[58] What prodded the IASC to revise its priorities was a forum on financial instruments organized by the Working Group on Accounting Standards of the Organisation for Economic Co-operation and Development (OECD) in Paris on 31 May–1 June 1988. IASC Chairman Georges Barthès de Ruyter attended the forum, as well as several other members of delegations to the IASC board. Barthès reported: 'At that Forum, a great deal had been expected of IASC; in particular, the Chairman of the OECD Working Group on Accounting Standards [Jean Dupont] had urged IASC to move quickly.'[59] On the spot, Barthès committed the IASC to speeding up its work on financial instruments, which was welcomed by the OECD.[60] Apart from the OECD, the IASC was also given encouragement to work on financial instruments by the Basel Committee of banking supervisors, who were concerned over the impact of accounting for financial instruments on capital adequacy ratios.[61]

The IASC board realized that it was undertaking a daunting project, one in which it could not rely on existing national standards. Many delegations were keen to be represented in the steering committee. As Secretary-General David Cairns noted wryly, all of the countries on the OPC, with the exception of Germany, made sure they had a member on the steering committee.[62] The steering committee's initial chairman was Arthur Wyatt (United States), who was succeeded by Ronald Murray (United States), when the former became chairman of the IASC in July 1990.[63]

Underlining the significance of the project, the steering committee was given its own consultative group, mainly formed by representatives from the member bodies of the IASC's 'main' Consultative Group with a particular interest in financial instruments, such as the International Chamber of Commerce, the joint international banking associations, the Basel Committee, and the OECD.

Given the IASC's slender resources and its ongoing commitment to other major projects, this new project might not have been feasible but for the offer by the CICA to provide staff support for a coordinated project. This offer, mediated by the Canadian staff observer, John Denman, was warmly welcomed by the IASC.[64] CICA staff member John Carchrae became the project manager of the joint project. This type of cooperation was unique for the IASC, as was the intention of the two bodies to consider and ultimately approve the same document. This intention was only partially realized. The CICA and the IASC did issue 'virtually identical' standards on disclosure and presentation but not on recognition and measurement.[65] The cooperation with the CICA, coupled with successive steering committee chairmen from the United States, brought its own operational challenges. The centre of gravity of the project was effectively in North America, with little dependence on the IASC's staff in London.[66]

The scope of the financial instruments project was defined very broadly. It was to deal with all aspects of recognition, derecognition, measurement, and disclosure, as well as with hedge accounting. It was to encompass all financial instruments and to be applicable to all types of enterprises.[67] Nevertheless, with proper resources and arrangements for broad-based consultation in place, it is perhaps understandable that the IASC displayed considerable optimism about the speed with which the project could be completed. The initial expectation was that a final, comprehensive standard might be issued late in 1992 or early in 1993.[68] The IASC maintained this prediction for several years and took pride in the leadership role it hoped to play.[69] In 1992, Chairman Wyatt repeatedly expressed the view in public that a standard was expected in 1993. A former FASB member, he remarked on one occasion that a 1993 date would mean that 'IASC will be years ahead of the FASB in the United States and other standard setting bodies, except, of course, the Canadians.'[70] Like others, Wyatt had by then realized that the issues were more complicated than initially expected. His public optimism was therefore a way of maintaining the pressure on the IASC itself. The primary objective was not speed, but 'to get it right'. If this could be combined with beating the FASB at its own game, so much the better, but it was not an overriding concern.[71]

11.5.2. Identifying the Issues

The IASC's efforts were first concentrated on the production of a statement of principles. Once this had been approved in November 1990, the board agreed swiftly and easily, by a unanimous vote, on the publication of an exposure draft (E40, 'Financial Instruments') in June 1991. The general approach and much of the actual text of E40 closely followed the statement of principles, a draft of which had been circulated among the IASC's member bodies for comment. The steering committee concluded that 'A significant majority of respondents support [the draft statement of principles] in most respects.'[72] This presumably helped the smooth progress towards E40.

E40 already contained the main elements around which the IASC's thinking on financial instruments throughout the 1990s would revolve. These main elements can be summarized as:

1. General definitions of financial assets and financial liabilities, based on cash and on rights and obligations to exchange cash or other financial instruments. From the beginning, the financial instruments project was not to deal just with the new or exotic financial instruments like many forms of derivatives, but also with 'traditional' instruments such as loans.

2. Scope exclusions. From the beginning, it was clear that accounting for interests in subsidiaries and associates should not be radically changed at this stage, and that most if not all of these investments would continue to fall under IAS 27 and IAS 28. But other exclusions, like insurance contracts, remained controversial throughout the project.

3. Presentation standards dealing with offsetting and classification. An important issue was the classification of financial instruments as between equity and liabilities.

4. Criteria for recognition and derecognition of financial instruments.

5. A 'benchmark' mixed-measurement model in which the measurement of financial instruments (fair value or historical cost) and the treatment of recognized gains and losses (in equity or through profit and loss) differed for several classes of financial instruments. In E40, financial instruments used for hedging were seen as one of these classes.
6. An alternative model by which all financial instruments were measured at fair value, with gains and losses reported in income.

In terms of charting the main issues and defining the basic concepts, subsequent developments did not move much beyond E40. In some respects, notably the definitions of financial assets and liabilities, the solutions of E40 were accepted at an early stage, and would find their way into the final standards. But in general, E40 merely marked the point at which the board had identified the relevant questions. From this point onwards, the project began to run into difficulties, and it became much more protracted than initially planned. By the time the board had to decide how to move forward following E40, that is, in the spring of 1993, it had become clear both what was the nature of the technical issues, and why it was difficult to resolve them.

Firstly, there were a few basic issues. Chief among these was whether it was proper to use management intent as the criterion to assign financial instruments to the various measurement categories. E40 generally was based on management intent, following traditional practices in many countries, including the United States. Those who opposed this traditional approach advocated the use of fair value measurement for as many financial instruments as possible. This, it was argued, would increase the relevance of the resulting information, and it would reduce the risk of earnings management inherent in reliance on management intent.

Fair value had already made a modest debut in the IASC standards in the early 1980s (*see* Section 5.12.1), following the example of US GAAP. As in the comparable US standards, fair value was used in IAS 16, 17, 18, and 22 in a supportive role, in order to determine the historical cost of an item acquired in a non-monetary transaction, or as a criterion for deciding whether a lease should be classified as an operating or a finance lease. Fair value was not mentioned in the IASC's Framework, and prior to the financial instruments project, the IASC standards showed little awareness that fair value might be used as the basis for periodic remeasurement of assets or liabilities. The exceptions were found in IAS 25 and 26 (approved in 1985 and 1986, respectively) where it was acknowledged that fair value was the proper basis for measuring investments for certain specialized investment enterprises and for the plan assets of retirement benefit plans. As in the United States, it was the financial instruments project which brought fair value into the mainstream of accounting by enterprises generally.

Within the IASC, the Australian delegation and in particular Warren McGregor were the most consistent advocates of a fair value approach. The Australian Accounting Research Foundation (AARF) had begun to work on financial instruments around the same time as the IASC, and in 1990 it published a commissioned study which advocated fair value measurement for all financial instruments.[73] Yet the idea found considerable support among other delegations as well. Indeed, the board had instructed the steering committee to prepare two versions of the exposure draft that would become E40, one in which full fair value was the benchmark treatment, and one in which it was an allowed alternative. In June 1991, the board chose the version in which the mixed-measurement, or modified historical cost basis, was the benchmark, which then became E40.[74] Related to this basic issue were others, such as the question of whether unrealized gains might be taken into income.

Secondly, there was a broad range of specific issues on which there was agreement in general terms, or on which there were shades of opinion rather than radically divergent views. Here, it often proved difficult to choose the exact wording of the standard. For instance, most board delegations agreed that the reclassification of financial instruments between the various measurement groups should be restricted to limited circumstances but not entirely ruled out. The problem was, of course, how to define the 'limited circumstances' in a way that was neither too restrictive nor too permissive. The financial instruments project raised a large number of problems like this, in which the consequences of small changes in wording had to be considered carefully.

In a general sense, these problems were not unique to financial instruments. When developing other standards, the IASC had also faced fundamental issues and problems of wording. But there were several reasons why they were more difficult to handle in the case of financial instruments.

First of all, the subject was new to most board members, and developments in financial engineering continued apace as the project went along. While it was not too difficult for board members to comprehend the issues at a high level of abstraction, many continued to have difficulties envisaging how the rules would work across the bewildering variety of specific financial instruments and situations that might be encountered in practice. Continuous fine-tuning of the drafts was necessary as the board gained more knowledge of financial instruments.[75]

Many companies and other interested parties, particularly outside North America, were following a similar learning curve as the board members. This meant that the significance and potential impact of the IASC's work on financial instruments were initially not widely understood or appreciated. As a result, it was difficult for the IASC to obtain a consistent view of what would be acceptable to its constituents and the users of its standards. For instance, the generally positive reactions to the IASC's draft statement of principles (1990), which had formed the basis of E40, had come almost exclusively from the English-speaking world, with a majority of 60 per cent coming from Canada alone.[76] Rather more critical views, especially from Japan, came in only after E40 had been published. Even after an already long response period for E40 (from September 1991 through May 1992), the Japanese Institute of Certified Public Accountants (JICPA) expressed its concern in early 1993 that many potential Japanese respondents had not had enough time to respond or were not yet fully aware of the issues.[77]

The financial instruments project was complicated by the unique position of the United States. In the case of most of the earlier standards, the United States had already issued a domestic standard on the issue when the IASC added the topic to its agenda, but so would have several other member countries. This made the search for an IASC standard a relatively straightforward process of striking a balance between several co-existing national approaches. With financial instruments, however, the United States was the only country where substantial progress had been made, yet by the time the IASC began seriously to consider how to move forward with E40, in the spring of 1993, the course to be taken in the United States was by no means settled, particularly in the thorny areas of derecognition and hedge accounting. In contrast to the IASC, which was seeking to develop a comprehensive standard dealing with all aspects of all types of financial instruments, the FASB had adopted a piecemeal approach. By early 1993, the FASB had issued two standards on disclosure, FAS 105, *Disclosure of Information about Financial Instruments with Off-Balance-Sheet Risk and Financial Instruments with Concentration of Credit Risk* (March 1990), and FAS 107, *Disclosures about Fair Value of Financial Instruments* (December 1991). It was about to issue a standard on recognition and measurement for a limited range of non-derivative financial instruments, FAS 115, *Accounting for Certain Investments in Debt and Equity Securities* (May 1993). In these standards, the FASB, encouraged by the Securities and Exchange Commission (SEC) and the AICPA, was moving gradually towards a more extensive use of fair value to measure financial instruments.[78] Fair value accounting had attracted the attention of the SEC, a body which had, with few exceptions, always championed historical cost accounting, if only because of the failure of historical cost accounting to reveal massive unrealized losses in mortgage portfolios until after many savings and loans associations in the United States had entered bankruptcy. In November 1991, SEC Chairman Richard C. Breeden convened the SEC's first-ever conference on accounting standards, entitled 'Relevance in Financial Reporting: Moving Towards Market Value Accounting'.

In FAS 115, which it considered to be an interim standard, the FASB had arrived at a mixed-measurement model, with management intent as the criterion for classifying financial instruments. However, the FASB recognized the shortcomings of this approach and expected it to be modified on the basis of further work and experience.[79] On behalf of the FASB, Vice-Chairman Jim Leisenring wrote to David Cairns to express his concern that an IASC standard on financial instruments might become an impediment to the FASB's progress. Leisenring wrote that the benchmark proposals of E40

closely reflect practice which has prevailed for a considerable number of years in the U.S. The financial instruments project was added to our agenda in 1986 as a result of requests from constituents (including the Securities and Exchange Commission) based on what were perceived to be inadequacies in existing accounting and reporting requirements for financial instruments. Therefore, it could be expected that our project will result in substantive changes to current practice over time. Such changes would inevitably be in conflict with proposals made in E40.[80]

As Leisenring had suggested, the SEC also expressed itself critically about E40 in its comment letter, written by Chief Accountant Walter Schuetze. But whereas the FASB's letter could be read as an invitation to the IASC to delay its project, Schuetze, a fair value advocate, emphasized the possibility of making it more radical and less dependent on management intent, for instance by making fair value measurement the benchmark treatment.[81]

11.5.3. Failure to Issue a Comprehensive Standard

After spending most of 1992 on the Improvements project, and after allowing time for the analysis of the comment letters which continued to come in well after the May 1992 deadline, the board discussed the project in March 1993.[82] In addition to the critical views of the FASB and the SEC discussed above, the 192 comment letters showed that there was far stronger opposition to the IASC's proposals than could have been surmised from the responses to the preceding draft statement of principles. Yet the steering committee concluded that there was no need to depart from the approach of E40, nor to delay or break up the project as many respondents had suggested.[83] Instead, the steering committee guided the board through a long list of detailed amendments. Most delegations, including the US delegation, supported the steering committee in its overall approach to move towards a standard based on E40. The amendments as approved by the board left the structure of E40 largely unchanged, although there were many carefully considered changes in the wording of the proposed standard. It was agreed, for instance, that financial instruments might be derecognized, not if 'all' (as in E40), but 'substantially all', risks and rewards of the instrument had been transferred to another party.

At this point, the question arose whether these changes justified a new exposure draft. This step would cause a substantial delay and would make it impossible to meet the IASC's self-imposed target of publishing a standard in 1993. In its March 1993 meeting in Tokyo, the board dodged the question by instructing the steering committee to prepare a draft of a standard for consideration in June and possible approval later that year. Meanwhile, an extensive summary of the proposed changes to E40 was published in May 1993 in a special issue of *IASC Insight*. The status of this publication was left vague. *IASC Insight* merely asked for comments without specifying whether a formal exposure draft would follow, or even what the next step in the process would be. By the June 1993 board meeting, it had become clear that there was widespread dissatisfaction outside the IASC with this departure from due process. Through various channels, the IASC had been given to understand that re-exposure was essential for the IASC's credibility, that *IASC Insight* did not attract the same level of comment as regular exposure drafts, and that the time allowed for comment on the May issue was extremely short.[84] However, the board still could not bring itself to decide on re-exposure. It was agreed to invite more comments on the May issue of *IASC Insight* and to make a final decision on re-exposure in November 1993.

Behind the board's reluctance to re-expose in June 1993 was its perception that IOSCO wanted to see swift progress on financial instruments. Unfortunately, the board did not get the right signals from IOSCO on this matter. At this time, no IOSCO observers were attending board meetings. IOSCO was represented on the Consultative Group and on several steering committees. At its June 1993 meeting, preceding the meeting of the board, the Consultative Group had voted in favour of re-exposure of E40 in a straw poll, but IOSCO's representative, Secretary-General Paul Guy, had voted against. This strengthened Deputy Chairman Michael Sharpe's conviction that it was important to IOSCO that the IASC approve a financial instruments standard well before IOSCO's annual conference of October 1994 (in Tokyo) during which the endorsement of IASC standards by IOSCO would be considered.[85] In fact, WP1 and its Accounting and Auditing Subcommittee were not at all concerned about possible delays in publishing a financial instruments standard, and were strongly in favour of re-exposure. When it became clear to WP1 that the IASC was dithering on re-exposure, it informed the IASC that, while there might be differences of views on the substance of E40 within the working party, there was unanimity on the need for further opportunity for public comment.[86]

It appears that it was particularly in Japan that opposition to E40 had begun to develop at a late stage. Apart from the JICPA's generally supportive letter, there had been no comment letters from Japan on E40.[87] The exposure period had ended in May 1992, but as late as October 1993 the Japanese argued in WP1 that the interested parties in Japanese financial circles were 'highly frustrated' with E40 and should be given another opportunity to comment. Moreover, it was pointed out that there had not been a Japanese translation of the May 1993 issue of *IASC Insight*.[88]

When the IASC board met again in November 1993, it could do little else but agree to publish a new exposure draft, E48 'Financial Instruments'. E48 was published in January 1994 with a relatively short comment period, closing on 31 July 1994. The CICA published a parallel exposure draft which differed in several respects from E48.[89] E48 essentially followed the changes proposed in the May 1993 issue of *IASC Insight*, and it was therefore a modified version of E40. Apart from the modified rules for derecognition mentioned above, there were numerous other changes such as the exclusion of insurance contracts and related assets, the requirement to designate financial instruments specifically as hedging instruments, and modified impairment rules.

Although E48 did not differ fundamentally from E40, it was not accepted as easily by the board. Whereas E40 had been approved unanimously, E48 was passed with two abstentions. Three delegations made known that they would not support a standard along the lines of the exposure draft.[90] The problem for the IASC was that objections to the approach taken in E40 and E48 came from two diametrically opposed directions. On the one hand, countries like Germany and Japan were not keen to move in the direction of more fair value, especially if this entailed recognizing unrealized gains in income. On the other hand, the SEC's Walter Schuetze had publicly urged the IASC in October 1993 to move further in the direction of fair value measurement and away from management intent.[91] When the IASC approved E48 in November 1993, the SEC's representatives on WP1 made known their concern to the IASC about the way it had 'ignored' Schuetze's comments.[92]

In 1994, the IASC board met only twice, in June and November. At its June meeting in Edinburgh, the board organized a two-day discussion with representatives of national accounting standard setters (including governmental bodies in charge of accounting) on E48. Standard-setting bodies from twelve countries were represented, as well as the European Commission and the Fédération des Experts Comptables Européens (FEE). All but three of the standard setters came from countries that were represented on the IASC board. Several board members and technical advisers switched roles during the meeting, to act as representatives of their national standard setters.[93] As might be expected, a wide range of opinions was expressed. On valuation, for instance, the Australians thought that the alternative treatment ('full fair value') was preferable to the benchmark mixed-measurement treatment. The FASB was sympathetic to fair value measurements, although it noted that this did not solve all hedge accounting issues. The Canadian standard setter, on the other hand, had omitted the full fair value option from its own exposure draft, which had been published in tandem with E48. European standard setters pointed out that the Fourth Directive limited the use of fair value and did not allow the inclusion of unrealized gains in income. But despite the many different points of view, a common thread running through many of the comments was that the standard setters preferred to see the IASC proceed more slowly and allow more ample discussion. The FASB's Jim Leisenring and the UK ASB's Allan Cook expressed the concern that an IASC standard might 'set in stone' unsatisfactory approaches and impede progress on domestic standards.[94] A particularly unsatisfactory approach, they said, was the IASC's reliance on management intent for the classification of financial instruments, for offsetting, and for hedging.[95] The FASB expressed the view that using management intent to classify financial instruments into groups with different measurement rules was 'fundamentally flawed', even though it admitted that this was the approach used in FAS 115.[96] As it happened, the FASB continued to rely on management intent throughout the 1990s, and it was asking the IASC to keep the road clear down which it was not yet ready to travel itself.

The standard setters repeated the suggestion, made before in numerous comment letters on E40, that the IASC should split the project into two or more parts so that it could begin with issuing a relatively non-controversial standard on disclosure. The board tentatively agreed to do that when, at the same June meeting, it instructed the steering committee to identify the elements of E48 that could be turned into separate standards.[97] In November, the final step was taken. By then, the combined opposition by those who thought that E48 would further entrench an unsatisfactory approach to financial instruments, as well as by those who thought it was already departing too much from current practice, was enough to bring about a 'very painful' decision to split the project into two.[98] The board agreed to publish the materials from E48 dealing with definitions, classification as between equity and liabilities, presentation, offsetting, and disclosure as a separate standard. This was done in March 1995, when the board unanimously adopted IAS 32, *Financial Instruments: Disclosure and Presentation*. The CICA published a virtually identical standard, and the Australian Accounting Standards Board (AASB) promptly issued an exposure draft based on IAS 32.[99]

The publication of IAS 32 followed on the heels of the dramatic collapse of Barings Bank in February 1995 as a result of uncontrolled trading in derivatives. This circumstance helps to explain why the world at large did not see IAS 32 as a climbdown, but rather welcomed it as a timely and credible step in solving a difficult issue to which no one had yet found a fully satisfactory answer.[100] The FASB had just added another disclosure standard to its collection of standards on accounting for financial instruments, by issuing FAS 119, *Disclosure about Derivative Financial Instruments and Fair Value of Financial Instruments* (October 1994). After that, it would take the FASB another four years to issue a standard on the recognition and measurement of derivatives.

11.5.4. Reorganization of the Project

The board's reluctant decision in November 1994 to split the project also included an instruction to the steering committee to continue work on recognition and measurement issues. The executive committee was authorized to review the composition of the steering committee in consultation with the steering committee chairman.[101] The executive committee interpreted this mandate in the broadest possible way. In January 1995, it decided to disband the steering committee upon the completion of IAS 32, and to appoint a new chairman with the charge of forming a new committee. While this was probably a disappointment for some members of the steering committee, there was a general feeling that there was a need to take a fresh look at the issues.[102]

The new steering committee chairman was Alex Milburn, until the middle of 1995 the chairman of the CICA's Accounting Standards Board, and there was no doubt that he became the steering committee's driving force.[103] In 1997, he retired from his (part-time) position with Ernst & Young to work on the project on a full-time basis. Together with Ian Hague, who in 1996 succeeded John Carchrae as the CICA's lead staff member on the project, Milburn prepared many of the steering committee's documents and maintained the momentum of the project.[104]

11.5.5. The IASC Makes Time for a Fundamental Study

With the formation of a new steering committee came the decision not to proceed on the basis of E48. The new committee advised the board to prepare a discussion paper first, which could also serve as a statement of intent. Apart from helping the board to formulate its thoughts, this approach would give 'advance notice' of the board's intentions, so that some of the due process problems of E40 and

E48 might be avoided.¹⁰⁵ Something similar had already been suggested at the June 1994 meeting with national standard setters, when the FASB had urged the IASC to produce 'a comprehensive educational document... so that the benefits of the learning process to date are not lost'.¹⁰⁶ Accordingly, the board charged the steering committee in November 1995 with preparing—by the end of 1996— a 'comprehensive discussion paper', examining 'the reasoning and assumptions underlying significant alternative approaches' and setting out 'proposed principles that will provide the framework for development of specific standards'.¹⁰⁷ In other words, the board deliberately chose to take the long road by way of a study of the basic principles, even though it faced a tight target date to deliver a set of core standards to IOSCO, including one on financial instruments.

In June 1996, Milburn informed the board that the steering committee was working on a discussion paper based on the measurement of all financial assets and liabilities at fair value. In effect, the steering committee was planning to place the 'alternative treatment' of E40 and E48 at the centre of its proposals. Notwithstanding the radical nature of these intentions, the board expressed its support.¹⁰⁸ The outside world was duly informed of developments in the project through articles in *IASC Insight*, which contained standing invitations to comment.¹⁰⁹

Choosing fair value measurement as a basic principle represented a considerable simplification compared to the intent-based classifications of E40 and E48. Nevertheless, it did not automatically provide solutions to some difficult issues, such as derecognition of financial assets and liabilities, and hedging of anticipated transactions. The steering committee worked on these issues through the remainder of 1996 and into 1997, and published its discussion paper, 'Accounting for Financial Assets and Financial Liabilities', in March 1997. Being a discussion paper, it was published on the authority of the steering committee, without formal approval by the board.

The steering committee tried to ensure that the paper would indeed be discussed. Between March and July 1997, members of the committee met preparers, users, and regulators in a number of countries in an intensive programme of special consultations.¹¹⁰ All of this had to take place under heavy time pressure. Comments on the discussion paper were due by 15 July 1997, and a draft standard was scheduled to be submitted to the board in October/November 1997.

11.5.6. The Core Standards Target Date Necessitates an Interim Solution

During the summer of 1997, while the steering committee was looking ahead to the next stage of preparing an exposure draft, uneasiness over the project began to develop in the executive committee.¹¹¹ In its July meeting, the executive committee noted that the programme of special consultations had been very successful in creating good lines of communication between the IASC and its constituents, and that the high quality of the discussion paper had been widely noted.¹¹² Among other things, the executive committee was informed that the SEC's Chief Accountant, Michael Sutton, had praised the document, and had expressed the hope that the IASC would stand its ground, as this would encourage the FASB to go further.[113] Nonetheless, it had also become clear that an attempt to complete the project along the lines of the discussion paper would bring serious difficulties. Strong opposition was said to be widespread in the banking industry, and some aspects caused general concern, particularly the reporting of unrealized gains and losses in income, and the valuation of debt at fair value. The executive committee noted that the target date for completing the standard (at that time, April 1998) 'was looking unrealistic'. In the course of this discussion, Chairman Sharpe raised the possibility of adopting the FASB's standards and other norms on financial instruments as an interim solution, and to cooperate with the leading national standard setters to develop a more permanent standard.[114] Sharpe argued that the FASB was the only standard setter which was 'even close to' having a complete set of standards, and that 'Better standards than those currently adopted by FASB would be difficult for any standard setter to develop on its own.' He also explained that his proposal was only an interim solution, by pointing out that the FASB did not consider its current standards as the last word on the subject either, but had expressed the wish to move towards a different standard in the long run.

After debating this new perspective at length, the executive committee authorized Secretary-General Carsberg to study the idea more closely and to make a proposal for the board to discuss at its next meeting. Carsberg thereupon asked Paul Pacter, a former FASB staff member who had joined the IASC's staff in 1996, to develop an IASC exposure draft on the basis of a compilation of US GAAP on financial instruments. With the help of Jim Leisenring and the FASB staff, Pacter completed this arduous task with a speed that few, if any, people could have matched. The result was a voluminous draft standard, longer by far than any draft standard the IASC had ever considered, in which the relevant sections of many different documents from the body of US GAAP were copied almost verbatim. Pacter's editorial work was limited to rearranging, cross-referencing to other IAS, and bringing the text into line with the IASC's customary style. This document was submitted to the board for its October/November meeting in Paris.[115]

This development came as a surprise to many people, both within and without the IASC, including most members of the board and the financial instruments steering committee. It was announced in a press release issued and simultaneously circulated to the board members by Carsberg on 8 September.[116] In addition, the steering committee members learned that their committee was to be disbanded.[117] Carsberg realized that dropping the proposal like a bombshell without prior consultation with the board and the steering committee would spark controversy. Yet he thought that the alternative was worse, because there would then be a risk that the news about this sensitive issue would leak uncontrollably, necessitating the IASC to make an official statement prior to the board meeting anyway.[118]

The proposal stirred up an international flurry of questions, exchanges of opinions, negotiations, and press comments lasting from early September to the next board meeting on 30 October.[119] The central element of adopting US GAAP was not difficult to understand, and therefore easy to like or dislike. The proposal was said to have caused 'outrage' among Continental Europeans.[120]

The European Commission's John Mogg reacted in a strongly worded letter to Carsberg:

[The proposal] has been understood by many in Europe as a clear choice in favour of US GAAP. This has occurred at a time when many large companies in Europe are hesitating whether they should opt for US GAAP rather than for IAS. There can be no doubt that the cause of IASC risks being severely damaged as a result of this initiative, if we cannot put the discussion back on a firm basis very quickly.[121]

Equally predictable was the point of view of the FASB's chairman, Edmund Jenkins, who welcomed the IASC's plans as 'evidence of the FASB's leadership role in the cooperative effort to harmonize accounting standards throughout the world'.[122]

Yet beyond this basic point were more complex issues. The main question was whether the proposal was necessary, or even helpful, to bring about the endorsement of IASC standards by IOSCO. There were several uncertainties on this score.

The first was the firmness of the target date for completing the core standards, which at that time was April 1998.[123] The date was not set in stone, but it was clearly not desirable to exceed it by too much, given the pressure from European and other companies that wanted to access the US capital markets (see Section 10.13). Moreover, there was a risk that delays beyond 1998 could lead to a disintegration of the core standards agreement, as personnel changes in IOSCO and its member bodies might lead to loss of momentum and commitment.

A second uncertainty was whether IOSCO would be willing to take financial instruments out of the core standards set. Several IASC board delegations suggested this to Bryan Carsberg, probably encouraged by the fact that the European members of WP1 also favoured this approach. However, this was resolutely opposed by the SEC, and it was something that could be decided only at a higher level within IOSCO.[124] As early as June 1997, Carsberg had already been given to understand by SEC Chief Accountant Michael Sutton that it would be unacceptable to the SEC to remove financial instruments from the core standards. So when the IASC board met at the end of October, it was acting on a very remote hope when it instructed Carsberg to sound out IOSCO about this possibility at its next annual conference, which was to take place in Taipei shortly after the board meeting.[125]

On the more realistic assumption that the IASC simply had to deliver a standard on financial instruments before long, the idea of using US GAAP as an interim solution definitely had its attractions. However, as was clear from the press comments, it carried reputational risks. Although it might not actually 'blow the IASC's credibility out of the water',[126] it was certainly not a sign of strength. Moreover, success was not guaranteed. On the one hand, the IASC board knew that the European IOSCO members were by no means enthusiastic about the idea of importing US GAAP, and certainly not about the voluminous draft prepared by Paul Pacter.[127] For its part, the SEC had been critical of the FASB's approach and as recently as the summer of 1997 had encouraged the IASC to proceed along the lines of its March 1997 discussion paper. At the same time, it was known that the IASC was vulnerable to criticism for the quality of its due process, particularly in the United States, where some members of the FASB did not tire of raising this point (*see* Section 10.17). An abrupt change of course made without consulting the steering committee was hardly going to improve the IASC's image in this regard. On balance, it was not very likely that the SEC would disown the FASB's work if it was adopted by the IASC, but nothing could be taken for granted.

A further uncertainty was what the proposal signified for progress on financial instruments worldwide and in the longer term. It could be argued that adopting US GAAP would be a way of supporting the FASB, which was under heavy fire from the banking industry because of its work on financial instruments.[128] In this light, the proposal was attractive to those who favoured some progress on financial instruments, but not too radical a departure from current practice. Others, though, who favoured the full fair value approach of the March 1997 discussion paper, feared that an interim standard, once in place, would be difficult to change. This view was held in particular by the UK and Australian delegations.

Apart from these strategic considerations, the board delegations raised a number of critical questions about specific aspects of the proposal. With all of this in mind, the board rejected the proposal when it was tabled in October. Although there was widespread admiration for Pacter's herculean work, only the US delegation expressed a willingness to concur with the proposal.[129] The board nonetheless accepted the idea of an interim standard. Paul Pacter was, in effect, turned into a one-man steering committee when the board decided that a draft should be prepared by the IASC staff for the April 1998 meeting. This draft was to be based not only on US GAAP but also on the IASC's own E48 and other sources. The board also agreed that the IASC should work together with other standard setters to develop a more permanent comprehensive solution.[130]

11.5.7. IAS 39 Completes the Set of Core Standards

The IASC had to work under intense pressure to complete the interim standard. It had publicly committed itself to the goal of completing the core standards in 1998. Even though IOSCO would not refuse to consider the standards for endorsement if they were completed early in 1999, 'Finalisation of a standard in 1998 would have a high presentational value,' as Secretary-General Carsberg wrote to the executive committee.[131] To meet that target, the board had to approve an exposure draft at its meeting in April 1998. So, in the course of just two meetings (January and April), the board discussed and approved E62, 'Financial Instruments: Recognition and Measurement'. The April meeting was a six-day marathon in Kuala Lumpur. During this meeting, Pacter three times produced a new draft overnight on the basis of the board's discussions that day.[132]

E62 was based on a slimmed-down and slightly modified version of the lengthy compilation of US GAAP that had been rejected by the board in October/November.[133] In a general sense, this meant that E62 reverted to the intent-based, mixed-measurement model of E48, with many modifications in substance and style reflecting the draft's origins in US GAAP. But despite E62's kinship with US GAAP, FASB Chairman Edmund Jenkins wrote to the US delegation on the IASC, calling on them not to support the draft to be put before the April 1998 board meeting.[134] Jenkins pointed out some internal contradictions and criticized the insufficient implementation guidance provided in the draft. But the letter did not go deeply into the technical details. The main point of the letter was the assertion that 'a standard as flawed as this one' would be unlikely to be endorsed by IOSCO, and that it would call into question the IASC's commitment to issue high-quality standards. Jenkins asked the IASC to wait until a permanent standard were to be developed by the national standard setters, and in effect repeated the point the FASB had made on E48: the IASC should wait until the problem was solved elsewhere. However, the IASC could not afford to wait, and for that reason the US delegation voted in favour of E62.[135]

One of the features that had distinguished E48 from US GAAP, but which had fallen by the wayside in E62, was the option to value all financial instruments at fair value. This was a principal reason why the UK and Australian delegations voted against E62.[136] According to the Australian delegation, which 'really opposed IAS 39 from day one', E62 embodied a retrograde approach which partially undid earlier moves towards fair value accounting, both voluntary and forced, across the Australian financial industry.[137] Both delegations also objected because it feared the interim standard would, in the words of David Tweedie, be 'stuck on with superglue because it has a lot of soft options which people won't want to give up'. But most other board members were said to be strongly in favour of the proposals, which were seen as reflecting best current practice.[138]

E62 was published in June 1998, with a short comment period lasting to the end of September. To facilitate the comment process, the exposure draft was, for the first time, published on the IASC's website, and comments were invited 'preferably' by email.[139] As there had been no steering committee for this project since the autumn of 1997, a new steering committee, chaired by Secretary-General Carsberg, was installed to review the comment letters.[140]

The board discussed drafts of a final standard at its meeting in November in Zurich and at an extra meeting in December, in Frankfurt am Main, called specifically for this purpose. There were still many issues on which the board struggled to find the right wording, for instance regarding the 'reliability exception', which allowed valuation at historical cost for certain financial instruments whose fair value cannot be measured reliably. Whereas there was a consensus that there should be an exception of that kind, there was ample scope for disagreement about the strictness of the criteria governing the exception.[141]

The UK delegation made a final attempt to introduce a full fair value option, but within the steering committee, reactions ranged from 'ambivalence' (one member) to 'hostility' (several members), and to 'strong disagreement' (the majority view).[142] The reaction by the board was also negative: in a straw poll, a fair value option was rejected by eight votes to six, with two abstentions.[143] Another issue that had come to the fore during 1998 was macro-hedging. This referred to the practice of hedging combined positions representing multiple risks. The French delegation argued to the end that hedge accounting should be allowed in such cases,[144] but the board decided against. It wanted to limit hedge accounting—essentially a departure from the normal treatment—to specific hedged risks.[145]

At the December 1998 board meeting, in a vote that remained unpredictable until the end, IAS 39, *Financial Instruments: Recognition and Measurement*, was approved with twelve votes in favour, the minimum number required. Australia voted against, and France, the United Kingdom, and the United States abstained (which counted as a negative vote). The reasons of the objectors differed: Australia objected in principle to departures from full fair value; the United Kingdom was still concerned that, without a full fair value option, a flawed interim standard could become deeply entrenched; France was concerned about a lack of reliability and prudence, and the United States had procedural objections, in particular to the speed with which the proposal was rushed through.[146]

The standard was given a distant effective date, with application to financial years starting after 1 January 2001. This was a compromise, allowing some delegations to justify their yes-vote with the expectation that the standard might never have to be applied. After all, the intention was that, by then, the collaborative effort of the national standard setters would have produced a permanent solution.[147]

After it published IAS 39, the IASC took the unusual step to provide detailed implementation guidance in the form of published questions and answers. This step highlighted the complex nature of the standard. It was perhaps also taken with the concerns of the SEC in mind, which had criticized the lack of detailed guidance on the application of IASC standards.[148] In 1998, the FASB had set up a Derivatives Implementation Group to provide similar guidance on the implementation of FAS 133. In the case of the IASC, the guidance was prepared by the staff, exposed for comment, and published in final form on the IASC's website after approval by an IAS 39 interpretations committee set up for that purpose in March 2000.[149]

As it happened, the IASC brought its project on financial instruments to a provisional end shortly after the FASB issued FAS 133, *Accounting for Derivative Instruments and Hedging Activities*, in June 1998. This standard covered some of the major recognition and measurement issues addressed by IAS 39. After a decade of sometimes competitive and sometimes cooperative development, the FASB and the IASC completed their respective projects in a virtual dead heat.

11.5.8. The Joint Working Group and the 'Permanent Solution'

Of the two key elements in the IASC's decision in October/November 1997, one was to issue an interim standard (IAS 39), and the other was to work with national standard setters towards a long-term solution on financial instruments. As with the proposal to adopt US GAAP, the cooperative approach to a fundamental solution had already been announced in Secretary-General Carsberg's press release of 8 September 1997, that is, before the IASC board had had a chance to discuss it. Also prior to the board meeting, concrete steps were taken to move along this track. On 24 September, the G4+1 group of standard setters from Australia,

Canada, New Zealand, the United Kingdom, and the United States (*see* Section 12.6), together with the IASC's Carsberg, met and agreed 'to join their efforts to work to agree a harmonised international standard by 2000'.[150] Initially, it may have been intended to limit the participation in this project to the members of the G4+1.[151] This was not implausible, as the G4+1 had already issued a relevant discussion paper, *Major Issues Related to Hedge Accounting*, in November 1995. In the run-up to the board meeting, though, the executive committee modified the proposal by suggesting a wider range of participating countries.[152]

In the closing months of 1997, a committee known as the Joint Working Group of Standard Setters (JWG) was formed, charged with developing a comprehensive standard for financial instruments. Alex Milburn, chairman of the now-defunct steering committee that had produced the IASC's March 1997 discussion paper, accepted the invitation to represent the IASC, and to serve as the JWG's chairman. Apart from the four original G4 standard setters, the Group included representatives from France, Germany, Japan, and the Nordic Federation (Denmark, Norway, and Sweden). In 1997, Germany did not yet have a standard setter, so that its representative was sent by the Institut der Wirtschaftsprüfer. New Zealand was subsequently added at the initiative of the JWG itself.[153] Ian Hague (CICA), who had served as a project manager on the IASC's financial instruments project, became project manager for the JWG. Although the CICA had decided not to follow the IASC in seeking an interim solution, the Canadian involvement in the search for a financial instruments standard remained strong.[154]

The JWG worked independently of the IASC board, despite the existence of an IASC steering committee set up to liaise with the JWG.[155] It regularly briefed the board about its progress and asked its opinion on numerous issues, but there was some concern within the board that it was unable to devote as much of its attention to the JWG as it should.[156] In December 2000, the 300-page JWG report, *Recommendations on Accounting for Financial Instruments and Similar Items* was published by the participating standard setters. Like the other standard setters, the IASC provided the report with its own 'wraparound' introductory text.

The JWG's report contained the text of a draft standard reminiscent of the full fair value approach of the 1997 discussion paper. However, the intention that this might soon lead to a definitive standard which would cut short the life of the interim standard, IAS 39, has so far proven unfounded. This confirmed the prediction made in 1997 by the South African Institute of Chartered Accountants, when the plan for an interim standard was first raised: 'We believe that once a standard has been issued it will be extremely difficult to change, even if it is stated that it is an interim measure, especially if the change will require more financial instruments to be measured at fair value and gains and losses included in net profit or loss at an earlier stage.'[157] This led to the ironic situation that David Tweedie, the chairman of the IASC's successor body, had to defend IAS 39 against strong opposition in Europe during his first years in office, even though he had consistently opposed the standard as a member of the UK delegation to the IASC.[158]

11.6. INTANGIBLE ASSETS AND IMPAIRMENT

Although no match for financial instruments, the project to develop a standard on intangible assets was also lengthy and complex. The topic was added to the agenda in April 1989. It had not been among the possible topics mentioned in the strategy review paper discussed at the March 1987 board meeting in Sydney, but by 1989 accounting for intangible assets had become an area in urgent need of attention.

During the second half of the 1980s, the first signs had become visible of a shift away from the traditional conservative approach to intangible assets, by which these assets were either not capitalized at all, or amortized over relatively brief periods. In the United Kingdom and in Australia, several prominent companies—including Cadbury Schweppes, Grand Metropolitan, News Corporation, Rank Hovis MacDougall, and Rowntree—explored new territory by ceasing to amortize intangible assets, by revaluing intangibles to some measure of current value, or by capitalizing internally generated intangible assets such as brands. The accounting practices of these companies attracted widespread attention and were recognized as a radical break with the past. The new forms of 'brand accounting' were controversial, not merely because they were new, but also because they were often presented as forms of earnings management used in the context of contested takeovers or aggressive financial management.[159] In the United Kingdom, where the ASC was replaced by the ASB in 1990, dealing with intangibles was seen as the critical test for the new body.[160] When the topic was adopted by the IASC, David Cairns described it as 'the most significant gap in International Accounting Standards that is not covered by an existing project'.[161]

However urgent, the project was not completed until July 1998. One reason for the delay was simply that, initially, most of the IASC's resources were tied up in the Comparability and Improvements projects.[162] More importantly, accounting for intangibles was inextricably linked to accounting for business combinations and goodwill, research and development costs, and asset impairment. It took the IASC some time to develop a coordinated approach to these related issues.

11.6.1. An Unsatisfactory First Exposure Draft

The steering committee on intangibles installed in 1989 was chaired by Peter Stilling, a member of the ASC and a partner in Touche Ross in the United Kingdom, the country where the debate on intangibles was most intense.[163] Initially, staff support was provided by the ASC, and some initial board discussions took place during 1990. In August 1990, the UK support was withdrawn, presumably in connection with the formation of the ASB.[164] For lack of resources, the project lay dormant during 1991 and 1992.[165] When it was resuscitated in 1993, *World Accounting Report* hailed it as a new project.[166] But resources remained a problem. In August 1994, David Cairns observed ruefully that a presentation by the ASB's project director on intangibles 'confirmed the immense difference between the nature and quantity of ASB staff work and IASC staff work.... Such differences do not result from a lack of effort or expertise on the part of the IASC staff. They do have major implications for the credibility of IASC's work.'[167] The intangibles project also suffered to some extent from disagreement over the division of responsibilities on technical issues between the board, the steering committees, and the staff.[168]

The main technical issues were: whether to allow the revaluation of intangibles, whether to require amortization, whether to impose a maximum amortization period, and if so, of what length, and how to ensure that the carrying amount of intangibles did not exceed their recoverable amount. None of these issues was particularly novel. For instance, the original version of IAS 16, on property, plant, and equipment (approved in October 1981) already had simple rules on testing assets for impairment. But in relation to the high but uncertain intangible asset values that some companies now carried in their balance sheets, these familiar issues acquired a new significance. In addition, determining the scope of the project was a thorny issue. The IASC already had standards on research and development costs and on goodwill (IAS 9 and IAS 22). Both had been revised as part of the Improvements project, and neither revision had been without problems. In the June 1994 Shiratori letters, IOSCO required the IASC to reconsider the mandatory capitalization of development costs meeting certain criteria (IAS 9). On the other hand, the revised IAS 22 with its mandatory capitalization of goodwill coupled with a short default amortization period of five years had been acceptable to IOSCO, but was proving to be 'extremely controversial' in several countries.[169] This was particularly so in France where companies were threatening to abandon IASC standards for this reason.[170] As France was one of the few developed countries where IASC standards were gaining relatively widespread acceptance in practice (*see* Section 12.2.1), this could not be ignored.

The IASC attempted to deal with these related issues throughout 1994 and into 1995. In order to help the project along, the IASC board held a one-day meeting with national standard setters on intangibles in March 1995, in Düsseldorf, just as it had done the year before on financial instruments. As with financial instruments, a wide range of opinions was expressed, and several standard setters pointed out potential conflicts with their own national standards or proposals.[171] In contrast to financial instruments, though, the IASC decided to go ahead, and it approved an exposure draft at its next meeting in May 1995.

E50, 'Intangible Assets' was approved in May 1995 with eleven votes (out of fourteen) in favour.[172] It was, inevitably, in many respects a compromise. It excluded goodwill and research and development costs from its scope. However, the IASC simultaneously added a project on goodwill to the core standards work programme that was being negotiated with IOSCO at that time, even though a revision of IAS 22 was not requested by IOSCO.[173] On the principal issues, E50 proposed to prohibit the capitalization of most internally generated intangible assets, and to establish measurement at cost less accumulated amortization as the benchmark approach. Despite the recently completed Comparability and Improvements projects to eliminate options in standards, E50 would have introduced measurement at fair value, with mandatory amortization, as an allowed alternative to measurement at historical cost. E50 proposed a maximum amortization period of twenty years, with exceptions in limited cases (particularly in cases where an active secondary market for the asset exists). With respect to impairment testing, E50 deliberately took no position on the use of discounting in calculating the recoverable amount, and offered only very brief guidance on the grouping of assets whose recoverable amounts could not be determined individually. In sum, E50 offered a limited solution, leaving out major classes of intangible assets. It did reflect some of the recent changes in accounting practice in countries like the United Kingdom and Australia, but in a way that was guaranteed not to satisfy the demands for more radical change.

Predictably, the ninety-two comment letters on E50 showed deep divisions, in particular over amortization. Most company respondents opposed any limit to amortization other than useful life, and many argued that some assets should not be amortized at all. But opposition did not come from companies only. The Dutch and French national standard setters also argued in favour of assets with indefinite useful lives. One thing that emerged clearly from the comment letters was that the IASC could not isolate intangible assets from goodwill and research and development costs. Many respondents pointed out the inconsistencies between E50 and other extant standards. The SEC emphatically urged the IASC to take a more comprehensive look at the issues in order to avoid creating opportunities for accounting arbitrage.[174]

11.6.2. Impairment First: IAS 36

It took until the end of 1996 to work out how the IASC should go forward through the thicket of issues related to intangibles, a problem that was further complicated by the March 1996 decision to accelerate the target completion date of the core standards. The final solution was, first, to grasp the nettle and consider all related issues together, and, second, to recognize that drafting a standard on asset impairment was not something that had to be done simply because it was on the IOSCO list of core standards, but because it was the key to solving the intangibles puzzle.[175] A rigorous impairment test might provide the middle ground on which proponents of capitalizing intangibles and those advocating the more traditional conservatism could meet. In June 1996, the board instructed the intangibles steering committee to prepare a revised exposure draft on intangibles as well as exposure drafts of revised versions of IAS 9 and IAS 22. At the same time, it set up a new steering committee to prepare an exposure draft on impairment. The final push towards the integration of all projects occurred, as it happened, after the death of Peter Stilling, the chairman of the intangibles steering committee, shortly after the June board meeting. At Carsberg's suggestion, the two steering committees were combined under the chairmanship of Gilbert Gélard, who had attended board meetings as the French delegation's staff observer since 1988.[176]

Under the new arrangements, the IASC made fast progress. The board approved an exposure draft on impairment (E55) in April 1997. In April 1998 it approved

IAS 36, *Impairment of Assets*, which differed only in minor respects from E55.[177] Apart from the original IAS 1, the IASC had never before completed a project so quickly. Secretary-General Carsberg had declared impairment of assets to be a revision of standards rather than a new topic, so that the fast-track procedure approved in March 1996 could be applied.[178] This was perhaps formally true, as standards like IAS 16, IAS 22, and IAS 25 did contain elementary rules on impairment testing, but to call the proposed standard a 'revision' stretched the meaning of that word to the limit.

Although IAS 36 applied to nearly all non-financial assets, its main impact was expected to be in the area of intangibles.[179] IAS 36 reflected the growing sophistication with which impairment was being treated by national standard setters, such as the emphasis on discounted cash flows to determine recoverable amounts and the grouping of assets into cash generating units. In fact, an important reason why the IASC could make such fast progress was because much of the conceptual ground had recently been cleared.[180] In 1995, the FASB had published FAS 121, *Accounting for the Impairment of Long-Lived Assets and for Long-Lived Assets to be Disposed Of.* In 1996, the UK ASB had published a discussion paper, 'Impairment of Tangible Fixed Assets', and an exposure draft, FRED 12, 'Goodwill and Intangible Assets'. The G4+1 was also working on a related discussion paper (published in 1997).

Developments in the United Kingdom were of particular importance for the IASC. The United Kingdom was one of the few countries where it was still common to charge goodwill directly to reserves.[181] This was the preferred approach under SSAP 22 (1984). The failure of the ASC to eliminate this practice had contributed to its demise in 1990.[182] Not least because of UK insistence, IAS 22 (1983) also allowed charging goodwill to reserves (*see* Section 5.13.2). This option was eliminated when a revised version of IAS 22 was approved in 1993 as part of the Comparability and Improvements projects. This increased the UK's international isolation, but during the next few years the ASB moved the United Kingdom from the rear to a position of leadership on goodwill accounting. It did so by introducing the idea that goodwill amortization might be replaced by annual impairment tests. This was the approach of FRED 12, which inspired the IASC in 1996 to address intangibles by dealing with impairment first.[183]

The FASB had not worked on impairment with a view to changing accounting for goodwill, which, according to APB Opinion No. 17, *Intangible Assets* (issued in 1970), was based on systematic amortization over a period not exceeding forty years. Although at a general level the approach to impairment in FAS 121 was similar to what was being developed in the United Kingdom, there were important differences. One difference was whether the test for impairment should be based on a comparison of the book value of an asset with the value of its undiscounted future cash flow (FAS 121) or with the discounted value of these cash flows (as in the United Kingdom). Another controversy occurred over the measurement of the impairment loss, that is, the determination of the new value to which the book value of an impaired asset had to be written down. The FASB, in FAS 121, had defined this recoverable amount in terms of the asset's fair value. The ASB, on the other hand, was strongly in favour of defining recoverable amount as the higher of net realisable value and value in use. In the ASB's approach, a reporting company was explicitly required to take its own circumstances into account when determining value in use, whereas the FASB opposed this kind of entity-specific measurement as a matter of principle.[184] In both E55 and IAS 36, the IASC chose to go with the ASB, despite concerns expressed by IOSCO's WP1.[185] Although IAS 36 was not developed in formal cooperation with the ASB, the ASB and the IASC worked effectively in tandem, so that IAS 36 was rather closer to the ASB's FRED 15 'Impairment of Fixed Assets and Goodwill' (1997) than to FAS 121.[186]

Notwithstanding the fast-track procedure, the IASC found time for a procedural innovation. For the first time, the proposals in an exposure draft were submitted to a field test. In the second half of 1997, twenty-two multinational companies agreed to apply the requirements of E55 to recently impaired assets and other assets. The results were reported in replies to questionnaires and discussed in visits to the companies by staff and steering committee members. Most of the companies came from eight European countries, together with one or two companies each from Australia, Canada, Japan, South Africa, and the United States. The steering committee concluded that a large majority of the participating companies supported the proposals.[187]

11.6.3. Goodwill and Other Intangibles

As mentioned above, the task given to the intangibles steering committee in June 1996 was to prepare a standard on intangible assets, as well as coordinated revisions of IAS 9 on research and development costs, and of IAS 22 on business combinations and goodwill. The three issues were obviously interrelated, as research and development expenditure could give rise to intangible assets, and as any unrecognized intangible assets acquired in a business combination would automatically end up as goodwill. In January 1997, the board took this logic one step further when it decided that there should no longer be a separate standard on research and development. In July 1997, the board approved two exposure drafts, E60, 'Intangible Assets', and E61 'Business Combinations'. This was followed in July 1998 by the approval of the corresponding standards, IAS 38, *Intangible Assets*, and IAS 22 (revised), *Business Combinations*. Again this was fast progress.

Although the knowledge that a state-of-the-art impairment standard was in preparation helped to take some of the pressure off the IASC's concurrent debate on goodwill and other intangible assets, there were still some hard choices to make: should capitalization of internally generated intangibles be allowed? Should there be an upper limit to the amortization period of intangible assets, or should companies be allowed to assume that some assets have an indefinite useful life? The debate on these issues crystallized around the two opposing positions of the SEC and the ASB.

The SEC was very reluctant to allow the capitalization of internally generated intangibles such as brand names, and it did not want unlimited amortization periods. On various occasions, Chief Accountant Michael Sutton made his concerns clear to Bryan Carsberg.[188] Sutton attended three board meetings in 1996 and 1997 as one of the IOSCO observers in order to express these and other concerns with IASC standards, and the board certainly noted the significance of the attendance of the SEC chief accountant in person.[189] The US delegation and the financial analysts tended to support the more conservative SEC position. David Tweedie, on the other hand, argued passionately that, in limited cases, intangibles and goodwill should be accounted for on the basis of indefinite useful life.[190]

The final agreement hammered out with considerable difficulty at the board meeting of July 1998 (Niagara-on-the-Lake, Canada) tended towards the UK position. IAS 38 and the revised IAS 22 aligned the amortization periods of goodwill and other intangibles. In both cases, as in the ASB's FRS 10, *Goodwill and Intangible Assets* (December 1997), a 'rebuttable presumption' was introduced that the useful life of both types of assets does not exceed twenty years. Hence, in contrast to the US position, there was no fixed maximum amortization period. But whereas FRS 10 allowed the assumption of an indefinite useful life both for goodwill and other intangible assets, IAS 38 and IAS 22 (revised) required the useful life to be finite. Both IAS 38 and FRS 10 allowed some scope for the capitalization of internally generated intangibles, whereas US GAAP allowed none. As with IAS 9, IAS 38 required rather than allowed the capitalization of development expenditure meeting certain conditions. Nevertheless, Australia and France thought that IAS 38 was too restrictive on the capitalization of internally generated intangible assets.

In all, IAS 38 and IAS 22 (revised) were finely balanced compromises, which mustered just enough votes to pass. In the case of IAS 22, the compromise included a discrepancy with IAS 37 on provisions, approved at the same meeting (*see* Section 11.7.4). The Australian, French, and financial analysts' delegations voted against IAS 38, and the United States abstained, but these four negative votes represented contrasting views on the proper treatment of intangibles.[191]

IAS 38 went against some of the SEC's stated positions on capitalizing intangible assets. It is significant that the IASC, which was exerting itself to the utmost to obtain IOSCO's endorsement, did not simply concur with the clearly expressed views of IOSCO's most powerful member.

11.7. OTHER CORE STANDARDS ON NEW TOPICS

Apart from financial instruments and impairment, there were four other areas where the IASC covered new, or largely new, territory during the 1990s: earnings per share, interim reporting, discontinuing operations, and provisions. These are discussed in the following sections.

11.7.1. IAS 33: Earnings per Share

Both the IASC's exposure draft and its standard on earnings per share were approved unanimously, which suggests that it was not a controversial topic. It was nevertheless a significant project, as IAS 33, *Earnings per Share* (approved in January 1997) was the IASC's only standard produced in a bilateral cooperative project with the FASB. This was not yet envisaged at the start of the project. Earnings per share was added to the IASC's agenda in March 1990, with some informal prompting by IOSCO.[192]

The small steering committee on earnings per share was chaired by Doug Brooking, a chartered accountant and financial analyst who was a member of the South African delegation. The steering committee had a somewhat unusual composition in that, next to Brooking, and apart from the subsequently added FASB representative, the other members represented financial analysts rather than national accountancy member bodies.[193] The steering committee was also unusual in that IOSCO sent no observers to its meetings. IOSCO did include a standard on earnings per share in its core list, but was apparently not greatly concerned about its contents.[194]

Like the project on intangibles, earnings per share made very slow progress until the middle of 1993 because of the Comparability and Improvements projects. But unlike intangibles, it ranked very low in the board's priorities.[195] Meanwhile, in August 1991 the FASB published its 'Plan for International Activities' in which it announced its intention to initiate cooperative international standard-setting projects (*see* Section 12.4.5). Shortly afterwards, in October 1991, David Mosso, a former FASB board member who had joined the FASB's senior staff, wrote to David Cairns: '[Earnings per share] is not a high priority item for the FASB agenda, but international comparability is. . . . Starting with a narrow, low-profile issue seems to us like a good way to get some cooperative mechanisms tested and in place.'[196] Following further contacts, and after completing its own due process required to approve new projects, the FASB began a project on earnings per share in March 1994. It announced its intention to cooperate with the IASC, but made it clear that the intention was not to publish identical documents.[197] An FASB staff member, Kimberly Petrone, began to attend the meetings of the IASC's steering committee.

The IASC welcomed the cooperation, and, given that the IASC's ambitions were persistently greater than its resources, it was very helpful that Petrone and the FASB staff bore a large fraction of the burden.[198] Yet the IASC had to accept in the course of the project that its views carried little weight once the FASB had followed its due process and made up its mind. The FASB had concluded in 1993 that earnings per share was a suitable candidate for international cooperation, because 'It would not involve profound or divisive theoretical issues.'[199] The IASC board members initially thought the same, and may well have underestimated the extent to which earnings per share calculations involved conceptual issues at all.[200] But by the end of 1994, it had emerged that the views of the FASB on the one hand, and the IASC board and steering committee on the other, had diverged over the objective of calculating diluted earnings per share.²⁰¹ After a thorough review of the issue, the FASB had come to see diluted earnings per share as a 'historic' number, reflecting, like basic earnings per share, a weighted average of conditions during the reporting period. In most countries represented on the IASC board, however, diluted earnings per share was seen, more traditionally, as a forward-looking 'warning signal', calculated on the basis of conditions on the balance sheet date. AIMR, the main North American financial analysts group, had initially supported the warning signal view but was persuaded early in 1995 to adopt the FASB's point of view. In a meeting of the steering committee with the FASB, also in January 1995, the steering committee 'was left with no illusions that a complete reversal of the FASB tentative view is possible'.²⁰² Gradually, however, the steering committee and the board allowed themselves to be persuaded by the FASB's arguments, and the IASC agreed with just a little reluctance that its exposure draft E52, 'Earnings per Share' (approved in November 1995), should be based on the FASB's view.²⁰³

The FASB was willing, as a concession, to propose additional disclosures based on the warning signal approach. These disclosures were included in E52 and in the FASB's corresponding exposure draft published in January 1996.²⁰⁴ However, more than half of the respondents to the FASB's exposure draft objected to the disclosure requirement, and the FASB proposed to eliminate it. The IASC agreed, even though a substantial majority of respondents to E52 did not object to the disclosure.²⁰⁵ IAS 33 was largely similar to FAS 128, *Earnings per Share* (published in February 1997), although FAS 128 called for more disclosure and included additional guidance.²⁰⁶

11.7.2. IAS 34: Interim Reporting

A project on interim reporting was included in the work programme underlying the July 1995 core standards agreement, and in November 1995 the IASC installed a steering committee. It was chaired by Sigvard Heurlin, a Swedish member of the Nordic delegation and a partner in Öhrlings Coopers & Lybrand.²⁰⁷ IAS 34, *Interim Financial Reporting*, was approved just over two years later, in January 1998. This followed an exposure draft, E57, approved in July 1997.

The IASC decided at an early stage of the project that it should not determine which companies should publish interim reports, or how frequently and when they should be issued, as these were matters for securities regulators or national legislation.²⁰⁸ The remaining point of discussion was whether interim financial statements should be seen as 'stand-alone' documents, prepared according to the same accounting policies as the annual financial statements and on the basis of information available on the interim balance sheet date only. The alternative to this so-called discrete approach was to allow modifications of accounting policies on the basis of anticipated or actually available information at other points during the financial year. Put this way, there were few proponents of a rigorously applied discrete approach, but there was a spectrum of opinions on which 'modifications' were acceptable, ranging all the way to various forms of income smoothing and computational short cuts.[209]

On the whole, the US delegation, supported by the financial analysts, were closest to the discrete or stand-alone view, even though APB Opinion No. 28, *Interim Financial Reporting* (1973), recognized several exceptions to the general principle that the same accounting policies should apply to annual and interim financial statements. The UK delegation, among others, were of the opinion that this could lead to incorrect financial statements, for instance when an asset found to be impaired in one quarter was no longer found to be impaired in a subsequent quarter of the same year.[210]

As on intangibles, the position adopted in both E57 and IAS 34 leaned more towards to the position the ASB was about to take than towards the US view.[211] IAS 34 prescribed a 'year-to-date' approach, by which the same accounting policies were used for interim and annual financial statements, but by which remeasurements might take place on the basis of new information.

IAS 34 reflected the demands of the financial analysts' delegation for rather extensive disclosures, including a condensed cash flow statement and certain disclosures by segment. This, in turn, prompted IAFEI and the Federation of Swiss Industrial Holding Companies to vote against the final standard.[212]

11.7.3. IAS 35: Discontinuing Operations

The project on discontinuing operations was launched with considerable ambition, but as the project progressed its scope was significantly reduced, resulting in a standard described by Secretary-General Carsberg as 'pretty non-contentious'.[213]

On the basis of the core standards work programme, the board agreed in November 1995 to add a project on discontinued operations to its agenda. The project proposal noted that IAS 8, *Net Profit or Loss for the Period, Fundamental Errors and Changes in Accounting Policies* (revised in 1993), included limited guidance on disclosure, but that 'There is no existing or proposed Standard dealing with the measurement issues surrounding discontinued operations, and for this reason further guidance is necessary.'[214] Although the board was already considering the possibility of fast-track procedures for revisions, and it was expected that the project would lead to a revision of IAS 8 rather than to a new standard, it was agreed that this project should follow the IASC's normal due process.[215] This was prior to the acceleration of the core standards programme. As discussed above, the board would subsequently and under increased time pressure approve a fast-track procedure for impairments, even though that project had perhaps a less valid claim to the status of a revision than the project on discontinued operations.

The steering committee, chaired by Christopher Nobes (United Kingdom), a professor of accounting at the University of Reading and a member of the UK delegation, proposed a further widening of the scope of the project in June 1996.[216] The board agreed with the proposal, originating with Nobes, that the project should deal with 'discontinuing' rather than 'discontinued' operations, to emphasize that the relevant accounting issues arise during a process of discontinuation or disposal, rather than merely at the end.[217] The board also agreed that the project should deal with disclosures on newly acquired operations, consistent with the steering committee's view that users should be provided with information on the financial position, performance, and cash flows of continuing operations. At this stage it was also noted that the project was related to several other projects on the IASC's agenda, including impairment, provisions, segment reporting, and the presentation of financial statements.[218] As it turned out, this potential overlap would be resolved by narrowing the scope of discontinuing operations rather than of the other projects.

In September 1996, the steering committee presented the board with a quite radical proposal. It proposed to 'mark-to-market' assets and liabilities classified as part of discontinuing operations, and to take gains and losses arising on the initial classification and on subsequent remeasurement through profit and loss. Discontinuing operations were to be presented separately in the balance sheet and income statement.[219] Although the work on financial instruments had gradually accustomed the members of the IASC board to the idea of recognizing unrealized gains in income, the proposals, including the measurement of liabilities at estimated settlement amount, represented a considerable step forward in the direction of the balance-sheet approach to which the IASC was converting. It was a step too far for the board, which began the process of paring down the project. The board decided that gains should not be recognized until actual disposal. The steering committee was also instructed to explore a 'more conventional' approach than mark-to-market, in which the measurement and recognition criteria were aligned as much as possible with other existing or proposed standards. The suggestion was also made that the standard might be limited to presentation only. Underlying these decisions was a growing awareness of the interactions with other projects, including impairment and provisions but also employee benefits, all of which dealt with aspects of the discontinuation of operations under troubled circumstances.[220] The steering committee and the secretary-general still favoured a mark-to-market approach, but in April 1997 it became evident that a majority of the respondents to the draft statement of principles supported the board's preference for a more 'conventional' approach to recognition and measurement. Many also questioned whether a separate standard was really necessary. The steering committee therefore asked the board to decide whether the project should be abandoned, or limited to presentation issues only. The board opted for the latter course, encouraged by the IOSCO representatives.[221] As the board also decided that the presentation of discontinuing operations did not necessarily have to be on the face of the balance sheet and income statement, the principal remaining issues were to determine the extent of disclosure and to ensure that the language of the standard was consistent with that used in the other related projects.[222] Although this did raise some points for debate, both the exposure draft E58 (approved in July 1997) and the standard IAS 35, *Discontinuing Operations* (approved in April 1998), were passed by a unanimous vote of the board.

11.7.4. IAS 37: Provisions

IOSCO had not included 'provisions' in its list of core standards, although it had asked for a revision of the guidance on contingencies in IAS 10, *Contingencies and Events Occurring After the Balance Sheet Date*. One reason why provisions was not separately listed by IOSCO may have been that US GAAP did not use a comprehensive term to identify the various liabilities, contingencies, and other accruals collectively described as provisions in the European tradition, as reflected in the Fourth Directive. In US GAAP, comparable items were treated across several pronouncements rather than in a single accounting standard.[223] Yet, by the time of the core standards agreement of July 1995, the subject of provisions was no longer an alien concept for the FASB. In November 1995, a G4+1 paper was published entitled *Provisions: Their Recognition, Measurement, and Disclosure in Financial Statements*. In terms of procedure, the IASC's provisions project was significant for being the clearest example of a G4+1 project which led directly to a corresponding IASC standard. In terms of substance, IAS 37, *Provisions, Contingent Liabilities and Contingent Assets* (approved in July 1998) represented a notable break with the traditional income-statement oriented approach to provisions known in many European countries, and a further move towards the balance-sheet orientation characteristic of the G4 group of standard setters.

The IASC's provisions project began in March 1996 with the installation of a steering committee chaired by David Tweedie.[224] The ASB had offered to provide staff support for the project on the same basis as that provided by the CICA for financial instruments.[225] The ASB's Andrew Lennard, who had authored the G4+1 paper together with Sandra Thompson, served as the project manager of the IASC project as well as of a parallel ASB project on provisions. In September 1998, the ASB published FRS 12, *Provisions, Contingent Liabilities and Contingent Assets*, which was substantially identical to IAS 37.

As might have been expected on the basis of the ASB's earlier work on provisions, the steering committee proposed an approach to the board in which provisions were to be recognized only in cases where the reporting enterprise had an obligation on the balance sheet date. This requirement was justified on the basis of the IASC's Framework, which allowed no credit-side balance-sheet items other than equity and liabilities. The essential characteristic of a liability was the existence of a legal or constructive obligation.[226] This was a rather more restricted approach to provisions than what was customary in Europe, including the United Kingdom. The Fourth Directive (article 20) allowed the formation of provisions for liabilities likely to arise in the future, as well as for expected future costs and losses originating prior to the balance sheet date. This wider definition had traditionally been justified on the basis of the prudence principle, but during the 1990s there were growing concerns in several European countries over excessive conservatism and over the use of provisions for income smoothing and other forms of earnings management.[227] The IASC board agreed relatively easily to the general principle that provisions should be restricted to present obligations, even though the French delegation continued to have misgivings on this point.[228]

However, there was considerable controversy over how this principle should be applied in the case of restructuring provisions. The question at issue was at what stage, or under what conditions, does a decision on restructuring by the board of directors of a company give rise to a constructive obligation. The Australian, US, and UK delegations tended to see restructuring provisions as an area of notorious earnings management and wanted to impose strict limitations. The Federation of Swiss Industrial Holding Companies, as well as the French and Dutch delegations, emphasized the need to allow legitimate prudence. These delegations pointed towards differences in company law among countries, which might mean that a board of directors was committed to a restructuring at an earlier stage than most of the English-speaking delegations would allow.[229] Nevertheless, the IASC board was in the end able to agree on a set of criteria that was, as indicated above, also acceptable to the ASB and used in FRS 12.

At the board meeting of July 1998 (Niagara-on-the-Lake), where IAS 37 was approved, the revised IAS 22, *Business Combinations*, also came up for the final vote. This standard also dealt with restructuring provisions, in the context of determining the amount of goodwill recognized in an acquisition. This reopened the debate on restructuring provisions. Following the logic of IAS 37, restructuring provisions could be formed (and hence, goodwill increased), only if an obligation existed at the time of the acquisition. However, the Swiss and Dutch delegations insisted on a more flexible treatment in this case. In order to approve IAS 22, it was necessary to allow a three-month period following the date of acquisition during which the acquiring company could develop the restructuring plan and form a provision by debiting goodwill rather than the profit and loss account. As the final decision on IAS 22 took place after Tweedie had left the board meeting, he was outraged when he learned about, as he saw it, this dilution of the standard.[230]

The debates on provisions show that the IASC was changing. The pervasive influence of the definition of a liability shows that many delegations had accepted the approach embodied in the IASC's Framework, even though this resulted in significant conflicts with their local rules and practices. However, the case of restructuring provisions also illustrates that the more traditional horse-trading was by no means a thing of the past.[231]

IAS 37 also dealt with contingent assets and liabilities which had originally been part of IAS 10. In November 1997, the IASC started a minor project to revise the remaining sections of IAS 10, dealing with events after the balance sheet date. No steering committee was appointed for this project. On the basis of work by the staff, the board approved an exposure draft (E63) in November 1998, and a revised standard, IAS 10, *Events After the Balance Sheet Date*, in March 1999.

11.8. REVISIONS OF STANDARDS

The core standards programme included the revision of several extant standards apart from IAS 10. This section discusses the major revisions of IAS 1, 14, and 19, and the minor revision of IAS 17. The revisions of IAS 1, *Disclosure of Accounting Policies* (1975) and IAS 14, *Reporting Financial Information by Segment* (1981) were originally seen as part of the work of the Improvements steering committee. As discussed in Section 9.3.5, the Improvements steering committee was soon forced to restrict its task to completing the revision of the ten standards affected by the *Statement of Intent*. In 1992 and 1993, separate steering committees were set up to deal with the revision of IAS 14 and IAS 1, respectively.

11.8.1. IAS 1: Presentation of Financial Statements

A project on 'presentation of financial statements' was set up in March 1993. This project was intended to result in a revised and expanded version of IAS 1. Apart from the disclosure of accounting policies, which was the subject matter of the original IAS 1, the new standard was to incorporate IAS 5, *Information to be Disclosed in Financial Statements*, and IAS 13, *Presentation of Current Assets and Current Liabilities*, as well, and so was to deal comprehensively with presentation and disclosure at a general level. The steering committee formed in 1993 was chaired by German delegate Heinz Kleekämper, a partner in Datag Deutsche Allgemeine Treuhand, Munich.[232] The project resulted in an exposure draft, E53, approved in June 1996, and a final standard, IAS 1, *Presentation of Financial Statements*, approved in July 1997.

IAS 1 had not been revised since it was issued in 1975. It had merely been reformatted in 1994, and therefore it still contained at least one strong reminder of the IASC's early days.[233] Prior to the revision, it proclaimed that 'There are many different accounting policies in use even in relation to the same subject; judgement is required in selecting and applying those which, in the circumstances of the enterprise, are best suited to present properly its financial position and the results of its operations' (paragraph 6). Such acceptance of accounting diversity was clearly no longer acceptable. The sentence was eliminated and replaced by strict guidance on how to choose accounting policies in the absence of a relevant IASC standard. The 'circumstances of the enterprise' were no longer mentioned as a relevant consideration (IAS 1 (revised in 1997), paragraph 20–2).

Apart from this change, which was effected without apparent discussion, and apart from numerous uncontroversial improvements, the revision of IAS 1 was characterized by extensive discussions on a pair of issues, which are discussed in the next two sections.

11.8.1.1. The True and Fair Override

The first issue involved the so-called 'true and fair override', that is, whether IAS 1 should instruct an enterprise to depart from the requirements of specific IASC standards in situations where adherence to the standard would conflict with the overall objectives of financial reporting. The prototypical override was the one contained in the UK Companies Act 1948, which stated, as the overall objective, that the financial statements should give a 'true and fair view' of the state of affairs of the company. It added that the detailed requirements of the act 'shall be without prejudice' to this general requirement.[234] Both the general true and fair view requirement and the override were included in the Fourth Directive of 1978, mainly because of UK insistence.[235] By the 1990s, the idea of an override had become widely accepted in Europe even though its practical significance might vary among countries. In the UK delegation to the IASC, David Tweedie was a passionate defender of the true and fair override, but his fellow delegate, Chris Nobes, was sceptical.[236] In contrast to the European situation, the ostensibly similar formula used in US audit reports of 'present fairly in conformity with generally accepted accounting principles' does not imply that the explicit requirements of US GAAP may be departed from for the sake of a 'fair presentation'.[237] In 1991, Australia moved towards the US position when an override clause in the Corporations Law, inherited from the UK tradition, was modified into a requirement for additional disclosure rather than a departure from accounting standards in the financial statements. In the view of Warren McGregor, the executive director of the AARF who had been an active participant at IASC board meetings since 1983, true and fair had become 'an accounting anachronism' with the advent of explicit conceptual frameworks.[238]

In the early stages of the project, the proposals did not include an overall requirement such as giving a true and fair view. When the idea of such a requirement did emerge, late in 1995, the board agreed easily to use fair presentation—the US wording—to describe the overall requirement, but it rejected the idea of an override.[239] This position was reiterated when E53 was unanimously approved in June 1996, and the board was careful to explain that it had considered the issue but 'could not foresee a situation where the...requirements in IAS could result in financial statements that were misleading'.[240]

A majority of the comment letters on E53, however, expressed a preference for an override. The steering committee noted that a simple counting of reactions in favour or against might not be appropriate, as most responses in favour of an override came from enterprises or business organizations who accounted for most of the comment letters, while the smaller number of users and user organizations tended to oppose an override.[241] Nevertheless, the steering committee did recommend a compromise to the board by which an override would be allowed in rare circumstances, with additional disclosures. Bryan Carsberg, who usually did not intervene directly in debates on technical issues, added his support for a compromise by pointing out to the board the importance of avoiding a conflict with the Fourth Directive.[242] This was unpalatable to the US and Australian delegations, who had been quite content with the proposals so far.[243] The SEC also expressed its concerns and wrote rather threateningly that an override 'would suggest that there is a fundamental weakness in the relevant standards and call into question the quality, and therefore, acceptability of those standards'.[244] At the July 1997 board meeting in Beijing, Michael Sutton, the SEC chief accountant, repeated these concerns. Nevertheless, the board, over the dissents of Australia and the United States, voted in favour of IAS 1, including an override in narrowly restricted circumstances.[245] Apparently, no serious consideration was given to re-expose the standard, presumably with an eye on the core standards target date. Opinions differed on whether the override was a purely theoretical point or not, but there was no question that the IASC's willingness to ignore the SEC's clearly expressed views was another significant indication that the IASC was not merely taking its cue from the United States in order to secure IOSCO endorsement.[246]

11.8.1.2. Comprehensive Income and Performance Reporting

The second major issue in IAS 1 was whether it should expand the definition of a set of financial statements to include a statement of comprehensive income in addition to the balance sheet, the income statement, and the cash flow statement. Comprehensive income, defined as all changes in equity apart from transactions with owners, had been introduced in the FASB's Statement of Financial Accounting Concepts No. 3 (December 1980). It had remained a mere concept until the evolving standards on financial instruments introduced significant new direct changes in equity, bypassing the income statement. Responding to similar developments, the ASB in 1992 published FRS 3, *Reporting Financial Performance*, which introduced a 'statement of total recognized gains and losses'. In 1997, the FASB issued FAS 130, *Reporting Comprehensive Income*. In between, the IASC worked on the revision of IAS 1, and, like the national standard setters, it struggled to find a way to make movements in equity more transparent. The IASC's staff recognized that a properly defined statement of comprehensive income had the potential to help resolve controversial accounting problems relating to the remeasurement of assets and liabilities. Such problems were becoming more frequent and more significant as the IASC extended the use of fair value as a balance-sheet measurement basis in areas such as financial instruments, agriculture, and retirement benefits. Reporting enterprises tended to objected to the resulting increase in earnings volatility, and in some countries the reporting of unrealized gains in income was rejected as a violation of the prudence principle. A 'second level of income' might help to alleviate both kinds of concerns and smooth the move to fair value.[247] The steering committee and the board were generally in favour of introducing a second performance statement next to the income statement. Highlighting the absence of an internationally agreed name for such a statement, it proposed, in E53, to introduce yet another name: the 'statement of non-owner movements in equity'.

The board might have known that its proposals would not be universally welcomed. Respondents to the steering committee's earlier draft statement of principles had rejected a statement of comprehensive income—under whatever name—by four to one.[248] This pattern was repeated with E53, when seventy-five out of one hundred respondents opposed a new separate financial statement.[249] Bryan Carsberg concluded that the 'climate of opinion' showed that a separate statement 'does not yet command sufficient support'.[250] The board therefore agreed to include in IAS 1 a less ambitious requirement to present a statement of changes in equity. Enterprises that wished to do so would not be prevented from presenting this as a performance statement, while others could choose a less prominent form of presentation such as a reconciliation of opening and closing equity.[251] This change occurred almost at the same time as the FASB, under pressure from industry, allowed in FAS 130 that unrealized gains and losses could be shown in the statement of changes in shareholders' equity, rather than, as stated in its exposure draft, in the income statement or in a statement of comprehensive income.[252]

In the IASC board, the change of emphasis was perhaps not greatly deplored, as doubts about the conceptual soundness of the proposals in E53 had already begun to emerge before the comment letters came in. E53 had been rather sketchy about the precise contents of the statement of non-owner movements in equity, and it appeared that there were differences of opinion about the way various specific movements in equity should be reported. Moreover, the financial analysts' delegation, in particular David Damant, pressed for a more fundamental study of performance reporting. In April 1997, the board agreed to set up a working party on performance reporting, chaired by Damant and consisting of the chairmen of the steering committees, for which movements in equity were an important issue, such as financial instruments, agriculture, and insurance. Although the working party was upgraded to a steering committee, with the intention to produce a draft exposure draft by October 1997, little progress was made.[253] Damant reported in January 1998 that the time was 'not propitious' for making further progress.[254] By then, the IASC had effectively thrown in its lot with the G4+1, which published a discussion paper on performance reporting, also in January 1998.[255] The main—though unintended—result was a straining of relations between the IASC and the G4 standard setters, which believed that the IASC, in its press release announcing the G4+1 discussion paper, gave insufficient credit to the principal authors, Todd Johnson of the FASB and Andrew Lennard of the ASB.[256] In fact, none of the national standard setters was able to make much progress with a fundamental review of performance reporting, and the IASC decided to suspend work on the issue. In July 1999, as the G4+1 had just published a second discussion paper on performance reporting,[257] the IASC board tentatively agreed to start a new project, but this did not result in any publications by the IASC during its final year.[258]

11.8.2. IAS 14: Segment Reporting

Patricia McConnell, a member of the financial analysts' delegation who was with Bear, Stearns & Co., New York, was the chair of a steering committee formed in 1992 to revise IAS 14, *Reporting Financial Information by Segment* (approved in 1981).[259] McConnell was a logical choice, as she also chaired a committee of the AIMR, which, in 1993, published a report advocating, among other things, a revision of the FASB's standard on segment reporting.[260] The US and Canadian standard setters were indeed beginning to move. Following the publication of separate research reports in 1992 and 1993, the FASB and the Accounting Standards Board (AcSB) of the CICA agreed in March 1993 to join forces on segment reporting.[261] Owing to the Improvements project's persistent demands on staff time, the IASC had moved slowly so far and began to pick up speed only in the course of 1993, when it was able to contract out the staff work to Paul Pacter. Pacter had been closely involved with the FASB's earlier standard on segment reporting (FAS 14, issued in 1976), and had written the FASB's 1993 research report on the subject.[262]

As the IASC and the FASB/AcSB were tackling segment reporting virtually simultaneously, the idea of harmonizing arose naturally, and it became the major theme of the IASC's project. As might be expected, given their backgrounds, Pacter and McConnell had no difficulty keeping in touch with the FASB, but full harmonization turned out to be impossible. The split occurred over the so-called management approach to segmentation, that is, over the principle of basing externally reported segment information on the structure and content of information reported to top management. The management approach had been advocated by AIMR in its 1993 report, and gained additional prominence as one of the more eye-catching recommendations in the September 1994 report of the AICPA's Jenkins Committee on improving financial reporting.[263]

The FASB embraced the management approach with conviction. However, the IASC steering committee was thinking originally along the lines of identifying segments on the basis of differences in risks and returns among activities. Because of this difference, the FASB and the AcSB were urging the IASC to defer its project, at the same time (during the summer of 1994), when the FASB was urging the IASC to suspend its work on financial instruments. David Cairns nevertheless advised the steering committee to proceed, with the result that the IASC and the FASB/AcSB issued diverging discussion papers in September 1994 and February 1995, respectively.[264] Over the next few years, the projects continued to run in tandem. The IASC's exposure draft (E51, approved in November 1995) was followed shortly afterwards by the FASB/AcSB joint exposure drafts of January 1996. Intensive consultations helped to narrow the gap. In E51, the IASC accepted a limited version of the management approach, under which the identification of segments should be based on the internal reporting structure, but with certain minimal requirements to ensure reporting of information on lines of business as well as geographical areas.[265] Unlike the FASB and the AcSB, though, the IASC remained unwilling to the end to accept that reported segment results would be based on internal measurements rather than on the accounting policies applied in the consolidated financial statements.[266] This was the most important remaining difference between IAS 14 (revised), *Segment Reporting*, which the IASC approved in January 1997, and the subsequent US and Canadian standards. Canada was the only board member to vote against, but the US delegation did not follow the line of its national standard setter. In order to allow a last attempt at harmonization, the IASC board agreed to postpone publication of its standard for half a year.[267] This did lead to some modifications but not to the resolution of the main sticking point. A modified version of IAS 14 was again, and this time finally, approved in July 1997. One of the modifications was an explicit permission to disclose additional segment information prepared according to other accounting policies, which would allow companies to comply with the North American model as well.[268] The Canadian delegation again provided the only no-vote. The FASB and the CICA issued their standards in June and September 1997, respectively.[269]

11.8.3. IAS 19: Employee Benefits

Even before the receipt of the Shiratori letters in June 1994, David Cairns had identified a revision of IAS 19 as a high priority in dealing with IOSCO's list of core standards.[270] In November 1994, the board agreed to start a project on retirement benefits and other employee costs. A steering committee was set up, chaired by Jan Klaassen, a partner in KPMG in the Netherlands and a professor of accounting in Amsterdam.[271]

The Improvements project had resulted in limited revisions to IAS 19, *Retirement Benefit Costs*. Like the original IAS 19 (1982), the revised version of 1993 was oriented towards the income statement. For defined benefit plans, the pièce de résistance of any standard on pension accounting, the standard included several options in the calculation of retirement benefit costs for the period, which allowed these costs to be smoothed over the expected period of service of the employees. The impact of IAS 19 on the balance sheet was limited to an asset or liability representing the accrued difference between these costs and the amounts funded. In other words, the balance sheet would not include the defined benefit obligation, nor the value of any plan assets, although disclosure of both items was required. The Shiratori letters confirmed that IOSCO's principal concerns were the inclusion of a minimum liability in the balance sheet, as well as the need for additional guidance on making the all-important actuarial assumptions underlying the estimate of a defined benefit obligation.[272]

Phrased in this way, IOSCO's concerns were an apparent request to modify IAS 19 according to the example of the relevant US standard, FAS 87, *Employers' Accounting for Pensions* (issued in 1985). FAS 87 had introduced more specific guidance on actuarial assumptions and on changes in actuarial assumptions, and it required the recognition of a minimum liability in the case of underfunded pension plans. When the revised version of IAS 19 was approved in January 1998, it did indeed show considerable similarity to the US approach, but the IASC had not been allowed to ignore the situation in other countries. More than any other subject, accounting for pensions inspired special pleading, as countries sought to argue that their national situation required a different treatment. Even the Shiratori letters mentioned Japanese welfare pension plans and stated, in the typical anonymous style of WP1, that 'One member country would like the IASC to consider an exemption from the application of IAS 19 and an acceptance of the treatment in Japan.'[273] A more general concern was that the approach underlying FAS 87 and the revised IAS 19 might not be universally applicable because it reflected the pension situation in Anglo-American countries.[274]

In general, the IASC did not allow itself to be greatly distracted by comments like these. From the point outline onwards and in line with its exposure draft (E54, approved in September 1996) it worked consistently towards an approach that was inspired by, but not identical to, FAS 87.[275] The steering committee characterized this approach as 'market-based', which meant essentially that, for defined benefit plans, the periodic expense item would be based on movements in a defined benefit obligation remeasured at each balance sheet date using market discount rates, and on movements in the fair value of plan assets. The balance sheet would include a net asset or liability based on the difference between the obligation and the plan assets. While this meant an important shift in the direction of a balance-sheet approach, the income statement approach remained visible in the treatment of actuarial gains and losses. These changes in the value of the obligation and the plan assets, other than changes expected on the basis of actuarial assumptions, should, on the basis of a pure balance-sheet approach, be recognized immediately in income. As this would expose companies to great earnings volatility, particularly in response to interest changes, the FASB had decided that such gains and losses should be deferred and amortized gradually once the cumulative total exceeds a certain minimum (following the so-called 'corridor' approach). The IASC adopted a similar approach.

At this point, the rather specialist project on employee benefits touched on issues with a wider significance. It was obvious that the deferral of actuarial gains and losses was a pragmatic solution, and that the resulting balance-sheet items did not meet the definition of assets and liabilities of the Framework. For that reason, the approach was opposed by the United Kingdom and Australia, which saw it as a lamentable condoning of income smoothing, and for this reason they voted against the standard.[276] The ASB was at work on a different approach, which was to recognize the gains and losses outside income in a statement of comprehensive income, or, as it was known in the United Kingdom, a statement of total recognized gains and losses. As a result, the employee benefits project became entangled with the IASC's inconclusive project on performance reporting (see Section 11.8.1). In the end, however, most delegations voted to maintain the corridor approach, not only because it would reduce earnings volatility, but also because it would reduce the significance of US GAAP reconciliations.[277] The United Kingdom gained little more than an acknowledgement in IAS 19's 'basis for conclusions' that the UK approach was, perhaps, better and might be considered in due course.[278] The Nordic delegation voted against because it believed that the standard allowed too many options for dealing with amounts outside the corridor.[279]

One of the most intractable issues of the revision of IAS 19 was the choice of discount rate.[280] Given fairly general agreement that a market rate should be used, it was still possible to differ vehemently over whether this should be a risk-free rate, a rate based on corporate bond yields, a rate based on the actual or planned composition of the portfolio of plan assets, or a rate reflecting the enterprise's own cost of capital. As with the actuarial gains and losses, this was an issue in which pragmatic concerns over the size of the recognized liability and the volatility of results were intermingled with theoretical issues such as whether the measurement of a retirement obligation should take into account the enterprise's own credit risk.

In line with FAS 87, and in face of opposition from the United Kingdom—but not from the UK delegation—and most actuarial associations, the IASC decided to maintain its original position that the discount rate should be based on the yield of high-quality corporate bonds.[281]

IAS 19, as revised in 1998, had the more general title of *Employee Benefits*. It therefore dealt not merely with pensions but also with other forms of compensation. Most of the requirements in this area were not particularly controversial. One potentially explosive subject was equity compensation benefits, such as employee stock options. The FASB had suffered a painful defeat in 1994 when it attempted to require that the fair value of such options be shown as an expense in the income statement.[282] The IASC decided at an early stage to limit itself to disclosure requirements.[283] Given the time pressure, the choice was perhaps not courageous, but certainly wise.

An innovation introduced with E54 and the revised IAS 19 was that, following long-standing US practice, they contained a basis for conclusions outlining the history of the standard and explaining the reasoning underlying the board's choices. The IASC's early standards had included an 'explanation' section preceding the standard proper, which frequently did give information on the board's views of alternative approaches. During the Improvements project, the explanation sections became an integral part of the standards in response to criticism, particularly from the United States, that the status of the explanation was ambiguous (*see* Section 9.3.7). As a result, the explanation sections, set in plain type and alternating with the boldfaced main paragraphs, lost some of their capacity to provide background information. As mentioned above, a background paper had been published with E49, Income Taxes, in October 1994, but this was not republished with the final standard. The IASC's decision to include a basis for conclusions was partly a response to calls for an improved due process,[284] but the response was made in a pragmatic fashion. Of the IASC's subsequent standards, IAS 36, IAS 38, IAS 40, and IAS 41 included similar appendices, but IAS 37 and IAS 39 did not.

11.8.4. IAS 17: Leases

When, in January 1996, the IASC's executive committee debated how it should proceed with the revision of IAS 17, called for by the core standards agreement, Carsberg noted that the G4 standard setters were considering major revisions of their standards on leasing.[285] At that time, the G4+1 was concluding work on its discussion paper *Accounting for Leases: A New Approach*, which was written by Warren McGregor and published in June 1996. The new approach set out in the discussion paper was to abolish the distinction between operating and finance leases, which characterized most national standards as well as IAS 17. Instead, the rights and obligations of all leases that met the definitions of assets and liabilities would be recognized on the balance sheet, and differences between types of leases would be reflected in measurement.

The executive committee had become wary of the G4+1. Its recent paper on provisions (November 1995) was seen to move beyond stating the issues and towards taking strong positions, and therefore in the direction of standard setting. Carsberg counselled that the G4 standard setters would continue regardless of the IASC's participation, and that it was better for the IASC to stay in touch. Therefore, the executive committee should wait to see what the G4+1 would do before defining the scope of the revision of IAS 17.[286]

In June 1996, however, the IASC board agreed to start a limited revision of IAS 17, intended merely to deal with the issues raised by IOSCO.[287] One assumes that the acceleration of the core standards programme agreed in March 1996 had made it imperative to complete the project as fast as possible. The IASC did not fall very much behind the G4 standard setters, because the latter did not make fast progress with the more fundamental revision of their leasing standards.[288] A second G4+1 discussion paper on leases was published in February 2000.

The limited revision was prepared by a steering committee chaired by Thomas Jones, of Citicorp, New York, a member of the IAFEI delegation which had just joined the board.[289]

Given the fast-track process appropriate for a revision, the project was completed in a short time. An exposure draft, E56, was approved in April 1997, and a revised standard, IAS 17, *Leases*, in November 1997. The main changes were an expansion of required disclosures and a settlement of the issue of revenue recognition by lessors. This latter issue had already bedevilled the IASC when it worked on the original IAS 17 in the early 1980s, and its continued inability to settle this question prompted the IASC to remove IAS 17 from the scope of the *Statement of Intent* in 1990. The problem was throughout that the United Kingdom preferred the so-called net cash investment approach for reasons related to its tax system, whereas most other countries preferred the net investment approach. The original IAS 17 had left a free choice between the two methods. In 1997, the IASC was finally prepared to cut the knot and to require the net investment approach in all cases. Even though UK respondents to E56 continued to argue that the IASC had chosen to eliminate the wrong method, the board was not impressed.[290] In the final vote, the Swiss delegation abstained because of the disclosure requirements, and the Canadian and UK delegations voted against. In the case of the United Kingdom, the net investment method was an obstacle, but, more importantly, both delegations believed that accounting for leases should be reformed more thoroughly.[291]

11.9. POST-CORE TECHNICAL WORK

The approval of IAS 39, on financial instruments, in December 1998 was regarded by the IASC as the effective completion of the core standards programme. Also in December 1998, the IASC issued the first discussion paper prepared by its Strategy Working Party with proposals for a major restructuring of the IASC (*see* Chapter 13). After a year of intense negotiations, the board agreed in November 1999 that the IASC should be replaced by a different type of organization, which would subsequently be called the IASB. In December 2000, the IASC board held its last meeting. Hence, after the completion of the core standards the IASC continued to operate for another two years, at first with an increasing likelihood and then with the certain knowledge that it had to hand over its work in the near future to a new body. This prospect did not discourage the board from continuing its technical work, and it held another eight meetings during 1999 and 2000. During 1997 and 1998, it had prepared for the post-core phase by gradually taking up a number of new projects, and during 1999 and 2000 it added several more. Of course, it could not hope to complete all of these projects. Hence, the IASC concentrated its efforts on the small number of projects on which there was a good chance of completing a standard, or a revised standard, by the end of 2000. The result was the issue of two new standards (IAS 40 and 41) as well as minor revisions of IAS 10, 12, 19, and 39. The fruits of the remaining energy of the board and the staff found an outlet in a range of publication formats, including approved SIC interpretations, discussion papers published by the IASC alone or in concert with the G4+1 or the standard setters cooperating in the JWG on financial instruments, implementation guidance on financial instruments, and an omnibus 'legacy' document in which the board transmitted its views on a wide range of accounting issues to its successor.[292] The next sections will discuss the IASC's last two standards as well as review the other technical work, to the extent that this has not been covered elsewhere in this chapter.

11.9.1. IAS 40: Investment Property

As shown in Section 9.3.1, the board decided in 1990 to exclude a revision of IAS 25, *Acccounting for Investments*, from its Comparability project, in order to await the results of its work on financial instruments. While the latter project dragged on, the revision of IAS 25 continued to be marked for future action. In the end, IAS 32 and IAS 39 dealt with most of the issues covered by IAS 25, so that a rump standard was left dealing with investment properties and other non-financial investments only. In July 1997, the executive committee believed that it would take only a limited amount of work to turn this remainder into a separate standard reflecting contemporary practice. In November, the board agreed to entrust the required preparations to the staff rather than to a steering committee.[293] It soon became apparent, however, that revising the standard might require more than just editorial work. As in 1985, when the original IAS 25 had been approved, the central accounting issues were simple: whether to allow or require remeasurement of investment properties, and, if so, (*a*) whether value changes should pass through the income statement or be recorded directly in equity, and (*b*) whether depreciation should be required in the case of periodic remeasurement.

What had changed since 1985 was that the world in general and the IASC board in particular had gone through an intense process of reflection on fair value in the context of accounting for financial instruments, leading in general to a greater willingness to accept fair value measurements, or other forms of current value, as well as the recognition in income of unrealized value changes.[294] These changed attitudes became apparent in proposals prepared by the staff in the autumn of 1997. These would change IAS 25 to require yearly remeasurement of all investment properties, even though gains would still be credited to a revaluation reserve rather than to income.[295] Even though the board tentatively went along with the staff's thinking, misgivings developed during the spring of 1998 that the IASC's due process might be compromised if such comparatively major changes would simply be prepared by means of staff work.[296] However, a complicating factor was that proper due process might interfere with the timely completion of the core standards. The IASC therefore sought IOSCO's views on whether the topic of investment properties was part of the core standards, and, if so, whether retaining the original provisions of IAS 25 would be acceptable. Uncertainty on these issues arose because IOSCO's original core standards list of August 1993 and the agreement of July 1995 referred to 'investments' and 'revision of IAS 25', without explicitly mentioning investment properties. IOSCO's initial position, communicated in July 1998, was that it expected investment properties to be addressed as part of the core standards.[297] Thereupon, Bryan Carsberg proposed that the staff would prepare an exposure draft of a revised IAS 25 for approval by the board in November, following which a steering committee would be appointed with the limited role of reviewing the responses. A similar approach had been used in the financial instruments project, following the approval of E62.[298] However, by November it emerged that IOSCO had agreed to start the evaluation of the core standards before the completion of a standard on investment properties, provided that the IASC were to show 'a sense of urgency in dealing with the project'.[299] This cleared the way for the board to set up a regular steering committee, charged with developing an exposure draft on the basis of the staff's prior work.

The steering committee created in November 1998 was chaired by Per Gunslev, a member of the Nordic Federation delegation, a partner in KPMG (Denmark), and chairman of the Danish Accounting Standards Committee.[300] It did not have much time in which to complete its work. The original intention was to approve an exposure draft at the March 1999 (Washington, DC) board meeting, but at that meeting the board was unable to agree. Several delegations, particularly the Australian delegation, pushed hard for a full fair value approach, including recognition of unrealized gains and losses in income.[301] For other delegations, this was going too far, too quickly. The agriculture standard, which was being developed simultaneously, was moving in the same direction, giving rise to the observation by the German delegate Jochen Pape that 'We are in danger here of adopting a comprehensive fair value model on the basis of a discussion of a few minor items.'[302] There were indeed important issues at stake, but Chairman Stig Enevoldsen believed it was imperative that an exposure draft be approved at the next meeting in June (in Warsaw). The board did agree on an exposure draft but only after protracted debate and after some recrimination that, because of the time pressure, the proper division of responsibilities between the board, the staff, and the steering committee had not been observed.[303]

Given the controversy, it is remarkable that the board chose the most radical approach possible. E64, 'Investment Property', was a draft of a completely new standard, not merely a revision of IAS 25. It proposed to measure all investment property at fair value. This was the IASC's first proposal to apply fair value measurement systematically to non-financial assets. After some zigzagging, the deeply divided board decided in the end to recognize all changes in fair value in the income statement, rather than allow the option of taking them directly to equity as well.[304] The French, German, and Swiss Industrial Holding Companies delegations voted against E64, and India/Sri Lanka abstained.[305]

The voting in the board, as well as the responses to E64, seemed to provide support for those who saw developments in financial reporting in terms of a simple conflict between Anglo-American and 'Continental' accounting traditions. More than 80 per cent of respondents from the G4 countries were in favour of mandatory measurement at fair value, whereas more than 70 per cent of those opposed were from Continental Europe and Japan.[306] Yet there were some notable departures from the stereotyped roles. The AICPA argued strongly that the historical cost model was the appropriate one for investment properties. The European Commission, on the other hand, thought that 'E64 has reached the right answer on a number of the crucial conceptual issues,' and it urged the IASC not to introduce a choice between recording value changes in income or equity. The body that for some—rightly or wrongly—was the epitome of compromised standard setting, observed that 'For the IASC to introduce a new standard that incorporated options would be a retrograde step.'[307]

On the whole, the comment letters showed strong divisions of opinion on the main issues. The board therefore went over the same ground again in lengthy discussions during its November and December 1999 meetings, and it finally agreed to introduce a major option in the standard. IAS 40, *Investment Property*, tentatively approved in December and confirmed in March 2000, allowed an enterprise-wide choice between a historical cost model, as in IAS 16, and measurement at fair value with changes taken through income. This satisfied the various concerns of the board delegations who had voted against E64, but this time the United Kingdom and the United States voted against, as they believed that the introduction of the option seriously lowered the quality of the standard.[308]

11.9.2. IAS 41: Agriculture

IAS 41, *Agriculture*, was the last standard issued by the IASC, and it was approved at the board's last meeting in December 2000, in London. The agriculture project had long been a sideshow, while all attention had been focused on the all-important core standards. In the end, though, the standard was a fitting finale for the IASC, as it became a showcase of the IASC's move towards a balance-sheet-oriented approach based on fair value measurement.

The project on agriculture emerged out of the IASC's long-standing belief that it should do some work with special relevance for developing countries (*see* Sections 9.4.2 and 11.9.3.3). The IASC's contacts with the World Bank provided the direct impetus. The Bank had joined the IASC's Consultative Group in 1981 with considerable enthusiasm, but, in the wake of staff changes, its contacts with the IASC had been reduced to a low level of intensity. These contacts were revived around 1990, and from then onwards Randolph Andersen, the chief of the division for central and operational accounting, became the IASC's main contact at the Bank. Andersen made it known to David Cairns that the World Bank was interested in improving accountability and transparency by its developing-country borrowers and that the Bank would probably be willing to fund a relevant IASC project.[309] Cairns supplied outlines of several possible projects, and the discussion soon focused on a standard on agricultural issues. During the spring of 1994, agreement was reached between Cairns and the Bank on a proposal involving a World Bank grant of $531,000. The IASC board approved the project at its June 1994 meeting.[310] According to Cairns, the board's approval was not given enthusiastically, and then mainly because of the World Bank grant. Several delegations questioned whether the IASC should take up agriculture, and in November 1994 Cairns wrote to Shiratori: 'Are we sure we want to do this project? I have not heard a good word about it (apart from the South Africans).'[311] Nevertheless, a steering committee was set up in November 1994, initially chaired by Narendra P. Sarda (India), followed briefly by Hank Howarth (Canada), and from 1996 to 2000 by Reyaz Mihular, chairman of the Sri Lankan Accounting Standards Committee and a member of the India/Sri Lanka delegation.[312]

Compared to the IASC's other technical work, the agriculture project initially developed at a leisurely pace. During 1996, the steering committee identified accounting for biological assets and their transformation as the main issue, that is, accounting for living animals and plants as opposed to the agricultural produce derived from them. For biological assets, the steering committee proposed measurement at fair value. As with all cases of periodic remeasurement to fair value, this raised the question of what to do with the value changes, and this then linked the project to the IASC's difficulties over comprehensive income.[313] During this stage, the board commented on the steering committee's reports but otherwise took a detached view. Meanwhile, the original developing-country background of the project had already largely disappeared from view. The IASC's project proposal to the World Bank had made it clear that the IASC would seek to draft a standard that would be applicable to enterprises in all countries, yet it had also strongly emphasized the practical relevance of the project to developing countries.[314] By 1996, the emphasis had shifted to a challenge of a more intellectual nature, that is, to deal with the unique features of biological assets in a way that was consistent with the IASC's evolving interpretation of its own Framework.[315] The project which it had adopted without enthusiasm had acquired an internal significance for the IASC as one more piece in the puzzle of developing a consistent approach to recognition, fair value measurement, and performance reporting. In October 1997, when the board discussed responses to a draft statement of principles issued earlier that year by the steering committee, it might have noticed that hardly any reactions had been received from developing countries.[316] Instead, the steering committee concentrated its attention on the conceptual problems:

> Some commentators recognised that some of the issues the Steering Committee are grappling with were likely 'to set precedents and to have influence beyond its own subject area'. The Steering Committee recognised that in terms of general support for the recommendations contained in the [draft statement of principles] a number of comments were circumscribed by the consequential impacts beyond the immediate sphere of agriculture.[317]

Several board delegations began to express reservations about the proposed approach, both because of its wider implications as well as because of concerns over the reliability of fair value measurements for biological assets.[318] The final push to complete the core standards kept agriculture largely off the IASC's agenda during 1998. It came back in March 1999, at the same time as a draft exposure draft on investment properties. As discussed above, both projects seemed to be harbingers of a fundamental change in financial accounting, and, as with investment properties, the IASC had difficulty reaching agreement on an exposure draft. E65 was approved with no-votes from the Swiss Industrial Holding Companies, Canada, and the United States, with India and Germany abstaining. These delegations doubted whether it was appropriate to measure biological assets at fair value, and whether such a measurement would be reliable. They also questioned whether the case against measurement at historical costs had properly been made.[319] This was one of two occasions in the IASC's history when an exposure draft was passed with just the required minimum of two-thirds of the votes.[320]

The Australians had been the main champions of the exposure draft. The thinking underlying the IASC's draft statement of principles was quite similar to that in ED 83, issued by the AARF in August 1997. The correspondence between the two projects was not coincidental, as the IASC's initial project manager was Ian Kirton, a New Zealander who was much attuned to the AARF's line of thinking.[321] In August 1998, the AASB issued AASB 1037, *Self-Generating and Regenerating Assets*. The main difference with the IASC's evolving approach was that the Australian standard required the recognition of changes in the fair value of biological assets in income, while the IASC was as yet undecided on this point. The Australian delegation staunchly, and successfully, defended their own standard in the IASC board from this point onwards.[322] As acknowledged by Bryan Carsberg, both E65 and IAS 41, *Agriculture*, were very similar to AASB 1037.[323] Conversely, the AASB pointed to the IASC's adoption of the Australian standard to defend its approach against criticism coming from the Australian corporate sector.[324] For IAS 41 to be approved, a reluctant Canada had to be persuaded by several changes which left the overall approach of E65 intact. The changes included an exception for biological assets whose fair value cannot be measured reliably.[325] What also helped, presumably, was that the final vote was taken at the last board meeting. There was a strong feeling that, in the light of the World Bank grant, it would not do for the IASC to leave the project unfinished.[326] The other delegations voted as on E65, with the result that IAS 41 passed with the smallest possible majority.

11.9.3. Unfinished Projects

11.9.3.1. Insurance

A project on insurance accounting had been on the IASC's lists of possible projects at least since the early 1980s. At that time, the IASC board was still reluctant to take up industry issues.[327] By the early 1990s, the board had become more willing to consider insurance accounting, but for many years it was not feasible to start a project, owing to lack of resources. Fortunately for the IASC, FEE set up a working party on insurance accounting to prepare a draft statement of principles, which, when finished, might serve as the starting point for an IASC steering committee.[328] In May 1995, a statement of principles was presented to the board by FEE.[329]

David Damant, a member of the IASC's executive committee, took initiatives to attract the insurance industry's interest and to raise funds.[330] Yet, despite continuous discussions, the IASC hesitated to take action. The executive committee had noted, with evident trepidation, that a project on insurance accounting 'would be similar in scale to the project on Financial Instruments', which was probably sufficient reason not to take up such a project immediately.[331] In April 1997, though, the time was clearly ripe and the board agreed to add the subject to its agenda, with the proviso that work should not, initially, take much of the board's time.[332] A sizeable steering committee was set up with, in the end, no fewer than thirteen members and observers. The committee was chaired by Warren McGregor (Australia).[333] Other than for the approval of a point outline, the project took very little of the board's time.[334] The steering committee produced and published, in its own name, a substantial issues paper of more than 450 pages in November 1999.[335] The paper focused on insurance contracts, rather than on insurance enterprises, which meant that many assets and liabilities of insurance enterprises would be covered by other IASC standards, particularly IAS 32 and IAS 39. In the paper, the steering committee proposed to move the accounting treatment of insurance contracts towards a balance-sheet approach in line with the IASC's Framework. The committee referred to the parallel attempt by the JWG to develop a standard for financial instruments to replace IAS 39. It expressed its belief that, if full fair value accounting were to be introduced for most financial assets and liabilities, insurance contracts should also be measured at fair value. Yet the steering committee also recognized the possibility that IAS 39 might not be replaced for some time, and that the deferral and matching approach, rather than the balance-sheet approach, was still the basis of accounting practice in many countries. Therefore, the paper discussed accounting issues both in the context of the more traditional forms of insurance accounting, as well as under the assumption of more radical change.

Although the paper generated a substantial volume of comment letters, the board did not have the opportunity to take the project any further before the end of 2000.

11.9.3.2. Extractive Industries

Extractive industries was another area that had long attracted the IASC's attention but on which it had never taken any action. Apart from a resource constraint, there must have been an awareness in the IASC that this was a topic with many pitfalls. Countries with highly developed extractive industries included Australia, Canada, South Africa, and the United States. All had developed their own approaches, often different between the oil and gas sector on the one hand and the mining sector on the other, and the resulting standards were not infrequently shaped by strong pressure from industry lobbies.[336] In 1995 and 1996, the IASC was occasionally sounded out by companies in the industry about a possible standard. In 1997, the executive committee noted that some of the more controversial accounting practices of South African mining companies had been modified, which, presumably, removed at least some obstacles from the way towards an IASC standard.[337] In April 1998, the board agreed to set up a steering committee, chaired by Ken Spencer, of the Australian delegation.[338] As with the insurance project, the steering committee produced a lengthy discussion paper of more than 400 pages with relatively little involvement of the board.[339] The paper was published in November 2000, which meant that the IASC had no occasion to take the project further.

11.9.3.3. Other Projects

Apart from several projects mentioned earlier in this chapter, the IASC set up steering committees on four projects in 1998–2000, none of which resulted in any publications.

In April 1998, a project was begun on discounting. Like other standard setters, particularly the G4, the IASC had come across discounting in a number of projects, including impairment, financial instruments, provisions, employee benefits, and income taxes. Like them, the IASC felt the need to develop a framework to ensure that discounting was applied consistently across standards.[340] A steering committee was created, chaired by Patricia Walters, of the financial analysts' delegation.[341] The steering committee intended to publish an issues paper early in 2001 but did not succeed in doing so. Some of its tentative conclusions were published in *IASC Insight*.[342] In April 2001, the IASB decided to incorporate the project into its more general consideration of measurement issues.[343]

Also in April 1998, when it became clear that new projects were needed to fill the post-core gap, a project was set up on developing countries and countries in transition. The immediate cause was another donation by the World Bank, granted in 1997 with the condition that it be linked to work that was relevant for developing countries.[344] More generally, the idea that the IASC had an obligation to pay special attention to the needs of developing countries had been present ever since the 1970s. Between 1989 and 1993 the IASC had run an earlier, unsuccessful project on the reporting needs of developing countries (*see* Section 9.4.2). Undeterred by that experience, the IASC approached the topic afresh. At first it set up a preparatory committee to explore the issues, transformed in November 1998 into a full-dress steering committee chaired by Tony Seah (Malaysia).[345] The steering committee included, for the first time, representatives from the People's Republic of China and the Russian Federation. Nevertheless, the status of the project remained unclear. Although the IASC's *Annual Review* continued to include the committee in its list of steering committees, the date at which the 'preparatory committee' was expected to begin work receded ever further into the future, according to the reports in *IASC Insight* during 1999 and 2000.[346] In June 2000, the board agreed that the preparatory committee should conduct a study to assess the extent of barter transactions.[347] In the end, developing countries were not mentioned in the IASC's 'legacy document' addressed to its successor. As before, the views of those who did not believe that developing countries had special reporting needs seem to have prevailed. The IASC did urge its successor to consider standards for small enterprises, a project which was indeed taken up by the IASB.

A project on business combinations began in November 1998, when a steering committee was formed to review the responses received by the IASC on the G4+1 discussion paper, 'Methods of Accounting for Business Combinations: Recommendations of the G4+1 for Achieving Convergence', which was published in December 1998. The paper was notable for its recommendation that the pooling of interests method should no longer be allowed. Just a few months before, the IASC had with great difficulty approved a revised version of IAS 22, *Business Combinations*, which allowed pooling of interests in the 'exceptional circumstances' where a business combination could be classified as a 'uniting of interests' rather than an acquisition. After noting the steering committee's report on the comment letters, the board instructed the committee to investigate the conceptual justification of the pooling of interests method.[348] The steering committee, chaired by Sigvard Heurlin, did report to the board in March 2000.[349] By that time the FASB had already proposed the abolition of pooling (in an exposure draft dated 7 September 1999). The IASC board was said to be 'split, but it may lean towards the abolition of pooling...if the FASB does this'.[350] The IASC board took no further action on the issue, but the IASB did eliminate pooling of interests with IFRS 3, *Business Combinations* (March 2004) after the FASB had done so in FAS 141, *Business Combinations* (June 2001).

The IASC board installed its final steering committee during its meeting of June 2000. The committee was to deal with disclosures in the financial statements of banks, leading to a possible revision of IAS 30 to bring it in line with IAS 1, IAS 32, and IAS 39. Just before, the Basel Committee had pointed out the desirability of revising IAS 30.[351] The committee was chaired by Geoffrey Mitchell, a former IASC secretary-general who by then had joined Barclays bank in the United Kingdom.[352] Although the steering committee did meet in 2000, it had no impact on the work of the IASC. In 2006, the IASB approved

IFRS 7, *Financial Instruments: Disclosures*, which superseded IAS 30 and parts of IAS 32.

In addition to these four projects, the board discussed a range of miscellaneous topics during 1999 and 2000 on the basis of papers prepared by the staff. As a result, the board was able to give its opinion, in its legacy document to the IASB, on, among others, accounting for share-based payments, narrative discussion of financial results by management, public sector accounting, and financial reporting on the Internet.[353] The last topic had also been the subject of a discussion paper published by the IASC staff in November 1999.[354]

11.10. CONCLUSION

In 1989, Ralph Walters, the chairman of the IASC's Comparability steering committee, remarked that he had often compared the IASC to the Jamaican bobsleigh team: 'We were aware that [it] existed, but it was hard to take it seriously.'[355] It is likely that Walters' view was shared by many at that time, including people who might, on closer inspection, have conceded that the IASC's standards were not necessarily inferior to their national accounting standards. By 2000, there was no longer any doubt that the IASC deserved to be taken seriously as an accounting standard setter. By intense effort, it had produced a body of standards that, in coverage and rigour, exceeded or equalled the national standards in almost all countries. However, throughout the IASC's life the question whether it could produce high-quality standards was different from the question whether these would be accepted in practice. As is shown in Chapter 12, an affirmative answer to the first question did not automatically settle the second.

12

The World Wakes Up to the IASC

12.1. INTRODUCTION

As concluded in Chapter 6, the IASC's impact on accounting practice and regulation was still fairly limited by the late 1980s. In none of the developed countries were companies required to comply with IASC standards, nor were companies allowed to prepare their financial statements in accordance with IASC standards instead of in conformity with national standards or accounting law. Given the permissive nature of IASC standards at that time, it must not have been unduly onerous for most companies to comply both with local standards and IASC standards. Nevertheless, voluntary references to compliance with IASC standards in financial statements or audit reports were rare, with the exception of Canada. In the developing world, the IASC's standards had gained a higher degree of acceptance, but it is not likely that strict compliance was widespread. This chapter discusses how, during the 1990s, the IASC achieved considerably more success in gaining recognition for its standards in the developed world.

We have not attempted to undertake a comprehensive survey of the degree to which the IASC standards were applied in practice around the world. Instead, we have drawn on the extensive study by David Cairns of compliance with IASC standards in different countries, published in 2000, to which we refer the reader for further details.[1]

This chapter is organized as follows. Section 12.2 reviews developments in selected European board member countries. Section 12.3 traces the origins of the IASC's greatest success, the decision in June 2000 by the European Commission to propose the required application of IASC standards in the consolidated financial statements of all listed companies in the European Union (EU), starting in 2005. Section 12.4 discusses the different responses to the IASC in several non-European board member countries, while Section 12.5 treats the support given to the IASC by international financial institutions such as the World Bank. Finally, Section 12.6 shows how several national standard setters created an intensive form of cooperation among themselves, known as the G4+1, which some saw as a potential rival of the IASC.

12.2. A MIXED RECORD OF ACCEPTANCE IN EUROPE

The 1990s were a decade of growing acceptance of IASC standards in Europe. In 1995, the IASC secretariat reported that seventy-seven companies from the fifteen member states of the EU disclosed compliance with IASC standards.[2] In June 2000, the European Commission claimed that 275 EU companies applied IASC standards.[3] It was clear that the degree of acceptance of IASC standards in Europe was higher than it had ever been before.

The rise of IASC standards in Europe occurred in a regulatory setting marked by a confusing uncertainty over the applicability of national accounting norms in relation to IASC standards.[4] As will be seen in the following sections, the European Commission, as well as national governments and standard setters, were reconsidering and re-negotiating their roles in accounting regulation in response to pressures from the globalizing capital market. At the same time, the IASC standards themselves were rapidly being transformed to become less permissive and more detailed. It was not always clear in every country and at all times whether a company was allowed to comply fully with the IASC standards of the day. Sometimes it was clear that they could not, but some companies claimed compliance with IASC standards nevertheless. At the same time, concerns were frequently expressed that companies applied IASC standards selectively, or with less than the appropriate rigour, and the phrase 'IAS-lite' made its appearance in this context.[5]

The impact of the IASC in Europe was far from uniform. Traditionally, Europe has been seen as divided between the Continental and Anglo-American accounting traditions. Countries like France, Germany, and Italy were firmly in the Continental camp; Ireland, the Netherlands, and the United Kingdom were in the 'Anglo-American' camp, with the Nordic countries occupying the middle ground. As the IASC has always been seen as a body that was dominated by the Anglo-American point of view, it is interesting to see that, during the 1990s, some of the Continental countries began to show evidence of considerable enthusiasm for IASC standards, while some of the countries associated with the Anglo-American tradition were slow to respond to the IASC's rapid increase in international stature. The next sections review how these different trajectories developed in the European countries represented on the IASC board during most of the 1990s.

12.2.1. France

The fact that a Frenchman, Georges Barthès de Ruyter, chaired the IASC from 1987 to 1990 had led to an enhanced awareness of the IASC in France.[6] Yet, at the end of the 1980s, the regulation of financial reporting in France was still very much based on a national approach, embodied, as it had been for several decades, by legal requirements and by the Plan Comptable Général (PCG). A limited degree of internationalization had been introduced with France's adoption of the Seventh Directive in 1986. Most importantly, companies were then allowed to choose different accounting policies in their consolidated and in their parent company financial statements. The corresponding sections of the PCG dealing with consolidated financial statements included several options that were international, not traditionally French, in character, such as the capitalization of leased assets. These changes were made with an eye to the future, for there were as yet few French companies with international listings.[7] The listing of Rhône-Poulenc on the New York Stock Exchange (NYSE) in 1989 marked the beginning of a widening interest in international capital markets, although the change was gradual. By 2000, eighteen French companies were listed in New York. Before the early 1990s, it was taken as given in France that foreign companies listing in the United States had to apply US generally accepted accounting principles (US GAAP). Yet French companies quickly began to take an interest in IASC standards as a potential alternative to US GAAP.[8] In 1992, Bernard Jaudeau of Thomson became the first financial executive to serve in the French IASC delegation. About forty multinational companies set up a supporting infrastructure in the form of an 'Association for the Participation of French Enterprises in the International Harmonization of Accounting' and provided it with a sufficient budget to hire a small technical staff. Among other activities, this group coordinated the responses of the associated French enterprises to IASC exposure drafts. In 1995, the IASC secretariat noted that twenty-eight French companies were already affirming compliance with IASC standards in their annual reports,[9] the highest in absolute terms for any European country apart from Switzerland.

Yet the consolidated financial statements of these companies still had to be prepared according to French requirements, which meant that companies either had to issue two sets of consolidated financial statements or had to combine French and IASC standards, increasing the risk of IAS-lite. The fast pace of change in IASC standards increased these difficulties and made a modernization of the French options for consolidated financial statements, as introduced in 1986, ever more urgent. In 1996, the Minister of Economics and Finance, Jean Arthuis, a former partner of Arthur Andersen, appointed Georges Barthès—another former Andersen partner—as chairman of the Conseil National de la Comptabilité (CNC), the body responsible for maintaining the PCG and advising the government on accounting matters. The mission given to Barthès was simple: to move towards IASC standards as fast as possible.[10] The result was a major revision of the section of the PCG dealing with consolidated financial statements, completed in April 1999.[11] The PCG was brought much closer to IASC standards, but differences were allowed to persist.[12]

A more radical step was taken, at least in principle, with the creation of the Comité de la Réglementation Comptable (CRC) in 1998. This body was set up to centralize the government's authority to issue accounting regulations, previously diffused among several ministries.[13] Henceforth, it would be the CRC which would formally endorse and promulgate the CNC's recommendations. The law creating the CRC also allowed it to adopt 'international [accounting] rules' and to set the conditions under which listed French companies could use these rules, rather than the requirements of French company law, in preparing their consolidated financial statements. To be adopted by the CRC, 'international rules' had to be translated into French and had to respect, in effect, the European accounting Directives.[14] The former condition was an elegant way of ruling out the application of US GAAP which, because of its bulk and complexity, would never be translated into French. IASC standards, on the other hand, were available in French because, unlike some other founder member bodies, the Ordre des Experts Comptables had persisted in preparing translations. In addition, the compatibility of IASC standards with the European Directives had been established by the European Commission in 1996 (*see* Section 12.3.3). Yet the CRC never formally adopted IASC standards, and the European Commission's initiative of June 2000 to require all listed companies to apply IASC standard made such a move redundant. Nevertheless, an interim measure stated that, prior to the adoption of any rules by the CRC and until the end of 2002, listed companies could use 'recognized international rules' that met the same two conditions. While this gave a more explicit legal status to the application of IASC standards, several French companies stopped referring to IASC standards in their financial statements in 1998 and 1999.[15]

12.2.2. Germany

Until the early 1990s, the IASC had made very little impact in Germany. It was hardly mentioned in the professional literature, and there was no domestic standard setter which could ensure that IASC standards were introduced through their incorporation in national accounting standards. The Institut der Wirtschaftsprüfer (IdW) did issue non-binding recommendations on accounting, but these dealt mainly with narrow issues and by no means matched the range of topics covered by IASC standards.[16] The IdW, a founding member of the IASC, had few formal powers. As it knew that a strong advocacy of the IASC would not be favourably received, its promotion of the IASC was muted. Around 1990, the IASC was little known among listed German companies.[17] By 1993, the IdW had ceased to translate IASC standards into German.[18]

As explained in Section 10.8.5, the early 1990s saw important changes in the German capital markets, and German companies began to look abroad for finance. This led some of the larger companies to make limited changes in accounting policies used in their consolidated financial statements. This was the case, for instance, with Schering when it listed in London in 1989. To do so, these companies exploited the formerly little-used possibility to use different accounting policies in the consolidated financial statements than were used in the parent company financial statements, which were linked to the tax system.[19] Nevertheless, the consolidated statements still had to be prepared according to German accounting regulations and norms, mainly included in the Commercial Code (Handelsgesetzbuch, HGB). While these initial forays abroad focused attention on the fact that German financial reporting was quite different from the Anglo-American tradition, the initial conclusion by companies, academics, and the government was that there was no reason why German financial reporting had to change. Instead, all attention was focused on justifying German reporting practices as appropriate in the light of the German socio-economic system,[20] and of seeking agreement with the United States on the mutual recognition of each other's financial reporting.²¹ A small group of leading companies took concerted action, together with the Ministry of Justice, to argue with the US Securities and Exchange Commission (SEC) in favour of mutual recognition, but to no avail. Then, in March 1993, Daimler-Benz broke away from this group and announced that it would list as the first German company on the NYSE. As discussed in Section 10.8.5, it accepted the need to reconcile to US GAAP, with the result that it was revealed that its 1993 HGB profit turned into a loss when restated according to US GAAP.²² The Daimler listing sent shock waves through the German corporate world and the accounting establishment. It brought home that mutual recognition was a dead end. Moreover, the fact that German accounting appeared to be less conservative than US GAAP led to serious questioning of the traditional arguments in favour of a distinctive German approach to accounting. On closer inspection, it should have been clear that the adverse translation of the Daimler results was caused by specific circumstances, and should by no means have called into question the generally prudent nature of German accounting. Nevertheless, the Daimler case led to a rapid erosion of political support for the maintenance of a separate German accounting system.²³ Already in April 1994, representatives from German business, the accountancy profession, the government, and academe came together at a major symposium with the eloquent title, 'Do the German Accounting Rules Still Have a Chance?'²⁴

Not all German companies were willing to follow Daimler all the way to Canossa. Some, like Bayer and Schering in 1994, opted instead to modify their HGB-based consolidated financial statements so that they could claim compliance with IASC standards as well, in the hope that IASC standards would before long be accepted by the SEC.²⁵ Deutsche Bank, in its 1995 financial statements, was another and very prominent convert to IASC standards. From that point onwards, the major German companies gradually began to split into two groups, one favouring US GAAP and the other using IASC standards. The result was that some prepared a double set of accounts, as Daimler did from 1996 onwards, while others had to use considerable creativity to prepare financial statements that complied both with German legal requirements and with IASC standards.²⁶ Whether that was, legally speaking, possible was an open question, and one that was ever less likely to be answered affirmatively as the IASC standards evolved towards a wider use of fair value.²⁷

Early in 1995, the German government recognized the inevitable, and it announced its intention to draft legislation that would formally allow the preparation of consolidated financial statements according to both US GAAP and IASC standards, instead of according to German law.²⁸ This radical change in policy was announced, as a complete surprise to the other delegations, at the April 1995 meeting of Working Party 1 (WP1) of the International Organization of Securities Commissions (IOSCO) by the German government's senior civil servant in charge of accounting issues, Herbert Biener of the Ministry of Justice.²⁹ Biener, who for most of the 1980s and 1990s personified the official German position on accounting, had until 1995 taken a critical line on the applicability of IASC standards in Europe, and especially in Germany.³⁰ From this point onwards, Biener was able to take a constructive attitude towards the IASC in WP1 and in the many other settings where he represented the German government.

The proposal to change the HGB ran into political difficulties, however, not least because the business community was split over the question whether US GAAP should be allowed. US GAAP was clearly favoured by companies like Daimler, but an opposition led by Bayer argued that this would weaken the position of the IASC in which Germany, at least, had a chance to participate.[31] Another issue was which companies would be allowed to use the option not to account according to German law.[32] It was not until April 1998 that the 'Law to Facilitate Raising Capital' (Kapitalaufnahmeerleichterungsgesetz or KapAEG) was enacted. This law allowed all listed companies, under relatively simple conditions, to prepare consolidated accounts according to 'internationally recognized principles of accounting'.[33] In contrast to the simultaneously enacted French law of April 1998 (see Section 12.2.1), this provision did not require additional government action to take effect. By 1999, almost 100 major German companies referred to compliance with IASC standards.[34]

When the KapAEG was passed, the traditionally tight regimentation of financial reporting in Germany was already in a state of flux, and both US GAAP and IASC standards had gained a considerable foothold in practice. An important factor was the launch, by Deutsche Börse, of the Neue Markt (New Market) in March 1997, a stock exchange segment for small, high technology enterprises. Among the listing requirements for this segment was the obligation to provide quarterly and annual reporting on the basis of US GAAP or IASC standards, or on the basis of German accounting with a reconciliation to either.[35] There was probably no other country, certainly not among those represented on the IASC board, which did not allow some of its companies to use their own country's accounting standards without a reconciliation to accounting standards developed outside the country.

The KapAEG was explicitly intended to create a limited period of experimentation, as it was to lapse by the end of 2004. To provide a focus for the development of opinions during this unsettled period, the Ministry of Justice persuaded Parliament to authorize it to set up a private-sector deliberative body on accounting.[36] In addition, such a body was expected to enable Germany to participate more effectively in international accounting harmonization. This last reason was explained by some commentators in terms of the ongoing discussions on the restructuring of the IASC (see Chapter 13). At the time, these discussions seemed likely to result in an IASC set up as a body of national standard setters, and for that reason it might be desirable to create a German standard setter.[37] The Deutsche Rechnungslegungs Standards Committee (initially known in English as German Accounting Standards Board, and currently as Accounting Standards Committee of Germany) was set up in March 1998 and formally recognized by the Ministry of Justice under the new legal provisions in September 1998.[38] However, the period of experimentation was cut short, and the potential significance of the new standard setter considerably diminished, by the European Commission's decision in June 2000 to recommend the required application of IASC standards by all listed European companies in their consolidated financial statements by

2005. Contrary to expectations, the IASC was not restructured as an organization of national standard setters either. Nevertheless, in just a few years, the traditional German accounting model, rooted deeply in the needs of the tax authorities and creditors, had taken on an Anglo-American hue, at least in companies' consolidated statements.

12.2.3. The Netherlands

Throughout the 1990s, the Netherlands maintained its traditionally flexible financial reporting environment. The Guidelines issued by the national standard setter, the Council on Annual Reporting (CAR), were not binding on companies, and auditors did not report on compliance with these Guidelines. There was no regulatory body that oversaw compliance with legal requirements, let alone the Guidelines. A company's accounting practices could be challenged by interested parties in a specialized court, but at considerable expense and following a cumbersome procedure.[39] In 1990, only two of 109 listed companies were found to refer to the CAR's Guidelines in their financial statements. In this situation, it was perhaps not surprising that only one company then referred to IASC standards.[40]

The Ministry of Justice, which regulated the financial reporting requirements of the Civil Code, was generally willing to tolerate a flexible interpretation of the European Directives and Dutch law so as to allow the application of IASC standards, but no steps were taken to encourage their adoption or to ensure a rigorous application.[41]

The traditional view of financial reporting was still very much in evidence in 1989, when the CAR commented critically on the IASC's E32, 'Comparability of Financial Statements'. Its comment letter, in which it pointed out that a company's right to select accounting policies appropriate for its circumstances was more important than comparability, was published prominently in the Netherlands.[42] In subsequent years, the CAR showed itself more attuned to the way the IASC was changing, and it tended to incorporate new IASC standards in its Guidelines. Yet it allowed itself to depart from the IASC's standards when it believed they were 'not acceptable' in the Netherlands.

Although this flexible environment was favourable to experimentation with elements of IASC standards, it was hardly a propitious climate in which to nourish a spirit of strict compliance. Prior to the IASC's Comparability and Improvements projects, and prior to the drive to complete the core standards, it might have been reasonable to believe that compliance with local standards implied compliance with IASC standards. But in 1998, the panel of judges that bestowed the country's leading award for the year's 'best annual report' accused the listed companies of 'complacency' in developing their reporting practices and urged them to adopt the more stringent regime of IASC standards.[43] But by 1999 there were still only few listed companies that claimed to use IASC standards.[44] Meanwhile, about a dozen of the largest companies, most with listings in the United States, became more and more oriented towards US GAAP.

Perhaps in the belief that there were few significant legal obstacles to the use of either US GAAP or IASC standards, the government was slow to respond to the European Commission's policy from 1995 onwards to remove formal restrictions on the use of IASC standards (*see* Section 12.3.3). It was not until 1999 that the government announced its intention to enact the necessary Civil Code amendments to allow multinational companies to use either US GAAP or IASC standards, provided that there was no conflict with the Directives.[45] The legislation was finally passed in 2005.

12.2.4. Nordic Countries

Denmark, Norway, and Sweden made up the IASC's Nordic delegation during the 1990s. Each of the three countries moved closer to IASC standards during this period but in different ways. In each of the countries, accounting was traditionally based on company law. During the 1990s, Sweden and Norway were still in the process of separating consolidated financial reporting from tax accounting, whereas Denmark had already broken that link with the adoption of the Fourth Directive in 1981.

The Danish accountancy body, Foreningen af Statsautoriserede Revisorer (FSR) published Danish translations of IASC standards, with a commentary, well before it decided, in 1986, to begin issuing national accounting standards. The IASC standards had no formal status, and, at least until the early 1990s, the impact of IASC standards was said to be limited and smaller than the FSR had expected.[46] When the FSR began to publish its national standards, these were imposed as a requirement on listed companies by the Copenhagen Stock Exchange. From the beginning, the FSR's standards were accompanied by an appendix indicating the degree of conformity with the relevant IASC standards. Initially, the degree of conformity was high, as the FSR began with relatively simple subjects, and the IASC had not yet completed its Comparability and Improvements projects. Yet in 1992, the FSR ruled out the use of last-in, first-out (LIFO), which it called 'misleading',[47] even though the IASC would later that year reverse its tentative decision to eliminate LIFO (*see* Section 9.3.3.3). As the IASC's technical work accelerated during the 1990s, the FSR had to make a more determined effort to bring its standards into line with IASC standards. As if to underscore the differences, a few Danish companies began to publish financial statements on the basis of IASC standards, in order to improve their access to capital markets.[48]

In Norway, a private-sector accounting standard setter (the Norwegian Accounting Standards Board, NASB) was created in 1989, whose standards were said to be based 'to a certain degree' on US GAAP.[49] Because of the oil industry, Norwegian accounting was receptive to the influence of US GAAP. Accounting education at business schools was also orientated to the United States. However, from the beginning the NASB was also clearly focused on the IASC.[50] The Oslo Stock Exchange, a co-founder of the NASB, took an active interest in accounting standards and exercised a degree of compliance monitoring. In 1998, a new accounting law was enacted in order to adopt the EU's accounting Directives (because of Norway's membership of the European Economic Area). Although this law did not by itself give IASC standards a legal footing in Norway, compatibility with IASC standards was an important underlying principle.[51] The drafting history of the law made it clear that Parliament expected Norwegian accounting standards to be set on the basis of harmonization with IASC standards.[52]

As in Norway, Swedish legislation was adapted to the European Directives. An amendment of the Companies Act to this effect came into force in 1997. Because of remaining tax influences, the new law was said to be not completely in line with the Directives. It was acknowledged that adherence to the law might result in material differences from IASC standards and US GAAP.[53] With respect to accounting standards, Sweden offered a complicated picture. The Swedish Accounting Standards Board, a government-sponsored body, but with a broad range of organizations represented in its membership, was set up in 1976. In addition, the main accountancy body, Föreningen Auktoriserade Revisorer (FAR), issued recommendations as it had done since 1949. In 1989, the Swedish Financial Accounting Standards Council (Redovisningsrådet) was created. It was a cooperative effort between the FAR and Swedish business, and once it was created the FAR all but ceased work on its own recommendations. The objective of the Redovisningsrådet was to issue recommendations for public companies. For listed companies, these recommendations were considered mandatory, and from the outset the intention was to adapt the recommendations 'as much as possible to international practice, including in particular the IASC standards'.[54] The Redovisningsrådet was from 1989 onwards the main vehicle for introducing IASC standards into Sweden.[55]

In each of the three countries, one can therefore see an ongoing and deliberate process by which national law and accounting standards were adjusted to IASC standards. By the end of the decade, however, it appears that in all three countries the process of adjustment had to some extent fallen behind, as the IASC's productivity surged during the core standards programme. The increasing domestication of IASC standards, or, more likely, the gap between national standards and IASC standards, may have been the reason why the number of companies referring explicitly to IASC standards remained small.[56] Cairns' 1999 survey showed that only seven out of forty-four selected companies from the three countries claimed to use IASC standards, sometimes partially, sometimes as supplementary information.[57]

12.2.5. Switzerland

Even though Swiss accounting may once have epitomized everything that was contrary to the capital-market orientation of accounting in the Anglo-American world, Swiss multinationals became the most prominent adopters of IASC standards during the 1990s. The seeds for this were sown in the 1980s, when the view gained currency that financial reporting in Switzerland was in need of modernization. In 1984, this led to the creation of a standard-setting body, inspired by the example of the English-speaking countries and the Netherlands.[58] The capital needs of the Swiss multinational companies did the rest. In 1989, Nestlé announced that it would switch to IASC standards, after it began to allow foreigners to hold registered stock, and following its listing on the London Stock Exchange.[59] Other Swiss multinationals, such as Roche and Ciba-Geigy, followed suit during the next few years in a wider movement of corporate governance and stock exchange reforms which included more transparent financial reporting.[60] The financial reporting requirements of Swiss company law, not very stringent to begin with, were modernized in 1991, but in a way that would not prevent the application of IASC standards.[61] In 1995, when financial reporting requirements were introduced for the first time in the stock exchange listing criteria, both US GAAP and IASC standards were recognized as acceptable, in addition to Swiss accounting standards.[62] In 1999, thirty-three out of forty-two large Swiss companies were reported to be using IASC standards, a degree of impact unmatched in any other European country.[63]

12.2.6. United Kingdom

The UK Accounting Standards Board (ASB) had a strong domestic position which it used to develop a recognizably British approach to financial reporting. The ASB was generally regarded, both within and outside the United Kingdom, as one of the leading standard-setting bodies in the world. This was not a situation that was conducive to the application of IASC standards by UK companies. Of 109 UK companies surveyed by David Cairns, only three referred at all to IASC standards in their 1999 financial statements.[64]

As far as can be ascertained, there was never any pressure from UK companies to be allowed to apply IASC standards rather than UK GAAP. In theory, such pressure might have arisen because foreign companies listed in London could use IASC standards. Yet, even though UK GAAP was generally seen as more demanding than IASC standards, this was not seen as an unfair advantage of foreign over domestic companies. IASC standards were seen as more demanding than the national accounting standards in many member states of the EU that had to be accepted as equivalent to UK GAAP under the principle of mutual recognition.[65]

Although there were a few instances in which standards of the ASB were influenced by the IASC, the impact was more often in the opposite direction. With this in mind, David Cairns predicted in 1998 that, following IOSCO's endorsement of the IASC's standards, the ASB would remain the most important standard setter for UK companies. He expected the ASB and the IASC to continue their cooperation, 'with the ASB giving to the IASC rather more than it takes from the IASC'.[66]

12.3. THE EUROPEAN COMMISSION'S GRADUAL CONVERSION TO IASC STANDARDS

Overall, one can conclude from the preceding review of developments in individual European countries that, although IASC standards were clearly in the ascendant during the 1990s, their overall dominance was hardly assured. In most countries, only a minority of companies explicitly referred to IASC standards, although it should be taken into account that the IASC's actual impact was also felt through the increasing incorporation of IASC standards into national standards. Yet in some countries, notably the United Kingdom, there was little sign of a movement towards IASC standards, and in other countries US GAAP remained a strong competitor. However significant the developments in individual European countries may have been, the IASC's fate was ultimately decided at the level of the EU. This section recounts the interaction between the European Commission and the IASC, which began in the 1980s.

12.3.1. Warming of Relations Between the IASC and the European Commission

As reported in Section 6.22, the IASC leadership and representatives of the European Commission had met both formally and informally since 1981. The European Commission has been the executive body of the European Economic Community (EEC) until 1993 and of the EU since then.[67] Historically, the Commission had been cool towards the IASC, and the initiative to hold bilateral meetings always came from the IASC side.[68] The Commission regarded its Fourth and Seventh Directives on Company Law, to be adapted into legislation by all of the member states of the Community, as the centrepiece of accounting harmonization in Europe. It did not welcome the challenge to its primacy by the private-sector IASC, which could not claim any legal force behind its standards. By 1990, however, the Directives-based approach began to show signs of obsolescence. The Directives, especially the Fourth, admitted of numerous optional accounting treatments, because their promulgation required the unanimous agreement of the member states. Such an approach to harmonization might have suited the 1970s and the 1980s, very much as the IASC's standards during that same period also were rife with options. But the times had changed, and in the 1990s the increasing globalization of capital markets, especially in Europe, demanded a higher level of comparability across countries. The IASC and IOSCO were alive to this development, but it took some time before the Commission, and some of the member states, became fully convinced that a different approach in Europe was in order.

During the 1980s, the major influence on the Commission's policies was exercised by Hermann Niessen, the head of the accounting unit with the European Commission's Directorate General XV (Internal Market). Niessen, however, was not enamoured of the investor-orientated financial reporting norms reflected in the IASC's standards.[69] In 1986, the first formal meeting between the Commission and the IASC since 1983 was held when IASC Chairman John Kirkpatrick and Secretary-General David Cairns visited Niessen. Yet Niessen apparently kept the IASC at a distance, and some intermediation was necessary. In 1987, Jean Dupont, the chairman of the CNC, probably at the suggestion of IASC Chairman Georges Barthès de Ruyter, had a long discussion with Niessen about the need for a closer relationship between the European Commission and the IASC. Although Niessen was said to be reluctant, he did admit that it was in everyone's interest to develop such a relationship.[70]

In 1988, the IASC offered membership on the Consultative Group to both the Financial Accounting Standards Board (FASB) and the European Commission, departing from the IASC's original policy that the Group would be for worldwide organizations only.[71] The times required a more flexible policy. The FASB accepted, but the European Commission was not prepared at that time to come on board. Niessen was, however, willing to attend the IASC board's meeting in November 1988, in Copenhagen, as a guest.[72] In his address to the board, Niessen was careful to explain the limits of the shared interests of the European Community and the IASC. Their common interest was in 'accounting harmonization'.[73] Yet, he said, while the IASC talks about the 'harmonization of accounting standards', the Community prefers the term 'harmonization of accounting legislation'. This reflected a fundamental difference between the two. The IASC, especially in the context of its programme to respond to IOSCO, was pursuing harmonization in order to promote comparability in world capital markets. From this perspective, a higher degree of comparability was always preferable, and Niessen characterized it as 'harmonization for the sake of harmonization'. The European Commission, by contrast, was carrying out its mandate to achieve the harmonization of company law within the European Community as part of the creation of an Internal Market. Here, the focus was on the basic level of harmonization required 'to give equivalent safeguards to shareholders or members and third parties'. Niessen also cited other differences. One was 'territorial': the worldwide aspirations of the IASC versus the twelve member states of the Community. He described another as a 'constitutional' difference: the IASC was composed of representatives of the accountancy profession, while the Community achieved harmonization via an elaborate process of approving Directives and implementing them in national legislation. In other words, Niessen saw the IASC as an arm of the accountancy profession alone and as a private-sector entity without any trappings of legal authority. Indeed, Karel Van Hulle, a member of Niessen's staff at that time, recalled that the European Commission viewed the IASC as a 'boys' club'.[74]

Yet, regardless of Niessen's views, by 1989 the European Commission could no longer treat the IASC as a marginal phenomenon. Within Europe, interest in the IASC had developed to such an extent that it became an unavoidable factor in discussions about the future direction of European accounting regulation. These discussions began in earnest in 1989 and continued until the European Commission's decision, taken in 2000, to require compliance with IASC standards of all European listed companies.

One of the parties that made sure that the European Commission paid attention to the IASC was the Fédération des Experts Comptables Européens (Federation of European Accountants, FEE). FEE was formed in 1987 to succeed two bodies: the Union Européenne des Experts Comptables, Economiques et Financiers (UEC) and the Groupe d'Études des Experts Comptables de la CEE (Groupe d'Études). One of FEE's stated objectives was to be the sole consultative organization of the European accountancy profession in relation to the European Community. During its early years, FEE was riven by many controversies, and one of them concerned the future of accounting harmonization in Europe. One view held that FEE should support the IASC and that FEE should encourage the European Commission to grant recognition to the work of the IASC.[75] Another view was that FEE should promote the development of European accounting standards, although not necessarily in competition with the IASC. These standards should be set by an officially recognized private-sector body, tentatively known as a Council for Annual Reporting in Europe (CARE), in which preparers and users of financial information should be represented as well as the accountancy profession, represented by FEE.[76] The idea of a European standard setter had occasionally surfaced before,[77] but during the 1990s it was continually present. Some saw it as a real threat or as a viable strategy for Europe, but others saw it as an impracticable idea that just refused to go away. One observer characterized it as the 'Loch Ness monster' of European accountancy.[78]

In early 1989, if not before, it became known that Niessen and Van Hulle favoured a CARE-like body, as they tentatively put forward the idea to various parties.[79] This gave rise to speculation that an intergovernmental conference on the future of accounting harmonization in Europe, to be organized by the European Commission towards the end of 1989, was in fact an attempt by the Commission to obtain a mandate to create a European accounting standard setter.[80] Against this background, FEE President Hermann Nordemann came out strongly in favour of the IASC, and against European accounting standards, in a speech at the IASC board's meeting in April 1989 in Brussels.[81] In the current climate of increasing globalization, Nordemann said, FEE 'is not favorably disposed towards the creation of an introverted European Community accounting standards zone' (iii) and instead 'recognizes that the worldwide harmonization of accounting standards is imperative' (i). The Directives programme, he said, was born of the needs of an earlier era and had not been a success. The Directive-setting process took too long, it allowed too many options to the member states, and it had failed to deal with a number of important accounting issues. He said that FEE supported the IASC because 'a faster and more responsive organization must take the lead' (iii), but, he cautioned, FEE's support of IASC standards 'is conditional upon there being a strong European input into their preparation in order to ensure that the specific needs and characteristics of the European financial reporting environments are taken into account and addressed in a satisfactory manner' (iii–iv). That the IASC's leadership welcomed Nordemann's speech is borne out by its reproduction in full in a four-page insert in the July 1989 issue of *IASC News*.

Nordemann spoke without prior consultation within FEE, and his widely publicized speech was controversial.[82] Speaking out in public against the views of the European Commission was a novelty for some former members of the Groupe d'Études who were now participants in FEE.[83] Asked for his reaction, Karel Van Hulle dismissed it as the point of view of the 'Anglo-Saxon' faction in FEE, which naturally supported the IASC. He described the IASC in turn as 'largely an Anglo-Saxon club, whether you like it or not'.[84]

Nevertheless, consultations between FEE and the European Commission, as well as between the Commission and the IASC, continued during 1989. A new element in the Commission's thinking was that it became concerned over what it saw as the SEC's increasing influence over the IASC.[85] This apparently prompted the Commission to take a more active interest in the IASC. Although the difficulties which Niessen had outlined to the IASC board in November 1988 continued to be mentioned, the European Commission found itself more closely engaged than ever in the work programme of the IASC.[86] During a meeting on 15 December 1989, Niessen and Van Hulle discussed at length the E32 proposals, standard by standard, with six representatives of the IASC.[87]

Meanwhile, Nordemann's speech had certainly helped to enliven discussions going on across Europe. In preparation for the Commission's intergovernmental conference, which, after a postponement, was held on 17–18 January 1990, the EEC member states were asked for their views on the future of accounting harmonization in Europe. This placed the question of the relationship between the IASC and accounting regulation in Europe squarely on the agenda of national governments and the national interest groups which they consulted. It soon became clear that there was little support in the European private sector for a European layer of accounting standards.[88]

The January 1990 conference, held in Brussels, marked a change in the relations between the IASC and the European Commission.[89] The conference agreed that close cooperation between Europe and the IASC was of great importance, especially for European enterprises operating outside Europe. Although the IASC was not to be given a 'blank cheque', the applicability of its standards in Europe had to be considered, and the European Community was to participate in the development of new international standards. The Commission also announced that it would accept the IASC's invitation to participate in the IASC's work on the same terms as the FASB.[90]

Shortly afterwards, Niessen confirmed to the IASC that he would attend the next meeting of the Consultative Group, set for March. In addition, Niessen and Van Hulle confirmed their interest in participating in the work of the IASC's steering committees, because it would be ineffective for the Commission to react to issues only at the board or Consultative Group level.[91] Van Hulle soon began attending meetings of the Improvements steering committee as an observer. In March 1990 Niessen attended a board meeting as a guest. Later that year, he retired from the Commission. Although Niessen was not, strictly speaking, succeeded by Van Hulle, the latter did become the dominant influence on the Commission's policy on accounting issues during the 1990s.[92] Van Hulle continued to attend board meetings as a guest. At the March 1992 meeting, the European Commission and FASB representatives were both accorded status as observers at board meetings, entitling them to participate in the dialogue.

At the January 1990 conference, the Commission also announced plans to create, not a European standard setter, but an Accounting Advisory Forum, thus enlarging the part that the European private sector would play in the deliberations leading to improved harmonization of accounting standards.[93] The role of the Forum, Van Hulle has written, was to 'advise the Commission on technical solutions for problems which have not been dealt with in the Accounting directives and provide guidance on the position to be taken in international accounting harmonization debates'. He added, 'The Forum should also provide a platform for discussions between users and preparers and national standards setting bodies on accounting issues and developments.'[94] The Forum, he said, was to be the private-sector counterpart of the Contact Committee (an advisory body on issues relating to the Directives, composed of representatives from the member state governments). The first meeting of the Forum was in January 1991. The members and accompanying experts of the first Forum included a number of current and former IASC board members and staff observers, as well as a former IASC secretary, attending in other capacities.[95]

12.3.2. The European Commission Seeks to Reinforce the European Voice in the IASC

The more positive stance towards the IASC that became apparent in 1990 did by no means imply that the European Commission renounced its own role as an accounting regulator. Rather, the Commission sought to enhance its role, at the same time as it sought to ensure that a more coordinated European point of view was put forward in the IASC.

At the 'Festival of Accounting', organized by the Institute of Chartered Accountants of Scotland, held in March 1991 in Edinburgh, Karel Van Hulle made strong and controversial claims for the exclusive competence of the European Commission in the area of accounting harmonization.[96] He also mentioned a proposal, that was being developed for submission to the Council of Ministers, which would allow the application of the so-called 'comitology' procedure in the area of financial reporting. This would mean that, in future, limited 'technical' amendments to the accounting Directives might be made by a special regulatory committee consisting of representatives of the member states and chaired by the Commission. In this way, the cumbersome route by way of the European Parliament and the Council of Ministers might be avoided. However, the proposal foundered primarily because of the resistance by Germany and the United Kingdom.[97] The view of the German Ministry of Justice in the early 1990s was that, with the completion of the accounting Directives, there was no legal basis for further European activity in the area of accounting harmonization. The Ministry also saw such activity as undesirable, because it was likely to upset the delicate historical balance in the Fourth Directive between the shareholder- and creditor-oriented approaches to accounting.[98] According to Van Hulle, the United Kingdom opposed further changes to the Directives, with or without comitology, because it wanted no European interference in the work of its newly created standard setter, the ASB.[99]

Different views held by the Commission and the member states, both on substantive accounting issues and on the role of the Commission, help to explain why the Accounting Advisory Forum was generally seen as a disappointment. Although the participants in the Forum agreed that more effective European input into the IASC was required, and that the Forum might play this role, there was no agreement on the precise arrangements. FEE and its members complained that the Commission was treating the Forum as an advisory body whose views it was free to ignore. On the other hand, the Commission might point out that the Forum had been unable to reach agreement on any of the accounting topics discussed during its first meetings.[100]

When the Commission began sending representatives to attend IASC board meetings as guests or observers from 1990 onwards, it became more impressed than ever with the need for a more effective European contribution, drawing on the Directives. Karel Van Hulle was perplexed both by the lack of coordination he observed among the European delegations and by their willingness to approve standards that were contrary to their domestic regulation or the European Directives.[101]

The Commission's anxiety grew as it saw the increasing attractiveness of the US capital market for European companies as well as the US influence in IOSCO and the influence of IOSCO in the IASC. It did not want Europe, directly or through the IASC, to be taken over by US GAAP.[102]

12.3.3. The Commission Places the IASC at the Centre of Its Harmonization Effort

The urgent need to do something for European companies seeking listings in the United States, as well as the disappointing performance of the Accounting Advisory Forum led the Commission to reconsider all of its options, including the possibility of European accounting standards.[103] At least as early as 1993, Van Hulle made it clear in public that the Commission considered the situation with regard to accounting harmonization in Europe as unsatisfactory, and that the Commission was casting about for a new strategy.[104] During the first half of 1995, these efforts intensified as Van Hulle conducted a round of consultations with member state governments, while proposals and counter-proposals continued to be floated in public.

Early in 1995, John Mogg, director-general of DG XV of the European Commission, announced that the Commission was giving thought to asking the Contact Committee to review and approve the IASC's standards for use in the EU.[105]

In May 1995, Van Hulle, in a speech to 18th Annual Congress of the European Accounting Association, acknowledged that agreement on updating the Fourth and Seventh Directives had proved 'impossible', and that the Accounting Advisory Forum had not achieved as much as had been hoped. He confirmed that the Commission was preparing to adopt a more interventionist stance in standardizing accounting practice.[106]

Responding to the Commission's suggestions, Jens Røder, the FEE president, urged the Commission to accept IASC standards for use by EU companies, so long as they did not contravene the Directives. He warned Mogg that 'There is a real risk that Europe will irretrievably lose the initiative to influence developments in accounting standards to the detriment of the competitive position of major companies in Europe.' He added that EU companies that were reluctant to change to US GAAP would nonetheless do so 'if obstacles are placed in the way of using an acceptable alternative or if European endorsement is slow and unpredictable'.[107]

Røder agreed with the European Commission's concern over the European contribution to the IASC. In a letter to Mogg dated 7 June 1995, Røder wrote, 'There is a risk that financial reporting in Europe will be dominated by requirements which result from a standard-setting process [i.e., in the US] in which there is little likelihood that the views and interests of European preparers and users will be taken into account. To counteract this risk, a mechanism should be developed to ensure both that the needs of Europe are properly considered and that access by European companies to foreign capital markets is facilitated.' Røder argued that 'The best way forward is to permit those listed European companies which so wish to prepare their consolidated financial statements in accordance with International Accounting Standards, provided that the role and influence of Europe within IASC are strengthened.'[108] He proposed two reforms: a 'European coordination panel', which would bring together the European members of the IASC board to facilitate an exchange of views, with advice from 'national governments, standard setters and securities markets regulators, as well as the preparers, users and auditors'; and a 'European research centre', a kind of 'think tank' that would serve to counter the 'substantial' US influence in the development of IASC standards. 'Its primary role', he said, 'would be to address accounting issues of relevance to a capital markets context, and to play a leadership role in developing proposals for the treatment of such accounting issues *before* they appear on IASC's agenda.'[109] As will be seen, both of these proposals were soon to be carried forward.

By the middle of 1995, it was clear to the Commission that the member states, most of all the United Kingdom, would not support a European standard setter. Moreover, some of the resistance to IASC standards had disappeared. The German government in particular had, in the early months of the same year 1995, changed its course and embraced IASC standards in principle (*see* Section 12.2.2).[110] Finally, the agreement between the IASC and IOSCO, announced in July 1995 (*see* Section 10.12) became an important element in the Commission's thinking. At the time, the Commission's staff believed that it was highly probable that IOSCO would in due course endorse the IASC's standards, opening the prospect of access to US capital markets without the need to apply, or reconcile to, US GAAP.[111]

The first clear indication of how these facts were shaping the views of the Commission was given in a widely reported speech by Mario Monti, the EU's financial services commissioner, at IOSCO's annual conference in July 1995. On behalf of the Commission, Monti welcomed the just-announced agreement between the IASC and IOSCO, and he denied that the Commission was thinking of creating a European Accounting Standards Board, 'nor', he said, 'is it our intention to create a new layer of European accounting standards on top of the existing layers (national standards and international standards)'.[112]

Later that year, the Commission gave its position in full in a major policy statement published in November 1995. In this Communication, the Commission proposed a policy 'of putting the Union's weight behind the international harmonization process which is already well under way in the International Accounting Standards Committee'.[113]

In announcing this policy, the Commission showed that there had been a major shift in its thinking. Until around 1990, the Commission had thought of accounting harmonization in terms of company law. The particular reporting needs of companies with global listings were seen as peripheral. In 1989, Van Hulle had characterized their number as 'peanuts' compared to the total number of limited liability companies subject to the Directives. He had observed that it was 'unthinkable' that the globally listed companies could be the Commission's frame of reference.[114] In its 1995 Communication, however, the Commission cited the needs of these companies as the principal reason for reconsidering the EU's approach to accounting harmonization:[115]

Large European companies seeking capital on the international capital markets, most often on the New York Stock Exchange, are obliged to prepare a second set of accounts for that purpose. This is burdensome and costly and constitutes a clear competitive disadvantage. Producing more than one set of accounts also causes confusion. Moreover, it involves companies in conforming with [US GAAP] which are developed without any European input. As more and more Member States are implementing important privatization programmes and as the capital needs of the companies concerned are increasing, the number of companies facing this problem is growing.

The Commission warned:[116]

The most urgent problem is that concerning European companies with an international vocation [i.e., listing].... There is a risk that large companies will be increasingly drawn towards US GAAP. They and the Member States are looking to the Union for a solution that can be implemented rapidly.

The Commission explained that, to deal with the needs of these companies as well as with some of the inherent difficulties of its previous approach based on Directives, it had considered and rejected several possibilities. These included exempting large, listed companies from the scope of application of the Directives, updating the Directives, and the creation of a European Accounting Standard Setting Body. The Commission had also attempted to initiate discussions with the United States on mutual recognition of accounts, 'but has found little interest on the American side' (paragraph 4.3). The Commission therefore concluded that, 'Of the various international bodies working on accounting standards, for the time being only the IASC is producing results which have a clear prospect of recognition in the international capital markets within a timescale which corresponds to the urgency of the problem' (paragraph 4.4).

On the basis of this conclusion, the Commission proposed a two-pronged policy. The first prong was to eliminate barriers to the application of the IASC's standards in the consolidated financial statements of large companies. This would require an analysis of the Directives and IASC standards to identify conflicts, and to amend either the Directives or the standards, according to the result of consultations with the IASC. It would then be up to the member states to amend their legislation in order to allow the application of IASC standards.

The second prong was not new, as it consisted of ensuring an appropriate European input into the work of the IASC. This time, the Commission emphasized the role of the Contact Committee, which, the Commission hoped, would be able to establish 'an agreed [European] Union position' on future exposure drafts issued by the IASC. The Accounting Advisory Forum was to continue as a consultative body to the Commission and the Contact Committee.

IASC Secretary-General Bryan Carsberg welcomed the Commission's new policy, and John Hegarty, the secretary-general of FEE, said, 'This is a radical step forward. It's what we have been working towards for a long time.'[117] Although the Commission bravely asserted that it was not abandoning the field of accounting harmonization,[118] it was clearly placing less emphasis on the Directives which hitherto had been paramount in its thinking. The new policy could therefore also be interpreted as an admission of defeat.

To implement the first element of its new policy, a technical subcommittee of the Contact Committee was created. It swiftly completed an inventory of conflicts between IASC standards and the Directives, and it concluded that such conflicts were essentially non-existent. Karel Van Hulle reported that, basing its decision on 'a dynamic interpretation of the Directives', the Commission concluded that 'It was possible for a European company to prepare its consolidated statements in conformity with IAS without being in conflict with the Accounting Directives.'[119] In fact, at least one member state had instructed its representative on the subcommittee that this would be the preferred outcome of the review.[120] Clearly, the Commission and some of the member states were stretching to make compatibility a reality. By the spring of 1996, John Mogg was fully committed to the objective of allowing European companies to use IASC standards in their consolidated accounts, and the attention of his Directorate was now focused on motivating the member states to support and implement this policy in order to fend off the domination of US GAAP.[121]

In line with the objective of reinforcing the European contribution to the work of the IASC, the European Commission strengthened its presence at board meetings. In August 1996, it appointed Allister Wilson, a partner and director of financial reporting in the UK firm of Ernst & Young, as a technical adviser.[122] Van Hulle wrote, 'His main role is to help the Commission in the technical formulation of positions to be defended within IASC.'[123] Beginning in September 1996, Wilson accompanied Van Hulle as an observer to meetings of the IASC board.

12.3.4. FEE Promotes a 'European Accounting Research Foundation'

Meanwhile, FEE moved ahead with the European research centre proposal described in Jens Røder's letter to John Mogg of 7 June 1995. FEE shared the Commission's concerns over the strong influence exerted by the SEC and IOSCO on the IASC board, and it believed that the European private sector had to assert itself as a countervailing force in the IASC's process. FEE could see that European accounting practice was heading in the direction of US GAAP and that Europe would not have any influence over the setting of US accounting standards. It also wanted a stronger role for the European private sector in relation to such government regulatory bodies as the SEC and the European Commission, and, derivatively, IOSCO.

In the Spring of 1996, FEE proposed that a body, to be called the European Accounting Research Foundation, should be created to coordinate the preparation of research projects in order to exert an influence on the IASC board early in its deliberative process. The overall aim of the Foundation was to marshal Europe's resources to counter the heavy hands of the Americans and of government regulators in general. It was stated in the prospectus that, 'With the possible exception of the United Kingdom, no one European country alone can compete with the other G4 countries [United States, Canada and Australia].'[124] Six delegations to the IASC board—France, Germany, the Netherlands, the Nordic Federation of Public Accountants, the United Kingdom, and the Federation of Swiss Industrial Holding Companies—came from Europe, the European Commission was represented by an observer, and Europeans were influential in the financial analysts and financial executives delegations. But their collective influence had been limited owing to 'a failure to coordinate the views of the different delegations' and to their 'inability to mobilize sufficient resources for research and deliberation'.[125]

The Foundation would have a governing board and a part-time research director. Half of its proposed annual budget of ten million Belgian francs (approximately US$315,000) was to be for the cost of carrying out research by academics and practitioners.

On 6 June 1996, FEE presented its proposal to a meeting of interested parties, including representatives from the European Commission, UNICE,[126] the European Round Table, the European Federation of Financial Executives Institutes (EFFEI), the Federation of European Stock Exchanges, and a number of members of delegations from Europe serving on the IASC board. At the meeting, the reactions ranged from scepticism to varying degrees of support. Karel Van Hulle, of the Commission, and Bernd-Joachim Menn, representing EFFEI (but also a member of the German delegation to the IASC board), were among the strongest supporters. But the proposal foundered on the matter of finance. The representatives of UNICE and the stock exchange federation declined interest in providing finance.[127]

After FEE had made enquiries about sources of finance from industry, it decided in February 1997 that the plan for a Foundation had to be abandoned. While it felt that the European accountancy profession would provide as much as half of the funding, it concluded that no more than an additional 11 per cent could be counted on from industry.[128] As will be seen, FEE's Foundation initiative resurfaced in the form of meetings of the European delegations to the IASC, known as E5+2 (see Section 12.6.3).

12.3.5. The Pace of European Companies Listing in New York Drives the European Commission's Evolving Accounting Policy

The European Commission reported in a major policy statement issued in October 1998 that 'The number of European companies with NYSE [New York Stock Exchange] and NASDAQ listings in the United States has increased nearly fivefold since 1990 to almost 250 in 1998, with a cumulative market capitalization of about $300 billion. There is thus growing pressure to bring our directives in line with international accounting standards to avoid having to apply different standards to produce different financial statements.'[129] Sounding very much like the SEC or IOSCO and underscoring its policy change in 1995 to think of accounting in terms of the global capital markets, the Commission added, 'The objective is to stimulate cross-border investment through more transparency and better comparability of accounts. The Commission will consider whether any of the options provided for by our accounting directives are no longer necessary or appropriate. In addition the Commission will review whether listed companies should be required to prepare their financial statements in conformity with a more harmonised framework such as IAS.'[138] This was the first sign that the Commission was contemplating an embrace of IASC standards as a requirement for listed companies in the EU, rather than merely as an option, as in the 1995 Communication.

As it turned out, the policy announced in the 1995 Communication had not solved all problems. While it might have been plausible to claim in 1996 that IASC standards were more or less compatible with the Directives, the IASC standards were changing fast. Already in May 1997 Commissioner Monti suggested that the compatibility assumption required that the Directives be 'bent beyond the limits of reasonable interpretation'.[131] Moreover, it appeared that the 1995 Communication had not assured the ascendancy of IASC standards over US GAAP in Europe. Only a minority of member states had changed their legislation to allow the use of IASC standards in consolidated accounts. Moreover, some of the countries that had introduced an option to use the IASC's standards had also permitted to use US GAAP. As discussed in Section 12.2.2, legislation was passed in Germany in 1998 to allow domestic companies with listings outside the EU to prepare their consolidated statements in accordance with accounting standards accepted internationally, so long as they did not contravene the EU Directives.[132] A similar law was enacted in Austria in 1998. These laws were influenced by the demand from major companies that their governments act to facilitate their listings in New York, enabling them either to use US GAAP or IASC standards. The decision by Germany to break with long tradition and establish an accounting standard-setting board in March 1998 was another development that may have prompted the Commission to act.[133] Otherwise, it might see its authority in the area of accounting dissolve under the combined influence of US GAAP and a proliferation of national standard setters. Within the Commission, a requirement for all listed companies to use IASC standards began to be seen as the most effective way of stopping US GAAP.[134]

For the time being, this was a bridge too far. In May 1999, the European Commission issued an Action Plan to move towards an integrated European market for financial services. Comparable financial reporting was included in the plan as one of the essential ingredients of an integrated capital market. In this document it was announced that 'Consideration is currently being given to a possible solution which would provide companies with an option (as the sole alternative to preparing financial statements in accordance with national laws transposing EU accounting Directives) to publish financial statements on the basis of IAS standards.'[135]

It was reported in the accountancy press that the May 1999 Action Plan represented a retreat from the more 'radical' proposal, hinted at in the October 1998 Communication, to impose IASC standards on all listed companies. This was reported to have been the Commission's preferred option, but its impact on the status of national standard setters such as the UK ASB was believed to be an important obstacle.[136] The proposals of the Action Plan would have stopped the use of US GAAP, as allowed by, for instance, the German legislation referred to above. In May 1999, the Commission referred only to the use of IASC standards and did not even mention US GAAP.

It may be noted in passing that the Action Plan again showed how far the Commission's views on accounting had developed. The harmonization of accounting, or rather, 'financial reporting' as it was now called, was no longer seen in terms of harmonizing company law at a basic level in order to facilitate a free market in goods and services generally, but redefined in terms of a high degree of comparability, required in the specific context of capital markets and financial services.

12.3.6. FEE Proposes a 'Financial Reporting Strategy within Europe'

In October 1999, when the restructuring of the IASC had reached the stage of heated debate, FEE proposed a middle ground between allowing or requiring the use of IASC standards by European companies. As in the Commission's May 1999 proposal, it recommended that EU listed companies be allowed to use IASC standards as an option in addition to their national GAAP. However, EU listed companies that continued to use their national GAAP would be required to reconcile to IASC standards. This allowance 'could be seen as a temporary regime leading to a requirement for certain companies to use IASs'.[137]

The Commission's May 1999 Action Plan had suggested that a 'screening mechanism' might have to be developed 'in order to ensure that IAS output conforms with EU rules and corresponds fully with EU public policy concerns'.[138] FEE elaborated on this suggestion by urging the creation of a European Financial Reporting Coordination and Advisory Council, a private-sector body composed of 'the key players in the European financial reporting scene': national standard setters, the cooperating of national capital and financial markets regulators, preparers (UNICE and the European Round Table, and the audit profession (FEE). It would replace the Accounting Advisory Forum and, probably, the study group of EU member country representatives on the IASC board known as E5+2 (*see* Section 12.6.3). Its functions would include working with the national standard setters to promote the integration of full IASC standards into national standards; enhancing the influence of country voices in the IASC board; coordinating and advising on the creation by regulators of a mechanism to enforce compliance with standards, at the European or country level; and giving advice to the European Commission on changes in the Directives so as to facilitate the use by all companies of IASC standards. According to FEE, its task would emphatically not be to select or adapt IASC standards for use in the EU or to issue interpretations of IASC standards: 'Any modifications to IASs involve a departure from truly global standards.'[139]

12.3.7. The European Commission Calls for a Required Use of IASC Standards by EU Listed Companies

In November 1999 and May 2000, the European Commission issued six-monthly progress reports on its Action Plan of May 1999, but no progress was reported on financial reporting.[140] The May 2000 Communication was issued in the wake of the Lisbon European Council, which 'took an important political step in March [2000] towards an integrated financial services and capital market in the European Union' and called for the EU's Financial Services Action Plan to be completed by 2005.[141]

And indeed, in June 2000, the Commission issued a strategy statement on financial reporting, which was a document of historic importance for the future of the IASC.[142] This time, the Commission took the step it had not yet dared to take in May 1999. It proposed that, beginning in 2005, all EU companies listed on a regulated market, including banks and other financial institutions, would be required to adopt IASC standards in their consolidated statements and preferably as well in their statutory individual (or parent company) financial statements.[143] The estimated number of listed companies was 6,700, of which 275 claimed to be using IASC standards already.[144] By this new strategy, the European Commission assured the IASC of a large market, the fifteen countries of the EU, for its standards.

The European Commission said that the central objective of its revised strategy 'is that the policy should ensure that securities can be traded on EU and international financial markets on the basis of a single set of financial reporting standards'.[145] Contrary to what might have seemed possible only five years before, this was a strategy statement that was entirely compatible with the aims of

IOSCO. The Commission's proposal was, as Karel Van Hulle has written, 'a radical change'.[146]

In its strategy statement, the Commission made mention of the IASC's decision the previous November to restructure itself, which it said was 'driven by a clear determination to make IAS the highest quality, comprehensive accounting standards for use in capital markets throughout the world.'[147] Yet there was no hint that the European Commission had strongly opposed the new structure finally adopted by the IASC under pressure from the SEC (*see* Chapter 13). Karel Van Hulle was quoted as saying that the new strategy was 'good news for the IASC, and a vote of confidence in it'.[148]

Yet another section of the European Commission's new strategy provoked controversy. Taking up the idea of a screening mechanism from the May 1999 Action Plan, the Commission said, 'This strategy will need to take full account of public policy interests. The European Union cannot delegate responsibility for setting financial reporting requirements for listed EU companies to a non-governmental third party.'[149] It then proposed a two-tier endorsement mechanism, at both the political and technical levels. It said, 'The IAS used in the EU will be the standards endorsed by this mechanism.'[150] 'The technical level', it said, 'will need to be under control set at a political level.'[151] At the technical level, a 'group of highly qualified experts' would submit comments on the IASC's drafts and would scrutinize the final standards.[152] It added, 'Recommendations made at the technical level on a particular IAS standard will need ratification at the political level. To avoid such a situation concerns about emerging IAS will need to be expressed at the earliest stage in the IASC's drafting process.'[153] As FEE had feared, the wording in this section seemed to leave open the possibility that the European Commission, based on the screening advice received, might substitute its judgement for that of the IASC or of the latter's Standing Interpretations Committee.

As a matter of principle, it was hard to object to the Commission's wish to establish some form of political oversight. The IASC may have chafed at the extremely cautious attitude of the US SEC towards endorsing the IAS core standards as a whole, but the SEC's authority was rarely questioned. Indeed, in its February 2000 concept release (*see* Section 10.20), the SEC reaffirmed its policy towards the FASB as well as, apparently, towards the IASC: 'Our willingness to look to the private sector...has been with the understanding that we will, as necessary, supplement, override or otherwise amend private sector accounting standards.'[154] Yet in Europe there was clear apprehension that the European Commission might not use its powers wisely. The *Financial Times* editorialized that 'The commission seems to want to pick and choose its standards through use of a filter mechanism to vet IASC rules. These will be scrutinised at a technical and political level and amended or rejected as desired.... In promoting its plan, the commission must avoid applying too heavy a hand, and must bear in mind the impact its actions will have outside Europe.'[155] Graham Ward, the president of the Institute of Chartered Accountants in England and Wales, said that it is 'disappointing that the Commission remains wedded to an endorsement mechanism'.[156] *The Accountant* quoted the UK head of assurance of one of the Big Five accountancy firms, saying, 'This mechanism could well be used to develop IAS into a separate body of European accounting standards which would be applied solely within the EU'.[157] Was the enforcement mechanism to be a European Accounting Standards Board in new dress?

The criticism of the European Commission's proposed screening mechanism was so troubling to the Commission that John Mogg, the director-general for the Internal Market, wrote a letter to the *Financial Times*, denying that the Commission 'will pick and choose between [IASC standards]. Nor is it determined to create a rival set of regional standards at global level.'[158] He added that the Commission's proposal for an endorsement mechanism 'is motivated by the need to ensure that IAS enjoy the necessary legal certainty and technical approval to allow them to become obligatory within the EU'.[159] Following the appearance of Mogg's letter, the secretary-general of FEE was quoted as saying that he was uncertain whether the Commission's proposal would lead to EU GAAP.[160] Karel Van Hulle counselled, 'If the experts (from the private sector) deliver high quality work, the chance that a standard would be found unacceptable diminishes considerably.'[161]

The screening mechanism at the technical level, created by the private sector in 2001, became known as the European Financial Reporting Advisory Group (EFRAG), which might be seen as the outgrowth of a range of initiatives in the 1990s, including E5+2 and FEE's 1996 plan for a European Accounting Research Foundation.[162] The Accounting Regulatory Committee, set up by the EU's IAS Regulation in 2002, became the screening mechanism at the political level.

Later in the statement of its new strategy, the European Commission provided for enforcement: 'Only IAS that are properly and rigorously enforced will improve the functioning of the EU securities market. Enforcement comprises a cascade of different elements including (1) clear accounting standards (2) timely interpretations and implementation guidance, (3) statutory audit, (4) monitoring by supervisors and (5) effective sanctions.'[163]

In July 2000, the EU's Council of European Economic and Finance Ministers (ECOFIN) endorsed the European Commission's new strategy for financial reporting.[164] The proposal was implemented by a Regulation of the European Parliament and the Council of Ministers of 19 July 2002.[165]

As for the European private sector, it was reported that, at a two-day conference in November 2000, 'Both the level of support and intensity of debate suggested that companies and their advisers are alert to the potentially substantial impact of the new Commission policy.'[166] Clearly, under this new strategy, Europe removed itself from the fringes of the IASC's attention to a central position.

12.4. IMPACTS OUTSIDE OF EUROPE

The IASC's record of achievement from 1987 to 2000, beginning with E32, and continuing with the Improvements project and the steady stream of core standards issued as part of the agreement with IOSCO, registered an impact in countries beyond Europe. We believe that four of the founder members of the board and the longest-serving non-founder member should be singled out for particular attention: Australia, Canada, Japan, South Africa, and the United States.

12.4.1. Australia

Beginning in 1992, Australia's largest corporation, Broken Hill Proprietary Company (BHP), stated that its annual accounts were prepared in compliance with IASC standards, except, in most years for IAS 28 on the equity method for associated companies. Few companies joined BHP in referring in their annual accounts to IASC standards.

Since the 1970s, the Australian Accounting Standards Board (AASB) had been appending to its standards a section commenting on each standard's compatibility with IASC standards. In 1994, the AASB announced in a discussion paper that it would pursue internationalization through a series of policies, including: 'to consider for adoption, where possible, the appropriate International Accounting Standards Committee (IASC) or other overseas accounting standards (for example, the accounting standards issued in Canada, New Zealand, the United States of America and the United Kingdom) when addressing an issue'.[167] This statement was issued at a time when some influential members of the Group of 100, an organization of senior finance executives from business enterprises, favoured Australian adoption of US GAAP.[168]

In a further policy statement, issued in April 1996, the AASB and its sister body, the Public Sector Accounting Standards Board (PSASB), said, much in the same vein, that they would 'use existing IASs as the basis for developing Australian accounting standards when addressing topics' and would 'work with the IASC to identify an acceptable approach to removing incompatibilities' between IASC standards and Australian standards. They asserted, however, that 'There does not presently exist a single internationally accepted set of accounting standards which, if adopted in Australia, would increase the comparability of Australian financial reports with those prepared in countries such as the United States of America, the United Kingdom, Canada or New Zealand.'[169] To some, such as the Australian Stock Exchange (ASX), neither of these statements may have been viewed as a strong enough commitment to international harmonization.

The ASX was concerned that the legal requirement to use Australian accounting standards was costly to Australian companies seeking secondary listings overseas. It feared that the requirement might even lead companies to abandon a primary listing in Australia, and that it was an impediment to foreign investment in Australian company shares. Therefore, the ASX took steps in 1996 to bring IASC standards to Australia. Richard Humphry, ASX's managing director, cited a comparative study by Brigid Curran as the turning point in the debate over whether Australian accounting standards should be harmonized with international standards.[170] It had been alleged, he said, that Australian standards were 'far superior' to international standards, yet Humphry wrote that Curran's study had found that, 'with few exceptions, IASC standards are more rigorous than, or at least as rigorous as, Australian standards'.[171]

Humphry, strongly supported by IASC Chairman Michael Sharpe (a member of the ASX board of directors and chairman of its audit committee), urged a plan on the AASB to adopt or adapt (which, it was not clear) IASC standards in Australia. ASX would raise $1 million—approximately the size of the AASB's annual budget[172]—by a levy on listed companies in 1997 and 1998 to fund a two-year programme by the AASB to harmonize to IASC standards.[173] ASX had allowed foreign companies to list by using IASC standards in their accounts for many years, but this accommodation did not address Humphry's problem. Humphry took note of IOSCO's July 1995 agreement with the IASC, which pointed towards an endorsement of the latter's core standards by 1999, as well as the US SEC's push in early 1996 to accelerate the IASC's target date for completing the core standards, which became March 1998 (see Section 10.13). ASX's programme, once accepted by the AASB, was announced in August 1996, in which it was stated that 'Companies surveyed by ASX registered their overwhelming support for the project.'[174] The AASB and PSASB, for their part, said that the programme's objective 'is to change Australian accounting standards and influence the development and change of IASC standards so that by the end of 1998 an Australian reporting entity complying with Australian standards would also be complying with IASC standards'.[175]

Tensions began to develop between the advocates of a more accelerated replacement of Australian accounting standards by IASC standards, which presumably included Humphry, and leading figures in the Australian standard-setting community, who preferred a more graduated approach. In March 1998, Ken Spencer, the AASB chairman, argued that 'committing to the adoption of IASC standards without amendment is premature'.[176] He believed that the IASC standards were too loosely drafted. Moreover, his board disagreed with some of the technical elements in the IASC standards, and its standards had not yet been adopted in any major jurisdictions. For these reasons, together with the uncertainty over the restructuring of the IASC, he said, some years later, 'Those of us involved in the AASB at the time weren't prepared to throw our lot in irrevocably with international standards.'[177] Nonetheless, by the end of 1998 both sides agreed that a great deal was accomplished.

In September 1997, the federal Treasurer released the first Corporate Law Economic Reform Programme (CLERP1), which included a proposal that the setting of accounting standards for entities in the private and public sectors be moved into the federal government as an Australian Accounting Standards Committee (AASC) under the oversight of a Financial Reporting Council (FRC).[178] The aim was to harmonize (adopt, not adapt) Australian standards with those of the IASC. From 1 January 1999, the AASC was to begin issuing exposure drafts and final standards that were identical to those issued by the IASC.[179] Brown and Tarca wrote, 'There can be no doubt that the ASX was a central party in determining the content of CLERP #1.'[180]

The CLERP1 proposals were debated for a considerable period, and their implementation was postponed because of a general election.[181] In October 1999, the federal Parliament enacted the Corporate Law Economic Reform Programme Act 1999, embodying the CLERP1 proposals, as amended. The provision about adopting IASC standards verbatim in the short term was relaxed, but the eventual adoption of IASC standards was still very strongly etched in the proposals. The new law took effect on 1 January 2000, when the new federal government agency, named the AASB, replaced the old AASB and PSASB, both of which had existed under the aegis of the Australian Accounting Research Foundation.

Among the founder member countries of the IASC, Australia thus became one of the first whose standard setter was charged by law to harmonize with IASC standards. In July 2002, the FRC, following the example recently set by the EU, announced that Australia would adopt the IASB's International Financial Reporting Standards (IFRS) by 1 January 2005.[182]

12.4.2. Canada

As noted in Section 6.8, in the early and middle 1980s the Canadian Institute of Chartered Accountants (CICA), working with the Toronto Stock Exchange, had succeeded in persuading as many as 100 companies to refer in their financial statements to compliance with IASC standards. By 1994, fifty companies were still doing so, a record that no other founder member of the IASC board could come close to matching.[183]

Canadian accounting standards and practice have been profoundly influenced by US standards and practice, not only because of proximity but also because the United States is Canada's major supplier of capital. Hundreds of Canadian companies are publicly traded in US capital markets and are thus subject to SEC regulation. Questions have periodically arisen in Canada, given its relatively small population base, whether it might not be better to give up national standard setting and instead adopt US GAAP. For some years, the CICA had, through its standard-setting committee, sought to harmonize as much as practicable with US GAAP, while nonetheless issuing standards on the basis of its own independent research and analysis. Yet the progress made by the IASC since the late 1980s prompted the question of whether Canada should shift its focus more to IASC standards than US GAAP, both in the short and long terms. In 1998, the CICA's Task Force on Standard Setting (TFOSS), following a two-year study, concluded that, in the long term, the CICA should 'accelerate its harmonization programme with FASB standards and increase its involvement with the IASC and other international groups, with the objective of reaffirming Canada's significant role in establishing international accounting standards'.[184] TFOSS signalled a tighter relationship with the FASB, for it said, 'in working to eliminate differences with US GAAP, Canadian standard setters would adopt FASB standards unless they can justify reasons for not doing so.' This conclusion was reached even though the task force said it envisioned, in the long term, that there will be one set of internationally accepted standards in the private sector. It was evident that TFOSS was straddling the fence.

The following year, the Certified General Accountants Association of Canada (CGA-Canada), another of the sponsors of the Canadian delegation to the IASC board, published a comprehensive study by two accounting academics, which disputed the TFOSS recommendations.[185] The authors went one step further than the task force by predicting that 'The IASC will emerge as the source of international accounting standards.' They said that IASC and FASB standards were 'broadly similar and converging', which means that 'The choice between these bodies in terms of their consequences for Canadian businesses and the accounting profession is moot.' They foresaw that, one day, IASC standards would be acceptable to the SEC. The authors concluded that Canada should commit to the use of IASC standards. In July 1999, CGA-Canada adopted a policy statement calling for the adoption of IASC standards for profit-seeking companies in Canada. This position did not secure much support in Canada at the time. In 2006, however, the CICA finally decided to converge with IFRS such that Canadian GAAP, as determined by its standard setter, would become the same as IFRS, a process which is to take effect in stages over a five-year period.[186]

Canada's long-standing commitment to IASC standards had thus become solid, notwithstanding the pull of US GAAP.

12.4.3. Japan

For decades in Japan, company financial reporting was governed by a 'triangular legal system', embracing the Commercial Law, the Securities and Exchange Law, and the Corporate Income Tax Law, with the Commercial Law in the centre.[187] Consolidated statements were uncommon before the 1990s, and individual companies' financial statements determined the amount of tax to be paid and were the basis for deciding on the amount of the dividend. Japanese accounting standards, which were set by the Business Accounting Deliberation Council (BADC), an advisory body to the Ministry of Finance, were, prior to the 1990s, little influenced by international trends and developments.

In November 1988, the securities bureau of the Ministry of Finance joined IOSCO, and its representatives began attending meetings of IOSCO's WP1 early in the 1990s, assisted by Atsushi Kato, technical adviser to the Ministry's representative and an audit partner of Chuo Audit Corporation (affiliated with Coopers & Lybrand) in Tokyo. The Ministry of Finance became impressed during these meetings with accounting developments overseas, which were more advanced than in Japan. Its involvement in WP1 changed the Ministry's mindset.

The IASC's E32, issued in 1989, was widely perceived in Japan as a watershed event, and the IASC began to be regarded as a body whose standards had to be taken more seriously, especially because of the interest being expressed in its work by IOSCO.[188] The Japanese Institute of Certified Public Accountants (JICPA) formed a special project committee to conduct a full review of E32 in comparison with Japanese accounting standards, and the JICPA organized a committee broadly representative of preparers and users, including the Ministry of Finance, to meet and discuss E32 and its possible implications.[189]

Increasingly, the BADC, which has always been much influenced by the Ministry of Finance, began harmonizing its standards with those of the IASC.[190] In 1992, the Ministry of Finance approached the US SEC to arrange the mutual recognition of accounting standards between the two countries, but no agreement resulted.[191]

In 1990, the Corporation Finance Research Institute (COFRI) was formed, with approval from the Minister of Finance. COFRI, a private-sector body financed by donations from private corporations, 'undertakes research into corporate financial reporting, with the objective of contributing to the improvement and enhancement of Japanese reporting and disclosure systems and accounting standards'.[192] From the outset, COFRI has been attuned to accounting developments overseas. Its research reports sometimes include recommendations on policy.

The cumulative effect of these developments, coupled with the increasing pace of globalization and Japan's desperate need to be able to compete more effectively with the New York and London capital markets, led to the 'financial big bang' announced by Prime Minister Ryutaro Hashimoto in November 1996, which called for 'free', 'fair', and 'global' financial markets.[193]

Even before the announcement of the financial big bang, the BADC had proposed in June 1996 an ambitious programme for conforming its standards more closely with IASC standards. In February 1997, as part of the financial big bang, the Ministry of Finance changed the organization of the BADC to make it more flexible and therefore more efficient.[194] Between 1997 and 1999, a period of intense activity, the BADC revised previous standards or issued new standards on such subjects as consolidated statements, research and development costs, retirement benefits, deferred taxes, financial instruments, and foreign currency transactions.[195] Collectively, these developments since 1997 have been called the 'accounting big bang'.[196]

Finally, as a result of the restructuring of the IASC, which was approved in 1999–2000, forces were set in motion to create the Financial Accounting Standards Foundation in July 2001, which promptly established the Accounting Standards Board of Japan, composed of three full-time and ten part-time members, and assisted by a large technical staff. The setting up of this independent, private-sector body was to make Japan eligible to contribute a liaison board member to the newly formed International Accounting Standards Board.[197]

12.4.4. South Africa

A pivotal decision was made in 1993 by the Council of the South African Institute of Chartered Accountants (SAICA), just as the country was emerging from a long period of international isolation and was re-entering the business and economic world. For some years prior to then, South Africa had been increasingly producing accounting standards patterned on IASC standards, but there were salient differences. By 1993, the South African business community and accountancy profession had come to accept IASC standards as sufficiently comprehensive and of suitably high quality to replace the South African standards.[198] The Council recommended to the Accounting Practices Board (APB), the independent body that approves the final standards, that in future it adopt IASC standards as 'generally accepted accounting practice' (GAAP), amending them only as necessary to tailor them to South African circumstances.[199] After receiving advice from SAICA's Accounting Practices Committee (APC), which drafts proposed standards, the APB endorsed the Council's recommendation.[200] The APB and APC then proceeded to develop a set of guidelines to facilitate the adaptation of IASC standards to South African conditions.

This action by SAICA and the APB had become imperative for South Africa in order that its companies might present their financial statements in a manner comparable with that of companies trading in world capital markets. It was also costly for South Africa to continue setting its own standards. The standards being set by the IASC were a known quantity to leading members of the South African accountancy profession, as SAICA had continuously sent a delegation to the board since 1978.

The mining companies were initially resistant to following IASC standards, but in 1997 the country's largest mining group, Anglo American Corporation, switched to IASC standards and was shortly followed by the other mining companies. As the Johannesburg Stock Exchange had revised its rules to allow listed companies to use either IASC standards or South African GAAP in their annual accounts, Anglo American seized the opportunity to adopt the international standards.[201]

In 2004, the APB took the next step by deciding that International Financial Reporting Standards will henceforth, subject to prior local due process, be issued in South Africa without amendment. Where there is a local need for guidance on an issue not yet covered by IFRS, South Africa will continue to issue its own standards and interpretations in the expectation that these will be replaced in due course by IASB guidance.[202]

12.4.5. United States

The comparatively few major US companies that, in the 1980s, began indicating that their financial statements were in compliance with IASC standards had all discontinued doing so by 1994, by which time the IASC had made considerable progress towards reducing or eliminating the number of allowed alternative methods in its standards. In this respect, the attitude and interest of the US corporate sector stood in marked contrast to that of Canadian companies, which had been disclosing compliance with IASC standards in considerable numbers since the 1980s, and to companies in Germany and Switzerland, which began doing so in the 1990s.

12.4.5.1. FASB 'Signs On' to an International Role in Its Mission Statement

Beginning in the late 1980s, the FASB, following years of indifference, marked out a greater international role for itself. In 1991, the FASB's oversight body, the Financial Accounting Foundation, apparently with prompting from the SEC (see below), revised the FASB's Mission Statement to declare, for the first time, its interest in the international sphere. The 1991 revision included the following cautiously worded charge to the board: 'Promote the international comparability of accounting standards concurrent with improving the quality of financial reporting'.[203] The wording made it clear that the board was not to dilute its standards in an effort to achieve international comparability.

Also in 1991, the FASB adopted an ambitious and multifaceted programme of active collaboration with the IASC, some of which was already under way, as well as 'to build a network for bilateral and multilateral cooperation' with other national standard setters.[204] In its new 'Plan for International Activities', the FASB took note of the increasing role of IOSCO and observed,

Until the decade of the eighties, the focus was on comparability among U.S. companies financing themselves in U.S. capital markets. Then, as a result of an explosive growth of cross-border financing and investing, the focus began to shift to comparability among companies of different nationalities. Consequently, the FASB has been urged in recent years to become more actively involved in international accounting matters.[205]

The FASB characterized the dual aim of its new strategy as follows: 'To make financial statements more useful for investor and creditor decision making by increasing the international comparability of accounting standards concurrently with improving the quality of accounting standards' and to enhance the board's standard-setting process 'by gaining new insights and ideas from other national and international standard setters and from financial statement users, preparers, auditors, and educators in other countries'.[206]

What precipitated this newly charted course? Surely, as the board said, the march of globalization in the capital markets and its obvious implications for financial reporting had become manifest. Also, Dennis Beresford, the FASB's chairman since 1987, had served as a member of the US delegation to the IASC board in 1982–4, a term that was cut short by his appointment to the FASB's newly established Emerging Issues Task Force.[207] In March 1987, when IASC Chairman John Kirkpatrick and Secretary-General David Cairns paid a call on the FASB, Beresford enquired whether the FASB might perhaps participate more directly in the IASC's work; he referred to previous FASB attendance at IASC board meetings (as a guest in 1984 and 1985) and their joint task forces on deferred tax, foreign currency, and pension costs (see Chapter 5).[208] When approached by the IASC the following year, during Georges Barthès de Ruyter's chairmanship, Beresford agreed to have a representative of the FASB serve on the IASC's Consultative Group and attend meetings of the IASC board as a guest, because FASB members could not, under the policy by which the FASB operates, participate as voting members of another body. He also was instrumental in proposing and planning what was to be the first in a series of annual conferences of world standard setters, held in June 1991 in Brussels, and which was organized by FEE.[209]

But another impelling factor may have been the swift rise of the SEC's interest in international harmonization and specifically in the role being played by the IASC. The SEC's staff have always been a major player in the development, and especially the implementation, of US GAAP, because the SEC alone possesses the legal authority to compel companies whose securities are traded in US securities markets to adhere to GAAP. Although in the late 1980s the FASB had begun a rapprochement towards the IASC and international harmonization, in the eyes of some SEC commissioners, it was not enough. The FASB, they believed, must formally go on record as participating actively and constructively in the international harmonization process. In an important speech in May 1991, SEC Commissioner Philip Lochner made explicit his personal view of the Commission's expectation that the FASB become a proactive player in international harmonization: 'FASB, at the very least, has a duty seriously to consider IASC positions and the international consensus they represent.... To the extent the U.S. appears to be simply stonewalling the [harmonization] process in hopes that its own standards will prevail, other countries will rightfully be suspicious that, for the U.S., harmonization means that every other country must harmonize to the U.S. tune.' Lochner noted that the FASB's Mission Statement, as adopted in 1973, 'does not even mention international considerations, much less direct FASB to work towards harmonization of accounting standards or to consider the international ramifications of its actions'. His message of reform was bluntly worded: 'FASB's Mission Statement is in urgent need of updating.'[210] SEC Chairman Richard Breeden has subsequently said that he and Lochner agreed that the FASB was far too insular, far too unresponsive, and slow-moving in the face of changing markets.[211]

Beginning in 1994, the FASB worked jointly with the IASC in developing a project on earnings per share and with Canada's Accounting Standards Board on segment reporting. This former collaboration led the two boards to promulgate virtually identical standards, IAS 33 and FAS 128, both issued in February 1997 (*see* Section 11.7.1).[212]

The FASB revised and reaffirmed its Plan for International Activities in January 1995, emphasizing the many points of cooperation between the FASB and the IASC. The 1991 and 1995 plans differed mainly in nuance, but in the latter the FASB added the statement in two places that it looks to the IASC as the 'focal point' for developing international standards. The FASB also affirmed that, since 1991, 'It has become apparent that international issues are so intertwined with domestic issues that there is no way to clearly separate the two.'[213]

As the IASC board accelerated its process of completing the core standards in 1996–7, FASB Chairman Beresford and board member Jim Leisenring were publicly critical of an apparent dilution in quality of the IASC's output. In 1996, the FASB published a comprehensive analysis—also with a critical undertone—of the differences between US GAAP and IASC standards (*see* Section 10.17).

12.4.5.2. FASB and SEC Hold European Financial Reporting Conferences

In April 1999, the FASB and SEC jointly sponsored the first in a series of three annual European Financial Reporting Conferences in Frankfurt, Germany, having two aims: 'One focus of this conference is to identify key accounting problems European companies face when they adopt US GAAP, especially when preparing for listing on US stock exchanges. The development of globally acceptable high-quality financial accounting standards is the second focus.'[214] In terms of the time allotted to the two focuses in the conference programme, the first one very much predominated.[215] The principal object of the conferences was to make registering with the SEC and dealing with US GAAP less of a mystery.[216] The conferences were organized by two FASB members, Gerhard Mueller and Jim Leisenring, and by Prof. Dr. Günther Gebhardt, of the Johann Wolfgang Goethe-Universität Frankfurt.

All three conferences succeeded in attracting large audiences of company representatives, as well as accounting practitioners and academics.[217]

No one from the IASC's leadership was a featured speaker on the programme in 1999, but IASC Chairman Stig Enevoldsen formed part of a panel of speakers at a session to discuss 'The Future Structure of International Accounting Standard Setting'.

12.5. SUPPORT FOR THE IASC FROM INTERNATIONAL FINANCIAL INSTITUTIONS

12.5.1. Impact of the World Bank on the Diffusion of IASC Standards among Developing Countries[218]

Behind many of the efforts taken in Third World countries to develop the accountancy profession, install IASC and auditing standards, and prepare students and members of the accountancy profession to use them has been the formidable international development agency, the World Bank. In a story that has seldom been told, the Bank has provided major financial support to stimulate and facilitate the use of IASC standards in its borrower countries.[219]

The World Bank is arguably one of the largest users of financial statements. Randolph Andersen, who has led the Bank's efforts to build an accounting, auditing, and financial management infrastructure and knowledge base in developing countries since 1993, when he became the manager of the Bank's Central Accounting, is quoted as saying, 'We have 5,000 sets of audited financial statements coming in every year. It is in our interests to have a common basis of accounting. We also did want to see developing countries go through the business of evolving a standard-setting process, which is being handled very well by the IASC.'

About a quarter of the financial reports received by the Bank are from commercial enterprises, the others coming from governmental or non-profit entities.

For the governmental entities, the International Federation of Accountants' Public Sector Committee, supported by funding from the Bank, has been developing a set of international public sector accounting standards which are modelled on the IASC's accounting standards.[220]

The Bank has not only been making loans to fund the development of an accountancy infrastructure, including training programmes, in borrower countries, but also has prepared extensive instructional materials. In 1995, the Bank published a manual, *Financial Accounting, Auditing, and Reporting Handbook*, now available in other languages as well, which states emphatically that 'In the absence of any superior national standards, the Bank requires the use of IASs in the preparation of financial statements because their use facilitates comparability between projects and countries, ensures consistent presentation of financial statements, and facilitates their interpretation.'[221]

In the World Bank's 1989 annual report, its auditors, Price Waterhouse, affirmed in their opinion that the Bank's financial statements conformed with International Accounting Standards. In the 1990 report, both the Bank and Price Waterhouse attested to this conformity.

The World Bank was one of the charter members of the IASC's Consultative Group in 1981, and Andersen attended its meetings from 1993 to 1996. In 1999, he was appointed to the IASC's steering committee on accounting in developing countries and countries in transition, chaired by Tony Seah, of Malaysia (*see* Section 11.9.3.3).[222]

12.5.2. The International Financial Stability Forum

The World Bank's view, or perhaps more aptly, the view of the Bank's Central Accounting department, that IASC standards were an important part of corporate governance and accountability, and hence a significant condition for economic development, suddenly gained wider currency in the aftermath of the Asian crisis of 1998. In response to the crisis, national and international financial supervisory bodies and international financial institutions set up the Financial Stability Forum in order to improve international cooperation and to strengthen the international financial system. Even before the Forum met for the first time in April 1999, the finance ministers and central bank governors of the G7 countries had issued a declaration on 30 October 1998. Among numerous other measures to be taken, the declaration included a call on the IASC 'to finalize by early 1999 a proposal for a full range of internationally agreed accounting standards. IOSCO, IAIS [International Association of Insurance Supervisors], and the Basel Committee should complete a timely review of these standards'.[223] The IASC had had, for many years, contacts with the Basel Committee and the World Bank, but this declaration marked an important enhancement of the IASC's stature in the international financial community. It was noted with satisfaction in the IASC board that UK Prime Minister Tony Blair and other G7 leaders 'had spoken positively about IASC as the financial crisis in Asia had shown the need for greater transparency'.[224]

Representatives of the Basel Committee were welcomed as guests at the same meeting.

In March 2000, the Financial Stability Forum identified 'Twelve Key Standards for Sound Financial Systems', selected from a large number of standards issued by bodies such as the International Monetary Fund, the Organisation for Economic Co-operation and Development, and the Basel Committee. Improved implementation of these standards was regarded as a priority for the members of the Financial Stability Forum. The IASC's International Accounting Standards were included among the twelve.[225] Although this listing did not, by itself, endow any of the 'key standards' with additional authority, it was a clear signal that the IASC was now taken seriously at a governmental level in the developed world. IOSCO's endorsement of the IASC's core standards in May 2000, although it had been in preparation well before the creation of the Financial Stability Forum, could now also be presented as one of its first specific results. The same was true for a declaration by the Basel Committee in April 2000, in which it expressed general support for the fifteen IASC's standards that had a significant effect on banks.[226]

12.6. THE G4+1[227]

In the 1990s, standard setters from countries with active equity capital markets began to realize that the IASC was becoming a major player in the eyes of IOSCO. Consequently, they felt a need for collaboration among themselves, drawing on their common conceptual frameworks, to try to influence the future course of the IASC's work. It is not an exaggeration to say that these standard setters felt in some sense threatened by an IASC that was seen as a potential world standard setter by IOSCO.

12.6.1. Early Evolution of the G4+1

Under its international plan announced in 1991 (*see* Section 12.4.5.1), the FASB began to engage in more international activities. It hosted the second annual conference of world standard setters, in October 1992 in Norwalk,[228] which led to a decision to hold a follow-up conference in a year's time to focus on a single technical issue. The UK ASB agreed to host the conference, and a working group composed of United States, United Kingdom, Canadian, and Australian standard setters and support staff met in April 1993 in London to discuss the planned topic, accounting for future events. A common approach was agreed, and Todd Johnson, a senior FASB staff member, offered to draft a discussion paper on the subject. The draft was discussed and revised at a meeting of the group in August and was debated at the third annual conference of world standard setters in November 1993.[229] As this collaborative venture was seen as a success, the members of the group decided to continue meeting regularly to exchange ideas on technical issues with a view towards trying to explore and resolve differences among them. In 1994, the group became known as the G4+1.[230] The '+1' was an IASC representative, usually the secretary-general (and sometimes the chairman), who attended the group's meetings. The G4 standard setters came from countries with similar objectives of financial statements and similar conceptual frameworks.

12.6.2. The Continuing Development of the G4+1

In the early years, meetings of the G4+1 were rotated among the countries represented by its members, and each meeting, until 1996, was led by someone from the host country delegation. Eyebrows were raised in March 1996, when the G4+1 chose David Tweedie as its first chairman, less than a year after he had joined the UK delegation to the IASC board. Tweedie was one of the founding members of the G4+1, but questions were raised about whether this new position tested his loyalty.[231] The subsequent G4+1 chairmen were Ken Spencer (AASB), 1998–9, and Jim Leisenring (FASB), 1999–2001.

In 1996, the New Zealand standard setter became a member. All of the participating standard setters and staff invested a great deal of time in its meetings, which were held three and then four times a year.

The G4+1's impressive output of publications included seven research studies, four position papers, and a discussion paper, mostly covering topics that were on the IASC board's agenda. The authors of the papers were members of the research staff of the five participating national standard setters. At its meeting in January/February 2001, the G4+1 decided to disband and cancel its future activities, at the time of the announcement of the members of the restructured IASC, which became known as the IASB. It was felt that the G4+1 was no longer needed and that it might get in the way of the IASB.[232]

The G4+1's deliberations and initiatives may have served to prod the IASC board into moving faster on a number of common projects.[233] Some believed that its impact seemed to be more on the board's agenda than on the content of its drafts.[234] Yet the IASC's chairman and secretary-general said in the IASC's *Annual Review 1998* that the G4+1 'demonstrates a challenge to IASC. IASC must plan its work to ensure that views on accounting issues do not become crystallized as a result of G4+1 projects and before the views of the nearly 100 other IASC member countries, which are not members of G4+1, are taken into account.'[235] While Secretary-General Carsberg did not anticipate that the G4+1 might itself issue any accounting standards based on common agreement, he began to foresee that 'Each of the country members would undertake to put the agreed proposals through a national due process with a view to adopting identical or almost identical standards at the national level.' Any such collaboration, he added, 'would be reached without the participation of the "non-English-speaking world" but it would be more difficult for IASC to produce a different standard'.[236] Indeed, Warren McGregor, an Australian representative in the G4+1, wrote in 1999 that in recent times [G4+1] has begun to act more and more like a *de facto* international standard-setting body. This is reflected in its establishment, in conjunction with the IASC, of a Joint Working Group to develop an accounting standard on financial instruments, and its decisions to issue invitations to comment on business combinations, accounting for joint ventures and reporting financial performance.[237]

The G4+1 had its detractors, particularly in Europe.[238] Some representatives from the European Continent viewed the G4+1 with suspicion, as an attempt by the Anglo-American countries' standard setters to gain undue leverage in the work of the IASC and in the harmonization movement generally. As a counter ploy, a European Accounting Study Group, known as E5+2 was formed, which is discussed next.

12.6.3. European Interests Establish E5+2 to Counter the G4+1

FEE's Research Foundation initiative (*see* Section 12.3.4) was followed in 1996 by the setting up of what became known as the European Accounting Study Group, dubbed E5+2. Like the Foundation initiative, it was a response to concerns over the lack of European influence in the IASC. Specifically, it was intended to counter the increasingly influential G4+1 and to offer the European delegations to the IASC board the opportunity to operate more as a unit.[239] While the Anglo-Americans exchanged ideas and coordinated their positions on standards issues in the G4+1 meetings, the Continental European delegations to the board developed their individual positions in isolation, much to the despair of Karel Van Hulle, of the European Commission.

The Study Group originated in 1996, when the Nederlands Instituut van Registeraccountants (NIVRA) proposed that the five EU country delegations to the IASC board (France, Germany, the Netherlands, the Nordic Federation, and the United Kingdom) meet informally together with the European Commission's observer on the IASC board to discuss a number of current IASC projects.[240] In 1997, the group was formalized by a written agreement, and representatives of the national standard setters, and of FEE, were asked to participate as well. The NIVRA provided most of Study Group's motive power.

Because the United Kingdom was also part of the G4+1 and was the only E5 member with a standard setter of international repute, it was the member least willing to commit itself to a common European position. But the UK representatives were willing to participate in order to keep informed. Partly owing to the United Kingdom's unique position but also because the other E5 members did not agree easily among themselves, the meetings of the Study Group were limited to an exchange of views. Gatherings of the Study Group continued to be held prior to each IASC board meeting until December 2000, when the outgoing board met for the final time. The Study Group then disbanded, as the G4+1 itself did about a month later.

The plan had been for all of the participating bodies to select a topic and conduct research as the basis for discussion papers to be published under the Group's name, much as the G4+1 had been doing, but only the NIVRA fulfilled. Therefore, the Study Group issued only one position paper, in early 2000, which was financed and published by the NIVRA.[241] The topic of the paper, the presentation in the company annual report of management's analysis of the business, was one that the IASC never seriously considered adding to its agenda, which may exemplify the Study Group's limited impact on the IASC. The European delegations continued to operate independently, and concerns about the weakness of the 'European voice' in the IASC continued until the end. In contrast, as is seen in Chapter 13, the standard setters composing the G4+1 formed a formidable bloc in the discussions and negotiations over the restructuring of the IASC that began in 1997.

13

Towards a World Standard Setter: The Restructuring of the IASC

It became evident in the 1990s that the IASC board had gone as far as it could as presently constituted, drawing mainly on the volunteer resources of the accountancy profession. This chapter recounts the politically charged process by which the board restructured itself in order to reinforce its credentials as a legitimate world accounting standard setter.[1]

13.1. FORMATION OF THE STRATEGY WORKING PARTY AND ITS MEMBERSHIP

As early as January 1996, Secretary-General Bryan Carsberg apprised the Advisory Council of his view that 'An organisation like IASC should plan to have a strategic review every five years or so—as, for example, do the FASB—although the depth of the review may well need to vary according to the circumstances.'[2] Carsberg had spent three years, 1978–81, on the technical staff of the Financial Accounting Standards Board (FASB) and was much impressed with its competence as a standard setter.[3] He noted that the last such review was undertaken in October 1992, when the Foundation Working Party was set up (*see* Section 8.15), and he thought that the Advisory Council or a special working party might be invited to conduct the next review sometime in 1997. His views at this stage are worth noting:

Assuming that, when the next review begins, IASC is well on the way to achieving successful completion of the IOSCO programme with the continuing expectation that it will obtain acceptance in all the major stock exchanges of the world for cross-border listings, we shall need to look at the question of what kind of organization IASC needs to be for the next phase in its development. If IASC is to become the leading standard setter in accounting and gradually take more of a leadership role in relation to the national standard setters, is some change in its structure needed?

...

Are we secure in our position as the international setter of accounting standards or is there some danger of a challenge from an unexpected source? Is it possible that a national standard setter might reconstitute itself in order to challenge for international leadership?

His thinking, he said, was stimulated 'by the unofficial discovery that the trustees of the [Financial Accounting Foundation (FAF)] which oversees FASB are about to embark on a strategic review of FASB with particular focus on international developments'. Several months later, with Carsberg's encouragement, Thomas Jones, the lead member of the financial executives delegation to the board and vice-chairman of the FAF, arranged a meeting in London between several of the FAF trustees, including Jones, David Ruder, Charles Bowsher, and Michael Cook (as well as FASB member Tony Cope) with Carsberg, IASC Chairman Michael Sharpe, IASC Deputy Chairman Stig Enevoldsen, and David Tweedie. Carsberg wanted to open a direct line to the FASB's trustees.[4] The trustees in turn were interested in the FASB and the FAF becoming a partner in creating international accounting standards. It was the first real discussion between the FAF trustees and those involved in the IASC.[5] Carsberg was also aware of pressure on its standards programme emanating from the G4+1, and the latter's decision in March 1996 to name David Tweedie as its first chairman was interpreted by some as heightening its challenge to the IASC, although Tweedie disavowed that view (see Section 12.6).[6]

Carsberg and Sharpe, who was a major force in this initiative, carried forward the plan for the strategy review. At its September 1996 meeting, the IASC board unanimously approved a recommendation from the executive committee and the Advisory Council to set up a Strategy Working Party (SWP) to 'advise on strategies to be pursued by IASC after completion of the current work programme in 1998',[7] a reference to the completion of the core standards for submission to the International Organization of Securities Commissions (IOSCO). It was to address a number of important issues:

- 'whether a major focus of the work of IASC after 1998 should be to narrow further the differences between national standards and international standards', and the procedures that would be appropriate to this task;
- 'whether some new form of association, agreement, or working arrangement between IASC and national standard setters is desirable'; and
- 'whether changes in procedures are needed to reconcile the conflicting requirements of efficient decision-making in a group which has already become very large for the purposes of technical discussions and the requirements of being a highly representative body in which more and more nations have strong claims to be included'.[8]

The SWP was also asked 'to consider what role IASC should take in educational and training activities relating to its Standards' and to 'review arrangements for funding IASC taking account of the success of the fund-raising programme over the last two years and the needs implied by the proposed strategy for IASC'. The working party was to furnish the board with a draft recommendation by the end of September 1997 and to produce a final report, with recommendations, by the end of March 1998.[9] Peter Clark has said, 'Bryan's original objective was to get the whole thing through, together with the IOSCO endorsement—he thought it would be quite a critical factor in the IOSCO endorsement. I think he felt that the [US Securities and Exchange Commission, SEC] probably wouldn't sign up to the process unless the constitutional changes were far advanced.'[10] The board's timetable, as it turned out, proved to be naively optimistic. The controversy and intense negotiations sparked by the working party's initial proposals, reflecting a philosophical chasm between the SEC (and Anglo-Americans) and the European Commission (and Continental Europeans), led to a series of further proposals and negotiations that inevitably put off its final report until the end of 1999.

As with any body constituted for a specific purpose, the composition of its membership can have a profound impact on the result. The IASC clearly wanted a working party chairman from North America who understood the demands and expectations of the SEC and in turn enjoyed the SEC's respect. The IASC initially invited Arthur Wyatt, a former IASC chairman, to chair the working party. But because he was then serving as an adviser to the SEC on international accounting standards, Wyatt declined on the justifiable ground that 'My appointment to this post could be interpreted negatively in many quarters given my present involvement with the SEC.'[11] The IASC then approached Edward Waitzer, a Toronto securities lawyer who had served as chairman of both the Ontario Securities Commission (OSC) and IOSCO's Technical Committee. He accepted. To a considerable degree, the working party was being asked to bridge the financial reporting and regulatory cultures of the United States and Continental Europe, and who better than a Canadian to manage and lead the challenging assignment. The other members of the working party, chosen by Chairman Sharpe, Deputy Chairman Enevoldsen, and Secretary-General Carsberg in consultation with the executive committee,[12] were announced as follows:[13]

Georges Barthès de Ruyter—chairman of France's Conseil National de la Comptabilité, former chairman of the IASC, and former partner in Arthur Andersen, Paris

Sir Bryan Carsberg—secretary-general of the IASC

Anthony Cope—member of the FASB and former financial analyst, and an observer on behalf of the FASB at IASC board meetings

Stig Enevoldsen—deputy chairman of the IASC

Birgitta Kantola—vice-president, finance and planning, International Finance Corporation

Frank Harding—president of the International Federation of Accountants (IFAC) and former partner in KPMG, London

Kazuo Hiramatsu—professor of accounting, Kwansei Gakuin University, Osaka, and member of the Business Accounting Deliberation Council

Jacques Manardo—chairman of the European 'Contact Group' of the Big Six accounting firms, and chairman of the European region of Deloitte Touche Tohmatsu, based in Paris

David S. Ruder—trustee of the Financial Accounting Federation (parent body of the FASB), a former chairman of the SEC, and law professor at Northwestern University, Chicago

Werner Seifert—chief executive officer, Deutsche Börse

Michael Sharpe—chairman of the IASC

Peter Sjöstrand—Swedish venture capitalist, partner of the BZ Group (Switzerland), and board member of Pharma Vision

Sir David Tweedie—chairman of the UK Accounting Standards Board, member of the UK delegation to the IASC board, and former partner in KPMG, London

Half of the working party's fourteen members, including the chairman, came from the United States, United Kingdom, Canada, and Australia, all being G4 countries. Werner Seifert and Peter Sjöstrand withdrew from active participation following the first meeting of the working party, apparently for personal reasons, although Seifert maintained contact with the project and agreed to support the working party's discussion paper of December 1998. They were not replaced, and their absence from the deliberations probably deprived the Continental European viewpoint of support. Peter Clark served as the project manager until the end of 1998. Sue Harding succeeded him in 1999.

Following each of the working party's meetings, the secretariat drafted a discussion paper—essentially a draft working party report—based on the exchange of views among the working party members. Peter Clark and thereafter Sue Harding drafted the succession of versions of the discussion paper, which were then reviewed and revised by Secretary-General Carsberg and working party Chairman Ed Waitzer.[14] It is important to point out that this series of internal drafts following the working party meetings were not agreed-upon documents, but were the secretariat's rendering of the ongoing deliberations. The first agreed draft was the discussion paper published in December 1998.

13.2. MEETINGS DURING 1997 AND SUCCESSIVE DRAFTS OF THE DISCUSSION PAPER[15]

13.2.1. July 1997 Meeting

At its first meeting, on 21–2 July in London, the working party held a wide-ranging discussion of the current aims and operation of the IASC.[16] After Carsberg described the IASC's core standards agreement with IOSCO and the SEC's response, David Ruder discussed the likelihood of the SEC's acceptance of the IASC's core standards once they were completed, and he emphasized that the SEC will act cautiously and wish to retain oversight authority over the setting of accounting standards used in the US securities market.

The working party then considered a lengthy memorandum prepared by Bryan Carsberg, after he had received comments from the executive committee and Advisory Council, in which he raised a host of issues.[17] Among the broader policy questions were: what is meant by 'harmonization', should the IASC's objective be to establish uniform global standards, and should the IASC tailor standards for developing countries, small businesses, particular industries, and public sector and non-profit organizations? But the issue of the IASC's future structure was paramount. In the memo, Carsberg underscored the dilemma of the size of board meetings:

> At one and the same time, [the] Board seems to be both too big and too small. It is too big in the sense that about 70 individuals might attend a Board meeting and this is too large a number for the most effective discussion to decide on the contents of accounting standards. However, more and more countries and other organizations have an interest in participating in IASC activities and have a legitimate claim on doing so.... Perhaps these conflicting pressures can be reconciled in some new structural arrangement.

Carsberg, who was both the IASC's secretary-general and a member of the working party, cited the 'critical success factors' in the work of the IASC:

- IASC should be recognised as having high quality professional skills. Board members and staff should be regarded as having excellent technical knowledge and analytical skills to provide assurance of high quality output.
- IASC needs to be efficient in producing good standards quickly and cost-effectively. Accounting standards are always needed urgently and the ability to make sound decisions and achieve closure on projects reasonably expeditiously is important.
- IASC must be perceived as being independent, that is its decisions must not be dominated by particular sectional interests or favour such sectional interests.
- IASC must be seen as fair and reasonable. It must listen to comments and provide good opportunities for differing views to be expressed.
- IASC must be seen as having legitimacy which must come from reasonable representation of countries and functions (users, preparers, the accounting profession, academics and so on).

As will be seen, the clash of views inside and outside the working party on structure turned on the relative degree of emphasis that was placed on efficiency, independence (and how it is defined), and legitimacy as regards geographical representation.

Carsberg presented the working party with a proposal for a bicameral structure, consisting of a small Board and an overarching General Assembly. He suggested consideration of a Board of nine to eleven individuals. 'This would provide for membership of one individual from each of several major accounting nations and a few others. It could include representation of users, preparers, academics, and others....' It would replace the steering committees as the body that drafts the proposed standards. But such a Board alone would not overcome 'the difficulty of providing participation to many countries which currently wish to be involved'. He then suggested a General Assembly that 'might include 100 or more individuals with a larger number of countries than included in the current Board'. The General Assembly would debate the standards proposals sent to it by the Board. 'If it did not agree with them, it might have the right to advise the Board to make a change or it might have the right to delay the issue of a standard or, at an extreme, it might have the right to veto a standard.' Carsberg saw the merit of the bicameral structure as taking account 'of the need to achieve high quality, efficiency and legitimacy with appropriate representation'. In connection with its choice of structure, whether bicameral or otherwise, Carsberg challenged the working party with a series of questions:

- Does the working party favour a bicameral structure, and, if so, how should the relative powers of each body be defined? If not, what structure would the working party favour?
- What authority should appoint members to the Board and the Assembly, and should the new structure distance itself from the accountancy profession?
- What role, if any, should be played by national standard setters in the new structure?
- Should any or all of the members of the Board be full-time or part-time?
- Should the IASC hold public hearings and hold its meetings 'in the sunshine'?
- How should the new structure be financed?
- Should there be a place for issuing interpretations in the new structure?
- Should the IASC do anything to promote good enforcement of its standards?

Carsberg's sweeping charge to the working party was daunting indeed, raising every conceivable question about the structure and operation of the IASC.

The working party preferred the top body to be called the IASC Board, and the lower body should be the Technical Board. (Technical Committee was also a favoured name.) Each of the major national standard setters would be invited to designate one of its members to serve on the Technical Board. The countries mentioned were the United States, United Kingdom, France, Canada, Australia, and perhaps Mexico. Major countries without a standard setter, namely Germany and Japan, would be encouraged to establish one (which Germany did the following year). There would also be 'at large' members. The national standard setters would agree to follow the Technical Board's agenda, and they would publish and seek comments on the Technical Board's draft standards. The Technical Board would then approve a standard, which then would need to be ratified by the IASC Board or sent back to the Technical Board for further consideration. Following ratification of a standard by the IASC Board, each national standard setter would adopt or reject the standard, or adopt a different standard on the same subject. The IASC would continue to have a secretary-general, a technical director, and a small technical staff.

The working party took up numerous other issues at the meeting. It thought that the Advisory Council, Consultative Group, and the Standing Interpretations Committee (SIC) would be retained. Questions were raised about funding and about the steps necessary to secure compliance with the IASC's standards. The working party was in favour of opening IASC Board meetings and perhaps even Technical Board meetings to the public. The working party's acceptance of this view, together with Carsberg's earlier suggestion that the IASC Board should meet in the sunshine, prompted the executive committee to recommend that the current board adopt this practice (*see* Section 8.7).

The working party agreed to meet with relevant constituencies, including the G4 standard setters in September, and it anticipated that a publishable discussion paper might be available in time for the IFAC Council meeting in October (at the time of the World Congress of Accountants in Paris) or at the latest by the end of November. It expected that the final recommendations would be ready for the meeting of the IASC member bodies scheduled for May 2000. These meetings were held every two-and-a-half years, when the same bodies met as the IFAC general assembly, and any restructuring of the IASC would have to be approved at such a meeting. Because the terms of the IASC board members were scheduled to end in June 2000, it was necessary to secure the approval of any restructuring at the next one of these meetings.

The G4+1 had already begun to address the restructuring issue. In March, 1997, three months prior to the working party's first meeting, the G4+1 resolved unanimously to support a proposal to replace the IASC with a smaller board of up to nine representatives of national standard setters that could demonstrate the expertise and resources to contribute to the process. The board would be supported by a general assembly composed of country representatives and interested parties, but the G4+1 did not contemplate that the assembly could overrule the board on standards.[18]

Following the July meeting, Peter Clark produced a series of draft discussion papers to 'flesh out' the proposals discussed by the working party. Each draft was revised on the basis of comments received from Carsberg and others. In the final iteration of the draft paper emerging from the inaugural meeting, the version dated 8 September 1997,[19] the Technical Committee (renamed from Technical Board) was to have from eight to eleven members, with a full-time chairman and perhaps one or two other full-time members, which would meet every one to two months. 'Most of its members would be full-time members of their national standard setters, as part-time members of national standard setters could not devote sufficient time to IASC as well' (paragraph 56). The Technical Committee would require more than a simple majority to submit exposure drafts or final standards to the Board for approval (paragraph 58). The membership of the Board would be expanded to perhaps twenty-five delegations, drawing not only from professional accountancy bodies but also from other organizations. The size of each delegation would be limited to two individuals, so as to reduce the number of persons attending its meetings. The Board would possess authority to approve exposure drafts and final standards by a three-fifths majority (compared to the current required majority of two-thirds for exposure drafts and three quarters for final standards), but it would not debate the technical details in as much depth as the IASC board presently did, and it would need to meet only two or three times a year, as an oversight body. Its chairman would serve part-time (paragraphs 61–5). A fourteen-member Foundation would replace the Advisory Council and would appoint the Board delegations and their members, the members of the Technical Committee, and the chairmen of the Board and the Technical Committee. It would also raise the funds. The Foundation would mediate any conflicts arising between the Board and the Technical Committee (paragraph 66), although 'The Foundation would not participate in the technical decisions of the Board and would do nothing to impair the independence and objectivity of the Board' (paragraph 67). Two or three of the Foundation members would come from the Big Six accounting firms, while the others would be broadly representative of other constituencies (paragraph 68). The draft was silent on the desired size and composition of the technical staff.

In this initial draft, the working party gave currency to the term 'convergence', which eventually came to supplant 'harmonization' in the IASC's deliberations and publications (paragraph 53(a)). The term convergence had been broached during the meeting. It was thought to connote a process rather than an end point and to acknowledge the continuing involvement of national standard setters. The working party equivocated on whether open meetings were desirable (paragraph 72). It was noted in the draft that the secretary-general estimated 'that IASC needs to increase its annual funding to around £3 million at current prices' to support the proposed structure (paragraph 79).

The burning question became: which body should possess the authority to approve the exposure drafts and final standards for publication? Would technical experts be willing to serve on a Technical Committee if its final drafts could be overruled by a non-expert body? Would professional accountancy bodies and other organizations send delegations to a Board that did not have the authority to approve exposure drafts and final standards?

13.2.2. September 1997 Meeting

Carsberg took the initiative to schedule an informal meeting of the working party for 26 September 1997 to coincide with a meeting the previous day of the G4+1 at the FASB's offices in Norwalk. As he had called the meeting on short notice, it was difficult for several of the members to arrange to be there, and thus the meeting was lightly attended, with only eight of its fourteen members present.[20] The aim was to obtain the reactions of the G4 members to the secretariat's draft discussion paper of 8 September, because they were the most prominent among the national standard setters that would be invited to send representatives to the proposed Technical Committee. At the joint meeting with the G4 standard setters, the latter agreed that the most critical issue in the proposed structure was the balance of power between the Board and the Technical Committee. Some national standard setters, it was said, would be reluctant to serve on the Technical Committee if its recommendations could be overruled by the Board. Yet it was believed that a Board composed of a membership similar to that of the current IASC board would be reluctant to give too much power to the Technical Committee. It was suggested that the working party might want to present more than one model in its discussion paper. One of the standard setters' criticisms was directed at the name, Technical Committee, because it might suggest that the body lacks real power and thus would discourage national standard setters from belonging. It was thought that the term 'Standards' would be an improvement. Some felt that all of the members of the Technical Committee should be involved in standard setting on a full-time basis, either at the IASC alone or at the IASC together with work in a national standard setter.[21]

At the working party's own meeting later in the day, after hearing out the G4 standard setters, it retreated from defining the power relationship between the Board and the Technical Committee so categorically.[22] For the next draft, it considered providing for three different models of the relationship: the one already outlined; a second, authorizing the Technical Committee to promulgate standards without obtaining Board approval, but after seeking the Board's advice; and a third, empowering the Board, or perhaps a 'super-minority' of the Board, to delay a proposed standard but not reject it. The working party's inclination was to give the Board more authority over final standards than over exposure drafts. As to the Technical Committee, all of the nominees from the national standard setters 'should be involved on a full-time basis, either at IASC alone or at IASC and domestically', incorporating the view expressed at the G4 meeting. But the Technical Committee should also have a preparer and a user, and perhaps an academic. Its members should come predominantly from countries with major capital markets. In a change in its position, the working party decided that the Foundation should not mediate differences between the Board and the Technical Committee. The chairman of the Technical Committee, who would be full-time, should be the IASC's CEO, replacing the secretary-general and becoming the IASC's chief spokesperson. The working party also considered different names for the Technical Committee, taking a cue from the G4 members.

In the next draft composed by the secretariat and sent to the working party, dated 17 October,[23] the three principal bodies were renamed: the Board became the Council, the Technical Committee was renamed the Standards Committee, and the Foundation became the Trustees. The composition of the Council and Standards Committee membership in the 8 September draft was modified by the conclusions reached at the working party's meeting of 26 September. On the critical issue of the relative powers of the Council and the Standards Committee to approve exposure drafts and final standards, the draft abandoned the single model presented in the previous draft and instead offered, not the three mentioned in the minutes, but four models, but it did not signify which one the working party favoured (paragraphs 107–14), paraphrased as follows:

- The Council will approve exposure drafts and final standards by a three-fifths majority.
- The Council will approve final standards but not exposure drafts, but the Standards Committee would seek the Council's views before issuing drafts.

- The Council, or perhaps a super-minority of the Council (say, 25 per cent of its members), could delay a proposed standard (and perhaps an exposure draft) but not reject a standard indefinitely; the Standards Committee would then have the power to issue the standard but only by a 'super-majority' (say, not more than two votes against).
- The Standards Committee has the power to issue exposure drafts and final standards but would be required to consult the Council thoroughly on all significant issues before doing so.

As before, the choice depended on what was required to achieve 'legitimacy' of the process, in order to secure the broad support of constituents, balanced by the need to recruit capable individuals to serve on the Council and the Standards Committee, depending on where the power is centralized. In this draft, the need for geographical diversity was invoked for the Standards (or Technical) Committee: its membership would include 'representation from emerging markets and developing countries' (paragraph 89). On the subject of interpretations, the SIC would submit final Interpretations to the Standards Committee for approval, but it must inform the Council of the issues so that it can comment (paragraphs 115–18). The composition and authority of the Trustees paralleled that of the old Foundation, except that it was no longer to attempt to resolve any conflicts between the Council and the Standards Committee (paragraphs 119–20). The draft called for 'a core of high-quality technical staff (at least 8), at a central location', which would be appointed by, and report to, the secretary of the Standards Committee (paragraphs 123–4). The draft came down in favour of open meetings of the Council, the Standards Committee, and the Trustees (paragraph 128(a)). It also favoured more frequent use of public hearings and field tests (paragraph 129). The estimate of annual funding was raised from about £3 million to £5.2 million (paragraph 153), an amount that reappeared in all of the drafts in 1998. This figure was ventured even though a provision appeared in this draft saying that 'national standard setters should be persuaded to pay' the salaries and travel costs of their members serving on the Standards Committee, as well as the costs of technical and any other of their staff assigned to assist the member (paragraph 85). On most other important matters, this draft was similar to its predecessor.

In this draft, the idea of convergence was given even greater emphasis, now elevated to a boldface subhead (paragraph 70).[24] In this regard, an important philosophical issue was raised in the draft, under the heading, 'Objectives of IASC':

Should IASC be a harmoniser or innovator? IASC was originally conceived as a harmoniser—a body that selected an accounting treatment from among the treatments that already existed at the national level in some countries. In recent years, IASC has become more of an innovator.... The role of an innovator will inevitably require greater resources, and will probably demand more significant changes to IASC's structure and working methods, than the role of harmoniser. For the rest of this discussion paper, the Working Party has assumed that IASC will continue to play an innovatory role, in close partnership with national standard setters. (paragraph 22)

The draft expanded upon this 'close partnership', intended to achieve convergence, by proposing an elaborate plan under which the IASC would coordinate its due process with that of national standard setters (paragraph 138). This section, which seems to have achieved ready agreement, foreshadowed one on 'Coordination with National Due Process' in the working party's final report issued in November 1999.[25] The IASC and national standard setters would coordinate their work plans and timetables with a view towards promoting the elimination of as many divergences as practicable between their respective exposure drafts and final standards.

On 17 November 1997, Carsberg transmitted to the working party another draft, of that date, reflecting only minor changes.[26] This draft made a point of saying that the working party believed that it was no longer appropriate for the accountancy profession, through IFAC, to control appointments to the Board (paragraph 120A). In a covering memorandum, Carsberg wrote that the IASC executive committee had seen the previous draft and was concerned over the role of the proposed Council 'and particularly the suggestion that the Council might have only an advisory role'.[27] He said that the same draft would be tabled for discussion at the board meeting in January. He attached a list of questions prepared by the FASB on the draft of 8 September (evidently prepared after the meeting in Norwalk). One of the FASB's concerns was the suggestion that the Board would not be expected to discuss detailed technical issues in as much depth as at present. The FASB said that, under the structure in the 8 September draft, the Board should debate such technical details in even more depth than at present, else how could it sit in judgement on the Technical Committee's decision to endorse a final standard?

The 17 November draft was circulated within the IASC to obtain the reactions of the board, the Advisory Council, and the Consultative Group. It was, however, leaked to a number of outsiders: the European Commission, the SEC, the FASB, the Big Six accounting firms, IOSCO, and perhaps others.[28] Stig Enevoldsen was reported as saying that he regretted that the working party's draft paper had been so widely distributed before it had completed its deliberations.[29]

13.2.3. Reactions to the 17 November Draft from Outside the Working Party

At the Advisory Council's meeting on 8 January 1998, only a limited amount of time was available to discuss the working party's draft. The Advisory Council believed that it was important for the working party to signify its preferred option for the balance of power between the proposed Council and the Standards Committee. Members of the Advisory Council thought it would be a mistake for the same body to prepare and approve the standards. The Advisory Council divided over whether the meetings of the proposed Council should be open and public hearings might be held.[30]

The 9–10 January meeting of the Consultative Group was poorly attended, and most of the debate over the working party's draft was critical. Some members, mostly Continental Europeans, did not see a need to change the present structure; to them, legitimacy, or representativeness, was paramount. There was concern over an apparent diminution in the role of preparers. The majority believed that the Council must possess the final authority.[31]

During the board meeting on 12–16 January 1998, at the outset of the discussion of the working party's draft, several delegations, mostly European, read prepared statements in opposition to the proposals. The majority of the speakers during the discussion, though not necessarily a consensus, favoured a change that was more 'evolutionary' than the working party had in mind. They were more satisfied than the working party with the IASC's process and standards.[32] Most delegations believed strongly that the ultimate authority should reside in the proposed Council. There was a suspicion that standard setters were mere technicians, not attuned to the real world. One board member was reported to have said, 'Standard setting is too important to be left to experts.' More representation, or power, was sought by smaller countries.[33] A board member who wrote an article on the meeting said, 'It is clear that several Board members (e.g. India, Malaysia, Mexico, the Netherlands, South Africa) see [a small decision-making body as] a threat to their influence on the IASC.'[34]

Over lunch during the board meeting, *Accountancy* conducted a colloquy among a number of board members. Jan Klaassen, of the Dutch delegation, said that leaving all of the decision-making to the national standard setters 'would mean the end of the IASC'.[35] Peter Zurbrügg, of the Federation of Swiss Industrial Holding Companies' delegation, largely agreed with Klaassen and said he liked the technical and political balance of the IASC board as it was.[36] Stig Enevoldsen agreed that the IASC needs more involvement by national standard setters, as the draft recommended, 'But it doesn't mean that they necessarily should take the whole thing over, which is one of the solutions in the paper.'[37] David Tweedie, of the UK delegation and a member of the working party, said, 'We need to tie the standard-setters in, because you don't actually want a G4 or a European independent group going off and doing its own thing.' He added, 'The way the paper is phrased at the moment, it looks as if the top body has no power at all and that is quite clearly unacceptable.'[38] Tweedie later said, 'The blunt fact was that the G-4 was going to be the international standard setter unless IASC changed itself. And I think IASC was quite aware that that was going to happen.'[39]

Warren McGregor, a member of the Australian delegation, subsequently wrote,

Reactions to early drafts of the [working party's] proposals from potentially disaffected parties have ranged from lukewarm support to hostile rejection. A common theme emanating from a number of IASC board member countries, in particular some of the Continental European countries, is 'if it isn't broken why fix it?' This reflects a deeply held concern that a number of countries will be excluded from participation in the [Standards Committee] under the new structure because they either do not currently have a national standard-setting body or because their standard-setting body lacks the necessary international recognition.[40]

A representative of IOSCO attending the IASC board meeting in January 1998 was minuted as reporting that, at a recent Working Party 1 meeting, a majority expressed concern over any 'drastic structure changes'. IOSCO members 'place a high value on a close and direct involvement in each project and would not want this to be lost in any new structure'. Open meetings would not be a solution if the IOSCO members in attendance 'were not able to inject comments into the debate'.[41]

The deliberations and internal drafts of the working party were no secret from the accountancy press. In its February 1998 issue, *The Accountant* reported that the IASC's 'plans to overhaul its constitution are in disarray. Incoming Chairman Stig Enevoldsen has revealed that the recommendations of its strategy working group have met with stiff resistance from non–English-speaking countries. They fear the so-called "G4" cadre of standard-setters from the US, UK, Australia and Canada would become too dominant under the proposed new structure.'[42] Enevoldsen himself was quoted as saying that he prefers 'evolutionary development, not a "big bang" switch to an unknown and unpredictable new system'.[43]

In its February 1998 issue, *Accountancy* reported that the biggest surprise at the IASC board's January meeting 'was the ferocious criticism that greeted the preliminary proposals on the board's future strategy'.[44] 'Delegates from continental Europe, the Far East and South Africa all criticised the proposals.' Karel Van Hulle, of the European Commission, was quoted as saying that the bicameral structure was 'undemocratic and dangerous.... You cannot say that the IASC should set standards for the world and at the same time exclude the world from active participation in the standard-setting.' Tony Seah, of the Malaysian delegation, was reported as saying that he was happy with the IASC as it was: 'It just needs refining.' Yet Ken Spencer, of the Australian delegation, said he supported the smaller standard-setting body. The following view was attributed to Spencer, 'If a larger oversight body had power of veto over the smaller group, the US would never buy into it. And if that happened, he hinted that the largest professional standard-setters such as Australia, Canada and the UK would throw in their lot with FASB rather than the IASC.'

Jim Leisenring, the outspoken FASB vice-chairman and a leading member of the G4+1, agreed with Spencer. He was quoted as saying, 'I wouldn't be interested in working my butt off to understand a technical issue and write a standard so that a bunch of politicians can vote yes or no on it. Final authority must be in the technical committee. The board should have an advisory role.'[45]

13.3. THE WORKING PARTY'S DELIBERATIONS DURING 1998

During 1998, the working party held meetings in January, April, and July. Bryan Carsberg's original timetable for the working party to complete its assignment by March 1998 had been discarded months earlier. In April, the executive committee hoped that the working party would agree a consultative document in July for publication in late August or September, probably with a comment period of six months.⁴⁶ In July, Carsberg said he hoped that the draft discussion paper could be published by October 1998 with a deadline for comments to be received by March 1999. The working party's final report, he hoped, would enable the IASC board to vote on the final restructuring in time for the next meeting of IASC/IFAC member bodies, which was scheduled for May 2000.⁴⁷ In the end, as will be seen below, the discussion paper was not published until December 1998, the deliberations and drafting having consumed a period of almost eighteen months.

From the beginning of the working party's meetings, two schools of thought emerged. The working party came to call them the 'independent expert model', supported by the Anglo-Americans, and the 'constituency model', largely reflecting Continental European views. These polar positions bedevilled the working party throughout its deliberations, and, as will be seen, they persisted as a fundamental disagreement until the very end of the process in late 1999.

Periodically, some members of the Anglo-American group would inject forebodings into the deliberations, during periods when advocacy for the constituency model gathered momentum in the working party's meetings. David Ruder, a former SEC chairman, would intone, 'The SEC will never accept that.' David Tweedie was known for saying that the G4 standard setters were prepared to enter the breach if the IASC were unable to restructure itself to become an effective standard setter. Carsberg and Enevoldsen heard the same message when they attended G4+1 meetings. Indeed, David Cairns reported that, at the G4+1's meeting in October 1997, it decided, for the first time, to try to develop a common standard rather than just a discussion paper.⁴⁸ In 1999, Warren McGregor, an Australian representative in the G4+1 meetings, wrote, 'The G4 has begun to act more like a standard-setting body than a discussion group.' He predicted that the restructured IASC 'will emerge from the G4'.⁴⁹

13.3.1. January 1998 Meeting

At its meeting on 18 January in London, the working party had a better attendance, ten of the fourteen members being present.⁵⁰ It had been the plan that the working party would put the finishing touches on its final draft discussion paper at the January meeting, but the critical reception of its proposals forced a deferral of that approval until July.⁵¹ Prior to the January meeting, Jacques Manardo, who had missed the working party's last meeting in September, submitted a lengthy set of critical comments on the 17 November draft.⁵² Manardo, who was a senior partner in Paris with Deloitte Touche Tohmatsu, did attend the 18 January meeting. He wanted the Council to be renamed the Board, much like the IASC board, as a way of underscoring its possession of real powers, which would include 'control over the work plan of the Standards Committee and approval of standards as a minimum'. He believed that the Standards Committee should include representatives from large audit firms, preparers, and users. Not all of the members of the Standards Committee, he said, needed to be involved full-time in national standard setting, else the Committee members would lose touch with their constituency, 'large audit firms or corporate world and users'.

On the first issue taken up at the meeting, funding, the working party believed that stock exchanges would be the most logical source, and some of those in attendance agreed to sound out several of the exchanges.

The names of two of the bodies were again changed: the Council reverted to the Board, and the Standards Committee became the Standards Development Committee (SDC), evidently to emphasize that, while the Committee would develop the standards, it would not necessarily be the body to approve them. Apart from funding, the working party agreed that the key issue was the balance of power between the Board and the SDC. The SDC should have eleven members (at the high end of the previous range of eight to eleven), a majority (probably seven or eight) should be standard setters, and at least seven of the eleven should be full time. The terms of SDC members should be five years. Pointedly, it was stated in the secretariat's note of the meeting: 'There should be no permanent seats for any particular standard setters or other constituents.' The working party favoured having a few observers, for example IOSCO and the European Commission, at Board meetings, with the right to speak. SDC members would also be able to attend as observers. The working party defined the required majority of the SDC to recommend an exposure draft or standard as seven out of the eleven members. The Board's required majority for approval was to remain at three-fifths, but it was added that the Board could not amend proposals from the SDC and it should give its reasons for rejection. Thereafter, if the SDC reconfirms its proposal with at least nine affirmative votes, the Board would require only a simple majority for approval. This approval procedure for exposure drafts and standards was, after a few modifications, urged on the working party by David Ruder and Tony Cope.[53] The number of Trustees was reduced from fourteen to twelve, of whom six should be delegates from organizations: two from IFAC and one each from the International Association of Financial Executives Institutes, the International Co-ordinating Committee of Financial Analysts Associations, the Fédération Internationale des Bourses de Valeurs (FIBV), and the International Association for Accounting Education and Research. The other six members of the Trustees should be chosen 'at large' by the Trustees as a whole, with a possible role in their selection given to the chairman and deputy chairman of the Board and to the chairman of the SDC.

Based on the views expressed at the working party's January meeting, the secretariat prepared a further draft discussion paper, dated 20 March 1998.[54] The World Trade Organization and the World Bank, as well as other development agencies that impose financial reporting obligations on borrowers or recipients of aid, were added to the list of interested parties in the development of IASC standards (paragraphs 1–6). The UN and the OECD were also mentioned in this context for the first time (paragraphs 20–1). To appease some of the critics, the draft characterized the needed changes as evolutionary (paragraph 91 and also in the executive summary, paragraph 12). Of the eleven members of the SDC, at least seven were to come from developed economies, at least two from countries in transition or developing countries (the geographical criterion), and at least seven should be involved in standard setting on a full-time basis (paragraphs 102–57). SDC members could be appointed for a maximum of two five-year terms.

The Board delegations would be drawn from twenty countries and five interested organizations. While the Board delegations would be selected by the Trustees, the composition of each delegation would be chosen by the country or organization in consultation with the Trustees, who would have a veto. As before, there would be a provision for observers. The draft was ambivalent about legitimacy: in paragraph 98, it was achieved through high quality, yet in paragraph 113 it was defined, in effect, as political acceptability. The composition of the Trustees was unchanged from the agreement reached during the 18 January meeting (paragraph 125). The very important balance of power between the SDC and the Board was also unchanged from the agreement reached in January (paragraphs 130, 136–7). Interpretations coming from the Standing Interpretations Committee (SIC) would be acted upon by the SDC without involvement by the Board, with seven votes required for approval. A provision, which Tony Cope said he could not recall being discussed by the working party, would create an executive committee of the Trustees, which would be responsible for appointing senior technical staff and handling all 'commercial' matters. He disliked this provision, because, he said, the Trustees should have oversight, not direct responsibility for administration. More important, he believed that an executive committee should be drawn from the Board, thus increasing the status and prestige of the Board in the power relation with the SDC.[55]

13.3.2. April 1998 Meeting

The working party met again on 3 April in New York City and on 12 July in Toronto. Because the secretariat believed that the minutes for the latter would do no more than duplicate the changes in the next version of the draft discussion paper, it did not prepare any minutes for that meeting. At the former, it was reported that two members' approaches to the New York Stock Exchange and the FIBV about possible funding had not yet borne fruit.[56] As to the draft, it was agreed that 'technical competence, integrity, objectivity, a commitment to the Framework and ability to make an active contribution to the IASC's work and attend meetings regularly' should be the primary criteria for membership on the SDC. The SDC 'should have at least two members from developing countries, but *only if* suitably qualified'. These changes reflected a shift from the constituency model towards the independent expert model. Another change was that the chairman of the SDC should not be the main spokesperson on technical issues. The working party decided that the executive committee should be a committee of the Board, not of the Trustees, a change that Tony Cope would have advocated (*see* above) and that the SIC should be appointed by the executive committee, not the Trustees.

The secretariat issued a further draft discussion paper dated 19 June, which was discussed at the meeting on 12 July. In the new paper, the SDC was to be supported by a Standards Development Advisory Committee (paragraph 108(ii)). Its purpose was 'to advise the Standards Development Committee whether its proposals were likely to be appropriate and operational in the domestic environment of the countries concerned' (paragraph 144). The advisory committee was to respond to the concerns of 'countries in transition and developing and newly industrialized countries' (paragraph 145). It was also stated that the SDC should have a full-time chairman (paragraph 113).

13.3.3. July 1998 Meeting

At the 12 July meeting,[57] the working party members disagreed whether they should make a firm recommendation on the power sharing between the Board and the SDC or whether a range of options, as in the 17 November draft, should be presented. Some believed that a firm recommendation with a clearly expressed minority opinion would encourage more useful responses. In regard to the composition of delegations appointed to the Board, should the Trustees have the right to veto an appointed member of any Board delegation who, in their view, does not possess the requisite qualities or experience to serve effectively? It was agreed that such a veto should require the agreement of nine of the twelve Trustees. A question was raised about the number of countries that should be represented on the eleven-member SDC. Some favoured as many as eight or ten countries.

Following the July meeting, the working party conducted a series of conference calls to iron out the members' remaining differences in a further succession of drafts.

13.4. THE DISCUSSION PAPER PUBLISHED IN DECEMBER 1998

The final draft of the discussion paper, entitled *Shaping IASC for the Future*, was released on the Internet on 7 December 1998 and shortly thereafter was published in hard copy. It was an extensive document of 114 pages.[58] The paper was styled as an 'invitation to comment' on the issues raised in a series of questions. Comments were to be submitted by 30 April 1999.

The membership of the SDC, the Board, and the Trustees was unchanged from previous drafts: eleven individuals, twenty-five delegations, and twelve individuals, respectively. The SDC would replace the steering committees and do the drafting. As before, the twenty-five delegations on the Board would consist of twenty country seats for accountancy bodies and five seats for other organizations with an interest in financial reporting (paragraph 137). For the first time, it was stated that 'there shall be a reasonable geographical spread' of the membership on all three bodies (paragraphs 128(f), 138(c), 150(e)), evidently to accommodate those who believed that legitimacy required a broadly representative membership.

The SDC would have a full-time chairman and would be composed of six to eight individuals from national standard setters, and two to four individuals from other groups, such as preparers, users, practising accountants, and academics (paragraph 127). If suitably qualified candidates were available (see below), at least two SDC members should come from 'developing countries or countries in transition to a market economy' (paragraph 128(d)). The SDC's members would have a staggered, five-year term, renewable for an additional term, and they would 'probably need to meet every one to two months' (paragraphs 134–5). The SDC would require a super-majority of seven votes to approve exposure drafts and standards (paragraph 154). The provision in the 17 October 1997 draft that the collaborating national standard setters should pay the salaries and travel costs of their members serving on the SDC reappeared in this draft (paragraph 131).

The overall funding estimate descended slightly from the £5.2 million in earlier drafts to £5 million, which was still considerably higher than the approximately £2 million for the existing IASC (paragraph 229). On the subject of staff, the draft stated, 'To play an equal role in partnership with national standard setters, IASC needs a core of high-quality technical staff (at least eight), at a central location' (paragraph 195).

As agreed in the working party's July 1998 meeting, the draft provided that the Trustees, with at least nine members in agreement, could veto an unsuitable individual appointed to a Board delegation (paragraphs 140, 142). Each Board delegation would be composed of two individuals, compared to mostly three in the then existing IASC board (paragraph 140). Board delegations would have two-and-a-half-year terms, which would be renewable at the discretion of the Trustees (paragraph 144). The Board would be headed by a non-executive, part-time chairman (paragraph 145). Six of the Trustees would be chosen by particular constituencies: three from IFAC, and three from other organizations such as those represented on the Consultative Group. The other six Trustees would be elected 'at large' by the Trustees as a whole (paragraph 149).

To be eligible for membership on the SDC, candidates would need to be 'people of proven technical competence in standard setting, integrity, and objectivity. They should not regard themselves as representing sectional interests but should be guided by the need to act in the public interest' (paragraph 128(a)).

While there were many elements in the discussion paper that would stimulate controversy and elicit lively comments from interested parties, the critical issue, as in the deliberations of the working party, was the power sharing between the Board and the SDC. The draft candidly acknowledged the daunting challenge of persuading the IASC's constituents to accept a two-tier, private-sector body (paragraph 165–6):

IASC cannot force anyone to use its Standards and so must rely on persuasion. It can persuade its constituents to use its Standards only if the Standards are of high quality and meet their needs. Also, IASC's constituents are more likely to use its Standards if they have a stake in, and play a meaningful part in, their development....

One way to persuade IASC's constituents to accept its due process and its Standards would be to set up an autonomous body of independent full-time and highly skilled experts, with a relatively small number of members for the sake of efficiency (an independent expert model). Another route would be to create a more broadly-based group from a larger number of countries and backgrounds (a constituency model).

The working party proceeded to say that neither of these two extremes would be feasible and that its proposal combined a mix of elements drawn from both models (paragraph 167). The working party acknowledged that talented and well-qualified individuals would not agree to serve on a body unless it were to have genuine decision-making authority. The problem facing the working party was one of achieving a compromise position which would assure members serving on both the Board and the SDC that they would possess this authority.

The working party then displayed a compass of four options which illustrated different balances of power between the Board and the SDC, paraphrased as follows (paragraph 170):

(a) the Board may approve exposure drafts and final standards by either a simple majority or a super-majority;

(b) the Board may reject exposure drafts or final standards by a specified majority or specified minority.

(c) the Board may, by a specified majority or specified minority, return exposure drafts or final standards without amendment to the SDC for further consideration;

(d) the SDC must consult the Board, but the Board has no authority to delay or reject exposure drafts or final standards approved by the SDC.

Indicative of the division of opinion within the working party, the draft revealed that some members preferred (a), while some preferred (d). The latter would have been consistent with the views of the G4 standard setters.

The working party emphasized that the precise voting arrangements were less important than the need for the Board and the SDC to 'work together constructively' (paragraph 171). Then the working party averted a dissent from David Ruder and Tony Cope, who favoured (d), by agreeing to a delicately weighed, consensus proposal, which was a variation on (b) and (c). If the Board were unable to secure a three-fifths majority to approve an exposure draft or final standard coming from the SDC, it would send the draft back to the SDC together with its reasons. The SDC could then vote to resubmit the draft or amend it. If nine or more members of the eleven-member SDC were to vote to resubmit the same draft to the Board, the Board would need only a simple majority (thirteen out of twenty-five delegations) for approval. If only seven or eight members of the SDC were to vote to resubmit the same draft, the Board would require the usual three-fifths majority to approve. If the SDC were to submit an amended draft, the Board would require a three-fifths majority for approval (paragraph 173). There was no provision for the Board to draft documents itself, and it would not have the power to amend the SDC's exposure drafts or standards (paragraph 174), which was an important concession to the Anglo-Americans.

The earlier suggestion of a Standards Development Advisory Committee was repeated in the discussion paper (paragraphs 160–3). It was envisaged that meetings of the advisory committee 'would replace the meetings of world standard setters that currently take place from time to time with IASC involvement'. In addition, there would be an SIC and a Consultative Group, both being essentially the same as the current ones (paragraphs 161, 184–9, 190). The working party was divided on whether the Board or the SDC should approve the SIC's final interpretations. The latter was stated as the majority's preference (paragraph 185). The draft said that an executive committee would no longer be needed (paragraph 192).

Shortly after the discussion paper was issued, Chris Nobes, in his periodic report on board meetings and developments at the IASC, pronounced the following judgement on the discussion paper:

> [The proposal for approving drafts] seems to give substantial powers to the SDC. However, the US and UK standard setters may still think that the part-time political Board has too much power to meddle in the work of the full-time independent technocrats. On the other hand, the majority of the present Board may feel that it would be giving too much power away to an unrepresentative group.
>
> If the standard setters do not feel committed to the proposals, they may set up their own smaller version and side-line the IASC. If the majority of the Board feels disenfranchised, the member bodies may withdraw support from the IASC. With luck, the compromise will avoid these alternative threats which might fatally damage the IASC and its work.[59]

13.5. COMMENT LETTERS ON THE DECEMBER 1998 DISCUSSION PAPER

By June 1999, the IASC had received a total of eighty-six comment letters on the December 1998 discussion paper.[60] More than half of them came in after the 30 April deadline. For the IASC leadership and the working party, there may have been little 'news' in the comment letters, because most of the commentators whose views carried the greatest weight had already conveyed their reactions, both orally and in writing, to the 17 November 1997 draft. Nevertheless, it is useful to review these letters, as they are the only well-documented source for the views of a wide range of respondents on the issues involved in restructuring the IASC.

The comment letters expressed virtually unanimous agreement with the proposed objective of developing standards for high-quality reporting for the benefit of capital markets, as well as with the proposal that the IASC should do so by entering into a partnership with national standard setters to bring about a convergence of accounting standards for listed enterprises. Beyond this general level, however, opinions diverged profoundly. Given the nature of the proposals in the discussion paper, it was not difficult for the respondents to come up with a bewildering variety of modifications in terms of the size, composition, appointment, and relative authority of the various components of the proposed new organization. The following paragraphs treat comments that might be accommodated within the overall structure as put forward in the discussion paper, followed by a consideration of comments suggesting more radical disagreements with the discussion draft.

Accepting the discussion paper's main premise that the IASC should function as a harmonizer or catalyst for convergence alongside national standard setters, many respondents commented on the place of the national standard setters in the new organization. In the discussion paper's proposal, between 60 and 80 per cent of the members of the SDC would be nominated by national standard setters. To some respondents, this was far too high a proportion. The Federation of Swiss Industrial Holding Companies characterized this as an unacceptable ' "takeover" of the IASC by national standard setters'. Other respondents used more restrained language, but there were numerous suggestions that the SDC should have a more balanced composition or in one way or another give users and preparers of financial statements a hand in the drafting of standards.[61] On the whole, however, most respondents agreed that the national standard setters should play a significant role in the SDC.

The question then became: which standard setters should be eligible for membership? The discussion paper had said little apart from proposing that the eligible standard setters should have 'the technical, human and financial resources to make a significant contribution'. Some of the national standard setters who responded, notably the Australian Accounting Standards Board (AASB), argued for rather more explicit restrictions. The AASB believed that the SDC should be open to standard setters 'that have an established record of setting high quality accounting standards and have access to staff with strong technical skills'. These standard setters 'should have experience with developing accounting standards in the light of a conceptual framework, consistent with the IASC's framework, and in an environment where the application of their standards has been tested by preparers and regulators of financial reports.' Although the AASB did not say so, this would have limited the SDC's membership to the G4 standard setters (which included New Zealand). The FASB made similar comments, and it added a little more bluntly that there should be permanent seats on the SDC, as well as on the Board and among the Trustees: 'It does not seem realistic or rational to exclude countries with significant capital markets like the United States, for example, because of a need to rotate representation.' As if anticipating the FASB's and AASB's comments, IOSCO's Technical Committee warned that 'The IASC should not be dominated by the G-4 or other blocks [sic] of standard setters.' Similar warnings against G4 dominance came from the European Commission and the Ordre des Experts Comptables. The former thought that the criteria in the discussion paper were 'almost guaranteed to produce a dominant "G4" membership', while the latter advocated reserving five out of the eleven seats on the SDC for Europe.

As to the composition of the Board, suggestions for the appropriate number of members ranged from sixteen to 'fifty or more'. There were numerous proposals to modify the representation of various groups, including some special pleading. The

Financial Executives Institute (FEI), for instance, argued for a permanent seat for the United States, while all of the other seats should rotate. The FEI wrote, 'Making the United States a standing member of the Board would provide permanent representation of a major portion of the global economy.' Most respondents, though, appeared reasonably satisfied with the composition of the Board.

As expected, the most contentious issue was the relationship between the Board and the SDC. Sixteen of the sixty-six respondents who expressed a definite opinion on this subject disagreed with the proposal that the Board should have the authority to approve the standards. Thirteen of these respondents were the G4 standard setters (apart from Canada's CICA) as well as the SEC, the main accountancy bodies of Ireland (ICAI), New Zealand (ICANZ), Scotland (ICAS), and the United States (American Institute of Certified Public Accountants, AICPA), and assorted individuals and organizations from these countries. It was an almost purely Anglo-American line-up.[62] Among respondents who accepted some form of approval by the Board of the SDC's recommendations, there was a comparable geographical split. Respondents from Europe and Japan, including the European employers' federation UNICE, mostly wanted a further increase of power of the Board, while a group of accountancy bodies from Australia (ICAA), Canada (CICA), South Africa (SAICA), the United Kingdom (ACCA), and the United States (IMA) advocated various reductions in power. Employers' groups from Australia (G100), the United Kingdom (The Hundred Group), and the United States (FEI) emphasized that the Board's right to approve standards should be used in exceptional cases only, or that consideration should be given to take away the Board's powers in this respect after a transition period. One argument that was often used by both sides was that a strengthening of the Board, or the SDC, was necessary in order to ensure that qualified individuals would be willing to take up a position on the body that should be strengthened.

Of the discussion paper's other proposals, the ideas for funding attracted relatively few comments. The respondents were evenly divided over whether there should be a Standards Development Advisory Committee. Few seem to have greeted the proposal with enthusiasm.

Perhaps more important than suggestions for modifications within the general framework envisaged in the discussion paper was a number of responses that reflected significant disagreement with the proposals on a more fundamental level. Put simply, the point made in these comment letters was that the IASC should not be structured as an organization coordinating the work of national standard setters, but as an international standard setter in its own right. This point was raised in letters from the European Commission and the SEC, as well as in the joint letter from the FASB and the FAF (referred to hereafter as the FASB). But whereas the Americans drew the conclusion that this meant that the IASC should become more like the FASB, the European Commission argued that the discussion proposals were already far too much like the FASB.

Both the SEC and the FASB criticized the discussion paper for the lack of a long-term vision or plan for turning the IASC, as the FASB put it, into 'a single, worldwide, self-sustaining standard setter'.[63] Both emphasized that the structure of such a standard setter should be expected to produce 'high quality' standards which required, as the SEC put it, 'an independent decision making body, an active advisory function, a sound due process, an effective interpretive function, independent oversight representing the public interest, and adequate staffing'. The FASB used largely similar wording, and referred to a list of 'five essential characteristics of a quality international standard setter' in its recently published report, *International Accounting Standard Setting: A Vision for the Future*.[64] Both the FASB and the SEC referred the IASC to the AICPA's 1972 Wheat Study report, which laid the basis for the creation of the FASB. The SEC went as far as to provide the IASC with a copy of the report 'which you may find useful as it reflects valuable insights and recommendations for the establishment of a private sector standard setter'. The most important comments of both bodies centred on the need to make the actual standard-setting body, the SDC, completely independent. This meant not only that the Board should have no powers to approve or veto standards, but also that the members of the SDC should be full-time standard setters, 'free from any commercial and political interests' (SEC).

In its *Vision* report, the FASB advanced the view that there were other options if the IASC were not structurally changed into a quality international standard setter: 'A successor international organization might emerge and build on what the IASC has done, perhaps based on the G4+1; or the FASB might be modified to become more acceptable internationally.'[65]

One notable difference between the letters from the FASB and the SEC was that the latter believed that national standard setters should remain indispensable, as 'Each jurisdiction must continue to have the ability to decide the extent to which international accounting standards satisfy its need for decision useful information for cross-border offerings and listings.' The FASB, on the other hand, allowed that there might come a day 'when national sovereignty might no longer be appropriate', but the condition for that was having an international standard setter that embodies the FASB's own qualities and character.

The comment letters from the UK ASB and the AASB generally supported the SEC and FASB positions. The AASB declared that it agreed with the essential functions and characteristics of a quality international standard setter as set out in the FASB's vision booklet mentioned above. The ASB did not refer to the US paradigm, but it did emphasize that the IASC should move from being a 'catalyst for convergence' to being 'a standard setter in its own right' and indeed, in the long term, 'an international standard setter effective throughout the world'. Both the ASB and the AASB argued for an SDC composed exclusively of standard setters. The Board was to be reduced to an advisory function.

The European Commission also took a long-term view. It criticized the discussion paper for focusing too much on the short-term needs of convergence, and paying too little attention to the ultimate objective of the IASC becoming 'the predominant global accounting standards setter'. In the light of that objective, the Commission argued that the key issue for the IASC was to ensure for itself the required political legitimacy, that is, the support from national governments, international bodies such as the IMF and the World Bank, and regulators. The

Commission said that the proposals in the discussion paper would actually impair rather than enhance the IASC's political legitimacy: 'For it to be trusted to safeguard the wider public interest, the IASC must be independent of, and be seen to be independent of, any one national standard setter or any group of national standard setters.' The Commission would dispense with the SDC altogether and give the entire authority to a single body, the Board. This Board would consist of a geographically balanced roll of country delegations, in which national standard setters would replace the accounting bodies. The Board would include as well a minority of voting seats for other organizations interested in financial reporting.[66]

Both the SEC and the European Commission argued for the centrality of legitimacy. But legitimacy to the SEC meant placing the emphasis on technical expertise, due process, and independence. To the European Commission it meant responsiveness to the IASC's constituency, which, in the end, consisted of national governments and intergovernmental bodies that possessed the authority to impose the standards.

13.6. THE ADVISORY COUNCIL, EXECUTIVE COMMITTEE, AND BOARD TAKE UP THE WORKING PARTY'S PROPOSALS IN MARCH 1999

On 9 March 1999, the Advisory Council spent half of its meeting on the working party's proposals. Many questions were raised.[67] Council Chairman Stephen Eccles recalls that the discussion paper was 'awfully received. It was a disaster.' Particularly, the Advisory Council believed that if the lower tier body was to be answerable to an oversight board, the right calibre of people from the national standard setters would not agree to serve.[68]

At the IASC executive committee meeting on 15 March 1999 in Washington, Chairman Stig Enevoldsen reported that Secretary-General Carsberg had attended a meeting of the G10 in New York the previous week to discuss the working party's proposals.[69] The G10 was an informal gathering of fourteen major professional accountancy bodies from ten countries. It was said that the debate at the G10 meeting was constructive in tone, but that there was no clear consensus.

The executive committee held a wide-ranging discussion of the working party's proposals and about the way forward. Even though only a few letters of comment on the discussion paper had been received by then, the executive committee knew the obstacles that lay ahead. The point was made that Enevoldsen and Carsberg—the only members of the executive committee who were also members of the working party—should hold discussions with the 'key interested parties', which included the IASC's member bodies, the European Commission, the SEC, and the FASB, to determine 'where flexibility exists in their positions with a view to identifying proposals to which everyone may be able to agree'. This marked the beginning of a new phase, in which Enevoldsen and Carsberg were given a role independent of the working party to try to forge a consensus on the restructuring.

A concern was expressed that the 'danger that the United States would stand aside from an international consensus and face international isolation on accounting issues would be regarded as serious'. Issues were raised about certain facets of the working party's proposals, mostly dealing with the relation between the Board and the SDC. Would the former be able to do more than vote 'yes' or 'no' on proposed standards? Was there a risk of a 'deadlock' between the Board and the SDC? Should standards require a vote of only 50 per cent instead of 60 per cent by the Board?

At the IASC board's meeting on 16–19 March, it held a one-and-a-half-hour 'preliminary' discussion, in a session closed to public attendance, of the working party's proposals, as it was scheduled to meet with the working party during its June/July meeting in Warsaw.[70] The discussion was spirited. A concern over the power sharing between the proposed Board and SDC was raised by several members, on both sides of the issue. How would the SDC members react if the Board were to reject one of its proposed standards? Contrasting Anglo-American and Continental European views were much in evidence. The SDC, it was argued, must be composed of standard setters who accept International Accounting Standards, an allusion to the fact that the US and Canadian standard setters did not do so. Everyone agreed that national standard setters had to be brought formally into the IASC's decision-making process, but was something like the SDC the best way? Gilbert Gélard, of the French delegation, remarked, 'The profession is the standard setter in a diminishing number of countries, and that trend will continue. It's already a fiction that the Institutes set the standards. The present structure of IASC is a remnant of the past, but the proposals go too fast in the other direction.'[71] The board's present standards were borrowed and not created afresh, it was argued, and a smaller body was needed to develop the right kind of standards. Others argued that the IASC board was already too large, yet more people wanted to join. After board members and observers had voiced their anxious views on one side or the other of the working party's proposals, Michael Crooch, of the US delegation, recapitulated the discussion as follows:

This is a classic negotiation, driven by fears:

- Fears that the United States will have too much power
- Fears that Europe will have too much power
- Fears that [national standard setters] will have too much influence
- Fears that small countries will have too much or too little influence
- Fears that the process will move too fast or too slowly
- Fears that the SDC will have too much or too little independence

We have to find a mechanism to allay those fears. We will have to choose something that nobody really likes, go with it, and review it after a while. More detail in the paper would help to allay fears.[72]

13.7. ENEVOLDSEN AND CARSBERG TABLE THEIR OWN PROPOSAL IN WARSAW IN JUNE/JULY 1999

13.7.1. The Proposals

A turning point in the restructuring debate occurred at the board's meeting in Warsaw in June/July 1999: Enevoldsen and Carsberg shelved the working party's bicameral proposals and instead presented a unicameral proposal of their own. They were concerned that the working party's compromise proposals had not secured sufficient support from key interested parties as a viable way forward, especially in view of their desire to secure board approval in time for the next meeting of the IASC member bodies in May 2000. They had recently held meetings with the FASB as well with other national standard setters represented on the G4, with John Mogg and Karel Van Hulle at the European Commission, with representatives of the SEC, and with the IFAC Council. On the basis of those and other consultations and a review of the comment letters, they began to formulate their own proposal as a way forward.

Enevoldsen and Carsberg took advantage of their attendance at the G4+1 meeting on 8–10 June 1999 in Port Douglas, Australia to deliberate and agree the content of what was to be their joint proposal. After returning to London, Carsberg composed a note setting out all of the agreed points. The proposal was to be presented in Warsaw to the executive committee and, with its approval, also to the board at the end of June and to the working party on 1 July.[73] Because the agenda and accompanying papers, including the note on their joint proposal, had to be dispatched to the members of the executive committee by 18 June, Carsberg did not have time to secure the reactions to the proposal from the members of the working party in advance of the Warsaw meetings. The working party had not held a meeting since July 1998, but one was scheduled to coincide with two days of the IASC board's Warsaw meeting.

Central to Enevoldsen and Carsberg's proposal, which they styled as a recommendation to the working party, was rejection of the bicameral structure in favour of a single board with some full-time and some part-time members.[74] They then straddled the issue of board size but gave a partial voting edge in the proposed body to those, such as the SEC and the national standard setters, who favoured full-time over part-time members. They envisaged a board of two possible sizes, probably for bargaining purposes: a twenty-five-member board composed of fifteen full-time members and ten part-time members, with fifteen votes required to approve a standard, or a board of ten full-time members and seven part-time members, with ten votes required to approve a standard. A standard could therefore pass if it had the support of all of the full-time members. Although they asserted that a standard 'could be blocked if it was opposed by a majority of the full-time members', in fact these blocking majorities would require the votes of 73 and 80 per cent, respectively, of the full-timers. They wrote, 'This would give a high degree of protection exercised by the full-time members against undesirable effects of vested interests.' Some of the full-time members would also be members of the boards of national standard setters or be nominated by standard setters but not be members of their boards. Some might have no connection with national standard setting.

Enevoldsen and Carsberg proposed a novel link between certain full-time board members and national standard setters, which was the forerunner of 'liaison' board members of the International Accounting Standards Board. For full-time members who were not involved in national standard setting, the IASC board would ask the national standard setter in their home country to allow them to participate as 'observer members' in its meetings. 'The purpose of this arrangement would be to improve the level of coordination of activities of IASC with those of national standard setters and to secure a flow of views about technical issues in both directions.'

As between the two optional board sizes, the larger body would have broader representation on its side, while the smaller body would arguably be more efficient. Reflecting the views of Continental Europeans, Enevoldsen and Carsberg recommended that both the full- and part-time members be drawn about equally from Europe, North America, and the rest of the world, including perhaps three to five from emerging markets. The selection of members would also reflect an array of functional backgrounds. The board chairman would be full-time, and a secretary-general would be 'head of the staff'. They proposed a 'professional staff' of about fifteen at the outset, which was much higher than the eight envisaged by the working party in its draft discussion paper of December 1998. A committee composed of senior IASC officials and the leading national standard setters would coordinate agendas and arrange for other forms of cooperation leading towards a convergence of standards.

Who would choose the board members? Enevoldsen and Carsberg proposed that twelve trustees should be appointed by named organizations, a departure from the working party's recommendation of an equal number of constituency and 'at large' trustees. The trustees would have fixed terms and term limits. Half of the trustees should be appointed by international organizations, such as the World Bank and IOSCO, which would be presumed to represent the public interest.

At the conclusion of their paper, Enevoldsen and Carsberg raised a major strategic issue. They warned the IASC member bodies that, if they were unwilling to surrender their present control over the board, thus standing in the way of an agreement on the restructuring, the G4 was ready to enter the field:

We have received clear indications that, if we do not succeed in restructuring IASC in a manner that is sufficiently acceptable to the national standard setters, some of them would move to establish an alternative body through which they would seek international harmonisation of accounting.

13.7.2. The Executive Committee Considers the Proposal

The executive committee discussed their proposal, and it was observed that 'A part-time Board member would still be independent if he or she had no other connections which produced a conflict of interest.'[75] This point brought out a fundamental difference in the public policy decision-making culture between the United States and Continental Europe. To the SEC and the FASB, independence would not exist if the decision-maker were not to sever all previous ties and thus become a full-time member of the standard setter. To Continental Europeans, a professional with an unquestioned reputation for serving the public interest could serve as a part-time member and still be regarded as independent.

The executive committee agreed that the paper embodying Enevoldsen and Carsberg's proposal be circulated to the board for discussion 'provided that every possible effort was made beforehand to check that the chairman of the Strategy Working Party saw no objection to this'. It was rather late in the day for such a proviso. This was 28 June, and the board was scheduled to discuss the Carsberg and Enevoldsen proposal and the letters of comment on 30 June. Accordingly, Enevoldsen met with working party Chairman Ed Waitzer over a light dinner on the evening of his arrival in Warsaw.

13.7.3. The Board Meets with the Working Party in June 1999

By the slimmest majority, 9–8, the board voted to open its meeting with the working party on 30 June to public attendance. Interestingly, the US delegation sided with those from Japan, Malaysia, Mexico, the Netherlands, South Africa/Zimbabwe, and the European Commission, as well as the financial executives delegation, to meet in executive session.[76] The board was evidently still a bit anxious about open meetings, as the Warsaw board meeting was only the second that was open to the public.

All of the active members of the working party were present during the board's discussion, as they were to hold their own meeting in Warsaw on 1–2 July. During the working party's four-hour meeting with the board, there was general agreement by all who spoke that the Enevoldsen and Carsberg proposal for a single board was superior to the two-tier proposal in the working party's discussion paper.[77] UK board member Chris Nobes observed that the working party's December 1998 proposals had apparently been 'comprehensively dumped' because of opposition within and without the board.[78]

In his remarks at the onset of the meeting, working party Chairman Ed Waitzer said that a 'high level consensus' within the working party supported the need for a partnership between the new body and national standard setters.

The independence of the proposed standard-setting body came in for considerable comment. It was mentioned that the United States (mainly the SEC) attitude towards part-time membership was at variance with attitudes in other parts of the world. Speakers from Australia, Canada, and the United Kingdom, where standard setters were wholly or mostly part-time, argued that part-timers did not necessarily lack independence, and that the personal qualities of the board members were paramount. Part-timers, it was argued, provided 'real world' experience. Jan Klaassen, of the Dutch delegation, said that he agreed with the view that the members of the proposed body should be independent, but he also believed that this should include independence from national standard setters. This was an important point, as the working party had believed in 1998 that SDC members might also be members of national standard setters and be paid by their national body. From July 1999 onwards, this belief was modified to stipulate that such members must owe their sole allegiance to the SDC and not have a split loyalty between the board and their country's standard setter. Indeed, several other speakers argued that the new body's members should be chosen as individuals, not as nominees of professional accountancy bodies, national standard setters, or other interested parties.

The speakers at the meeting differed on numerous particulars. In general, the Continental Europeans preferred the larger board, with twenty-five members, because of global legitimacy, while the Anglo-Americans favoured the smaller board, with seventeen members—or one even smaller than that—because of efficiency of operation. A few commentators believed that steering committees should be retained to do the drafting, but others disagreed.

Enevoldsen mentioned that he and Carsberg envisaged the trustees as performing similar functions as the US FAF, the parent body of the FASB. Questions were raised about funding such a board and its staff.

13.7.4. The Working Party Meets in July to Consider the 'Single Board' Proposal

On 1–2 July 1999, following its joint meeting with the board, the working party held a pivotal meeting of its own. In view of the many and varied criticisms made of the bicameral model, the working party was probably relieved to turn its attention to the Enevoldsen and Carsberg proposal for a single board to be overseen by trustees, and with an advisory group.[79]

The discussion moved almost immediately to the structure and composition of the board. A consensus coalesced around a board of between fifteen and twenty members, although David Tweedie, David Ruder, and Tony Cope argued for fewer. In the end, it was agreed that the board should have twenty members, at least five of whom, including the chairman and a vice-chairman, would be full-time board members based in the IASC's London office. If possible, these members should have had previous national standard-setting experience. At least seven members would occupy 'national standard setter' positions: they would serve part-time on the new body and would spend their remaining time with their national standard setter. They would be full-time employees of the IASC, and their time spent with their national standard setter would be invoiced by the IASC to the standard-setting body. Each of these members would come from a different country. The other eight members would be part-time members coming from various professional backgrounds.

The issue of board composition provoked a lengthy debate over geographical representation. Parity between North America and Europe was finally agreed, a concession to those who favoured a 'representative' approach. Europe and North America would have six seats each. For Europe, these would include single national standard setter seats for Germany, France, and the United Kingdom. The North American allotment would include four seats for the United States and one each for Canada and Mexico. One US seat and the Canadian seat would fall into the national standard setter category, and the other US seats would be drawn from various professional backgrounds. Ruder and Cope indicated that only one seat for the FASB would be acceptable. In addition, four seats would come from Asia-Pacific, including one national standard setter seat each for Japan and Australia. The rest of the world would be allotted three seats, including one for South Africa.

The functional backgrounds were more easily agreed upon. Apart from the chairman and the seven national standard setter members, the other twelve should possess professional backgrounds as follows: at least five (25 per cent) as practicing accountants or auditors; at least four (20 per cent) as preparers of financial statements; and the remaining three as financial analysts (say, two) or academics (say, one).

An advisory group, with a large and broadly constituted membership, would include the representatives of national standard setters expressing a desire to be involved in the work of the IASC. Its members would be selected by the trustees, and it would meet four times a year. The SIC would continue.

The working party agreed on the board's procedures, including voting thresholds. Thirteen votes (65 per cent) would be needed to approve a standard. After consulting the advisory group, the board could approve an exposure draft by a simple majority. Dissenting opinions on standards, as well as anonymous alternative views on exposure drafts, should be published. All other decisions would require only a simple majority.

Funding, it was believed, would come from voluntary contributions, although it was hoped that governments and multinational agencies might contribute. Commercial Director Kurt Ramin was asked to prepare a budget. Rough estimates of US$10 million for staff costs and an additional US$5 million for board costs were mentioned. The technical staff should be increased to fifteen, and there should be a sizeable administrative staff, including those concerned with fund-raising. Funding should be guaranteed for the first five years. The sources of funding would be the G7 governments (one-third); the accountancy profession (one-third); and the stock markets, companies, and financial institutions, including the central banks (one-third). Manardo indicated that the Big Five audit firms would be willing to bear a significant portion of the share expected from the accountancy profession.

There would be a mandatory review after about three years so that the viability of the model could be assessed.

Anxiety was expressed over the remaining timetable. Stig Enevoldsen insisted that the new structure must be installed no later than 2001. As already planned in 1997, this meant that the IASC member bodies had to vote at their next meeting, in May 2000. Working backward, this implied that the final proposals had to be exposed to the IFAC Council by its next semi-annual meeting, in November. Wide consultation on the proposed model would be necessary, because there would not be time to publish another draft paper for public comment.

Assuming that these proposals were to find widespread support, there was a need to set up a nominating committee to select the trustees. Carsberg, Enevoldsen, and Frank Harding (representing IFAC) were to propose names for the nominating committee by September.

The draft discussion paper, prepared shortly afterwards by the secretariat, gave effect to the working party's agreements in Warsaw, albeit with some modifications. It reported that the board should consist of twenty members, of whom twelve would be full-time.[80] The full-time members would include a chairman, who would also be the IASC's chief executive, and seven members having 'direct liaison responsibilities for one or more designated national standard setters' (paragraph 36). The notion of liaison responsibilities had emerged from the suggestion for observer members in the Enevoldsen and Carsberg proposal. It was also an outgrowth of the working party's earlier view that national standard setters should be given seats on the SDC, but now they were not to be employed by the national standard setters. The geographic origins of the board members would be six from North America (United States, Canada, and Mexico), six from Europe, four from Asia-Pacific, and three from elsewhere; the chairman would be 'stateless'. As to functional backgrounds, at least 25 per cent should be practising auditors, at least 20 per cent should be preparers, and a minimum of 10 per cent should be users. At least one member was to have an academic background. The board's required voting majority for all decisions would be 65 per cent, thirteen out of the twenty members. In comparison with the majorities required in the Enevoldsen and Carsberg proposal, this threshold was higher than the 60 per cent for their larger board size, but slightly lower than the two-thirds specified for their smaller board.

In a section of the draft entitled 'Independence', it stated that all of the twelve full-time members 'must sever all employment relationships with current employers and must not hold any position giving rise to perceived economic incentives which might interfere with their role on the IASC Board. As a result, secondments and any rights to return to an employer would not be permitted' (paragraph 48). As will be seen, this provision was not well received by the European Commission.

There would be twelve trustees, but no geographical origins were stipulated. The initial group of trustees would be selected by a nominating committee to be appointed by the current board to represent the public interest. IFAC would suggest five of the twelve trustees, and then IFAC would engage in a mutual consultation with the nominating committee to determine the suitability of each candidate prior to formal nomination as a trustee. The SIC would be continued, and an advisory council of at least thirty persons would 'provide a forum in which to test ideas and debate technical issues with groups and constituencies not represented on the Board and to provide a formal vehicle for participation of such groups' (paragraph 62). Nothing was said in the draft about a budget or funding. On 16 August 1999, Carsberg wrote to the working party with his and

Ramin's outline budgets for the proposed board. Their estimates ranged between £7.6 million and £11.2 million.[81]

Apparently, this draft was circulated only internally. Yet one supposes that copies found their way into the hands of key interested parties.

13.8. DEVELOPMENTS FOLLOWING WARSAW

Although they managed to collaborate in June 1999 in the development of a proposal for a single board, Enevoldsen and Carsberg were hardly of one mind on the desirable direction in which the board should restructure. Both desired the board to be a credible international standard setter. However, to achieve this end, Enevoldsen strongly favoured the constituency model associated with the European Continent. He believed fervently in the importance of part-time membership and broad geographical representation. Carsberg was sympathetic to the independent expert model if only because of his respect for the FASB after serving on its research and technical staff in 1978–81. Above all, however, Carsberg wanted to get the restructuring accomplished, and commitment from the international community to move the IASC into position as a global standard setter. During the autumn of 1999, their partnership was fragile, partly because of differences in personality, partly owing to philosophical differences. But Enevoldsen was the IASC chairman, while Carsberg was employed as its secretary-general, his chief of staff. The relationship had its tensions.

13.8.1. Consultations

The spring, summer, and early autumn of 1999 were a period of intense consultations on all sides. Together or individually, Enevoldsen and Carsberg made frequent trips to the United States, Japan, and Australia, as well as around Europe, to take soundings and secure support. They paid a call on Jules Muis, the vice-president and controller of the World Bank. They made a point of meeting several times with SEC Chief Accountant Lynn Turner and with John Mogg, the European Commission's director-general of the Internal Market and Financial Services Directorate. The European Commission in turn consulted with its member states. Jacques Manardo was in touch with the Big Five audit firms and held consultations as well with other principals. The FASB and the SEC's accounting staff regularly exchanged views, sometimes bringing in the FAF trustees and the AICPA. David Ruder reported on developments to the FAF trustees and to the FASB's advisory council, and he and Ed Waitzer frequently talked by telephone with Lynn Turner at the SEC. Tony Cope rendered reports to the FASB. Lynn Turner and other SEC staff went to Toronto to meet with Waitzer and the chairman of the OSC, David Brown, who was also vice-chairman of IOSCO's Technical Committee, and they took a major trip to Europe.

The SEC also paid calls on the White House, the President's Council of Economic Advisers, and the Treasury and Commerce Departments to explain the importance to the markets of International Accounting Standards and the IASC's restructuring project and to convey its views about the most desirable outcome. These meetings were intended both to educate and to ensure support for the public policy positions the SEC was taking. The SEC also conferred with the World Bank and the International Monetary Fund to secure support for its position.

The SEC's Turner, who was uncompromising in his support of the small, full-time, independent expert model exemplified in the FASB's structure and process, had emphatically said to Enevoldsen and Carsberg, when they visited the SEC prior to Warsaw, that the SEC would reject the constituency model categorically.

In a conference call during July, several FASB members and staff exchanged views with Turner and Associate Chief Accountant Mary Tokar on the direction in which the working party was headed. There was a general expression of concern over the size of the board and the involvement of other than full-time members. Turner was concerned that the liaison members and part-timers could block a standard. He wanted a board of no more than twelve to fifteen members, else he saw the G4 or internationalization of the FASB as realistic alternatives to a restructured IASC. He believed there was a need to gather support for a counter-proposal to the model currently being considered by the working party.[82]

In a meeting with several FASB members three weeks later, Turner conceded that part-timers were acceptable so long as they could not control the vote and were very limited in number—not more than two. On the composition of the trustees, there was a concern over the influence of IFAC, yet it was stated that the Europeans viewed IFAC as a counterweight to US dominance. Turner was opposed to government funding and continued to want a smaller board. Support was expressed for a quality full-time staff and an advisory board. Turner made it known that he, Tokar, and Marisa Lago, director of the SEC's Office of International Affairs who was attending meetings of IOSCO's Technical Committee, were planning a series of visits to key parties, mostly securities market regulators, in Europe and Canada to build support for their position.[83]

On their trip to Europe, the three SEC representatives met with the G4+1 at its meeting in Dublin in September 1999, a meeting attended as well by Enevoldsen and Carsberg. The G4 members in attendance supported a full-time board and opposed the European Commission's preference for a representative body.[84] The SEC tour continued with visits to the UK Financial Services Authority (FSA) in London; France's Commission des Opérations de Bourse (COB), the securities commission, in Paris; the Bundesaufsichtsamt für den Wertpapierhandel (BAWe), Germany's federal securities and futures regulator, and the German Accounting Standards Board in Berlin; and the European Commission in Brussels. The head of the Hong Kong Securities and Futures Commission flew to Europe to meet with them. At the COB, they met with Chairman Michel Prada, who was the chairman of IOSCO's Technical Committee. In Brussels, they met with representatives of the European Commission, with which they knew they would disagree, and they did. Their final stop was in Toronto to meet with Ed Waitzer and David Brown. With

13.8.2. Turner's Letter

On 21 September 1999, Turner dispatched a five-page letter to Waitzer in care of the IASC office in London, with copies to Enevoldsen and Carsberg, in which he set out the specific attributes that were required for the reconstituted IASC to protect the public interest.[86] The working party's next meeting was to begin on the following day in London. In his letter, Turner said that the SEC's staff had just concluded discussions 'with a broad range of parties including national and international professional bodies, standard setters and regulators. These discussions have been very helpful in shaping our thoughts. They have highlighted substantial support for a structure that realizes the IASC's goal of developing high quality standards that will have authority and legitimacy, with investors in world-wide capital markets.'

In the letter, he argued against the twenty-member board proposed by the working party, urging that the board be composed of between eight and twelve members who would serve full-time and be expert and independent. The board should have 'the ultimate authority to set its own agenda and issue its own proposals and standards'. On the composition of the board, he wrote, 'While the Trustees should strive to select Board members with a broad range of perspectives and experience, including different national backgrounds, geographic diversity should not be the predominant selection criterion. The first priority of the Trustees should be selecting Board members with the greatest expertise and ability to contribute to the development of high quality accounting standards.' To counter the argument that a board composed solely of full-time members would not be sensitive to the practical issues of financial reporting, he proposed that the working party 'should look to an active advisory body and the use of project working groups (like steering committees) that could work with the Board on an issue-by-issue basis to bring in current hands-on experience with reporting issues'. He also said that there should be a 'robust due process that encourages participation in each project'.

Turner did leave the door ajar to admit part-time board members: 'If the SWP decides that a limited number of part-time Board members is necessary as an interim step, Board members with ongoing commercial ties must not be able either to pass or block a proposal if they voted as a group.'

He regarded the proposal that only two of the twelve trustees should be designated 'at large' as 'a profound, and ultimately fatal, flaw'. SEC Chairman Arthur Levitt had only recently fought a significant battle over the composition of the board of trustees for the FAF, which oversees the FASB, and both he and Turner were not willing to accept an international board with the same inherent flaws they believed existed in the United States.[87] A majority of the trustees, he said, should 'exclusively represent the public interest' and 'should not be appointed by specific organizations'. Turner supported a nominating committee of six to eight members from a broad pool of individuals 'with a deep commitment to establishing a high quality international standard setter'. He favoured a review of the effectiveness of the new structure after three years.

Because of the various consultations which the SEC's staff had been having with the FASB and its trustees and with the G4+1 and others, the general contents of Turner's letter would have come as no surprise. Some of the specifics in the letter may have been news. It was important to the working party and the IASC's leadership that any restructuring proposal have the support of the body that regulated the world's largest capital market.

13.8.3. Mogg's Letter

Another letter reached the working party just in time for its 22–3 September 1999 meeting. The seven-page letter addressed to Bryan Carsberg was from John Mogg, at the European Commission.[88] His letter was in reaction to the secretariat's draft discussion paper based on the proposals agreed by the working party at its meeting in early July. He said that Enevoldsen and Carsberg's Warsaw paper contained 'changes that we viewed as positive because they reflected our views on the need for more representation and legitimacy. This impression was reinforced by the tenor of your comments at our meeting. However, this latest paper in practice did not fulfil our optimism and, indeed, represents something of a set-back.' He added,

I continue to believe that your proposals will not deliver the added credibility and acceptance that are the prerequisites to the IASC making the step change to being the predominant global accounting standards setter. As I indicated to you previously the European Union is implementing a series of measures designed to facilitate integration of European capital markets in which internationally comparable financial information plays an important role. Discussions with our Member States have considered the possibility of giving added support to IAS. At the present time this is not possible. I hope that you will reflect further to avoid the risk that the Union moves more visibly against the strategy you suggest.

As Turner had re-emphasized in his letter the points made in his comment letter on the working party's December 1998 discussion paper, Mogg's letter synthesized the main points in his twenty-five-page comment letter on the discussion paper and elaborated upon in a letter from Karel Van Hulle to Stig Enevoldsen of 26 July 1999.[89]

Mogg's concern was apparently ignited by the working party draft's proposed board size of twenty instead of as many as twenty-five in the Enevoldsen and Carsberg proposal. The draft also specified a formal link with seven national standard setters. In addition, as was noted above, the larger role accorded to IFAC in the selection of the trustees provoked him. Shortly before the date of Mogg's letter, Turner and his SEC colleagues had held a meeting in Brussels with Mogg and Van Hulle, which ended in a profound disagreement. Mogg had perhaps felt a need to emphasize his points of disagreement with the direction the proposals were taking, as if to offset the apparently increasing impact of the SEC.

Mogg argued that the acceptance of international accounting standards 'is not dependent on adopting a structure which is independent in form, rather it is linked to the representativeness and legitimacy of the decision-making process'. He contended that IFAC retained too much influence in the latest draft, because IFAC would advance the names of candidates for five of the twelve trustees. He wrote, 'If the IASC is to take its place in the global financial architecture as *the* global standard setter it needs to introduce public accountability at the top of the organisation to complement its profession based knowledge. That inevitably means the profession giving up its control and influence.'

Reacting to the provision on independence in the draft, Mogg argued, not without some justification, that, 'Although it might be possible to get people to formally sever their ties with other organisations with no right of return, in practice the individuals will always have half an eye on some sort of life after the IASC which will have at least a subliminal influence over their relationship with national standards setters.' In fact, two members of the FASB had returned to their accountancy firms immediately following their board service in the 1970s and 1980s.[90] Mogg believed that independence of mind did not automatically follow from severing one's ties with a former employer. He argued that 'The IASC with its supposed lack of independence in form has now produced standards on goodwill, intangible assets and on impairment of assets which are at least the equal of the equivalent US standards in technical quality.'

Mogg viewed the current proposal as 'very largely a re-packaged SDC under a different name' and as 'very close to the suggestions put forward by the SEC in their response to the original proposal'.

He expressed concern that the working party had not addressed the question of the enforcement of the IASC's standards. He said that, in Van Hulle's letter of 26 July, the Commission advocated a Compliance Monitoring Unit 'that would establish links or "regulatory partnerships" with national regulators. The unit would monitor the application of IAS in practice and would alert the regulators to cases of perceived non-compliance.'[91]

13.8.4. Prada's Letter

A still further letter was sent by Michel Prada, the chairman of IOSCO's Technical Committee, to Waitzer in time for the working party meeting.[92] Prada argued that the trustees should be accountable to the global public interest and therefore the process of their selection should include 'consultation with international bodies that reflect the global public interest'. He said that the Technical Committee wanted to 'reiterate our support for having half of the trustees (the "at large" Trustees) be representatives of the global public interest rather than a designated group (e.g., the accounting profession)'. As with Mogg, this was a reaction to the large role given to IFAC in the selection of the trustees.

13.9. WORKING PARTY MEETS IN SEPTEMBER 1999

At the working party's meeting of 22–3 September in London, keen disappointment was expressed by some at the negative tone of Mogg's letter, especially at his implied threat to scuttle the restructuring.[93] Yet Mogg's implied threat was matched by Turner's implied threat to throw in his lot with the G4 or an internationalized FASB.

Mogg's critical tone had the unintended consequence that one member of the working party who had been fairly neutral on the issue of expert versus 'constituency' swung the discussion more in the direction to the expert view.

At the meeting, Chairman Stig Enevoldsen reported on his visits in Europe. He observed that the country views differed, depending on whether they perceived they would have a place in the restructured IASC. This was a continuing concern of the smaller countries, such as the Netherlands and the Scandinavian countries. The European accountancy bodies, he said, were generally supportive and recognized the reality of their loss of control. They did believe, however, that the trustees should be geographically balanced. There were no particular concerns about the full-time versus part-time issue. But they believed that the new organization must be truly international and not US-dominated.

As the working party knew it was entering the home stretch, the discussions became intense and lengthy. When discussing implementation issues, the possible reactions by the SEC, IOSCO, the European Commission, and IFAC were given consideration by working party members, because it was seen as necessary that the SEC, IOSCO, and the European Commission be brought on board, and the IFAC Council would have to endorse the restructuring plan. The views of the FASB and Japan's Ministry of Finance were also considered during the discussion. During one meeting with the European Commission's Mogg in the middle of 1999, Carsberg heard Mogg dangle the 'glittering prize' of the possibility that European listed companies might be required to use IASC standards.[94] Yet, Carsberg believed that the European Commission had nowhere else to go but to IASC standards. The Commission was no longer contemplating a European Accounting Standards Board (*see* Section 12.3), and it would have rejected US GAAP categorically.

It was agreed that a nominating committee should be appointed by the IASC board. It would be small and composed of key international players so as to endow it with legitimacy. It was felt to be essential to have SEC Chairman Arthur Levitt on the nominating committee.

The working party decided to increase the number of trustees from twelve to nineteen, representing the following constituencies: four from IFAC; two from the Big Five audit firms' senior executives; one each from preparers, users, and academics; and ten 'at large'. In this new proposal for the trustees, IFAC and the Big Five firms would nominate six of nineteen, compared with IFAC's five of the twelve in the July draft. The trustees themselves would select the preparer, user, and academic. The trustees could serve for two three-year terms. It was agreed that the trustees should be representative of the world's capital markets and come from a diversity of geographic and professional backgrounds.

After a robust exchange of views, the working party decided to reduce the maximum size of the board from twenty to sixteen, of whom no more than four might be part-time. Sixteen, being the same size as the IASC's then current board, was a compromise, as some preferred more and others less. Some of the full-time members would have significant liaison responsibilities with one or more designated standard setters. One full-time member would be designated as the chairman and the IASC's chief executive, and another would serve as technical director. Ten votes would constitute a majority to approve exposure drafts, standards, and final interpretations. Stig Enevoldsen did much to steer the working party towards consensus positions on these critical issues. It was felt that participation on the advisory council and as members of project task forces would mollify external parties preferring a larger board. The foremost qualification was technical competence. Board members could serve two five-year terms. The working party provided that the board members should come from functionally diverse backgrounds: at least five from the practice of auditing, at least three each with experience as preparers and users, and at least one academic. There was general agreement on a geographical balance: a minimum of three from the Americas, three from Europe, and three from Asia-Pacific, with no more than two to come from any country. It was questioned whether the latter provision might allow as many as eight, or even ten, members from G4 countries. While some believed that the SEC was averse to geographical considerations because its experience was in a setting with one language and one culture, the SEC has always insisted that it was interested only in the very best standard setters regardless of where they were from.

There was no provision for the attendance of observers at board meetings who would have the privilege of the floor, but the board's due process would allow for extensive consultation with interested parties, including the possibility, as suggested in the December 1998 discussion paper, of public hearings and field tests.

On the subject of enforcement, the working party took steps in the direction of Mogg's Compliance Monitoring Unit by recommending that the IASC work with IOSCO and the European Commission to ensure that national regulators take their enforcement responsibility seriously and that the IASC refer obvious cases of non-compliance to the appropriate authorities, including professional bodies and regulators. This provision, with only minor changes, survived for inclusion in the working party's final draft discussion paper.

For the first time, the working party proposed the annual salaries of board members: £400,000 for the chairman, £325,000 for the other full-time members, and £162,500 for the part-time members. The proposed salaries were based on the existing FASB salaries to ensure that the levels would be on a par between the two boards. The chairman of the trustees would receive US$40,000 a year, with the other trustees receiving half of that amount. These proposed salaries were arrived at in consideration that the board members would enjoy no fringe benefits. The working party provided for a technical staff of fifteen, and it estimated the annual budget for the IASC at £10 million, double the £5 million proposed in its December 1998 discussion paper. The working party recommended that funds be raised from end beneficiaries, such as the Big Five audit firms and corporations, as well as from intermediaries and government organizations. Concern was expressed that fund-raising in the United States might be difficult, leading to uncertainty whether sufficient funds could be raised.

At the end of the two-day meeting, the working party turned its attention to the steps needed to consult immediately with key external parties on its decisions taken at the meeting, and to issue a discussion paper embodying these decisions for public comment. The timetable was more tight than ever, as the IFAC Council (at its 3–4 November meeting), the IASC board (at its mid-November, mid-December, and March 2000 meetings), and the IASC member bodies (in May 2000) had to act on the final recommendations very soon. It was anticipated that the nominating committee would hold its first meeting in January and would approve the trustees by June, and that the new board would come into being on 1 January 2001. To say the least, this was an ambitious plan. A new draft discussion paper, entitled 'Draft Report on Shaping IASC for the Future', was produced by the secretariat in early October. Although the intention apparently was to publish the document and invite public comment by 15 December 1999, it promptly became subject to further changes and was never published as a draft. Pressures from outside parties, notably the SEC, continued to prompt changes in the draft recommendations.

13.10. RUN-UP TO THE BOARD'S NOVEMBER 1999 MEETING IN VENICE

13.10.1. The Working Party Confers to Make Further Revisions

On 10 October, the working party held a conference call.[95] Enevoldsen and Carsberg reported on their recent meetings at the European Commission, the French COB, the SEC, the AICPA, and with the FASB chairman. Apparently, Ed Waitzer had conferred with Lynn Turner. The Brussels visit, they said, 'wasn't easy'. John Mogg was very disappointed and said that the working party had 'caved in to the SEC'. He believed that the working party had gone so far from what the European Commission favours that further discussion would not be useful. It was said that Michel Prada, at the COB, continued to be concerned over the manner of selecting the trustees, but he was still supportive.

Although it was reported that the SEC contended that the sixteen-member board was too large, Lynn Turner's chief objection was believed to be the prescription of geographical origins for board members: a minimum of three from each of the Americas, Europe, and Asia-Pacific. It was clear that the SEC was adamant that any reference to geographical backgrounds for board members be deleted, although the SEC would accept geographical criteria for the trustees. Then the bargaining over geographical criteria for board members began in earnest in the working party, pitting the Anglo-Americans—Cope, Ruder, Sharpe, and Tweedie—against the Continental Europeans—principally Enevoldsen, but to a degree also Manardo and Barthès. As IFAC president, Frank Harding had an interest in representing IFAC views. Some, such as Enevoldsen, revulsed at an SEC-imposed solution, yet the worry was again expressed that, if changes were not made that the SEC could accept, the SEC would instead support a competing group to set international standards, an allusion to the G4 or an internationalized FASB. In the end, the working party agreed to a prescription of geography for the trustees as an acceptable trade-off for the removal of any such prescription for the board members. Carsberg redrafted the provisions relating to board members (paragraphs 54 and 55). The new version modified somewhat the minimum number of board members whose functional backgrounds were to be as auditors, preparers, and users (including an academic). The geographical issue was finessed by the following general language in paragraph 54, which placed the burden of achieving an appropriate balance in the hands of the trustees:

The foremost qualification for Board membership would be technical expertise. Trustees would select Board Members so the Board will be composed of a group of people representing within that group the best available combination of technical skills and background experience of relevant international business and market conditions in order to contribute to the development of high quality, international accounting standards. The selection of Board Members would not be based on geographical representation. The Trustees would exercise their best judgement to ensure that the Board is not dominated by any particular constituency or regional interest.

Correspondingly, Carsberg revised paragraph 30 on the selection of the trustees to stipulate an explicit geographical distribution:

To ensure a broad international base, Trustees would be appointed so that there would be six (6) from North America, six (6) from Europe, four (4) from Asia Pacific, and three (3) others from any area, as long as geographical balance is maintained.

The working party also approved a provision that the Standards Advisory Council (the new name of the advisory council) 'would be selected to ensure a diversity of geographical and functional backgrounds', an accommodation to those favouring a broad base of participation in the work of the board.

All three of these provisions survived into the working party's final report, *Recommendations on Shaping IASC for the Future*, which was published in early December 1999.

13.10.2. Enevoldsen and Carsberg Pre-Empt the Working Party

During the last week of October, Enevoldsen and Carsberg were in the United States for a final round of consultations. They met in New York with the G10 accountancy bodies and in Washington with the SEC. On 22 October, they had sent a summary statement of the working party's recommendations to the G10 bodies as a briefing paper.⁹⁶ The statement was also sent to the SEC, and it came to the attention of members of the working party as well. Michael Sharpe was nettled by their assertion in the statement that the proposed model, which paralleled that of the working party, 'is the model called for by the SEC in order for them to accept and support the reorganised IASC'. Sharpe countered in an email to Enevoldsen and Carsberg that this was not the model called for by the SEC, which wanted a board of no more than twelve members, and that it was not helpful to imply that the working party had caved in to the SEC.⁹⁷ Tony Cope was troubled by Enevoldsen and Carsberg's remark in the statement, 'We have agreed not to express an opinion on the proposed structure at the present time....' In an email to Carsberg, Cope wrote, 'Do you and Stig intend to not support the work of the Working Party?' He added, 'The model we are proposing is not an "SEC model". It is an SWP model.'⁹⁸

At the end of the 22 October summary statement of what Enevoldsen and Carsberg called 'the SEC model' was an italicized section that read like a lengthy dissent. It was said to be 'The case for rejecting the SEC's model' and raised issues (size and composition of the board, and geography) that Enevoldsen himself had advanced in the working party but on which he was outvoted. Originally, the remarks in italics were Enevoldsen's editorial comments on Carsberg's initial draft. In the end, it was decided, but apparently without Enevoldsen's consent, that the original draft and the editorial comments should be shown separately in the same paper.

On 29 October, just after the meeting at the SEC, Carsberg alone (but with Enevoldsen's agreement) dispatched a rather different summary statement to the IFAC Council. In this version, he altered the size of the board from sixteen to fourteen members, of whom at least ten, and perhaps twelve, would be full-time. A simple majority of eight votes would be required to approve drafts and standards, down from the 65 per cent agreed by the working party in July. One supposes that the demands Carsberg heard expressed at the SEC drove him to rewrite the recommendations to make them more SEC-friendly. This was the statement that was considered by the IFAC Council at its meeting in Cape Town, but it seems likely that neither the working party nor the board ever saw this document.

Whether Carsberg had consulted Ed Waitzer before making these changes in the board's size, composition, and operation is not known, but at around the same time the working party itself was reconsidering these same issues via two conference calls and a stream of emails. When Waitzer found that the IASC's secretariat in London had abruptly stopped responding with revised drafts to the working party's initiatives, it fell to him, with major drafting assistance from David Ruder, to compose and circulate several further versions himself. He transmitted the drafts electronically to the other working party members, and he incorporated their comments, all within the space of two weeks. The last of these drafts, dated 12 November, a scant three days before the board meeting was to begin in Venice, endorsed a proposed board of twelve full-time and two part-time members, with a simple majority required for voting.

13.11. THE EXECUTIVE COMMITTEE'S AND BOARD'S NOVEMBER 1999 MEETINGS IN VENICE

13.11.1. The Enevoldsen and Carsberg Note: Circumventing the Working Party

The IASC board's historic meeting of 15–19 November was held in Venice. It was to be the 'showdown' meeting for the restructuring proposals. But it was not the working party's draft report of its recommendations that was included in the board's agenda papers but instead a model proposed in a note to the board from Enevoldsen and Carsberg.[99] The working party had always believed that the board would receive its report in Venice, and the agenda sent out in advance of the meeting confirmed this belief.[100] Ed Waitzer was not amused at this abrupt change in plan, which was adopted without consulting the working party.[101] It was, however, noted at the outset of the section dealing with the restructuring proposals in the minutes of the board's meeting that 'The Strategy Working Party had not had time to finalize its report although it was on the verge of doing so'.[102]

Enevoldsen and Carsberg wrote that their recommended model 'has not yet been finally adopted by IASC's SWP although we hope that the Working Party will do so'. The only members of the working party who were to attend the board meeting were Tony Cope, the FASB observer; David Tweedie, of the UK delegation; and Enevoldsen and Carsberg. The working party's chairman, Ed Waitzer, was not invited.

It was evident that Enevoldsen and Carsberg were attuned to the demands of the SEC, for they wrote in the opening remarks in their note:

We hope that the SEC will support the recommended model. We believe that it has the main features which the SEC sees as essential to an acceptable international standard setter. It does not incorporate the first choice of SEC on every parameter but we believe that it is close enough to satisfy its reasonable requirements. The FASB appears to have the same views as the SEC.

Curiously, their note called for a board of sixteen members, of whom four would be part-time, and a voting majority of ten, which were the parameters in the working party's draft of three weeks earlier. As only Carsberg had signed the 29 October communication to the IFAC Council, had Enevoldsen insisted, in their joint communication to the board, that the original size of sixteen should prevail? As noted above, the working party had since moved to the model of fourteen board members, including two part-time, and a simple majority. Enevoldsen and Carsberg also inserted a provision in their note for a trustee from Africa, which had never been mentioned in the working party's drafts. Enevoldsen and Carsberg had only recently returned from meeting with the IFAC Council, which 'agreed in principle to support the IASC proposals'.[103] Concern was expressed at the Council that there was no provision for a member of the trustees from the African Continent.

This note by Enevoldsen and Carsberg served to apprise board members that a model similar to the one they reviewed in Warsaw would be presented for their consideration. But by the time the board meeting began, the executive committee had itself taken over and remade the entire approach to presenting the proposals to the board.

13.11.2. Fateful Decision at the Executive Committee Meeting

At its meeting on 14 November, the executive committee 'unanimously supported the broad tenor of the proposals' set out in Enevoldsen and Carsberg's agenda note, but its members wanted to be sure that the SEC would go along.[104] During the discussion, Enevoldsen pressed his own case but finally gave in. In view of the dominant Anglo-American composition of the executive committee, Enevoldsen was probably a minority of one.[105] The decision was taken that someone other than Enevoldsen, who was out of sympathy with the restructuring proposals insisted upon by Lynn Turner, had to conduct the presentation to the board. Michael Crooch, a member of the executive committee and of the US delegation to the board and who knew Turner, was tapped to take on the assignment, and he agreed. First, however, it was important to the executive committee that Crooch telephone Turner in order to gain assurance that the proposals to be presented would be acceptable to the SEC. This was the first of numerous calls from Crooch and others at the board to Turner, in which the terms of the final proposals were, in effect, negotiated. Turner insisted on a board no larger than fourteen, which could include two part-time members. He knew that these were the terms already set out in the working party's latest draft. Other changes were discussed as well, and finally Turner assured Crooch that the SEC would put out a news release supporting the restructuring proposals once the agreed terms were approved by the board. In addition, it was agreed that the SEC would play a role in selecting the nominating committee for new trustees. Crooch also called Waitzer, who affirmed that 'the deal', as it was known, would be acceptable to the working party. Tony Cope and D. J. Gannon, a member of the SEC's accounting staff who was in the IOSCO delegation to the board, also participated in the calls to one or more of Turner, Waitzer, and David Ruder. The executive committee agreed that the proposals, when finally agreed after the necessary consultations by telephone, should be presented to the board as its recommendation.

No one knew how the board would react to the proposed structure. The executive committee therefore decided to postpone the board's agenda item on the proposals for a few days in order to give Tom Jones and Patricia McConnell (the two vice-chairmen), assisted by Mike Crooch, sufficient time in which to meet with all of the delegations, in the corridors during the board's technical sessions and until late in the evenings, in order to explain the imperative need for the proposed structure and to apprise them of the adverse consequences of not adopting it. Another reason for the postponement was to allow Chairman

Enevoldsen, who had to return to Copenhagen for one day to attend an urgent meeting with an audit client, to be present to chair the session at which the new structure would be placed before the board. The pressure on the delegations, on some more than others, was intense.

Upon his return to Venice the following day, Enevoldsen learned from Jones and McConnell that they were confident they had secured majority voting support for the proposal worked out with the SEC. They said they hoped he would support the proposed structure in the board meeting. For Stig Enevoldsen, the IASC's chairman, it was a low point during his many years of service on the IASC board. He had lost the confidence of the executive committee on this one vital matter. Although he briefly contemplated resigning his chairmanship, in the end he was determined to carry on as best he could in the circumstances and support the majority view.

13.11.3. 'The Deal'

'The deal' was very similar to the latest version of the working party's drafts, but there were a few differences.[106] There would be a nominating committee, which would choose its chairman. The number of trustees would be nineteen, but five (instead of four in the working party's latest draft) would be nominated by IFAC, with eleven 'at large' and one each from users, preparers, and academe. The geographic distribution of the trustees was unchanged from the working party's most recent draft: six from North America, six from Europe, four from Asia-Pacific, and three others to provide balance. The board, as noted above, was to have fourteen members, of whom only two would be part-time, which the working party had already accepted. The board members' functional backgrounds were the same as in the working party's latest draft: at least five from auditing practice, a minimum of three each with experience as preparers and users, and at least one academic. It was made clear that the selection of board members would be based on their expertise and not geography. Seven of the board members would have liaison responsibilities with designated national standard setters, whereas the working party's latest position was that 'some' members would have such responsibilities. A simple majority would be required to approve exposure drafts and standards, also in line with the latest working party draft.

There would be an advisory council, a continuation of the SIC, technical staff, and adequate due process (including steering committees), but no details were given about any of them.

The criteria for selecting board members would be as follows:

- demonstrated technical competency and knowledge of financial accounting
- ability to analyse
- communication skills
- judicial decision-making

- awareness of financial reporting environment
- ability to work in a collegial atmosphere
- integrity, objectivity, and discipline
- commitment to the IASC's mission and public interest

These were identical to the criteria the working party had specified in Appendix A to its 12 November draft.

13.11.4. The Board Meeting

The foregoing elements were the totality of the proposals placed before the board on 17 November, on the third day of the board's five-day meeting. The meeting was open to the public. The elements were no more than an outline, a series of bullet points. This was what Mike Crooch presented orally to the board in a much-anticipated session, following opening remarks by Chairman Enevoldsen.[107] The board was given nothing in writing. To relieve the tension, Crooch began with some self-deprecating humour, saying that he wished he could speak English and not in just his native Oklahoman. In presenting the outline, he said that it had been cleared with Lynn Turner at the SEC and that the SEC's support of the restructured IASC was essential to its success. The terms of the outline, he said, were fixed and non-negotiable. They were a package on which the board must vote up or down. He emphasized the importance of having a unanimous vote. One board member who wrote a report on the meeting said, 'This is rather like getting turkeys to vote for Thanksgiving.'[108]

During the discussion, which consumed almost an entire day, the board was informed of the working party's strong support for the proposals.[109] But the actual contents of the working party's latest draft were known only to Cope, Tweedie, and Carsberg because of their membership on the working party.[110] Tony Cope informed the board that the FASB supported the proposals, and David Tweedie assured the board of the G4's support as well.[111] Lynn Turner's message of support, which was to appear in the SEC's news release, was read to the meeting. All of the 'big guns' were thus rolled out.

During the discussion, board members raised concerns about a number of the elements in 'the deal', including especially whether, and from what sources, adequate funding could be secured for the new body. Apparently, the working party's estimate of the annual funding requirement of £10 million was revealed during the meeting.[112] A number of board members said that they must consult their sponsoring bodies before casting a definitive vote. Sigvard Heurlin said that he was on the board to do the technical work, but this was strategic, and he wanted to consult on such a matter with the Swedish Institute.[113] Board members had many questions and concerns about how the various organs would function in the proposed structure, but no answers could be given at this time. A number said they wanted to see supporting language in a fully fledged draft before committing themselves. Yet there was only the outline of 'the deal'. Some enquired how the various numerical benchmarks were arrived at, such as the simple majority to approve an exposure draft or standard and the geographic distribution of the trustees.

Some members of delegations, particularly from Continental Europe, were highly uncomfortable with the board being confronted with the proposal on a 'take it or leave it' basis. Their criticism during the debate might have been muted because they realized that there was no viable alternative but to go along.

Karel Van Hulle, who was an observer from the European Commission, made one of the strongest negative comments about 'the deal'. In his remarks, he sarcastically likened the SEC to the pigs in George Orwell's famous dictum in *Animal Farm*, 'All animals are equal, but some animals are more equal than others.'[114]

Enevoldsen, who spoke on behalf of the proposals, said that the approval in principle by the IFAC Council meant that the accountancy profession was prepared to dissolve its relationship with the IASC. At several points, he responded to restive board members that there was no room for any substantive change, and he urged them to vote their conscience and not according to instructions from home.

The final tally stunned everyone: 16–0. The executive committee's strategy proved to be successful. It was a victory for the SEC and for those of the board members who preferred the independent expert model. Likewise, it was a defeat for those, like the European Commission, who preferred the constituency model. For its part, the IASC could take comfort in the belief that its standards potentially would gain recognition in the world's most important capital market. But some delegations regarded this as no more than a straw vote, subject to consultation with their sponsoring bodies and an opportunity to discuss and debate the working party's final draft at the board's December meeting in Amsterdam. Carsberg made it clear that the Constitution of the new IASC would not be voted on by the board until its March meeting.

As Lynn Turner had promised, the SEC issued a news release, dated 17 November, in which he applauded the board's decision and thanked both the working party and the board for their hard work. He was quoted in the release as saying, 'I am enthusiastic about this approach and look forward to working to support adoption and implementation of this revised structure.'[115] Also on 17 November, the FASB issued a public statement in which Chairman Edmund Jenkins called the board's decision 'a historic milestone for the future of financial reporting that will benefit investors around the world'.[116]

On 19 November, the IASC itself issued a press release, in which Enevoldsen was quoted as saying,

We have achieved what we have dreamt of for a long time. We have reached agreement on a proposed structure which will take IASC a giant step in the direction of being *the* global standard setter. The proposal has broad support not only from our Board, but from several national standard setters, leading professional accountancy bodies, and the Council of the International Federation of Accountants. The proposal is also strongly supported by IASC's Executive Committee and of course by myself.[117]

Although Enevoldsen put a good face on the outcome, his words would not have been easily put to paper.

In the eyes of the board's leadership, the decisive vote had been taken. The result had been trumpeted on both sides of the Atlantic. The working party was given the task of quickly incorporating 'the deal' into its discussion paper. Yet not a few delegations expected to hold a substantive discussion of the fleshed-out proposals during the board's December meeting in Amsterdam.

13.12. TRANSITION FROM THE OLD TO THE NEW IASC

13.12.1. Development and Issue of the Working Party's Final Report

The working party went immediately to work, as Secretary-General Carsberg felt strongly that its report should be made available to the board delegations as far in advance of the 13–16 December 1999 meeting as possible.[118] Because the working party's 12 November draft had so closely matched 'the deal', the redrafting dealt mostly with issues on which agreement was easily reached. The working party negotiated numerous changes in wording, mainly through a series of emails with Sue Harding at the secretariat.[119] The two interim drafts, dated 22 and 27 November, were cleared, word for word, with Lynn Turner at the SEC. Finally, in a conference call on 29 November, the working party members signed off on the final draft, and on 6 December the thirty-three-page report of the working party, entitled *Recommendations on Shaping IASC for the Future*, was published.[120]

13.12.2. The Selection of Members of the Nominating Committee

It was essential to get the nominating committee off and running so that the trustees and eventually the members of the new board could be chosen in time for the planned launch of the board by 1 January 2001. The committee was to consist of between five and eight members, and its assignment was to appoint the initial group of trustees. In the working party's final report, it was suggested that the nominating committee should draw on 'senior members of regulatory bodies, major international organizations, major global corporations, and the accounting profession' (paragraph 21). It was made known that Arthur Levitt, the SEC chairman, was interested in being a member. The committee was to elect its own chairman, and he would have been the leading candidate. Once the vote in Venice had been secured, Carsberg immediately began the process of identifying the candidates for the committee, whom the board would be asked to approve in Amsterdam. With the SEC's help in persuading key individuals to serve on the committee, acceptances were received from the following individuals: Levitt; Michel Prada, chairman of France's COB; Howard Davies, chairman of the UK FSA; Andrew Sheng, chairman of the Hong Kong Securities and Futures Commission; James D. Wolfensohn, president of the World Bank; and James E.

Copeland, Jr., chief executive of Deloitte Touche Tohmatsu. Carsberg very much wanted to include a senior figure from the European Commission, which had opposed the proposals approved by the board in Venice. He had approached the Commission, but there was a long delay in securing a response. Finally, at the board's meeting in Amsterdam, Karel Van Hulle made it known that Commissioner Frits Bolkestein decided not to serve on the nominating committee.[121] Evidently, the Commission had no taste for being represented on the committee. Instead, Carsberg secured the acceptance of Karl-Hermann Baumann, the deputy chairman of the German Accounting Standards Board and the chairman of the supervisory board of Siemens.[122]

In Amsterdam, as is noted below, the board unanimously appointed these seven members to the nominating committee, and the committee proceeded to choose Arthur Levitt as its chairman.

13.12.3. The Board's December Meeting in Amsterdam

Now in possession of the working party's report, the board delegations raised some tough issues at its meeting on 13–16 December 1999, in Amsterdam.[123] In his introductory remarks, Chairman Stig Enevoldsen said that he, Carsberg, and the executive committee unanimously, all supported the proposals set out in the working party's report.

Questions were raised about the role to be performed by the full-time board members who were to liaise with a designated national standard setter. The board expressed a preference that such liaison members should not also be a voting member of the national standard setter, else that could impair their independence.

It was asked whether the board was bound by its vote in Venice. Others asked whether the provision for eight votes to approve standards, or the absence of a provision on geographical criteria for board members, could be changed. Enevoldsen replied that those were 'deal breakers'. He said that the entirety of proposals voted upon in November was not subject to change. One member then asked what purpose was served by this discussion.

Questions were raised about the role of steering committees in the board's due process. Members disagreed over the past effectiveness of the steering committees. A working party member said that it was planned to use steering committees for all main projects.

There was scepticism that the trustees could raise the £10 million funding. A reply from a member of the executive committee was that major financial support was already being generated and that the proposed budget was less than that of the FASB.

It was asked what would happen if the SEC were to differ with SIC over an interpretation, an issue that remains today.

Questions were raised about the commitment expressed in paragraph 53, which required board members to 'agree conceptually to act in the public interest and apply the IASC Framework in deciding on and revising standards'. Should there be a provision in place for saying how the Framework can be revised?

Several members urged that the Constitution not be laden with great detail, so that the IASC could evolve in the light of changed conditions.

At the conclusion of the discussion, the members again voted 16–0 to approve the report and to instruct the secretariat to prepare resolutions for a change in the Constitution based on the report. In a closed session, the board then voted unanimously to appoint the members of the nominating committee.[124] The membership was announced in the December 1999 issue of *IASC Update*.

13.12.4. IASC Nominating Committee Selects the Trustees for the New Regime

The nominating committee's first meeting was at the SEC offices in Washington, DC. After that meeting, the committee sent out requests for nominations. In February, the committee met again in Paris at the offices of the COB. In Paris, it was felt that the calibre of the nominations received thus far was disappointing. SEC Chairman Levitt, who chaired the nominating committee, opened the meeting by emphasizing that the board of trustees had to be composed of international figures of the highest standing. They needed to have the power and dignity such that prospective candidates for membership on the new board would have great difficulty saying no. The others readily agreed, and it was decided to restart the process, aiming even higher. Levitt argued for trustees of the equivalent of Paul Volcker, the highly respected former chairman of the board of governors of the US Federal Reserve System. Some wondered if Volcker could be interested in the position. In the end, with broad support, Levitt personally recruited Volcker to chair the trustees and was active in recruiting many of the other trustees as well.

On 22 May 2000, the nominating committee announced the selection of nineteen trustees to oversee the newly restructured IASC board, including Volcker as chairman.[125] All of the continents, three of the Big Five audit firms, major industrial enterprise and financial institutions, the legal profession, securities market regulators, and standard-setting bodies were represented on the trustees group. That the chairman and four other trustees were Americans did not go unnoticed in the accountancy press.[126]

Howard Davies, chairman of the UK's FSA and a member of the nominating committee, said in a speech, 'We have managed to assemble an outstanding group of people. Paul Volcker ... will bring real authority and clout to the exercise, as will the other trustees in their own constituencies and countries.'[127]

13.12.5. Funding Requirements

The IASC reported that it was 'undertaking a feasibility and planning study to determine whether it can raise a capital pool of £50–£60 million, the amount thought necessary to supply the estimated [annual] operating budget of £10 million'.[128] Towards this end, the IASC secured advice from the London office of a New York firm, Community Counselling Service Ltd, which specialized in developing fund-raising programmes. The advice received was that the IASC should place emphasis on 'the global private sector of industry', specifically the major international accountancy firms, stock exchanges, international banks, international insurance companies and securities firms, and multinational firms. Of the sixty-two individuals interviewed, who were with such institutions mostly in Europe and North America, forty-eight indicated they would support a campaign in a financial capacity.[129] The trustees were assigned the task of fund-raising. Paul Volcker chaired the trustees' finance committee.

13.12.6. IASC Board Approves the Constitution

Approval of a new Constitution required a three-quarters majority of the board. On 16 March 2000, the IASC board, meeting in São Paulo, Brazil, unanimously approved the new Constitution for the restructured IASC.[130] The objectives of the new body were to develop 'a single set of high quality, understandable and enforceable global accounting standards ... ; to promote the use and rigorous application of those standards; and to bring about convergence of national accounting standards and International Accounting Standards to high quality solutions' (article 2).

13.12.7. IASC Member Bodies Approve the IASC's Restructuring

A simple majority vote was required for approval by the IASC's 143 professional accountancy bodies (that is, member bodies) in 104 countries.[131] Yet on 24 May 2000, during the meeting of IFAC's assembly of members, held in Edinburgh, the IASC's member bodies unanimously approved the restructuring of the IASC, marking the final stage in the process of consummating this major overhaul.[132] By this vote, the IASC was finally cut loose from the accountancy profession.

The task of convincing the member bodies to vote for the restructuring was not as easily achieved as the final vote would imply. After Chairman Stig Enevoldsen's prepared address to the large assemblage, there was a lengthy debate, during which some delegates raised critical and not supportive comments. The IASC's leadership became nervous about the outcome. There was more opposition than they had expected. Then Enevoldsen gave a ten-minute unscripted presentation in which he strongly defended the model approved by the board and argued, with ultimate success, that the time was past when the accountancy profession could own a global accounting standard setter.

13.12.8. The Trustees Choose the New Members of the Restructured Board

Before the newly appointed trustees could hold their first meeting, it became an urgent matter to decide whether David Tweedie, chairman of the UK Accounting Standards Board, should be persuaded to become the chairman of the newly restructured board. Word spread quickly that Tweedie had been offered the vice-chancellorship of a prestigious Scottish university, and the fear immediately arose that he would be lost to the IASC. Tweedie held a Ph.D. from the University of Edinburgh, where he was a part-time visiting professor. In a flurry of phone calls, the Americans engineered the appointment. SEC Chairman Levitt, SEC Chief Accountant Lynn Turner, and FASB Chairman Edmund Jenkins each telephoned Tweedie and urged him to take the chairmanship. Howard Davies also played a major role in this effort. Levitt and Turner discussed with Volcker the credentials and stature that Tweedie would bring to the board.[133] In the end, the trustees, in their first meeting on 28 June, unanimously extended the offer, and Tweedie accepted.[134] The trustees followed normal due process for the other appointments to the board: after announcing a search for candidates and receiving applications, they conducted interviews. The nominating committee was chaired by Trustee Ken Spencer. The names of the fourteen board members were announced on 25 January 2001, and they included eight former IASC board delegates or observers (marked with an asterisk), as follows:[135]

> Chairman: Sir David Tweedie*—full-time chairman of the Accounting Standards Board and former partner in KPMG Peat Marwick McLintock, London (United Kingdom)
>
> Vice-Chairman: Thomas Jones*—retired executive vice-president, Citigroup and former trustee of the US FAF (United States)
>
> Mary Barth (part time)—professor of accounting, Stanford University, and former audit partner in Arthur Andersen (United States)
>
> Hans-Georg Bruns—chief accounting officer, DaimlerChrysler (Germany)
>
> Anthony Cope*—member of the FASB and a former security analyst (United States)
>
> Robert Garnett—executive vice-president of finance, Anglo-American (South Africa)
>
> Gilbert Gélard*—partner in KPMG, Paris, formerly the chief accounting officer of two industrial groups and on the staff of the Ordre des Experts Comptables (France)

498   Towards a World Standard Setter

Robert Herz (part time)—technical partner in PricewaterhouseCoopers, New York (United States)

James Leisenring*—director of international activities and former vice-chairman of the FASB (United States)

Warren McGregor*—partner in Stevenson McGregor, Melbourne, and former executive director of the Australian Accounting Research Foundation (Australia)

Patricia O'Malley—full-time chairman of the Accounting Standards Board of Canada and former partner in KPMG, Toronto (Canada)

Harry Schmid*—retired senior vice-president, Nestlé (Switzerland)

Geoffrey Whittington—professor of financial accounting, Cambridge University, and member of Accounting Standards Board (United Kingdom)

Tatsumi Yamada*—partner in ChuoAoyama Audit Corporation (affiliated with PricewaterhouseCoopers), Tokyo and was a member of the Business Accounting Deliberation Council (Japan)

Jones and Cope were British citizens, although they had pursued their professional careers mainly in the United States. Those, like the European Commission, which favoured a board with broad geographical representation could not fail to notice that nine of the fourteen board members, more than the simple majority required to approve exposure drafts and standards, came from the G4 countries.

At its meeting on 30 January–1 February 2001, the G4+1 decided, because the newly restructured IASC board was ready to begin operations, to disband and cancel its planned activities.[136] Indeed, David Tweedie and Jim Leisenring, two former G4+1 chairmen, as well as Warren McGregor, another long-serving G4+1 member, had been appointed to the restructured board. Ken Spencer, also a former chairman of the G4+1, was a member of the board of trustees.

13.12.9. The IASC Reaches the End of Its Life

The IASC board conducted no further business following its meeting on 11–13 December 2000, held in London. Only some staff work remained to be done. On the evening of the final day of the board meeting, the IASC held a celebratory, farewell dinner in Goldsmiths' Hall, London, attended by the members and observers of the board, the staff, several guests, and six former chairmen: John Hepworth, Hans Burggraaff, Stephen Elliott, John Kirkpatrick, Georges Barthès de Ruyter, and Stig Enevoldsen. Twenty-seven and one-half years from its founding on 28 June 1973, the IASC, which was an unincorporated association, terminated its existence on 21 January 2001, the date on which the trustees resolved to put the new Constitution in force.

As discussed in Section 12.3.7, in June 2000 the European Commission announced that it would seek legislation to require all listed EU companies to adopt International Accounting Standards in their consolidated statements beginning in 2005. The decision was a big boost for the new board.

The IASC's founder, Sir Henry Benson, got it right when he prophesied in 1975 that the effects of the IASC's work would become evident by the year 2000 (*see* Section 3.2). Changes in world capital markets had finally overcome the resistance by many countries that sought to preserve their sovereignty over the setting of accounting standards.

APPENDIX 1

Text of the 1973 Agreement and Constitution

An Agreement to establish an International Accounting Standards Committee

London, Friday 29 June 1973

Agreement

1. The professional accountancy bodies which are signatories hereto, hereby collectively agree:

    (*a*) to establish and maintain an International Accounting Standards Committee, with the membership and powers set out below, whose function will be to formulate and publish in the public interest, basic standards to be observed in the presentation of audited accounts and financial statements and to promote their worldwide acceptance and observance;

    (*b*) to support the standards promulgated by the Committee;

    (*c*) to use their best endeavours:

    (i) to ensure that published accounts comply with these standards or that there is disclosure of the extent to which they do not and to persuade governments, the authorities controlling securities markets and the industrial and business community that published accounts should comply with these standards;

    (ii) to ensure that the auditors satisfy themselves that the accounts comply with these standards. If the accounts do not comply with these standards the audit report should either refer to the disclosure of non-compliance in the accounts, or should state the extent to which they do not comply;

    (iii) to ensure that, as soon as practicable, appropriate action is taken in respect of auditors whose audit reports do not meet the requirements of (ii) above;

    (*d*) to seek to secure similar general acceptance and observance of these standards internationally.

2. The professional accountancy bodies which are signatories hereto, further agree that the International Accounting Standards Committee, with the objectives, functions, powers, composition, organisation and financial arrangements set out in its Constitution, shall be a part of the International Co-ordination Committee for the Accountancy Profession established by the Heads of Delegations to the Xth International Congress of Accountants in Sydney but shall be autonomous in the issue of exposure drafts and standards. The Constitution of the International Accounting Standards Committee shall not be reviewed until the end of 1976 without the agreement of the International Accounting Standards Committee and the International Co-ordination Committee for the Accountancy Profession.

Constitution

Membership

1. (*a*) The membership of the International Accounting Standards Committee will consist of not more than 2 members per country (and for the purposes of this Constitution the United Kingdom and the Republic of Ireland shall be treated as though they were one country), nominated by the accountancy bodies thereof which are signatories to this Constitution. The members may be accompanied at meetings of the Committee by a staff observer.

   (*b*) An accountancy body of a country not represented on the Committee under (*a*) above may, on request, become an Associate Member provided that the Committee is satisfied that it is prepared to subscribe to the objectives set out in the Agreement; is representative of the profession in that country; has standards and resources which would enable it to contribute towards the work of the Committee; and is willing, on the invitation of the Committee, to nominate members to carry out particular assignments or to join working parties or groups constituted to undertake tasks allotted by the Committee. Associate Members would not be entitled to attend meetings of the Committee nor to vote but may attend the meetings of the Committee by invitation.

   (*c*) The members of the Committee and the persons nominated by Associate Members shall not regard themselves as representing sectional interests but shall be guided by the need to act in the public interest and the general interest of the accountancy profession as a whole.

Officers

2. The Committee shall be presided over by a Chairman elected by a simple majority for two years by the members of the Committee from amongst their numbers and shall not be eligible for re-election.

Voting

3. Each country represented on the Committee shall have one vote which may be taken by a show of hands or by postal ballot. Except where otherwise provided, the decisions of the Committee shall be taken on a simple majority.

Powers

4. (*a*) The Committee shall have power, subject to a vote of two-thirds in favour, to issue proposals (including amendments to existing statements) in its own name in the form of exposure drafts for comment. Exposure drafts shall be addressed to professional accountancy bodies entitled to participate in International Congresses. They may also be addressed to such governments, securities markets, regulatory and other agencies as the Committee may determine.

   (*b*) After a suitable period has been allowed for comment, the Committee shall review such proposals and approve, amend or abandon them as it may consider fit. No standard shall be issued for publication unless it is approved, on a vote, by at least three-quarters of the total voting rights. Every standard so approved shall be published by the participating professional accounting bodies, which are signatories hereto, and in the countries to which Associate Members belong. The standards will also be addressed to other professional accountancy bodies entitled to participate in International Congresses. They may also be addressed to such governments, securities markets, regulatory and other agencies as the Committee may determine.

(c) Dissentient opinions will not be included in any exposure drafts or standards promulgated by the Committee. Exposure drafts will however include the arguments for and against the adoption of a particular standard.

Operating Procedures

5. (a) The Committee shall determine its operating procedures so long as they are not inconsistent with the terms of this Constitution.

(b) The definitive text of any exposure draft or standard shall be that published in the English language. The Committee shall give authority to the individual participating bodies to prepare translations of exposure drafts and standards. The responsibility for and cost of translating, publishing and distributing copies in any country shall be borne by the professional bodies of the country concerned.

Financial Arrangements

6. (a) An annual budget for the ensuing calendar year will be prepared by the Committee and submitted in August each year to the Councils of the accountancy bodies which are signatories hereto.

(b) Each country shall contribute on 1st January each year a sum equal to one-ninth of the annual budget for that year.

(c) The following expenses will be a charge against the revenues of the Committee:

    (i) costs of staff employed in, and the operating costs of, the permanent office of the Committee *excluding* the rent, rates and any taxes of the permanent office which shall be borne by the professional body or bodies of the country where the permanent office is located;

    (ii) the travelling, hotel and incidental expenses of one member of each of the countries represented on the Committee;

    (iii) the travelling, hotel and incidental expenses of the permanent staff who are required to attend meetings of the Committee.

(d) Any surplus of revenue over expenditure in anyone year shall be retained by the Committee and carried forward to the following year.

(e) The travelling, hotel and incidental expenses of the second member of the Committee and of the staff observer from each of the countries represented shall be borne by the professional body(ies) of the country concerned. The same arrangement will apply to persons nominated by Associate Members to working parties constituted by the Committee or to carry out specific assignments on behalf of the Committee.

Meetings

7. Meetings of the Committee shall be held at such times and in such places as the members of the Committee may mutually agree.

Permanent Office

8. The location of the permanent office of the Committee shall be London.

Secretariat

9. The accountancy bodies in the United Kingdom and the Republic of Ireland will be responsible, subject to the approval of the Committee, for recruiting staff for the permanent office in London.

signed for and on behalf of
The Institute of Chartered Accountants in Australia
Australian Society of Accountants
E. H. BURGESS

signed for and on behalf of
The Canadian Institute of Chartered Accountants
P. HOWARD LYONS

signed for and on behalf of
Ordre des Experts Comptables et des Comptables Agréés
ROGER CAUMEIL

signed for and on behalf of
Institut der Wirtschaftsprüfer in Deutschland e V
Wirtschaftsprüferkammer
DR. KRAFFT FRHR. VON DER TANN

signed for and on behalf of
The Japanese Institute of Certified Public Accountants
SHOZO TATSUMI

signed for and on behalf of
Instituto Mexicano de Contadores Públicos, A.C.
J. FREYSSINIER

signed for and on behalf of
Nederlands Instituut van Registeraccountants
J. W. SCHOONDERBEEK

signed for and on behalf of
The Institute of Chartered Accountants in England and Wales
The Institute of Chartered Accountants of Scotland
The Institute of Chartered Accountants in Ireland
The Association of Certified Accountants
The Institute of Cost and Management Accountants
The Institute of Municipal Treasurers and Accountants
HENRY BENSON

signed for and on behalf of
American Institute of Certified Public Accountants
WALLACE E. OLSON

APPENDIX 2
Chairmen and Senior Staff

Chairmen

June 1973–July 1976	Sir Henry Benson (Coopers & Lybrand) (United Kingdom)
July 1976–June 1978	Joseph Cummings (Peat, Marwick Mitchell) (United States)
July 1978–June 1980	John Hepworth (Yarwood Vane/Deloitte) (Australia)
July 1980–October 1982	Hans Burggraaff (Binder Dijker Otte) (The Netherlands)
November 1982–March 1985	Stephen Elliott (Arthur Andersen) (Canada)
April 1985–October 1987	John Kirkpatrick (KMG Thomson McLintock) (United Kingdom)
October 1987–June 1990	Georges Barthès de Ruyter (Arthur Andersen) (France)
July 1990–December 1992	Arthur Wyatt (Arthur Andersen) (United States)
January 1993–June 1995	Eiichi Shiratori (IONA International Corporation) (Japan)
July 1995–December 1997	Michael Sharpe (Coopers & Lybrand) (Australia)
January 1998–June 2000	Stig Enevoldsen (Deloitte & Touche) (Nordic Federation of Public Accountants)
July 2000–February 2001	Thomas Jones (Citigroup) (United States)

Deputy Chairmen and Vice-Chairmen

Deputy Chairmen

Michael Sharpe, elected in October 1992
Stig Enevoldsen, elected in May 1995

Vice-Chairmen

Patricia McConnell (United States), elected in October/November 1997 for a term beginning in January 1998
Thomas Jones (United States), elected in October/November 1997 for a term beginning in January 1998

Secretaries

June 1973–June 1975	Paul Rosenfield (AICPA)
July 1975–November 1977	John Brennan (University of Saskatchewan)
December 1977–September 1979	Roy Nash (Arthur Young, New York)
October 1979–December 1981	Allan Cook (Unilever, London)

January 1982–December 1983   Geoffrey Mitchell (Flinders University of South Australia)

All were seconded from their firms or universities.

Secretaries-General

January 1984–March 1985	Geoffrey Mitchell
April 1985–December 1994	David Cairns (Stoy Hayward, London)
January 1995–May 1995	Liesel Knorr (KPMG, Köln)(acting secretary-general)
May 1995–December 2000	Sir Bryan Carsberg (UK Office of Fair Trading)

Assistant Secretaries

July 1973–June 1975	Richard Simmons (Arthur Andersen, London)
July 1975–March 1977	Christopher Relleen (Deloitte, London)
April 1977–May 1979	Hugh Richardson (Coopers & Lybrand, London)
June 1979–May 1981	Peter Akins (Yarwood Vane/Deloitte, Sydney)
June 1981–May 1983	Brian Shearer (Grant Thornton, London)
June 1983–September 1985	John Bloxsome (Spicer and Pegler, London)
October 1985–March 1987	Brian Rutherford (University of Kent at Canterbury)

The first six were seconded from their firms. Rutherford resigned from his university upon joining the IASC staff.

Technical Directors

1991	Robert Langford
1991–1992	Brigid Curran
1994–1999	Liesel Knorr
1999–2000	James Saloman

Affiliations are shown as of the time when the individuals took up their indicated position with the IASC.

APPENDIX 3

Members of the Delegations to the IASC, 1973–2000

Notes: This list does not include substitute members or incidental visitors. The staff observer was renamed technical adviser in 1990. Affiliations are shown as of the time when the individuals joined the IASC board.

Founding Delegations

Australian Delegation

Dick Burgess	1973–4 (Arthur Young)
Ron Munro	staff observer 1973–5 (Australian Society of Accountants)
John Hepworth	1974–80 (Yarwood Vane & Co.)
Tony Kewin	staff observer 1974–5 (Hungerfords)
Phillip Cox	1978–80 (Phillip C.E. Cox)
John Bishop	1980–3 (Peat Marwick)
Kenneth Spencer	1983–5; 1998–2000 (Peat Marwick)
Ronald Cotton	1985–7 (John Fairfax)
Warren McGregor	staff observer/technical adviser 1986–99 (AARF)
David Boymal	1988–90; 1998–9 (Arthur Young)
Brigid Curran	1990–1 (Coopers & Lybrand)
Jan McCahey	deputy technical adviser 1991–3; 1995–8 (AARF)
Michael Sharpe	1990–7 (Coopers & Lybrand)
Ian Hammond	1995–2000 (Price Waterhouse)
Geoffrey Heeley	1995–7 (BHP)
Angus Thomson	technical adviser 1999–2000 (AARF)
Brian Morris	2000 (Edwards Marshall & Co.)

Canadian Delegation

Howard Lyons	1973–7 (Haskins & Sells)
Doug Thomas	1973–81 (CICA)
Morley Carscallen	1976–9 (Coopers & Lybrand)
Stephen Elliott	1979–85 (Arthur Andersen)
Douglas Hagerman	1981–5 (NOVA Corporation)
Doug Thomas	staff observer 1982–3 (CICA)
John Denman	staff observer 1983–95 (CICA)
Bruce Irvine	1984–7; 1996–7 (University of Saskatchewan)
Michael Dawson	1986–9 (Consolidated-Bathurst, Inc.)
Arthur Guthrie	1988–92 (A. Guthrie & Associates)
Paul Cherry	1989–95; 1999–2000 (Coopers & Lybrand)

Members of the Delegations to the IASC, 1973–2000

Hank Howarth	1993–6 (JHD Associates)
Alex Milburn	1995–8 (Ernst & Young)
Robert Rutherford	technical adviser 1996–2000 (CICA)
James Gaa	1997–2000 (University of Alberta)

French Delegation

Robert Mazars	1973–8 (Mazars)
Alfred Cordoliani	staff observer 1973–6 (Ordre des Experts Comptables)
André Henrot	1973–4 (Fiduciaire de l'Est)
Camille Bodès	1976–7 (sole practitioner)
Dominique Ledouble	staff observer 1976–81 (Ordre des Experts Comptables)
François Capelo	1979–83 (Arthur Young)
Patrice Cardon	staff observer 1980–5 (Ordre des Experts Comptables)
Georges Barthès de Ruyter	1982–90 (Frinault Fiduciaire/KMG)
Jean-Pierre Lagarrigue	1984–5 (Pavie & Associés)
Jean-Claude Scheid	staff observer 1985–7 (Ordre des Experts Comptables)
Jean-Luc Dumont	1985–97 (Salustro, Vincent, Gayet & Associés)
Raymond Béthoux	1988–92 (Béthoux, Burner & Associés A.T.H.)
Marc Ghiliotti	staff observer 1988 (Ordre des Experts Comptables)
Gilbert Gélard	staff observer 1988–97 (Ordre des Experts Comptables)
Gilbert Gélard	1998–2000 (KPMG)
Bernard Jaudeau	1992–7 (Thomson)
Jean Keller	1997–2000 (Lafarge)
Annie Moutardier-Mersereau	technical adviser 1997–9 (Ordre des Experts Comptables)
Christophe Patrier	technical adviser 1999–2000 (Ordre des Experts Comptables)

German Delegation

Krafft Freiherr von der Tann	1973–80 (sole practitioner)
Horst Kaminski	staff observer 1973–8 (IdW)
Hans Havermann	1973–5 (DTG Vereinigte Deutsche Treuhandgesellschaft)
Otto Grünewälder	1975–80 (sole practitioner)
Peter Marks	staff observer 1978–90; 1991–2 (IdW)
Henner Schmick	1980–3 (Wohnungswirtschaftliche Prüfungs- und Treuhand)
Peter Meyer	1981–4 (BDO Deutsche Warentreuhand)
Wilhelm Tjaden	1984–9 (Deutsche Baurevision)
Manfred Bolin	staff observer 1989–90 (IdW)
Dietz Mertin	1989–91 (Coopers & Lybrand Treuarbeit Deutsche Revision)
Heinz Kleekämper	1991–7 (Schitag Ernst & Young)
Bernd-Joachim Menn	1993–8 (Bayer)
Albrecht Ruppel	technical adviser 1993–9 (IdW)
Jochen Pape	1998–2000 (PricewaterhouseCoopers)
Helmut Berndt	1999–2000 (Henkel)
Klaus-Peter Naumann	technical adviser 1998–2000 (IdW)

Japanese Delegation

Junichi Kawaguchi	1973–5 (Asahi & Co.)
Shozo Tatsumi	1973–5 (Tatsumi & Associates)
Seigo Nakajima	staff observer 1973–5 (International Christian University)
Seigo Nakajima	1975–88 (International Christian University/Ferris Jogakuin)
Yukio Fujita	staff observer 1976–9; 1981 (Waseda University)
Eiichi Shiratori	staff observer 1982–3 (Arthur Andersen/Asahi)
Eiichi Shiratori	1983–8; 1990–5 (Arthur Andersen/Asahi)
Toshiaki Katsushima	staff observer 1983–7 (Deloitte Haskins & Sells)
Tadaaki Tokunaga	1985–92 (Shinko Management Services)
Noriaki Kinoshita	1988–9 (Inoue Chuo Kyodo audit corporation)
Etsuo Sawa	technical adviser 1992–9 (JICPA)
Yukio Ono	1992–5 (Deloitte Touche Tohmatsu)
Ikuo Nishikawa	1993–8 (KPMG Century Audit Corporation)
Tatsumi Yamada	1996–2000 (Chuo Audit Corporation/Coopers & Lybrand)
Shozo Yamazaki	1998–2000 (Deloitte Touche Tohmatsu)

Mexican Delegation

Manuel Galván Cebrián	1973–8 (Gonzalez Vilchis/Price Waterhouse)
Luis Nieto Martínez	1979–81 (DH&S)
Leopoldo Romero Escobar	1979–83 (Galaz, Carstens/Touche Ross)
Rolando Ortega Vázquez	staff observer 1981 (Despacho Roberto Casas Alatriste/Coopers & Lybrand)
Rolando Ortega Vázquez	1982–6 (Coopers & Lybrand)
Jesús Hoyos Roldán	staff observer 1982–3 (Price Waterhouse)
Jesús Hoyos Roldán	1984–7 (Price Waterhouse)
Alfonso Campaña Roiz	1986–7 (Ernst & Whinney)

NO DELEGATION FROM 1988 TO 1994

Rafael Gómez Eng	1995–7 (Cárdenas Dosal/KPMG)
María Estela Imamura Ogushi	1995–7 (Galaz, Gómez Morfin/Deloitte & Touche)
Juan Gras Gas	1996–8 (Ruiz, Urquiza/Arthur Andersen)
Luis Moirón Llosa	1998–2000 (Gonzalez Vilchis/ PricewaterhouseCoopers)
Carlos Buenfil	technical adviser 1998–2000 (Ruiz, Urquiza/Arthur Andersen)

Netherlands Delegation

Pieter Louwers	1973–4 (Philips)
Henk Treffers	1973–8 (Moret & Limperg)
Henk Volten	staff observer 1973–87 (NIVRA)
Is Kleerekoper	1975–9 (Klynveld Kraayenhof)

Hans Burggraaff	1979–82 (Dijker en Doornbos)
Jan Uiterlinden	1980–1 (Klynveld Kraayenhof)
Herman Marseille	1982–90 (Dijker Van Dien)
Frans Graafstal	1982–8 (Klynveld Kraayenhof)
Johan van Helleman	1988–97 (Royal Dutch/Shell)
Cor Regoort	technical adviser 1990–3 (NIVRA)
Jan Klaassen	1991–2000 (KPMG)
Cees Dubbeld	technical adviser 1993–8 (NIVRA)
Jean den Hoed	1998–2000 (Akzo Nobel)
Ruud Vergoossen	technical adviser 1998–2000 (NIVRA)

United Kingdom & Ireland Delegation (United Kingdom from 1988 onwards)

Sir Henry Benson	1973–6 (Coopers & Lybrand)
Alexander Mackenzie	1973–8 (Whinney Murray & Co.)
Jeremy Winters	staff observer 1973–6 (ICAEW)
John Grenside	1976–80 (Peat Marwick)
Nick Reece	staff observer 1976–9 (ICAEW)
John Kirkpatrick	1978–83, 1984–7 (Thomson McLintock)
David Tweedie	staff observer 1979–81 (ICAS)
David Hobson	1980–5 (Coopers & Lybrand)
Simon Timms	staff observer 1980–3 (ICAEW)
Jeff Pearcy	1983 (ICI)
Susan Baker	staff observer 1983–6 (ICAEW)
Gerard Murphy	1985–9 (Anglo Irish Bank, Dublin)
Christopher Stronge	1985–90 (Deloitte)
Geoffrey Mitchell	staff observer 1986–90 (ICAEW)
Peter Stilling	1990–5 (Touche Ross)
Stanley Thomson	1991–3 (Ford Motor Company)
Henry Gold	technical adviser 1991–5 (ICAEW)
Christopher Nobes	1993–2000 (University of Reading)
Sir David Tweedie	1995–2000 (ASB)
Bruce Picking	technical adviser 1995–7 (ICAEW)
David Perry	technical adviser 1997–2000 (ICAEW)

United States Delegation

Joseph Cummings	1973–8 (Peat Marwick)
Robert Sempier	staff observer 1973–7 (AICPA)
Eugene Minahan	1976–9 (Atlantic Richfield)
Donald Hayes	1978–81 (Arthur Young)
Paul Rosenfield	staff observer 1978–85 (AICPA)
Willis Smith	1979–82 (CPC International)
Roger Cason	1981–2 (Main Hurdman)
Ralph Harris	1982–5 (IBM)
Dennis Beresford	1982–4 (Ernst & Whinney)
Ralph Walters	1984–7 (Touche Ross)
Thomas McRae	staff observer 1985–9 (AICPA)

John Chironna	1986–92 (IBM)
Arthur Wyatt	1988–92 (Arthur Andersen)
John Hudson	technical adviser 1990–5 (AICPA)
Arlene Rodda Thomas	1990–4 (Coopers)
Ronald Murray	technical adviser 1993, 1995 (AICPA)
Jay Perrell	1994–7 (American Express)
Barry Robbins	1994–7 (Price Waterhouse)
Richard Stuart	technical adviser 1995–6 (AICPA)
Jane Adams	technical adviser 1996–7 (AICPA)
Michael Crooch	1997–2000 (Arthur Andersen)
Mitchell Danaher	1997–2000 (General Electric)
Elizabeth Fender	technical adviser 1997–2000 (AICPA)
Fred Gill	joint technical adviser 1998–9 (AICPA)
John Smith	2000 (October and December) (Deloitte & Touche)

Non-Founding Delegations

South African Delegation (from 1995 onwards the South African/Zimbabwe Delegation)

Warwick Thorby	1978–86 (Peat Marwick)
Jock Porteous	1978–83 (Goldby, Compton & Mackelvie/Touche Ross)
Derrick Robson	staff observer 1978–82 (National Council/SAICA)
Rick Cottrell	1983–9 (Coopers)
Peter Wilmot	1988–93; 1997–2000 (Pim Goldby/Touche Ross)
Douglas Brooking	1990–1; 1992–5; (Ivor Jones, Roy & Co.)
Monica Singer	technical adviser 1993–5 (SAICA)
Ian Somerville	1993–7 (South African Breweries)
Peter Bailey	technical adviser 1995–7 (KPMG, Zimbabwe)
Rosanne Blumberg	technical adviser 1996–7 (SAICA)
Erna Swart	1998–9 (SAICA)
Leslie Anderson	technical adviser 1997–2000 (Deloitte & Touche, Zimbabwe)
Erna Swart	technical adviser 2000 (SAICA)

Nigerian Delegation

Adedoyin Ogunde	1979–83 (Peat Marwick)
Oyeniyi Oyediran	1979–82 (Coopers)
Michael Ayodeji Oni	1983–7 (Ernst & Young)
Chief Olusegun Osunkeye	1984–7 (Nestlé Nigeria)

Italian Delegation

Giancarlo Tomasin	1983–94 (Studio Tomasin Commercialisti)
Mario Zappalà	1983–6 (Arthur Andersen)
Giuseppe Verna	1987–92 (Studio Verna)
Ambrogio Picolli	staff observer 1988–9 (Studio Associato Picolli)
Fabrizio Ferrentino	technical adviser 1992–3 (Consiglio Nazionale)

International Co-Ordinating Committee of Financial Analysts Associations (International Council of Investment Associations from 1988 onwards)

David Damant	1986–2000 (Quilter Goodison Company, London/ MAP Fund Managers/Credit Suisse/European Federation of Financial Analysts' Societies)
Rolf Rundfelt	1989–2000 (KPMG Bohlins, Stockholm)
Patricia McConnell	1990–2000 (Bear, Stearns, New York)
Ray De Angelo	technical adviser 1992–95 (AIMR)
Patricia McQueen (Walters)	technical adviser 1996–2000 (AIMR)
Nobuaki Kemmochi	1996–8 (Security Analysts Association of Japan)
Toshihiko Amano	1999–2000 (Security Analysts Association of Japan)

Federation of Swiss Industrial Holding Companies

Harry Schmid	1995–2000 (Nestlé)
Peter Zurbrügg	1995–9 (Hoffmann-La Roche)
Philipp Hallauer	technical adviser 1995–2000 (KPMG Fides Peat)
Malcolm Cheetham	1999–2000 (Novartis)

International Association of Financial Executives Institutes

Thomas Jones	1996–2000 (Citicorp, New York)
David Potter	1996–2000 (British American Tobacco, London)
Luis Nelson Carvalho	technical adviser 1996–7 (Universidade de São Paulo)
Luis Nelson Carvalho	1999–2000 (Universidade de São Paulo)
Martin Noordzij	1999–2000 (VNO-NCV, The Hague)

Taiwanese Delegation

S. T. Chiang	1984–7 (Chiang, Lai, Lin & Co.)

Korean Delegation

In Ki Joo	1988–91 (Yonsei University)
Doo Hwang Kim	1988–92 (Sae Dong & Co.)
Soo Keun Kwak	1991–2 (Seoul National University)

Danish Delegation

Morten Iversen	1988–9 (Price Waterhouse)
Stig Enevoldsen	1989–90 (Deloitte & Touche)

Jordanian Delegation

Talal Abu-Ghazaleh	1989–90 (Talal Abu-Ghazaleh & Co.)
Fouad Alaeddin	1988–94 (Dajani & Alaeddin/Arthur Andersen)

Munir Al-Borno	staff observer 1988–9 (Talal Abu-Ghazaleh & Co.)
Munir Al-Borno	1990–5 (Talal Abu-Ghazaleh & Co.)

Nordic Federation of Public Accountants' Delegation

Erik Mamelund (N)	1990–2000 (Oslo Stock Exchange)
Stig Enevoldsen (DK)	1991–8 (Deloitte & Touche)
Sigvard Heurlin (S)	1992–2000 (Öhrlings Coopers & Lybrand)
Per Gunslev (DK)	1996–2000 (KPMG)

Indian Delegation (from 1995 Onwards, the Indian/Sri Lankan Delegation)

Narendra Sarda	1993–5 (P.C. Hansotia & Company)
Yashodhan Kale	1995–7 (A.F. Ferguson/ICAI)
Reyaz Mihular	1995–2000 (Ford, Rhodes, Thornton & Co., KPMG, Sri Lanka)
Thekkiam Sitaram Vishwanath	1998–2000 (ICAI)
Narain Dass Gupta	2000 (ICAI)

Malaysian Delegation

Mohammad Bin Abdullah	1995–6 (AOM Management Services)
Yap Kim Len	technical adviser 1995–6 (Malaysian Institute of Accountants)
Tony Seah Cheoh Wah	technical adviser 1995–7 (SQ Associates)
Tony Seah Cheoh Wah	1997–2000 (SQ Associates)
Katharene Expedit	1999–2000 (Malaysian Institute of Accountants)

APPENDIX 4

Technical Projects, Exposure Drafts, and Standards

Topic, start of project	Steering committee chairman	Exposure draft, date of approval	Standard, date of approval	Comments
Disclosure of accounting policies including the basis of valuation of assets June 1973	A. I. Mackenzie (UK & Ireland)	E1 'Disclosure of Accounting Policies' January 1974	IAS 1 *Disclosure of Accounting Policies* November 1974	Replaced by IAS 1 (revised in 1997)
Valuation of stock and work in progress June 1973	P. H. Lyons (Canada)	E2 'Valuation and Presentation of Inventories in the Context of the Historical Cost System' July 1974	IAS 2 *Valuation and Presentation of Inventories in the Context of the Historical Cost System* July 1975	Superseded by IAS 2 (revised in 1993)
Consolidated accounts June 1973	J. P. Cummings (United States)	E3 'Consolidated Financial Statements and the Equity Method of Accounting' November 1974	IAS 3 *Consolidated Financial Statements and the Equity Method of Accounting* March 1976	Superseded by IAS 27 and IAS 28
Depreciation of fixed assets January 1974	A. H. Kewin (Australia)	E4 'Depreciation Accounting' April 1975	IAS 4 *Depreciation Accounting* July 1976	Partially superseded by IAS 16 (revised in 1993) and by IAS 38; withdrawn November 1999
Basic disclosure in financial statements January 1974	M. Galván (Mexico)	E5 'Information to be Disclosed in Financial Statements' April 1975	IAS 5 *Information to be Disclosed in Financial Statements* July 1976	Replaced by IAS 1 (revised in 1997)
Translation of foreign accounts in financial statements January 1974	H. Treffers (The Netherlands) S. Nakajima (Japan)	E11 'Accounting for Foreign Transactions and Translation of Foreign Financial Statements' July 1977		

Appendix 4 *Cont.*

Topic, start of project	Steering committee chairman	Exposure draft, date of approval	Standard, date of approval	Comments
Accounting in the face of inflation April 1974	P. H. Lyons (Canada)	E23 'Accounting for the Effects of Changes in Foreign Exchange Rates' October 1981 E6 'Accounting Treatment of Changing Prices' October 1975 Discussion Paper: 'Treatment of Changing Prices in Financial Statements: A Summary of Proposals' November 1976	IAS 21 *Accounting for the Effects of Changes in Foreign Exchange Rates* March 1983 IAS 6 *Accounting Responses to Changing Prices* March 1977	Superseded by IAS 21 (revised in 1993) Superseded by IAS 15
Source and application of funds November 1974	R. Mazars (France) H. F. A. Cordoliani (France)	E7 'Statement of Source and Application of Funds' March 1976	IAS 7 *Statement of Changes in Financial Position* July 1977	Superseded by IAS 7 (revised in 1992)
Presentation of the income statement November 1974	J. P. Cummings (United States)	E8 'The Treatment in the Income Statement of Unusual Items and Changes in Accounting Estimates and Accounting Policies' July 1976	IAS 8 *Unusual and Prior Period Items and Changes in Accounting Policies* October 1977	Superseded by IAS 8 (revised in 1993)
Research and development November 1974	R. D. Thomas (Canada)	E9 'Accounting for Research and Development Costs' November 1976	IAS 9 *Accounting for Research and Development Activities* March 1978	Superseded by IAS 9 (revised in 1992)

Events occurring after the balance sheet date, and accounting for contingencies July 1975	A. I. Mackenzie (UK & Ireland)	E10 'Contingencies and Events Occurring After the Balance Sheet Date' March 1977	IAS 10 *Contingencies and Events Occurring After the Balance Sheet Date* June 1978	Superseded by IAS 10 (revised in 1999)
Accounting for certain types of long-term contracts July 1975	L. Nieto (Mexico)	E12 'Accounting for Construction Contracts' July 1977	IAS 11 *Accounting for Construction Contracts* November 1978	Superseded by IAS 11 (revised in 1993)
Accounting for taxation in financial statements July 1975	J. A. Hepworth (Australia)	E13 'Accounting for Taxes on Income' October 1977	IAS 12 *Accounting for Taxes on Income* March 1979	Superseded by IAS 12 (revised in 1996)
Accounting for diversified operations July 1976	E. J. Minahan (United States)	E15 'Reporting Financial Information by Segment' October 1979	IAS 14 *Reporting Financial Information by Segment* March 1981	Superseded by IAS 14 (revised in 1997)
The treatment of leases in financial Statements July 1976	P. Rutteman (UK & Ireland)	E19 'Accounting for Leases' June 1980	IAS 17 *Accounting for Leases* March 1982	Superseded by IAS 17 (revised in 1997)
Working capital November 1976	M. P. Carscallen (Canada)	E14 'Current Assets and Current Liabilities' March 1978	IAS 13 *Presentation of Current Assets and Current Liabilities* June 1979	Replaced by IAS 1 (revised in 1997)
A 'watching brief' on developments in inflation accounting March 1977	J. P. Grenside (UK & Ireland)	E17 'Information Reflecting the Effects of Changing Prices' March 1980	IAS 15 *Information Reflecting the Effects of Changing Prices* June 1981	Status reduced to non-mandatory October 1989
Banking March 1977	E. L. Larkin (Unite States) C. I. Brown (UK & Ireland)	Discussion paper: 'Disclosures in the Financial Statements of Banks' October 1979		Project resumed October 1984

Appendix 4 *Cont.*

Topic, start of project	Steering committee chairman	Exposure draft, date of approval	Standard, date of approval	Comments
Accounting for pension costs and commitments July 1977	R.D. Thomas (Canada) D. Page (Canada)	E16 'Accounting for Retirement Benefits in the Financial Statements of Employers' October 1979	IAS 19 *Accounting for Retirement Benefits in the Financial Statements of Employers* June 1982	Superseded by IAS 19 (revised in 1993)
Accounting for fixed assets June 1978	L. Romero (Mexico)	E18 'Accounting for Property, Plant and Equipment in the Context of the Historical Cost System' March 1980	IAS 16 *Accounting for Property, Plant and Equipment* October 1981	Superseded by IAS 16 (revised in 1993)
Business combinations, mergers and takeovers and treatment of goodwill June 1978	P. C. E. Cox (Australia)	E22 'Accounting for Business Combinations' March 1981	IAS 22 *Accounting for Business Combinations* June 1983	Superseded by IAS 22 (revised in 1993)
Revenue recognition June 1978	S. Elliott (Canada)	E20 'Revenue Recognition' November 1980	IAS 18 *Revenue Recognition* June 1982	Superseded by IAS 18 (revised in 1993)
Accounting for government grants June 1979	W. G. Thorby (South Africa)	E21 'Accounting for Government Grants and Disclosure of Government Assistance' March 1981	IAS 20 *Accounting for Government Grants and Disclosure of Government Assistance* November 1982	
Accounting for interest costs June 1979	W. A. Smith (United States)	E24 'Accounting for the Capitalisation of Borrowing Costs' June 1982	IAS 23 *Capitalisation of Borrowing Costs* October 1983	Superseded by IAS 23 (revised in 1992)
Related party transactions June 1980	P. Meyer (Germany)	E25 'Disclosure of Related Party Transactions' November 1982	IAS 24 *Related Party Transactions* March 1984	

Appendix 4   517

Topic	Person	Steering Committee report	Exposure Draft	Standard	Notes
Accounting for deferred income tax June 1981	M. Vallas (France)	Unpublished report to board October 1984			Project resumed March 1987
Accounting for marketable securities October 1981	F. Capelo (France) G. Barthès (France)		E26 'Accounting for Investments' June 1984	IAS 25 Accounting for Investments October 1985	Superseded by IAS 39 and IAS 40
Review of existing International Accounting Standards March 1982	J. Hoyos (Mexico)	Unpublished reports to board on revision of IAS 1–8 June 1983–March 1985			
Accounting for pension plans March 1982	R. L. Harris (United States)		E27 'Accounting and Reporting by Retirement Benefit Plans' March 1985	IAS 26 Accounting and Reporting by Retirement Benefit Plans June 1986	
Aspects of the objectives of financial statements November 1982	M. A. Oni (Nigeria)				Merged into Conceptual Framework project November 1986
Review of IAS 3 March 1983	S. Nakajima (Japan)		E30 'Consolidated Financial Statements and Accounting for Investments in Subsidiaries' March 1987	IAS 27 Consolidated Financial Statements and Accounting for Investments in Subsidiaries June 1988	
Accounting for joint ventures June 1983	D. R. Hagerman (Canada)		E28 'Accounting for Investments in Associates and Joint Ventures' March 1986	IAS 28 Accounting for Investments in Associates November 1988	New project on joint ventures started November 1988
Accounting in high inflation economies October 1983	W. Tjaden (Germany)		E31 'Financial Reporting in Highly Inflationary Economies' July 1987	IAS 29 Financial Reporting in Hyper-inflationary Economies April 1989	
Liabilities March 1984	R. G. Cottrell (South Africa)				Merged into Conceptual Framework project November 1986

Appendix 4 *Cont.*

Topic, start of project	Steering committee chairman	Exposure draft, date of approval	Standard, date of approval	Comments
Owners' equity June 1984	G. Tomasin (Italy)			Merged into Conceptual Framework project November 1986
Disclosures in financial statements of banks October 1984	D. C. Hobson (UK & Ireland) A. G. Murphy (UK & Ireland)	E29 'Disclosures in the Financial Statements of Banks' November 1986		
		E34: Disclosures in the Financial Statements of Banks and Similar Financial Institutions April 1989	IAS 30 *Disclosures in the Financial Statements of Banks and Similar Financial Institutions* June 1990	
Asset recognition June 1985	R. J. Cotton			Merged into Conceptual Framework project November 1986
International harmonization of accounting for pension costs October 1985	H. Marseille (the Netherlands)	Unpublished report to board March 1986		
Framework for financial reporting November 1986	J. M. Dawson (Canada)	ED 'Framework for the Preparation and Presentation of Financial Statements' March 1988	*Framework for the Preparation and Presentation of Financial Statements* April 1989	
To recommend on the status of IAS 15 March 1987	F. Graafstal (the Netherlands)			Status of IAS 15 reduced to non-mandatory October 1989

Project	People	Exposure Draft	Standard	Notes
Revision of IAS 12 March 1987	R. Béthoux (France) B. Jaudeau (France)	E33 'Accounting for Taxes on Income' November 1988	IAS 12 (revised 1996) Accounting for Taxes on Income September 1996	
		E49 'Income Taxes' June 1994		Amended as IAS 12 (revised in 2000)
Comparability of financial statements March 1987	R. E. Walters (United States)	E32 'Comparability of Financial Statements' November 1988	Statement of Intent on the Comparability of Financial Statements June 1990	
Financial instruments June 1988	A. R. Wyatt (United States) R. J. Murray (United States)	E40 'Accounting for Financial Instruments' June 1991		
		E48 'Financial Instruments' November 1993	IAS 32 Financial Instruments: Disclosure and Presentation March 1995	Project continued March 1996
Undivided interests and investments in joint ventures November 1988	A. Guthrie (Canada)	E35 'Financial Reporting of Interests in Joint Ventures' October 1989	IAS 31 Financial Reporting of Interests in Joint Ventures November 1990	
Improvements to International Accounting Standards April 1989	R. Walters (United States) P. Cherry (Canada)	E37 'Accounting for Research and Development Activities' February 1991	IAS 9 (revised in 1993) Research and Development Costs October 1992	Superseded by IAS 38
		E38 'Inventories' June 1991	IAS 2 (revised in 1993) Inventories October 1992	
		E39 'Capitalisation of Borrowing Costs' June 1991	IAS 23 (revised in 1993) Capitalisation of Borrowing Costs October 1992	

Appendix 4 *Cont.*

Topic, start of project	Steering committee chairman	Exposure draft, date of approval	Standard, date of approval	Comments
		E45 'Business Combinations' November 1991	IAS 22 (revised in 1993) *Business Combinations* July 1993	Amended with IAS 36
		E41 'Revenue Recognition' November 1991	IAS 18 (revised in 1993) *Revenue* July 1993	
		E42 'Construction Contracts' November 1991	IAS 11 (revised in 1993) *Construction Contracts* July 1993	
		E43 'Property, Plant and Equipment' March 1992	IAS 16 (revised in 1993) *Property, Plant and Equipment* July 1993	Amended with IAS 36
		E44 'The Effects of Changes in Foreign Exchange Rates' March 1992	IAS 21 (revised in 1993) *The Effects of Changes in Foreign Exchange* November 1993	
		E46 'Extraordinary Items, Fundamental Errors and Changes in Accounting Policies' June 1992	IAS 8 (revised in 1993) *Net Profit or Loss for the Period, Fundamental Errors and Changes in Accounting Policies* July 1993	
		E47 'Retirement Benefit Costs' October 1992	IAS 19 (revised in 1993) *Retirement Benefit Costs* July 1993	Superseded by IAS 19 (revised in 1998)
Intangibles April 1989	P. J. Stilling (United Kingdom)	E50 'Intangible Assets' May 1995		Merged with impairment project September 1996

Appendix 4   521

Topic	Steering Committee Chair (country)	Exposure Draft	IAS	Notes
Statement of changes in financial position April 1989	P. Wilmot (South Africa)			Project discontinued July 1993
Financial reporting needs of developing and newly industrialized countries April 1989	T. Abu-Ghazaleh (Jordan) A. A. Dieye (France)			
		E36 'Cash Flow Statements' February 1991	IAS 7 (revised in 1992) *Cash Flow Statements* October 1992	
Earnings per share March 1990	D. Brooking (South Africa)	E52 'Earnings per Share' November 1995	IAS 33 *Earnings per Share* January 1997	
Financial information by segment March 1992	P. McConnell (Financial Analysts)	E51 'Reporting Financial Information by Segment' November 1995	IAS 14 (revised in 1997) *Segment Reporting* January 1997	
Presentation of financial statements March 1993	H. Kleekämper (Germany)	E53 'Presentation of Financial Statements' June 1996	IAS 1 (revised in 1997) *Presentation of Financial Statements* July 1997	
Agriculture June 1994	N. P. Sarda (India) H. D. Howarth (Canada) M. R. Mihular (Sri Lanka)	E65 'Agriculture' July 1999	IAS 41 *Agriculture* December 2000	
Retirement benefits and other employee benefit costs November 1994	J. Klaassen (The Netherlands)	E54 'Employee Benefits' September 1996	IAS 19 (revised in 1998) *Employee Benefits* January 1998	Amended as IAS 19 (revised in 2000)
Discontinued operations November 1995	C. W. Nobes (United Kingdom)	E58 'Discontinuing Operations' July 1997	IAS 35 *Discontinuing Operations* April 1998	
Interim reporting November 1995	S. Heurlin (Nordic Federation)	E57 'Interim Financial Reporting' July 1997	IAS 34 *Interim Financial Reporting* January 1998	
Provisions and contingencies March 1996	D. Tweedie (United Kingdom)	E59 'Provisions, Contingent Liabilities and Contingent Assets' July 1997	IAS 37 *Provisions, Contingent Liabilities and Contingent Assets* July 1998	

Appendix 4 *Cont.*

Topic, start of project	Steering committee chairman	Exposure draft, date of approval	Standard, date of approval	Comments
Financial instruments March 1996	J. A. Milburn (Canada)	Discussion Paper: 'Accounting for Financial Assets and Financial Liabilities' March 1997		Project reorganized October 1997
Impairment June 1996	G. Gélard (France)	E55 'Impairment of Assets' April 1997	IAS 36 *Impairment of Assets* April 1998	
		E60 'Intangible Assets' July 1997	IAS 38 *Intangible Assets* July 1998	
		E61 'Business Combinations' July 1997	IAS 22 (revised in 1998) *Business Combinations* July 1998	
Leases June 1996	T. Jones (IAFEI)	E56 'Leases' April 1997	IAS 17 (revised in 1997) *Leases* November 1997	
Insurance April 1997	W. McGregor (Australia)	Issues Paper: 'Insurance' November 1999		
Financial instruments October 1997	IASC staff	E62 'Financial Instruments: Recognition and Measurement' April 1998	IAS 39 *Financial Instruments: Recognition and Measurement* December 1998	Amended as IAS 39 (revised in 2000)
Events after the balance sheet date November 1997	IASC staff	E63 'Events after the Balance Sheet Date' November 1998	IAS 10 (revised 1999) *Events after the Balance Sheet Date* March 1999	
Investment properties November 1997	P. Gunsley (Nordic Federation)	E64 'Investment Property' July 1999	IAS 40 *Investment Property* March 2000	
Discounting April 1998	P. McQueen-Walters (Financial Analysts)			No publication by end of 2000

Developing countries April 1998	T. Seah (Malaysia)		No publication by end of 2000
Extractive industries April 1998	K. Spencer (Australia)	Issues Paper: 'Extractive Industries' November 2000	
Business combinations November 1998	S. Heurlin (Nordic Federation)		No publications by end of 2000
Reporting Financial Performance July 1999	P. McConnell (Financial Analysts)		No publication by end of 2000
Limited amendments to IAS 19 July 1999	IASC staff	E67: Pension Plan Assets June 200	IAS 19 (revised 2000) *Employee Benefits* October 2000
Bank disclosures and presentation July 1999	G. Mitchell (United Kingdom)		No publication by end of 2000
IAS 39 Implementation Guidance March 2000	J. T. Smith (United States)	Draft 'Staff Implementation Guidance on IAS 39' June 2000	
		E66 'Financial Instruments: Recognition and Measurement—Limited Revisions to IAS 39' June 2000	IAS 39 (revised in 2000) *Financial Instruments: Recognition and Measurement* October 2000
Limited amendments to IAS 12 March 2000	IASC staff	E68 'Income Tax Consequences of Dividends: Proposed Limited Revisions to IAS 12 (revised)' June 2000	IAS 12 (revised in 2000) *Income Taxes* October 2000

APPENDIX 5
Venues and Dates of Board Meetings

1973
29 June   London
15–16 November   London

1974
14–15 January   Paris
8–9 April   London
15–17 July   London
5–6 November   London

1975
15–16 January   London
9–11 April   Montreal
9–10 July   London
8–10 October   London

1976
9–11 March   London
6–8 July   London
9–11 November   Washington, DC

1977
1–3 March   Amsterdam
29–30 June, 1 July   Edinburgh
18–20 October   London

1978
7–9 March   London
14–16 June   Perth, Australia
7–9 November   London

1979
27–8 February, 1 March   Mexico City
19–21 June   London
23–5 October   London

1980
11–13 March   London
24–7 June   Berlin
4–6 November   Dublin

1981
24–7 March   Tokyo
23–6 June   London
14–16 October   London

Venues and Dates of Board Meetings

1982
24–6 March	London
22–5 June	Amsterdam
24–6 November	London

1983
23–5 March	Edinburgh
14–16 June	London
26–8 October	Paris

1984
14–16 March	London
19–21 June	Toronto
17–19 October	Düsseldorf

1985
6–8 March	Rome
25–7 June	New York
16–18 October	London

1986
5–7 March	Dublin
17–19 June	Amsterdam
5–7 November	London

1987
24–7 March	Sydney
1–3 July	Edinburgh

1988
29 February and 2–4 March	Düsseldorf
22–4 June	Toronto
9–11 November	Copenhagen

1989
12–14 April	Brussels
24–5 October	New York

1990
7–9 March	Amsterdam
20–2 June	Paris
7–9 November	Singapore

1991
27–8 February	London
12–14 June	Milan
5–8 November	Seoul

1992
4–6 March	Madrid
16–18 June	Amman
7–9 October	Chicago

1993
23–6 March	Tokyo
30 June–2 July	London
2–5 November	Oslo

1994
13, 15–17 June	Edinburgh
1–4 November	Budapest

1995
28–31 March	Düsseldorf
8–10 May	Amsterdam
1–4 November	Sydney

1996
27–30 March	Brussels
11–14 June	Stockholm
23–8 September	Barcelona

1997
6–9 January	London
7–11 April	Johannesburg
8–12 July	Beijing
30 October–4 November	Paris

1998
12–16 January	London
20–6 April	Kuala Lumpur
6–10 July	Niagara-on-the-Lake, Ontario
9–13 November	Zurich
14–16 December	Frankfurt am Main

1999
16–19 March	Washington, DC
28 June–2 July	Warsaw
15–19 November	Venice
13–16 December	Amsterdam

2000
13–17 March	São Paulo
19–23 June	Copenhagen
16–20 October	Tokyo
11–13 December	London

APPENDIX 6
Interviewees

Australia
John Bishop, David Boymal, Ian Hammond, John Hepworth, Warren McGregor, Malcolm Miller, Paul Phenix, Michael Sharpe, Ken Spencer, Kevin Stevenson, and Angus Thomson.

Belgium
Karel Van Hulle.

Canada
John Adams, John Carchrae, Paul Cherry, James Gaa, Gertrude Mulcahy, James Saloman, Doug Thomas, and Edward Waitzer.

Denmark
Stig Enevoldsen.

France
Georges Barthès de Ruyter, Philippe Danjou, Jean-Luc Dumont, Gilbert Gélard, Dominique Ledouble, Jacques Manardo, and Jean-Claude Scheid.

Germany
Herbert Biener, Hans Havermann, Heinz Kleekämper, Liesel Knorr, Peter Marks, Bernd-Joachim Menn, Louis Perridon, and Albrecht Ruppel.

Italy
Giancarlo Tomasin.

Japan
Yukio Fujita, Kazuo Hiramatsu, Atsushi Kato, Noriaki Kinoshita, Seigo Nakajima, Etsuo Sawa, Kiichiro Tobari, Tadaaki Tokunaga, Tatsumi Yamada, and Shozo Yamazaki.

Mexico
Jorge Barajas, Rafael Gómez Eng, Jesús Hoyos, Luis Moirón, and Leopoldo Romero.

Netherlands
Gijs Bak, Hans Burggraaff, Frans Graafstal, Johan van Helleman, Jan Klaassen, Herman Marseille, Jules Muis, Aad Tempelaar, Jan Schoonderbeek, and Ruud Vergoossen.

Norway
Harald Brandsås and Erik Mamelund.

South Africa
Doug Brooking, Rick Cottrell, Jock Porteous, Monica Singer, Ian Somerville, Erna Swart, Graham Terry, Warwick Thorby, and Peter Wilmot.

Sweden
Sigvard Heurlin and Rolf Rundfelt.

Switzerland
Harry Schmid.

United Kingdom
Randolph Andersen, John Barrass, David Cairns, Sir Bryan Carsberg, Peter Clark, Allan Cook, David Damant, Howard Davies, Gavin Fryer, Sir John Grenside, Frank Harding, David Hobson, John Hough, Jeffrey Knight, Christopher Nobes, Geoffrey Mitchell, Sir Douglas Morpeth, Michael Renshall, Richard Simmons, Christopher Stronge, David Swanney, Richard Thorpe, Sir David Tweedie, John Williams, and Allister Wilson.

United States
Michael Alexander, Dennis Beresford, Richard Breeden, Anthony Cope, James Copeland, Edmund Coulson, Michael Crooch, Stephen Eccles, Edward Greene, Sara Hanks, Trevor Harris, John Hegarty, Edmund Jenkins, Thomas Jones, Sandra Kinsey, Susan Koski-Grafer, Marisa Lago, James Leisenring, Arthur Levitt, Patricia McConnell, Michael Mann, Robert L. May, Eugene Minahan, Gerhard Mueller, Wallace Olson, Paul Pacter, Irving Pollack, Linda Quinn, Barry Robbins, Paul Rosenfield, David Ruder, Walter Schuetze, Robert Sempier, Willis Smith, Michael Sutton, Mary Tokar, Lynn Turner, Ralph Walters, and Arthur Wyatt.

APPENDIX 7
Use of, and References to, Unpublished Sources

IASC Archive

The IASC archive, held at the offices of the International Accounting Standards Board, London, has been the main archival source for this study. At the time of our research, the archive was not indexed. A small number of older files were numbered according to a filing system that has long been discontinued. These numbers have not been used. In general, we have identified the location of documents by including a 'file' name, which is normally the name indicated on the folder, binder or box in which the documents are contained. In cases where documents have been preserved in electronic format only, the file name indicates the main folder for the project or organizational unit within the IASC, with the note '(electronic)'.

Agenda papers of the IASC board were consecutively numbered from 1 upwards for each meeting. These papers are referred to as AP 3/1986 paper 5, meaning agenda paper 5 for the meeting of March 1986.

Other Archives

The main other archives consulted are:

ICAS   Archive of the Institute of Chartered Accountants of Scotland, held at ICAS's offices, Edinburgh.
          References are limited to Council minutes and agenda papers which are referred to by date and (consecutive) minute number.

NIVRA   Archive of the Nederlands Instituut van Registeraccountants, held at the Nationaal Archief, The Hague, and at NIVRA's offices, Amsterdam.
          The location of documents is identified either by the inventory number of the materials deposited in The Hague, or (for more recent documents held in Amsterdam) by their file name.

Authors' Collections

Documents referred to as in the authors' collections consist mainly of:

— Written communications to the authors by principals in the IASC history, written in response to specific queries by the authors.

— Copies of unpublished documents such as letters, memoranda, speeches etc. supplied to the authors by various parties. The originals of these documents typically are held in collections that are not accessible to the public and/or for which no specific archival references can be given. In such cases, we indicate the nature of the document and the party by which the document was supplied.

Notes

NOTES TO CHAPTER 2

1. John H. Dunning, 'Capital Movements in the Twentieth Century', in John H. Dunning (editor), *Studies in International Investment* (London: George Allen & Unwin Ltd, 1970), 16–48.
2. Jean-Jacques Servan-Schreiber, *Le défi americain* (Paris: Denoël, 1967); the English translation was published as *The American Challenge* (New York: Atheneum, 1968). See also 'Companies Outgrow Countries', *The Economist*, October 1964.
3. John H. Dunning, 'Transatlantic Foreign Direct Investment and the European Economic Community', in John H. Dunning (editor), *The Globalization of Business: The Challenge of the 1990s* (London: Routledge, 1993), 167–89.
4. Throughout this book, we use 'Germany' and 'German' to refer to the German Federal Republic, both before and after reunification with the German Democratic Republic.
5. See Peter Walton (editor), *European Financial Reporting: A History* (London: Academic Press, 1994).
6. 'U.E.C.—*Union Européenne des Experts Comptables, Economiques et Financiers*', *The Accountant*, 149/4628 (31 August 1963), 246–8; see also E. H. Victor McDougall, 'Regional Accountancy Bodies', in W. John Brennan (editor), *The Internationalization of the Accountancy Profession* (Toronto: Canadian Institute of Chartered Accountants, 1979).
7. See Juan R. Herrera, 'La Asociación Interamericana de Contabilidad', in Jorge Tua Pereda (coordinator), *La Contabilidad en Iberoamérica* (Madrid: Instituto de Contabilidad y Auditoría de Cuentas, Ministerio de Economía y Hacienda, 1989), 17–32. Also see Lyle E. Jacobsen, 'Multinational Accounting: Research Priorities for the Eighties—Latin America', in Frederick D. S. Choi (editor), *Multinational Accounting: A Research Framework for the Eighties* (Ann Arbor, MI: UMI Research Press, 1981), 230–1.
8. Frederick D. S. Choi and Gerhard G. Mueller, *An Introduction to Multinational Accounting* (Englewood Cliffs, NJ: Prentice-Hall, 1978), 171.
9. Khalid Amin Abdulla and Donald L. Kyle, 'Conferences of Asian and Pacific Accountants', *The Australian Accountant*, 43/4 (May 1973), 235. At the second conference, held in 1960, Clifford V. Andersen, the executive director of the Australian Society of Accountants, issued a similar plea.
10. *Proceedings of the Seventh International Congress of Accountants 1957* (Amsterdam: Seventh International Congress of Accountants 1957, no year), 69.
11. Jacob Kraayenhof, 'International Challenges for Accounting', *The Journal of Accountancy*, 109/1 (January 1960), 34–8.
12. Kraayenhof, 'International Challenges for Accounting', 37.
13. Kraayenhof, 'International Challenges for Accounting', 38.
14. Memo from Gerhard G. Mueller to the authors, dated 23 July 2003.
15. Interview with Robert L. May (during the 1960s an Arthur Andersen & Co. partner and an active member of the AICPA's committee on international relations), 20 June 2003.

16. John L. Carey (editor), *The Accounting Profession: Where Is It Headed?* (New York: American Institute of Certified Public Accountants, 1962).
17. *Proceedings, Eighth International Congress of Accountants* (New York: American Institute of Certified Public Accountants, 1963), 20.
18. *Proceedings, Eighth International Congress of Accountants*, 21.
19. *Proceedings, Eighth International Congress of Accountants*, 27.
20. *Proceedings, Eighth International Congress of Accountants*, 52.
21. Alvin R. Jennings, 'International Standards of Accounting and Auditing', *The Journal of Accountancy*, 114/3 (September 1962), 36–42.
22. 'The Need for International Standards in Accounting', editorial, *The Canadian Chartered Accountant*, 83/2 (August 1963), 83.
23. John L. Carey, *The Rise of the Accounting Profession: To Responsibility and Authority 1937–1969* (New York: AICPA, 1970), 370.
24. *Professional Accounting in 25 Countries* ([New York:] American Institute of Certified Public Accountants, 1964), vii. See also James J. Mahon, 'Some Observations on World Accounting', *The Journal of Accountancy*, 119/1 (January 1965), 33–7.
25. *Professional Accounting in 25 Countries*, vii.
26. *Professional Accounting in 25 Countries*, vii–viii.
27. This represented a major advance, in terms of international awareness, beyond the book *The Accounting Profession: Where Is It Headed?*, published three years earlier, which was also an outgrowth of the committee's deliberations.
28. John L. Carey, *The CPA Plans for the Future* (New York: American Institute of Certified Public Accountants, 1965), 103.
29. See *The Professional School and World Affairs* (Albuquerque: University of New Mexico Press, 1967/68), 41–51.
30. See the articles in Part One of Kenneth B. Berg, Gerhard G. Mueller, and Lauren M. Walker (editors), *Readings in International Accounting* (Boston: Houghton Mifflin Company, 1969).
31. This was the first in a series of quinquennial international conferences on accounting education that have been held in conjunction with international congresses of accountants.
32. They were entitled *Accounting Practices in...* and were published in a Series in Accounting by the College of Business Administration, University of Washington.
33. In 1911, Henry Rand Hatfield was the first US accounting academic to present a paper on comparative accounting practices and norms, although it was not published until well after his death. See 'Some Variations in Accounting Practice in England, France, Germany and the United States', *Journal of Accounting Research*, 4/2 (Autumn 1966), 169–82.
34. Gerhard G. Mueller, *International Accounting* (New York: Macmillan, 1967).
35. See Thomas R. Dyckman and Stephen A. Zeff, 'Two Decades of the *Journal of Accounting Research*', *Journal of Accounting Research*, 22/1 (Spring 1984), 225–97.
36. See the chapters on Great Britain, the United States, and Canada in Stephen A. Zeff, *Forging Accounting Principles in Five Countries* (Champaign, IL: Stipes Publishing Co., 1972).
37. For a review of the 1959 volume in the CICA's series, see Thomas F. Keller, 'Financial Reporting in Canada' (book review), *The Accounting Review*, 35/3 (July 1960), 570.

38. See Stephen A. Zeff, *Forging Accounting Principles in Australia* (Melbourne: Australian Society of Accountants, 1973), and Stephen A. Zeff, *Forging Accounting Principles in New Zealand* (Wellington: Victoria University Press, 1979).
39. Peter Standish, *The French Plan Comptable: Explanation and Translation* (Paris: Expert Comptable Média, 1997), chapter 2.
40. Dieter Ordelheide and Dieter Pfaff, *European Financial Reporting: Germany* (London: Routledge, 1994), 85–93.
41. Stephen A. Zeff, Frans van der Wel, and Kees Camfferman, *Company Financial Reporting: A Historical and Comparative Study of the Dutch Regulatory Process* (Amsterdam: North-Holland, 1992), chapters 3 and 4.
42. Zeff, *Forging Accounting Principles in Five Countries*, 26–7.
43. Geoffrey Holmes, 'Sir Henry Benson Moves on from Coopers', *Accountancy*, 86/981 (May 1975), 47.
44. Obituary, *The Times*, 7 March 1995, 19.
45. In November 1968, the editor of *The Accountant* wrote, 'There is no doubt that the gentle wind of change that commenced to blow through the Institute a few years ago has developed into a strong refreshing breeze.' 'More Publicity for Chartered Accountants', *The Accountant*, 159/4902 (30 November 1968), 731. Also see Zeff, *Forging Accounting Principles in Five Countries*, 27–32.
46. Zeff, *Forging Accounting Principles in Five Countries*, 30.
47. Chartered accountants practicing in Northern Ireland, which is part of the United Kingdom, were then, as now, required to be members of the Institute of Chartered Accountants in Ireland, based in Dublin.
48. *Annual Conference Papers 1966* (Toronto: Canadian Institute of Chartered Accountants, 1966), 14.
49. Henry Benson, 'Establishing Standards through a Voluntary Professional Process across National Boundaries', in John C. Burton (editor), *The International World of Accounting, Challenges and Opportunities* (Reston, VA: Council of Arthur Young Professors, 1981), 29.
50. Interview with Doug Thomas (the CICA's executive director and director of research in 1966, who conversed with Trueblood and Wilson in Regina and attended the AICPA annual meeting in Boston), 18 February 2003. This coolness is perhaps borne out by the omission of any reference to the Study Group in Wilson's presidential address to CICA members at the annual conference in September 1967. *Annual Conference Papers, 1967* (Toronto: Canadian Institute of Chartered Accountants, 1967), 10–14. Nor was there a mention of the Study Group in the 1967 report of the AICPA Council to the Institute's membership in September 1967. See *Strengthening the Professional Practice of Certified Public Accountants* (New York: American Institute of Certified Public Accountants, 1967).
51. Benson, 'Establishing Standards', 40.
52. *Accounting and Auditing Approaches to Inventories in Three Nations* (Accountants International Study Group, 1968), Foreword.
53. 'International Study Group Formed', *The Accountant*, 156/4806 (28 January 1967), 125.
54. 'International Study Group Begins Work', *The Accountant*, 156/4819 (29 April 1967), 571; John G. Arthur, 'International Study Group', *World*, 3/2 (Spring 1969), 59.
55. Henry Benson, 'The Future Role of the Accountant in Practice', *The Accountant*, 139/4373 (11 October 1958), 434.

56. Henry Benson, 'The Story of International Accounting Standards', *Accountancy*, 87/995 (July 1976), 34.
57. The first and fourth motivations were suggested in the interview with Doug Thomas, 18 February 2003, and in a communication from Thomas to the authors, dated 29 August 2003. Benson's strong interest in a project on the audit of inventories has been confirmed in an interview with Michael Renshall (secretary in charge of drafting the inventories booklet, on behalf of the ICAEW), 28 April 2003, and 'Interview, Bob Rennie', *Accountancy Age*, 4/7 (16 February 1973), 14. Rennie, a Canadian partner in Touche Ross & Co., was chairman of the Study Group in 1972–3.
58. Letter from J. M. Renshall, under-secretary of the ICAEW, dated 10 January 1968, ICAS archive, AISG file, no. 1369.
59. Appendix I to the minutes for the 13th plenary session of the Accountants International Study Group, 18–19 June 1973, ICAS archive, AISG file, no. 1369H.
60. *Accounting and Auditing Approaches to Inventories in Three Nations* (1968), paragraph 100.
61. 'Auditors' Attendance at Stock-taking', *The Accountant*, 159/4882 (13 July 1968), 36–8. The executive vice-president of the AICPA observed that the guidance statement 'takes a strong position on the necessity for auditors to physically inspect inventories, thus bringing English practice into line with North American standards'. Leonard M. Savoie, 'International Dimensions of Accounting', *The International Journal of Accounting Education and Research*, 5/1 (Fall 1969), 83.
62. For a description of the working procedures, see R. Douglas Thomas, 'The Accountants International Study Group—The First Three Years', *The International Journal of Accounting Education and Research*, 6/1 (Fall 1970), 60–3.
63. Thomas, 'The Accountants International Study Group', 64.
64. Among the subjects requiring the attention of the ICAEW's staff between 1969 and 1974 were a fruitless effort to integrate the UK accountancy bodies, the launch of the UK accounting standards programme, its heightened activities in the UEC, the consequences of the UK's accession to the EEC, and the start of the IASC. On 26 January 1973, the president of the ICAS said at Council that 'He viewed with some concern [the] signs of overstrain on the English Institute's organisation.' ICAS Council, Minute 5030.
65. This was the project on foreign currency translation. See note from Victor McDougall to Peter McMonnies, dated 10 May 1972, ICAS archive, AISG file, no. 1369E.
66. Memorandum from Alister Mason (CICA Research Studies Director from 1973 to 1975) to the authors, dated 17 August 2003. Mason was the draftsman for three of the booklets published in 1975. He wrote that the pipeline of projects was 'full to overflowing' when he came on as director in 1973.
67. Memorandum from Alister Mason to the authors, dated 17 August 2003.
68. Interview with A. F. Tempelaar (1967–8 president of the NIVRA), 21 January 2003.
69. Benson, 'The Story of International Accounting Standards', 36.
70. Minutes of the Third Plenary Meeting of AISG, London 10–11 June 1968, paragraph 5, ICAS archive, AISG file, no. 1369. Also see Thomas, 'The Accountants International Study Group—The First Three Years', 64.
71. Benson, 'The Story of International Accounting Standards', 36.
72. 'Auditors' Reporting Standards', *The Accountant*, 160/4930 (14 June 1969), 830.

73. Gerhard G. Mueller, book review, *The Accounting Review*, 51/3 (July 1976), 692. The draftsman for this booklet was Alister Mason.
74. Letter from J. M. Renshall to members of the Study Group, dated 12 May 1970, ICAS archive, AISG file, no. 1369A.
75. Note by G. D. H. Dewar on AISG meeting of 2–4 December 1973, ICAS archive, AISG file, no. 1369H.
76. The CICA used the Study Group's booklets in setting its accounting and auditing standard-setting agendas. Communication from William W. Buchanan (retired senior vice-president, studies & standards for the CICA) to the authors, dated 1 July 2003.
77. John L. Carey, *The CPA Plans for the Future*, 103–4. Carey's reference may have been to a proposal in a recent article by Washington SyCip, a leading practitioner in the Philippines, who had become one of numerous consultants to the Institute's committee on long-range objectives: 'Auditors in a Developing Economy', *The Journal of Accountancy*, 116/1 (July 1963), 46–8.
78. *9e Congrès international de Comptabilité* (Paris: Comité de Direction du 9e Congrès International de Comptabilité, 1967), 126, 128.
79. J. W. de Koning, 'Tussen Place d'Etoile en Place de la Concorde, Het negende internationale accountantscongres Parijs, 6 tot 12 september 1967', *De Accountant*, 74/8 (January 1968), 437.
80. J. W. Schoonderbeek and P. E. de Hen, *Getuigen van de geschiedenis van het Nederlandse accountantsberoep* (Assen: Van Gorcum, 1995), 80; interview with A. F. Tempelaar, 21 January 2003.
81. Interview with A. F. Tempelaar, 3 April 2003.
82. 'The World of Accounting Beyond our Shores', paper by Robert L. May on behalf of AICPA Committee on Overseas Relations for Council of AICPA, 4 October 1969, ICAS archive, AISG file, 1369A.
83. Wallace E. Olson, *The Accounting Profession, Years of Trial: 1969–1980* (New York: AICPA, 1982), 224.
84. Olson, *The Accounting Profession*, 224; interview with A. F. Tempelaar, 3 April 2003.
85. *Final Report to Participating Bodies at International Congresses of Accountants* (n.p., International Working Party to be renamed International Co-ordinating Committee for the Accountancy Profession, December 1971), paragraph 21.
86. Mueller, *International Accounting*, 123.
87. Interview with Gerhard G. Mueller, 22 July 2003.
88. Paul Rutteman, 'Contribution by the Groupe d'Études des Experts Comptables to Harmonization of Accounting Standards in Europe', in *Harmonization of Accounting Standards* (Paris: Organisation for Economic Co-operation and Development, 1986), 83; Louis Perridon, 'Die berufliche Zusammenarbeit in Europa—Einige Gedanken zum fünfundzwanzigjährigen Bestehen der UEC', *Journal UEC*, 11/4 (October 1976), 222.
89. McDougall, 'Regional Accountancy Bodies', 18.
90. Interview with Louis Perridon (then UEC secretary-general), 19 March 2003.
91. W. Elmendorff. 'Geleitwort des Präsidenten.' *La Vie de l'UEC*, December 1963, 4; P. E. de Hen, J. G. Berendsen, and J. W. Schoonderbeek, *Hoofdstukken uit de geschiedenis van het Nederlandse accountantsberoep* (Assen: Van Gorcum, 1995), 19.
92. Louis Perridon, 'Professional Co-operation in Europe—Some Reflections on the Occasion of the Silver Jubilee of U.E.C.' *Journal UEC*, 11/4 (October 1976), 263.
93. 'News from the UEC,' *Journal UEC*, 1/1 (1966), 72.

94. Wilhelm Elmendorff, 'Coordination of the Legal Accounting Requirements in the Various Countries of the European Economic Community', *Journal UEC*, 2/4 (October 1971), 238.
95. 'Six and Three Become One', *The Economist*, 21 July 1973.
96. Reinhard Goerdeler, ' "A True and Fair View—or Compliance with the Law and the Company Statutes" ', *Die Wirtschaftsprüfung*, 26/19 (1 October 1973), 521.
97. Rudolf Niehus, 'Zur Entwicklung von Grundsätzen ordnungsmäßiger Bilanzierung in den Vereinigten Staten und in England', *Die Wirtschaftsprüfung*, 25/16 (15 August 1973), 442.
98. As suggested by Olson, *The Accounting Profession*, 224.
99. Schoonderbeek and de Hen, *Getuigen*, 53; interview with Louis Perridon, 19 March 2003.
100. Interview with Louis Perridon, 19 March 2003; 'Terugblik internationale contacten', memo from A. F. Tempelaar to Hans Burggraaff, dated 26 January 1977, NIVRA archive, 481, 62–8.
101. Henry Benson, 'Harmonization of Accountancy Practice', *The Accountant*, 167/5113 (14 December, 1972), 758.
102. A. F. Tempelaar, 'Harmonization of Accounting Practice', *The Accountant*, 168/5121 (8 February 1973), 176.
103. 'The UK Profession and Europe', editorial, *The Accountant*, 169/5155 (4 October 1973), 425.
104. Edward Stamp, 'The EEC and European Accounting Standards: A Straitjacket or a Spur?' *Accountancy*, 83/957 (May 1973), 10.
105. A. F. Tempelaar, 'Reorganisation of the U.E.C', *Journal UEC*, 7/2 (April 1972), 89.
106. NIVRA board (dagelijks bestuur), minutes of 23 November 1972, NIVRA archive, no. 67.
107. Interviews with A. F. Tempelaar, 3 April 2003, and with Louis Perridon, 19 March 2003. In November 1971, ICAS Secretary Victor McDougall advised the ICAS Council that 'UEC is...going through a very difficult phase, and some whose opinions are worthy of respect consider it to be dying.' E. H. Victor McDougall, 'The Accountancy Profession in Europe, Some Thoughts on the Occasion of the United Kingdom's Adherence to the Treaty of Rome', agenda paper for ICAS Council meeting of 30 November 1971, minute 4749, ICAS archive.

NOTES TO CHAPTER 3

1. LeRoy Layton, 'Beyond the Tenth International Congress', *The Australian Accountant*, December 1972, 413.
2. 'The Tenth International Congress of Accountants: Report by the President and Secretary of the Scottish Institute', dated 12 November 1972, agenda paper for ICAS Council, meeting of 17 November 1972, ICAS archive.
3. Interview with John P. Hough, 4 October 2003.
4. Published accounts of this meeting can be found in R. D. Thomas, 'The Closer We Get the Better We'll Look', *The Australian Accountant*, 46/7 (August 1976), 401 and Wallace E. Olson, *The Accounting Profession, Years of Trial: 1969–1980* (New York: American Institute of Certified Public Accountants, 1982), 226–7. Douglas Morpeth has asserted that the idea of convening the meeting occurred to him during the congress, while listening to Benson's presentation of the final report of the

International Working Party. According to Morpeth, he then suggested to Benson to call a meeting on the spot (Peter Walton, 'It All Started with a Phone Call', *World Accounting Report*, October 2003, 12; interview with Sir Douglas Morpeth, 28 April 2003). This view of events is further elaborated in Claude Bocqueraz and Peter Walton, 'Creating a Supranational Institution: The Role of the Individual and the Mood of the Times', *Accounting History*, 11/3 (2006), 271–88. Morpeth's recollection is not borne out by information from other interviewees who remember that the meeting was convened in advance by Henry Benson. Interviews with Doug Thomas and Gert Mulcahy, 18 February 2003, and with John P. Hough (secretary of the ICAEW), 4 October 2003. In this interview, Hough also recalled that there were as many as three of these informal meetings in Sydney 'to thrash out' the details of the proposal on international accounting standards. These multiple meetings have not been confirmed by other interviewees. In their report on the congress to the ICAS Council, Alec Mackenzie and Victor McDougall mentioned a single meeting, but added that this issue 'occupied much time and thought in Sydney'. 'The Tenth International Congress of Accountants: Report by the President and Secretary of the Scottish Institute', dated 12 November 1972, agenda paper for ICAS Council, meeting of 17 November 1972, ICAS archive.

5. Olson, *The Accounting Profession*, 227 and Thomas, 'The Closer We Get', 401, suggest that it was agreed at this meeting to set up a new body alongside the AISG. However, the agenda for the December 1972 London meeting summarized the results of the Sydney meeting in terms of reorganizing the AISG. 'Basic Accounting Standards—An Urgent International Need', version dated 21 November 1972, IASC archive, board minutes file.

6. Henry Benson, *Accounting for Life* (London: Kogan Page, 1989), 106.

7. 'Basic Accounting Standards—An Urgent International Need', version dated 4 December 1972, IASC archive, board minutes file.

8. The Association of Certified Accountants, the Institute of Cost and Management Accountants, and the Institute of Municipal Treasurers and Accountants. See 'Minutes of the Meeting of the Presidents of UK and Republic of Ireland Accountancy Bodies at Chartered Accountants' Hall on Friday 2nd February, 1973', IASC archive, miscellaneous files relating to founding of IASC.

9. Derek Matthews and Jim Prie, *The Auditors Talk: An Oral History of a Profession from the 1920s to the Present Day* (New York: Garland Publishing, 2000), 318. Wallace Olson (interview, 13 March 2003) surmised that the initiative for setting up the IASC came from Morpeth. On the other hand, John Hepworth (interview, 25 May 2003), Doug Thomas (interview, 18 February 2003), and John Hough (interview, 4 October 2003) have emphasized how much the IASC was seen as Benson's initiative from the start.

10. Cited in 'New Effort to Defuse Accountancy Minefield', *Birmingham Post*, 2 July 1973.

11. 'Basic Accounting Standards—An Urgent International Need', version dated 4 December 1972, IASC archive, board minutes file. See also Benson, *Accounting for Life*, 106; 'Benson Unbends on the Standards in His Life', interview with David Simpson, *Accountancy Age*, 6/3 (17 January 1975), 12–13. For similar views, see Thomas, 'The Closer We Get', 401.

12. Stephen A. Zeff, *Forging Accounting Principles in Five Countries: A History and an Analysis of Trends* (Champaign, IL: Stipes Publishing Co., 1972), 27–50.

13. This point was allegedly raised by the ICAEW in contacts with the NIVRA. Minutes Algemeen Bestuur, 28 March 1973, NIVRA archive, no. 68.

14. In particular see Anthony G. Hopwood, 'Some Reflections on "The Harmonization of Accounting Within the EU" ', *The European Accounting Review*, 3/2 (1994), 243–4. This view of the IASC's origins was also expressed by Karel Van Hulle, in Georges Timmerman, 'Zand in het Europese raderwerk' [interview with Karel Van Hulle], *Accountancy & Bedrijfskunde*, 9/4 (May 1989), 29.
15. Wallace Olson (interview, 13 March 2003) inferred from statements by John Hough (ICAEW secretary) that this was the prominent motive behind the formation of the IASC. See also Olson, *The Accounting Profession*, 226. Robert Sempier (interview, 19 April 2003) has asserted that the IASC was 'a British effort to cut [the French and the Germans] off at the pass'. See also Defliese's observation that 'The IASC ... offered a way to inject authoritative accounting thought into the EEC deliberations.' Philip L. Defliese, 'British Standards in a World Setting', in Sir Ronald Leach and Edward Stamp (editors), *British Accounting Standards: The First 10 Years* (Cambridge: Woodhead-Faulkner, 1981), 111. Joseph Cummings has asserted that the EEC's programme of Directives 'probably was the impetus' for the founding of the IASC. *The 4th Ross Institute Seminar in Accounting, International Accounting Standards—The Outlook* (New York: Vincent C. Ross Institute of Accounting Research, 1976), 4. On the other hand, Doug Thomas (interview, 18 February 2003), Dominique Ledouble (interview, 5 June 2003), and A. F. Tempelaar (interview, 21 January 2003) have stated their belief that the EEC was a secondary consideration. It was mentioned as a secondary consideration by Benson himself. Henry Benson, 'Commentaar Sir Henry Benson', in *Stormen rond normen: De jaarrekening in nationaal, regionaal en mondiaal perspectief* (Amsterdam: NIVRA, 1976), 52.
16. The suggestion that concern over the OECD and UN played a role in the initiative to form the IASC was made by Allan Cook in 1981, 'Cook Sets Standards for International Accounts', *Accountancy Age*, 27 November 1981, 14.
17. Interviews with Doug Thomas and Gert Mulcahy, 18 February 2003, and with David Hobson (Benson's partner in Coopers), 29 April 2003.
18. 'Le programme d'harmonisation des principes et méthodes comptables à l'échelon international: la tâche de l'I.A.S.C.', *Revue Française de Comptabilité*, no. 56 (December 1975), 672. A comparable statement by Benson ('My aim is to see a huge dramatic change in the presentation of financial accounts and in their enforcement within general international accountancy by the year 2000') is reported in Simpson, 'Benson unbends', 12.
19. No specific information was available to the authors about the reactions of the Australian and Canadian bodies.
20. Olson, *The Accounting Profession*, 227.
21. Interview with Dominique Ledouble, 5 June 2003.
22. Interview with David Hobson, 29 April 2003.
23. Letter from E. Potthoff and R. Goerdeler to Morpeth, dated 26 February 1973, NIVRA archive, no. 477.
24. Interview with Peter Marks and Albrecht Ruppel, 4 June 2003.
25. Interview with Kiichiro Tobari, 1 July 2004.
26. Interview with Seigo Nakajima, 30 June 2004.
27. Interviews with Jesús Hoyos Roldán (staff observer and board representative 1982–7), 1 March 2004, and with Jorge Barajas Palomo (executive director of the Mexican Institute in the late 1960s and early 1970s and president 1983–4), 2 March 2004. According to Barajas, Julio Freyssinier, the Institute's president, attended the March 1973 meeting in London without prior consultation with his Council.

Although the Council objected strongly to the arrangement by which the budget would be shared equally among the IASC's members, it accepted that membership of the IASC was in keeping with the international status sought by the Institute.

28. *Nederlands Instituut van Registeraccountants: Jaarverslag 1972–73*, 31.
29. NIVRA board (dagelijks bestuur), minutes 7 March 1973, NIVRA archive, no. 68.
30. In the initial drafts, the founding document of the IASC was to consist of a Constitution only. For unknown reasons, this text was split into an 'Agreement' and a 'Constitution' between the 19 March and 28 June 1973 meetings.
31. Olson, *The Accounting Profession*, 226. Independently of the AICPA, Doug Thomas also argued with Benson in favour of Japanese membership (interview with Doug Thomas, 18 February 2003). Morpeth reportedly said that a position for Japan was 'exacted in particular by the U.S.' Note of a meeting between Douglas Morpeth and J. W. Schoonderbeek (president of the NIVRA), dated 20 February 1973, NIVRA archive, no. 489.
32. It was later said that the JICPA 'could not dispatch members to the preliminary meeting in London on 19 March because of the lack of preparation'. Masato Kikuya, 'International Harmonization of Japanese Accounting Standards', *Accounting, Business & Financial History*, 11/3 (November 2001), 351.
33. NIVRA board (dagelijks bestuur), minutes 2 May 1973, NIVRA archive, no. 68.
34. Japan was not proposed as an ICCAP member in the IWP report, but it was invited to join between the Sydney congress and ICCAP's first meeting in April 1973.
35. Henk Volten, report on London meeting of 19 March 1973, NIVRA archive, no. 477; 'Minutes of a Meeting Held at Chartered Accountants' Hall on 19th March 1973', minute 6, IASC archive, board minutes file.
36. Memorandum by J. W. Schoonderbeek on meeting with H. B. Dhondy, dated 13 July 1973, NIVRA archive, no. 477. At the same time, it was reported that the Indian profession was 'somewhat upset' at not being invited to join the IASC, 'Americans Opposed IASC's Birth', *Accountancy Age*, 4/28 (13 July 1973), 1.
37. Strictly speaking, the 1973 Constitution referred to the accountancy bodies as 'signatories' who could send 'members' to the Committee. Since 1977, the bodies were referred to as members who could send 'representatives' to the Board.
38. The Wirtschaftsprüferkammer is the body charged by law with supervising the public accountancy profession. Membership is mandatory for auditors engaged in legal audits. The IdW is a voluntary association representing the interests of the auditing profession.
39. See also 'Americans Opposed IASC's Birth', *Accountancy Age*, 4/28 (13 July 1973), 1.
40. Olson, *The Accounting Profession*, 226.
41. 'Basic Accounting Standards—An Urgent International Need', 21 November 1972, IASC archive, board minutes file.
42. Letter from Michael Chetkovich (AICPA representative on ICCAP) to E. Potthoff (IdW chairman), dated 15 January 1973; letter from Gordon Cowperthwaite (CICA) to IdW, dated 13 February 1973, quoted in letter from E. Potthoff and R. Goerdeler to Douglas Morpeth, dated 26 February 1973; letter from Michael Chetkovich to E. Potthoff, dated 28 February 1973, NIVRA archive, no. 477.
43. Memo by Henk Volten, dated 20 March 1973, NIVRA archive, no. 477; Minutes of NIVRA board (dagelijks bestuur), 28 March 1973, NIVRA archive, no. 68.
44. On 7 March 1973, a meeting was arranged 'late in the evening' after the Presidents' Dinner of the ICAEW. Present were 'among others': Morpeth, Benson, Hough, and Carrel (ICAEW); Mackenzie and McDougall (ICAS); Géniaux and Cordoliani

(Ordre); Potthoff and Dieterich (IdW); Schoonderbeek and Volten (NIVRA). No common position was reached. Memo by Schoonderbeek, dated 11 March 1973, NIVRA archive, no. 477. The minutes of the ICAS Council recorded that the plan of the AICPA to establish an international secretariat 'did not commend itself to (*inter alios*) the Presidents and Vice-Presidents of the three chartered bodies, who had discussed it at a meeting in Ireland on 25 March, and steps were taken with a view to combating it'. ICAS Council, meeting of 30 March 1973, minute 5096.

45. Olson, *Accounting Profession*, 231; memo from Henk Volten to NIVRA board, dated 27 April 1973, NIVRA archive, no. 477; circular letter from Henry Benson to accountancy bodies participating in IASC, dated 7 May 1973, IASC archive, board minutes file.
46. Benson, *Accounting for Life*, 108.
47. 'International Accounting Standards Committee—Constitution', draft dated 4 December 1972, IASC archive, board minutes file.
48. 'Basic Accounting Standards—An Urgent International Need', version dated 14 November 1972, IASC archive, board minutes file.
49. NIVRA board (dagelijks bestuur), minutes of 28 March 1973, NIVRA archive, no. 68.
50. e.g. 'Accountants in 9 Countries Link to Agree on Standards', *Financial Times*, 2 July 1973.
51. Basic Accounting Standards—An Urgent International Need', version dated 4 December 1972, IASC archive, board minutes file.
52. Memo by Henk Volten on meeting of 19 March 1973, London, dated 20 March 1973, NIVRA archive, no. 477.
53. 'Constitution—Proposed Amendments', memo dated 8 June 1973, IASC archive, board minutes file.
54. Letter from P. C. Louwers to J. W. Schoonderbeek dated 15 March 1973, NIVRA archive, no. 489.
55. IASC meeting of 28 June 1973, minute 4.
56. 'Constitution—Proposed Amendments', AP 6/1973, unnumbered paper.
57. 'Minutes of the Meeting Held on 19th March 1973', AP 6/1973 paper 3.
58. IASC meeting of 28 June 1973, minute 4.
59. Henk Volten, notes on a meeting between representatives of ICAEW and NIVRA, dated 20 February 1973, NIVRA archive, no. 489. Letter from Douglas Morpeth to E. Potthoff, dated 6 March 1973, NIVRA archive, no. 477.
60. Memo from Henk Volten to NIVRA board, dated 1 May 1973, NIVRA archive, no. 477.
61. Henry Benson, 'Harmonization of Accountancy Practice', *The Accountant*, 167/5113 (14 December 1972), 757.
62. 'Reflections on a Momentous Event', *Accountancy Age*, 4/2 (12 January 1973), 14–15.
63. 'Morpeth Pleads for Co-operation', *Accountancy Age*, 4/11 (23 March 1973), 32.
64. Cited in 'Historic Agreement', *The Accountant*, 169/5142 (5 July 1973), 2.
65. 'Move Welcomed', *Accountants Weekly*, 6 July 1973.
66. 'Committee Formed to Streamline International Accounting Methods', *The Times*, 2 July 1973.
67. 'New Effort to Defuse Accountancy Minefield', *Birmingham Post*, 2 July 1973.
68. 'Panel Aims to Unify Accounting Methods Across Globe, Sees Strong Effect by 1983', *The Wall Street Journal*, 2 July 1973.
69. 'International Panel Seeks Basic Accounting Standard', *The New York Times*, 2 July 1973.

70. 'International Standards Are Important Must', *Accountancy Age*, 4/27 (6 July 1973), 7.
71. 'Historic Agreement', *The Accountant*, 169/5142 (5 July 1973), 1–3.
72. J. W. Schoonderbeek, 'Op weg naar internationaal aanvaarde normen voor de jaarrekening', *De Accountant*, 80/1 (September 1973), insert. The NIVRA also took the initiative for a publication in the main financial newspaper in the Netherlands, 'Accountants werken aan internationale normen jaarrekening', *Het Financieele Dagblad*, 4–6 August 1973.
73. 'Internationale Zusammenarbeit der Accountants-Organisationen', *Die Wirtschaftsprüfung*, 26/24 (15 December 1973), 673.
74. 'Nine Nations Establish Joint Standards Panel', *Journal of Accountancy*, 136/2 (August 1973), 14–16; 'Nine Countries Form International Accounting Standards Committee', *The CPA*, July–August 1973, 16.
75. 'Création du comité international pour les principes comptables (I.A.S.C.)', *Revue Française de Comptabilité*, no. 33 (December 1973), 418–22; 'An Agreement to Establish an International Accounting Standards Committee', *The Australian Accountant* 43/7 (August 1973).
76. Letter from E. Potthoff and R. Goerdeler to D. Morpeth, dated 26 February 1973, NIVRA archive, no. 477.
77. Memo from Henk Volten to NIVRA management board, dated 1 May 1973, NIVRA archive, no. 477.
78. See International Working Party, *Final Report* (n.p., 1971), 11.
79. ICAEW Overseas Relations Committee, minutes of meeting of 23 January 1973, IASC archive, miscellaneous files relating to founding of IASC.
80. France's Ordre was not a UEC member.
81. Letter from P. C. Louwers to J. W. Schoonderbeek, dated 15 February 1972, NIVRA archive, no. 489.
82. NIVRA board (dagelijks bestuur), minutes of meeting 10 April 1973, NIVRA archive, no. 489.
83. Memo by Henk Volten, dated 19 May 1973, NIVRA archive, no. 477.
84. W. Dieterich, 'Towards Professional Standards in the International Field', *Journal UEC*, 8/4 (October 1973), 249–50; 'Statement on UEC Accounting and Auditing Recommendations', *Journal UEC*, 9/1 (January 1974), 76–7.
85. 'Six and Three Become One', *The Economist*, 21 July 1973; circular letter from Louis Perridon to UEC member bodies, dated 31 August 1973, NIVRA archive, no. 478.
86. Interviews with Louis Perridon (then UEC secretary-general), 19 March 2003, and with Aad Tempelaar (then UEC president), 3 April 2003.
87. Accountants International Study Group, minutes of 12th session, 4–5 December 1972, ICAS archive, AISG file, no. 1369G.
88. Thomas, 'The Closer We Get', 401.
89. Interview with John W. Adams, 29 June 2003. Adams pointed to the stock exchanges, especially the New York Stock Exchange, which were reluctant to support the IASC.
90. ICAS insisted that the Study Group not be disbanded until it was clear that IFAC was going to be established. ICAS Council, 26 November 1976, Minute 6322.
91. Alison Rooper, 'How the Success of AISG Led to Its Death', *Accountancy Age*, 23 September 1977, 9.
92. Alister K. Mason, *The Development of International Financial Reporting Standards*, ICRA Occasional Paper no. 17 (Lancaster: University of Lancaster, ICRA, 1978), 98.

Mason, a staff member of the CICA during the 1970s, was responsible for drafting three of the Study Group's booklets. See also Edward Stamp, 'International Standards to Serve the Public Interest', in W. John Brennan (editor), *The Internationalization of the Accountancy Profession* (Toronto: Canadian Institute of Chartered Accountants, 1979), 118.

93. Joseph P. Cummings, 'The Emergence of International Accounting Standards in the Face of Diverging National Accounting Standards', *Accountants' Journal*, November 1976, 343.

NOTES TO CHAPTER 4

1. For more about Benson, see his entry in David J. Jeremy (editor), *Dictionary of British Biography* (London: Butterworths, 1984), 287–9.
2. IASC meeting of 15–17 July 1974, minute 14(2). Benson's three years as chairman facilitated a staggering of terms of the chairman and the secretary, as Paul Rosenfield, the initial secretary, departed in July 1975.
3. See the obituary in *IASB Insight*, January 2003, 2–3.
4. See the obituary in *IASB Insight*, January 2003, 3.
5. Interview with David Cairns, 8 June 2003.
6. The Mexican delegation was keenly disappointed at the outcome, as it had been assured of voting support for Ortega that, in the end, was not delivered. They believed that the board was an 'Anglo-Saxon' body that was not prepared to have a 'non-Anglo-Saxon' as chairman. This setback is one reason why the Mexican Institute was not more forthcoming when it was negotiating with the IASC for financial relief following the big Mexican devaluation of 1982. Interviews with Jesús Hoyos Roldán, 1 March 2004, and with Jorge Barajas Palomo, 2 March 2004. As it happened, Rolando Ortega died in December 1986, which would have prevented him from completing a term as chairman.
7. The only exception was Harry Levy, in the Australian delegation, who was employed in a company. He came to London with Ron Munro to represent the Australian Society of Accountants at the signing ceremony on 28 June, and he remained to attend the inaugural meeting of the IASC the following day.
8. Tony Kewin, of Australia, was employed in industry, and Seigo Nakajima, of Japan, was an academic.
9. Under the Constitution, the United Kingdom & Ireland were treated as though they were one country. In 1988, Ireland was removed from the name of the delegation, although the delegation continued to represent the Irish Institute. There was always a member of the Scottish Institute in the delegation until 1985, and an ICAEW member served in the delegation continually until 1995. A member of the Irish Institute based in Dublin sat in the delegation from 1985 to 1989. A member of the Chartered Association of Certified Accountants (today the Association of Chartered Certified Accountants) formed part of the delegation from 1991 to 2000.
10. See 'The International Accounting Standards Committee', comment in *Management Accounting*, 55/11 (May 1974), 6; 'Are We Pulling Together?' comment in *Management Accounting* (the United States), 56/12 (June 1975), 6.
11. Interviews with Wallace Olson, 13 March 2003, and with Robert Sempier, 19 April 2003.
12. Interview with Eugene Minahan, 13 January 2004.
13. IASC board meeting of 11–13 March 1980, minute 13(i).

14. The Accounting Principles Board (1959–73) was a senior technical committee of the AICPA. It was succeeded in 1973 by the FASB, which was an independent standard-setting body.
15. With respect to the IASC, SMAC and CGAA agreed to work in conjunction with the CICA in July 1974. They did not formally join the IASC as members until March 1978.
16. Insights into the intricate composition of the Australian delegation come from several sources, but mainly from the interview with John N. Bishop, 28 May 2003. Also see Geoff Burrows, *The Foundation: A History of the Australian Accounting Research Foundation 1966–91* (Caulfield, Vic.: Australian Accounting Research Foundation, 1996), 140.
17. Interview with Peter Marks and Albrecht Ruppel, 4 June 2003.
18. Interview with Jesús Hoyos Roldán, 1 March 2004.
19. IASC board meeting of 5–7 March 1986, minute 1.
20. Letter from John Kirkpatrick to Francisco Alcalá, president of the Instituto Mexicano de Contadores Públicos, dated 7 November 1986, IASC archive, 'Mexico' file. The contributions in arrears were paid in 1987.
21. IASC board meeting of 18–20 October 1977, minute 13.
22. IASC board meeting of 7–9 March 1978, minute 12.
23. IASC board meeting of 14–16 June 1978, minute 14.
24. IASC board meeting of 24–6 November 1982, minute 5(d).
25. Communication from Antonio Castilla (until recently past president of the Colegio de Contadores de Chile) to the authors, dated 21 September 2003.
26. IASC board meeting of 14–16 June 1983, minute 10(a); *IASC News*, 12/4 (June 1983), 5.
27. It has been suggested that there was a dispute from time to time in the Italian profession as to whether the representatives should come from large or small firms. Communication from David Cairns to the authors, dated 22 January 2004.
28. IASC board meeting of 24–7 March 1987, minute 7(iii).
29. Letter from Kirkpatrick to Benson, dated 5 November 1987, IASC archive, 'Kirkpatrick' file.
30. David Cairns's notes of a telephone conversation with Kirkpatrick, dated 17 September 1985, IASC archive, 'Kirkpatrick' file.
31. IASC meeting of 29 June 1973, minute 11.
32. The first associate members approved by the Committee, at its meeting in April 1974, were professional accountancy bodies from Belgium, India, Israel, New Zealand, Pakistan, and Rhodesia (later Zimbabwe).
33. IASC meeting of 14–15 January 1974, minute 10(2). At that meeting, it was reported that the Institute of Chartered Accountants of Trinidad and Tobago asked the IASC 'to reconsider the level of contributions for Associate Membership since a fee of £1,000 would constitute a significant percentage of their budget' (minute 10(1)(c)).
34. Wallace E. Olson, *The Accounting Profession, Years of Trial 1969–1980* (New York: AICPA, 1982), 229.
35. Communication from Richard J. Simmons to the authors, dated 9 December 2003.
36. *IASC News*, 7/5 (September 1979), 2.
37. Memorandum from Hans Burggraaff to the authors, dated 22 April 2004.
38. IASC board meeting of 14–16 June 1983, minute 6(i).
39. *IASC News*, 12/5 (September 1983), 1–2.
40. IASC board meeting of 25–7 June 1985, minute 7(h).

41. Cairns wanted the assistant secretary to be renamed as research manager. He asked Rutherford to accept this re-designation in title, but he declined. Conversation with Brian Rutherford, 5 November 2005.
42. David Cairns, 'The Future Shape of Harmonization: A Reply', *The European Accounting Review*, 6/2 (1997), 321.
43. 'Basic International Accounting Standards', minutes of a meeting held at Chartered Accountants' Hall on 19 March 1973, minute 10, IASC archive, board minutes file.
44. 'Constitution—Proposed Amendments', item 4 for the meeting of 28 June 1973, 7(b), IASC archive, board minutes file.
45. 'Basic International Accounting Standards', minutes of a meeting held in London on 28 June 1973, minute 4 on article 5(b) of the Constitution. Also see IASC meeting of 29 June 1973, minute 4.
46. IASC meeting of 15–16 November 1973, minute 13(9)(c).
47. IASC meeting of 15–17 July 1974, minute 18.
48. Interview with Giancarlo Tomasin, 7 April 2003.
49. Later, this obligation was assumed by the Consultative Committee of Accountancy Bodies (CCAB). In 1986, the CCAB notified the IASC board that 'It had decided to discontinue its subsidy of the rent, rates and service charge of the office premises of IASC with effect from 31 December 1987.' The board 'expressed its appreciation to the United Kingdom and Ireland for providing the subsidy over the last 15 years'. IASC board meeting of 5–7 November 1986, minute 6(iix).
50. Memorandum from Hans Burggraaff to the authors, dated 22 April 2004.
51. Communication from Roy Nash to the authors, dated 1 October 2003.
52. IASC board meeting of 22–5 June 1982, appendix 2, point 5.
53. IASC meeting of 29 June 1973, minute 8(j).
54. IASC meeting of 8–9 April 1974, minutes 7(2) and 9.
55. IASC meeting of 15–17 July 1974, minute 11(3)(c).
56. The lone exception occurred in 1976, when Paul Rutteman, a London partner in Arthur Young, became chairman of the steering committee on leases. At that time, he also was chairing an ASC committee on the same subject. Rutteman never served on the IASC board.
57. 'Report on Activities on Behalf of IASC for the Year Ended 30 June 1983', *1983 Annual Report* of the International Federation of Accountants, 11.
58. *International Accounting Standards*, the full texts of all International Accounting Standards extant at 1 September 1987 (London: The Institute of Chartered Accountants in England and Wales, [1987]).
59. David Cairns, *Applying International Accounting Standards* (London: Butterworths, second edition 1999), 32.
60. 'IASC Publishes its First Annual Report', *IASC News*, 16/5 (October 1987), 6.
61. IASC meeting of 15–16 November 1973, minute 12(a).
62. IASC board meeting of 27–8 February and 1 March 1979, minute 10(4).
63. IASC board meeting of 24–7 March 1981, minute 12(1). An enumeration of the series of guests invited by successive chairmen between 1983 and 1986 is given in Section 6.21.
64. These amounts were the gross expenditure, before drawing on reserves, on annual donations from charitable foundations, or on the fees paid by non-board members.
65. IASC meeting of 29 June 1973, minute 7, and IASC meeting of 8–9 April 1974, minutes 12(1) and 12(6)(d); the £7,000 grant from the Leverhulme Trust was the

first of three annual installments, and it was doubtless engineered by Benson, whose accounting firm had long been the auditors of Unilever Ltd. IASC meeting of 5–6 November 1974, minute 15(3); IASC meeting of 15–17 July 1974, minutes 10(3), 11(2), and 12(1), (3).
66. IASC meeting of 15–17 July 1974, minute 8(2).
67. IASC meeting of 15–17 July 1974, minute 9.
68. For the first time, the board held four-day meetings in June 1980 and in March and June 1981.
69. Under the 1973 Constitution, the costs of associate members serving on steering committees were not reimbursed at all.
70. *The Making of Accounting Standards: Report of the Review Committee under the Chairmanship of Sir Ron Dearing CB* (London: The Institute of Chartered Accountants in England and Wales, 1988), 40.
71. *The Making of Accounting Standards*, 40.
72. *Annual Report 1986/1987*, The Canadian Institute of Chartered Accountants, 22. To find the gross budgeted expenditure of Can$745,000, the Can$17,000 contribution from Financial Executives Institute Canada was added to the line item, Can$728,000.
73. *Establishing Standards for Financial Reporting*, Annual Report 1987 of the FAF, FASB, and GASB, 8.
74. For the entire list, see *International Accounting Standards Committee: Objectives and Procedures*, appendix 5.
75. On more than one occasion, members of the board raised the question whether the IASC could be accorded charitable status so that it could attract more donations from the private sector. In 1984, a reply to an enquiry made of the UK Charity Commission led the board to conclude 'The application should not be pursued further at the present time.' IASC board meeting of 17–19 October 1984, minute 6(g).
76. IASC meeting of 15–17 July 1974, minutes 15(4) and (5).
77. IASC meeting of 15–16 January 1975, minute 6(2).
78. *IASC News*, 4/7 (24 November 1976), 2–3; *IASC News*, 5/2 (18 March 1977), 4; IASC board meeting of 14–16 June 1978, minute 9(2)(b).
79. IASC meeting of 15–17 July 1974, minute 14.
80. The following extracts from the committee's recommendations were reported in minute 9 from the IASC meeting of 8–10 October 1975.
81. IASC meeting of 1–3 March 1977, minute 7(2).
82. IASC board meeting of 18–20 October 1977, minute 11.
83. Communication from David Cairns to the authors, dated 22 January 2004.
84. IASC board meeting of 7–9 March 1978, minute 10.
85. IASC board meeting of 18–20 October 1977, minute 11(b).
86. In 1977, Grenside succeeded Sir Ronald Leach as senior partner of Peat, Marwick, Mitchell & Co. Grenside sat on the ICAEW's Council from 1966 to 1983, an unusually long period.
87. IASC board meeting of 23–6 June 1981, minute 11.
88. IASC board meeting of 24–7 June 1980, minute 10; interview with Allan V. C. Cook, 30 April 2003. David Cairns has written, 'These people did not want to be listed as members as such because their views could not bind the members of their respective organizations. This was, of course, true of everybody else in the Consultative Group, but it was a more sensitive issue for inter-governmental organizations.' Communication from David Cairns to the authors, dated 22 January 2004.

89. For reports on the first meeting, see *IASC News*, 10/6 (October 1981), 1–2; 'Active IASC Convenes Meeting of Consultative Group', *World Accounting Report*, November 1981, 8.
90. Interview with Allan V. C. Cook, 30 April 2003.
91. Stephen Elliott, 'IASC Sets Sights on "Spirit of Partnership"', *The Accountants' Journal*, 61 (December 1982), 440.
92. Interview with Allan V. C. Cook, 30 April 2003. See also Susan Baker, 'Growing Prestige of the IAS Setters', *Certified Accountant* (England), May 1986, 10–11.
93. The IASC/IFAC Mutual Commitments pact, the revised IASC Agreement and Constitution, and the revised 'Preface to International Accounting Standards' were reproduced in the brochure *International Accounting Standards Committee: Objectives and Procedures*. It succeeded *The Work and Purpose of the International Accounting Standards Committee* (London: IASC, September 1975).
94. Memorandum from Hans Burggraaff to the authors, dated 22 April 2004.
95. Christopher Nobes, 'Is the IASC Successful?' *The Accountant*, 183 (21 August 1985), 20.
96. IASC board meeting of 24–6 November 1982, minute 5(e)(1). Kirkpatrick's selection probably signified that Elliott anticipated his election as the next chairman-designate.
97. *1983 Annual Report* of the International Federation of Accountants, 12.

NOTES TO CHAPTER 5

1. IASC meeting of 29 June 1973, minute 8.
2. Communication to the authors from David Cairns, dated 16 January 2004. The board minutes report the discussions on individual projects as if they were uninterrupted, and therefore do not necessarily represent the actual order of the meetings.
3. AP 6/1981 paper 13.
4. IASC board meeting of 7–9 March 1978, minute 7(2). See also *IASC News*, 6/4 (July 1978), 4.
5. Communication from David Cairns to the authors, dated 26 January 2004. Cairns estimated that towards the end of the 1980s several hundreds of people had access to the IASC's agenda papers.
6. The information on steering committees given here is mainly based on the IASC board minutes, references in board agenda papers, and, for later periods, IASC annual reports. In addition, information from interviewees and from miscellaneous archival sources has been used for corrections and additions.
7. IASC board meeting of 24–7 June 1980, minute 9(d).
8. Early in 1984, the joint membership of the IASC and the International Federation of Accountants (IFAC) was reported to consist of 88 member bodies from 65 countries. *IASC News,* 13/1 (February 1984). Of these countries nine or ten would be founder member countries, depending on whether Ireland would be classified as a separate country.
9. Interview with Allan Cook, 30 April 2003, and with Hans Burggraaff, 24 May 2004.
10. Appendix A (dated 14 November 1972) to 'Basic Accounting Standards—An Urgent International Need', version dated 21 November 1972, IASC archive, board minutes file.
11. Interview with Sir Douglas Morpeth, 28 April 2003.

12. As shown by a letter from Dr. Kenntemich (of the IdW) to Philip Carrel (of the ICAEW), dated 30 May 1973, IASC archive, IAS 2 documentation file. The four subjects were disclosure of accounting policies, the minimum information to be included in published accounts, consolidated accounts, and minimum audit requirements and the form and contents of audit reports.
13. The other members of the committee were Robert Mazars (France) and Pieter Louwers (the Netherlands).
14. Joe Cummings wrote that IAS 1 was 'very similar to Accounting Principles Board Opinion No. 22'. Joseph Cummings, 'The International Accounting Standards Committee: Current and Future Developments', *International Journal of Accounting Education and Research,* 11/1 (Fall 1975), 32.
15. 'International Accounting Standard 1—Note by the Chairman', AP 11/1973, unnumbered paper.
16. Interview with Richard J. Simmons, 25 September 2003. See also Henry Benson, *Accounting for Life,* 86–7.
17. The influence of Louwers is mentioned by Henk Volten, 'IASC en NIVRA', *De Accountant,* 82/10 (June 1976), 577–8. See also P. Sanders, G. L. Groeneveld, and R. Burgert, *De jaarrekening nieuwe stijl* (Alphen aan den Rijn: Samsom, 1975), 123–4.
18. For the French amendments see AP 11/1973 paper 4. It was reported in 1980 that 'it is still not yet general practice for comparative figures to be given in the accounts' in France. *Comparative Reporting and Accounting Practices in France* (Paris: Deloitte Haskins & Sells, France, 1980), 18.
19. AP 11/1974 paper 8. See also Hans Havermann, 'Organisation und Thematik der internationalen Facharbeit und ihre Auswirkung auf die tägliche Berufsausübung', *Die Wirtschaftsprüfung,* 28/1–2, 1/15 January 1975, 16.
20. IASC meeting of 5–6 November 1974, minute 7.
21. Memorandum from Richard Simmons to Henry Benson, dated 21 November 1974, IASC archive, file 'Sir Henry Benson'.
22. 'International Accounting Standards Committee News Release', 16 January 1975, IASC archive, history file.
23. 'Business Diary: High-Speed Sir Henry', *The Times,* 17 January 1975.
24. 'Accounting Group Issues First Standard in Planned Uniform International Rules', *The Wall Street Journal,* 17 January 1975.
25. Joseph P. Cummings observed in 1976 that there was 'nothing in the official literature in the U.S. which requires comparative financial statements [as required by IAS 1], although it is a requirement with the SEC, and of the stock exchanges'. At that time, the AICPA considered whether to bring this matter to the attention of the FASB. *International Accounting Standards—The Outlook,* 4th Ross Institute Seminar in Accounting (New York: Vincent C. Ross Institute of Accounting Research, 1976), 5.
26. See Benson's statement that 'The impact [of IAS 1] belongs to the sheer fact that an international standard is to be issued at all.' Quoted in: David Simpson, 'Benson Unbends on the Standards in His Life', interview with Sir Henry Benson, *Accountancy Age,* 6/3 (17 January 1975), 12.
27. 'International Accounting Standards Committee News Release', 16 January 1975, IASC archive, history file.
28. See Henry Benson, 'The Work and Purpose of the International Accounting Standards Committee', *The Australian Accountant* (January/February 1975), 24–9.

Essentially the same text was read as a speech to a meeting of the Ordre des Experts Comptables on 23 April 1975, 'Le programme d'harmonisation des principes et méthodes comptables à l'échelon international: la tâche de l'I.A.S.C.', *Revue Française de Comptabilité*, no. 56 (December 1975), 668–7.
29. 'A Step Toward Uniform Accounting', *The Financial Times of Canada*, 11 March 1974. See also 'How We're Moving Towards Worldwide Accounting Rules', *The Financial Post*, 23 March 1974; 'First Hurdle Passed', *Accountants Weekly*, 8 March 1974, and 'International Accounting Group Moves Toward Setting Up Uniform Global Rules', *The Wall Street Journal*, 6 March 1974.
30. D. Ledouble, 'Quelques remarques sur la première recommendation emise par l'I.A.S.C.', *Revue Française de Comptabilité*, no. 43 (October 1974), 375–80.
31. Henk Volten, 'IASC en NIVRA', *De Accountant*, 82/10 (June 1976), 578.
32. AP 1/1974 paper 11.
33. A. I. Mackenzie, 'The Progress of the International Accounting Standards Committee: The First Two Years', *The Accountant's Magazine*, 80/4 (April 1976), 137.
34. The transcript of comment letters on E1 have not been preserved. An unfortunate consequence of the IASC's reliance on transcripts is that the identity of the senders can often not be determined. With minor exceptions, the original comment letters received prior to the 1990s have not been preserved. In the transcripts, the country from which individual responses were received is noted, but in most cases prior to 1985 the identity of the sender is not, although it can often be deduced.
35. IASC meeting of 29 June 1973, minute 9(c).
36. AP 4/1974 paper 3, and reaction by the NIVRA in AP 7/1975 paper 3.
37. *Accounting Principles and Reporting Practices: A Survey in 38 Countries* (Price Waterhouse International, 1973), Table 138.
38. The other members were Seigo Nakajima (Japan) and Manuel Galván (Mexico).
39. When LIFO was used, the difference between the LIFO carrying amount and the FIFO or current cost carrying amount had to be disclosed. Compare first and second drafts (AP 4/1974 paper 4 and 7/1974 paper 3) and steering committee cover letter on second draft (AP 7/1974 paper 2). In Accounting Series Release No. 141, issued on 15 February 1973, the SEC had imposed a similar disclosure requirement on companies that were using LIFO.
40. AP 7/1975 paper 3.
41. In 1974, the AICPA's annual survey of 600 industrial and commercial corporations, *Accounting Trends & Techniques* (New York: AICPA, 1974), 90–1, reported that 150 of the 600 companies used LIFO for some or all of their inventories in 1973.
42. Havermann, 'Organisation und Thematik der internationalen Facharbeit', 16.
43. 'World Standard Ammunition for Critics of SSAP 9', *Accountancy Age*, 6/40 (10 October 1975), 1.
44. Comisión de Principios de Contabilidad, *Principios Aplicables a Partidas o Conceptos Específicos: Boletín C4 Inventarios* (Instituto Mexicano de Contadores Públicos, October 1973), paragraph 21; D2 'Treatment of Stock-in-Trade and Work in Progress in Financial Accounts' (issued in December 1963), paragraph 8.
45. The ASSC's exposure draft, ED 6, 'Stocks and Work in Progress' of May 1972 explicitly ruled out variable costing in its appendix I.
46. On the United States, see R. G. Walker, *Consolidated Statements: History and Analysis* (New York: Arno Press, 1978), chapter 13. In France, mandatory consolidation was introduced by Law 85-11 of 3 January 1985, implementing the EEC Seventh Directive, and the accompanying changes in the Plan Comptable

of 1986. In Japan, consolidation became mandatory for listed companies in 1977.
47. AP 4/1974 paper 5 (cover note to first draft). Apart from Cummings, the steering committee consisted of Noel Buckley (Australia) and Krafft von der Tann, followed by Hans Havermann (Germany).
48. In the United Kingdom, segment reporting by line of business had been introduced with the Companies Act 1967. In the United States, the SEC had required line of business segmentation from new registrants since 1969, extending the requirement to Form 10-K reports in 1970 and to annual reports to stockholders in 1974.
49. For instance, in the Netherlands, see '(Gewijzigd) voorstel voor vierde EEG-richtlijn—Rapport van de Commissie Ondernemingsrecht', *De Accountant,* 81/5 (January 1975), 319. Nevertheless, the final text of the Fourth Directive did contain a requirement to segment sales revenues (paragraph 43.8).
50. Letter from Leach to Benson, dated 22 April 1975, reproduced in AP 10/1975 paper 2(b). Section 150(2)(b)(iii) of the 1947 Companies Act allowed the directors not to include a subsidiary in the group accounts if they were of the opinion that 'the business of the holding company and that of the subsidiary are so different that they cannot reasonably be treated as a single undertaking'.
51. Joseph Cummings, cited in *International Accounting Standards—The Outlook,* 5.
52. IAS 3 was singled out as 'one of the most important standards' by Allan Cook, cited in 'Cook Sets Standards for International Accounts', *Accountancy Age,* 27 November 1981, 14. It was described as 'one of our most succesful standards' by John Kirkpatrick in John N. Slipkowsky, 'IASC Chairman Kirkpatrick on International Standards', *Management Accounting* (NAA), 68 (October 1986), 29.
53. Interview with Richard Simmons, 25 September 2003.
54. AP 7/1974 paper 23.
55. AP 11/1974 paper 13.
56. AP 4/1975 paper 1. The other members of the steering committee were Doug Thomas (Canada) and Robert Mazars (France).
57. AP 7/1976 paper 2.
58. AP 7/1976 paper 6.
59. AP 7/1976 paper 2.
60. Letter from J. P. Carty (ASC secretary) to Allan Cook, dated 2 July 1980, IASC archive, IAS 4 documentation file.
61. AP 7/1976 paper 12.
62. The other members were Krafft von der Tann (Germany) and Alexander Mackenzie (UK & Ireland).
63. AP 11/1974 paper 15.
64. The final version of E3 was approved by a postal ballot in October 1974.
65. AP 7/1976 paper 12.
66. Jean-Claude Scheid and Peter Standish, 'Accounting Standardisation in France and International Accounting Exchanges', in Anthony G. Hopwood (editor), *International Pressures for Accounting Change* (Hemel Hempstead: Prentice-Hall International, 1989), 168.
67. Anonymous US observer, quoted in Alister K. Mason, *The Development of International Financial Reporting Standards,* ICRA Occasional Paper No. 17 (Lancaster: International Centre for Research in Accounting, 1978), 111.
68. Joseph P. Cummings, 'Bringing the World Together at IASC', *World* (Peat, Marwick, Mitchell & Co.), Winter 1976, 6.

69. Interview with Georges Barthès, 5 June 2003.
70. Hans Burggraaff, 'Setting a Standard for the Whole World', *Accountants Weekly*, 26 September 1980, 22–5; 'IASC: Obstacles and Opportunities', speech at the occasion of the annual meeting of the American Accounting Association, 7 August 1981.
71. See, for instance, Alexander I. Mackenzie, 'The Progress of the International Accounting Standards Committee: The First Two Years', *The Accountant's Magazine*, April 1976, 138; 'Benson Bangs the Drum', *Accountancy Age*, 7/20 (21 May 1976), 9; and John Grenside, 'Search for Worldwide Harmony', *Accountancy Age*, 5 December 1980, 18.
72. Henry Benson, 'Establishing Standards Through a Voluntary Professional Process across National Boundaries', in John C. Burton (editor), *The International World of Accounting: Challenges and Opportunities*, 1980 proceedings of the Arthur Young Professors' Roundtable (Reston, VA: The Council of Arthur Young Professors, 1981), 32.
73. 'Unifying Rules in Accounting', *The New York Times*, 4 June 1980, section D, 2.
74. AP 1/1974 paper 11.
75. Erwin Pougin, 'UEC's New Concept', *Journal UEC*, 10/1 (January 1975), 10–12. See also IASC meeting of 5–6 November 1974, minute 14.
76. There is no reference to this issue in the minutes of the IASC meeting of 9–11 March 1976. In a letter to R. D. Galpin (Bank of England) dated 16 March 1976, Benson summarized the position taken by the IASC during its March meeting.
77. Letter from G. Blunden to J. P. Cummings, dated 14 September 1976, AP 11/1976 paper 19.
78. See David Tweedie and Geoffrey Whittington, *The Debate on Inflation Accounting* (Cambridge: Cambridge University Press, 1984), for a comprehensive treatment of worldwide developments on inflation accounting.
79. Inflation rates in this section are based on the International Monetary Fund World Economic Outlook Database. While the use of other price indices may result in different inflation percentages, the pattern described here is generally supported in the literature.
80. AP 1/1974 paper 11. In a letter to C. Croxton-Smith (ICAEW president), dated 10 March 1971, in the authors' collection, Benson raised the issue of 'producing accounts under inflationary conditions'. He wrote that 'The matter has now become urgent and important.... I believe that the accounting profession is doing positive harm to the economy by not taking a lead in this field.'
81. IASC meeting of 8–9 April 1974, minute 9.
82. The other members were A. Fass (Israel), Wessel van Bruinessen (the Netherlands), I. C. P. Hogg (UK & Ireland), and Eugene J. Minahan (United States).
83. 'The Numbers Game: Tower of Babel?', *Forbes*, March 1975, 75.
84. W. van Bruinessen, 'Een IASC-ontwerp over de behandeling van prijsfluctuaties met een begeleidende notitie', *De Accountant*, 82/5 (January 1976), 258.
85. In the United States, the FASB and the SEC had by 1975 come out in favour of general price level accounting and supplementary data on the basis of replacement cost, respectively. In the United Kingdom, the ASSC had issued an exposure draft calling for supplementary general price level disclosures in January 1973. See for a review of initiatives on inflation accounting in ten countries: Stephen A. Zeff, 'Response', in *Economic Calculation Under Inflation* (Indianapolis: Liberty Press, 1976), 135–48.
86. AP 4/1975 papers 5–8.

87. IASC meeting of 9–11 April 1975, minute 6.
88. AP 7/1975 paper 7.
89. Nevertheless, a New Zealand exposure draft on general price level accounting was published in March 1975, and a Canadian exposure draft on general price level accounting in July 1975.
90. 'Entwurf einer Verlautbarung "Zur Berücksichtigung der Substanzerhaltung bei der Rechnungslegung" ', *Die Wirtschaftsprüfung*, 27/24 (15 December 1974), 666–7.
91. Preliminary Exposure Draft, 'A Method of Current Value Accounting', Australian Accounting Research Foundation, June 1975.
92. Proposed Amendment to Regulation S-X, 'Disclosure of Certain Replacement Cost Data in Notes to Financial Statements', 21 August 1975. Regulation S-X was amended with Accounting Series Release 190 of March 1976.
93. *Inflation Accounting: Report of the Inflation Accounting Committee, F.E.P. Sandilands Esq CBE, Chairman* (London: Her Majesty's Stationery Office, 1975).
94. Van Bruinessen, 'Een IASC-ontwerp', 259.
95. AP 3/1977 paper 4.
96. 'IASC Steering Committee Changing Prices, Stratford on Avon, 8, 9 en 10 december 1976', memo by Henk Volten, dated 10 December 1976, NIVRA archive, no. 481.
97. NIVRA Management Board, minutes of 27 April 1977, NIVRA archive, no. 73.
98. AP 3/1976 paper 13.
99. Christopher Nobes and Robert Parker, *Comparative International Accounting*, 5th edition (Hemel Hampstead: Prentice-Hall Europe, 1998), 399–400.
100. IASC meeting of 1–3 March 1977, minute 4. The committee consisted of John Grenside (UK & Ireland, chairman), Is Kleerekoper (the Netherlands), and Philip Defliese (United States).
101. AP 11/1978 paper 11.
102. For instance, IAS 15, paragraph 24(d) called for disclosure of the impact on 'results', which might be read either as 'net income' in the United Kingdom or 'income from continuing operations' in the United States. See AP 10/1979 paper 7; AP 3/1980 paper 2.
103. See James Carty, 'Accounting Standards in 1984', *World Accounting Report*, December 1984, 7, where the August 1983 remark was repeated and it was added, 'This year saw the corpse decomposing.'
104. By FAS 82 (1985) and FAS 89 (1986), respectively.
105. See 'Report on the Fourth Year's Experience with Section 4510 of the CICA Handbook', issued by the CICA in November 1987. The percentage of companies providing information about the effects of changing prices, not necessarily according to section 4510, had fallen from 23 in 1983 to just 4 in 1986.
106. Interview with Frans Graafstal, 15 November 2004.
107. See also IASC board meeting of 24–5 October 1989, minute 3. Eleven votes were in favour, with one against and two abstentions. IAS 15 was finally withdrawn by the International Accounting Standards Board in 2003.
108. Interviews with Hans Burggraaff, 24 May 2004; and with Geoffrey Mitchell, 19 February 2004.
109. AP 11/1974 paper 2.
110. Kees Camfferman, *Voluntary Annual Report Disclosure by Listed Dutch Companies, 1945–1983* (New York: Garland, 1997), 258–61. See also *The Funds Statement: Current Practice in Canada, the United Kingdom and the United States*

(n.p.: Accountants International Study Group, 1973), paragraph 2, and Stephen A. Zeff, introduction to chapter 3, 'Financial Statements', in Stephen A. Zeff and Bala G. Dharan, *Readings and Notes on Financial Accounting*, 4th edition (New York: McGraw-Hill, 1994), 131–2 for a summary of relevant accounting standards.
111. Initially, Robert Mazars (France) had been designated as chairman. The other members of the steering committee were Ian Vassie (Australia) and Jock Porteous (South Africa).
112. The steering committee had wanted to specify cash and cash equivalents as the required funds concept, with working capital an allowed alternative. AP 4/1975 paper 10.
113. IASC meeting of 5–6 November 1974, minute 3; AP 11/1974 paper 2.
114. The other members of the steering committee were Hans Havermann (Germany) and Seigo Nakajima (Japan).
115. The relevant pronouncements were APB Opinion No. 9, *Reporting the Results of Operations* (December 1966) and APB Opinion No. 20, *Accounting Changes* (July 1971). On Opinion 9, five of the twenty members (not including Cummings) assented with qualification. Opinion No. 20 required three years and two exposure drafts to emerge, and the vote was twelve to six, the barest majority as two-thirds was required.
116. AP 7/1975 paper 12.
117. The other exceptions were prior period items and the effects of accounting changes. AP 10/1975 paper 8.
118. AP 10/1977 paper 4.
119. The word 'fairer' had been used in auditor's reports in the 1950s by the US firm Arthur Andersen & Co. to describe the effect of fair value depreciation applied as a departure from US GAAP. See Stephen A. Zeff, 'Arthur Andersen & Co. and the Two-Part Opinion in the Auditor's Report: 1946–1962', *Contemporary Accounting Research*, 8/2 (Spring 1992), 457–9.
120. AP 10/1977 paper 4. Several UK & Irish commentators observed that E8 was less restrictive than SSAP 6. The comments from Denmark were the most negative and included among other things one of the earliest references to the lowest common denominator.
121. The other members of the steering committee were Manuel Galván followed by Leopoldo Romero (Mexico) and Graham Edgar (New Zealand).
122. AP 10/1975 paper 10 and AP 3/1976 paper 9.
123. On the developments in the United Kingdom, see Tony Hope and Rob Gray, 'Power and Policy Making: The Development of an R&D Standard', *Journal of Business Finance and Accounting*, 9/4 (Winter 1982), 531–58.
124. AP 11/1976 papers 3 and 4.
125. AP 3/1978 paper 4. Similar comments were made by some US respondents.
126. AP 7/1975 paper 6.
127. IASC meeting of 9–11 July 1975, minute 5.
128. AP 6/1978 paper 4.
129. The steering committee was chaired by Alexander Mackenzie (UK & Ireland). The other members were Seigo Nakajima (Japan) and Karel Van Oostveldt (Belgium).
130. In fact, IAS 10 was slightly stricter than FAS 5, as the latter stated that gain contingencies are 'usually' not accrued (paragraph 17), whereas the former merely stated that they 'should not' be accrued (paragraph 29).

131. Sanders, Groeneveld, and Burgert, *De jaarrekening nieuwe stijl*, 185. See also Wieland Geese, 'Sind bewertungsmäßige Anpassungen notwendig, damit ein französischer Jahresabschluß einen sicheren Einblick in die Vermögens- und Ertragslage einer Gesellschaft gewährt?', *Die Wirtschaftsprüfung*, 31/10 (15 May 1978), 290.
132. The members were Luis Nieto (Mexico, chairman), Robert Mazars followed by J. Raffegeau (France), and Y. H. Malegam (India).
133. Both the point outline (AP 7/1976 paper 18) and the steering committee's first draft (AP 11/1976 paper 12) proposed to require the percentage of completion method unless its application was prevented by uncertainty.
134. AP 7/1977 papers 7 and 8.
135. AP 11/1978 papers 8 and 8A.
136. AP 11/1978 paper 8A.
137. AP 11/1976 paper 13. See also AP 3/1977 paper 15.
138. Christopher Nobes, 'Cycles in UK Standard Setting', *Accounting and Business Research*, 21/83 (Summer 1991), 268; Michael Renshall, 'The Economics and Politics of Standard Setting', in *Standard Setting for Financial Reporting* (n.p: KPMG Peat Marwick Main & Co., 1987), 90–1; Stephen A. Zeff, ' "Political" Lobbying on Proposed Standards: A Challenge to the IASB', *Accounting Horizons*, 16/1 (March 2002), 46–8; interview with David C. Hobson, 29 April 2003.
139. J. A. Burggraaff, quoted in 'IASC', *De Accountant*, 84/1 (September 1977), 5. The other steering committee members were John Hepworth (Australia, chairman) and Robert Hampton III (United States).
140. AP 10/1977 paper 5.
141. Countries where the taxes payable method was common typically did not take a strong position on partial allocation, as they saw it as a practical half-way house towards comprehensive allocation. Interview with Hans Burggraaff, 24 May 2004.
142. AP 2/1979 papers 4 and 4A. See also *World Accounting Report*, April 1978, 7, for a critical assessment. However, see Bill N. Schwartz, 'Income Tax Allocation: It Is Time for a Change', *Journal of Accounting, Auditing and Finance*, 4 (Spring 1981), 238–47 for a favourable assessment by a US academic.
143. AP 2/1979 paper 1.
144. See AP 10/1977 paper 4 for the point outline and AP 3/1978 paper 6 for the draft exposure draft.
145. AP 6/1979 paper 1. See AP 6/1979 paper 4 for the comment letters. In total, 54 transcript pages of comment letters were received.
146. The other members of the steering committee were Peter Meyer (Germany) and H. Edenhammer (Sweden).
147. AP 6/1979 paper 1. Nevertheless, the US Committee on Accounting Procedure had already pronounced on this subject in Accounting Research Bulletin No. 30 (August 1947). It was reissued as chapter 3(a) in Accounting Research Bulletin No. 43 (1953). The latter referred to the 'normal operating cycle' rather than a one-year criterion to distinguish current from non-current assets. However, the interpretive comments in 3(a) make it clear that the committee was thinking of one year.
148. Roy C. Nash, 'Why Global Harmony of Accounting Standards Is a Long Way Off', *Financial Times*, 20 February 1980, 14. The discussion papers mentioned are the discussion papers on inflation accounting (*see* Section 5.7.2) and on accounting by banks (*see* Section 5.10).

149. Between March 1978 and June 1981, the IASC's minutes simply record that standards were 'approved'. Before and after that period, the vote is explicitly recorded. For all standards prior to March 1978, the vote was unanimous. For exposure drafts, the minutes always record the nature of the vote. The first recorded abstention, in any vote, appears in 1980 (on E19, accounting for leases), the first recorded no-vote in 1981 (on E23, on foreign currency translation). On the basis of the recollections of participants, we assume that the votes that were not explicitly recorded were unanimous, or at least made unanimous. Communications from Hans Burggraaff and Allan Cook to the authors, dated 31 May 2004 and 7 June 2004, respectively.
150. In March 1978, three delegations were against a requirement in IAS 9 to disclose total research and development costs, and for that reason they would not vote for the standard. At the time, this constituted a blocking minority. In the end the Netherlands, one of the three, decided to change its vote and the standard was passed. The minutes record simply that the standard was 'approved'. See 'IASC Board 7–9 maart 1978, Londen', memo by Henk Volten, dated 10 March 1978, NIVRA archive, no. 482.
151. From the beginning, it seems to have been a regular practice to ask all member countries to send in information on relevant domestic legislation or standards at the start of new projects. Several instances of the resulting correspondence can be found in the documentation files on individual standards in the IASC archive.
152. Mason, *The Development of International Financial Reporting Standards*, 112.
153. The other members of the steering committee were Seigo Nakajima (Japan) and Robert Sempier followed by Donald Hayes (United States). Nakajima chaired the committee from 1981 onwards. In 1975 the United Kingdom, represented by a succession of members, was added, and in 1978 Morley Carscallen (Canada) joined the committee.
154. AP 7/1974 papers 25 and 26.
155. AP 3/1976 paper 7.
156. In January 1975, the Committee decided to add a UK member to the steering committee 'with practical experience in these matters'. IASC meeting of 15–16 January 1975, minute 3. The steering committee chairman, Henk Treffers, was the senior partner of one of the major Dutch audit firms and would presumably have had some relevant experience.
157. By the late 1970s, the closing rate method was used by a majority of listed companies in the Netherlands and the United Kingdom. See Christopher Nobes and Robert Parker, *Comparative International Accounting*, 7th edition (Harlow: Pearson Education, 2002), 404; *Onderzoek Jaarverslagen 1979* (Amsterdam/Deventer: NIVRA/Kluwer, 1981), 87. In Germany, on the other hand, there was a tendency to use historical rate methods. The closing rate method was used as well. See Jörg Bankmann, 'Der internationale Konzernabschluß (Weltabschluß)', *Betriebswirtschaftliche Forschung und Praxis*, 33/6 (November 1981), 510–19.
158. AP 6–7/1977 paper 6; see also IASC meeting of 1–3 March 1977, minute 6.
159. AP 11/1978 paper 4.
160. AP 11/1978 paper 1.
161. IASC board meeting of 7–9 November, 1978, minute 5. A Canadian member was added to the committee.
162. In November 1978, a revised draft was planned for submission to the board in June 1979. No draft was submitted until November 1980, but the minutes do not record a decision to suspend the project. That it was in fact suspended, and that

the suspension was linked to the revision of FAS 8, can be inferred from statements by US board representative Donald J. Hayes, 'The International Accounting Standards Committee—Recent Developments and Current Problems', *The International Journal of Accounting* 16 (Fall 1980), 9, and by Dutch staff observer Henk Volten, 'Vreemde valuta: FASB eindelijk door de bocht?', *De Accountant*, 86/8 (April 1980), 485.

163. Interview with Allan V. C. Cook, 30 April 2003; memo from Cook to Burggraaff, 16 August 1980, IASC archive, 'Burggraaff' file. See also FAS 52, Basis for Conclusions, paragraph 157.
164. FAS 52 and IAS 21 reflected the methods developed by Unilever. Prior to his service as IASC secretary, Allan Cook had worked for Unilever, and he advocated the line of reasoning developed in that company before the task force. Interview with Allan Cook, 30 April 2003; interview with Hans Burggraaff, 13 December 2002.
165. Letter from E. Salustro (president, Ordre des Experts Comptables) to Hans Burggraaff, received 2 November 1980; telex of Dr. Nebendorf (president, Wirtschaftsprüferkammer) and Dr. Broenner (president, IdW), 28 October 1980, both attached to minutes of the meeting of the IASC board of 4–6 November 1980.
166. Interview with Allan V. C. Cook, 30 April 2003; Geoffrey B. Mitchell, 'The United Kingdom Response to International Pressures for Accounting Change' in Anthony G. Hopwood (editor), *International Pressures for Accounting Change* (Hemel Hempstead: Prentice-Hall International, 1989), 154; Harold Ainsworth, 'Sharp Suggests a Standard Setting Body', *World Accounting Report*, July 1981, iv; David Cairns, 'The Future Shape of Harmonization: A Reply', *European Accounting Review*, 6/2 (1997), 329.
167. 'French Attack on US "Chauvinism"', *Accountancy Age*, 8 August 1980, 3; 'Développements internationaux des règles d'établissement des comptes d'entreprise', *Bulletin Mensuel COB*, July 1980, 6–8.
168. This was a point of view expressed by Henk Volten, 'Vreemde valuta: FASB eindelijk door de bocht?', 485.
169. This possibility is raised in 'IASC', *De Accountant*, 87/4 (December 1980), 215. *Accountancy Age* ('Forming a Triumvirate', 5 August 1980, 12) had reported 'misty talk' about possible cooperation on current cost accounting and leasing.
170. Letter from T. R. Watts to H. Niessen (European Commission), dated 8 September 1980. Copy in NIVRA archive, no. 484. The letter was brought to the attention of the European IASC member bodies when it was distributed by the UK representative in the Groupe d'Études in September 1980. For comments by Watts on the IASC, see for instance 'The Search for International Agreement Goes On', *Accountancy Age*, 11/11 (14 March 1980), 15; and Michael Lafferty, 'Tom Watts: A Personal View', *World Accounting Report*, January 1981, 2.
171. Michael Lafferty, 'Do We Still Have an Anglo-Saxon Accounting World?', *World Accounting Report*, September 1980, 3.
172. IASC board meeting of 4–6 November 1980, minute 8.
173. 'IASC Board, Dublin, 4–6 november 1980', memo by Henk Volten, dated 10 November 1980. NIVRA archive, no. 484.
174. IASC board meeting of 14–16 October 1981, minute 3. No comment letters on E23 were received from Mexico.
175. IASC board meeting of 23–5 March 1983, minute 2; 'IASC-Board, 23–25 maart 1983, Edinburgh' memo by Henk Volten, dated 28 March 1983, NIVRA archive, no. 486.

176. Note by R. D. Galpin (Bank of England) to Benson, no date (February 1976 according to a letter from Benson to Galpin, dated 16 March 1976), IASC archive, file 'Banks—Liaison with Group of Ten Committee'.
177. The steering committee was chaired, apparently in succession, by E. L. Larkin (United States) and C. I. Brown (UK & Ireland). The other members were W. Scholtz (Germany), A. A. Soetekouw (the Netherlands), and W. J. Dolan (United States).
178. AP 3/1978 papers 10 (draft standard) and 11 (cover note).
179. Letter from W. P. Cooke (chairman of Basel Committee) to J. P. Cummings, 7 July 1978, AP 11/1978 paper 13.
180. See AP 6/1978 paper 5 and 'IASC Set to Publish Controversial Discussion Paper', *World Accounting Report*, August 1979, 6.
181. AP 10/1979 paper 16B paragraph 28.
182. Analyst David Andrews, quoted in 'Backdown on Bank Disclosure by IASC', *Accountancy Age*, 5 June 1981, 3.
183. 'Surprise Attack on Leading Banks' Accounting', *World Accounting Report*, June 1979, 4 and Michael Lafferty, 'The Iron Age of Bank Accounting Around the World', *World Accounting Report*, June 1980, 2.
184. 'The IASC Banking Proposals: An Early Look at the Response', *World Accounting Report*, Special Feature, August 1981.
185. The March 1980 banking discussion paper attracted seventy-seven transcribed pages of comment letters. The comparable figure was fifty-four for E14 (current assets and liabilities, July 1978), forty for E15 (segment reporting, March 1980), eighty-four for E16 (retirement benefits, April 1980), thirty-three for E17 (changing prices, August 1980), and seventy-two for E18 (property, plant, and equipment, August 1980). Cook's remark is reported in 'IASC Presses on Despite Apathy on Bank Paper', *Accountancy Age*, 11 September 1981, 3. It may be noted that around 1980 the FASB regularly received several hundreds of letters on its exposure drafts.
186. The relatively low response rate to IASC exposure drafts is also discussed in Roy A. Chandler, 'The International Harmonization of Accounting: In Search of Influence', *International Journal of Accounting Education and Research*, 27/3 (1992), 226.
187. IASC board meeting of 23–6 June 1981, minute 5(2).
188. For criticism of the IASC's standards on this point, see David Cairns, 'The Battle to Get Better Reporters', *Accountancy Age*, 11/32 (8 August 1980), 16; 'The Declining Role of the IASC', *Accountancy Age*, 17 October 1980, 15; 'Grenside Tells IASC to Stop Being Defeatist', *Accountancy Age*, 19 September 1980, 3.
189. The Swedish requirement was introduced with the Companies Act 1944. The UK requirement was contained in the Companies Act 1967, and the French requirement was in the Decree of 23 March 1967, article 148.
190. Prior to FAS 14, APB Statement No. 2, *Disclosure of Supplemental Financial Information by Diversified Companies*, called for voluntary disclosure of segmental information. After FAS 14 was published, Canada and Australia followed suit in 1979 and 1984, respectively.
191. The other members were Robert Mazars, followed or assisted by Dominique Ledouble and Yves Bernheim (France) and P. J. Kjaer (Denmark). AP 3/1977 paper 16 noted: 'M. Bertrand d'Illiers of the Commission des Opérations de Bourse participated actively and supportively.'

192. AP 3/1977 paper 17.
193. AP 6–7/1977 paper 9 (cover note) and 10 (point outline).
194. AP 6/1978 paper 9.
195. Taken from one of the Dutch reactions in the comment letters, transcribed in AP 3/1981 paper 4. See also the other Dutch, German, and UK reactions.
196. Peter Mantle, 'IASC Standard on Segment Reporting Imminent', *World Accounting Report*, March 1981, 2. The standard proposed in E15 was called 'a significant step' by Ralph T. Bartlett, 'Current Developments at the IASC', *The CPA Journal*, 51 (May 1981), 24. For some of the subsequent criticism, see Jenice Prather-Kinsey and Gary K. Meek, 'The Effect of Revised IAS 14 on Segment Reporting by IAS Companies', *The European Accounting Review*, 13/2 (2004), 213–34.
197. 'Standard Threat to Trade Secrets', *Accountancy Age*, 20 March 1981, 1.
198. 'Segmental Reporting Standard on the Way', *Accountancy Age*, 21 August 1981, 2.
199. As in other respects, IAS 3 was exceptional in this regard as well, with twelve definitions. The average for IAS 1–2 and 4–16 was just under two.
200. The other members of the IASC steering committee were Seigo Nakajima (Japan) and P. H. Wong (Hong Kong).
201. Robert Bruce, 'Interview: John Brennan', *Accountancy Age*, 8/40 (7 October 1977), 20–1.
202. See 'IASC Publishes Leasing Draft', *Accountancy Age*, 31 October 1980, 1; 'International Boost for UK Leasing Draft', *Accountancy Age*, 15 April 1982, 2.
203. AP 6–7/1977 paper 12.
204. See, for instance, 'Leasing Draft Faces Troubled Exposure', *Accountancy Age,* 19 June 1981, 1.
205. AP 3/1982 paper 5. For the 1973–87 period, IAS 17 ranked second after IAS 3 in terms of the volume of comment letters received.
206. Chairman's letter to accompany IAS 17, AP 6/1982 additional paper.
207. 'Leasing Standard "Illegal" Claim', *Accountancy Age*, 16 January 1981, 2.
208. Mason, *The Development of International Financial Reporting Standards*, 170.
209. Article 43 paragraph 7 contained a generally worded requirement to disclose pension liabilities in the notes to the financial statements, without any attempt to define such liabilities.
210. According to Doug Thomas (communication to the authors, dated 29 August 2003), this was one of the subjects on which the CICA 'streamed' its own project with that of the IASC. Other countries represented on the steering committee were Australia (Geoffrey Heeley), the Philippines (several representatives), and the Netherlands (Herman Marseille).
211. The comment letters transcribed in AP 6/1981 paper 4 total eighty-four transcribed pages.
212. AP 10/1979 paper 3.
213. AP 6/1981 paper 4. A similar response was obtained from Norway. The single German response was also in favour of the draft even though the Consultative Group of Actuarial Associations from the European Community Countries had pointed out particular problems in Germany.
214. See also 'IASC First with Draft on Pensions', *Accountancy Age*, 11/14 (4 April 1980), 2.
215. 'Londen, IASC Board, 16–18 oktober 1985', memo by Henk Volten, NIVRA archive, No. 48.

216. AP 10/1985 paper 8(j) and IASC board meeting of 16–18 October 1985, minute 6.
217. 'Kort verslag bijeenkomst I.A.S.C. in Dublin 4–7 maart 1986', memo by Frans Graafstal, dated 21 March 1986, NIVRA archive, no. 49; interview with Herman Marseille, 27 October 2004.
218. AP 3/1986 paper 14 and IASC board meeting of 5–7 March 1986, minute 8.
219. AP 3/1980 paper 10A.
220. IASC board meeting of 11–13 March 1980, minute 9. Subsequently, the definition was expanded to cover the settlement of liabilities as well as the exchange of assets, and simplified by combining the buyer and the seller into 'parties'.
221. AP 10/1981 paper 11; IASC board meeting of 14–16 October 1981, minute 6.
222. TIAVSC's objective echoed the IASC's Constitution when it aspired 'to formulate and publish, in the public interest, valuation Standards for property valuation and to promote their worldwide acceptance'. Since 1994, it has been known as the International Valuation Standards Committee.
223. The other members of the steering committee were S. Weirich (Germany) and E. Oke and/or A. Mbanefo (Nigeria).
224. AP 3/1980 paper 3.
225. The other members of the steering committee were Yukio Fujita (Japan) and I. Husain (Pakistan).
226. See AP 10/1979 paper 10 (point outline).
227. AP 3/1980 paper 8 (draft exposure draft).
228. AP 6/1982 paper 4, in particular the responses from Denmark and one from the United Kingdom. The responses from Germany and Austria were quite positive. The Austrian response, after a ringing endorsement of the prudence principle, concluded that the criteria of E20 'practically have a similar content as Austrian accounting standards'.
229. AP 6/1982 paper 1.
230. AP 10/1983 paper 10.
231. Frederick D. S. Choi and Vinod B. Bavishi, 'Financial Accounting Standards: A Multinational Synthesis and Policy Framework', *International Journal of Accounting Education and Research*, 18 (Fall 1982), 159–83.
232. 'Report from the Ad Hoc Advisory Committee to the Organisation and Planning Committee', no date [early 1984], IASC archive, file 'Plans and Future Work', 1981–91.
233. Rudolph Niehus (IdW president), speech to IASC board and Consultative Group, 16 October 1984, IASC archive, Consultative Group agenda papers (post-October 1984).
234. Hilary Abbott, 'Meeting the IASC Chairman', *Accountancy*, 192 (25 April 1985), 16–17. Similar statements by Kirkpatrick can be found in Susan Baker, 'Growing Prestige of the IAS Setters', *Certified Accountant* (England), May 1986, 10–11.
235. David Cairns, 'Notes on Telephone Conversation with Henk Volten on 28 May, 1985', IASC archive, 'Netherlands' country file.
236. 'Een nieuwe verspreidingswijze voor internationale discussie-ontwerpen en uitspraken', *De Accountant*, 90/10 (June 1984), 742–3.
237. AP 3/1980 paper 3.
238. Interview with Allan V. C. Cook, 30 April 2003, and with Benjamin S. Neuhausen (then an FASB professional accounting fellow), 18 August 2003.
239. AP 6/1980 paper 5.

240. See also 'The History of the Pooling-of-Interests Method in the Jurisdictions of G4+1 Member Organizations', appendix to *G4+1 Position Paper: Recommendations for Achieving Convergence on the Methods of Accounting for Business Combinations* (London: IASC, December 1998).
241. Interview with Hans Burggraaff, 24 May 2004.
242. See Stephen A. Zeff, *Forging Accounting Principles in Five Countries: A History and an Analysis of Trends* (Champaign, IL: Stipes Publishing Co., 1972), 212–16 and Frank R. Rayburn and Ollie S. Powers, 'A History of Pooling of Interests Accounting for Business Combinations in the United States', *Accounting Historians Journal*, 18/2 (September 1991), 155–92.
243. The other members of the steering committee were Raymond Béthoux (France) and a succession of members from Singapore.
244. AP 6/1980 paper 2.
245. Interview with John N. Bishop, 28 May 2003.
246. Peter Holgate, 'Foreign Accounts Moves Can Hit Close to Home', *Accountancy Age*, 24 November 1983, 16.
247. The new entity method first appears in AP 6/1979 paper 12 (point outline). At that stage, the steering committee merely recognized it as a theoretical alternative, and proposed not to include it in the standard.
248. AP 11/1980 paper 4.
249. Comments from member bodies on a 1979 draft had shown that both pooling and new entity were rare. Curiously, only the Dutch reaction indicated that new entity was common in the Netherlands, but this is likely to be based on a misunderstanding. See AP 6/1980 paper 2.
250. AP 3/1983 papers 5 and 8.
251. Peter Holgate, 'How IAS 22 Will Affect UK Law', *Accountancy Age*, 1 December 1983, 16.
252. 'IASC-Board, 23–25 maart 1983, Edinburgh', memo by Henk Volten, NIVRA archive, no. 486; interview with Frans Graafstal, 15 November 2004.
253. AP 6/1980 paper 3 (revised draft) and 2 (cover note).
254. AP 11/1980 paper 4.
255. IASC board meeting of 14–16 June 1983, minute 2; 'IASC-Board, 14–16 juni 1983, Londen', memo by Henk Volten, NIVRA archive, no. 486. E22 had been approved with a single dissenting vote by Nigeria and one abstention, IASC board meeting of 24–7 March 1981, minute 3.
256. IASC board meeting of 26–8 October 1983, minute 3.
257. Interview with Willis A. Smith, 13 January 2004. The other members of the steering committee were Morris Kanne (Israel) and R. Martinez (Mexico).
258. On developing countries, see AP 11/1980 paper 6. On UK & Irish objections, see AP 3/1981 paper 9.
259. AP 10/1983 paper 4 (transcript of comment letters).
260. IASC board meeting of 24–7 June 1980, minute 9(d). The members were Peter Meyer (Germany, chairman), L. U. do Nascimento (Brazil), H. H. A. Appelo (the Netherlands), and C. O. O. Oyediran (Nigeria).
261. AP 6/1981 paper 13 (issues paper).
262. See AP 6/1981 paper 12 and AP 3/1984 paper 1.
263. AP 6/1981 paper 13 (issues paper).
264. AP 3/1984 paper 1.
265. AP 3/1984 paper 2 (comment letters), quotation from page 4.12.

266. IASC board meeting of 14–16 March 1984, minute 2.
267. Interview with Georges Barthès de Ruyter, 5 June 2003. Barthès took over the chairmanship of the steering committee from François Capelo (France). The other members were Giancarlo Tomasin (Italy), Eiichi Shiratori (Japan), and Peter Bailey (Zimbabwe).
268. AP 10/1985 paper 2.
269. AP 6/1982 paper 7 (issues paper).
270. IASC board meeting of 19–21 June 1984, minute 2. The no-votes are recorded in 'IASC-Board, 19–21 juni 1984, Toronto', memo by Henk Volten, dated 28 June 1984, NIVRA archive, no. 48.
271. AP 10/1985 paper 4 (comment letters) and paper 2 (steering committee recommendations).
272. 'Londen, IASC Board, 16–18 oktober 1985', memo by Henk Volten, dated 18 October 1985, NIVRA archive, no. 48.
273. 'IASC to Cut Choices in Standards', *World Accounting Report,* June 1987, 3.
274. Interviews with Georges Barthès de Ruyter, 5 June 2003; with Warren McGregor, 9 June 2003; and with Herman Marseille, 27 October 2004.
275. AP 3/1982 paper 13. This meant that the topic had not been supported during the previous twelve months by either a member of the board or the Consultative Group.
276. The other members were E. Aldeweireldt (Belgium), J. B. Hindin (New Zealand), and C. F. Sleigh (UK & Ireland).
277. AP 3/1985 papers 1 and 4; AP 6/1986 papers 1 and 4.
278. See also Susan Baker, 'Pensions Statement Approaches Majority', *Accountancy Age,* 27 June 1985, 17.
279. AP 3/1983 paper 9; AP 6/1986 paper 1.
280. See for a recent comment of this nature: Barry J. Epstein and Abbas Ali Mirza, *IAS 2004 Interpretation and Application of International Accounting and Financial Reporting Standards* (Hoboken, NJ: John Wiley & Sons, 2004), 9.
281. Hans Burggraaff, 'Setting a Standard for the Whole World', *Accountants Weekly,* 26 September 1980, 22–5
282. David Cairns, cited in 'Guess Who's Coming to Dinner? The Secretary General of the IASC Talks to the Editor', *The Accountant's Journal,* March 1986, 4.
283. Quoted in 'IASC Developments: An Update', *Journal of Accountancy,* 154/3 (September 1982), 104.
284. John N. Slipkowsky, 'IASC Chairman Kirkpatrick on International Standards', *Management Accounting* (NAA), 68 (October 1986), 30.

NOTES TO CHAPTER 6

1. IASC meeting of 9–11 April 1975, minute 9(5).
2. IASC meeting of 9–11 April 1975, minute 9(6).
3. 'Enforcement of Standards', note by the chairman, AP 11/1974 paper 25.
4. Henk Volten, 'IFAC en IASC in Mexico', *De Accountant,* 89/3 (November 1982), 154.
5. Quoted in the Research Department of *CAmagazine,* 106/1 (January 1975), 52.
6. *Acceptance and Observance of International Accounting Standards* (London: IASC, September 1977), paragraph 11.
7. IASC meeting of 5–6 November 1974, minute 13(1).

8. Letter from Benson to Sr. Don P. Rodríguez Ponga y Ruiz de Salazar, dated 25 January 1974, IASC archive, file 'International Federation of Stock Exchanges FIBV'. It was recorded in the IASC minutes that Benson had provided the London Stock Exchange with 'a paper giving background information' before the Exchange developed its own approach to the FIBV. IASC meeting of 15–17 July 1974, minute 16(6).
9. Joseph P. Cummings and Michael N. Chetkovich, 'World Accounting Enters a New Era', *Journal of Accountancy*, 145/4 (April 1978), 56.
10. Michael Lafferty with David Cairns and James Carty, *1979 Financial Times Survey of 100 Major European Companies' Reports & Accounts* (London: The Financial Times, 1979); Michael Lafferty and David Cairns, *Financial Times World Survey of Annual Reports 1980* (London: The Financial Times Business Information, 1980); David Cairns, Michael Lafferty, and Peter Mantle, *Survey of Accounts and Accountants 1983–84* (London: Lafferty Publications, 1984).
11. For a reference to other such surveys adopting IASC standards as their yardstick, see 'IASC Welcomes Studies', *World Accounting Report*, September 1984, 1.
12. Cairns, Lafferty, and Mantle, *Survey of Accounts and Accountants 1983–84*, 20. Also see 'IASC Comes of Age (And It's Only 10!)', *Accountancy*, 94/1079 (July 1983), 24.
13. Cairns, Lafferty, and Mantle, *Survey of Accounts and Accountants 1983–84*, 21.
14. R. D. Thomas, 'Support for International Accounting Standards Continues to Grow', *CAmagazine*, 115/9 (September 1982), 72.
15. *World Accounting Report*, May 1976, 2.
16. Peter Stilling, Richard Norton, and Leon Hopkins, *Financial Times World Accounting Survey 1984* (London: Financial Times Business Information, 1984), 19. Stilling, a partner in Touche Ross & Co., was to serve as a member of the UK delegation to the IASC board from 1990 to 1995.
17. R. D. Fitzgerald, A. D. Stickler, and T. R. Watts, *International Survey of Accounting Principles and Reporting Practices* (n.p., Price Waterhouse International, 1979), 8–9.
18. S. J. Gray, L. G. Campbell, and J. C. Shaw (editors), *International Financial Reporting: A Comparative International Survey of Accounting Requirements and Practices in 30 Countries* (Basingstoke, Hampshire, UK: Macmillan Publishers, 1984), 24.
19. Lafferty with Cairns and Carty, *1979 Financial Times Survey of 100 Major European Companies' Reports & Accounts*, 19.
20. Lafferty and Cairns, *Financial Times World Survey of Annual Reports 1980*, 9.
21. The survey results were reported in AP 3/1980 paper 19A. References will be made in the following sections to the results of this survey.
22. Letter from Roy C. Nash to the authors, dated 8 February 1978.
23. *IASC News*, 16/5 (October 1987), 12.
24. In 1976, Steering was dropped from the name.
25. These latter three bodies are now known as the Association of Chartered Certified Accountants, the Chartered Institute of Management Accountants, and the Chartered Institute of Public Finance and Accountancy, respectively.
26. 'Introduction to Statements of International Accounting Standards' (authorized December 1974), Section W of the *Members' Handbook* (ICAEW).
27. Michael Renshall, Preface, 'Handbook for the Accounting Standards Committee Archive', Working Paper 93/1, Centre for Empirical Research in Accounting and Finance, Department of Accounting and Finance, University of Manchester, iii.
28. e.g. 'Application in the UK and Ireland of International Accounting Standard No. 1, Disclosure of Accounting Policies', in *International Accounting Standards: The Full Text of All International Accounting Standards Extant at 1 September 1987* (London:

ICAEW, [1987]), 352. The CCAB's prefaces for the first twenty-six IASC standards were reproduced in this book.
29. Peter Taylor and Stuart Turley, *The Regulation of Accounting* (Oxford: Basil Blackwell Ltd, 1986), 161.
30. Edward Stamp, 'Does the English Institute Have a Death Wish?' in Stanley Weinstein and Michael A. Walker (editors) *Annual Accounting Review*, volume 1, 1979 (Chur: Harwood Academic Publishers, 1979), 203.
31. Brian Underdown and Peter J. Taylor, *Accounting Theory & Policy Making* (London: Heinemann, 1985), 44, 55.
32. Ian Hay Davison, *The Accounting Standards Committee 1982–1984*, 1985 Julian Hodge Accounting Lecture at the University of Wales on 18 February 1985 (London: Arthur Andersen & Co.), 17.
33. See 'Companies Caught by International Depreciation Rule', *Accountancy Age*, 8/4 (28 January 1977), 1.
34. 'Preface to Statements of International Accounting Standards' (authorized March 1978), Section W of the *Members' Handbook* (ICAEW).
35. *Survey of Published Accounts 1979* (London: ICAEW, 1980), 31.
36. *Survey of Published Accounts 1978* (London: ICAEW, 1979), 89. See 'Depreciation Bites', *Accountancy Age*, 27 May 1977, where it was reported that one company, Woolworth, adopted IAS 4 and thus depreciated its long-leasehold properties, because, its finance director said, 'If the English ICA handbook states that the council expects members to follow the international standards then we have to follow them'. SSAP 12, the first UK and Irish standard on depreciation, was not issued until almost a year after IAS 4 took effect.
37. Paul Rutteman, 'Demands of a Different Environment', *Accountancy*, 100/1130 (October 1987), 18.
38. Rutteman, 'Demands of a Different Environment', 18.
39. 'Explanatory Foreword', *Accounting Standards 1986/87: The Full Texts of all UK Exposure Drafts and Accounting Standards Extant at September 1986* (London: ICAEW, 1986), 115. After quoting the last of these three sentences from the Explanatory Foreword, Taylor and Turley (*The Regulation of Accounting*, 161) added, 'and there is no suggestion that non-compliance with international standards should be regarded as a significant consideration by auditors when preparing their report, unlike SSAPs, where non-compliance could lead to an audit qualification'.
40. Interview with David C. Hobson, 29 April 2003.
41. 'International Harmony of Accounting Standards?' *World Accounting Report*, December 1979, 2.
42. Geoffrey Holmes, 'Tom Watts—Still at the ASC Helm', *Accountancy*, 90/1035 (November 1979), 75.
43. IASC Organization & Planning Steering Committee meeting of June 1980, agenda paper VI.
44. Interview with Allan V. C. Cook, 30 April 2003.
45. *International Accounting Standards 1981: The Full Texts of All International Accounting Standards Extant at 1 March 1981* (London: ICAEW, 1981).
46. The Stock Exchange's Council said that 'It will request companies who wish to maintain their listing to renew their [listing] agreement upon the occasion of any future amendment to the terms of the current Listing Agreement or the related notes'. Thus, until the agreement was renewed, the compliance

obligation was an expectation, not a requirement. Quoted in *Survey of Published Accounts 1973–74* (London: ICAEW, 1972), 257. At this early stage, the Institute of Municipal Treasurers and Accountants had not yet joined in the work of the ASSC.

47. Quoted in *Survey of Published Accounts 1975* (London: ICAEW, 1975), 175. For a news report, see *The Accountant*, 171/5212 (14 November 1974), 630.
48. Statement of London Stock Exchange listing requirements applicable to accounting standards (supplied to the authors by the UK Financial Services Authority). See 'Foreign Companies Told to Apply IASC Rules', *Accountancy Age*, 5/43 (1 November 1974), 1.
49. William M. K. Slimmings, 'The Rôle and Responsibility of the Accounting Profession', in *Financial Reporting and Accounting Standards*, Conference Papers (n.p., University of Glasgow Press, 1978), 60.
50. The *Financial Times*'s accounting correspondent Michael Lafferty wrote, 'It was Benson's personal initiative that got The Stock Exchange to enforce international standards on listed companies without the agreement of the UK accountancy bodies'. *World Accounting Report*, August 1977, 9.
51. Interview with Gavin Fryer, 18 May 2004.
52. *Survey of Published Accounts 1979*, 293–4.
53. See *Submissions on the Accounting Standards Committee's Consultative Document: Setting Accounting Standards* (n.p., The Accounting Standards Committee, 1979), 76, 103, 118, 145, 150. Also see Edward Stamp, 'A View from Academe', in Ronald Leach and Edward Stamp (editors), *British Accounting Standards: The First 10 Years* (Cambridge: Woodhead-Faulkner, 1981), 243–6.
54. Amendments to 'Admission of Securities to Listing', Quotations Department, The Stock Exchange, July 1983; circular letter to foreign listed companies from G. H. Fryer, head of the Exchange's Quotations Department, dated November 1983, IASC archive, 'F.I.B.V.' file. Gavin Fryer recalls that he had written a letter of comment to the IASC, saying that its segment reporting proposal would not work, as the Exchange had encountered stiff opposition from companies when it had proposed its own segment reporting obligation in the 1960s. Interview with Gavin Fryer, 18 May 2004. The Exchange's lengthy letter of comment to the IASC is the anonymous communication numbered G.23 in AP 3/1981 paper 4.
55. 'Founder Members of IASC: Enforcement of International Accounting Standards', summary of responses to the IASC's survey conducted in early 1975, dated 30 April 1975, IASC archive, 'Enforcement—Steering Committee' file.
56. *Survey of the Use and Application of International Accounting Standards 1988* (London: IASC, 1988), 21–69.
57. Interview with Wallace E. Olson, 13 March 2003.
58. Alister K. Mason, 'The Evolution of International Accounting Standards', in Frederick D. S. Choi (editor), *Multinational Accounting: A Research Framework for the Eighties* (Ann Arbor, MI: UMI Research Press, 1981), 164.
59. Interview with Philip D. Ameen (GE's vice-president and comptroller), 9 September 2003.
60. David H. Cairns, 'The Harmonization of Accounting Standards: The Role and Achievements of the International Accounting Standards Committee', in *Standard Setting for Financial Reporting: An International Conference Sponsored by the American Accounting Association with Klynveld Main Goerdeler*, August 17–20, 1986 (n.p., Peat, Marwick, Main & Co., 1987), 118.

61. Communications from David C. Fisher to the authors, dated 3 January and 4 January 2006. From 1988 to 1993, Fisher was the controller at Salomon.
62. The AICPA inserted the IASC standards in its annual publication, *AICPA Professional Standards*.
63. 'Founder Members of IASC: Enforcement of International Accounting Standards', summary of responses to the IASC's survey conducted in early 1975, dated 30 April 1975, IASC archive, 'Enforcement—Steering Committee' file.
64. *Survey of the Use and Application of International Accounting Standards 1988*, 21–69.
65. Letter dated 10 June 1975 from Burton to Robert N. Sempier. The letters cited and quoted in this section, with one exception, are in the 'SEC' and 'AICPA' files in the IASC's archive. The letter from Marshall Armstrong was obtained from the FASB's archive.
66. Letter dated 26 June 1975 from Armstrong to Garrett.
67. Letter dated 29 April 1975 from Hornbostel to Defliese.
68. Minutes of the December 1974 meeting of the AICPA's Board of Directors (furnished by the AICPA).
69. Quoted in Thomas G. Evans and Thomas D. Leddy, 'Can American Accountants Serve Two Masters: FASB and IASC?' *The CPA Journal*, 46/1 (January 1976), 7.
70. Letter dated 19 May 1975 from Defliese to Hornbostel.
71. Letter dated 30 July 1975 from Hornbostel to Defliese.
72. Letter dated 29 July 1975 from Hornbostel to Garrett.
73. Letter dated 8 September 1975 from Benson to Garrett.
74. Letter dated 3 October 1975 from Garrett to Armstrong.
75. Garrett was not the first SEC chairman to advocate the international harmonization of accounting standards. In May 1972, even before the IASC was founded, William J. Casey, Garrett's immediate predecessor as SEC chairman, spoke at a conference in Paris in favour of 'achieving some acceptable level of accounting uniformity on an international basis'. 'Toward Common Accounting Standards', *The Journal of Accountancy*, 134/4 (October 1972), 70. On 25 September 1973, in only his second month as SEC Chairman, Garrett looked favourably on an effort 'to resolve the important differences in financial reporting around the world'. Ray Garrett, Jr., 'The Internationalization of our Securities Markets', an address to the Boston Stock Exchange, p. 12 (available at: http://www.sechistorical.org/collection/papers/1970/1973_0925_Garrett_BSE_Speech.pdf).
76. Letter dated 9 October 1975 from Garrett to Hornbostel.
77. Letter dated 14 August 1975 from Defliese to Benson.
78. 'Moving Toward Worldwide GAAP', *In Perspective: Current Accounting Developments* (July 1975), third page.
79. 'One Cook Too Many?' *Accounting Events and Trends*, 2/1 (15 February 1975), 5, 6.
80. Harvey E. Kapnick, 'We Must Reorganize our Efforts in Establishing Internationally Recognized Accounting Standards', *Executive News Briefs*, 3/8 (May 1975), third page.
81. Quoted in Joseph P. Cummings, letter to the editor, *The CPA Journal*, 46/6 (June 1976), 5. Also see *The CPA Letter* (semi-monthly newsletter of the AICPA), 55/14 (August 1975), 2. For the original, see the minutes of the 24 July 1975 meeting of the AICPA board of directors, pages 2–3 (copy supplied to the authors by the AICPA). For the full statement of the AICPA's commitment under the best endeavours clause, see *AICPA Professional Standards, As of June 1, 1989* (New York: AICPA, 1989), 11001–2.

82. Letter from Defliese to Hans Reintges, dated 29 August 1975, IASC archive, 'Enforcement—Founder Members' file.
83. Letter from Defliese to Grenside, dated 1 August 1975; letter from Defliese to Benson, dated 1 August 1975, IASC archive, file 'AICPA 1973–83'.
84. *Report of the Public Review Board 1986* (n.p., Arthur Andersen & Co., 1986), 4.
85. Letter from Mackenzie to Cummings, dated 12 April 1976, IASC archive, 'Enforcement—Steering Committee' file.
86. Henry P. Hill, 'International Accounting Standards—The Outlook', *The 4th Ross Institute Seminar on Accounting*, New York University, May 1976, 14.
87. Analysis dated 10 November 1976 by George J. Staubus; letter from Hauworth to Armstrong, dated 11 July 1977 (in the authors' files).
88. 'Recent FASB Responses to Requests for Action', *Status Report*, no. 60 (5 January 1978), 3.
89. 'New Standard for Foreign Currency Translation Replaces Statement 8', *Status Report*, no. 123 (7 December 1981), 4.
90. 'Accounting Regulation in the US: The Growing Debate', *International Accounting Bulletin*, 7, supplement (January 1984), S/5. Kirk's term of office ended on 31 December 1986.
91. Cairns, Lafferty, and Mantle, *Survey of Accounts and Accountants 1983–84*, 7.
92. Ralph E. Walters, 'From National to International Standards: Can the FASB Bridge the GAAP?', *Status Report*, no. 154 (12 March 1984), 6, 7.
93. Donald J. Kirk, 'Some Comments on the Prospects for International Harmonization', *Status Report*, no. 154 (12 March 1984), 8.
94. See Robert Van Riper, *Setting Standards for Financial Reporting: FASB and the Struggle for Control of a Critical Process* (Westport, CT: Quorum Books, 1994), 46–7.
95. Donald J. Kirk, 'The United States Approach', in *Harmonization of Accounting Standards: Achievements and Prospects* (Paris: Organisation for Economic Co-operation and Development, 1986), 79.
96. Communication from David Cairns to the authors, dated 22 January 2004.
97. IASC board meeting of 23–6 June 1981, minute 18; IASC board meeting of 14–16 October 1981, minute 14(e).
98. IASC board meeting of 17–19 October 1984, minute 7.
99. See 'Compatibility of Australian Accounting Standards and International Accounting Standards: Statement of Policy' (K3/300-03), issued in November 1976, and APS 1 (K1/300), amended in September 1978.
100. Communication from Warren McGregor to the authors, dated 27 October 2003. Kenneth Spencer, in a communication to the authors dated 14 October 2003, confirms that 'Companies and auditors made no mention in financial statements or audit reports identifying departures from IAS.'
101. Communications from John Hepworth to the authors, dated 17 October 2003 and 3 February 2004.
102. *Survey of the Use and Application of International Accounting Standards 1988*, 21–69.
103. See 'New Status for GAAP', *CICA/ICCA Dialogue*, 4/6 (January 1973), 1. The action taken by the securities commissions was known as National Policy No. 27.
104. 'References to CICA Handbook in Canadian Legislation and Regulations', memorandum prepared by the CICA as of October 1987. Also see George J. Murphy, 'Financial Statement Disclosure and Corporate Law: The Canadian Experience', *The International Journal of Accounting Education and Research*, 15/2 (Spring 1980),

97; and R. Douglas Thomas, 'Establishing Accounting and Auditing Standards', *CAmagazine*, 109/6 (December 1976), 56.
105. 'Canadian Review Procedures', memorandum dated 30–1 March 1977, IASC archive, 'Enforcement—Founder Members' file.
106. Communication from Doug Thomas to the authors, dated 30 August 2003.
107. 'Revenue', *Proposed Accounting Recommendations* (Toronto: CICA, October 1985), 3.
108. Written by Alan D. Stickler, of Price Waterhouse, it was entitled *Financial Reporting in an International Environment: A Comparison of International Accounting Standards with Canadian Practice*. See 'Canadian GAAP Harmonize with International Standards', *Dialogue* (membership newsletter of the CICA) (April 1984), 3.
109. Communication from Gert Mulcahy (then the CICA's accounting research director) to the authors, dated 2 September 2003.
110. *CICA Handbook* paragraph 1501.05.
111. See *Financial Reporting in Canada*, fourteenth edition (Toronto: CICA, 1981), 13.
112. IASC meeting of 24–7 June 1980, minute 13. See also AP 6/1979, paper 20.
113. For an extract from the letter sent by Toronto Stock Exchange president and CEO J. Pearce Bunting to the CEOs of listed companies, see *IASC News*, 14/2 (March 1985), 4; also see *Survey of the Use and Application of International Accounting Standards 1988*, 70–1. The CICA carefully maintained a record of the companies signifying their compliance with IASC standards and looked into instances in which companies dropped their reference to IASC standards in a subsequent year. The CICA's energetic management of this process of encouraging company compliance is borne out by the contents of a CICA file, '6719 IAS Reference to Annual Reports', supplied to the authors by the CICA.
114. *Survey of the Use and Application of International Accounting Standards 1988*, 71.
115. 'Activities on Compliance with IAS', report submitted by the CICA, addendum to minutes of the IASC board meeting of 14–16 March 1984.
116. See 'Support for International Accounting Standards Continues to Grow', *CAmagazine*, 115/9 (September 1982), 72; CICA Special Committee on Standards-Setting, Report to CICA Board of Governors (19 December 1980), 86; *Financial Reporting in Canada*, fifteenth edition (Toronto: CICA, 1983), 15–6; and *Financial Reporting in Canada*, sixteenth edition (Toronto: CICA, 1985), 17–8.
117. *Survey of the Use and Application of International Accounting Standards 1988*, 71. Extracts from several company annual reports are presented.
118. *Survey of the Use and Application of International Accounting Standards 1988*, 21–69.
119. Gilbert Mourre, 'La C.O.B. et l'harmonisation des comptes à l'échelon national et international', *Revue Française de Comptabilité*, supplement to no. 68 (January 1977), 26–7.
120. Alain Mikol, 'The History of Financial Reporting in France', in Peter Walton (editor), *European Financial Reporting: A History* (London: Academic Press, 1994), 91–122.
121. Interview with Dominique Ledouble, 5 June 2003.
122. Robert Mazars, 'Le travail de l'International Accounting Standards Committee (I.A.S.C.)', *Revue Française de Comptabilité*, supplement to no. 68 (January 1977), 4, 8.
123. AP 3/1980 paper 19A, pages 48–57.
124. Mazars, 'Le travail', 7.

125. See for the relation of early IASC standards and French domestic requirements: Jean-Claude Scheid and Peter Standish, 'Accounting Standardisation in France and International Accounting Exchanges' in Anthony G. Hopwood (editor), *International Pressures for Accounting Change* (Hemel Hempstead: Prentice-Hall International, 1989), 166–8.
126. *IASC News*, 4/7 (24 November 1976), 3.
127. Interview with Philippe Danjou, 14 February 2005.
128. Mourre, 'La C.O.B. et l'harmonisation', 25.
129. 'The Emergence of the International Accounting Standards Committee', 8, submitted to the meeting on 10 October 1977 of all IASC member accountancy bodies in Munich, AP 10/1977 paper 8B. The COB made statements to this effect both in its *Bulletin Mensuel* (February 1976) and in its 1975 Annual Report. See Mourre, 'La C.O.B. et l'harmonization', 25.
130. 'COB Endorses IASC Standards', *World Accounting Report*, May 1976, 21. For the COB's statement, see 'Normalisation Internationale des Principes Comptables', *Bulletin Mensuel de la Commission des Opérations de Bourse*, no. 79 (February 1976), 9.
131. Fitzgerald, Stickler, and Watts, *International Survey of Accounting Principles and Reporting Practices*, 9.
132. Mazars, 'Le travail', 5.
133. Interview with Dominique Ledouble, 5 June 2003.
134. See 'French Attack on US "Chauvinism" ', *Accountancy Age*, 5 August 1980, 3.
135. 'Développements internationaux des règles d'établissement des comptes d'entreprise', *Bulletin Mensuel COB* (July 1980), 6–8.
136. Interview with Jean-Claude Scheid, 18 February 2004.
137. See on this transformation: Mikol, 'The History of Financial Reporting in France', 119–20 and Scheid and Standish, 'Accounting Harmonization', 183–4.
138. Philippe Danjou, 'La consolidation des comptes: comparaison du texte Français et des textes internationaux', *Revue Française de Comptabilité*, 162 (November 1985), 162.
139. *IASC News*, 12/6 (November 1983), 3–4.
140. Dang Pham, 'Group Accounting in France', in S. J. Gray, A. G. Coenenberg, and P. D. Gordon, *International Group Accounting: Issues in European Harmonization*, 2nd edition (London: Routledge, 1993), 80.
141. *IASC News*, 13/1 (February 1984), 1.
142. Danjou, 'La consolidation des comptes', 15.
143. The *Revue Française de Comptabilité* featured very few articles on the IASC between 1980 and 1987. In his essay, 'Financial Reporting in France', published in 1985, Robert Parker did not mention the IASC. The essay is included in Christopher Nobes and Robert Parker (editors), *Comparative International Accounting*, 2nd edition (Oxford: Philip Allan, 1985), 75–96.
144. Ernst & Whinney, *The Impact of the Seventh Directive* (London: The Financial Times, 1984), 27.
145. *IASC News*, 15/6 (December 1986), 2; and *IASC News*, 16/1 (February 1987), 1.
146. *Survey of the Use and Application of International Accounting Standards 1988*, 21–69.
147. Hans Havermann, 'Organisation und Thematik der internationalen Facharbeit und ihre Auswirkung auf die tägliche Berufsausübung'. *Die Wirtschaftsprüfung*, 28/1–2 (1/15 January 1975), 14.
148. Havermann, 'Organisation und Thematik', 16.

149. Communication from Heinz Kleekämper to the authors, dated 22 June 2006.
150. Hans Havermann, 'IASC-Statements und EG-Richtlinien', *Die Wirtschaftsprüfung*, 31/13 (1 July 1978), 369.
151. Interview with Peter Marks and Albrecht Ruppel, 4 June 2003.
152. Reply to the IASC, dated 25 September 1979, reproduced in AP 3/1980 paper 19A, pages 58–63. It was reported in 1977 that the German delegation to the FIBV's meeting in Johannesburg in October 1975 made it clear 'that compliance with international accounting standards may not be considered as long as there are certain aspects left which are not in agreement with the law presently prevailing in Germany'. Letter from H. Kaminski to W. J. Brennan, dated 11 March 1977, in the IASC's archive, 'Enforcement—Steering Committee' file.
153. Rudolf J. Niehus, 'Die Vierte Gesellschaftsrechtliche Richtlinie: Harmonisierung des Jahresabschlusses vor internationalem Hintergrund', *Die Wirtschaftsprüfung*, 31/17 (1 September 1978), 473.
154. With respect to both France and Germany, Nobes wrote in 1985 that 'the *Ordre* and the *Institut* have little room (and inadequate authority) to influence accounting practice because of the strength and detail of company law and the *plan comptable*'. Christopher Nobes, 'Harmonization of Financial Reporting', in Nobes and Parker (editors), *Comparative International Accounting* (1985), 337.
155. *Survey of the Use and Application of International Accounting Standards 1988*, 21–69.
156. *Survey of the Use and Application of International Accounting Standards 1988*, 5.
157. James J. Quinn, 'Multinational Enterprises and the SEC', in Dhia D. AlHashim and James W. Robertson (editors), *Accounting for Multinational Enterprises* (Indianapolis: Bobbs-Merrill Educational Publishing, 1978), 97; also see Jill Lorraine McKinnon, *The Historical Development and Operational Form of Corporate Reporting Regulation in Japan* (New York: Garland Publishing, 1986), 268 (n. 14), 292; and Roy C. Nash, 'Why Multinationals Should Support IASC', *World Accounting Report*, February 1980, 2. *World Accounting Report* said that the IASC's exposure draft on consolidated statements 'has been copied extensively in the new Japanese requirements for consolidated accounts which take effect from April 1977'. *World Accounting Report*, June 1976, 5.
158. Memorandum from T. E. Cooke to the authors, dated 2 January 2003.
159. Letter from Bunsuke Itoh (assistant secretary, JICPA) to Paul Rosenfield, dated 24 February 1975, IASC archive, 'Enforcement—Founder Members' file.
160. Letter from Munehiro Watanabe (assistant secretary, JICPA) to E. P. Akins (assistant secretary, IASC), dated 21 December 1979, reproduced in AP 3/1980 paper 19A, page 69.
161. 'Compliance reports', AP 3/1986 paper 17, page 12; and *IASC News*, 14/4 (July 1985), 4. The authors are grateful to Kazuo Hiramatsu, in a communication dated 18 March 2006, for confirming the disclosure in Sasebo's annual report for the financial year ending 31 March 1985. The authors are also grateful to Masato Kikuya, in a letter dated 9 March 2006, for further information in this regard.
162. *Survey of the Use and Application of International Accounting Standards 1988*, 21–69.
163. Les Campbell, 'Financial Reporting in Japan', in Nobes and Parker (editors), *Comparative International Accounting* (1991), 239–40. This identical passage also appeared in Campbell's chapter on Japan in the second edition of the Nobes and Parker book, published in 1985 by Philip Allan Publishers Limited, 158.
164. Submission by the Instituto Mexicano de Contadores Públicos to the IASC, dated 21 March 1975, IASC archive, 'Enforcement—Founder Members' file.

165. Submission by the Instituto Mexicano de Contadores Públicos to the IASC, dated 30 November 1979, reproduced in AP 3/1980 paper 19A, pages 72–5.
166. *Survey of the Use and Application of International Accounting Standards 1988*, 21–69.
167. *Survey of the Use and Application of International Accounting Standards 1988*, 5.
168. Henk Volten, *Challenges to Financial Reporting in the Netherlands: How Corporate Reporting is Monitored by Social Pressure Groups*, PILOT (the Netherlands) 9 (Amsterdam: Nederlands Instituut van Registeraccountants, 1979), 8–9.
169. The change was in preparation by early 1975; see IASC meeting of 15–16 January 1975, minute 7(3).
170. Stephen A. Zeff, Frans van der Wel, and Kees Camfferman, *Company Financial Reporting: A Historical and Comparative Study of the Dutch Regulatory Process* (Amsterdam: North-Holland, 1992), 241–4, 249–52.
171. See e.g. *Richtlijnen voor de Jaarrekening* (Amsterdam: Tripartiete Overleg, 1980), Appendix 2.
172. *Survey of the Use and Application of International Accounting Standards 1988*, 21–69.
173. Memorandum to the authors from Hans Burggraaff, dated 22 April 2004.
174. Submission by Henk Volten on compliance with IASC standards, addendum to Minutes of the IASC board meeting of 14–16 June 1983.
175. *Onderzoek Jaarverslaggeving 1984*, NIVRA geschrift 39 (Amsterdam/Deventer: NIVRA/Kluwer, 1985), 110; *Onderzoek Jaarverslaggeving 1986*, NIVRA geschrift 42 (Amsterdam/Deventer: NIVRA/Kluwer, 1987), 108.
176. 'Een nieuwe verspreidingswijze voor internationale discussie-ontwerpen en uitspraken', *De Accountant*, 90/10 (June 1984), 742.
177. 'Regeling Gelijkwaardigheid van Voorschriften voor Jaarrekeningen', 15 January 1986, reproduced in *Documentatie Rond de Jaarrekening* (Deventer: Kluwer), 7.01-31-3.
178. IASC board meeting of 5–7 March 1986, minute 11.
179. 'Netherlands: International Standards Equivalent to Seventh Directive', *IASC News*, 15/2 (April 1986), 1; letter from Cairns to Herman Marseille, dated 3 February 1986, IASC archive, file 'the Netherlands'.
180. 'Hopes Raised for IAS Recognition'. *Accountancy*, 102/1142 (October 1988), 1; interview with Karel Van Hulle, 17 February 2004.
181. Kamerstukken (parliamentary papers), 19813, no. 9, 18 May 1988.
182. The Institute's reply to the IASC, dated 30 September 1979, reproduced in AP 3/1980 paper 19A, pages 76–7.
183. R.S. Olusegun Wallace, *Accounting and Financial Reporting in Nigeria* (London: ICAEW, 1989), 94–100.
184. 'Compliance reports', AP 3/1986 paper 17, page 18.
185. *Survey of the Use and Application of International Accounting Standards 1988*, 21–69.
186. J. A. Porteous, 'Accounting Standards in South Africa', *CAmagazine*, 107/4 (October 1975), 66.
187. The National Council's reply to the IASC, dated 30 September 1979, reproduced in AP 3/1980 paper 19A, pages 78–83.
188. Interviews with Doug Brooking, 18 March 2004, with Rick Cottrell, 15 March 2004, and with Ian Somerville, 15 March 2004.
189. 'Compliance reports', AP 3/1986 paper 17.
190. *Survey of the Use and Application of International Accounting Standards 1988*, 21–69.
191. *Survey of the Use and Application of International Accounting Standards 1988*, 5.
192. Cairns, Lafferty, and Mantle, *Survey of Accounts and Accountants 1983–84*, 21.

193. Cairns, Lafferty, and Mantle, *Survey of Accounts and Accountants 1983–84*, 105. Also see Stefano Zambon and Chiara Saccon, 'Accounting Change in Italy: Fresh Start or *Gattopardo*'s Revolution', *The European Accounting Review*, 2/2 (September 1993), 250; Angelo Riccaboni and Rosanna Ghirri, *European Financial Reporting: Italy* (London: Routledge, 1994), 98; 'CONSOB's Big Move', *World Accounting Report*, April 1982, 3; and *IASC News*, 11/3 (May 1982), 1, where it was said, 'This decision in Italy is being reported as the most important step CONSOB has taken and one of great significance for the accounting world in general, not just for Italy'.
194. 'Activities on Compliance with IASC in Italy', submitted by the Consiglio Nazionale dei Dottori Commercialisti, addendum to the minutes of the IASC board meeting of 14–16 June 1983; in 1986, it was said that 'most auditors' reports make reference to IASC statements', 'Compliance Reports', AP 3/1986 paper 17, page 11.
195. *Survey of the Use and Application of International Accounting Standards 1988*, 21–69.
196. *Survey of the Use and Application of International Accounting Standards 1988*, 5.
197. 'Compliance reports', AP 3/1986 paper 17, pages 24–8.
198. Anne Wu, 'Taiwan', in Ronald Ma (editor), *Financial Reporting in the Pacific Asia Region* (Singapore: World Scientific, 1997), 273–9.
199. *Survey of the Use and Application of International Accounting Standards 1988*, 21–69.
200. *Survey of the Use and Application of International Accounting Standards 1988*, 5.
201. Interview with Allan V. C. Cook, 30 April 2003. Nobes has identified Kenya, Malaysia, Nigeria, Pakistan, Singapore, and Zimbabwe as countries where 'a ready-made IASC set [of standards] has proved attractive'. Nobes, 'Harmonization of Financial Reporting', in Nobes and Parker (editors), *Comparative International Accounting* (1991), 79.
202. *IASC News*, 6/3 (May 1978), 2.
203. Dara F. Dastoor, 'Financial Reporting in Pakistan', *The Pakistan Accountant* (April–June 1976), 5–6.
204. *IASC News*, 9/2 (March 1980), 2.
205. *IASC News*, 15/1 (February 1986), 1; Companies Ordinance, 1984, paragraph 234(3)(i).
206. Bhabatosh Banerjee, 'Harmonization of Accounting Standards in Some SAARC Countries—A Study with Special Reference to India', in Bhabatosh Banerjee (editor), *Contemporary Issues in Accounting Research* (Calcutta: Indian Accounting Association Research Foundation, 1991), 204.
207. *Survey of the Use and Application of International Accounting Standards 1988*, 21–69.
208. Bhabatosh Banerjee, *Regulation of Corporate Accounting and Reporting in India* (Calcutta: The World Press, 2002), 42.
209. Kamal Gupta, 'Harmonization of Accounting Standards: The Indian Experience', in *Standard Setting for Financial Reporting: An International Conference Sponsored by the American Accounting Association with Klynveld Main Goerdeler*, Princeton, New Jersey, 17–20 August 1986, 136.
210. D. K. Chakravorty, *Development of Corporate Accounting in India* (New Delhi: Venus Publishing House, 1994), 113.
211. Letter from P. S. Gopalakrishnan to W. J. Brennan, dated 4 November 1976, IASC archive, 'Enforcement—Associate Members' file.
212. *Survey of the Use and Application of International Accounting Standards 1988*, 21–69. On page 14 of the survey, however, it is affirmed that IASC standards are used more widely than the detailed analysis by standard would suggest.
213. For the procedure used, see *IASC News*, 11/4 (July 1982), 5.

214. Foo See Liang and Ng Shwn Yng, 'Singapore', in T. E. Cooke and R. H. Parker (editors), *Financial Reporting in the West Pacific Rim* (London: Routledge, 1994), 270, 275–8, 296–7.
215. *Survey of the Use and Application of International Accounting Standards 1988*, 21–69.
216. Communication from David Cairns to the authors, dated 22 January 2004.
217. P. Phenix, 'Hong Kong', in Cooke and Parker (editors), *Financial Reporting in the West Pacific Rim*, 174–5.
218. Pak Auyeung, 'Hong Kong', in Ma (editor), *Financial Reporting in the Pacific Asia Region*, 293–8.
219. *Survey of the Use and Application of International Accounting Standards 1988*, 21–69.
220. J. S. W. Tay, 'Malaysia', in Cooke and Parker (editors), *Financial Reporting in the West Pacific Rim*, 236, 241–2, 261. Also see Hai Yap Teoh and Soon Guan Chuah, 'Malaysia', in Ma (editor), *Financial Reporting in the Pacific Asia Region*, 336–40.
221. *IASC News*, 9/2 (March 1980), 2.
222. Paul Phenix, 'International Accounting Standards and the Regulation of Corporate Business', *The Malaysian Accountant* (July 1986), 11.
223. Interview with Paul Phenix, 26 May 2003.
224. *Survey of the Use and Application of International Accounting Standards 1988*, 21–69.
225. Stephen A. Zeff, *Forging Accounting Principles in New Zealand* (Wellington: Victoria University Press, 1979), 59.
226. AP 4/1975 paper 12.
227. *Survey of the Use and Application of International Accounting Standards 1988*, 21–69.
228. IASC Chairman-Designate Arthur R. Wyatt said in 1989, 'The absence of representatives from South or Central America on the Board of IASC is a notable gap'. 'Absence of Latin America—A Gap on the IASC Board', *IASC News*, 18/4 (December 1989), 4–5.
229. IASC meetings of 5–6 November 1974, minute 11(11); of 8–10 October 1975, minute 11(3); of 9–11 March 1976 minute 10(4). Galván was a partner in Price Waterhouse & Co., which was strongly linked with Price Waterhouse Peat & Co. (PWP), the dominant accounting firm in both Argentina and Brazil, as well as in Uruguay, Bolivia, and Peru. Cummings was a partner in Peat, Marwick, Mitchell & Co., which was also affiliated with PWP.
230. Of the forty-one, ten were in Asia and six were in Africa.
231. Gray, Campbell, and Shaw (editors), *International Financial Reporting: A Comparative International Survey of Accounting Requirements and Practices in 30 Countries*.
232. Fitzgerald, Stickler, and Watts, *International Survey of Accounting Principles and Reporting Practices*.
233. *Survey of the Use and Application of International Accounting Standards 1988*. Ecuador joined IFAC in 1983.
234. IASC board meeting of 5–7 March 1986, minute 7(xiii)(b).
235. Communication from Howard P. Keefe (formerly president of the Inter-American Accounting Association) to the authors, dated 22 October 2003. It is of some interest that the leading Argentine accountancy body was reported to have said in 1974 that it did not intend to apply for associate membership because 'its international relations are dealt with through the Interamerican Accounting Conference'. IASC meeting of 5–6 November 1974, minute 11(11).
236. *Survey of the Use and Application of International Accounting Standards 1988*, 53.
237. Interview with Ralph E. Walters, 18 October 2003.

238. 'IASC-Board, 24–27 maart 1981, Tokyo', memo by Henk Volten dated 6 April 1981, NIVRA archive, no. 485. According to this memo, letters had been sent to companies in the Canada, the Netherlands, and the United Kingdom, and companies had been approached orally in Australia and the US. France was said to be studying the matter, and Germany and South Africa had reported that the 'time was not yet ripe' to take action.
239. *IASC News*, 4/5 (2 August 1976), 3.
240. Quoted in *IASC News*, 15/5 (October 1986), 4.
241. Memorandum from Hans Burggraaff to the authors, dated 22 April 2004.
242. Quoted in *IASC News*, 12/6 (November 1983), 1–2.
243. Interview with Richard J. Simmons, 25 September 2003.
244. Rutteman, 'Demands of a Different Environment', 17. Other studies which highlighted the IASC's limited impact include Thomas G. Evans and Martin E. Taylor, ' "Bottom Line Compliance" with the IASC: A Comparative Analysis', *International Journal of Accounting Education and Research*, Fall 1982, 115–28, and S. M. McKinnon and Paul Janell, 'The International Accounting Standards Committee: A Performance Evaluation', *International Journal of Accounting Education and Research*, Spring 1984, 19–34.
245. e.g., Chairman Cummings invited the SEC chairman, the FASB chairman, the AICPA president, the SEC chief accountant, and the vice-president of the New York Stock Exchange to a dinner he gave in Washington, DC on 10 November 1976 on the occasion of the board's first meeting in the United States. See *IASC News*, 4/7 (24 November 1976), 1–2. The NIVRA gave a dinner for the IASC in March 1977, when the board was meeting in Amsterdam, to which several Dutch dignitaries were invited. Hans Burggraaff was at that time the president of the NIVRA. *IASC News*, 5/2 (18 March 1977), 2.
246. *IASC News*, 6/2 (February 1978), 4; *IASC News*, 6/4 (July 1978), 4.
247. On Burggraaff's proposal for outreach see IASC board meeting of 24–7 June 1980, minute 10. See IASC board meeting of 14–16 March 1984, minute 5(g) for Chairman Stephen Elliott's plans for visits. Also see *IASC News*, 12/6 (November 1983), 4–5; *IASC News*, 15/3 (June 1986), 2; and *IASC News*, 15/4 (August 1986), 3.
248. *IASC News*, 10/1 (February 1981), 1.
249. *IASC News*, 10/6 (October 1981), 5; *IASC News*, 11/1 (February 1982), 2; *IASC News*, 12/1 (February 1983), 2. These visits were reported in the IASC's presentation to the SEC on 26 March 1984 (*see* Section 6.23). For visits in 1985, see *IASC News*, 14/3 (May 1985), 1.
250. 'International Accounting Standards Committee: Report on Activities for the Year Ended 30 June 1986', *1986 Annual Report* of the International Federation of Accountants, 16.
251. See *IASC News*, 15/5 (October 1986), 4; and *IASC News*, 16/1 (February 1987), 2, 4.
252. Communication from David Cairns to the authors, dated 22 January 2004.
253. Extracts from some of their remarks to the board were appended to the minutes. Extracts from, and a summary of, Spinosa Cattela's talk appears in *IASC News*, 15/4 (August 1986), 1.
254. IASC board meeting of 14–16 June 1983, minute 6(j)(i).
255. IASC meetings of 14–15 January 1974, minute 13; 15–17 July 1974, minute 16(3); and 15–16 January 1975, minute 11(1).
256. Letter from Kramer to Cook, dated 11 March 1980, IASC archive, file 'Liaison—Groupe d'Études, UEC & IASC'.

257. Memorandum to the authors from Hans Burggraaff, dated 22 April 2004.
258. The correspondence between the IASC and the European Commission, and minutes of the meetings, may be found in the 'EEC' file in the IASC archive.
259. *IASC News*, 15/4 (August 1986), 3.
260. John L. Kirkpatrick, typescript of a speech to be presented at the Accounting Standards—International Conflict Conference on 10 December 1980, IASC archive, speeches file.
261. Quoted in *IASC News*, 13/2 (March 1984), 4. Also see 'IASC to Meet SEC for First Time', *International Accounting Bulletin*, no. 9 (March 1984), 7; and 'Chenok, Kirk Comment at SEC Open Meeting on International Accounting Rules', *Journal of Accountancy*, 157/5 (May 1984), 12. Shad's testimony was reproduced in *International Bank Lending: Hearings before the Subcommittee on Financial Institutions Supervision, Regulation and Insurance of the Committee on Banking, Finance and Urban Affairs*, House of Representatives, Ninety-eighth Congress, First Session, 20–1 April 1983 (Serial No. 98-16), 358–9.
262. Kirk, 'Some Comments on the Prospects for International Harmonization'.
263. 'Comments by Donald J. Kirk at the SEC Meeting March 26, 1984', copy in IASC archive, SEC file.
264. 'No Breakthrough at SEC/IASC Summit', *International Accounting Bulletin*, no. 10 (April 1984), 12.
265. *IASC News*, 13/2 (March 1984), 4.
266. 'No Breakthrough at SEC/IASC Summit', *International Accounting Bulletin*, no. 10 (April 1984), 12.
267. In September 1984, Paul Rosenfield telephoned Clarence Staubs to ask if the SEC would consider responding to IASC exposure drafts. Staubs replied that this would not be possible, as the SEC did not even respond to the FASB's exposure drafts. Memorandum from Geoffrey Mitchell dated 26 September 1984, IASC archive, SEC file. In the 1990s, however, the SEC did begin to comment on IASC exposure drafts, either directly or through IOSCO.
268. *IASC News*, 14/4 (July 1985), 5; letter from David Cairns to John Wheeler (SEC), dated 12 July 1985, IASC archive, SEC file.
269. *Internationalization of the Securities Markets,* chapter IV-51.
270. *Internationalization of the Securities Markets*, chapter IV-52. Report of the Staff of the U.S. Securities and Exchange Commission to the Senate Committee on Banking, Housing and Urban Affairs and the House Committee on Energy and Commerce, dated 27 July 1987 (available at: http://www.sechistorical.org/collection/papers/1980/1987_IntSecMarketsRep).
271. *Internationalization of the Securities Markets*, chapter IV-50.

NOTES TO CHAPTER 7

1. Edward Stamp, 'Uniformity in International Accounting Standards', *Journal of Accountancy*, 133/4 (April 1972), 67.
2. 'UN Calls Summit over Accounting', *Accountancy Age*, 2/45 (17 December 1971), 1. The 1971 conference was organized from 7 to 10 December by the ILO's International Centre for Advanced Technical and Vocational Training in Turin.
3. *The Impact of Multinational Corporations on Development and on International Relations* (New York: United Nations, 1974), 32.
4. *The Impact of Multinational Corporations*, 95–6.

5. IASC meeting of 5–6 November 1974, minute 12.
6. Klaus A. Sahlgren, 'The Work of Non-Accountant International Bodies: The United Nations', in W. John Brennan (editor), *The Internationalization of the Accountancy Profession* (Toronto: The Canadian Institute of Chartered Accountants, 1979), 67.
7. See, e.g. 'IASC Upstaged by UN', *Accountancy Age*, 8/42 (21 October 1977), 4.
8. IASC meetings of 9–11 March 1976, minute 17, and of 6–8 July 1976, minute 17.
9. *International Standards of Accounting and Reporting for Transnational Corporations: Report of the Group of Experts on International Accounting and Reporting* (E/C 10/33) (New York: United Nations Publications, 1978).
10. 'UN Body Prepares Rules for Multinationals', *Accountancy Age*, 8/34 (26 August 1977), 7; 'The U.N. May "Audit" Business', *Business Week* (26 June 1978), 98. See also Donald J. Hayes, 'The International Accounting Standards Committee: Recent Developments and Current Problems', *International Journal of Accounting Education and Research*, 16 (Fall 1980), 5–6.
11. 'The UN Plan for World Reporting Standards', *World Accounting Report*, April 1978, 2–3; 'Multinationals Spurn UN Plan', *World Accounting Report*, May 1978, 5–10.
12. Henry Benson, 'Flaws in the UN's Disclosure Proposals', *Financial Times*, 22 March 1978. John Grenside, 'Search for Worldwide Harmony', *Accountancy Age*, 5 December 1980, 18, commented that some of the disclosure requirements tended 'to reflect emotional and political motivation particularly by developing country governments suspicious about a [transnational corporation's] local activities'.
13. Edward Stamp, 'Why Opposition to the UN's Disclosure Plans is Misguided', *Financial Times*, 10 May 1978. See also Stamp's letter to the editor, 'Disclosure Proposals', *Financial Times*, 14 April 1978.
14. IASC board meeting of 7–9 November 1978, minute 11.
15. Circular letter from O. Van der Meulen to Heads of Delegations, dated 13 October 1977, attached to AP 6/1978 paper 16. See also 'Secretary's Notes on Meeting [of Alec Mackenzie and John Brennan with O. Van der Meulen and K. Van Oostveldt] 15 December 1977', AP 3/1978 paper 18B; letter from J. A. Hepworth to O. Van der Meulen, dated 12 July 1978, IASC archive, file 'Belgium'; see correspondence with Scandinavian bodies in AP 6/1978 paper 16.
16. Letter from Ata Ullah to Roy C. Nash, dated 27 March 1978, attached to AP 6/1978 paper 18, and related correspondence in IASC archive, 'Pakistan' country file.
17. AP 6/1978 paper 18.
18. AP 6/1978 paper 18. See also letter from H. F. Richardson to A. C. I. Mbanefo, dated 8 September 1978, IASC archive, file 'Nigeria'.
19. 'Review of Existing IAS's', AP 6/1982 paper 13. In the end, the steering committee consisted of representatives from Malaysia, Mexico, South Africa, and the Netherlands.
20. See Sheikh F. Rahman, 'International Accounting Regulation by the United Nations: A Power Perspective', *Accounting, Auditing & Accountability Journal*, 11/5 (1998), 593–623, for an analysis of the tensions over financial reporting between the G77 and OECD countries.
21. See comments by Washington SyCip in 'Informal Notes on a Discussion at the IFAC Council, 14 May 1980', IASC archive, file 'Mutual Commitments'; Peter Mantle, 'IASC Seeks Links with UN and OECD', *World Accounting Report*, October 1980, 6.
22. Hans Burggraaff, quoted in 'Informal Secretariat Notes of an IFAC/IASC Working Party meeting', 2 November 1981, IASC archive, file 'Mutual Commitments'.

23. Memo from John Denman to R. D. Thomas, dated 26 November 1980, IASC archive, file 'United Nations 1979–1983'. See also Peter Mantle, 'Mexico Congress a Forum for World Debate', *Financial Times*, 17 June 1982, 32: 'The UN in particular seems quite impressed with the level of co-operation afforded by the accountants [i.e. the IASC]'.
24. James Carty, 'Accounting Standards and the United Nations', *World Accounting Report*, September 1982, 9–15.
25. 'Notes on Telephone Conversation with George Smith by Geoffrey Mitchell' dated 26 November 1982, IASC archive, file 'United Nations 1979–1983'.
26. Letter from John Denman to Stephen Elliott, dated 20 October 1982, IASC archive, file 'United Nations 1979–1983'.
27. Geoffrey B. Mitchell, 'IASC—A Decade of Success and Achievement', *World Accounting Report*, October 1982, 4.
28. *International Standards of Accounting and Reporting: Report of the Ad Hoc Intergovernmental Working Group of Experts on International Standards of Accounting and Reporting* (E/C 10/1982/8) (New York: United Nations Centre on Transnational Corporations, 1982).
29. Richard D. Fitzgerald, 'International Accounting and Reporting: Where in the World Are We Headed?', *The Price Waterhouse Review*, 27/2 (1983), 22.
30. UN Economic and Social Council, resolution 1982/67.
31. Communication from Lorraine Ruffing to the authors, dated 19 August 2005.
32. 'International Group of Experts—Notes on First Session', undated memo, IASC Archive, file 'United Nations 1979–1983'.
33. As in 'Minutes of the Fifth Meeting of the IASC/IFAC Coordinating Committee . . . 5 June 1987', minute 4. IASC Archive, file 'IASC/IFAC Coordinating Committee 1982–1995'.
34. 'NIVRA Position Paper Regarding IASC-Proposals', memo by Henk Volten, dated 9 April 1973, NIVRA archive, no. 477.
35. In a 25 September 1973 speech, SEC Chairman Ray Garrett remarked: 'The head of our Division of Corporation Finance is working with senior officials from foreign countries under the auspices of the Organization for Economic Cooperation and Development to establish minimum standards [for offering and trading securities] and the Commission's Chief Accountant is participating in the work of the American Institute of Certified Public Accountants and various international groups to resolve the important differences in financial reporting around the world.' Ray Garrett, 'The Internationalization of our Securities Markets', typescript (in the authors' files), 12.
36. Interview with Allan V. C. Cook, 30 April 2003.
37. The genre seems to have started with P. N. McMonnies, 'EEC, UEC, ASC, IASC, AISG, ICCAP-IFAC, Old Uncle Tom Cobbleigh and All', *Accounting and Business Research*, 7/28 (Summer 1977), 162–7. See also 'OECD Enters Accounting Standards Ring', *World Accounting Report*, May 1979, 6; Sean Heath, 'Who is Meddling in Worldwide Accounting?', *Accountancy Age*, 10/37 (28 September 1979), 13; Michael Renshall, 'Serving Six Masters', *Accountancy Age*, 11/6 (8 February 1980), 18; Kate Moore, 'World Standard-Setters Look to 1982—But Will It All Be Simpler?', *Accountancy*, 86/1047 (November 1980), 18.
38. See, e.g. J. C. Shaw, 'Multinational Corporations and International Standards', *World Accounting Report*, July 1980, 2–3, and the response by John H. Denman, 'Canadian Support for IASC', *World Accounting Report*, August 1980, 5–7.

39. In 1978, the Financial Executives Institute wrote to the US Secretary of State that international corporate disclosure standards should be issued by the OECD rather than the UN, if this could not be left to 'existing groups of professionals who are well qualified to do this work'. Letter from Charles C. Hornbostel to Cyrus R. Vance, dated 8 May 1978, IASC archive, file 'OECD Working Group to 1983'. See also Grenside, 'Search for Worldwide Harmony', 18.
40. See 'Accounting Standards Shake Up Urged by World Body', *Accountancy Age*, 10/36 (21 September 1979), 1.
41. Interview with Allan V. C. Cook, 30 April 2003. The possibility that the OECD might set standards was suggested by Michael Lafferty, 'OECD May Issue Accounts Standards', *Financial Times*, 22 March 1979. Referring to this article, David Hoddinott, the chairman of the OECD Ad Hoc Working Group, wrote to IASC board member John Grenside to deny that the OECD considered issuing accounting standards for multinational enterprises (letter dated 26 March 1979). Yet, at the meeting of the Working Group in April 1979, some members of the OECD Secretariat expressed themselves rather more in favour of a standard-setting role. See letter from Willis A. Smith to John Hepworth, dated 31 July 1979 and attached to report on OECD Working Group meeting. All letters in IASC archive, file 'OECD Working Group to 1983'.
42. AP 6/1979 paper 20; interview with Allan V. C. Cook, 30 April 2003.
43. IASC board meeting of 19–21 June 1979, minute 12.
44. The Canadian and US government representatives gave 'pretty solid support' to the view that 'the OECD should be kept out of standard-setting'. Letter from R. D. Thomas to Hepworth, dated 3 October 1979. During the fall of 1979, the US delegates, Willis Smith and Donald Hayes, were in touch with the US State Department themselves and liaised with companies and organizations who did the same. IASC archive, file 'OECD Working Group to 1983'.
45. Meeting of IASC board of 23–5 October 1979, minute 14.
46. See also 'Future OECD Work on Accounting Standards', report by the Ad Hoc Working Group on Accounting Standards, 9 November 1979, OECD, IME(79).17 (1st revision), paragraph 27(ii).
47. Arnold Kransdorff, 'Co-ordinating Role Seen for OECD in Financial Reporting', *World Accounting Report*, October 1979, 12–14; John H. Denman, 'The OECD and International Accounting Standards', *CAmagazine*, 113 (February 1980), 56–9.
48. See, e.g. Roy Nash, 'Why Multinationals Should Support IASC', *World Accounting Report*, February 1980, 2–4; John L. Kirkpatrick, 'International Harmonization Needs Help of Big Audit Firms', *World Accounting Report*, July 1981, 2–3.
49. IASC board meeting of 24–7 June 1980, minute 10.
50. AP 3/1981 paper 16.
51. 'Future OECD Work on Accounting Standards', report by the Ad Hoc Working Group on Accounting Standards, 9 November 1979, OECD, IME(79).17 (1st revision), paragraph 30(i).
52. See for instance letter from A. V. C. Cook to D. P. Tweedie, dated 14 July 1980, IASC archive, file 'OECD Working Group to 1983'.
53. Interview with Geoffrey Mitchell, 19 February 2004.
54. *Harmonization of Accounting Standards: Achievements and Prospects* (Paris: OECD, 1986). The significance of the support expressed for the IASC at the conference is reported in H. Marseille, 'Jaarverslaggeving en harmonisering van standaarden', *De Accountant*, 91/11 (July/August 1985), 610–12; and Susan Baker, 'Growing

Prestige of the IAS Setters', *Certified Accountant* (United Kingdom), May 1986, 10–11.
55. The wording 'part of' was deliberately chosen. A proposal by the ICAEW had included the phrase that the IASC should be 'under the aegis' of ICCAP. The German representative Krafft von der Tann jokingly questioned the use of Latin when it had just been agreed that the official language of the IASC was English. But the serious underlying point was taken up, and the more explicit 'part of' was used. Note by John Williams, attached to letter from Elliott to Burggraaff, Kirkpatrick, and Cook, dated 13 January 1981, IASC archive, file 'Mutual Commitments'.
56. Wallace E. Olson, *The Accounting Profession, Years of Trial: 1969–1980* (New York: American Institute of Certified Public Accountants, 1982), 232–6. See also 'ICCAP Plan Hits Trouble', *Accountancy Age*, 6/13 (4 April 1975), 1; 'Preparing to Meet the Challenge of the New World', *Accountancy Age*, 6/28 (18 July 1975), 7.
57. AP 10/1975 paper 21.
58. Letter from Reinhard Goerdeler to Benson, dated 3 October 1975, IASC archive, file 'Organisation and Future Work'.
59. Olson, *The Accounting Profession*, 236, suggests that the organizations sponsoring the IASC and ICCAP could have decided the fate of the IASC by themselves, but that 'it was believed that obtaining the agreement of the individuals serving on the IASC would avoid any bruised feelings'.
60. IASC meeting of 8–10 October 1975, minute 14.
61. See Henry Benson, 'Note of a Meeting in Frankfurt . . . 26th January 1976', IASC archive, file 'IFAC General Correspondence'; AP 3/1976 paper 25; AP 11/1976 paper 7b; correspondence between Benson and Goerdeler, March–November 1976, IASC archive, files 'IFAC General Correspondence' and 'Correspondence re IASC & ICCAP'.
62. *Interim Report of the International Coordination Committee of the Accountancy Profession*, March 1976, paragraph 20; *Final Report of the International Coordination Committee of the Accountancy Profession*, March 1977, paragraph 45.
63. Gordon Cowperthwaite, 'Chronology of Events Relating to Relationship Between ICCAP, IFAC and IASC', January 1981. The attribution of this unsigned note to Cowperthwaite is based on equating it to the 'paper' by Cowperthwaite referred to in Allan Cook's memo 'IASC/IFAC Working Party 14 January 1981'. Both papers in IASC archive, file 'Mutual Commitments'.
64. This working party was the predecessor of the Organisation and Planning Committee (OPC).
65. 'Agreement and Constitution of IASC', 10 May 1976, IASC archive, file 'Organisation and Future Work'.
66. Letter from Mackenzie to Cummings, dated 2 September 1976, IASC archive, file 'Organisation and Future Work'.
67. Letter from H. F. A. Cordoliani to W. J. Brennan, dated 29 June 1976; telex from H. Kaminski to W. J. Brennan, dated 26 July 1976; letter from Cummings to Mackenzie, dated 20 August 1976; letter from Mackenzie to Cummings, dated 2 September 1976. All documents in IASC archive, file 'Organisation and Future Work'.
68. Subsequent meetings were also attended by Hans Burggraaff for the IASC and Wallace Olson, Washington SyCip, and Russell Palmer for IFAC.
69. 'Meeting of the Joint IASC/IFAC Working Party, 13 June 1979', IASC archive, file 'Mutual Commitments'.

70. 'Meeting of the Joint IASC/IFAC Working Party, 13 June 1979'; letter from Olson to Robert Sempier, dated 22 August 1979; telex from Hepworth to Nash and Cook, dated 4 September 1979; letter from Cook to Sempier, dated 7 September 1979. All documents in IASC archive, file 'Mutual Commitments'.
71. AP 10/1979 paper 13.
72. See Stephen A. Zeff, Frans van der Wel, and Kees Camfferman, *Company Financial Reporting, A Historical and Comparative Study of the Dutch Regulatory Process* (Amsterdam: North-Holland, 1992), chapter 5.
73. 'IASC/IFAC Working Party Recommendations, Informal Secretariat Notes of IASC Board Discussion, October 1979', IASC archive, file 'Mutual Commitments'.
74. 'IFAC Council, 6 November 1979, Mexico City', IASC archive, file 'Mutual Commitments'.
75. J. A. Burggraaff, 'Notes on Conversation with G. Cowperthwaite', October 1980, IASC archive, file 'Mutual Commitments'.
76. AP 3/1980 papers 15–17.
77. IASC board meeting of 11–13 March 1980, minute 12.
78. 'United Kingdom and Irish Position on the Proposed IASC/IFAC Merger', IASC archive, file 'Mutual Commitments'.
79. 'Informal Secretariat Notes on Joint IASC/IFAC Working Party, 14 March 1980', IASC archive, file 'Mutual Commitments'.
80. See also Peter Mantle, 'IASC/IFAC Merger Now Unlikely', *World Accounting Report*, December 1980, 3.
81. J. A. Burggraaff, 'Notes on Conversation with G. Cowperthwaite', October 1980, IASC archive, file 'Mutual Commitments'.
82. 'The future of IASC, Informal Secretariat Notes on IASC Board Discussion 26 June 1980', IASC archive, file 'Mutual Commitments'.
83. Meeting of IASC board of 4–6 November 1980, minute 10.
84. Letter from Cook to Michael H. J. Hornby, dated 18 February 1981, IASC archive, file 'Mutual Commitments'.
85. Communication from J. A. Burggraaff to the authors, dated 22 April 2004.
86. Interview with Allan V. C. Cook, 30 April 2003.
87. Allan Cook, 'IASC/IFAC Working Party 14 January 1981 Toronto', IASC archive, file 'Mutual Commitments'. Unless otherwise indicated, the discussion of this meeting is based on this memo. It is assumed that the pages of this handwritten memo are incorrectly numbered and that the order of the meeting is reflected by reading the pages in the following order: 1, 4 (two pages), 2, 3, 5.
88. Or 'Institutes'. Burggraaff may not necessarily have been thinking of the US FEI alone.
89. See Peter Mantle, 'IFAC and IASC: A New Relationship', *World Accounting Report*, February 1981, 21.
90. 'IASC/IFAC Mutual Commitments', paragraph 8.
91. That the formation of the Consultative Group was purely a response to outside pressure is suggested in 'IASC's Future Hangs on Tokyo Decisions', *Accountancy Age*, 13 January 1981, 9.
92. Henk Volten, 'NIVRA Position Paper Regarding IASC-Proposals', 9 April 1973, NIVRA archive, no. 477.
93. IASC meeting of 15–16 November 1973, minute 16(1).
94. Telex from Galván to Rosenfield, dated 7 March 1974, IASC archive, file 'IAFEI'.
95. Note from Benson to Rosenfield, dated 17 April 1974, IASC archive, file 'IAFEI'.

96. This list consisted of: World Bank, International Finance Corporation, International Monetary Fund, OECD, European Commission, International Chamber of Commerce, International Confederation of Free Trade Unions, World Confederation of Labour, Fédération Internationale des Bourses de Valeurs, European Federation of Financial Analysts' Societies, International Bar Association, ICCAP, UEC, Groupe d'Études, International Labour Organisation, Association Nationale des Directeurs Financiers et de Contrôle de Gestion, US Agency for International Development, Confederation of Asian and Pacific Accountants, International Association of Financial Executives Institutes. AP 1/1974 paper 10; AP 4/1974 paper 2; IASC meeting of 14–15 January 1974, minute 7.
97. As shown by an analysis of IASC contacts by the secretariat, AP 10/1979 paper 18.
98. NIVRA General Director Henk Volten did so in a November 1976 conference on international standards, hosted by the English Institute. See 'What Standards Now for International Standards?', *Accountancy Age*, 7/46 (26 November 1976), 8.
99. Interview with Allan V. C. Cook, 30 April 2003.
100. Meeting of IASC board of 23–5 October 1979, minute 15; AP 10/1979 paper 18.
101. A secretariat paper on these issues was discussed at the board meeting of 24–7 June 1980 (Minute 10). See also AP 6/1980 paper 14 and 'The Future of IASC, Informal Secretariat Notes 26 June 1980', IASC archive, file 'Mutual Commitments'. The idea of a consultative group had in fact been suggested by Wallace Olson in 1979: 'IASC/IFAC Working Party, 7 November 1979', IASC archive, file 'Mutual Commitments'.
102. Peter Godfrey, 'Why the ASC Should Go It Alone', *Accountancy*, 98/1117 (September 1986). Godfrey, the ASC chairman from 1984 to 1986, added, 'This facility has never been used to the full and I consider that to be unfortunate'. Indeed, only two of the twenty ASC members appointed in 1985 and only one of the twenty-one in 1987 were not members of the CCAB accountancy bodies, and were users. *Accountancy*, 96/1107 (November 1985), 23; *Accountancy*, 100/1127 (July 1987), 38.
103. 'Informal Notes on a Discussion at the IFAC Council, 14 May 1980', IASC archive, file 'Mutual Commitments'. On French reservations to involve 'non-professionals' see also letter from Burggraaff to Cowperthwaite, 26 February 1981, IASC archive, file 'Mutual Commitments'.
104. The list consisted of: International Chamber of Commerce, International Association of Financial Executives Institutes, Fédération Internationale des Bourses de Valeurs, International Council of Free Trade Unions, World Confederation of Labour, World Bank, and 'a group representing the international interests of commercial banks, if an appropriate body could be identified'. 'International representation by financial analysts should also be sought if it was established that they would not overlap with any of the other groups that were being approached'. IASC board meeting of 24–7 June, 1980, minute 10.
105. See also Peter Mantle, 'IASC to Form New Consultative User Group', *World Accounting Report*, January 1981, 8–9.
106. *Establishing Financial Accounting Standards: Report of the Study on Establishment of Accounting Principles* (New York: American Institute of Certified Public Accountants, 1972), 75–7.
107. *Accounting Standards 1978: The Full Texts of all UK Exposure Drafts and Accounting Standards Extant at 1 May 1978* (London: The Institute of Chartered Accountants in England and Wales, 1978), 3.

108. Burggraaff cited from 'IASC/IFAC Working Party, 7 November 1979', IASC archive, file 'Mutual Commitments'. The idea of seats for outside organizations had already been included in the draft integration agreement presented by the JWP in March 1980, see AP 3/1980 papers 15–17.
109. Interview with Allan V. C. Cook, 30 April 2003; communication from J. A. Burggraaff to the authors, dated 22 April 2004.
110. In June 1981, IASC Chairman Stephen Elliott mentioned the Fédération Internationale des Bourses de Valeurs, the International Confederation of Free Trade Unions, the World Bank, and the International Association of Financial Executives Institutes as possible board members, but not the financial analysts. 'IASC and IFAC Formalize Relationship', *CAmagazine*, 114 (June 1981), 20.
111. Letter from Damant to Rosenfield, dated 19 November 1973, IASC archive, file 'Financial Analysts'.
112. IASC board meeting of 24–7 March 1981, minute 11. See also letter from Damant to Cook, dated 12 March 1980, IASC archive, file 'Financial Analysts'.
113. IASC board meeting of 19–21 June 1984, minute 6(r)(iii); IASC board meeting of 6–8 March 1985, minute 7(l); IASC board meeting of 25–7 June 1985, minute 7(g); IASC board meeting of 16–18 October 1985, minute 8. See also *IASC News*, 14/6 (November 1995), 1.
114. The two quotations are taken from an interview with David Cairns, 8 June 2003. In a number of countries in Western Europe as late as the 1980s, company executives did not regard auditors as being on the same social plane. Also see minute 7(iv) from the IASC board meeting of 5–7 March 1986.
115. Appendix I to Mutual Commitments, annex I.
116. See, e.g. 'IASC Takes Stock of Relationship with IFAC', *Accountancy*, 96/1107 (November 1985), 7; 'May Surveys World Scene', *World Accounting Report*, November 1986, 3.
117. Starting with the 1987 congress, what was previously known as the International Congress of Accountants was referred to as the World Congress of Accountants.
118. Letter from Raymond G. Harris to Heads of Institutes represented on the IFAC Council and the IASC Board, dated 7 August 1987, IASC archive, 'Bishop Working Party' file.
119. Letter from Raymond G. Harris to Heads of Institutes, dated 15 September 1987, IASC archive, 'Bishop Working Party' file.
120. Ray Harris, letter to the editor, *Accountancy Age*, 29 October 1987.
121. The ICAEW's attitude to Wilkes is discussed in 'Note of Telephone Conversation with Georges Barthès 2 December 1988', memo by David Cairns, IASC archive, 'Bishop Working Party' file.
122. Letter from Henk Volten to David Cairns, dated 14 January 1986; letter from Henk Volten to Raymond Harris, dated 24 August 1987. See for comments on the significance of Volten's change of mind 'Notes of a Meeting at the Institute of Chartered Accountants in England and Wales', memo by David Cairns, dated 11 February 1988. All documents in IASC archive, 'Bishop Working Party' file. For Volten's views on the IASC's strategic discussions in March 1987, see 'De toekomst van het IASC', memo by Henk Volten, dated 19 February 1987, NIVRA archive, no. 49.
123. 'The Changing World of the Accountant', *Accountancy Age*, 22 October 1987, 1.
124. The working party itself recognized that merger 'had been the thrust of the Canadian initiative in convening the Tokyo meeting..., but that the terms of reference adopted in Tokyo—whilst not excluding merger considerations—did not focus

on this question'. 'Points from Meeting—June 1988', attached to letter from John Bishop to Marc Ghiliotti, 3 August 1988, IASC archive, 'Bishop Working Party' file.
125. Interview with John N. Bishop, 28 May 2003.
126. Robert Bruce, 'Political Strife in International Arena', *Accountancy Age*, 22 October 1987, 5.
127. Letter from John Bishop to Ray Harris, dated 18 April 1988, copy supplied by Bishop to the authors.
128. 'Unofficial Secretariat Notes of the Meeting of the IASC Board and Consultative Group—Tuesday 21 June, 1988', memo by David Cairns, IASC archive, 'Bishop Working Party' file.
129. Letter from David Cairns to Rainer Geiger (OECD), dated 21 September 1988, IASC archive, 'Bishop Working Party' file.
130. Letter from Georges Barthès to John Bishop, dated 2 May 1989, IASC archive, 'Bishop Working Party' File.
131. 'IFAC/IASC: Review of Aims, Activities and Organisation', Working Party Report, December 1989. The quotation is taken from page 12.
132. Circular letter from Raymond G. Harris to Heads of Institutes and Associations Represented on IFAC Council and IASC Board, dated 19 February 1991, IASC archive, 'Bishop Working Party' File.

NOTES TO CHAPTER 8

1. In 1987, Barthès' former firm of Frinault Fiduciaire, which had been part of KMG, merged with Arthur Andersen, when KMG became part of KPMG.
2. Interview with Georges Barthès de Ruyter, 5 June 2003; 'Appointment of Deputy Chairmen (a Note from the Secretary-General)', IASC executive committee meeting of June 1994, agenda paper VI.
3. Interview with Michael Sharpe, 29 May 2003. Also see 'Sharpe Response to Challenges', *IASC Insight*, June 1995, 1.
4. For an interview with Enevoldsen several months after he became IASC chairman, see 'A Look Back and A Look Forward', *IASC Insight*, June 1998, 15–17.
5. 'IASC Board Restructured to Widen Representation', *IASC Insight*, June 1995, 4.
6. In 1998, Citicorp became part of Citigroup.
7. A reason given for adding the title of deputy chairman was that two years was a long time for a chairman-designate to serve in waiting. Communication from David Cairns to the authors, dated 1 March 2004.
8. 'Review by Chairman and Secretary-General', IASC's *Annual Review 1997*, 11.
9. For Sharpe's views on the importance of integrating national standard setters into the work of the board, see 'Statement by Chairman and Secretary-General', IASC's *Annual Review 1995*, 4, and Michael Sharpe, 'A Review of IASC's Progress', *IASC Insight*, October 1997, 2.
10. Interview with Michael Sharpe, 29 May 2003.
11. Letter from Cairns to Shiratori and Sharpe, dated 3 February 1993, IASC archive, file, 'Michael Sharpe (Deputy Chairman)'.
12. Interview with David Cairns, 8 June 2003. Also see, David Cairns, 'The Future Shape of Harmonization: A Reply', *The European Accounting Review*, 6/2 (1997), 324.
13. Interview with Harry K. Schmid, 15 March 2004.

14. IASC's *Annual Review 1995*, 3. Yet two members of the board voted against seating the Federation. There was apparently a concern that the invitation to the Swiss Federation would set a precedent for other preparer groups from individual countries to seek board membership. IASC board meeting of 8–10 May 1995, minute 12.
15. See 'Financial Executives Join the IASC Board', *IASC Insight*, December 1995, 2.
16. Interview with Ian Somerville, 15 March 2004.
17. Interview with Monica Singer, 15 March 2004.
18. A member of the South African delegation criticized the IASC's pursuit to become 'politically correct' as diluting its mission to set standards at a high level of high quality. Interview with Monica Singer, 15 March 2004.
19. Minutes of IASC/IFAC Coordinating Committee, 15 November 1994.
20. IASC board meeting of 12–14 April 1989, minute 10.
21. Communication from David Cairns to the authors, dated 20 June 2006.
22. IASC board meeting of 12–14 April 1989, minutes 1, 10 and the appendix.
23. Interview with David Cairns, 27 January 2004.
24. Interview with Arthur R. Wyatt, 9 August 2004.
25. Interviews with David Cairns, 8 June 2003 and 27 January 2004, with Arthur R. Wyatt, 9 August 2004, and with Peter Clark, 15 October 2004.
26. Interview with David Cairns, 8 June 2003.
27. Memorandum from Bryan Carsberg to the authors, dated 17 June 2005.
28. Interview with Rafael Gómez Eng, 30 June 2005.
29. Minutes of IASC/IFAC Coordinating Committee, 15 November 1994; IASC executive committee meeting of 27 March 1995, minute 6.
30. Cairns, 'The Future Shape of Harmonization: A Reply', 324.
31. The change was not reflected in the IASC's Constitution until it was revised in October 1992.
32. The voting record prior to 1995 cannot be reconstructed completely, as the votes were at that time not recorded in the minutes of board meetings. The votes between 1995 and 2000 have been reconstructed on the basis of notes taken by the delegation of the Federation of Swiss Industrial Holding Companies (supplied to the authors by Harry Schmid), supplemented by information from interviews.
33. Interview with Etsuo Sawa, 5 July 2004.
34. The single exception occurred in November 1998, on E63, 'Events after the Balance Sheet Date'.
35. Interviews with Heinz Kleekämper, 14 July 2004, and with Bernd-Joachim Menn, 18 August 2004; also interviews with Herbert Biener, 13 July 2004, with Michael Sharpe, 29 May 2003, with Karel Van Hulle, 16 February 2005, and with Gijs Bak, 8 December 2004.
36. Something similar could be said of the Nordic Federation of Public Accountants.
37. See Dieter Ordelheide and Dieter Pfaff, *European Financial Reporting: Germany* (London: Routledge, 1994), 82–93.
38. IASC board meeting of 9–11 November 1988, minute 11(d).
39. 'Standard Setting Bodies (A Note from the Secretariat)', IASC executive committee meeting of October 1994, agenda paper V.
40. IASC board meetings of 9–11 November 1988, minute 11(d); of 12–14 April 1989, minute 9(a); and of 7–9 March 1990, minute 9(g).
41. 'E32 is Only the Beginning in a Continuous Process of Harmonisation' [an interview with Arthur R. Wyatt], *Corporate Accounting International*, 22 (October 1991), 11.

42. See David Cairns, 'IOSCO Member's Attack on IASC was Ill-conceived', *Accountancy* (international edition), 122/1262 (October 1998), 62.
43. Communication from Bryan Carsberg to the authors, dated 10 June 2006. See Section 10.13 for a discussion of the decision to accelerate the core standards programme.
44. The IASC had made its first official contact with China in February 1992, when a delegation headed by Chairman Wyatt participated in an International Symposium of Accounting Standards in Shenzhen, which was organized by the Ministry of Finance and the CICPA. See 'International Symposium of Accounting Standards', *IASC Insight*, March 1992, 10–14. In December 1994, Eiichi Shiratori addressed a similar symposium held in Shanghai. See 'China Hosts World Experts', *IASC Insight*, March 1995, 3.
45. Minutes of the meetings of IFAC Council of 15–17 May 1996, and of 7–9 May 1997, in the IFAC archive.
46. Interview with Michael Sharpe, 29 May 2003.
47. 'Observer Membership of the Board', AP 6/1996 paper 21.
48. IASC board meeting of 11–14 June 1996, minute 13.
49. See, e.g. Stig Enevoldsen, 'A Look Back and A Look Forward', *IASC Insight* June 1998, 17.
50. See, e.g. the IASC's *Annual Review 1987*, 5.
51. Christopher Nobes, 'Life is Definitely Not a Beach at the IASC', *Accounting & Business*, 1/6 (June 1998), 18.
52. Interview with Stig Enevoldsen, 16 February 2005.
53. 'Paper from the Secretary-General', IASC Advisory Council meeting of 31 January 1996, agenda paper 3.
54. 'G4+1—First Open Meeting', *World Accounting Report*, April 1997, 13.
55. 'Shaping IASC for the Future: A Discussion Paper Issued by the Strategy Working Party of the International Accounting Standards Committee', draft 17 November 1997, AP 1/1998 paper 28, paragraph 128(a).
56. 'Opening IASC Meetings to Public Attendance', paper prepared by the secretary-general, AP 11/1998 paper 4A. The Advisory Council is discussed in Section 8.16.
57. IASC board meeting of 9–13 November 1998, minute 3.
58. See 'IASC Lets the Sunshine in on Its Meetings', *Accountancy* (international edition), 122/1264 (December 1998), 13; and 'International Accounting Standards Committee Board Holds First Open Meeting', *The CPA Journal*, 69/5 (May 1999), 12.
59. Dennis R. Beresford, 'A Former FASB Chairman's Take on International Accounting Standard Setting', *Financial Executive*, 13/5 (September/October 1997), 22.
60. Arthur Levitt, 'CPAs and CEOs: A Relationship at Risk', remarks at The Economic Club of Detroit, Detroit, Michigan, 19 May 1997 (available at: http://www.sec.gov/news/speech/speecharchive/1997/spch157.txt).
61. Christopher Nobes, 'IASC Meets the World', *Accounting & Business*, 2/4 (April 1999), 34.
62. Communication from Angus Thomson to the authors, dated 21 February 2006; also see *AASB Action Alert*, no. 26 (September 1999).
63. On a few previous occasions, interested parties sat in on steering committee meetings.
64. IASC executive committee meeting of 31 October 1994, minute 12.
65. Letter from Cairns to Board Representatives and Technical Advisers, dated 30 December 1994, IASC archive, file 'Board/Executive Committee Mailings'.

66. For a judgement on Carsberg's credentials for his new position, see 'Carsberg Nemesis', *World Accounting Report*, May 1995, 1. For an interview with Carsberg conducted shortly after he joined the IASC, see 'Back and Able', *Accountancy*, 116/1225 (September 1995), 24.
67. Communication from Michael Sharpe to the authors, dated 30 March 2006.
68. Rutherford had resigned from his university upon becoming assistant secretary in October 1985.
69. Memorandum from David Cairns to the authors, dated 12 December 2003. See also Cairns, 'The Future Shape of Harmonization: A Reply', 321–2.
70. AARF also seconded Paul Sutcliffe to the IASC staff in 1993–4. AARF's successive executive directors, Kevin Stevenson and Warren McGregor (the staff observer/technical adviser of the Australian delegation from 1986 to 1999), were robust supporters of the IASC.
71. That a board meeting scheduled for March 1994 in South Africa had to be cancelled because 'there would be no technical items ready for consideration by the Board' may have been due in part to the lack of staff to prepare the items. Minutes of an unofficial meeting of members of the executive committee held in London on 9 November 1993, IASC executive committee meeting of March 1994, agenda paper IA.
72. Interview with Liesel Knorr, 29 March 2005. Paul Sutcliffe had already returned to Australia, and Paul Pacter was servicing a project on a part-time basis.
73. The CICA, chiefly because of John Denman, the accounting standards director and a long-time member of the Canadian delegation to the board, was, like AARF, a major supporter of the IASC.
74. 'New Technical Director for IASC', *IASC Insight*, October 1999, 2.
75. 'The Role of OPC and the Board', IASC board meeting of June 1991, agenda paper VI; *Annual Report 1990*, International Federation of Accountants, 5. The IFAC reform had been recommended by the Bishop Working Party.
76. 'The Role of OPC and the Board'.
77. IASC board meeting of 30 June–2 July 1993, minute 18.
78. IASC board meeting of 23–8 September 1996, minute 2(d); 'Interpretations of International Accounting Standards', *IASC Update*, October 1996, 1. See also 'Interpretations Body Approved', *Accountancy* (international edition), 118/1238 (October 1996), 7; Peter Clark, 'What Does It All Mean?' *Accountancy* (international edition) 119/1244 (April 1997), 68.
79. 'Standing Interpretations Committee', *IASC Update*, June 1997, 1.
80. Arthur R. Wyatt, speech to the congress of the Asociación Interamericana de Contabilidad in Asunción, Paraguay, in September 1989; typescript in IASC archive, file 'Wyatt'.
81. The FASB's figures are taken from the annual reports of the Financial Accounting Foundation, which are broken down between the FASB and the Governmental Accounting Standards Board. The FASB's US$14,368 for 1992 is translated at the rate of $2 per pound. The FASB's US$15,734 for 1995 is translated at the rate of $1.60 per pound. The ASB's figures are those for the Financial Reporting Council taken from the *Reports and Financial Statements* issued by the Financial Reporting Council Limited. Virtually all of the FRC's costs related to the work of the ASB. The figures for 1995 are actually for 1995/96.
82. Interview with David Cairns, 27 January 2004.

83. *IFAC/IASC: Review of Aims, Activities and Organisation*, Working Party Report (December 1989), 18.
84. Conversation with Robert Mednick, 21 June 2006; communication from David Cairns to the authors, dated 20 June 2006; and IASC board meeting of 20–22 June 1990, minute 9(h).
85. IASC board meeting of 7–9 November 1990, minute 8(h); board meeting of 4–6 March 1992, minute 9.
86. Letter from Cairns to John Denman, dated 17 July 1991, IASC archive, file 'IOSCO Working Party 1'. Not all board members believed that it was necessary to raise additional long-term funding. See Cairns, 'The Future Shape of Harmonization: A Reply', 335.
87. 'IASC Constitution', AP 2/1991 paper 11.
88. Communication from David Cairns to the authors, dated 20 June 2006.
89. 'Working Party on the International Accounting Standards Foundation and the Future Structure and Organization of IASC', dated January 1993, a background paper from the secretariat, IASC archive, file 'IOSCO Working Party 1'.
90. IASC board meeting of 7–9 October 1992, minute 11, and reproduced in *IASC Insight*, December 1992, 4.
91. IASC board meeting of 23–6 March 1993, minute 10.
92. The Working Party's report is included in the file 'IASC Foundation Working Party 3', IASC archive.
93. David Cairns strongly favoured a closer involvement with national standard setters. See David Cairns, 'The IASC Must Move Closer to National Bodies', *Accountancy*, 116/1224 (August 1995), 70.
94. IASC executive committee meeting of 24–5 March 1994, minute 9; AP 6/1994 paper 12.
95. IASC executive committee meeting of 11–12 June 1994, minute 8.
96. At the IASC board meeting of 13, 15–17 June 1994 in Edinburgh, minute 7 reflected this reluctance: 'Various Board Representatives and Technical Advisers emphasised the need for the Board to remain independent and argued that less emphasis should be placed on the supervisory role of the Advisory Council.'
97. Cairns, 'The Future Shape of Harmonization: A Reply', 336.
98. Cairns, 'The Future Shape of Harmonization: A Reply', 336.
99. IASC board meeting of 13, 15–17 June 1994 in Edinburgh, minute 7. This was not really an amendment, as the working party's report went no further than to 'encourage' such participation. The other two amendments did not concern the operation of the Advisory Council.
100. Cairns, 'The Future Shape of Harmonization: A Reply', 337.
101. Quoted in the IASC's *Annual Review 1995*, 5.
102. Letter from Eiichi Shiratori to Al Sommer, dated 9 May 1995, IASC archive, file 'Advisory Council'.
103. See the IASC's *Annual Review* 1995, 5.
104. See the IASC's *Annual Review 1997*, 13, and *Annual Review 1998*, 11.
105. These figures and the country breakdown below appear in agenda paper II for the executive committee meeting of November 1999, and agenda paper IC for the executive committee meeting in March 2000. The IASC's annual reports on fund-raising show the figures for 1995 and 1996 as £414,000 and £802,000, respectively, which sum to the same as the figures reported here for 1995 and 1996. We do not understand the discrepancy. We have decided to alter the figures for 1995 and 1996

to agree with those in the 1995 and 1996 issues of the *Annual Review* and with Table 8.1.
106. Interview with Bryan Carsberg, 26 May 2005.
107. Most of the remainder of this section is based on the interview with Stephen D. Eccles, 5 January 2005.
108. *IFAC/IASC: Review of Aims, Activities and Organisation*, Working Party Report (December 1989), 5.
109. 'Minutes of Meeting of the Member Bodies of the International Accounting Standards Committee held at the Grand Hyatt Hotel, Washington, D.C., U.S.A. on Sunday 11th October 1992 at 9:00 a.m.', IASC archive, file 'Advisory Council'.
110. The relevant correspondence is included in the file, 'Board/Executive Committee Mailings [1994–96]', in the IASC archive.
111. IASC executive committee meeting of 9/10 July 1995, minute 8; also 'Future Strategy of IASC', IASC executive committee meeting of July 1995, agenda paper VII.
112. Communication from David Cairns to the authors, dated 20 June 2006.
113. Interviews with Allan V. C. Cook, 30 April 2003, with Rick Cottrell, 15 March 2004, with David Damant, 19 May 2004, and with Christopher Stronge, 27 May 2004.
114. 'Procedures for Board and Consultative Group' [written by the secretary-general], IASC executive committee meeting of June 1996, agenda paper V.
115. Interview with Bryan Carsberg, 26 May 2005; and with David Damant, 19 May 2004.
116. See 'Accounting Academics Join the IASC Consultative Group', *IASC Insight*, December 1995, 2.
117. IASC board meeting of 1–4 November 1995, minute 10(b).

NOTES TO CHAPTER 9

1. AP 11/1978 paper 4.
2. AP 6/1979 paper 20.
3. John A. Hepworth, 'International Accounting Standards Committee—The Future', in W. John Brennan (editor), *The Internationalization of the Accountancy Profession* (Toronto: Canadian Institute of Chartered Accountants, 1979), 53. Hepworth's paper bears a June 1979 date.
4. Michael Renshall, 'Satisfying Six Masters', *Accountancy Age*, 11/6 (8 February 1980), 18.
5. The list in Hepworth, 'International Accounting Standards Committee', 52, is taken from one of these secretariat papers.
6. AP 11/1982 paper 2. At the meeting, the Netherlands 'objected to objectives'. The other recorded views were those of France ('objectives is fine'), the United States ('objectives okay if concise') and Mexico ('we like objectives'). 'Unofficial Secretariat Notes of Discussion at November 1982 IASC Board on New Topics', IASC archive, file 'New Topics 1980–1993'.
7. The attitude of the Consultative Group is mentioned in 'Selection of a New Topic for Study', AP 3/1983 paper 11. From the minutes of the Consultative Group meeting of 23 November 1982 it appears that Elliott himself was in favour of Objectives, while only four out of nine members of the Consultative Group expressed support.
8. IASC board meeting of 24–6 November 1982, minute 5(b); 'Unofficial Secretariat Notes of Discussion at November 1982 IASC Board on New Topics', IASC archives, file 'New Topics 1980–1993'. In public, Elliott emphasized that the project was

'not to be confused' with a conceptual framework: 'New Objectives for the IASC', *Accountancy*, 94/1073 (January 1983), 26.
9. AP 10/1983 paper 10.
10. IASC board meeting of 14–16 June 1983, minute 6(g). The members of the committee were Rolando Ortega (Mexico, chairman), Dennis Beresford (United States), Herman Marseille (the Netherlands), and Kenneth Spencer (Australia).
11. 'Report from the Ad Hoc Advisory Committee to the Organisation and Planning Committee', no date, IASC archive, file 'IASC Plans and Future Work'. It is assumed that this is the final report, underlying the paper 'Summary of Conclusions & Recommendations' (agenda paper I for the OPC's March 1984 meeting). The wording of the quoted paragraph is closely related to the opinions of Spencer and Beresford recorded in the informal secretariat notes of the ad hoc advisory committee's meeting on 25 October 1983, IASC archive, file 'IASC Plans and Future Work'. That Spencer keenly wanted the IASC to move towards a framework has also been suggested by Kevin Stevenson (interview, 27 January 2004). Beresford, however, was sceptical about the merits of the FASB's conceptual framework. See Stephen A. Zeff, 'The Evolution of the Conceptual Framework for Business Enterprises in the United States', *The Accounting Historians Journal*, 26/2 (December 1999), 113.
12. Interviews with Warren McGregor, 9 June 2003, and with Kevin Stevenson, 26 January 2004. See also Geoff Burrows, *The Foundation: A History of the Australian Accounting Research Foundation 1966–91* (Caulfield, Vic: Australian Accounting Research Foundation, 1996), 160–1.
13. AP 3/1984 paper 12; AP 6/1984 paper 9; IASC board meetings of 14–16 March 1984, minute 5(d), and of 19–21 June 1984, minute 6(c).
14. AP 10/1984 paper 10.
15. In 1985, the board followed a new procedure by which it would make a preliminary selection of topics. Those who had suggested the selected topics would then write briefing papers which were the basis for the final decision during a following meeting. The briefing paper on assets and expenses was written by Spencer. IASC board meeting of 6–8 March 1985, minute 7(g); AP 6/1985 paper 12.
16. The other members were Kenneth Spencer (Australia), A. A. Couto (Brazil), and M. Cvetanovic (Yugoslavia).
17. AP 3/1984 paper 9.
18. AP 10/1984 paper 2; AP 6/1985 paper 2; AP 6/1986 paper 5; IASC board meeting of 17–19 June 1986, minute 4.
19. AP 10/1984 paper 1; AP 6/1985 paper 2; IASC board meeting of 25–7 June 1985, minute 3.
20. AP 6/1986 paper 8, p. 6.
21. AP 6/1985 paper 8. The other members of the steering committee were H. Reiter (Austria), A. Shawki (Egypt), and J. Eskilson (Sweden).
22. The issue of deferred credits was raised by the steering committee in AP 6/1985 paper 8, and further developed in AP 3/1986 paper 6. See also IASC board meetings of 25–7 June 1985, minute 6, and of 5–7 March 1986, minute 5.
23. AP 10/1985 paper 10. The other members of the steering committee were N. Farstad (Norway), Ian Brindle (UK & Ireland), and C. Odreman (Venezuela).
24. AP 10/1985 paper 10; IASC board meeting of 16–18 October 1985, minute 4.
25. The other members of the steering committee were Francis Bastien (France), E. S. H. Dahodwala (Pakistan), and U. H. Palihakkara (Sri Lanka, with G. Fonseka as a substitute or successor).

26. Interview with Warren McGregor, 9 June 2003.
27. A similar anthology was included in Malcolm C. Miller and M. Atiqul Islam, *The Definition and Recognition of Assets*, Accounting Theory Monograph 7 (Caulfield, Vic: Australian Accounting Research Foundation, 1988).
28. AP 6/1986 paper 9.
29. IASC board meeting of 5–7 November 1986, minute 5(e).
30. Interviews with Rick Cottrell, 15 March 2004, and with Giancarlo Tomasin, 7 April 2003.
31. The views of the board expressed in June are summarized in AP 11/1986 paper 14.
32. The regular attendees were M. A. Oni (OPC chairman) and O. Osunkeye (both from Nigeria), Ron Cotton and Warren McGregor (Australia), John Kirkpatrick (UK & Ireland, IASC chairman), and Georges Barthès (IASC chairman-designate). The secretariat was represented by Secretary-General David Cairns and Assistant Secretary Brian Rutherford. Responding to the invitation to attend were Michael Dawson and John Denman (Canada), Rick Cottrell (South Africa), and Ralph Walters (United States). Italy was also a member of the OPC at the time, but the Italian representatives rarely attended, and none did so at this meeting.
33. Interview with Warren McGregor, 9 June 2003.
34. David H. Cairns, 'The Harmonization of Accounting Standards: The Role and Achievements of the International Accounting Standards Committee', in *Standard Setting for Financial Reporting: An International Conference Sponsored by the American Accounting Association with Klynveld Main Goerdeler*, August 17–20, 1986 (n.p., Peat Marwick Main & Co., 1987), 119.
35. 'The Future Work of IASC', AP 11/1986 paper 14, p. 5.
36. Minutes of OPC meeting of 3 November 1986; IASC board meeting of 5–7 November 1986, minute 6(ii).
37. AP 11/1986 paper 14, p. 7–8.
38. Frans Graafstal, of the Dutch delegation, understood the choice of Dawson as a consequence of the fact that Canada had provided the chairmanship of the steering committee on revenue recognition, which initially was also seen as one of the building blocks. 'Kort verslag IASC meeting Londen 4–7 november 1986', memo by Frans Graafstal, dated 25 November 1986, NIVRA archive, no. 49.
39. Interviews with Rick Cottrell, 15 March 2004, with Kevin Stevenson, 26 January 2005, and with Angus Thomson, 27 May 2003.
40. SFAC 1, *Objectives of Financial Reporting by Business Enterprises*; SFAC 2, *Qualitative Characteristics of Accounting Information*; SFAC 3, *Elements of Financial Statements of Business Enterprises*; SFAC 5, *Recognition and Measurement in Financial Statements of Business Enterprises*.
41. AP 11/1986 paper 14, p. 6.
42. AP 3/1987 paper 4; see also IASC board meeting of 24–7 March 1987, minute 7(xii).
43. Interview with David Cairns, 8 June 2003.
44. Interview with Jean-Luc Dumont, 15 February 2005.
45. Communication from Michael Dawson to the authors, dated 1 February 2003.
46. See, e.g. Surendra P. Agrawal, Paul H. Jensen, Anna Lee Meador, and Keith Sellers, 'An International Comparison of Conceptual Frameworks of Accounting', *The International Journal of Accounting*, 24/3 (1989), 243; Heinz Kleekämper, 'Rechnungslegung aus der Sicht des IASC', in Jörg Baetge (editor), *Die deutsche Rechnungslegung vor dem Hintergrund internationaler Entwicklungen*

(Düsseldorf: IDW-Verlag, 1994), 47; and Pelham Gore, *The FASB Conceptual Framework Project 1973–1985: An Analysis* (Manchester: Manchester University Press, 1992), 126–7.

47. For a summary of the various conceptual framework projects of the 1980s, see Gore, *The FASB Conceptual Framework Project*, 124–30; and Paul Ebling, 'Accountants and the Seven Year Itch', *Accountancy*, 103/1150 (June 1989), 22.
48. Interview with David Cairns, 27 January 2004.
49. 'Canadian Chairs IASC Conceptual Framework Committee', *CAmagazine*, 120/2 (February 1987), 11.
50. Communication to the authors from Michael Dawson, dated 1 February 2003; interview with Georges Barthès, 5 June 2003; Raymond Béthoux and François Kremper, 'Le cadre conceptuel de l'IASC: contexte et contenu', *Revue Française de Comptabilité*, June 1989, 59–80.
51. See Jörg Baetge, 'Begrüßung anläßlich des 10. Münsterischen Tagesgespräches am 29. April 1994', in Baetge (editor), *Die deutsche Rechnungslegung vor dem Hintergrund internationaler Entwicklungen*, 2–5; communication from Michael Dawson to the authors, dated 1 February 2003.
52. Minutes of meeting of NIVRA IASC delegation with CAJ-working party, 17 March 1989, NIVRA archive, file CAJ-IASC, 73.
53. AP 4/1989 paper 11 (comment letters) and minutes of meeting of IASC board and Consultative Group, 1 March 1988.
54. AP 11/1986 paper 14, p. 4; AP 3/1987 paper 9, p. 12.
55. AP 3/1987 paper 9, p. 12.
56. AP 4/1989 paper 11, p. 14.
57. David Cairns, 'Providing the User with a Useful Statement', *Accountancy*, 102/1139 (July 1988), 26–7. See also David Cairns, cited in Guy Carter, 'Setting the Standards: A Framework for the Future', *Corporate Finance*, June 1988, 42; Christopher Stronge, 'Financial reporting: Disturbing Lack of a Common Language', *The Accountant*, 196/5813 (July 1988), 22–3.
58. On the asset and liability view expressed in the FASB's Conceptual Framework, see Paul B. W. Miller, 'The Conceptual Framework as Reformation and Counterreformation', *Accounting Horizons*, 4/2 (June 1990), 26–7. In 1985, SFAC 3 was replaced by SFAC 6, *Elements of Financial Statements*, in order to include not-for-profit organizations.
59. AP 3/1987 paper 5, p. 22.
60. Peter Wilmot, 'A Framework for Financial Statements', *Accountancy SA*, July 1987, 209.
61. AP 4/1989 paper 11, p. 12.
62. The views from Arthur Young and the ASC are largely similar to those expressed by Ron Paterson (of both Arthur Young and the ASC) in 'Building the Right Framework', *Accountancy*, 102/1142 (October 1988), 26–7.
63. AP 4/1989 paper 11, p. 14.
64. AP 4/1989 paper 9.
65. Michael Lafferty and David Cairns, *Financial Times World Survey of Annual Reports 1980* (London: The Financial Times Business Information, 1980), 14. See also David Cairns, 'The Battle to Get Better Reporters', *Accountancy Age*, 11/32 (8 August 1980), 16.
66. IASC board meeting of 24–6 March 1982, minute 5. For support by the Consultative Group, see AP 6/1982 paper 13.

67. South Africa was added to the steering committee in June 1982 as 'an additional English-speaking country'. Finland had initially been asked to provide a member but did not participate. IASC board meetings of 24–6 March 1982, minute 5, and of 22–5 June 1982, minute 7.
68. AP 6/1983 paper 6.
69. IASC board meeting of 26–8 October 1983, minute 4. No decisions by the board on the true and fair override and LIFO are recorded. These are inferred from a comparison of the steering committee's point outline (AP 6/1983 paper 6) and its draft standard (AP 10/1983 papers 7 and 8).
70. That was true for the Ordre des Experts Comptables. Interview with Dominique Ledouble, 5 June 2003. In 1984, the NIVRA decided no longer to prepare translations, partly for financial reasons (see Section 6.13).
71. IASC board meeting of 17–19 October 1983, minute 2. This was done 'with the acquiescence' of the steering committee chairman, Jesús Hoyos (AP 3/1985 paper 10).
72. AP 3/1985 paper 10; IASC board meeting of 25–7 June 1985, minute 5.
73. AP 3/1985 paper 10.
74. IASC board meeting of 25–7 June 1985, minute 5.
75. AP 3/1985 paper 10; IASC board meeting of 23–5 March 1985, minute 5.
76. OPC meeting of 24 October 1983, minute 2.
77. AP 3/1986 paper 13; IASC board meeting of 5–7 March 1986, minute 7(ix).
78. The other members were Morten Iversen (Denmark), A. N. Mattar (Lebanon), and Manuel Galván Cebrián (Mexico).
79. The other members came from Indonesia (Witadinata Sumantri), Spain (several members in succession), and Taiwan (S. T. Chiang).
80. AP 6/1982 paper 13; IASC board meeting of 22–5 June 1982, minute 7.
81. Karel van Hulle and Leo van der Tas, chapter 13, 'European Union: Group Accounts', in Dieter Ordelheide and KPMG, *Transnational Accounting* (London: Macmillan, 1995). The importance of IAS 3 for the Seventh Directive is also asserted in Herbert Biener, 'Auf dem Weg zum Europäischen und zum internationalen Jahresabschluss', in *Wirtschaftsprüfung und Wirtschaftsrecht: Beiträge zum 75 Jährigen Bestehen der Treuhand-Vereinigung Aktiengesellschaft* (Stuttgart: Poeschel, 1980), 77.
82. AP 6/1984 paper 6. In addition, a survey of member bodies (AP 6/1982 paper 13) had revealed that, in contrast to IAS 1 and 2, 'IAS 3 was not well reflected in local standards or law'. When it was agreed to revise IAS 3, the start of the project was delayed until the completion of the Seventh Directive (AP 3/1983 paper 15). On the relationship between IAS 3, IAS 27, and the Seventh Directive, see also David Cairns, 'What is the Future of Mutual Recognition of Financial Statements and is Comparability Really Necessary?', *The European Accounting Review*, 3/2 (1994), 351.
83. AP 6/1988 paper 1; communication from David Cairns to the authors, dated 21 January 2004; interview with Karel Van Hulle, 17 February 2004.
84. In IAS 24, *Related Party Disclosures*, the IASC had already taken one step in this direction by using a mixed definition based on both voting power and power to control financial and operating policies.
85. Communication from David Cairns to the authors, dated 20 June 2006.
86. AP 6/1984 paper 7.
87. Communication from David Cairns to the authors, dated 20 June 2006.
88. *A Survey and Analysis of Consolidations/Equity Accounting Practices* (New York: Price Waterhouse, 1990).

89. AP 6/1988 paper 5. E28 attracted a total of thirty-five transcribed pages of comment letters, see AP 6/1988 paper 8.
90. AP 10/1989 paper 1. The other members were Peter Day (Australia), Arthur Wyatt (United States), and Jens Røder (Fédération des Experts Comptables Européens).
91. 'New IASC Draft for Different Forms of Joint Ventures', *IASC News*, 18/4 (December 1989), 7.
92. The comment letters (AP 11/1990 paper 4) are discussed extensively in Sara York Kenny and Robert K. Larson, 'Lobbying Behaviour and the Development of International Accounting Standards: The Case of the IASC's Joint Venture Project', *The European Accounting Review*, 2/3 (December 1993), 531–54. See also 'International Standard on Joint Ventures', *World Accounting Report*, December 1990/January 1991, 3.
93. AP 10/1990 paper 1.
94. Gilbert Gélard, letter to the editor, *World Accounting Report*, 1 April 1991, 11.
95. Communication from David Cairns to the authors, dated 7 November 2003.
96. AP 11/1986 paper 14 and AP 3/1987 paper 9, both entitled 'The Future Work of IASC'.
97. IASC board meeting of 24–7 March 1987, minute 6 (a)–(c) and (k).
98. AP 3/1987 paper 9, paragraph 8.
99. See Louis Bisgay and Susan Jayson, 'Ralph Walters on Harmonization', *Management Accounting* (NAA), August 1989, 22–4.
100. 'IOSCO' and 'Steering Committee's Work Programme', memos by David Cairns, dated 28 October and 16 November 1987, respectively, IASC archive, 'Comparability' file.
101. Donald E. Wygal, David E. Stout, and James Volpi, 'Reporting Practices in Four Countries', *Management Accounting* (NAA), December 1987, 37–42. Cairns took note of the study in 'One Giant Compromise', *CAmagazine*, 122/7 (September 1989), 40.
102. Andy Simmonds and Olivier Azières, *Accounting for Europe—Success by 2000 AD?* (London: Touche Ross Europe, 1989).
103. 'Major Options in International Accounting Standards', memo by David Cairns dated 18 June 1987, IASC archive, 'Comparability' file.
104. 'Unofficial Secretariat Notes of Steering Committee Meeting on 3rd July, 1987', memo by David Cairns, IASC archive, 'Comparability' file. [feasible in] is inserted as a conjecture.
105. 'Unofficial Secretariat Notes of Steering Committee Meeting on 3rd July, 1987', memo by David Cairns, IASC archive, 'Comparability' file; IASC board meeting of 22–4 June 1988, minute 4(h).
106. Ralph Walters, cited in 'IASC to Cut Choices in Standards', *World Accounting Report*, June 1987, 3–4.
107. Interview with Herman Marseille, 27 October 2004.
108. Memorandum from Paul Cherry to the authors dated 8 October 2004. See also fax message from Walters to Cairns, dated 12 April 1988, and 'IASC Board meeting notes—2 March 1988', both in IASC archive, 'Comparability' file.
109. Interview with Angus Thomson, 27 May 2003.
110. See, e.g. 'IASC Board Meeting Notes—2 March 1988', IASC archive, 'Comparability' file.
111. Communication from David Cairns to the authors, dated 7 November 2003.

112. In January 1988, Paul Cherry noted that 'the official posture will endeavour to be neutral.' 'IOSCO Working Group No. 2, Progress Report #1', January 1988, IASC archive, 'Comparability' file.
113. 'Unofficial Secretariat Notes of Steering Committee Meeting on 3rd July, 1987' memo by David Cairns, and draft agenda paper, dated 28 March 1988, both in IASC archive, 'Comparability' file.
114. *IASC News*, however, described the preferred treatments as 'the most appropriate and practicable ways of achieving greater comparability'. 'IASC Proposals on Free Choices of Accounting Treatments', *IASC News*, 18/1 (January 1989), 8.
115. Interview with Herman Marseille, 27 October 2004.
116. In an earlier proposal, 'conformity with the proposed Framework' was listed as the last of four criteria. 'Minutes of the Meeting of the Steering Committee on Comparability of Financial Statements Held in London on 9th and 10th December 1987', IASC archive, 'Comparability' file.
117. 'Unofficial Secretariat Notes of Discussions at the Board Meeting Held in New York on 23rd and 24th October, 1989', IASC archive, 'Comparability' file.
118. The Fourth Directive (articles 34.1.a and 37.1) limited the default amortization period to five years, but did not set an upper limit to the amortization period that might be used in the case of a demonstrably longer useful life.
119. IASC board meeting of 9–11 November 1988, minute 2.
120. Memorandum to the authors from Ralph Walters, dated 18 October 2003.
121. Communication from Tadaaki Tokunaga to the authors, dated 30 June 2004.
122. AP 11/1988 paper 1; letter from Michael Bromwich to Cairns, dated 5 September 1988, IASC archive, 'Comparability' file.
123. See, e.g. 'IASC Board Seeks to Reduce Alternatives in International Accounting Standards', *IASC News*, 16/3 (June 1987), 1; comments by Ralph Walters reported in 'IASC to Cut Choices in Standards', *World Accounting Report*, June 1987, 3–4; David Cairns, 'Calling All National Standard Setters', *Accountancy*, 101/1134 (February 1988), 13–14; and Georges Barthès, quoted in 'IASC Moves to Unite Worldwide Standards', *Journal of Accountancy*, 165/6 (June 1988), 22, 26.
124. Relevant correspondence between Cairns and the member bodies in IASC archive, 'Comparability' file.
125. Notes, transcripts, and correspondence relating to these visits in IASC archive, 'Comparability' file. Several of these visits were reported in the 1989 issues of *IASC News*.
126. E32 was the last occasion when the IASC staff prepared a transcript of the comment letters as it had done from the first standards onwards. The transcript for E32 amounted to 280 pages, excluding some letters received subsequently. For E3, the comparable total was 183 pages. IASC archive, 'Comparability' file.
127. Letter from Cairns to steering committee members, dated 4 January 1990, IASC archive, 'Comparability' file.
128. The number of 160 letters is reported in *Statement of Intent* (paragraph 6). The bound volume of comment letters issued by the IASC in July 1990 contains 139 letters. Since the decision to publish the letters was made after the publication of E32, the difference may have been caused by some respondents withholding permission to publish their letter.
129. See Kenny and Larson, 'Lobbying behaviour', 533, for a discussion of response volumes to FASB and IASC exposure drafts.
130. AP 3/1990 paper 5, p. 4.

131. IASC board meeting of 20–2 June 1990, minute 3.
132. 'E32, Comparability of Financial Statements', *IASC News*, 19/2 (July 1990), 5. This issue of the *IASC News* contains a summary of the comment letters on E32.
133. E32 comment letters, bound volume, 60–1 and 199–200.
134. See, for instance, comments from the Japanese Institute of Certified Public Accountants and the Gesellschaft für Finanzwirtschaft in der Unternehmensführung (Germany), E32 comment letters, bound volume, 61 and 256, respectively. For the allegation that E32 was biased against Continental European accounting traditions, see also Herbert Biener, 'What is the Future of Mutual Recognition of Financial Statements and is Comparability Really Necessary?', *The European Accounting Review*, 3/2 (1994), 337.
135. Of the 139 letters reproduced in the bound volume of comment letters, ninety-six were from Australia, Canada, New Zealand, South Africa, the United Kingdom, and the United States. A total of twenty-four came from Continental Europe.
136. 'Meeting the Expectations of Global Capital Markets', *IASC News*, 18/3 (July 1989), 1.
137. AP 10/1989 paper 5 summarizes due process concerns expressed in the comment letters. See also 'Issues Paper: E32 Comparability of Financial Statements' prepared by the secretariat for the Comparability steering committee and 'CICA Forum on International Harmonisation of Financial Statements', IASC archive, 'Comparability' file.
138. AP 3/1990 paper 6; 'Future work', memo by David Cairns, dated 4 January 1990, IASC archive, 'Comparability' file.
139. AP 3/1990 paper 4.
140. AP 4/1989 paper 22.
141. IASC board meeting of 7–9 March 1990, minute 4.
142. Letter from Morley Carscallen to Cairns, dated 18 August 1989, E32 comment letters, bound volume, 700.
143. See 'IASC Move to Standardised Global Results', *World Accounting Report*, 14 June 1990, 3, for comments on UK opposition to E32's goodwill proposal.
144. See, for instance, the comments by Walter Meier Holding (Switzerland) and Lafarge Coppée (France). E32 Comment letters, bound volume, 581, 548–51.
145. Letter from Cherry to Walters, dated 14 March 1990, IASC archive, 'Comparability' file.
146. That this was a real 'sticking point' for the United Kingdom is noted in 'Financial Reporting Discussion Group Meeting 18 May 1989', memo by IASC staff member Mark Wovsaniker (IASC archive, 'Comparability' file). From this meeting with the UK standard setter and other interested parties, Wovsaniker concluded that a concession to the United Kingdom on this point might secure UK agreement on other controversial issues in E32.
147. See 'Financial Instruments: First Meeting of IASC Steering Committee', *IASC News*, 18/2 (April 1989), 3.
148. AP 3/1990 paper 7. The IOSCO observers participated in the vote.
149. Letter from Cherry to Cairns, dated 23 January 1990. Commenting on this letter, Edmund Coulson, the chief accountant of the SEC, wrote to Cairns (letter dated 1 February 1990), 'I basically agree with the points made.' IASC archive, 'Comparability' file.
150. Count based on the 139 published comment letters only.

151. Letter from Cherry to Walters, dated 14 March 1990, IASC archive, 'Comparability' file.
152. The principled and pragmatic arguments came from predictable sources. Bodies like the AARF and the South African Institute of Chartered Accountants argued on the basis of the IASC's Framework, while bodies like Keidanren (Japan) and enterprises like Hydro Québec (Canada) took a pragmatic line. Nevertheless, a number of enterprises and enterprise associations, such as the Canadian Bankers Association, argued along conceptual lines and the IASC's Framework. See E32 comment letters, bound volume.
153. IASC board meeting of 7–9 March 1990, minute 4.
154. See, for instance, file notes by David Cairns on meetings with the OECD Working Group on Accounting Standards on 26 April 1989, and on meetings in the United Kingdom on 27–9 June 1989, dated 10 May 1989 and 9 August 1989, respectively. IASC archive, 'Comparability' file.
155. Interview with Paul Cherry, 8 October 2004.
156. 'Unofficial Secretariat Notes of Discussions at the Board Meeting Held in New York on 23rd and 24th October, 1989', 2–3, IASC archive, 'Comparability' file.
157. The decision is not reported in the IASC's minutes, but it can be inferred that the decision was tentatively taken in October 1989 and confirmed in March 1990. See 'Unofficial Secretariat Notes of a Meeting at the European Commission, 15 December 1989', memo by David Cairns, dated 22 December 1989, IASC archive, 'Comparability' file. Henk Volten, 'Het IASC en de regelgevers', *De Accountant*, 96/6 (6 February 1990), 309, wrote that Chairman Barthès, speaking publicly in November 1989, hinted that the IASC would not require reconciliations. See 'IASC Comparability Climbdown', *World Accounting Report*, March 1990, 2, for the view that the IASC would decide on reconciliations during its March 1990 meeting.
158. See secretariat note 'E32, Comparability of Financial Statements', January 1990, IASC archive, 'Comparability' file.
159. IASC board meeting of 7–9 March 1990, minute 4.
160. *Annual Report 1988*, International Organization of Securities Commissions, 8.
161. AP 4/1989 paper 22, p. 4, refers to 'A recent Policy Statement of the U.S. Securities and Exchange Commission' and 'similar comments from other regulators and the international business community'.
162. AP 4/1989 paper 22; IASC board meeting of 12–14 April 1989, minute 11(l).
163. The September 1990 meeting is referred to as the second steering committee meeting in 'Vergadering Steering Group Improvements... Toronto 17 en 18 september 1990', memo by Cor Regoort dated 25 September 1990, NIVRA archive, CAJ-IASC (March–December 1990), 167. There may have been a preliminary meeting in the course of 1989. Plans for a 1989 meeting are mentioned in 'Notes on a Meeting with John Denman and Ron Salole, CICA, Toronto, 13th March, 1989', IASC archive, 'Comparability' file.
164. Over time, several IOSCO observers from Canada, France, the United Kingdom, and the United States attended. Karel Van Hulle was the first observer for the European Commission, followed by Leo van der Tas.
165. AP 11/1990 paper 14. Quotations in this paragraph are taken from this document.
166. Note from Cairns to board representatives and technical advisers, dated 11 January 1991, AP 2/1991, unnumbered paper.
167. By November 1991, six exposure drafts had been approved, compared to a planned total of twelve according to the November 1990 work plan. See for revisions of

the work programme 'Comparability of Financial Statements—Revised Implementation Programme', *IASC Insight*, July 1991, 2–3 and 'IASC Work Programme—1992/93 Plans', *IASC Insight*, December 1991, 6–9.
168. Interviews with Paul Cherry, 8 October 2004, and with Ralph Walters, 18 October 2003.
169. For an outline of the package vote issue, see 'Comparability—A Critical Stage', *IASC Insight*, July 1992, 1, and AP 10/1992 paper 4.
170. The names of the delegations voting against are not recorded in the board meetings. Votes are reconstructed on the basis of: 'Bijeenkomst in Milaan van de IASC-Board 10 tot 14 juni 1991', memo by Cor Regoort, dated 28 June 1991, NIVRA archive, file CAJ-IASC, 220; communication from David Cairns to the authors, dated 10 June 2005; pre-board comment letters (IASC archive, filed with June 1991 agenda papers). On LIFO in Germany, see Dieter Ordelheide and Dieter Pfaff, *European Financial Reporting: Germany* (London: Routledge, 1994), 147.
171. In April 1992, Wyatt surmised that IOSCO's intervention on this issue 'may well cause us to reverse our position'. Letter from Wyatt to Cairns, dated 29 April 1992, IASC archive, file 'Arthur Wyatt'. A subsequent secretariat note (AP 6/1992 paper 7) reported that a minority of the Improvements steering committee, including the IOSCO observers, believed that LIFO should be retained as allowed alternative. It was reported in *IASC Insight* ('Comparability of Financial Statements', December 1992, 1) that 'IOSCO also strongly supported the retention of LIFO'. Retrospectively, David Cairns claimed that 'Had IOSCO not sent that last minute message, I have no doubt that the vote would have gone the other way.' David Cairns, 'IOSCO Member's Attack on IASC was Ill-Conceived', *Accountancy*, 122/1262 (October 1998), 62.
172. IASC board meeting of 16–18 June 1992, minutes 4–5.
173. 'Comparability—A Critical Stage', *IASC Insight*, July 1992, 1; Georgette Thompson, 'The Crunch Comes for International Harmonization', *Accountancy*, 110/1190 (October 1992), 90.
174. Interview with Dennis Beresford, no title, *Controllers Update* (IMA), no. 87 (March 1992), 4.
175. Letter from Norman N. Strauss, AICPA Accounting Standards Executive Committee, to Cairns, dated 22 January 1992, IASC archive, E38 comment letters.
176. Letter from Patricia McConnell to David Damant, dated 5 June 1991, pre-board comment letters filed with AP 6/1991.
177. Heinz Kleekämper, 'Rechnungslegung aus der Sicht des IASC', in Baetge (editor), *Die deutsche Rechnungslegung vor dem Hintergrund internationaler Entwicklungen*, 56–7; see also Herbert Biener, 'Bedeutung und Chancen der IASC-Vorschriften als internationale Rechnungslegungsnormen', in Dietrich Dörner and Peter Wollmert (editors), *IASC-Rechnungslegung: Beiträge zu Aktuellen Problemen* (Düsseldorf: IDW-Verlag, 1995), 17–18.
178. Dennis R. Beresford, 'What's the FASB Doing about International Accounting Standards?', *Financial Executive*, 6/3 (May/June 1990), 23. Beresford mentioned the abolition of LIFO, the proposed five-year amortization period of goodwill, restrictions on completed contract accounting, and the requirement to take translation adjustments on long-term monetary items to income.
179. AP 10/1992 paper 9.
180. Pre-board comment letters filed with AP 10/1992.

181. Interview with Heinz Kleekämper, 14 July 2004.
182. 'Het IASC zet een belangrijke stap voorwaarts in de "windy city"', memo by Cor Regoort (staff observer to the Dutch delegation), dated 29 October 1992, NIVRA archive, file CAJ-IASC, 308.
183. IASC board meeting of 7–9 October 1992, minute 3. There was, in fact, some uncertainty before and after the board meeting what should be, or had been, agreed concerning the voting on the package. See letter from Wyatt to Cairns, dated 19 August 1992 (file 'Arthur Wyatt'); letter from Cairns to Shiratori, dated 2 September 1992 (file 'Shiratori'); letter from Gilbert Gélard to Cairns, dated 14 January 1993 and letter from Cairns to Gélard, dated 14 January 1993 (file 'France'), all in the IASC archive.
184. Kleekämper, 'Rechnungslegung aus der Sicht des IASC', 57. See for a similar view of these events: Wienand Schruff, 'Die internationale Vereinheitlichung der Rechnungslegung nach den Vorschlägen des IASC—Gefahr oder Chance für die deutsche Bilanzierung?', *Betriebswirtschaftliche Forschung und Praxis*, 45/4 (July 1993), 405–6.
185. IASC board meeting of 2–5 November 1993, minute 6.
186. See AP 11/1991 paper 1 for the additional materials proposed for IAS 22.
187. P.G., 'Les normes révisés IAS 2, 9 et 23 prennent en compte l'approche européenne', *Revue Française de Comptabilité*, April 1993, 23–4.
188. Memorandum from Paul Cherry to the authors, dated 8 October 2004; communication from David Cairns to the authors, dated 20 June 2006; interview with Johan van Helleman, 1 December 2004. One member of a board delegation was cited in support of a different status in 'IASC Changes Valuation Rules', *World Accounting Report*, October 1998, 2.
189. Paul Pacter, 'It's All Black and White', *World Accounting Report*, May 2000, 9.
190. IASC board meeting of 1–4 November 1994, minute 7; letter from Cairns to board representatives and technical advisers, dated 7 January 1994, IASC archive, file 'Board/Executive Committee Mailings'.
191. The total length of the revised standards increased from 115 to 196 pages.
192. AP 11/1991 paper 1, p. 3.
193. AP 11/1991 paper 1, p. 3; interviews with Johan van Helleman, 1 December 2004, and with David Cairns, 8 June 2003.
194. 'Approval of Ten Revised Standards Completes Project', *IASC Insight*, December 1993, 8. The note on the completion of the project in the November 1993 issue of *IASC Update* was equally sober.
195. e.g. 'IASC Completes Comparability Project, Receives IOSCO Endorsement', *Journal of Accountancy*, 177/1 (January 1994), 23. The reference in the title to IOSCO endorsement relates to IAS 7.
196. See the analysis of the ten revised standards by Jan Klaassen and Johan van Helleman, 'Het IASC en internationale vergelijkbaarheid van jaarrekeningen', *De Accountant*, 100/9 (May 1994), 626–30; see also James R. Peterson, 'Bourse Regulators Endorse IASC Cash-Flow Standard', *Corporate Accounting International*, no. 42 (November 1993), 1.
197. Arthur Wyatt, 'International Accounting Standards: A New Perspective', *Accounting Horizons*, 3/3 (September 1989), 107.
198. AP 3/1988 paper 4.
199. The other members of the steering committee were Jens Elling (Denmark), K. V. Jamias (Philippines), and A. C. Sondhi (financial analysts).

200. IASC board meeting of 27–8 February 1991, minute 3, and of 7–9 October 1992, minute 2.
201. A discussion of the revision of IAS 7 can be found in 'Cash Flow Statements', *IASC Insight*, July 1991, 5–9.
202. Other cash-flow standards were issued in Australia (1983), Canada (1985), New Zealand (1987), and the United Kingdom (1991).
203. David Cairns, 'Aid for the Developing World', *Accountancy*, 105/1159 (March 1990), 82; 'IASC', *De Accountant*, 90/5 (January 1984), 296.
204. 'Notes of a Telephone Conversation with Maurice Mould on Wednesday, 24 July, 1985', undated memo by David Cairns, IASC archive, 'World Bank' file.
205. The members were C. P. García (Argentina), A. Fass (Israel), Jésus Hoyos Roldán (Mexico), and Ralph Walters (United States). Walters recalled that the technical contributions from the United States were largely made by Paul Rosenfield, the staff observer of the US delegation. Communication from Ralph Walters to the authors, dated 18 October 2003.
206. AP 6/1985 paper 4; AP 4/1989 paper 4.
207. IASC board meeting of 24–7 March 1987, minute 4.
208. IASC board meeting of 1–3 July 1987, minute 3. At the same meeting, it was decided to include in the explanatory section that a cumulative rate of 100% could be seen as a characteristic of a hyperinflationary environment. Whether to include such a quantitative element in the definition of high inflation had been extensively discussed in earlier stages of the project.
209. IASC board meeting of 12–14 April 1989, minute 11(l)(iv).
210. The other members were A. A. Dieye (from Senegal, but representing France), Giancarlo Tomasin (Italy), Khoo Eng Choo (succeeded by Soon Kwai Choy, Malaysia), E. F. Oke (Nigeria), Lorraine Ruffing (United Nations), P. Rashid (World Bank), J. C. N. Tetley (International Finance Corporation), Paul Phenix (Fédération Internationale des Bourses de Valeurs), and Juan Herrera (International Federation of Accountants).
211. AP 3/1990 paper 9.
212. Communication from David Cairns to the authors, dated 20 June 2006.
213. 'Planning Committee IFAC, Curaçao, 22 en 23 februari 1990', memo by Henk Volten, dated 23 February 1990, NIVRA archive, file B-Int (1988/1990), 56–7.
214. 'Study of the Financial Reporting Needs of Developing and Newly Industrialised Countries', memo by the Jordanian delegation to the IASC, dated 7 March 1990, attached to minutes of IASC board meeting of 7–9 March 1990.
215. IASC board meeting of 7–9 March 1990, minute 5; IASC board meeting of 20–2 June 1990, minute 5; AP 6/1990 paper 10.
216. IASC board meeting of 20–2 June 1990, minute 5. According to Henk Volten, Abu-Ghazaleh announced his resignation from the board already in March 1990. 'IASC Board, 7–9 maart 1990, Amsterdam', memo by Henk Volten, dated 9 March 1990, NIVRA archive, file B-Int (1988/1990), 59.
217. AP 6/1992 paper 11; IASC board meeting of 16–19 June 1992, minute 13.
218. David Cairns, cited in Pratap Chatterjee, 'Survey Examines Need for Special Standards', *Financial Times*, 18 October 1990; IASC board meeting of 16–19 June 1992, minute 15(d).
219. AP 6/1992 paper 11, which notes in particular the support for these projects in the Council of the Eastern, Central and Southern African Federation of Accountants (ECSAFA).

220. See, e.g. Nick Sciulli, 'IASC out of Touch', letter to the editor, *Australian Accountant*, 63/11 (December 1993), 8; David Chitty, 'Has the IASC Lost the Plot?', *Accountancy*, 121/1257 (May 1998), 56; 'The IASC to Look at Developing Countries', *World Accounting Report*, February 1999, 15. See for a rebuttal of this type of criticism: David Cairns, 'Developing Countries Always on the Agenda', *Accountancy*, 119/1244 (April 1997), 62–3, and the remarks by Bryan Carsberg and other board members cited in 'Back Chat: Round Table on International Accounting Standards', *Accountancy*, 121/1258 (June 1998), 20–1.
221. 'Disclosures in Financial Statements of Banks', *IASC News*, 13/6 (November 1984), 1.
222. Untitled speech by A. G. Murphy to the Conference of the International Savings Bank Institute (Bonn), 18 June 1991, IASC archive, speeches file.
223. The other members of the steering committee were E. Dieter Nolte (Germany), P. A. Nair (India), T. Kasuga (Japan, as well as T. Myata and M. Ichii), and W. J. Dolan (United States). David Swanney (Basel Committee), and M. Marker (American Bankers Association) also attended meetings of the steering committee.
224. Interview with David Swanney, 9 February 2006; communication from David Cairns to the authors, dated 20 June 2006.
225. 'New Bank Exposure Draft', *IASC News*, 18/2 (April 1989), 2–3.
226. IASC board meeting of 12–14 April 1989, minute 4.
227. Council Directive 86/635/EEC of 8 December 1986, article 37.
228. Interview with Herman Marseille, 27 October 2004; H. Marseille, 'ED 34 van het IASC en de jaarverslagen van Nederlandse banken', *De Accountant*, 95/11 (July/August 1989), 560; 'Notulen vergadering NIVRA-gedelegeerden in het IASC met de CAJ-werkgroep IASC', 17 March 1989, NIVRA archive, file CAJ-IASC, 73.
229. IASC board meeting of 5–7 November 1986, minute 4; IASC board meeting of 12–14 April 1989, minute 4.

NOTES TO CHAPTER 10

1. IASC board meeting of 24–7 March 1987, minute 6.
2. David Marsh, 'Planned Reforms Sharpen IASC Regulatory Teeth', *Financial Times*, 17 July 1986, 1, and 'Watchdogs to Bark in Tune', *Financial Times*, 21 July 1986, 16. Also see 'Conference Creates Panel to Promote Securities Law Enforcement Worldwide', *BNA Securities Regulation & Law Report*, 18 July 1986, 1049–50.
3. 'The International Association of Securities Commissions—Notes of a Telephone Conversation with Clarence Staubs, Securities and Exchange Commission, 24 July 1986', written by David Cairns, IASC archive, IOSCO file.
4. 'The International Association of Securities Commissions—Note of a Conversation with Don Calvin, New York Stock Exchange, 24 July 1986', written by David Cairns, IASC archive, IOSCO file. Calvin had attended the July conference in Paris.
5. There is no written history of IOSCO for the years prior to 1988. The authors have developed this historical trail with the assistance of emails from Jean-Pierre Cristel, the deputy secretary-general of IOSCO, dated 13 and 16 January 2006. For a view of IOSCO from 1988 onwards, see A. A. Sommer, Jr., 'IOSCO: Its Mission and Achievement', *Northwestern Journal of International Law & Business*, 17/1 (Fall 1996), 15–29.
6. This quotation and the next are from Marsh, 'Planned Reforms Sharpen IASC Regulatory Teeth'.

7. Interview with Linda Quinn, 11 September 2003.
8. Bank for International Settlements, *68th Annual Report* (1998), table VI.1.
9. Letter from Cairns to Barthès de Ruyter, dated 28 July 1986, IASC archive, IOSCO file.
10. At the outset of his service as IOSCO secretary-general in July 1986, Paul Guy was président of the Commission des Valeurs Mobilières du Québec (Quebec Securities Commission), which housed IOSCO's secretariat from 1986 to 1999, when it moved to Madrid. Guy served as secretary-general from 1986 to 1994. See 'Report from the Secretary General', *Annual Report 1994* of the International Organization of Securities Commissions, 2.
11. 'Report from the Secretary General', *Annual Report 1994* of the International Organization of Securities Commissions, 2, as well as the *Annual Reports* for 1990 and 1995.
12. The proceedings were published as *Standard Setting for Financial Reporting: An International Conference Sponsored by the American Accounting Association with Klynveld Main Goerdeler*, Princeton, New Jersey, 17–20 August 1986.
13. Quoted in *IASC News*, 16/5 (October 1987), 9.
14. Interview with Michael Mann (in the 1990s the director of the SEC's Office of International Affairs), 25 June 2003.
15. 'Notes of Visit to the Securities and Exchange Commission, Washington 11th March 1987', IASC archive, SEC file. Also see *IASC News*, 16/2 (April 1987), 3.
16. 'Notes of Visit to the Securities and Exchange Commission, Washington 11th March 1987', IASC archive, SEC file. Also, letter from Cairns to Cox, dated 9 April 1987, IASC archive, IOSCO file.
17. 'Acceptable Global GAAP Still Far Off, Audit Rules Moving Ahead, Sampson Says', *BNA Securities Regulation & Law Report*, 19/15 (10 April 1987), 505.
18. Interview with Edmund Coulson, 12 September 2003.
19. *IASC News*, 16/2 (April 1987), 3.
20. 'Visit to FASB and SEC, March 1987', AP 3/1987, additional paper.
21. The quotations and paraphrases in this paragraph and the next are taken from minute 6 of the IASC board meeting of 24–7 March 1987. Also see *IASC News*, 16/3 (June 1987), 1, and the IASC's 'Report on Activities for the Year Ended 30 June 1987', in the *1987 Annual Report*, International Federation of Accountants, 21.
22. Memorandum from Paul Cherry to the authors, dated 8 October 2004.
23. Memorandum from Ralph Walters to the authors, dated 18 October 2003.
24. IASC board meeting of 24–7 March 1987, minute 7(iii).
25. *IASC News*, 16/3 (June 1987), 3.
26. Quoted in John Kirkpatrick, 'IASC, Rosetta Stone of Financial Reporting', *Accountancy*, 101/1133 (January 1988), 17.
27. *IASC News*, 16/5 (October 1987), 2.
28. *Annual Report 1988*, International Organization of Securities Commissions, 14. Cherry has written that its formation was 'a major milestone' for, without it, 'IOSCO would never have made any real progress or had any influence on IASC.' Memorandum from Paul Cherry to the authors, dated 8 October 2004.
29. Memorandum from Paul Cherry to the authors, dated 22 April 2004.
30. *Annual Report 1991*, International Organization of Securities Commissions, 6.
31. *Annual Report 1988*, International Organization of Securities Commissions, 4.
32. D'Illiers' formal title was chef du service des affaires comptables.

33. Memorandum from Ralph Walters to the authors, dated 18 October 2003. It was reported that d'Illiers, with IASC support, invited Karel Van Hulle, of the European Commission, to attend meetings of the Comparability steering committee as an observer; David Cairns reiterated the invitation and said that it applied as well to Hermann Niessen. But they evidently did not accept the invitation. Letter from Cairns to Van Hulle, dated 25 April 1988, IASC archive, EEC file.
34. Letter from Cherry to Coulson and Cairns, dated 30 June 1988, IASC archive, IOSCO file.
35. Memorandum from Ralph Walters to the authors, dated 18 October 2003.
36. Interview with Edmund Coulson, 12 September 2003. Richard Breeden, the SEC chairman from 1989 to 1993, has said that, if foreign companies were permitted to have far less disclosure than is required of, say, Ford and General Motors in the US capital market, the SEC would have to reduce the disclosure standards for Ford and General Motors to make them equal. Interview with Richard Breeden, 12 November 2004.
37. Linda Quinn, in the proceedings from a colloquy in June 1989: Helen Gernon, S. E. C. Purvis, and Michael A. Diamond, *An Analysis of the Implications of the IASC's Comparability Project*, Topical Issues Study No. 3 ([Los Angeles:] School of Accounting, University of Southern California, 1990), 48.
38. Attachment to letter from Cherry to Paul Guy, dated 6 September 1988, IASC archive, IOSCO file.
39. Letter from Coulson to Cherry, dated 29 September 1988, IASC archive, IOSCO file.
40. 'Statement of Support for International Accounting Standards Committee Initiative', dated 4 October 1988, attached to a letter from Paul Guy to Georges Barthès de Ruyter, dated 12 October 1988, IASC archive, IOSCO file; it was published in *IASC News*, 18/1 (January 1989), 2–3.
41. IASC board meeting of 9–11 November 1988, minute 2.
42. E32, paragraph 19. Of interest is the use in point (a) of 'generally accepted accounting principles', a term that was widely employed in the United States, Canada, and Mexico but was little used elsewhere.
43. Memorandum from Paul Cherry to the authors, dated 8 October 2004.
44. Letter from Meagher to Cairns, dated 29 September 1989, in E32 comment letters, bound volume, 232.
45. Memorandum from Donald Moulin to the authors, dated 26 May 2004. Moulin had himself attended the 1984, 1986, and 1987 IOSCO annual conferences as a registered observer, and a partner in his firm from the Bogotá office attended the 1985 conference.
46. *Annual Report 1988*, International Organization of Securities Commissions, 12. One infers that 'common standards' includes accounting standards, but one cannot be sure.
47. Memorandum from Donald Moulin to the authors, dated 26 May 2004.
48. Memorandum from Donald Moulin to the authors, dated 26 May 2004. Except where otherwise noted, the discussion of Moulin's initiative is drawn from this memorandum.
49. Communication from Edmund Coulson to the authors, dated 20 July 2004.
50. Donald J. Moulin, 'Practical Means of Promoting Common Accounting and Auditing Standards', Workshop 4—Harmonization of Accounting and Auditing Standards, for presentation at the 13th Annual Conference of IOSCO, 16 November

1988—Melbourne, Australia (copy supplied by Moulin). An almost identical version of the paper was published under the names of Moulin and his partner, Morton B. Solomon, 'Practical Means of Promoting International Standards', *The CPA Journal*, 59/12 (December 1989), 38–40, 45–6, 48.

51. *IASC News*, 18/1 (January 1989) 2; interview with Donald Moulin, 20 April 2004, and his memorandum. The conference programme showed the Australian participant as Ken Rennie, the president of the Institute of Chartered Accountants in Australia, but Spencer replaced him at the last minute. With Barthès and Walters, the panel was weighted in favour of the IASC. As indicated in the previous section, Cherry admired the progress the Comparability steering committee had made.
52. 'Report of Workshop No. 4: Harmonization of Accounting and Auditing Standards, 13th Annual Conference of IOSCO' (supplied by IOSCO). An account of the Workshop's deliberations appears in *IASC News*, 18/1 (January 1989), 2.
53. 'Report of Workshop No. 4: Harmonization of Accounting and Auditing Standards, 13th Annual Conference of IOSCO' (supplied by IOSCO).
54. 'Report of Workshop No. 4: Harmonization of Accounting and Auditing Standards, 13th Annual Conference of IOSCO' (supplied by IOSCO) and *Annual Report 1988*, International Organization of Securities Commissions, 8.
55. Paul Cherry confirms that Ruder was the one who cast the veto. Memorandum from Paul G. Cherry to the authors, dated 8 October 2004.
56. 'Note of Telephone Conversation with Georges Barthes, 2 December 1988', by David Cairns, IASC archive, IOSCO. SEC Chief Accountant Coulson was unable to attend the IOSCO conference; hence, he did not attend the Workshop. Interview with Coulson, 12 September 2003. Moulin recalls in his memorandum that Ruder attended most of the Workshop but did not comment. The Presidents Committee made its decisions by unanimous vote.
57. 'Note of Telephone Conversation with Georges Barthes, 2 December 1988', by David Cairns, IASC archive, IOSCO file. Paul Cherry, who was then the chairman of IOSCO's Working Party 2, has written: 'IASC were also disturbed that IOSCO was urging IASC to commit to major endeavours without any corresponding commitment [on its part]. Also, IOSCO seemed to be holding IASC to a much higher standard of performance than it expected/accepted of its own working parties'. Memorandum from Paul G. Cherry to the authors, dated 8 October 2004.
58. 'Regulation of International Securities Markets', Policy Statement (Release No. 33-6807, 34-26284, IC-16636, IA-1143, S7-25-88), dated 21 November 1988, Sec. III; also see 'SEC Seeks Continued Efforts on International Accounting Standards', *IASC News*, 18/1 (January 1989), 3. Two years later, the SEC's Office of the Chief Accountant completed a 116-page staff study comparing IASC disclosure standards with those of US GAAP, which was transmitted to the IASC by Chief Accountant Edmund Coulson under cover of a letter dated 14 August 1990. Clearly, the SEC's accounting staff wanted to probe the differences between IASC standards and US GAAP. The IASC acquired two copies for its library.
59. *International Equity Offers* (IOSCO, 1989), 75. Among the members of Douglas-Mann's Working Party 1 was Linda Quinn, director of the SEC's Division of Corporation Finance, who would become the major interlocutor between the SEC and the IASC during the first half of the 1990s.
60. *Accountancy Age* reported, 'By withdrawing the reconciliation rules the IASC is trying to remove obstacles which might prevent companies from complying with the bulk of the new standards.' See 'IASC Comparability Climbdown', *Accountancy*

Age, 1 March 1990, 2. But the IASC board, in its *Statement of Intent*, did say that it 'will continue to support the efforts of IOSCO which are to encourage individual securities regulators to allow or require each foreign issuer' to reconcile 'its financial statements prepared in conformity with its domestic requirements' to the IASC's benchmark treatments, or to present its financial statements in conformity with the benchmark treatments. *Statement of Intent*, paragraph 19.

61. Memorandum from Paul Cherry to the authors, dated 8 October 2004.
62. Interview with Edmund Coulson, 12 September 2003.
63. IASC board meeting of 12–14 April 1989, minute 11(l)(ii) and (m).
64. *International Equity Offers* (IOSCO, 1989), 45.
65. Paul G. Cherry, 'Perspective: International Accounting Standards in the Post-Cold War Era', *Journal of Corporate Accounting and Finance*, Summer 1991, 504.
66. Interview with Richard Breeden, 12 November 2004.
67. Interview with Richard Breeden, 12 November 2004.
68. *Annual Report 1991*, International Organization of Securities Commissions, 6.
69. Breeden served as chairman of the Technical Committee from November 1990 to November 1992. Successor chairmen and the months in which their terms began were Jean Saint-Geours, chairman of the COB (October 1992), Edward Waitzer, chairman of the OSC (October 1994), Anthony Neoh, chairman of the Hong Kong Securities and Futures Commission (September 1996), Michel Prada, chairman of the COB (September 1998), and David Brown, chairman of the OSC (May 2000). The new terms began at the time of IOSCO's annual conference. Communication from Jean-Pierre Cristel, deputy secretary-general of IOSCO, to the authors, dated 5 November 2004.
70. This is the unit that reviews financial statements and complementary disclosures in prospectuses and annual and quarterly filings by SEC registrants.
71. In the IOSCO annual reports, WP1 carried the name 'Multinational Disclosure and Accounting'. In 1996, the working parties were renamed working groups.
72. The SEC had a special relationship with the OSC and was confident that it shared the SEC's values. As will be seen, in 1991 the SEC announced a 'multijurisdictional agreement' with Canada, by which US and Canadian prospectuses would be accepted in the other country.
73. Testimony of Richard C. Breeden on 2 May 1991 before the Subcommittee on Telecommunications and Finance of the Committee on Energy and Commerce, *SEC Reauthorization*, House of Representatives, 102nd Congress, 1st Session, Serial No. 102–17 (Washington: U.S. Government Printing Office, 1991), 17.
74. Yet, in late 1988, David Walker, the chairman of the SIB, called for 'a convergence by regulators and stock exchanges in the major markets on common minimum or benchmark standards of information disclosure in financial statements'. 'Convergence on Common Standards of Disclosure Highly Desirable', *IASC News*, 18/1 (January 1989), 4.
75. Interviews with David Cairns, 8 June 2003, and with Geoffrey Mitchell, dated 19 February 2004; 'IOSCO', note by David Cairns, AP 6/1992, additional paper. Mitchell says he urged the SIB to become active in IOSCO because of the important role that the IASC was likely to play in the future development of accounting standards.
76. Interview with Atsushi Kato, 2 July 2004.
77. Letter from Meagher to Cairns, dated 7 July 1993, IASC archive, file 'IOSCO Core Standards Liaison'.

78. See the correspondence the file 'IOSCO Core Standards Liaison', IASC archive.
79. Edward J. Waitzer, 'International Securities Regulation—Coping with the "Rashomon Effect"', *Ontario Securities Commission Bulletin*, 17 (22 April 1994), 1845; and 'Towards the Endorsement of International Accounting Standards', *IASC Insight*, June 1994, 5.
80. 'Notes on a Confidential Telephone Conversation with Stuart Grant, Australian Securities Commission, 3rd December 1993', by David Cairns, IASC archive, file 'IOSCO Core Standards Liaison'.
81. See 'Meeting of IOSCO Working Party 1 held on 2nd December 1993 in Rome, Italy', by David Cairns, IASC archive, file 'IOSCO Core Standards Liaison'.
82. See, for example, the Subcommittee's view that E40, on financial instruments, be re-exposed, contrary to the IASC's intention and, indeed, to the view expressed by the IOSCO representative at a recent meeting of the IASC's Consultative Group. 'Notes of a Telephone Conversation with Richard Reinhard, Securities & Exchange Commission, and Michael Meagher, Chairman IOSCO Accounting Sub-Committee, 17th September 1993'. The Subcommittee's view was unanimously supported by WP1 the following month. Letter from Quinn and Meagher to Cairns, dated 23 October 1993. Both documents in IASC archive, file 'IOSCO Core Standards Liaison'.
83. 'Meeting of IOSCO Working Party 1 Held on 2nd December 1993 in Rome, Italy', by David Cairns, IASC archive, file 'IOSCO Core Standards Liaison'.
84. 'IOSCO', ES/MS Meeting, January 1993, IASC archive, file 'IOSCO Core Standards Liaison'.
85. Cherry has written (memorandum to the authors, dated 8 October 2004), 'Linda was hugely helpful and deserves a lot of credit for working behind the scenes to bring other IOSCO members along. Also, she worked hard to make the SEC's commitment more substantive in terms of resources and public awareness. She was a very senior person and carried tremendous influence.'
86. Memorandum from Paul Cherry to the authors, dated 8 October 2004.
87. Much of the content of this paragraph and the next is based on communications to the authors from David Cairns, dated 6 and 9 May 2004. Also see David Cairns, 'The Future Shape of Harmonization: A Reply', *The European Accounting Review*, 6/2 (1997), 346–7, and 'IOSCO (A note from the Secretary-General)', IASC executive committee meeting of June 1994, agenda paper III.
88. Cairns has argued that, 'Had IOSCO not sent that last minute message [at the April 1992 meeting of the Improvements steering committee], I have no doubt that the vote [in October] would have gone the other way.' David Cairns, 'IOSCO Member's Attack on IASC was Ill-conceived', *Accountancy* (international edition), 122/1262 (October 1998), 62. For a summary of some of the views for and against LIFO by commentators on E38, on inventories, see 'Board Approves First Three Revised Standards', *IASC Insight*, December 1992, 14–15.
89. David Cairns, 'Can International Accounting Standards Improve Financial Reporting?', paper presented at the 1994 Financial and Auditing Research Conference, sponsored by the Research Board of the ICAEW and held at the London Business School, 18 July 1994, 4, IASC archive, speech file.
90. Arthur Wyatt, 'Harmonization's Future', in Mark E. Haskins, Kenneth R. Ferris, and Thomas I. Selling, *International Financial Reporting and Analysis: A Contextual Analysis*, fourth edition (Chicago: Irwin, 1996), 836. Indeed, two US accounting firms, Arthur Andersen and Coopers & Lybrand, publicly supported the

elimination of LIFO 'in the interest of harmonization of international standards'. 'C&L's and AA's US Firms Support Elimination of LIFO', *Corporate Accounting International*, 25 (February 1992), 1.
91. 'World Congress Report', *World Accounting Report*, November 1992, 4–5.
92. The data in this section are derived from *World Stock Exchange Fact Book 2001* (Plano TX: Meridian Securities Markets, 2001). Data for the US are for the New York Stock Exchange only.
93. See Sara Hanks, 'Globalization of World Financial Markets: Perspective of the U.S. Securities and Exchange Commission', in Frederick D. S. Choi (editor), *International Accounting and Finance Handbook* (New York: John Wiley & Sons, 1997), 2-17 and 2-18.
94. 'Multijurisdictional Disclosure and Modifications to the Current Registration and Reporting System for Canadian Issuers', Securities Act Release No. 6902, Exchange Act Release No. 29354 (13 June 1991) [56 FR 30036]. For a description of the MJDS, see 'The Multijurisdictional Disclosure System with Canada', Office of International Corporate Finance, Division of Corporation Finance, US Securities and Exchange Commission (17 January 1995). See also 'SEC Approves Multijurisdictional Agreement with Canada', *Corporate Accounting International*, 19 (June 1991), 1, 13, and Hanks, 'Globalization of World Financial Markets: Perspective of the U.S. Securities and Exchange Commission', 2-13 to 2-16. Generally, see Roberta S. Karmel, *National Treatment, Harmonization and Mutual Recognition—The Search For Principles for the Regulation of Global Equity Markets: A Discussion Paper* (Capital Markets Forum, Section on Business Law, International Bar Association, 1993).
95. Interview with Sara Hanks, 27 February 2004. Hanks was chief of the SEC's Office of International Corporate Finance from 1988 to 1990. Also see the remarks by Karel Van Hulle and Sarah E. Brown, in *Festival of Accounting: Proceedings* (Edinburgh: The Institute of Chartered Accountants of Scotland, 1991), 31.
96. The proposing rules for the MJDS were issued in 1989, in Securities Act Release No. 6841 (July 24, 1989) [54 FR 32226].
97. Interview with Sara Hanks, 27 February 2004.
98. Interview with Atsushi Kato, 2 July 2004. Kato attended the discussions as an accounting adviser to the Ministry of Finance.
99. See 'International Accounting Standard Endorsed by IOSCO', IASC press release, 28 October 1993, and 'Agreement on Cash Flow Statements and Core Standards', *IASC Insight*, December 1993, 4, and James R. Peterson, 'Bourse Regulators Endorse IASC Cash-flow Standard', *Corporate Accounting International*, 42 (November 1993), 1. The SEC issued its notice of proposed rulemaking in Release Nos. 33-7029, 34-33139, International Series Release No. 608, File No. S7-30-93 (30 November 1993).
100. 'SEC Tries to Ease Disclosure Rules for Foreign Firms', *The Wall Street Journal*, 4 November 1993, A11. Also see Kenneth N. Gilpin, 'The S.E.C. is Welcoming Foreign Stocks, But Will They Come?' *The New York Times*, 3 May 1994, D10, and 'SEC Initiatives for Foreign Companies', *IASC Insight*, December 1993, 3.
101. Interviews with Linda Quinn, 11 September 2003, and with Michael Mann, 25 June 2003. Mann recalls, 'The question was, how do you start [the negotiation over IASC standards] and say we really believe it. So, as soon as IAS 7 was done, we were the first country in the world to say, "we'll accept it". That was intentional.' WP1 recommended the endorsement to the Technical Committee. Letter from Quinn and Meagher to Shiratori, dated 16 August 1993, IASC archive, file 'IOSCO Core Standards Liaison'.

102. Interview with Richard Breeden, 12 November 2004.
103. Interview with Linda Quinn, 11 September 2003. In the same interview, Quinn observed that, by accepting IAS 7, the SEC sought to avoid foreign issuers pointedly asking the SEC, 'why do we have to prepare a US GAAP cash flow statement?'
104. Quoted in 'SEC Proposes Endorsement of Three More International Accounting Standards', IASC press release, 28 April 1994, 2.
105. Quoted in 'SEC Initiatives for Foreign Companies', *IASC Insight*, December 1993, 3.
106. 'Internationalising Accounting' (an interview with Trevor Harris), *Corporate Accounting International*, 58 (May 1995), 14; reproduced in *IASC Insight*, June 1995, 17–18.
107. Interviews with Bernd-Joachim Menn, 18 August 2004, and with Richard Breeden, 12 November 2004. See David Waller, 'Germans Draw Line at Two Sets of Accounts', *Financial Times*, 19 March 1992, 33. In April 1992, an official of the Federation of German Stock Exchanges argued for the direct listing of German stocks on US stock exchanges. See Jonathan Fuerbringer, 'S.E.C. Says No on German Stocks', *The New York Times*, 26 April 1992, F15.
108. Interview with Linda Quinn, 11 September 2003; also, interview with Edmund Coulson, 12 September 2003.
109. See 'Daimler Drives into Trouble', *World Accounting Report*, May 1993, 2–3.
110. Two years later, Daimler financial executives came to the realization that the law regulated only companies' filings of their audited financial statements at the public register, not the contents of their annual report to shareholders. Therefore, beginning in its annual report for 1996, Daimler expressed its consolidated financial statements in US GAAP and referred readers who were interested in its consolidated statements in German GAAP to the filing at the public register.
111. Interview with Richard Breeden, 12 November 2004.
112. James L. Cochrane, 'Are U.S. Regulatory Requirements for Foreign Firms Appropriate?' *Fordham International Law Journal*, 17 (1994 Symposium), S61. Columnist Floyd Norris wrote that the Daimler Benz listing would 'cap a bitter battle' between Donaldson and SEC Chairman Richard C. Breeden. 'Daimler-Benz is Ready to Sign Up with Wall St.', *The New York Times*, 25 March 1993, D1.
113. Interview with Edmund Coulson, 12 September 2003. He added, 'in that time frame, there was an absolute rise in the German and Japanese market, and the London Stock Exchange was outpacing Nasdaq and New York.' William H. Donaldson, who was the chairman of the New York Stock Exchange from 1991 to 1995, applied the pressure through numerous speeches. See 'IOSCO', note by David Cairns, AP 6/1992, additional paper.
114. Peter Norman and John Gapper, 'Germany Seeks US Concession on Listings', *Financial Times*, 27 September 1993, 21. For early signs of this development, see Axel Haller, 'International Accounting Harmonization: American Hegemony or Mutual Recognition with Benchmarks? Comments and Additional Notes from a German Perspective', *The European Accounting Review*, 4/2 (1995), 238.
115. Breeden was quoted in Fuerbringer, 'S.E.C. Says No on German Stocks', F15.
116. Schapiro was quoted in Norman and Gapper, 'Germany Seeks US Concession on Listings', 21. For the similar view of Richard Breeden, who had just departed as SEC chairman, see his 'Foreign Companies and U.S. Securities Markets in a Time of Economic Transformation', *Fordham International Law Journal*, 17 (1994 Symposium), S89. For a triptych of articles on 'The Politics of Mutual Recognition', by Walter P.

Schuetze, Herbert Biener, and David Cairns, see *The European Accounting Review*, 3/2 (1994), 329–52.

117. 'Statement by William H. Donaldson', news release, New York Stock Exchange, 30 March 1993, AP 3/1993, additional paper. Also see Fuerbringer, 'S.E.C. Says No on German Stocks', F15, where Donaldson was said to claim that there were 2,500 foreign companies that could be listed on the Exchange.

118. Breeden, 'Foreign Companies and U.S. Securities Markets in a Time of Economic Transformation', S95. The pressure from the NYSE on the Commission continued into the middle 1990s by the provision on international accounting standards the Exchange lobbied into Congressional legislation in 1996 (*see* Section 10.16).

119. Interviews with Michael Mann, 25 June 2003 and with Sara Hanks, 27 February 2004.

120. Edward F. Greene, Daniel A. Braverman, and Sebastian R. Sperber, 'Hegemony or Deference: U.S. Disclosure Requirements in the International Capital Markets', *The Business Lawyer*, 50/2 (February 1995), 423, ftn. 49.

121. Memorandum from Michael Sutton to the authors, dated 25 June 2004. Also see Breeden, 'Foreign Companies and U.S. Securities Markets in a Time of Economic Transformation'.

122. 'Daimler-Benz Figures Highlight Need for International Accounting Standards', IASC press release, 24 September 1993.

123. Cochrane, 'Are U.S. Regulatory Requirements for Foreign Firms Appropriate?', S65.

124. Cochrane, 'Are U.S. Regulatory Requirements for Foreign Firms Appropriate?', S65.

125. Trevor S. Harris, *International Accounting Standards versus US-GAAP Reporting: Empirical Evidence Based on Case Studies* (Cincinnati: South-Western, 1995). For a report on Harris' study, see James R. Peterson, 'Satisfying the Gatekeeper', *Corporate Accounting International*, 57 (April 1995), 9. Also, interview with Trevor Harris, 22 July 2005.

126. As quoted in 'Internationalising Accounting' (an interview with Trevor Harris), *Corporate Accounting International*, 58 (May 1995), 15. Harris and two co-authors found in an empirical study that there was very little difference between the United States and Germany in the associations between prices or returns and earnings and changes in earnings. Trevor S. Harris, Mark Lang, and Hans Peter Möller, 'The Value Relevance of German Accounting Measures: An Empirical Analysis', *Journal of Accounting Research*, 32/2 (Autumn 1994), 187–209.

127. Some of the views and data contained in this section and elsewhere in this chapter were first reported in Stephen A. Zeff, 'The Coming Confrontation on International Accounting Standards', *The Irish Accounting Review*, 5/2 (Autumn 1998).

128. See 'SEC Proposes Endorsement of Three More International Accounting Standards', IASC press release, 28 April 1994. Also see Wayne E. Carnall, 'International Reporting Issues in the Division of Corporation Finance', speech at the AICPA's Twenty-Third Annual Conference on Current SEC Developments, Washington, DC, 16 February 1996 (available at: http://www.sec.gov/news/speech/speecharchive/1996/spch082.txt). The SEC issued its notice of proposed rulemaking on IAS 22 in Release Nos. 33-7056, 34-33921, International Series Release No. 656, File No. S7-13-94 (26 April 1994). The SEC's notice of proposed rulemaking for IAS 21 and 29 was Release No. 33-7054 (19 April 1994).

129. SEC staff member Wayne Carnall has said, 'In certain instances, the staff did not object to these companies using amounts that were first adjusted for inflation prior to translation as a surrogate for the remeasurement principles of paragraphs

10 & 11 of SFAS 52 to determine the historical cost basis of non monetary items—for example, property, plant and equipment.' See Carnall, 'International Reporting Issues in the Division of Corporation Finance'.

130. For the SEC's final rule, see 'Selection of Reporting Currency for Financial Statements of Foreign Private Issuers and Reconciliation to U.S. GAAP for Foreign Private Issuers with Operations in a Hyperinflationary Economy', International Series Release No. 757 (13 December 1994). In 1997, the Commission wrote that it 'does not require reconciliation of inflation adjustments if the financial statements of a foreign private issuer include a comprehensive measure of inflation. Inflation adjusted financial statements often are prepared by Latin American and Israeli companies.' See *Report on Promoting Global Preeminence of American Securities Markets*, pursuant to section 509(5) of the National Securities Markets Improvement Act 1996, by the United States Securities and Exchange Commission (October 1997), 27–8. It is the authors' understanding that this policy was in place even before the Commission's action on IAS 29 in 1994.

131. Interview with Edmund Coulson, 12 September 2003. For the SEC's final rule, see 'Reconciliation of the Accounting by Foreign Private Issuers for Business Combinations', International Series Release No. 759 (13 December 1994). See the remarks by SEC Professional Accounting Fellow Chris M. Holmes to the 21st Annual National Conference on Current SEC Developments (11 January 1994): 'Registrants and their auditors can expect the SEC staff to question extended amortization periods for goodwill in light of evidence suggesting that a shorter amortization period is warranted.' Jim Leisenring, the former FASB vice-chairman, recalled (interview, 16 August 2004) the SEC's previous pressure to reduce the life of goodwill from forty to twenty years. Arthur Wyatt (interview, 9 August 2004) recalled that the SEC's staff position applied mostly to the goodwill of financial institutions. Yet Michael Sutton (interview, 4 January 2005) has said that, as the former senior technical partner of Deloitte & Touche, he cannot remember such an SEC staff position.

132. 'Internationalising Accounting', 14.

133. Interview with Michael Sutton, 4 January 2005.

134. Interview with Linda Quinn, 11 September 2003.

135. Interviews with Linda Quinn, 11 September 2003, and with Walter Schuetze, 6 February 2004.

136. *Report on Promoting Global Preeminence of American Securities Markets*, pursuant to section 509(5) of the National Securities Markets Improvement Act 1996, by the United States Securities and Exchange Commission (October 1997), 28. Also see Carnall, 'International Reporting Issues in the Division of Corporation Finance'. The SEC issued its notice of proposed rulemaking in Release Nos. 33-7029, 34-33139, International Series Release No. 608, File No. S7-30-93 (15 November 1993).

137. The following quotations are taken from Michael Meagher, 'Dynamics of Change in Financial Reporting for the 1990's: A Securities Regulatory Perspective', Fordham University, 23 March 1993; typescript in IASC archive, file 'Michael Sharpe (deputy chairman)'. Meagher advises that he was speaking as a regulator, not as someone from the private sector. Communication from Meagher to the authors, dated 7 May 2004.

138. Memorandum from Paul Cherry to the authors, dated 8 October 2004.

139. Paul Pacter, 'It's all Black and White', *World Accounting Report*, May 2000, 9; reprinted in *IASC Insight*, June 2000, 14.

140. Examples included the insurance, oil and gas, mining, property development, motion picture, and transportation industries. See 'Meeting with David Cairns—IASC Secretary-General', memo prepared by the SEC, dated 25 May 1993, IASC archive, file 'IOSCO Core Standards Liaison'.
141. For the correspondence, see IASC archive, file 'IOSCO Core Standards Liaison'.
142. Letter from Quinn and Meagher to Shiratori, dated 16 August 1993, attached to AP 11/1992, paper 1.
143. See the correspondence in part H, 'IOSCO Core Standards Liaison', in the IASC archive.
144. Letter from Cairns to Shiratori and Sharpe, dated 24 August 1993, IASC archive, file 'IOSCO Core Standards Liaison'. Cairns went on to suggest that the list had an American bias because of such topics as impairment.
145. David Cairns, 'International Equity Offerings: The Role of International Accounting Standards' (in the authors' files).
146. See Cairns, 'International Equity Offerings: The Role of International Accounting Standards'; also, a communication from Cairns to the authors, dated 19 June 2006.
147. 'Agreement on Cash Flow Statements and Core Standards', *IASC Insight*, December 1993, 5.
148. This view was repeated in Paul Guy, 'International Regulatory Initiatives', in Frederick D. S. Choi, and Richard Levich (editors), *International Capital Markets in a World of Accounting Differences* (Homewood, IL: Richard D. Irwin, 1994), which in turn was quoted in Cairns, 'The Future Shape of Harmonization: A Reply', 341.
149. Meagher, 'Dynamics of Change in Financial Reporting for the 1990s', 4.
150. See 'IOSCO to Consider International Accounting Standards', *IASC Insight*, September 1993, 5; and IASC board meeting of 30 June–2 July 1993, minute 3(c). Also see Cairns, 'The Future Shape of Harmonization: A Reply', 341.
151. Waitzer, 'International Securities Regulation—Coping with the "Rashomon Effect" ', quoted in Cairns, 'The Future Shape of Harmonization: A Reply', 343.
152. Interview with Bernd-Joachim Menn, 18 August 2004.
153. Interview with Paul Cherry, 8 October 2004.
154. AP 6–7/1993, paper 24, page 3.
155. Interviews with Atsushi Kato, 2 July 2004, and with Herbert Biener, 13 July 2004.
156. 'Notes of a Telephone Conversation with George Barthes', by David Cairns, IASC archive, file 'IOSCO Core Standards Liaison'.
157. 'Notes of a Meeting with Linda Quinn, Chairman of IOSCO WP1, SEC, Washington, USA, 10 January [1994]', IASC archive, file 'IOSCO Core Standards Liaison'.
158. IASC board meeting of 23–6 March 1993, minute 2; 'IASs Must be Used, Pledges New Chief', *Accountancy*, 111/1194 (February 1993), 16. Also see the English translation of an excerpt from Shiratori's article, 'Upon Assuming Chairmanship of the International Accounting Standards Committee', *JICPA Journal*, 453 (April 1993), 4–5, in Kiyomitsu Arai, *Accounting in Japan*, IRBA Series No. 25 (Tokyo: Institute for Research in Business Administration, Waseda University, 1994), 80.
159. Letter from Sharpe to Cairns, dated 10 February 1994, IASC archive, file 'IOSCO Core Standards Liaison'. In the same place, see the memorandum from Cairns to Shiratori and Sharpe, dated 12 January 1994, in which he reported that Linda Quinn said the letter in question 'should be approved by the Working Party at its February 1994 meeting'.
160. Both letters in IASC archive, file 'IOSCO Liaison/Core Standards (2)'.

161. IAS 20 and 31, it was reported, were acceptable to all but one member of WP1, and the working party may permit an accounting treatment not allowed by IAS 20.
162. Eiichi Shiratori, 'Time for a Different Approach from IOSCO', *IASC Insight*, December 1994, 10.
163. Memorandum from Cairns to members of the Consultative Group, dated 30 September 1994; letter from Cherry to Cairns, dated 5 July 1994; letter to Cairns from Sharpe, dated 1 August 1994. IASC archive, file 'IOSCO Liaison/Core Standards (2)'.
164. 'Conversation with Linda Quinn, EFFAS Congress, Edinburgh, 22 September 1994', note prepared by David Cairns, attached to the Shiratori letter to Quinn and James Saloman, dated 28 December 1994, in the file 'IOSCO Liaison Core Standards (2)', IASC archive.
165. 'IOSCO Deals Blow to IASC', *World Accounting Report*, November 1994, 1.
166. Interview with Peter Clark, 15 October 2004.
167. Shiratori, 'Time for a Different Approach from IOSCO'. Subsequent quotations are from this published version of the speech. The title used in the final typescript version of the speech was 'Efficiencies in Multinational Securities Offerings: How to Promote International Harmonisation of Accounting Standards', speech at the Twenty-First Conference [should read Nineteenth Conference] of the International Organisation of Securities Commissions, in Tokyo, Japan, October 1994, AP 11/1994, additional paper. For a news report, see 'IOSCO Comes in for Strong Criticism', *Accountancy*, 114/1215 (November 1994), 18. Stig Enevoldsen, then a member of the board delegation representing the Nordic Federation of Public Accountants, later said, several months after becoming IASC chairman, that his 'biggest disappointment' was the failure to secure IOSCO's endorsement in 1994. 'A Look Back and A Look Forward', *IASC Insight*, June 1998, 15.
168. Cairns, 'The Future Shape of Harmonization: A Reply', 344.
169. 'IOSCO (A Note from the Staff)', IASC archive, file 'Executive Committee 1994–1995'.
170. Interview with Linda Quinn, 11 September 2003.
171. Interviews with Edmund Coulson, 12 September 2003, and with Richard Breeden, 12 November 2004. Trevor Harris, who counselled Daimler-Benz on its US listing, has said, 'I think part of the difficulty of the SEC [supporting an IOSCO endorsement of the IASC's standards as they then were] is that it is concerned about what that could mean to US registrants, as opposed to non-US registrants.' 'Internationalising Accounting' (an interview with Trevor Harris), *Corporate Accounting International*, 58 (May 1995), 14.
172. See Nathaniel C. Nash, 'Stretching the S.E.C.'s Reach', *The New York Times*, 13 July 1986, Sec. 3, 4; and Linda Quinn, in Gernon, Purvis, and Diamond, *An Analysis of the Implications of the IASC's Comparability Project*, 48.
173. Memorandum from David Cairns to Board Representatives and Technical Advisers, dated 5 September 1994, contained in the file 'IOSCO Liaison Core Standards (2)', IASC archive.
174. IASC board meeting of 1–4 November 1994, minute 11. A copy of Shiratori's letter is contained in the file 'IOSCO Liaison Core Standards (2)', IASC archive.
175. Interview with James Saloman, 8 October 2004.
176. Interview with Linda Quinn, 11 September 2003.
177. 'IASC and IOSCO Reach Agreement', *CAmagazine*, 128/8 (October 1995), 13.

178. Interview with James Saloman, 8 October 2004.
179. Memorandum from Sharpe to the authors, dated 22 May 2003.
180. Interview with Linda Quinn, 11 September 2003.
181. Except where indicated, the developments related in this paragraph are based on correspondence contained in the file 'IOSCO Liaison Core Standards (2)', IASC archive.
182. Interview with John Barrass, 10 February 2006.
183. IASC executive committee meeting of 27 March 1995, minute 2.
184. Letter from Eiichi Shiratori to James Saloman, dated 9 May 1995, copy in the authors' files.
185. Interview with Michael Sharpe, 29 May 2003.
186. Interview with Bryan Carsberg, 14 January 2005; IASC executive committee meeting of 9/10 July 1995, minute 2.
187. 'IASC and IOSCO Reach Agreement', IASC press release, 11 July 1995. Also see 'Important Milestone for IASC and IOSCO', *IASC Insight*, August 1995, 1, and 'Target 1999: Global Approval', *IASC Insight*, September 1995, 1, 4–5.
188. 'Important Milestone for IASC and IOSCO', *IASC Insight*, August 1995, 1
189. IASC Advisory Council meeting of 8 July 1995, minute 3.
190. 'IASC: Edging Towards the Ultimate Vision', supplement on 'The Standard-Setters', *World Accounting Report*, August/September 1995, x.
191. IASC Advisory Council meeting of 8 July 1995, minute 3.
192. 'IASC Team in IOSCO Endgame', *World Accounting Report*, August/September 1995, 1.
193. Michael Sutton, 'International Accounting Issues: Challenges and Opportunities', a speech to the American Accounting Association annual meeting in August 1996; an adaptation of the speech was published by the FASB in its *Status Report*, no. 280 (20 September 1996), 4. It was unusual for *Status Report* to contain articles or speeches by persons other than FASB members and staff. A member of the Price Waterhouse Europe technical team called the agreement 'a significant milestone in [the IASC's] 23-year history'. Robert Dove, 'IASC Ambitions', *Accountancy* (international edition), 117/1233 (May 1996), 74.
194. P. Leder, 'IOSCO Assessment: A View from Within', *Maandblad voor Accountancy en Bedrijfseconomie*, 73/9 (September 1999), 467.
195. Interview with Gijs Bak, 8 December 2004.
196. '"It's Time to Deliver" says Sharpe', *World Accounting Report*, August/September 1995, 3.
197. David Cairns, 'The Future of the IASC and the Implications for UK Companies', in *Financial Reporting Today—Current and Emerging Issues, The 1998 Edition* (London: The Institute of Chartered Accountants in England and Wales, 1997), 133.
198. 'Supplementary Secretary-General's Report', AP 3/1996, supplement to paper 1.
199. 'IASC Accelerates Work Programme', IASC press release, 3 April 1996.
200. IASC Advisory Council meeting of 10 June 1996, minute 3.
201. 'IASC Accelerates Work Programme', IASC press release, 3 April 1996. Also see 'Fast-track IASC Seeks Extra Funding', *Accountancy* (international edition), 117/1232 (April 1996), 7; Liesel Knorr, 'Fast Track? Good News', *Accountancy* (international edition), 117/1234 (June 1996), 66–7; and Liesel Knorr, 'IASC Accelerates its Work Programme', *IASC Insight*, July 1996, 9–12.
202. Interview with John Barrass, 10 February 2006.
203. *New York Stock Exchange Fact Book*, 1993–7.

204. *Foreign Companies Registered and Reporting with the U.S. Securities and Exchange Commission December 31, 1997* (New York: Office of International Corporate Finance, Securities and Exchange Commission, [1998]); and data supplied by the SEC's Office of International Corporate Finance.
205. 'Selling the Nasdaq', *The Wall Street Journal*, 16 March 1998, A22. The European Commission reported in 1998 that 'The number of European companies with NYSE and NASDAQ listings in the US has increased nearly fivefold since 1990 to almost 250 in 1998, with a cumulative market capitalization of about $300bn.' *Financial Services: Building a Framework for Action*, Communication of the Commission [28 October 1998], 10.
206. *Accounting Harmonisation: A New Strategy vis-a-vis International Harmonisation*, Communication from the Commission, COM 95 (508)/EN (November 1995), paragraph 1.3.
207. Allister Wilson, 'Harmonisation: Is It Now or Never for Europe?' *Accountancy*, 114/1215 (November 1994), 98.
208. *Global Stock Markets Factbook 2003* (New York: Standard & Poor's, 2003), 25.
209. 'By mid-1995, the banks declared that they had already spent their "banking billions"' to aid the privatization process in eastern Germany. Susanne Lütz, 'From Managed to Market Capitalism? German Finance in Transition', *German Politics*, 9/2 (2000), 163. Lütz also reports that the big German banks were 'deliberately disengaging themselves from industry in an effort to improve their international reputation as security traders and business consultants', 161 (footnote omitted).
210. Breeden, 'Foreign Companies and U.S. Securities Markets in a Time of Economic Transformation', S80.
211. See Lütz, 'From Managed to Market Capitalism? German Finance in Transition', 156, 160–1. Also, interview with Herbert Biener, 13 July 2004.
212. Interview with Bernd-Joachim Menn, 18 August 2004.
213. Gerhard Liener, Daimler-Benz's finance director at the time, 'was regarded as a traitor by some elements of Germany's financial establishment ... which had hoped that by presenting a united front in negotiations with the Securities and Exchange Commission (SEC) they could have won exemption from the more rigorous requirements of US GAAP'. 'Daimler-Benz' US GAAP Pioneer Found Dead', *Corporate Accounting International*, 65 (January 1996), 3. Lütz reports that Daimler 'came under heavy fire in Germany', Lütz, 'From Managed to Market Capitalism? German Finance in Transition', 161.
214. By 1995, the German multinationals Bayer and Hoechst were already preparing their consolidated statements following IASC standards, and in March 1996 Veba said it was following Daimler-Benz's lead and filing its consolidated statements in US GAAP. Niall Brady, 'Trying to Agree on Global Standards', *Corporate Accounting International*, 65 (January 1996), 14. In December 1995, Deutsche Bank announced that it would henceforth produce group accounts in accordance with IASC standards. Laura Covill, 'Deutsche Bank Switch to IASC Standards Fuels Hopes for Greater Banking Transparency', *Corporate Accounting International*, 66 (February 1996), 1. See Karel Van Hulle, 'Bridging the GAAP in Europe?', *IASC Insight*, June 1995, 7, and 'Increased International Harmonisation', *World Accounting Report*, May 1996, 2. For a discussion of the factors that precipitated this general development, see Axel Haller, 'Financial Accounting Developments in the European Union: Past Events and Future Prospects', *The European Accounting Review*, 11/1 (2002), 160–3.

215. 'Supplementary Secretary-General's Report', AP 3/1996, supplement to paper 1.
216. Trevor Harris has been quoted as saying that Arthur Levitt was more open than his predecessor, Richard Breeden, to the possible acceptance of IASC standards 'as long as there is not a compromise in quality'. Breeden, he said, did help develop more flexible SEC rules for foreign registrants but insisted that they nonetheless meet US GAAP standards. See 'SEC is Now More Amenable', *Corporate Accounting International*, 58 (May 1995), 15. SEC Chief Accountant Walter Schuetze was reported as saying in late 1993, 'Arthur Levitt has made international standard setting one of his important goals.... The probability for international standards has been enhanced by the push of foreign firms wanting to list in New York.' James R. Peterson, 'International Accounting Standards Imminent—SEC Head', *Corporate Accounting International*, 43 (December 1993), 7.
217. News release, 'Mary B. Tokar Designated Senior Associate Chief Accountant (International)', dated 26 September 1997 (supplied by Mary Tokar).
218. 'SEC Engages Arthur Wyatt as International Accounting Expert', SEC news release, 13 May 1996. See James R. Peterson, 'SEC Hires Former IASC Chairman as Adviser', *Corporate Accounting International*, 69 (May 1996), 3.
219. Memorandum from Michael Sutton to the authors, dated 25 June 2004. See 'NYSE Chief Complains that Standards Deter Foreign Companies', *Corporate Accounting International*, 70 (June 1996), 4.
220. 'SEC Statement Regarding International Accounting Standards', news release 96–61, Securities and Exchange Commission, 11 April 1996. The bulleted points are taken verbatim from the release. This release is reproduced in the SEC's *Report on Promoting Global Preeminence of American Securities Markets* (October 1997), appendix 5. Much of the discussion in this section is drawn from Zeff, 'The Coming Confrontation on International Accounting Standards'.
221. Memorandum from Bryan Carsberg to members of the Advisory Council and executive committee, dated 18 April 1996, AP 6/1996, additional paper.
222. Memorandum from Michael Sutton to the authors, dated 25 June 2004.
223. The following year, a senior member of the SEC's Office of the Chief Accountant illustrated the meaning of this new term: 'High quality accounting standards produce financial statements where events are reflected in the period in which they occur, not before or after. This means that there are no extra "rainy day" reserves, no deferment of loss recognition; and actual volatility is not "smoothed away" to create an artificial picture of steady and consistent growth.' 'Capital Market Standards for Financial Reporting: Perspectives from the Securities and Exchange Commission', remarks by Mary B. Tokar, senior associate chief accountant, Hanover, Germany, 1 October 1997 (available at: http://www.sec.gov/news/speech/speecharchive/1997/spch177.txt).
224. 'SEC Statement Regarding International Accounting Standards', news release 96–61, Securities and Exchange Commission, 11 April 1996.
225. Arthur Levitt, 'The Accountant's Critical Eye', remarks at the 24th Annual National Conference on Current SEC Developments, 10 December 1996 (available at: http://www.sec.gov/news/speech/speecharchive/1996/spch122.txt); extracts from Levitt's speech were published in 'US SEC Makes No Promises', *Accountancy* (international edition), 119/1242 (February 1997), 67. For a reaction by IASC's Deputy Chairman Stig Enevoldsen, see 'The IASC's Long March Towards Harmonisation', *Accountancy* (international edition), 119/1243 (March 1997), 17. In 1994, Levitt had said, 'My strategy is to see if we can use the tools available to us to embrace

[IASC] standards that are close enough to U.S. standards to be acceptable.' Kenneth N. Gilpin, 'The S.E.C. is Welcoming Foreign Stocks, But Will They Come?' *The New York Times*, 3 May 1994, D10. In October 1997, Michael Sutton himself pointedly remarked that 'the Commission's participation [in the IASC's core standards project] does not mean that it is obliged to accept the resulting product.' Michael H. Sutton, 'Financial Reporting and Investor Protection' (20 October 1997), *The Emanuel Saxe Distinguished Lectures in Accounting 1997* ([New York] Baruch College), 34. An elaboration of the SEC's policy appears in 'International Harmonization of Accounting Standards: Perspectives from the Securities and Exchange Commission', remarks by Michael H. Sutton at the 1997 Annual Meeting, American Accounting Association, Dallas, Texas, 17 August 1997 (available at: http://www.sec.gov/news/speech/speecharchive/1997/spch174.txt).

226. 'IASC "Confident" of SEC's Support', *Accountancy* (international edition), 118/1238 (October 1996), 14. As indicated above, Michael Sharpe had expressed confidence in an IOSCO endorsement once the standards were revised, implying a vote of support from the SEC. Carsberg reacted by saying, 'I am still confident that the spirit of agreement with the SEC has not changed'. 'IASs—The Quality Debate Continues....' *Accountancy* (international edition), 119/1244 (April 1997), 7.

227. Securities and Exchange Commission, *Report on Promoting Global Preeminence of American Securities Markets*, 31.

228. 'Note of Meetings at SEC, 16 June 1997', IASC executive committee meeting of July 1997, agenda paper II. According to Carsberg, the meeting between Carsberg and Sutton was 'a rather strained affair' because of the negative reaction within the SEC to press reports of Carsberg's speech. 'Report on Activities from mid-June 1997 to end November 1997', IASC Advisory Council meeting of January 1998, agenda paper 2A.

229. Sutton, 'International Accounting Issues: Challenges and Opportunities', 5.

230. Sutton, 'International Accounting Issues: Challenges and Opportunities', 5.

231. See Bryan Carsberg, 'Interpreting the Standards', *IASC Insight*, July 1996, 8. For an alternative view of how the IASC should deal with interpretations of its standards, see David Cairns, 'The Need for an Interpreter', *Financial Times*, 19 September 1996.

232. Communication from Bryan Carsberg to the authors, dated 31 August 2004.

233. 'Issuing IASC "Interpretations"', AP 6/1996, paper 1. The agenda paper is not signed, but it is evidently from the secretary-general. Even though WP1 raised this matter three months before the SEC issued its news release, the SEC would have had it under consideration for some time. For the same reasons, IASC Chairman Michael Sharpe was also an advocate of an interpretations committee. See 'Increased International Harmonisation', *World Accounting Report*, May 1996, 2.

234. Gijs Bak, a member of WP1, recalled (interview, 8 December 2004) that the SIC originated with the SEC.

235. Interview with Paul Cherry, 8 October 2004.

236. Remarks of Edward J. Waitzer, 'Crisis Performance & Collaboration in Financial Regulation', dated 16 May 1996, *Ontario Securities Commission Bulletin*, 19 (24 May 1996), 2789.

237. James R. Peterson, 'SEC Suffers Another Blow as Quinn Leaves', *Corporate Accounting International*, 67 (March 1996), 5. Quinn was succeeded as WP1 chairman by Meredith Cross, her deputy at the Commission. Cross was followed in 1997

by Paul Leder, of the SEC's Office of International Affairs, and by Mary Tokar in 1999.
238. The SEC's Office of International Affairs, headed by Michael D. Mann and later by Marisa Lago, continued to be involved throughout the 1990s.
239. Interview with Richard Thorpe, 10 February 2006.
240. IASC Advisory Council meeting of 10 June 1996, minute 3.
241. 'NYSE Rings Out Record 1997', *The Exchange*, January 1998, 8.
242. Comparisons between Exchanges can be misleading. Former SEC Chairman Breeden has said, 'the number of foreign companies listed in London is often a bit overstated, because many of the foreign companies listed in London are from various former British colonies and dependencies. No matter what our rules might be, it's not very likely that we will have eighty-five South African companies trading in the United States'. Breeden, 'Foreign Companies and U.S. Securities Markets in a Time of Economic Transformation', S83. On the other side, some sixty of the foreign companies listed on the New York Stock Exchange were from one country, Canada.
243. The term 'billion' refers to nine zeroes. The figures were supplied by the exchanges. The London Stock Exchange figures were translated at an exchange rate of US$1.60/£1. The figures for foreign companies do not reflect an adjustment for cross-holdings in Japanese companies. For evidence that the New York Stock Exchange was eyeing the London Stock Exchange as an international competitor, see Cochrane, 'Are U.S. Regulatory Requirements for Foreign Firms Appropriate', S58–S9.
244. As early as 1991, the Exchange said that the SEC's required reconciliation was '[t]he major hurdle, even for the strongest and most stable foreign companies', to becoming listed in the United States. See the letter from the chairman and the president, *Entering the Third Century*, 1991 Annual Report of the New York Stock Exchange, 9. Also see James L. Cochrane, James E. Shapiro, and Jean E. Tobin, 'Foreign Equities and U.S. Investors: Breaking Down the Barriers Separating Supply and Demand', *Stanford Journal of Law, Business & Finance*, 2/2 (Spring 1996), 241–63; and James L. Cochrane, 'Helping to Keep U.S. Capital Markets Competitive: Listing World-Class Non-U.S. Firms on U.S. Exchanges', in Choi and Levich (editors), *International Capital Markets in a World of Accounting Differences*, 233–8. Cochrane was then senior vice-president and chief economist of the New York Stock Exchange. Also see 'Notes of a Meeting at the New York Stock Exchange, 12th March 1992', by David Cairns, IASC archive, New York Stock Exchange file.
245. This assertion is based on interviews held in 1998 with parties on both sides of the transaction.
246. National Securities Markets Improvement Act 1996 (Public Law 104-290), sec. 509. The full text of the provision appears in *IASC Insight*, December 1996, 3, and in an appendix to Zeff, 'The Coming Confrontation on International Accounting Standards'.
247. For news coverage of the report, see David Cairns, 'The SEC's Report on IASs', *World Accounting Report*, November 1997, 2–3.
248. Securities and Exchange Commission, *Report on Promoting Global Preeminence of American Securities Markets*, pursuant to Section 509(5) of the National Securities Markets Improvement Act 1996 (October 1997), 23.
249. Securities and Exchange Commission, *Report on Promoting Global Preeminence of American Securities Markets*, 23.

250. Securities and Exchange Commission, *Report on Promoting Global Preeminence of American Securities Markets*, 17.
251. Securities and Exchange Commission, *Report on Promoting Global Preeminence of American Securities Markets*, 10 and 24, respectively.
252. See Stephen A. Zeff, 'A Perspective on the U.S. Public/Private-Sector Approach to the Regulation of Financial Reporting', *Accounting Horizons*, 9/1 (March 1995), 57–60. In 1965, the Commission dictated an accounting norm when the APB declined to act on a contested issue. See 'Balance Sheet Classification of Deferred Income Taxes Arising from Installment Sales', *Accounting Series Release No. 102* (SEC: 7 December 1965).
253. 'What Is Going to Happen in the US?', remarks by Mary B. Tokar at the 2nd International Accounting Standards Conference, Brussels, 10 March 1998, <http://www.sec.gov/news/speech/speecharchive/1998/spch207.htm>.
254. See Stephen A. Zeff, 'The Evolution of U.S. GAAP: The Political Forces Behind Professional Standards', *The CPA Journal*, 75/1 (January 2005), 18–27, and Stephen A. Zeff, *Forging Accounting Principles in Five Countries: A History and an Analysis of Trends* (Champaign, IL: Stipes Publishing, 1972), 173–221.
255. James R. Peterson, 'Sharpe Enthusiasm', *Corporate Accounting International*, 57 (April 1995), 8.
256. James R. Peterson, 'FASB Chief Attacks "Hopelessly Optimistic" IASC', *Corporate Accounting International*, 72 (August 1996), 3. Also see ' "Friendly" FASB Savaging for IASC', *Accountancy* (international edition), 118/1236 (August 1996), 9; 'IASC Culture Clash is Cause for Concern', *Accountancy* (international edition), 118/1237 (September 1996), 7; Jim Kelly, 'A Foot on the Brake', *Financial Times*, 13 March 1997; and 'High Noon at Connecticut', *Accountancy* (international edition), 118/1238 (October 1996), 18.
257. See 'Departing Chief Beresford Stiffens Assault on IASC', *The Accountant*, 5920 (April 1997), 5.
258. Interview with Barry Robbins, 1 April 2005. A member of the Australian delegation in 1998 said, 'I think towards the end they were cutting corners'. Interview with Kenneth Spencer, 26 May 2003.
259. 'IASC Culture Clash is Cause for Concern', *Accountancy* (international edition), 118/1237 (September 1996), 7.
260. James J. Leisenring, 'FASB Perspectives on the Development of International Accounting Standards' (9 March 1998), in *The Emanuel Saxe Distinguished Lectures in Accounting 1998* ([New York] Baruch College), 8.
261. IASC executive committee meeting of July 1997, agenda paper II. On this meeting, *see also* Section 10.14.
262. Carrie Bloomer, *The IASC-U.S. Comparison Project: A Report on the Similarities and Differences Between IASC Standards and U.S. GAAP* (Norwalk, CT: Financial Accounting Standards Board, 1996), 23. The FASB issued a revised version of this volume in 1999, which played down the number and significance of the 'variations' between IASC standards and US GAAP.
263. Bloomer, *The IASC-U.S. Comparison Project: A Report on the Similarities and Differences Between IASC Standards and U.S. GAAP*, iii.
264. *Apples to Apples: Accounting for Value in World Markets* ([New York:] Morgan Stanley Dean Witter, 6 February 1998), 2.
265. 'US GAAP v IASs', *Accountancy* (international edition), 119/1241 (January 1997), 9.

266. IASC Advisory Council meeting of 10 January 1997, minute 2.
267. 'Accounting Standards: America v the World', *The Economist*, 346/8051 (17 January 1998), 59.
268. 'IASs Are Not up to Scratch, Says FASB Member', *Accountancy* (international edition), 123/1265 (January 1999), 9.
269. 'Big Talk' [a dialogue among six members of the IASC board], *Accountancy* (international edition), 121/1254 (February 1998), 26.
270. Interview with Ralph Walters, 18 October 2003.
271. 'IASC's Core Standards Finalised', *Accountancy*, 123/1266 (February 1999), 10. For a discussion of IOSCO's and the SEC's expected roles once the core standards were completed, see Paul Pacter, 'IOSCO and the SEC Bite into the Core', *IASC Insight*, March 1999, 6–7; also see David Cairns, 'IOSCO: The Decisions to be Made', *World Accounting Report*, 2/7 (September 1999), 12–14.
272. See 'IASC Admits Defeat on Global Code Deadline', *The Accountant*, 5927 (November 1997), 1. Not all board members were sanguine about how long it would take to complete the financial instruments project. A member of the UK delegation, writing in January 1998, predicted that the financial instruments project 'cannot possibly be completed until at least the year 2000'. Christopher Nobes, 'Prospects for World Standards by 2000?' *Accounting & Business*, 1/1 (January 1998), 10.
273. Letter from Carsberg to Enevoldsen, dated 21 November 1997, IASC archive, Advisory Council file.
274. Letter from Carsberg to Enevoldsen, dated 21 November 1997, IASC archive, Advisory Council file.
275. For an overview of listed German companies' use of IASC standards and US GAAP in 1997–9 see Jürgen Spanheimer and Christian Koch, 'Internationale Bilanzierungspraxis in Deutschland—Ergebnisse einer empirischen Untersuchung der Unternehmen des DAX und MDAX sowie des Neuen Marktes', *Die Wirtschaftsprüfung*, 53/7 (1 April 2000), 301–10.
276. 'IASC Approves IAS 39—The Last Major Core Standard', *IASC Insight*, December 1998, 1–2.
277. Warren McGregor, 'An Insider's View of the Current State and Future Direction of International Accounting Standard Setting', *Accounting Horizons*, 13/2 (June 1999), 160.
278. Interviews with John Carchrae, 8 October 2004, with Gijs Bak, 8 December 2004, and with Mary Tokar, 18 May 2004.
279. In 2000, the members of the Technical Committee represented the sixteen most developed capital markets.
280. *IASC Standards—Assessment Report*, Report of the Technical Committee of the International Organization of Securities Commissions, May 2000 (available at: http://www.iosco.org/library/pubdocs/pdf/IOSCOPD109.pdf).
281. *IASC Standards—Assessment Report*, ftn. 7 under C1.
282. *IASC Standards—Assessment Report*, fourth paragraph under C1.
283. Interview with Philippe Danjou, 14 February 2005, with Gijs Bak, 8 December 2004, and with Richard Thorpe, 10 February 2006.
284. 'IASC Standards', IOSCO press release, 17 May 2000 (available at: http://www.iosco.org/news/pdf/IOSCONEWS26.pdf). See 'IOSCO Endorsement', *World Accounting Report*, 3/5 (June 2000), 3; 'IOSCO Report on IAS', *World Accounting Report*, 3/6 (July 2000), 9–10; and Tom Ravlic and Paul Rogerson, 'IOSCO Endorses 30 Global Core Standards', *The Accountant*, 5958 (May 2000), 1. For an analysis of IOSCO's

endorsement and the European Commission's June 2000 decision to require all EU listed companies to adopt IASC standards in their consolidated statements, see Ted Awty, 'The Glass is Half Full', *Accountancy*, 126/1283 (July 2000), 98.
285. Mary Tokar, 'A Regulator's Perspective on the Needs of the Capital Markets', speech at the International Federation of Accountants conference, in Edinburgh, 22 May 2000 (available at: http://www.sec.gov/news/speech/spch385.htm).
286. *IASC Standards—Assessment Report*, second paragraph under D5.
287. 'IASC Standards', IOSCO press release, 17 May 2000 (available at: http://www.iosco.org/news/pdf/IOSCONEWS26.pdf).
288. Interviews with John Carchrae, 8 October 2004, and with Philippe Danjou, 14 February 2005.
289. Tokar, 'A Regulator's Perspective on the Needs of the Capital Markets'.
290. Interview with Richard Thorpe, 10 February 2006.
291. Interview with John Barrass, 10 February 2006.
292. 'Relationships with IOSCO', by Bryan Carsberg, IASC executive committee meeting of November 1998, agenda paper IV.
293. Lynn E. Turner, 'Initiatives for Improving the Quality of Financial Reporting', remarks to the New York Society of Security Analysts, New York, N.Y., 10 February 1999 (available at: http://www.sec.gov/news/speech/speecharchive/1999/spch252.htm).
294. Lynn E. Turner, 'A Vision for the 21st Century', speech to the 26th Annual National Conference on Current SEC Developments, 9 December 1998 (available at: http://www.sec.gov/news/speech/speecharchive/1998/spch242.htm).
295. Interviews with Lynn Turner, 19 November 2004 and 17 March 2005.
296. For press reports on the criticisms, see Melody Petersen, 'U.N. Report Faults Big Accountants in Asia Crisis', *The New York Times*, 24 October 1998, C1, C4; Jim Kelly, 'Big Five Criticised Over Global Audit Standards', *Financial Times*, 19 October 1998, 1; 'World Bank Asks Big 5 to Ensure the Quality of Globe's Accounting', *The Wall Street Journal*, 20 October 1988, B20. For the UNCTAD study, see M. Zubaidur Rahman, 'The Role of Accounting in the East Asian Financial Crisis: Lessons Learned?' in *Transnational Corporations*, 7/3 (December 1998), 1–52.
297. Marisa Lago, 'Building an Infrastructure for Financial Security', speech before the Federal Reserve Bank of Boston, 22 June 2000 (available at: http://www.sec.gov/news/speech/spch389.htm). Lago was the SEC's director of the Office of International Affairs.
298. Communication from Mary Tokar to the authors, dated 8 March 2004.
299. Interview with Lynn Turner, 19 November 2004.
300. 'International Accounting Standards', Release Nos. 33-7801, 34-42430, International Series No. 1215, File No. S7-04-00, 16 February 2000) (available at: http://www.sec.gov/rules/concept/34-42430.htm). For a news report, see 'SEC Concept Release', World Accounting *Report*, March 2000, 10. For an analysis of the release, see Stephen Zeff, 'What Is the SEC Looking For?' *World Accounting Report*, April 2000, 10–11.
301. 'International Accounting Standards', Section I.
302. David Cairns, *The FT International Accounting Standards Survey 1999* (Financial Times, 1999). For a summary, see David Cairns, 'Compliance with International Standards', *World Accounting Report*, November 1999, 8–10.
303. Isaac C. Hunt, Jr., 'Financial Reporting and the Global Capital Markets', speech at the 2nd European FASB–SEC Financial Reporting Conference, Frankfurt, Germany, 23 March 2000 (available at: http://www.sec.gov/news/speech/spch363.htm).

For a news report on the speech, see James R. Peterson, 'Global Stumbling Block', *The Accountant*, 5957 (April 2000), 13.
304. 'Accounting: Holier than Thou', *The Economist*, 366/8310 (8 February 2003), 69.
305. Interview with Lynn Turner, 19 November 2004. The occurrence of this meeting was recorded in Anthony T. Cope's notes of a conference call with Lynn Turner and Mary Tokar, dated 19 July 1999 (supplied by Cope). Turner refers to the occurrence in 'Major Issues Conference: Securities Regulation in the Global Internet Economy', sponsored by the Securities and Exchange Commission Historical Society in cooperation with the United States Securities and Exchange Commission with the support of Northwestern University Law School, held in Washington on 15 November 2001, p. 107 (available at: http://www.sechistorical.org/collection/papers/2000/2001_1115_SECHS_Conf.PDF).
306. Interview with Hans Havermann, 29 March 2005.
307. 'A Tentative First Step', *IASC Insight*, March 2000, 1.
308. Hunt, 'Financial Reporting and the Global Capital Markets'. In an interview the previous year, Chief Accountant Lynn Turner had made the same point, and added, 'Some IASs are better than US standards'. 'In the Hot Seat at the SEC', *Accountancy* (international edition), 122/1261 (September 1998), 19.
309. 'A Tentative First Step', *IASC Insight*, March 2000, 2.
310. John M. Morrissey, 'International Reporting: The Way Forward', remarks at the 28th National Conference on Current SEC Developments (5 December 2000) (available at: http://www.sec.gov/news/speech/spch443.htm). The Business Roundtable is an association of chief executive officers of approximately 150 leading US companies.
311. Letter from Edmund Jenkins and Manuel Johnson to Jonathan G. Katz, Securities and Exchange Commission, dated 5 June 2000 (available at: http://www.sec.gov/rules/concept/s70400/jenkins1.htm).
312. Letter from Barry Melancon and Robert Elliott to Jonathan G. Katz, secretary, Securities and Exchange Commission, dated 1 June 2000 (available at: http://www.sec.gov/rules/concept/s70400/melanco1.htm).
313. See, e.g., Donald T. Nicolaisen, remarks before the 2004 AICPA National Conference on Current SEC and PCAOB Developments, 6 December 2004 (available at: http://www.sec.gov/news/speech/spch120604dtn.htm).
314. Interviews with Christopher Nobes, 13 January 2005, and with Patricia McConnell, 21 July 2005.
315. Interviews with James Saloman, 8 October 2004, and Tatsumi Yamada, 5 July 2004.

NOTES TO CHAPTER 11

1. AP 3/1987 paper 9.
2. The numbers in the text are based on the following classification. Revisions of standards (nine projects): intangible assets (including revision of IAS 9 and 22), revisions of IAS 1, IAS 7, IAS 10, IAS 14, IAS 17, IAS 19, and the unfinished projects on business combinations (IAS 22) and bank disclosures (IAS 30). Sixteen new projects were: IAS 31, IAS 32/39, IAS 33, IAS 34, IAS 35, IAS 36, IAS 37, IAS 38, IAS 40, IAS 41, and the unfinished projects on developing countries (1989–93), insurance, emerging markets (1998), discounting, extractive industries, and reporting financial performance.
3. Communication from David Cairns to the authors, dated 20 June 2006.
4. AP 3/1993 paper 23.

5. In 1993, the Public Sector Committee assumed that the IASC did not want to be reappointed as it had sent a representative to only one meeting during the last three years. Letter from Peter Agars (IFAC) to Eiichi Shiratori, dated 4 May 1993, IASC archive, file 'IASC/IFAC Coordinating Committee'.
6. 'IASC Strategic Plan', memo by David Cairns, dated 5 January 1993, IASC archive, file 'ES/MS/DHC Meetings 1993'.
7. Communication from David Cairns to the authors, dated 20 June 2006.
8. Fax message from Cairns to Shiratori and Sharpe, dated 7 December 1993, IASC archive, file 'ES/MS/DHC Meetings 1993'.
9. 'IASC and IOSCO Reach Agreement', IASC press release, 11 July 1995.
10. The relationship between the proposed core standards work programme, IOSCO's demands, and the IASC's existing plans and activities is discussed in 'IASC Work Programme', staff memo dated 12 June 1995, IASC executive committee meeting of July 1995, attachment to agenda paper II.
11. IASC board meeting of 12–14 April 1989, minute 7. Initially, practice varied as to whether it was the draft or the approved statement of principles which was circulated (e.g. IASC board meetings of 7–9 March 1990, minute 2, and of 7–9 November 1990, minute 4). In June 1994 the rule was established that steering committees would publish a draft statement of principle without approval by the board. See AP 6/1994 paper 14 and IASC board meeting of 13 and 15–17 June 1994, minute 8(e).
12. Arthur Wyatt, 'International Accounting Standards: A New Perspective', *Accounting Horizons*, 3/3 (September 1989), 105–8.
13. Interview with Johan van Helleman, 1 December 2004; communication from David Cairns to the authors, dated 20 June 2006.
14. AP 3/1996 supplement to paper 1; IASC board meeting of 27–30 March 1996, minute 2. At its meeting of 1–4 November 1995 (minute 2(e)), the board had already approved the use of a simplified process for revisions of standards.
15. Liesel Knorr, 'Fast Track? Good News', *Accountancy*, 117/1234 (June 1996), 66–7.
16. See, e.g. 'IASs–The Quality Debate Continues', *Accountancy*, 119/1244 (April 1997), 7; remarks by Jim Leisenring, cited in Sarah Grey, 'Sparring with a World Heavy-Weight', *Accountancy*, 121/1256 (April 1998), 20; letter from John Mogg to Bryan Carsberg, dated 3 April 1998, IASC archive, 'EEC' file; remarks by John Mogg, cited in 'IASC Due Process Slammed', *Accountancy*, 121/1257 (May 1998), 9; 'IASC Changes Valuation Rules', *World Accounting Report*, October 1998, 2.
17. IASC executive committee meeting of March 1996, paper V.
18. AP 6/1994 paper 14; IASC board meeting of 13 and 15–17 June 1994, minute 8(e).
19. AP 3/1996 paper 16.
20. See, e.g. letter from David Cairns to Eiichi Shiratori, dated 18 October 1993 and the related fax message from Michael Sharpe to David Cairns, dated 22 October 1993, IASC archive, file 'ES/MS/DHC Meetings 1993'. See also IASC board meeting of 2–5 November 1993, minute 2, and IASC executive committee meeting of 9 June 1996, minute 2.
21. IASC executive committee meeting of 24–5 March 1994, minute 16; AP 6/1994 paper 14; IASC board meeting of 13 and 15–17 June 1994, minute 8(e).
22. Interviews with Bryan Carsberg, 14 January 2005, with Jean-Luc Dumont, 15 February 2005, with David Tweedie, 12 January 2005, and with Karel Van Hulle, 16 February 2005; communication from David Cairns to the authors, dated 20 June 2006.

23. The analysis is based on the bound volumes of comment letters published by the IASC, supplemented with information from board agenda papers. Counts of comment letters are ambiguous within a small range because of varying treatment of late responses, joint responses, and confidential letters.
24. The exceptions were the exposure drafts dealing with limited revisions of standards (particularly E66–E68) and the drafts on employment benefits (E54) and investment properties (E64), on both of which the IASC received around 120 letters.
25. Interview with Bryan Carsberg, 26 May 2005.
26. Background information on most of the standards discussed in this chapter can also be found in David Cairns, *Applying International Accounting Standards*, 2nd edition (London: Butterworths, 1999).
27. An extensive discussion of the revision of IAS 12 can be found in Anja Hjelström, *Understanding International Accounting Standard Setting: A Case Study of the Process of Revising IAS 12 (1996), Income Tax* (Stockholm: EFI/Stockholm School of Economics, 2005).
28. From 1981 to 1984, a special working party, consisting of M. Vallas (France, chairman), Jan Schoonderbeek (the Netherlands), David Hobson (United Kingdom), and Robert Sprouse (United States) had also considered IAS 12, but its recommendation to revise IAS 12 was shelved. See AP 3/1993 paper 10. See also IASC board meeting of 17–19 October 1984, minute 7; IASC board meeting of 24–7 March 1987, minute 5.
29. AP 3/1987 paper 7, a report by French delegate Jean-Luc Dumont on the responses received from the member bodies on a questionnaire on IAS 12.
30. AP 3/1987 paper 7.
31. Initially, the other members of the steering committee were: E. R. Gelbcke (Brazil), N. Iordanides (Greece), and C. E. Bohlin (Sweden). Hong Kong had originally been chosen to provide a member, but was replaced by Greece. Subsequently, Greece was represented by G. P. Samothrakidis followed by C. Varvatsoulis. In 1993, Barry Robbins (United States) and F. Ulrich (International Chamber of Commerce) joined the committee. IOSCO sent an observer from 1995 onwards. Steven Leonard, Liesel Knorr, and Peter Clark served successively as project managers.
32. See AP 6/1988 paper 11 and AP 11/1988 paper 4, for the steering committee's reasoning.
33. AP 6/1988 paper 11.
34. Robert Sprouse, the vice-chairman of the FASB, had already informed the 1981–4 IASC working party on deferred taxation that the FASB had concluded that APB Opinion No. 11 was not consistent with the definition of a liability. 'Deferred Income Taxes', undated memo by R. T. Sprouse, IASC archive, documentation file IAS 12/E33.
35. See, e.g. Paul Rosenfield, 'The Fatal Flaws of FASB Statement 96', *Accounting Horizons*, 4/3 (September 1990), 98–100.
36. AP 6/1990 paper 6.
37. Gilbert Gélard, 'Révision de l'IAS 12 "Comptabilisation de l'Impôt sur les Bénéfices"', *Revue Française de Comptabilité*, November 1993, 11.
38. Jan Klaassen and Cees Dubbeld, cited in 'Accountants willen greep op derivaten', *Het Financieele Dagblad*, 26 October 1994, 15; Robert Dove, 'IASC's E49 Leaves UK in the Cold', *Accountancy*, 115/1218 (February 1995), 79–80; Bryan Carsberg, cited in 'The Last Word on IASs', *Accountancy* (international edition), 119/1245 (May 1997), 21–2.

39. Interview with Barry Robbins, 1 April 2005.
40. AP 11/1993 paper 5.
41. IASC board meeting of 2–5 November 1993, minute 4(a)–(b).
42. Letter from Cairns to Shiratori, dated 22 August 1993, IASC archive, file 'ES/MS/DHC Meetings 1993'. See also IASC board meeting of 2–5 November 1993. The background paper, 'Income Taxes', was published in October 1994.
43. AP 3/1993 paper 10.
44. 'United Kingdom v the Rest of the World', *Accountancy*, 118/1235 (July 1996), 7; 'IASC Turns Up the Heat on the ASB', *Accountancy*, 118/1239 (November 1996), 7.
45. Interviews with Barry Robbins, 1 April 2005, and with David Tweedie, 12 January 2005. *See also* Section 5.8.6.
46. 'Spectre of Deferred Tax Split Looms', *World Accounting Report*, December 1995/January 1996, v–vi.
47. Interview with Barry Robbins, 1 April 2005. See also Hjelström, *Understanding International Accounting Standard Setting*, 237–56.
48. Agenda paper 1 for the steering committee meeting of July 1995, IASC archive, file 'IAS 12' (electronic).
49. Compare AP 11/1995 paper 4(a), AP 3/1996 paper 10, and AP 6/1996 paper 6.
50. AP 9/1996 paper 5; interview with Ian Somerville, 15 March 2004.
51. Interview with Ian Somerville, 15 March 2004.
52. Interviews with Sigvard Heurlin and Rolf Rundfelt, 31 March 2003, with Monica Singer, 15 March 2004, with Barry Robbins, 1 April 2005, and with Patricia McConnell, 21 July 2005.
53. Cited in Liz Fisher, 'Small Country, Big Voice', *World Accounting Report*, October 1998, 7.
54. Peter Clark, 'Farewell, Deferral Method', *Accountancy* (international edition), 118/1239 (November 1996), 59–60.
55. Gunter Dufey and Ian H. Giddy, 'Innovation in the International Financial Markets', *Journal of International Business Studies*, 12/2 (supplement, Autumn, 1981), 33–51; Merton H. Miller, 'Financial Innovation: The Last Twenty Years and the Next', *Journal of Financial and Quantitative Analysis*, 21/4 (December 1986), 459–71.
56. See remarks by Georges Barthès cited in 'Call for Greater Bank Disclosure', *World Accounting Report*, December 1987, 3.
57. AP 3/1988 paper 13; IASC board meeting of 29 February and 2–4 March 1988, minute 6(x).
58. AP 6/1988 paper 20.
59. 'Minutes of the Sixth Meeting of the IASC/IFAC Coordination Committee, London, Thursday, 30 June 1988', IASC archive, Bishop Working Party file.
60. *New Financial Instruments, Disclosure and Accounting* (Paris: OECD, 1988), 232. The significance of the OECD conference for the IASC's project is also indicated in John Carchrae, 'Financial Instruments', *IASC Insight*, July 1991, 10.
61. Carchrae, 'Financial Instruments', 10; speech by Arthur Wyatt, 'ICAEW Seminar, January 29, 1992, London, England', IASC archive, speech file.
62. Memo by David Cairns, 'The role of OPC and the Board', OPC meeting of June 1991, agenda paper VI.
63. The other members were David Boymal (Australia), G. K. Rutledge (Canada), D. Marteau and/or C. Vulliez, subsequently Yves Bernheim (France), R. Costaguta (Italy), Atsushi Kato (Japan), Philip Maat (the Netherlands), and Peter Stilling

(United Kingdom). Wyatt continued as chairman of the steering committee until its meeting of September 1990, see AP 11/1990 paper 11.
64. Interview with John Carchrae, 8 October 2004.
65. *CICA Handbook* Section 3860 'Financial Instruments—Disclosure and Presentation' (published 1995) was said by John Carchrae to be virtually identical to IAS 32. John Carchrae, 'Statement of Principles in 1996', *IASC Insight*, December 1995, 8. The CICA did not include a matching section in its *Handbook* when IAS 39 was published in 1999.
66. Interview with John Carchrae, 8 October 2004. On some of the occasional problems this caused, see letter from David Cairns to Eiichi Shiratori and Michael Sharpe, dated 7 May 1993, IASC archive, file 'IASC/IFAC Coordinating Committee'.
67. IASC board meeting of 12–14 April 1989, minute 7.
68. IASC board meeting of 24–5 October 1989, minute 6.
69. David Cairns, 'A Long Haul to Harmony', *Certified Accountant*, July 1991, 36; Colin Parker, 'Interview—David Cairns', *Australian Accountant*, 64/10 (November 1994), 26.
70. Arthur Wyatt, 'Financial Instruments', *IASC Insight*, March 1992, 4. See also Arthur Wyatt, 'Report of the Chairman of IASC to the Assembly of the International Accounting Standards Committee Member Bodies', 11 October 1992, IASC archive, file 'IASC Constitution 1992'.
71. Interview with Arthur Wyatt, 9 August 2004.
72. AP 11/1990 paper 13.
73. Phil Hancock, *Financial Reporting for Financial Institutions and Accounting for Financial Instruments*, discussion paper no. 14 (Caulfield, Vic: Australian Accounting Research Foundation, 1990).
74. IASC board meeting of 7–9 November 1990, minute 3; IASC board meeting of 12–14 June 1991, minute 5. Dutch delegate Herman Marseille reported that, in November 1990, the full fair value model obtained 'relatively much support'. Herman Marseille, 'IFAC en IASC in Singapore', *De Accountant*, 97/5 (January 1991), 308–9.
75. Interviews with Johan van Helleman, 1 December 2004, and with Heinz Kleekämper, 14 July 2004.
76. Analysis of comment letters, AP 11/1990 paper 13.
77. E40 had been approved in June 1991, but publication was delayed in order to achieve simultaneous publication with the CICA's exposure draft. For the Japanese reaction, see fax message of JICPA to Cairns, dated 18 March 1993, filed with AP 3/1993.
78. FAS 115, 'Background Information and Basis for Conclusions', paragraphs 29–38.
79. FAS 115, 'Background Information and Basis for Conclusions', paragraphs 86–9.
80. Letter from Leisenring to Cairns, dated 5 June 1992, IASC archive, E40 comment letters.
81. Letter from Schuetze to Cairns, dated 5 January 1993, IASC archive, E40 comment letters.
82. The IASC received 192 comment letters, of which only seventy-four were sent directly to the IASC. The others were collected by the CICA and were from Canadian respondents. See 'E40, Financial Instruments—Progress Report', *IASC Insight*, May 1993, 1. See also John Carchrae, 'Financial Instruments—New IASC and Canadian Exposure Draft', *IASC Insight*, March 1994, 13.
83. AP 3/1993 paper 12.

84. IASC board meeting of 30 June–2 July 1993, minute 12(b) and 12(e).
85. Letter from Sharpe to Shiratori, dated 6 July 1993, IASC archive, file 'ES/MS/DHC meetings 1993'. See also IASC board meeting of 30 June–2 July 1993, minute 12(a).
86. Letter from Linda Quinn and Michael Meagher to David Cairns, dated 23 October 1993, IASC archive, file 'IOSCO Core Standards'. See also 'Notes of a Telephone Conversation with Richard Reinhard, Securities & Exchange Commission, and Michael Meagher, Chairman IOSCO Accounting Sub-Committee, 17 September 1993', memo by David Cairns, IASC archive, file 'IOSCO Core Standards'.
87. Nevertheless, in March 1993, the IASC was informed of the 'concerns of the members of the JICPA' on E40 during a visit by Shiratori, Sharpe, Cairns, and Murray. 'Notes of Meeting with International Advisory Committee of JICPA, Thursday 25 March 1993 in Tokyo, Japan', IASC archive, file 'JICPA-Japan'.
88. Memo from Richard Reinhard to David Cairns, dated 26 October 1993, IASC archive, file 'IOSCO Core standards'.
89. The differences are listed in John Carchrae, 'Financial Instruments—New IASC and Canadian Exposure Draft', *IASC Insight*, March 1994, 14.
90. IASC board meeting of 2–5 November 1993, minute 7.
91. 'SEC Advises the World to Go for Mark to Market', *Thomson's International Bank Accountant*, 3/43 (15 November 1993), 1.
92. 'Meeting of IOSCO Working Party 1 held on 2nd December 1993 in Rome, Italy', memo by David Cairns, dated 3 December 1993, IASC archive, file 'ES/MS/DHC meetings 1993'.
93. At the meeting, the standard setters from Australia, Belgium (not a board member), Canada, Denmark, France, Germany, Mexico (not a board member), the Netherlands, New Zealand (not a board member), Norway, Sweden, the United Kingdom, and the United States were represented.
94. David Cairns, 'Standard Setting Bodies—E48 Concerns', *IASC Insight*, September 1994, 5–6; 'Meeting of the IASC Board with Representatives of National Standard-Setting Bodies Edinburgh—June 1994', IASC staff note, AP 11/1994 unnumbered paper.
95. ICAEW Technical Director Henry Gold, quoted in 'Growing Instruments of Power', *The Times*, 2 June 1994; interview with John Carchrae, 8 October 2004.
96. 'Meeting of the IASC Board with Representatives of National Standard-Setting Bodies Edinburgh—June 1994', IASC staff note, AP 11/1994 unnumbered paper.
97. IASC board meeting of 15–17 June 1994, minute 6(a).
98. Liesel Knorr, cited in 'Worst is Yet to Come', *Accountancy*, 115/1221 (May 1995), 16.
99. Gundi Jeffrey, 'Canadian Institute Sticks with IASC Approach', *Corporate Accounting International*, no. 58 (May 1995), 3; Mark Lawson, 'Australia Follows IASC Line on Derivatives', *Corporate Accounting International*, no. 60 (July/August 1995), 9.
100. Gerry Acher, 'A Force to Be Reckoned With', *Corporate Accounting International*, no. 65 (January 1996), 11.
101. IASC executive committee meeting of 31 October 1994, minute 11; IASC board meeting of 1–4 November 1994, minute 3.
102. Interview with John Carchrae, 8 October 2004.
103. The composition of the steering committee varied considerably over time. The following is an approximate reconstruction of its membership: Ian Hammond (Australia), Gilbert Gélard, followed by G. Gil (France), M. Sakamoto (Japan), C. C. van der Sluis (the Netherlands), Erik Mamelund (Norway), W. J. Woodwark (United Kingdom), Barry Robbins (United States), David Damant and Rolf

Rundfelt (financial analysts), A. Dangerfield (Federation of Swiss Industrial Holding Companies), David Swanney (Basel Committee), and C. Morson followed by C. A. McDonough (World Bank). IOSCO, the FASB, and the ASB sent observers. IASC board meeting of 27–30 March 1996, minute 4; AP 11/1995 paper 2; AP 3/1996 paper 4.

104. Interviews with John Carchrae, 8 October 2004, with Barry Robbins, 1 April 2005, and with Jan Klaassen, 28 April 2005.
105. AP 11/1995.
106. 'Meeting of the IASC Board with Representatives of National Standard-Setting Bodies Edinburgh—June 1994', IASC staff note, AP 11/1994 unnumbered paper, p. 16.
107. IASC board meeting of 1–4 November 1995, minute 4.
108. IASC board meeting of 11–14 June 1996, minute 6.
109. Ian Hague, 'Financial Instruments: the Measurement Issue', *IASC Insight*, July 1996, 4–5.
110. A schedule of over forty meetings in twelve countries is mentioned by Alex Milburn, 'The Discussion Stage', *IASC Insight*, June 1997, 7.
111. Unless otherwise indicated, this paragraph is based on, and citations are taken from, IASC executive committee meeting of 7, 10, and 11 July 1997, minute 2.
112. On the reception of the discussion paper, see also ' "Radical" IASC Proposals Hailed', *Accountancy* (international edition), 119/1245 (May 1997), 8; 'Accounting: IASC', *World Accounting Report*, June 1997, 4.
113. 'Notes of Meetings with SEC, 16 June 1997' memo by Bryan Carsberg, IASC executive committee meeting of July 1997, agenda paper II.
114. The identification of Sharpe as the source of the proposal is based on interviews with Bryan Carsberg, 26 May 2005, and with Liesel Knorr, 29 March 2005.
115. AP 10–11/1997 paper 9A. Interview with Paul Pacter, 10 July 2004.
116. Press release and letter attached to AP 10–11/1997 paper 9B.
117. Interview with Barry Robbins, 1 April 2005. There appears to have been no formal decision by the board to disband the steering committee. The decision was apparently implied in the executive committee's decision to set up the Joint Working Group (*see* Section 11.5.7). IASC executive committee meeting of 29 October 1997, minute 2.
118. Interview with Bryan Carsberg, 26 May 2005; circular letter from Bryan Carsberg to IASC board members and technical advisers, dated 21 October 1997, copy in NIVRA archive, file 'Vaktechniek IASC Board meetings'.
119. For a review of some of the reactions, see: 'Playing for High Stakes', *The Accountant*, no. 5925 (September 1997), 13; David Cairns, 'IASC, G4+1 and US Congress', *World Accounting Report*, October 1997, 3–4; 'Derivatives Valuation Proposals Attacked', *Financial Times*, 18 September 1997, 9; 'Bilanzen aus der Provinz', *Börsen Zeitung*, no. 189 (2 October 1997), 7; 'IASC Proposals in for a Rough Ride', *Accountancy*, 120/1251 (November 1997), 8.
120. Christopher Nobes, 'Prospects for World Standards by 2000?', *Accounting & Business*, January 1998, 11.
121. Letter from John Mogg to Bryan Carsberg, dated 22 October 1997, IASC archive, October 1997 pre-board letters.
122. Edmund Jenkins, quoted in 'IASC Staff to Propose Adoption of US Standards on Financial Instruments, including Derivatives', *Status Report*, no. 293 (22 September 1997), 1. The proposal was also interpreted as 'a shot in the arm' for

the FASB in 'IASC Offers Support for the FASB', *CFO Alert*, 4/35 (15 September 1997), 1.
123. See 'IASC Accelerated Work Programme', *IASC Insight*, March 1997, 14.
124. Memo from Jan Klaassen to other members of the Dutch IASC delegation, on conversation with Gijs Bak (Dutch representative in WP1), dated 23 October 1997, NIVRA archive, file 'Vaktechniek, IASC Board meetings'. See also letter from Carsberg to Enevoldsen, dated 21 November 1997, IASC archive, 'Advisory Council' file.
125. 'Notes of Meetings with SEC, 16 June 1997' memo by Bryan Carsberg, IASC executive committee meeting of July 1997, agenda paper II. In January 1998, Carsberg reported to the board that there had been 'no consensus in IOSCO's technical committee' in favour of removing financial instruments from the core standards. See IASC board meeting of 12–16 January 1998, minute 2(a).
126. Sarah Grey, 'O Ye of Little Faith', *Accountancy* (international edition), 120/1250 (October 1997), 6.
127. Memo from Jan Klaassen to other members of the Dutch IASC delegation, dated 23 October 1997, NIVRA archive, file 'Vaktechniek, IASC Board meetings'.
128. Sarah Grey, 'O Ye of Little Faith', 6; Robert Bruce, 'A Fudge that Could Lead to an Alliance', *The Times*, 18 September 1997. On opposition in the United States, see 'US Bankers Step Up War over Derivatives Plans', *The Accountant*, October 1997, 1; 'Opposing the FASB', *World Accounting Report*, September 1997, 10–11.
129. Pre-board comment letters, notably from the South African Institute of Chartered Accountants, dated 20 October 1997, the Australian Accounting Standards Board, 21 October 1997, and the French Compagnie Nationale des Commissaires aux Comptes and the Ordre des Experts Comptables, 24 October 1997, IASC archive, file '1997 Board Comments'. For a summary of the board discussion see also Bryan Carsberg, 'Report on Activities from Mid-June 1997 to End November 1997', IASC Advisory Council meeting of 8 January 1998, agenda paper 2A.
130. IASC board meeting of 30 October–4 November 1997, minute 6(a) and (d).
131. 'Financial Instruments—A Note on Timing', undated paper by Bryan Carsberg, IASC executive committee meeting of April 1998, unnumbered agenda paper.
132. Interview with Paul Pacter, 10 July 2004.
133. For instance, E62 included the option to recognize fair value changes of available-for-sale financial assets in income, whereas US GAAP required these to go directly to equity.
134. Letter from Edmund Jenkins to Michael Crooch, Mitchell Danaher, and Elizabeth Fender (US IASC delegation), dated 1 April 1998, copy supplied to the authors by Anthony Cope. See also IASC executive committee meeting of 19 April 1998, minute 2. Extracts from the letter can be found in 'IASC "At a Critical Point in its History" ', *Accountancy*, 121/1257 (May 1998), 7.
135. Mitchell Danaher, member of the US delegation, quoted in 'Back Chat', *Accountancy*, 121/1258 (June 1998), 21–2.
136. In addition, Canada and India/Sri Lanka abstained.
137. Interview with Ian Hammond, 29 May 2003.
138. 'Financial Instruments Standard Inches Closer', *Accountancy*, 121/1258 (June 1998), 9; see also 'Back Chat', *Accountancy*, 121/1258 (June 1998), 20–2.
139. In December 1997, the IASC had begun the electronic publication of documents by placing a number of draft SIC interpretations on its website. *IASC Insight*, December 1997, 4.

140. IASC board meeting of 6–10 July 1998, minute 10. The other members were Alex Milburn (Canada), Tatsumi Yamada (Japan), Sigvard Heurlin (Sweden), Michael Crooch and John T. Smith (United States), and Martyn Taylor (FEE). Apart from Smith and Taylor, all others were members of board delegations.
141. IASC board meeting of 9–13 November 1998, minute 9; 'Interim Standard Causes Controversy', *Accountancy*, 122/1264 (December 1998), 12.
142. AP 12/1998 paper 6, p. 13.
143. IASC board meeting of 9–13 November 1998, minute 9.
144. See the pre-board comment letters by the Ordre des Experts Comptables, dated 8 December 1998, and the French delegation, dated 11 December 1998, IASC archive, file '1998 Board Comment Letters'.
145. IASC board meeting of 9–13 November 1998, minute 9.
146. Christopher Nobes, 'IASC Nears the End of the Core Standards', *Accounting & Business*, 2/1 (January 1999), 34; Ruud Vergoossen, 'IASC Quo Vadis?', *De Accountant*, 105/6 (February 1999), 378; interview with David Tweedie, 12 January 2005.
147. Interviews with Jan Klaassen, 28 April 2005, and with Christopher Nobes, 13 January 2005.
148. The guidance is linked to the SEC's concerns in 'International News', *World Accounting Report*, April 2000, 2.
149. 'IAS 39—Staff Implementation Guidance', *IASC Insight*, June 2000, 5. A compilation of the implementation guidance as of July 2001 was published in *Accounting for Financial Instruments: Standards, Interpretations, and Implementation Guidance* (London: IASB, 2001).
150. AP 10–11/1997 paper 2 ('IASC Work Programme'); see also AP 10–11/1997 paper 9B where the meeting is explicitly presented as a G4+1 meeting.
151. What was to become the Joint Working Group was characterized as a G4+1 activity by David Cairns, 'IASC, G4+1 and US Congress', *World Accounting Report*, 1 October 1997, 3–4. The JWG was called a G4+1 initiative by Warren McGregor, 'An Insider's View of the Current State and Future Direction of International Accounting Standard Setting', *Accounting Horizons*, 13/2 (June 1999), 165.
152. IASC executive committee meeting of 29 October 1997, minute 2.
153. Communication from Peter Clark to the authors, dated 21 May 2006.
154. 'Canada: No Interim Solution', *World Accounting Report*, February 1998, 6.
155. Interviews with Jan Klaassen, 28 May 2005, and with Allister Wilson, 11 January 2005.
156. 'International News', *World Accounting Report*, September 1999, 3.
157. Memo from South African Institute of Chartered Accountants to Bryan Carsberg, dated 20 October 1997, IASC archive, file '1997 Board Comments'.
158. See, e.g. 'Tweedie Speaks Out', *Accountancy*, 133/1325 (January 2004), 51–3.
159. 'No Accounting for Taste', *The Economist*, 25 June 1988; Terry Smith, *Accounting for Growth: Stripping the Camouflage from Company Accounts* (London: Century Business, 1992), chapter 11; Michael Power, 'The Politics of Brand Accounting in the United Kingdom', *European Accounting Review*, 1/1 (May 1992), 39–68.
160. 'New Regime Sets High Compliance Standards', *Financial Times*, 2 August 1990, 10.
161. Circular letter from David Cairns to IASC member bodies, dated 2 May 1989, IASC archive, file 'IASC plans and future work'.
162. IASC board meeting of 4–6 March 1993, minute 7.
163. Other members who served during the whole or part of the steering committee's six-year life were Hank Howarth (Canada), Ambrogio Picolli and

G. Strada (Italy), and John Hagen (New Zealand). The European Commission and IOSCO provided observers from 1993 and 1995 onwards, respectively. The project managers were, successively, Paul Sutcliffe, Terry Harding, and Laurence Rivat.

164. 'History Sheet: Accounting for Long Term Intangibles', undated memo [1994], IASC archive, (electronic) file 'IAS 38'.
165. IASC board meetings of 7–9 March 1990, minute 3, of 20–2 June 1990, minute 4, and of 7–9 November 1990, minute 5.
166. 'Brand New Ideas', *World Accounting Report*, May 1993, 1.
167. Fax message from Cairns to Shiratori, dated 31 August 1994, IASC archive, file 'ES/MS/DHC meetings 1993'.
168. Letter from Cairns to Shiratori, dated 18 October 1993 and fax message from Sharpe to Cairns, dated 22 October 1993, both in IASC archive, 'ES/MS/DHC meetings 1993' file.
169. IASC executive committee meeting of 30 October 1995, minute 2.
170. Letter from Patrick Rochet (Association Française des Entreprises Privées) to Carsberg, dated 13 March 1995, IASC archive, file 'France'.
171. IASC board meeting of 28–31 March 1995, minute 5.
172. IASC board meeting of 8–10 May 1995, minute 4.
173. See David Cairns, 'Can the IASC Cope with Goodwill?', *Accountancy* (international edition), 117/1232 (April 1996), 62–4.
174. Based on AP 3/1996 paper 8 (analysis of comment letters).
175. AP 9/1996 paper 22, paragraph 9; Liesel Knorr, 'IASC Accelerates its Work Programme', *IASC Insight*, July 1996, 10.
176. AP 9/1996 paper 3A; IASC board meeting of 23–8 September 1996, opening remarks. The other members of the steering committee were Peter Day (Australia), Ahmad Ghazali followed by Goh Joon-Hai (Malaysia), Peter Holgate (United Kingdom), Walter Schuetze followed by Michael Crooch (United States), Patricia McQueen (financial analysts), Philippe Gaberell (Federation of Swiss Industrial Holding Companies), and Ed Milan (IAFEI). IOSCO and the European Commission sent observers. Laurence Rivat served as project manager.
177. Laurence Rivat, 'New IAS on Impairment of Assets Issued', *IASC Insight*, June 1998, 18–19.
178. AP 6/1996 paper 17.
179. Henri Giot, 'IASC: Décisions et projets', *Revue Française de Comptabilité*, May 1997, 7.
180. 'Impairment of Long-lived assets: A Background Issues Paper for the IASC Steering Committee on Impairment', dated August 1996, IASC archive, file 'IAS 36' (electronic).
181. *FEE European Survey of Published Accounts 1991* (London: Routledge, 1991), 54.
182. See B. A. Rutherford, 'Narrowing the Areas of Difference: A History of the Accounting Standards Committee 1969–1990', manuscript dated October 2004 (forthcoming from Routledge), chapter 10 'Group Accounting and Intangibles'.
183. Sonia Bonnet-Bernard and Gilbert Gélard, 'Goodwill et immobilisations incorporelles: Du Royaume-Uni à l'IASC', *Revue Française de Comptabilité*, November 1996, 35–7.
184. Anne McGeachin, 'Bringing Impairment under One Umbrella', *Accountancy* (international edition), 120/1247 (July 1997), 66.
185. IASC board meeting of 7–11 April 1997, minute 7.

186. Christopher Nobes, 'The Continuing Merger of UK and IASC Standard Setting', *Accounting & Business*, May 1998, 25; interview with David Tweedie, 12 January 2005.
187. AP 1/1998 paper 15B.
188. 'Note of Meetings at SEC, 16 June 1997', IASC executive committee meeting of July 1997, agenda paper II; IASC executive committee meeting of 29 October 1997, minute 2.
189. Interview with Tom Jones, 13 January 2005.
190. 'Three of the IASC's Most Controversial Standards Finalised at Last', *Accountancy*, 122/1260 (August 1998), 8–9.
191. 'Three of the IASC's Most Controversial Standards Finalised at Last', 8–9; interview with Warren McGregor, 9 June 2003. On Australian views of IAS 38, see also Geoff Harris, 'A Changing View from Down Under', *World Accounting Report*, October 1999, 7–8.
192. Liesel Knorr, 'IASC and FASB Speak with One Voice on EPS', *Accountancy*, 119/1244 (April 1997), 67, mentions the suggestion by IOSCO. Paul Cherry suggested the topic in 1989, in a meeting with David Cairns: 'Notes of Meeting with Paul Cherry, Toronto, 12th March 1989', IASC archive, 'Comparability' file.
193. The other members were F. Tokumasu (Japan), Rolf Rundfelt (Europe), and Peter Knutson (United States), all three representing financial analysts. In November 1990, a representative of the Korean member body, T. K. Moon, was added, but he apparently did not participate after 1992. Tokumasu apparently no longer participated by 1994. Interview with Liesel Knorr, 29 March 2005. G. Thompson and Liesel Knorr served as project managers.
194. IASC executive committee meeting of 27 March 1995, minute 2.
195. IASC board meeting of 4–6 March 1992, minute 7.
196. Letter from Mosso to Cairns, dated 24 October 1991, IASC archive, AP 11/1991, unnumbered paper.
197. 'FASB Joins IASC in Earnings-Per-Share Project', *Journal of Accountancy*, 177/6 (June 1994), 19–20. In a circular letter to board members, dated 6 April 1994 (IASC archive, file 'Board/Executive Committee Mailings'), David Cairns also emphasized that it was not the intention to publish common documents.
198. Interview with Paul Pacter, 10 July 2004.
199. FAS 128, *Earnings Per Share*, appendix B, paragraph 68.
200. Interview with Rolf Rundfelt, 31 March 2003.
201. Unless otherwise indicated, this paragraph is based on AP 3/1995 paper 5, a staff note on Earnings Per Share.
202. AP 3/1995 paper 5, paragraph 8.
203. Communication from Doug Brooking to the authors, dated 1 March 2006.
204. FASB exposure draft 'Earnings per Share and Disclosure of Information about Capital Structure', issued in January 1996.
205. AP 9/1996 paper 13 (analysis of comment letters).
206. Liesel Knorr, 'IAS 33, Earnings Per Share', *IASC Insight*, March 1997, 15.
207. The other members of the steering committee were Paul Phenix (Hong Kong), B. E. Abrahams (South Africa), C. Gatto (IAFEI), R. Fischer followed by Malcolm Cheetham (ICC), and E. T. Doran followed by P. Morton (FIBV). IOSCO sent an observer. Paul Pacter served as project manager.
208. IASC board meeting of 11–14 June 1996, minute 8(a); see Paul Pacter, 'Interim Reports: Who, What and When?', *Accountancy* (international edition),

118/1235 (July 1996), 70–2, for the steering committee's early thoughts on the subject.
209. Interview with Sigvard Heurlin, 31 March 2003.
210. Ingrid Tighe and Sarah Grey, 'Concerted US Opposition Bodes Ill for Eventual SEC Acceptance of IASs', *Accountancy* (international edition), 120/1248 (August 1997), 18–19.
211. Nobes, 'The Continuing Merger of UK and IASC Standard Setting', 24–5. The ASB issued a non-binding statement, *Interim Reports*, in September 1997.
212. Notes prepared by the delegation of the Federation of Swiss Industrial Holding Companies (Swiss delegation) on IASC board meeting of 12–16 January 1998. These notes, as well as those referred to subsequently, were kindly supplied to the authors by Harry Schmid. See on an earlier phase of the debate on disclosure: Henri Giot, 'Board de l'IASC à Beijing', *Revue Française de Comptabilité*, September 1997, 10.
213. Cited in 'IASC Workload Proves too Much for the Board', *Accountancy* (international edition), 121/1258 (June 1998), 8.
214. AP 11/1995 paper 17.
215. IASC board meeting of 1–4 November 1995, minute 2(d) and 9; see also AP 11/1995 paper 17.
216. The other members were Keith Rushbrook (New Zealand), Maritza Izquierdo (Peru), Aw Cheok-Huat (Singapore), and A. Baldi (Federation of Swiss Industrial Holding Companies). IOSCO and the European Commission sent observers. The project manager was Laurence Rivat, succeeded by Paul Pacter.
217. Interview with Christopher Nobes, 13 January 2005.
218. AP 6/1996 paper 14.
219. AP 9/1996 paper 19.
220. IASC board meeting of 23–8 September 1996, minute 12. A summary of the board's discussion is included in AP 4/1997 paper 4.
221. Fax message from Paul Pacter to steering committee members, dated 9 October 1996, IASC archive, IAS 35 file (electronic); AP 4/1997 paper 4; IASC board meeting of 7–11 April 1997, minute 4.
222. This decision is referred to retrospectively in AP 4/1998 paper 7. It is not clear when the decision was taken, but the most likely date is the April 1997 board meeting.
223. See Wayne Upton, 'Comparative Analysis of IAS 37 (1998), *Provisions, Contingent Liabilities and Contingent Assets*, and Related U.S. GAAP', in Carrie Bloomer (editor), *The IASC-U.S. Comparison Project: A Report on the Similarities and Differences between IASC Standards and U.S. GAAP*, 2nd edition (Norwalk, CT: FASB, 1999), 433–49.
224. The other members of the steering committee were John Andersen (Denmark), Eberhard Dreissig (Germany), Yüksel Koç Yalkin (Turkey), Freddy Méan (IAFEI), and Trevor Harris (UNCTAD). IOSCO and the European Commission sent observers.
225. IASC executive committee meeting of 30 January 1996, minute 2.
226. AP 3/1996 paper 15; AP 9/1996 paper 20.
227. C. P. M. Overboom and R. G. A. Vergoossen, 'Voorzieningen en Jaarrekeningbeleid', *Maandblad voor Accountancy en Bedrijfseconomie*, 71/9 (September 1997), 405–16; Walter Busse von Colbe, 'Zur Anpassung der Rechnungslegung von Kapitalgesellschaften an Internationale Normen', *Zeitschrift für Betriebswirtschaftliche Forschung und Praxis*, 1995, 373–91.

228. Jean-Claude Scheid, 'Le projet de norme IASC sur les provisions', *Revue Française de Comptabilité*, April 1997, 9–10; see comments by the French delegation filed with AP 7/1998.
229. 'Informal Notes of Johannesburg Board Discussion, April 1997', IASC archive, file 'IAS 37' (electronic).
230. Interviews with Warren McGregor, 9 June 2002, and with David Tweedie, 12 January 2005; 'Three of the IASC's Most Controversial Standards Finalised at Last', *Accountancy*, 122/1260 (August 1998), 8–9.
231. Interviews with Heinz Kleekämper, 14 July 2004, and with Ken Spencer, 16 May 2003.
232. In January 1995 Datag merged into Schitag Ernst & Young Deutsche Allgemeine Treuhand. The other members of the steering committee were Karel Van Oostveldt (Belgium), S. K. Choy followed by Tony Seah (Malaysia), Ian Somerville (South Africa), and David Damant (financial analysts). The European Commission and IOSCO sent observers. The project manager was Terry Harding.
233. Interview with Hans Burggraaff, 24 May 2004.
234. Companies Act 1948 (consolidated), section 149 (1) and (3).The clause was introduced with the Companies Act 1947.
235. See R. H. Parker and C. W. Nobes, *An International View of True and Fair Accounting* (London: Routledge, 1994), 61–87 and the articles included in the special section 'A European True and Fair View?', *European Accounting Review* 2/1 (May 1993), 47–104.
236. David Tweedie, 'The True and Fair View—A Standard-Setter's Perspective', Foreword to Parker and Nobes, *An International View of True and Fair Accounting*, ix–xii; interview with David Tweedie, 12 January 2005.
237. Nevertheless, the AICPA Code of Professional Conduct (rule 203) did allow an opinion of conformity with generally accepted accounting principles when 'in unusual circumstances' compliance with promulgated GAAP would be misleading. As far as can be ascertained, this rule has rarely been applied in the case of any listed company. See Stephen A. Zeff, 'The Primacy of "Present Fairly" in the Auditor's Report', manuscript dated June 2006 (forthcoming in *Accounting Perspectives*).
238. Parker and Nobes, *An International View of True and Fair Accounting*, 108–9; interview with Ian Hammond, 29 May 2003.
239. 'Fair presentation' was presented as the general requirement in the final version of the statement of principles completed following the November 1995 board meeting. However, neither the agenda papers for that meeting nor the minutes indicate that a decision on this point was expected or taken. Compare AP 11/1995 paper 13 with 'Statement of Principles: Presentation of Financial Statements', 20 December 1995, IASC archive, file 'IAS 1' (electronic).
240. E53, 'Presentation of Financial Statements', 3–4.
241. AP 4/1997 papers 22 and 23.
242. AP 4/1997 paper 22A.
243. See pre-board comment letters by the Australian and US delegations, IASC archive, April and July 1997 agenda papers.
244. Letter from Michael Sutton to Bryan Carsberg, dated 31 March 1997, IASC archive, April 1997 agenda papers.
245. See for a characterization of the final standard: Peter Clark (IASC project manager), 'Bomb Disposal Continues at the IASC', *Accountancy*, 120/1252 (December 1997), 69.

246. 'Concerted US Opposition Bodes Ill For Eventual SEC Acceptance of IASs', *Accountancy* (international edition), 120/1248 (August 1997), 18–19; interview with Heinz Kleekämper, 14 July 2004.
247. AP 11/1995 paper 12; see also AP 4/1997 paper 22A.
248. AP 11/1995 paper 14. The numbers refer to the forty-one respondents (out of sixty-six) who expressed an opinion on this subject.
249. AP 4/1997 paper 23.
250. AP 4/1997 paper 22A.
251. AP 4/1997 paper 22.
252. See Stephen A. Zeff, ' "Political" Lobbying on Proposed Standards: A Challenge to the IASB', *Accounting Horizons*, 16/1 (March 2002), 46–8.
253. IASC board meeting of 8–12 July 1997, minute 11.
254. IASC executive committee meeting of 11 January 1998, minute 2.
255. L. Todd Johnson and Andrew Lennard, *Reporting Financial Performance: Current Developments and Future Directions* (AASB, AcSB, IASC, FRSB, ASB, FASB, 1998).
256. Interview with David Tweedie, 12 January 2005.
257. Kathryn Cearns, *Reporting Financial Performance: Proposals for Change* (AASB, AcSB, IASC, FRSB, ASB, FASB, 1999). The report was subtitled *A Proposed Approach* in the version published by the FASB. The ASB's version was published in June 1999, the IASC's version in August.
258. The steering committee, installed in March 2000, consisted of Patricia McConnell (chairman, financial analysts), Tricia O'Malley (Canada), Jean Keller (France), Adir Inbar (Israel), Kwon-Jung Kim (Korea), Egbert Eeftink (the Netherlands), John Spencer (New Zealand), and Anthony Cope (United States). IOSCO and the European Commission sent observers.
259. The other members of the steering committee were Bernard Jaudeau (France), Yashodan Kale (India), Robert Padgett (United Kingdom), Geoff Harris (followed by J. Eagan and D. Ashby, for the ICC), and Geoffrey Mitchell (since 1995, for IOSCO). Project managers were Paul Sutcliffe (until 1993), followed by Paul Pacter.
260. Peter H. Knutson, *Financial Reporting in the 1990s and Beyond: A Position Paper* (Charlottesville, VA: AIMR, 1993).
261. John M. Boersema and Susan J. Van Weelden, *Financial Reporting for Segments* (n.p.: CICA, 1992); Paul Pacter, *Reporting Disaggregated Information* (Norwalk CT: FASB, 1993).
262. Interview with Paul Pacter, 10 July 2004.
263. *Improving Business Reporting—A Customer Focus: Meeting the Information Needs of Investors and Creditors* (New York: AICPA, 1994).
264. Fax from Cairns to Shiratori, dated 11 August 1994; fax from Shiratori to Cairns dated 17 August 1994, both in IASC archive, file 'ES/MS/DHC Meetings 1993'. See also AP 1/1997 paper 5A for brief project history.
265. See AP 11/1995 paper 8 for a review of developments during 1995.
266. Interview with Patricia McConnell, 21 July 2005. See AP 7/1997 paper 21 for a summary of the final remaining differences, as well as an overview of the preceding consultations between FASB/AcSB and IASC.
267. IASC board meeting of 6–9 January 1997, minute 5.
268. IASC board meeting of 8–12 July 1997, minute 12(i).
269. FAS 131, *Disclosures about Segments of an Enterprise and Related Information*;*CICA Handbook* Section 1701, revision no. 93.
270. IASC executive committee meeting of 11–12 June 1994, agenda paper III.

271. The other members of the steering committee were Graham Peirson (Australia), Jochen Pape (Germany), Etsuo Sawa (Japan), Reyaz Mihular (Sri Lanka), John Dirks (United States), and David Morgan (ICC). IOSCO and the International Forum of Actuarial Associations sent observers. The project manager was Peter Clark.
272. Appendix I to letter from Linda Quinn and Michael Meagher to Shiratori, dated 17 June 1994, IASC archive, 'IOSCO' file.
273. Appendix I to letter from Linda Quinn and Michael Meagher to Shiratori, dated 17 June 1994, IASC archive, 'IOSCO' file.
274. AP 3/1996 paper 5.
275. Compare AP 3/1996 and IASC board meeting of 27–30 March 1996, minute 5 with IAS 19 (1998).
276. Interview with David Tweedie, 12 January 2005; 'IAS 19 Is an "Unhappy Compromise"', *Accountancy*, 121/1254 (February 1998), 9.
277. Interview with Christopher Nobes, 13 January 2005.
278. IAS 19 (1998), appendix 3, paragraph 2.
279. Communication from Sigvard Heurlin to the authors, dated 13 April 2006.
280. AP 4/1997 paper 5; IASC executive committee meetings of 6 April 1997, minute 2, of 7, 10, and 11 July 1997, minute 2, and of 29 October 1997, minute 2; interview with Etsuo Sawa, 5 July 2004.
281. Christopher Nobes, 'Prospects for World Standards by 2000?', *Accounting & Business*, January 1998, 10; Peter Clark, 'Counting the Cost of Pensions', *Accountancy* (international edition), 121/1255 (March 1988), 70.
282. See Stephen A. Zeff, 'The U.S. Senate Votes on Accounting for Employee Stock Options', in Stephen A. Zeff and Bala G. Dharan (editors), *Readings & Notes on Financial Accounting*, 5th edition (New York: McGraw-Hill, 1997), 507–17.
283. IASC board meeting of 27–30 March 1996, minute 5(a).
284. E54 included a basis for conclusions in order to make up for the lack of a draft statement of principles which had been omitted with the acceleration of the core standards programme. On the basis of the comment letters, the board decided to retain the basis for conclusions in the standard. Communcation from Peter Clark to the authors, dated 21 May 2006.
285. IASC executive committee meeting of 30 January 1996, minute 2.
286. IASC executive committee meeting of 30 January 1996, minute 2.
287. AP 6/1996 paper 15; IASC board meeting of 11–14 June 1996, minute 10(a).
288. For the opposition to the AASB's attempt to reform accounting for leases in Australia, see Geoff Burrows, *The Foundation: A History of the Australian Accounting Research Foundation 1966–91* (Caulfield, Vic: Australian Accounting Research Foundation, 1996), 196–9.
289. The other members of the steering committee were Kevin Stevenson (Australia), Roberto Tizzano (Italy), Antonio Lucio-Villegas (Fédération Bancaire de l'Union Européenne), Philippe Malaquin (International Valuation Standards Committee), and H.-G. Schulz (European Federation of Equipment Leasing Associations). The European Commission and IOSCO sent observers. The project was managed by Liesel Knorr.
290. AP 10/1997 paper 13A.
291. Interviews with Christopher Nobes, 13 January 2005, and with David Tweedie, 12 January 2005; notes prepared by Swiss delegation on IASC board meeting of 30 October–4 November 1997.

292. 'Statement by the Board of the International Accounting Standards Committee—December 2000', *IASC Insight*, December 2000, 9–16.
293. IASC executive committee meeting of 7, 10, and 11 July 1997, minute 2; AP 10/1997 paper 11; IASC board meeting of 30 October–4 November 1997, minute 7.
294. See Chris Nobes, 'The Beginning of the End of Conventional Accounting', *Accounting & Business*, 2/8 (September 1999), 48–50.
295. AP 10/1997 paper 11.
296. IASC board meetings of 30 October–4 November 1997, minute 7, and of 20–6 April 1998, minute 3.
297. 'Investment Properties', staff note, agenda paper 1 for steering committee meeting of December 1998. IASC archive, file 'IAS 40' (electronic).
298. 'Investment Properties', note from Bryan Carsberg to board representatives and technical advisers, dated 14 August 1998, IASC archive, file 'IAS 40' (electronic).
299. IASC executive committee meeting of 8 November 1998, minute 2; see also 'IASC Approves IAS 39—The Last Major Core Standard', *IASC Insight*, December 1998, 2; 'IASC Can't Celebrate Yet', *Accountancy*, 123/1265 (January 1999), 14.
300. The other steering committee members were P. F. Winkelmann (Hong Kong), Shozo Yamazaki (Japan), D. Hilton (United Kingdom), L. Mayshak (United States), and Rolf Rundfelt (financial analysts). The European Commission, IOSCO, and the International Valuation Standards Committee sent observers. Project managers were, in succession, Liesel Knorr and Peter Clark.
301. Interview with Ian Hammond, 29 May 2003.
302. Jochen Pape, quoted in 'Sun Shines on IASC Troubles', *Accountancy International*, 123/1268 (April 1999), 7.
303. Letter from Karel Van Hulle to Bryan Carsberg re AP 6/1999 paper 24, dated 22 June 1999, IASC archive, filed with June/July 1999 agenda papers; 'Investment Property Squeezes Through', *Accountancy International*, 124/1272 (August 1999), 5.
304. IASC board meeting of 16–19 March 1999, minute14(f); AP 6/1999 papers 22 and 24; IASC board meeting of 28 June–2 July 1999, minute 5.
305. Notes prepared by Swiss delegation on IASC board meeting of 28 June–2 July 1999.
306. AP 11/1999 papers 13 and 13A.
307. Letter from David B. Kaplan and Cassandra Camp to Bryan Carsberg, dated 29 October 1999; letter from Karel Van Hulle to Bryan Carsberg, dated 3 November 1999, IASC archive, E64 comment letter file.
308. Notes of Swiss delegation on December 1999 and March 2000 IASC board meetings; 'Second Class Standard Won't Do', *Accountancy International* 125/1277 (January 2000), 7; Christopher Nobes, 'One Small Step Back for IAS 40, but a Giant Leap for the IASC', *Accounting & Business*, 3/2 (February 2000), 12–13.
309. Letter from Eccles to Cairns, dated 13 October 1993; 'Meeting with Randolph Andersen, World Bank, London, 15th November 1993', memo by David Cairns dated 16 November 1993, IASC archive, 'World Bank' file.
310. 'Meeting at World Bank, Washington, 10 January 1993 [sic]', memo by Cairns, dated 20 January 1994; letter from Eccles to Cairns dated 21 June 1994, IASC archive, 'World Bank' file. See also IASC board meeting of 13 and 15–17 June 1994, minute 2 and 8(d).
311. 'Chairman's Briefing', memo from Cairns to Shiratori, dated 28 October 1994, IASC archive, file 'Board/Executive Committee Mailings'. See also 'Meetings with Eiichi Shiratori, Tokyo, 25–7 July 1994', memo by Cairns, IASC archive, file 'ES/MS/DHC Meetings 1993'.

312. The other members who served during all or part of the steering committee's life were Pierre Dumont, followed by J. Allimant (France), J. van Ham (the Netherlands), B. A. Monopoli (New Zealand), K. Narongdej followed by A. Priebjrivat (Thailand), S. Dedman (United Kingdom), and J. A. Atkinson (Zimbabwe). G. Russel acted as observer for the World Bank. The project managers were, in succession, Ian Kirton, Paul Pacter, and Rieko Yanou.
313. AP 3/1996 paper 9; AP 9/1996 paper 15; notes of Swiss delegation on IASC board meetings of March and September 1996.
314. Project proposal, appendix A to AP 3/1996 paper 9. The original proposal of January 1994 was not found in the IASC archive.
315. AP 3/1996 paper 9.
316. AP 10/1997 paper 3A. Out of forty-two letters, three were received from countries that might perhaps be classified as developing countries: Argentina, Malaysia, and Zimbabwe.
317. AP 10/1997 paper 3A.
318. See letters from the UK CCAB, the IdW, and the Canadian Advisory Group on International Accounting Standards, filed with October/November 1997 agenda papers.
319. Interview with Paul Cherry, 8 October 2004.
320. The only other instance was E41, 'Revenue Recognition', approved in November 1991 with ten votes in favour out of fourteen.
321. Interviews with Bryan Carsberg, 26 May 2005, and with Allister Wilson, 11 January 2005.
322. Interviews with Ian Hammond, 29 May 2003, and with David Tweedie, 12 January 2005.
323. Carsberg cited in 'Mixed Reactions to Agriculture Draft', *World Accounting Report*, September 1999, 9.
324. 'Mixed Reactions to Agriculture Draft', *World Accounting Report*, September 1999, 9.
325. Memorandum from Paul Cherry to the authors, dated 8 October 2004.
326. Interviews with Bryan Carsberg, 26 May 2005, and with Allister Wilson, 11 January 2005.
327. See, e.g. 'Report from the Ad Hoc Advisory Committee to the Organisation and Planning Committee', no date [early 1984], IASC archive, 'Plans and Future Work' file.
328. IASC executive committee meeting of 31 October 1993, minute 3(b).
329. IASC board meeting of 8–10 May 1995, minute 7.
330. IASC executive committee meetings of 9–10 July 1995, minute 2, of 30 January 1996, minute 2, and of 25 March 1996, minute 3.
331. IASC executive committee meeting of 30 January 1996, minute 2.
332. IASC executive committee meeting of 22 September 1996, minute 7; IASC board meeting of 7–11 April 1997, minute 3.
333. The other members who served during part or all of the steering committee's life were J. le Douit (France), G. Geib (Germany), E. Tachibana (Japan), J. W. Schoen (the Netherlands), D. Allvey (United Kingdom), H. E. Dalton and W. Freda (United States), A. Cowell (financial analysts), and David Potter (IAFEI). The European Commission, the International Forum of Actuarial Associations, IOSCO, the FASB, and the International Association of Insurance Supervisors sent observers. Peter Clark and Martin Faarborg served as project managers.

334. IASC board meeting of 9–13 November 1998, minute 11.
335. *Insurance: An Issues Paper Issued for Comment by the Steering Committee on Insurance* (London: IASC, 1999).
336. See Robert Van Riper, *Setting Standards for Financial Reporting: FASB and the Struggle for Control of a Critical Process* (Westport, CT: Quorum Books, 1994), 55–71 for a review of the FASB's problems over oil and gas accounting.
337. IASC executive committee meetings of 30 January 1996, minute 2, of 25 March 1996, minute 3, and of 6 April 1997, minute 2.
338. The other members of the committee were J. A. Gordon (Canada), H.-W. Ufer, followed by B. J. Breloer (Germany), R. Roy (India), Robert Garnett (South Africa), K. Klaver (United States), Patricia McQueen followed by F. Wellings (financial analysts), B. Fuchs followed by K. Cameron (Federation of Swiss Industrial Holding Companies), David Potter followed by A. Mazzoni (IAFEI), and C. Wright (academic). IOSCO and the UK Oil Industry Accounting Committee sent observers. Paul Pacter served as project manager.
339. *Extractive Industries: An Issues Paper Issued for Comment by the IASC Steering Committee on Extractive Industries* (London: IASC, 2000).
340. See Peter Clark, 'Building a Framework for Discounting', *IASC Insight*, September 2000, 15–16. The ASB published a working paper, 'Discounting in Financial Reporting', in April 1997. The FASB had been studying present value measurements since 1988, resulting in Statement of Financial Accounting Concepts No. 7, *Using Cash Flow Information and Present Value in Accounting Measurements* (February 2000).
341. The other members of the steering committee were: Dominique Thouvenin (France), Jörg Baetge (Germany), Rahul Roy (India), Shinichi Tanimoto (Japan), Eric Phipps (United Kingdom), Malcolm Cheetham (Federation of Swiss Industrial Holding Companies), Nelson Carvalho (IAFEI), and Sam Gutterman (International Actuarial Association). The Basel Committee, the European Commission, the FASB, the International Association of Insurance Supervisors, and IOSCO sent observers. The project was managed by Peter Clark.
342. Clark, 'Building a Framework for Discounting', 15–16.
343. Peter Clark, 'Narrowing the Range for Measurement', *IASB Insight*, October 2001, 13.
344. Letter from Carsberg to Stephen D. Eccles, dated 17 October 1997, IASC archive, 'World Bank' file.
345. The other members of the steering committee were Chen Yugui (China), Khaled Hegazy (Egypt), S. Castillon (France), C. Muchene (Kenya), L. Gorbatova (Russian Federation), G. Ee (Singapore), David Perry (United Kingdom), F. Vasquez (Venezuela), David Damant (financial analysts), M. Smith (IAFEI), and Peter Walton (UNCTAD). The European Commission, the International Finance Corporation, IOSCO, and the World Bank sent observers. Project managers were, in succession, Liesel Knorr and Colin Fleming.
346. See also 'The IASC to Look at Developing Countries', *World Accounting Report*, February 1999, 15.
347. IASC board meeting of 19–23 June 2000, minute 9.
348. IASC board meetings of 28 June–2 July 1999, minute 3, and of 15–19 November 1999, minute 2.

349. The other members of the steering committee were: Enrique Fowler Newton (Argentina), M. Tambosso (Canada), C. Lopater (France), Jörg Baetge (Germany), M. Sato (Japan), Ron Paterson (United Kingdom), and Malcolm Cheetham (Federation of Swiss Industrial Holding Companies). The European Commission, the FASB, and IOSCO sent observers. The project managers were Susan Harding, followed by Frank Palmer.
350. Christopher Nobes, 'Work Continues at the Old IASC while the New IASC Takes Shape', *Accounting & Business*, 3/4 (April 2000), 14.
351. 'Basel Committee Supports IAS', *World Accounting Report*, May 2000, 2. The board had already agreed to add the project to its agenda in July 1999. IASC board meeting of 28 June–2 July 1999, minute 7.
352. The other members of the steering committee were: Chris Begy (Canada), Wolfgang Kolb (Germany), Tadayuki Matsushige (Japan), Steve Ball (South Africa), and Russel Picot (Fédération Bancaire de l'Union Européenne). The Basel Committee, the European Commission, and IOSCO sent observers. Magnus Orrell served as project manager.
353. 'Statement by the Board of the International Accounting Standards Committee—December 2000', *IASC Insight*, December 2000, 9–16.
354. Andrew Lymer, Roger Debreceny, Ashaq Rahman, and Glen Gray, *Business Reporting on the Internet*. The project was managed for the IASC by Paul Pacter.
355. 'Ralph Walters on Harmonization', *Management Accounting* (NAA), 71 (August 1989), 24.

NOTES TO CHAPTER 12

1. David Cairns, *International Accounting Standards Survey 2000* (Henley-on-Thames, UK: David Cairns, International Financial Reporting, 2001), chapters 7–10. Also see David Cairns, *Applying International Accounting Standards*, second edition (London: Butterworths, 1999), appendix to chapter 5; Alan J. Richardson and Ian R. Hutchinson, *The Case for International Accounting Standards in Canada, A Detailed Report* (Vancouver, BC: Certified General Accountants Association of Canada, 1999), appendix B; and Corinne Ollier, 'Accounting Standards in Africa', *Accounting & Business*, March 1998, 18–20.
2. IASC Advisory Council meeting of July 1995, agenda paper VIII, annex C.
3. 'Update of the Accounting Strategy Frequently Asked Questions', MEMO/00/34, dated 14 June 2000, appended to 'Europe Moves Closer towards Global Financial Reporting Standards', European Commission press release IP/00/606, 14 June 2006.
4. For a general review, see Axel Haller, 'Financial Accounting Developments in the European Union: Past Events and Future Prospects', *The European Accounting Review*, 11/1 (2002), 153–90.
5. See, for instance, Karel Van Hulle cited in 'Brussels Abandons Low-Key Approach', *European Accountant*, June 1995, 8, and David Cairns, 'IAS Soft and IAS Supersoft', *Accountancy* (international edition) 120/1248 (August 1997), 64–5. For specific examples of selective application of IASC standards see 'Non-Compliance Hurts', *World Accounting Report*, June 1997, 7, and Cairns, *International Accounting Standards Survey 2000*, 185–96.
6. Interview with Jean-Luc Dumont, 15 February 2005.

7. Peter Standish, *The French Plan Comptable: Explanation and Translation* (Paris: Expert-Comptable Média: 1997), 104–5; Peter Standish, *Developments in French Accounting and Auditing 2000* (Paris: Expert-Comptable Média 2001), 27.
8. Interview with Georges Barthès, 7 June 2005.
9. IASC Advisory Council meeting of July 1995, agenda paper VIII, annex C.
10. Interview with Georges Barthès, 7 June 2005.
11. CRC Regulation 99-02 of 29 April 1999.
12. 'Le CNC cale les comptes consolidés sur les standards internationaux', *La Tribune*, 18 December 1998, 32.
13. Interview with Georges Barthès, 7 June 2005; see also 'France—Towards a Genuine Standard Setting Body', *World Accounting Report*, January 1997, 9–10.
14. Law 98-261 of 6 April 1998, article 6.
15. Cairns, *International Accounting Standards Survey 2000*, 83; *100 Groupes industriels et commerciaux: Doctrine et pratiques européennes* (Paris: CPC Meylan, 2000), 51–2.
16. See Dieter Ordelheide and Dieter Pfaff, *European Financial Reporting: Germany* (London: Routledge, 1994), 90–1 for a listing of the IdW's recommendations up to 1992.
17. Interview with Bernd-Joachim Menn, 18 August 2004. In 1992 Cairns was informed that 'German industry is very negative about IASC' and that German banks were 'totally uninformed about IASC'. 'Meeting with Peter Marks and Albrecht Ruppel, IDW, Dusseldorf, Germany, 15 September 1992', memo by David Cairns, dated 20 September 1992, IASC archive, file 'Germany'.
18. In the 1993 bound volume of IASC standards, 'German' is no longer included in the list of languages in which IASC standards have been translated either completely or in part. In 1998, the publication of an 'official' German translation of IASC standards was announced without reference to an existing translation. *IASC Insight*, March 1998, 22.
19. Ordelheide and Pfaff, *European Financial Reporting: Germany*, 82.
20. An example is the joint paper by a group of nineteen German academics, 'German Accounting Principles: An Institutionalized Framework', *Accounting Horizons*, 9/3 (September 1995), 92–9.
21. For the position of the German Ministry of Justice in 1992–93, see Herbert Biener, 'Möglichkeiten und Grenzen der internationalen Harmonisierung der Rechnungslegung', speech on the occasion of the award of the Dr. Kausch Prize at the Hochschule St. Gallen, 21 January 1992; Herbert Biener, 'What Is the Future of Mutual Recognition of Financial Statements and Is Comparability Really Necessary?', *European Accounting Review*, 3/2 (1994), 335–42.
22. For commentary see 'Daimler Bends', *The Economist*, 3 April 1993, 76; 'Why Daimler Went Red Over a Share Quote in New York', *The Times*, 7 October 1993.
23. Interview with Heinz Kleekämper, 14 July 2004.
24. The proceedings were published as Jörg Baetge (editor), *Die deutsche Rechnungslegung vor dem Hintergrund internationaler Entwicklungen: Vorträge und Diskussionen aus nationaler und internationaler Sicht zum 10. Münsterischen Tagesgespräch, "Haben die deutschen Rechnungslegungsvorschriften noch eine Chance?"* (Düsseldorf: IDW-Verlag, 1994).
25. See the comments by Bayer's CEO in 'Bayer kurz für Akquisition in USA', *Börsen Zeitung*, 14 January 1995, 7; 'Deutsche Bilanzierung: Abschied vom HGB', *Börsen Zeitung*, 30 December 1995, 21.

26. Kurt Ramin, 'Deutsche Bilanzen im Umbruch', *Börsen Zeitung*, 28 December 1995, 5; 'A Change of Culture', *World Accounting Report*, June 1997, 3; 'Understanding a Variety of GAAP', *World Accounting Report*, March 1998, 6.
27. See Jochen Pape und Sebastian Heintges, 'Verhältnis von US-GAAP und IAS zur Rechnungslegung nach deutschem Handelsrecht', in Rüdiger von Rosen und Werner Seifert (editors), *Zugang zum US-Kapitalmarkt für deutsche Aktiengesellschaften* (Frankfurt am Main: Deutsches Aktieninstitut/Deutsche Börse, 1998), 201–5. For a further discussion of the problem of 'dual' financial statements see *Berichte über die 38. Arbeitstagung 1996 des IDW vom 13.–15. November 1996 in Baden-Baden* (Düsseldorf: IDW-Verlag, 1996), Thema D.
28. Herbert Biener, 'The Relationship between IOSCO and IASC', statement to the IASC board, 9 May 1995; Herbert Biener, 'Öffnung des deutschen Rechts für internationale Konzernabschlüsse?', undated paper [1995] (copies supplied to the authors by Herbert Biener). See also Brigite Eierle, 'Differential Accounting in Germany: A Historical Analysis', *Accounting, Business & Financial History*, 15/3 (November 2005), 291–2.
29. Minutes of the meeting of WP1 on 3–4 April 1995 (in the authors' files); interviews with Herbert Biener, 13 July 2004, with John Barras, 10 February 2006, and with Geoffrey Mitchell, 19 February 2004.
30. See, e.g. Herbert Biener, 'Die Rechnungslegungsempfehlungen des IASC und deren Auswirkungen auf die Rechnungslegung in Deutschland', *Betriebswirtschaftliche Forschung und Praxis*, 4/1993, 345–56.
31. 'Industrie uneins über HGB-Öffnung', *Börsen Zeitung*, 21 October 1995, 1; 'Germany: Double Book-Keeping for Daimler as Regulators Refuse US GAAP', *Corporate Accounting International*, January 1996, 1; 'GAAP Opponents Scuttle Last Attempt at Compromise', *Corporate Accounting International*, March 1996, 3.
32. 'Koalition will den Finanzplatz Deutschland starken', *Frankfurter Allgemeine Zeitung*, 31 October 1997.
33. HGB paragraph 292a.2.2.a as inserted by KapAEG of 20 April 1998; see also Lita Olbrich, 'Bundestag Sanctions Accounting Reform Law', *The Accountant*, issue 5931 (March 1998), 1, 11.
34. Cairns, *International Accounting Standards Survey 2000*, 87–8. For a review of the switch to US GAAP and IASC standards by listed companies during 1997–9, see also Jürgen Spanheimer and Christian Koch, 'Internationale Bilanzierungspraxis in Deutschland—Ergebnisse empirischen Untersuchung der Unternehmen des DAX und MDAX sowie des Neuen Marktes', *Die Wirtschaftsprüfung*, 53/7, 1 April 2000, 301–10.
35. 'Voraussetzungen für ein Listing am Neuer Markt', *Börsen Zeitung*, 19 April 1997, B10.
36. HGB paragraph 342 as insterted by KontrAG of 27 April 1998.
37. Peter Wolmert, 'Internationalising German Accounts', *World Accounting Report*, September 1998, 7.
38. 'Rechnungslegungskomitee gegründet', *Börsen Zeitung*, 31 March 1998; 'Fears Over Remit of German Standard-setter', *The Accountant*, issue 5933 (May 1998), 1.
39. Stephen A. Zeff, Frans van der Wel, and Kees Camfferman, *Company Financial Reporting: A Historical and Comparative Study of the Dutch Regulatory Process* (Amsterdam: North-Holland, 1992), 335–7.

40. *Onderzoek Jaarverslaggeving 1990*, NIVRA Geschriften no. 60 (Amsterdam: NIVRA, 1992), 152,
41. Interview with Gijs Bak, 8 December 2005.
42. 'Commentaar op ED 32 "Comparability of Financial Statements" ', *De Accountant*, 96/2 (October 1989), 71–3.
43. 'Prof. Traas wil aanscherping boekhoudregels', *Het Financieele Dagblad*, 25 November 1998, Supplement, 7.
44. Cairns, *International Accounting Standards Survey 2000*, 95.
45. Kamerstukken (parliamentary papers), 25732 no. 8, 10 May 1999.
46. Jens O. Elling, 'Denmark', in John Flower (editor), *The Regulation of Financial Reporting in the Nordic Countries* (Stockholm: Fritzes, 1994), 49.
47. Regnskabsvejledning no. 8, *Varebeholdninger* (March 1992), paragraph 29.
48. 'Trying to Struggle Loose', *The Accountant*, 22 February 1999, 17.
49. David Alexander and Hans R. Schwencke, 'Accounting Change in Norway', *The European Accounting Review*, 12/3 (1993), 554–5.
50. Interview with Erik Mamelund and Harald Brandsås, 8 April 2005.
51. 'Financial Accounting in Norway', speech by Finn Berg Jacobsen, 19th Annual Congress of the European Accounting Association, Bergen, Norway, 2–4 May 1996, copy in IASC archive, 'Norway' documentation file.
52. Alexander and Schwencke, 'Accounting Change in Norway', 557.
53. *Swedish Accounting and Auditing 1998* (Stockholm: Föreningen Auktoriserade Revisorer, 1998), 15.
54. *Information Redovisningsrådet* (Stockholm: Redovisningsrådet, 1991), 7.
55. *Swedish Accounting and Auditing 1998*, 28.
56. Communication from Sigvard Heurlin to the authors, dated 19 June 2006.
57. Cairns, *International Accounting Standards Survey 2000*, 79–80; 98; 102–3.
58. Giorgio Behr, 'Swiss GAAP oder das Schweizer Konzept der Fachempfehlungen zur Rechnungslegung FER', *Die Wirtschaftsprüfung*, 47/24 (15 December 1994), 832–6.
59. 'Nestlé Expects 15% Growth in Earnings', *Financial Times*, 23 November 1989, 38; 'Stepping Out onto a Wider Stage', *Financial Times*, 6 February 1992, 21.
60. 'Angst in the Alps', *Financial Times*, 1 August 1991, 14; 'More Swiss Companies "May Adopt IAS" ', *Financial Times*, 10 December 1991, 26; 'Mehr Transparanz der Schweizer Geschäftsberichte', *Neue Zürcher Zeitung*, 3 March 1993, 31; 'Swiss Finance: On Deaf Ears', *The Economist* (UK edition), 28 August 1993, 66.
61. On developments in Swiss company law, see Ann-Kristin Achleitner, 'The History of Financial Reporting in Switzerland', in Peter Walton (editor), *European Financial Reporting: A History* (London: Academic Press, 1995), 241–58.
62. 'Den Trends der Rechnungslegung auf der Spur', *Neue Zürcher Zeitung*, 21 November 1995, 33.
63. Cairns, *International Accounting Standards Survey 2000*, 105; see also Giorgio Behr, 'Switzerland Survey—Accounting Reforms', *World Accounting Report*, March 1997, 10–11.
64. Cairns, *International Accounting Standards Survey 2000*, 106–9.
65. Interview with Christopher Nobes, 13 January 2005; see also David Cairns, 'The Future of the IASC and the Implications for UK Companies', in *Financial Reporting Today—Current and Emerging Issues: The 1998 Edition* (Milton Keynes: Accountancy Books, [1998]), 146.
66. Cairns, 'The Future of the IASC and the Implications for UK Companies', 149.

67. By the Treaty of Maastricht (1992), the name of the European Economic Community was changed to 'European Community'. By the same treaty, the European Union was created as the overarching structure of the European Community, the European Coal and Steel Community, and the European Atomic Energy Community.
68. The historical coolness of the Commission is noted in 'IASC Team in IOSCO Endgame', *World Accounting Report*, August/September 1995, 1. For a review of developments in the Commission's policy during the 1990s, see also Haller, 'Financial Accounting Developments in the European Union'.
69. Interview with Georges Barthès de Ruyter, 5 June 2003.
70. 'Notes of a Telephone Conversation with Georges Barthès 15/12/87', preparer's name not known, IASC archive, file 'EEC'.
71. Letter from Cairns to Van Hulle, dated 25 April 1988, IASC archive, file 'EEC'.
72. Letter from Niessen to Barthès, dated 12 October 1988, IASC archive, file 'EEC'.
73. 'Speech by H. Niessen, Head of Division of the European Communities at the meeting of the Board of IASC held on the 9th of November 1988 in Copenhagen', typescript in both English and French versions, IASC archive, file 'EEC'. Quotations and paraphrasings in this paragraph are from this speech.
74. Interview with Karel Van Hulle, 17 February 2004.
75. 'FEE Strategy—A Discussion Paper', unsigned draft dated 3 February 1988 attached to letter from John Hegarty to members of FEE's Coordination Committee, dated 23 February 1988, NIVRA archive, file B-Int (1987–8), 76–81.
76. 'The E.C. and the European Profession', memo by Henk Volten (NIVRA), dated May 1988, NIVRA archive, file CIB-FEE A4800.
77. In 1979, Paul Rutteman proposed the formation of a European Accounting Standards Committee. See 'Rutteman Calls for European Standards Committee', *Accountancy Age*, 10/25 (29 June 1979), 1. Rutteman was then the UK member of the Groupe d'Études.
78. Interview with Gilbert Gélard, 27 May 2004.
79. Letter from Allan Cook (Shell), to David Cairns, dated 9 January 1989, IASC archive, file 'EEC'. See also 'Meeting with Commission Officials—13 July 1989', report on a meeting of Hermann Nordemann, Edouard Salustro, and John Hegarty (FEE) with Hermann Niessen and Karel Van Hulle, NIVRA archive, B-Int (1988–90), 74–81.
80. Georges Timmerman, 'Zand in het Europese raderwerk', *Accountancy en Bedrijfskunde*, 9/4 (May 1989), 28.
81. Worldwide Harmonisation in Europe's Best Interests', *IASC News*, 18/3 (July 1989), i–iv. The quotations are keyed to their respective page numbers.
82. Undated memo by Kees Meijer (NIVRA) on meeting of FEE Coordinating Committee of 5 June 1989, NIVRA archive, file CIB-FEE, A4842; letter of Jacques Potdevin (president, Compagnie Nationale des Commissaires aux Comptes) and François Fournet (president, Ordre des Experts Comptables et des Comptables Agrées) to J. L. M. J. Obers (chairman, NIVRA), dated 29 May 1989, NIVRA archive, file B-Int (1988–9), 58. For a report on the reverberations following on the Commission's threat to add a third tier of accounting standards in Europe, see 'Standards Threat Looms', *Accountancy*, April 1989, 5.
83. Interview with John Hegarty, 17 August 2004.
84. Karel Van Hulle, cited in Timmerman, 'Zand in het Europese raderwerk', 28.

85. Notes on a meeting between G. E. Fitchew, Hermann Niessen, and Karel Van Hulle (European Commission) with Georges Barthès, Christopher Stronge, Herman Marseille, Wilhelm Tjaden, David Cairns, and Mark Wovsaniker (IASC), memo by Wovsaniker, dated 21 April 1989, IASC archive, file 'EEC'.
86. 'Meeting with Commission Officials—13 July 1989', report on a meeting of Hermann Nordemann, Edouard Salustro and John Hegarty (FEE) with Hermann Niessen and Karel Van Hulle, NIVRA archive, B-Int (1988–90), 74–81.
87. 'E32, Comparability of Financial Statements/Unofficial Secretariat Notes of a Meeting at the European Commission—15th December 1989', prepared by David Cairns, IASC archive, file 'EEC'.
88. In particular at a KPMG-sponsored forum on 'International Comparability of Company Accounts', held on 21 November 1989. See Henk Volten, 'Het IASC en de regelgevers', *De Accountant*, 96/6 (February 1990), 309.
89. See *The Future of Harmonisation of Accounting Standards within the European Communities: Conference, 17–18 January 1990, Brussels* (Luxemburg: Office for Official Publications of the European Communities, 1990).
90. Volten, 'Het IASC en de regelgevers', 309.
91. 'Unofficial Notes of a Meeting with the European Commission, 15th February 1990, Brussels', prepared by David Cairns, IASC archive, file 'EEC'.
92. Niessen was succeeded as head of the company law unit by the German Gisbert Wolff. Van Hulle was subsequently made head of a new unit, 'Financial Information—Accounting Standards'.
93. The idea for such a forum was elaborated in a paper by Anthony Hopwood, 'Harmonization of Accounting Standards within the EC: A Perspective for the Future', which formed the basis of the discussions during the January 1990 conference. See *The Future of Harmonisation of Accounting Standards within the European Communities*, 73–6. Hopwood's paper was also published as 'The Future of Accounting Harmonization in the Community', *European Accounting*, 1991, 12–21.
94. Karel Van Hulle, 'Harmonization of Accounting Standards: A View from the European Community', *The European Accounting Review*, 1/1 (May 1992), 167–8.
95. Among those present were: Gerard Murphy, Morten Iversen, Horst Kaminsky, Herman Marseille, and David Tweedie (former IASC board members), Rolf Rundfelt and Stig Enevoldsen (current board members), and Allan Cook (former IASC secretary). See the letter from Niessen to Nordemann, dated 22 November 1990, IASC archive, file 'EEC'.
96. Karel Van Hulle, 'The E.C.'s Contribution to Making Corporate Reports Valuable: Variations on a Melody', in *Festival of Accounting, Proceedings* ([Edinburgh:] Institute of Chartered Accountants of Scotland, 1991), 4–8. The Commission's proposals are described and criticized in Herbert Probst, 'Mehr angloamerikanische Rechnungslegung in der EG durch geänderte Verfahren?', *Zeitschrift für Betriebswirtschaftliche Forschung und Praxis*, 44/5 (1992), 426–40.
97. See remarks by Karel Van Hulle, cited in 'Rechnungslegung im Spannungsfeld von Tradition, Globalisierung und europäischer Integration', *Zeitschrift für Betriebswirtschaftliche Forschung und Praxis*, 55/1 (1998), 78–9.
98. For a review of the position of the German Ministry of Justice, see Dieter Ordelheide, 'Notwendigkeiten und Probleme der Weiterentwicklung der EG-Bilanzrichtlinien und des deutschen Konzernabschlußrechts', in Baetge (editor), *Die deutsche Rechnungslegung vor dem Hintergrund internationaler Entwicklungen*,

18–23. See also Biener, 'Möglichkeiten und Grenzen der internationalen harmonisierung der Rechnungslegung'.
99. Van Hulle, 'Rechnungslegung im Spannungsfeld von Tradition, Globalisierung und europäischer Integration', 79–80.
100. A report on the first meetings of the Forum and expressions of disappointment are found in a draft FEE report 'EC Accounting Advisory Form—Assessment of Performance to Date and Recommendations for Future Improvement', dated 13 January 1993. IASC archive, file 'EEC'.
101. Interview with Karel Van Hulle, 17 February 2004.
102. Memorandum from Liesel Knorr, dated 7 July 1995, reporting on a meeting with John Mogg, Karel Van Hulle and others present on 3 July 1995, IASC archive, file 'EEC'. In a speech to FEE, Mogg was quoted as saying, 'It would not be acceptable for Europe to delegate the setting of accounting standards to the US.' 'Signs of a More Active Role', *Corporate Accounting International*, 56 (March 1995), 9.
103. Interview with Karel Van Hulle, 16 February 2005. See also Karel Van Hulle, 'The European Commission's Strategy for the Harmonisation of Financial Reporting', presented at the 2nd International Accounting Standards Conference, held on 10 March 1998 in Brussels, 2, published in Italian as 'La strategia della Commissione Europea per l'armonizzazione contabile', in *Economia & Management: La rivista di direzione aziendale*, 5 (September 1998), 63–71.
104. Karel Van Hulle, 'Harmonization of Accounting Standards in the EC: Is It the Beginning or Is It the End', *The European Accounting Review*, 2/2 (September 1993), 387–96.
105. 'Europe: A Study in Standard-setting Ambiguity', in 'The Standard-Setters', a supplement to *World Accounting Report*, August/September 1995, xii.
106. 'Europe Prepares to Re-enter International Harmonisation Arena', *Corporate Accounting International*, issue 59 (June 1995), 1, 6.
107. The quotations attributed to Røder appear in 'Europe: A Study in Standard-Setting Ambiguity', xii. Also see 'Profession Fights to Avoid Third Tier', *Accountancy*, 114/1222 (June 1995), 18.
108. Letter from Røder to Mogg, dated 7 June 1995 (supplied to the authors by FEE).
109. Letter from Røder to Mogg, dated 7 June 1995.
110. IASC Secretary-General Carsberg reported in early July 1995 that Mogg had told him that the 'toleration' in Germany of the use of IASC standards in consolidated financial statements had been helpful to the Commission's attitude towards IASC standards. IASC Advisory Council meeting of 8 July 1995, minute 3.
111. Interviews with Karel Van Hulle, 17 February 2004 and 16 February 2005.
112. 'EC Embraces International Accounting Standards', *World Accounting Report*, August/September 1995, 2. Also see 'European Set of Standards Ruled Out by EU Commission', *European Accountant*, issue 58 (August 1995), 1.
113. *Accounting Harmonisation: A New Strategy vis-a-vis International Harmonisation*, COM 95 (508), paragraph 1.4. See also paragraph 4.6. Karel Van Hulle, in a paper published in June 1995, foreshadowed the Commission's evolving accounting policy. Karel Van Hulle, 'Bridging the GAAP in Europe?', *IASC Insight*, June 1995, 5–7. See also 'Europe Makes the Right Move', *World Accounting Report*, December 1995/January 1996, 1; 'European Standards Idea Dropped by EC', *World Accounting Report*, December 1995/January 1996, 2, and 'EU Puts Weight Behind IASC', *IASC Insight*, March 1996, 1, 3.

114. Timmerman, 'Zand in het Europese raderwerk', 29. The changing position was intimated in a meeting of IASC representatives with John Mogg in September 1993. While Mogg reiterated the Commission's responsibility for some three million limited liability companies in the Community, he acknowledged the demands placed on Community legislation by globalization. 'Notes of Meeting at European Commission, Brussels, 14th September 1993', memo by David Cairns, IASC archive, file 'EEC'.
115. *Accounting Harmonisation: A New Strategy vis-a-vis International Harmonisation*, paragraph 1.3.
116. *Accounting Harmonisation: A New Strategy vis-a-vis International Harmonisation*, paragraph 3.3.
117. 'EC Admits Defeat', *Accountancy*, 116/1228 (December 1995), 13.
118. 'Communication from Mr. Monti to the Commission', appended to *Accounting Harmonisation: A New Strategy vis-a-vis International Harmonisation*.
119. Karel Van Hulle, 'From Accounting Directives to International Accounting Standards', in Christian Leuz, Dieter Pfaff, and Anthony Hopwood (editors), *The Economics and Politics of Accounting: International Perspectives on Research Trends, Policy, and Practice* (Oxford: Oxford University Press, 2004), 360. See also 'Satisfying Global Demand', *World Accounting Report*, December 1996, 2.
120. Interview with Gijs Bak, 8 December 2004.
121. Minutes of meeting of John Mogg and Karel Van Hulle (European Commission) with Frank Harding (IFAC), David Darbyshire and John Williams (FEE), 16 April 1996, NIVRA archive, file B-Int (1996), 23.
122. 'E&Y to Advise EC on IASs', *Accountancy* (international edition), 118/1237 (September 1996), 7, and memorandum from Allister Wilson to the authors, dated 5 May 2005.
123. Van Hulle, 'The European Commission's Strategy for the Harmonisation of Financial Reporting', 8.
124. 'Prospectus for a European Accounting Research Foundation [Draft] May 1996', IASC archive, file 'FEE', 3. Until 1996, the G4 countries were the United States, the United Kingdom, Canada and Australia, represented by their respective standard setters. During 1996, the New Zealand standard setter became a member of the G4.
125. 'Prospectus for a European Accounting Research Foundation', 3.
126. UNICE (Union des Confédérations de l'Industrie et des Employeurs d'Europe, or Union of Industrial and Employers' Confederations of Europe) is the major body speaking on behalf of European industry.
127. See 'Round Table on the Establishment of a European Research Foundation, Brussels—6 June 1996, Draft Minutes', IASC archive, file 'FEE'.
128. Letter from David Darbyshire to Carsberg, dated 12 February 1997, IASC archive, file 'FEE'.
129. *Financial Services: Building a Framework for Action*, Communication of the Commission, COM (1998) 625 (28 October 1998), 10.
130. *Financial Services: Building a Framework for Action*, 10
131. 'Changes to EU 4th Directive?', *World Accounting Report*, May 1997, 3.
132. By the middle of 2000, Austria, Belgium, Germany, Finland, France, Italy, and Luxembourg had acted to allow their domestic companies listed in foreign markets to use IASC standards or US GAAP. See *Global Financial Reporting: IAS or US GAAP? European Survey—April 2000* (KPMG International, 2000), 4, and 'Major Reform Ahead', *World Accounting Report*, July 2000, 3. For a discussion of these

developments by a member of the UK delegation to the IASC board, see Christopher Nobes, 'European Moves Towards International Harmonisation', *Accounting & Business*, 1/11–12 (November/December 1998), 32–3.
133. See 'Internationalising German Accounts', *World Accounting Report*, September 1998, 6–7, and 'Fears Over Remit of German Standard-setter', *The Accountant*, 5933 (May 1998), 1, 4.
134. Interview with Karel Van Hulle, 16 February 2005.
135. *Financial Services: Implementing the Framework for Financial Markets: Action Plan*, Communication of the Commission, COM (1999) 232 (11 May 1999), 7.
136. 'Commission in Retreat on Imposition of Global Rules', *The Accountant*, issue 5946 (May 1999), 1.
137. Fédération des Experts Comptables Européens (FEE), *Discussion Paper on A Financial Reporting Strategy Within Europe*, 8 October 1999, 13 (available at: http://www.fee.be/publications). See Paul Rogerson, 'FEE Backs IASs in New Accounting Strategy', *The Accountant*, 5951 (October 1999), 3.
138. *Financial Services: Implementing the Framework for Financial Markets: Action Plan*, 7.
139. FEE, *Discussion Paper on A Financial Reporting Strategy Within Europe*, 12–13.
140. *Financial Services Action Plan, Progress Report* (29 November 1999) and *Progress on Financial Services, Second Report*, COM (2000) 336 (31 May 2000).
141. *Progress on Financial Services, Second Report*, 2.
142. *EU Financial Reporting Strategy: The Way Forward*, Communication from the Commission to the Council and the European Parliament, COM (2000) 359 (13 June 2000).
143. *EU Financial Reporting Strategy: The Way Forward*, paragraphs 16, 17, 30. The EU Commissioner for the Internal Market, wrote a 'personal view' column: Frits Bolkestein, 'One Currency, One Accounting Standard', *Financial Times*, 14 June 2000, 23.
144. *EU Financial Reporting Strategy: The Way Forward*, paragraph 16 and n. 7; also see Deborah Hargreaves and Michael Peel, 'Plan for Common EU Accounting Standards', *Financial Times*, 14 June 2000, 10.
145. *EU Financial Reporting Strategy: The Way Forward*, paragraph 7.
146. Van Hulle, 'From Accounting Directives to International Accounting Standards', 362.
147. *EU Financial Reporting Strategy: The Way Forward*, paragraph 6.
148. 'EU Financial Reporting Strategy', *IASC Insight*, June 2000, 9.
149. *EU Financial Reporting Strategy: The Way Forward*, paragraph 19.
150. *EU Financial Reporting Strategy: The Way Forward*, paragraph 20.
151. *EU Financial Reporting Strategy: The Way Forward*, paragraph 22.
152. *EU Financial Reporting Strategy: The Way Forward*, paragraph 22.
153. *EU Financial Reporting Strategy: The Way Forward*, paragraph 25.
154. 'International Accounting Standards', Release Nos. 33-7801, 34-42430, International Series No. 1215, File No. S7-04-00, 16 February 2000, <http://www.sec.gov/rules/concept/34-42430.htm>, section IV.A.3.(b).(iv)
155. 'Accounting Rules,' *Financial Times*, 15 June 2000, 22.
156. Graham Ward, 'No Need for Endorsement Mechanism' (letter), *Financial Times*, 20 June 2000, 26
157. 'Commission Sparks Fears of EU GAAP Creation', *The Accountant*, issue 5959 (June 2000), 1.

158. John Mogg, 'Brussels Leads Way on Rules for Accounting' (letter), *Financial Times* (22 June 2000), 24. Karel Van Hulle defended the screening mechanism in 'Towards Global Standards', *Accountancy*, 126/1284 (August 2000), 108.
159. Mogg, 'Brussels Leads Way on Rules for Accounting', 24.
160. 'Mogg Rebuts "EU GAAP" Claim', *The Accountant*, issue 5960 (July 2000), 2.
161. Van Hulle, 'Towards Global Standards', 108.
162. In November 2000, it was reported that FEE was already working on a 'European Financial Reporting Advisory Group' (EFRAG) to become the screening mechanism at the technical level. See 'The IASC and Europe', *World Accounting Report*, November 2000, 12. John Hegarty (interview, 17 August 2004), who was then the secretary-general of FEE, saw EFRAG as the successor to the ill-fated European Accounting Research Foundation of 1996, discussed in Section 12.3.4. Ruud Vergoossen (interview, 22 June 2005) saw EFRAG as evolving out of FEE's involvement with E5+2.
163. *EU Financial Reporting Strategy: The Way Forward*, paragraph 26.
164. 'Ministers Back Use of IAS', *World Accounting Report*, September 2000, 7.
165. Regulation (EC) No. 1606/2002 on the applicability of international accounting standards.
166. 'The IASC and Europe', *World Accounting Report*, November 2000, 12
167. Australian Accounting Standards Board, *Towards International Comparability of Financial Reporting*, Policy Discussion Paper No. 1 (Caulfield, Vic.: Australian Accounting Research Foundation, 1994), 2.
168. Interview with Ken Spencer, 26 May 2003.
169. AASB and PSASB, *International Harmonisation Policy* (Caulfield, Vic.: AASB and Australian Accounting Research Foundation, 1996), paragraphs 5.3(a), 5.3(d), and 4.2, respectively.
170. Richard Humphry, 'The Competitive Imperative of Harmonisation with International Accounting Standards', *Australian Accounting Review*, 7/2 (October 1997), 29. For the study, see Brigid T. Curran, *A Comparative Study of Australian & International Accounting Standards—Challenges for Harmonisation* (Sydney: Coopers & Lybrand, 1996).
171. Humphry, 'The Competitive Imperative of Harmonisation with International Accounting Standards', 29.
172. The total budget for the AASB for 1995/96 was slightly over $1 million. Australian Accounting Standards Board, *Annual Report 1996–97*, 17.
173. See Humphry 'The Competitive Imperative of Harmonisation with International Accounting Standards', 29. Communication from Michael Sharpe to the authors, dated 11 April 2006. Ken Spencer (interview, 26 May 2003), Warren McGregor (interview, 9 June 2003), then the executive director of the Australian Accounting Research Foundation, (AARF), and Angus Thomson (interview, 27 May 2003), then a senior staff person at the AARF, held the view that Sharpe was influential behind Humphry's initiative. This view is supported in Philip Brown and Ann Tarca, 'Politics, Processes and the Future of Australian Accounting Standards', *Abacus*, 37/3 (October 2001), 277.
174. 'ASX Pushes Support for New Accounting Standards', Australian Stock Exchange news release, dated 28 August 1996. Also see 'Standards Levy Gets Harmonious Response', *Business Review Weekly*, 26 August 1996, 92.

175. 'Australia to Harmonise with IASC Standards', *The Standard* (newsletter of the AARF and AASB), 3 (December 1996), 1. The table of tentative programme timing was announced in the same issue of *The Standard*.
176. Ken Spencer, 'The View from the AASB: Take It Easy, Get It Right', *Australian Accountant*, 68/2 (March 1998), 20–2.
177. Interview with Ken Spencer, 26 May 2003. Similar views were expressed in the interviews with Warren McGregor, 9 June 2003, and Angus Thomson, 27 May 2003.
178. *Accounting Standards: Building International Opportunities for Australian Business*, Corporate Law Economic Reform Programme, Proposals for Reform: Paper no. 1 (Commonwealth of Australia, 1997), part 6. Also see Philip Brown and Bryan Howieson, 'Capital Markets Research and Accounting Standard Setting', *Accounting and Finance*, 38/1 (March 1998), 13–4.
179. 'First Release of Corporate Law Economic Reform Proposals—Building International Opportunities for Australian Business', press release, no. 105, by the Treasurer, dated 8 September 1997. Also see *Accounting Standards: Building International Opportunities for Australian Business*, Corporate Law Economic Reform Programme, Proposals for Reform: Paper no. 1, part 5.
180. Brown and Tarca, 'Politics, Processes and the Future of Australian Accounting Standards', 277.
181. For a discussion of the debate precipitated by the CLERP1 proposals, see Brown and Tarca, 'Politics, Processes and the Future of Australian Accounting Standards'.
182. 'Adoption of International Accounting Standards by 2005', bulletin of the Financial Reporting Council, 2002/4, 3 July 2002 (available at: http://www.iasplus.com/resource/ausfrc.pdf).
183. IASC Advisory Council meeting of July 1995, agenda paper VIII, annex C.
184. This and the next quotation are taken from *CICA Task Force on Standard Setting, Final Report* (Toronto: Canadian Institute of Chartered Accountants, May 1998), 4. One of the members of the task force was Edward J. Waitzer, a Toronto lawyer who was, since July 1997, the chairman of the IASC's Strategy Working Party.
185. Richardson and Hutchinson, *The Case for International Accounting Standards in Canada*. The quotations and views drawn from this study in this paragraph are from pages 20–2. In the preface, Guy Legault, CGA-Canada's president and chief operating officer, stated that this study was the source of the July 1999 policy statement, mentioned below.
186. Lawrence Richter Quinn, 'Closing the Gap', *CAmagazine*, 136/6 (August 2003), 16–22, and 'Canada's Accounting Standards Board Ratifies its Strategic Plan, Approves Convergence with International Reporting Standards', CICA media release, dated 10 January 2006. Also see 'Canadian Accounting Standards—Global Positioning: The New Direction', *Bulletin #1* of the Accounting Standards Board of Canada [May 2006].
187. Kiyomitsu Arai, *Accounting in Japan*, IRBA Series No. 25 (Tokyo: Institute for Research in Business Administration, Waseda University, 1994), 5.
188. Interviews with Atsushi Kato, 2 July 2004, with Noriaki Kinoshita, 2 July 2004, with Seigo Nakajima, 30 June 2004, with Etsuo Sawa, 5 July 2004, and with Tatsumi Yamada, 5 July 2004. Kinoshita reported that Professor Kiyomitsu Arai, who was then the chairman of the BADC, wrote a book on E32 and publicized the importance of E32 among Japanese academics.
189. Memorandum from Tadaaki Tokunaga to the authors, dated 30 June 2004.

190. Masato Kikuya, 'International Harmonization of Japanese Accounting Standards', *Accounting, Business & Financial History*, 11/3 (November 2001), 357–8, 365, 366.
191. Interview with Atsushi Kato, 2 July 2004.
192. *COFRI Corporation Finance Research Institute, Japan* (Tokyo: COFRI, 1992), 2.
193. Kazuo Hiramatsu, 'The Financial Big Bang and the Accounting-Auditing Reforms in Japan', *International Review of Business*, 3 (December 1998), 10.
194. Hiramatsu, 'The Financial Big Bang and the Accounting-Auditing Reforms in Japan', 12–13.
195. Kikuya, 'International Harmonization of Japanese Accounting Standards', 360–2.
196. Kenji Shiba, *'Accounting Big Bang' and Corporate Behaviour in Japan*, Discussion Paper Series No. 4 (Osaka: The Institute of Economic and Political Studies, Kansai University, March 2003), 2.
197. Kazuo Hiramatsu, 'Problems of Accounting Standard-Setting in Japan', *International Review of Business*, 6 (March 2003), 1.
198. Interview with Doug Brooking, 18 March 2004.
199. This section is based on the following three articles: G. V. Terry, 'Going the International Route', *Accountancy SA*, August 1993, 3; Monica Singer, 'SA Goes International', *Accountancy SA*, November/December 1993, 36; and Rosanne Blumberg, 'International Accounting Standards—The Way to Go?' *Accountancy SA*, May 1995, 3. The authors are grateful to Erna Swart for furnishing these three articles.
200. Interview with Monica Singer, 15 March 2004.
201. Interview with Erna Swart, 15 March 2004.
202. Interview with Doug Brooking, 18 March 2004.
203. 'The Mission of the Financial Accounting Standards Board', in *Facts about FASB*, 1993–4 edition (FASB), 1.
204. 'FASB's Plan for International Activities', *FASB Status Report*, no. 223 (31 August 1991), 6. For a commentary, see 'FASB Goes Global?' *World Accounting Report*, October 1991, 1.
205. 'FASB's Plan for International Activities', 6.
206. 'FASB's Plan for International Activities', 7. Also see 'FASB Goes Global?', 1.
207. Interview with Dennis R. Beresford, 8 August 2004.
208. 'Visit to FASB and SEC, March 1997', AP 3/1987 additional agenda paper.
209. See 'Standard Setters Are Getting Together', *World Accounting Report*, July 1991, 1.
210. Philip R. Lochner, Jr., 'The U.S. Role in Achieving International Harmonization of Accounting Standards', The 10th Annual SEC and Financial Reporting Institute Conference, Los Angeles, California, 16 May 1991, 19–20, SEC Library. For an extract from the speech, see 'Worth Repeating', *Journal of Accountancy*, 172/4 (September 1991), 108–9. Lochner had attended a meeting of the FASB's advisory council in July 1990, when he raised questions whether the benefits justified the costs to companies of differences between US and IASC accounting standards. Minutes of meeting, Financial Accounting Standards Advisory Council, 24 July 1990 (supplied by the FASB).
211. Interview with Richard Breeden, 12 November 2004.
212. See Liesel Knorr, 'IASC and FASB Speak with One Voice on EPS', *Accountancy* (International edition), 119/1244 (April 1997), 67.
213. 'FASB's Plan for International Activities', *Highlights of Financial Reporting Issues* (Financial Accounting Standards Board, January 1995), 1. For a news report on this revised Plan, see James R. Peterson, 'FASB Supports Global Accounting Standards', *Corporate Accounting International*, 56 (March 1995), 8.

214. Announcement of the [First] European FASB-SEC Financial Reporting Conference, 8–9 April 1999, Centre for Financial Studies, University of Frankfurt, Germany (available at: http://www.ifk-cfs.de/English/content/veranstaltungen/data/19990408Europe.htm).
215. This much heavier weighting on the first focus was made evident in the FASB's own report on the conference. See 'FASB/SEC Hold Joint European Conference', *FASB Status Report*, no. 313 (18 May 1999), 2.
216. Interview with Edmund Jenkins, 7 June 2005.
217. Interviews with Edmund Jenkins, 7 June 2005, with Jim Leisenring, 16 August 2004, and with Gerhard Mueller, 10 August 2004.
218. This section benefited considerably from an interview with Randolph Andersen, 3 November 2005.
219. See Peter Walton, 'There's More to It Than Just Lending $20bn', an interview with Randolph A. Andersen, *Accounting & Business*, April 1998, 11–12, 16. Except where noted, much of this section is based on this article. Also see Cairns, *International Accounting Standards Survey 2000*, 56–7.
220. Randolph A. Andersen, Preface to Hennie van Greuning and Marius Koen, *International Accounting Standards, A Practical Guide* (The World Bank, 1998), v.
221. The World Bank, *Financial Accounting, Reporting, and Auditing Handbook* (The World Bank, January 1995), 7.
222. See Peter Walton, 'The IASC to Look at Developing Countries, *World Accounting Report*, 2/1 (February 1999), 15.
223. 'Declaration of G7 Finance Ministers and Central Bank Governors', 30 October 1998 (available at: http://www.fsforum.org/attachments/Declaration-G7financeministers_centrabank30_10_98.pdf).
224. IASC board meeting of 9–13 November 1998, chairman's introduction.
225. Press release 'Third Meeting of the FSF (Singapore, 25–6 March 2000)' (available at: http://www.fsforum.org/press/press_releases_31.html).
226. *Report to G7 Finance Ministers and Central Bank Governors on International Accounting Standards* (Basel: Basel Committee on Banking Supervision, April 2000), paragraph 26.
227. For an extensive study on the G4+1, see Donna L. Street, *Inside G4+1: The Working Group's Role in the Evolution of the International Accounting Standard Setting Process* (London: The Institute of Chartered Accountants in England and Wales, 2005). Also see Dennis R. Beresford, 'G4+1: A Newcomer on the International Scene', *The CPA Journal*, March 2000, 14–19.
228. See 'FASB Hosts Meeting of World Standard Setters', *FASB Status Report*, no. 237 (30 November 1992), 2–3, and 'Meeting of World Standard Setters', *IASC Insight*, March 1993, 8–11.
229. For reports on the conference, see 'Standard-setters Strive for Unified Purpose', *World Accounting Report*, December 1993/January 1994, 2–4, and 'London Conference of Standard Setting Bodies—What is the Role of Future Events in Financial Reporting?' *IASC Insight*, December 1993, 6–7. The paper was jointly published by the four countries' standard-setting bodies and the IASC in 1994 under the title, *Future Events: A Conceptual Study of their Significance for Recognition and Measurement*.
230. Memorandum from L. Todd Johnson to the authors, dated 12 January 2004.
231. See 'G4 Seeks to Influence Standards', *The Accountant*, issue 5908 (May 1996), 11, and 'G Force on IASC', *World Accounting Report*, May 1996, 1.

232. Interview with Edmund Jenkins, 7 June 2005.
233. Paul Cherry views the G4+1 as having a huge impact on the work of the IASC board. Memorandum from Paul Cherry to the authors, dated 8 October 2004.
234. Interviews with Tatsumi Yamada, 5 July 2004, with Etsuo Sawa, 5 July 2004, and with Christopher Nobes, 13 January 2005.
235. IASC's *Annual Review 1998*, 6.
236. 'Report on Activities from Early January 1998 to End May 1998', IASC Advisory Council meeting of July 1998, agenda paper 2A.
237. Warren McGregor, 'An Insider's View of the Current State and Future Direction of International Accounting Standard Setting', *Accounting Horizons*, 13/2 (June 1999), 165.
238. The IASC's participation in G4+1 meetings was evidently resented by some members of IASC board delegations. Interview with Jim Leisenring, 16 August 2004. Also, interview with Bernd-Joachim Menn, 18 August 2004.
239. See David Cairns, 'A Louder Voice for Europe', *World Accounting Report*, February 1998, 2, and 'G4+1 Gets a Rival', *Accountancy* (international edition), 121/1263 (January 1998), 8. The content of much of this section is drawn from an interview with Ruud Vergoossen (NIVRA technical director), 22 June 2005.
240. Letter from Cees Dubbeld to European members and technical advisers of the IASC board, no date [April 1996], NIVRA archive, file 'Vaktechiek/IASC board meetings'.
241. The position paper was *Management's Analysis of the Business*, Focus 3 (Amsterdam: Koninklijk NIVRA, 2000).

NOTES TO CHAPTER 13

1. Much of the rendering of the deliberations and negotiations in this chapter is based on the authors' interviews with the following principals: Georges Barthès de Ruyter, John Carchrae, Bryan Carsberg, Paul Cherry, Peter Clark, Anthony Cope, Michael Crooch, David Damant, Philippe Danjou, Howard Davies, Stig Enevoldsen, James Gaa, Gilbert Gélard, Ian Hammond, Frank Harding, Sigvard Heurlin, Kazuo Hiramatsu, Thomas Jones, Jan Klaassen, Arthur Levitt, Erik Mamelund, Jacques Manardo, Patricia McConnell, Warren McGregor, Jules Muis, Christopher Nobes, David Ruder, Rolf Rundfelt, Etsuo Sawa, Harry Schmid, Michael Sharpe, Ken Spencer, Angus Thomson, Mary Tokar, Lynn Turner, David Tweedie, Karel Van Hulle, Edward Waitzer, Allister Wilson, and Tatsumi Yamada. Except in a few instances, these interviews will not be cited as support for the developments and views discussed below. In addition, more than a dozen of these interviewees commented on an early draft of this chapter. The authors are grateful to Tony Cope, David Ruder, and Jacques Manardo, as well as to Peter Clark, for providing useful documents and notes in support of this chapter.
2. 'Paper from the Secretary-General', IASC Advisory Council meeting of 31 January 1996, agenda paper 3. The next two quotations are also from this paper.
3. Interview with Bryan Carsberg, 14 January 2005.
4. Interview with Bryan Carsberg, 14 January 2005.
5. Interview with Thomas Jones, 13 January 2005.
6. See Jim Kelly, 'UK Aims to Influence Search for Global Accounting Code', *Financial Times*, 22 April 1996; and 'G Force on IASC', *World Accounting Report*, May 1996, 1.
7. IASC board meeting of 23–8 September 1996, minute 2(c).
8. IASC board meeting of 23–8 September 1996, minute 2(c).

9. IASC board meeting of 23–8 September 1996, minute 2(c).
10. Interview with Peter Clark, 15 October 2004. As will be seen, Clark staffed the working party until December 1998.
11. Letter from Carsberg to Wyatt, dated 7 October 1996, and letter from Wyatt to Carsberg, dated 18 October 1996, IASC archive, Strategy Working Party file.
12. IASC executive committee meeting of 5–8 January 1997, minute 7.
13. 'Strategy Working Party', *IASC Insight*, June 1997, 3.
14. For his views, see Edward J. Waitzer, 'Strategic Tasks the IASC has to Tackle', *Accountancy* (international edition), 120/1251 (November 1997), 77, where he expresses sympathy for a bicameral structure. In Edward Waitzer, 'What Should IASC Look Like After 1998?' *IASC Insight*, December 1997, 10, he writes that 'The Working Party believes that the most vital challenge is to engage national standard setters more directly in IASC's process and, at the same time, to draw in other constituents who, to date, have not been active contributors to the process'.
15. A review of the evolution of the working party's thinking, based on published reports, may be found in Donna L. Street, *Inside G4+1: The Working Group's Role in the Evolution of the International Accounting Standard Setting Process* (London: The Institute of Chartered Accountants in England and Wales, 2005), 67–80.
16. No official minutes were recorded for this meeting. David Ruder and Tony Cope separately took notes of the meeting and have furnished them to the authors.
17. 'Issues for the Strategy Working Party', Strategy Working Party (SWP) meeting of 21–2 July 1997, agenda paper 3, IASC archive, Strategy Working Party file. The quotations in the next two paragraphs are taken from this source.
18. David Cairns, 'G4+1—First Open Meeting', *World Accounting Report*, April 1997, 15.
19. 'Shaping IASC for the Future: A Discussion Paper Issued by the Strategy Working Party of the International Accounting Standards Committee', draft dated 8 September 1997, IASC archive, 'Strategy' file (electronic). Paragraph references in this and the next paragraph are to this draft.
20. Memorandum from Carsberg to members of the SWP, dated 20 August 1997 (in the authors' files). He mentioned in the memorandum that some members of the working party, who were members of the G4+1 (Carsberg, Cope, and Tweedie), would be in Norwalk at the time of the meeting anyway.
21. 'IASC Strategy Working Party—Notes of Meeting with National Standard Setters (Australia, Canada, New Zealand, UK, USA), 25 September 1997, at the Financial Accounting Standards Board, Norwalk, USA', IASC archive, Strategy Working Party file. The accountancy press reported the meeting. See 'G4 Pledge Support for the IASC', *Accountancy* (international edition), 120/1251 (November 1997), 9, and 'A New IASC', *World Accounting Report*, October 1997, 4.
22. 'IASC Strategy Working Party—Notes of Second Meeting, 26 September 1997, Norwalk, USA', IASC archive, Strategy Working Party file.
23. 'Shaping IASC for the Future: A Discussion Paper Issued by the Strategy Working Party of the International Accounting Standards Committee', draft dated 17 October 1997, IASC archive, 'Strategy' file (electronic). Paragraph references in this and the next two paragraphs are to this draft.
24. The point that 'convergence' was taking precedence over 'harmonisation' was also noted by Tony Cope. See Memorandum from Anthony Cope to [FASB] Board, Lucas, Seidman, Bloomer, dated 18 November 1997 (in the authors' files).

25. *Recommendations on Shaping IASC for the Future, A Report of the International Accounting Standards Committee's Strategy Working Party: Recommendations to the IASC Board* (November 1999), paragraph 80.
26. 'Shaping IASC for the Future: A Discussion Paper Issued by the Strategy Working Party of the International Accounting Standards Committee', draft dated 17 November 1997, AP 1/1998 paper 28. Paragraph references in this paragraph are to this draft.
27. Covering memorandum from Carsberg to members of SWP, dated 17 November 1997, IASC archive, Strategy Working Party file.
28. Chairman Waitzer complained that early versions of the draft 'were leaked last January and there was fairly vigorous resistance'. See 'Balancing Powers' [interview with Waitzer], *The Accountant*, issue 5942 (January 1999), 12.
29. Stig Enevoldsen, in 'Big Talk', *Accountancy* (international edition), 121/1254 (February 1998), 26.
30. IASC Advisory Council meeting of 8 January 1998, minute 7.
31. Memorandum from Anthony Cope to FAF Trustees, dated 22 January 1998 (in the authors' files); IASC Consultative Group meeting of 9–10 January 1998, minute 2.
32. Memorandum from Anthony Cope to FAF Trustees, dated 22 January 1998 (in the authors' files).
33. Memorandum from Anthony Cope to FAF Trustees, dated 22 January 1998 (in the authors' files). For a recitation of the points made at the meeting, see IASC board meeting of 12–16 January 1998, minute 15.
34. Christopher Nobes, 'IASC's Brave New World', *Accounting & Business*, 1/2 (March 1998), 23.
35. Jan Klaassen, in 'Big Talk', 26.
36. Peter Zurbrügg, in 'Big Talk', 26.
37. Stig Enevoldsen, in 'Big Talk', 26.
38. David Tweedie, in 'Big Talk', 26.
39. David Tweedie, in 'Major Issues Conference: Securities Regulation in the Global Internet Economy', sponsored by the Securities and Exchange Commission Historical Society in cooperation with the United States Securities and Exchange Commission with the support of Northwestern University Law School, held in Washington on 15 November 2001, p. 133 (available at: http://www.sechistorical.org/collection/papers/2000/2001_1115_SECH_Conf.PDF).
40. Warren McGregor, 'An Insider's View of the Current State and Future Direction of International Accounting Standard Setting', *Accounting Horizons*, 13/2 (June 1999), 162.
41. IASC board meeting of 12–16 January 1998, minute 15.
42. 'Row Erupts over IASC Restructuring Plan', *The Accountant*, 5930 (February 1998), 5.
43. 'Row Erupts over IASC Restructuring Plan', 5; also see 'Setting the Standard', an interview with Stig Enevoldsen, *The Accountant*, 5930 (February 1998), 16.
44. 'Board's Strategy Crisis', *Accountancy* (international edition), 121/1254 (February 1998), 8. The quotations and attributions in this paragraph were taken from this article.
45. 'Sparring with a World Heavyweight' [interview with Jim Leisenring], *Accountancy* (international edition), 121/1256 (April 1998), 20.
46. IASC executive committee meeting of 19 April 1998, minute 8.
47. IASC Advisory Council meeting of 14 July 1998, minute 6.

48. David Cairns, 'IASC, G4+1 and US Congress', *World Accounting Report*, October 1997, 4.
49. McGregor, 'An Insider's View of the Current State and Future Direction of International Accounting Standard Setting', 167. Also see 'G4's Warning to IASC', *Accountancy* (international edition), 122/1264 (December 1998), 9.
50. As noted above, Werner Seifert and Peter Sjöstrand had stopped attending after the first meeting in July 1997. Most of the contents of this section are drawn from 'IASC Strategy Working Party, Notes of Third Meeting, 18 January 1998, London', IASC archive, Strategy Working Party file. A memorandum on the meeting from Tony Cope to the FAF trustees, dated 22 January 1998 (in the authors' files), agreed in substance with the official notes.
51. The plan was to publish the discussion paper 'early in the New Year'. See Waitzer, 'What Should IASC Look Like After 1998?'
52. Letter from Jacques Manardo to Carsberg and Clark, dated 12 January 1998, IASC archive, Strategy Working Party file. Quotations in this paragraph were taken from the memorandum attached to the letter.
53. Memorandum from Anthony Cope to [FASB] Board, Lucas, Ruder, dated 25 March 1998 (in the authors' files).
54. 'Shaping IASC for the Future: A Discussion Paper Issued by the Strategy Working Party of the International Accounting Standards Committee', draft dated 20 March 1998', IASC archive, 'Strategy' file (electronic). Paragraph references in this and the next paragraph are to this draft.
55. Memorandum from Anthony Cope to [FASB] Board, Lucas, Ruder, dated 25 March 1998 (in the authors' files).
56. 'IASC Strategy Working Party, Notes of Fourth Meeting, 3 April 1998, New York', IASC archive, Strategy Working Party file. Quotations in this paragraph were taken from these notes.
57. Tony Cope prepared handwritten notes during the meeting (in the authors' files).
58. *Shaping IASC for the Future: A Discussion Paper Issued for Comment by the Strategy Working Party of the International Accounting Standards Committee* (December 1998). (Available at: http://www.iasb.org/about/history_restructure.asp). Paragraph references in the next several paragraphs refer to this discussion paper.
59. Chris Nobes, 'Compromise at IASC: The Shape of Things to Come?' *Accounting & Business*, 2/2 (February 1999), 48.
60. See the summaries of comment letters in AP 6/1999 papers 27, 28, and 28A. Observations about numbers of respondents supporting particular positions are based on these summaries. The comment letters referred to in this section are letters to Bryan Carsberg from Ed Jenkins and Manuel H. Johnson (FASB/Financial Accounting Foundation), dated 10 March 1999; Dirk Hudig (UNICE), 13 April; Bryce Denison (G100—Australia), 12 April; Michael Butcher (UK ASB), 22 April; Basel Committee on Banking Supervision, 26 April; Arnold Knechtle and Jan Attlesander (Federation of Swiss Industrial Holding Companies), 28 April; John Mogg (European Commission), 28 April; Ken Spencer (Australian Accounting Standards Board), 29 April; Michel Prada (IOSCO Technical Committee), 30 April; David Perry (ICAEW), 30 April; Rosemary Thorne (The Hundred Group—UK); Lynn E. Turner (SEC staff), 14 May; Dominique Ledouble and Michel Leclerq (Ordre des Experts Comptables/CNCC), 19 May; Susan Koski-Grafer (FEI), 21 May; and Ernst & Young LLP (United States), 28 May 1999. IASC archive, 'Strategy' file (electronic).

61. See responses by the ICAEW, IOSCO's Technical Committee, the Basel Committee, Ernst & Young (United States), and several companies and business organizations.
62. The other three respondents who saw no role for the Board in approving standards were the Malaysian Securities Commission, the Malaysian Accounting Standards Board, and the Arab Society of Certified Accountants.
63. For a discussion of the FASB's letter, see James R. Peterson, 'FASB Pulls Apart IASC Restructuring Proposals', *The Accountant*, 5944 (March 1999), 1, 3.
64. *International Accounting Standard Setting: A Vision for the Future* (Norwalk CT: FASB, 1999), appendix C.
65. *International Accounting Standard Setting: A Vision for the Future*, 7. See also Christopher Nobes, 'Strategy Wars: The Future of IASC', *Accounting & Business*, 3/1 (January 2000), 11.
66. Also see Karel Van Hulle, 'Shaping IASC for the Future', *World Accounting Report*, 2/6 (July 1999), 8–9.
67. IASC Advisory Council meeting of 9 March 1999, minute 6.
68. Interview with Stephen D. Eccles, 5 January 2005.
69. IASC executive committee meeting of 15 March 1999.
70. IASC board meeting of 16–19 March 1999, minute 10. The official minutes reported nothing of what was discussed, but Tony Cope, the FASB observer at board meetings, took extensive notes.
71. This quotation was recorded by Cope in his notes. Gélard has confirmed its accuracy and has permitted the attribution to him.
72. This quotation was recorded by Cope in his notes. Crooch has confirmed its accuracy and has permitted the attribution to him.
73. IASC executive committee meeting of 28 June 1999, minute 7.
74. 'A Note on the Proposals of the Strategy Working Party', by Stig Enevoldsen and Bryan Carsberg', IASC executive committee meeting of June 1999, agenda paper II.
75. IASC executive committee meeting of 28 June 1999, minute 7.
76. It is not known why the European Commission, as an observer delegation, was entitled to vote on the question. See SWPVOTE.doc, IASC archive, June/July 1999 board meeting file (electronic).
77. This section is based on Tony Cope's notes taken during the board meeting. For a résumé of the points discussed during the meeting, see IASC board meeting of 28 June–2 July 1999, minute 1.
78. Chris Nobes, 'The Beginning of the End of Conventional Accounting', *Accounting & Business*, 2/8 (September 1999), 50.
79. This rendering of the discussions during the meeting is based on notes taken by Jacques Manardo at the meeting as well as on a memo from Anthony Cope to the authors, dated 27 January 2006. The memo was in turn based on notes he had taken during the meeting. No official notes or minutes were taken at the meeting. For Carsberg's report on the developments in Warsaw, including the meeting of the working party, see 'IASC's Strategy', *IASC Insight*, October 1999, 6–7.
80. The basis for this rendering is 'IASC Strategy Working Party—Draft Report Outline Reflecting Discussions at the Warsaw Meeting', undated, and a draft 'Report on Shaping IASC for the Future', undated, both in IASC archive, 'Strategy' file (electronic).
81. Memorandum from Bryan Carsberg to the members of the Strategy Working Party, dated 16 August 1999 (in the authors' files).

82. Notes by Tony Cope of a conference call on 19 July 1999. In a communication dated 20 February 2006, to the authors, Turner recalls that he mentioned only a small board of twelve members.
83. Notes by Tony Cope of a meeting on 9 August 1999.
84. Street, *Inside G4+1: The Working Group's Role in the Evolution of the International Accounting Standard Setting Process*, 76.
85. Interviews with Mary Tokar, 18 May 2004, and with Lynn E. Turner, 19 November 2004.
86. Letter from Lynn E. Turner to Ed Waitzer, dated 21 September 1999, in the authors' files.
87. See Paul B. W. Miller, Rodney J. Redding, and Paul R. Bahnson, *The FASB: The People, the Process, and the Politics* (Burr Ridge, IL: Irwin/McGraw-Hill, 1998), 186–92.
88. Letter from John F. Mogg to Sir Bryan Carsberg, dated 20 September 1999 (in the authors' files).
89. Letter from Karel Van Hulle to Stig Enevoldsen, dated 26 July 1999 (in the authors' files).
90. In 1976, Walter Schuetze returned to Peat, Marwick, Mitchell & Co., and in 1987 Arthur Wyatt returned to Arthur Andersen & Co.
91. Letter from Van Hulle to Enevoldsen, dated 26 July 1999 (in the authors' files).
92. Letter from Prada to Waitzer, dated 21 September 1999 (in the authors' files).
93. This rendering of the discussions during the meeting is based on notes taken during the meeting by Anthony Cope, as well as on official notes taken during the meeting by Sue Harding, IASC archive, 'Strategy' file (electronic). The agreements reached at the meeting were confirmed in the draft discussion paper produced by the IASC secretariat in October, entitled 'Draft Report on Shaping IASC for the Future'.
94. Interview with Bryan Carsberg, 14 January 2005.
95. The rendering of this discussion is based on notes taken during the conference call by Anthony Cope.
96. The statement was styled as a draft communication to the IFAC Council and was entitled, 'The Reorganisation of IASC: A Note to IFAC Council, by Stig Enevoldsen and Bryan Carsberg', dated 22 October 1999 (in the authors' files).
97. Email message from Sharpe to Enevoldsen and Carsberg, dated 25 October 1999 (in the authors' files).
98. Email from Cope to Carsberg, dated 22 October 1999, IASC archive, 'Strategy' file (electronic).
99. 'The Reorganisation of IASC—A Note from the Chairman and Secretary-General', AP 11/1999 paper 12.
100. See AP 11/1999 paper 1.
101. Memorandum from Edward Waitzer to the SWP, dated 11 November 1999, IASC archive, 'Strategy' file (electronic).
102. IASC board meeting of 15–19 November 1999, minute 10.
103. Minutes of meeting, IFAC Council, Cape Town, 4/5 November 1999, minute 4 (supplied by IFAC). These were, of course, the proposals set out in Carsberg's communication sent to the Council.
104. IASC executive committee meeting of 14–15 November 1999, minute 2.
105. The members of the executive committee were, in addition to Chairman Enevoldsen, Michael Crooch (United States), David Damant (financial analysts), Gilbert Gélard (France), Thomas Jones (financial executives, vice-chairman), Jan Klaassen

(the Netherlands), Patricia McConnell (financial analysts, vice-chairman), and Peter Wilmot (South Africa).
106. Crooch's notes on 'the deal' were photocopied by Tony Cope (in the authors' files). For a narrative summary of 'the deal', see IASC board meeting of 15–19 November 1999, minute 10.
107. This rendering of the discussions during the meeting is based on notes taken during the meeting by Tony Cope.
108. Nobes, 'Strategy Wars: The Future of IASC', 11.
109. Message sent to the members of the SWP on behalf of Bryan Carsberg, from Susan Harding, dated 22 November 1999, IASC archive, 'Strategy' file (electronic).
110. Enevoldsen did not know the contents of the working party's latest draft.
111. Memorandum from Enevoldsen to the SWP members, dated 25 November 1999, IASC archive, 'Strategy' file (electronic).
112. See Nobes, 'Strategy Wars: The Future of IASC', 11, and 'IASC Agrees Future Structure', *World Accounting Report*, 2/10 (December 1999/January 2000), 2.
113. Interview with Sigvard Heurlin, 31 March 2003.
114. Van Hulle repeated this remark in an interview with a BNA reporter. See Steve Burkholder, 'IASC Resolves to Change Structure; FASB Backs Change "100 Percent"', *BNA Securities Regulation & Law Report*, 31/45 (19 November 1999), 1555.
115. 'Statement of SEC Chief Accountant Lynn E. Turner on IASC Board Decision to Support Restructuring Plan', SEC news release no. 99-152, dated 17 November 1999 (available at: http://www.sec.gov/news/press/pressarchive/1999/99-152.txt).
116. 'Statement of Edmund L. Jenkins, FASB Chairman on the Revised Proposal to Restructure the IASC', dated 17 November 1999 (in the authors' files). Also see Anthony Cope, 'FASB Supports Proposed New Structure for IASC Board', FASB *Status Report*, 320 (27 December 1999), 2–3.
117. 'IASC Board Reaches Momentous Decision on its Future Structure', IASC press release, dated 19 November 1999 (available at: http://www.iasb.org/uploaded_files/documents/8_210_99pr1119.pdf). See Burkholder, 'IASC Resolves to Change Structure; FASB Backs Change "100 Percent"', 1554–5, and 'Strategy Working Party', *IASC Update*, November 1999, 1.
118. Message to the members of the SWP on behalf of Bryan Carsberg, from Susan Harding, dated 22 November 1999, IASC archive, 'Strategy' file (electronic).
119. The emails are reproduced in the 'Strategy' file (electronic), IASC archive.
120. 'IASC's Strategy Working Party Issues Report to the IASC Board "Recommendations on Shaping IASC for the Future"', IASC press release, dated 6 December 1999, IASC archive, 'Strategy' file (electronic) (available at: http://www.iasb.org/uploaded_files/documents/8_210_swp_rep.pdf).
121. Communication from Karel Van Hulle to the authors, dated 1 March 2006.
122. Interview with Bryan Carsberg, 14 January 2005.
123. IASC board meeting of 13–16 December 1999, minute 5, and notes taken during the meeting by Tony Cope. See 'New Structure for a New Century', *IASC Insight*, December 1999, 1–3.
124. IASC board meeting of 13–16 December 1999, minute 11.
125. 'Shaping IASC for the Future: IASC Nominating Committee Selects Initial Trustees of Restructured IASC', IASC press release, dated 22 May 2000 (available at: http://www.iasb.org/uploaded_files/documents/8_210_2000pr25.pdf). See 'Key Stages Accomplished', *IASC Insight*, June 2000, 8.

126. 'US Influence Weighs Heavy in IASC Trustee Choice', *The Accountant*, 5959 (June 2000), 8.
127. Howard Davies, remarks at IFAC 2000 Conference, Edinburgh, 25 May 2000 (available at: http://www.fsa.gov.uk/Pages/Library/Communication/Speeches/2000/sp48.shtml).
128. 'Funding the Restructured IASC', *IASC Insight*, March 2000, 8.
129. Final report, Fund Raising Feasibility and Planning Study, rendered by Community Counselling Service Ltd, April 2000, 7 (in the authors' files).
130. 'Shaping IASC for the Future: IASC Board Approves New Constitution', IASC press release, dated 24 May 2000 (available at: http://www.iasb.org/uploaded_files/documents/8_210,2000). See IASC board meeting of 13–17 March 2000, minute 1. For a report on the meeting, see Christopher Nobes, 'Work Continues at the Old IASC While the New IASC Takes Shape', *Accounting & Business*, 3/4 (April 2000), 13–14.
131. 'IASC Constitution', *IASC Update*, undated (probably April 2000), 1.
132. 'Shaping IASC for the Future: IASC Members Approve Restructuring', IASC press release, dated 24 May 2000 (available at: http://www.iasb.org/docs/press/2000pr16.pdf).
133. Interviews with Arthur Levitt, 20 April 2005, with Lynn Turner, 19 November 2004, with Edmund Jenkins, 7 June 2005, and with Howard Davies, 10 February 2006.
134. 'First Meeting of IAS Trustees and Appointment of New IASC Board Chair', IASC press release, dated 29 June 2000 (available at: http://www.iasb.org./uploaded_files/documents/8_210_2000pr18.pdf). See 'IASC Chairman Named', *World Accounting Report*, 3/7 (September 2000), 3; 'Tweedie to Chair IASC', *Accountancy*, 126/1284 (August 2000), 8; Andrew Bolgor, 'New Role for Accounts Watchdog', *Financial Times*, 30 June 2000, 25; and 'Cabinetmaking', *IASC Insight*, September 2000, 7.
135. 'IASC Trustees Announce New Standard-Setting Board to Reach Goal of Global Accounting Standards', IASC press release, dated 25 January 2001 (available at: http://www.iasb.org/uploaded_files/documents/8_210_2001pr01.pdf).
136. See Deloitte's IAS PLUS Website, 12 February 2001 (available at: http://www.iasplus.com/pastnews/2001feb.htm).

Index

Abbott, Hilary 557
Abdulla, Khalid Amin 530
Abrahams, B. E. 627
absorption costing 99
Abu-Ghazaleh, Talal 223, 289, 290, 512, 520
Accountants International Study Group (AISG) 6, 22, 26–36, 43–4, 47–55, 122
  disbandment 36, 57–8
  formation 29–30
  motivations for 30–1
  work of 31–6
    Inventories Booklet 31–2
    publications 32
Accounting and Auditing Approaches to Inventories in Three Nations 31–2
accounting policies
  changes in *see* IAS 8
  disclosure of *see* IAS 1
Accounting Principles Board (APB), US 542
  APB Opinion No. 8 (*Accounting for the Costs of Pension Plans*) 129
  APB Opinion No. 9 (*Reporting the Results of Operations*) 551
  APB Opinion No. 11 (*Accounting for Income Taxes*) 116, 358, 619
  APB Opinion No. 16 (*Business Combinations*) 131, 136, 317
  APB Opinion No. 17 (*Intangible Assets*) 136, 317, 381
  APB Opinion No. 20 (*Accounting Changes*) 551
  APB Opinion No. 28 (*Interim Financial Reporting*) 386
  APB Opinion No. 29 (*Accounting for Nonmonetary Transactions*) 131
accounting standards 2
  calls for uniformity 23–5
  national programmes 27–9
  see also International Accounting Standards (IAS)
Accounting Standards Board (AcSB), Canada 393–4
Accounting Standards Board (ASB), UK 83, 236, 239, 386, 417, 423, 443, 623
  cooperation with IASC 355, 378, 388–9
  restructuring of IASC 429, 469
  technical work 360–1, 381–2, 388, 392, 396, 634
Accounting Standards Committee (ASC), UK 66, 68–9, 83, 102, 109, 113, 116, 127–8, 152–4, 269, 360, 378, 381, 578
Accounting Standards Steering Committee (ASSC), UK 45, 46, 99–100, 150, 154
Adams, John W. 34, 57, 540
Agars, Peter 69
agriculture *see* IAS 41
Akins, E. Peter 75
Alaeddin, Fouad 238, 281
Aldeweireldt, E. 559
Alexander, David 638
Allimant, J. 633
Allvey, D. 633
American Institute of Certified Public Accountants (AICPA) 23–4, 25–6, 49, 66, 74, 155, 161, 358, 542
  Accounting Research Bulletins 28
  reactions to IASC proposal 46
  responses to IASC's surveys 157
Amsterdam Stock Exchange 145, 173
Andersen, Clifford V. 530
Andersen, Randolph 247, 402, 441–2, 628, 647
Anderson, Leslie 220
Andrews, David 555
APB Opinions *see* Accounting Principles Board (APB), US
Appelo, H. H. A. 558
Arab Society of Certified Accountants 223, 652
Arai, Kiyomitsu 607, 645
Archer, Gerry 622
Armstrong, Marshall S. 158–9, 162
Argentina 180, 288, 570
Arthuis, Jean 410
Arthur Andersen & Co. 51, 63, 74, 156, 160–1, 213, 410, 449, 497, 530, 551, 580, 602, 653
Arthur Young & Company 68, 75, 588
Ashby, D. 630
Asociación Interamericana de Contabilidad 23
assets 258–9
associate companies *see* IAS 28
associate members *see* International Accounting Standards Committee
Association for Investment Management and Research (AIMR) 356, 385, 393–4
Association of Chartered Certified Accountants 49, 66, 541

Atkinson, J. A. 633
auditing standards 23–6, 28–9, 51, 104–5, 301–4, 315, 331, 344–5, 441
Australia
  delegation to the IASC 64–5, 66–7, 69–70, 506
  impact of IASC standards 164, 433–5
  national accounting principles 28
Australian Accounting Research Foundation (AARF) 255–6, 364–5, 403, 498, 583
Australian Accounting Standards Board (AASB) 183, 403, 433–5, 467
Australian Society of Accountants 49, 66, 164
Australian Stock Exchange (ASX) 433–4
Austria 22, 23, 133, 428, 557, 642
Auyeung, Pak 570
Azières, Olivier 590

Baetge, Jörg 588, 634, 635, 636
Bahnson, Paul R. 653
Bailey, P. 559
Baker, Susan 545, 559, 567, 575
balance sheet approach 13, 263–4, 359, 387, 396, 404
Baldi, A. 628
Ball, Steve 635
Balmford, John 69
Banerjee, Bhabatosh 569
Bankmann, Jörg 553
banks
  discussion paper 123–5
  financial statements project 84, 105, 406–7
  see also IAS 30
Barajas Palomo, Jorge 537, 541
Barings Bank 370
Barthès de Ruyter, Georges 12, 69, 86, 213, 409–10, 498, 559, 580, 587, 620
  financial instruments project and 362
  financing issues 208, 242, 244
  IOSCO relations 303
  Strategy Working Party involvement 449
  work on IAS 25 140
Barth, Mary 497
Basel Committee 105, 123–4, 230–2, 291, 306, 362, 406, 442–3
  steering committee participation 597, 623, 634, 635
base stock method 98–9
BASF 314
Bastien, Francis 261, 586
Batzer, R. Kirk 34
Baumann, Karl-Hermann 345, 494
Bavishi, Vinod 134, 557
Bayer 227, 314, 412, 413, 610
Begy, Chris 635
Behr, Giorgio 638
Belgium 21, 23, 79, 113, 148, 190, 308, 642

Benelux Customs Union 21
Benson, Sir Henry 1, 6, 65, 180, 181–2, 499, 538, 541, 560
  Accountants International Study Group and 26–7, 29–34, 43–4, 48
  compliance issues 145–7
  as IASC chairman 61, 63
  IASC formation 50, 51, 54, 56, 57
  motivation for 44–6
  interest in auditing standards 105
  International Working Party and 37–8
  opposition to integration with IFAC 196–7
  policy issues 104, 159
  promotion of IASC standards 154, 182, 184, 203
  publications 532, 533, 535, 536, 539, 546, 549, 573, 576
  reaction to UN involvement 189
  role in drafting of standards 93–6, 101
  UEC involvement 40–2
Bentsen, Lloyd 315
Beresford, Dennis R. 68, 255, 262, 283, 338, 439–40, 582, 586, 594
Berg, Kenneth B. 531
Bernheim, Yves 555, 620
Bertol, Gillian 236, 240
'best endeavours' undertaking 52–3, 74, 85, 88, 129, 130, 144–6, 152, 155, 169–70, 175, 203, 285
Béthoux, Raymond 358, 558
Biancheri, Carlo 308
Biener, Herbert 183, 229, 308, 412–13, 581, 589, 592, 594, 605, 607, 636, 637, 641
biological assets see IAS 41
Bisgay, Louis 590
Bishop, John 69, 207, 208, 542, 558, 580
  work on IAS 22 136
Bishop Working Party 206–9, 242, 244, 249, 349
Bloomer, Carrie 614
Bloxsome, John R. 75–6
Bocqueraz, Claude 536
Boersema, John M. 630
Bohlin, C. E. 619
Bolivia 180, 570
Bolkestein, Frits 494, 643
Bonnet-Bernard, Sonia 626
borrowing costs see IAS 23
Bosch, Henry 301, 302, 303
Botswana 178
Boymal, David 69, 70, 237, 620
Braverman, Daniel A. 605
Brazil 139, 180
Breeden, Richard 306–7, 315, 330, 331, 366, 440, 601, 605, 610, 613
  endorsement of IASC standards 313, 316
Breloer, B. J. 634

Brennan, W. John 75, 128, 569
Brindle, Ian 586
Broken Hill Proprietary Company (BHP) 356, 433
Bromwich, Michael 275
Brooking, Doug 220, 384, 568, 627, 646
Brown, C. I. 555
Brown, David 478, 479
Brown, Gordon 340–1
Brown, Philip 434, 644, 645
Brown, Sarah E. 603
Bruce, Robert 556, 580, 624
Bruns, Hans-Georg 497
Buckley, Noel 548
Bunting, J. Pearce 565
Burgess, Dick 64, 66
Burggraaff, Hans 7, 9, 63, 67, 78, 220, 498, 549, 552, 558, 559, 571, 573, 577, 579
  constitutional changes and 88
  Consultative Group formation and 204, 205
  guest attendance at board meetings and 82
  IASC strategy and 104, 143, 191
  IFAC relations 199, 200–2
  OECD relations 192
  promotion of IASC standards 173, 183, 184
Burton, John C. 157–8, 160
Business Accounting Deliberation Council (BADC), Japan 67, 171, 214, 436, 437
business combinations project 406
  see also IAS 22

Cairns, David 7, 12, 76, 233, 417, 542, 545, 557, 559, 579, 580, 584, 587, 596, 601, 602, 607, 618
  agriculture project and 402
  compliance issues 156, 174, 182, 345
  core standards and 320–1
  executive committee involvement 238
  Framework project 259–60
  funding issues 239, 240–6
  IFAC relations 207
  intangible assets project and 378–9
  IOSCO relations 294, 295–8, 302, 307, 316, 323–5, 328
  promotion of IASC standards 183, 184–5
  publications 543, 555, 562, 564, 568, 569, 582, 584, 587, 588, 589, 596, 597, 602, 607, 608, 609, 616, 621, 622, 626, 635, 636, 637, 638, 648, 649, 651
  technical work involvement 354
    Comparability project 270–1, 275, 280
    Improvements project 264, 280, 282, 286, 310
    planning 349
Cameron, K. 634

Camfferman, Kees 532, 550, 568, 577, 637
Campala, Alfonso 65
Campbell, L. G. 148–9, 172, 180, 560, 567, 570
Canada
  delegation to the IASC 65, 66, 69, 506–7
  impact of IASC standards 149, 165–6, 181, 435–6
  compliance 7, 145
  national programmes for accounting principles 28
  SEC's MJDS arrangement 312–13
Canadian Institute of Chartered Accountants (CICA) 3, 7, 25, 28, 29, 30, 33, 49, 52, 63, 165–6, 260, 355, 435
  financial instruments project and 362, 622
  Task Force on Standard Setting (TFOSS) 435–6
Capelo, F. 559
Carchrae, John 229, 236, 362, 615, 616, 620, 621, 622, 623, 648
Cardon, Patrice 69
Carey, John L. 25–6, 37, 531, 534
Carnall, Wayne 605
Carrel, Philip 538, 546
Carsberg, Sir Bryan 12, 15, 233–5, 426, 583, 612, 623, 641
  Consultative Group and 250–1
  FASB's comparative study and 339
  financial instruments project and 372, 373, 374, 375, 376
  funding issues 248, 249
  G4+1 involvement 14, 398
  IAS 1 revision and 391, 392
  impairment project and 380, 381
  IOSCO relations 229, 325, 327, 329, 332–4, 335
  SEC relations 343
  Strategy Working Party involvement 447–54, 457, 459–60, 470–8, 481–90, 492
    restructuring 493–4
  technical work and 354
Carscallen, Morley 69, 118, 278, 553
Carter, Guy 588
Carty, James 550, 560, 574
Carvalho, L. Nelson 222, 634
Casey, William J. 563
cash flow statement *see* IAS 7
Cason, Roger 68
Castillon, S. 634
Cearns, Kathryn 630
Central American countries, non-participation 180–1
Certified General Accountants Association of Canada (CGA-Canada) 436, 542, 645

Chakravorty, D. K. 569
Chambers, R. J. 26
Chandler, Roy A. 555
Chaput, Pierre 308
Cheetham, Malcolm 222, 627, 634, 635
Chen, Yugui 634
Chenok, Philip B. 185
Cheok-Huat, Aw 628
Cherry, Paul 270, 279, 298–9, 302, 303, 323, 326–7, 590, 591, 595, 598, 600, 601, 602, 648
  Improvements project involvement 281, 305, 306, 307, 309, 321
  Standing Interpretations Committee involvement 238, 334
Chetkovich, Michael N. 560
Chiang, S. T. 73, 176
Chile 72, 73
China 229, 290, 406, 582
Chinese Institute of Certified Public Accountants (CICPA) 229
Chironna, John F. 66, 67, 237
Chitty, David 597
Choi, Frederick 134, 530, 557, 562
Choo, Khoo Eng 264, 596
Choy, Soon Kway 596, 629
Citicorp/Citigroup 216, 222, 497
Clark, Peter 236, 448, 453, 581, 583, 608, 620, 625, 629, 631, 648
  project manager 354, 450, 619, 632, 633, 634, 649
Cochrane, James 247, 249, 315, 316, 317, 604, 605, 613
Coleman, Robert 147
Comité de la Réglementation Comptable (CRC), France 410–11
Commission des Opérations de Bourse (COB), France 166–9, 229, 294, 479
Commission Saxe 39
Commissione Nazionale per la Società e la Borsa (Consob), Italy 148, 176, 308, 341
compliance issues 7–8, 13–14, 52, 144
  'best endeavours' undertaking 52–3, 85, 88, 144–6
  see also specific countries
comprehensive income 392–3
Conference of Asian and Pacific Accountants 23, 578
Conferencia Interamericana de Contabilidad 23
Congresses of Accountants
  International 22, 37, 61, 74, 531, 579
    1957 (Amsterdam) 23–4
    1962 (New York) 24–5, 37
    1967 (Paris) 37, 49
    1972 (Sydney) 38, 43–5, 54
    1977 (Munich) 84, 189, 196, 198, 202
    1982 (Mexico City) 47, 80, 87
  World 531, 579
    1987 (Tokyo) 206–7
    1992 (Washington DC) 208–9, 243
    1997 (Paris) 453
Conseil National de la Compatibilité (CNC), France 167–9, 410
Consiglio Nazionale dei Dottori Commercialisti, Italy 176
consolidated financial statements 3, 99
  AISG booklet 35
  see also IAS 3; IAS 27
construction contracts *see* IAS 11
Consultative Committee of Accountancy Bodies (CCAB) 66, 151, 543, 578
  response to IASC standards 151–3
contingent assets and liabilities *see* IAS 10; IAS 37
Cook, Allan 9, 75, 554, 557, 569, 575, 577, 579
  banking discussion paper and 125
  consultative group and 205
  financial instruments project and 369
  mutual commitments and 200
  promotion of IASC standards 153, 184
  work on IAS 21 121
Cook, Michael 247
Coopers & Lybrand 61, 68, 70, 72, 75, 215, 281, 299, 307, 308, 316, 385, 436, 602
Cope, Anthony 228, 630, 651, 653
  restructuring of IASC 449, 461, 462, 465, 475, 476, 478, 487, 489
  membership of restructured board 497
Copeland, James E., Jr. 493–4
Cordoliani, Alfred 65, 66, 69, 78, 538
  work on IAS 7 111
core standards *see* International Accounting Standards (IAS)
corporate income taxes
  AISG booklet 35 *see also* IAS 12
Corporation Finance Research Institute (COFRI), Japan 437
Costaguta, R. 620
Cotton, Ronald J. 69–70, 258, 587
Cottrell, Rick G. 71, 257, 264, 568, 585, 587
Coulson, Edmund 270, 295, 298–9, 301, 302, 305, 315, 599, 604, 606
Council for Annual Reporting in Europe (CARE) 420
Council on Annual Reporting, Netherlands 173, 276, 414
Couto, A. A. 586
Cowan, Tom K. 37
Cowell, A. 633
Cowperthwaite, Gordon 197, 199, 201–2, 576

Cox, Charles C. 186, 294–6
Cox, Phillip C. E. 69
CPC International 156, 249
Crooch, Michael 220, 228, 471, 489, 491, 625, 626, 648, 653
Cummings, Joseph 65, 66, 68, 180, 188, 220, 541, 546, 548, 560, 563, 571
  as IASC chairman 7, 58, 61, 63, 104
  promotion of IASC standards 182
  work on IAS 3 100, 101
  work on IAS 8 112
  work on IAS 21 121
Curran, Brigid 235, 286, 433–4, 644
current assets and liabilities see IAS 13
current cost accounting 132, 289, 317 see also IAS 6, IAS 15
Cvetanovic, M. 586
Cyprus 178

Dahodwala, E. S. H. 586
Daimler-Benz 11, 227, 312, 314–16, 328, 330, 412–13
Dalton, H. E. 633
Damant, David C. 73, 205–6, 220, 579, 585, 622, 629, 634, 648, 653
  Framework steering committee involvement 260
  insurance project and 404
  performance reporting issue 393
Dangerfield, A. 623
Danjou, Philippe 566
Dastoor, Dara 569
Davies, Howard 493, 495, 497, 648, 655
Davison, Ian Hay 152, 153, 561
Dawson, J. Michael 69, 260, 261, 587, 588
Day, Peter 590, 626
Debreceny, Roger 635
Dedman, S. 633
deferred tax accounting 35, 116–17, 357 see also IAS 12
Defliese, Philip L. 158–9, 160, 161, 537, 550, 564
de Koning, J. W. 534
Deloittes 68, 71, 74, 149, 215, 236, 449, 460, 494, 606, 655
den Hoed, Jean 220
Denman, John 69, 191, 220, 225–6, 244, 327, 362, 574, 576, 583, 587
Denmark 22, 23, 40, 92, 113, 148, 201, 215, 223, 248, 415–16, 551, 622 see also Nordic Federation of Public Accountants
depreciation see IAS 4; IAS 16; IAS 40
Desmarchelier, Francis 229
Deutsches Rechnungslegungs Standards Committee (DRSC), Germany 345, 413, 479, 494

Deutsche Telekom 329–30
developing countries 189–90, 288–91, 405–6
  agriculture project 402
  hyperinflation 288–9
  impact of IASC standards 182, 441–2
  reporting needs 289–91
de Wael, Jean-Guy 247
Dewar, George D. H. 34, 36, 534
Dieterich, W. 539, 540
Dieye, A. A. 596
d'Illiers, Bertrand 208, 270, 298, 309, 555, 598, 599
direct costing 99
Dirks, John 631
disclosure see IAS 1; IAS 5
discontinuing operations see IAS 35
discounting project 405
diversified companies, AISG booklet 35 see also IAS 14
Dolan, W. J. 555, 597
Donaldson, William 315, 604, 605
Doran, E. T. 627
Dörner, Dietrich 594
Douglas-Mann, Stewart 304
Dove, Robert 609
Drake, M. 135
Dreissig, Eberhard 628
Dubbeld, Cees 619
Dufey, Gunter 620
Dumont, Jean-Luc 69, 270, 587, 618, 635
Dumont, Pierre 633
Dunning, John H. 530
Dupont, Jean 169, 362, 419
Dyckman, Thomas R. 531

E5+2 group 428, 430, 432, 445–6, 644
Eagan, J. 630
earnings per share see IAS 33
Ebling, Paul 588
Eccles, Stephen 246–7, 248–9, 470, 585, 652
economic integration 21–2
Edenhammer, H. 552
Edgar, Graham 551
Eeftink, Egbert 630
Ee, G. 634
Elling, Jens O. 595, 638
Elliott, Stephen 7, 63, 65, 69, 86, 87, 89, 98, 166, 220, 255, 498, 545, 579, 585
  promotion of IASC standards 184, 185–6
  work on IAS 18 133
Elmendorff, Wilhelm 39, 40, 534, 535
Enevoldsen, Stig 15, 213, 215, 216–17, 220, 223, 231, 235, 498, 650
  Advisory Council involvement 247
  executive committee involvement 238

Index 661

IAS 40 and 400–1
Strategy Working Party involvement 449, 457–60, 470–8, 481, 483–90
restructuring of IASC 492, 494, 496–7
Epstein, Barry J. 559
equity method *see* IAS 3; IAS 27
Ernst & Whinney 68, 72, 169
Ernst & Young 72, 330, 652
Eskilson, J. 586
European Accounting Research Foundation 427, 432, 644
European Accounting Study Group 445–6 *see also* E5+2
European Coal and Steel Community (ECSC) 21–2, 38–9
European Commission 4, 5, 122, 147, 174, 330, 409, 578
Accounting Advisory Forum 422–3, 426, 430
accounting harmonization in Europe and 39, 419, 420, 422, 429
endorsement of IASC standards 11, 16–17, 316, 328, 347, 411, 418–32
IASC restructuring and 15, 431, 449, 457, 459, 461, 467–72, 477–81, 483–5, 492, 494, 498
participation in IASC's work 11, 183, 184, 228–9, 232, 238, 251, 268, 275, 281, 353, 356, 369, 401, 419, 426, 445, 474, 652
steering committee membership 593, 599, 626, 628–35
seeking access to US capital markets 425, 428–9, 610
European Economic Community (EEC) 22, 553
accounting harmonization 38–41, 45, 422–6
Directives on Company Law 167, 184–5, 410, 414, 416, 419–20, 422–5, 428–9
compatibility with IAS 411, 415, 426
First Directive 39
Fourth Directive 39, 40, 136, 369, 388, 391
Seventh Directive 39, 99, 136, 267–8
European Free Trade Association 22
Evans, Thomas G. 563, 571
events after balance sheet date *see* IAS 10
extractive industries project 405
Exxon Corporation 156, 249

fair value 13, 14, 131–2, 141, 226, 364–6, 369, 371, 375–7, 382, 392, 396–7, 400–4, 412, 551, 621, 624 *see also* financial instruments

Farstad, N. 586
FAS *see* Financial Accounting Standards Board (FASB), US
Fass, A. 549, 596
Fédération des Experts Comptables Européens (FEE) 57, 232, 369, 404, 420, 427–8, 429–30, 431, 440, 445, 625, 644
Fédération Internationale des Bourses de Valeurs (FIBV) 86, 232, 461–2, 560, 578, 579, 627
endorsement of IASC standards 146–7, 170
Federation of Swiss Industrial Holding Companies 11, 87, 221–2, 238, 251, 340, 357, 386, 389, 427, 458, 467, 581, 634, 635, 651
Fiji 148
Financial Accounting Foundation (FAF) US 447–8, 475, 544, 583
Financial Accounting Standards Advisory Council (FASAC) 205
Financial Accounting Standards Board (FASB), US 4, 6, 11, 16, 214, 439–41, 544
ambivalence towards international standards 11, 162–4
conceptual framework of 587, 588, 619
conflict over IASC's E3 157–61
FAS 2 (*Accounting for Research and Development Costs*) 113
FAS 5 (*Accounting for Contingencies*) 114, 551
FAS 8 (*Accounting for the Translation of Foreign Currency Transactions and Foreign Currency Financial Statements*) 120, 121, 554
FAS 13 (*Accounting for Leases*) 128, 131
FAS 14 (*Financial Reporting for Segments of a Business Enterprise*) 126–7, 394, 555
FAS 33 (*Financial Reporting and Changing Prices*) 109
FAS 34 (*Capitalization of Interest Cost*) 138
FAS 35 (*Accounting and Reporting by Defined Benefit Pension Plans*) 142
FAS 36 (*Disclosure of Pension Information*) 129
FAS 52 121, 123, 554
FAS 87 (*Employers' Accounting for Pensions*) 129, 395–7
FAS 94 (*Consolidation of All Majority-Owned Subsidiaries*) 267
FAS 95 (*Statement of Cash Flows*) 266, 287, 314
FAS 96 (*Accounting for Income Taxes*) 358, 359

FASB (cont.)
  FAS 105 (*Disclosure of Information about Financial Instruments with Off-Balance-Sheet Risk and Financial Instruments with Concentration of Credit Risk*) 366
  FAS 107 (*Disclosures about Fair Value of Financial Instruments*) 366
  FAS 109 (*Accounting for Income Taxes*) 358, 359, 360
  FAS 115 (*Accounting for Certain Investments in Debt and Equity Securities*) 366, 369
  FAS 119 (*Disclosure about Derivative Financial Instruments and Fair Value of Financial Instruments*) 370
  FAS 121 (*Accounting for the Impairment of Long-Lived Assets and for Long-Lived Assets to be Disposed Of*) 381, 382
  FAS 128 (*Earnings per Share*) 385, 440
  FAS 130 (*Reporting Comprehensive Income*) 392
  FAS 133 (*Accounting for Derivative Instruments and Hedging Activities*) 376
  FAS 141 (*Business Combinations*) 406
  financial instruments project and 226, 361, 363, 366, 367, 370–4, 375–6, 630
  Mission Statement 439–40
  origin and operations 6, 542, 555, 583, 591
  on comparative financial statements 546
  on inflation accounting 549
  relations with IASC 161–2, 283, 296, 354–5
    guest/observer attendance at IASC meetings 11, 14, 81, 228–9, 251, 270, 354–5, 419, 422, 633, 634, 635
    members join IASB 497, 498
    questioning of IASC's due process 15, 338–40
  relations with SEC 572, 646
  Statements of Financial Accounting Concepts (SFAC) 256, 260
    SFAC 1 (*Objectives of Financial Reporting by Business Enterprises*) 254
    SFAC 2 (*Qualitative Characteristics of Accounting Information*) 256
    SFAC 3 (*Elements of Financial Statements of Business Enterprises*) 263
  Strategy Working Party involvement
    comments on Discussion Paper 467–70
    consultations 468, 472, 474–6, 481, 482–6
    IASC's Venice meeting 488, 491, 492
    inception of 447–50
    meetings of 454, 457, 459
    run-up to the IASB 494, 497

Financial Accounting Standards Foundation, Japan 437
financial analysts 220
financial executives 220–2
Financial Executives Institute (FEI), US 67, 157–60, 201, 262, 264, 468, 575
financial instruments 356, 361–77
  discussion paper 370–1
  issues 363–7
  see also IAS 32; IAS 39
financial reporting 3, 22
  AISG booklet 35–6
  developing countries 289–91
  surveys 147–9
  see also IAS; IAS 34
Financial Services Agency, Japan 341
Financial Stability Forum 442–3
financial statements, objectives of 254–5, 256–7
Financial Times
  survey of financial reports 147–8
Finland 589, 642
First-in, first-out (FIFO) system 98, 104, 279
Fischer, R. 627
Fisher, David C. 563
Fitzgerald, R. D. 560, 566, 570, 574
Fleming, Colin 634
FMC Corporation 156, 249
Fonseka, G. 586
Foo, See Liang 570
foreign currency translation *see* IAS 21
Foreningen af Statsautoriserede Revisorer (FSR), Denmark 415
Föreningen Auktoriserade Revisorer (FAR), Sweden 416
Fowler Newton, Enrique 635
France
  financial instruments project 375–6, 622
  impact of IASC standards 95, 149, 166–9, 379, 409–11
  national accounting principles 28, 47, 99
  see also Ordre des Experts Comptables
Freda, W. 633
Freyssinier, Julio 65, 537
Frielink, A. B. 264
Fryer, Gavin 154, 562
Fuchs, B. 634
Fujinuma, Tsuguoki 244
Fujita, Yukio 70, 557
funds statement, AISG booklet 35 *see also* IAS 7

G4+1 group 14–15, 231, 376–7, 393, 397–8, 443–6, 450, 498
  development of 444–5
  early evolution 443–4
  restructuring of IASC 448, 453, 460, 465–9, 472–3, 479, 483, 491, 498

Gaberell, Phillipe 626
Galpin, R. D. 555
Galván, Manuel 65, 67, 70, 180, 203, 547, 551, 589
　work on IAS 5 103
Gannon, D. J. 229, 489
Gapper, John 604
García, C. P. 596
Garnett, Robert 497, 634
Garrett, Ray 158, 159–60, 563, 574
Gatto, C. 627
Geib, G. 633
Gélard, Gilbert 225, 269, 471, 497, 590, 619, 622, 626, 639, 648, 653
　work on IAS 36 380
Gelbcke, E. R. 619
General Electric (GE) 156, 249
German Accounting Standards Board
　see Deutsches Rechnungslegungs Standards Committee
Germany 530
　adoption of US GAAP in 330, 340, 412–13
　impact of IASC standards 169–71, 227, 411–14
　national accounting principles 14, 28, 40, 99, 105, 109, 111, 119, 132, 146, 314–5, 409
　see also Institut derWirtschaftsprüfer (IdW), Germany
Ghazali, Ahmad 626
Giddy, Ian H. 620
Gil, G. 622
Gilpin, Kenneth N. 612
Giot, Henri 626, 628
Godfrey, Peter 130, 183, 578
Goerdeler, Reinhard 47, 50, 196–7, 535, 576
Goh, Joon-Hai 626
Gold, Henry 127, 622
Gómez Eng, Rafael 219, 581
goodwill 136–7, 278, 379, 381, 382–3
　AISG booklet 36
　see also IAS 22; IAS 38
Gopalakrishnan, P. S. 569
Gorbatova, L. 634
Gordon, J. A. 634
Governmental Accounting Standards Board (GASB), US 583
government grants *see* IAS 20
Graafstal, Frans 67, 550, 558, 587
Grady, Paul 24
Gramm, Phil 331, 336
Grant, Stuart 308
Grant Thornton 75
Grasso, Richard 247, 249, 331
Gray, Glen 635
Gray, Rob 551

Gray, S. J. 148–9, 180, 560, 570
Greene, Edward F. 605
Grenside, John P. 38, 68–9, 86, 153, 193, 201, 254, 544, 549, 550, 573, 575
　role in Joint Working Party 197–8
Grey, Sarah 618, 624, 628
Groupe d'Etudes des Experts Comptables de la C.E.E. 39, 57, 94, 184, 420–1, 578
Grünewälder, Otto 70
Gunslev, Per 220, 400
Gupta, Kamal 178, 569
Guthrie, Arthur 269
Gutterman, Sam 634
Guy, Paul 294, 598, 607
　financial instruments project and 368
　IASC relations 208, 297–8
　endorsement issues 304, 321

Hagen, John 626
Hagerman, Douglas R. 69, 166, 220, 267
Hague, Ian 236, 370, 377, 623
Haller, Axel 604, 610, 635, 639
Hammond, Ian 219, 622, 624, 629, 632, 633, 648
Hampton, Robert 552
Hancock, Phil 621
Hanks, Sara 603, 605
Harding, Frank 244, 247, 248, 449, 477, 486, 648
Harding, Susan 450, 493, 635
Harding, Terry 236, 354, 626, 629
Harris, Geoff 627, 630
Harris, Ralph L. 67, 142, 185
Harris, Raymond G. 206–7, 579
Harris, Trevor 314, 316, 317, 339, 605, 608, 611, 628
Hashimoto, Ryutaro 437
Haskins & Sells 69
Hatfield, Henry Rand 531
Hauworth,William P. 162
Havermann, Hans 65, 66, 70, 84, 169–70, 345, 546, 547, 548, 551, 566, 567, 617
Hayes, Donald J. 68, 162, 553, 554, 573, 575
Heath, Sean 574
hedge accounting 120–1, 376
Heeley, Geoffrey 221, 356, 556
Hegarty, John 426, 639, 644
Hegazy, Khaled 634
Heidelberger Zement, 227
Heintges, Sebastian 637
Henrot, André 65
Hepworth, John A. 7, 61–3, 65, 69, 81, 84, 147, 201, 254, 498, 536, 552, 585
　promotion of IASC standards 182
　role in JointWorking Party 197

Herrera, Juan R. 244, 247, 530, 596
Herz, Robert 498
Heurlin, Sigvard 220, 250, 385, 406, 491, 620, 625, 628, 648, 654
Hill, Henry P. 162, 564
Hilton, D. 632
Hindin, J. B. 559
Hiramatsu, Kazuo 449, 646, 648
Hobson, David C. 68, 153, 220, 552, 561, 619
  work on IAS 30 291
Hoddinott, David 575
Hoechst 314, 610
Hogg, I. C. P. 549
Holgate, Peter 558, 626
Holmes, Chris M. 606
Holmes, Geoffrey 532, 561
Hong Kong 148, 177, 179, 298, 328, 358, 619
Hong Kong Society of Accountants 179
Hope, Tony 551
Hopkins, Leon 560
Hopwood, Anthony G. 537, 554, 640
Hornbostel, Charles C. 158–9
Hough, John P. 535, 536, 537, 538
Howard, Donald S. 156
Howarth, Hank 402, 625
Hoyos Roldán, Jesús 70, 264, 537, 541, 542, 596
Humphry, Richard 433–4, 644
Hunt, Isaac C., Jr. 345, 346, 616
Husain, I. 557
Hutchinson, Ian R. 635, 645
Hyde Committee Guidelines 109
hyperinflation, accounting for *see* IAS 29

IAS 1 (*Disclosure of Accounting Policies*) 57, 93–6, 104, 115, 513, 546
  revision 238–9, 257, 260, 264, 265, 390–3, 521
IAS 2 (*Valuation and Presentation of Inventories under the Historical Cost System*) 96–9, 179, 226, 513
  revision 264, 265, 278, 283, 310, 519
IAS 3 (*Consolidated Financial Statements and the Equity Method of Accounting*) 99–101, 151, 160, 169, 171, 513, 548, 556, 589
  revision 264–5, 266–7, 357
IAS 4 (*Depreciation Accounting*) 101–2, 140, 152–3, 513, 561
  revision 264
IAS 5 (*Information to be Disclosed in Financial Statements*) 102–3, 513
  revision 264, 274, 390
IAS 6 (*Accounting Responses to Changing Prices*) 106–9, 514

IAS 7 (*Statement of Changes in Financial Position*) 111, 514
  IOSCO endorsement of 313–14, 321, 604
  revision 264, 266, 287–8, 313–14, 520
IAS 8 (*Unusual and Prior Period Items and Changes in Accounting Policy*) 111–13, 514
  revision 264, 266, 285, 386, 520
IAS 9 (*Accounting for Research and Development Activities*) 113–14, 164, 165, 259, 514, 553
  revision 279, 284, 322, 379, 382, 519
IAS 10 (*Contingencies and Events Occurring after the Balance Sheet Date*) 114, 514, 551
  revision 388–9, 522
IAS 11 (*Accounting for Construction Contracts*) 114–15, 515
  revision 266, 274, 519
IAS 12 (*Accounting for Taxes on Income*) 115–17, 130, 157, 515
  revision 164, 266, 357–61, 518, 523, 619
IAS 13 (*Presentation of Current Assets and Current Liabilities*) 117–18, 515
  revision 390
IAS 14 (*Reporting Financial Information by Segment*) 126–7, 155, 515
  revision 355, 393–5, 521
IAS 15 (*Information Reflecting the Effect of Changing Prices*) 109–10, 289, 515, 550
IAS 16 (*Accounting for Property, Plant and Equipment*) 131–3, 379, 516
  revision 520
IAS 17 (*Accounting for Leases*) 127–9, 131, 515, 556
  revision 278, 397–8, 522
IAS 18 (*Revenue Recognition*) 131–2, 133, 165, 256, 263, 516
  revision 519
IAS 19 (*Accounting for Retirement Benefits in the Financial Statements of Employers*) 129–30, 515
  revision 322, 395–7, 520, 521, 522
IAS 20 (*Accounting for Government Grants and Disclosure of Government Assistance*) 135, 516, 608
IAS 21 (*Accounting for the Effects of Changes in Foreign Exchange Rates*) 119–23, 176, 317, 514, 554
  revision 285, 520
IAS 22 (*Accounting for Business Combinations*) 131, 135–8, 317, 516
  revision 274, 285, 379, 381–3, 389, 519, 521
IAS 23 (*Capitalisation of Borrowing Costs*) 138, 272, 279, 516
  revision 284, 519

IAS 24 (*Related Party Transactions*) 92, 138–9, 516, 589
IAS 25 (*Accounting for Investments*) 140–1, 153, 269, 364, 516
  revision 271, 274, 278, 281, 351, 399–401
IAS 26 (*Accounting and Reporting by Retirement Benefit Plans*) 141–2, 323, 517
IAS 27 (*Consolidated Financial Statements and Accounting for Investments in Subsidiaries*) 266–8, 363, 517
IAS 28 (*Accounting for Investments in Associates*) 266–7, 268, 363, 433, 517
IAS 29 (*Financial Reporting in Hyper-inflationary Economies*) 288–9, 317, 323, 517
IAS 30 (*Disclosures in the Financial Statements of Banks and Similar Financial Institutions*) 230, 291–2, 323, 518
  revision 406–7
IAS 31 (*Financial Reporting of Interests in Joint Ventures*) 266–7, 268–9, 318, 519
IAS 32 (*Financial Instruments: Disclosure and Presentation*) 361–70, 399, 406–7, 519
IAS 33 (*Earnings per Share*) 384–5, 520
IAS 34 (*Interim Financial Reporting*) 385–6, 521
IAS 35 (*Discontinuing Operations*) 386–7, 521
IAS 36 (*Impairment of Assets*) 349, 380–2, 397, 521
IAS 37 (*Provisions, Contingent Liabilities and Contingent Assets*) 13, 383, 388–9, 397, 521
IAS 38 (*Intangible Assets*) 349, 382–3, 397, 521
IAS 39 (*Financial Instruments: Recognition and Measurement*) 13, 230, 340, 342, 361–77, 397, 404, 406, 522
  implementation guidance 376
  revision 523
IAS 40 (*Investment Property*) 342, 399–401, 522
IAS 41 (*Agriculture*) 13, 401–4, 521
IASC Insight 239, 286, 367
IASC News 80, 239
Ichii, M. 597
impairment *see* IAS 36
Inbar, Adir 630
income tax, accounting for *see* IAS 12
India 37, 48, 79, 100, 178, 458
  delegation to the IASC 223
Indonesia 148
industry standards 8, 124, 134, 141, 290, 339, 404–5

inflation accounting 105–6
  hyperinflation *see* IAS 29
  see also IAS 6; IAS 15
Institut derWirtschaftsprüfer (IdW), Germany 49, 55, 66, 94
  delegation to the IASC 65, 66, 70, 227–8, 507
  reaction to IASC proposal 47, 55–6 IAS 21 122–3
  support of IASC standards 169–71, 411
Institute of Chartered Accountants in Australia 49, 66, 164
Institute of Chartered Accountants in England and Wales
  in Accountants International Study Group 26–30, 31–4, 36, 533
  development of national accounting principles 28, 99, 109, 261
  joins IASC 49
  membership with ICAI on the IASC board 541
  relations with IASC 74, 78–9, 93
  role in founding of IASC 43–6, 50, 53, 54, 56, 203, 536, 538–9
  role in IASC/IFAC relations 37, 38, 50, 195–7, 207, 576
  role in the IASC's early going 93, 99, 109, 150–5, 203, 207, 576
  support for IASC standards 80, 150–5
  UK and Irish IASC delegation *see* United Kingdom
Institute of Chartered Accountants of India (ICAI) 178, 223
Institute of Chartered Accountants in Ireland (ICAI) 30, 32, 150, 468, 532, 541
Institute of Chartered Accountants of Nigeria 72, 174, 190
Institute of Chartered Accountants of Pakistan 71, 177, 190
Institute of Chartered Accountants of Scotland (ICAS) 30, 33, 37, 49, 56, 150, 195, 435, 468, 541
Institute of Chartered Accountants of Sri Lanka 223
Institute of Chartered Accountants of Zimbabwe 223
Institute of Cost and Management Accountants 49
Institute of Municipal Treasurers and Accountants 49
Instituto dos Auditores Independentes do Brasil 180
Instituto Mexicano de Contadores Públicos
  delegation to the IASC 65, 67, 70–1, 80–1, 508
  financial problems 70–1, 225

Instituto Mexicano ... (cont.)
  position in restructured IASC 452, 458, 474, 476, 477
  reaction to IASC proposal 47, 49, 67, 199, 541
  support of IASC standards 172
insurance project 404–5
intangible assets 378–80, 382–3
  see also goodwill; IAS 38
Inter-American Accounting Association 23
Inter-American Accounting Conference 23
Intergovernmental Working Group of Experts on International Standards of Accounting and Reporting (ISAR) 190–2
interim reports
  AISG booklet 36
  see also IAS 34
International Accounting Research Foundation (IARF) 242, 243–4
International Accounting Standards (IAS)
  compliance issues 7–8, 13–14, 52
    'best endeavours' undertaking 52–3, 85, 88, 144–6
  core standards 12–13, 350–2
    acceleration of target date 328–31
    completion of 340–1, 374–6, 398
    expectations of IOSCO 320–1
  early plan 79
  endorsement of
    European Commission 16–17, 347, 418–32
    FIBV 146–7
    IOSCO 16, 313–14, 318–19, 341–3
    New York Stock Exchange 316–17
    SEC 15–16, 313–14, 317–18, 331–4
    World Bank 441–2
  impact of 149–81, 408–17, 432–41
    Australia 164, 433–5
    Canada 165–6, 181, 435–6
    developing countries 182
    France 166–9, 409–11
    Germany 169–71, 411–14
    Hong Kong 179
    India 178
    Italy 176
    Japan 171–2, 436–7
    Malaysia 179
    Mexico 172
    Netherlands 172–4, 414–15
    New Zealand 179–80
    Nigeria 174–5
    Nordic countries 415–16
    Pakistan 177–8
    Singapore 178–9
    South Africa 175, 437–8
    Switzerland 416–17
    Taiwan 176–7
    United Kingdom 150–5, 417
    United States 155–64, 438–41
  promotion of 182–6
  revisions 264–6, 285–6, 351, 389–98
    Comparability project 253–4, 262, 269–70, 275–6, 277–80, 282–4, 298–300, 305, 519
    format 285–6
    Improvements project 253–4, 280–6, 305–6, 309–11, 318–19
  standard-setting process 90–3, 352–7
    comment letters 355–7
    due process 11, 15, 232, 245, 276, 277, 329, 338, 340, 352–3, 374, 397, 400
    involvement of national standard setters 354–5
    steering committees 90–3, 353–4
    technical staff 353–4
    translations of 77–8, 96, 122, 134, 150, 173, 236, 265, 272, 368, 410–11, 415, 589, 636
  see also specific IAS standards
International Accounting Standards Board (IASB) 1–2, 399, 497–8
International Accounting Standards Committee (IASC)
  Advisory Council 12, 244–7, 447, 448, 450, 452, 454, 457, 470
  associate members 8, 48, 73–4, 79–80, 83–5, 91–2, 182, 189, 542, 544 see also specific countries
  board/committee meetings 80–2, 230–1, 524–6
    guests and observers 228–30, 334–5, 421–2
    opening meetings to the public 231–2
  chairmen 61–3, 213–17, 504
  constitution and agreement 48–53, 500–3
    'best endeavours' undertaking 52–3, 85, 88, 144–6
    changes in 1977 84–5
    changes in 1982 87–8
    changes in 1992 243, 249–50
    changes in 2000 496
    objectives 51
    participating countries 48–9
    voting 53, 228
  Consultative Group 9, 86–7, 202, 250–2, 452, 457–8, 464, 466
    formation of 204–5
  delegations 11, 64–73, 220–5
    added after 1987 71–3
    evolution to 1987 67–71
    financial analysts 220
    financial executives 220–4

original delegations 64–7
see also specific countries
Executive Committee 237–8, 470–1
financing 11–12, 53, 82–4
 fund-raising 240–9
 growth in budget 239–40, 241
 restructuring 496
Foundation Working Party 240–6
founding of 1, 5–6, 43–58, 203
 founder members 48–9
 initiative 43–4
 motivation 44–6
 reactions to 46–8, 54–8
 stage for 41–2
Framework project 253, 254–6, 259–63, 518
 balance-sheet approach 263–4
 Building Block projects 256–9
 reduction of options 262
IASC/IFAC Co-ordinating Committee 89, 250
location 53
 premises 78–9, 236–7
national standard setters' involvement 219–20
Nominating Committee 493–4, 495
non-participation by Central and South American countries 180–1
official language(s) 77–8
Organisation and Planning Committee (OPC) 85–6, 237
re-election/rotation of board members 201–2
relations with other organizations *see specific organizations*
restructuring 447–99
 transition to new regime 493–9
 see also Strategy Working Party (SWP) (below)
staff observers 225–6
Standing Interpretations Committee (SIC) 238–9, 333–4, 342, 399, 452, 456, 462, 466, 476, 477, 490, 494
Statement of Intent see Comparability Project steering committees 353–4
 composition 79–80, 91–3
 observers on 232–3
 working arrangements 90–3
 see also specific projects and standards
Strategy Working Party (SWP) 15, 230, 447–50
 July 1997 meeting 450–4
 September 1997 meeting 450–4
 November 1977 draft 457–9
 January 1998 meeting 460–2
 April 1988 meeting 462–3
 July 1988 meeting 463

December 1988 discussion paper 463–70
Enevoldsen and Carsberg proposal 472–8, 481
developments followingWarsaw 478–82
September 1999 meeting 483–5
run-up to 1999 Board meeting 485–7
November 1999 Board meeting 488–93
transition to new regime 493–9
technical advisers 225–6
technical agenda development 96–7, 110–11, 348–52
technical staff 74–7, 235–6
International Assets Valuation Standards Committee 132, 251
International Association of Financial Executives Institutes (IAFEI) 73, 86, 203, 206, 222, 578, 579
International Association of Securities Commissions (IASC) 293
see also International Organizaton of Securities Commissions (IOSCO)
International Bar Association 87, 251
International Chamber of Commerce (ICC) 86, 204, 205, 222, 232, 578
International Confederation of Free Trade Unions 87, 203, 578, 579
International Co-ordinating Committee of Financial Analysts Associations (ICCFAA) 73, 87, 206, 461, 511–12
International Co-ordination Committee for the Accountancy Profession (ICCAP) 38, 43, 46–48, 55, 66
 relations with IASC 49–51, 195–7
International Federation of Accountants (IFAC) 8, 61, 66, 69, 157
 founding of 22, 195–7
 proposed name change 250
 relations with IASC 8–9, 195, 197–202, 250
 Bishop Working Party 206–9
 failure of proposed integration agreement 197–200
 IASC/IFAC Co-ordinating Committee 89
 Joint Working Party (JWP) 197–200, 201
 Mutual Commitments 9, 72–3, 74, 80, 83, 87–8, 176, 180, 200–2, 206
 restructuring of IASC 453, 457, 477, 479, 482, 483, 487, 496–7
International Finance Corporation (IFC) 182, 232, 578, 634
International Labour Organisation (ILO) 188, 578
International Monetary Fund (IMF) 443, 469, 479, 578

International Organization of Securities
    Commissions (IOSCO) 87, 306–9,
    623
  Accounting and Auditing
      Subcommittee 306, 308
    activities 308, 318, 322, 326, 368
    composition 236, 307, 325, 326, 334
    emergence of 293–5
    endorsement of IASC standards
      final endorsement (2000) 16, 341–3
      partial endorsement (IAS 7) 313–14,
        321
      refusal to endorse (1994) IASC 321–5
    relations with IASC 10–11, 12, 270,
        295–335
      core standards agreement with
        IASC 320–1, 325–6, 349, 350
      financial instruments project and 340,
        368, 373
      guest attendance at IASC meetings 229
      initial contact 186, 295–8
      observers on IASC steering
        committees 232
      role in Improvements project 309–11,
        318–19, 321
    resolutions at 1988 annual
        conference 300–5
    Technical Committee
      composition 298, 306, 321
      views on endorsement 299, 322, 326–7,
        342
    Working Party 1 (WP1)
      assessment of core standards 341, 603
      composition and mode of
        operation 306, 307, 308, 319, 326,
        334, 436, 612
      contacts with IASC 235, 324, 335
      lack of unanimity in 309, 324, 395, 608
      precursor 298, 306
      restructuring of IASC 459
      views on endorsement 308, 320, 322–3,
        327
International Working Party (IWP) 37–8,
    49–50, 56
inventories
  AISG booklet 31–2, 34–5
  see also IAS 2
investment property see IAS 25; IAS 40
investments see IAS 25
Iordanides, N. 619
Ireland, impact of IASC standards 148, 150–5
Irvine, Bruce 69, 266
Islam, M. Atiqul 587
Italy
  delegation to the IASC 73, 138, 225,
    282–3, 510
  impact of IASC standards 148, 176

Iversen, Morten 589
Izquierdo, Maritza 628

Jaafar, Azizah Mohd 225
Jacobsen, Lyle E. 530
Jamias, K. V. 595
Janell, Paul 571
Japan
  financial instruments project and 365,
    368
  impact of IASC standards 171–2, 436–7
Japanese Institute of Certified Public
    Accountants (JICPA) 49, 226, 248,
    436–7
  delegation to the IASC 65, 67, 70, 81, 184,
    226, 276, 282–3, 285, 508, 538
  financial instruments project and 365,
    368
  joins IASC 47–9
  support of IASC standards 171–2
Jaudeau, Bernard 221, 358, 410, 630
Jayson, Susan 590
Jeffrey, Gundi 622
Jenkins, Edmund 373, 375, 492, 497, 623,
    647, 648, 654, 655
Jennings, Alvin R. 24–5
Johnson, Todd 393, 443, 630
joint ventures see IAS 31
JointWorking Group of Standard Setters
    (JWG) 377, 399, 404, 625
Jones, Thomas 16, 213, 216, 217, 222, 448,
    489–90, 497, 627, 648, 653
  IAS 17 revision 398
Jordanian delegation 223, 290

Kale, Yashodan 630
Kaminski, Horst 65, 66, 70
Kanne, Morris 558
Kantola, Birgitta 449
KapAEG law, Germany 413
Kapnick, Harvey E. 161, 563
Kasuga, T. 597
Kato, Atsushi 308, 436, 601, 603, 607, 620,
    645, 646
Kawaguchi, Junichi 65
Keefe, Howard P. 570
Keller, Jean 630
Keller, Thomas F. 531
Kenmochi, Toshiyuki 229
Kenny, Sara York 590, 591
Kewin, Tony 65, 67, 541
  work on IAS 4 102
Kikuya, Masato 538, 646
Kim, Kwon-Jung 630
Kinzonzi, M. N. K. 183
Kirk, Donald J. 162–3, 183, 185, 564,
    572

Kirkpatrick, John L. 7, 63, 69, 73, 86, 134, 143, 213, 302, 498, 557, 572, 575, 587, 598
   IASC/IFAC Co-ordinating Committee involvement 89
   initial contact with IOSCO 295–8
   promotion of IASC standards 184–5
Kirton, Ian 403, 633
Kjaer, P. J. 555
Klaassen, Jan 395, 458, 474–5, 595, 619, 623, 625, 648, 653
Klaver, K. 634
Kleekämper, Heinz 284–5, 390, 581, 587, 594, 595, 621, 629, 630, 636
Kleerekoper, Is 65, 66, 67, 550
Knorr, Liesel 236, 326, 339, 354, 583, 618, 619, 627, 634, 641, 646
Knutson, Peter 627, 630
Kolb, Wolfgang 635
Korean delegation 225, 280–3
KPMG *see* Peat Marwick
Kraayenhof, Jacob 23–4, 530
Kramer, G. J. 184
Kransdorff, Arnold 575
Kremper, François 588
Krumnow, Jürgen 247, 248
Kyle, Donald L. 530

Lafferty, Michael 147–8, 264, 554, 560, 564, 568, 569, 575, 588
Lagarrigue, Jean-Pierre 69
Lago, Marisa 479, 613, 616
Langford, Robert 235
Larkin, E. L. 555
Larson, Robert 590, 591
Last-in, first-out (LIFO) system 98, 156, 226
   proposed elimination of 265, 278–9, 283–5, 305, 310
Lauver, Raymond C. 183, 228
Layton, LeRoy 43, 48, 50, 535
Leach, Sir Ronald 34, 46, 100, 154, 537, 544, 562
leases *see* IAS 17
Leddy, Thomas D. 563
Leder, Paul 328, 341, 343, 609, 613
Ledouble, Dominique 69, 96, 122, 168, 537, 547, 555, 565, 566, 589
le Douit, J. 633
Legault, Guy 645
LeGrange, Ulyesse 244
Leisenring, James 228, 361, 441, 606, 614, 618, 647, 648
   criticism of IASC 338, 339–40, 440
   financial instruments project and 366–7, 369
   G4+1 involvement 444
   restructuring of IASC 459, 498

Lennard, Andrew 388, 393, 630
Leonard, Steven 619
Le Portz, Yves 294
Leroy-Lewis, David 54
Levitt, Arthur 232, 313, 314, 315, 316, 329, 331, 333, 336, 480, 582, 611, 648, 655
   Nominating Committee involvement 483, 493, 494, 495, 497
Levy, Harry 64, 66–7, 541
liabilities 257–8
Liener, Gerhard 610
Limerick, Lord 54
Lochner, Philip R., Jr. 440, 646
London Stock Exchange 145, 248, 294, 304, 307, 311, 336, 560
   support for IASC standards 127, 147, 148, 154–5, 335–6
Lopater, C. 635
Louwers, Pieter 52, 65, 66, 67, 546
   work on IAS 1 94
Lucio-Villegas, Antonio 631
Lütz, Susanne 610
Luxembourg 21, 22, 23, 291, 308, 642
Lymer, Andrew 635
Lyons, Howard 65, 66, 69
   work on IAS 2 98
   work on IAS 6 106

Ma, Ronald 569
Maat, Philip 620
McConnell, Patricia 217, 220, 489–90, 630
   IAS 14 revision 393, 394
McDougall, E. H. Victor 39, 530, 534, 536, 538
MacFarlane, Selwyn 175
McGeachin, Anne 626
McGregor, Warren 70, 220, 225, 341, 564, 587, 615, 648, 650, 651
   financial instruments project and 364
   Framework project 258, 259, 260, 261
   G4+1 involvement 444–5, 460
   insurance project 404
   restructuring of IASC 458, 498
   true and fair override issue 391
McDonough, C. A. 623
Mackenzie, Alexander 65, 69, 84, 161–2, 197, 536, 538, 547, 549, 551, 564
   work on IAS 1 93
McKinnon, Jill Lorraine 567
McKinnon, S. M. 571
McMonnies, P. N. 574
McQueen (Walters), Patricia 238, 405, 626, 634
Macrae, Edwin W. 34
Malaquin, Philippe 631
Malawi 178
Malaysia 148, 177, 178, 179, 225

Malaysian Accounting Standards Board 652
Malaysian Association of Certified Public
    Accountants 179
Malaysian Securities Commission 225, 652
Malegam, Y. H. 552
Mamelund, Erik 622, 638, 648
Manardo, Jacques 449, 460, 476, 478
Mann, Michael 313, 315, 332
Mantle, Peter 163, 176, 556, 560, 564, 568,
    574, 577, 578
Marker, M. 597
Marks, Peter 70, 537, 542, 567
Marseille, Herman 67, 130, 174, 270, 556,
    557, 559, 575, 586, 590, 591, 597, 621,
    640
Marsh, David 597
Marteau, D. 620
Martinez, R. 558
Mason, Alister 119, 533, 534, 540–1, 548,
    553, 556, 562
Matsushige, Tadayuki 635
Mattar, A. N. 589
Matthews, Derek 536
May, Robert L. 38, 183, 530, 534
Mayshak, L. 632
Mazars, Robert 65, 66, 95, 167, 168, 546, 548,
    551, 552, 555, 565, 566
Mazzoni, A. 634
Mbanefo, A. 557
Meagher, Michael 300, 306, 307–10, 318–19,
    321, 322–3, 325, 606, 607
Méan, Freddy 628
Mednick, Robert 242, 584
Menn, Bernd-Joachim 221, 222, 227,
    427, 581, 604, 607, 610, 636,
    648
Mexico 175, 183, 187, 622
    impact of IASC standards 172
    see also Instituto Mexicano de Contadores
        Públicos
Meyer, Peter 552, 558
Mihular, Reyaz 219, 223, 402, 631
Mikol, Alain 565, 566
Milan, Ed 626
Milburn, Alex 219, 623, 625
    financial instruments project and 370,
        371
    Joint Working Group involvement 377
Miles, John 183
Miller, Malcolm C. 587
Miller, Merton H. 620
Miller, Paul B.W. 588, 653
Minahan, Eugene J. 67, 126, 541, 549
Mirza, Abbas Ali 559
Mitchell, Geoffrey 7, 75, 191, 550, 554, 574,
    575, 601, 630, 637
    banks project 406–7
    Framework project 255–6, 259

IOSCO relations 307, 308
    promotion of IASC standards 184, 185
Mogg, John 373, 423–4, 426, 432, 472, 646
    restructuring of IASC 472, 478, 481–2,
        483
Monopoli, B. A. 633
Monti, Mario 424–5, 428
Moore, Kate 574
Morgan, David 631
Morpeth, Douglas S. 34, 38, 44, 53, 54, 196,
    535–6
Morrissey, John M. 346, 617
Morson, C. 623
Morton, P. 627
Mosso, David 384
Moulin, Donald J. 301–4, 599–600
Mourre, Gilbert 565, 566
Muchene, C. 634
Mueller, Gerhard G. 24, 26, 36, 38, 441, 530,
    531, 534, 647
Muis, Jules 478, 648
Mulcahy, Gert 536, 537
multijurisdictional disclosure system
    (MJDS) 312–13
multinational corporations, growth of 21,
    329–31
Munro, Ron 65, 67, 541
Murphy, George J. 564
Murphy, Gerard 69, 640
    work on IAS 30 291
Murray, Ronald 362, 622
Myata, T. 597

Nair, P. A. 597
Nakajima, Kimiaki 247
Nakajima, Seigo 65, 67, 70, 86, 184, 201, 220,
    537, 541, 547, 551, 553, 556
    revision of IAS 3 267
Nakaune, Mikio 229
Napier, Christopher 275
Narongdej, K. 633
Nascimento, L. U. do 558
Nash, Nathaniel C. 608
Nash, Roy C. 75, 78, 118, 182–3, 190, 552,
    567, 575
National Association of Accountants, US 66,
    257
National Council of Chartered Accountants,
    South Africa 71, 175
Nederlands Instituut van Registeraccountants
    (NIVRA) 53, 55, 56, 66, 98, 134–5,
    192, 203, 536
    compliance issue 52
    delegation to the IASC 65, 66, 67, 508–9
    European Accounting Study Group and
        445–6
    options in standards and 358
    reaction to IASC proposal 47

replacement value accounting issue 106–8
support of IASC standards 172–4
Nestlé 222, 356, 417, 498
Netherlands, 183, 248, 409, 622
  impact of IASC standards 172–4, 414–15
  national accounting principles 28
  see also Nederlands Instituut van Registeraccountants (NIVRA)
Neuhausen, Benjamin S. 557
New York Stock Exchange (NYSE)
  acceleration in listings of overseas companies 311–12, 329, 428–9
  Daimler-Benz listing 314–16
  IASC Advisory Council and fund-raising 247–9
  support for IASC standards 316–17, 335–8
New Zealand 179–80, 183, 433, 444, 622
  national accounting principles 28
New Zealand Society of Accountants 179–80
Ng, Shwn Yng 570
Nicolaisen, Donald T. 617
Niehus, Rudolf 535, 557, 567
Niessen, Hermann 183, 184–5, 228, 418–21, 599, 640
Nieto, Luis 552
Nigeria
  delegation to the IASC 71, 72, 86, 510
  impact of IASC standards 148, 174–5
Nigerian Accounting Standards Board (NASB) 174
Nobes, Chris 220, 231, 232, 244, 545, 550, 552, 553, 567, 569, 582, 623, 625, 627, 628, 629, 631, 635, 650, 651, 652, 654
  restructuring of IASC 466, 474
  true and fair override issue 391
  work on IAS 35 386–7
Nolte, E. Dieter 597
Nordemann, Hermann 420–1
Nordic Federation of Public Accountants
  delegation to IASC 213, 223, 284, 377, 400, 415–16, 427, 445
Norman, Peter 604
Norton, Richard 560
Norway 22, 23, 223, 415–16
Norwegian Accounting Standards Board (NASB) 415–16
not-for-profit accounting 349

Odreman, C. 586
Ogunde, Adedoyin 174
Oke, E. 557
Olson, Wallace E. 46, 48, 50, 54, 57, 155, 196, 537, 541, 576, 578
  publications 534, 535, 536, 537, 538, 539, 542
O'Malley, Patricia 498, 630
Oman 178
Oni, Michael Ayodeji 72, 86, 256, 587

Ontario, 298, 334
Ontario Securities Commission 4
  involvement with
    Comparability project 270, 281, 298–300
    Improvements project 309, 318–19, 321, 323
    Strategy Working Party 15, 449, 478–9
    the SEC's MJDS arrangement with Canada 312–13
  on IOSCO's observer delegation to IASC 229
  on IOSCO's Technical Committee 306, 325, 327, 329, 331, 601
  on IOSCO's Working Party 1 236, 243, 307, 308, 326, 341
options in IASC standards 142–3, 269
  reduction of 253, 262, 269–80, 285, 298
  IAS 12 357–8
Ordelheide, Dieter 532, 581, 589, 594, 636, 640
Ordre des Experts Comptables, France 49, 167–9, 411, 467, 497, 540, 578
  delegation 65, 66, 69, 507
  reaction to IAS 21 122–3
  reaction to IASC proposal 47
Organisation for Economic Co-operation and Development (OECD)
  Ad Hoc Working Group 192–4, 199
  Forum on harmonization of accounting standards (1985) 87, 130, 163, 195
  IASC Consultative Group 87, 204, 578
  influence on IASC 126–7, 139, 183, 190, 192–5, 198, 201, 204, 297, 362
  as potential standard setter 573, 575
Orrell, Magnus 635
Ortega, Rolando 63, 70, 86, 541, 586, 541
Osunkeye, O. 587
Otten, P. F. S. 24
Overboom C. P. M. 628
Oyediran, C. Oyeniyi O. 72, 174, 558

Pacter, Paul 236–7, 319, 354, 583, 595, 599, 606, 615, 623, 624, 627, 628, 630, 633, 634, 635
  financial instruments project and 372, 373–4
  IAS 14 revision 394
Padgett, Robert 630
Pakistan 71, 190, 542
  impact of IASC standards 148, 177–8, 569
Pakistan Institute of Industrial Accountants 177
Palihakkara, U. H. 586
Palmer, Frank 635
Palmer, Russell E. 89, 576
Pape, Jochen 400, 631, 632, 637
Parker, Colin 621

Parker, Robert 550, 553, 566, 567, 569, 570, 629
partial tax allocation 116–17, see also IAS 12
Paterson, Ron 281, 588, 635
Pearcy, Jeff 63, 69
Pears, John 46
Peat Marwick / KMPG 61, 68, 71, 222, 301, 318, 395, 400, 544, 580
 members of IASB 497, 498
 members of Strategy Working Party 449, 450
Peirson, Graham 631
performance reporting 392–3
Perridon, Louis 534, 535, 540
Perry, David 634
Peru 180, 223, 570, 628
Peterson, James R. 595, 603, 605, 611, 612, 614, 646, 652
Petrone, Kimberley 384
Pfaff, Dieter 532, 581, 594, 636, 642
Pham, Dang 566
Phenix, Paul. 570, 596, 627
Philips Gloeilampenfabrieken 24, 52, 66, 106, 183
Phipps, Eric 634
Picolli, Ambrogio 625
Picot, Russel 635
Plan Comptable Général (PCG), France 28, 409
pooling of interests see IAS 22
Porteous, J. A. 71, 551, 568
Portugal 22, 23
Potter, David C. 222, 633, 634
Potthoff, E 539
Pougin, E. 184, 549
Prada, Michel 479, 482, 485, 493, 601
Price Waterhouse 24, 26, 67, 70, 74, 359, 570
 criticism of IASC 160–1
 survey of financial reporting practices 148, 149
Priebjrivat, A. 633
Prie, Jim 536
provisions see IAS 37
public sector accounting 349
Public Sector Accounting Standards Board (PSASB), Australia 433, 434, 435

Québec 298
Quebec Securities Commission 598
Quinn, James J. 567
Quinn, Lawrence Richter 645
Quinn, Linda 247, 299, 306–9, 313–15, 317, 320, 322–7, 599, 608

Raffegeau, J. 552
Rahman, Ashaq 635
Rahman, Sheikh F. 573

Ramin, Kurt 236, 237, 476, 478, 637
Rashid, P. 596
Rayburn, Frank R. 558
Redding, Rodney J. 653
regional accountancy bodies 22
 creation of 23
Reinhard, Richard 307, 309
Reiter, H. 586
related party transactions see IAS 24
Relleen, Christopher J. 74, 75
Rennie, Robert M. 34, 533
Renshall, Michael 151, 533, 552, 560, 574, 585
replacement value accounting 98, 106–7 see also IAS 6; IAS 15
research and development costs see IAS 9; IAS 38
retirement benefits see IAS 19; IAS 26
revenue recognition see IAS 18
Reydel, A. 184
Richard, François-Maurice 37, 204
Richardson, Alan J. 635, 645
Richardson, Hugh F. 75
Rickard, Douglas 69
Rivat, Laurence 236, 354, 626, 628
Robbins, Barry 338, 359, 614, 619, 620, 622, 623
Røder, Jens 244, 424, 427, 590
Romero, Leopoldo 70, 551
 work on IAS 16 132
Rooper, Alison 540
Rosenfield, Paul 68, 74, 80, 91, 220, 572, 596, 619
Roy, Rahul 634
Royal Dutch/Shell Group of Companies 75, 173, 262, 264, 356
Ruder, David S. 304, 306, 315
 restructuring of IASC 448, 449, 450, 460, 461, 465, 475, 476, 478, 486, 487, 489, 600, 648
Ruffing, Lorraine 596
Rundfelt, Rolf 620, 622–3, 627, 632, 640, 648
Ruppel, Albrecht 537, 542, 567
Rushbrook, Keith 628
Russia 229, 406
Rutherford, Brian A. 76, 235, 543, 583, 587, 626
Rutledge, G. K. 620
Rutteman, Paul 128, 152–3, 165, 182, 534, 543, 561, 571, 639

Sahlgren, Klaus A. 573
Saint-Geours, Jean 247, 320, 321, 601
Sakamoto, M. 622
Saloman, James 229, 236, 325, 326–7, 608, 609, 617

Salomon Inc. 156, 249
Samothrakidis, G. P. 619
Sampson, Clarence 185, 186, 295–6
Sarda, Narendra P. 402
Sasebo Heavy Industries Co. 171
Sato, M. 635
Savoie, Leonard M. 533
Sawa, Etsuo 226, 281, 581, 631, 645, 648
Saxe, Léon 39
Schapiro, Mary L. 315, 604
Scheid, Jean-Claude 69, 548, 566, 629
Schering 227, 411, 412
Schmid, Harry K. 222, 238, 251, 356, 498, 580, 648
Schoen, J. W. 633
Scholtz, W. 555
Schoonderbeek, Jan 55, 183, 534, 535, 539, 540, 619
Schuetze, Walter 320, 605, 606, 611, 626, 653
 financial instruments project and 367, 368–9
Schulz, H.-G. 631
Schwartz, Bill N. 552
Schwencke, Hans R. 638
Sciulli, Nick 597
Seah, Tony 225, 406, 442, 459, 629
Securities and Exchange Commission (SEC), US 10, 144, 311–18, 440–1, 549
 concept release 343–7
 conflict over IASC's E3 157–60
 endorsement of IASC standards 15–16, 317–18
  IAS 7 313–14
  pressure from New York Stock Exchange 335–8
  three key elements required 331–4
 MJDS arrangement 312–13
 relations with IASC contacts 185–6
 Rule 144A 312
 Strategy Working Party discussion paper responses 468–9
Securities and Investments Board (SIB), UK 307–8, 309, 601
Security Analysts Association, Japan 356
segment reporting see IAS 14
Seifert, Werner 450, 637, 651
Sempier, Robert 65, 66, 84, 160, 183, 206, 302, 541, 553, 537
 work on IAS 21 121
Servan-Schreiber, Jean-Jacques 21, 530
Shad, John S. R. 185–6, 294, 572
Shapiro, James E. 613
Sharpe, Michael 12, 213, 215, 216–17, 234–5, 250, 434, 537, 580, 581, 582, 609, 644, 648
 board membership and 219, 220
 executive committee involvement 238
 financial instruments project and 368, 372, 622
 funding issues 244, 245–6, 247
 involvement of China 229
 IOSCO relations 322, 323, 325–8, 612
 Strategy Working Party and 448, 449, 450, 486, 487
Shaw, J. C. 148–9, 180, 560, 570, 574
Shawki, A. 586
Shearer, Brian R. 75
Shell see Royal Dutch/Shell Group of Companies
Sheng, Andrew 493
Shiba, Kenji 646
Shiratori, Eiichi 12, 213, 214, 216, 559, 608
 Advisory Council involvement 247
 Comparability project involvement 270
 executive committee involvement 238
 involvement of China 229, 582
 IOSCO endorsement issues 311, 320–7, 334, 349–50
Shiratori letters 322–5, 326, 350, 379, 395
Simmonds, Andy 590
Simmons, Richard J. 74, 182, 546, 548, 571
Singapore 117, 148, 178–9, 248, 558, 569
Singapore Society of Accountants 178
Sjöstrand, Peter 450, 651
Slator, Gerry 65, 66
Sleigh, C. F. 559
Slimmings, Sir William 154, 562
Slipkowsky, John N. 548, 559
Smith, George 191
Smith, John T. 238, 625
Smith, M. 634
Smith, Terry 625
Smith, Willis A. 67–8, 138, 185, 558, 575
Society of Management Accountants of Canada (SMAC) 542
Soetekouw, A. A. 555
Solomons, David 261
Somerville, Ian 221, 356, 568, 581, 620, 629
Sommer, Al, Jr. 247, 597
Sondhi, A.C. 595
Sony Corporation 47
South Africa
 financial contributions 248
 impact of IASC standards 148, 175, 437–8
 mining companies 405
South African Breweries 175, 221, 356
South African Institute of Chartered Accountants (SAICA) 175, 222–3, 377, 437–8, 593
 delegation to the IASC 71–2, 137, 191, 222–3, 227, 510, 581
 steering committee participation 79, 92, 573, 589
 voting in IASC 141, 199, 201, 250, 360

South American countries,
    non-participation 180–1
Spain 23, 47, 298, 589
Spencer, John 630
Spencer, Kenneth 69, 220, 258, 303, 434, 564,
    586, 629, 630, 644, 645, 648
    extractive industries project 405
    Framework project and 255, 256, 262, 586
    G4+1 involvement 444
    restructuring of IASC 459, 497, 498
Sperber, Sebastian R. 605
Spinosa Cattela, Robert C. 183, 571
Sprouse, Robert T. 164, 619
Sri Lanka 100, 223, 401, 624
SSAP *see* Statement of Standard Accounting
    Practice (SSAP), UK
Stamp, Edward 41, 151–2, 187–8, 189, 535,
    541, 561, 562, 572, 573
Standish, Peter 532, 548, 566, 636
Statements of Standard Accounting Practice
    (SSAP), UK 151–5, 561
    SSAP 9 (*Stocks and Work in Progress*) 99,
        115
    SSAP 10 (*Statements of Source and
        Application of Funds*) 115
    SSAP 11 (*Accounting for Deferred Tax*) 116
    SSAP 12 (*Accounting for Depreciation*) 102
    SSAP 14 (Group Accounts) 151
    SSAP 16 (*Current Cost Accounting*) 109,
        110
    SSAP 19 (*Accounting for Investment
        Properties*) 102, 152–3
    SSAP 20 (*Foreign Currency
        Translation*) 121
    SSAP 21 (*Accounting for Leases and Hire
        Purchase Contracts*) 128
    SSAP 22 (*Accounting for Goodwill*) 381
    SSAP 24 (*Accounting for Pension Costs*) 129
    SSAP 25 (*Segmental Reporting*) 127
Statements of Financial Accounting Standards
    (SFASs), Taiwan 176–7
Staubs, Clarence 185, 295–96, 572
Staubus, George J. 564
Stevenson, Kevin 260, 583, 586, 587, 631
Stickler, A. D. 560, 565, 566, 570
Stilling, Peter 220, 238, 560, 620
    intangible assets project involvement 378,
        380
Stout, David E. 590
Strada, G. 626
Stronge, Christopher J. 68–9, 153, 242, 585,
    588
subsidiaries *see* IAS 27
Sutcliffe, Paul 354, 583, 626, 630
Sutton, Michael 229, 317, 328, 331–4, 338,
    346, 605, 606, 609, 612
    financial instruments project and 371–2,
        373

IAS 1 revision and 391
intangible assets project and 383
Swanney, David 597, 623
Sweden 22, 23, 55, 298
    contribution to IASC work
        programme 92, 100, 133, 377, 622
    delegation to the IASC 223
    impact of IASC standards 415–16
    national accounting principles 126, 555
    see also Nordic Federation of Public
        Accountants
Switzerland 11, 13, 22, 23, 248, 298, 308
    impact of IASC standards 416–17
    national accounting principles 125
SyCip,Washington 23, 89, 183, 199, 534, 573,
    576

Tachibana, E. 633
Taiwan 229
    delegation to the IASC 73, 81, 191
    impact of IASC standards 176–7
Tambosso, M. 635
Tanimoto, Shinichi 634
Tatsumi, Shozo 65
taxation, accounting for *see* IAS 12
Tay, J. S.W. 570
Taylor, Martin I. 571
Taylor, Martyn 625
Taylor, Peter 561
Tempelaar, Aad 41, 56, 533, 534, 535, 537,
    540
Tetley, J. C. N. 596
Thiele, Rex 69
Thomas, R. Douglas 33, 193, 532, 533, 535,
    536, 537, 538, 540, 548, 556, 560, 565
    member of Canadian delegation 65, 66,
        69, 220
    work on IAS 9 113
    work on IAS 19 129
Thomas, R. D. 560
Thompson, Georgette 594, 627
Thompson, Sandra 388
Thomson, Angus 235, 582, 590, 644, 645, 648
Thorby, Warwick G. 71, 86
    work on IAS 20 135
Thouvenin, Dominique 634
Tighe, Ingrid 628
Timmerman, Georges 537, 639, 642
Tizzano, Roberto 631
Tjaden, Wilhelm 135, 237
    work on IAS 29 288
Tobari, Kiichiro 537
Tobin, Jean E. 613
Tokar, Mary 229, 331, 334–5, 337, 341–4,
    479, 613, 614, 615, 616, 648, 653
Tokumasu, F. 627
Tokunaga, Tadaaki 281
Tomasin, Giancarlo 258, 543, 559, 587, 596

Toronto Stock Exchange 145, 166, 435
Touche Ross & Co. 68, 70, 71, 160, 271, 533, 560
Treffers, Henk 65, 66, 67
    work on IAS 21 119, 553
Trinidad and Tobago 148, 542
Tripartite Study Group, Netherlands 63, 173, 199 *see also* Council on Annual Reporting, Netherlands
Trueblood, Robert M. 29–30, 34, 532
true and fair override 390–2 *see also* IAS 1
Tua Pereda, Jorge 530
Turley, Stuart 561
Turner, Lynn E. 343–4, 345, 616, 617
    restructuring of IASC 478, 479, 480–1, 485, 489, 491, 492, 493, 497, 648, 653, 654, 655
Tweedie, David 69, 219, 220, 228, 549, 618, 630, 631, 633, 640, 650
    financial instruments project and 375, 377, 625
    G4+1 involvement 444, 448
    intangible assets project and 383
    objections to revised IAS 12 360–1, 620
    restructuring of IASC 448, 450, 458, 460, 475, 486, 488, 491, 498, 648, 649
        chairmanship of restructured board 497
    true and fair override issue 391, 629
    work on IAS 37 388–9, 627, 629

Ufer, H.-W. 634
Uiterlinden, Jan 67, 173
Ulrich, F. 619
Underdown, Brian 561
Unilever 75, 544, 554
Union Européenne des Experts Comptables Economiques et Financiers (UEC) 23, 38, 78, 93, 184, 420, 533, 553
    reactions to IASC founding 55–7
    relations with IASC 105, 184, 578
    role in accounting harmonization 39–41, 50, 55–7, 93, 94
United Kingdom (UK)
    auditing standards 28–9
    delegation to the IASC 65, 66, 68–9, 82, 84, 200, 237, 355, 509, 541
        on specific accounting issues 106, 137, 360, 375, 377, 386, 389, 391, 397, 398
    impact of IASC standards 150–5, 417
    national programmes for accounting principles 28, 29
    see also Institute of Chartered Accountants in England andWales (ICAEW); Institute of Chartered Accountants of Scotland (ICAS); Institute of Chartered Accountants in Ireland (ICAI)

United Nations (UN) 45, 87, 127, 187–9
    Ad Hoc Working Group 190–2
    Group of Eminent Persons 188
    Group of Experts 188–9, 192–3
    influence on IASC 127, 139, 191, 192, 461, 537
    Intergovernmental Working Group of Experts on International Standards of Accounting and Reporting (ISAR) 191–2
    as potential standard setter 134, 139, 168, 187–8, 192, 193, 201, 297
    UNCTAD 232, 344, 628, 634
United States (US)
    auditing standards 28–9
    delegation to the IASC 65, 66, 67–8, 82, 220, 228, 509–10, 596
        stance on specific issues 98, 106, 226, 283, 297, 310, 367, 375, 383, 386, 389, 391, 575
    financial instruments project and 366
    Generally Accepted Accounting Principles (US GAAP) 10–11, 28, 29, 35, 45, 100, 306, 338, 483
        comparisons with IAS 96, 100, 101, 110, 269, 283, 316, 339, 600, 614
    influence on IASC standards 115, 119, 131, 138, 261, 268, 279
    international influence of 45, 122, 169, 173, 227, 314, 316, 324, 328–31, 340, 410–11, 412–13, 417, 418, 424–6, 428, 429, 435–6
    reconciliation to 186, 296, 299, 311, 314, 315, 329, 335–6, 342, 396, 424, 441
    see also Accounting Principles Board (APB), US; Financial Accounting Standards Board (FASB), US
    impact of IASC standards 108, 117, 155–64, 438–41
    international accounting in 25–6
    see also American Institute of Certified Public Accountants (AICPA)
Upton,Wayne 628
Uruguay 180, 570

Vallas, M. 619
van Bruinessen,Wessel 106–8, 549, 550
Van der Meulen, O. 189–90, 573
van der Sluis, C. 622
van der Wel, Frans 532, 568, 577, 637
van Ham, J. 633
van Helleman, Johan 281, 595, 618, 621
Van Hulle, Karel 184–5, 228, 419–26, 427, 431–2, 445, 537, 568, 581, 589, 593, 599, 603, 610, 618, 635, 639, 640–4, 652
    IASC restructuring and 459, 472, 481, 492, 648

van Ittersum, Boudewijn F. Baron 247
Van Oostveldt, Karel 551
Van Riper, Robert 564, 634
Van Weelden, Susan J. 630
Varvatsoulis, C. 619
Vasquez, F. 634
Vassie, Ian 551
Venezuela 180–1
Verhagen, Ger 244
Volcker, Paul 495–6, 497
Volpi, James 590
Volten, Henk 55, 65, 67, 97, 134, 146, 173, 207, 538, 539, 540, 546, 547, 554, 559, 568, 577, 578, 579, 640
Von der Tann, Krafft Freiherr 65, 66, 70, 548, 576
Vulliez, C. 620

Waigel, Theo 315
Waitzer, Edward J. 15, 308, 321, 325, 327, 329, 331, 334, 602, 607, 612, 645, 649
  Strategy Working Party involvement 449, 450, 474, 478, 479, 487
Walker, David 601
Walker, Lauren M. 531
Walker, Michael A. 561
Walker, R. G. 547–8
Wallace, R. S. Olusegun 289, 568
Walters, Patricia *see* McQueen (Walters), Patricia
Walters, Ralph E. 68, 163, 181, 220, 302, 303, 340, 407, 564, 587, 590, 596, 599
  Comparability project 141, 270, 271–2, 274, 297, 298
Walton, Peter 530, 536, 565, 634, 638, 647
Ward, Graham 431, 643
Watanabe, Munehiro 567
Watts, Thomas R. 122, 153, 183, 554, 560, 566, 570
Weinstein, Stanley 561
Weirich, S. 557
Wellings, F. 634
Whittington, Geoffrey 498, 549
Wild, Kenneth 307
Wilkes, Richard 207, 579
Wilkinson, Theodore L. 34
Wilmot, Peter 220, 238, 263, 270, 271, 588, 654
  work on IAS 7 revision 287

Wilson, Allister 229, 330, 426, 610, 625, 633, 648
Wilson, J. R. M. (Jack) 30, 34
Winkelmann, P. F. 632
Winters, Jeremy 65, 66
Wirtschaftsprüferkammer 49, 122, 169–70, 538, 554
Witadinata, Sumantri 589
Wolfensohn, James 493
Wong, Eng Howe 147
Wong, P. H. 556
Woodwark, W. J. 622
Wootton, Charles G. 147
World Bank 25
  financial support of IASC 246, 350, 402–3, 405–6
  participation in IASC's work 87, 232, 288, 289, 402, 578, 579, 596, 623, 633, 634
  restructuring of IASC 461, 469, 473, 478–9, 493
  support for IAS 182, 441–2
Worms, Gérard 247
Wright, C. 634
Wu, Anne 569
Wyatt, Arthur 12, 213–14, 229, 311, 353, 570, 581, 582, 583, 590, 594, 595, 599, 602, 606, 618, 621, 653
  advises SEC 331, 335, 449
  Comparability and Improvements projects 282, 286
  financial instruments project 362, 363
  financing issues 239, 242
  Strategy Working Party and 449
Wygal, Donald E. 590

Yalkin, Yüksel Koç 628
Yamada, Tatsumi 498, 617, 625, 645, 648
Yamazaki, Shozo 632
Yanou, Rieko 633

Zambia 148
Zambian Association of Accountants 102, 103
Zeff, Stephen A. 531, 532, 536, 549, 551, 552, 558, 568, 570, 577, 586, 605, 611, 613, 614, 616, 629, 630, 631, 637
Zimbabwe 148, 178, 182, 223, 542, 569, 633
Zoido, Antonio 247
Zurbrügg, Peter 222, 340, 458, 650

Lightning Source UK Ltd.
Milton Keynes UK
UKHW020642190223
417171UK00003B/104